PRODUCTS LIABILITY

EDITORIAL ADVISORS

Erwin Chemerinsky
Sydney M. Irmas Professor of Public Interest Law, Legal Ethics, and Political Science
University of Southern California

Richard A. Epstein
James Parker Hall Distinguished Service Professor of Law
University of Chicago
Peter and Kirsten Bedford Senior Fellow
The Hoover Institution
Stanford University

Ronald J. Gilson
Charles J. Meyers Professor of Law and Business
Stanford University
Marc and Eva Stern Professor of Law and Business
Columbia University

James E. Krier
Earl Warren DeLano Professor of Law
University of Michigan

Richard K. Neumann, Jr.
Professor of Law
Hofstra University School of Law

Kent D. Syverud
Dean and Garner Anthony Professor
Vanderbilt University Law School

Elizabeth Warren
Leo Gottlieb Professor of Law
Harvard University

EMERITUS EDITORIAL ADVISORS

E. Allan Farnsworth
Alfred McCormack Professor of Law
Columbia University

Geoffrey C. Hazard, Jr.
Trustee Professor of Law
University of Pennsylvania

Bernard Wolfman
Fessenden Professor of Law
Harvard University

PRODUCTS LIABILITY
Problems and Process
Fifth Edition

James A. Henderson, Jr.
Frank B. Ingersoll Professor of Law
Cornell Law School

Aaron D. Twerski
Newell DeValpine Professor of Law
Brooklyn Law School

1185 Avenue of the Americas, New York, NY 10036
www.aspenpublishers.com

© 2004 James A. Henderson, Jr. and Aaron D. Twerski

All rights reserved. No part of this publication may be reproduced or transmitted in any form or by any means, electronic or mechanical, including photocopy, recording, or any information storage and retrieval system, without permission in writing from the publisher. Requests for permission to make copies of any part of this publication should be mailed to:

Permissions
Aspen Publishers
1185 Avenue of the Americas
New York, NY 10036

Printed in the United States of America.

1 2 3 4 5 6 7 8 9 0

ISBN 0-7355-4031-4

Library of Congress Cataloging-in-Publication Data

Henderson, James A., 1938–
    Products liability : problems and process / James A. Henderson, Jr., Aaron D. Twerski—
5th ed.
        p. cm.
    Includes index.
    ISBN 0-7355-4031-4
        1. Products liability—United States—Cases.   I. Twerski, Aaron D.   II. Title.

KF1296.A7H43   2004
346.7303′8—dc22   2003063656

About Aspen Publishers

Aspen Publishers, headquartered in New York City, is a leading information provider for attorneys, business professionals, and law students. Written by preeminent authorities, our products consist of analytical and practical information covering both U.S. and international topics. We publish in the full range of formats, including updated manuals, books, periodicals, CDs, and online products.

Our proprietary content is complemented by 2,500 legal databases, containing over 11 million documents, available through our Loislaw division. Aspen Publishers also offers a wide range of topical legal and business databases linked to Loislaw's primary material. Our mission is to provide accurate, timely, and authoritative content in easily accessible formats, supported by unmatched customer care.

To order any Aspen Publishers title, go to *www.aspenpublishers.com* or call 1-800-638-8437.

To reinstate your manual update service, call 1-800-638-8437.

For more information on Loislaw products, go to *www.loislaw.com* or call 1-800-364-2512.

For Customer Care issues, e-mail *CustomerCare@aspenpublishers.com*; call 1-800-234-1660; or fax 1-800-901-9075.

Aspen Publishers
A Wolters Kluwer Company

To Marcie and Kreindel

Summary of Contents

Contents		xi
Preface to the Fifth Edition		xxi
Acknowledgments		xxiii

PART I
Liability for Manufacturing Defects — 1

Chapter One	Manufacturers' Strict Liability for Defect-Caused Harm	3
Chapter Two	Assigning Responsibility Inside and Outside the Commercial Chain of Distribution	67
Chapter Three	Causation	117

PART II
Liability for Generic Product Risks — 159

Chapter Four	Liability for Defective Design	161
Chapter Five	Liability for Failure to Warn	315
Chapter Six	Express Warranty and Misrepresentation	397
Chapter Seven	Federal Preemption	423
Chapter Eight	Affirmative Defenses	453

PART III
Special Problem Areas — 503

Chapter Nine	Special Products and Product Markets	505
Chapter Ten	Special Elements of the Plaintiff's Recovery	577

PART IV
Institutional Perspectives — 649

Chapter Eleven	Special Features Reflecting the Fact That Most Products Defendants Are Corporations	651
Chapter Twelve	Adjusting the Liability System to the Demands of a National Economy	677
Chapter Thirteen	International Perspectives on Products Liability	699

Table of Cases	721
Table of Statutes and Other Authorities	733
Index	739

Contents

Preface to the Fifth Edition	xxi
Acknowledgments	xxiii

PART I
Liability for Manufacturing Defects — 1

CHAPTER ONE   Manufacturers' Strict Liability for Defect-Caused Harm — 3

A. The Role of Negligence in the Formative Period	4
1. Negligence from First-Year Torts	4
2. The Fall of the Privity Rule	6
3. The Rise of Res Ipsa Loquitur	8
Escola v. Coca Cola Bottling Co.	9
Authors' Dialogue 1	13
B. The Modern Rule of Strict Liability in Tort	14
1. Implied Warranty as a Bridge to Strict Liability in the 1950s and Early 1960s	14
Greenman v. Yuba Power Products, Inc.	16
2. Adoption of §402A of the Restatement (Second) of Torts in 1965	19
Pulley v. Pacific Coca-Cola Bottling Co.	21
Practical Implications: What Does Strict Liability Actually Accomplish?	23
Problem One	24
3. Policy Objectives Supporting Strict Liability in Tort	25
James A. Henderson, Jr., Coping with the Time Dimension in Products Liability	26
Problem Two	28
4. Why Strict Liability for Manufacturing Defects Is Workable	30
James A. Henderson, Jr., Why Negligence Dominates Tort	30
C. Defect as the Linchpin of Strict Products Liability	33
1. What Makes a Product Defective? (The Conceptual Dimension)	33
Cronin v. J. B. E. Olson Corp.	33
Problem Three	38
2. How Does the Plaintiff Prove Original Defect? (The Practical Dimension)	39
Speller v. Sears, Roebuck & Co.	41
Problem Four	44

D.	The Boundaries of Strict Products Liability		45
	1. What Are (and What Are Not) Products?		45
		Winter v. G. P. Putnam's Sons	*49*
		Problem Five	53
		Postscript on Blood and Other Human Tissue	53
	2. Which Commercial Activities Constitute "Selling or Otherwise Distributing"?		55
		Magrine v. Krasnica	*59*
	3. When Is a Product Seller or Other Distributor "In the Business of Selling or Distributing"?		64
		Authors' Dialogue 2	65

CHAPTER TWO Assigning Responsibility Inside and Outside the Commercial Chain of Distribution 67

A.	Allocating Responsibility Between Product Distributors and Other Defendants and Among Members of the Distributive Chain		67
	1. Joint and Several Liability		67
	2. Letting Retailers and Wholesalers Out of the Litigation		70
		Authors' Dialogue 3	72
		Problem Six	74
	3. Contribution Among Members of the Distributive Chain		74
	4. Indemnity Rights up the Distributive Chain		76
	5. Settlement and Release Between the Plaintiff and Members of the Distributive Chain		78
B.	Assigning Responsibility Collectively to the Distributive Chain		80
	1. Holding Members of the Distributive Chain Liable Collectively in the Normal Course of Events		81
	2. Special Circumstances that May Justify a More Aggressive Approach to Shifting Responsibility to the Entire Chain		82
		Anderson v. Somberg	*82*
		Problem Seven	88
		Charles W. Wolfram, Modern Legal Ethics	93
C.	Assigning Responsibility for Product-Related Workplace Accidents		95
	1. Direct Attack by the Employee Against the Employer		95
		a. The Worker Compensation Bar to Employer Tort Liability	95
		b. The Intentional Tort Exception to the Worker Compensation Bar	95
		Laidlow v. Hariton Machinery Co., Inc.	*99*
		c. The Dual Capacity Doctrine	107
	2. Allocating Responsibility Between the Employer (the Worker Compensation System) and the Product Manufacturer (the Products Liability System)		109
		Kotecki v. Cyclops Welding Corp.	*109*
		Authors' Dialogue 4	114

CHAPTER THREE Causation	117
A. Did the Product Actually Cause the Plaintiff's Harm?	118
1. But-For Causation in General	118
2. Special Problems of Proof: Reliance on Experts	119
Rider v. Sandoz Pharmaceutical Corp.	*123*
Authors' Dialogue 5	128
Problem Eight	130
B. Did the Defendant Supply the Product?	131
1. Defendant Identification in General	131
2. Creative Attempts to Solve a Unique Problem: Market Share	131
Problem Nine	136
C. Did the Defect in the Defendant's Product Contribute to Harming the Plaintiff?	137
1. All-or-Nothing Causation	137
Midwestern V.W. Corp. v. Ringley	*137*
Problem Ten	139
Authors' Dialogue 6	140
2. Enhanced Injury	140
Lahocki v. Contee Sand & Gravel Co., Inc.	*140*
Authors' Dialogue 7	146
3. Loss-of-a-Chance	147
Problem Eleven	148
D. Did the Defective Product Proximately Cause the Plaintiff's Harm?	149
Union Pump Co. v. Allbritton	*149*
Authors' Dialogue 8	153
Problem Twelve	157

PART II
Liability for Generic Product Risks   159

CHAPTER FOUR Liability for Defective Design	161
A. Do We Need Judicial Review of Product Designs?	163
B. Do We Need the Defect Requirement? What About Broad Enterprise Liability?	164
James A. Henderson, Jr., Why Negligence Dominates Tort	165
C. Do We Need an External Standard to Determine Design Defect? Inferring Defect from Product Malfunction	167
D. Risk-Utility Standards for Determining Design Defect	169
1. The Reasonable Alternative Design Standard for Determining Design Defect	169
a. Defining the Standard for Determining Design Defect	172
Smith v. Louisville Ladder Co.	*172*
Problem Thirteen	181
Authors' Dialogue 9	182
Problem Fourteen	182

	b. From Which Perspective Should the Product Be Judged? Time of Sale or Time of Trial?	184
	(1) Manufacturers' Responsibility for Post-Sale Increases in Knowledge of Risk	186
	(2) Manufacturers' Responsibility for Post-Sale Improvements in Risk-Avoidance Techniques	187
	(a) State of the Art as a Defense	187
	Boatland of Houston, Inc. v. Bailey	*188*
	(b) Subsequent Remedial Measures	195
	(3) Manufacturers' Responsibility for Post-Sale Shifts in Public Attitudes Toward Risk	199
	c. Should Reasonable Alternative Design Claims Be Submitted to Juries on Both Negligence and Strict Liability Grounds?	201
	Lecy v. Bayliner Marine Corporation	*201*
	d. Can a Warning Substitute for a Reasonable Alternative Design?	206
	Uniroyal Goodrich Tire Company v. Martinez	*206*
	2. Risk-Utility Balancing Without Requiring a Reasonable Alternative Design	213
	Vautour v. Body Masters Sports Industries, Inc.	*213*
	3. Product Category Liability	218
	O'Brien v. Muskin Corp.	*219*
	James A. Henderson, Jr. & Aaron D. Twerski, Closing the American Products Liability Frontier: The Rejection of Liability Without Defect	227
	Ellen Wertheimer, The Smoke Gets in Their Eyes: Product Category Liability and Alternative Feasible Designs in the Third Restatement	230
	Carl T. Bogus, War on the Common Law: The Struggle at the Center of Products Liability	233
	Dawson v. Chrysler Corp.	*234*
	Authors' Dialogue 10	240
E.	The Consumer Expectations Standard for Determining Design Defect	243
	1. Consumer Expectations as a Sword to Impose Liability	244
	Heaton v. Ford Motor Co.	*244*
	Potter v. Chicago Pneumatic Tool Company	*248*
	Problem Fifteen	255
	The Uniform Commercial Code and the Consumer Expectations Test	256
	2. Consumer Expectations as a Shield Against Liability	259
	Halliday v. Strum, Ruger & Co., Inc.	*259*
	Authors' Dialogue 11	266
F.	The Two-Prong Standard for Determining Design Defect	269
	Soule v. General Motors Corporation	*269*
	Authors' Dialogue 12	279
	Problem Sixteen	280
G.	Idiosyncratic Standards for Determining Design Defect	280
H.	Special Duty Problems in Design Litigation	282
	1. Whether and to What Extent Should Courts Defer to Markets?	282

	Linegar v. Armour of America, Inc.	282
	Scarangella v. Thomas Built Buses, Inc.	285
2.	Whether and to What Extent Should Courts Defer to Safety Statutes or Administrative Regulations?	290
	Authors' Dialogue 13	292
3.	Beyond the Pale: High Profile No-Duty Cases	294
	Hamilton v. Beretta U.S.A. Corp.	295
	In re September 11 Litigation	300
I.	Relying on Expert Testimony to Prove Design Defect: *Daubert* Revisited	304
J.	Special Problems of Misuse, Alteration, and Modification	305
	Morguson v. 3M Co.	307

CHAPTER FIVE — Liability for Failure to Warn — 315

A.	The Basic Duty to Warn at Time of Sale	316
1.	The General Rule	316
2.	No Duty to Warn of Obvious, Generally Known Risks	318
	Jamieson v. Woodward & Lothrop	319
	Problem Seventeen	327
	To Speak or Not to Speak; Or, "Digging Your Own Grave with the Best of Intentions"	328
	Problem Eighteen	329
3.	No Duty to Warn of Unknowable Risks	329
	Anderson v. Owens-Corning Fiberglas Corp.	329
	Liability Insurance and Long-Tail, Unknowable Risks	337
	Olson v. Prosoco, Inc.	338
4.	Informed Choice Warnings	340
	Problem Nineteen	342
	Liriano v. Hobart Corp.	343
	Authors' Dialogue 14	348
B.	Who Must Warn Whom?	349
	Persons v. Salomon North America, Inc.	349
C.	The Sufficiency of the Defendant's Warning	355
	Tesmer v. Rich Ladder Co.	355
	Problem Twenty	359
	Lewis v. Sea Ray Boats, Inc.	361
	James A. Henderson, Jr. & Aaron D. Twerski, Doctrinal Collapse in Products Liability: The Empty Shell of Failure to Warn	365
	Broussard v. Continental Oil Co.	368
D.	Post-Sale Warnings	372
	Lovick v. Wil-Rich	373
E.	Special Problems with Proximate Cause	379
1.	Would the Plaintiff Have Heeded an Adequate Warning?	379
	Golonka v. General Motors Corp.	382

	2. When the Defendant's Failure to Warn Causes Plaintiff to Suffer Harm from Another Product		387
	Powell v. Standard Brands Paint Co.		*387*
	Authors' Dialogue 15		388
	3. Did the Plaintiff Suffer the Sort of Harm that an Adequate Warning Would Have Aimed at Preventing?		392
	Problem Twenty-One		392
F.	Other Forms of Defective Marketing		393

CHAPTER SIX   Express Warranty and Misrepresentation   397

A. Express Warranty		397
1. What Is Warranted		397
Baxter v. Ford Motor Co.		*398*
Problem Twenty-Two		400
2. Basis of the Bargain—The Reliance Controversy		401
Cipollone v. Liggett Group, Inc.		*401*
Yarusso v. International Sport Marketing, Inc.		*408*
Note: The Implied Warranty of Fitness for Particular Purpose		412
B. Misrepresentation		413
Crocker v. Winthrop Laboratories		*415*
Authors' Dialogue 16		421
Note: Representations as the Mood Music for Determining Product Defect Under Existing Law		422

CHAPTER SEVEN   Federal Preemption   423

A. Federal Preemption of Warning Claims		424
Cipollone v. Liggett Group, Inc.		*425*
Note: Drugs and Pesticides: Preemption or Not?		435
Authors' Dialogue 17		436
B. Federal Preemption of Design Defect Claims		437
Geier v. American Honda Motor Company, Inc.		*439*

CHAPTER EIGHT   Affirmative Defenses   453

A. Conduct-Based Defenses		453
1. Background Principles		453
a. Introduction		453
b. Contributory Negligence		454
c. Comparative Fault		455
(1) Multiple Defendants		456
(a) Unit Rule		456
(b) Modified Unit Rule		456
(c) Individual Rule		457

	(2) Assumption of the Risk and Last Clear Chance	457
	(3) Superseding Cause	457
	Barry v. Quality Steel Products, Inc., et al.	457
2.	Application of Comparative Fault in Products Liability	462
	a. Can Fault and Defect Be Compared?	463
	(1) Manufacturing Defects: Comparing Apples and Oranges	463
	(2) Generic Defects: Comparing Fault Under Risk-Utility Balancing	464
	b. Should Fault and Defect Be Compared?	464
	(1) Are Products Liability Cases Different?	464
	Webb v. Navistar Int'l 1994 Transportation Corp.	464
	Social Control of Product-Related Accidents: The Seat Belt Defense and Governmental Control of Drivers' Behavior	476
	(2) The Crashworthiness Imbroglio: Should Fault Be Compared with Enhanced Injury?	477
	D'Amario v. Ford Motor Company	477
	(3) Should Plaintiff's Fault Be Compared with Defendant's Breach of Express Warranty?	483
	(4) No Duty/Primary Assumption of Risk: Reintroducing Plaintiff's Conduct as a Total Bar	484
	Andren v. White-Rodgers Co.	485
	Problem Twenty-Three	488
B. Non-Conduct-Based Defenses		489
1.	Time-Based Defenses	489
	a. Open-Ended Time Bars	489
	Authors' Dialogue 18	490
	(1) Knowledge of Injury as a Trigger	491
	(2) Knowledge of the Causal Connection Between the Injury and the Product as a Trigger	492
	(3) Knowledge of the Defendant's Identity as a Trigger	493
	b. Fixed-Period Time Bars	494
	Problem Twenty-Four	495
	Note: Constitutionality of Statutes of Repose	496
2.	Contract-Based Defenses	498
3.	Worker Compensation Barriers	498
4.	Governmental Immunity	498
5.	Government Contractor Defense	499

PART III
Special Problem Areas   503

CHAPTER NINE   Special Products and Product Markets   505

A.	Component Parts and Raw Materials	505
	Zaza v. Marquess & Nell, Inc.	505
	Authors' Dialogue 19	513

	B.	Prescription Drugs and Medical Devices	514
		1. Liability Based on Failure to Warn	514
		a. Warning the Health Care Provider	514
		Sterling Drug, Inc. v. Yarrow	*516*
		b. Warning the Patient Directly	522
		Perez v. Wyeth Laboratories Inc.	*524*
		2. Liability for Defective Drug Designs	534
		Brown v. Superior Court (Abbott Laboratories)	*534*
		Authors' Dialogue 20	535
		James A. Henderson, Jr. & Aaron D. Twerski, Drug Designs *Are* Different	544
		George W. Conk, The True Test: Alternative Safer Designs for Drugs and Medical Devices in a Patent-Constrained Market	550
		3. Pharmacists' Liability for Prescription Products	553
	C.	Used Products	556
		1. The Tort Rules Governing Liability	556
		Crandell v. Larkin and Jones Appliance Co.	*556*
		Note: Tort and Contract—Something Old, Something New	559
		2. The Role of Disclaimers in Determining Liability for Used Products	561
		Problem Twenty-Five	566
		Authors' Dialogue 21	567
	D.	Food, Nonprescription Drugs, and Cosmetics	568
		1. Food Products	568
		2. Nonprescription Drugs and Cosmetics	572

CHAPTER TEN   Special Elements of the Plaintiff's Recovery   577

A.	Recovery of Compensatory Damages	577
	1. Limitations on Noneconomic Damage Awards	577
	2. Modifications of the Collateral Source Rule	578
	3. Reforms Allowing Periodic Payment of Damages	579
B.	Recovery for Pure Emotional Upset	579
	Kennedy v. McKesson Co.	*581*
C.	Recovery for Pure Economic Loss	586
	East River Steamship Corp. v. Transamerica Delaval, Inc.	*587*
	Jimenez v. The Superior Court	*595*
	Problem Twenty-Six	603
	C. Wolfram, Modern Legal Ethics	604
D.	Special Problems in Toxic Torts Litigation	605
	1. Increased Risk of Future Injury	605
	Mauro v. Raymark Industries, Inc.	*606*
	2. Recovery for Emotional Upset	610
	Metro-North Commuter R.R. Co. v. Buckley	*610*
	3. Medical Monitoring	616
	Bower v. Westinghouse Elec. Corp.	*617*
	Authors' Dialogue 22	626

E.	Recovery of Punitive Damages	627
	1. Standard Limitations Imposed by the States	627
	Wangen v. Ford Motor Co.	*627*
	2. Federal Constitutional Control of Punitive Damages	636
	State Farm Mutual Automobile Ins. Co. v. Campbell	*636*
	Authors' Dialogue 23	646

PART IV
Institutional Perspectives — 649

CHAPTER ELEVEN   Special Features Reflecting the Fact That Most Products Defendants Are Corporations — 651

A. The General Rule of Limited Shareholder Liability (and Exceptions Thereto) — 651
   Nelson v. International Paint Co., Inc. — *654*
   Problem Twenty-Seven — 661
B. A Special Extension of Liability: Successor Corporations — 668
   Martin v. Abbott Laboratories — *668*

CHAPTER TWELVE   Adjusting the Liability System to the Demands of a National Economy — 677

A. The Patchwork Quilt of Existing State Law — 677
B. Uniform Laws Approach — 679
C. The New Restatement (Third) of Torts: Products Liability — 681
D. Federal Legislative Solutions — 681
  1. Substantive Law Reform — 681
  2. Insurance Availability: The Risk Retention Act — 682
E. Are Judicial Solutions Viable? — 682
  1. Federal Common Law — 683
     In re "Agent Orange" Product Liability Litigation — *683*
  2. Federal Preemption of State Law — 689
  3. National Management of Mass Tort Litigation — 689
F. Areas of Special Federal Competence — 691
  1. The Federal Bankruptcy System — 691
     Note, The Manville Bankruptcy: Treating Mass Tort Claims in Chapter 11 Proceedings — 692
  2. Admiralty — 696

CHAPTER THIRTEEN   International Perspectives on Products Liability — 699

A. Foreign Products Liability Law — 699
   Gary T. Schwartz, Product Liability and Medical Malpractice in Comparative Context, in The Liability Maze — 699

Hideyuki Kobayashi & Yoshimasa Furuta, Products Liability
Act and Transnational Litigation in Japan 707
B. Does the American Liability System Put American Firms at a
Competitive Disadvantage? 713
1. Effects of the American Liability System on Costs and Prices
of American Products 713
2. Effects of the American Products Liability System on Product
Innovation 717

Table of Cases 721
Table of Statutes and Other Authorities 733
Index 739

Preface to the Fifth Edition

This edition of the casebook represents a substantial revision from earlier editions. Frankly, we found ourselves reorganizing the syllabus over the past two years to reflect a sequencing of the materials that was both more economical to the student and intellectually more sound. It became clear to us that as painful and as difficult as it was to abandon a familiar structure and reorganize this edition we simply had to do it.

Substantively we have sharpened the debate regarding the appropriate test for design defect. We include cases that agree and disagree with the position of the Restatement (Third) of Torts: Products Liability that, in order to establish a prima facie case, one must prove the availability of reasonable alternative design. Furthermore, we are now encountering cases in which courts that adopt various of the Restatement sections disagree as to how they are to be applied to a given fact pattern. As the co-reporters for the Products Liability Restatement we follow the debates with regard to the Restatement with great interest. It will not surprise you to learn that we believe that we got it right. Indeed, members of the plaintiffs' bar who were critical of some of the positions that we took in the Restatement are finding that some of the so-called pro-plaintiff theories they advocated have a decidedly wicked pro-defendant aspect to them. This edition includes cases that reflect the double-edged sword of these supposedly pro-plaintiff theories of liability.

The Restatement test for drug design defect liability has been criticized by some commentators and courts. We have set forth the criticism and our response to them. We have mounted a spirited defense of our position. The student will have to decide who has the better of it.

We have also separated out for discussion the cutting-edge issues attendant to toxic tort litigation. Issues such as liability for increased risk, mental distress absent physical manifestation of injury, and medical monitoring have taken center stage and must be understood by all who seek expertise in the field of products liability.

Finally, if we have not communicated to the student our passion and love for this field of law, we will have failed. More than anything we hope that you like learning from this book. Enjoy. Enjoy.

James A. Henderson, Jr.
Aaron D. Twerski

February 2004

Acknowledgments

The authors wish to thank Jylanda Diles, at Cornell, and Rose Patti, at Brooklyn, who helped to prepare the manuscript. We could not have seen this through without them.

Research assistants provided invaluable help in assembling these materials. John Baumann (Cornell '86), Jay Bohn (Cornell '88), and Grace Lee (Brooklyn '87) helped us on the first edition. On the second edition, Ron Jenkins and David Ludwick (Cornell '93), Claire Kelly (Brooklyn '93), and Marni Schlissel (Brooklyn '92) provided invaluable assistance. On the third edition, Jordan Anger (Cornell '98), Hanna Liebman (Brooklyn '98), Allison Sealove (Brooklyn '97), and Victoria Ostrovsky (Brooklyn '97) were all of great help to us. On the fourth edition, Thomas Ciarlone (Cornell '01), Jesse Eggert (Cornell '01), Debbie Sternberg Tyler (Brooklyn '00), Kim Houghton (Brooklyn '01), and Michael Heydrich (Brooklyn '00) helped us meet very tight deadlines. On the fifth edition, Mason Barney (Brooklyn '05), Erez Davy (Brooklyn '05), Jennifer Lee (Brooklyn '05), Daniel London (Brooklyn '05), Carl Berry (Cornell '05), and Katharine Burns (Cornell '05) helped us to complete a very substantial revision of these materials. We are grateful to them for their contributions.

Deans John Siliciano at Cornell and Joan Wexler at Brooklyn also deserve thanks for their generous support.

We would like to thank the authors and publishers of the following works for permitting us to include excerpts from these works:

American Bar Association, Model Rule of Professional Conduct, Rule 3.3 Candor Toward the Tribunal (1983). Model Code of Professional Responsibility, Disciplinary Rule 7-102, Representing a Client Within the Bounds of the Law (1980). Copyright © 1983 by the American Bar Association. Reprinted by permission of the American Bar Association. Copies of the ABA Model Rules of Professional Conduct and the ABA Model Code of Professional Responsibility are available from the Service Center, American Bar Association, 750 North Lake Shore Drive, Chicago, IL 60611, (800) 285-2221.

American Law Institute, Restatement of Torts (Second), §310, §311, §402A, and Comments *f, i, k,* and *n*; §402B and Comment *b*; §520. Copyright © 1965, 1977 by The American Law Institute. Reprinted with permission.

American Law Institute, Restatement of Torts (Third): Products Liability, §1, §2, and Comments *c, d, e, f, g, I, j, k, m,* and *n*; §3 and Comments *b, c,* and *d*; §4 and Comments *a, b, d,* and *e*; §5, §6, and Comments *b, d, h,* and *f*; §7 and Comments *a* and *b*; §8, §9, and Comments *a* and *b*; §10 and Comments *a* and *j*; §15, §16, §17, §18, §19, §20, §21, and Comment *e*. Copyright © 1998 by The American Law Institute. Reprinted with permission.

American Law Institute, Restatement of Torts (Third): Apportionment of Liability §22, §23. Reporters Note to §7, §32, §33. Copyright © 2000 by The American Law Institute. Reprinted with permission. U.C.C. §2-302 and Comment *1*; §2-313 and Comments *3* and *8*; §2-316 and Comment *1*; §2-719 and Comment *3*; §2-725. Copyright © 1995 by the American Law Institute and the National Conference of Commissioners on Uniform State Laws. Proposed Amendments to Article 2, §2-313A and Preliminary Official Comment *1*; §2-313B and Preliminary Official Comments *1* and *3*. Copyright © 2001 by the American Law Institute and the National Conference of Commissioners on Uniform States Laws. Reprinted with permission.

Bogus, C., War on the Common Law: The Struggle at the Center of Products Liability, 60 Mo. L. Rev. 1, 30-34. Copyright © 1995 by the Curators of the University of Missouri. Reprinted with permission.

Casenote, Successor Liability in Washington, 6 U. Puget Sound L. Rev. 323, 313-333. Copyright © 1983 by University of Puget Sound School of Law. Reprinted with permission.

Comparative Negligence: Law and Practice §19.10[6]. Copyright © by Matthew Bender & Co., Inc. Reprinted by permission of Comparative Negligence: Law and Practice.

Conk, G., The True Test: Alternative Safer Designs for Drugs and Medical Devices in a Patent-Constrained Market, 49 UCLA L. Rev. 737, 738-739, 756-758, 783-784, 787-788. Copyright © 2002 by the Regents of the University of California. Reprinted by permission of the Regents of the University of California.

Davis, M., Design Defect Liability: In Search of a Standard of Responsibility, 39 Wayne L. Rev. 1217, 1236-1237 (1993). Reprinted by permission.

Hansmann & Kraakman, Toward Unlimited Shareholder Liability for Corporate Torts. Copyright © 1991 by the Yale Law Journal. Reprinted by permission of the authors, the Yale Law Journal Company, Inc., and the Fred B. Rothman Company from the Yale Law Journal, vol. 100, pages 1879-1934.

Henderson, Why Negligence Dominates Tort, 50 UCLA L. Rev. 377, 390-400. Copyright © 2002 by the Regents of the University of California. Reprinted by permission of the Regents of the University of California.

———, Coping with the Time Dimension in Products Liability. Copyright © 1981 by the California Law Review. Reprinted from California Law Review, vol. 69, No. 4, 919, 931-939 by permission of the Review.

———, Judicial Review of Manufacturers' Conscious Design Choices: The Limits of Adjudication. Copyright © 1973 by The Directors of Columbia Law Review Association, Inc. All rights reserved. This Article originally appeared at 73 Colum. L. Rev. 1531, 1534-1536, 1538-1542, 1552, 1558, 1578 (1973). Reprinted by permission.

Henderson & Twerski, Drug Designs *Are* Different. Copyright © 2001 by The Yale Law Journal Company, Inc. Reprinted by permission of the authors, The Yale Law Journal Company, and Fred B. Rothman & Company from The Yale Law Journal, vol. 111, No. 1, pages 151-153, 155-157-159, 162-164, 168-169, 171-172, 180-181.

———, Closing the American Products Liability Frontier: The Rejection of Liability Without Defect, 66 N.Y.U. L. Rev. 1263, 1298-1300, 1305-1306, 1316-1318. Copyright © 1991 by the New York University Law Review. Reprinted by permission of the New York University Law Review.

———, Doctrinal Collapse in Products Liability: The Empty Shell of Failure to Warn, 65 N.Y.U. L. Rev. 265, 292-294. Copyright © 1990 by the New York University Law Review. Reprinted by permission of the New York University Law Review.

Huber, P., Liability: The Legal Revolution and Its Consequences, pp.1-2, 157. Copyright © 1988 by Peter Huber. Reprinted by permission.

Keeton, P., Products Liability — Design Hazards and the Meaning of Defect. Reprinted by permission of the author and the Cumberland Law Review from the Cumberland Law Review, vol. 10, No. 2, p.310. Copyright © 1979 by the Cumberland Law Review. This article was originally published at 10 Cumb. L. Rev. 293 (1979) and is reprinted with permission.

Kobayashi & Furuta, Products Liability Act and Transnational Litigation in Japan, 34 Tex. Int'l Law J. 93, 94-101. Copyright © 1999 by University of Texas at Austin School of Law Publications, Inc. Reprinted by permission.

Kraakman, Corporate Liability Strategies and the Costs of Legal Controls. Copyright © 1984 by The Yale Law Journal Company, Inc. Reprinted by permission of the author, The Yale Law Journal Company, Inc., and Fred B. Rothman & Company from the Yale Law Journal, vol. 93, pages 857, 897.

Kysar, D., The Design of Products Liability: A Reply to Professors Henderson and Twerski. Copyright © 1981 by The Directors of the Columbia Law Review Association, Inc. All rights reserved. This Article originally appeared at 103 Colum. L. Rev. 1700, 1763-1764, 1767, 1773-1774. Reprinted by permission.

Litan, R., The Liability Explosion and American Trade Performance: Myths and Realities, in Tort Law and the Public Interest: Competition, Innovation and Consumer Welfare, pp.130, 140 (Schuck, P., ed.). Copyright © 1991 by The American Assembly. Reprinted by permission.

LoPucki, L., Virtual Judgment: A Rejoinder. Copyright © 1998 by the Yale Law Journal Company, Inc. Reprinted by permission of the author, The Yale Law Journal Company, Inc. and Fred B. Rothman & Company from the Yale Law Journal, vol. 107, No. 5, pages 1413-1434.

———, The Death of Liability. Copyright © 1996 by The Yale Law Journal Company, Inc. Reprinted by permission of the author, The Yale Law Journal Company, Inc., and Fred B. Rothman & Company from The Yale Law Journal, vol. 106, pages 23-28, 88-90.

Note, The Manville Bankruptcy: Treating Mass Tort Claims in Chapter 11 Proceedings, 96 Harv. L. Rev. 1121, 1121-1131. Copyright © 1983 by the Harvard Law Review Association. Reprinted by permission.

Posner, R., A Theory of Negligence, 1 J. Legal Stud. 29, 32. Copyright © 1972 by the University of Chicago. Reprinted with permission of the author and the publisher.

Schwartz, G., Product Liability and Medical Malpractice in Comparative Context, in Huber and Litan, The Liability Maze, 36-51, 63-67, 70-75 (Huber and Litan eds.). Copyright © 1991 by the Brookings Institution. Reprinted with permission of the author and The Brookings Institution.

Stayin, R., The U.S. Product Liability System: A Competitive Advantage to Foreign Manufacturers, 14 Can.–U.S.L.J. 193, 199, 206. Copyright © 1988 by the Canada–United States Law Journal. Reprinted by permission of the author and the Canada–United States Law Journal.

Twerski, Weinstein, Donaher, & Piehler, The Use and Abuse of Warnings in Product Liability: Design Defect Litigation Comes of Age, 61 Cornell L. Rev. 495, 526 (1976). Reprinted by permission of The Cornell Law Review.

Van Tassel, K., Adding Biotech Foods to the Torts System, The Western Massachusetts Law Tribune (2003). Reprinted with permission of the author and publisher.

Viscusi & Moore, Rationalizing the Relationship between Product Liability and Innovation, in Tort Law and the Public Interest, p.123 (Schuck, P., ed.). Copyright © 1991 by The American Assembly. Reprinted by permission.

Wertheimer, E., The Smoke Gets in Their Eyes: Product Category Liability and Alternative Feasible Designs in the Third Restatement, 61 Tenn. L. Rev. 1429. Copyright © 1994 by The Tennessee Law Review Association, Inc. Reprinted by permission of the Tennessee Law Review Association, Inc.

Wheeler, M., The Use of Criminal Statutes to Regulate Product Safety, 13 J. Legal Stud. 593, 618. Copyright © 1984 by the University of Chicago. Reprinted with permission of the author and the publisher.

White, J., Corporate Judgment Proofing: A Response to Lynn M. LoPucki's The Death of Liability. Copyright © 1998 by The Yale Law Journal Company, Inc. Reprinted by permission of the author, The Yale Law Journal Company, Inc., and Fred B. Rothman & Company from The Yale Law Journal, vol. 107, No. 5, pages 1369, 1412.

Wolfram, C., Modern Legal Ethics 594-596, 653-657. Copyright © 1986 by West Publishing Co. Reprinted with permission of the author and the West Group.

PRODUCTS LIABILITY

PART I
Liability for Manufacturing Defects

Part I serves two purposes. First, it sets forth the law governing the liability of manufacturers for harm caused by manufacturing defects (Chapter One). And second, it introduces basic subjects, such as allocation of responsibility among potential defendants (Chapter Two) and causation (Chapter Three), that cut across the entirety of American products liability. Although most of the materials in Part I involve manufacturing defects, not all of them do. Because some of the important doctrinal issues to be addressed in this part — for example, issues of causation — can best be illustrated by cases and problems involving generically defective products, some of the materials in this part involve such alternative examples of defectiveness. Consistent with our basic plan of attack, however, whenever the defectiveness issue is central to the analysis we will limit ourselves to manufacturing defects. In those instances involving generically defective products we will assume away the problems of defining "defectiveness" and focus instead on other issues of doctrine and policy concerning how courts do, and should, deal generally with questions of liability for defective products. We will wait to wrestle with the conceptual problems of generic defectiveness — defective design and failure-to-warn — until Part II.

CHAPTER ONE
Manufacturers' Strict Liability for Defect-Caused Harm

To recover for harm (personal injury and property damage) caused by a defective product, American tort law demands that at the very least plaintiff establish: (1) that the plaintiff's harm results from a product defect; and (2) that the product was defective when it left the hands of the defendant-distributor. Before the onset of the products liability revolution in the early 1960s, it was also necessary to establish that the defendant-distributor of the defective product had been negligent in either manufacturing or distributing the defective product. As we shall see shortly, courts have dispensed with the need to prove negligence in at least one significant category of products liability cases. When the plaintiff can establish a manufacturing defect such that the product unit does not conform to the manufacturer's own intended design, the plaintiff is no longer required to prove that the distributor was at fault. It is sufficient to prove that the product was defective and that the defect caused the plaintiff's harm.

In this chapter we will briefly (very briefly) review the basic principles of negligence from first year torts and then turn our attention to a problem that continues to haunt both litigants and courts in seeking to fairly adjudicate product liability claims. When products cause harm, victims often suspect that a product defect was the culprit. Let us assume that the plaintiff is correct. The product that caused the injury was indeed defective at the time of the accident. Plaintiff is only halfway home. The plaintiff must also establish that the product was defective when it left the hands of the defendant. Surely a defendant who distributed a perfectly good product that was rendered defective by someone else afterwards does not bear legal responsibility for the plaintiff's harm.

One's first impression may be that proving that the defect originated at the time of distribution is not likely to be a serious problem. There are, after all, few genies whose principal task is to introduce defects into products post-distribution. We assure you that the problem is most serious. Once the distributor lets a product out of its hands the product is at the mercy of a host of people. Consumers can be counted on to abuse and misuse products. Merchants and repairers have access to the innards of a product. Age and heavy use can take a serious toll on product integrity. As you will see, proving that a defect originated at time of sale may at times be even more difficult than proving that a product defect caused the accident.

A. THE ROLE OF NEGLIGENCE IN THE FORMATIVE PERIOD

1. Negligence from First-Year Torts

These materials assume that you have taken the basic first-year torts course and that you are generally familiar with the principles governing liability for negligent conduct. You will recall that Judge Learned Hand articulated a classic formulation of the negligence standard in United States v. Carroll Towing Co., 159 F.2d 169 (2d Cir. 1947). Judge Hand took the position that whether an actor's injury-causing conduct was negligent depended on three variables: (1) the probability that injury would result from the actor's conduct; (2) the gravity of the harm that could be expected to result should injury occur; and (3) the burden of adequate precautions to avoid or minimize injury. In one of the most famous (or infamous, depending on your philosophical weltanschauung) tort quotes, Hand suggested that his test could be reduced to algebraic terms: "If the probability be called P; the injury L [loss]; and the burden B [i.e., the burden of precaution to avoid the risk of loss]; liability depends upon whether B is less than L multiplied by P: i.e., whether $B < PL$." Id. at 173.

After *Carroll Towing,* a quarter of a century passed before Professor (now Judge) Richard Posner pointed out that the Learned Hand negligence tort formula was in lockstep with an economic test of negligence. In what has come to be recognized as a landmark article expressing the law-and-economics perspective on the subject, Posner argued that the Learned Hand formula stood for the following proposition:

> Discounting (multiplying) the cost of an accident if it occurs by the probability of occurrence yields a measure of the economic benefit to be anticipated from incurring the costs necessary to prevent the accident. The cost of prevention is what Hand meant by the burden of taking precautions against the accident. It may be the cost of installing safety equipment or otherwise making the activity safer, or the benefit forgone by curtailing or eliminating the activity. If the cost of safety measures or of curtailment — whichever cost is lower — exceeds the benefit in accident avoidance to be gained by incurring that cost, society would be better off, in economic terms, to forgo accident prevention. A rule making the enterprise liable for the accidents that occur in such cases cannot be justified on the ground that it will induce the enterprise to increase the safety of its operations. When the cost of accidents is less than the cost of prevention, a rational profit-maximizing enterprise will pay tort judgments to the accident victims rather than incur the larger cost of avoiding liability. Furthermore, overall economic value or welfare would be diminished rather than increased by incurring a higher accident-prevention cost in order to avoid a lower accident cost. If, on the other hand, the benefits in accident avoidance exceed the costs of prevention, society is better off if those costs are incurred and the accident averted, and so in this case the enterprise is made liable, in the expectation that self-interest will lead it to adopt the precautions in order to avoid a greater cost in tort judgments. [Posner, A Theory of Negligence, 1 J. Legal Stud. 29, 32 (1972).]

Implicit in the negligence concept as applied to manufacturing defects is the notion that a reasonable manufacturer would not invest unlimited resources in preventing defects, even if it were to bear all defect-related costs. Instead, a reasonable manufacturer would invest up to, but not beyond, the point at which an additional dollar invested in quality control (efforts by producers to prevent defects) returns a dollar in accident costs avoided. Beyond this point, society (including our reasonable manufacturer) is better off incurring defect-related accident costs than paying for quality control aimed at avoiding those costs. This may seem a bit heartless to some of you. If a manufacturer could eliminate even more defects, together with the accident costs those defects cause, shouldn't the manufacturer spend additional money on quality control even if the savings in accident costs prevented by further spending are less than the costs of preventing them? We defer this and related questions until we reach the section below on strict liability. For now, let us consider negligence for what it is, even if some of you harbor doubts about its ethical adequacy as a liability standard.

Some writers who agree that negligence is an appropriate liability standard have insisted that Learned Hand's approach in *Carroll Towing* rests on unrealistic assumptions about the rationality of human decisionmaking. An earlier treatment is William H. Rodgers, Jr., Negligence Reconsidered: The Role of Rationality in Tort Theory, 54 S. Cal. L. Rev. 1 (1980). On the subject of rationality in reaching reasonableness decisions, see generally Gregory C. Keating, Reasonableness and Rationality in Negligence Theory, 48 Stan. L. Rev. 311 (1996). For a comprehensive survey of the literature, reaching the conclusion that some Learned Hand critics have overstated the case against rational choice, see Jeffrey J. Rachlinski, The Uncertain Psychological Case for Paternalism, 97 Nw. L. Rev. 1165, 1168 (2003) ("[T]he primary lesson that legal scholars have taken from the cognitive rationality psychology of judgment and choice, the notion that people make systematically erroneous choices, is mistaken.") See generally Paul Slovic, *Perception of Risk,* in The Perception of Risk 220, 231 (Paul Slovic ed. 2001) ("basic conceptualization of risk is much richer than that of experts and reflects legitimate concerns that are typically omitted from expert risk assessments"). In any event, Judge Hand himself expressed doubt over the wisdom of trying to reduce the negligence concept to precise mathematical formulas. See Moisan v. Loftus, 178 F.2d 148 (2d Cir. 1949). But the basic idea that Hand tried to capture with his "B < PL" formulation has come to be recognized as an appropriate way of expressing the basis for liability for negligently caused harm. Although some judges prefer to express the negligence test in the more humanistic terms of "what a reasonable person would have done," even that formulation is consistent with the notion that reasonable persons weigh the costs of activities against their benefits in deciding upon courses of action.

From whatever perspective one measures the interests at stake in making the necessary cost-benefit trade-offs, this much is clear: If a manufacturer fails to invest in quality control at least to the point where the next incremental investment in safety would not save more than it would cost to make it — if the manufacturer fails to take all cost-effective safety measures — the manufacturer is negligent and is liable for all of the harm that its defective products cause. Concommitantly, if the manufacturer takes all cost-effective quality control measures, the injured plaintiff will not be able to point to a further safety measure that the manufacturer could have taken where "B < PL," and the manufacturer is not negligent (and thus is not liable to the injured plaintiff). This will result even if a considerable number of victims, like the plaintiff, are being harmed because of product defects. The negligence system leaves it to the victims, themselves, to insure against the defect-related accident costs that are not worth preventing. These so-called "residual accident costs" remain where they have fallen — on the accident victims and their casualty loss insurers. Thus, the only accident-related costs that reasonable manufacturers bear under a negligence regime are the costs of the quality control measures that they must take to avoid being negligent. (Defect-related accidents also hurt their reputations in the market; but the market imposes those costs, not the tort system.)

Strictly speaking, these costs of quality control are not "insurance" costs so much as they are "prevention" costs. One incurs prevention costs in trying to stop accidents from happening. In contrast, casualty loss insurance serves to spread the costs of accidents that are cheaper to incur than to prevent. Those at risk of loss transfer the risk to commercial insurers, who aggregate, or "pool," similar risks of loss, charging an appropriate premium, thereby spreading the high costs of individual losses among all the insureds in the relevant risk pool. Spreading such "primary accident costs" lowers the social dislocations, or "secondary costs," of the residual accidents that are not worth preventing. Under negligence, manufacturers engage in accident prevention and accident victims insure against the residual accident losses that are too costly for the manufacturer to prevent by the exercise of care. Of course, victims also play a secondary role in accident prevention under the rules governing contributory negligence; we will address that aspect at the end of Part I.

Why would a rational tort system adopt negligence as the basis of manufacturers' liability for manufacturing defects? Traditional notions of fairness play an important role. Certainly it is fair to impose liability on manufacturers who unreasonably expose users and consumers to risks of harm. Likewise, it is only fair, the supporters of traditional negligence will argue, that a manufacturer who does all that a reasonable person would do to prevent defects should not be held liable for accidents that it is in the best interests of society, including product users and consumers, to allow to happen. People who purchase and use products have a right to expect that manufacturers will behave reasonably. But purchasers know that some defects are unavoidable and should take that possibility into account in deciding whether to purchase and use such products. Moreover, each individual purchaser understands better than anyone else his or her own tolerance toward risk and is in the best position to know how much dislocation costs a defect-related accident will cause and thus how much casualty loss insurance coverage to obtain. Moreover, each consumer pays her own premiums for her own insurance; a rock star who wants 50 million dollars coverage should pay her own premiums, and not expect law students who buy the same products she does to help pay her insurance costs. A system of negligence-based liability, therefore, is not only fair to everyone involved but is also efficient, in that it achieves the proper levels of both accident prevention and casualty loss insurance.

We will return to reconsider the merits of this assessment when we reach the subject of strict tort liability.

2. *The Fall of the Privity Rule*

An interesting chapter in the development of negligence-based liability for defective products, now chiefly of historical interest, involved the question of whether the negligent manufacturer of a defective product could be held liable to an injured person with whom the manufacturer had not directly contracted. The question should seem odd to you. *Of course* a negligent manufacturer's responsibility extends beyond its immediate buyers. Indeed, a negligent manufacturer should be liable for all the harms that a reasonable person would have foreseen at the time of original sale of the defective product. But what seems clear to us today was not always so clear. Beginning in England in the first half of the nineteenth century, courts adopted a general rule that the negligent supplier of a defective product was liable only to those with whom he had directly dealt in the supply contract; anyone not in "privity of contract" with the supplier could not recover for the supplier's negligence no matter how directly and foreseeably his injuries were causally linked to that negligence.

This strange rule limiting a product supplier's tort liability is generally referred to as the "privity rule." By common consent, its origins are traced to the opinion of Lord Abinger, C.B., in Winterbottom v. Wright, 10 M. & W. 109 (Exch. 1842), in which the plaintiff sought to recover in negligence for injuries suffered when a horse-drawn mail coach collapsed while plaintiff was driving it. The defendant had supplied the coach in question, along with others, to the Postmaster General pursuant to a contract that called for the defendant to keep the coach in good repair. The plaintiff alleged that the defendant negligently failed to fulfill his contractual promise to keep the coach in repair, causing it to collapse and injure the plaintiff.

In granting judgment for defendant, the English court concluded that, given the absence of any contractual relationship between the defendant and the plaintiff, no recovery could be had in negligence. Refusing to permit the contract between the defendant and the Postmaster General to be turned into a tort, Lord Abinger observed:

> There is no privity of contract between [the plaintiff and the defendant]; and if the plaintiff can sue, every passenger, or even any person passing along the road, who was injured by the upsetting of the coach, might bring a similar action. Unless we confine the operation of such contracts as this to the parties who entered into them, the most absurd and outrageous consequences, as to which I can see no limit, would ensue. [10 M. & W. at 114.]

Although the privity rule in *Winterbottom* came generally to be recognized by American courts, by the end of the nineteenth century a number of exceptions were developed judicially. In an early New York case, Thomas v. Winchester, 6 N.Y. 307 (1852), falsely labeled poison was sold to a druggist, who in turn sold it to a customer. The customer, who was seriously injured due to the mislabeling, recovered damages from the defendant who had affixed the erroneous label even though the injured plaintiff had no direct privity relationship with the defendant. The defendant's negligence, the court said, "put human life in imminent danger." Once the privity barrier had been overcome for products that created "imminent danger," injured plaintiffs besieged courts with claims against remote manufacturers, contending that, indeed, their injuries were brought about by products whose danger levels were very high and thus met the threshold test for bypassing the privity rule.

The seeming arbitrariness of the privity rule, together with the conceptual confusion surrounding exceptions to the rule, finally came to an end with the decision of the New York Court of Appeals in MacPherson v. Buick Motor Co., 111 N.E. 1050 (N.Y. 1916). The case involved an allegedly defective wooden wheel on a 1911 Buick Runabout automobile that collapsed and caused an accident that injured the plaintiff. The plaintiff's negligence-based complaint against Buick was dismissed for lack of privity, whereupon the intermediate appellate court remanded for trial, holding that the privity rule did not bar plaintiff's claim. On remand, the jury found for the plaintiff on the grounds that Buick had been negligent in failing to inspect the wheel for defects and a manufacturing defect had caused the accident. The trial court entered judgment for the plaintiff. The intermediate court affirmed and Buick appealed to the Court of Appeals, New York's highest court. Judge Benjamin N. Cardozo, one of America's greatest appellate judges and the author of a number of famous opinions on the subject of tort law, wrote for the majority in affirming the judgment below:

> The defendant is a manufacturer of automobiles. It sold an automobile to a retail dealer. The retail dealer resold it to the plaintiff. While the plaintiff was in the car, it suddenly collapsed. He was thrown out and injured. One of the wheels was made of defective wood, and its spokes crumbled to fragments. . . . The wheel was not made by the defendant. It was bought from another manufacturer. There is evidence, however, that its defects could have been discovered by reasonable inspection, and that inspection was omitted. . . . [The defendant] was not at liberty to put the finished product on the market without subjecting the component parts to ordinary and simple tests. . . . We hold, then, that the principle of Thomas v. Winchester is not limited to poisons, explosives, and things of like nature, to things which in their normal operation are implements of destruction. If the nature of a thing is such that it is reasonably certain to place life and limb in peril when negligently made, it is then a thing of danger. Its nature gives warning of the consequences to be expected. If to the element of danger there is added knowledge that the thing will be used by persons other than the purchaser, and used without new tests, then, irrespective of contract, the manufacturer of this thing of danger is under a duty to make it carefully. . . . There must be knowledge of a danger, not merely possible, but probable. It is *possible* to use almost anything in a way that will make it dangerous if defective. That is not enough to charge the manufacturer with a duty independent of his contract. Whether a given thing is dangerous may be sometimes a question for the court and sometimes a question for the jury. There must also be knowledge that in the usual course of events the danger will be shared by others than the buyer. Such knowledge may often be inferred from the nature of the transaction. . . . We have put aside the notion that the duty to safeguard life and limb, when the consequences of negligence may be foreseen, grows out of contract and nothing else. We have put the source of the obligation where it ought to be. We have put its source in the law. . . . (111 N.E. at 1053).

The holding in MacPherson v. Buick eventually gained widespread acceptance and is now universally recognized. See generally W. Prosser & P. Keeton, Law of Torts 683 (5th ed. 1984); Restatement (Second) of Torts, §395, Comment *a* (1965). See generally James A. Henderson, Jr., *MacPherson v. Buick Motor Co.: Simplifying the Facts While Reshaping the Law*, in Tort Stories 41 (Robert L. Rabin & Stephen D. Sugarman eds. 2003). Today, lack of privity is not a bar to negligence-based recovery for personal injuries against suppliers of defective products. The privity doctrine does, however, retain considerable vitality in products liability cases when recovery is sought for economic harm, reflecting the fact that plaintiffs in those cases must base their claims on contract, rather than tort. We shall consider such instances in Chapter Ten, Section C, infra.

3. *The Rise of Res Ipsa Loquitur*

During the period following the fall of the privity rule, American courts increasingly relied on the doctrine of res ipsa loquitur in negligence-based manufacturing defect cases. Res ipsa loquitur ("the thing speaks for itself") allows an inference of negligence to be drawn from the occurrence of an accident involving an instrumentality (in a products liability case, the product itself) within the defendant's control under circumstances where such an accident would not ordinarily occur in the absence of negligence. See generally Fleming James, Proof of Breach in Negligence Cases, 37 Va. L. Rev. 179 (1951); W. Page Keeton, Products Liability—Proof of Manufacturer's Negligence, 49 Va. L. Rev. 675 (1963).

Thus, from the fact that a defective product failed in use and caused an accident, courts allowed triers of fact to infer that the manufacturer of the product negligently caused the defect to occur. One difficulty with res ipsa loquitur from the plaintiff's perspective was proving that the defect was present when the product left the hands of the manufacturer—that is, that the product was in the defendant's control when it became defective. Direct proof was sometimes available, but not always. In these latter instances, if the product failed immediately after first distribution, when practically new, and if the product was being used normally, the inference could be drawn that the defect originated with the manufacturer. But if the product was not new or had been subjected to rough handling after purchase, or if the plaintiff could not account for what had happened between distribution of the product and its subsequent failure in use, then the plaintiff faced more substantial difficulties.

One aspect of the res ipsa doctrine that has caused some confusion over the years is the frequently repeated statement that the accident must be an event that does not ordinarily happen if the defendant is exercising due care. Some plaintiffs have sought to prove this by demonstrating that when an actor in the same position as was the defendant exercises care, the event rarely happens—for example only once in a thousand times—whereas when actors behave negligently the event occurs only once in a hundred times. In theory, this ought not to be sufficient to reach the jury, because although the event occurs more frequently when the actor is negligent, there is no indication regarding the relative frequency with which the actor behaves negligently. If negligence only rarely is present, then in any given instance an absence of negligence may be the more likely explanation. Thus, in the words of the Oregon Supreme Court's opinion in Brannon v. Wood, 444 P.2d 558, 562 (Or. 1968) (a medical malpractice case), "[t]he test is not whether a particular injury rarely occurs, but rather, when it occurs, is it ordinarily the result of negligence." See generally David Kaye, Probability Theory Meets Res Ipsa Loquitur, 77 Mich. L. Rev. 1456 (1979).

The following well-known products liability decision by the California Supreme Court addresses these issues.

Escola v. Coca Cola Bottling Co.
150 P.2d 436 (Cal. 1944)

GIBSON, C.J.

Plaintiff, a waitress in a restaurant, was injured when a bottle of Coca Cola broke in her hand. She alleged that defendant company, which had bottled and delivered the alleged defective bottle to her employer, was negligent in selling "bottles containing said beverage which on account of excessive pressure of gas or by reason of some defect in the bottle was dangerous . . . and likely to explode." This appeal is from a judgment upon a jury verdict in favor of plaintiff. . . .

. . . [B]eing unable to show any specific acts of negligence [plaintiff] relied completely on the doctrine of res ipsa loquitur.

Defendant contends that the doctrine of res ipsa loquitur does not apply in this case, and that the evidence is insufficient to support the judgment. . . .

Res ipsa loquitur does not apply unless (1) defendant had exclusive control of the thing causing the injury and (2) the accident is of such a nature that it ordinarily would not occur in the absence of negligence by the defendant.

Many authorities state that the happening of the accident does not speak for itself where it took place some time after defendant had relinquished control of the instrumentality causing the injury. Under the more logical view, however, the doctrine may be applied upon the theory that defendant had control at the time of the alleged negligent act, although not at the time of the accident, *provided* plaintiff first proves that the condition of the instrumentality had not been changed after it left the defendant's possession. As said in Dunn v. Hoffman Beverage Co., 126 N.J.L. 556 [20 A.2d 352, 354], "defendant is not charged with the duty of showing affirmatively that something happened to the bottle after it left its control or management; . . . to get to the jury the plaintiff must show that there was due care during that period." Plaintiff must also prove that she handled the bottle carefully. The reason for this prerequisite is set forth in Prosser on Torts, supra, at page 300, where the author states:

> Allied to the condition of exclusive control in the defendant is that of absence of any action on the part of the plaintiff contributing to the accident. Its purpose, of course, is to eliminate the possibility that it was the plaintiff who was responsible. If the boiler of a locomotive explodes while the plaintiff engineer is operating it, the inference of his own negligence is at least as great as that of the defendant, and res ipsa loquitur will not apply until he has accounted for his own conduct.

It is not necessary, of course, that plaintiff eliminate every remote possibility of injury to the bottle after defendant lost control, and the requirement is satisfied if there is evidence permitting a reasonable inference that it was not accessible to extraneous harmful forces and that it was carefully handled by plaintiff or any third person who may have moved or touched it. If such evidence is presented, the question becomes one for the trier of fact and, accordingly, the issue should be submitted to the jury under proper instructions.

In the present case no instructions were requested or given on this phase of the case, although general instructions upon res ipsa loquitur were given. Defendant, however, has made no claim of error with reference thereto on this appeal.

Upon an examination of the record, the evidence appears sufficient to support a reasonable inference that the bottle here involved was not damaged by any extraneous force after delivery to the restaurant by defendant. It follows, therefore, that the bottle was in some manner defective at the time defendant relinquished control, because sound and properly prepared bottles of carbonated liquids do not ordinarily explode when carefully handled.

The next question, then, is whether plaintiff may rely upon the doctrine of res ipsa loquitur to supply an inference that defendant's negligence was responsible for the defective condition of the bottle at the time it was delivered to the restaurant. Under the general rules pertaining to the doctrine, as set forth above, it must appear that bottles of carbonated liquid are not ordinarily defective without negligence by the bottling company. . . .

An explosion such as took place here might have been caused by an excessive internal pressure in a sound bottle, by a defect in the glass of a bottle containing a safe pressure, or by a combination of these two possible causes. The question is whether under the evidence there was a probability that defendant was negligent in any of these respects. If so, the doctrine of res ipsa loquitur applies.

The bottle was admittedly charged with gas under pressure, and the charging of the bottle was within the exclusive control of defendant. As it is a matter of common knowledge that an overcharge would not ordinarily result without negligence, it follows under the doctrine of res ipsa loquitur that if the bottle was in fact excessively charged an inference of defendant's negligence would arise. If the explosion resulted from a defective bottle containing a safe pressure, the defendant would be liable if it negligently failed to discover such flaw. If the defect were visible, an inference of negligence would arise from the failure of defendant to discover it. Where defects are discoverable, it may be assumed that they will not ordinarily escape detection if a reasonable inspection is made, and if such a defect is overlooked an inference arises that a proper inspection was not made. A difficult problem is presented where the defect is unknown and consequently might have been one not discoverable by a reasonable, practicable inspection. In [an earlier] case we refused to take judicial notice of the technical practices and information available to the bottling industry for finding defects which cannot be seen. In the present case, however, we are supplied with evidence of the standard methods used for testing bottles.

A chemical engineer for the Owens-Illinois Glass Company and its Pacific Coast subsidiary, maker of Coca Cola bottles, explained how glass is manufactured and the methods used in testing and inspecting bottles. He testified that his company is the largest manufacturer of glass containers in the United States, and that it uses the standard methods for testing bottles recommended by the glass containers association. A pressure test is made by taking a sample from each mold every three hours — approximately one out of every 600 bottles — and subjecting the sample to an internal pressure of 450 pounds per square inch, which is sustained for one minute. (The normal pressure in Coca Cola bottles is less than 50 pounds per square inch.) The sample bottles are also subjected to the standard thermal shock test. The witness stated that these tests are "pretty near" infallible.

It thus appears that there is available to the industry, a commonly-used method of testing bottles for defects not apparent to the eye, which is almost infallible. Since Coca Cola bottles are subjected to these tests by the manufacturer, it is not likely that they contain defects when delivered to the bottler which are not discoverable by visual inspection. Both new and used bottles are filled and distributed by defendant. The used bottles are not again subjected to the tests referred to above, and it may be inferred that defects not discoverable by visual inspection do not develop in bottles after they are manufactured. Obviously, if such defects do occur in used bottles there is a duty upon the bottler to make appropriate tests before they are refilled, and if such tests are not commercially practicable the bottles should not be re-used. This would seem to be particularly true where a charged liquid is placed in the bottle. It follows that a defect which would make the bottle unsound could be discovered by reasonable and practicable tests.

Although it is not clear in this case whether the explosion was caused by an excessive charge or a defect in the glass, there is a sufficient showing that neither cause would ordinarily have been present if due care had been used. Further, defendant had exclusive control over both the charging and inspection of the bottles. Accordingly, all the requirements necessary to entitle plaintiff to rely on the doctrine of res ipsa loquitur to supply an inference of negligence are present.

It is true that defendant presented evidence tending to show that it exercised considerable precaution by carefully regulating and checking the pressure in the bottles and by making visual inspections for defects in the glass at several stages during the bottling process. It is well settled, however, that when a defendant produces evidence to rebut the inference of negligence which arises upon application of the doctrine of res ipsa loquitur, it is ordinarily a question of fact for the jury to determine whether the inference has been dispelled.

The judgment is affirmed.

SHENK, J., CURTIS, J., CARTER, J., and SCHAUER, J., concurred.

TRAYNOR, J.

I concur in the judgment, but I believe the manufacturer's negligence should no longer be singled out as the basis of a plaintiff's right to recover in cases like the present one. In my opinion it should now be recognized that a manufacturer incurs an absolute liability when an article that he has placed on the market, knowing that it is to be used without inspection, proves to have a defect that causes injury to human beings. MacPherson v. Buick Motor Co., 217 N.Y. 382 [111 N.E. 1050], established the principle, recognized by this court, that irrespective of privity of contract, the manufacturer is responsible for an injury caused by such an article to any person who comes in lawful contact with it.

. . . Even if there is no negligence, however, public policy demands that responsibility be fixed wherever it will most effectively reduce the hazards to life and health inherent in defective products that reach the market. It is evident that the manufacturer can anticipate some hazards and guard against the recurrence of others, as the public cannot. Those who suffer injury from defective products are unprepared to meet its consequences. The cost of an injury and the loss of time or health may be an overwhelming misfortune to the person injured, and a needless one, for the risk of injury can be insured by the manufacturer and distributed among the public as a cost of doing business. It is to the public interest to discourage the marketing of products having defects that are a menace to the public. If such products nevertheless find their way into the market it is to the public interest to place the responsibility for whatever injury they may cause upon the manufacturer, who, even if he is not negligent in the manufacture of the product, is responsible for its reaching the market. However intermittently such injuries may occur and however haphazardly they may strike, the risk of their occurrence is a constant risk and a general one. Against such a risk there should be general and constant protection and the manufacturer is best situated to afford such protection.

The injury from a defective product does not become a matter of indifference because the defect arises from causes other than the negligence of the manufacturer, such as negligence of a submanufacturer, of a component part whose defects could not be revealed by inspection or unknown causes that even by the device of res ipsa loquitur cannot be classified as negligence of the manufacturer.

authors' dialogue 1

JIM: You know, the thing that bugs me about *Escola* is how the plaintiff got away with her claim that the bottle was defective when it was delivered to the restaurant. I buy Traynor's point about applying strict liability instead of negligence. But how can he and the rest of the court practically assume away the defect issue?

AARON: I'm not sure they did that, Jim. The plaintiff introduced proof that the bottle had been handled normally, including when she retrieved it, herself, from the cooler. Why shouldn't that suffice?

JIM: It's proving a negative, Aaron. In effect, the court in *Escola* not only allows a presumption of manufacturer's negligence, but also a presumption of original defect. And *Escola* isn't the only case we've considered thus far that's done that.

AARON: What do you mean?

JIM: I wrote a "tort story" about *MacPherson*,[1] and I read the trial transcript in that case.

AARON: And?

JIM: Cardozo says in his opinion in *MacPherson* that the plaintiff was driving his nearly new Buick down the road when all of a sudden the wheel collapsed due to defective wooden spokes. He assumes a manufacturing defect and goes on to demolish the privity defense.

AARON: That makes sense to me. I assume plaintiff's experts examined the spokes and found them to be defective, and the jury bought their story. What's the problem?

JIM: The problem is that the car was more than a year old when the accident happened; had been driven safely many miles on rough country roads, hauling heavy gravestones (MacPherson was a stone carver); and had hit a telephone pole at fairly high speed when the accident happened. The odds of the wheel actually being rotten when MacPherson originally bought the car were nil.

AARON: What's your point in telling me this? It doesn't change the law in either *MacPherson* or *Escola*, does it?

JIM: No, it doesn't. Cardozo and Traynor were so bent on changing the law that they winked at the facts. But the defect issue will come back to haunt them, mark my words.

AARON: Get down of the soapbox, Jim, before it collapses under you. We'll get to the defect issue soon enough. (See Section C, infra.)

---

1. See James A. Henderson, Jr., *MacPherson v. Buick Motor Co.:* Simplifying the Facts While Reshaping the Law, Tort Stories 41 (Robert L. Rabin & Stephen D. Sugarman eds. 2003).

The inference of negligence may be dispelled by an affirmative showing of proper care. . . . An injured person, however, is not ordinarily in a position to refute such evidence or identify the cause of the defect, for he can hardly be familiar with the manufacturing process as the manufacturer himself is. In leaving it to the jury to decide whether the inference has been dispelled, regardless of the evidence against it, the negligence rule approaches the rule of strict liability. It is needlessly circuitous to make negligence the basis of recovery and impose what is in reality liability without negligence. If public policy demands that a manufacturer of goods be responsible for their quality regardless of negligence there is no reason not to fix that responsibility openly. . . .

As handicrafts have been replaced by mass production with its great markets and transportation facilities, the close relationship between the producer and consumer of a product has been altered. Manufacturing processes, frequently valuable secrets, are ordinarily either inaccessible to or beyond the ken of the general public. The consumer no longer has means or skill enough to investigate for himself the soundness of a product, even when it is not contained in a sealed package, and his erstwhile vigilance has been lulled by the steady efforts of manufacturers to build up confidence by advertising and marketing devices such as trade-marks. Consumers no longer approach products warily but accept them on faith, relying on the reputation of the manufacturer or the trade mark. Manufacturers have sought to justify that faith by increasingly high standards of inspection and a readiness to make good on defective products by way of replacements and refunds. The manufacturer's obligation to the consumer must keep pace with the changing relationship between them. . . .

B. THE MODERN RULE OF STRICT LIABILITY IN TORT

Strict products liability is liability in tort for harm caused by defective products without any necessity for the plaintiff to show negligence on the part of the defendant. Although it was many decades in the making, it finally came into American products liability law in the early 1960s. We shall consider, in Section D, the categories of commercial product suppliers to whom strict tort liability applies. In the discussions that follow we will assume that it applies to product manufacturers, wholesalers, and retailers. We shall also consider in Chapter Ten the elements of harm that may, and may not, be recovered under strict liability. For the purposes of this chapter, we will assume that the elements of harm for which plaintiffs may recover include personal injuries and property damage.

1. Implied Warranty as a Bridge to Strict Liability in the 1950s and Early 1960s

Strict products liability evolved out of two different bases of liability: negligence and implied warranty. Prior to recognition of strict products liability by American courts in the 1960s, each of these theories of liability had a "good news, bad news" quality for products plaintiffs. Thus, while the privity requirement had been eliminated in negligence cases by the 1940s, due mainly to Cardozo's opinion in MacPherson v. Buick Motor Co., discussed in Section A, supra, it remained necessary for plaintiffs to prove negligence. Res ipsa loquitur was frequently available, as in Escola v. Coca Cola Bottling Co., reprinted in the preceding Section. But even there the jury could, in any given instance, refuse to draw an inference of negligence from the mere fact of a product defect. Historically, an alternative method of recovery that required the plaintiff to establish only defect (not fault) was available. Plaintiff could bring an action for breach of the implied warranty of merchantability. Under the Uniform Sales Act and later under the U.C.C. §2-314(2)(c), accompanying every sale of goods (unless disclaimed) is a warranty that the product is "reasonably fit for the ordinary purposes for which such goods are used." Defective products satisfy the statutory definition of unmerchantability and provide a predicate for a cause of action. Very simply, the implied warranty of merchantability can be characterized as "strict liability in contract."

But along with the "good news" that accompanied Code warranties, the "bad news" was quite substantial. First, since the cause of action was contractual, the requirement that the parties to the suit be in privity with each other was a necessary requisite for standing to sue. *MacPherson,* supra, dealt the death blow to privity in causes of action based on negligence. The privity doctrine remained very much alive, however, in cases involving implied warranties. Admittedly, plaintiffs could sue immediate sellers with whom they were in privity, such as retailers, for breach of implied warranty. However, this right was often a mirage. Retail sellers were often judgment-proof. In some cases they disclaimed liability as allowed by the U.C.C. §2-316. Furthermore, the U.C.C. statute of limitations provides for a maximum of four years from tender of delivery (sale), U.C.C. §2-725. By contrast, a tort statute of limitations generally runs from the time of injury, thus in many cases providing a longer time to bring suit.

The landmark decision that stripped the implied warranty action of its contractual impediments involved an action for breach of the implied warranty of merchantability. In Henningsen v. Bloomfield Motors, Inc., 161 A.2d 69 (N.J. 1960), plaintiff brought suit for injuries sustained when a new Plymouth that her husband had purchased two weeks earlier went out of control. Mrs. Henningsen was driving when she heard a loud noise "from the bottom, by the hood." It "felt as if something cracked." The steering wheel spun in her hands; the car veered sharply to the right and crashed into a highway sign and a brick wall. The trial judge dismissed negligence counts against Chrysler, the manufacturer of the car. The judge submitted the issue of breach of implied warranty of merchantability to the jury, which found against both the retailer and the manufacturer.

The auto manufacturer, Chrysler, appealed the verdict against it on the grounds that it was not in privity with the injured plaintiff. In striking down the privity defense the court said:

> Under modern conditions the ordinary layman, on responding to the importuning of colorful advertising, has neither the opportunity nor the capacity to inspect or to determine the fitness of an automobile for use; he must rely on the manufacturer who has control of its construction, and to some degree on the dealer who, to the limited extent called for by the manufacturer's instructions, inspects and services it before delivery. In such a marketing milieu his remedies and those of persons who properly claim through him should not depend "upon the intricacies of the law of sales. The obligation of the

manufacturer should not be based alone on privity of contract. It should rest, as was once said, upon 'the demands of social justice.'"...

Accordingly, we hold that under modern marketing conditions, when a manufacturer puts a new automobile in the stream of trade and promotes its purchase by the public, an implied warranty that it is reasonably suitable for use as such accompanies it into the hands of the ultimate purchaser. Absence of agency between the manufacturer and the dealer who makes the ultimate sale is immaterial. 161 A.2d at 83-84.

We are pleased to report that either by judicial decision or through legislative enactment[2] lack of privity is no longer a viable defense in personal injury litigation. As we shall see in a later chapter, in cases involving pure economic loss the privity defense retains considerable vitality.

After clearing the way for plaintiff's recovery by eliminating privity as a requirement for suit, the *Henningsen* court went on to invalidate the disclaimer of tort liability that was part of the standard automobile contract of sale. We defer discussion of the efficacy of disclaimers to later in this book.

The *Henningsen* decision, as important as it was, sought to impose strict liability against manufacturers within the terminology framework of the Uniform Commercial Code. Only a short time elapsed before American courts recognized that the language used by the U.C.C. to talk about liability provided a clumsy tool to utilize for prosecuting personal injury cases. Only two years after *Henningsen,* the time had come to announce that strict liability was a purely tort doctrine. As fate would have it, the task of authoring the landmark opinion accomplishing this change fell to Justice Traynor, whose concurrence in *Escola* earlier had urged the replacement of res ipsa loquitur with strict liability in tort.

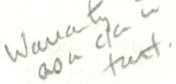

Greenman v. Yuba Power Products, Inc.
377 P.2d 897 (Cal. 1962)

TRAYNOR, J.

Plaintiff brought this action for damages against the retailer and the manufacturer of a Shopsmith, a combination power tool that could be used as a saw, drill, and wood lathe. He saw a Shopsmith demonstrated by the retailer and studied a brochure prepared by the manufacturer. He decided he wanted a Shopsmith for his home workshop, and his wife bought and gave him one for Christmas in 1955. In 1957 he bought the necessary attachments to use the Shopsmith as a lathe for turning a large piece of wood he wished to make into a chalice. After he had worked on the piece of wood several times without difficulty, it suddenly flew out of the machine and struck him on the forehead, inflicting serious injuries. About 10½ months later, he gave the retailer and the manufacturer written notice of claimed breaches of warranties and filed a complaint against them alleging such breaches and negligence.

---

2. U.C.C. §2-318 (Alternative C) provides that both express and implied warranties extend "to any person who may reasonably be expected to use, consume, or be affected by the goods and who is injured in person by breach of the warranty."

The Modern Rule of Strict Liability in Tort

After a trial before a jury, the court ruled that there was no evidence that the retailer was negligent or had breached any express warranty and that the manufacturer was not liable for the breach of any implied warranty. Accordingly, it submitted to the jury only the cause of action alleging breach of implied warranties against the retailer and the causes of action alleging negligence and breach of express warranties against the manufacturer. The jury returned a verdict for the retailer against plaintiff and for plaintiff against the manufacturer in the amount of $65,000. The trial court denied the manufacturer's motion for a new trial and entered judgment on the verdict. The manufacturer and plaintiff appeal. Plaintiff seeks a reversal of the part of the judgment in favor of the retailer, however, only in the event that the part of the judgment against the manufacturer is reversed.

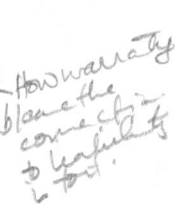

Plaintiff introduced substantial evidence that his injuries were caused by defective design and construction of the Shopsmith. His expert witnesses testified that inadequate set screws were used to hold parts of the machine together so that normal vibration caused the tailstock of the lathe to move away from the piece of wood being turned permitting it to fly out of the lathe. They also testified that there were other more positive ways of fastening the parts of the machine together, the use of which would have prevented the accident. The jury could therefore reasonably have concluded that the manufacturer negligently constructed the Shopsmith. The jury could also reasonably have concluded that statements in the manufacturer's brochure were untrue, that they constituted express warranties,[2] and that plaintiff's injuries were caused by their breach.

The manufacturer contends, however, that plaintiff did not give it notice of breach of warranty within a reasonable time and that therefore his cause of action for breach of warranty is barred by section 1769 of the Civil Code. Since it cannot be determined whether the verdict against it was based on the negligence or warranty cause of action or both, the manufacturer concludes that the error in presenting the warranty cause of action to the jury was prejudicial.

Section 1769 of the Civil Code provides:

> In the absence of express or implied agreement of the parties, acceptance of the goods by the buyer shall not discharge the seller from liability in damages or other legal remedy for breach of any promise or warranty in the contract to sell or the sale. But, if, after acceptance of the goods, the buyer fails to give notice to the seller of the breach of any promise or warranty within a reasonable time after the buyer knows, or ought to know of such breach, the seller shall not be liable therefor.

Like other provisions of the Uniform Sales Act (Civ. Code, §§1721-1800), section 1769 deals with the rights of the parties to a contract of sale or a sale. It does not provide that notice must be given of the breach of a warranty that arises independently of a contract of sale between the parties.

Such warranties are not imposed by the sales act, but are the product of

---

2. In this respect the trial court limited the jury to a consideration of two statements in the manufacturer's brochure. (1) "When Shopsmith Is in Horizontal Position — Rugged construction of frame provides rigid support from end-to-end. Heavy centerless-ground steel tubing insures perfect alignment of components." (2) "Shopsmith maintains its accuracy because every component has positive locks that hold adjustments through rough or precision work."

common-law decisions that have recognized them in a variety of situations. It is true that in many of these situations the court has invoked the sales act definitions of warranties (Civ. Code, §§1732, 1735) in defining the defendant's liability, but it has done so, not because the statutes so required, but because they provided appropriate standards for the court to adopt under the circumstances presented.

The notice requirement of section 1769, however, is not an appropriate one for the court to adopt in actions by injured consumers against manufacturers with whom they have not dealt.

> As between the immediate parties to the sale [the notice requirement] is a sound commercial rule, designed to protect the seller against unduly delayed claims for damages. As applied to personal injuries, and notice to a remote seller, it becomes a booby-trap for the unwary. The injured consumer is seldom "steeped in the business practice which justifies the rule," [James, Product Liability, 34 Texas L. Rev. 44, 192, 197] and at least until he has had legal advice it will not occur to him to give notice to one with whom he has had no dealings. (Prosser, Strict Liability to the Consumer, 69 Yale L.J. 1099, 1130, footnotes omitted.)

It is true that in [prior decisions] the court assumed that notice of breach of warranty must be given in an action by a consumer against a manufacturer. Since in those cases, however, the court did not consider the question whether a distinction exists between a warranty based on a contract between the parties and one imposed on a manufacturer not in privity with the consumer, the decisions are not authority for rejecting the rule of the [decision based on tort.] We conclude, therefore, that even if plaintiff did not give timely notice of breach of warranty to the manufacturer, his cause of action based on the representations contained in the brochure was not barred.

Moreover, to impose strict liability on the manufacturer under the circumstances of this case, it was not necessary for plaintiff to establish an express warranty as defined in section 1732 of the Civil Code. A manufacturer is strictly liable in tort when an article he places on the market, knowing that it is to be used without inspection for defects, proves to have a defect that causes injury to a human being. Recognized first in the case of unwholesome food products, such liability has now been extended to a variety of other products that create as great or greater hazards if defective.

Although in these cases strict liability has usually been based on the theory of an express or implied warranty running from the manufacturer to the plaintiff, the abandonment of the requirement of a contract between them, the recognition that the liability is not assumed by agreement but imposed by law, and the refusal to permit the manufacturer to define the scope of its own responsibility for defective products make clear that the liability is not one governed by the law of contract warranties but by the law of strict liability in tort. Accordingly, rules defining and governing warranties that were developed to meet the needs of commercial transactions cannot properly be invoked to govern the manufacturer's liability to those injured by its defective products unless those rules also serve the purposes for which such liability is imposed.

We need not recanvass the reasons for imposing strict liability on the manufacturer. They have been fully articulated in the cases cited above. The purpose of such liability is to insure that the costs of injuries resulting from defective products are borne by the manufacturers that put such products on the market rather than by the injured persons who are powerless to protect themselves. Sales warranties serve this purpose fitfully at best. (See Prosser, Strict Liability to the Consumer, 69 Yale L.J. 1099, 1124-1134.) In the present case, for example, plaintiff was able to plead and prove an express warranty only because he read and relied on the representations of the Shopsmith's ruggedness contained in the manufacturer's brochure. Implicit in the machine's presence on the market, however, was a representation that it would safely do the jobs for which it was built. Under these circumstances, it should not be controlling whether plaintiff selected the machine because of the statements in the brochure, or because of the machine's own appearance of excellence that belied the defect lurking beneath the surface, or because he merely assumed that it would safely do the jobs it was built to do. It should not be controlling whether the details of the sales from manufacturer to retailer and from retailer to plaintiff's wife were such that one or more of the implied warranties of the sales act arose. (Civ. Code §1735.) "The remedies of injured consumers ought not to be made to depend upon the intricacies of the law of sales." To establish the manufacturer's liability it was sufficient that plaintiff proved that he was injured while using the Shopsmith in a way it was intended to be used as a result of a defect in design and manufacture of which plaintiff was not aware that made the Shopsmith unsafe for its intended use.

The manufacturer contends that the trial court erred in refusing to give three instructions requested by it. It appears from the record, however, that the substance of two of the requested instructions was adequately covered by the instructions given and that the third instruction was not supported by the evidence.

The judgment is affirmed.

GIBSON, C.J., SCHAUER, J., MCCOMB, J., PETERS, J., TOBRINER, J., and PEEK, J., concurred.

2. *Adoption of §402A of the Restatement (Second) of Torts in 1965*

Rarely has a single provision of any Restatement of the law had a greater impact on courts than did the adoption in 1965 of the strict liability rule in §402A. And rarely has a single individual been so closely associated with the development of a legal doctrine as was Professor William Prosser with the development of strict products liability. In what are perhaps the two best-known law review articles on the subject, Prosser developed the reasoning leading up to, and immediately following, judicial recognition of strict privity-free liability. See William S. Prosser, The Assault upon the Citadel (Strict Liability to the Consumer), 69 Yale L.J. 1099 (1960); Prosser, The Fall of the Citadel (Strict Liability to the Consumer), 50 Minn. L. Rev. 791 (1966). Prosser was in a unique position to predict the future path of American products liability law. As Reporter for the Restatement of Torts (Second) he played a leadership role in getting the American Law Institute to include a general strict products liability provision in its restatement of tort law. Based primarily on the *Greenman* decision and designated §402A, the new rule of strict tort liability was destined to dominate, and in some instances to confuse and confound, the law of products liability to the present day.

Restatement (Second) of Torts
(1965)

§402A. SPECIAL LIABILITY OF SELLER OF PRODUCT FOR PHYSICAL HARM TO USER OR CONSUMER

(1) One who sells any product in a defective condition unreasonably dangerous to the user or consumer or to his property is subject to liability for physical harm thereby caused to the ultimate user or consumer, or to his property, if
    (a) the seller is engaged in the business of selling such a product, and
    (b) it is expected to and does reach the user or consumer without substantial change in the condition in which it is sold.

(2) The rule stated in Subsection (1) applies although
    (a) the seller has exercised all possible care in the preparation and sale of his product, and
    (b) the user or consumer has not bought the product from or entered into any contractual relation with the seller.

COMMENT:

b. History. Since the early days of the common law those engaged in the business of selling food intended for human consumption have been held to a high degree of responsibility for their products. As long ago as 1266 there were enacted special criminal statutes imposing penalties upon victualers, vintners, brewers, butchers, cooks, and other persons who supplied "corrupt" food and drink. In the earlier part of this century this ancient attitude was reflected in a series of decisions in which the courts of a number of states sought to find some method of holding the seller of food liable to the ultimate consumer even though there was no showing of negligence on the part of the seller. These decisions represented a departure from, and an exception to, the general rule that a supplier of chattels was not liable to third persons in the absence of negligence or privity of contract. In the beginning, these decisions displayed considerable ingenuity in evolving more or less fictitious theories of liability to fit the case. The various devices included an agency of the intermediate dealer or another to purchase for the consumer, or to sell for the seller; a theoretical assignment of the seller's warranty to the intermediate dealer; a third party beneficiary contract; and an implied representation that the food was fit for consumption because it was placed on the market, as well as numerous others. In later years the courts have become more or less agreed upon the theory of a "warranty" from the seller to the consumer, either "running with the goods" by analogy to a covenant running with the land, or made directly to the consumer. Other decisions have indicated that the basis is merely one of strict liability in tort, which is not dependent upon either contract or negligence.

Recent decisions, since 1950, have extended this special rule of strict liability beyond the seller of food for human consumption. The first extension was into the closely analogous cases of other products intended for intimate bodily use, where, for example, as in the case of cosmetics, the application to the body of the consumer is external rather than internal. Beginning in 1958 with a Michigan case involving cinder building blocks, a number of recent decisions have discarded any limitation to intimate association with the body, and have extended the rule of strict liability to cover the sale of any product which, if it should prove to be defective, may be expected to cause physical harm to the consumer or his property.

Pulley v. Pacific Coca-Cola Bottling Co.
415 P.2d 636 (Wash. 1966)

FINLEY, J.

Foreign matter occasionally found, or allegedly found, in bottles of CocaCola is a perpetual provoker of legal controversy. The nature of the foreign or deleterious material allegedly ingested by consumers has ranged from the expectable to the totally unpredictable. Thus, despite the investment of large sums of money, manpower, and scientific expertise, the manufacturers of this carbonated beverage apparently have as yet been unable to develop a bottling or manufacturing process which is *infallible* in terms of the purity and wholesomeness of the manufactured product. Lawsuits by consumer plaintiffs have involved such incidents as alleged swallowing of pieces of broken glass, or unconsumed portions of a bottle containing residual matter such as a rusted bottle cap and dirt. But "the pause that refreshes" has also been rudely disturbed by the asserted discovery of such bizarre objects as a dead mouse, "three dead flies and other foreign matter," and even a "dead oriental cockroach." By comparison, the cigarette allegedly involved in the instant case would seem relatively innocuous.

The plaintiff-respondents herein, husband and wife, purchased a carton of six "king-size" bottles of Coca-Cola from the defendant-appellant retailer, Lucky Stores, Inc., on the night of May 24, 1962. The respondents went home immediately and placed the six-pack carton on its side in the family refrigerator. On the following day, Mrs. Pulley removed an apparently sealed bottle from the refrigerator, uncapped it, and took a swallow. She noted that the beverage seemed to have an odd taste, but she took a second swallow. At the trial Mrs. Pulley described her reactions as follows:

> Immediately thought this tasted like, it didn't taste like coke, it tasted like tobacco or tobacco smoke, and it was bitter, and it was a little slimy.

Mrs. Pulley examined the remaining contents of the bottle. She noticed a cigarette and floating bits of loose tobacco. Immediately thereafter, she became violently ill. During the course of her ensuing three-day period of intermittent regurgitation and nausea, she unfortunately lost her dentures in the commode!

The plaintiffs subsequently brought this action against the retailer, Lucky Stores, Inc., and the bottler, Pacific Coca-Cola Bottling Co., on a [strict liability theory that did not require them to prove fault]. At the close of the plaintiff's case, the defendants made an offer of proof concerning the modern methods utilized by the defendant bottler to prevent contamination by foreign objects or material. The trial court refused to allow such testimony; whereupon, the defendant rested its case. The jury returned a verdict in favor of the plaintiffs in the amount of $2,100.00. . . .

The appellants' third assignment of error concerns the exclusion by the trial court of the appellants' proffered testimony relating to the methods utilized by appellant Pacific Coca-Cola Bottling Company in processing and bottling its product. The gravamen of appellants' theory in this respect is that the exclusion of such testimony deprives them of their only possible defense. In other words, by the very nature of food products liability cases the manufacturers and/or the retailer will generally be unable to dispute by direct eyewitness testimony the alleged presence in the food product and the ingestion of a particular object or deleterious substance. Frequently, the plaintiff will have consumed the product while alone or with members of the immediate family, and hardly ever when in the presence of strictly objective and disinterested witnesses. The appellants assert that their only possible course of action — and defense — is to impeach the credibility of the plaintiff's story by demonstrating the improbability of a foreign object escaping the assorted methods and techniques utilized to insure the wholesomeness of the finished product. Admittedly, the argument is persuasive. However, we must recall that the plaintiffs' theory of recovery is [strict liability] and not negligence. The proffered testimony as to the bottling methods employed would obviously be admissible if the question was whether or not Pacific Coca-Cola Bottling Company exercised due care in the manufacturing of its product. But the question is not whether Pacific Coca-Cola Bottling Company was negligent, but whether or not it and Lucky Stores, Inc., breached [their duty to supply] Coca-Cola [that] was fit for human consumption. . . . An assertion . . . by a consumer-plaintiff, . . . that he or she was harmed by the presence of some foreign object in food or drink, in practical effect thrusts a burden upon the defendant manufacturer and the defendant retailer to show who contaminated the particular food product — and will not permit a showing by indirect and circumstantial evidence that it was improbable or even impossible that the defendants were responsible for the presence of the harmful object.

It is thus our view, under the existing authorities, that the trial court properly excluded the proffered evidence as to the bottling methods utilized by the defendant bottling company. One cannot impeach the credibility of an opposing party's testimony by testimony collateral to the issues of the case. The proffered testimony was collateral because it was not directly refutative of the plaintiff's relation of the incident involved. The appellants made no claim as to the infallibility of their particular bottling process. They attempted to demonstrate that it was *highly improbable* that a cigarette could have found its way into a bottle of "king-size" Coca-Cola in the absence of tampering by a third party. Obviously, the appellants were unable to disprove the presence of the cigarette. The ultimate question is whose *inadvertence* or *intentional act* produced the uncontroverted contamination of the bottle of Coca-Cola. As a matter of public policy the burden of proof in this respect is placed by law upon food manufacturers and retailers and not upon the consumer. The particular evidence of the appellants was properly excluded.

The judgment of the trial court should be affirmed. . . .

[ROSELLINI, C.J., DOWORTH and WEAVER, JJ., and LANGENBACH, J., concurred.]

PRACTICAL IMPLICATIONS: WHAT DOES STRICT LIABILITY ACTUALLY ACCOMPLISH?

How much is accomplished, as a practical matter, by moving from negligence/implied warranty to strict liability? Certainly, if one focuses on the comparison between full-blown res ipsa loquitur (à la *Escola,* supra, p.9) and liberal implied warranty (à la *Henningsen,* supra) on the one hand, and strict liability, on the other, one's answer is apt to be "not much." Justice Traynor's concurrence in *Escola is* technically correct—under strict liability juries would be required, not merely allowed, to find for the plaintiff once the elements of defect-at-sale, causation, and lack of contributory fault are found. Thus, in theory, the "residual accident costs" (the costs remaining after optimal investments in accident avoidance) that were borne by victims under negligence are shifted to manufacturers under strict liability. But as Professor Prosser remarked in his seminal essay, moving the last step to strict liability probably doesn't make much practical difference in terms of outcomes in actual cases. William L. Prosser, The Assault on the Citadel (Strict Liability to the Consumer), 69 Yale L.J. 1099, 1114 (1960). Indeed, manufacturers' liability insurance rates do not appear to have risen significantly during the period in which strict products liability came to be generally recognized. Insurance rates appear only in the mid-1970s to have risen dramatically enough to be widely perceived to be a problem. See Inter-Agency Task Force on Product Liability, United States Dept. of Commerce, Final Report at VI-11 to VI-24 (1977).

So what is the big deal? Part of the answer may lie in the effects of the move to strict liability on nonmanufacturing commercial product sellers—wholesalers and retailers. Under earlier tort law, they were liable only if the plaintiff could prove negligence, often an especially difficult thing to do vis-à-vis nonmanufacturers. Of course, retailers were liable to buyer/plaintiffs for breaches of implied warranties, assuming no disclaimers. But nonbuyer plaintiffs—users and bystanders—faced the privity problem against retailers under warranty. And even buyer/plaintiffs faced the same problem against wholesalers and others further up the chain. So the movement to strict liability, which holds all commercial sellers strictly liable, presumably affected the liability exposures of middlemen in the distribution chain.

In addition, even with respect to manufacturers, adoption of strict liability would prove to have longer-run effects in connection with the availability to defendants of doctrines such as contributory negligence. How, courts would ask themselves, can that defense properly be raised in a strict liability action? The move to strict liability thus generated significant changes, over time, in the satellite doctrines and concepts that surround the underlying conceptual basis of liability. Moreover, as will be made clear in later chapters, the move to strict liability would have profound consequences as courts in the 1970s and 1980s began to address the issues of product sellers' liabilities for defective designs and improper marketing.

PROBLEM ONE

Your firm represents Hilda Brooks, age 58, in a products liability action against Zonar Manufacturing Co. Zonar manufactures surgical implants. Ms. Brooks underwent surgery on her leg about a year ago, during which her doctor implanted a surgical pin known as a Schneider intramedullary rod into her fractured bone to provide support and stabilization during the healing process. Ms. Brooks remained in a wheelchair for approximately six months after surgery and was then permitted to place partial weight on the affected leg, first while using a single crutch and later a cane. Several months after she began walking on the leg a routine X ray revealed a break in the rod, which, according to one of the doctors, had probably occurred several days earlier.

Because of the breaking of the intramedullary rod, Ms. Brooks's doctors recommended surgery to correct the situation. As it turned out the breaking of the rod led the doctors to perform two separate operations. The first operation was not wholly successful and a second surgical intervention was necessary.

The case is in the midst of trial. Plaintiff presented the testimony of two metallurgists and a mechanical engineer. The metallurgists' analyses revealed the presence of various imperfections in the rod, including a small crack about a quarter-inch from the break, pitting on the surface of the rod, and inclusions (foreign objects in the steel). Their testimony indicated that any of these imperfections could have existed at the time the rod left the manufacturer and that their presence could initiate a crack in the metal and create areas of stress concentration, weakening the metal so that fatigue failure would occur at a stage considerably below the ordinary anticipated endurance level. It was the opinion of both metallurgists that, if the rod was properly designed for implantation in the human body and not bent prior to use, the failure resulted from a defect that existed at the time of manufacture. The mechanical engineer took measurements of the rod and of plaintiff, ascertained weight distribution, and determined the stress placed upon the rod in walking and in rising from a sitting position. Given the tensile strength of the rod and its endurance limit, the rod, in his opinion, could not have fractured unless a defect existed.

Defendants' expert, qualified both in the fields of metallurgy and mechanical engineering, testified that fracture of the rod occurred as a result of fatigue failure. Her extensive research in the field of implants had shown that because maximum stress occurs at the point of non-union of the bone, fatigue failure of the implant commonly occurs at that same point. It was this witness's opinion that the computations of plaintiff's expert were inaccurate because, in determining the endurance limit of the implanted rod, consideration had not been afforded the additional stresses brought by muscle pull, which, in her experience, can surpass the stresses of bodily weight. She further testified that no defect existed in the rod; its failure, rather, resulted from the stress of a cyclic load over an extended period of time in the area of non-union of the bone.

Defendant's counsel, Robert Best, is seeking to bolster his expert's opinion by introducing the testimony of Allen Franklin, the director of quality control at Zonar. The trial judge excused the jury and heard Best's offer of proof. Best told the court that Franklin will testify that, unlike most quality control procedures that merely test random samples of the product to assure quality, Zonar submits every surgical implant to rigorous inspection which, Franklin insists, would have caught any defect.

Defendant's attempt to introduce this testimony came late this afternoon. Judge Moses decided to recess for the day and has requested both sides to brief the issue and to present her with memos in the morning.

New California has adopted strict liability in tort. It has not specifically ruled on the issue of the admissibility of quality control techniques in a strict liability case. Mr. Young, the partner who is trying the case, has asked you to prepare a memo arguing against the admissibility of Franklin's testimony. Young also wants you to anticipate Best's arguments and prepare rebuttals to them.

3. Policy Objectives Supporting Strict Liability in Tort

The place to begin the analysis is with Judge Roger Traynor's concurrence in *Escola,* supra, the exploding Coke bottle case from California decided in 1944. You will recall that Judge Traynor urged his colleagues to stop relying on res ipsa loquitur in favor of adopting strict liability in tort. It is worth setting forth his reasoning verbatim (150 P.2d 462):

> . . . Even if there is no negligence, however, public policy demands that responsibility be fixed wherever it will most effectively reduce the hazards to life and health inherent in defective products that reach the market. It is evident that the manufacturer can anticipate some hazards and guard against the recurrence of others, as the public cannot. Those who suffer injury from defective products are unprepared to meet its consequences. The cost of an injury and the loss of time or health may be an overwhelming misfortune to the person injured, and a needless one, for the risk of injury can be insured by the manufacturer and distributed among the public as a cost of doing business. It is to the public interest to discourage the marketing of products having defects that are a menace to the public. If such products nevertheless find their way into the market it is to the public interest to place the responsibility for whatever injury they may cause upon the manufacturer, who, even if he is not negligent in the manufacture of the product, is responsible for its reaching the market. However intermittently such injuries may occur and however haphazardly they may strike, the risk of their occurrence is a constant risk and a general one. Against such a risk there should be general and constant protection and the manufacturer is best situated to afford such protection.

Several aspects of Judge Traynor's analysis may seem, at least at first glance, somewhat puzzling. First, he says responsibility should be fixed wherever it will reduce the hazards inherent in defective products. But doesn't a negligence rule, properly administered, achieve that risk-reduction objective? That is, doesn't the traditional negligence rule require manufacturers to prevent all the defects that are worth preventing? How will strict liability improve on that situation? Another potential puzzlement arises in connection with Traynor's observation that, with respect to defects that do reach the market and cause harm despite the manufacturer's reasonable efforts at quality control, "the manufacturer is best situated to afford general and constant protection." What sort of protection does strict liability in tort afford the product purchaser who, on Traynor's assumption, has already been injured by the product defect? Consider the following observations by one of this book's authors regarding the policy objectives generally recognized as supporting strict manufacturers' liability in tort.

James A. Henderson, Jr., Coping with the Time Dimension in Products Liability
69 Calif. L. Rev. 919, 931-939 (1981)

In general, strict liability is thought to be preferable to negligence because it better enhances social utility by reducing the costs associated with accidents and because it promotes fairness. Strict liability is believed to increase utility by satisfying four major objectives: encouraging investment in product safety, discouraging consumption of hazardous products, reducing transaction costs, and promoting loss spreading. The relevance of these utility-related objectives to tort law has been explored elsewhere and will be discussed only briefly here.

Strict liability promotes investment in product safety, the so-called "risk control" objective, by imposing liability rules that encourage manufacturers to find ways to reduce or eliminate avoidable product risks. Although in theory this same objective is satisfied by holding manufacturers liable only for their negligence, those who advocate strict liability suggest that manufacturers escape a significant portion of negligence-based liability. An action sounding in negligence presents the plaintiff with difficult issues of proof, such as what a manufacturer with expertise in the field should have known. Manufacturers also may be able to destroy adverse test results and frustrate plaintiffs' attempts to demonstrate that the defendant knew of the hazards. Knowing that the average plaintiff has difficulty in establishing negligence, manufacturers may be willing to bet on escaping liability, or at least large judgments, and thus may limit their efforts to reduce product risks. A regime of strict liability, which does not consider the manufacturer's knowledge, eliminates the practical difficulties involved in litigating a negligence claim. Manufacturers will be less likely to escape liability and will have a greater incentive to invest in efforts to reduce product risks.

Strict liability has also been justified on the ground that it reduces the consumption of risky products by increasing their cost and so placing them at a disadvantage in the market. This second objective, frequently referred to as "market deterrence," rests on the assumption that consumers tend to underassess the risks associated with various products. Unless consumers are reminded of these risks by price increments reflecting manufacturers' liability insurance costs, including the costs of insuring against accidents not worth trying to prevent, they will overconsume relatively risky products. Lowering consumption of risky products will result in fewer accidents, thereby reducing the costs of product liability insurance. Unlike the risk control objective, market deterrence is not achieved to the same extent, even in theory, by imposing liability only for negligence: A relatively hazardous product will escape liability if its benefits are sufficient to justify its risks and a reasonable person would not have made it safer at the time of its distribution. In that event, the product will reflect the relevant avoidance costs, but will not reflect the costs of insuring against those accidents that are not worth trying to prevent.

The third objective traditionally thought to be promoted by strict liability is the reduction of transaction costs, which include the costs of operating the accident reparation system. Strict liability reduces these costs by simplifying the proof necessary to establish liability. Since the plaintiff need not put forward evidence of the defendant's negligence, often a difficult, costly, and time consuming process, the costs of trials under a strict liability rule should be lower than they would be under a negligence rule.

The final utility objective concerns reducing dislocation costs that occur when a single individual or business must bear the full accident loss. The costs of repairing the damage or replacing what has been lost, whether borne by an unsuccessful plaintiff or by a liable defendant, may financially destroy the loss bearer. The additional social costs represented by the uncompensated victim who becomes a public charge, or by the manufacturer who goes into bankruptcy, must also be counted as costs of accidents. These dislocation costs can be reduced by spreading accident losses among a large number of persons by means of insurance. In general, manufacturers are believed to be better able to obtain insurance than are consumers, and are assumed to be able to pass on most, if not all, of the insurance costs by raising the prices of products. Under a negligence approach, manufacturers who are not negligent escape liability; even very large accident costs caused by dangerous products will not be shifted to defendants who have acted reasonably. Under strict liability, more of such costs are shifted to manufacturers and their insurers, thus decreasing dislocation costs to the extent of the increased liability.

In addition to the first four objectives aiming at the promotion of social utility, strict products liability traditionally has been supported on the ground that it responds to shared notions of fairness. . . .

First, strict liability may be justified on fairness grounds because the product that contains a hidden manufacturing defect that causes harm disappoints the consumer's or user's reasonable expectations with regard to safety. The producer may not have been negligent, and the plaintiff may have understood as a general proposition that mistakes can happen. However, when the plaintiff has paid value for the product, he has a right to expect that it will not fail dangerously in its intended use. Moreover, producers typically try to communicate impressions of infallibility that create consumer confidence in the product. Intuitively it seems appropriate to allow the plaintiff in such a case to claim compensation based on the unfair disappointment of his reasonable expectations.

Second, strict liability for manufacturing defects may be justified because in distributing its products, some of which contain hidden manufacturing defects, the producer may be said to be deliberately taking the physical well-being of those who are injured by the product. The producer is like an actor who shoots into a crowd. The producer, like the shooter, does not know who will be injured; but as surely as the shooter knows that someone will be shot, the producer knows that someone will be injured. Both the shooter and the producer can also estimate the number of victims. The shooter loads his gun with a certain number of bullets, and the producer accepts a certain defect rate when setting the level of quality control for its products. Having set a defect rate, the producer can predict the number of accidents, and thus, the number of accident victims. Choosing to limit quality control means accepting a certain number of accidents; so in a sense, the eventual victims of this choice are harmed deliberately. Of course, the shooter is presumably not privileged, and thus commits a battery when he shoots into the crowd. In contrast, the producer is here assumed to have made the economically reasonable decision in choosing to limit quality control. Consequently, the producer can be said to be privileged in the sense that it will not be found liable under a system of negligence even though its conduct caused harm to others. However, there is precedent for holding an actor liable to others for harm deliberately inflicted even when the actor is privileged to act. The best that can be said for the manufacturer is that it has behaved in an economically rational manner; but that does not alter the fact that its deliberate decision has condemned users and consumers to suffer harm. On this view, the manufacturer should in fairness be required to compensate the injured victims.

Finally, strict liability for manufacturing defects may be justified on fairness grounds because it causes the financial burden of accidents to be borne by those who use, and therefore benefit directly from, the product. From this perspective, the producer is a conduit through which accident costs are shifted from injured persons who do not directly benefit from the product to those persons who do. When a defective product distributed by a nonnegligent producer causes an accident in which a nonuser or nonconsumer bystander is injured, the producer who is held strictly liable shifts the costs to those who purchase and use or consume the product. The bystander-plaintiff's claim is supported by the fairness principle that "those who benefit should pay." Of course, the principle applies only crudely. Some nonusers and nonconsumers benefit indirectly from the use and consumption of the products that cause them injury. Also, spreading the costs pro rata on a per-product rather than on a per-use basis causes some users and consumers to bear more, and some less, than their fair share of the burden. Moreover, recovery on the basis of strict liability is not restricted to bystanders; users and consumers also recover for harm caused by manufacturing defects. However, within these narrow limitations strict liability for manufacturing defects seems to be supported by the "benefits/burdens" fairness principle.

All three fairness rationales represent responses to situations in which accident costs are imposed on certain persons without their express or tacit consent. The "benefits/burdens" rationale, with its concern for bystanders who in no way consent to being victims, is most clearly concerned with consent. The other rationales reflect similar perspectives. The "consumer expectations" rationale relies on the assumption that producers, through advertising, entice purchasers into a misplaced sense of security so that the consent seemingly given by purchasers to their exposure to product-related risks is more properly viewed as involuntary. Finally, the "deliberate taking" rationale, although it purports to focus on the deliberateness of the manufacturer's quality control decision, relies on the idea of nonconsensual "taking."

PROBLEM TWO

Assume that a manufacturer produces products that occasionally contain defects that cause injury. Quality control measures in the form of inspection for defects are available by which to reduce the incidence of defects, each successive measure costing more than the last. Without any inspection (quality control), there will be 10 defect-caused accidents per 100,000 product units, at an expected cost of $1,000/accident. Assume that the manufacturer's costs of investments in quality control and the corresponding reductions in accidents are reflected in the chart set forth in Figure 1, infra. Assume further that the only costs associated

Figure 1

(1) reduction in flaw-caused accidents (per 100K prod's)	marginal accident cost reduction (per unit quality control)	(2) total accident cost reduction (cumulative)	(3) total residual accident costs (per 100K prod's)	(4) marginal costs of quality control (per unit quality control)	(5) total costs quality control (cumulative)	(6) total social costs of quality control and accidents (3+5)	(7) total producer's cost (quality control and liability) under negligence	(8) total producer's costs (quality control and liability) under strict liability (3+5)
10 → 9	1,000	1,000	9,000	100	100	9,100	9,100	9,100
9 → 8	1,000	2,000	8,000	300	400	8,400	8,400	8,400
8 → 7	1,000	3,000	7,000	700	1,100	8,100	8,100	8,100
7 → 6	1,000	4,000	6,000	1,200	2,300	8,300	1,100	8,300
6 → 5	1,000	5,000	5,000	1,900	4,200	9,200	4,200	9,200
5 → 4	1,000	6,000	4,000	2,800	7,000	11,000		
4 → 3	1,000	7,000	3,000	5,400	12,400			
3 → 2	1,000	8,000	2,000	11,000	23,400			

(handwritten annotations:)

3+5 until no longer — 100 < 9100

this amount of accidents would never be incurred

cost avoidance < P * cost of injury

at this pt 1200 to save 1000 — not table equiv

with manufacturing defects are those included in the chart, and that negligent manufacturers are liable for "residual accident costs." How far would a rational manufacturer invest in quality control under a negligence rule perfectly and costlessly applied? How far, under strict liability? See if you can answer these questions on the data given in the chart in Figure 1. Then fill in columns (6), (7), and (8), either to help reach the answers or to confirm their validity. Surprised? Might there even be an argument that a manufacturer will provide greater quality control under a negligence regime than under strict liability?

Before turning to the question of whether a strict liability/loss insurance system of the sort envisioned here is workable, it is useful to consider the fairness implications of the move from negligence to strict liability. Under negligence, it will be recalled, accident victims bear the burden of insuring against the residual accident losses that are not worth avoiding. (See p.5, supra.) Under strict liability, manufacturers insure against those residual losses and pass on the insurance costs to purchasers as part of the prices paid for the products. Observe that the premiums charged for the insurance are priced on a pro-rata, per product basis. A rock star who buys a bottle of soda pays the same loss insurance premium as does a law student. And yet the loss insurance is worth much, much more to the rock star than to the law student. (Do you see why?) Under negligence, where each would-be victim buys his own insurance, the rock star pays much more in premiums, reflecting the fact that the rock star's insurance is worth much more. But under strict liability, both the rock star and the law student pay the same premium. In effect, under strict liability the law student subsidizes the rock star. Is this fair?

4. Why Strict Liability for Manufacturing Defects Is Workable

Policy rationales for strict products liability rest on the unstated premise that shifting responsibility for insuring against residual accident losses from accident victims to manufacturers will result in a workable liability system. This premise rests, in turn, on the assumption that manufacturers are able to function as insurers against defect-caused losses, in effect selling casualty loss insurance policies to product purchasers and charging premiums as part of the prices for those products. While this assumption of viability is intuitively reasonable, it will pay dividends to consider more explicitly how such an insurance system maintains its viability. Consider the following excerpts.

James A. Henderson, Jr., Why Negligence Dominates Tort
50 UCLA L. Rev. 377, 390-398 (2002)

A. An Overview of the Necessary Conditions for Maintaining a System of Strict Liability

To be viable, a strict liability system must satisfy two necessary conditions: The liability disputes that it generates must be adjudicable, and the risks for which it holds commercial enterprises strictly responsible must be insurable. The first requirement of adjudicability reflects the fact that courts are called upon to resolve liability disputes in our torts system. Adjudicability is a matter of degree. It depends on the extent to which the applicable rules of decision allow the parties on both sides to work through the relevant issues at trial, insisting upon a favorable outcome as a matter of right. For disputes under strict liability to be adjudicable, the boundaries of the liability system—the descriptions of harm-causing activities for which the system holds enterprises strictly responsible—must be relatively specific and must not depend on fact-sensitive risk-utility calculations. The reasons why these boundary descriptions must be crisp rather than fuzzy relate in part to strict liability's self-proclaimed objective of achieving a non-fault-based liability regime at relatively low transaction costs. But even if a strict liability system avoided self-defeating reliance on notions of fault, as long as the boundary descriptions are indeterminate, the disputes they present will defy rational, consistent resolution by means of adjudication. . . .

The second fundamental condition required for viability—insurability—reflects the reality that strict enterprise liability constitutes an insurance-compensation system whose primary objectives include loss shifting and spreading rather than risk management and control. Enterprises held strictly liable function as insurers; victims who receive compensation are the insureds. For any insurance system to be viable, the risks insured against must be ascertainable and quantifiable ahead of time. Moreover, insureds must pay premiums—in connection with strict enterprise liability, by means of increments included in the prices of goods and services supplied by the enterprise—that proportionally reflect their contributions to the relevant risk pools. In connection with commercial insurance, insurers must classify risks to keep premiums proportional to insureds' contributions to the risk pools. Risk classification reduces adverse selection, which otherwise occurs when high-risk insureds do not pay appropriately higher premiums—when they are undercharged relative to lower-risk insureds. When lower-risk insureds are thus overcharged, they leave the insurance pools, forcing the insurer to raise premiums to cover the higher-risk insureds who remain. Such premium increases cause a new set of relatively lower-risk insureds to leave the pools, requiring further premium increases, and so on. Insurers protect against this unraveling of insurance pools by classifying risks—by requiring that insureds pay premiums that are proportional to the risks of loss those participants bring with them. If for any reason—as with most strict liability systems—the premiums charged are uniform across insureds, either the risks contributed by insureds must also be uniform or the choice of whether to be covered must not be within individual insureds' control. Without adequate classification, insurance pools will disproportionately attract high-risk insureds, threatening the viability of those pools. As a subsequent discussion makes clear, these conditions are difficult for a strict liability system to satisfy.

Another threat to the viability of any insurance scheme is moral hazard—the natural tendency for insureds to increase their risks of incurring covered losses by risky conduct after the insurance takes effect. Like adverse selection, moral hazard threatens to allow higher-risk insureds to pay less than they should for coverage. Thus, it tends to drive lower-risk insureds, who pay more than they should, out of the insurance pools, thereby threatening the insurance scheme with crushing liabilities generated by the higher-risk insureds who remain. Commercial insurers combat moral hazard by excluding from coverage losses resulting from high-risk conduct by insureds. When strict liability requires enterprises to function as insurers, it must somehow prevent those who are covered from significantly increasing the risk of covered losses once the enterprise's obligation to insure is in place. Putative victims, in other words, must play a generally passive role in a strict liability system. When the insured can manipulate the risks, the insurance scheme is seriously threatened.

B. Strict Liability [for Manufacturing Defects Is] Viable Because It ... Generates Adjudicable Disputes

Courts impose strict liability on product manufacturers for harm caused by manufacturing defects. ... The strict liability [for manufacturing defects] portion of our products liability system rests on relatively bright-line boundaries — "commercial sellers and other distributors of products containing manufacturing defects" — that courts have, over time, established with substantial formality. While determining what is and is not a "product sold and distributed" is an ongoing project, the definition of "manufacturing defect" is straightforwardly unambiguous and mechanical in nature, relying on the bright-line standard of physical departures from the manufacturer's intended design. No case-by-case risk-utility calculus is involved in either instance, and courts have borrowed the cause-in-fact and proximate causation triggers, with only minor adjustments, from traditional negligence analysis.

C. Strict Products Liability [Is] Viable Because the Risks It Assigns to Commercial Enterprises [Are] Insurable

An earlier discussion of the insurability requirement noted that, to achieve viability, a ... strict liability system must assure that the risks are ascertainable ahead of time and that the commercial enterprises held strictly liable as insurers are adequately protected from the potentially devastating effects of adverse selection and moral hazard. [Clearly,] strict liability [for manufacturing defects has] managed to achieve insurability. Recall that the key to protecting enterprises in this regard is to prevent those who obtain insurance coverage from significantly increasing the risk of covered losses once the enterprise's insurance obligation is in place. Essentially, this means that, once a commercial enterprise is insuring the risk, the enterprise and not the putative victim who may suffer harm must control the risk.

[S]everal features of the strict liability regime covering manufacturing defects combine to place post-sale control of the relevant risks exclusively in the hands of product distributors. Most importantly, courts require that the defect that eventually causes harm must have been present at the original time of distribution — and release of control — by the defendant. Commercial distributors are not strictly liable for physical defects that occur after distribution, and courts deny recovery to plaintiffs who discover defects and proceed to use or consume the defective product units. With respect to the risks presented by manufacturing defects, the purchase of a new product unit resembles the placement of a wager on a toss of dice. No one knows whether the particular unit contains a defect, but the manufacturer knows the odds almost exactly. Once the purchase is made — once the dice are tossed — no player may deliberately affect the outcome without forfeiting the right to recover. When a purchaser's number comes up — when an original defect causes accidental harm — a tort/insurance payout is due. Courts and commentators from the very start have understood the insurance implications of strict liability for manufacturing defects and have self-consciously explained and justified it in these terms. [Citing to Traynor's concurrence in *Escola*.]

C. DEFECT AS THE LINCHPIN OF STRICT PRODUCTS LIABILITY

Strict liability for manufacturing defects is settled law in every jurisdiction in this country. This might lead you to think that all the problems are behind us, and that products liability plaintiffs harmed by manufacturing defects "have got it made in the shade." Well, think again. While courts no longer require plaintiffs to show that a manufacturer was negligent in allowing a defect to escape into the stream of commerce, they continue to require plaintiffs to prove that a defect caused the accident and that the defect existed when the defendant sold or otherwise commercially distributed the product. Proving an "original defect" (a defect that existed at the time of original distribution) is as difficult now as it was back in Judge Traynor's day. To understand the role of defect as the linchpin of strict products liability, two questions must be answered: (1) What, exactly, makes a product defective? and (2) How does the plaintiff prove original defect? This section seeks to answer these questions.

1. What Makes a Product Defective? (The Conceptual Dimension)

Without defining the term "defect," §402A of the Restatement (Second) of Torts (1965) refers to "any product in a defective condition unreasonably dangerous to the user or consumer." (See p.20, supra.) What purpose does the "unreasonably dangerous" modifier serve? Consider the following case.

Cronin v. J. B. E. Olson Corp.
501 P.2d 1153 (Cal. 1972)

SULLIVAN, J.

In this products liability case, the principal question which we face is whether the injured plaintiff seeking recovery upon the theory of strict liability in tort must establish, among other facts, not only that the product contained a defect which proximately caused his injuries but also that such defective condition made the product unreasonably dangerous to the user or consumer. We have concluded that he need not do so. Accordingly, we find no error in the trial court's refusal to so instruct the jury. Rejecting as without merit various challenges to the sufficiency of the evidence, we affirm the judgment.

On October 3, 1966, plaintiff, a route salesman for Gravem-Inglis Bakery Co.

(Gravem) of Stockton, was driving a bread delivery truck along a rural road in San Joaquin County. While plaintiff was attempting to pass a pick-up truck ahead of him, its driver made a sudden left turn, causing the pick-up to collide with the plaintiff's truck and forcing the latter off the road and into a ditch. As a result, plaintiff was propelled through the windshield and landed on the ground. The impact broke an aluminum safety hasp which was located just behind the driver's seat and designed to hold the bread trays in place. The loaded trays, driven forward by the abrupt stop and impact of the truck, struck plaintiff in the back and hurled him through the windshield. He sustained serious personal injuries.

The truck, a one-ton Chevrolet stepvan with built-in bread racks, was one of several trucks sold to Gravem in 1957 by defendant Chase Chevrolet Company (Chase), not a party to this appeal. Upon receipt of Gravem's order, Chase purchased the trucks from defendant J. B. E. Olson Corporation (Olson), which acted as sales agent for the assembled vehicle, the chassis, body, and racks of which were manufactured by three subcontractors. The body of the van contained three aisles along which there were welded runners extending from the front to the rear of the truck. Each rack held ten bread trays from top to bottom and five trays deep; the trays slid forward into the cab or back through the rear door to facilitate deliveries.

Plaintiff brought the present action against Chase, Olson and General Motors Corporation[3] alleging that the truck was unsafe for its intended use because of defects in its manufacture, in that the metal hasp was exceedingly porous, contained holes, pits and voids, and lacked sufficient tensile strength to withstand the impact. Defendants' answers denied the material allegations of the complaint and asserted the affirmative defense of contributory negligence. Subsequently, upon leave of court, the additional defense of assumption of the risk was asserted.

At the trial, plaintiff's expert testified, in substance, that the metal hasp broke, releasing the bread trays, because it was extremely porous and had a significantly lower tolerance to force than a non-flawed aluminum hasp would have had. The jury returned a verdict in favor of plaintiff and against Olson in the sum of $45,000 but in favor of defendant Chase and against plaintiff. Judgment was entered accordingly. This appeal by Olson followed.

Defendant attacks the sufficiency of the evidence to support the verdict and the trial court's instruction on strict liability. The challenge to the evidence is multi-pronged, claiming in effect that plaintiff produced no evidence on several essential issues. We first turn to this challenge, considering defendant's arguments in the order presented.

[The court concludes that the plaintiff introduced sufficient evidence to support the conclusion that the hasp was defective when originally supplied by the defendant. A collision of the sort involved here is reasonably foreseeable, and the hasp was intended to prevent what happened here. Plaintiff's expert testified that if the hasp had not been weak and porous, it would have prevented the plaintiff's injuries. The court next turns to the question of whether the trial judge erred in instructing the jury that it might find the hasp defective, and the defendant liable, without finding the hasp to have been unreasonably dangerous.]

The history of strict liability in California indicates that the requirement that

---

3. Defendant General Motors Corporation, manufacturer of the chassis, was voluntarily dismissed by plaintiff prior to trial.

Defect as the Linchpin of Strict Products Liability

the defect made the product "unreasonably dangerous" crept into our jurisprudence without fanfare after its inclusion in section 402A of the Restatement (Second) of Torts in 1965. The question raised in the instant matter as to whether the requirement is an essential part of the plaintiff's case is one of first impression.

We begin with section 402A itself. According to the official comment to the section, a "defective condition" is one "not contemplated by the ultimate consumer, which will be unreasonably dangerous to him." Rest. 2d Torts, §402A, com. g.) Comment i, defining "unreasonably dangerous," states, "The article sold must be dangerous to an extent beyond that which would be contemplated by the ordinary consumer who purchases it, with the ordinary knowledge common to the community as to its characteristics." Examples given in comment i make it clear that such innocuous products as sugar and butter, unless contaminated, would not give rise to a strict liability claim merely because the former may be harmful to a diabetic or the latter may aggravate the blood cholesterol level of a person with heart disease. Presumably such dangers are squarely within the contemplation of the ordinary consumer. Prosser, the reporter for the Restatement, suggests that the "unreasonably dangerous" qualification was added to foreclose the possibility that the manufacturer of a product with inherent possibilities for harm (for example, butter, drugs, whiskey and automobiles) would become "automatically responsible for all the harm that such things do in the world." (Prosser, Strict Liability to the Consumer in California (1966) 18 Hastings L.J. 9, 23.)

The result of the limitation, however, has not been merely to prevent the seller from becoming an insurer of his products with respect to all harm generated by their use. Rather, it has burdened the injured plaintiff with proof of an element which rings of negligence. As a result, if, in the view of the trier of fact, the "ordinary consumer" would have expected the defective condition of a product, the seller is not strictly liable regardless of the expectations of the injured plaintiff. If, for example, the "ordinary consumer" would have contemplated that Shopsmiths posed a risk of loosening their grip and letting the wood strike the operator, another Greenman might be denied recovery. In fact, it has been observed that the Restatement formulation of strict liability in practice rarely leads to a different conclusion than would have been reached under laws of negligence.

Of particular concern is the susceptibility of Restatement section 402A to a literal reading which would require the finder of fact to conclude that the product is, first, defective and, second, unreasonably dangerous. A bifurcated standard is of necessity more difficult to prove than a unitary one. But merely proclaiming that the phrase "defective condition unreasonably dangerous" requires only a single finding would not purge that phrase of its negligence complexion. We think that a requirement that a plaintiff also prove that the defect made the product "unreasonably dangerous" places upon him a significantly increased burden and represents a step backward in the area pioneered by this court.

We recognize that the words "unreasonably dangerous" may also serve the beneficial purpose of preventing the seller from being treated as the insurer of its products. However, we think that such protective end is attained by the necessity of proving that there was a defect in the manufacture or design of the product and that such defect was a proximate cause of the injuries. Although the seller should not be responsible for all injuries involving the use of its products, it should be liable for all injuries proximately caused by any of its products which are adjudged "defective."

We can see no difficulty in applying [this] formulation to the full range of products liability situations, including those involving "design defects." A defect may emerge from the mind of the designer as well as from the hand of the workman.

Although it is easier to see the "defect" in a single imperfectly fashioned product than in an entire line badly conceived, a distinction between manufacture and design defects is not tenable.

The most obvious problem we perceive in creating any such distinction is that thereafter it would be advantageous to characterize a defect in one rather than the other category. It is difficult to prove that a product ultimately caused injury because a widget was poorly welded — a defect in manufacture — rather than because it was made of inexpensive metal difficult to weld, chosen by a designer concerned with economy — a defect in design. The proof problem would, of course, be magnified when the article in question was either old or unique, with no easily available basis for comparison. We wish to avoid providing such a battleground for clever counsel. Furthermore, we find no reason why a different standard, and one harder to meet, should apply to defects which plague entire product lines. We recognize that it is more damaging to a manufacturer to have an entire line condemned, so to speak, for a defect in design, than a single product for a defect in manufacture. But the potential economic loss to a manufacturer should not be reflected in a different standard of proof for an injured consumer.

In summary, we have concluded that to require an injured plaintiff to prove not only that the product contained a defect but also that such defect made the product unreasonably dangerous to the user or consumer would place a considerably greater burden upon him than that articulated in *Greenman*. We believe the *Greenman* formulation is consonant with the rationale and development of products liability law in California because it provides a clear and simple test for determining whether the injured plaintiff is entitled to recovery. We are not persuaded to the contrary by the formulation of section 402A which inserts the factor of an "unreasonably dangerous" condition into the equation of products liability.

We conclude that the trial court did not err by refusing to instruct the jury that plaintiff must establish that the defective condition of the product made it unreasonably dangerous to the user or consumer.

The judgment is affirmed.

WRIGHT, C.J., MCCOMB, J., PETERS, J., TOBRINER, J., MOSK, J., and BURKE, J., concurred.

Some of the *Cronin* court's confidence that "unreasonably dangerous" is not necessary may lie in the relative ease with which manufacturing defects may be conceptualized. As reflected in all of the materials considered up to this point, manufacturing defects are imperfections in a few product units out of many, which cause the few units to fail dangerously during use. As we shall discover in later chapters dealing with liability for defective product design, courts encounter conceptual difficulties trying to construct objective legal standards of reasonableness with which to determine the adequacy of product designs.

In any event, in 1992 the American Law Institute began the task of revision §402A by commissioning a project to write the Restatement (Third) of Torts:

Products Liability. The authors of this casebook were the Reporters for the project, which was finally approved and promulgated in 1998. In its finished form it provides a systematic formulation of American products liability in the familiar "black letter/comment" format. Courts have been reacting to the new Restatement since the late 1990s, for the most part favorably. We will include portions of it, where relevant, throughout these materials. Here are the first two sections which serve as the linchpins for the entire Products Liability Restatement project.

Restatement (Third) of Torts: Products Liability
(1998)

§1. LIABILITY OF COMMERCIAL SELLER OR DISTRIBUTOR FOR HARM CAUSED BY DEFECTIVE PRODUCTS

One engaged in the business of selling or otherwise distributing products who sells or distributes a defective product is subject to liability for harm to persons or property caused by the defect.

§2. CATEGORIES OF PRODUCT DEFECT

A product is defective when, at the time of sale or distribution, it contains a manufacturing defect, is defective in design, or is defective because of inadequate instructions or warnings. A product:

(a) contains a manufacturing defect when the product departs from its intended design even though all possible care was exercised in the preparation and marketing of the product;

(b) is defective in design when the forseeable risks of harm posed by the product could have been reduced or avoided by the adoption of a reasonable alternative design by the seller or other distributor, or a predecessor in the commercial chain of distribution, and the omission of the alternative design renders the product not reasonably safe;

(c) is defective because of inadequate instructions or warnings when the foreseeable risks of harm posed by the product could have been reduced or avoided by the provision of reasonable instructions or warnings by the seller or other distributor, or a predecessor in the commercial chain of distribution, and the omission of the instructions or warnings renders the product not reasonably safe.

COMMENT:

c. Manufacturing defects. As stated in Subsection (a), a manufacturing defect is a departure from a product unit's design specifications. More distinctly than any other type of defect, manufacturing defects disappoint consumer expectations. Common examples of manufacturing defects are products that are physically flawed, damaged, or incorrectly assembled. In actions against the manufacturer, under prevailing rules concerning allocation of burdens of proof plaintiff ordinarily bears the burden of establishing that such a defect existed in the product when it left the hands of the manufacturer.

Occasionally a defect may arise after manufacture, for example, during shipment or while in storage. Since the product, as sold to the consumer, has a defect that is a departure from the product unit's design specifications, a commercial seller or distributor down the chain of distribution is liable as if the product were defectively manufactured. As long as the plaintiff establishes that the product was defective when it left the hands of a given seller in the distributive chain, liability will attach to that seller. Such defects are referred to in this Restatement as "manufacturing defects" even when they occur after manufacture.

One critic of the Products Liability Restatement noted that liability would ensue under §2(a) if a defective connection of a wire in a car radio caused static and diverted the attention of the driver to fiddle with the dial, thus taking the driver's eye off the road and resulting in an accident. Was the critic right? Why were the Reporters so bullheaded in their insistence, with regard to manufacturing defects, that there be no requirement that the defect render the product "not reasonably safe?"

PROBLEM THREE

John Mutkowski called you two weeks ago and asked you to represent his 23-year-old son, Randy, in an action to recover damages for injuries Randy suffered in an accident three months ago in John's basement. Two subsequent interviews with the Mutkowskis and follow-up investigation reveal the following facts. The accident occurred during a weekend family get-together when a chair collapsed under Randy, causing him to fall and sustain injuries to his lower back. John had bought the chair, along with three others just like it, four weeks earlier from Fernrock Furniture Sales, Inc., a large furniture retailer in your city. "I was looking for something sturdy — we're big people, you know," John explained. The chairs are made of wood and do, indeed, appear heavy and sturdy. They were on sale at Fernrock's, at a price about 25 percent lower than comparably sized and finished wooden chairs. "I needed four of 'em for my basement family room," John tells you. "They were just what I was looking for, at a good price, so I got four of 'em."

Investigation reveals that the chairs in question were manufactured by the Ole Hickory Furniture Company, a medium-sized manufacturer in the southern part of your state. The chairs had been manufactured on special order for the Buffalo Bullfinches Football Club, an original franchise of the now-defunct Federal Football League. The Bullfinches had ordered the chairs to special specifications of higher strength and sturdiness for use in their team dining room. (The players were very large people who did not treat furniture gently.) The Bullfinches Club folded with the League a year ago, before taking delivery of the 200 chairs they had ordered. Ole Hickory sold the chairs "as is," at a deep discount, to Fernrock, who cleared them out quickly at an attractive retail price. Fernrock insists that it never mentioned to anyone the background regarding the chairs, and sold them as regular merchandise.

After John Mutkowski bought four of the chairs and put them in his basement family room, they were subjected to normal use and caused no problems. On the night of the accident four weeks later, Randy was sitting on one of the chairs watching T.V. He had rocked the chair back on its two hind legs and was leaning against the wall. Howie, Randy's 19-year-old brother, asked if he could borrow the chair to take upstairs and Randy refused. Howie thereupon walked over and sat on Randy's lap. John admits that Howie "sort of flopped down on Randy's lap." The two sat for about ten seconds, engaged in friendly wrestling, when the right rear leg of the chair snapped with the sound of a pistol shot and the two young men fell to the floor. Randy cracked several vertebrae and has just now gotten out of the hospital. His injuries are serious.

Inspection of the chair by an expert reveals that the wooden leg that broke contained a latent defect near where the leg joins the bottom of the chair. The expert says that the chair probably would have lasted a normal lifetime of ordinary use. "Even with the defect, the higher strength specifications made the leg as strong as the legs on most wooden chairs of this size and overall design," he explains. "The two Mutkowski boys weighed nearly 500 pounds together. All that weight on the two back legs, at an angle to the floor, was more than most chairs could stand."

Mildly exasperated that the expert seemed to be passing some kind of moral judgment on what you view to have been the innocent horseplay of the Mutkowski brothers, you pressed him on the role of the defect in causing the accident. "Oh yes, you're right," he replied, "I'm almost certain that the chair would not have broken if it hadn't been defective. I've run tests on one of the other chairs that Mr. Mutkowski bought, and with its strength specifications the chair that broke would have held up just fine if it hadn't had the defect."

Pressing John Mutkowski regarding the terms of his purchase of the chairs, he recalls nothing being said to him about the chairs having been designed to be extra-strong. You have talked to two other persons who also purchased the same chairs at Fernrock's and it is clear that they were sold as ordinary wooden chairs, with no mention of the background facts. The best you can get out of John Mutkowski is that they looked sturdy to him, and he was looking for sturdy chairs. "We're big people, you know."

Based on these facts, together with any reasonable inferences or assumptions, what are your chances of reaching a jury with strict liability claims against Fernrock and Ole Hickory? In making your assessment, you should assume that your state has adopted pure comparative fault in these cases, and that the question of the plaintiff's contributory fault, as a defense independent of how his and his brother's conduct may relate to the issue of the defendants' breach of duty, will be for the jury. The main question for you to answer, therefore, is whether a jury could find that the chair in this case was "in a defective condition, unreasonably dangerous to the user." In this regard you are to assume that the courts in your state have not yet confronted the issue decided in the *Cronin* case, supra.

2. How Does the Plaintiff Prove Original Defect? (The Practical Dimension)

One obvious way for a plaintiff to prove an original product defect is through the testimony of an expert who has examined the product and is able to opine that a defect at time of sale caused the accident. *Cronin,* supra, involved such testimony in connection with the failure of a metal hasp in a bread truck. Experts in that case examined the hasp and found the metal to be dangerously porous. This sort of direct evidence of original defect appears in many of the reported decisions in this and subsequent chapters. Even more important to plaintiffs is circumstantial proof of defect. Typically, the product malfunctions under circumstances that support an inference of original defect. The Products Liability Restatement addresses this phenomenon in the following way:

Restatement (Third) of Torts: Products Liability
(1998)

§3. CIRCUMSTANTIAL EVIDENCE SUPPORTING INFERENCE OF PRODUCT DEFECT

It may be inferred that the harm sustained by the plaintiff was caused by a product defect existing at the time of sale or distribution, without proof of a specific defect, when the incident that harmed the plaintiff:
(a) was of a kind that ordinarily occurs as a result of product defect; and
(b) was not, in the particular case, solely the result of causes other than product defect existing at the time of sale or distribution.

COMMENT:

b. Requirement that the [harmful incident] be of a kind that ordinarily occurs as a result of product defect. The most frequent application of this Section is to cases involving manufacturing defects. When a product unit contains such a defect, and the defect affects product performance so as to cause a harmful incident, in most instances it will cause the product to malfunction in such a way that the inference of product defect is clear. From this perspective, manufacturing defects cause products to fail to perform their manifestly intended functions. Frequently, the plaintiff is able to establish specifically the nature and identity of the defect and may proceed directly under §2(a). But when the product unit involved in the harm-causing incident is lost or destroyed in the accident, direct evidence of specific defect may not be available. Under that circumstance, this Section may offer the plaintiff the only fair opportunity to recover.

When examination of the product unit is impossible because the unit is lost or destroyed after the harm-causing incident, a somewhat different issue may be presented. Responsibility for spoliation of evidence may be relevant to the fairness of allowing the inference set forth in this Section. In any event, the issues of evidence spoliation and any sanctions that might be imposed for such conduct are beyond the scope of this Restatement, Third, Torts: Products Liability. . . .

ILLUSTRATIONS:

1. John purchased a new electric blender. John used the blender approximately 10 times exclusively for making milkshakes. While he was making a milkshake, the blender suddenly shattered. A piece of glass struck John's eye, causing harm. The incident resulting in harm is of a kind that ordinarily occurs as a result of product defect.

2. Same facts as Illustration 1, except that John accidentally dropped the blender, causing the glass to shatter. The product did not fail to function in a manner supporting an inference of defect. Whether liability can be established depends on whether the plaintiff can prove a cause of action under §§1 and 2 [based on direct proof of defect.]

c. No requirement that plaintiff prove what aspect of the product was defective. The inference of defect may be drawn under this Section without proof of the specific defect. Furthermore, quite apart from the question of what type of defect was involved, the plaintiff need not explain specifically what constituent part of the product failed. For example, if an inference of defect can be appropriately drawn in connection with the catastrophic failure of an airplane, the plaintiff need not establish whether the failure is attributable to fuel-tank explosion or engine malfunction.

d. Requirement that the incident that harmed the plaintiff was not, in the particular case, solely the result of causes other than product defect existing at the time of sale. To allow the trier of fact to conclude that a product defect caused the plaintiff's harm under this Section, the plaintiff must establish by a preponderance of the evidence that the incident was not solely the result of causal factors other than defect at time of sale. The defect need not be the only cause of the incident; if the plaintiff can prove that the most likely explanation of the harm involves the causal contribution of a product defect, the fact that there may be other concurrent causes of the harm does not preclude liability under this Section. But when the harmful incident can be attributed solely to causes other than original defect, including the conduct of others, an inference of defect under this Section cannot be drawn.

Evidence may permit the inference that a defect in the product at the time of the harm-causing incident caused the product to malfunction, but not the inference that the defect existed at the time of sale or distribution. Such factors as the age of the product, possible alteration by repairers or others, and misuse by the plaintiff or third parties may have introduced the defect that causes harm.

ILLUSTRATION:
6. While driving a new automobile at high speed one night, Driver drove off the highway and crashed into a tree. Driver suffered harm. Driver cannot remember the circumstances surrounding the accident. Driver has brought an action against ABC Company, the manufacturer of the automobile. Driver presents no evidence of a specific defect. However, Driver's qualified expert presents credible testimony that a defect in the automobile must have caused the accident. ABC's qualified expert presents credible testimony that it is equally likely that, independent of any defect, Driver lost control while speeding on the highway. If the trier of fact believes the testimony of Driver's expert, then an inference of defect may be established under this Section. If, however, ABC's expert is believed, an inference of product defect may not be drawn under this Section because Driver has failed to establish by a preponderance of the evidence that the harm did not result solely from Driver's independent loss of control at high speed.

Speller v. Sears, Roebuck & Co.
790 N.E.2d 252 (N.Y. 2003)

GRAFFEO, J.

In this products liability case, [the trial court denied defendants' motion for summary judgement and defendants brought interlocutory appeal to the Apellate Division, who reversed and] granted summary judgment dismissing plaintiffs' complaint. Because we conclude that plaintiffs raised a triable issue of fact concerning whether a defective refrigerator caused the fire that resulted in plaintiffs' injuries, we reverse and reinstate the complaint against these defendants.

Plaintiffs' decedent Sandra Speller died in a house fire that also injured her seven-year-old son. It is undisputed that the fire originated in the kitchen. Plaintiffs commenced this action against Sears, Roebuck and Co., Whirlpool Corporation and the property owner alleging negligence, strict products liability and breach of warranty. Relevant to this appeal, plaintiffs asserted that the fire was caused by defective wiring in the refrigerator, a product manufactured by Whirlpool and sold by Sears. After discovery, defendants Sears and Whirlpool moved for summary judgment seeking dismissal of the complaint. Relying principally on a report issued by the New York City Fire Marshal, defendants rejected the refrigerator as the source of the fire, instead contending that a stovetop grease fire was the cause of the conflagration. Thus, they argued that their product was outside the chain of causation that resulted in plaintiffs' damages.

In opposition to defendants' motion for summary judgment, plaintiffs submitted excerpts from the depositions of two experts and an affidavit from a third, as well as other materials. Plaintiffs' experts refuted the conclusions reached in the Fire Marshal's report, opining that the fire started in the upper right quadrant of the refrigerator, an area with a concentration of electrical wiring. All three rejected the stove as the source of the fire. Plaintiffs also submitted portions of the deposition of a Whirlpool engineer retained as an expert by defendants. Although the engineer disputed that the fire originated in the refrigerator, he acknowledged that a fire would not occur in a refrigerator unless the product was defective.

Supreme Court denied defendants' request for summary judgment, holding that plaintiffs' submissions raised a triable issue of fact as to whether the fire was caused by a defect in the refrigerator. The Appellate Division reversed and granted the motion, dismissing the complaint as against Sears and Whirlpool. The Court reasoned that defendants' evidence suggesting an alternative cause of the fire shifted the burden to plaintiffs to come forward with specific evidence of a defect. Characterizing the submissions of plaintiffs' experts as "equivocal," the Court concluded that plaintiffs failed to satisfy their burden of proof to withstand summary judgment. (294 A.D.2d 349, 350 [2002].) This Court granted plaintiffs leave to appeal.

A party injured as a result of a defective product may seek relief against the product manufacturer or others in the distribution chain if the defect was a substantial factor in causing the injury. "A product may be defective when it contains a manufacturing flaw, is defectively designed or is not accompanied by adequate warnings for the use of the product" (Liriano v. Hobart Corp., 92 N.Y.2d 232, 237 [1998]; Robinson v. Reed-Prentice Div. of Package Mach. Co., 49 N.Y.2d 471, 478 [1980]).

In this case, plaintiffs' theory was that the wiring in the upper right quadrant of the refrigerator was faulty, causing an electrical fire which then spread to other areas of the kitchen and residence. Because that part of the refrigerator had been consumed in the fire, plaintiffs noted that it was impossible to examine or test the wiring to determine the precise nature of the defect. Thus, plaintiffs sought to prove their claim circumstantially by establishing that the refrigerator caused the house fire and therefore did not perform as intended.

New York has long recognized the viability of this circumstantial approach in products liability cases. Indeed its origins can be traced back to Codling v. Paglia (32 N.Y.2d 330, 337 [1973]), where this Court stated that a plaintiff "is not required to prove the specific defect" and that "[p]roof of necessary facts may be circumstantial." In order to proceed in the absence of evidence identifying a specific flaw, a plaintiff must prove that the product did not perform as intended and exclude all other causes for the product's failure that are not attributable to defendants (Halloran v. Virginia Chems., 41 N.Y.2d 386, 388 [1977]; see generally Kreindler, Rodriguez, Beekman and Cook, New York Law of Torts §16.64, at 519-522 [15 West's N.Y. Prac Series 1997]). In this regard, New York law is consistent with the Restatement, which reads: [The court sets out §3, supra.]

Of course, if a plaintiff's proof is insufficient with respect to either prong of this circumstantial inquiry, a jury may not infer that the harm was caused by a defective product unless plaintiff offers competent evidence identifying a specific flaw (see Shelden v. Hample Equip. Co., 59 N.Y.2d 618 [1983], *affg* 89 A.D.2d 766, 453 N.Y.S.2d 934 [3d Dept 1982]).

Here, in their motion for summary judgment, defendants focused on the second prong of the circumstantial inquiry, offering evidence that the injuries were not caused by their product but by an entirely different instrumentality — a grease fire that began on top of the stove. This was the conclusion of the Fire Marshal who stated during deposition testimony that his opinion was based on his interpretation of the burn patterns in the kitchen, his observation that one of the burner knobs on the stove was in the "on" position, and his conversation with a resident of the home who apparently advised him that the oven was on when the resident placed some food on the stovetop a few hours before the fire.

In order to withstand summary judgment, plaintiffs were required to come forward with competent evidence excluding the stove as the origin of the fire. To meet that burden, plaintiffs offered three expert opinions: the depositions of an electrical engineer and a fire investigator, and the affidavit of a former Deputy Chief of the New York City Fire Department. Each concluded that the fire originated in the refrigerator and not on the stove.

In his extensive deposition testimony, the electrical engineer opined that the fire started in the top-right-rear corner of the refrigerator, an area that housed the air balancing unit, thermostat, moisture control and light control. He stated that the wiring in this part of the appliance had been destroyed in the fire, making it impossible to identify the precise mechanical failure and, thus, he could only speculate as to the specific nature of the defect. He testified that the "most logical probability" was that a bad connection or bad splice to one of the components in that portion of the unit caused the wire to become "red hot" and to ignite the adjacent plastic. He tested the combustibility of the plastic and confirmed that the "plastic lights up very easily, with a single match" and continues to burn like candle wax. The engineer observed that the doors of the refrigerator were "slightly bellied out," indicating they were blown out from the expanding hot gases inside the refrigerator. The wall behind the refrigerator was significantly damaged and the upper right quadrant was burned to such a degree that it was not likely to have been caused by an external fire. Interpreting the burn patterns differently from the Fire Marshal, the electrical engineer found that the cabinets above the stove, although damaged, were not destroyed to the extent he expected to find if there had been a stovetop grease fire.

Plaintiffs' fire investigator similarly opined that the fire originated in the refrigerator's upper right corner, in part basing his conclusion on his observations of the scene three days after the fire and his examination of the appliances. He also interviewed a witness to the fire. He testified that he eliminated the stove as the source of the fire after his examination of that appliance and the cabinets above it. Contrary to the testimony of the Fire Marshal, he observed that all of the burner knobs on the stove were in the same position, either all "off" or all "on." He further examined the burn patterns, noting that if the blaze had been caused by a grease fire on the stove, the cabinets directly above would have been consumed in the fire. Instead, they were merely damaged. He acknowledged that he did not know exactly how the fire started inside the refrigerator but indicated he suspected there had been a poor connection in the wiring that caused the wire to smolder until it ignited the highly combustible foam insulation inside the unit.

The former Deputy Chief of the New York City Fire Department asserted in his affidavit that the "fire damage to the area around the refrigerator when compared to that of the stove clearly shows the longer and heavier burn at the refrigerator," indicating the fire originated there. He also stated that he had ruled out all other possible origins of the fire. Upon review of these expert depositions and affidavit, we conclude that plaintiffs raised a triable question of fact by offering competent evidence which, if credited by the jury, was sufficient to rebut defendants' alternative cause evidence. In other words, based on plaintiffs' proof, a reasonable jury could conclude that plaintiffs excluded all other causes of the fire.

We therefore disagree with the Appellate Division's characterization of plaintiffs' submissions as equivocal. Plaintiffs' experts consistently asserted that the fire originated in the upper right quadrant of the refrigerator and each contended the stove was not the source of the blaze. Both parties supported their positions with detailed, nonconclusory expert depositions and other submissions which explained the bases for the opinions.

Defendants contend that after they came forward with evidence suggesting an alternative cause of the fire, plaintiffs were foreclosed from establishing a product defect circumstantially but were then required to produce evidence of a specific defect to survive summary judgment. We reject this approach for two reasons. First, such an analysis would allow a defendant who offered minimally sufficient alternative cause evidence in a products liability case to foreclose a plaintiff from proceeding circumstantially without a jury having determined whether defendant's evidence should be credited. Second, it misinterprets the court's role in adjudicating a motion for summary judgment, which is issue identification, not issue resolution. Where causation is disputed, summary judgment is not appropriate unless "only one conclusion may be drawn from the established facts" (Kriz v. Schum, 75 N.Y.2d 25, 34 [1989]). That is not the case here where plaintiffs directly rebutted defendants' submissions with competent proof specifically ruling out the stove as the source of the blaze. Because a reasonable jury could credit this proof and find that plaintiffs excluded all other causes of the fire not attributable to defendants, this case presents material issues of fact requiring a trial.

Accordingly, the order of the Appellate Division should be reversed, with costs, and the motion of defendants Sears, Roebuck and Co. and Whirlpool Corporation for summary judgment denied.

. . .

Chief Judge KAYE and Judges SMITH, CIPARICK, WESLEY, ROSENBLATT and READ concur.

Order reversed, etc.

PROBLEM FOUR

Hanna Liebman was driving to the supermarket in her three-year-old, four-door Stardom Sedan manufactured by BMC Inc. Liebman was driving on her side of the road when she was suddenly hit head-on by a car driven by Sheldon Varik.

Varik had apparently dozed off for a few seconds. His car veered over the center line and collided with Liebman. She was seriously injured in the accident when her face hit the windshield of her BMC Stardom. Varik carries the minimum $20,000 liability insurance policy mandated by the State of New California; Liebman's injuries are in excess of one million dollars. All events transpired in New California and its law will govern the case.

Liebman insists that she was wearing her seat belt at the time of the accident. She has a clear and unmistakable recollection of buckling up before embarking on her trip. Furthermore, she insists that she always wears her seat belt. Her contention is that the seat belt malfunctioned and did not restrain her at the time of impact. All experts in the case agree that if Liebman had been wearing her seat belt and if her seat belt had been working properly, Liebman's head would not have hit the windshield and almost all of her injuries would have been avoided. However, experts who examined the seat belt mechanism after the crash can find no defect in the retraction mechanism. The mechanism works perfectly.

You are the trial judge in the case of Liebman v. BMC Inc. BMC has moved for directed verdict on the grounds that the seat belt was not defective. Liebman's lawyers argue that, if Liebman was telling the truth and she did, in fact, wear her seat belt, then the seat belt mechanism must have failed in some unexplained fashion. The issue of Liebman's credibility, they contend, is for the jury to decide. Will you grant the defendant's motion for directed verdict?

D. THE BOUNDARIES OF STRICT PRODUCTS LIABILITY

An earlier excerpt from the UCLA Law Review on the workability of the strict liability system for manufacturing defects (see p.30, supra) characterized the boundaries of strict liability as sufficiently definite to render disputes arising in that system adjudicable. The materials in this section will help you assess the accuracy of that observation. Whether a plaintiff's claim falls within or without the boundaries determines whether the defendant is strictly liable or liable only for negligence. Plaintiffs whose claims fall outside the boundaries are not necessarily without remedy in tort; but they must prove that the defendant was at fault. Of course, proving negligence may not be possible on the facts, so in many cases the boundary determination will determine liability. The operative language in §1 of the Products Liability Restatement, setting the boundaries of the subject, is: "One engaged in the business of selling or otherwise distributing products who sells or distributes a defective product is subject to liability. . . ." The materials that follow are designed to answer the following questions: (1) What are (and what are not) products?; (2) What commercial activities constitute "selling or otherwise distributing?"; and (3) When is a product seller or distributor "in the business of selling or distributing?"

1. What Are (and What Are Not) Products?

The place to begin is with the definition of "product" in the Products Liability Restatement:

Restatement (Third) of Torts: Products Liability
(1998)

§19. Definition of "Product"

For purposes of this Restatement:

(a) A product is tangible personal property distributed commercially for use or consumption. Other items, such as real property and electricity, are products when the context of their distribution and use is sufficiently analogous to the distribution and use of tangible personal property that is appropriate to apply the rules stated in this Restatement.

(b) Services, even when provided commercially, are not products.

(c) Human blood and human tissue, even when provided commercially, are not subject to the rules of this Restatement.

The baseline principle that products are tangible personal property is straightforward enough, though some tangible personalty cases present interesting factual variations. For example, in Sease v. Taylor's Pets, Inc., 700 P.2d 1054 (Or. Ct. App. 1985), *rev. denied,* 704 P.2d 514 (Or. 1985), the Oregon appellate court had no trouble holding a pet shop strictly liable for having sold a rabid skunk.

Before proceeding to consider extensions of the "product" concept beyond tangible personalty, it will be helpful to consider those commercial activities that clearly do *not* involve the sale or distribution of products: the purveyors of pure "services," referred to in subjection 19(b), supra. Examples of these commercial activities include services furnished by health care providers, architects, attorneys, engineers, and others. In Milford v. Commercial Carriers, Inc., 210 F. Supp. 2d 987 (N.D. Ill. 2002), the court refused to impose strict liability on a company that provided blueprints and designs for the construction of — but did not, itself, construct — an automobile carrier that injured its operator. Other examples of judicial refusals to extend strict liability to service providers include Truglio v. Hayes Construction Co., 785 A.2d 1153 (Conn. App. Ct. 2001) (builder of sidewalk using liquid concrete, as opposed to preformed slabs, held to have performed service); and Jackson v. L.A.W. Contracting Corp., 481 So. 2d 1290 (Fla. Dist. Ct. App. 1986) (road resurfacing company). In many instances, service providers are associated closely enough with the distribution of defective products that strict liability claims against them are at least arguable. But once the court concludes that these defendants are essentially providing services, the plaintiffs must prove negligence.

A frequently litigated example of this type of case involves repairers, who may arguably be viewed as placing a repaired product into commerce, whether or not they actually supply any parts. Repairers who furnish no replacement parts in the course of their work have been treated as providers of services, liable only if found negligent. Ayala v. V. & O. Press Co., 126 A.D.2d 229 (N.Y. App. Div. 1987). The *Ayala* decision also limited the negligence-based liability of a repairer, holding that a repairer was not required to warn the user of a design defect in the machine he was repairing when he restored the machine to the condition of its original design. See also Seo v. All-Makes Overhead Doors, 119 Cal. Rptr. 2d 160 (Cal. Ct. App. 2002) (finding no duty on the part of repairer of remote-controlled gate to correct or warn of defects). Courts, however, have held repairers who supply allegedly defective parts strictly liable for harm caused by defects in those replacement parts. See, e.g., Bell v. Precision Airmotive Corp., 42 P.3d 1971 (Alaska 2002). Similarly, strict liability has been applied to product rebuilders. See Michalko v. Cooke Color and Chemical Corp., 451 A.2d 179 (N.J. 1982) (rebuilder of machine strictly liable for defects, including design defects, despite fact that rebuilder merely followed buyer's specifications.) But see Barry v. Stevens Equipment Co., 335 S.E.2d 129 (Ga. Ct. App. 1985) (summary judgment for defendant product rebuilder in strict liability action affirmed).

Returning to the examples of "products" not involving tangible personalty referred to in subjection 19(a), supra, a generally accepted extension of strict products liability doctrine is the inclusion of commercial sellers of new housing in the category of commercial sellers of products. Historically, the major impediment to the inclusion of such sellers was the notion that the term "product" implied personalty, and did not readily apply to real property. See, e.g., Lowrie v. City of Evanston, 365 N.E.2d 923 (Ill. App. Ct. 1977). Additionally, courts assumed that purchasers of real property were as able as sellers to inspect for defects, and most of the cases did not involve personal injuries. The widespread development of mass-production techniques in the housing industry in the decades following World War II provided the factual basis for the eventual elimination of these conceptual impediments. Real estate developers began manufacturing tract houses, and courts came to realize that the individual purchasers of mass-produced homes are typically in no better position to inspect for defects than are the purchasers of mass-produced automobiles. Moreover, in many cases the structural components alleged to have been defective at time of sale were manufactured items that clearly would have qualified as "products" had they not been attached to realty when sold by the defendant.

Early in the development of products liability, the Supreme Court of New Jersey extended the boundaries of strict liability to include commercial sellers of mass-produced housing. See Schipper v. Levitt & Sons, Inc., 207 A.2d 314 (N.J. 1965); Patitucci v. Drelich, 379 A.2d 297 (N.J. Super. Ct. App. Div. 1977). See generally Sean M. O'Brien, Note, Caveat Venditor: A Case for Granting Subsequent Purchasers a Cause of Action Against Builder-Vendors for Latent Defects in the Home, 20 J. Corp. L. 525 (Spring 1995); Jonathan M. Goodman, Survey, Developments in Maryland Law, 1992-93: Real Property, 53 Md. L. Rev. 986 (1994). With few exceptions, courts in other states have followed New Jersey's lead, even in cases involving the commercial sale of new, custom-built homes. See, e.g., Bastian v. Wausau Homes Inc., 620 F. Supp. 947 (N.D. Ill. 1985); Elderkin v. Gaster, 288 A.2d 771 (Pa. 1972); Rutledge v. Dodenhoff, 175 S.E.2d 792 (S.C. 1970). But see Oliver v. Superior Court, 259 Cal. Rptr. 160 (Cal. Ct. App. 1989) (holding that strict liability did not apply against the developer who had built only two homes and was thus not a mass producer of homes).

Controversy has also surrounded the question of whether subcontractors should be subject to strict liability. In La Jolla Village Homeowners' Assn. v. Superior Court, 261 Cal. Rptr. 146 (Cal. Ct. App. 1989), one court held that subcontractors who did not have ownership or control over mass-produced homes or over their portion of the project being built could not be held strictly liable. The court noted that the subcontractor customarily performs one narrow task that is integrated into the whole. Developers and general contractors are better capitalized and better able to carry the substantial burden of strict liability. But see Bednarski v. Hideout Homes & Realty Inc., 711 F. Supp. 823 (M.D. Pa. 1989), holding an electrical subcontractor to strict liability under Pennsylvania law. In Wooldridge v. Rowe, 477 So. 2d 296 (Ala. 1985), the Alabama Supreme Court held that the builder/seller's liability, even for negligence, did not extend to subsequent purchasers from the first purchaser. See generally Paul G. Haskell, The Case for an Implied Warranty of Quality in Sales of Real Property, 53 Geo. L.J. 633 (1965).

An area in which quite a lot of judicial activity has occurred is the generation and delivery of electrical power. A small number of courts have refused to consider electricity a product. See, e.g., Curtiss v. Northeast Utilities, 1994 WL 702690 at 3 (Conn. Super. Ct. 1994) (plaintiff's cattle were injured by coming into contact with defendant's electricity lines; court found that "it strains credibility to hold a utility company strictly liable unless negligence is involved" and added that electricity cannot be "defective" because it is natural and not manufactured as such); Bowen v. Niagara Mohawk Power Corp., 183 A.D.2d 293 (N.Y. App. Div. 1992); Wyrulec Co. v. Schutt, 866 P.2d 756 (Wyo. 1993).

The majority position considers electricity a product once it has passed through a consumer's meter, as that indicates that it has been harnessed and made safe for consumer use and been placed into the stream of commerce. See Bryant v. Tri-County Electric Membership Corporation, 844 F. Supp. 347 (W.D. Ky. 1994); Otte v. Dayton Power & Light Co., 523 N.E.2d 835 (Ohio 1988). A few courts have demonstrated uneasiness with a bright-line rule that makes liability dependent on whether the electricity passes through a meter. In Monroe v. Savannah Electric and Power Co., 471 S.E.2d 854 (Ga. 1996), electricity in an overhead power line that fed a dock came in contact with a metal stanchion on plaintiff's shrimp boat, delivering a high-voltage shock. The electricity had not passed through the meter. The court held the majority rule's requirement that the electricity have passed through a meter to be too rigid. As long as the product has been placed in the stream of commerce, even short of an actual metered sale, the court reasoned, the electricity should be considered a product and strict liability should adhere. On the facts of the case, the court held that strict liability was inappropriate because the electricity in the power line had not been rendered safe for consumer use (and hence was unmarketable) at the time of the accident. Electricity becomes safe for consumer use only when it has passed through transformers that reduce the voltage to marketable levels. Similarly, in Priest v. Brown, 396 S.E.2d 638, 641 (S.C. Ct. App. 1990), a deputy sheriff arrived at an auto accident scene and tried to move a downed power line that was allegedly defective. The court noted that "a sale need not occur in the literal sense for strict liability to apply as long as the product is injected into the stream of commerce by other means." As in *Monroe,* supra, the court held that the extremely high-voltage electricity had not yet been placed in the stream of commerce and had not reached the stage where it was safe for immediate consumer use. For more on this subject see Roger W. Holmes, Strict Products Liability for Electric Utility Companies: A Surge in the Wrong Direction, 29 Suffolk U.L. Rev. 161 (1995).

One area of products liability that poses some particularly interesting conceptual questions involves the sale of information. As the following decision illustrates, the physical manifestations of a book fall neatly within the definition of a product because they are "tangible." Thus, poisonous glues used in the binding will bring strict liability. But what about the allegedly poisonous ideas within?

Winter v. G. P. Putnam's Sons
938 F.2d 1033 (9th Cir. 1991)

SNEED, Circuit Judge:

Plaintiffs are mushroom enthusiasts who became severely ill from picking and eating mushrooms after relying on information in The Encyclopedia of Mushrooms, a book published by the defendant. Plaintiffs sued the publisher and sought damages under various theories. The district court granted summary judgment for the defendant. We affirm.

Facts and Proceedings Below

The Encyclopedia of Mushrooms is a reference guide containing information on the habitat, collection, and cooking of mushrooms. It was written by two British authors and originally published by a British publishing company. Defendant Putnam, an American book publisher, purchased copies of the book from the British publisher and distributed the finished product in the United States. Putnam neither wrote nor edited the book.

Plaintiffs purchased the book to help them collect and eat wild mushrooms. In 1988, plaintiffs went mushroom hunting and relied on the descriptions in the book in determining which mushrooms were safe to eat. After cooking and eating their harvest, plaintiffs became critically ill. Both have required liver transplants.

Plaintiffs allege that the book contained erroneous and misleading information concerning the identification of the most deadly species of mushrooms. In their suit against the book publisher, plaintiffs allege liability based on products liability, breach of warranty, negligence, negligent misrepresentation, and false representations. Defendant moved for summary judgment asserting that plaintiffs' claims failed as a matter of law because 1) the information contained in a book is not a product for the purposes of strict liability under products liability law; and 2) defendant is not liable under any remaining theories because a publisher does not have a duty to investigate the accuracy of the text it publishes. The district court granted summary judgment for the defendant. Plaintiffs appeal. We affirm.

Discussion

A book containing Shakespeare's sonnets consists of two parts, the material and print therein, and the ideas and expression thereof. The first may be a product, but the second is not. The latter, were Shakespeare alive, would be governed by copyright laws; the laws of libel, to the extent consistent with the First Amendment; and the laws of misrepresentation, negligent misrepresentation, negligence, and mistake. These doctrines applicable to the second part are aimed at the delicate issues that arise with respect to intangibles such as ideas and expression. Products liability law is geared to the tangible world.

A. Products Liability

The language of products liability law reflects its focus on tangible items. In describing the scope of products liability law, the Restatement (Second) of Torts lists examples of items that are covered. All of these are tangible items, such as tires, automobiles, and insecticides. The American Law Institute clearly was concerned with including all physical items but gave no indication that the doctrine should be expanded beyond that area.

The purposes served by products liability law also are focused on the tangible world and do not take into consideration the unique characteristics of ideas and expression. Under products liability law, strict liability is imposed on the theory that "[t]he costs of damaging events due to defectively dangerous products can best be borne by the enterprisers who make and sell these products." Prosser & Keeton on The Law of Torts, §98, at 692-93 (W. Keeton ed. 5th ed. 1984). Strict liability principles have been adopted to further the "cause of accident prevention . . . [by] the elimination of the necessity of proving negligence." Id. at 693. Additionally, because of the difficulty of establishing fault or negligence in products liability cases, strict liability is the appropriate legal theory to hold manufacturers liable for defective products. Id. Thus, the seller is subject to liability "even though he has exercised all possible care in the preparation and sale of the product." Restatement §402A comment *a*. It is not a question of fault but simply a determination of how society wishes to assess certain costs that arise from the creation and distribution of products in a complex technological society in which the consumer thereof is unable to protect himself against certain product defects.

Although there is always some appeal to the involuntary spreading of costs of injuries in any area, the costs in any comprehensive cost/benefit analysis would be quite different were strict liability concepts applied to words and ideas. We place a high priority on the unfettered exchange of ideas. We accept the risk that words and ideas have wings we cannot clip and which carry them we know not where. The threat of liability without fault (financial responsibility for our words and ideas in the absence of fault or a special undertaking or responsibility) could seriously inhibit those who wish to share thoughts and theories. As a New York court commented, with the specter of strict liability, "[w]ould any author wish to be exposed . . . for writing on a topic which might result in physical injury? e.g., How to cut trees; How to keep bees?" Walter v. Bauer, 109 Misc. 2d 189, 191, 439 N.Y.S.2d 821, 823 (Sup. Ct. 1981) (student injured doing science project described in textbook; court held that the book was not a product for purposes of products liability law), aff'd in part & rev'd in part on other grounds, 88 A.D.2d 787, 451 N.Y.S.2d 533 (1982). One might add: "Would anyone undertake to guide by ideas expressed in words either a discrete group, a nation, or humanity in general?"

Strict liability principles even when applied to products are not without their costs. Innovation may be inhibited. We tolerate these losses. They are much less disturbing than the prospect that we might be deprived of the latest ideas and theories.

Plaintiffs suggest, however, that our fears would be groundless were strict liability rules applied only to books that give instruction on how to accomplish a physical activity and that are intended to be used as part of an activity that is inherently dangerous. We find such a limitation illusory. Ideas are often intimately linked with proposed action, and it would be difficult to draw such a bright line. While "How To" books are a special genre, we decline to attempt to draw a line that puts "How To Live A Good Life" books beyond the reach of strict liability while leaving "How To Exercise Properly" books within its reach.

Plaintiffs' argument is stronger when they assert that The Encyclopedia of Mushrooms should be analogized to aeronautical charts. Several jurisdictions have held that charts which graphically depict geographic features or instrument approach information for airplanes are "products" for the purpose of products liability law. See Brocklesby v. United States, 767 F.2d 1288, 1294-95 (9th Cir. 1985) (applying Restatement for the purpose of California law), *cert. denied,* 474 U.S. 1101 (1986); Saloomey v. Jeppesen & Co., 707 F.2d 671, 676-77 (2d Cir. 1983) (applying Restatement for the purpose of Colorado law); Aetna Casualty & Surety Co. v. Jeppesen & Co., 642 F.2d 339, 342-43 (9th Cir. 1981) (applying Nevada law); Fluor Corp. v. Jeppesen & Co., 170 Cal. App. 3d 468, 475, 216 Cal. Rptr. 68, 71 (1985) (applying California law). Plaintiffs suggest that The Encyclopedia of Mushrooms can be compared to aeronautical charts because both items contain representations of natural features and both are intended to be used while engaging in a hazardous activity. We are not persuaded.

Aeronautical charts are highly technical tools. They are graphic depictions of technical, mechanical data. The best analogy to an aeronautical chart is a compass. Both may be used to guide an individual who is engaged in an activity requiring certain knowledge of natural features. Computer software that fails to yield the result for which it was designed may be another. In contrast, The Encyclopedia of Mushrooms is like a book on how to use a compass or an aeronautical chart. The chart itself is like a physical "product" while the "How to Use" book is pure thought and expression. Given these considerations, we decline to expand products liability law to embrace the ideas and expression in a book. We know of no court that has chosen the path to which the plaintiffs point. . . .[5]

[The court's discussion of misrepresentation and negligence is omitted. In connection with plaintiff's claim that Putnam negligently failed to discover the alleged errors in the book, the court has held that a publisher has no duty to investigate the accuracy of an author's statement in published works.]

Winter continues to draw support. In Garcia v. Kusan, Inc., 655 N.E.2d 1290 (Mass. App. Ct. 1996), the court held that the instructions and rule book for indoor hockey are not a product for purposes of applying strict liability. Plaintiff was struck in the eye by a hockey stick during a game that took place at his elementary school. He could not identify the stick as one sold by the defendant manufacturer. Instead, he claimed that the instructions and rules accompanying

---

5. See Jones v. J. B. Lippincott Co., 694 F. Supp. 1216, 1217-18 (D. Md. 1988) (nursing student injured treating self with constipation remedy listed in nursing textbook; court held that Restatement 402A does not extend to dissemination of an idea of knowledge); Herceg v. Hustler Magazine, Inc., 565 F. Supp. 802, 803-04 (S.D. Tex. 1983) (person died after imitating "autoerotic asphyxiation" described in magazine article; court held that contents of magazines are not within meaning of Restatement 402A); Walter v. Bauer, 109 Misc. 2d 189, 190-91, 439 N.Y.S.2d 821, 822-23 (Sup. Ct. 1981) (student injured doing science project described in textbook; court held that the book was not a defective product for purposes of products liability law because the intended use of a book is reading and the plaintiff was not injured by reading), *aff'd in part & rev'd in part on other grounds,* 88 A.D.2d 787, 451 N.Y.S.2d 533 (1982); Smith v. Linn, 386 Pa. Super. 392, 398, 563 A.2d 123, 126 (1989) (reader of Last Change Diet book died from diet complications, court held that book is not a product under Restatement §402A), *aff'd,* 587 A.2d 309 (1991), cf. Cardozo v. True, 342 So. 2d 1053, 1056-57 (Fla. Dist. Ct. App.) (transmission of words is not the same as selling items with physical properties so that where a bookseller merely passes on a book without inspection, the thoughts and ideas within the book do not constitute a "good" for the purposes of a breach of implied warranty claim under the U.C.C.), *cert. denied,* 353 So. 2d 674 (Fla. 1977).

hockey sticks sold to the school constituted a defective product. The court held that the rule book sans the hockey sticks was not a defective product. See also Smith v. Linn, 563 A.2d 123 (Pa. Super. Ct. 1989), *aff'd,* 587 A.2d 309 (1991) (diet book not a product for purposes of products liability); Way v. Boy Scouts of America, 856 S.W.2d 230 (Ct. App. Tex. 1993) (advertising supplement in *Boys' Life* magazine describing shooting and firearms is not a product; decedent, a young boy killed after he was encouraged to experiment with guns as a result of advertisement, could not bring an action for products liability); Birmingham v. Fodor's Travel Publications, Inc., 833 P.2d 70 (Haw. 1992) (products liability claim cannot be brought by vacationer injured while swimming at the beach against the publisher of a travel guide that described the beach but did not warn of dangers lurking in the waters). See also Note, Read at Your Own Risk: Publisher Liability for Defective How To Books, 45 Ark. L. Rev. 699 (1992).

Just as information contained within printed materials can cause harm, so too, as the last paragraph in *Winter* suggests, can information contained within computer software. The caselaw addressing the question of whether information contained within software is a product appears to be underdeveloped. See Proof of Manufacturer's Liability for Defective Software, 68 Am. Jur. P of. 3d 333, 353 (2002) (noting that to date, "no cases have been found applying strict liability to software"); but see Hou Tex, Inc. v. Landmark Graphics, 26 S.W.3d 103 (Tex. App. 2000) (accepting for purposes of defendant's motion for summary judgment that graphics software that models data resembles a navigational chart and is arguably a product; citing *Winter,* supra). Early on, courts deliberating a related question under the Uniform Commercial Code found business software to be a "good" rather than a "service." See RRX Industries, Inc. v. Lab-Con Inc., 772 F.2d 543 (9th Cir. 1985) (software is a good under the U.C.C.); Triangle Underwriters, Inc. v. Honeywell, Inc., 604 F.2d 737 (2d Cir. 1979). Yet exceptions have been made for custom-made software. See Data Processing v. L. H. Smith Oil Corp., 492 N.E.2d 314 (Ind. App. 1986); see also Michael R. Maule, Comment, Applying Strict Products Liability to Computer Software, 27 Tulsa L.J. 735 (1992) (arguing strict liability should be imposed on mass-produced software but should be applied to other kinds only on a case-by-case basis, depending on policy considerations). Nonetheless, in 2003 the American Law Institute and the National Conference of Commissioners on Uniform State Laws complicated matters by approving a complete revision of the Uniform Commercial Code, Article 2, which is now written to exclude "information" from the definition of "goods." U.C.C. §2-103 (Proposed Amendment April 18, 2003).

In at least one area of software the question of whether or not information falls under the definition of a product for strict liability purposes appears to have been answered firmly in the negative. The information contained within interactive video game software does not constitute a product for strict liability purposes. In Wilson v. Midway Games, Inc., 198 F. Supp. 2d 167 (D. Conn. 2002), a mother sued the producers of Mortal Kombat, a console video game in which human opponents brutally slaughter one another, when her son was fatally stabbed by his adolescent friend shortly after playing Mortal Kombat. The stabbing occurred in a manner eerily resembling an episode contained within the game. Citing *Winter,* supra, the *Wilson* court conceptually divided commercial information into two categories: instruction manuals, cookbooks, navigational charts, etc. on the one hand; and exhortation, inspiration, and suggestion, on the other. The court opined that it is at least arguable that information falling within the first category should be considered a product, whereas information falling within the second category should not. Dismissing the mother's complaint for failure to state a claim upon which relief could be granted, the court reasoned that, because information contained within video game software is closer to the second category, it should not be considered a product for strict liability purposes. Other courts have reached similar results. See Sanders v. Acclaim Entertainment, 188 F. Supp. 2d 1264 (D. Colo. 2002) (Columbine victims' families failed to state a strict liability claim against game software makers, who allegedly inspired school shooting because intangible thoughts and ideas are not products); James v. Meow Media, Inc., 300 F.2d 683 (6th Cir. 2002) (Parents of school shooting victim failed to state a strict liability claim against game software makers, movie producers, and parties maintaining pornographic websites because those parties did not deal in "products.")

PROBLEM FIVE

Claire Kelly has asked you to represent her in an action against Exotic Eating Magazine. Claire became critically ill after eating a batch of muffins that she made following a recipe in Exotic Eating Magazine. Exotic Eating always requests new recipes from its readers. One reader, Marni Schlissel from Michigan, decided to submit her recipe for muffins, which had always been a big hit at family gatherings. The recipe for Marni's Marvelous Muffins called for an unusual amount of extract of wintergreen, one-half cup, to give them that special something. Extract of wintergreen is a tasty ingredient readily available in markets in the Midwest.

The magazine's testers in New York always check the availability of the recipe ingredients. When the testers couldn't find extract of wintergreen, they published the recipe with what they considered to be a reasonable substitute, oil of wintergreen. Unfortunately, oil of wintergreen is really methyl salicylate and is used primarily to rub sore muscles. Taken internally in anything more than minute quantities it becomes very toxic.

Claire made a big batch of Marni's Marvelous Muffins following the magazine's recipe step by step. As she was very hungry when she made them, she proceeded to eat three of the muffins, which she actually enjoyed before she passed out and was rushed to the hospital with toxic poisoning.

You've just read the *Winter* decision and it controls in your jurisdiction. Does Ms. Kelly have a cause of action?

POSTSCRIPT ON BLOOD AND OTHER HUMAN TISSUE

Before leaving the question of "What are products?," it remains to consider the issue addressed in subsection 19(c) of the Products Liability Restatement, supra. When a hospital or a blood bank sells a unit of blood contaminated with hepatitis or the HIV virus, and the recipient-purchaser contracts hepatitis or AIDS, should the seller be strictly liable in tort? Except for the fact that these viruses cannot be detected and eliminated, the appropriate answer would seem to be "yes"—the defendant sold a product with a defect that caused harm to the plaintiff. Hepatitis and HIV viruses are arguably "foreign" rather than "natural" ingredients in the human bloodstream, and thus constitute defects. What, then, of the fact that there is no foolproof method to detect them? On one view, that should not matter; as a practical matter, manufacturers of fabricated products such as automobiles cannot find and eliminate all "theoretically detectable" manufacturing defects, either. See, e.g., Rostocki v. Southwest Florida Blood Bank, Inc., 276 So. 2d 475, 477 (Fla. 1973).

Reacting to the possibility that courts might impose (or have imposed) strict liability in these "bad blood" cases, states have, nearly without exception, enacted shield statutes aimed at preventing such outcomes. Borne of a legislative perception that strict liability would threaten sources of these vital products, shield statutes protect sellers of blood from strict products liability and have even been interpreted to implicitly shield distributors of other parts of the human body. See, e.g., Condos v. Muskoloskeletal Transplant Foundation, 208 F. Supp. 2d 1226 (C.D. Utah 2002) (legislature intended to shield distributors of bone tissue by enacting Utah's Blood Shield Statute). The decisions are collected in Products Liability Reporter (CCH) ¶1630 (updated periodically). Some jurisdictions distinguish between commercial and non-profit sellers of blood products and human tissue. See, e.g., Ariz. Rev. Stat. Ann. §32-1481(B) (1992); La. Rev. Stat. Ann. §9:2797 (West 1991). Most have held that the policy protecting non-profit sellers extends to commercial sellers as well. See, e.g., Doe v. Travenol Laboratories, 698 F. Supp. 780 (D. Minn. 1988). Observe that the Products Liability Restatement preserves these immunities by fiat—without saying that blood is not a product, §19(c) simply places blood and other human tissue outside the scope of the Restatement. Why do you suppose the Institute handled the issue in that way?

Quite apart from the question of strict liability, suppliers of bad blood are everywhere liable for harm caused by their negligence. In this connection, careful donor selection and special handling can reduce, but not eliminate, the relevant risks. Thus, sellers who fail to take these steps may be held liable for negligently causing injury to recipients who contract hepatitis. The hot question dividing the courts concerns the standard to which blood banks will be held in administering the negligence rule. The blood bank industry has argued that they should be held to the professional standard of care that governs medical care providers. Under this approach, adherence to customary practice constitutes an absolute defense to liability. See, e.g., Osborn v. Irwin Memorial Blood Bank, 7 Cal. Rptr. 2d 101 (Cal. Ct. App. 1992); Goss v. Oklahoma Blood Institute, 856 P.2d 998 (Ct. App. Okla. 1990). Several courts, however, have refused to recognize adherence to custom as a blanket defense for blood banks. See, e.g., Vuono v. New York Blood Center, 696 F. Supp. 743 (D. Mass. 1988); Hernandez v. Nueces County Medical Society Community Blood Bank, 779 S.W.2d 867 (Tex. Ct. App. 1989).

In United Blood Services v. Quintana, 827 P.2d 509 (Colo. 1992), a plaintiff who contracted the HIV virus from contaminated blood brought suit against United Blood Services for its negligence in screening and testing the blood. After extensive discussion, the court concluded that a blood bank should be held to a professional standard of care. The court took note of the important role of custom in deciding whether a blood bank was negligent. It said:

> To be sure, there is a presumption that adherence to the applicable standard of care adopted by a profession constitutes due care for those practicing that profession. The presumption, however, is a rebuttable one, and the burden is on the one challenging the standard of care to rebut the presumption by competent evidence. . . . 827 P.2d at 521.

The embattled blood industry is facing a new threat of liability. In Snyder v. American Association of Blood Banks (AABB), 676 A.2d 1036 (N.J. 1996), the New Jersey Supreme Court affirmed liability on the part of the AABB, an organization that inspects and accredits blood banks and sets policy and standards of practice for the industry. The defendant was held liable for failing to take reasonable steps to require more vigorous testing for the HIV virus in the early 1980s. The defendant argued that it was entitled to immunity from tort liability because it performs a quasi-governmental task in regulating blood banks. The court rejected the immunity claim and found adequate evidence of negligence on the part of AABB to support the jury's verdict.

For discussion of the AIDS blood contamination cases, see Ross D. Eckert, The AIDS-Blood Transfusion Cases: A Legal and Economic Analysis of Liability, 29 San Diego L. Rev. 203 (1992); Kathryn W. Pieplow, AIDS, Blood Banks and the Courts: The Legal Response to Transfusion-Acquired Disease, 38 S.D.L. Rev. 609 (1993).

2. Which Commercial Activities Constitute "Selling or Otherwise Distributing"?

Once again, consider the Products Liability Restatement's definitions of these terms:

Restatement (Third) of Torts: Products Liability
(1998)

§20. DEFINITION OF "ONE WHO SELLS OR OTHERWISE DISTRIBUTES"

For purposes of this Restatement:

(a) One sells a product when, in a commercial context, one transfers ownership thereto either for use or consumption or for resale leading to ultimate use or consumption. Commercial product sellers include, but are not limited to, manufacturers, wholesalers, and retailers.

(b) One otherwise distributes a product when, in a commercial transaction other than a sale, one provides the product to another either for use or consumption or as a preliminary step leading to ultimate use or consumption. Commercial nonsale product distributors include, but are not limited to, lessors, bailors, and those who provide products to others as a means of promoting either the use or consumption of such products or some other commercial activity.

(c) One also sells or otherwise distributes a product when, in a commercial transaction, one provides a combination of products and services and either the transaction taken as a whole, or the product component thereof, satisfies the criteria in Subsection (a) or (b).

Subsection 20(a) describes the paradigm, the commercial product seller, to which most of the cases in these materials conform. The term "sells" implies a consideration; but in the commercial setting even gifts for which no price is charged are really transfers of title for a tacit consideration in the form of customer good will. Thus, when a business supplies free samples by way of advertising, courts apply strict liability in such cases. See, e.g., McKisson v. Sales Affiliates, Inc., 416 S.W.2d 787 (Tex. 1967). See also Levondsky v. Marina Associates, 731 F. Supp. 1210 (D. N.J. 1990) (defective glass in which free drink was served by casino). Observe that the operative concept here is "sells;" all sellers in the commercial chain, from manufacturers down to retailers, are strictly liable for defects existing at the time of sale.

Subsection 20(b) is also quite straightforward, though more interesting. As indicated in the black letter, commercial product lessors have been included in the category of suppliers held strictly liable for product defects. See, e.g., Cintrone v. Hertz Truck Leasing & Rental Service, 212 A.2d 769 (N.J. 1965); Francioni v. Gibsonia Truck Corp., 372 A.2d 736 (Pa. 1977). In *Cintrone,* the Supreme Court of New Jersey held the commercial lessor of a truck fleet strictly liable for injuries to a driver-employee of the lessee. Relying on implied warranty concepts, the court concluded that "the relationship between the parties fairly calls for an implied warranty of fitness for use, at least equal to that assumed by a new car manufacturer." 212 A.2d at 777. In Kemp v. Miller, 453 N.W.2d 872 (Wis. 1990), the court gave a ringing endorsement to *Cintrone.* The Wisconsin court held that the commercial lessor "impliedly represents that those products will be fit for use throughout the term of the lease." The court specifically held that the lessor's liability extended "not only to design and manufacturing defects but also to defects which arise after the product leaves the manufacturer's control." 453 N.W.2d at 879. The plaintiff is, however, required to establish that the product was defective when it left the lessor's control. Similarly, in Samuel Friedland Family Enterprises v. Amoroso, 630 So. 2d 1067 (Fla. 1994), a hotel guest was injured when a rented sailboat's crossbar broke. The court held that strict liability for defective products applies to commercial lessors. See also Ghionis v. Deer Valley Resort Co., 839 F. Supp. 789 (D. Utah, C.D. 1993) (ski rental); Richard C. Ausness, Strict Liability for Chattel Leasing, 48 U. Pitt. L. Rev. 273 (1987).

Subsection 20(b) also explicitly includes commercial bailors. Thus, courts have applied strict liability to suppliers of demonstration models loaned out to promote product sales. See Delaney v. Townmotor Corp., 339 F.2d 4 (2d Cir. 1964); Thorpe v. Bullock, Inc., 348 S.E.2d 55 (Ga. App. 1986) (where defendant supplier allowed a restaurant to use a deep fryer free of charge as an inducement for the restaurant to buy the fryer, supplier was just as liable as if it had sold the fryer, in that it had placed it in the stream of commerce); Beatie v. Martin Chevrolet-Buick, Inc., 786 A.2d 549 (Del. 2001) (court cites Restatement (Third) of Torts: Products Liability in holding car dealership strictly liable for harm caused by defect in promotional vehicle used by employee as a perquisite, though not in a technical bailment relationship, because vehicle was supplied for the purpose of promoting the sale or lease of other vehicles.) Defective products that cause harm prior to actual purchase receive the same treatment. See Barker v. Allied Supermarket, 596 P.2d 870 (Okla. 1979) (product harmed plaintiff before purchase in self-service store). The Eleventh Circuit, interpreting Florida law, was less charitable. In McQuiston v. K-Mart Corp., 796 F.2d 1346 (11th Cir. 1986), plaintiff suffered permanent injuries to her wrist when she lifted the lid of a cookie jar sitting on a display shelf and the lid came apart. Plaintiff had not decided to buy the cookie jar; she was just looking for a price tag on the inside of the lid. The court held that there was no action against the retailer for breach of the implied warranty of merchantability because the purchaser had not yet formed an intent to purchase. The court differentiated this case from an injury caused when plaintiff had taken the item off the shelf in a self-service store with the definite intent to purchase the item.

Commercial actors whose conduct facilitates the sale and distribution of products by others without themselves providing products for use and consumption, are generally excluded from strict products liability. Thus, trademark licensors who provide promotional material but do not supply products are held strictly liable only when they actively control or participate substantially in the design, manufacture, or distribution of the licensee's product. See Products Liability Restatement §14, Comment *d* (1998). The case law supports this proposition. For example, in Torres v. Goodyear Tire & Rubber Company, Inc., 786 P.2d 939 (Ariz. 1990), the Arizona Supreme Court held Goodyear, a trademark licensor who was actively involved in its licensee's operation, strictly liable for plaintiffs' injuries resulting from a defective Goodyear tire produced and distributed by its licensee. The court relied on Goodyear's extensive degree of control over its licensees' manufacture and production of tires. However, strict liability may not be imposed where the licensor's involvement with the licensee is tenuous. See, e.g., Tyler v. Pepsico, 400 S.E.2d 673 (Ga. 1990), where Pepsico, a soft drink franchisor, was not held strictly liable for injuries sustained by a plaintiff struck in the eye by the aluminum cap of an exploding bottle. The Georgia court reasoned that although Pepsico supplied syrup to the bottler, Pepsico and the bottler operated as distinct and separate entities, and the bottler exclusively received the proceeds from bottle sales. See generally David J. Franklyn, The Apparent Manufacturer Doctrine, Trademark Licensors and the Third Restatement of Torts, 49 Case W. Res. L. Rev. 671 (1999); Margaret Frankel Goldstein, Products Liability and the Trademark Owner: "When a Trademark Is a Warranty," 32 Bus. Law. 957 (1977); Sandrock, Tort Liability of a Non-Manufacturing Franchisor for Acts of Its Franchisee, 48 U. Cin. L. Rev. 699 (1979); Arthur Schwartz, The Foreign Trademark Owner Living with American Products Liability Law, 12 N.C.J. Intl. L. & Com. Reg. 375 (1987); Robert W. Emerson, Franchisors' Liability When Franchisees Are Apparent Agents: An Empirical and Policy Analysis of "Common Knowledge" about Franchising, 20 Hofstra L. Rev. 609 (Spring 1992).

An interesting wrinkle involving sales facilitators is presented when plaintiffs seek to include product certifiers such as Good Housekeeping and Underwriters Laboratories, who give their seals of approval to the products, as defendants in strict liability actions. The very purpose of such a seal is to induce consumer confidence in the safety and the quality of the product. Might not this be a component part of the product? Nonetheless, the few cases extant have permitted only causes of action based in negligence and have refused to impose strict liability against such certifiers. See Hempstead v. General Fire Extinguishing Corp., 269 F. Supp. 109 (D. Del. 1967); Hanbery v. Hearst Corp., 81 Cal. Rptr. 519 (Cal. Ct. App. 1969); accord United States Lighting Service v. Llerrad Corp., 800 F. Supp. 1513 (N.D. Ohio, E.D. 1992) (after defective energy-saving lights caused damages, plaintiff installer sought to recover from defendant independent testing laboratory, which had rated the product as adequate. Summary judgment was denied so that issues of negligence of the testing laboratory in rating the product could be litigated); FNS Mortgage Service Corp. v. Pacific General Group, Inc., 29 Cal. Rptr. 2d 916 (Cal. Ct. App. 1994) (summary judgment in favor of non-profit plumbing association reversed where association-approved pipe was defective and caused damage; there was a negligence claim for failing to properly assess whether the approved pipe met appropriate standards and for failing to delist it based on its substandard condition). However, a product certifier's liability extends only so far as its specific "undertaking." See the Restatement (Second) of Torts §324A (1965); Dekens v. Underwriters Laboratories Inc., 132 Cal. Rptr. 2d 699 (Cal. Ct. App. 2003) (finding that defendant could not be liable for negligence under "negligent undertaking doctrine" where it did not undertake to test product's safety with respect to asbestos content, but rather certified the product for safety with respect to fire, heat or electrical shock.)

Auctioneers are another category of sales facilitators excluded from strict products liability. In refusing to apply strict liability against an auctioneering firm that auctioned some 90 used tractors, the court, in Musser v. Vilsmeier Auction Co., 562 A.2d 279 (Pa. 1989), analogized the role of the auctioneer to that of a financier: They both help facilitate the sale of the product but neither has any role in the selection of goods for sale. It is not surprising that courts are reluctant to impose strict liability on a party whose role in marketing or producing the equipment is so far removed from the traditional role of the product seller.

Consistent with the foregoing, courts refuse to hold commercial actors who finance sales transactions, even when the financing party plays a role that formally makes it part of the distributive chain. In Abco Metals Corp. v. J.W. Imports Co., Inc., 560 F. Supp. 125, 131 (N.D. Ill. 1982) aff'd sub nom. Abco Metals Corp. v. Equico Lessors, Inc., 721 F.2d 583 (7th Cir. 1983), the court described the role of financial lessors:

> [It] does not actually provide the equipment to the lessee, but rather provides the money which allows the user of already selected equipment to purchase it. To a substantial extent, a financial lessor may be analogized to a bank that loans money to its clients. Rather than simply loaning the money for the purchase to the ultimate user of the equipment, the transaction is set up as a "lease," with the lessor "purchasing" the equipment for the specific purpose of "renting" it to the user. . . . Normally the lessor has no familiarity with the particular equipment involved and rarely does the lessor intend to take possession of the equipment when the lease term is completed.

The court went on to explain why it was inappropriate to hold financial lessors liable as a member of the distributive chain:

> The inescapable conclusion is that Equico had no input into the production or marketing of this machine. It was not, therefore, in the original chain of distribution and was not a party capable of preventing a defective product from entering the stream of commerce.

Id. at 585. See Potts v. UAP-GA AG CHEM, Inc., 567 S.E.2d 316 (Ga. 2002); D'Huyvetter v. A. O. Smith Harvestore Products, 475 N.W.2d 587 (Wis. Ct. App. 1991); Rivera v. Mahogony Corp,, 494 N.E.2d 660 (Ill. App. Ct. 1986); Bickram v. Case I.H., 712 F. Supp. 18 (E.D.N.Y. 1989).

Magrine v. Krasnica
227 A.2d 539 (N.J. 1967), *aff'd sub nom.* Magrine v. Spector,
241 A.2d 637, *aff'd,* 250 A.2d 129 (N.J. 1969)

LYNCH, J.S.C. (temporarily assigned).

The novelty of this case lies in the attempt by plaintiff, a patient of defendant dentist, to extend the rule of "strict liability" against defendant for personal injuries caused by the breaking of a hypodermic needle in plaintiff's jaw while being used by defendant in an injection procedure. The break was due to a latent defect in the needle.

Novelty, of itself, does not foreclose consideration of plaintiff's contentions in this field of developing tort law. Neither does it justify a headlong leap to impose strict liability unless, based on proper policy considerations and reason, such liability should be found. Plaintiff concedes that there is no precedent — anywhere — holding a dentist, or any other "user" of an article, strictly liable for injuries caused by a latent defect therein. Since the case is one of first impression, the court feels impelled to set forth its reasoning at some length.

The case is submitted for decision on a stipulation setting forth the following facts: On November 22, 1963 plaintiff was a patient of defendant. He was administering a local anesthetic with a hypodermic needle inserted in the left temporomandibular space, a point at the extreme end of the lower gum beyond the last tooth. The needle extended 1⅝″ beyond the syringe. It had been assembled by the doctor just before the injection and had been used approximately eight times for about three weeks prior to the accident. It is the custom of the doctor to use about four needles a month and to discard them at the end of the month. As the injection was being made the needle "separated" at the hub, the place where the needle entered the syringe, leaving the entire 1⅝″ length of the needle in plaintiff's jaw. Defendant does not know what caused the needle to break, but he believes there must have been some sort of defect in it. He does not know from whom he purchased the needle. However, he testified on oral deposition that the needle was manufactured by a certain Precision Bur Company of New York, but in answers to interrogatories he had suggested other possible manufacturers.

> Paragraph 22 of the stipulation of facts reads as follows:
> Plaintiffs make no assertion or claim that defendant failed to do what a reasonably prudent person would have done under the circumstances or that defendant did what a reasonably prudent person would not have done. Plaintiffs rely upon strict liability, breach of warranty and breach of contract to recover. They do not assert the negligence of defendant except insofar as negligence may be included in the above theories of liability.

We have seen the rapid development of the "strict liability" concept in the products liability field. . . . [W]e in New Jersey have seen it move from [Henningsen v. Bloomfield Motors, Inc., 32 N.J. 358, 161 A.2d 69 (1960)] (holding liable a manufacturer of automobiles), to [Santor v. A & M Karagheusian, 44 N.J. 52, 207 A.2d 305 (1965)] (manufacturer of rugs), to [Schipper v. Levitt & Sons, Inc., 44 N.J. 70, 207 A.2d 314 (1965)] (mass seller of homes) and, finally, moving out of the "sales" field, to [Cintrone v. Hertz Truck Leasing & Rental Service, 45 N.J. 434, 212 A.2d 769 (1965)] (lessor of a "U-Drive-It" truck held strictly liable for injuries caused by a defect in the vehicle).

Inspired by the holding in *Cintrone,* and the authorities cited therein, to the effect that "strict liability" is not confined to "sales" transactions, plaintiff conceives that the gates are wide open, at least to the extent that the doctrine should be applied "to service contracts, and particularly to those involving the use of manufactured implements in the performance of the service."

Plaintiff's argument moves from the major premise that "strict liability" is not confined to "sales," through the minor premise that the basic policy considerations of the doctrine apply to the use of a needle by a dentist, and concludes that he should be held liable though free from negligence. Since the major premise is established (*Cintrone*), it therefore remains for us to analyze the policy considerations projected by our decisions and other authorities and determine to what extent, if any, they postulate a judgment for plaintiff.

Quoting from 2 Harper and James, Law of Torts, §28.19, p. 1576 (1956), plaintiff asserts that the relevant policy considerations are as follows:

> Warranties may be imposed or annexed to a transaction by law, because one party to the transaction is in a better position than another (1) "to know the antecedents that affect . . . the quality of the thing . . . dealt with; (2) to control those antecedents; (3) and to distribute losses which occur because the thing has a dangerous quality; (4) when that danger is not ordinarily to be expected; (5) so that other parties will be likely to assume its absence and therefore refrain from taking self-protective care."

At first glance it would appear that, indeed, defendant dentist is in a "better position" "to know the antecedents that affect . . . the quality" of the needle he used and "to control those antecedents" than his patient — this for the reason that he selected his own supplier and presumably the particular needle. *Literally,* therefore, the first policy consideration would appear to be satisfied. But does the statement of Harper and James coincide with the sense of the concept as applied by our Supreme Court?

[A discussion of prior case law is omitted.]

Thus, in all of our recent cases strict liability was imposed (except with respect to a retail dealer) upon those who were in "a better position" in the sense that they *created* the danger (in making the article—*Henningsen, Santor, Schipper* and [Jakubowski v. Minnesota Mining and Manufacturing, 80 N.J. Super. 184, 193 A.2d 275 (App. Div. 1963), *rev'd on other grounds,* 42 N.J. 177, 199 A.2d 826 (1964)]), or possessed a better capacity or expertise to control, inspect and discover the defect (*Henningsen, Santor, Schipper, Jakubowski* and *Cintrone*) than the party injured. In these respects the dentist here was in no better position than plaintiff. He neither created the defect nor possessed any better capacity or expertise to discover or correct it than she.

It is further very clear that strict liability was imposed in our New Jersey cases for the *essentially basic reason* that those so held liable put the product "in the stream of trade and promote its purchase by the public." . . . Defendant dentist did not put the needle in the stream of commerce or promote its purchase.

It may be logically argued that the foregoing analysis does not effectively distinguish defendant from the retail dealer who, for example, sells food in a sealed container, or otherwise has no opportunity to discover a defect in the article he sells, and who nevertheless is liable for breach of warranty. In this respect such retail dealer is in no better position to discover the defect than the dentist here. Nevertheless, the situations are distinct. In the first place, the Uniform Sales Act and the Uniform Commercial Code, *legislative* enactments, apply to sales and there can be no judicial construction which could deny a warranty against a retail seller. At common law the implied warranty was originally confined to food. Even so, several courts have refused to impose warranty liability on the "innocent" retailer who has no means of discovering the defect in the goods. Such reasoning is not without a concept of fairness. Prosser suggests that other courts may follow this position but that he would hold such a dealer liable. Of more meaningful significance is a recognition that the *essence of* the transaction between the retail seller and the consumer relates to the *article sold.* The seller is *in the business* of supplying the product to the consumer. It is that, and that alone, for which he is paid. A dentist or a physician offers, and is paid for, his professional services and skill. That is the *essence* of the relationship between him and his patient.

Plaintiff also invokes the policy consideration of "spreading of the risks"—the concept which suggests that defendant could cover his liability by insurance, or he could be held harmless by impleading his supplier or manufacturer. The "risk distributing theory" is a relevant consideration. But again, we must appreciate the context in which it has been applied in our cases. In *Henningsen, Santor, Schipper* and *Cintrone* it was considered in holding liable the manufacturer or lessor, who put the goods in the stream of commerce. Such a party may fairly be assumed to have substantial assets and volume of business, and a large area of contacts over which the risk can be widely spread. It is the "large-scale" enterprise which should bear the loss. The impact of liability upon such a defendant is minuscule in comparison with that of an individual dentist or physician. His means of "spreading the risk" could be by insurance or impleading his supplier or manufacturer. "Malpractice" insurance, however, does not cover implied warranty unless the policy "expressly covers contract claims." In this very case defendant dentist is represented not only by counsel for his insurance carrier but also by his personal counsel because the carrier denies coverage. In any event, there are definite limits as to how far the argument of "risk-spreading" by insurance can go. As Prosser says in "The Assault":

> What insurance can do, of course, is to distribute losses proportionately among a group who are to bear them. What it cannot do and *should not do is to determine whether the group should bear them in the first instance*—and whether, for example, consumers shall be compelled to accept substantial price increases on everything they buy in order to compensate others for their misfortunes. Even the distribution of the losses through insurance may be a process that has its flaws. (at p. 1121; emphasis added)

So, here, if the dentist or physician were to obtain insurance covering strict liability for equipment failure, the risk would be spread upon his patients by way of increased fees. Can anyone gainsay the fact that medical and dental costs, and insurance therefore, are already bearing hard there? Witness the constant cry over increasing medical-surgical insurance premiums in New Jersey. As a matter of principle, the spreading of losses to their patients subverts, rather than supports, the policy consideration that the loss should be imposed on those best able to withstand it, i.e., the manufacturer or other entity which puts the article into the stream of commerce. . . .

Something can be said, by way of logical argument, in plaintiff's favor, for the policy consideration that if the dentist be held liable he, as the retail seller of food in a sealed container, can implead the manufacturer and thus be used as a conduit to place the loss where it belongs. This, too, should be regarded as only a "makeweight" argument. While we fully appreciate the appeal of the suggestion that the retail dealer — or the dentist here — is the most convenient conduit to "fight out" liability with the ultimate manufacturer, we are not satisfied that in this case such circuity of action is appropriate. . . . Here, as the stipulation says, defendant "does not know from whom the needle was purchased; he testified on oral depositions that the needle was manufactured by a certain Precision Bur Co. of New York, New York, but in answers to interrogatories Dr. Krasnica had suggested other possible manufacturers." Thus, plaintiff is not without remedy to reach the supplier by proper use of discovery procedures. If it be shown that identification of the supplier does not eventuate in this particular case, and *both* plaintiff and defendant are denied recourse to him, then our answer is that this is a "hard case" from which bad law should not flow. It is not the usual situation, for ordinarily the manufacturer can be reached. In our view it would be bad law to sustain plaintiff's contentions because the relevant policy considerations do not justify imposition of strict liability upon a dentist in the first, or last, instance. Further, the vast body of malpractice law, presumably an expression of the public policy involved in this area of health care, imposes upon a dentist or physician liability only for negligent performance of his services-negligent deviation from the standards of his profession. In the performance of his professional skill he has control of what he does. As to the instrument he uses, he has no control with respect to a latent defect therein. Why, then, should he be held strictly liable for the instruments he uses, as to which he has no control over latent defects, and liable only for negligence in the performance of his professional services, which he does control? "Suggestive analogy" is useful, but reason and consistency of principle should not be totally disregarded. . . .

We must consider, also, the consequences if we were to adopt the rule of strict liability here. The same liability, in principle, should then apply to any user of a tool, other equipment or any article which, through no fault of the user, breaks due to a latent defect and injures another. It would apply to any physician, artisan or mechanic and to any user of a defective article — even to a driver of a defective automobile. In our view, no policy consideration positing strict liability justifies application of the doctrine in such cases. No more should it here. . . .

Judgment for defendant.

As *Magrine* suggests, providers of medical services are generally not treated as commercial sellers of the medical products they use and otherwise provide in the course of treatment. Thus, hospitals are not considered sellers of medical supplies utilized during surgery. See, e.g., *In Re* Breast Implant Product Liability Litigation, 503 S.E.2d 445 (S.C. 1998) (breast implants); Cafazzo v. Central Medical Health Services, Inc., 668 A.2d 521 (Pa. 1995) (defective mandibular prosthesis implanted in plaintiff); Easterly v. HSP of Texas, Inc., 772 S.W.2d 211 (Tex. Ct. App. 1989) (catheter included in an epidural kit during the administration of anesthesia broke and was left in the patient's spine). But see Bell v. Poplar Bluff Physicians Group, Inc., 879 S.W.2d 618, 620 (Mo. Ct. App. 1994), *overruled by* Budding v. SSM Healthcare Sys., 19 S.W.3d 678 (Mo. 2000) (court refused to apply strict liability against hospital that supplied temporomandibular interpositional joint implant. Statute requires that negligence be established against health-care providers).

Magrine is an example of the type of case described in Subsection 20(c), supra, often referred to as a "sales-service hybrid" or "nonsale supplier transaction." In general, other than in the medical context, courts have been willing to impose strict liability on providers of services as long as a product-sale component can be identified. In Newmark v. Gimbel's Inc., 258 A.2d 697 (N.J. 1969), a well-known decision involving an allegedly defective hair treatment product used on a beauty parlor customer, the Supreme Court of New Jersey reversed the trial court's refusal to give a strict liability instruction to the jury. The court likened the defendant's position to that of a retailer and distinguished *Magrine,* supra, on several grounds, among them that the beauty parlor operator was a nonprofessional offering a mechanical and routine service; that he advertised for customers; and that he charged customers directly for the products consumed in the course of treatment.

A good example of the sort of sales-service hybrid in which courts are likely to find that the service component dominates, and thus are likely to refuse to impose strict liability, is Ferrari v. Grand Canyon Dories, 38 Cal. Rptr. 2d 65 (Cal. Ct. App. 1995), *rev. denied,* 1995 Cal. LEXIS 2964 (Cal. 1995) in which the plaintiff was a passenger on a white water rafting trip arranged by the defendant commercial tour provider. Plaintiff was injured when she hit her head on the raft's metal frame, and alleged that the raft was defective in that the frame was not buffered by padding and no helmets were provided. In rejecting plaintiff's claim that the tour supplier was subject to strict liability as lessor of the raft, the court analogized the situation to an airline passenger suing the airline rather than the plane manufacturer for a defect in the plane. The court explained the various roles: "The manufacturer's role is that of a provider of a product, the airplane. On the other hand, the airline operating the plane would be primarily involved in providing a service, i.e., transportation. The airline is itself the end user of the product and imposition of strict liability would be inappropriate." Id. at 71. For a further look at the sale-service issue, see Ellen Taylor, Applicability of Strict Liability Warranty Theories to Service Transactions, 47 S.C. L. Rev. 231 (1996).

Nonsale suppliers may conveniently be divided into two subcategories: those who charge their customers specifically and directly for the use of the product provided, and those who treat the costs of furnishing the product as part of their overhead, to be reflected in the prices they charge for their other products and services. Several courts have imposed strict products liability on nonsale suppliers in the first subcategory. For example, the Superior Court of Delaware imposed strict liability on the operator of a skating rink for injuries to a patron caused by an alleged defect in a pair of rented roller skates. Wilson v. Dover Skating Center, Ltd., 566 A.2d 1020 (Del. Super. Ct. 1989). The court concluded that the rink was the owner-lessor of the skates and that, as such, it was in the best position to inspect the skates for defects and take defective pairs out of circulation. The court also determined that the rental of the skates was an integral part of the rink's business and was used as an inducement to garner additional customers.

Compared with the preceding group, nonsale suppliers in the second subcategory, who do not specifically charge customers for using the products, are involved in many more reported cases across a broader range of fact patterns. The comparative abundance and variety of these decisions stems in part from the fact that many commercial enterprises furnish products for the temporary use and convenience of their customers. Examples of non-liability include supermarkets that provide shopping carts (see, e.g., Keen v. Dominick's Finer Foods, Inc., 364 N.E.2d 502 (Ill. App. Ct. 1977)) and hotels that supply bathmats in their bathrooms (see, e.g., Wagner v. Coronet Hotel, 458 P.2d 390 (Ariz. Ct. App. 1969)). A similar result obtained in a recent case where an aerobatics flight student was killed in a crash. Cook v. Gran-Aire, Inc., 513 N.W.2d 652 (Wis. Ct. App. 1994), *rev. denied,* 520 N.W.2d (Wis. 1994). The court found that no sale or lease had taken place despite a separate charge for the use of the plane, because the plane had never left the possession or control of the flight school insofar as the instructor at all times had access to separate flight controls. See also Feik v. Sieg Company, 823 F. Supp. 588 (C.D. Ill. 1993) (auto parts store that lent a compressor vise to a customer so that he could self-install new struts not strictly liable; the loan was not part of the consideration for the purchase, nor was the use of a compressor a necessary incident to the sale).

Although commentators have urged extension of the boundaries of strict products liability to include nonsale suppliers in this second subcategory (see, e.g., John C. Love, Landlord's Liability for Defective Premises: Caveat Lessee, Negligence, or Strict Liability?, 1975 Wis. L. Rev. 19), courts have been reluctant to impose strict liability on this group. In part, this reluctance reflects an unwillingness to overturn the rules limiting the liability of commercial enterprises for harm suffered by persons coming onto business premises. The plaintiffs in these nonsale supplier cases are typically business invitees to whom the invitor owes a duty of reasonable care. In such cases, proof of negligence has traditionally been a prerequisite to invitor liability.

In an early case, California held a defendant landlord to strict liability when a defective glass shower door broke and injured a tenant. Becker v. IRM Corp., 698 P.2d 116 (Cal. 1985). However, in Peterson v. Superior Court, 899 P.2d 905 (Cal. 1995), the Supreme Court overruled *Becker* and joined the majority of courts, holding that strict liability was not available against a landlord to a plaintiff tenant who had slipped in an allegedly defective bathtub.

3. When Is a Product Seller or Other Distributor "In the Business of Selling or Distributing"?

The general rule that strict liability applies only to commercial product distributors can be traced back to the origins of products liability law in commercial sales warranties. The limitation was built into §402A of the Restatement (Second) of Torts, considered the wellspring of American products liability law. In its terms, that section applies to product distributors "engaged in the business of selling" such products. (§402A(1)(a)). Comment *f* states that strict liability:

> applies to any manufacturer of such a product, to any wholesale or retail dealer or distributor, and to the operator of a restaurant. It is not necessary that the seller be engaged solely in the business of selling such products. Thus the rule applies to the owner of a

The Boundaries of Strict Products Liability

> **authors' dialogue 2**
>
> **JIM:** You remember Judge Vincent McKusick, an advisor to the Products Liability Restatement project?
>
> **AARON:** How could I not remember Vince? He had recently retired as Chief Justice of the Supreme Judicial Court of Maine. He was one of the most helpful, thoughtful advisors we had.
>
> **JIM:** Do you remember what he told us at the very beginning of the Restatement project, in early 1993, about trying to define the boundaries—what are products, and who can be said to have sold or distributed them?
>
> **AARON:** Yeah. He said it would be harder than trying to nail a jellyfish to the wall. Was he right?
>
> **JIM:** Having just finished reorganizing the boundaries material for the fifth edition, I'd say he exaggerated a bit. I'll stick with what we said at the outset of this Section: The boundaries are clear enough to make the system workable. But they're flexible enough to make it interesting.

motion picture theatre who sells popcorn or ice cream, either for consumption on the premises or in packages to be taken home.

The rule does not, however, apply to the occasional seller of food or other such products who is not engaged in that activity as a part of his business. Thus it does not apply to the housewife who, on one occasion, sells to her neighbor a jar of jam or a pound of sugar.

As noted at the beginning of this Section, the new Products Liability Restatement applies to "one engaged in the business of selling or otherwise distributing products." Two categories of product suppliers are excluded from coverage: (1) those who supply unsafe and defective products, but in noncommercial contexts; and (2) those who supply unsafe and defective products in a commercial context, but are not in the business of selling the type of product supplied. In cases involving the first type of supplier, courts unanimously refuse to impose strict liability, even when the supplier sells the product. See, e.g., Elley v. Stephens, 760 P.2d 768 (Nev. 1988) (Husband and wife sellers not strictly liable for harm caused to buyers by manufacturing defect in their "prefab" home). Inevitably, some cases come close to the line between commercial and noncommercial activity, but most are fairly easy to categorize. Thus, when someone gives, lends, or sells to a neighbor a defective product that subsequently causes an injury, the transferor is liable in tort only if the injured party can prove negligence.

In contrast to the product suppliers in the first category just considered, the suppliers in the second category who routinely escape strict liability are those who, although clearly commercial, are not in the business of supplying the type of product that injured the plaintiff. Thus, courts refuse to apply strict liability to isolated sales of products by commercial enterprises not in the business of selling the same type of product as those causing injury. (These cases are frequently said to involve "casual sales.") See, e.g., Ridenhour v. Colson Caster Corp.,

687 S.W.2d 938 (Mo. App. 1985) (contractor not strictly liable for lending defective scaffolding as a matter of convenience to plaintiff's employer, subcontractor); Suklijian v. Ross & Son Co., 503 N.E.2d 1358 (N.Y. 1986) (sale of an old industrial mill found to be "casual" because completely incidental to defendant's business producing space technology). However, one should not assume that a one-time sale of a particular product will necessarily be found to be casual. In Sprung v. MTR Ravenburg, Inc., 788 N.E.2d 620 (N.Y. 2003), the New York Court of Appeals found that a strict liability claim against a specialty sheet metal manufacturer for a defective retractable floor should not be precluded by the fact that the manufacturer had not ever produced such a floor. The court justified this holding in that the sale was "not incidental" to the manufacturer's normal business, but rather a regular sort of sale for the manufacturer. Id. at 623-624.

CHAPTER TWO
Assigning Responsibility Inside and Outside the Commercial Chain of Distribution

A. ALLOCATING RESPONSIBILITY BETWEEN PRODUCT DISTRIBUTORS AND OTHER DEFENDANTS AND AMONG MEMBERS OF THE DISTRIBUTIVE CHAIN

1. Joint and Several Liability

At early common law, two situations in which defendants acted tortiously toward the plaintiff gave rise to what is now referred to as joint and several liability: (1) where the defendants acted in concert to cause the harm, and (2) where the defendants acted independently but caused indivisible harm. Liability in the case of concerted action is a form of vicarious liability, in which all the defendants will be responsible for the harm actually caused by only one of them. An example of this is where A and B engage in an automobile race on a public street and A runs over the plaintiff. B will be liable to the plaintiff just as much as A, although B did not actually hit the plaintiff. Joint and several liability will also be imposed if the defendants act independently, each actually causing harm to the plaintiff but under circumstances in which it is impossible to apportion harm between defendants. Thus, if the plaintiff were a passenger in A's automobile, which collided with B's automobile due to the fault of both drivers, A and B will be jointly and severally liable for the harm to the plaintiff.

Because of the procedural limitations relating to the circumstances under which two or more defendants could be joined in a single action, the common law distinguished between these two types of cases. Where the defendants acted in concert, they were joint tortfeasors and could be joined in one action, or sued separately, hence the phrase joint and several liability. But where defendants acted independently to cause indivisible harm, courts would not allow joinder. In those cases, defendants were severally liable only. Technically, only defendants acting in concert were called joint tortfeasors. However, modern rules of procedure permit joinder in indivisible harm cases (see Fleming James et al., Civil Procedure 557, 5th ed., 2001), and today courts refer to defendants causing such harm as joint tortfeasors. The term "joint and several liability" has now become a shorthand phrase to reflect a substantive rather than a procedural rule. It means that each joint tortfeasor can be held responsible for the totality of the plaintiff's judgment. A plaintiff cannot, of course, recover more, in total, than the amount of his judgment and any interest owing at the time of satisfaction. Furthermore, there is no requirement that jointly and severally liable defendants be joined as defendants. There is also no requirement that the defendant from whom the judgment is collected be substantially at fault.

As the following materials indicate, modern tort law provides opportunities for the defendant initially singled out by the plaintiff to shift some (or all) of the liability to other defendants who should share (or bear entirely) the financial burden. Given these more recent developments, of what significance, today, is the theoretical "jointness" of the defendant's liability to the plaintiff? The most important implication is a practical one: If the other defendants are judgment proof, the jointly liable defendant against whom the plaintiff successfully proceeds ends up holding the entire financial bag. Thus, in an egregious case that catalyzed reform efforts, a defendant adjudged one percent at fault footed 86 percent of the damages bill. Walt Disney World Co. v. Wood, 515 So. 2d 198 (Fla. 1987).

With the adoption of comparative fault by most American jurisdictions, the question arises whether joint tortfeasors should be limited to the allocated fault apportionments, thus eliminating traditional joint tortfeasor liability. In other words, a defendant would be "severally liable," i.e., liable for only the percentage of harm allocated to him or her by the fact finder. The legislatures have been busy enacting statutes to deal with apportionment issues, and by now, a majority of states have adopted some form of limitation on joint and several liability. Fourteen jurisdictions—Alabama, Arkansas, Delaware, the District of Columbia, Maine, Maryland, Massachusetts, North Carolina, Pennsylvania, Rhode Island, South Carolina, South Dakota, Virginia, and West Virginia—still adhere to the common law joint and several system. See Reporters' Notes to §§17, A18, Restatement (Third) of Torts: Apportionment of Liability (2000).

Eighteen states have abolished joint and several liability. They are Alaska, Arizona, Colorado (with an exception for concerted action), Idaho (with an exception for concerted action), Indiana (with an exception for medical malpractice claims), Kansas, Kentucky, Louisiana, Michigan (with an exception for medical malpractice claims among other exceptions), Minnesota (with an exception for concerted action), Montana (with certain exceptions), Nevada, New Mexico, North Dakota, Tennessee, Utah, Vermont, and Wyoming. See Reporters' Notes to §§17, B18, Restatement (Third) of Torts: Apportionment of Liability (2000).

Most of the reform has been effected through legislation; very few states have abolished joint and several judicially, though a few did so initially and then followed up with statutory codification. Tennessee, however, rejected the common law joint and several doctrine by case law when it adopted comparative fault. McIntyre v. Balentine, 833 S.W.2d 52 (Tenn. 1992). Later, in Owens v. Truckstops of America, Inc., 915 S.W.2d 420 (Tenn. 1996), the Tennessee Supreme Court distinguished the entire distributive chain from other tortfeasors in the context of products liability cases. Thus, in Tennessee, all tortfeasors are severally liable only, but retailers, manufacturers, and other members of the distributive chain are jointly and severally liable for the percentage of fault allocated to the entire distributive chain.

While retention of the common law rule and outright abolition constitute the polar extremes, many states have adopted middle-ground positions by statute, limiting in some fashion the plaintiff's recovery to the percentage of fault assigned to each defendant. The statutes are often byzantine in their complexity. Many contain myriad qualifications — e.g., abolishing joint and several only when defendants meet a threshold percentage of fault (Illinois), or only when the plaintiff is not at fault, or for some causes of action and not others, or for only non-economic loss (pain and suffering). Many states employ combinations of these conditions. For summaries of these statutes, see Reporters' Notes to §§17, D19, E18, Restatement (Third) of Torts: Apportionment of Liability (2000).

A common feature of joint and several reform measures is application of a percentage threshold that triggers a reversion to joint liability. If the defendant is determined to be more than, say, 50 percent at fault, then liability is joint and several rather than several only. For example, in Montana and New Hampshire, if a defendant is more than 50 percent at fault, he is jointly and severally liable; otherwise several liability applies. Wisconsin's threshold is 51 percent (Wis. Stat. Ann. §895.045 (West Supp. 1995) (amended 1995)) and New Jersey's is 60 percent; 1995 N.J. Stat. Ann. §2A:15-5.3 (West Supp. 1995). Minnesota limits the liability of defendants 15 percent or less at fault to four times their share, Minn. Stat. Ann. §604.01 (West 1988 and Supp. 1995).

Five states — Georgia, Ohio, Missouri, Oklahoma, and Washington — tie several recovery to a plaintiff's fault (i.e., only a faultless plaintiff will be entitled to a joint and several award).

Many of the statutes include exceptions for certain types of torts. An interesting example is New Mexico's law, N.M. Stat. Ann. §41-3A-1 (Michie repl. pamp. 1989), which retains joint and several liability for intentional torts claims, claims of vicarious liability, strict products liability claims, and claims that the courts find implicate a "sound basis in public policy" that demands application of the joint and several rule.

A few other states except intentional torts; some retain the common law doctrine for products liability; and one reverts to joint and several for all strict liability claims (Nevada). And, echoing the modern concerns about the environment, five states make exceptions for toxic torts, environmental torts, or cases involving solid waste disposal sites. Idaho, Nevada, and Washington (which, notably, preserves joint and several for business torts and manufacturers of generic products as well as toxics and acting in concert), along with New Mexico, supra, are the most laden with exceptions. Something about that area of the country?

Eight states — California, Connecticut, Florida, Hawaii, Nebraska, New York, Ohio, and Oregon — have abolished joint and several for noneconomic damages (e.g., pain and suffering) only. Of these, Hawaii is most riddled with exceptions, ranging from intentional torts, toxic torts, and environmental pollution to aircraft and motor vehicle accident claims, strict and products liability claims, and claims based on maintenance and design of highways where the tortfeasor had notice of similar accidents. Also in Hawaii, if a defendant is at fault 25 percent or more, he is jointly liable. H.R.S. §663-10.9 (repl. 1993). Florida, New York, and Oregon maintain percentage thresholds for noneconomic loss. See Reporters' Notes to §§17, C21, Restatement (Third) of Torts: Apportionment of Liability (2000).

Several states (Connecticut, Michigan, Minnesota, Missouri, Montana, New Hampshire, Oregon) have opted for a kinder, gentler modification of the common law joint tortfeasor doctrine, patterned after the Uniform Comparative Fault Act. According to this model, in the event of an insolvent tortfeasor, the forfeited share is reallocated among the remaining parties, including the plaintiff, if the plaintiff was negligent. Michigan limits any reallocated amount to no more than the proportion of the defendant's negligence.

A related issue that has received attention in recent years is whether to allocate fault to nonparties. Some states allow the factfinder to take into account the fault of nonparties, including settling tortfeasors and immune parties. Supporters of this position point out that without considering the fault of nonparties or immune parties, the goal of limiting a defendant's liability to his percentage of fault is undercut. Defendants will pay more than their several shares of awards since the fault of nonparties will be borne by the available defendants. Detractors retort that plaintiffs may not be fairly compensated for their losses when recovery is reduced based on the fault of a nonparty. Furthermore, plaintiffs complain that it is difficult to litigate the fault of nonparties who are not identified. Nonparty defenses are included in many of the reform statutes. See, e.g., Burns Ind. Code Ann. §34-51-2-7 (Supp. 2003); New Mexico, supra (calculation of nonparty fault permitted, not required); Utah Code Ann. §78-27-38 (1992 and Supp. 1995) (amended 1994); Colo. Rev. Stat. Ann. §13 21 111.5 (West 1989 and Supp. 1995) (requires statutorily defined notice before the nonparty defense can take hold).

The pace and vigor that have characterized joint and several liability reform have led to understandable complexity; it is often hard to keep track of even one state's frenetic activity in this arena. Many jurisdictions have developed a patchwork of case-law-based clarifications and amendments on top of intense activity on the part of legislatures. To trace these developments, useful discussions of the joint tortfeasor tort reform movement can be found in Kathleen M. O'Connor and Gregory P. Sreenan, Apportionment of Damages: Evolution of a Fault-Based System of Liability for Negligence, 61 J. Air L. & Com. 365 (1996) (includes a complete rundown of each jurisdiction's overarching scheme); Gregory C. Sisk, Comparative Fault and Common Sense, 30 Gonz. L. Rev. 29 (1994/1995); Edward J. Kionka, Recent Developments in the Law of Joint and Several Liability and the Impact of Plaintiff's Employer's Fault, 54 La. L. Rev. 1619 (1994).

2. *Letting Retailers and Wholesalers Out of the Litigation*

One interesting development has been the movement (or at least the beginnings of a movement) to let retailers and wholesalers off the strict liability hook (or at least partway off). Later in this chapter we consider the rules governing contribution and indemnity among the various members in the distributive chain. The tendency in that connection is for the liability to be passed up the chain from retailers and wholesalers to the manufacturer by means of implied rights of indemnity. Although this tendency reduces the ultimate exposures to liability of retailers and wholesalers, those categories of sellers are routinely joined as defendants and, even if eventually they (or their insurers) escape liability to the plaintiff, they incur substantial costs defending against liability and otherwise protecting their interests.

Earlier, in the days when implied warranty and res ipsa loquitur were the vehicles by which product sellers' liabilities were expanded, some jurisdictions recognized exceptions for retailers and wholesalers to whom products came wrapped in packaging that prevented inspection for defects. Despite the fact that these "sealed package," or "sealed container," exceptions for retailers and wholesalers were not recognized by the Second (or Third, for that matter) Restatement of Torts, §402A, a number of states have retained them, often by statute. See Del. Code Ann. Tit. 18 §7001 (1999) (product sold in "sealed container" and in "unaltered form" provides a defense to action for manufacturing or design defect); Md. Code Ann. Cts. & Jud. Proc. §5-405(b) (2001) (using virtually identical language).

The "sealed container" doctrine has even been extended to shield defendants from strict liability in cases where products are sold outside of their containers. In Jones v. GMRI, Inc., 551 S.E.2d 867 (N.C. Ct. App. 2001) the North Carolina Court of Appeals applied that state's "sealed container" statute, G.S. §99B-2(a), which provides that:

> No product liability action, except an action for breach of express warranty, shall be commenced or maintained against any seller when the product was acquired and sold by the seller in a sealed container or when the product was acquired and sold by the seller under circumstances in which the seller was afforded no reasonable opportunity to inspect the product in such a manner that would have, or should have, in the exercise of reasonable care, revealed the existence of the condition complained of, unless the seller damaged or mishandled the product while in his possession. . . .

At trial, the jury had found that contaminated meatballs served by the defendant restaurant had arrived in a "sealed container" and been promptly cooked, giving the defendant "no reasonable opportunity to inspect," and judgment had been entered on that verdict. The appellate court affirmed because defendant was entitled to judgment by the "plain meaning" of the statute given the jury's findings.

Some observers feel that imposing strict liability on retailers and wholesalers is unfair, at least when the manufacturer is available to be a defendant. Consider the Model Uniform Product Liability Act, 44 Fed. Reg. 62,714 (1979).

§105. Basic Standards of Responsibility for Product Sellers Other than Manufacturers

(A) A product seller, other than a manufacturer, is subject to liability to a claimant who proves by a preponderance of the evidence that claimant's harm was proximately caused by such product seller's failure to use reasonable care with respect to the product.

Before submitting the case to the trier of fact, the court shall determine that the claimant has introduced sufficient evidence to allow a reasonable person to find by a preponderance of the evidence that such product seller has failed to exercise reasonable care and that this failure was a proximate cause of the claimant's harm.

In determining whether a product seller, other than a manufacturer, is subject to liability under Subsection (A), the trier of fact shall consider the effect of such product seller's own conduct with respect to the design, construction, inspection, or condition of the product, and any failure of such product seller to transmit adequate warnings or instructions about the dangers and proper use of the product.

Unless Subsection (B) or (C) is applicable, product sellers shall not be subject to liability in circumstances in which they did not have a reasonable op-

authors' dialogue 3

JIM: The MUPLA provision letting wholesalers and retailers off the hook unless they themselves were negligent or expressly warranted the product seems to make good sense. I can see why so many state legislatures have enacted such legislation.

AARON: In general I agree with you. Letting them out makes a lot of sense. But neither MUPLA nor the state statutes are sensitive to problems that plaintiffs will face once the middlemen are taken out of the picture. Here, as elsewhere, legislators cannot foresee all the fallout from the rules that they enact into law.

JIM: I don't see the problem. The legislation allows for recovery when the manufacturer is not subject to the jurisdiction of the court of the claimant's domicile and also allows recovery when the manufacturer is insolvent or when it is highly probable that it will become insolvent.

AARON: But that's not enough protection for plaintiffs. Consider the following scenario. Plaintiff files suit against XYZ Corp. in January 2000 for the sale of a defective product that caused her injury. The wholesaler and retailer move to dismiss because they were not negligent nor did they expressly warrant the product. In January 2000 there is no hint that XYZ is in financial trouble, so the trial court grants the middlemen's motions. The case muddles along in state court for five years before it comes to trial. In January, 2005, XYZ Corp. files for Chapter 11. Thus when the case is ready for trial, XYZ is no longer a solvent defendant. The wholesaler and retailer,

portunity to inspect the product in a manner which would or should, in the exercise of reasonable care, reveal the existence of the defective condition.

(B) A product seller, other than a manufacturer, who makes an express warranty about a material fact or facts concerning a product is subject to the liability set forth in Subsection 104(D) [dealing with liability for express warranty].

(C) A product seller, other than a manufacturer, is also subject to the liability of manufacturer under Section 104 if:

(1) The manufacturer is not subject to service of process under the laws of the claimant's domicile; or

(2) The manufacturer has been judicially declared insolvent in that the manufacturer is unable to pay its debts as they become due in the ordinary course of business; or

(3) The court determines that it is highly probable that the claimant would be unable to enforce a judgment against the product manufacturer.

(D) Except as provided in Subsections (A), (B), and (C), a product seller, other than a manufacturer, shall not otherwise be subject to liability under this Act.

however, were dismissed from the suit in 2000. If plaintiff tries to sue them in 2004-5, the tort statute of limitations will have run. Plaintiff is out of luck.

JIM: By gosh you're right, Aaron. But there is an easy fix. The MUPLA-based statute should be changed so that the statute of limitations against the middlemen is tolled and that, if the manufacturer becomes insolvent at any time before trial, the wholesaler and retailer can be brought back into the litigation.

AARON: If the middlemen cannot close their books on the case at the time suit against the manufacturer is brought, what good does the MUPLA-based legislation do them? They have to insure against products liability losses. And what is worse, they will be forced to reenter a case four years from the original time of suit. They would have to reopen discovery so that they could properly defend themselves. It's no fun to have to enter a case many years after the injury event.

JIM: I think that middlemen could purchase insurance rather cheaply if their only exposure were that they would be held liable if the manufacturer subsequently became insolvent. As for discovery, it is unlikely that the manufacturer who sought to defend the case when it was still solvent, would not have developed sufficient information to mount a defense. Why would they not share such information with their middlemen? I'm not making light of the problem you raised. With major companies going into insolvency, the problem is real. But with the change in legislation that I suggest, it seems to me that plaintiffs will have adequate protection and middlemen would not be hurt too badly. No legislative resolution on this issue will be letter perfect. But middlemen legitimately want out of products liability suits in which they are truly nonplayers and the law ought to accommodate them.

The Model Uniform Product Liability Act (MUPLA), one of the most significant proposals at the state level for reform of American products liability law, was developed by a special task force of the United States Department of Commerce. Promulgated in 1979, MUPLA is aimed at bringing uniformity to what has increasingly become a confusing patchwork of varying state law. One of the interesting aspects of §105, supra, is that such a reform may stand a better chance of enactment into law than reform aimed at helping manufacturers, because wholesalers and retailers represent a large and politically powerful group, better able than are manufacturers to present the "little guy" image at legislative hearings. Evidence that these groups wield considerable clout is the fact that a large number of states have passed legislation along the line of MUPLA §105. See, e.g., Idaho Code §6-1407 (Michie Supp. 1985) (adopting MUPLA largely verbatim); N.J. STAT. ANN. §2A:58C-8 (West 2000) (product seller subject to strict liability if: manufacturer is unknown, or manufacturer has no presence in the U.S., or has no attachable assets, or has been adjudicated bankrupt and a judgment is not otherwise recoverable from the assets of the bankrupt estate); Ohio Rev. Code Ann. §2307.78 (Anderson 2001) (product "supplier" subject to products liability as if a manufacturer only if: manufacturer is not subject to process within the state, manufacturer is not subject to enforcement mechanisms, supplier owned the manufacturer at time of manufacture or vice versa, supplier furnished designs, supplier altered or failed to maintain the product after gaining possession, supplier marketed the product under its own label, or supplier neglected to furnish name and address of manufacturer upon request in a timely manner). Legislation embodying the basic provisions of MUPLA §105 has also been included in proposed (but vetoed) federal legislation. See The Common Sense Product Liability Legal Reform Act of 1996, H.R. Conf. Rep. No. 481, 104th Cong., 2d Sess. (1996).

PROBLEM SIX

Florence Green wants you to represent her in a products liability action. Ms. Green's story is simple and straightforward. The week before her parents' anniversary she went to Jack's Liquor Mart to buy several bottles of Shangri-La Champagne. She took the bottles home and refrigerated them in preparation for the anniversary party she was giving. When the party was in full swing she went to the refrigerator and removed a bottle of champagne. When she tried to open the bottle it suddenly exploded and caused disfiguring cuts to her face. Jack's Liquor Mart is a high-volume discount liquor supermarket. It purchased 100 cases of Shangri-La Champagne from Triangle Liquor Distributors, who had purchased the champagne from the Shangri-La Winery. The bottles used by the Winery were manufactured by Glass Perfect, Inc. to the specifications of Shangri-La.

Your initial investigation reveals that Jack's Liquor Mart is a frequent litigant in exploding champagne bottle cases. The problem stems from the self-service aspect of the store. Customers have free access to the bottles and bottle abuse by customers who think it rather funny to shake up a bottle of champagne or otherwise mishandle the bottle (for example, by scratching it with a pocket knife) is not uncommon. The owner of Jack's Liquor Mart (Jack Keehl) has done his best to cut down this practice by putting several guards on duty but he frankly admits that he cannot stop a prankster who is intent on doing damage. The expert who has examined this broken glass is certain that the bottle was defective when it exploded but he cannot determine where in the distributive chain such defect came into being.

In evaluating the case you discover that New California has enacted legislation identical to the provision of the Model Uniform Product Liability Act §105, set forth supra. You must now decide whether the case has sufficient merit for you to pursue it.

3. Contribution Among Members of the Distributive Chain

At early common law, if the plaintiff recovered against one of several joint tortfeasors, the liable tortfeasor was without legal recourse against the others to compel them to share the burden of liability. The harshness of this early rule has been ameliorated to some extent, and today most states provide for contribution among joint tortfeasors, either by statute or by judicial decision. A number of states have adopted the Uniform Contribution Among Tortfeasors Act, in either its 1939 or its 1955 version. See Reporters' Notes to §23 of Restatement (Third) of Torts: Apportionment of Liability (2000). The basic principles are contained in the following excerpts from the 1955 Uniform Act:

§1. [RIGHT TO CONTRIBUTION]

(a) Except as otherwise provided in this Act, where two or more persons become jointly or severally liable in tort for the same injury to person or property or for the same wrongful death, there is a right of contribution among them even though judgment has not been recovered against all or any of them.

(b) The right of contribution exists only in favor of a tortfeasor who has paid more than his pro rata share of the common liability, and his tort recovery is limited to the amount paid by him in excess of his pro rata share. No tortfeasor is compelled to make contribution beyond his own pro rata share of the entire liability.

(c) There is no right of contribution in favor of any tortfeasor who has intentionally [willfully or wantonly] caused or contributed to the injury or wrongful death.

(d) A tortfeasor who enters into a settlement with a claimant is not entitled to recover contribution from another tortfeasor whose liability for the injury or wrongful death is not extinguished by the settlement nor in respect to any amount paid in a settlement which is in excess of what was reasonable. . . .

§2. [PRO RATA SHARES]

In determining the pro rata shares of tortfeasors in the entire liability . . . their relative degrees of fault shall not be considered. . . .

The Uniform Act calls for the trier of fact initially to allocate fault among joint tortfeasors on a pro rata basis. Under that approach, if there are three such defendants, each is assigned one-third of the liability burden. In contrast to this pro rata approach, the majority of states have now adopted approaches that might be referred to as "equitable allocation," in which the share of liability initially allocated to each defendant is determined on the basis of that defendant's comparative share of the negligence, or fault. This is accomplished either by statute, or by judicial decision. See, e.g., Blazovic v. Andrich, 590 A.2d 222 (N.J. 1991); Schneider National, Inc., v. Holland Hitch Co., 843 P.2d 561 (Wyo. 1992). Thus, if defendant A is found by the judge or jury to have been 40 percent negligent; defendant B, 50 percent; and defendant C, 10 percent, and all of the defendants are solvent and nonimmune, they would owe $40,000, $50,000, and $10,000, respectively, of a $100,000 judgment. Note that the problem of contribution among tortfeasors is eliminated if a tortfeasor's liability is limited to the tortfeasor's percentage of the fault. Since a tortfeasor will not pay more than the equitable share assigned to that tortfeasor, that person will not be entitled to contribution.

In Zeller v. Cantu, 478 N.E.2d 930 (Mass. 1985), the Massachusetts Supreme Judicial Court concluded that its version of the Uniform Contribution Act, calling for pro rata contribution, had not been impliedly repealed by the enactment of the Comparative Fault Act. The court imposed pro rata liability on a doctor and a surgical blade manufacturer.

The Restatement (Third) of Torts: Apportionment of Liability §23 (2000) adopts the following approach:

§23. CONTRIBUTION

(a) When two or more persons are or may be liable for the same harm and one of them discharges the liability of another by settlement or discharge of judgment, the person discharging the liability is entitled to recover contribution from the other, unless the other previously had a valid settlement and release from the plaintiff.

(b) A person entitled to recover contribution may recover no more than the amount paid to the plaintiff in excess of the person's comparative share of responsibility.

(c) A person who has a right of indemnity against another person under §22 does not have a right of contribution against that person and is not subject to liability for contribution to that person.

An important difference between products liability cases and other kinds of tort cases is the fact that, in products cases, the defendants are usually members of the same commercial chain of distribution and thus have opportunities to address the contribution question ahead of time, by contract. These contract provisions tend to allocate on an "all-or-nothing" basis, and thus might be considered "contracts of indemnity." In any event, courts give them effect as between the contracting parties in the distributive chain. See generally Victor E. Schwartz, Comparative Negligence, Chap. 16 (1994); Henry Woods, Comparative Fault §13.12 (1987). See also William M. Landes & Richard A. Posner, Joint and Multiple Tortfeasors — An Economic Analysis, 9 J. Legal Stud. 517 (1980).

4. Indemnity Rights up the Distributive Chain

A plaintiff injured by a defective product typically sues all the members of the distributive chain who can be served. As we shall see, wholesalers and retailers may be held strictly liable for selling defective products even though they were not at fault and had no way of discovering that the product was defective. It is not surprising that these nonmanufacturing sellers seek indemnity from parties above them in the distributive chain. When the sellers are, in fact, totally free from fault, each seller is entitled to indemnity from any predecessor in the distributive chain. See, e.g., Promaulayko v. Johns Manville Sales Corp., 562 A.2d 202 (N.J. 1989). In Godoy v. Abamaster of Miami, Inc., the plaintiff brought an action for defective design against a retailer, a wholesale distributor, and an importer/distributor after she lost four fingers while operating a commercial meat grinder. 302 A.D.2d 57 (N.Y. App. Div. 2003). Although the jury apportioned 50 percent of the fault to the distributor and only 10 percent to the distributor/importer, the court found that the evidence did not support the finding that either defendant was more negligent than the other. Finding *Promaulayko*'s reasoning persuasive, the court held that in the absence of the manufacturer, the party closest to the manufacturer, the importer/distributor, should indemnify the distributor lower in the commercial chain of distribution. However, when the wholesaler or retailer has been negligent in its distribution of the product, there is little reason to allow full indemnity up the chain. Thus, in Frazer v. A.F. Munsterman, Inc., 527 N.E.2d 1248 (Ill. 1988), the Illinois Supreme Court denied indemnity in favor of the retail distributor of a trailer manufactured with defective brakes by the third-party defendant. Indemnity was inappropriate, the Illinois high court reasoned, because the distributor had been found negligent in providing its customer with an inadequate trailer hitch. The jury should apportion liability between the manufacturer and the retail distributor under the Illinois contribution act. Refusing to allow full "upstream" indemnity does not undermine the policies underlying strict products liability, the court concluded. (One Justice dissented vigorously.) And in Thatcher v. Commonwealth Edison Co., 527 N.E.2d 1261 (Ill. 1988), the Illinois Supreme Court applied the rule in *Frazer* to bar indemnity on behalf of a downstream purchaser/user who settled the injured tort-plaintiff's claim against it. Although the settlement prevented a jury finding on the issue of negligence, the high court held the settlement to be a sufficient admission of fault to bar the upstream claim of full indemnity. (One justice dissented, arguing that mere settlement is not the equivalent of an admission or finding of fault and that the issue of the settling defendant's culpability, if any, should be tried.) 527 N.E.2d at 1264.

Other courts, however, insist that a negligent actor whose fault contributed to the plaintiff's injury should be entitled to full indemnity against the manufacturer. In Schneider National, Inc. v. Holland Hitch Co., 843 P.2d 561 (Wyo. 1992), the operator of a trucking company was allowed full indemnity against the manufacturer of a defective trailer hitch that broke and caused the trailer to disengage and kill passengers in an oncoming car despite the claim by the hitch manufacturer that the trucker had acted negligently in failing to inspect the tractor and trailer. The trucking company impleaded the manufacturer of the hitch for full indemnity. The court held that it was appropriate to hold the hitch manufacturer for the entirety of the loss under strict liability since it was the "cheapest cost avoider." Similarly in East Penn Mfg. Co. v. Pineda, 578 A.2d 1113 (D.C. App. 1990), a retailer who was an experienced seller of batteries and was negligent in failing to place an adequate warning on a battery warning of dangers attendant to jumpstarting sought full indemnity from the battery manufacturer. The court found an implied duty to indemnity because the seller reasonably relied on the manufacturer's knowledge and skill in making a defect-free product and the seller's negligence consisted, at most, of a failure to discover the defect.

Where contribution rules allow joint tortfeasors to recover against each other based on the percentage of fault rather than on a pro rata basis, there seems to be no good reason to allow a defendant whose fault contributed to the injury to recover total indemnity. The majority of cases clearly point in that direction. See Debra T. Landis, Annotation, Products Liability: Seller's Right to Indemnity From Manufacturer, 79 A.L.R.4th 278 (1990). The Restatement (Third) of Torts: Apportionment of Liability §22 (2000) provides:

§22. INDEMNITY

(a) When two or more persons are or may be liable for the same harm and one of them discharges the liability of another in whole or in part by settlement or discharge of judgment, the person discharging the liability is entitled to recover indemnity in the amount paid to the plaintiff, plus reasonable legal expenses, if:

(1) the indemnitor has agreed by contract to indemnify the indemnitee, or
(2) the indemnitee
(i) was not liable except vicariously for the tort of the indemnitor, or

(ii) was not liable except as a seller of a product supplied to the indemnitee by the indemnitor and the indemnitee was not independently culpable.

(b) A person who is otherwise entitled to recover indemnity pursuant to contract may do so even if the party against whom indemnity is sought would not be liable to the plaintiff.

5. Settlement and Release Between the Plaintiff and Members of the Distributive Chain

It is most often to the advantage of both plaintiff and defendant to settle out of court. Indeed, without pervasive settlement practice the litigation system, which is already overburdened, would bog down completely. When joint tortfeasors are involved, the plaintiff may be able to reach agreement with only one of the tortfeasors. At common law, if the plaintiff settled with one joint tortfeasor, all were automatically released. This rule discouraged settlements since plaintiffs would be unwilling to settle with one party for a reasonable dollar amount if it might require abandoning claims against the remaining tortfeasors. The automatic release rule has now been rejected by all states, and plaintiff is able to release one tortfeasor and retain actions against the others. See generally William L. Prosser and W. Page Keeton, The Law of Torts, §49 (5th ed. 1984). See also Restatement (Third) of Torts: Apportionment of Liability §40(b) (2000).

Another problem has arisen, however. Does the defendant who settles with the plaintiff and receives a release from liability remain open to a contribution action by the defendant who decides to eschew settlement and litigate? May the litigating defendant who loses the lawsuit turn to the settling defendant and demand contribution for the damages paid out as a result of the judgment? There are no easy solutions to these problems. If contribution against the settling defendant is permitted, defendants will be discouraged from entering into settlements; under such a rule, settlement may not buy the settling party peace, but may only delay the lawsuit for a later day. On the other hand, if contribution against the settling defendant is not allowed and the judgment is reduced only by the dollar amount of the settlement, a "sweetheart settlement" between friendly parties may leave the nonsettling tortfeasor holding the bag. A succession of Uniform Contribution Among Tortfeasor Acts have dealt with this problem in different ways. The 1939 Act left the settling tortfeasor liable for contribution and the 1955 Act adjusted the rule slightly by releasing the settling tortfeasor from contribution if, but only if, the settlement had been made in good faith. Section 23 of the Restatement (Third) of Torts: Apportionment of Liability (2000), reproduced supra, bars contribution against the settling party who obtains a release from the plaintiff.

The Uniform Comparative Fault Act, promulgated in 1979, takes a markedly different approach to resolving this problem. The act provides for allocation of fault for each party in the action. Section 6 of the Act provides:

> A release, covenant not to sue, or similar agreement entered into by a claimant and a person liable discharges that person from all liability for contribution, but it does not discharge any other persons liable upon the same claim unless it so provides. However,

the claim of the releasing person against other persons is reduced by the amount of the released person's equitable share of the obligation, determined in accordance with the provisions of [another] Section.

A simple hypothetical demonstrates how this works. Consider the following example propounded in a leading treatise:*

> Assume plaintiff (P) has suffered $100,000 in damages because of the combined negligence of two defendants (D1 and D2). Plaintiff settles with D1 for $10,000 and proceeds to trial against D2. In a jurisdiction following the Uniform Act, the jury finds P 10% at fault, D1 60% at fault, and D2 30% at fault. Had P not settled with D1, P would have received a judgment against both defendants for 90% of P's damages (D1's 60% plus D2's 30%) or $90,000. Under the Uniform Act's principle of joint-and-several liability, P could have recovered $90,000 from either joined defendant. But because P has settled with D1, P's judgment under the Uniform Act is reduced by D1's share of the fault; thus P receives a judgment not for 90% of the damages but only for 90% less 60% (D1's share), or 30%. This amounts to a $30,000 judgment against D2; when added to the $10,000 received in settlement from D1, P has received a total of $40,000 — as opposed to the $90,000 P would have received had P not settled. Settling with D1 has cost plaintiff $50,000. [Comparative Negligence: Law and Practice §19.10[6](1995).]

In short, plaintiff settled out of not only the dollar amount of the claim with the settling tortfeasor but also the percentage of fault that will ultimately be attributed to him. Under this approach, which is adopted in §16 of the Restatement (Third) of Torts: Apportionment of Liability (2000), plaintiff can no longer profitably enter into a sweetheart settlement with the settling tortfeasor. If the defendant's fault percentage is higher than plaintiff has estimated, the difference comes out of the plaintiff's pocket.

Although the solutions under the Uniform Comparative Fault Act and the new Restatement governing allocation of liability have merit, they can discourage some legitimate settlements from taking place because a plaintiff may be unwilling to barter away a hitherto undetermined percentage of the lawsuit. Consider, for example, a plaintiff injured as a result of the combined fault of automobile driver error and defective brakes. Assume that the driver has low liability insurance limits and no assets otherwise available to pay a judgment. The insurer might be willing to tender the face value of the policy in settlement and close the case, but the plaintiff may not be willing to accept the settlement and issue the release. By releasing the settling tortfeasor from liability the plaintiff forgoes the right subsequently to collect that defendant's percentage of fault from the solvent, otherwise jointly and severally liable tortfeasor. Is there any sensible way out of this morass?

Another problem that requires resolution concerns a tortfeasor who settles out and receives a release but does not discharge other defendants from liability. The remaining tortfeasor goes to trial and it is determined in the ensuing litigation that the settling torfeasor paid more than his or her equitable share in settling the case. Is the settling torfeasor entitled to contribution against the nonsettling

---

*Copyright © 1995 by Matthew Bender & Co., Inc. Reprinted with permission from Comparative Negligence: Law and Practice. All rights reserved.

tortfeasor? Most states do not allow contribution. Where, however, the settling tortfeasor gets a full release for the entirety of the claim against all defendants, most states grant the settling tortfeasor the right of contribution against the nonsettling defendants. See, e.g., Ariz. Rev. Stat. §12-2501 (d) (2003); Iowa Code §668.5(2) (2003); Ore. Rev. Stat. §18.440 (3) (2001). A few states take the position that a settling tortfeasor waives all contributions rights. See, e.g., N.Y. General Obligations Law §15-108(c) (McKinney 2001). Some commentators question the wisdom of this position. Why should a settling torfteasor not be entitled to contribution against a nonsettling tortfeasor who is totally protected from a lawsuit by the plaintiff? The defendant has, so to speak, bought out the lawsuit by his settlement with the plaintiff. Why should the norsettling defendants receive a windfall?

For treatments of the problems attendant on settlement see Lewis A. Kornhauser and Richard L. Revesz, Settlements Under Joint and Several Liability, 68 N.Y.U. L. Rev. 427 (1993); Jean Macchiaroli Eggen, Understanding State Contribution Laws and Their Effect on the Settlement of Mass Torts Actions, 73 Tex. L. Rev. 1701 (1995); Daniel Klerman, Settling Multidefendant Lawsuits: The Advantage of Conditional Setoff Rules, 25 J. Legal Stud. 445 (1996).

B. ASSIGNING RESPONSIBILITY COLLECTIVELY TO THE DISTRIBUTIVE CHAIN

This section examines techniques whereby an injured victim may overcome difficulties in establishing where in the commercial distributive chain (manufacturer, wholesaler, retailer, etc.) the product came to be defective. For the purpose of this discussion, we will assume that the product was defective when the purchaser bought it from the retailer, but that it is not clear when the defect arose. A diagram will help to clarify the analysis. Figure 1 sets forth a diagram of a verti-

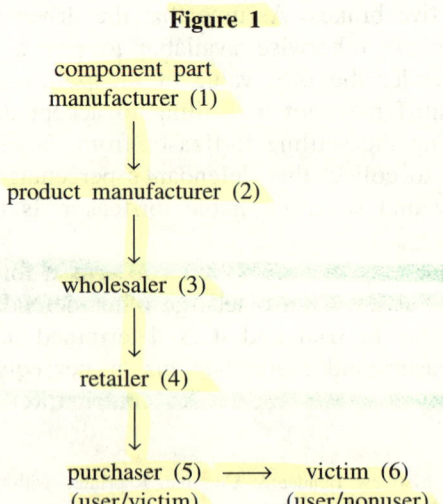

Figure 1

cal distributive chain from top to bottom, coupled with a horizontal chain across the bottom from left to right. Note that the diagram presents two variations regarding the horizontal chain. The first is that the user/victim is the direct purchaser of the product from the vertical chain ((5) in the diagram). The second is that the victim is not the purchaser but rather is a third party, either a user or a nonuser in the horizontal chain ((6) in the diagram). Both variations can present the plaintiff with serious problems in identifying the defect in the hands of a financially solvent and legally responsible party.

In order to recover in negligence against one or more defendants in the chain, the plaintiff must prove that it (or they) acted negligently in causing the defect to occur or remain undetected. Even if the plaintiff can prove that some defendants' efforts at quality control were negligently inadequate, each defendant will point to the others as the source of the defect. The manufacturer (1), wholesaler (2), and retailer (3) will insist that "A member of the chain above me caused the defect, and I could not reasonably be expected to have discovered it." The component part manufacturer, manufacturer, and wholesaler will argue that "A member of the chain below me caused the defect." All four defendants will also argue, of course, that the defect occurred after the last commercial sale of the product; while it was being used, but we have assumed away that possibility in our hypothetical in order to simplify the analysis of "gap in the chain" problems that persist even when the plaintiff can prove that he bought a dangerously defective product.

Under strict liability, some, but not all, of the finger pointing is eliminated. Strict liability holds the defendant liable for commercially selling a defective product. Whether the defect is discoverable or not by the seller is irrelevant. Thus, the parties down the distributive chain (i.e., manufacturer, wholesaler, retailer) cannot point up the chain and contend that the defect was created before the product came into their hands. That might be the basis of a defense under negligence but it is not under strict liability. However, the finger pointing down the chain continues to be a viable line of defense under strict liability. Remember, it is almost always legitimate for a defendant to contend that the product was nondefective when the defendant distributed it and that the defect was introduced after the product left the defendant's hands. Thus, if any member of the distributive chain is insolvent, underinsured, or immune from suit, the plaintiff may be forced to seek recovery up the chain. The classic answer by defendants up the chain will be that the product was tampered with or otherwise became defective down the chain.

The materials that follow consider several approaches by which plaintiffs may be able to overcome these difficulties of proof by holding the entire commercial chain jointly and severally liable for harm caused by a defect existing at the time the product was finally delivered to the plaintiff or to the plaintiff's predecessor in the horizontal chain of use and consumption.

1. Holding Members of the Distributive Chain Liable Collectively in the Normal Course of Events

The phrase "in the normal course of events" should not convey the impression that courts routinely allow a plaintiff who can prove that a product was defective when he bought it to join the entire commercial chain, including the manufacturer, without also proving that the product was defective from the very beginning. Most courts will not do that. However, a minority of states have been more generous to injured plaintiffs and have allowed them to join the members of the chain as defendants without identifying the original source of the defect existing at the time of retail sale. Some of these decisions pre-date adoption of §402A. See, e.g., Nichols v. Nold, 258 P.2d 317 (Kan. 1953); Loch v. Confair, 93 A.2d 451 (Pa. 1953). William L. Prosser, the author of §402A, criticized these decisions in The Fall of the Citadel, 50 Minn. L. Rev. 791, 847 (1966). Subsequent decisions have followed this same course. See, e.g., Snider v. Bob Thibodeau Ford, Inc., 202 N.W.2d 727 (Mich. Ct. App. 1972).

In Prutch v. Ford Motor Co., 618 P.2d 657 (Colo. 1980), the Colorado Supreme Court held that plaintiff need not establish where in the distributive chain the defect arose. The court said:

> To impose an impossible or unreasonably onerous burden of proof is to deny many consumers a meaningful remedy. Thus, the plaintiff's burden should be no more than to establish that the defect arose in the course of manufacture-distribution and before the plaintiff purchased the item. . . . A plaintiff . . . therefore, should be able to satisfy the burden of proof by evidence that at the time of purchase or acquisition the product was flawed, . . . and damages resulted. . . .
>
> Manufacturers, distributors and sellers in the chain usually have greater access to information identifying a defect's source than does the buyer. Moreover, they are in a position to protect themselves against losses from conduct of another in the chain, as by "hold harmless" and indemnity agreements or other contractual arrangements. . . .
>
> Requiring each defendant in the chain of distribution to show that the product was not defective when it left its control imposes no unreasonable burden on defendants. Such a procedure simply redistributes the burden to those who have superior knowledge of the truth and better access to evidence. [Id. at 660.]

An Arizona appellate court added its endorsement. Mineer v. Atlas Tire Co., 806 P.2d 904 (Ariz. Ct. App. 1990).

Notwithstanding these decisions, the general rule remains that the plaintiff must establish that the product was defective in the hands of each defendant sought to be held strictly liable. When a gap cannot be covered by evidence sufficiently probative to point the finger at a particular defendant, the plaintiff loses against that defendant. See, e.g., Moreno v. Sayre, 208 Cal. Rptr. 444 (Cal. Ct. App. 1984); SCM Corp. v. Letterer, 448 N.E.2d 686 (Ind. Ct. App. 1983); Marderosian v. The Stroh Brewery Co., 333 N.W.2d 341(Mich. Ct. App. 1983).

2. *Special Circumstances that May Justify a More Aggressive Approach to Shifting Responsibility to the Entire Chain*

Anderson v. Somberg
338 A.2d 1 (N.J.), *cert. denied*, 423 U.S. 929 (1975)

PASHMAN, J.

These negligence-products liability actions had their inception in a surgery performed in 1967 on the premises of defendant St. James Hospital (Hospital).

Assigning Responsibility Collectively to the Distributive Chain

Plaintiff was undergoing a laminectomy, a back operation, performed by defendant Dr. Somberg. During the course of the procedure, the tip or cup of an angulated pituitary rongeur, a forceps-like instrument, broke off while the tool was being manipulated in plaintiff's spinal canal. The surgeon attempted to retrieve the metal but was unable to do so. After repeated failure in that attempt, he terminated the operation. The imbedded fragment caused medical complications and further surgical interventions were required. Plaintiff has suffered significant and permanent physical injury proximately caused by the rongeur fragment which lodged in his spine.

Plaintiff sued: (1) Dr. Somberg for medical malpractice, alleging that the doctor's negligent action caused the rongeur to break; (2) St. James Hospital, alleging that it negligently furnished Dr. Somberg with a defective surgical instrument; (3) Reinhold-Schumann, Inc. (Reinhold), the medical supply distributor which furnished the defective rongeur to the hospital, on a warranty theory; and (4) Lawton Instrument Company (Lawton), the manufacturer of the rongeur, on a strict liability in tort claim, alleging that the rongeur was a defective product. In short, plaintiff sued all who might have been liable for his injury, absent some alternative explanation such as contributory negligence.

Dr. Somberg testified that he had not examined the rongeur prior to the day of surgery. He inspected it visually when the nurse handed it to him during the operation, and manipulated its handles to make certain it was functional. The doctor stated that he did not twist the instrument, and claimed that the manner in which the instrument was inserted in plaintiff's body precluded the possibility of twisting. He noted the absence of one of the rongeur's cups when he withdrew the instrument from plaintiff's spinal canal, but his efforts to retrieve the fragment proved of no avail.

Dr. Graubard, a general surgeon, testified as an expert witness for plaintiff. He stated that the rongeur was a delicate instrument, a tool not to be "used incorrectly or with excessive force or to be used against hard substances." He claimed that a twisting of the instrument might cause it to break at the cups. Dr. Graubard stated that a "rongeur used properly and not defective would not break." The deposition of the operating room supervisor of defendant hospital, Sister Carmen Joseph, was read into the record. She was responsible for visually examining and sterilizing all instruments prior to surgery. The rongeur in question was used about five times a year, and had been used about 20 times before this operation. She did not know who had taken out the rongeur for this operation; she had not worked the day of plaintiff's operation.

The hospital's purchasing agent testified that the rongeur had been purchased from the distributor, Reinhold, about four years prior to plaintiff's surgery and was received in a box bearing the name of the manufacturer, Lawton. The owner of Reinhold testified that the rongeur was not a stock item and had to be specially ordered from Lawton upon receipt of the hospital purchase order. The box was opened at Reinhold's warehouse, to verify that it was a rongeur and it was then forwarded to the hospital.

Defendant Lawton called a metallurgist, a Mr. John Carroll, as an expert witness. He testified that an examination of the broken rongeur revealed neither structural defect nor faulty workmanship. He said that the examination (conducted at an optical magnification 500 times normal size) revealed a secondary crack near the main crack but he could not suggest how or when that crack formed.

Mr. Carroll offered an opinion as to the cause of the instrument's breaking: the instrument had been strained, he said, probably because of an improper "twisting" of the tool. The strain, however, could have been cumulative, over the course of several operations, and the instrument could conceivably have been cracked when handed to Dr. Somberg and broken in its normal use.

In short, when all the evidence had been presented, no theory for the cause of the rongeur's breaking was within reasonable contemplation save for the possible negligence of Dr. Somberg in using the instrument, or the possibility that the surgeon had been given a defective instrument, which defect would be attributable to a dereliction of duty by the manufacturer, the distributor, the hospital or all of them. The case was submitted to a jury on special interrogatories, and the jury returned a finding of no cause as to each defendant. On appeal, the entire Appellate panel concurred in an order for a new trial. A majority held that the verdict represented a miscarriage of justice, and that on the facts of this case it was clear that one of the parties was liable and the jury should have been told that it had to return a verdict against at least one of the defendants. The concurring opinion writer argued that the jury had not been properly instructed on its prerogatives to find for plaintiff; but he felt that the order for a directed verdict against an unnamed defendant was an invitation to the jury to guess which defendant was liable. Accordingly, the concurrence urged that the case be remanded for trial, and that the jury be instructed that plaintiff had made out a very strong prima facie case.

First, we note that the suggestion in the concurring opinion that the case be sent back on "strengthened" instructions is little more than a pretext for giving plaintiff a second chance before a jury. Neither in the Appellate Division nor before this Court has it been alleged, let alone demonstrated, that the charge did not comport with the standard charge for a "strong" prima facie case made out by res ipsa loquitur (thought to be appropriate here). [The trial judge had instructed the jury as follows:

> The right of the defendants to have the plaintiff bear the required burden is a substantial one and not a mere matter of form. This burden may be sustained, however, on the basis of all of the evidence in this case and the legitimate inferences to be drawn from it. And in this connection you may consider that the defendants were the only ones shown to have any relationship with the pituitary rongeur which broke during the course of the operation. And you may infer that the breaking was attributable to dereliction on the part of one or other of the defendants in this case.]

The position adopted by the Appellate Division majority seems to us substantially correct: that is, at the close of all the evidence, it was apparent that at least one of the defendants was liable for plaintiff's injury, because no alternative theory of liability was within reasonable contemplation. Since defendants had engaged in conduct which activated legal obligations by each of them to plaintiff, the jury should have been instructed that the failure of any defendant to prove his nonculpability would trigger liability; and further, that since at least one of the defendants could not sustain his burden of proof, at least one would be liable. A no cause of action verdict against all primary and third-party defendants will be unacceptable and would work a miscarriage of justice sufficient to require a new trial.

In the ordinary case, the law will not assist an innocent plaintiff at the ex-

Assigning Responsibility Collectively to the Distributive Chain

pense of an innocent defendant. However, in the type of case we consider here, where an unconscious or helpless patient suffers an admitted mishap not reasonably foreseeable and unrelated to the scope of the surgery (such as cases where foreign objects are left in the body of the patient), those who had custody of the patient, and who owed him a duty of care as to medical treatment, or not to furnish a defective instrument for use in such treatment can be called to account for their default. They must prove their nonculpability, or else risk liability for the injuries suffered. . . .

The imposition of the burden of proof upon multiple defendants, even though only one could have caused the injury, is no novelty to the law, as where all defendants have been clearly negligent. Summers v. Tice, 33 Cal. 2d 80, 199 P.2d 1 (1948). As against multiple defendants where there is no evidence as to where culpability lies, the rule is not generally available, according to Prosser, because it might impose an equal hardship on an innocent defendant as on an innocent plaintiff. Prosser notes exceptional special cases, as where defendant owes a special responsibility to plaintiff, and in those instances the burden of proof can in fact be shifted to defendants. Prosser, Torts (4 ed. [1971]), pp. 243-244, 231, 223. The facts of this case disclose just such a special responsibility, and require a shifting of the burden of proof to defendants. . . .

In cases of this type, no defendant will be entitled to prevail on a motion for judgment until all the proofs have been presented to the court and jury. The judge may grant any motion bearing in mind that the plaintiff must recover a verdict against at least one defendant. Inferences and doubts at this stage are resolved in favor of the plaintiff. If only one defendant remains by reason of the court's action, then, in fact, the judge is directing a verdict of liability against that defendant.

The holding of the Court in this matter will, according to the dissenters, remove from the judicial process "any semblance of rationality" and reduce it to "trial by lot, or by chance." The objections which they raise, however, hardly justify this resplendently apocalyptic rhetoric. . . .

The dissenters . . . accuse the Court of deliberately and perversely ignoring the fact — known, they assert, by everyone associated with the case — that not all conceivable defendants are before the trial court. The accusation is, of course, true. Anyone with a moderately fertile imagination could conceive of other persons whose conduct might have caused the injury. Indeed, as the dissenters are at pains to note, two witnesses did speculate that another doctor might have damaged the rongeur within the preceding four years, and, while none of the witnesses or parties have thus far suggested the possibility, the Court on its own motion might note that it is also conceivable that some unknown enemy of Mr. Anderson might have slipped into the hospital prior to the operation and deliberately damaged the instrument or that some unknown disgruntled employee of Reinhold-Schumann or Lawton Instrument might have done so.

Nevertheless, the fact remains that involvement by any person other than the defendants actually before the court below has never been asserted as anything other than pure and undisguised speculation. None of the defendants introduced any evidence to actually support the claim of responsibility by other persons; they made no effort to join additional parties. It would be exceedingly unjust to deny plaintiff compensation simply because an imaginative defendant can conceive of other possible parties. On the record presently before the Court, the contention of the dissent, that the Court is "visiting liability . . . upon parties who are more probably than not totally free of blame," is, at best, an exercise in judicial hyperbole.

A wholly faultless plaintiff should not fail in his cause of action by reason of defendants who have it within their power to prove nonculpability but do not do so. In this case, the balance of equities requires no less.

The judgment of the Appellate Division is hereby affirmed, and the cause remanded for trial upon instructions consonant with this opinion.

JACOBS, J., concurs in the result but votes to affirm on the majority opinion rendered in the Appellate Division.

MOUNTAIN, J., dissenting. This Court has reached an extraordinary result in a very remarkable way. As I shall hope to make clear, the structure of argument as presented in the Court's opinion is rested upon an assumed factual premise which does not exist. In part because of this, the concluding and most significant part of the argument suffers from the defect of visiting liability, in a wholly irrational way, upon parties who are more probably than not totally free of blame. I respectfully dissent.

During the course of the Court's opinion there appear statements to the effect that all those who might have been in any way responsible for plaintiff's injury are before the court. Hence, the argument continues, a process of selection properly undertaken by the finder of fact cannot fail to implicate the true culprit or culprits. Indeed, as I read the opinion, the entire argument is made to rest upon this premise: each and every person who may have brought about the imperfection in the surgical instrument or who may have caused the injury by its misuse is before the court; it remains only to identify him.

And yet we know — and everyone who has been associated with this case has always known — that this assumption is not in fact true. The only four defendants in the case are: the surgeon, Dr. Harold Somberg, who performed the operation; St. James Hospital, the medical facility in which the operation took place; Lawton Instrument Co., which manufactured the rongeur; and Reinhold-Schumann, Inc., the distributor which sold it to the hospital. There is no other defendant in the case. And yet the record is replete with testimony that other surgeons — perhaps as many as twenty — have used the rongeur during the four years that it has formed part of the surgical equipment of the hospital, and that any one or more of them may perfectly well have been responsible for so injuring the instrument that it came apart while being manipulated in plaintiff's incision; or that it may have been weakened to near breaking point by cumulative misuse, entirely by persons not now before the court. In the face of this uncontroverted proof that the surgical instrument had been used upon approximately twenty earlier occasions and possibly by the same number of different surgeons, in the hands of any of whom it may have been fatally misused, how then can it be said that the wrongdoer is surely in court! There is a far greater likelihood that he is no party to this litigation at all and that his identity will never be established. . . .

The authorities which have adopted or espoused the view that res ipsa shifts the burden of proof have, as far as I can discover, understood this to mean that upon such a shift taking place, a defendant becomes obliged to offer evidence explaining his own conduct or throwing light upon the circumstances attending plaintiff's injury, which will be of sufficient probative force to establish his lack of fault by a preponderance of the evidence. The fact finder will then be called upon to decide whether the defendant's proofs have met this test or whether they have fallen short.

The view expressed by the Court in this case as to the effect of shifting the burden of proof appears to be something quite different. Under this new rule it is no longer enough that a defendant meet the standard described above. His role is no longer simply that of one who may hope to succeed if his proofs justify a verdict. Rather he now finds himself one of a band of persons from among whom one or more *must* be singled out to respond in damages to the plaintiff's claim. He is now a member of a group who must collectively, among themselves, play a game of *sauve qui peut*—and play it for rather high stakes. With all due respect I submit that at this point there has been complete departure from the rule of reason; the argument is now stripped of all rational basis.

Note, first, the role the jury is being called upon to play. The judge will give to the jury two potentially contradictory instructions. First the jurors will be told to arrive at a verdict by a preponderance of the evidence, each defendant having the burden of exculpating himself. Then a further direction will be given that they *must* bring in a verdict against some one or more of the defendants. But suppose the members of the jury cannot agree that the evidence will sustain a verdict against *any* defendant. What then! Each juror has taken an oath—no small matter—to reach a verdict only "according to the evidence." What does he now do? Presumably he poses his problem to the judge. And upon seeking the aid of the court, what further instructions is he to be given? . . .

Consider further the hypothesis last suggested, that a jury does undertake, despite a failure of adequate proof, to carry out the mandate of this instruction. How is a verdict to be reached? The absence of sufficient evidence upon which a verdict might justly rest, coupled with the compulsion to reach a verdict against *someone,* removes from the case any semblance of rationality. It then becomes a mere game of chance. There being no rational guide, each jury may proceed as the whimsy of the moment dictates. Thus we have trial by lot, or by chance — no more a rational process than were trial by ordeal or trial by combat. And yet it is the very essence of the judicial process that a determination reached by a court shall be the result of a rational study and analysis of applicable fact and law. . . .

I would vote to reverse the judgment of the Appellate Division and to reinstate the judgment of the trial court.

CLIFFORD, J., and COLLESTER, J., join in this dissenting opinion.

In an action brought by a patient injured by an implanted catheter, plaintiff joined the catheter manufacturer, tubing manufacturer, hospital, and surgeons under *Anderson.* The trial court granted summary judgment for defendants. The Appellate Division reversed, citing *Anderson.* Maciag v. Strato Medical Corp., 644 A.2d 647 (N.J. Super. Ct. App. Div. 1994). The court remanded the case for trial and held that each defendant should be required to explain why it should not be liable.

The Supreme Court of New Jersey applied the *Anderson* holding in an action brought on behalf of a decedent whose death was allegedly caused by a nitrogen gas embolism that occurred during surgery. See Estate of Chin v. St. Barnabas Medical Center, 734 A.2d 778 (N.J. 1999). The plaintiff joined as defendants: the surgeon, the nurses attending in the operating room, the hospital, and the manufacturer of the medical instrument used in the operation. The trial court ruled for the manufacturer as a matter of law. The jury returned a verdict against the remaining defendants for $2 million, allocating responsibility 20 percent to the surgeon, 20 percent to one nurse, 25 percent to another nurse, and 35 percent to the hospital. Judgment NOV was entered in favor of the nurses and the hospital. The defendant surgeon appealed from the judgment entered against him. The intermediate court reversed, reinstating the verdicts against all four defendants. The high court granted certification and affirmed the intermediate court's order.

The supreme court recognized that *Anderson* applies only in limited circumstances, namely, in "medical malpractice cases in which all the possible defendants are before the court." To this, however, the court added that "[a]lthough *Anderson* is applicable in a narrow set of factual circumstances, it is nonetheless firm in its application to those circumstances when they arise."

PROBLEM SEVEN

The law firm in which you are an associate represents Peter Nyhart for the purpose of bringing claims in tort for personal injuries he suffered recently in a workplace accident. The senior partner handling the case wants your help with certain aspects. No complaints have been filed; investigation is at the preliminary stage.

The file reveals that Mr. Nyhart is a 27-year-old, unmarried college graduate. At the time of the accident last December 31st, he was working as a waiter at The Green Parrot, a fairly large, quite successful restaurant in Huntsburg, New California, the city in which your law firm is located. Mr. Nyhart had worked at The Green Parrot for a little over three years; he has not returned to work since the accident. The client was injured while attempting to open a bottle of Antoine's Champagne for a customer having dinner at the restaurant on New Year's Eve. As Mr. Nyhart was removing the foil from the plastic cork, the neck of the bottle broke with explosive force. A flying glass chip lacerated the cornea of his left eye and the jagged edge of the broken bottle severed arteries and tendons in his right wrist. (The dinner companion of the customer who ordered the champagne was also injured, but we have no knowledge of claims she may have brought.) Mr. Nyhart spent eight days in the hospital, during which he underwent surgery on both his eye and his wrist. The eye appears to be healing properly and the doctors expect him to regain full vision. The wrist is more problematic. The doctors are uncertain whether he will ever regain the use of his right hand. (Mr. Nyhart is right-handed.)

The file contains a lengthy statement by the client describing the accident and the preceding events and surrounding circumstances. The Green Parrot seats about 150 persons and was operating at capacity on the New Year's Eve in question. The restaurant is a closely held corporation owned and operated by Nicholas Savros. All of his employees, including Mr. Nyhart, are covered by worker compensation insurance. The comp carrier has paid practically all of Mr. Nyhart's medical expenses arising from the accident. In addition, the same carrier has paid Mr. Nyhart disability benefits on a weekly basis amounting to approximately two-thirds of what he would have received had he continued working. The worker compensation statute contains the following language: "Employers who comply with [the statute] shall not be liable to respond in damages at common law . . . for any injury . . . received . . . by any employee in the course of . . . his employment."

The bottle of Antoine's Champagne (the remnants of which have been examined by an expert and are in our possession) had been purchased by Mr. Savros from Huntsburg Beverages Wholesalers, Inc. Huntsburg Beverages delivers a wide range of products to The Green Parrot every Monday morning. Due to limited record-keeping and the nature of the stock rotation system at the restaurant, it is impossible to determine exactly when the bottle in question was delivered. But it is fairly certain that it was delivered between one week and eight weeks prior to the accident.

When The Green Parrot receives a delivery from Huntsburg Beverages, the cartons are placed in a storage area. It appears that the restaurant employees who handle the cartons treat them fairly roughly, often not distinguishing between cartons of canned goods and cartons of bottled beverages. Mr. Savros indicates that bottles of wine, including Antoine's Champagne, have been found broken in cartons in recent years, a fact of which Nyhart disclaims any knowledge. Savros says that he discovered two broken bottles of Antoine's, on two different occasions, within a six-week period in October/November last year. He had no further problems with bottle breakage until Nyhart's accident, which was the first such incident to occur at the restaurant.

Sparkling wines, including Antoine's Champagne, are always served chilled. A large refrigerator near the dining area facilitates the cooling process. Each morning a busboy checks the inventory in the refrigerator, under instructions to rotate the stock and replenish supplies, as needed, from the storeroom. (It is not clear how reliably or carefully these tasks are performed.) Mr. Nyhart had served many bottles of sparkling wine, including Antoine's Champagne, without mishap during his tenure as a waiter at The Green Parrot. He insists that he was handling the bottle normally when it broke.

On the evening of the accident, after the customer had ordered the Antoine's from the wine list, Mr. Nyhart set up an ice bucket at the table and retrieved the unopened bottle from the refrigerator. Nothing about the bottle indicated that anything was wrong with it. After returning to the table with the bottle, Mr. Nyhart showed it to the customer to verify that it was the wine that he had ordered, and began to remove the foil that covered the cork. Mr. Nyhart says that he had the bottle in his left hand and pulled on the foil with his right hand, exerting moderate pressure on the bottle neck. "The next thing I knew, the neck broke off and there was a loud explosion. I must have fallen down because the next thing I knew, I was sitting on the floor with my left eye burning like crazy and blood all over my hands."

An expert who examined the remnants of the broken bottle at the partner's request has concluded that there can be no doubt that when Mr. Nyhart retrieved the bottle from the cooler, the neck of the bottle contained a fracture that weakened it and caused it to break when Mr. Nyhart exerted moderate lateral pressure on the neck. The expert cannot determine when the fracture occurred. It is possible that it was present when the bottle was first manufactured, prior to being filled with champagne. She explains that the fracture might have been present from the beginning, but might not have been large enough to cause the bottle to fail during the bottling process. Subsequent normal handling, including the cooling of the bottle prior to serving it, could have exacerbated the fracture to the point that it finally caused the bottle to break as Nyhart attempted to open it.

On the other hand, the expert continues, the bottle could have been normal when delivered to the champagne bottling company and then been fractured during bottling; or it could have been normal when delivered to the restaurant and then been fractured during subsequent rough handling. She states that there is no way to tell with certainty from the bottle remnants themselves when the fracture occurred. Everyone from The Green Parrot interviewed so far denies having mishandled the bottle or cartons of bottles, but it is possible that mishandling occurred. Employee turnover is fairly high, and it is possible that someone who mishandled the bottle in question is no longer employed at the restaurant and thus is unavailable to be interviewed.

The bottle of Antoine's Champagne that broke in the client's hands was produced by BMX Corporation, a large winery in the western part of the state.[1] BMX produces and distributes a line of sparkling wines bearing the "Antoine's" label. Huntsburg Beverages has exclusive distribution rights in the greater Huntsburg area and purchases directly from BMX. (We have not yet looked into Huntsburg Beverages's operations.) BMX purchases the wine bottles new (they are never reused) for its Antoine's Champagne from Molinar Glass Works, Inc., a company located near the wine-producing area of the state, catering especially to the needs of the wine industry. Molinar manufactures the bottles to design specifications established by BMX. BMX's specifications exceed the standards for strength and durability set by the state Beverage Commission's regulations governing such products. Molinar does not inspect every bottle, a process that its experts insist would be prohibitively expensive. It selects at random a percentage of bottles for inspection—a percentage Molinar maintains keeps its overall failure experience below the national average for similar glass containers.

Molinar ships empty bottles by truck to BMX in large cardboard containers reinforced to prevent damage in transit. BMX does not reinspect the empty bottles before filling them with wine. A BMX representative insists that reinspection at that time would constitute "a wasteful redundancy." After the bottles are filled, corked, sealed, and labelled, BMX inspects a certain percentage, chosen randomly, for defects. BMX insists that it would be prohibitively expensive to inspect every bottle of wine it produces. A BMX spokesman explains:

> We are trying to produce a high-quality champagne at a price that nearly everyone can afford. You must understand that there is a limit to how much we can invest in quality control. To inspect every bottle of sparkling wine before it is shipped would add so much to our costs that we could not compete with out-of-state producers. The mass-produced sparkling wine industry is highly competitive—it is the closest thing to a perfect market that you will ever see. Studies confirm that if we, or any other mass producer of sparkling wine, tried to produce a defect-free product, we would not survive.

Several weeks ago Mr. Nyhart called and asked to be briefed on the progress of the lawsuit. The senior partner was going on vacation and asked you to meet

---

1. Your state, New California, is an important producer of wine, both still and sparkling. It ranked third in the United States, behind California and New York, in total production last year.

Assigning Responsibility Collectively to the Distributive Chain

with the client and to discuss with him the problems that may prevent the successful prosecution of the case. He instructed you not to be overly pessimistic but remarked that, at the same time, "Nyhart's got to know that his case is on the thin side." At your meeting with Nyhart you discerned that he is a perceptive young man. In fact, his questioning was so good that you jokingly suggested that he might want to go to law school and try his own case. Notwithstanding attempts at humor, Nyhart was deeply disturbed by the picture you conveyed to him. He had thought his case was a sure winner. His injuries are extremely painful and the doctor has told him that he may never be able to carry significant weight in his right hand. He remarked, "There goes my job as a waiter." His ophthalmologist is also unhappy with the most recent examination of his eye, hinting that further surgery may be necessary. Nyhart remarked that something is wrong with the law if he cannot recover from someone. "I did nothing but open the bottle. Someone is at fault and it is not me."

You met again with Nyhart on Tuesday morning. On the previous Friday, Nyhart had called and asked to meet with you. At your Tuesday meeting, Nyhart began by saying, "I have good news. I may have discovered a good witness for our side." He went on to explain:

> This kid, Ray Small, used to work for us at the restaurant. He seemed like a good kid, so I convinced Savros to hire him to do odd jobs. Ray recently got another job, but I was able to run him down. He's out of town right now but will be back in a couple of weeks. Ray says that he remembers that for several months before my accident, each shipment of Antoine's had three or four broken bottles. He saw them when he unpacked the cases to refrigerate the bottles. That's a lot of broken bottles. Ray remembers mentioning the broken bottles to Savros, who told him to ignore it because it didn't really make much difference. We had such a good deal on Antoine's that three or four broken bottles for each 10-case shipment really didn't amount to much. Savros also told Ray not to tell anybody else about the broken bottles.

Nyhart then turned to you and said "This is important to our case — isn't it?"

At your Tuesday meeting, you questioned Nyhart closely on the matter and asked why he supposed that a stickler for details like Savros would have reacted that way. You also asked Nyhart why he hadn't told you about Ray Small earlier. He answered that it never occurred to him that it was important. You then asked Nyhart whether Ray Small would be a strong and forceful witness. Nyhart replied, "He better be, for all I've done for him. He may need some shoring-up but he'll do just fine."

Your immediate reaction was that Nyhart had fabricated a story. You told him so and suggested that it might not be such a good idea to call Small as a witness. Nyhart exploded. "Now just one #$*?& minute! Whose side are you on anyway? He's my witness. And he's going to testify whether you like it or not." You managed to calm Nyhart down with vague assurances that it would all work out one way or the other, and the meeting ended.

Upon further reflection over the past week, you are more troubled than ever about continuing to represent Nyhart. The senior partner returned from vacation three days ago, and you informed him of this new development. His first reaction was that Ray Small may not make a very convincing witness in any event, but he wants you to research the ethical issues raised. He also wants you to prepare an outline of the arguments that will support liability against one or more of the possible defendants whether or not you decide to rely on Ray Small's testimony. The partner wants you to assume in your analysis that the design specifications of the bottle — the thickness of the glass, the shape of the bottle, and the like — are all right. Furthermore, he does not want you to consider whether Molinar, BMX, or Huntsburg should have provided more adequate instructions or warnings. Thus, the partner wants you to focus on whether a defect in the wine bottle sold by one or more of the possible defendants might be found to have caused Nyhart's injuries. Regarding Savros's possible tort liability, the partner wants you to assume for the time being that Savros is immune from tort liability under the New California worker compensation statute, and thus cannot be sued directly.

In preparing your analysis, you are to assume that all events occurred in New California, whose law governing product sellers' liability conforms to the general descriptions preceding this problem, and you are also to assume that *Anderson,* supra, was decided by the highest court in your state and that your state has adopted the Federal Rules of Civil Procedure. If further factual inquiries should be undertaken, identify them and explain their relevance to your analysis.

Model Code of Professional Responsibility
(1980)

DR 7-102 Representing a Client Within the Bounds of the Law

(A) In his representation of a client, a lawyer shall not: . . .
(4) Knowingly use perjured testimony or false evidence. . . .

Model Rules of Professional Conduct
(1983)

Rule 3.3 Candor Toward the Tribunal

(a) A lawyer shall not knowingly: . . .
(4) offer evidence that the lawyer knows to be false. If a lawyer has offered material evidence and comes to know of its falsity, the lawyer shall take reasonable remedial measures. . . .
(c) A lawyer may refuse to offer evidence that the lawyer reasonably believes is false. . . .

COMMENT:
The advocate's task is to present the client's case with persuasive force. Performance of that duty while maintaining confidences of the client is qualified by the advocate's duty of candor to the tribunal. However, an advocate does not vouch for the evidence submitted in a cause; the tribunal is responsible for assessing its probative value.

False Evidence
When evidence that a lawyer knows to be false is provided by a person who is not the client, the lawyer must refuse to offer it regardless of the client's wishes.

Refusing to Offer Proof Believed to Be False

Generally speaking, a lawyer has authority to refuse to offer testimony or other proof that the lawyer believes is untrustworthy. Offering such proof may reflect adversely on the lawyer's ability to discriminate in the quality of evidence and thus impair the lawyer's effectiveness as an advocate. In criminal cases, however, a lawyer may, in some jurisdictions, be denied this authority by constitutional requirements governing the right to counsel.

Charles W. Wolfram, Modern Legal Ethics*
653-657 (1986)

The Problem of Perjury

Possible Divergence Between Client and Social Interest

A lawyer faced with perjurious testimony by a client or friendly witness confronts the choice between client interest and social interest in a most poignant form. One instinct might be to remain silent in order to protect the interests of the lawyer's client in the litigation. Possibly the lawyer's silence would also protect the client against disclosure as the source of the lawyer's knowledge or even as a perjurer. A powerfully conflicting instinct will be to resist the perjury because it is false and in order to preserve the truth-finding function of the trial and thereby the workability and validity of the law itself.

The perjury problem has troubled lawyers for a long time and has occasioned considerable scholarly interest. Despite the centrality and difficulty of the perjury problem, the professional regulations spoke in barely detectable whispers about it until the adoption of the 1983 Model Rules, which took a strong position against a lawyer's participation, even if unwillingly, in the presentation of perjury. The Model Rules comport with the great weight of decided cases but conflict with some recent lower court decisions on constitutional issues in criminal cases. The Model Rules also rejected a prior ABA "compromise" solution that has attracted some judicial attention. . . .

What Lawyers Know

Before inquiring into a lawyer's duty when confronted with perjury, it is well to attempt to define those circumstances that trigger an obligation on the part of a lawyer to react to perjury. Are reasonable suspicions sufficient, or, at the other extreme, is the standard that of knowledge beyond doubt?

Both of the ABA lawyer codes require certain knowledge. The 1969 Code, in DR 7-102(A)(4), states that a lawyer shall not "knowingly" use perjury. The 1983 Model Rules contain a similar standard, and a similar rule, in Rule 3.3(a)(4). The terminology section of the Rules states that such a level of knowledge "denotes actual knowledge of the fact in question. A person's knowledge may be inferred from circumstances." The latter sentiment makes it clear that a lawyer's denial of knowledge is not conclusive on the question. And, as in the criminal law, a law-

---

*Reprinted from C. Wolfram, Modern Legal Ethics (1986), with permission of the West Publishing Company.

yer's conscious avoidance of knowledge of the falsity of evidence should not prevent a finding of actual knowledge. For instances in which a lawyer's knowledge of the falsity of evidence does not rise to this level, Model Rule 3.3(c) states that a lawyer has professional discretion, but not a duty, to refuse to offer evidence that the lawyer "reasonably believes" to be false. If the lawyer's disquietude about a client's intended testimony is the result of mere conjecture or an unsubstantiated opinion, however, the lawyer should present the testimony. Importantly, even if the lawyer's suspicion permits formation of a reasonable belief that the evidence is false — and thus permits its nonintroduction under Rule 3.3(c) — this does not entitle, or require, the lawyer to make disclosure or take other remedial action under Rule 3.3(a)(4), because the lawyer does not "know" the evidence to be false. Disclosure of false evidence that results in revelation of confidential client information in these circumstances would violate Rule 1.6(a), just as it would violate DR 4-101(B).[2]

Dealing with False Testimony . . .
Perjury in Civil Cases

The duties of a lawyer confronted with a client or friendly witness intent on perjury can be analyzed in terms of remonstration, withdrawal, calling witnesses, eliciting testimony, arguing to the fact finder, and disclosure. A lawyer's obligations in these respects flow from the provisions of DR 7102(A)(4) of the 1980 Code, providing that a lawyer shall not "knowingly use perjured testimony or false evidence," and from 1983 Model Rule 3.3(a)(4), which provides that: "a lawyer shall not knowingly . . . offer evidence that the lawyer knows to be false. If a lawyer has offered material evidence and comes to know of its falsity, the lawyer shall take reasonable remedial measures."

Remonstration is clearly required: A lawyer must attempt to persuade a client not to present or, if it is presented, to correct, false testimony. Remonstration in most cases should cover the fact that perjury is a criminal offense, the risks of its detection, the importance of truthful testimony, the lawyer's duty to withdraw, and the extent of the lawyer's duty to disclose perjury. Cases very broadly agree that a lawyer whose client nonetheless insists on presenting false testimony is required to *withdraw* from the representation, if necessary, to avoid engaging in the presentation of the testimony. The rule is also clear with respect to a lawyer who *calls a witness* whose testimony the lawyer knows will be false. The lawyer controls access to the witness stand and may not call a witness if the lawyer knows that perjurious testimony will result. In the instance of a witness who will testify truthfully to some questions but falsely to others, a lawyer may not *put a question* to a witness knowing that the witness will respond with false testimony. That follows from the obligation not to call a perjurious witness to the stand. It also operates independently in the case of surprise perjury — when a friendly witness or client surprises a lawyer by beginning to testify falsely on the witness stand. By similar extension, a lawyer may not argue in *summation* that the fact finder should accept, as credible, evidence that the lawyer knows is false.

---

2. State v. Regier, 228 Kan. 746, 621 P.2d 431 (1980) (revealing unconfirmed suspicions about client perjury to two district judges in order to have court investigate suspicions violates DR 4-101).

C. ASSIGNING RESPONSIBILITY FOR PRODUCT-RELATED WORKPLACE ACCIDENTS

Mix together the following ingredients: (1) a steady stream of serious and often permanently disabling injuries to employees flowing from hundreds of thousands of workplace accidents in this country each year; (2) the growing expectation among our citizenry that whenever serious injury occurs in a commercially managed environment, the managers of that environment should probably be liable in tort to the injured person; and (3) a century-old tradition under American worker compensation statutes that the compensation remedy, which is typically only a monetary fraction of the potential tort remedy, is exclusive — the employee may not bring a negligence action against his employer for work-related accidental injuries. Stir these ingredients over a moderate flame and what have you got? A volatile and potentially explosive mixture. Add one further ingredient: Many of these workplace accidents occur in the context of employees using dangerous and allegedly defective machinery manufactured by corporations that are not immune from tort liability to the injured employees. Now what have you got? One of the fastest growing and most perplexing areas of modern American products liability law.

1. Direct Attack by the Employee Against the Employer

a. The Worker Compensation Bar to Employer Tort Liability

In connection with many of the products liability claims brought by employees against the manufacturers of products that have caused them to suffer workplace injuries, the employer has played a sufficiently substantial role in causing the accident to justify joining the employer as a co-defendant with the manufacturer. That such joinder almost never occurs reflects the reality that employers enjoy an immunity under worker compensation statutes from tort liability for all workplace injuries, including injuries caused by defective products. This bar to tort liability is subject to limited exceptions, which are identified in the subsections that follow. But in most instances, injured employees cannot recover in tort directly from their employers. The prevailing view is that the statutory bar is an appropriate quid pro quo for the employer's having provided a no-fault compensation remedy for workplace injuries.

b. The Intentional Tort Exception to the Worker Compensation Bar

The employer's worker compensation immunity from tort should be, and is, difficult to break. It was intended to provide broad-based protection, and courts have by and large interpreted the immunity so as to protect the employer from almost all tort-based suits. But dissatisfaction has arisen in some quarters with the all-encompassing sweep of immunity. A leading case recognizing an intentional tort exception to the worker compensation bar is Blankenship v. Cincinnati Milacron Chemicals, Inc., 433 N.E.2d 572 (Ohio), *cert. denied,* 459 U.S. 857

(1982). In that case, eight Milacron employees brought an action against their employer alleging that they were exposed to certain dangerous chemicals within the scope of their employment. They claimed that Milacron failed to correct the conditions, failed to warn them of the dangers, and failed to report the conditions to governmental agencies. Plaintiffs alleged that these failures were "intentional, malicious and in willful and wanton disregard of the health of [the employees.]" The trial court dismissed the complaint on the ground that the worker compensation statute barred direct actions in tort.

On appeal, the Ohio Supreme Court reversed and remanded for trial. The majority reasoned:

> Clearly, neither the relevant constitutional language [authorizing the Workers' Compensation Act] nor the pertinent statutory language expressly extend the grant of immunity to actions alleging intentional tortious conduct by employers against their employees. The General Assembly, however, in enacting R.C. 4123.95, established a rule of construction which is clearly of assistance in determining the scope of employer immunity. This section provides that:
>
>> Sections 4123.01 to 4123.94, inclusive, of [the Act,] shall be liberally construed in favor of employees and the dependents of deceased employees.
>
> It is with this requirement in mind that we . . . [conclude] that where an employee asserts in his complaint a claim for damages based on an intentional tort, ". . . the substance of the claim is not an 'injury . . . received or contracted by any employee in the course of or arising out of his employment' within the meaning of [our Workers' Compensation Act.]" No reasonable individual would equate intentional and unintentional conduct in terms of the degree of risk which faces an employee nor would such individual contemplate the risk of an intentional tort as a natural risk of employment. Since an employer's intentional conduct does not arise out of employment, [the Act] does not bestow upon employers immunity from civil liability for their intentional torts and an employee may resort to a civil suit for damages.
>
> The workers' compensation system is based on the premise that an employer is protected from a suit for negligence in exchange for compliance with the Workers' Compensation Act. The Act operates as a balance of mutual compromise between the interests of the employer and the employee whereby employees relinquish their common law remedy and accept lower benefit levels coupled with the greater assurance of recovery and employers give up their common law defenses and are protected from unlimited liability. But the protection afforded by the Act has always been for negligent acts and not for intentional tortious conduct. Indeed, workers' compensation Acts were designed to improve the plight of the injured worker, and to hold that intentional torts are covered under the Act would be tantamount to encouraging such conduct, and this clearly cannot be reconciled with the motivating spirit and purpose of the Act.

Locher, J., concurred and dissented on the ground that, while the case should be remanded for the building of an adequate factual record, evidence that the employer knew that work conditions were risky should not alone suffice to establish the employer's intent to cause injury. He concluded: "Every undertaking involves some risk. We should not circumvent the statutory framework for workers' compensation merely because a known risk existed. We should demand a virtual certainty." 433 N.E.2d at 580.

The Ohio legislature sought to limit the *Blankenship* doctrine by enacting Ohio Rev. Code Ann. §4121.80(G) (West Supp. 1987), which capped recovery in intentional tort cases against an employer at three times the total of worker compensation benefits with a maximum limit of $1 million. In 1991, Ohio's high court declared the statute unconstitutional, reaffirming *Blankenship*. Brady v. Safety-Kleen Corp., 576 N.E.2d 722 (Ohio 1991). In 1995, the Ohio legislature made one more attempt to limit *Blankenship* and *Brady* by enacting Ohio Rev. Code Ann. §2745.01 (Anderson 1999), which required clear and convincing proof that the employer deliberately committed all elements of an "employment intentional tort," which was defined as "an act committed by an employer in which the employer deliberately and intentionally injures, causes an occupational disease of, or causes the death of an employee." Section 2745.01 also declared that an employer was no longer liable for any other kind of intentional tort that occurred during the course of employment. In Johnson v. B.P. Chemicals, Inc., 707 N.E.2d 1107, 1111-12 (Ohio 1999), the Ohio Supreme Court scolded the legislature for attempting to circumvent its decision in *Brady:*

> In *Brady,* the court invalidated former R.C. 4121.80 in its entirety, and, in doing so, we thought that we had made it abundantly clear that any statute created to provide employers with immunity from liability for their intentional tortious conduct cannot withstand constitutional scrutiny. [citations omitted]. Notwithstanding, the General Assembly has enacted R.C. 2745.01, and, again, seeks to cloak employers with immunity. In this regard, we can only assume that the General Assembly has either failed to grasp the import of our holdings in *Brady* or that the General Assembly has simply elected to willfully disregard that decision.

The court went on to declare §2745.01 unconstitutional in its entirety, because it "creates an insurmountable obstacle for victims of 'employment intentional torts,'" id. at 1114, once again reaffirming *Blankenship* and its progeny. For a critique of §2745.01, see Mark A. Claybon, Ohio's "Employment Intentional Tort": A Workers' Compensation Exception, or the Creation of an Entirely New Cause of Action? 44 Clev. St. L. Rev. 381, 405-406 (1996). For a constitutional analysis of Ohio developments, see Stephen J. Werber, Ohio: A Microcosm of Tort Reform Versus State Constitutional Mandates, 32 Rutgers L.J. 1045 (2001). For a discussion of Florida's judicially created intentional tort exception, see John T. Burnett, The Enigma of Workers' Compensation Immunity: A Call to the Legislature for a Statutorily Defined Intentional Tort Exception, 28 Fla. St. U. L. Rev. 491 (2001).

The operative test in Ohio is whether the employer was "substantially certain" that the injury would take place. Accordingly, in Holtz v. Schutt Pattern Works Co., 626 N.E.2d 1029 (Ohio 1993), where an employee lost two fingers while using a machine without a safety guard, the court of appeals found error in the trial court's grant of summary judgment to the employer. In this case, the employer had informed the worker that "the sign of a good pattern maker is how many fingers are missing," confirming the fact that similar injuries had occurred before. An injured employee must also show that his employer required him to perform the dangerous task. In Wetmore v. American Guard Co., Inc., 2003 WL 1632970 (Ohio App. Dist.), the court upheld summary judgment for the employer where the employer had previously addressed plaintiff's concerns by installing a safety device at his request and the employee had not refused to operate the machine.

Several states have followed Ohio's lead in circumventing the worker compensation bar by allowing employees to sue their employers directly. A growing number of courts including Louisiana follow a substantial-certainty test, which sometimes is interpreted to allow certain actions that are not "true" intentional torts to sidestep exclusivity. See, e.g., Trahan v. Trans-Louisiana Gas Co., 618 So. 2d 30 (La. Ct. App. 1993) (exposure to chemicals); Wainwright v. Moreno's, Inc., 602 So. 2d 734 (La. Ct. App. 1992) (foreman ordered plaintiff to remain in a ditch despite warnings of an imminent cave-in); Rose v. XYZ Cable Co., Inc., 600 So. 2d 774 (La. Ct. App. 1992). Yet some states steadfastly adhere to the actual-intent standard, either by judicial decision or legislative enactment. In Mandolidis v. Elkins Indus Inc., 246 S.E.2d 907 (W.Va. 1978), the West Virginia Supreme Court held that allegations of willful, wanton, and reckless misconduct on the part of employers established intent. But in 1983, the West Virginia legislature cut back the *Mandolidis* rule by enacting amendments to the workers' compensation law that defined "intentional" as acting "with a consciously, subjectively, and deliberately formed intention to produce the specific . . . injury or death to an employee." W.Va. Code §23-4-2 (1994 repl. vol.). Despite these stringent statutory requirements, in Smith v. Monsanto Co., 822 F. Supp. 327 (S.D. W.Va. 1992), the court denied summary judgment because the defendant employer did not prove it had complied with industry standards regarding exposure to paraminobiphenyl (PAB), thus raising a fact issue on "deliberate intent."

Other states have had similar experiences involving court-legislature interaction. For example, shortly after the Michigan Supreme Court moved toward a substantially certain-type test with its decision in Beauchamp v. Dow Chemical Co., 398 N.W.2d 882 (Mich. 1986), the Michigan legislature amended its worker compensation statute to limit direct tort actions to cases where the employer is found to have "specifically intended an injury." Mich. Comp. Laws Ann. §418.131(1) (West Supp. 1996). Short of a malicious attack, most causes of action do not meet the tougher test of the new Michigan law; but some cases still go to trial on the statutory intentional tort issue. See, e.g., Travis v. Dreis & Krump Mfg. Co, 523 N.W.2d 818 (Mich. 1994); Golec v. Metal Exch. Corp., 528 N.W.2d 756 (Mich. 1995) (both courts reversed summary judgment in situations where management had been informed of imminent injuries and instructed workers to continue their shifts; the courts concluded there was enough evidence of actual knowledge of injury to proceed to trial).

Several state legislatures have moved to make direct actions easier by enacting statutes expressly providing for an intentional tort exception. For example, the New Jersey's Workers Compensation Act reads in part: "If an injury or death is compensable under this article, a person shall not be liable to anyone at common law or otherwise on account of such injury or death for any act or omission occurring while such person was in the same employ as the person injured or killed, except for intentional wrong." N.J. Stat. Ann. §34:15-8 (West 2003). In the following case, the Supreme Court of New Jersey considered what constitutes an "intentional wrong" within the meaning of the Act.

Laidlow v. Hariton Machinery Co., Inc.
790 A.2d 884 (N.J. 2002)

LONG, J.

The Workers' Compensation system has been described as an historic "trade-off" whereby employees relinquish their right to pursue common-law remedies in exchange for prompt and automatic entitlement to benefits for work-related injuries. Millison v. E. I. du Pont de Nemours & Co., 101 N.J. 161, 174, 501 A.2d 505 (1985). That characterization is only broadly accurate. In fact, not every worker injured on the job receives compensation benefits and not all conduct by an employer is immune from common-law suit. The Legislature has declared that certain types of conduct by the employer and the employee will render the Workers' Compensation bargain a nullity. Thus, for example, a worker whose death or injury is "intentionally" self-inflicted or results from a "willful" failure to make use of a safety device, furnished and required by the employer, will be ineligible for benefits. Likewise, an employer who causes the death or injury of an employee by committing an "intentional wrong" will not be insulated from common-law suit. N.J.S.A. 34:15-8; *Millison,* supra, 101 N.J. at 169.

The described limitations involve intentional wrongful conduct committed either by the worker or the employer. Underlying those limitations is the idea that such conduct neither constitutes "a natural risk of" nor "arises out of" the employment, the very notions at the heart of the Workers' Compensation bargain in the first instance.

The focus of this appeal is conduct by an employer that is alleged to constitute an intentional wrong under N.J.S.A. 34:15-8. We are called on to revisit our holding in *Millison;* resolve conflicting interpretations of it; and apply that decision to a case in which an injured employee claims that his employer has removed a safety device from a dangerous machine, knowing that the removal was substantially certain to result in injury to its workers and, in addition, deliberately and systematically deceived safety inspectors into believing that the machine was properly guarded. We hold that, in those circumstances, the employee's allegations, if proven, meet both the conduct and context prongs of *Millison,* thus entitling the employee to pursue his common-law remedies.

I

Rudolph Laidlow (Laidlow) suffered a serious and debilitating injury when his hand became caught in a rolling mill he was operating at his place of employment, AMI-DDC, Inc. (AMI). Laidlow sustained a crush and degloving injury resulting in partial amputations of the index, middle, ring and small fingers of his dominant left hand. Laidlow sued AMI on an intentional tort theory. He also named his supervisor, Richard Portman (Portman), in the suit for discovery purposes. AMI answered, denying the allegations of the complaint, and moved for summary judgment on the basis of the Workers' Compensation bar.

Under Rule 4:46-2, a movant will be granted summary judgment if the court finds, after reviewing the full motion record in the light most favorable to the adverse party, that there is no genuine issue of material fact. It is with that standard in mind that we view the facts presented on AMI's motion.

AMI is in the business of manufacturing electrical products. Laidlow has been employed by AMI since August 7, 1978. On December 11, 1992, Laidlow was performing his job as a "set up man," which required him to work with a rolling mill that changed the dimension of heated metal bars when they were inserted into the mill. Laidlow manually inserted the bars into a "channel" that guided them into the mill, and often had to apply pressure to the bars with his hand in order to feed them into the rollers. On the day of the accident, Laidlow's glove became caught by the unguarded nip point as he was pushing a bar of silver into the channel. His gloved hand was pulled toward the mill's rollers. An eyewitness, Laidlow's co-worker Steven Smozanek, described the incident as follows: "The rollers are approximately 18 inches in diameter, and as he was feeding the bar into the roller, it pulled his hand against the roller, not into the roller, and as it pulled the hand against the roller, it just ripped the glove and the skin right off his hand."

On a prior occasion, Laidlow's glove had also become hooked on a bar, but he was able to slip his hand out of the glove before it was pulled into the machine. Smozanek described a similar incident when he was working on the mill and his gloved hand had snagged on a bar, but he too was able to pull his hand out of the glove just in time to escape injury. Those close calls were reported to AMI.

After the rolling mill was purchased by AMI in 1978, the company arranged to have a safety guard installed. However, the safety guard was "never" engaged; from 1979 to the date of Laidlow's accident in 1992, the guard always was "tied up." According to Laidlow, the guard was placed in its proper position only when Occupational Safety and Health Administration (OSHA) inspectors came to the plant. On those occasions, Portman, Laidlow's supervisor, would instruct employees to release the wire that was holding up the safety guard. As soon as the OSHA inspectors left, the safety guard would again be disabled.

Laidlow operated the mill without the safety guard in place for approximately twelve to thirteen years. During that period, except for the "near misses" referred to earlier, there were apparently no accidents with the mill until Laidlow was seriously injured during the incident at issue here.

Laidlow spoke to Portman regarding the safety guard three times during the period immediately preceding his accident. Approximately two weeks prior to the accident, Laidlow asked Portman to restore the guard. Several weeks before that, he spoke to Portman because a new operator was going to work on the mill and Laidlow thought the guard should be restored to its operative position. Additionally, one week before the incident, Laidlow again expressed concern that a new, inexperienced operator would be working on the mill, and told Portman that it was dangerous not to use the guard. According to Laidlow, the guard was never restored. Portman responded to his requests by stating that "it was okay" and "not a problem," and by "walk[ing] away." Laidlow never refused to operate the mill without the safety guard in place nor spoke with any other superior in the company about the safety guard.

AMI concedes that the guard was removed for "speed and convenience." In addition, Gerald Barnes, a professional engineer retained by Laidlow, certified that AMI "knew there was a virtual certainty of injury to Mr. Laidlow or a fellow work[er] arising from the operation of the mill without a guard."

On those facts, the trial court concluded that Laidlow failed to demonstrate an "intentional wrong" under N.J.S.A. 34:15-8 and that Workers' Compensation was his exclusive remedy. Accordingly, the trial court granted AMI's motion for summary judgment, along with a similar motion filed by Portman.

The Appellate Division affirmed the dismissals, concluding that there was no evidence of an intentional wrong by AMI to warrant an exception from the Workers' Compensation bar. The panel relied on the lack of any accident over a twelve-year period and determined that OSHA violations alone, in the absence of proof of deliberate intent to injure, would not satisfy the intentional wrong standard. The court dismissed the suit against Portman because Laidlow failed to demonstrate any need to pursue discovery.

Judge Lintner dissented, contending that the record, fairly read, presented a jury issue regarding intentional wrong; that the lack of injuries over the twelve-year period was not dispositive of the issue of substantial certainty of injury; that, coupled with the guard's removal, AMI's deceptive practices with regard to OSHA provided conclusive evidence of "context" under *Millison;* and that Laidlow should have been allowed to obtain discovery from Portman because Portman was in a unique position to provide evidence of what the employer knew.

The appeal is before us as of right under Rule 2:2-1(a)(2) based on the dissenting opinion below. We granted Amicus status to the Trial Lawyers of America (ATLA-NJ) and New Jersey Manufacturer's Insurance Company (NJM).

II

In essence, Laidlow's argument is that the combination of the employer's disabling of the safety guard and deception of OSHA presents a triable issue on whether such conduct meets the definition of an "intentional wrong." AMI counters that under *Millison,* an intentional wrong requires a "deliberate intention to injure" and that Laidlow concedes that no one at AMI harbored such an intention. AMI also maintains that *Millison* specifically declared that the removal of a safety device fails to meet the intentional wrong standard. To the extent that recent Appellate Division decisions suggest the contrary, AMI argues that those cases should be disapproved. Furthermore, AMI argues that even if removal of a safety guard could qualify in some circumstances as an intentional wrong, the absence of any prior injury on its machine and Laidlow's successful experience in operating the machine without an accident for over twelve years obviates that possibility in this case.

NJM supports AMI's position that, under *Millison,* the standard for an intentional wrong requires proof of an employer's subjective intent to injure and that the deliberate removal or alteration of a safety guard does not constitute a "deliberate intent to injure." NJM also claims that the OSHA violations are legally irrelevant under *Millison.*

The heart of ATLA-NJ's position is that AMI and NJM totally mischaracterize *Millison.* ATLA contends that *Millison* specifically rejected the notion that an intentional wrong requires a deliberate intent to injure on the part of the employer; that *Millison* never declared that removal of a safety device failed to meet the standard for an intentional wrong; that the Appellate Division's reliance on the lack of prior accidents on the mill machine allows for "one free injury" contrary to our public policy; and that there is a jury question regarding whether the employer's actions constituted an intentional wrong.

III

Our decision in *Millison* is obviously at the root of this case and a review of our holding there is essential. In *Millison,* we were faced with the question of "what categories of employer conduct will be sufficiently flagrant so as to constitute an 'intentional wrong,' thereby entitling a plaintiff to avoid the 'exclusivity' bar of N.J.S.A. 34:15-8?" *Millison,* supra, 101 N.J. at 176, 501 A.2d 505. That statute reads:

> Such agreement shall be a surrender by the parties thereto of their rights to any other method, form or amount of compensation or determination thereof than as provided in this article and an acceptance of all the provisions of this article, and shall bind the employee and for compensation for the employee's death shall bind the employee's personal representatives, surviving spouse and next of kin, as well as the employer, and those conducting the employer's business during bankruptcy or insolvency.
>
> If an injury or death is compensable under this article, a person shall not be liable to anyone at common law or otherwise on account of such injury or death for any act or omission occurring while such person was in the same employ as the person injured or killed, except for intentional wrong. N.J.S.A. 34:15-8.

That is the so-called exclusive remedy provision of the Workers' Compensation Act, often referred to as the Workers' Compensation bar. *Millison* confronted that provision in the context of an occupational disease caused by exposure to asbestos during employment.

The appeal in *Millison* challenged a trial court's grant of summary judgment to an employer based on N.J.S.A. 34:15-8 in connection with plaintiffs' claim that the employer knowingly exposed them to an occupational disease. That court simultaneously denied summary judgment to the company doctors with respect to whom plaintiffs alleged the fraudulent concealment of their asbestos-related diseases. The Appellate Division affirmed the grant of summary judgment to the employer and reversed the denial of summary judgment to the physicians because there was no evidence that they "deliberately intended" to injure the workers.

We granted plaintiffs' petition for certification. Before us, plaintiffs argued that "their charges that defendants knowingly and deliberately exposed employees to a hazardous work environment and fraudulently concealed existing occupational diseases are sufficient to fall within the Act's limited 'intentional wrong' exception and to take their injuries outside the intended scope of the Compensation Act." *Millison,* supra, 101 N.J. at 170.

In addressing that contention, we recounted the history of the intentional wrong exception that had led the Appellate Division to its conclusion that only an employer's deliberate intent to injure was sufficient to vault the exclusivity bar. We also identified the precedents underlying the Appellate Division's ruling. [Description of earlier rulings requiring "deliberate intention" omitted.]

We recognized that those cases traced their rationale to Professor Larson's narrow and limited approach to intentional wrong and quoted extensively from his treatise. Specifically, we cited the following section:

Even if the alleged conduct goes beyond aggravated negligence, and includes such elements as knowingly permitting a hazardous work condition to exist, knowingly ordering claimant to perform an extremely dangerous job, willfully failing to furnish a safe place to work, or even willfully and unlawfully violating a safety statute, this still falls shorts of the kind of actual intention to injure that robs the injury of accidental character.

. . .

If these decisions seem rather strict, one must remind oneself that what is being tested here is not the degree of gravity or depravity of the employer's conduct, but rather the narrow issue of intentional versus accidental quality of the precise event producing injury. The intentional removal of a safety device or toleration of a dangerous condition may or may not set the stage for an accidental injury later. But in any normal use of the words, it cannot be said, if such an injury does happen, that this was deliberate infliction of harm comparable to an intentional left jab to the chin. 2A A. Larson, The Law of Workmen's Compensation §68.13 at 13-22 to 13-27 (1983) (footnotes omitted).

What is critical, and what often has been misunderstood, is that we cited Professor Larson and the cases relying on his approach for informational, not precedential, purposes. *Millison,* in fact, specifically rejected Professor Larson's thesis that in order to obtain redress outside the Workers' Compensation Act an employee must prove that the employer subjectively desired to harm him. In place of Larson's theory, we adopted Dean Prosser's broader approach to the concept of intentional wrong.

Under Prosser's approach, an intentional wrong is not limited to actions taken with a subjective desire to harm, but also includes instances where an employer knows that the consequences of those acts are substantially certain to result in such harm. See W. Prosser and W. Keeton, The Law of Torts, §80 at 569 (5th ed. 1984).

In abandoning Larson's purely subjective approach in favor of substantial certainty, we stated: "In adopting a 'substantial certainty' standard, we acknowledge that every undertaking, particularly certain business judgments, involve some risk, but that willful employer misconduct was not meant to go undeterred." Id. at 178.

Put another way, we recognized that Larson's "deliberate intent to injure" standard would sweep under its protection employer conduct that the Legislature never intended to insulate. By adopting Prosser's "substantial certainty" standard, we delineated another method by which a plaintiff could prove an intentional wrong. . . . Although noting in *Millison* that we were not repudiating earlier decisions [requiring deliberate intention,] we recognized that those decisions had been modified to the extent that an intentional wrong can be shown not only by proving a subjective desire to injure, but also by a showing, based on all the facts and circumstances of the case, that the employer knew an injury was substantially certain to result. In addition to adopting Prosser's "substantial certainty" test relative to conduct, in *Millison* we added a crucial second prong to the test:

Courts must examine not only the conduct of the employer, but also the context in which that conduct takes place: may the resulting injury or disease, and the circumstances in which it is inflicted on the worker, fairly be viewed as a fact of life of industrial employment, or is it rather plainly beyond anything the legislature could have contemplated as entitling the employee to recover only under the Compensation Act? Id. at 179, 501 A.2d 505.

By the addition of the context prong, *Millison* required courts to assess not only whether the employer acted with knowledge that injury was substantially certain to occur, but also whether the injury and the circumstances surrounding it were part and parcel of everyday industrial life or plainly outside the legislative grant of immunity. In other words, under *Millison,* if only the conduct prong is satisfied, the employer's action will not constitute an intentional wrong within the meaning of N.J.S.A. 34:15-8. That standard will be met only if both prongs of *Millison* are proved.

Applying the newly adopted standard to the facts in *Millison,* we concluded, with respect to the defendant employer, that:

> count one of plaintiffs' complaints seeking damages beyond those available through workers' compensation for their initial work-related occupational diseases must fall. Although defendants' conduct in knowingly exposing plaintiffs to asbestos clearly amounts to deliberately taking risks with employees' health, as we have observed heretofore the mere knowledge and appreciation of a risk — even the strong probability of a risk — will come up short of the "substantial certainty" needed to find an intentional wrong resulting in avoidance of the exclusive-remedy bar of the compensation statute. In the face of the legislature's awareness of occupational diseases as a fact of industrial employment, we are constrained to conclude that plaintiffs-employees' initial resulting occupational diseases must be considered the type of hazard of employment that the legislature anticipated would be compensable under the terms of the Compensation Act and not actionable in an additional civil suit. Ibid.

Regarding the defendant physicians' conduct, however, we reached a different conclusion:

> Plaintiffs have, however, pleaded a valid cause of action for aggravation of their initial occupational diseases under the second count of their complaints. Count two alleges that in order to prevent employees from leaving the workforce, defendants fraudulently concealed from plaintiffs the fact that they were suffering from asbestos-related diseases, thereby delaying their treatment and aggravating their existing illnesses. . . .
>
> These allegations go well beyond failing to warn of potentially-dangerous conditions or intentionally exposing workers to the risks of disease. There is a difference between, on the one hand, tolerating in the workplace conditions that will result in a certain number of injuries or illnesses, and, on the other, actively misleading the employees who have already fallen victim to those risks of the workplace. An employer's fraudulent concealment of diseases already developed is not one of the risks an employee should have to assume. Such intentionally-deceitful action goes beyond the bargain struck by the Compensation Act. . . . The legislature, in passing the Compensation Act, could not have intended to insulate such conduct from tort liability. . . .

Recapping, a number of principles relevant to the present inquiry can be distilled from *Millison*. First, although we recognized the need for a chary interpretation of the intentional wrong exception to the Workers' Compensation bar so that the exception would not "swallow up" the rule, we clearly rejected Larson's narrow and limited approach that required subjective intention to injure. Second, in rejecting that approach, we also declined to adopt Larson's conclusion concerning the effect of removal of a safety device. At the very least, that issue remained open after *Millison*.

Third, we adopted Prosser's substantial certainty test for intentional wrong, a test encompassing acts that the employer knows are substantially certain to produce injury even though, strictly speaking, the employer does not will that result. Fourth, although we did not repudiate [early caselaw] outright, our adoption of the "substantial certainty" standard as a complement to the "subjective desire" standard governing conduct plainly modified that line of cases. Fifth, under *Millison,* in order for an employer's act to lose the cloak of immunity of N.J.S.A. 34:15-8, two conditions must be satisfied: (1) the employer must know that his actions are substantially certain to result in injury or death to the employee, and (2) the resulting injury and the circumstances of its infliction on the worker must be (a) more than a fact of life of industrial employment and (b) plainly beyond anything the Legislature intended the Workers' Compensation Act to immunize. . . .

V

We turn now to the case at bar. . . . [W]e are satisfied that under our well-established standards for summary judgment . . . summary judgment should have been denied to AMI and the case sent to a jury on the issue of substantial certainty.

The evidence with inferences in favor of Laidlow is powerful. The rolling mill is a dangerous machine because it requires an employee to manually feed material into a nip point. . . . Apparently recognizing that principle, after its purchase AMI provided a safety guard for the rolling mill. Yet, for 13 years, from 1979 to 1992 when Laidlow was injured, the guard was inactivated by AMI nearly 100% of the time the machine was in use. During that period, Laidlow and a fellow employee had experienced close calls with the nip point of the unguarded mill. Those were potentially serious accidents in which the employees' gloves were ripped off by the machine and their fingers saved only by the cloth in the gloves. Those close calls were reported to AMI to no avail. They were persuasive evidence that AMI knew not only that injury was substantially certain to occur, but also that when it did occur it would be very serious, as Laidlow's injury turned out to be. Within the month prior to his accident, Laidlow asked his supervisor three times to restore the guard because the unguarded machine was dangerous and because new and inexperienced employees would be operating it. Nothing was ever done. . . .

AMI argues that the absence of prior accidents obviates a possible finding of "substantial certainty" by a jury. We disagree. To be sure, reports of prior accidents like prior "close-calls" are evidence of an employer's knowledge that death or injury are substantially certain to result, but they are not the only such evidence. Likewise, the absence of a prior accident does not mean that the employer did not appreciate that its conduct was substantially certain to cause death or injury. In short, we disagree with AMI and the Appellate Division that the absence of a prior accident on the rolling mill ended any inquiry regarding intentional wrong. That is simply a fact, like the close-calls, that may be considered in the substantial certainty analysis.

Turning to the facts in this record, we are satisfied that a reasonable jury could conclude, in light of all surrounding circumstances, including the prior close-calls, the seriousness of any potential injury that could occur, Laidlow's complaints about the absent guard, and the guilty knowledge of AMI as revealed by its deliberate and systematic deception of OSHA, that AMI knew that it was substantially certain that the removal of the safety guard would result eventually in injury to one of its employees. Thus, a jury question was presented on that issue.

A finding that the substantial certainty prong was satisfied does not end our inquiry. Laidlow's allegations, if proved, also must satisfy the context prong of *Millison* to preclude AMI from summary judgment. We have concluded that if Laidlow's allegations are proved, however, the context prong of *Millison* would be met. Indeed, if an employee is injured when an employer deliberately removes a safety device from a dangerous machine to enhance profit or production, with substantial certainty that it will result in death or injury to a worker, and also deliberately and systematically deceives OSHA into believing that the machine is guarded, we are convinced that the Legislature would never consider such actions or injury to constitute simple facts of industrial life. On the contrary, such conduct violates the social contract so thoroughly that we are confident that the Legislature would never expect it to fall within the Worker's Compensation bar.

Our holding is not to be understood as establishing a per se rule that an employer's conduct equates with an "intentional wrong" within the meaning of N.J.S.A. 34:15-8 whenever that employer removes a guard or similar safety device from equipment or machinery, or commits some other OSHA violation. Rather, our disposition in such a case will be grounded in the totality of the facts contained in the record and the satisfaction of the standards established in Millison and explicated here.

VI

In general, the same facts and circumstances will be relevant to both prongs of Millison. However, as a practical matter, when an employee sues an employer for an intentional tort and the employer moves for summary judgment based on the Workers' Compensation bar, the trial court must make two separate inquiries. The first is whether, when viewed in a light most favorable to the employee, the evidence could lead a jury to conclude that the employer acted with knowledge that it was substantially certain that a worker would suffer injury. If that question is answered affirmatively, the trial court must then determine whether, if the employee's allegations are proved, they constitute a simple fact of industrial life or are outside the purview of the conditions the Legislature could have intended to immunize under the Workers' Compensation bar. Resolving whether the context prong of Millison is met is solely a judicial function. Thus, if the substantial certainty standard presents a jury question and if the court concludes that the employee's allegations, if proved, would meet the context prong, the employer's motion for summary judgment should be denied; if not, it should be granted. . . .

VII

The judgment of the Appellate Division is reversed. The matter is remanded for trial after plaintiff is afforded a reasonable opportunity to complete discovery concerning Portman.

In two other cases, both involving summary judgment for the employer, the New Jersey high court remanded for reconsideration in light of *Laidlow*. In Crippen v. Central Jersey Concrete Pipe Co., 823 A.2d 789 (N.J. 2003), an employee suffocated after falling into a loading hopper. The intermediate court of appeals reaffirmed its grant of summary judgment for the employer, concluding that "Laidlow [did] not alter [its] prior analysis." Id. at 794. The supreme court disagreed and reversed, finding summary judgment inappropriate where the employer violated an OHSA directive to remedy dangerous conditions and intentionally deceived OHSA that the conditions had been abated. The supreme court also reversed summary judgment in Mull v. Zeta Consumer Products, 823 A.2d 782 (N.J. 2003), although the plaintiff did not allege OHSA deception. The court concluded, under the context prong, that the removal of safety devices, coupled with the employer's alleged knowledge of the machine's dangerous condition from prior accidents and employee complaints, and prior OHSA violation notices did not constitute simple facts of industrial life.

New Mexico appears to be charting a new path, rejecting the substantial-certainty test yet finding the actual-intent test too favorable to employers. In Delgado w. Phelps Dodge Chino, 34 P.3d 1148 (N.M. 2001), an employee died after following orders to remove, by himself, a 15-foot cauldron overflowing with molten slag during an emergency situation though he had never before removed the cauldron without assistance. His widow brought suit, alleging that the employer knew or should have known its employee would die or suffer great bodily harm while performing the task. The court reversed summary judgment for the employer, holding that employees may bring a tort action when "an employer wilfully or intentionally injures a worker." Many states continue to resist the expansion of employer tort liability. See Fenner v. Municipality of Anchorage, 53 P.3d 573 (Alaska 2002) (limiting intentional tort exception to instances where an employer has a subjective intent to injure an employee).

c. The Dual Capacity Doctrine

Products liability cases present plaintiffs with another stratagem for bypassing the exclusive remedy provision of worker compensation. In Douglas v. E & J Gallo Winery, 137 Cal. Rptr. 797 (Cal. Ct. App. 1977) (superseded by statute), employees were injured by a defective scaffold furnished by their employer from a supply it had manufactured for sale to others. The court held that an employer could function in a "dual capacity." In its employer capacity it was required to pay worker compensation benefits and was immune from tort liability. Receipt of such benefits would not, however, prevent the employee from suing the manufacturer in its parallel capacity as a product manufacturer. This dual capacity doctrine was expanded in Bell v. Industrial Vangas, Inc., 637 P.2d 266 (Cal. 1981), to impose tort liability on behalf of a route salesman who was injured while he was delivering flammable gas to the premises of a customer. The employer was not the manufacturer of the allegedly defective product but was involved in its marketing and distribution. Such a seller would be liable for strict liability in tort had the plaintiff been a nonemployee. *Bell* is discussed in Glen R. Olson, Note, Bell v. Industrial Vangas: The Employer-Manufacturer and the Dilemma of Dual Capacity, 34 Hastings L.J. 461 (1982).

The dual capacity doctrine has been controversial. Larson impugns the dual capacity exception, concluding that no state retains a dual capacity doctrine along the lines of the *Douglas* case. 2A Arthur Larson, Workmen's Compensation §72.81 (1993). The California legislature responded to *Bell* by mandating that worker compensation be the exclusive remedy even if the employer functioned in a dual capacity. Cal. Liab. Code §3602 (West 1986). The statute reflects concern that an unlimited dual capacity doctrine would swallow the entirety of the exclusivity doctrine. The dissenters in *Bell* observed that the potential for abuse was substantial: "If an employer is to be held civilly liable to injured workers in the employer's capacity as a 'manufacturer,' what compelling reason can exist for denying similar liability for injuries attributable to the employer's other relationships, including his status as 'Landowner,' 'motor vehicle operator' or 'cafeteria proprietor?'" 637 P.2d at 278. See also Byrd v. Munsey Products of Tennessee, No. 47 C.A. (Tenn. Ct. App. July 26, 1985).

The Supreme Court of Ohio reacted differently from the *Bell* Court, supra, in a case involving the dual capacity doctrine. In Schump v. Firestone Tire and Rubber Company, 541 N.E.2d 1040 (Ohio 1989), the plaintiff, who worked for a tire manufacturer, received injuries while driving a truck equipped with his employer's tires. The Ohio high court refused to apply the dual capacity doctrine, holding that the truck was equipped with the employer's tires in accordance with company policy and that any injury resulting from a defective tire was sustained as an employee and not as a consumer. The court held that the dual capacity doctrine would only be applicable when there was a showing that an employer occupied two independent and unrelated relationships with an employee and that it had assumed a role other than that of an employer. In Jessop v. Angelo Benedetti, Inc., 2003 WL 23114 (Ohio), the plaintiff was severely injured after his boot became caught in the blade of a piece of paving equipment. The court upheld summary judgment, finding no liability under the dual capacity doctrine where the employer designed and developed the machine solely for the business use of its employees and not for sale or lease. Illinois, which also recognizes the dual capacity doctrine, rejected an injured employee's contention that the employer acted as a "quasi-manufacturer" by modifying a trim press in Murcia v. Textron, Inc., 2003 WL 21089071 (Ill. App. Dist.). The court found that the dual capacity doctrine did not apply where the modification was incident to the employer's business of manufacturing machine parts and was undertaken in its capacity as employer.

Many states either reject the dual capacity doctrine altogether or explicitly state their reluctance to apply it. See Kaczorowska v. National Envelope Corp., 777 A.2d 941 (N.J. Super. Ct. App. Div. 2001) (stating that the doctrine is "disfavored, if not outright disapproved" in New Jersey); Tolley v. ACF Industries, Inc., 575 S.E.2d 158 (W.Va. 2002) (quoting the lower court that the state "has never adopted and applied the doctrine" and finding no reason to do so in this case); Suburban Hospital, Inc. v. Kirson, 763 A.2d 185 (Md. 2000) (describing the doctrine as "not compatible with Maryland law").

Some states recognize the dual persona doctrine, a variant of the dual capacity doctrine. The Supreme Court of South Carolina suggested the following doctrinal distinction: The dual persona doctrine recognizes different legal entities, whereas the dual capacity doctrine recognizes different activities or relationships. Tatum v. Medical University of South Carolina, 552 S.E.2d 18 (S.C. 2001). In

Martinez v. Callahan Mfg., Inc., 2003 WL 42527 (Wash. Ct. App.), the court found the dual persona doctrine inapplicable where the defendant's "manufacturer" persona was dependent upon and related to his "employer persona" so as to amount to the same legal entity. *Martinez* acknowledged that the Washington Supreme Court had applied the dual persona doctrine before, but observed that the doctrine has not been applied to products liability actions.

2. *Allocating Responsibility Between the Employer (the Worker Compensation System) and the Product Manufacturer (the Products Liability System)*

Kotecki v. Cyclops Welding Corp.
585 N.E.2d 1023 (Ill. 1991)

MORAN, J.

Mark A. Kotecki (Kotecki) brought an action in LaSalle County for personal injury, allegedly caused by defendant Cyclops Welding Corporation's (Cyclops) negligence in the design and construction of an agitator, used on the premises of Carus Chemical Company (Carus), Kotecki's employer. Cyclops then filed a third-party complaint against Carus, seeking contribution. Carus moved to strike the ad damnum clause of the third-party claim for contribution. The trial court denied the motion. . . . [Interlocutory-appeal followed.]

The sole issue on appeal is whether an employer, sued as a third-party defendant in a product liability case, is liable for contribution in an amount greater than its statutory liability under the Workers' Compensation Act.

As this is an interlocutory appeal, all of the facts are gleaned from the pleadings. Kotecki, in his complaint, alleges that he sustained personal injury when he caught his hand in the motor of an agitator; that the injury occurred while he was acting in the scope of his employment with Carus; and that Cyclops negligently designed, constructed, and installed the agitator on the Carus property without sufficient guarding devices for the motor and drive system.

Cyclops then filed a third-party complaint against Carus, alleging various acts of negligence. Cyclops thus sought contribution from Carus under the Contribution Act (Ill. Rev. Stat. 1987, ch. 70, par. 301 et seq.), in an amount proportionate with the degree of fault attributable to Carus' culpability, if it is found liable to Kotecki at trial. . . .

Any discussion of the effect of workers' compensation on the Contribution Act must begin with Skinner v. Reed-Prentice Division Package Machinery Co. (1977), 70 Ill. 2d 1. In *Skinner,* the court held that a defendant manufacturer sued in strict tort liability had a right of contribution against the employer (whose conduct may have contributed to the injury) of an injured worker. The plaintiff, Rita Skinner, was injured while she was using an injection molding machine and she sued the machine's manufacturer under strict product liability. The manufacturer filed a third-party action against her employer for contribution, alleging negligence. This court found that the trial court's dismissal of the third-party action was error. (*Skinner,* 70 Ill. 2d at 16.) It additionally found that there is a right of contribution among joint tortfeasors, and that the doctrine would apply prospectively only. *Skinner,* 70 Ill. 2d at 16.

110   2. Assigning Responsibility Inside and Outside the Commercial Chain of Distribution

Following this court's decision in *Skinner,* the legislature passed the Contribution Among Joint Tortfeasors Act (Ill. Rev. Stat. 1989, ch. 70, pars. 301 through 305) (Contribution Act). For the purposes of this case, the statute states in pertinent part:

> [W]here 2 or more persons are subject to liability in tort arising out of the same injury to person or property, or the same wrongful death, there is a right of contribution among them, even though judgment has not been entered against any or all of them. Ill. Rev. Stat. 1989, ch. 70, par. 302(a). . . .

Carus essentially argues that although it is clear that an employer can be held liable for contribution to a manufacturer, this court has never stated if that amount is limited by the employer's workers' compensation liability. Cyclops . . . argues that . . . a manufacturer has a right to contribution from the employer, and the amount that the employer can be required to pay is limited only by the extent of the damages that are attributable to the employer's negligence. . . .

Cyclops . . . argues that this court should not examine any potential limitations on the amount that an employer could be required to contribute because the legislature is currently considering various pending bills in this area of the law. (Cyclops cited potential legislative amendments to the Workers' Compensation Act or the Contribution Act which would bar a third party from filing a third-party complaint against an employer. However, all of the bills that Cyclops cites either were tabled or left pending at the end of the legislative term.) Nevertheless, as this court has noted:

> We believe that the proper relationship between the legislature and the court is one of cooperation and assistance in examining and changing the common law to conform with the ever-changing demands of the community. There are, however, times when there exists a mutual state of inaction in which the court awaits action by the legislature and the legislature awaits guidance from the court. Such a stalemate is a manifest injustice to the public. When such a stalemate exists and the legislature has, for whatever reason, failed to act to remedy a gap in the common law that results in injustice, it is the imperative duty of the court to repair that injustice and reform the law to be responsive to the demands of society. (Alvis v. Ribar (1981), 85 Ill. 2d 1, 23-24 (despite the presence of six bills in the legislature, the court abolished the doctrine of contributory negligence).) . . .

The underlying controversy between workers' compensation and contribution was succinctly stated by the Minnesota Supreme Court:

> If contribution or indemnity is allowed, the employer may be forced to pay his employee — through the conduit of the third-party tortfeasor — an amount in excess of his statutory workers' compensation liability. This arguably thwarts the central concept behind workers' compensation, i.e., that the employer and employee receive the benefits of a guaranteed, fixed-schedule, nonfault recovery system, which then constitutes the exclusive liability of the employer to his employee. [Citation.] If contribution or indemnity is not allowed, a third-party stranger to the workers' compensation system is made to bear the burden of a full common-law judgment despite possibly greater fault on the part of the employer. This obvious inequity is further exacerbated by the right of the employer to recover directly or indirectly from the third party the amount he has paid in compensation regardless of the employer's own negligence. [Citations.] Thus, the third party is forced to subsidize a workers' compensation system in a proportion greater than his own fault and at a financial level far in excess of the workers' compensation sched-

ule. (Lambertson v. Cincinnati Corp. (1977), 312 Minn. 114, 119-20, 257 N.W.2d 679, 684.) . . .

The majority (45) of other jurisdictions do not allow a contribution action against an employer, from a defendant sued in tort, by an injured employee. (See Sherman, Contribution from Employers: Availability, Good Faith Settlements and What the Future May Hold, 75 Ill. B.J. 568, 572 n.52 (June 1987) (collecting cases).) At the other end of the spectrum, only New York allows a defendant to recover unlimited contribution from negligent employers. (See Dole v. Dow Chemical Co. (1972, 30 N.Y.2d 143, 381 N.Y.S.2d) 382, 282 N.E.2d 288.) . . .

The Minnesota Supreme Court adopted a rule finding that, as in Illinois, an employer could be required to contribute, but that the amount of an employer's contribution would be limited by its workers' compensation liability. (*Lambertson,* 312 Minn. at 130, 257 N.W.2d at 689.) . . . The Minnesota rule arguably strikes a balance between the competing interests of the employer, as a participant in the workers' compensation system, and the equitable interests of the third-party defendant in not being forced to pay more than its established fault. Notably, this approach has been adopted by legislation in Idaho. See Runcorn v. Shearer Lumber Products, Inc. (1984), 107 Idaho 389, 395, 690 P.2d 324, 330. . . .

We find that the Minnesota rule provides the fairest and most equitable balance between the competing interests of the employer and the third-party defendant. . . . Limiting the amount of contribution of an employer to its liability under workers' compensation:

> allows the third party to obtain limited contribution, but substantially preserves the employer's interest in not paying more than workers' compensation liability. While this approach may not allow full contribution recovery to the third party in all cases, it is the solution we consider most consistent with fairness and the various statutory schemes before us. *Lambertson,* 312 Minn. at 130, 257 N.W.2d at 689.

The language of the Workers' Compensation Act clearly shows an intent that the employer only be required to pay an employee the statutory benefits. These limited benefits are paid in exchange for a no-fault system of recovery. The Contribution Act . . . requires that the employers contribute to tort judgments if they are partially responsible for an employee's injuries. . . .

Reversed and remanded, with directions.

The injured employee's ability to recover worker compensation benefits against the employer and then to prosecute a products liability claim against the manufacturer has raised questions regarding the proper method for allocating the liabilities between the two systems. According to an early study, employer negligence is implicated in more than half of all employment-related products liability claims. See Insurance Services Office, Product Liability Closed Claim Survey: A Technical Analysis of Survey Results Report 10, 64-66 (1977). Even when employer negligence is established, states differ sharply as to how the losses are to be allocated. Among the major positions one finds:

(1) No Contribution. The majority rule places the entirety of the loss on the manufacturer of the defective product, with no right of contribution against the

employer. See, e.g., Landry v. Union Pacific Railroad, 631 So. 2d 623 (La. Ct. App. 1994) (refusing to allow a third-party action against the employer). In fact, in most states the employer who pays (or whose insurer pays) benefits to the injured employee has a subrogation lien against the ultimate tort recovery. Manufacturers are justifiably angered by the majority position, because the no-fault worker compensation system ends up bearing no responsibility whatsoever for harm caused, at least in part, by the employers' faulty conduct. By denying manufacturers contribution rights against employers and allowing subrogation, courts do more than protect the worker compensation system from tort recovery — they protect worker compensation from its own underlying obligation to the employee. Given the high level of dissatisfaction with the no contribution rule, its majority status is likely to change. Both courts and legislatures will be forced to acknowledge the legitimate complaints of manufacturers.

(2) Total Contribution. For many years New York permitted a manufacturer of a defective product to bring a third-party claim for contribution based on the proportionate fault of the parties. See Dole v. Dow Chemical Co., 282 N.E.2d 288 (N.Y. 1972). New York stood alone in this regard; no other state allowed total contribution. The New York approach drew heavy criticism because it exposed an employer to tort damages in excess of its liability under worker compensation law. In 1996 the New York legislature cut back significantly on *Dole.* New York Workers' Compensation Law §11 (McKinney 2001) now provides that the right to contribution by a third party against an employer for injuries suffered by an employee acting within the scope of his or her employment will only be allowed if the employee suffered a "grave injury." The statue defines "grave injury" to mean only one or more of the following:

> . . . death, permanent and total loss of use or amputation of an arm, leg, hand or foot, loss of multiple fingers, loss of multiple toes, paraplegia or quadriplegia, total and permanent blindness, total and permanent deafness, loss of nose, loss of ear, permanent and severe facial disfigurement, loss of an index finger or an acquired injury to the brain caused by an external physical force resulting in permanent total disability. [Ch. 635, Laws of 1996.]

After some initial indications that the gravity of the employee's injuries might be a question of fact for the jury, it now appears that the New York courts will not permit contribution unless the employee's injuries are expressly listed in the statute. See, e.g., Castro v. United Container Machinery Group, Inc., 761 N.E.2d 1014 (N.Y. 2001) (holding that the loss of multiple fingertips did not meet the "loss of multiple fingers" requirement and thus was not a "grave injury" under §11); Meis v. ELO Organization, LLC, 767 N.E.2d 146 (N.Y. 2002) (finding that the loss of a thumb is not listed in §11 as a "grave injury" and plaintiff failed to demonstrate that he suffered a "permanent and total loss of use" of the hand); Ibarra v. Equipment Control, Inc., 256 A.D.2d 13 (N.Y. App. Div. 2000) (finding that employee's loss of vision in one eye, even if total, does not constitute "total and permanent blindness").

(3) Limited Contribution. Kotecki, supra, is a leading case. As noted in *Kotecki,* Minnesota adopted a rule allowing third parties to seek contribution from negligent employers in Lambertson v. Cincinnati Corp., 257 N.W.2d 679 (Minn. 1977).

The court applied comparative fault principles and held that the amount to be contributed must reflect the negligent employers' percentage of fault, but cannot exceed the total worker compensation liability for the injury. Illinois courts continue to apply *Kotecki* even where the employee did not pursue his workers' compensation rights, Pavelich v. All Am. Homes, Inc., 606 N.E.2d 859 (Ill. App. 2d Dist. 1992) or where willful and wanton employer misconduct is alleged, Lannom v. Kosco, 616 N.E.2d 731 (Ill. App. Ct. 1993). The *Kotecki* limit can, however, be waived contractually. West Bend Mutual Insurance Co. v. Mulligan Masonry Co., Inc., 786 N.E.2d 1078 (Ill. App. Ct. 2003). The limited contribution approach was adopted in the Draft Uniform Product Liability Act but was rejected in the final draft of the Act because establishing the percentage of employer fault imposed significant transaction costs.[2] A strong endorsement of this position is found in Paul C. Weiler, Worker's Compensation and Product Liability: The Interaction of a Tort and a Non-Tort Regime, 50 Ohio St. L.J. 825, 844 (1989).

(4) Severing the Systems. An interesting approach to resolving the conflict between the worker compensation system (which provides the employee limited benefits) and the tort system (which provides the employee total recovery) is to apportion fault between the parties and then to hold the manufacturer liable for its share of damages in tort, and the employer (or its insurer) for the worker compensation benefits. For example, in a case where the worker compensation recovery is $10,000 and the total tort damages are $200,000, if the manufacturer is held 75 percent at fault and the employer is held 25 percent at fault, the employee recovers $150,000 from the manufacturer and $10,000 from the employer. This approach was adopted by the district court in Shellman v. United States Lines, Inc., only to be promptly reversed, 528 F.2d 675 (9th Cir. 1975), *cert. denied,* 425 U.S. 936 (1976). A similar holding involving the Longshoremen and Harbor Workers' Compensation Act was reversed by the United States Supreme Court. Edmonds v. Compagnie Generale Transatlantique, 577 F.2d 1153 (4th Cir. 1978) (en banc), *rev'd,* 443 U.S. 256, *reh'g denied,* 444 U.S. 880 (1979). For a discussion of the alternative solutions, see Jayne F. Lynch, The Clash between Strict Products Liability Doctrine and the Worker's Compensation Exclusivity Rule: The Negligent Employer and the Third-Party Manufacturer, 50 Ins. Couns. J. 35 (1983). The reasoning behind severing the systems is that the employee has made his bargain with the worker compensation system, and should be limited to that system's measure of damages against the employer. Thus, this approach severs the joint tortfeasor doctrine and allocates damages according to the provisions of the two differing systems. Although courts and scholars have expressed interest in the solution, it is not the governing law in any jurisdiction that retains the joint tortfeasor doctrine. Many states have abrogated joint and several liability and limit a defendant's liability to the defendant's proportional share of fault. See Section C, infra.

(5) Dollar-for-Dollar Reduction of Plaintiff's Tort Recovery. The solution that has engendered the most support in debates over a federal products liability act

---

2. Model Uniform Product Liability Act §114, Analysis 44 Fed. Reg. at 62,740 (1979).

authors' dialogue 4

JIM: At the end of the day, I can't help thinking that our courts and legislatures have made a mess of the interface between worker compensation and products liability. I think they may be going too far in allowing employees to sue employers in tort, and not far enough in allowing manufacturers to interplead employers for contribution.

AARON: Your preference for contribution seems a bit arbitrary. If you want the employer to bear some (all) of the tort liability, why not let it happen directly, via an intentional tort action?

JIM: First of all, courts are distorting the concept of intentionality in allowing employees to sue their employers directly. These doctrinal distortions may spill over into other areas and, suddenly, almost every negligence action becomes an intentional tort. Heck, even selling perfectly good knives can be an intentional tort, given that it is certain that people will cut themselves. The better way to handle the employer's role in creating unreasonable product-related risks in the workplace is via the allocation of responsibility by juries under comparative fault, as part of the products liability action against the manufacturer. Juries can assess the appropriate responsibilities as between manufacturers who commercially design and market the machinery and employers who manage the workplaces in which the accidents occur.

AARON: If your idea is sound, why haven't more states adopted it?

JIM: I don't know, really. Maybe it's politics. Most states deny tort recovery against the employers and deny contribution on behalf of manufacturers, leaving products liability to bear all the tort-measured losses. Most states even pay back the worker comp carriers out of the plaintiff's products recovery, holding the employer's side completely harmless for what, in many instances, is clearly the employer's fault.

AARON: But then, why the beginnings of a trend in favor of allowing knowledge-based intentional tort recoveries against employers?

JIM: Maybe it's more acceptable, politically. Who can argue against allowing tort recovery for *intentional* wrongdoing?

would allow the defendant manufacturer to deduct the plaintiff's worker compensation benefits from the amount of any tort judgment. Under this proposal, it would make no difference whether the employer was negligent. Worker compensation benefits would be assessed exclusively against the compensation system. No subrogation lien would be allowed and no contribution action against the employer could be brought. The drafters of the Model Uniform Product Liability Act (MUPLA) have backed this approach as does the leading authority on worker compensation. See Arthur Larson, Third Party Action Over Against Workers' Compensation Employer, 1982 Duke L.J. 483, 540-541. The approach has been enacted into law in Connecticut. Section 114(a) of MUPLA provides:

In the case of any product liability claim brought by or on behalf of an injured person entitled to compensation under a state Worker Compensation statute, damages shall be reduced by the amount paid as Worker Compensation benefits for the same injury plus the present value of all future Worker Compensation benefits payable for the same injury under the Worker Compensation statute.

It might be argued that the proposed statute would accomplish "mirror image" injustice. Just as current law shifts employer-caused costs onto manufacturers, the proposal would allow the manufacturer to shift partial liability to the no-fault system for an injury that was entirely the fault of the manufacturer. Such a reaction, however, is probably not justified. The worker compensation system, which was established to provide limited recovery for a work-related injury, would, in fact, be paying for a work-related injury. To deny the employer who was truly not at fault his third-party action against the manufacturer may appear to be somewhat unfair. But does it violate basic principles of fairness to recognize that when a no-fault system operates side-by-side with a fault system, it is best to permit each system to work separately? It might be possible to "fine tune" the proposal and allow dollar-for-dollar reduction only when the employer is at fault, and even to allow the subrogation lien when he is not. But that would require that fault be tried and apportioned between the employer and manufacturer. Such an approach would increase transaction costs, presenting apportionment questions for jury resolution in the workplace setting where apportionment of fault may be especially difficult.

For discussions of the various positions, see Nicholas B. Clifford, Jr., Note, Kotecki v. Cyclops Welding Corp.: The Efficacy of a Limited Contribution Rule and Its Effect on Good Faith Settlements, 68 Chi.-Kent. L. Rev. 479 (1992); George H. Singer, Workers' Compensation: The Assault on the Shield of Immunity — Coming to Blows with the Exclusive-Remedy Provisions of the North Dakota Workers' Compensation Act, 70 N.D. L. Rev. 905 (1994); Dale T. Hansen, Note, Sullivan v. Scoular Grain Co.: Apportioning the Fault of Immune Employers, 1994 B.Y.U. L. Rev. 187 (1993).

CHAPTER THREE
Causation

It should come as no surprise that the plaintiff in a products liability case must establish a causal connection between the defendant's defective product and the plaintiff's harm. In products cases sounding in tort, courts approach the causation issue very much as they do in non-products cases studied in the first-year torts course; and in cases sounding in warranty, all of the relevant Code sections impose causation requirements. Beyond this, generalizations are difficult. For one thing, the relevant terminology tends to be confusing. Some courts distinguish between cause-in-fact and proximate cause, others employ only one (or the other) of these terms, while still others rely on phrases such as "direct cause," or "substantial cause." Notions of "intervening cause" and "superceding cause" also generate considerable mischief. The best advice to the student regarding terminology is to be aware that jurisdictions differ in the ways they talk about causation, and to use the terminology appropriate to the jurisdiction in which he or she is briefing or arguing a given case. We have organized the following causation materials around the persistent substantive issues presented in the cases, rather than around the vicissitudes of terminology.

Several distinct (or at least distinguishable) questions arise in connection with the causation issue. Suppose that the plaintiff suffers harm after using or consuming a product that she can show was defective at time of sale, and seeks to hold the defendant manufacturer liable for the harm. Four questions must be answered in the affirmative for the plaintiff to establish causation:

(1) Did the product harm the plaintiff?
(2) Did the defendant supply the product?
(3) Did the defect in the defendant's product contribute to harming the plaintiff?
(4) Did the defective product proximately cause the plaintiff's harm?

These questions provide the structure for this chapter. All of them can arise in cases involving manufacturing defects; but typically some of them — for example, the first question involving whether the product, in fact, caused the plaintiff's harm — are easily answered in the affirmative. Thus, when a plaintiff buys a new bicycle that suddenly breaks because of a defect while being used normally and causes personal injury, typically no one disputes that the bicycle in question harmed the plaintiff. Instead, the first causation question will usually be contested only in cases involving generic product hazards. For example, did the misleadingly marketed cigarettes that plaintiff smoked for 20 years cause plaintiff's lung cancer? Notwithstanding the fact that some of the causation issues considered in this chapter involve generic product risks rather than manufacturing defects, all

117

four causation issues are considered here for convenience. The existence of a defect may be assumed in all of these cases for purposes of considering causation, and therefore "defect" does not present problems that will confuse the analysis.

Restatement (Third) of Torts: Products Liability
(1998)

§15. GENERAL RULE GOVERNING CAUSAL CONNECTION BETWEEN PRODUCT DEFECT AND HARM

Whether a product defect caused harm to persons or property is determined by the prevailing rules and principles governing causation in tort.

Notwithstanding this attempt to treat the issue of causation in products liability as part of the broader law of torts, products cases present enough peculiar wrinkles to make this chapter interesting.

Speaking of "the broader law of torts," the American Law Institute has undertaken a revision of that subject in the Restatement (Third) of Torts: Liability for Physical Harm (Basic Principles) (hereafter Restatement of Basic Principles). Begun in 1998, the year the Restatement of Products Liability was completed and published, this broader torts project continued during the preparation of the fifth edition of this casebook. Tentative Drafts No. 2 and No. 3, dated March 25, 2002 and April 7, 2003, respectively, address the subject of causation. We will refer to relevant provisions in these materials. Although these drafts do not change the substance of what follows in this chapter, it should be noted that §26 of the new Restatement of Basic Principles lumps the first and third questions in subsections A and C, infra, into the single issue of "factual cause." And §29 abandons the traditional "proximate cause" terminology employed in subsection D. For an analysis of the Restatement's treatment of causation see Richard L. Cupp, Jr., Proximate Cause, the Proposed Basic Principles Restatement, and Products Liability, 53 S. Car. L. Rev. 1085 (2002).

A. DID THE PRODUCT ACTUALLY CAUSE THE PLAINTIFF'S HARM?

1. But-For Causation in General

But-for causation in products liability (and tort law generally, for that matter) comes into play in two different, but related, contexts. The first, of concern in this Section, tests whether the product was a necessary condition to the plaintiff suffering harm. The second, of concern in Section C, infra, tests whether the defective aspect of the product, rather than simply the product itself, was a necessary condition. The first but-for issue is universally dealt with as part of cause-in-fact. As for the second, while many courts also treat it as part of cause-in-fact, some deal with it as part of proximate cause. Section 26 of the Restatement of Basic Principles, mentioned supra, falls into the first camp. Thus, it asserts that tortious conduct "is a factual cause of harm when the harm would not have occurred absent the [tortious] conduct." In the cause-in-fact context considered in this Section, the question is whether the plaintiff would have suffered the same harm if the product had never been produced in the first instance. That is, but-for the product, itself (rather than the product defect), would the plaintiff have been harmed anyway? If the answer is "Yes, the plaintiff would have been harmed even if the product had never existed," the product is not a cause-in-fact of the plaintiff's harm.

But-for actual causation breaks down logically into two components. The first, sometimes referred to as "general," or "generic," causation, concerns whether the product sold by the defendant is generally (generically) capable of causing the sort of harm suffered by the plaintiff. If it is not, the defendant wins the actual causation issue as a matter of law. The second cause-in-fact issue is specific causation—whether the product actually harmed this particular plaintiff. Most products liability cases involve only specific causation; the general causation issue is not raised by the facts. When, for example, an allegedly defective automobile runs over the plaintiff and the issue is whether a defect in the vehicle caused the accident, general causation is not an issue—no one questions that automobiles are generally capable of physically harming people. But what if the plaintiff claims that fumes from the automobile's exhaust caused him to contract lung cancer? In that instance, the manufacturer may argue not only that the automobile was not defective, but also that exhaust fumes from a single vehicle are not capable, as a general matter, of causing lung cancer. Indeed, even if the defendant in the "fumes hurt the plaintiff" case admits that the vehicle's exhaust system was defective, it may still have the general causation argument that, in any event, vehicles generally cannot—and, therefore, this particular vehicle did not—cause people to contract lung cancer. Even if it were clear as a general matter that toxic exhaust fumes from motor vehicles can cause people to contract cancer, the manufacturer may still argue that the particular automobile involved in the case did not cause the plaintiff's illness. This second actual causation issue in our exhaust fumes hypothetical—whether the particular automobile in question harmed the plaintiff—is the issue of specific causation, the issue presented in most products liability cases involving actual causation.

2. Special Problems of Proof: Reliance on Experts

Regarding the issue of specific causation, in most cases the facts speak for themselves. As has been observed already, no one questions that the allegedly defective automobile in which the plaintiff was riding caused his traumatic injuries in the accident resulting from the defect. But cases do arise in which the plaintiff must rely on expert testimony to prove specific causation. Suppose that the plaintiff is driving his automobile on a city street and inadvertently loses control and crashes into the car in front of him. Moments after the crash, the driver of a third car, following behind the plaintiff, loses control because of an original defect in the brakes and crashes into the plaintiff's car. The plaintiff ends up with a broken neck. In the plaintiff's products liability action against the manufacturer of the third car, the plaintiff claims that the first crash caused no harm and that it was the subsequent rear-end crash due to defective brakes that broke his neck.

The defendant manufacturer argues that the first crash, which the manufacturer did not cause, broke the plaintiff's neck, not the second crash from behind. Not surprisingly, both sides must rely on experts to opine regarding whether the second crash, allegedly caused by a defect in the brakes, was the cause-in-fact of plaintiff's neck injury. In an actual case quite similar to this hypothetical, the federal district court for the Northern District of Illinois entered summary judgment for the defendant automobile manufacturer when the only evidence was that plaintiff's decedent had died of a sudden cardiac arrest moments before the accident rather than because the airbag failed to deploy. See Klootwyk v. Daimler-Chrysler Corp., 2003 WL 21038417 (N.D. Ill.).

By contrast, the issue of generic, or general, causation raises very interesting issues regarding the proper use of expert testimony. The reason for this is that questions of general causation tend to arise at the fringes of scientific knowledge and often involve expert testimony that is questionable from the standpoint of scientific methodology. Defendants frequently challenge the admissibility of plaintiff's expert proof as well as its adequacy. To understand how these issues get resolved it will be necessary to trace a bit of history. In 1923, in Frye v. United States, 293 F. 1013 (D.C. Cir. 1923), the District of Columbia Court of Appeals was asked whether evidence derived from a lie-detector test was admissible against a defendant in a murder trial. The court devised a standard for admissibility of scientific evidence that would become the rule for most, if not all, American courts for the next 70 years:

> Just when a scientific principle or discovery crosses the line between the experimental and demonstrable stages is difficult to define. Somewhere in this twilight zone the evidential force of the principle must be recognized, and while courts will go a long way in admitting expert testimony deduced from a well-known scientific principle or discovery, the thing from which the deduction is made must be sufficiently established to have gained general acceptance in the particular field in which it belongs. 293 F. at 1014.

Thus, when faced with an objection to a party's scientific evidence, the court applying the *Frye* test must determine whether or not the method by which that evidence was obtained was generally accepted by experts "in the particular field in which it belongs." If the judge determines that the methodology is not generally accepted by the relevant field, the judge will disallow the evidence. If the plaintiff's cause of action depends on the disallowed evidence, this often marks the end of the case. In this way, the court tries to ensure that the scientific evidence admitted deserves the weight that jurors are likely to give it, while establishing that a field of experts is available from which the opposing party can obtain expert rebuttal.

No other area of products liability in recent years reflects more vividly the problems just described than cases involving the widely used prescription drug, Bendectin. Approved in 1956 by the F.D.A. as a safe treatment for morning sickness during pregnancy, Bendectin was used by over 30,000,000 women between 1957 and 1983. Richardson-Merrell, Inc., the manufacturer, withdrew the drug from the market in 1983 due to widespread fears that it caused severe birth defects in the children of women who ingested the drug while pregnant. Whether these fears were grounded in fact is still disputed; but the fears were real enough. A large number of tort claims had been filed based on scientific studies, including epidemiological studies, allegedly revealing the drug to be a teratogen, or birth defect-causing agent. By the mid-1980s, Bendectin litigation appeared to be a growth area for plaintiffs' lawyers. See, e.g., Oxendine v. Merrell Dow Pharmaceuticals, 506 A.2d 1100 (D.C. 1986) (Bendectin manufacturer held liable based on epidemiological proof of causation).

Notwithstanding the optimism that reigned in the early to mid-1980s among plaintiffs' lawyers regarding the future of Bendectin litigation, the tide began turning against them as the established scientific community concluded in a number of major research projects that the link between the drug and the birth defects had not been established at an adequate level of statistical significance — that is, observed correlations between ingestion and injury could, for all the data showed, have been the product of random chance. Courts began issuing summary judgments for the defendant, Merrell, with increasing frequency. Not all federal courts agreed with this trend, however, and a fair amount of confusion reigned. All of these developments culminated in an epochal Supreme Court decision.

In Daubert v. Merrell Dow Pharmaceuticals, Inc., 509 U.S. 579 (1993), the Supreme Court vacated the judgment of the court of appeals in favor of the defendant in a Bendectin case. The court of appeals had ruled for defendant after excluding plaintiff's expert's testimony based on *Frye*. The Supreme Court reversed and remanded, holding that "general acceptance" is not a necessary precondition to the admissibility of scientific evidence under the Federal Rules of Evidence:

> Faced with a proffer of expert scientific testimony . . . the trial judge must make a preliminary assessment of whether the testimony's underlying reasoning or methodology is scientifically valid and properly can be applied to the facts at issue. Many considerations will bear on the inquiry, including whether the theory or technique in question can be (and has been) tested, whether it has been subjected to peer review and publication, its known or potential error rate, the existence and maintenance of standards controlling its operation, and whether it has attracted widespread acceptance within a relevant scientific community. The inquiry is a flexible one, and its focus must be solely on principles and methodology, not on the conclusions that they generate. Throughout, the judge should also be mindful of other applicable Rules. . . . [C]ross examination, presentation of contrary evidence, and careful instruction on the burden of proof, rather than wholesale exclusion under an uncompromising "general acceptance" standard, is the appropriate means by which evidence based on valid principles may be challenged. Excerpted from official Syllabus, 509 U.S. at 580.

Rather than necessarily making it easier or more difficult for plaintiffs to get their scientific testimony admitted into evidence, the Supreme Court in *Daubert* appears to have aimed at giving federal courts more control over the admissibility issue, instead of deferring under *Frye* to the scientific community.

On remand from the Supreme Court, the court of appeals wrestled with the new test set forth in *Daubert*. In Daubert v. Merrell Dow Pharmaceuticals, Inc., 43 F.3d 1311 (9th Cir. 1995), the court affirmed the district court's grant of summary judgment, clearly echoing Chief Justice Rehnquist's assessment of vagueness and difficulty. Judge Kozinski's opinion begins:

> The first prong of *Daubert* puts federal judges in an uncomfortable position. . . . Though we are largely untrained in science and certainly no match for any of the witnesses whose testimony we are reviewing, it is our responsibility to determine whether those

experts' proposed testimony amounts to "scientific knowledge," constitutes "good science," and was "derived by the scientific method."

The task before us is more daunting still when the dispute concerns matters at the very cutting edge of scientific research, where fact meets theory and certainty dissolves into probability. As the record in this case illustrates, scientists often have vigorous and sincere disagreements as to what research methodology is proper, what should be accepted as sufficient proof for the existence of a "fact," and whether information derived by a particular method can tell us anything useful about the subject under study.

Our responsibility, then, unless we badly misread the Supreme Court's opinion, is to resolve disputes among respected, well-credentialed scientists about matters squarely within their expertise, in areas where there is no scientific consensus as to what is and what is not "good science," and occasionally to reject such expert testimony because it was not "derived by the scientific method." Mindful of our position in the hierarchy of the federal judiciary, we take a deep breath and proceed with this heady task. (43 F.3d at 1315-1316).

Perhaps the most important consideration in the court's analysis of the record below was the undisputed fact that none of the plaintiffs' experts based his testimony on preexisting or independent research:

> One very significant fact to be considered is whether the experts are proposing to testify about matters growing naturally and directly out of research they have conducted independent of the litigation, or whether they have developed their opinions expressly for purposes of testifying. That an expert testifies for money does not necessarily cast doubt on the reliability of his testimony, as few experts appear in court merely as an eleemosynary gesture. But in determining whether proposed expert testimony amounts to good science, we may not ignore the fact that a scientist's normal workplace is the lab or the field, not the courtroom or the lawyer's office. . . .
>
> We have examined carefully the affidavits proffered by plaintiffs' experts, as well as the testimony from prior trials that plaintiffs have introduced in support of that testimony, and find that none of the experts based his testimony on preexisting or independent research. While plaintiffs' scientists are all experts in their respective fields, none claims to have studied the effect of Bendectin on limb reduction defects before being hired to testify in this or related cases. (43 F.3d at 1317).

The court proceeds to recognize peer review of proffered expert testimony as the other important consideration in determining admissibility under the first prong of the Supreme Court's two-prong test. The court next turns to the second prong of the test advanced in *Daubert*—whether the testimony will assist the trier of fact in resolving the factual issue to which it purports to relate. In this case, the court observes, the crucial issue is specific causation. The court continues:

> California tort law requires plaintiffs to show not merely that Bendectin increased the likelihood of injury, but that it more likely than not caused their injuries. In terms of statistical proof, this means that plaintiffs must establish not just that their mothers' ingestion of Bendectin increased somewhat the likelihood of birth defects, but that it more than doubled it—only then can it be said that Bendectin is more likely than not the source of their injury. Because the background rate of limb reduction defects is one per thousand births, plaintiffs must show that among children of mothers who took Bendectin the incidence of such defects was more than two per thousand.[1] (43 F.3d at 1320).

---

1. No doubt, there will be unjust results under this substantive standard. If a drug increases the likelihood of birth defects, but doesn't more than double it, some plaintiffs whose injuries are attributable to

The court of appeals concludes that the plaintiffs' experts' testimony that Bendectin caused the birth defects in this case, even if it were admissible under the first prong, does not satisfy the requirement imposed by the second prong of *Daubert*.

Several state courts have rejected *Daubert*'s reconsideration of the Federal Rules of Evidence, opting instead to continue following *Frye*'s "general acceptance" principle. For example, in Goeb v. Tharaldson, 615 N.W.2d 800 (Minn. 2000), the Supreme Court of Minnesota declined to adopt the *Daubert* standard, stating that "[*Frye*] is more apt to ensure objective and uniform rulings as to particular scientific methods and techniques"; and that while "a key assumption to [*Daubert*] is that judges can . . . resolve disputes among qualified scientists who have spent years immersed in their field of study, . . . the *Frye* general acceptance standard ensures that the persons most qualified to assess scientific validity of a technique have the determinative vote." Id. at 813-814. But see Farm Bureau Mut. Ins. Co. v. Foote, 14 S.W.3d 512 (Ark. 2000) (adopting the *Daubert* standard and affirming the trial court's decision to exclude expert testimony that dogs allegedly have an ability to detect fire accelerants that is more effective than the chemical detectors used by forensic scientists).

The Supreme Court has revisited the *Daubert* principle in several recent decisions. See, e.g., General Elec. Co. v. Joiner, 522 U.S. 136 (1997) (holding that a court of appeals should utilize the "abuse of discretion" standard in reviewing a trial court's decision to exclude expert testimony under *Daubert*); Kumho Tire Co. v. Carmichael, 526 U.S. 137 (1999) (holding that a trial court correctly applied the *Daubert* standard when excluding the testimony of a witness who purported to be an expert in tire defects). These decisions are discussed further in Rider v. Sandoz, infra. For an informative account of the evolution of the *Daubert* principle, see Jean Macchiaroli Eggen, Clinical Medical Evidence of Causation in Toxic Tort Cases: Into the Crucible of Daubert, 38 Hous. L. Rev. 369 (2001). See also Mark Geistfeld, Scientific Uncertainty and Causation in Tort Law, 54 Vand. L. Rev. 1011 (2001). For a philosophical approach to general causation in toxic tort cases, see Danielle Conway-Jones, Factual Causation in Toxic Tort Litigation: A Philosophical View of Proof and Certainty in Uncertain Disciplines, 35 U. Rich. L. Rev. 875 (2002).

Rider v. Sandoz Pharmaceutical Corp.
295 F.3d 1194 (11th Cir. 2002)

Before ANDERSON, HULL and RONEY, Circuit Judges.

RONEY, Circuit Judge:

This case involves an issue that has repeatedly come before federal courts: whether expert testimony purporting to link the drug Parlodel with hemorrhagic stroke is admissible to prove causation. Bridget Siharath and Bonnie Rider (plain-

---

the drug will be unable to recover. There is a converse unfairness under a regime that allows recovery to everyone that may have been affected by the drug. Under this regime, all potential plaintiffs are entitled to recover, even though most will not have suffered an injury that can be attributed to the drug. One can conclude from this that unfairness is inevitable when our tools for detecting causation are imperfect and we must rely on probabilities rather than more direct proof. In any event, this is a matter to be sorted out by the states, whose legal standards we are bound to apply. Id.

tiffs) brought this action, alleging that their postpartum hemorrhagic strokes were caused by ingestion of Parlodel. Defendant Sandoz Pharmaceuticals Company (Sandoz), maker of Parlodel, moved to suppress the testimony of the plaintiffs' expert witnesses and for summary judgment. The district court [for the Northern District of Georgia] held that the plaintiffs' expert testimony was not sufficiently reliable to meet the standards established by Daubert v. Merrell Dow Pharm., 509 U.S. 579, 113 S. Ct. 2786, 125 L. Ed. 2d 469 (1993), and granted summary judgment in favor of Sandoz. Plaintiffs appeal. We affirm. . . .

I. Background

Bridget Siharath and Bonnie Rider both took the drug Parlodel to suppress lactation after childbirth. The active ingredient in Parlodel is bromocriptine, an ergot alkaloid compound. Both women subsequently suffered hemorrhagic strokes.

Siharath and Rider filed suit against Sandoz, alleging that Parlodel caused their hemorrhagic strokes. After discovery, Sandoz moved, in limine, to exclude the opinions and testimony of the plaintiffs' experts on causation, and for summary judgment. Because the motions, documentary evidence, experts, and issues were the same in both cases, the district court addressed the motions together. The district court held a *Daubert* hearing to determine whether the evidence was admissible.

The district court, in a three-day hearing, examined the evidence presented in great detail and found that the plaintiffs' claims were based on speculation and conjecture rather than the scientific method. The court drew a careful distinction between clinical process, in which conclusions must be extrapolated from incomplete data, and the scientific method, in which conclusions must be drawn from an accepted process, and concluded that the plaintiffs' experts were relying on the former. Accordingly, the district court excluded the evidence and granted summary judgment in favor of Sandoz. . . . This appeal followed.

II. The Legal Standard

Toxic tort cases, such as this one, are won or lost on the strength of the scientific evidence presented to prove causation. For many years the standard for admissibility of such evidence was the "general acceptance" test set forth in Frye v. United States, 293 F. 1013 (D.C. Cir. 1923). When the Federal Rules of Evidence were enacted in 1975, a question arose as to whether the "general acceptance" test had been supplanted by the reliability test articulated in Rule 702. The question was resolved in three cases decided by the Supreme Court. Daubert v. Merrell Dow Pharm., 509 U.S. 579, 113 S. Ct. 2786, 125 L. Ed. 2d 469 (1993); Gen. Elec. Co. v. Joiner, 522 U.S. 136, 118 S. Ct. 512, 139 L. Ed. 2d 508 (1997); Kumho Tire Co., Ltd. v. Carmichael, 526 U.S. 137, 119 S. Ct. 1167, 143 L. Ed. 2d 238 (1999). These cases are commonly referred to as the *Daubert* trilogy.

Since *Daubert,* courts are charged with determining whether scientific evidence is sufficiently reliable to be presented to a jury. The *Daubert* court made it clear that the requirement of reliability found in Rule 702 was the centerpiece of any determination of admissibility. The Supreme Court identified four factors used to determine the reliability of scientific evidence: 1) whether the theory can and has been tested; 2) whether it has been subjected to peer review; 3) the known or expected rate of error; and 4) whether the theory or methodology employed is generally accepted in the relevant scientific community.

In *Joiner,* the Supreme Court established the standard for reviewing trial court rulings of admissibility, and held that such rulings would be made under an abuse of discretion standard. The *Joiner* court also established the important test of analytical "fit" between the methodology used and the conclusions drawn. The court reasoned that just because a methodology is acceptable for some purposes, it may not be acceptable for others, and a court may not admit evidence when there is "simply too great an analytical gap between the data and the opinion proffered."

In *Kumho Tire,* the Supreme Court made it clear that testimony based solely on the experience of an expert would not be admissible. The expert's conclusions must be based on sound scientific principles and the discipline itself must be a reliable one. The key consideration is whether the expert "employs in the courtroom the same level of intellectual rigor that characterizes the practice of an expert in the relevant field." The court emphasized that judges have considerable leeway in both how to test the reliability of evidence and determining whether such evidence is reliable. . . .

III. *The Plaintiffs' Theory of Causation*

Plaintiffs sought to introduce the testimony of five experts. All five possessed impressive credentials and were found to be well qualified by the district court, three over the defendants' objection. . . . Two of the experts, Doctors Kulig and Dukes, testified at the *Daubert* hearing. The experts presented a detailed argument for the cause of the plaintiffs' hemorrhagic strokes that may be summarized as follows:

1) The active ingredient in Parlodel is bromocriptine, a member of the class of drugs known as ergot alkaloids.
2) Other ergot alkaloids can cause vasoconstriction, which suggests that bromocriptine causes vasoconstriction.
3) Animal studies also suggest that bromocriptine causes vasoconstriction.
4) Vasoconstriction can cause high blood pressure and ischemic stroke (stroke caused by decreased blood flow to the brain).
5) If vasoconstriction and high blood pressure can cause ischemic stroke, it can also cause hemorrhagic stroke (stroke caused by a rupturing of a blood vessel).
6) Thus, Parlodel caused the plaintiffs' hemorrhagic strokes.

IV. *The Evidence Presented*

The scientific evidence presented by plaintiffs in support of their theory of causation may be grouped into six categories: 1) epidemiological studies that, on the whole, may point weakly toward causation; 2) case reports in which injuries were reported subsequent to the ingestion of Parlodel; 3) dechallenge/rechallenge tests that implied a relationship between Parlodel and stroke; 4) evidence that ergot alkaloids (a class of drug that includes bromocriptine) may cause ischemic stroke; 5) animal studies indicating that under some circumstances, bromocriptine may cause vasoconstriction in dogs and other animals; and, 6) the FDA statement withdrawing approval of Parlodel's indication for the prevention of lactation.

A. Epidemiology

Epidemiology, a field that concerns itself with finding the causal nexus between external factors and disease, is generally considered to be the best evidence of causation in toxic tort actions. Plaintiffs presented four epidemiological studies. Three of the four appear to have found no relationship or a negative relationship between Parlodel and stroke. Another may suggest a positive relationship. Nonetheless, both parties agree that none of the studies present statistically significant results and that the epidemiological evidence in this case is inconclusive. . . .

It is well-settled that while epidemiological studies may be powerful evidence of causation, the lack thereof is not fatal to a plaintiff's case. . . . This Court has long held that epidemiology is not required to prove causation in a toxic tort case. Accordingly, this case presents the difficult question of whether the evidence submitted to prove causation, in the absence of epidemiology, was sufficient to meet the requirements of *Daubert*.

B. Case Reports

Much of the plaintiffs' expert testimony relied on case reports in which patients suffered injuries subsequent to the ingestion of Parlodel. Although a court may rely on anecdotal evidence such as case reports, courts must consider that case reports are merely accounts of medical events. They reflect only reported data, not scientific methodology. Some case reports are a very basic form report of symptoms with little or no patient history, description of course of treatment, or reasoning to exclude other possible causes. The contents of these case reports were inadequate, even under the plaintiffs' expert's standards, to demonstrate a relationship between a drug and a potential side effect.

Some case reports do contain details of the treatment and differential diagnosis. Even these more detailed case reports, however, are not reliable enough, by themselves, to demonstrate the causal link the plaintiffs assert that they do because they report symptoms observed in a single patient in an uncontrolled context. They may rule out other potential causes of the effect, but they do not rule out the possibility that the effect manifested in the reported patient's case is simply idiosyncratic or the result of unknown confounding factors. As such, while they may support other proof of causation, case reports alone ordinarily cannot prove causation. The record demonstrates that the district court carefully considered the case reports and properly concluded that the case reports did not by themselves provide reliable proof of causation.

C. Dechallenge/Rechallenge Data

Plaintiffs' experts provided dechallenge/rechallenge data that they argue suggests a link between Parlodel and stroke. A test is a "dechallenge" test when a drug that is suspected of causing a certain reaction is withheld to see if the reaction dissipates. The drug may then be reintroduced in a "rechallenge" to see if the reaction reoccurs. These reports, which may be analogized to controlled studies with one subject, can be particularly useful in determining whether a causal relationship exists. Nonetheless, because none of the studies involved a patient with the particular injury suffered by the plaintiffs, they do not provide data useful in determining whether Parlodel caused the plaintiffs' injuries. . . .

[T]hese dechallenge/rechallenge reports suggest at most a possibility that Parlodel may cause localized vasoconstriction, and may suggest that it causes hypotension. They cannot be considered reliable evidence of a relationship between Parlodel and stroke because neither of them involve stroke. Moreover, dechallenge/rechallenge tests are still case reports and do not purport to offer definitive conclusions as to causation. . . .

D. Chemical Analogies

Bromocriptine is one of many drugs in a class known as ergot alkaloids. Plaintiffs sought to introduce evidence that because other ergot alkaloids cause vasoconstriction, then it is proper to conclude bromocriptine must do so as well. There is an insufficient basis in the record for this Court to hold that the district court abused its discretion by not drawing such a conclusion. Ergot alkaloids encompass a broad class of drugs with great chemical diversity, and "[e]ven minor deviations in chemical structure can radically change a particular substance's properties and propensities." The district court, after a detailed review of the properties of ergot alkaloids, concluded that plaintiffs failed to come forward with even a theory as to why the mechanism that causes some ergot alkaloids to act as vasoconstrictors would more probably than not be the same mechanism by which bromocriptine acts to cause vasoconstriction. The district court did not abuse its discretion in doing so.

E. Animal Studies

Plaintiffs offered evidence of animal studies in which bromocriptine demonstrated vasoconstrictive properties in dogs and certain other animals. Plaintiffs did not offer any animal studies that suggest that bromocriptine causes stroke, or even high blood pressure. The district court discussed each of these studies and was within its discretion in concluding that plaintiffs offered insufficient evidence on which that court could base a conclusion that the effect of bromocriptine would be the same on humans as it is on animals.

F. FDA Findings

Plaintiffs presented evidence that the FDA issued a statement withdrawing approval of Parlodel's indication for the prevention of lactation. The district court concluded that the language in the FDA statement itself undermined its reliability as proof of causation. In the statement, the FDA did not purport to have drawn a conclusion about causation. Instead, the statement merely states that possible risks outweigh the limited benefits of the drug. This risk-utility analysis involves a much lower standard than that which is demanded by a court of law. A regulatory agency such as the FDA may choose to err on the side of caution. Courts, however, are required by the *Daubert* trilogy to engage in objective review of evidence to determine whether it has sufficient scientific basis to be con-

> **authors' dialogue 5**
>
> **AARON:** I don't like the way the lower courts are applying *Daubert*. Clearly the Supreme Court believed it was making things somewhat easier on plaintiffs by admitting expert testimony that satisfies its criteria even if the expert's methodology has not been generally accepted in the scientific community. But by making "general acceptance" one of the criteria, the new approach seems to have retained all the difficulties of the traditional *Frye* rule for plaintiffs, and added further hurdles for them to overcome. Now, even if an expert's methodology is accepted by part of the relevant scientific community, and thus the testimony might have been admissible under *Frye*, it can be excluded if the trial court concludes that the expert's methodology fails to meet the other *Daubert* criteria. At the very least, *Daubert* is adding greatly to the costs of bringing iffy causation claims into court. I guess I'm fearful that *Daubert* may be making it too difficult for plaintiffs to prove their claims.
>
> **JIM:** I followed you up until the last part. Why *shouldn't* we make it more difficult for plaintiffs to bring "iffy claims" into court? Without *Daubert,* plaintiffs can always get some voodoo doctor to come in and opine that the plaintiff's stomach cancer was caused by the defendant's pop-up toaster, or the microwave oven. Besides, I'm not sure that, in fact, courts are being all that hard on plaintiffs.
>
> **AARON:** Now *you've* gone too far. For all you know, a poorly designed microwave could very well cause cancer. Why not allow the plaintiff to try and prove it through a qualified expert, even if the expert's theories are not accepted by the scientific establishment?
>
> **JIM:** As I read the case, all *Daubert* asks is that the expert explain herself and show that she is relying on sound scientific method. Surely that is not too much to ask.
>
> **AARON:** Maybe what we're saying is that there's no middle ground. Courts have to choose between being too hard and too easy on expert theorizing that is out of the mainstream. You, a throwback to the Cro-Magnon period, prefer being too hard. And I, the quintessential Renaissance man, prefer being too easy, if that is the only alternative.
>
> **JIM:** I'm feeling queasy.

sidered reliable. The district court did not abuse its discretion in concluding that the FDA actions do not, in this case, provide scientific proof of causation.

V. Applying the Evidence to the Plaintiffs' Theory of Causation

The deficiencies in the evidence reveal three gaps in the causal argument advanced by the plaintiffs. First, plaintiffs suggest that because bromocriptine is an ergot alkaloid, it causes vasoconstriction. Although some other ergot alkaloids do cause vasoconstriction, plaintiffs offered insufficient evidence for the district court to find that bromocriptine does so as well. This is not a case where the Court finds the evidence offered to be unreliable. In this case the record contains no evidence at all of this hypothesis. Instead, it contains principally speculation and conjecture. . . .

Second, the plaintiffs urge the Court to extrapolate the results of animal studies to humans. As with the plaintiffs' evidence of chemical properties, the district court did not err in finding no basis for doing so. Plaintiffs' experts admitted that with respect to animal studies generally, what happens in an animal would not necessarily happen in a human being. Accordingly, it is necessary for plaintiffs to offer some rationale for the suggestion that the vascular structures of humans and animals are sufficiently similar in this context to conclude that bromocriptine's effects on animals may be extrapolated to humans. Plaintiffs have not done so. . . .

Third, plaintiffs argue that because there is some evidence that bromocriptine causes ischemic stroke, it also causes hemorrhagic stroke. This is the most untenable link in the causal chain. Strokes are broadly classified into two categories: ischemic and hemorrhagic. Ischemic strokes occur as a result of lack of blood flow to the brain. Hemorrhagic strokes occur as a result of bleeding within the brain. Thus, although the two conditions share a name, they involve a wholly different biological mechanism. The evidence that suggests that Parlodel may cause ischemic stroke does not apply to situations involving hemorrhagic stroke. This is a "leap of faith" supported by little more than the fact that both conditions are commonly called strokes. Plaintiffs argue that as a result of the vasoconstriction caused by Parlodel, blood pressure may increase to the point that blood vessels in the brain rupture. Plaintiffs have offered no reliable evidence that Parlodel increases blood pressure to such dangerous levels. Even if they had, they failed to offer proof of how such an increase in blood pressure can precipitate a hemorrhagic stroke.

Since the shortcomings in the evidence render the theory unreliable, the district court did not abuse its discretion in excluding the plaintiffs' evidence of causation.

VI. *Conclusion*

In the absence of epidemiology, plaintiffs may still prove medical causation by other evidence. In the instant case, however, plaintiffs simply have not provided reliable evidence to support their conclusions. To admit the plaintiffs' evidence, the Court would have to make several scientifically unsupported "leaps of faith" in the causal chain. The *Daubert* rule requires more. Given time, information, and resources, courts may only admit the state of science as it is. Courts are cautioned not to admit speculation, conjecture, or inference that cannot be supported by sound scientific principles. "The courtroom is not the place for scientific guesswork, even of the inspired sort. Law lags science; it does not lead it." Rosen v. Ciba-Geigy Corp., 78 F.3d 316, 319 (7th Cir. 1996). . . .

We hold that the district court did not abuse its discretion in concluding that the Plaintiffs' scientific proof of causation is legally unreliable and inadmissible under the standards set by the *Daubert* trilogy.

AFFIRMED.

PROBLEM EIGHT

Ilisa Mazarek, a 28-year-old woman, has come to see you about bringing an action against TFL Laboratories, the manufacturer of Perfect-Coil, an intrauterine device (IUD). Ilisa has been married for seven years and has been unable to conceive. She has consulted numerous obstetricians and has had a full battery of tests. Her husband, Michael, has been tested for sterility and his sperm has been found healthy.

In April of this year, Ilisa made an appointment with Dr. Suzanne Blanzer, who reviewed all the test results that had been gathered previously. Blanzer then asked Ilisa whether she had ever used an IUD. Ilisa said that while in college she had used a plastic IUD called Perfect-Coil. Dr. Blanzer then told her that it could well be that the IUD was the source of her trouble. She said that recent research performed at the Harvard Medical School and at the University of Washington in Seattle revealed that women who had used IUDs (especially plastic IUDs) had twice the risk of later infertility than non-IUD users. The studies were published in the most recent issue of a prestigious medical journal. According to the Harvard study, 89 of the 283 infertile women (31.4 percent) had used an IUD as compared with 646 of 3833 in the fertile control group (16.7 percent). The Seattle results were even more pronounced. The difference between infertile and fertile women was 35.2 percent to 13.8 percent.

Apparently, use of an IUD contributes to a higher than normal risk of pelvic inflammatory disease. These infections can damage the fallopian tubes, causing infertility. The head of the Harvard study clearly believes a causal relationship was established between IUDs and infertility because of the unlikelihood of chance or bias in the results and the consistency of the results with findings in other studies.

Dr. Blanzer told Ilisa that there was no way to determine with certainty whether her fallopian tubes had been damaged as a result of infections brought about by use of the IUD. "Although many fallopian tube inflections cause pain, it certainly is possible that you had one or more infections without realizing, or that you had some minor abdominal pain and paid little attention to it." Dr. Blanzer told Ilisa that she would treat her to help enhance her chances of conceiving. "Nonetheless," she said, "you must face the facts. The great likelihood is that you will not conceive." Dr. Blanzer then raised a question that Ilisa had never been asked before by any other obstetrician. She asked whether Ilisa had a number of different sexual partners before or during her marriage. The reason she asked was that the Boston researchers had found an increased risk of infertility for all IUD users who had several sexual partners as compared to monogamous users. In fact, regardless of the type of contraception used, the researchers found that women who had multiple sexual partners faced an increased risk of developing pelvic infection.

Ilisa told Dr. Blanzer that during marriage she had been totally faithful but that she had not been a paragon of virtue in her younger years. When you asked her to be more precise, she said, "I was far from promiscuous. In any event, it's my business and nobody else knows. That's the way it is. That's the way it's going to be."

You must decide whether to take the case. You are to assume that New California has adopted the *Daubert* approach to expert testimony. You have heard that

Did the Defendant Supply the Product?

a consortium of plaintiff's lawyers has filed thousands of law suits against TFL Laboratories. Nonetheless, considerable skepticism exists as to whether the claimants can prevail. Would other kinds of factual investigation might be helpful before you decide to proceed?

B. DID THE DEFENDANT SUPPLY THE PRODUCT?

1. Defendant Identification in General

This Section, like the first, focuses on gaps in the plaintiff's proof regarding what actually happened. In one kind of gap case, the plaintiff points to a product that was clearly defective at the time of distribution and that clearly harmed him, but cannot directly prove that the product was manufactured or distributed by the defendant, or by someone for whom the defendant is legally responsible. The plaintiff might try to overcome this obstacle by offering circumstantial evidence tending to show that the product was manufactured or distributed by the defendant. The plaintiff may offer testimony that the defective product bore the defendant's trademark, insignia or logo. See, e.g., Kim v. Ingersoll Rand Co., 921 F.2d 197 (8th Cir. 1990); Smith v. Ariens Co. 377 N.E.2d 954 (Mass. 1978). A plaintiff may also try to prove the defendant's identity as the manufacturer or distributor by showing design similarities between the defective product and those products known to be produced by the defendant. See, e.g., Lenherr v. NRM Corp., 504 F. Supp. 165 (D. Kan. 1980). Of course, the defendant can always offer contravening testimony, for example, by asserting that a third party manufactured or distributed the defective product as a "knockoff." Ultimately, if the plaintiff produces sufficient circumstantial evidence implicating the defendant, the issue of the manufacturer's or distributor's identity will go to the finder of fact. See, e.g., Smith v. Ariens Co., 377 N.E.2d 954 (Mass. 1978). Cf. Dura-Stilts Co. v. Zachry, 697 S.W.2d 658 (Tex. App. 1985), in which plaintiff succeeded in proving that a pair of defective stilts was manufactured by the defendant, even though the stilts bore no identifying label.

2. Creative Attempts to Solve a Unique Problem: Market Share

The most difficult gap-in-the-proof causation cases are those in which the plaintiff is harmed by a defective product that is both unidentified by trademark or insignia and cannot be directly linked to the defendant. In the classic example of such a defendant-identification case, the plaintiff is harmed by a defective unit of a type of product manufactured and distributed by many companies, under circumstances where the plaintiff cannot prove which company actually produced and distributed the defective, harm-causing product unit. These difficult causation cases usually involve generically dangerous products rather than manufacturing defects. Some of the best-known examples involve personal injuries allegedly resulting from plaintiffs' prenatal exposure to the prescription drug, diethylstilbestrol (DES). The plaintiffs in these cases are women whose mothers took DES many years earlier, while pregnant, to prevent miscarriage. Reliable expert testimony shows that the drug affected the plaintiffs while in their mothers' wombs, resulting in reproductive tract cancers in the plaintiffs many years later. Hundreds of thousands of women have been involved. Many of the plaintiffs cannot prove which drug company distributed the DES their mothers took. (As many as 300 companies may have produced the generic drug during the relevant period.) Some courts responded in ways that allow the injured plaintiffs to overcome otherwise fatal gaps in their proofs of actual causation by joining as defendants all, or most, of the companies manufacturing and distributing DES in the relevant geographical areas during the time periods relevant to their cases. The leading case is Sindell v. Abbott Labs., 607 P.2d 924 (Cal. 1980), *cert. denied*, 449 U.S. 912 (1980).

The California high court in *Sindell* considered and rejected the "alternative liability" theory from earlier California caselaw that would have held all the defendants jointly and severally liable unless they could prove that they did not market the DES that harmed the plaintiff. Not only did the companies lack any comparative advantage in determining which company's drug had caused the cancer, but the numbers of victims were much greater than in the earlier cases, and not all of the possible defendants could be joined in one legal action. And allocating liability pro rata among companies overlooked the reality that some companies produced many times the quantities of DES compared with other, smaller companies. To overcome these difficulties, the *Sindell* court adopted what has come to be known as the "market-share theory." According to the market-share approach, when a plaintiff joins the manufacturers who produced, in the aggregate, a substantial share of the relevant DES market, the burden shifts to each defendant to prove it did not produce the drug that the plaintiff's mother ingested. Those companies that do not carry this burden are held liable to the plaintiff for the percentage of damages approximating their individual share of the relevant DES market. The court reasoned that it was fair to shift the burden of proof on causation to the defendants in light of the fact that each defendant's market share, and therefore its share of the damages, would approximate the probability that it caused the plaintiff's injuries.

One of the difficulties facing plaintiffs under *Sindell*—the necessity of joining companies that manufacture a "substantial share" of the DES that may have harmed the plaintiff—caused the Supreme Court of Wisconsin to modify the *Sindell* approach a few years after that landmark decision. Thus, in Collins v. Eli Lilly Co., 342 N.W.2d 37, 50-52 (Wis. 1984), the court outlined its more liberal approach:

> Thus, the plaintiff need commence suit against only one defendant and allege the following elements: that the plaintiff's mother took DES; that DES caused the plaintiff's subsequent injuries; that the defendant produced or marketed the type of DES taken by the plaintiff's mother; and that the defendant's conduct in producing or marketing the DES constituted a breach of a legally recognized duty to the plaintiff. In the situation where the plaintiff cannot allege and prove what type of DES the mother took, as to the third element the plaintiff need only allege the use in preventing miscarriages during pregnancy....
>
> Once the plaintiff has proven a prima facie case, . . . the burden of proof shifts to the defendant to prove by a preponderance of the evidence that it did not produce or market the subject DES either during the time period the plaintiff was exposed to DES or in the relevant geographical market area in which the plaintiff's mother acquired the DES. In utilizing these defenses, the defendant must establish that the DES it produced

or marketed could not have reached the plaintiff's mother. We conclude that it is appropriate to shift the burden of proof on time and geographic distribution to the defendant drug companies because they will have better access to relevant records than the plaintiff. Further, if relevant records do not exist, we believe that the equities of DES cases favor placing the consequences on the defendants [who should bear liability based on their percentages of the market.]

We believe that this procedure will result in a pool of defendants which it can reasonably be assumed could have caused the plaintiff's injuries. We note in this regard that, in cases where the plaintiff's mother took DES over a period of time and had the prescription refilled, it is possible that DES from several drug companies may have contributed to the plaintiff's injuries. This still could mean that some of the remaining defendants may be innocent, but we accept this as the price the defendants, and perhaps ultimately society, must pay to provide the plaintiff an adequate remedy under the law.

In a footnote to the above-quoted excerpt from *Collins,* the opinion refers to defendant's argument that the sort of remedy adopted by the court "should be fashioned by the legislature." (342 N.W.2d at (52, n.12).) The court disagreed with the argument, saying that "It is the function of this court to modify the existing common law if that becomes necessary to promote justice under the law."

The courts that have adopted the market share approach have been forced to grapple with three difficult issues: (1) how to define the market; (2) whether a defendant who can prove that its product did not injure the plaintiff should escape liability under the market share theory; and (3) if only a given percentage of defendants who participated in the market at the time of injury can be accounted for, who should bear the loss for the missing market shares.

Several courts have held that market shares should be calculated based on the sales of all manufacturers of the product in the national market, whether or not particular defendants could have supplied the particular units that harmed the plaintiff. The New York Court of Appeals was the first to adopt this approach. In Hymowitz v. Eli Lilly Co., 539 N.E.2d 1069, 1077-78 (N.Y. 1989) the court said:

We are aware that the adoption of a national market will likely result in a disproportion between the liability of individual manufacturers and the actual injuries each manufacturer caused in this State. Thus our market share theory cannot be founded upon the belief that, over the run of cases, liability will approximate causation in this State (see, Sindell v. Abbott Laboratories). Nor does the use of a national market provide a reasonable link between liability and the risk created by a defendant to a particular plaintiff (see, Collins v. Lilly & Co.; Martin v. Abbott Laboratories). Instead, we choose to apportion liability so as to correspond to the over-all culpability of each defendant, measured by the amount of risk of injury each defendant created to the public-at-large. Use of a national market is a fair method, we believe, of apportioning defendants' liabilities according to their total culpability in marketing DES for use during pregnancy. Under the circumstances, this is an equitable way to provide plaintiffs with the relief they deserve, while also rationally distributing the responsibility for plaintiffs' injuries among defendants. . . .

Florida has opted for a much narrower definition of the market. In Conley v. Boyle Drug Co., 570 So. 2d 275, 283 (Fla. 1990) the court argued:

[T]he relevant market for determining liability should be as narrowly defined as the evidence in a given case allows. Thus, where it can be determined that the DES ingested by the mother was purchased from a particular pharmacy, that pharmacy should be considered the relevant market. Likewise, where the county or state of ingestion is as specific an area as can be established, that geographic area will serve as the relevant market. [D]efining the relevant geographic market in this manner is consistent with the fact that . . . a defendant may exculpate itself by showing that it did not market the DES in the geographic market area where the plaintiff's mother obtained the drug. Narrowing the relevant market is also consistent with the overall goal of market-share alternate liability. The narrower the market, the greater the likelihood that liability will be imposed only on those drug companies who could have manufactured the DES which caused the plaintiff's injuries.

Closely related to the market size question is whether a defendant can escape paying its market share if it can establish that it was not responsible for the harm to the particular plaintiff. Until *Hymowitz,* the courts had answered the question in the affirmative. Though *Hymowitz* is a minority view in denying the defendant the right to prove itself out of a market share, its position is defensible in principle. Market share posits the view that causation should be viewed writ large over a broad market. Of what importance is it that a defendant establishes that its pill was not sold to a particular patient? Switching back and forth between traditional causation and proportional causation in this class of cases seems odd. Furthermore, the transaction costs of litigating and establishing different market shares depending on the posture of any individual case are likely to be enormous.

As for the question of joint and several liability in the market-share setting, several courts have been troubled by the fact that, under *Sindell-Collins,* a defendant who had proved its market share would be liable to pay for the harm caused by unnamed or insolvent defendants. Most courts, including California, have now concluded that joint and several liability ought not to be applied against market share defendants. For example, in Martin v. Abbott Laboratories, 689 P.2d 368, 383 (Wash. 1984), the court explained how it would administer its rule of probabilistic causation:

> Application of this rule of apportionment is illustrated by the following hypotheticals. Assume that plaintiff's damages are $100,000 and defendants X and Y remain subject to liability after exculpation by other named defendants. If neither establishes its market share then they are presumed to have equal shares of the market and are liable respectively for 50 percent of the total judgment, X, $50,000 and Y, $50,000.
>
> Assume defendant X establishes that it occupies 20 percent of the relevant market, and defendant Y fails to prove its market share. Defendant X is then liable for 20 percent of the damages, or $20,000, and defendant Y is subject to the remaining 80 percent, or $80,000.
>
> Assume that defendant X establishes a market share of 20 percent and defendant Y a 60 percent market share. Then defendant X is subject to 20 percent of the judgment, $20,000, and defendant Y a 60 percent of the judgment, $60,000. The plaintiff does not recover her entire judgment because the remaining 20 percent of the market share is the responsibility of unnamed defendants.
>
> The defendants may implead third party defendants in order to reduce their presumptive share of the market or in order to establish an actual reduced market share.
>
> This ability of a defendant to reduce its liability reduces the disproportion between potential liability that a particular defendant caused the injury by imposing liability according to respective market shares. In the case where each party carries its burden of proof, no defendant will be held liable for more harm than it statistically could have caused in the respective market.

The controversy concerning the wisdom of applying market share has been even more shrill when plaintiffs have sought to apply the approach to manufacturing defects. In Sheffield v. Eli Lilly & Co., 192 Cal. Rptr. 870 (Cal. Ct. App. 1983), the plaintiff developed encephalitis as a result of being inoculated with defective polio vaccine. Plaintiff made exhaustive attempts to discover which drug manufacturer had made the particular batch of defective vaccine supplied to Wayne County, Indiana, where she took her shot. Since the plaintiff was unable to identify the manufacturer, she sought to apply the market-share theory against all the manufacturers of polio vaccine. In rejecting this extension of *Sindell*, the court explained:

> It is true that in each case the manufacturers were making a generic pharmaceutical product according to a uniform formula and a process approved by the federal government. Here, unlike *Sindell*, the injuries did not result from the use of a drug generally defective when used for the purpose it was marketed, but because some manufacturer made and distributed a defective product. The product that allegedly injured the plaintiffs was itself not a unit of a total generic pharmaceutical product but a deviant defective vaccine. 192 Cal. Rptr. at 876.

The court argued that such an extension could not be supported on policy grounds:

> The "deep pocket" theory may be socially desirable as a vehicle to insure that all victims of a defective product will be compensated from an industry-wide fund; but if applied indiscriminately to penalize the careful and careless producer alike it fails to act as a deterrent to the latter or provide an incentive to product safety industry-wide, and it may result in keeping beneficial but potentially dangerous products off the market. It may not be solely sufficient merely to say that it would be legally and morally irresponsible to hold manufacturers, who never produced a defective vaccine, to be liable on a market share basis for the damage caused by one manufacturer who did. It is clear, however, that one manufacturer cannot force its competitors to discover or guard against defects in its products. The imposition of such a liability over that portion of the pharmaceutical industry producing the beneficial safe product would inhibit drug research and development, unreasonably raise the cost of health care, and punish drug manufacturers who have done no wrong. 192 Cal. Rptr. at 876.

At least one court has not been so hesitant. The Supreme Court of Hawaii, in Smith v. Cutter Biological, Inc., 823 P.2d 717 (Hawaii, 1991), adopted market-share liability in an action in which a hemophiliac allegedly contracted the AIDS virus from a tainted blood product.

Attempts to extend the market-share approach beyond DES cases have been overwhelmingly rejected. See, e.g., Ferris v. Gatke, 132 Cal. Rptr. 2d 819 (Cal. Ct. App. 2003) (asbestos); Becker v. Baron Bros., 649 A.2d 613 (N.J. 1994) (asbestos); Hamilton v. Beretta, 750 N.E.2d 1055 (N.Y. 2001) (handguns); Brenner v. American Cyanamid Co., 263 A.D.2d 165 (N.Y. App. Div. 1999) (lead paint); Santiago v. Sherwin Williams Co., 3 F.3d 546 (1st Cir. 1993) (lead paint); Spencer v. Baxter Int'l, Inc., 163 F. Supp. 2d 74 (D. Mass. 2001) (AIDS); Mills v. Allegiance Healthcare Corp., 178 F. Supp. 2d 1 (D. Mass. 2001) (latex gloves). But see, e.g., In re Methyl Tertiary Butyl Ether (MTBE), 175 F. Supp. 2d 593 (S.D.N.Y. 2001) (permitting a market-share theory of liability to go forward for well owners who alleged that oil companies conspired to mislead the government and public that concentrations of MTBE were acceptable). See generally Frank J. Giliberti, Emerging Trends for Products Liability: Market Share Liability, Its History and Future, 15 Touro L. Rev. 719 (1999).

PROBLEM NINE

Your firm represents Louise Larkin, age 37, who seeks to recover for injuries sustained while undergoing surgery six months ago. Having suffered from ovarian cysts for several years, Ms. Larkin was advised by her physician, about a year ago, to undergo abdominal surgery to correct the condition. Both the surgeon and the anesthesiologist recommended spinal, rather than general, anesthesia. Fully informed of the benefits and risks associated with the surgery, Ms. Larkin consented to the operation. During the administering of the spinal anesthesia, the hypodermic needle broke off in Ms. Larkin's spine, causing serious complications that may lead to permanent partial paralysis. Investigation has revealed that the needle in question was new, and that it broke due to a latent manufacturing defect.

Efforts to trace the identity of the manufacturer of the needle have thus far proven futile. The hospital in which the surgery was performed supplied the needle in question, along with the other equipment to be used in the operation. The hospital purchases such needles in bulk, from several different medical supply distributors in your city. When items such as hypodermic needles come into the hospital supply department, they are treated as fungible goods, within appropriate categories of type, size, and the like. No effort is made to keep track of from whom, or when, any particular hypodermic needle was purchased. Given the need for standardization of items of this sort, no effort appears to have been made by manufacturers to allow products such as hypodermic needles to be distinguished from similar items produced by others. Thus, there appears to be no way by which the needle may be shown to have been produced by a particular manufacturer or sold to the hospital by a particular distributor. For the last several years the hospital has purchased this sort of hypodermic needle from three different distributors, who purchased their needle supplies from at least ten, and possibly as many as twenty, needle manufacturers. Two, at least, of the twenty manufacturers are foreign-based; one of the domestic manufacturers who may have produced the needle declared bankruptcy last month.

Assuming that Magrine v. Krasnica (Chapter One, supra) and Anderson v. Somberg (Chapter Two, supra) are decisions of the highest court in your state, and that Collins v. Eli Lilly, excerpted, supra, was decided by the court that actually decided it (and that your high court has not yet addressed the so-called "market share" issue), what are the chances of reaching the jury against one or more of the possible defendants in Ms. Larkin's case? In undertaking your analysis, make whatever reasonable assumptions of fact you believe are necessary.

C. DID THE DEFECT IN THE DEFENDANT'S PRODUCT CONTRIBUTE TO HARMING THE PLAINTIFF?

In the cases in this Section, the plaintiff can prove that the defendant produced the harm-causing product and that the product contained a dangerous defect, but has difficulty establishing that the presence of the defect in the product contributed to the product's having caused the harm. The inquiry is not into what actually happened, which is typically clear enough, but into what would have happened if the manufacturing defect had not been present. As explained earlier, this inquiry is frequently referred to as a but-for inquiry. The question to be answered is this: But for the presence of the defect, would the plaintiff have suffered the same (or similar) harm anyway? Again, this is a different question than is asked in the defendant-identification cases considered in the preceding section. Unlike the earlier-considered cases, gaps-in-proof are not typically present. In most cases, it is clear that the defendant's product (or conduct) has caused plaintiff's harm; what is at issue is what role, if any, the defective condition of the product played in causing the harm. As mentioned earlier, the new Restatement of general tort principles merges this question with the first question in Section A, supra, under the umbrella heading "factual cause." See Restatement (Third) of Torts: Liability for Physical Harm (Basic Principles §26 (Tentative Draft No. 2, 2002)).

1. All-or-Nothing Causation

Midwestern V.W. Corp. v. Ringley
503 S.W.2d 745 (Ky. 1973)

STEPHENSON, Justice.

A Hardin Circuit Court jury awarded Wanda Ringley damages for personal injuries and property damage as a result of an accident when her automobile skidded and struck a telephone pole. The verdict was against Kelly Vance Motors, Inc., the Volkswagen dealer from whom Wanda purchased the car, Volkswagenwerk Aktiengesell, the manufacturer of the car, Volkswagen of America, Inc., the importer, a wholly owned subsidiary of the factory, and Midwestern Volkswagen Corporation, the distributor who purchased the car from the importer and sold the automobile to Kelly Vance Motors. The manufacturer, importer, and distributor appeal from the judgment in favor of Wanda Ringley and also appeal from a joint and several judgment in favor of Kelly Vance Motors against them for indemnity. Kelly Vance Motors does not appeal.

Wanda purchased a new Volkswagen automobile from Kelly Vance Motors. The warranty against defects in manufacturing covered a period of twenty-four months. Shortly after Wanda purchased the automobile, while applying the brakes to come to an abrupt stop, . . . the automobile pulled to the right. Wanda returned the automobile to Kelly Vance Motors and reported the incident, and when she picked up the automobile, she was advised that it had been repaired. She testified she had no further difficulty until shortly thereafter when a similar incident occurred, and again the automobile was returned to Kelly Vance Motors and again she was advised that the car was repaired. Wanda testified that she had no further difficulty until a little more than a month after the car was purchased when a similar instance of the automobile's pulling to the right after the brakes were applied resulted in Wanda's again returning the automobile to Kelly Vance Motors for the assigned reason that the "brakes grab and pull to one side."

Eight days after picking up the automobile, Wanda undertook to pass an automobile on a wet road and, according to Wanda, she observed a pool of water in the road ahead of her. She testified that she applied the brakes, that the right-front wheel grabbed sending her automobile into a spin and out of control. The automobile struck a telephone pole resulting in severe personal injuries.

According to witnesses who testified for Wanda, it was discovered that the right-front brake drum was "out of round" to a degree exceeding factory specifications. They testified that this was a defect in the manufacturing process which would cause the automobile to pull to the right when the brakes were applied.

Wanda's version of the accident was contradicted, as was the testimony of the extent that the "out of round" condition of the brake drum exceeded factory specification, or that the brake drum was "out of round" at all. All of this presents no problem as a jury issue was presented. Numerous errors are asserted; however, we conclude that appellants' assertion that Wanda failed to prove causation is dispositive of the case.

All of Wanda's witnesses testified that an "out of round" brake drum on the right front would cause the automobile to pull to the right when the brakes were applied. On cross-examination, they testified that dirt and dust in the left brake lining would cause the automobile to pull to the right. There was testimony that the brake drums were blown out when the automobile was taken to Kelly Vance Motors. They further testified on cross-examination that water in the left brake lining would cause the automobile to pull to the right; that improper adjustment of the right-front brake drum would cause the automobile to pull to the right. There was testimony by one of the witnesses that an examination of the right-front brake after the accident revealed that it was adjusted too tightly. Wanda's witnesses further testified on cross-examination that improper tire pressure and improper alignment could cause pulling.

The voluminous transcript is composed chiefly of testimony attempting to establish a defect in manufacturing. None of Wanda's expert witnesses testified that the "out of round" brake drum "probably" caused the automobile to pull to one side at the time of the accident. The testimony was that an "out of round" brake drum was dangerous and would cause the automobile to pull when the brakes were applied, also that other conditions asked about would cause the automobile to pull when the brakes were applied.

The jury found for Wanda under an instruction based on the doctrine of manufacturer's strict liability. This doctrine of strict liability does not relieve Wanda from the plaintiff's burden of introducing evidence of causation. Although the jury may draw reasonable inferences from the evidence of a defect in manufacturing, it is incumbent on the plaintiff to introduce evidence that will support a reasonable inference that the defect was the 'probable' cause of the accident as distinguished from a 'possible' cause among other possibilities; otherwise, the jury verdict is based on speculation or surmise. . . .

The only evidence which would even tend to establish a probability is encompassed in one question and answer during the cross-examination of one of Wanda's witnesses:

Q. Likewise, is there any way of telling now whether, at the time of this accident Miss Ringley had, what the reason was for the car pulling to the right, or whichever direction it was, any way of telling what actually happened on that occasion?
A. The only thing I can tell what caused it is the brake drum being out of round and the lining has been chattering, and it will show chattering points just a little on the lining.

We conclude that this answer is so equivocal that it cannot be said that the witness was testifying as to a probability.

Finally, Wanda cites Gaidry Motors v. Bannon, Ky., 268 S.W.2d 627, as authority for submission of her case to the jury. There the purchaser of a used car drove only fourteen blocks from the used-car lot; and when applying the brakes at an intersection, the car brakes grabbed, causing the car to skid and injure a pedestrian. Mechanics testified that there was grease on one of the brake drums and that this condition would cause the brakes to grab. This court held that the evidence was sufficient to submit the case to the jury on the question of proximate cause. We feel that the brief interval of time between the purchase of the used car and the accident and the absence any other explanation for the mechanical failure are the distinguishing factors between *Gaidry* and the instant case.

We conclude that Wanda failed to establish a jury issue as to causation and that the trial court erred in not directing a verdict for the appellants.

The judgment is reversed with directions to enter a judgment dismissing the claim against the appellants.

In Henry v. Bridgestone/Firestone, Inc., 2003 WL 2013051 (7th Cir. Ind.), the plaintiff claimed an original defect in a tire caused tread separation, which caused a blowout that caused an accident that caused her injury. The district court ruled that the plaintiff's experts failed to offer testimony regarding other possible causes of the blowout related to maintenance and tire age. In affirming the judgment for defendant the court of appeals held the plaintiff failed to prove that the tire blowout was caused by a tread separation defect rather than by other common causes of sudden tire failure.

PROBLEM TEN

Milton Ratabush invited his mother, Belle, to come and live with him for a few months after the death of his father. Belle is an alert, but somewhat frail, 75-year-old woman. The first week she was at Milton's home she mentioned to Dotty (Milton's wife) that it was hard for her to use the shower because the bathtub surface was slippery. Milton immediately purchased a package of "No-Slip" Strips manufactured by Drydock, Inc. The package contained four 36-inch strips.

authors' dialogue 6

JIM: I know you disagree, but I think *Midwestern VW* was wrongly decided.

AARON: You are right.

JIM: *Midwestern VW* is wrong?

AARON: No. I do disagree with you. The plaintiff should be required to play by the rules. It shouldn't suffice for the plaintiff to have a one-car accident, hurt herself badly, and then find some small departure-from-the-specs in a brake drum on which to blame the manufacturer. The plaintiff's expert has got to be more precise and informative.

JIM: But all that means is that the plaintiff's lawyer was a little sloppy. Next time the expert will simply say the magic words and the plaintiff will reach the jury. Why punish Wanda Ringley?

AARON: Let's not forget *Daubert* and its progeny. (See pp. 121-129, supra.) Those cases, together with the holding in *Midwestern VW,* will help sort out the worthy claims from the unworthy. If you feel sorry for Wanda, let her sue her attorney.

JIM: Ouch!

Directions on the package indicated that two strips should be sufficient to provide the desired traction for the tub.

Two weeks after Milton installed two "No-Slip" strips in his bathtub, Belle fell and broke her hip while showering in the tub. When Milton examined the strips on the floor of the tub, he discovered that they had become loose around the edges at a number of places. An expert's examination of the two unused strips revealed gaps in the distribution of the glue-like substance that is supposed to provide adhesion to the tub.

This is not the first time that Belle has suffered injury due to a fall. Last year she suffered a momentary blackout while walking upstairs. She fell and broke her arm. Belle has no recollection of the accident in Milton's home. When Dotty found her in the bathtub, she had blacked out. Her doctor maintains that the blackout could have occurred after the fall as a result of the intense pain caused by the breaking of the hip. Belle does not remember what precipitated her fall.

Milton has consulted you about bringing suit against Drydock on his mother's behalf. Will you take the case?

2. Enhanced Injury

Lahocki v. Contee Sand & Gravel Co., Inc.
398 A.2d 490 (Md. Ct. Spec. App. 1979)

LOWE, J.

This appeal is from a judgment grounded upon a jury verdict in the Circuit Court for Prince George's County, wherein George E. Lahocki was awarded one million two hundred thousand dollars from General Motors Corporation, and he and his wife an additional three hundred thousand dollars to compensate them for injuries sustained by Mr. Lahocki when he was thrown from a General Motors Corporation van after its top detached in a one car accident. . . .

George E. Lahocki was the passenger in a General Motors Corporation (G.M.) van that had been equipped by its owner (Warner) with a make-shift plastic passenger seat affixed to the front floor, and on which Mr. Lahocki was seated. The owner had also equipped the van with pipes racked inside and out, and with interior bins full of plumbing supplies and tools. The van, driven by co-worker George Campbell, was proceeding between 40 and 55 miles per hour on a highway when it struck and "rode" heavy timber barricades placed there by the Contee Sand and Gravel Co., Inc. (Contee), a contractor repaving a portion of the road. The van "went up in the air and flipped," damaging 142 feet of barricade before its forward progress ended. It came to rest upside down separated from its roof panel which lay near by. Although the driver was still inside and relatively uninjured, Mr. Lahocki lay on the road some distance from both van and roof panel.

Based upon expert evidence, Mr. Lahocki contended that the roof panel came off because it was inadequately welded according to G.M.'s own standards, and that his broken back was the direct result of having been thrown out of the vehicle through the open roof. He argues that he would not have been so injured if the roof had remained intact. G.M. contends that the roof attachment defect was irrelevant because: 1) it would have come off anyhow, 2) Lahocki was probably injured inside the vehicle and, 3) he might have been ejected through other openings in a roll over accident even with the roof intact. . . .

Appellant showed through expert testimony that according to industry standards, and with reference to G.M.'s own specifications, the van's roof was not affixed by a requisite number of "good" welds. G.M.'s own specifications, as stated by G.M.'s expert Alan Thebert, required 234 welds. The Lahockis' expert based his own calculations on a requirement of only 212 welds. He stated that based on industry standards, and his own expertise, a diameter of at least .187 inches for each weld was necessary for a proper attachment of the roof. He found only 67 of the welds qualitatively met these standards. Because, as we have indicated, the focus in strict liability cases is upon the product, making it substantially easier to prove the breach of duty, [Phipps v. General Motors Corp., 278 Md. at 344, 363 A.2d 955 (1976)], sufficient evidence was produced to provide a jury question, i.e., whether the product placed upon the market by G.M. was unreasonably dangerous.

Appellant . . . contends that because the likelihood of injury within a contained vehicle is substantial, the defective roof does not unreasonably aggravate the risk of injury inherent in the accident. But this contention is supported, if at all, by the stability of a pronouncement by G.M. that:

> By far, the most common cause of injury in an accident is what is known as the second impact between an occupant and some surface.

Thus says G.M.:

> Common sense and experience indicate that a person who sits unrestrained in a van as it is rolled over heavy timber construction barricades at 50 miles per hour and who is

thrown around the inside of that van as it tears up 142 feet of those barricades has a very good chance of receiving a serious injury or being killed. If that occupant is to be heard to say that the manufacturer who had nothing to do with causing the accident, is responsible for his injuries, he should be prepared to prove it beyond speculation.

We cannot judicially proclaim as fact that upon which the argument rests. What G.M. fails to comprehend is that "experience and common sense" are jury arguments, not cognizable as matters of law, short of facts so common-place as to require judicial notice. The evidence introduced in this case is that Lahocki's sole injury, a broken back, occurred as a result of his having been thrown from the vehicle. Indeed, it was opined by an expert that generally the risk of *any* injury is greater when one is ejected in an accident rather than contained in the vehicle. There was sufficient evidence that the injury was directly related to the defect for a jury to so find.

A somewhat related argument by G.M. follows from the rather obvious premise that a defect in an automobile which does not *cause* an accident does not subject the manufacturer to liability for all injuries sustained in the accident, but only that portion caused by the defective condition over and above the damage or injury that would have occurred as a result of the collision, absent the defect, i.e., the "enhanced" injury. See Frericks, 274 Md. at 304, 336 A.2d 118; Larsen, 391 F.2d at 503. That principle, though somewhat obscured by the developing professional patois, is but a part of the necessary proofs of any traditional negligence or strict liability case, i.e., that there be some reasonable connection between the act or omission of the defendant and the damage or injury that the plaintiff has suffered. W. Prosser, The Law of Torts 236 (4th ed. 1971). In older judicial jargon that connection is referred to as "proximate cause" and is intended to depict the limitation placed upon the wrongdoer's responsibility for the consequences of his conduct. Because in strict liability "second injury cases" the initial injury is dependent upon some preceding primary negligence, the injury that was proximately caused by the design or construction defect is most often distinguished from that which would have occurred despite the defect, as the "enhanced" injury. We agree with G.M. that there must be evidence of such causal connection. We depart from G.M. on how much is enough.

We begin our departure from G.M.'s reasoning when it points to Huddell v. Levin, 537 F.2d 726 (3rd Cir. 1976), for the premise that the plaintiff not only must prove that his injury was enhanced by the defect attributable to G.M., but also must specifically set forth what precise injuries would have occurred absent the defect.

> Thus (says G.M.) . . . the plaintiffs also were required to prove, beyond speculation, what injuries Mr. Lahocki would have sustained had the alleged construction defect not been present, i.e., what injuries Mr. Lahocki would have received had the roof of the van stayed on during the accident sequence.

To state such a premise in this case points to its absurdity unless a plaintiff's experts could qualify as soothsayers. Mr. Lahocki had a single indivisible injury, a thoracic spine injury, a broken back. No other injury was asserted against G.M. One of Mr. Lahocki's experts in biomechanics was asked on direct examination precisely the question which appellant now contends was the necessary, but absent, proof for the Lahocki claim:

Q. Assume that the roof of this van stayed on during the roll sequence, and the driver, Mr. Campbell, was found in the van after it came to rest with little or no serious injuries. Do you have an opinion founded on the basis previously stated, including your inspection of the van and your observations that you made concerning it as to what injuries of a serious nature, if any, Mr. Lahocki would have received?

The answer, which was based upon the expert's knowledge of biomechanics, experience with anthropomorphic dummies and an inspection of the vehicle, came in over appellant's objections:

> That he would not have suffered a serious injury, and in particular, he would not have suffered a thoracic spine injury.

The validity of such an opinion, while arguable, was for a jury to decide. It was at least *some* evidence of causal connection between the defect and the injury. "Maryland has gone almost as far as any jurisdiction that we know of in holding that meager evidence of negligence is sufficient to carry the case to the jury." Fowler v. Smith, 240 Md. 240, 246, 213 A.2d 549, 554 (1965). That rule requires submission of the case to the jury if there be *any* evidence, "however slight," legally sufficient as tending to prove negligence (i.e., a breach of duty) the weight and value being left to the jury. The trial judge here submitted the issue with an appropriate instruction utilizing the distinguishing new language, "enhanced injury," and perhaps went even farther in G.M.'s favor than was necessary:

> The plaintiffs are required to prove by the weight of the evidence and not by speculation or conjecture what injuries would have resulted to Mr. Lahocki had the roof not separated, and you must compare those injuries with the injuries actually received by Mr. Lahocki in order to determine to what extent, if any, Mr. Lahocki's injuries were caused by or enhanced by any defect in the van.
> If you find that even if the roof had not separated Mr. Lahocki would have sustained the same injuries or a similar injury, or even a different but equally serious injury in the accident, either within the vehicle or due to ejection through another opening such as another opening other than the roof opening, such as the windshield area or the window area on the right door, or wherever else, then your verdict should be for the defendant General Motors Corporation because obviously the defect in the roof would have nothing to do with the injuries sustained in this case.

Although appellant set up hypothetical possibilities[15] on cross-examination which the witness could not positively exclude, such hypotheses go to the weight of his testimony, they do not remove the opinion expressed from the jury's consideration. Baltimore Transit Co. v. Smith, 252 Md. 430, 436, 250 A.2d 228 (1969). Thus, even if we agreed with appellant that it is a plaintiff's burden to prove what injuries would have been sustained had the defect not been present, that was done for purposes of this case. The answer was "none." But we do not agree that such specificity as G.M. demands is part of plaintiff's burden of proof.

---

15. The possibilities included: that Lahocki may have struck his head on various objects as the van turned over, and that "part of his upper torso may have gone out the window and been crushed between the van and the street as the van rolled over."

G.M. contends that the plaintiff must not only prove his injuries and connect those attributable to G.M. causally, but also that he must precisely apportion the injuries among the wrongdoers:

> In order to prove that Mr. Lahocki's injuries were enhanced by the alleged defect the plaintiffs were required to show what his injuries would have been had the roof remained attached. This could have been accomplished by reconstructing what his motion would have been and showing what injuries would have resulted. Despite having hired two witnesses professing expertise in these areas (Somerset and McElhaney), plaintiffs offered no such evidence.

[The court disagrees.] To require the plaintiff, in this manufacturing defect case, to prove how, and how much, he would have been injured "but for" the defect in the manufacturer's product, simply denies the application of strict liability to such cases.

The very purpose of strict liability is to ease an injured party's burden of proof where it was heretofore foreclosingly difficult. By focusing on the product rather than the conduct of the manufacturer, the "new law" is practically another form of negligence per se. *Phipps,* 278 Md. at 351, 363 A.2d 955. The "newness" of the concept obscures the fact that "strict liability" is not a radical departure from traditional tort concepts, and compares favorably to the doctrine of res ipsa loquitur. Res ipsa, of course, is the rebuttable presumption that a defendant is negligent, and arises from proof that the instrumentality causing the injury was in defendant's exclusive control. Potts v. Armour & Co., 183 Md. 483, 486 (1944). In *Phipps,* strict liability is described as:

> Proof of a defect in the product at the time it leaves the control of the seller implies fault on the part of the seller sufficient to justify imposing liability for injuries caused by the product. Where the seller supplies a defective and unreasonably dangerous product, the seller or someone employed by him has been at fault in designing or constructing the product. Id. at 352, 363 A.2d at 963.

The adoption of the concept of strict liability was intended to make it easier for injured parties "to comply with the proof requirements of negligence actions." Id. at 352-353, 363 A.2d at 963. Since damages are a requisite element of proof in negligence actions, it would be contradictory to adopt, for public policy reasons, a concept to ease proof requirements of one aspect of negligence actions (liability), and then to erect an unreasonable and all but impossible barrier to recovery upon another aspect of proof (damages). To do so in this manner would be contrary even to our older traditional concepts of assigning burdens of proof of damages. See Mullan v. Hacker, 187 Md. 261, 269-270, 49 A.2d 640 (1946).

We find no fault with the underlying premise that a plaintiff must prove that his injuries were "enhanced" (i.e., caused) by the defect. *Some* evidence of enhancement (causation) is prerequisite to engendering a jury issue of assignable damages, just as *some* evidence of liability is a prerequisite to overcoming a motion for directed verdict. But the court below found, and we agree, that there was sufficient evidence to serve that purpose. The evidence ascribed the entire injury to the defect. The burden of persuading the jury by minimizing the degree of enhancement or causation is the defendant's responsibility. . . .

G.M.'s enhancement concern ends with a Parthian dart; it contends that because it showed the possibility that Lahocki might have been ejected from "no less than four open portals," he did not satisfactorily establish that the alleged defect was the cause of his injury. The three additional possibilities for his departure were brought out in the defense case by G.M. and were adequate jury questions. However, in addition to the expert testimony indicating the likelihood of ejection through the absent roof area, mere common sense could have inferentially indicated that the enlarged aperture was a more likely possibility than the other three suggested by appellant, i.e., the open window next to the driver (who was not thrown out), the open window next to Lahocki or the windshield. . . .

Judgment affirmed.

The high court of Maryland reversed *Lahocki* on a ground unrelated to the merits but worth mentioning here. See General Motors Corp. v. Lahocki, 410 A.2d 1039 (Md. 1980). The plaintiff had originally joined as a defendant with G.M. the contractor who built the timber barricades into which the van collided. Prior to trial, the plaintiff reached an agreement with the contractor under which the contractor would guarantee a certain recovery by the plaintiff, which would be reduced in proportion to the plaintiff's success against General Motors. The agreement was not revealed to the court, and the contractor remained a defendant at trial. The trial judge had directed a verdict for the defendant contractor, and the agreement with the plaintiff was revealed only sometime after entry of judgment against General Motors. Referring to such agreements as "Mary Carter Agreements," the court held them to be against public policy unless revealed at trial, and reversed judgment and remanded for a new trial at which the jury would be fully informed as to the nature of the contractual agreement.

Restatement (Third) of Torts: Products Liability
(1998)

§16. INCREASED HARM DUE TO PRODUCT DEFECT

(a) When a product is defective at the time of sale and the defect is a substantial factor in increasing the plaintiff's harm beyond that which would have resulted from other causes, the product seller is subject to liability for the increased harm.

(b) If proof supports a determination of the harm that would have resulted from other causes in the absence of the product defect, the product seller's liability is limited to the increased harm attributable solely to the product defect.

(c) If proof does not support a determination under Subsection (b) of the harm that would have resulted in the absence of the product defect, the product seller is liable for all of the plaintiff's harm attributable to the defect and other causes.

(d) A seller of a defective product who is held liable for part of the harm suffered by the plaintiff under Subsection (b), or all of the harm suffered by

> **authors' dialogue 7**
>
> **AARON:** The rules in *Lahocki* and Section 16 of the Restatement hold out a false promise to auto manufacturers, don't they?
>
> **JIM:** In what way?
>
> **AARON:** Well, think about it. In most cases involving increased harm — all of them, really — the manufacturer will want to argue under §16(a) that there was no enhancement at all; that the plaintiff's irreversible brain injury would have occurred even if the vehicle had been more crashworthy. They will argue "in a high-speed crash that horrific, nothing we could have done would have helped the plaintiff."
>
> **JIM:** O.K. I'm with you so far.
>
> **AARON:** Given the benefit of the doubt that §16(c) gives plaintiffs once they succeed in showing *some* enhancement under (a), manufacturers will tactically decide not to try to apportion under §16(b). They don't want to undercut their "no enhancement" argument under (a) by appearing to concede the issue in order to preserve their apportionment rights under (b). So they will litigate most (all) of these cases on an "all or nothing basis." And the plaintiff certainly won't raise the possibility of apportionment.
>
> **JIM:** Come to think of it, that's exactly what the lawyers who opposed §16(c) argued: that it would turn all these crashworthiness cases into life-or-death struggles, leaving no middle ground of causal apportionment.
>
> **AARON:** But isn't that more or less inevitably going to happen, whether or not §16(c) is the tiebreaker?
>
> **JIM:** Not necessarily. If the plaintiff must prove how much enhancement occurred in order to recover anything, the plaintiff will have an incentive, not present given §16(c), to address the issue.
>
> **AARON:** But that is very difficult to do in most cases. So under a "plaintiff must prove the extent of enhancement" approach, plaintiffs will go for the whole enchilada and try to prove *all* the injuries were caused by the defect.
>
> **JIM:** Putting the enchilada issue to one side, if it's going to be all-or-nothing either way, why benefit the plaintiffs with §16(c)? Why not leave the burden on the plaintiff to prove 100% enhancement?
>
> **AARON:** Ask your students.

the plaintiff under Subsection (c), is jointly and severally liable with other parties who bear legal responsibility for causing the harm, determined by applicable rules of joint and several liability.

The Reporters to the new Restatement, the authors of this book, set forth the judicial authority supporting this position in the Reporters' Note to §16. Referring to the majority position as the *Fox-Mitchell* approach, the Reporters assert that, as of early 1995, twenty-two jurisdictions support the position espoused in §16(c). Referring to the view that the plaintiff takes nothing when causal apportionment is impossible, as in the *Huddell* approach, the Reporters assert that only five jurisdictions have so held. In Lally v. Volkswagen Aktiengesellschaft, 698 N.E.2d 28 (Mass. 1998), the appellate court affirmed verdicts and judgments for the defendant in an enhanced injury case, citing to §16 of the new Restatement.

3. Loss-of-a-Chance

A seminal decision on loss-of-a-chance causation is Herskovits v. Group Health Cooperative of Puget Sound, 664 P.2d 474 (Wash. 1983). Although not a products liability decision, it deserves consideration here because it deals forthrightly with the issue of whether there should be liability when all we can ever know is that the defendant's wrongful conduct contributed marginally to increase the risk that ultimately materialized in injury. *Herskovits* involved a wrongful death action against a hospital and its employees; plaintiff proved that the defendant's negligence reduced the decedent's chances of surviving cancer. At no point in time relevant to the liability issue did the decedent have better than a 50 percent chance of survival. No expert witness was able to testify that the defendant's negligent delay in diagnosis "probably" or "more likely than not" caused the decedent's death. The trial court granted defendant's motions for summary judgment. The Washington high court reversed, concluding:

> The ultimate question raised here is whether the relationship between the increased risk of harm and Herskovits' death is sufficient to hold Group Health responsible. Is a 36 percent (from 39 percent to 25 percent) reduction in the decedent's chance for survival sufficient evidence of causation to allow the jury to consider the possibility that the physician's failure to timely diagnose the illness was the proximate cause of his death? We answer in the affirmative. To decide otherwise would be a blanket release from liability for doctors and hospitals any time there was less than a 50 percent chance of survival, regardless of how flagrant the negligence. . . .
>
> Causing reduction of the opportunity to recover (loss of chance) by one's negligence, however, does not necessitate a total recovery against the negligent party for all damages caused by the victim's death. Damages should be awarded to the injured party or his family based only on damages caused directly by premature death, such as lost earnings and additional medical expenses, etc. 664 P.2d at 476-79.

One Justice in *Herskovits* concurred in a separate opinion pointing out that the crux of the case was determining the injury or disability caused by defendant's negligence. The concurrence observed:

> Therefore, although the issue before us is primarily one of causation, resolution of that issue requires us to identify the nature of the injury to the decedent. Our conception of the injury will substantially affect our analysis. If the injury is determined to be the death of Mr. Herskovits, then under the established principles of proximate cause plaintiff has failed to make a prima facie case. Dr. Ostrow was unable to state that probably, or more likely than not, Mr. Herskovits' death was caused by defendant's negligence. On the contrary, it is clear from Dr. Ostrow's testimony that Mr. Herskovits would have probably died from cancer even with the exercise of reasonable care by defendant. Accordingly, if we perceive the death of Mr. Herskovits as the injury in this case, we must affirm the trial court, unless we determine that it is proper to depart substantially from the traditional requirements of establishing proximate cause in this type of case.

If, on the other hand, we view the injury to be the reduction of Mr. Herskovits' chance of survival, our analysis might well be different. Dr. Ostrow testified that the failure to diagnose cancer in December 1974 probably caused a substantial reduction in Mr. Herskovits' chance of survival. 664 P.2d at 481.

The concurrence concluded that the proper way to value the plaintiff's loss is to allow recovery for a percentage of the value of plaintiff's loss due to decedent's death, based on the percentage by which his chance of survival was reduced by defendant's negligence. Presumably, if the loss due to death was $100,000, and defendant's negligence reduced his chances of survival from 39 percent to 25 percent, plaintiff would recover $14,000 ($100,000 × (.39 − .25) = $14,000).

One Justice dissented, arguing that the whole thing was too speculative for a court to countenance.

The new Restatement (Third) Torts: Liability for Physical Harm (Basic Principles) under consideration during the preparation of this fifth edition, recognizes the loss-of-chance cause of action in §26, comment *n* (Tentative Draft No. 2, 2002). After observing that a number of courts have reconceptualized the concept of plaintiff's harm so as to allow recovery in cases where the plaintiff is deprived of a less-than-fifty-percent chance of recovery, the comment opines regarding the possible future of the "loss opportunity" tort:

> To date, the courts that have accepted lost opportunity as cognizable harm have almost universally limited its recognition to medical-malpractice cases. Three features of that context are significant: 1) a contractual relationship exists between patient and physician (or physician's employer), in which the raison d'être of the contract is that the physician will take every reasonable measure to obtain an optimal outcome for the patient; 2) reasonably good empirical evidence is available about the general statistical probability of the lost opportunity; and 3) frequently the consequences of the physician's negligence will deprive the patient of a less-than-50-percent chance for recovery. Whether there are appropriate areas beyond the medical-malpractice area to which lost opportunity might appropriately be extended is a matter that the Institute leaves to future development.

For a useful summary of judicial developments in non-product settings, including scholarly commentaries, see *ibid,* Reporters' Note to comment *n*.

PROBLEM ELEVEN

Jon Brett was placed in the intensive care unit (ICU) of the local hospital after suffering a severe heart attack. His condition was critical, but did not require constant bedside attention because his condition was continually monitored by a Kardia Heart Monitor. The hospital relies on such monitoring machines for early warning of changes in the condition of ICU patients. Because of a manufacturing defect, the monitor malfunctioned and hospital personnel were not alerted immediately to the onset of Brett's second heart attack. By the time the hospital personnel became aware of the situation, Brett's condition was beyond remedy, and he died. Brett's wife and children seek to hold Kardia strictly liable for his death.

In general, early warnings increase survival rates of second heart attacks by about 20%. Factors such as advanced age, severity of the first heart attack, weight, and high blood pressure can reduce the chance of survival. Data are not available as to how much each of the factors reduce a given individual's chance of survival, and there are also no reliable statistics as to the synergistic effects of these factors. Although Brett was a trim age 45, his first heart attack was severe and he suffered from high blood pressure.

D. DID THE DEFECTIVE PRODUCT PROXIMATELY CAUSE THE PLAINTIFF'S HARM?

Union Pump Co. v. Allbritton
898 S.W.2d 773 (Tex. 1995)

OWEN, Justice.

The issue in this case is whether the condition, act, or omission of which a personal injury plaintiff complains was, as a matter of law, too remote to constitute legal causation. Plaintiff brought suit alleging negligence, gross negligence, and strict liability, and the trial court granted summary judgment for the defendant. The court of appeals reversed and remanded, holding that the plaintiff raised issues of fact concerning proximate and producing cause. Because we conclude that there was no legal causation as a matter of law, we reverse the judgment of the court of appeals and render judgment that plaintiff take nothing.

On the night of September 4, 1989, a fire occurred at Texaco Chemical Company's facility in Port Arthur, Texas. A pump manufactured by Union Pump Company caught fire and ignited the surrounding area. This particular pump had caught on fire twice before. Sue Allbritton, a trainee employee of Texaco Chemical, had just finished her shift and was about to leave the plant when the fire erupted. She and her supervisor Felipe Subia, Jr., were directed to and did assist in abating the fire.

Approximately two hours later, the fire was extinguished. However, there appeared to be a problem with a nitrogen purge valve, and Subia was instructed to block in the valve. Viewing the facts in a light most favorable to Allbritton, there was some evidence that an emergency situation existed at that point in time. Allbritton asked if she could accompany Subia and was allowed to do so. To get to the nitrogen purge valve, Allbritton followed Subia over an aboveground pipe rack, which was approximately two and one-half feet high, rather than going around it. It is undisputed that this was not the safer route, but it was the shorter one. Upon reaching the valve, Subia and Allbritton were notified that it was not necessary to block it off. Instead of returning by the route around the pipe rack, Subia chose to walk across it, and Allbritton followed. Allbritton was injured when she hopped or slipped off the pipe rack. There is evidence that the pipe rack was wet because of the fire and that Allbritton and Subia were still wearing fireman's hip boots and other firefighting gear when the injury occurred. Subia admitted that he chose to walk over the pipe rack rather than taking a safer alternative route because he had a "bad habit" of doing so.

Allbritton sued Union Pump, alleging negligence, gross negligence, and strict liability theories of recovery, and accordingly, that the defective pump was a proximate or producing cause of her injuries. But for the pump fire, she asserts, she would never have walked over the pipe rack, which was wet with water or firefighting foam.

Following discovery, Union Pump moved for summary judgment. To be entitled to summary judgment, the movant has the burden of establishing that there is no genuine issue of material fact and that it is entitled to judgment as a matter of law. A defendant who moves for summary judgment must conclusively disprove one of the elements of each of the plaintiff's causes of action. Lear Siegler, Inc. v. Perez, 819 S.W.2d 470, 471 (Tex. 1991). All doubts must be resolved against Union Pump and all evidence must be viewed in the light most favorable to Allbritton. Id. The question before this Court is whether Union Pump established as a matter of law that neither its conduct nor its product was a legal cause of Allbritton's injuries. Stated another way, was Union Pump correct in contending that there was no causative link between the defective pump and Allbritton's injuries as a matter of law?

Negligence requires a showing of proximate cause, while producing cause is the test in strict liability. Proximate and producing cause differ in that foreseeability is an element of proximate cause, but not of producing cause. Id. Proximate cause consists of both cause in fact and foreseeability. Cause in fact means that the defendant's act or omission was a substantial factor in bringing about the injury which would not otherwise have occurred. A producing cause is "an efficient, exciting, or contributing cause, which in a natural sequence, produced injuries or damages complained of, if any." Common to both proximate and producing cause is causation in fact, including the requirement that the defendant's conduct or product be a substantial factor in bringing about the plaintiff's injuries. . . . *Lear Siegler,* 819 S.W.2d at 472 n.1 (quoting Restatement (Second) of Torts 431 cmt. *e* (1965)).

At some point in the causal chain, the defendant's conduct or product may be too remotely connected with the plaintiff's injury to constitute legal causation. As this Court noted in City of Gladewater v. Pike, 727 S.W.2d 514, 518 (Tex. 1987), defining the limits of legal causation "eventually mandates weighing of policy considerations." See also Springall v. Fredericksburg Hospital and Clinic, 225 S.W.2d 232, 235 (Tex. Civ. App.—San Antonio 1949, no writ), in which the court of appeals observed:

> [T]he law does not hold one legally responsible for the remote results of his wrongful acts and therefore a line must be drawn between immediate and remote causes. The doctrine of "proximate cause" is employed to determine and fix this line and "is the result of an effort by the courts to avoid, as far as possible the metaphysical and philosophical niceties in the age-old discussion of causation, and to lay down a rule of general application which will, as nearly as may be done by a general rule, apply a practical test, the test of common experience, to human conduct when determining legal rights and legal liability."

Id. at 235 (quoting City of Dallas v. Maxwell, 248 S.W. 667, 670 (Tex. Comm'n App. 1923, holding approved)).

Drawing the line between where legal causation may exist and where, as a matter of law, it cannot, has generated a considerable body of law. Our Court has considered where the limits of legal causation should lie in the factually analogous case of Lear Siegler, Inc. v. Perez, supra. The threshold issue was whether causation was negated as a matter of law in an action where negligence and product liability theories were asserted. Perez, an employee of the Texas Highway Department, was driving a truck pulling a flashing arrow sign behind a highway sweeping operation to warn traffic of the highway maintenance. Id. at 471. The sign malfunctioned when wires connecting it to the generator became loose, as they had the previous day. Id. Perez got out of the truck to push the wire connections back together, and an oncoming vehicle, whose driver was asleep, struck the sign, which in turn struck Perez. Id. Perez's survivors brought suit against the manufacturer of the sign. In holding that any defect in the sign was not the legal cause of Perez's injuries, we found a comment to the Restatement (Second) of Torts, section 431, instructive on the issue of legal causation:

> In order to be a legal cause of another's harm, it is not enough that the harm would not have occurred had the actor not been negligent. . . . The negligence must also be a substantial factor in bringing about the plaintiff's harm. The word "substantial" is used to denote the fact that the defendant's conduct has such an effect in producing the harm as to lead reasonable men to regard it as a cause, using that word in the popular sense, in which there always lurks the idea of responsibility, rather than in the so-called "philosophic sense," which includes every one of the great number of events without which any happening would not have occurred.

Lear Siegler, 819 S.W.2d at 472 (quoting Restatement (Second) of Torts §431 cmt. *a* (1965)).

As this Court explained in *Lear Siegler,* the connection between the defendant and the plaintiff's injuries simply may be too attenuated to constitute legal cause. 819 S.W.2d at 472. Legal cause is not established if the defendant's conduct or product does no more than furnish the condition that makes the plaintiff's injury possible. Id. This principle applies with equal force to proximate cause and producing cause. Id. at 472 n.1.

This Court similarly considered the parameters of legal causation in Bell v. Campbell, 434 S.W.2d 117, 122 (Tex.1968). In *Bell,* two cars collided, and a trailer attached to one of them disengaged and overturned into the opposite lane. A number of people gathered, and three of them were attempting to move the trailer when they were struck by another vehicle. Id. at 119. This Court held that the parties to the first accident were not a proximate cause of the plaintiffs' injuries, reasoning:

> All acts and omissions charged against respondents had run their course and were complete. Their negligence did not actively contribute in any way to the injuries involved in this suit. It simply created a condition which attracted [the plaintiffs] to the scene, where they were injured by a third party.

Id. at 122.

In *Bell,* this Court examined at some length decisions dealing with intervening causes and decisions dealing with concurring causes. The principles underlying the various legal theories of causation overlap in many respects, but they are not coextensive. While in *Bell,* this Court held "the injuries involved in this suit were not proximately caused by any negligence of [defendants] but by an independent and intervening agency," id., we also held "[a]ll forces involved in or generated by the first collision had come to rest, and no one was in any real or apparent danger therefrom[,]" id. at 120, and accordingly, that the "[defendants'] negligence was not a concurring cause of [the plaintiffs'] injuries." Id. at 122. This reasoning applies with equal force to Allbritton's claims.

Even if the pump fire were in some sense a "philosophic" or "but for" cause of Allbritton's injuries, the forces generated by the fire had come to rest when she fell off the pipe rack. The fire had been extinguished, and Allbritton was walking away from the scene. Viewing the evidence in the light most favorable to Allbritton, the pump fire did no more than create the condition that made Allbritton's injuries possible. We conclude that the circumstances surrounding her injuries are too remotely connected with Union Pump's conduct or pump to constitute a legal cause of her injuries. See *Lear Siegler*, 819 S.W.2d at 472.

Accordingly, we reverse the judgment of the court of appeals and render judgment that plaintiff take nothing.

Union Pump generated both a concurring and a dissenting opinion. The concurrence chides the majority for "unnecessarily perpetuating confusion" by "conflat[ing] foreseeability and other policy issues with cause in fact." According to the concurrence, the causation analysis should include two steps. First, one must ask whether the defendant's actions, or the product's defect, was the cause-in-fact of the plaintiff's injury. This "but-for" prong is devoid of any policy considerations; the task is simply to determine whether the plaintiff's injury was "philosophically" caused by plaintiff's negligence. Once this hurdle has been passed, "the court should consider . . . whether the policies or principles at the heart of [the] cause of action dictate a further limitation on liability." While acknowledging that the pump defect was a but-for cause of the plaintiff's injury, indeed was a substantial cause of her injury, the concurrence concludes that policy considerations prevent the defect from being a legal cause:

> In this case, the injury to Allbritton was not foreseeable. [Her] injuries were all the result of a needlessly dangerous shortcut taken after the crisis had subsided. Holding Union Pump liable for Allbritton's failure to use proper care in exiting the area of the fire after the crisis ended is akin to holding it liable for an auto accident she suffered on the way home, even though the accident probably would not have occurred had she left after her normal shift. Foreseeability allows us to cut off Union Pump's liability at some point; I would do so at the point the crisis had abated or at the point Allbritton and Subia departed from their usual, safe path. 898 S.W.2d at 784.

The dissent declares that the defendant is not entitled to summary judgment:

> The record reflects that at the time Sue Allbritton's injury occurred, the forces generated by the fire in question had not come to rest. Rather, the emergency situation was continuing. The whole area of the fire was covered in water and foam; in at least some places, the water was almost knee-deep. Allbritton was still wearing hip boots and other gear, as required to fight the fire. . . .
>
> This case is markedly different from the two main cases on which the majority relies: Lear Siegler, Inc. v. Perez, and Bell v. Campbell. In each of those cases, a defendant's negligence simply created a condition that attracted an individual to the scene, where a negligent third party inflicted an injury. Here, in contrast, there was no negligent third party. To whatever extent Allbritton's own negligence may have contributed to

authors' dialogue 8

JIM: The dissent in *Union Pump* is right, isn't it?

AARON: I don't think so. It seems to me that the majority got it right on the money. What the plaintiff did by taking the shortcut was her own private frolic. As long as she had a safer way out of the fire area, and chose not to take it, the pump manufacturer should be off the hook.

JIM: But you aren't talking proximate cause. You're talking assumption of the risk, or plaintiff's contributory fault, aren't you?

AARON: What difference does it make what you call it? The manufacturer should not be liable for the risks she brought on herself.

JIM: The difference it makes is that if it's her own negligence that is doing the work for you, most states have adopted comparative fault. If you are right that she acted negligently, the jury should apportion responsibility between the parties, not bar her recovery altogether.

AARON: I see what you're saying, but I think I'm talking proximate cause, here. It is not reasonably foreseeable that a defect in a pump would lead to someone taking a dangerous shortcut after the defect-caused fire is out. When proximate cause is absent, defendant wins the whole enchilada – the plaintiff takes nothing.

JIM: What's with this "enchilada" schtick? (Cf. Dialogue 7, p. 146, supra). Anyway, what if the plaintiff had not taken the shortcut, and had slipped on the wet floor and hurt herself coming out the safer way?

AARON: Then I agree that the proximate cause issue should have been for the jury.

JIM: So the difference for you really is the element of plaintiff's fault, isn't it?

AARON: I don't think so. It's foreseeability. What if she had decided to perform handsprings to celebrate the fire being put out, and had suffered injury doing that? Defendant should win that case on proximate cause grounds as a matter of law, shouldn't it?

JIM: I guess so. But taking a more dangerous shortcut is the result of momentary inadvertence that the manufacturer should pay for once its defective pump causes a fire that causes commotion and requires fire fighting. Wilfully reckless conduct by the plaintiff may break the proximate cause link as a matter of law. But as long as she has her firefighting gear on and is walking out of the area through foamy water, proximate cause should not be an outright bar to recovery as a matter of law. Plaintiff should have reached the jury.

AARON: My goodness, Jim, you're actually on the plaintiff's side!

JIM: You won't tell anyone, will you?

her injury, a jury should be allowed to allocate comparative responsibility. 898 S.W.2d at 785-786.

The opinion in Lear Siegler, Inc. v. Perez, 819 S.W. 2d 470 (Tex. 1991), a Texas Supreme Court decision that the *Union Pump* court describes and upon which it relies, mentioned that instead of being hurt while on the highway the plaintiff might have been injured when he brought the malfunctioning sign back to headquarters early, only to have the roof cave in on him at that exact moment. In that hypothetical situation, the defective sign could not be considered a legal cause of the worker's injury, even if it is a cause-in-fact.

In Marshall v. Nugent, 222 F.2d 604 (1st Cir. 1955), the U.S. Court of Appeals addressed the same line-drawing problem as the court in *Lear Siegler* posed hypothetically. In that case, defendant's driver drove his truck in a dangerous manner around a curve on an icy mountain road. In doing so, he forced a car in which the plaintiff was a passenger off the road and into a snowbank. No one was hurt. The truck driver stopped to assist in extricating the car from the snowbank, and suggested that the plaintiff go up the hill to warn oncoming traffic. The plaintiff started up the hill, and within two minutes was struck and seriously injured by a car driven by co-defendant Nugent.

At trial, the jury found for the plaintiff. In upholding the trial court's decision to allow the question of the truck driver's liability to go to the jury, the Court of Appeals held that it is the jury who must decide the policy issues involved with causation analysis, that is "whether under all the circumstances the defendant ought to be recognized as privileged to do the act in question or to pursue his course of conduct with immunity from liability for harm to others which might result." 222 F.2d at 611. In such "borderline cases" the court leaves the issue of proximate cause to the jury "with appropriate instructions." As for the extent to which a jury might hold a negligent driver liable for injuries stemming from his actions, the court said:

> In a traffic mix-up due to negligence, before the disturbed waters have become placid and normal again, the unfolding of events between the culpable act and the plaintiff's eventual injury may be bizarre indeed; yet the defendant may be liable for the result. . . . In such a situation, it would be impossible for a person in the defendant's position to predict in advance just how his negligent act would work out to another's injury. Yet this in itself is no bar to recovery. 222 F.2d at 610.

The court then presented this hypothetical:

> If the Chevrolet had pulled back onto the highway, and Harriman and Marshall, having got in it again, had resumed their journey and had had a collision with another car five miles down the road, in which Marshall suffered bodily injuries, it could truly be said that such subsequent injury to Marshall was a consequence in fact of the earlier delay caused by the defendant's negligence. . . . But on such assumed state of facts, the courts would no doubt conclude, 'as a matter of law,' that [the defendant's] earlier negligence in cutting the corner was not the 'proximate cause' of this latter injury received by the plaintiff. That would be because the extra risks to which [plaintiff had been subjected by the defendant] were obviously entirely over; the situation had been stabilized and be-

come normal, and, so far as one could foresee, whatever subsequent risks the Chevrolet might have to encounter in its resumed journey were simply the inseparable risks . . . incident to the Chevrolet's being out on the highway at all. 222 F.2d at 612.

The approach in the *Marshall* decision appears more willing to give the issue of proximate causation to the jury than does the approach in *Union Pump.* Wherein, exactly, lies the difference?

Section 29 of the new Restatement (Third) of Torts: Liability for Physical Harm (Basic Principles) (Tentative Draft No. 2, March 25, 2002) jettisons the phrase "proximate cause" in favor of "limitations on liability." In a "Special Note" to Chapter 6, "Scope of Liability (Proximate Cause)," the Reporters include the following explanation:

> Although the term "proximate cause" has been in widespread use in judicial opinions, treatises, casebooks, and scholarship, the term is not generally employed in this Chapter because it is an especially poor one to describe the idea to which it is connected. See §29, Comment *b.* Hence, this Chapter is entitled "Scope of Liability." That terminology more accurately describes the concerns of this Chapter: Tort law does not impose liability on an actor for all harm factually caused by the actor's tortious conduct. With the exception of no-duty rules and affirmative defenses, limitations on liability are contained in this Chapter. Nevertheless, to communicate clearly with judges, lawyers, and academics who understand limitations on liability under the proximate-cause rubric, the term is included in a parenthetical following the Chapter's title. The Institute fervently hopes that the Restatement Fourth of Torts will not find this parenthetical necessary.

Section 29 simply asserts that "An actor is not liable for harm different from the harms whose risks made the actor's conduct tortious." Is this formulation helpful in working out sensible solutions to the causation issue presented in *Union Pump, Lear Siegler,* and *Marshall,* supra?

The plaintiff in Ford Motor Co. v. Eads, 457 S.W.2d 28 (Tenn. 1970), purchased a tractor with a defective ignition switch that rendered the tractor difficult — and at times impossible — to start. A safety mechanism incorporated into the switch prevented the tractor from being started while in gear. Plaintiff's brother borrowed the tractor and hot-wired the ignition, which coincidentally bypassed the safety mechanism. The brother failed to inform the plaintiff of the hot-wiring. In his brother's presence, the plaintiff, thinking the tractor was in neutral, started the tractor in gear while standing next to the tractor. The tractor moved forward, injuring the plaintiff's leg. The Tennessee Supreme Court reversed the decision in favor of the plaintiff. The court explained:

> It is undisputed that when plaintiff's brother, Ted Eads, was using the tractor, the tractor's engine was killed and could not be started. At this point it is evident that the tractor was an inert piece of machinery which could not be started at all. . . . [I]nstead of being a defective tractor and unreasonably dangerous, this defective tractor could not be started, and was dangerous to no one in its inert condition. . . .
>
> Plaintiff's position is that defendant should have reasonably foreseen that a user having difficulty in starting a tractor might, in order to complete his day's work, rewire the tractor in order to cause it to start.
>
> Defendant, on the other hand, urges that the tractor that could not be started had 'failed safe'; and that the 'hot-wiring' was an efficient intervening cause as a matter of law. . . .

> [F]oreseeability is an essential ingredient of proximate causation in the law of negligence. Here, it is much argued, pro and con, as to whether the defendant should have, or not, foreseen the 'hot-wiring' which occurred. That, however, becomes relatively insignificant in view of the fact that the plaintiff's own brother did the 'hot-wiring' and then neglected to inform plaintiff of such condition. This record shows that the 'hot-wiring' condition continued for some two to three weeks prior to Donald Eads' accident and injury. The record also shows that the plaintiff's brother was on the scene at the time of the casualty itself.
>
> For the reasons heretofore expressed, we hold that the 'hot-wiring' was a conscious agency, which unforeseeably intervened, and destroyed any causal connection between defendant and the ultimate injury sustained by the plaintiff. 457 S.W.2d at 31-32.

As the foregoing excerpts indicate, many courts sort out proximate cause issues by relying on the concept of foreseeability. (Indeed, earlier editions of this casebook employed the concept in the heading to this section D.) Section §29 of the Restatement (Third) of Torts: Liability for Physical Harm (Basic Principles) (Tentative Draft No. 3, 2003) limits the defendant's liability to harms that are similar to the harms whose risks made the actor's conduct tortious to begin with. Comment *k* contains the following observations regarding the usefulness of foreseeability in this context:

> Properly understood, both the [harms-within-the-] risk standard and a foreseeability test exclude liability for harms that were sufficiently unforeseeable at the time of the actor's tortious conduct that they were not among the risks — potential harms — that made the actor negligent. Negligence limits the requirement of reasonable care to those risks that are foreseeable. Thus, when scope of liability arises in a negligence case, the risks that make an actor negligent are limited to foreseeable ones, and the factfinder must determine whether the harm that occurred is among those reasonably foreseeable potential harms that made the actor's conduct negligent. . . .
>
> For the strict-liability bases for liability, the connection between a foreseeability standard and the standard in this section is a bit more complicated. Most strict-liability torts include some requirement of foreseeability, although it is more refined than that for negligence. Typically strict-liability torts require that some form of physical harm be foreseen. In the products-liability area, liability for design and warnings defects is limited to those risks that are foreseeable. See Restatement Third, Torts: Products Liability §2(b) and (c). Thus, in these products-liability cases, the foreseeability test has the same relationship to the risk standard of this section as exists for negligence claims. . . . [In contrast to the fault-based liability imposed for design and warnings defects], strict liability is imposed for manufacturing defects. Focusing on the risks created by a manufacturing defect, rather than attempting to manipulate the concept of foreseeability, provides greater illumination of the requisite analysis.

See generally John D. Rue, Note, Returning to the Roots of the Bramble Bush: The "But-For" Test Regains Primacy in Causal Analysis in the American Law Institute's Proposed Restatement (Third) of Torts, 71 Fordham L. Rev. 2679 (2003).

The so-called "rescuer doctrine," that allows rescuers who are injured during rescue to recover from those whose negligence created the need for rescue in the first place, is recognized in products liability cases. For example, in McCoy v. American Suzuki Motor Corp., 961 P.2d 952 (Wash. 1998), a defect in an SUV allegedly caused it to roll over. The plaintiff-passerby stopped his own vehicle to help the victims in the roll-over and was himself struck and injured by a hit-and-run driver. The rescue attempt and subsequent injuries could be found to have been reasonably foreseeable to the SUV manufacturer. See generally Restatement (Third) of Torts: Liability for Physical Harm (Basic Principles) §31 (Tentative Draft No. 2, 2002).

When a third party's conduct intervenes to cause harm, special problems are raised. Thus, in Hollenbeck v. Selectone Corporation, 476 N.E.2d 746 (Ill. App. Ct. 1985), a police officer was attacked and injured while attempting to arrest several suspects after the pager issued by his department failed to send a warning message to the precinct. The trial court dismissed the plaintiff's complaint against defendant pager manufacturer because the criminal acts perpetrated by the criminal suspects were not probable or foreseeable, thereby breaking the causal connection between the product's failure and the plaintiff's injury. The court of appeals reversed, holding:

> ... The intervening criminal acts were not so improbable and unforeseeable as to break the causal connection. ... The plaintiff has alleged that the defendant represented that its product was suitable for use by police agencies and that it marketed its product specifically for use by such agencies. ... It was objectively reasonable to expect that the pager would be utilized in a situation involving a criminal offense. 476 N.E.2d at 747-48.

See generally Restatement (Third) of Torts: Liability for Physical Harm (Basic Principles) §33 (Tentative Draft No. 2, 2002).

PROBLEM TWELVE

Unitop, Inc. manufactures a full line of commercial meat slicing machines. Its top-of-the-line unit, Model 505, is a sophisticated piece of machinery. One of the safety features on Model 505 is an automatic shut-off which closes down the slicer when the guard holding the meat to the slicer advances within ½ inch of the slicing blade. In Unitop's experience, even with the metal guard which holds the meat to the slicing blade, users who are momentarily distracted can get their hands near the blade and suffer injury. The automatic cut-off forces the user to engage a button (Single-Slice Button) for each slice to be made after the ½-inch level has been reached. Since users have to engage the button for each slice, they tend to focus attention on what they are doing and thus are more apt to avoid injury.

Mo's Deli purchased a Model 505 two years ago. Morris (Mo) Blitner liked the machine but detested the ½-inch automatic cut-off feature because it interrupted the smooth flow of work. Six months later, Mo discovered that the Single-Slice Button was not working. Apparently due to inadequate soldering, the wires loosened and then shorted out. Mo's one-year warranty on the Model 505 had run out. The cost of repairing the wiring of the Single-Slice Button would have been $150. It was much simpler for Mo to disengage the automatic cut-off mechanism and be done with it.

One week after removing the automatic cut-off, Mo, while slicing pastrami, was engaged in serious discussion with a customer (a stockbroker) who had a particularly good tip on some commodities futures. Mo was not paying sufficient attention to what he was doing and his fingers hit the blades. (The remaining piece of unsliced pastrami had reached a thickness where the automatic cut-off would have been operative if it were still connected.)

Mo subsequently brought a tort action against Unitop, which has moved for summary judgment based on the uncontested facts set forth herein. As the law clerk for Judge Malcolm Sweet, before whom the case is pending, you have been assigned to draft an opinion with regard to this matter. You are to assume that the Supreme Court of New California in a recent opinion expressed disagreement with the holding in Ford Motor Co. v. Eads, discussed and quoted in the text, supra.

PART II
Liability for Generic Product Risks

The phrase "generic product risks" embraces two important categories of products liability cases; those in which the plaintiff claims that the design of the defendant's product exposed her to unreasonable risks of injury ("defective design") and those in which the plaintiff claims that the defendant supplied a product without adequate instructions or warnings about nonobvious risks of injury ("defective marketing"). The issues in both categories involve generic product risks because every product unit designed and marketed in the same way shares the same risk potential. Unlike manufacturing defects, if you condemn one unit as generically defective, you condemn them all. That, of course, is why litigation over the adequacy of product design and marketing provides the impetus for reforming the products liability system; a manufacturer can wake up one morning and find itself confronted with the real possibility that all the products it has sold for the last 20 years (all 450 billion of them) are legally defective.

Why take up defective design before defective marketing? Given that it is easier for a manufacturer to provide adequate warnings and accurate portrayals of its products than it is to redesign its products, arguably warnings should come first. However, good engineering demands that a manufacturer's first responsibility is to reduce risk as much as reasonably possible by building hardware into products that eliminates the risk of injury. Warnings serve as a backup once one has, so to speak, maxed out with regard to design. Consider, for example, a punch press that is unguarded at the point of operation. An inattentive or forgetful plaintiff may stick his hand into the danger point and suffer serious injury. Even the boldest warning, "Danger—Keep Hands Away" will not eliminate the possibility that a forgetful employee may inadvertently get his hand caught. A safety guard is the preferable option since it prevents the accident from happening by blocking entrance to the danger point. As we shall see, the thesis that a manufacturer should undertake reasonable design as the first step in seeking to accomplish safer products is a governing principle in the Products Liability Restatement §2, Comment *l*. We thus direct our attention first to design because it really does come first. Not until we have exhausted available avenues for reasonable design do we look to whether further steps might have been taken to safeguard against residual risks through the mechanism of warning.

Chapter Four deals with liability for defective design. Chapter Five examines the legal standards by which defendants are held liable for failure to instruct or to warn. Although the distinction between design and marketing is clear enough in most cases, you should appreciate that it gives way under pressure. For example, plaintiffs frequently combine claims of defective design with claims of failure to warn: "You should have designed the top so that it would not fall off, or at least should have warned me that it might fall off." Or: "You should have made the top less likely to fall off, and should have warned me in any event." Whether juries in such cases keep straight the distinction between design and warning is open to question. Chapter Six considers the liability of sellers for express statements about product performance. Actions for breach of express warranty or misrepresentation are almost always generic to an entire product line. Finally, Chapters Seven and Eight deal with federal preemption and affirmative defenses, two subjects that are fundamentally involved in litigation over generically dangerous products.

CHAPTER FOUR
Liability for Defective Design

We begin this chapter with fair warning to the student. The material that follows is tough stuff. What will be frustrating to the student is trying to get a handle on the differing legal standards that determine when a product is defectively designed. Courts have given voice to several different standards. Many courts take the position that the plaintiff must proffer credible evidence that a reasonable alternative design was available that would have prevented the harm suffered by the plaintiff. The Products Liability Restatement also takes this position. Some courts appear to allow a plaintiff to establish design defect if the product that caused the harm disappointed consumer expectations. Under this view, the nature of the alternative design that should have been adopted remains vague and indeterminate. The rhetoric is often extreme in favor of one test or another. You will have to struggle with the cases to determine whether the rhetoric reflects important policy differences that have a significant impact on the outcome of cases or whether the rhetoric provides little more than good sound bites. In reality, there may be more fundamental agreement as to what it takes to make out a cause of action for design defect than meets the eye.

In seeking to fashion a legal standard for defective design, it will be useful to look at the problems that attend establishing a design for any complex system. Consider the decisions faced by a traffic engineer in regulating city traffic: where to place red lights, whether to stagger the lights so that drivers do not have to stop at every block, what speed limits to set on various thoroughfares, what parking restrictions to put in place, etc. A moment's reflection reveals that the engineer will have to concern herself with competing values. The more stoplights that are in place, the easier it will be to have safe pedestrian crossings. If she decides to stagger the lights and increase the speed limit to facilitate faster driving, pedestrians anxious to cross may encounter fast-moving cars if they are not willing to wait for a long light. The presence of parked cars complicates the picture. Though parking may be necessary to allow for access to shopping, parked cars may eliminate a lane of traffic essential to maintaining a steady flow of traffic.

If one were to ask what is a reasonable way to design a traffic system in a given neighborhood, the answer is not readily apparent. There may be five reasonable ways to design the system, depending on which values one wishes to give primacy. Is fast flow of traffic to come in first? Pedestrian access to shopping? Pedestrian safety? Staggering lights may require limiting the availability of parking. Limiting parking may then require adding crosswalks in order to facilitate pedestrian access to stores. However, increasing the number of pedestrian crosswalks may then require increasing the number of stop lights. And on it goes. The late Professor Lon Fuller labeled the decision-making process for this kind of problem as "polycentric." Such problems are ill-suited for litigation. If after the occurrence of an accident a claim was made that the traffic system was not reasonably designed, a court would have a devil of a time dealing with the issue. When each point for decision is related to all the others as are the strands of a spiderweb, if one strand is pulled, a complex patter of readjustment will occur throughout the web. As one issue is resolved another pops up. As the second is resolved a third must be confronted. And as the third issue is being resolved it may be necessary to go back and reexamine the first issue.

In an article written at the very outset of the design defect era, Professor Henderson argued that product design litigation is inherently polycentric. He contended that:

> [A]bsolute safety is not attainable and — in any event — is not the sole desirable objective of the product's design, the engineer must place relative values upon a multitude of factors. The decisions he must make regarding these factors are as interrelated and interdependent as the strands of an intricate web. [Changing one's assessment of any single factor changes one's assessment of all, or most, of the other factors.] Intelligent answers to the question of "How much product safety is enough?" — the question that will concern us throughout — can only be provided by a process that considers such factors as market price, functional utility, and aesthetics, as well as safety, and achieves the proper balance among them. Ultimately, the question reduces to "What portion of society's limited resources are to be allocated to safety, thereby leaving less to be devoted to other social objectives?"

James A. Henderson, Jr., Judicial Review of Manufacturers' Conscious Design Choice: The Limits of Adjudication, 73 Colum. L. Rev. 1531, 1540 (1973).

Henderson's critique of design defect litigation brought forth the following response from the coauthor of this casebook. In an article entitled The Use and Abuse of Warnings in Products Liability: Design Defect Litigation Comes of Age, 61 Cornell L. Rev. 495, 526 (1976), Professor Aaron D. Twerski, with colleagues Weinstein, Donaher, and Piehler, argued:

> In the cases discussed by Professor Fuller, courts are thrown a complex problem and asked to resolve it on no basis other than general notions of fairness and equity. Such litigation is unfocused and diffuse. There is no central focal point that becomes the axis about which all considerations must turn. In product design litigation the opposite is true. Admittedly, absolute safety is unattainable and is not the only consideration germane to a design defect case. But the focal point of the case is clearly defined. It revolves around the question of whether the product has met a minimal level of product safety acceptability, i.e., the product is not unreasonably dangerous. To the extent that factors such as cost, aesthetics and functional utility are examined, they are examined not in isolation but in relation to safety.

Suffice it to say that both authors have moderated their views. Twerski acknowledges that polycentricity can be a serious problem in design litigation. Henderson now believes that a well-formulated test for design defect that concentrates on marginal comparisons may reduce the justiciability concerns that he expressed in his early piece. In any event, design litigation is not a cakewalk. In analyzing the various tests propounded by the courts for defect, it is important to keep in mind the underlying difficulty in judging any complex design system and to ask how any suggested test for determining defect addresses the problem of evaluating the trade-offs that are inherent in design.

One further word of caution is in order. We have noted that the legal test for defect should be aimed at establishing the hitherto unimplemented standard against which to measure the product that caused the injury. Whatever the legal standard finally adopted, there is an inescapable reality: In the process of defining a legal standard, courts are creating ex nihilo. The hypotheticated alternative product may be something new, or at the very least something different. Bringing this kind of creative process to the courtroom is both exciting and frightening. It tests the limits of traditional adjudication in ways that have not often been confronted in litigation practice. The student is thus cautioned not to let the search for a legal test for design defect distract attention from the battle over how a hypothetical standard is proved in court. At the colosseum, the spectator should keep his eye first and foremost on the combatants, not the referee. With these admonitions in mind, we invite you to enter the arena. The gladiators are ready and the lions very hungry.

A. DO WE NEED JUDICIAL REVIEW OF PRODUCT DESIGNS?

The best place to begin one's consideration of judicial review of product designs is to ask why such review is needed. The risks with which courts are concerned are presumably generic — that is, we are not here talking about risks associated with manufacturing defects. Moreover, the risks we are referring to in design-defect cases are presumably either obvious or adequately warned about. That being the case, the market should function well to achieve appropriate levels of product safety. And if the risks are hidden and the warnings inadequate, plaintiff need not pursue a case for design defect. A failure to warn claim provides a much easier road to recovery. Thus, the question remains: Why must courts review product designs at all?

Suggesting that the answer to this question is anything but easy, one should be reminded that, until fairly recently, many courts did *not* review product designs when the generic risks were obvious. Referred to as the "patent danger rule," this single factor barrier to liability reigned in many jurisdictions. The leading case adopting the patent danger rule is Campo v. Scofield, 95 N.E.2d 802 (N.Y. 1950). The plaintiff in *Campo* had his hands crushed in the rollers of a piece of farm machinery. The plaintiff argued that the machinery was defectively designed in that the risk of user injury was unreasonably great. The New York high court held for the defendant as a matter of law on the basis that the risk was obvious to the user and therefore should be the user's, and not the defendant's, responsibility. The *Campo* decision was followed in many American jurisdictions, and at one time represented the majority view. Many courts adopting the rule used it to explain why someone who cuts himself with a sharp knife cannot recover from the knife manufacturer — the sharpness of the knife is obvious, therefore it is up to the user to be careful not to suffer injury.

California was one of the first jurisdictions to overturn the patent danger rule.

In Pike v. Frank G. Hough Co., 467 P.2d 229 (Cal. 1970), the court held that, although a blind spot due to the absence of rearview mirrors was obvious to the operator of a high earthmoving machine, such obviousness should not constitute an absolute bar to the defendant's liability in negligence toward a bystander run over by the mirrorless machine. That the patent danger rule's days were numbered was made clear in Micallef v. Miehle Co., 348 N.E.2d 571 (N.Y. 1976), in which the New York Court of Appeals overruled *Campo*. Since that time, a strong majority of states have rejected the patent danger rule. See, e.g., Byrns v. Riddel, Inc., 550 P.2d 1065 (Ariz. 1976); Auburn Mach. Works Co., Inc. v. Jones, 366 So. 2d 1167 (Fla. 1979); Ogletree v. Navistar Int'l Transp. Co., 500 S.E.2d 570 (Ga. 1998); Holm v. Sponco Mfg. Inc., 324 N.W.2d 207 (Minn. 1982); Sperry-New Holland v. Prestage, 617 So. 2d 248 (Miss. 1993). But see McCollum v. Grove Mfg. Co., 293 S.E.2d 632, *aff'd*, 300 S.E.2d 374 (N.C. 1983).

What is the theoretical basis for overturning the patent danger rule and embarking on what, in many jurisdictions, has become a vigorous and robust process of judicial review of product designs even when the risks are obvious? As is so often the case, the answer from an instrumental, efficiency-based standpoint is that courts recognize that users and consumers are sometimes unable to cope adequately with even obvious product-related risks. For example, a modern court confronted with the *Campo* fact pattern is likely to view the worker's plight more sympathetically than did the New York court in 1950. Sooner or later, people working with farm machinery are going to be inattentive. A machine designed so that a single moment's inadvertence may cost the user a finger or a hand is too unforgiving to pass muster. It is better, modern judges are apt to conclude, to design the machine so as to forgive a certain amount of momentary forgetfulness and inadvertence. And when the injured victim is not a user but a bystander, as in the *Pike* decision, supra, the argument for building greater safety into the design is even stronger.

The Products Liability Restatement §2, Comment *d* rejects the patent danger rule as an absolute defense to a claim for design defect. The obviousness of the danger is only one factor to be taken into account in deciding whether the product should have been more safely designed.

B. DO WE NEED THE DEFECT REQUIREMENT? WHAT ABOUT BROAD ENTERPRISE LIABILITY?

In part I, supra, dealing with manufacturing defects, it seemed intuitively correct to rely on the concept of defect as the trigger for the defendant seller's liability. At the very least, manufacturers should be liable when the product unit that harms the plaintiff fails to conform to the design intended by the manufacturer — when the purchaser, quite literally, does not get what he paid for and the defect proximately causes serious harm. But when the plaintiff *does* get what he paid for — when the product unit in question conforms to the intended design — the proper judicial response is less intuitively obvious. One response would be to deny liability altogether, at least when the risks inherent in the design are obvious and there has been no deceptive marketing. We considered that possibility in the previous Section and indicated that American courts have rejected it overwhelmingly. Even when a product unit conforms exactly to its intended design, courts will impose liability if the risks presented by the design exceed the legal standard to which the design must conform — if the design, itself, is "defective." In this Section, we want you to consider whether it should be necessary to ask whether a design is defective before imposing liability on the manufacturer. The question to be addressed is the one in the heading to this Section: "Do we really need defect?"

The alternative here to be considered is broad-based enterprise liability — liability based merely on the fact that the defendant's product has caused the plaintiff's harm. Such liability would truly be strict liability. All that a plaintiff would be required to show is that the defendant's product caused, presumably in a but-for sense, her harm. Instrumentally, such a system would be attractive in theory because it would "internalize" all the accident costs associated with product use and consumption, leaving manufacturers, operating out of self-interest, to work out the best designs and marketing schemes to achieve optimal levels of accident costs. And from a fairness standpoint, enterprise liability without defect would simply ask manufacturers to "pay for what they break." After all, manufacturers volunteer to distribute inherently risky products in order to make a profit; it is only fair that they compensate victims when the products cause harm. Plaintiff's comparative fault could be taken into account in measuring recoveries, but the plaintiff would not be required to prove defect in order to establish a prima facie case.

The question yet to be addressed is whether such a broad-based system of strict liability without any requirement of defect would be viable. Consider the following excerpt from a law review article written by one of the authors of this casebook.

James A. Henderson, Jr., Why Negligence Dominates Tort
50 UCLA L. Rev. 377, 393-400 (2002)

[It will be recalled from an excerpt from this same law review article reproduced in Chapter One (see pp. 30-33, supra) that two conditions must be satisfied for any strict liability system to be workable. First, the boundaries of the system must be sufficiently specific, and questions of causation sufficiently mechanical, to allow consistent resolution of liability disputes by means of adjudication. And second, the beneficiaries of the insurance system implicit in strict liability must not be allowed to increase the risks of injury and loss either by strategically seeking insurance coverage (the threat of adverse selection) or by engaging in highly risky activities after obtaining coverage (the threat of moral hazard). The earlier excerpt referred to the first condition as one of "adjudicability" and the second as one of "insurability." The earlier analysis concluded that the system of strict liability for manufacturing defects satisfies both conditions. The law review article proceeds, in the excerpts that follow, to consider the workability of a broad-based system of strict enterprise liability for generic product hazards, without requiring that the design or marketing of the products be defective in any way. The analysis considers, first, the requirement of adjudicability, and next, the requirement of insurability.]

B. Broad-Based Strict Liability Would Not Be Viable Because It Would Generate Unadjudicable Disputes

To appreciate the unadjudicability of liability disputes under a broad-based strict liability system, consider the boundary and causation problems that would arise in connection with a system in which product manufacturers were held strictly liable for all the harm their products cause, whether or not those products were defective. Indeed, the threshold policy question would be why courts should limit such a strict liability system to "products" in the first instance. Our existing products liability system maintains the boundary between products and services largely because commercial suppliers of services, in contrast to suppliers of products, are not held strictly liable. Thus, the products boundary exists primarily in order to support a viable regime of strict liability for manufacturing defects. If the decision were ever reached to abandon the defectiveness requirement and extend strict liability to all product-related risks, including . . . generic risks . . . the primary reason for the system limiting itself to products would vanish. And once the boundaries of strict liability were expanded to include all commercial activities, including the generic risks associated with products and services, the relevant causation triggers would be required to carry more weight conceptually than they can possibly bear. As noted earlier, most accidental losses in our society can be causally connected, on a but-for basis, to endless combinations of commercial activities. The issue of "Which commercial activities caused which harms?" has long been recognized as the most difficult part of comprehensive strict liability. Without the conceptual linchpins of "negligence" and "defect," courts administering a broad-based strict liability system could not possibly reach consistent, rational outcomes. . . .

A concrete example will help to clarify this important point. Suppose that the plaintiff is at home in his basement, working on a wood lathe. He has just finished a meal of pasta, washed down with two cold beers. At a critical juncture, the light over his head suddenly goes out and, drowsy from lunch, he steps on a roller skate on the floor next to where he is standing and falls, injuring his hand in the turning lathe mechanism. The plaintiff brings a tort action against the contractor who built the home, the subcontractor who installed the lighting, and the manufacturers and distributors of the pasta, the beer, the roller skate, and the power lathe, joining them all as defendants. Assuming that the activities of all these defendants are but-for causes of the accident, how would the court under a broad-based strict enterprise liability system decide which defendants should be liable for which portions of the plaintiff's harm? Under existing law, the court would identify the responsible party by applying the limiting principles of fault, product defect, and proximate causation. [Adoption of] a broad strict liability system that has abandoned these limiting principles would lead to conceptual chaos. . . .

C. Broad-Based Strict Liability Would Not Be Viable Because the Risks It Would Assign to Commercial Enterprises Would Be Uninsurable

An earlier discussion of the insurability requirement noted that, to achieve viability, a broad-based strict liability system must assure that the risks are ascertainable ahead of time and that the commercial enterprises held strictly liable as insurers are adequately protected from the potentially devastating effects of adverse selection and moral hazard. It will now be demonstrated that even if a broad-based strict liability system could somehow surmount problems of adjudicability, it would not be able to surmount intractable problems of uninsurability. Such a system could fairly easily limit itself to ascertainable risks, but even so, the risks assigned to defendant enterprises would be uninsurable. . . . Recall that the key to protecting enterprises in this regard is to prevent those who obtain insurance coverage from significantly increasing the risk of covered losses once the enterprise's insurance obligation is in place. Essentially, this means that, once a commercial enterprise is insuring the risk, the enterprise and not the putative victim who may suffer harm must control the risk. . . .

To appreciate the uninsurability of the risks that a broad-based strict liability system would assign to enterprises, it is useful to consider, as before, the problems that would arise in a system that held product manufacturers strictly liable for all the harm their products cause, whether or not those products are defective. Even if the system limited liability to ascertainable risks, manufacturers under such a liability regime could not hope to operate viable insurance systems covering all losses caused by their products. For one thing, product consumers could alter their general patterns of purchase, use, and consumption so as to take advantage of the flat-rate characteristics of insurance pricing in such a system. Moreover, unlike a game of dice, which does not allow players to increase their chances of winning or the amounts of their wagers after the dice have been tossed, under a broad-based strict liability regime, any product user or consumer could, after purchasing any given product, deliberately affect both variables with substantial impunity. Even if defenses such as contributory fault, product misuse, product modification, and the like were available to defendants, such rules could never adequately accommodate the variety of post-distribution product uses and modes of consumption that would dramatically affect an enterprise's exposure to liability. Adverse selection and moral hazard would surely combine to destroy the integrity of a broad-based strict liability system for all product-caused harms.

It follows that the concept of defect is a necessary condition to maintaining a viable system of products liability for generic product risks. As you work through the materials in this chapter, you should pause occasionally to ask whether the liability approach being considered is workable, judged by the criteria advanced in the foregoing analysis.

C. DO WE NEED AN EXTERNAL STANDARD TO DETERMINE DESIGN DEFECT? INFERRING DEFECT FROM PRODUCT MALFUNCTION

Before turning to complex design defect cases where we must go outside the manufacturer's design choice to discover a standard against which to measure the design chosen by the manufacturer, it is necessary to identify the easy design defect case. Indeed, the easy design defect case is so basic that often it is not even identified as one of design defect. You will recall that Chapter One set forth §3 of the Products Liability Restatement, p.40, supra, which provides that one can draw a res ipsa-like inference of defect without proof of the specific nature of the defect "when the incident that harmed the plaintiff: (a) was of a kind that ordinarily occurs as a result of product defect, and (b) was not, in the particular case, solely the result of causes other than product defect existing at the time of sale or distribution."

Most often these res ipsa-type inferences are drawn when a product contains a manufacturing defect that causes it to fail in circumstances under which an inference of defect is compelling. However, it is possible that when a product fails to perform its manifestly intended function the culprit was a design error. Like the manufacturing defect case where the built-in standard against which the product is measured is the product's "intended design," when the product fails in its core uses, the built-in standard against which it is measured is the product's "intended function." Comment *b* to §3 and several illustrations clarify this point.

Restatement (Third) of Torts: Products Liability
(1998)

§3. CIRCUMSTANTIAL EVIDENCE SUPPORTING INFERENCE OF PRODUCT DEFECT

. . .

COMMENT:

. . .

b. Requirement that the harm be of a kind that ordinarily occurs as a result of product defect. . . . Although the rules in this Section [allowing for an inference of defect to be drawn based on product malfunction] most often apply to manufacturing defects, occasionally a product design causes the product to malfunction in a manner identical to that which would ordinarily be caused by a manufacturing defect. Thus, an aircraft may inadvertently be designed in such a way that, in new condition and while flying within its intended performance parameters, the wings suddenly and unexpectedly fall off, causing harm. In theory, of course, the plaintiff in such a case would be able to show how other units in the same production line were designed, leading to a showing of a reasonable alternative design under §2(b). As a practical matter, however, when the incident involving the aircraft is one that ordinarily occurs as a result of product defect, and evidence in the particular case establishes that the harm was not solely the result of causes other than product defect existing at time of sale, it should not be necessary for the plaintiff to incur the cost of proving whether the failure resulted from a manufacturing defect or from a defect in the design of the product. Section 3 allows the trier of fact to draw the inference that the product was defective whether due to a manufacturing defect or a design defect. Under those circumstances, the plaintiff need not specify the type of defect responsible for the product malfunction. . . .

ILLUSTRATIONS:

3. Mary purchased a new automobile. She drove the car 1,000 miles without incident. One day she stopped the car at a red light and leaned back to rest until the light changed. Suddenly the seat collapsed backward, causing Mary to hit the accelerator and

the car to shoot out into oncoming traffic and collide with another car. Mary suffered harm in the ensuing collision. As a result of the collision, Mary's car was set afire, destroying the seat assembly. The incident resulting in the harm is of a kind that ordinarily occurs as a result of product defect. Mary need not establish whether the seat assembly contained a manufacturing defect or a design defect.

4. Same facts as in Illustration 3, except that the seat-back assembly failed when Mary, while stopped at the red light, was rear-ended by another automobile at 40 m.p.h. Mary cannot make out liability under this Section. The product did not fail to function in a manner supporting an inference of defect since the collapse of the seat is not the kind of incident that ordinarily occurs as a result of product defect. Liability must be established under the rules set forth in §§1 and 2.

Where to draw the line between cases that allow for an inference of defect without specifying the nature of the defect and cases that require proof of an external standard against which to measure the defendant's design is a matter of common sense. This problem has been with us for a long time. In the negligence context, courts have always had to struggle regarding how far one could push the res ipsa doctrine and when to require direct proof of defendant's fault. Nonetheless, no one can conclude that res ipsa eats up the entirety of negligence law. Similarly, the cases in which one can draw an appropriate inference of product defect from product failure will not eat up the entirety of design defect law. The cases where an inference of defect can clearly be drawn are usually factually compelling and intuitively apparent. When that is the case, a plaintiff should not be put through the pains of proving a reasonable alternative design or establishing defect by some other external standard. The circumstantial inference of defect should carry the day.

D. RISK-UTILITY STANDARDS FOR DETERMINING DESIGN DEFECT

1. The Reasonable Alternative Design Standard for Determining Design Defect

It should not be surprising that in searching for a test for design defect, courts would look to the risk-utility test developed by Learned Hand in United States v. Carroll Towing Co., 159 F.2d 169 (2d Cir. 1947) (see Chapter One). If that test is capable of determining whether a bargee was reasonable in leaving his vessel rather than incurring the costs occasioned by his remaining on board, it should also be able to determine whether a product is reasonably designed without certain safety features. Indeed, the *Carroll Towing* decision may be said to have involved the question of "How should a reasonable barge operation be designed?"

In Thibault v. Sears, Roebuck and Co., 395 A.2d 843 (N.H. 1978), the court indicated that when a warning could not eliminate the risk of harm, it would judge the adequacy of the design using risk-utility standards. In that case, the plaintiff had his foot caught under the housing of a power lawnmower while mowing up and down on a steep slope. Despite the instruction booklet warning not to mow up and down, the plaintiff thought he could do so, given the length of the slope. While mowing, he lost his balance and fell. He instinctively gripped the handle of the mower, and when he came to rest at the end of the slope, his foot was under the housing, badly mangled. The plaintiff contended that the injury could have been avoided had the mower been equipped with a rear trailing guard. In reviewing the elements of plaintiff's prima facie case, the court said:

> In a strict liability case alleging defective design, the plaintiff must first prove the existence of a "defective condition unreasonably dangerous to the user." In determining unreasonable danger, courts should consider factors such as social utility and desirability. The utility of the product must be evaluated from the point of view of the public as a whole, because a finding of liability for defective design could result in the removal of an entire product line from the market. Some products are so important that a manufacturer may avoid liability as a matter of law if he has given proper warnings. In weighing utility and desirability against danger, courts should also consider whether the risk of danger could have been reduced without significant impact on product effectiveness and manufacturing cost. For example, liability may attach if the manufacturer did not take available and reasonable steps to lessen or eliminate the danger of even a significantly useful and desirable product. Id. at 846.

As case law developed, it became clear that, in cases not involving malfunction, the availability of a reasonable alternative design was not merely a consideration to be taken into account in determining defect — it was a requisite for the imposition of liability for defective design.

Restatement (Third) of Torts: Products Liability
(1998)

§1. LIABILITY OF COMMERCIAL SELLER OR DISTRIBUTOR FOR HARM CAUSED BY DEFECTIVE PRODUCTS

One engaged in the business of selling or otherwise distributing products who sells or distributes a defective product is subject to liability for harm to persons or property caused by the defect.

§2. CATEGORIES OF PRODUCT DEFECT

A product

. . .

(b) is defective in design when the foreseeable risks of harm posed by the product could have been reduced or avoided by the adoption of a reasonable alternative design by the seller or other distributor, or a predecessor in the commercial chain of distribution, and the omission of the alternative design renders the product not reasonably safe.

COMMENT:

f. Design defects: factors relevant in determining whether the omission of a reasonable alternative design renders a product not reasonably safe. Subsection (b) states that a product is defective in design if the omission of a reasonable alternative design renders the product not reasonably safe. A broad range of factors may be considered in determining whether an alternative design is reasonable and whether its omission renders a product not reasonably safe. The factors include, among others, the magnitude and probability of the foreseeable risks of harm, the instructions and warnings accompanying the product, and the nature and strength of consumer expectations regarding the product, including expectations arising from product portrayal and marketing. See Comment g. The relative advantages and disadvantages of the product as designed and as it alternatively could have been designed may also be considered. Thus, the likely effects of the alternative design on production costs; the effects of the alternative design on product longevity, maintenance, repair, and esthetics; and the range of consumer choice among products are factors that may be taken into account. A plaintiff is not necessarily required to introduce proof on all of these factors; their relevance, and the relevance of other factors, will vary from case to case. Moreover, the factors interact with one another. For example, evidence of the magnitude and probability of foreseeable harm may be offset by evidence that the proposed alternative design would reduce the efficiency and the utility of the product. On the other hand, evidence that a proposed alternative design would increase production costs may be offset by evidence that product portrayal and marketing created substantial expectations of performance or safety, thus increasing the probability of foreseeable harm. Depending on the mix of these factors, a number of variations in the design of a given product may meet the test in Subsection (b). On the other hand, it is not a factor under Subsection (b) that the imposition of liability would have a negative effect on corporate earnings or would reduce employment in a given industry.

When evaluating the reasonableness of a design alternative, the overall safety of the product must be considered. It is not sufficient that the alternative design would have reduced or prevented the harm suffered by the plaintiff if it would also have introduced into the product other dangers of equal or greater magnitude.

While a plaintiff must prove that a reasonable alternative design would have reduced the foreseeable risks of harm, Subsection (b) does not require the plaintiff to produce expert testimony in every case. Cases arise in which the feasibility of a reasonable alternative design is obvious and understandable to laypersons and therefore expert testimony is unnecessary to support a finding that the product should have been designed differently and more safely. For example, when a manufacturer sells a soft stuffed toy with hard plastic buttons that are easily removable and likely to choke and suffocate a small child who foreseeably attempts to swallow them, the plaintiff should be able to reach the trier of fact with a claim that buttons on such a toy should be an integral part of the toy's fabric itself (or otherwise be unremovable by an infant) without hiring an expert to demonstrate the feasibility of an alternative safer design. Furthermore, other products already available on the market may serve the same or very similar function at lower risk and at comparable cost. Such products may serve as reasonable alternatives to the product in question.

In many cases, the plaintiff must rely on expert testimony. Subsection (b) does not, however, require the plaintiff to produce a prototype in order to make out a prima facie case. Thus, qualified expert testimony on the issue suffices, even though the expert has produced no prototype, if it reasonably supports the conclusion that a reasonable alternative design could have been practically adopted at the time of sale. . . .

A test that considers such a broad range of factors in deciding whether the omission of an alternative design renders a product not reasonably safe requires a fair allocation of proof between the parties. To establish a prima facie case of defect, the plaintiff must prove the availability of a technologically feasible and practical alternative design that would have reduced or prevented the plaintiff's harm. Given inherent limitations on access to relevant data, the plaintiff is not required to establish with particularity the costs and benefits associated with adoption of the suggested alternative design.

In sum, the requirement of Subsection (b) that a product is defective in design if the foreseeable risks of harm could have been reduced by a reasonable alternative design is based on the common-sense notion that liability for harm caused by product designs should attach only when harm is reasonably preventable. For justice to be achieved, Subsection (b) should not be construed to create artificial and unreasonable barriers to recovery.

The necessity of proving a reasonable alternative design as a predicate for establishing design defect is, like any factual element in a case, addressed initially to the courts. Sufficient evidence must be presented so that reasonable persons could conclude that a reasonable alternative could have been practically adopted. Assuming that a court concludes that sufficient evidence on this issue has been presented, the issue is then for the trier of fact. This Restatement takes no position regarding the specifics of how a jury should be instructed. So long as jury instructions are generally consistent with the rule of law set forth in Subsection (b), their specific form and content are matters of local law.

a. Defining the Standard for Determining Design Defect

Smith v. Louisville Ladder Co.
237 F.3d 515 (5th Cir. 2001)

W. EUGENE DAVIS, Circuit Judge:

This is an appeal from a judgment entered on a jury verdict for the plaintiff, Rodger Nelson Smith ("Smith"), in a products liability action against Louisville Ladder Corp. ("Louisville"). . . . We conclude that the record evidence does not support any of Smith's theories of recovery. We therefore reverse and render judgment for Louisville.

I.

Rodger Smith worked as a technician for Longview Cable Company ("Longview"), which provided cable television service in the Longview, Texas area. At the time of his accident in April 1995, Smith had been employed by Longview for approximately one and one-half years. Longview purchased the extension ladder and hook assembly in use at the time of Smith's accident from Louisville.

On the day of Smith's injury, he was assigned a routine repair job that required him to rest the ladder against a cable strand located some twenty feet off the ground. Smith placed the cable line inside the U-shaped hooks that extended from the top of the ladder and rested the ladder against the cable. The base of the ladder was on the ground approximately five feet from a utility pole to which the overhead cable was attached. Because of its weight, the cable sloped down slightly as it moved from the pole.

Smith climbed the ladder without securing the ladder to the pole or any other stationary object. Smith's plan was to secure himself to the ladder with his safety belt when he reached the top of the ladder and then use a hand line to attach the ladder to the utility pole. After Smith climbed to the top of the ladder, he reached for his safety belt and his weight shifted, causing the ladder to slide to his left down the natural slope of the cable. The ladder slid sideways for some distance with Smith hanging onto the ladder. When the ladder reached a position at or near the low point of the line between the two utility poles to which it was attached, one of the hooks came off the line, and the ladder twisted and came to an abrupt halt. Unable to maintain his grip on the ladder, Smith fell to the ground and was seriously injured.

Lateral slides of ladders along cables were well recognized risks in the telecommunications industry, and Smith, himself, had experienced several of these slides during his employment with Longview. However, in the earlier slides Smith had attached his safety belt to the ladder before the slide began and because he did not fall from the ladder he suffered no injury. . . .

Following trial, the jury found in favor of Smith . . . and after taking Smith's 15% contributory negligence into account, awarded Smith $1,487,500. The district court entered judgment on the verdict and denied Smith's post-judgment motions. This appeal followed.

II

A. Design Defect

Smith focused most of his time and attention at trial on his theory that the Louisville extension ladder with hook assembly was defective because of the hook's ability to come off the cable during a slide. Smith's expert, Dr. Packman, testified that when the hook disengaged from the cable near the end of Smith's slide, the ladder to which Smith was clinging twisted more violently than it would had the hook remained attached to the cable and he concluded that this additional twist contributed to Smith's fall. Packman introduced the concept of a simple latching device that, when engaged, would close the opening in the hook, encircle the cable and prevent the hook from disengaging from the strand. Under Dr. Packman's concept, the latch remains disengaged until the hook is placed over the cable and the ladder is resting on the cable. The operator, from his position on the ground, would then remotely activate a spring loaded latch by pulling a line running from the latch to the bottom of the ladder. Once the latch was engaged, the hook would no longer be open and in the event of a slide, the hook could not disengage from the cable.

Louisville Ladder argues that Smith did not establish that the hook with Dr. Packman's latch was a "safer alternative design" within the meaning of the Texas statute. To establish a design defect, Section 82.005 of the Texas Civil Practice and Remedies Code requires a claimant "to prove by a preponderance of the evidence that: (1) there was a safer alternative design; and (2) the defect was a producing cause of the personal injury property damage or death for which the claimant seeks recovery." Subsection (b) states:

> (b) In this section, "safer alternative design" means a product design other than the one actually used that in reasonable probability:
> (1) would have prevented or significantly reduced the risk of the claimant's personal injury, property damage, or death without substantially impairing the product's utility; and
> (2) was economically and technologically feasible at the time the product left the control of the manufacturer or seller by the application of existing or reasonably achievable scientific knowledge.

We found only one Texas case discussing the proof necessary to establish a safer alternative design under this statute. In General Motors Corp. v. Sanchez, 997 S.W.2d 584 (Tex. 1999), the plaintiff's expert testified that his alternative design of the General Motors transmission would prevent internal forces in the transmission from moving the gear selector toward "reverse" rather than "park" when the driver inadvertently leaves the lever in a position between "reverse" and "park." According to plaintiff's expert, his proposed design change would eliminate this spontaneous movement 99% of the time. The court held that this testimony was sufficient to allow the jury to conclude that plaintiff had established a safer alternative design. Id. at 592.

In our case, Smith completely relies on Dr. Packman's evidence and testimony to establish a safer alternate design. Packman testified that his spring loaded latch, by preventing the hook from disengaging from the cable, would make the jolt at the end of the slide less violent, and, therefore, the worker would have a better chance of hanging onto the ladder. He conducted videotaped experiments for the purpose of establishing this fact. In the first experiment, he placed a 200-pound weight on a ladder with hooks like those found on the Louisville Ladder and then precipitated a slide to demonstrate the jerk that would occur when one of the hooks disengaged from the strand. For the second experiment, Dr. Packman videotaped a slide involving hooks that encircled the cable. This experiment demonstrated a less violent jerk at the end of the slide.

The only conclusion Dr. Packman was able to reach was that his alternative design would result in a less violent jerk on the ladder at the end of slide. Unlike the expert who testified in *General Motors,* Dr. Packman was unable to quantify this reduction in force and was unable to say that Smith or another worker could stay on the ladder in a slide where the hook was prevented from disengaging from the cable. The most Dr. Packman could say was that his design alteration would diminish the possibility of the worker's falling off because there was some reduction in the jerk.

Furthermore, Dr. Packman's concept of the latching device to close the open end of the hook around the cable was a preliminary concept. At the time of trial he admitted that he had considered several possible ways a man on the ground (or some distance up the ladder) could operate the latch mechanism but had not settled on any particular method. He agreed that his design was preliminary and that he was not ready to recommend it to a manufacturer. In addition, Packman conceded that a person climbing the ladder would find his proposed mechanism somewhat awkward and that using the mechanism could cause the ladder to get out of balance and slide. He was also questioned about a concern that the line to operate the latch mechanism running the length of the ladder has the potential of being a hazard to the person climbing the ladder. Packman agreed that he never evaluated the risks associated with his proposed alternate design due in part to the fact that it was never completed. Packman also conceded that he did not purport to conduct a risk-benefit analysis of his proposed redesign. . . .

After careful review of the record, we conclude that no reasonable jury could have found from the evidence that the latching device Dr. Packman proposed adding to the hook assembly was a safer alternative design as defined by the Texas statute. Dr. Packman conceded that his proposed alternate design would not assist in preventing the hook from sliding on the cable. He also agreed that the only benefit a worker would derive from the alternate design was a reduced jerk at the end of the slide. He was therefore unable to say that his alternate design would have prevented Mr. Smith's fall. Therefore, we conclude that the evidence fails to establish that the alternative design would have "significantly" reduced the risk of Mr. Smith's injury.

Furthermore, Dr. Packman conceded that he made no risk-benefit analysis including what additional hazards would be created in implementing his proposed alternative design. Thus, Dr. Packman's testimony does not establish that his proposed design would not have substantially impaired the ladder's utility. The jury's finding of design defect, therefore, cannot stand. . . .

[The court's discussion of other grounds for liability is omitted.]

IV

For the above stated reasons, we conclude that Smith failed to present sufficient evidence at trial to support any of his theories of recovery. The district court's judgment is, therefore, reversed and judgment is rendered in favor of Louisville.

REVERSED and RENDERED.

DENNIS, Circuit Judge dissenting:. . . .

The Texas Supreme Court and appeals courts have drawn on common law, statutes, and the Restatements in expounding the state's products liability laws. . . .

In Turner v. General Motors Corp., the Texas Supreme Court discussed the strict liability standard of "defectiveness" as applied in design defect cases. The court held that, in a design defect case, evidence is admissible upon the factors of risk and utility, such as the product's utility to users and to the public as a whole balanced against the likelihood and severity of injury from its use; the availability of an alternative product that would fill the same need without being unsafe or unreasonably costly; the ability to eliminate the product's unsafe character without significantly impairing its utility or increasing its cost; the consumer's awareness of the product's inherent dangers; the avoidability of those dangers because of their obvious nature or because of warnings supplied by the manufacturer; and the ordinary consumer's expectations. However, the court also held that the jury must be instructed only in general terms to consider the utility of the product and the risks involved in its use, and that the jury should not be instructed to balance specifically enumerated factors. . . . "The Texas Supreme

Court has never explicitly made proof of each balancing factor a distinct element of a strict liability claim. . . . And certainly, that the jury is instructed in ultimate terms without detailing the criteria is at odds with the notion that proof of each is required." (citations, footnotes and internal quotations omitted). . . .

In 1993, Texas codified the safer alternative design factor, making it an essential element of a design defect claim. TPLA §82.005. Section 82.005 does not attempt to state all the elements of a design defect claim, however. For example, it does not define design defect or negate the common law requirement that such a defect render the product unreasonably dangerous. The statute was not intended to, and does not, supplant the Texas common law risk-utility analysis Texas has for years employed in determining whether a defectively designed product is unreasonably dangerous. That analysis still permits strict liability parties to direct their evidence to the various balancing criteria listed in *Turner,* while the jury can be instructed only in general terms and cannot be required to perform a balancing of enumerated factors. Id. at 256 n.6. The only change rendered by section 82.005 is that it converts two elements — a safer alternative design and producing cause — to necessary, though not sufficient, elements in proving a defective design claim. . . .

Subsequent to the enactment of section 82.005, the Texas Supreme Court, in expounding Texas's strict tort liability design defect law, has often relied upon other sources consistent with section 82.005, especially the Restatement (Third) of Torts: Products Liability. . . .

For all of the foregoing reasons, I believe that the Texas Supreme Court would follow Restatement Third: Products Liability §2 and its comments with respect to design defects, especially when those provisions are consistent with and complementary to Texas statutory and common law. In addition to those already adopted or followed by the Texas Supreme Court, other provisions of the section 2 comments have particular relevance in the present case.

[The court excerpts Comment *f* to §2(b), set out supra.]

The majority clearly errs in proceeding to decide this case as if, under Texas law, the plaintiff in a design defect case is absolutely required to present an expert to mathematically quantify risk and utility evidence and to balance risk and utility factors. In a Texas design defect case, evidence is admissible as to many factors, including risk and utility, such as utility of the product to the user, usefulness to the public, and the gravity and likelihood of injury from its use, availability of a suitable substitute product taking into consideration cost of production and any impairment to usefulness, public knowledge or obviousness of dangers of the product, suitable warnings, and expectations of the ordinary consumer. A plaintiff is not necessarily required to introduce proof on all of these factors; their relevance and the relevance of other factors, will vary from case to case. See Temple EasTex, Inc. v. Old Orchard Creek Partners, Ltd., 848 S.W.2d 724, 731 (Tex. App.-Dallas 1992); Restatement (Third) of Torts: Products Liability §2, comment *f* (1998); *accord Shipp,* 750 F.2d at 421. Moreover, under Texas law, it is *the jury's function* to weigh risks and utilities by deciding whether the product was defectively designed, taking into consideration the utility of the product and the risk involved in its use. . . . The jury can be instructed only in general terms, however, and cannot be required to balance specifically enumerated factors. . . . The notion of mathematical "quantification" appears to be the majority's own invention; no Texas case or law demands expert mathematical quantification of risk or utility factors as a sufficiency of evidence or proof requirement in a products liability case. . . .

The majority departs from Texas law again in holding that the alternative design presented by Dr. Packman was not valid because he had not introduced a model of a spring loaded cable hook. The Texas products liability law does not, however, require the plaintiff to produce a prototype in order to make out a prima facie case. "'Qualified expert testimony on the issue suffices, even though the expert has produced no prototype, if it reasonably supports the conclusion that a reasonable alternative design could have been practically adopted at the time of sale.'" *Sanchez,* 997 S.W.2d 584, 592 (Tex. 1999) (quoting Restatement (Third) of Torts: Products Liability §2, cmt. *f* (1998)) . . . .

Based on the foregoing data, Dr. Packman testified that in his opinion the alternative design that he proposed, consisting of a cable hook held closed during engagement by a spring latch, would have prevented or significantly reduced the risk of Mr. Smith's injury; that the alternative design was feasible because the technology of the spring latch was simple, well-known and had been in existence for a very long time; that spring latches were readily available — indeed, agreeing to the statement that they were "available in hardware stores pretty much everywhere" — when the ladder was manufactured; that its attachment to the cable hook would not have impaired the utility of the product significantly; and that a spring-loaded latch was already incorporated into the ladder's design by Louisville Ladder in the ladder's rung-lock mechanism, making the spring latch concept an "absolutely obvious" one of which the defendant was fully aware. Mr. Van Bree, the defendant's representative, testified that Louisville Ladder did, indeed, incorporate the spring-latch design into its rung-lock mechanism, though it had not tested the idea of incorporating the concept into the cable hook. . . .

[T]he evidence upon which the majority relies — that due to the imponderable variables none of the experts, including Dr. Packman, were able to mathematically quantify either the likelihood and gravity of the risk or the amount of risk reduction through the use of the alternative design; that Dr. Packman did not manufacture a prototype of his suggested alternative design; that Dr. Packman testified only that the alternative design would prevent cable hook disengagement and thereby reduce torsional forces and in turn reduce the risk and severity of accidents; and that Dr. Packman frankly conceded that he could not testify as to whether the alternative design would have prevented Mr. Smith's accident altogether — "although relevant, is certainly not dispositive." *Reeves,* 530 U.S. 133, . . . In concluding that this testimony so overwhelmed the evidence favoring Mr. Smith that no rational trier of fact could have found that Mr. Smith proved that the defendant's open cable hook was defectively designed for the purposes for which it was sold, the majority impermissibly substitutes its judgment concerning the weight of the evidence for the jury's. . . . I must dissent.

Many state legislatures and courts require that, in order to succeed in a case alleging defective design, a plaintiff must establish the availability of a reasonable alternative design. Mississippi, Ohio, Louisiana, and New Jersey have enacted reasonable alternative design statutes similar to that of Texas. Most states have adopted the reasonable alternative design requirement as part of their common law of products liability, even if they have not yet considered whether to recognize §2(b) of the Products Liability Restatement.

In Wright v. Brooke Group, Ltd., 652 N.W.2d 159 (Iowa 2002), in response to a certified question from the United States District Court requesting direction as to the appropriate standard for determining whether cigarettes are unreasonably dangerous, the Iowa Supreme Court adopted §2 of the Products Liability Restatement. The court held that the consumer expectations test was not appropriate for deciding whether a product was defectively designed. Instead, the court opted for a risk-utility test and held that such a test required plaintiff to prove a reasonable alternative design. The court said "[W]e think that it [the Restatement] sets forth an intellectually sound set of legal principles for product defect cases." Id. at 167. In another certified question case, Jones v. NordicTrack, Inc., 550 S.E.2d 101 (Ga. 2001), plaintiff tripped over a blunt chrome leg that protruded from a NordicTrack Ski Exerciser. Defendant argued that the machine was not "in use" at the time of the injury. The court held that there was no such requirement as a predicate to bringing a case for design defect in Georgia; the question instead was whether the product met risk-utility guidelines. Citing the Products Liability Restatement §2, the court acknowledged that under risk-utility standards "[T]he 'heart' of a design defect case is the reasonableness of selecting from among alternative product designs and adopting the safest feasible one." Id. at 103.

A number of other courts require plaintiff to prove a reasonable alternative design in order to make out a prima facie case. See, e.g., Vines v. Beloit Corp., 631 So. 2d 1003, 1006 (Ala. 1994) (summary judgment granted to defendant where plaintiff failed to show reasonable alternative design for machine which processes pulp wood into paper); Reeves v. Cincinnati, Inc., 439 N.W.2d 326, 329 (Mich. Ct. App. 1989) (to make a prima facie case "requires a showing of alternative safety devices . . . effective as a reasonable means of minimizing the foreseeable risk of danger"); Peck v. Bridgeport Machines, Inc., 237 F.3d 614 (6th Cir. 2001) (applying Michigan law) (summary judgment for defendant upheld due to plaintiff's failure to present sufficient evidence of reasonable alternative design); Cohen v. Winnebago Ind., Inc., 2000 WL 299459 at *4 (4th Cir. 2000) (applying South Carolina law) ("providing evidence of the existence of an alternative safer, feasible design is part of plaintiff's product liability case under South Carolina law"). Similar expressions are found in cases from Colorado, Delaware, Florida, Kentucky, Massachusetts, Montana, New York, Pennsylvania, Utah, and West Virginia.

With the adoption of the reasonable alternative design requirement, courts have had to face the problem that divided the Fifth Circuit in *Smith*. What quantum of proof is necessary to make out a reasonable alternative? It is rare in tort cases for courts to direct a verdict for a defendant on disputed issues of fact as the majority did in *Smith*. In products liability design defect cases, however, it is not unusual at all for courts to step in and declare that plaintiff has not provided sufficient credible evidence to make out a reasonable alternative design. The reason that courts police design defect cases more aggressively is that the stakes are much higher than they are in the run-of-the-mill negligence case. The societal impact of an erroneous risk-utility decision in the traditional negligence context is limited. Tort cases are fact-sensitive and each case has its own peculiar fact pattern upon which the jury must decide whether the defendant met the societal standard of reasonable care. In design defect cases, once a product has been declared defectively designed the entire product line of that genre of product is open to attack in repetitive litigation. A plaintiff's verdict that withstands appellate scrutiny sends a message to the manufacturer (and ofttimes to an entire industry) that its design standards are not up to snuff. Courts are reluctant to countenance design claims based on a weak factual predicate.

An early Oregon case has been influential. In Wilson v. Piper Aircraft Corp., 577 P.2d 1322 (Or. 1978), plaintiffs, representing their relatives who were killed in the crash of a small airplane, alleged that the fatal crash was caused by engine failure resulting from carburetor icing. The plaintiffs proffered an alternative design that would have eliminated the icing problem. They suggested that had the airplane been equipped with a fuel injection engine, the tragedy could have been averted. In reversing a jury verdict for the plaintiff, the court said:

> If liability for alleged design defects is to "stop somewhere short of the freakish and the fantastic," plaintiff's prima facie case of a defect must show more than the technical possibility of a safer design. . . . It is not proper to submit . . . allegations [of a defective design] to the jury unless the court is satisfied that there is evidence from which the jury could find the suggested alternatives are not only technically feasible but also practicable in terms of cost and the overall design and operation of the product. . . .
>
> There is not . . . any evidence about what effects the substitution of the fuel injected engine in this airplane design would have had upon the airplane's cost, economy of operation, maintenance requirements, over-all performance, or safety in respects other than susceptibility to icing. Id. at 1326-1327.

Similar sentiments were expressed by the court in Troja v. Black & Decker Mfg. Co., 488 A.2d 516 (Md. Ct. Spec. App. 1985). In that case, a radial saw was removed from its metal base in order to be used at a different work site. Once removed from its base the saw lacked the guide fence. Plaintiff amputated his thumb while operating the saw without the guide fence. He alleged that the radial saw was defective in that it did not have an interlock mechanism that would have prevented the saw from operating while not in its permanent fixture. The trial court directed a verdict for the defendant and the court affirmed on appeal. The court held that plaintiff's expert was unable to furnish a practical alternative design incorporating an interlock system, nor was he able to explain how such a system could be integrated into the saw without interfering with the functions for which the guide fence would normally not be employed.

Many courts continue to set a high threshold for proof of a reasonable alternative design. See, e.g., Honda of America Mfg., Inc. v. Norman, 104 S.W.3d 600, 608 (Tex. App. 2003) (insufficient evidence to support a jury verdict for plaintiff that seat-belt mechanism was defectively designed since plaintiff failed to show the economic feasibility of the alternative design or that the alternative design would not impose "equal or greater risk of harm under all relevant circumstances"); Quintana-Ruiz v. Hyundai Motor Corp., 303 F.3d 62 (1st Cir. 2002) (applying Puerto Rican law) (insufficient evidence to support a jury verdict for plaintiff that air bag should have had a higher deployment threshold; evidence of technological feasibility of alternative design does not suffice where there was evidence that the higher deployment threshold would have increased the risk of injury in lower intensity crashes); Wolf v. Stanley Works, 757 So. 2d

316 (Miss. Ct. App. 2000) (upholding summary judgment for defendant, noting that alternative design for automatic door-opening system unsustainable where competing model had shorter life expectancy, was expensive to implement, and likely to fail and cause injury); Austin v. Wil-Burt Co., 232 F. Supp. 2d 682 (N.D. Miss. 2002) (granting summary judgment to defendant where plaintiff unable to establish practical feasibility of RAD of broadcast mast designed to prevent contact with electrical wires); General Motors Corp. v. Harper, 61 S.W.2d 118 (Tex. App. 2001) (reversing jury verdict in favor of plaintiff where alternative seat-belt design would have introduced greater risk of impacting steering wheel during collision).

For the most part, however, the question of sufficiency of the evidence on reasonable alternative design is for the jury. See, e.g., Cacevic v. Simplimatic Eng'g Co., 645 N.W.2d 287 (Mich. Ct. App. 2001) (suggested alternative design of a plexiglass safety guard on palletizer machine that would have prevented plaintiff access to danger at point of operation was reasonable when the cost of the safety guard was $1000 on a $64,000 machine); Buongiovanni v. General Motors Corp., 1998 WL 1107329 (Pa. Com. Pl. 1998) (jury verdict for plaintiff of $28 million predicated on claim that seat of her Chevette was not sufficiently rigid and caused the seat to collapse backward when the car was struck from behind injuring the plaintiff was upheld; expert testimony supported the contention that reasonable alternative design could have been adopted and contention that the more rigid seat would create addition risks in other scenarios was for the jury to decide); Clay v. Ford Motor Co., 215 F.3d 663 (6th Cir. 2000) (applying Ohio law) (jury verdict upheld where "reasonable minds could differ" whether feasible alternative design of a car's beam suspension system would pose less risk than design adopted).

Scholarly commentary written prior to the Restatement project agrees overwhelmingly with the risk-utility/reasonable alternative design approach. See, e.g., M. Stuart Madden, Products Liability vol. 1 at 299 (2d ed. 1988) ("[T]he majority rules posits that plaintiff cannot establish a prima facie case of defective design without evidence of a technologically feasible, and practicable, alternative to defendant's product that was available at the time of manufacture."). See generally Sheila L. Birnbaum, Unmasking the Test for Design Defect: From Negligence [to Warranty] to Strict Liability to Negligence, 33 Vand. L. Rev. 593 (1980); Richard A. Epstein, Products Liability: The Search for the Middle Ground, 56 N.C. L. Rev. 643 (1976); Michael Hoenig, Product Designs and Strict Tort Liability: Is There a Better Approach?, 8 Sw. U. L. Rev. 109 (1976); W. Page Keeton, Products Liability—Design Hazards and the Meaning of Defect, 10 Cumb. L. Rev. 293 (1979); William Powers, Jr., A Modest Proposal to Abandon Strict Products Liability, 1991 U. Ill. L. Rev. 639 (1991); Gary T. Schwartz, Foreward: Understanding Products Liability, 67 Cal. L. Rev. 435 (1979); John W. Wade, On Product "Design Defects" and Their Actionability, 33 Vand. L. Rev. 551 (1980).

In the post-Restatement era, including law review articles written during the project, the commentators have been more shrill on either side of the RAD debate. See, e.g., Richard L. Cupp, Jr., Defining the Boundaries of "Alternative Design" Under the Restatement (Third) of Torts: The Nature and Role of Substitute Products in Design Defect Analysis, 63 Tenn. L. Rev. 329 (1996); Theodore S. Jankowski, Focusing on Quality and Risk: The Central Role of Reasonable Alternatives in Evaluating Design and Warning Decisions, 36 S. Tex. L. Rev. 283

(1995); Philip H. Corboy, The Not-So-Quiet Revolution: Rebuilding Barriers to Jury Trial in the Proposed Restatement (Third) of Torts: Products Liability, 61 Tenn. L. Rev. 1043 (1994); Marshall S. Shapo, In Search of the Law of Products Liability, The ALI Restatement Project, 48 Vand. L. Rev. 631 (1995); David G. Owen, Defectiveness Restated: Exploding the Strict Liability Myth, 1996 U. Ill. L. Rev. 743 (1996); James A. Henderson, Jr. & Aaron D. Twerski, Achieving Consensus on Defective Product Design, 83 Cornell L. Rev. 867 (1998).

PROBLEM THIRTEEN

Fun Playgrounds, Inc., one of your firm's clients, manufactures and markets playground systems to schools and municipalities in the State of New California. Rather than selling individual pieces of equipment such as slides, monkey bars, etc., they design and install the entire playground. This includes providing the layout for the playground equipment; the grass, walkways, benches, and protective padding; and fencing, signs, water fountains, and lighting. After a layout plan is agreed upon, Fun Playgrounds installs all the equipment.

New Country Day School, an upscale private elementary school, contracted with Fun Playgrounds to install an elaborate playground on its grounds. After completion, during the first week that the playground was put to use, Bobby Spark, a precocious 5-year-old, suffered severe brain damage while using the playground. Bobby had climbed up seven rungs of an eight-rung ladder attached to a slide. Scott Kenner, a classmate, was at the top of the ladder. Apparently, Bobby was impatient with Scott for taking too much time before getting on the slide, and gave Scott a push. Scott responded in kind. Bobby fell backwards off the ladder and landed on his head.

Bobby's parents have consulted with a plaintiff's law firm about the possibility of bringing a products liability action against Fun Playgrounds, Inc. The firm has notified the client of the pending claim in writing. The case has been assigned to you for evaluation, and you have conducted a preliminary investigation. Your experts tell you that Bobby's brain damage was almost certainly occasioned by the intensity of the contact of the playground surface with his head. The protective padding over the portions of the playground surface surrounding larger pieces of equipment is three inches of pulverized rubber material. The experts say that if the padding had been six inches thick Bobby would probably have escaped with only minor injuries. Your research as to the thickness of padding for young childrens' playgrounds reveals that standard padding in the playground industry is three inches thick. Playground safety regulations require only three inches; Fun's playgrounds conform to all applicable regulations. The classic text on playground design suggests that if you exceed three inches for padding, children find that the playground is too safe and unchallenging. If the children find the playground boring they will tend to avoid the playground and go and play in the street, where they tend to engage in more dangerous activities such as fighting or using slingshots. The text goes on to say that there are real limitations regarding the levels of safety that can, or should, be designed into playground equipment. The text strongly suggests that much of the residual risk of playground injury must be dealt with by providing adult supervision over children of tender age.

You have shared this information with a senior partner who asks you to write

> **authors' dialogue 9**
>
> **AARON:** Jim, as big boosters of the reasonable alternative design test for defect, we have taken our share of lumps from some courts and commentators that just don't like it. Why is it that reasonable people disagree with such a common sense test for defect?
>
> **JIM:** Well for one, the acronym (RAD) hasn't helped any. It sounds like some kind of disease.
>
> **AARON:** Come on, Jim, I'm serious.
>
> **JIM:** Okay, okay. It seems so foreboding, so "RADical." Just look at the majority decision in Smith v. Lousiville Ladder. If the test were some loosey-goosey risk-utility balancing, the majority might have let the jury verdict stand. But once they focused on Reasonable Alternative Design, the court felt that plaintiff had not proved enough to pass directed verdict muster.
>
> **AARON:** Aha, I get it. Some people (especially plaintiffs' trial lawyers) don't like what we did because we sort of rub their noses in the fact that plaintiffs must do more than merely assert defectiveness and let the jury decide. They've got to introduce evidence to support their claims. Being an Orthodox Jew, let me tell you one of my favorite jokes. One member of the clan decides that he wants once in his life to taste ham. (You know that ham is strictly forbidden under Jewish law). Anyway, this guy goes to the deli and points to the ham in the display counter and says, "Give me a half-pound of that." To which the salesperson responds, "Do you mean the ham, sir?" To which the guy with the guilty conscience says, "Who asked you to name it?" You get the point. I'm having enough trouble with eating ham. Don't rub my nose in it. Maybe that's why what we did is unpopular in some circles. We have made them face the music.
>
> **JIM:** I think that there is something to what you say. But it may be more than facing the music. Our critics think the music is too shrill and loud. I think

a memorandum as to whether a claim for reasonable alternative design against Fun Playgrounds, Inc., based on the adequacy of the padding would withstand a motion for summary judgment. He also asks whether the plaintiff might have some other ground for a design defect claim against Fun Playgrounds. The claims have not yet been filed, but he wants to know what may be coming. In preparing your analysis, you are to assume that Smith v. Louisville Ladder Corp., reprinted above, is a decision of the Supreme Court of New California.

PROBLEM FOURTEEN

Carmencita Castrol has consulted your law firm regarding a potential case against Chrysler. Your initial investigation and research reveals the following: Ms. Castrol suffered grievous injuries in a nighttime, head-on collision with a that they would like a "kindler, gentler" version of RAD, one that has a better chance of getting the judges away from directing verdicts and letting almost all cases go to juries.

AARON: Look, Jim, we tried to soften things up by saying that a plaintiff does not have to produce a prototype and that, in our view, risk-utility balancing is not an exact science. But I'll be damned if I want to present mush to courts.

JIM: Hey, wait a minute. I'm on your side. You asked me to explain why our critics don't like us and that's what I did. But let me make one argument against RAD that even I believe has some merit. Some courts have read *Daubert* very strictly and have precluded experts from testifying as to a RAD on the grounds that the RAD has not been subjected to testing. By demanding prototype testing, courts can put a screeching halt to some pretty good RAD cases.

AARON: The cure for that is to read *Daubert* with some common sense. Whether a scientific thesis has been tested and subjected to peer review is only one factor in *Daubert*. There is nothing wrong with RAD. There may be a whole lot wrong with judges who read *Daubert* as if it were the Ten Commandments.

JIM: Once again you're right. But, our test sure plays into the hands of the hard hats. I still believe that what we have done is right. RAD is the only intellectually honest way of dealing with the design standard. And you know, maybe the majority opinion in *Smith* was right. The expert expressed confidence in his RAD but then he said his design was preliminary and he was not prepared to recommend it to a manufacturer for implementation. Maybe the expert gets an "A" for honesty, but a RAD should certainly be more than a good idea. At the very least, the expert should testify that RAD could be immediately implemented. "I need to think about it some more" is a very sad RAD.

Chrysler automobile being driven by Norman Whitehead on a highway outside of Pittsburgh, New California. The state police tested Mr. Whitehead shortly after the collision, and his blood alcohol level was recorded at 0.19, well in excess of legal intoxication. An expert for the plaintiff testified that at that level most people would have been unconscious. Mr. Whitehead's intoxication caused him to drive his automobile across the median line of the highway into Ms. Castrol's lane, hitting Ms. Castrol's automobile head-on.

The potential case against Chrysler would be based on a claim that the auto manufacturer should have foreseen that drunken drivers would attempt to operate its automobiles, and should have accordingly provided one or another of three devices in its basic design that would have prevented Mr. Whitehead from starting his automobile on the night in question. The first of these devices is a chemical breath analysis test built into the dashboard of the vehicle, which the driver would have to pass (by blowing into a plastic tube) before the vehicle could be started. The second is a test of alertness in which the steering wheel would be used to keep a needle on the dashboard within certain marks before the car would start. The third anti-drunk-driver device is a system in which five digits are flashed for a brief time on a screen, after which the driver must key in the first three digits, depress the brake pedal, and then key in the last two digits before the car can be started. When a driver "flunks" one of these tests, he is given one more chance, after which he must wait an hour (regardless of whether he would be able to pass the test within a shorter time period) before being given another chance. All three devices are aimed at keeping intoxicated persons, whose alertness and coordination are presumably impaired, from being able to start their automobiles.

Anti-drunk-driver devices are clearly within existing technology. The literature on this subject in technological journals claim that any one of the devices would prevent 80 to 90 percent of legally intoxicated drivers from starting their cars. It is reasonable to assume that had an anti-drunk-driver device been installed in Whitehead's car, it would almost certainly have prevented him from starting his car on the night in question.

When the adoption of anti-drunk-driver devices was first suggested by People Against Drunk Driving (PADD), auto manufacturers dismissed the idea. They claimed that the reliability of the devices is questionable, and that their high cost of initial installation (in excess of $1,000 per vehicle) would be only a modest down-payment on the costs of maintenance and the aggravations caused by malfunctions. Moreover, subsets of the innocent driver population whose coordination and reflexes may be somewhat below normal (elderly drivers, nervous drivers, and the like) would be "trapped" by the devices, and denied their freedom of movement. Chrysler also argues that the breath analysis device would pick up "false signals" from various forms of perfumes and mouthwashes, and would be especially unreliable. And problems of bypassing the devices, including drunk drivers having the tests taken by less intoxicated passengers, or drivers starting their cars and then proceeding to get drunk, would reduce the utility of such devices.

The senior partner in your firm has misgivings about investing time in a contingent fee case that may go nowhere. He expects that Chrysler will move to dismiss, or if that fails, move for summary judgment. He asks you to prepare a memorandum addressing whether plaintiff could withstand either of these preliminary motions.

In preparing your memorandum you are to assume that Smith v. Louisville Ladder Co., reprinted above, is a decision of the Supreme Court of New California.

b. From Which Perspective Should the Product Be Judged? Time of Sale or Time of Trial?

Assuming that a risk-utility/reasonable alternative design standard has been adopted, one must establish the time as of when the manufacturer (or seller) is to be held accountable to the standard. As of what point in time, for example, should the reasonableness of the defendant's design choices be judged? At the original time of sale? At the time of the accident? At the time of trial? At first blush, it may seem odd that any such questions should arise. No one, it might be presumed, should be held liable for risk information or for technological developments that arose after the distribution of the product. The materials in Section A, supra, demonstrated why a no-fault enterprise liability system was unworkable for generic product hazards. Those materials indicated that, for any insurance system to work, the risks insured against must be ascertainable and quantifiable ahead of time. It follows that to impose liability on manufacturers for risks that were not knowable at the time the products were distributed would render products claims uninsurable. See generally Patricia Munch Danzon, Tort Reform and the Role of Government in Private Insurance Markets, 13 J. Legal Stud. 517 (1984); Alan Schwartz, Products Liability, Corporate Structure and Bankruptcy: Toxic Substances and the Remote Risk Relationship, 14 J. Legal Stud. 689 (1985).

However, before common sense can triumph, many obstacles have to be overcome. Doctrine has become an impediment to clear thinking. The problem is fundamental. Once courts began to focus on risk-utility balancing in conscious design choice cases, the question arose whether strict liability perceptibly differed from negligence. One obvious difference between the two might be the time when information became available to the manufacturer or seller. Negligence, with its focus on the conduct of the manufacturer, would impose liability only when the defendant knew, or a reasonable manufacturer should have known, of the relevant information. In contrast, it might be thought that strict liability would impose liability even though a reasonable manufacturer would not have had access to information that later became available. Thus, courts applying a strict liability standard might deem a product "unreasonably dangerous" even though the manufacturer had acted reasonably in designing and marketing the product.

The possibility of attributing to the manufacturer knowledge that could not have been acquired using reasonable care has created apprehension in the business community. Courts and legislatures have responded to this concern by allowing defendants to make "Who could have known?" arguments in response to strict liability claims based on post-sale knowledge of risk. Although the formulations of these arguments differ from jurisdiction to jurisdiction, in the end and for all practical purposes they reinstate the negligence standard as the operative rule in most cases.

In a 1983 treatment of the time dimension question, Dean Wade identified three separate kinds of knowledge that could be relevant to risk-utility balancing:

(1) knowledge of danger, hazards, or risks that arise from normal use of a product that a manufacturer could have learned of after marketing the product;
(2) scientific and technological developments that have occurred since marketing that could make the product safer; and
(3) product use and misuse that a manufacturer could not have reasonably foreseen at the time of marketing but that the actual experience of consumer use has made available.

See John W. Wade, On the Effect in Product Liability of Knowledge Unavailable Prior to Marketing, 58 N.Y.U. L. Rev. 734, 751-753 (1983). Wade notes that courts differ sharply on the issue of whether they should impute knowledge of dangers to the defendant. As to the issue of technological and economic feasibility, the issue most often dubbed "state of the art," most courts appear unwilling to impute post-marketing knowledge. Wade notes that "while product hazards exist independently of whether anyone knows about them, feasibility is, almost by definition, a function of contemporary perceptions and priorities." Id. at 757-758. Nonetheless, he finds no justification for distinguishing among the various kinds of knowledge.

*(1) Manufacturers' Responsibility for
Post-Sale Increases in Knowledge of Risk*

The problem of unknowable risk can theoretically arise in a design defect case. The analytical quandary this may pose is that if a risk is truly unforeseeable at the time of sale, how can the manufacturer design against it? Nonetheless, several courts have expressed the view that in design defect cases, the seller is charged with knowledge of even unforeseeable risks. See, e.g., Phillips v. Kimwood Mach. Co., 525 P.2d 1033, 1036-1037 (Or. 1974) ("A dangerously defective article would be one which a reasonable person would not put into the stream of commerce *if he had knowledge of its harmful character*"); Voss v. Black & Decker Mfg. Co., 450 N.E.2d 204, 208 (N.Y. 1983) (the standard for design defect is whether, "*if the design defect were known at the time of manufacture,* a reasonable person would conclude that the utility of the product did not outweigh the risk inherent in marketing [the product.]").

In the context of design defect cases we are convinced that debate concerning "foreseeability of risk" belongs to the realm of "how many angels can dance on the head of a pin." The problem almost never arises. In failure-to-warn litigation, the issue of risk foreseeability has practical significance. As we shall see in Chapter Five, all but a small minority of courts impose liability in failure-to-warn cases only when the risk of harm is reasonably foreseeable. However, the overwhelming majority of design defect cases concern mechanical problems whose risks are rarely unforeseeable; the principles of mechanics have not changed much since the time of Sir Isaac Newton. Admittedly, in cases of products that have toxic qualities such as drugs and chemicals, the problem of slumbering risks that suddenly appear after many years of exposure to the product is real. But toxic design defect cases are a rare breed. We search in vain for a standard design defect case in which the problem of risk foreseeability has any practical significance. See Products Liability Restatement §2, Comment *m.* Thus, the statements of courts, such as those set forth above, account for little more than dicta.

The Wisconsin Supreme Court appears to be one of the small minority discounting foreseeability of risk as a requisite for imposing design defect liability. Although we noted that toxic design defect cases are a rare breed, there has recently been some litigation in this area arising from the use of latex gloves. In Green v. Smith & Nephew AHP, Inc., 629 N.W.2d 727 (Wis. 2001), plaintiff brought suit against the manufacturer of latex gloves contending that the gloves contained an excessive level of allergy-causing latex proteins. As a precaution against contracting AIDS, plaintiff health care worker had begun using the latex gloves in 1986 when handling patients. Over the next several years she developed a serious rash over various parts of her body as well as an asthmatic condition. Although latex gloves sold by other manufacturers contained greatly reduced protein levels, there was no scientific knowledge of any allergic reaction to latex proteins at the time of manufacture and sale. The claim was thus that the gloves sold by the defendant with high latex protein were defective and unreasonably dangerous irrespective of the manufacturer's knowledge (or lack thereof) at the time of production. The defendant argued that it should not be held liable for designing gloves with a high latex protein content since it neither knew nor could have known of the risk of harm presented by condition of the product. The jury was instructed that whether defendant knew or could have know of the risk was irrelevant for a claim based in strict liability. On appeal the Wisconsin Supreme Court held that foreseeability of harm is an element of negligence and is not to be considered in a case based on strict liability. Most other jurisdictions disagree. On a nearly identical claim, a California appellate court in Morson v. Superior Court, 109 Cal. Rptr. 2d 343 (Ct. App. 2002) took the view that under risk-utility balancing it would be necessary to consider what was technologically knowable in order to decide whether latex gloves were defectively designed.

Most courts are aware that the issue of foreseeability almost never arises in design defect litigation. If and when such a case were to arise, we predict that the courts would resolve the issue of foreseeability in design cases identically to how they have decided the failure to warn cases. It is not likely that liability for unforeseeable risk will become a staple of either design or warning cases in the foreseeable future.

(2) Manufacturers' Responsibility for Post-Sale Improvements in Risk-Avoidance Techniques

(a) State of the Art as a Defense

The preceding Section deals with the fact that knowledge about product-related risks increases through time. In this Section, we confront the related phenomenon that knowledge regarding ways of reducing and avoiding such risks also increases through time. Thus, persons using or consuming a product known to be risky may do so in the reasonable belief that the risks are unavoidable, only to discover at some future time that a means of avoiding those risks (while still enjoying the benefits of use or consumption) is possible. The question presented by such after-the-fact discovery of risk-avoidance techniques is similar to the question of what to do with the fact that hitherto-unknown risks have subsequently been discovered. Is the manufacturer to be held to time-of-trial knowledge, when such knowledge would not have been available to the defendant earlier, despite the exercise of reasonable care?

If the answer is "yes," then the manufacturer will be held strictly liable for harm caused by its nonnegligent conduct. If the answer is "no," and the plaintiff must prove that a reasonably prudent manufacturer would have discovered the risk-avoidance technique advanced by the plaintiff at trial, then the test for liability will be negligence. A third possibility would be to make the discoverability of the risk-avoidance technique a relevant consideration, but to place upon the defendant the burden of proof on that issue. Presumably, plaintiffs would reach the jury with the issue in most, if not all, cases under such a "shift the burden" approach.

In any event, the issue thus framed has come to be referred to as the "state-of-the-art" issue in American products liability. As is so frequently the case, the phrase means different things to different people. In some jurisdictions, a defendant's product design conforms to the state of the art at the time of distribution if it includes all safety features available at that time that have proven themselves in the marketplace to be cost effective. In other jurisdictions, a defendant's design conforms to the state of the art only if it includes all safety features that were then available by the imaginative use of cutting-edge technology. Consider the position taken by the Texas Supreme Court in the following well-known decision.

Boatland of Houston, Inc. v. Bailey
609 S.W.2d 743 (Tex. 1980)

McGee, J.

This is a product defect case involving an alleged defect in the design of a 16-foot bass boat. The plaintiffs were the widow and adult children of Samuel Bailey, who was killed in a boating accident in May of 1973. They sued under the wrongful death statute, alleging that Samuel Bailey's death occurred because the boat he was operating was defectively designed. The boat had struck a partially submerged tree stump, and Bailey was thrown into the water. With its motor still running, the boat turned sharply and circled back toward the stump. Bailey was killed by the propeller, but it is unclear whether he was struck when first thrown out or after the boat circled back toward him.

Bailey's wife and children sought damages under a strict liability theory from the boat's seller, Boatland of Houston, Inc. At trial, they urged several reasons why the boat was defectively designed, including inadequate seating and control area arrangement, unsafe stick steering and throttle design, and the failure of the motor to automatically turn off when Bailey was thrown from the boat.

The trial court rendered a take-nothing judgment based on the jury's failure to find that the boat was defective and findings favorable to Boatland on several defensive issues. The court of civil appeals, with one justice dissenting, reversed and remanded the cause for a new trial because of errors in the admission of evidence and the submission of the defensive issues. We reverse the judgment of the court of civil appeals and affirm that of the trial court.

Evidence of Design Defect

The alleged design defects are causally related to Bailey's being thrown from the boat and struck by the propeller and not to the boat's hitting the stump. Nevertheless, the same rules of strict liability govern cases in which the defect caused the initial accident and cases in which the defect caused the injuries. Turner v. General Motors Corp., 584 S.W.2d 844, 848 (Tex. 1979).

In Turner v. General Motors Corp., this court discussed the strict liability standard of "defectiveness" as applied in design defect cases. Whether a product was defectively designed requires a balancing by the jury of its utility against the likelihood of and gravity of injury from its use. The jury may consider many factors before deciding whether a product's usefulness or desirability are outweighed by its risks. Their finding on defectiveness may be influenced by evidence of a safer design that would have prevented the injury. Turner v. General

Motors Corp., supra at 849. Because defectiveness of the product in question is determined in relation to safer alternatives, the fact that its risks could be diminished easily or cheaply may greatly influence the outcome of the case.

Whether a product was defectively designed must be judged against the technological context existing at the time of its manufacture. Thus, when the plaintiff alleges that a product was defectively designed because it lacked a specific feature, attention may become focused on the feasibility of that feature — the capacity to provide the feature without greatly increasing the product's cost or impairing usefulness. This feasibility is a relative, not an absolute, concept; the more scientifically and economically feasible the alternative was, the more likely that a jury may find that the product was defectively designed. A plaintiff may advance the argument that a safer alternative was feasible with evidence that it was in actual use or was available at the time of manufacture. Feasibility may also be shown with evidence of the scientific and economic capacity to develop the safer alternative. Thus, evidence of the actual use of, or capacity to use, safer alternatives is relevant insofar as it depicts the available scientific knowledge and the practicalities of applying that knowledge to a product's design. This method of presenting evidence of defective design is not new to the Texas law of product liability.

As part of their case-in-chief, the Baileys produced evidence of the scientific and economic feasibility of a design that would have caused the boat's motor to automatically shut off when Bailey fell out. According to the Baileys, the boat's design should have incorporated an automatic cut-off system or the boat should have been equipped with a safety device known as a "kill switch."

The deposition of J. C. Nessmith, president of Boatland, was read, in which he stated that there were presently several types of "kill switches" available, and that they were now installed by Boatland when it assembled and sold bass boats.

The deposition of Bill Smith, who was a passenger in the boat with Bailey at the time of the accident, was also read. Smith had not heard of automatic kill switches before the accident, but afterwards he got one for his own boat.

The deposition testimony of George Horton, the inventor of a kill switch designed for open-top carriers, was also introduced. Horton began developing his "Quick Kill" in November of 1972 and applied for a patent in January of 1973. According to Horton, his invention required no breakthroughs in the state of the art of manufacturing or production. He stated that his invention was simple: a lanyard connects the operator's body to a device that fits over the ignition key. If the operator moves, the lanyard is pulled, the device rotates, and the ignition switch turns off. When he began to market his "Quick Kill," the response by boat dealers was very positive, which Horton perceived to be due to the filling of a recognized need. He considered the kill switch to be a necessary safety device for a bass boat with stick steering. If the kill switch were hooked up and the operator thrown out, the killing of the motor would prevent the boat from circling back where it came from. Horton also testified that for 30 years racing boats had been using various types of kill switches. Thus, the concept of kill switches was not new.

Robert Swint, a NASA employee who worked with human factors engineering, testified that he had tested a bass boat similar to Bailey's. He concluded that the boat was deficient for several reasons and that these deficiencies played a part in Bailey's death. According to Swint, when the boat struck a submerged object and its operator became incapacitated, the seating and control arrangement caused the boat to go into a hard turn. If the operator were thrown out, the boat was capable of coming back and hitting him. Swint also stated that a kill switch would have cut off the engine and the motor would not have been operative when it hit Bailey.

Jim Buller, who was fishing in the area when Bailey was killed, testified that his own boat did not have a kill switch at that time, but he ordered one within "a matter of days."

Boatland elicited evidence to rebut the Baileys' evidence of the feasibility of equipping boats with kill switches or similar devices in March of 1973, when the boat was assembled and sold. The Baileys had been granted a running objection to all evidence of this nature. In response to the Baileys' evidence that kill switches were presently used by Boatland, Nessmith testified that he did not know of kill switches until the spring of 1973, and first began to sell them a year later.

In response to the Baileys' evidence that the "Quick Kill" was readily available at the time of trial, Horton stated on cross-examination that until he obtained the patent for his "Quick Kill" in 1974 he kept the idea to himself. Before he began to manufacture them, he investigated the market for competitive devices and found none. The only applications of the automatic engine shut-off concept in use at the time were homemade, such as on racing boats. He first became aware of competitive devices in August of 1974.

Boatland introduced other evidence to show that kill switches were not available when Bailey's boat was sold. The deposition of Jimmy Wood, a game warden, was read in which he stated that he first became aware of kill switches in 1975. He testified that he had a "Quick Kill" on his boat since 1976, and he thought it was the only kill switch made. Willis Hudson, who manufactured the boat operated by Bailey, testified that he first became aware of kill switches in 1974 or 1975 and to his knowledge no such thing was available before then. Ralph Cornelius, the vice-president of a marine appliance dealership, testified that kill switches were not available in 1973. The first kill switch he saw to be sold was in 1974, although homemade "crash throttles" or foot buttons had long been in use.

Apart from evidence of the feasibility of an automatic motor cut-off design, evidence was introduced pertaining to whether such a design would have prevented Bailey's injuries. After considering the feasibility and effectiveness of an alternative design and other factors such as the utility and risk, the jury found that the boat was not defective. The trial court rendered judgment for Boatland. The Baileys complained on appeal that the trial court erred in admitting Boatland's evidence that kill switches were unavailable when Bailey's boat was assembled and sold. The court of civil appeals agreed, holding that the evidence was material only to the care exercised by Boatland and thus irrelevant in a strict liability case.

In its appeal to this court, Boatland contends that the court of civil appeals misconstrued the nature and purpose of its evidence. According to Boatland, when the Baileys introduced evidence that kill switches were a feasible safety alternative, Boatland was entitled to introduce evidence that kill switches were not yet available when Bailey's boat was sold and thus were not a feasible design alternative at that time.

The primary dispute concerning the feasibility of an alternative design for Bailey's boat was the "state of the art" when the boat was sold. The admissibility and effect of "state of the art" evidence has been a subject of controversy in both negligence and strict product liability cases. In negligence cases, the reasonableness of the defendant's conduct in placing the product on the market is in issue. Evidence of industry customs at the time of manufacture may be offered by either party for the purpose of comparing the defendant's conduct with industry customs. An offer of evidence of the defendant's compliance with custom to rebut evidence of its negligence has been described as the "state of the art defense." In this connection, it is argued that the state of the art is equivalent to industry custom and is relevant only to the issue of the defendant's negligence and irrelevant to a strict liability theory of recovery.

In our view, "custom" is distinguishable from "state of the art." The state of the art with respect to a particular product refers to the technological environment at the time of its manufacture. This technological environment includes the scientific knowledge, economic feasibility, and the practicalities of implementation when the product was manufactured. Evidence of this nature is important in determining whether a safer design was feasible. The limitations imposed by the state of the art at the time of manufacture may affect the feasibility of a safer design. Evidence of the state of the art in design defect cases has been discussed and held admissible in other jurisdictions. In this case, the evidence advanced by both parties was relevant to the feasibility of designing bass boats to shut off automatically if the operator fell out, or more specifically, the feasibility of equipping bass boats with safety switches.

The Baileys offered state of the art evidence to establish the feasibility of a more safely designed boat: They established that when Bailey's boat was sold in 1973, the general concept of a boat designed so that its motor would automatically cut off had been applied for years on racing boats. One kill switch, the "Quick Kill," was invented at that time and required no mechanical breakthrough. The Baileys were also allowed to show that other kill switches were presently in use and that the defendant itself presently installed them.

Logically, the plaintiff's strongest evidence of feasibility of an alternative design is its actual use by the defendant or others at the time of manufacture. Even if a safer alternative was not being used, evidence that it was available, known about, or capable of being developed is relevant in determining its feasibility. In contrast, the defendant's strongest rebuttal evidence is that a particular design alternative was impossible due to the state of the art. Yet the defendant's ability to rebut the plaintiff's evidence is not limited to showing that a particular alternative was impossible; it is entitled to rebut the plaintiff's evidence of feasibility with evidence of limitations on feasibility. A suggested alternative may be invented or discovered but not be feasible for use because of the time necessary for its application and implementation. Also, a suggested alternative may be available, but impractical for reasons such as greatly increased cost or impairment of the product's usefulness. When the plaintiff has introduced evidence that a safer alternative was feasible because it was used, the defendant may then introduce contradictory evidence that it was not used.

Thus in response to the Baileys' evidence of kill switch use in 1978, the time of trial, Boatland was properly allowed to show that they were not used when the boat was sold in 1973. To rebut proof that safety switches were possible and feasible when Bailey's boat was sold because the underlying concept was known and the "Quick Kill," a simple, inexpensive device had been invented, Boatland was properly allowed to show that neither the "Quick Kill" nor any other kill switch was available at that time.

It could reasonably be inferred from this evidence that although the underlying concept of automatic motor cut-off devices was not new, kill switches were not as feasible an alternative as the Baileys' evidence implied. Boatland did not offer evidence of technological impossibility or absolute nonfeasibility; its evidence was offered to show limited availability when the boat was sold. Once the jury was informed of the state of the art, it was able to consider the extent to which it was feasible to incorporate an automatic cut-off device or similar design characteristic into Bailey's boat. The feasibility and effectiveness of a safer design and other factors such as utility and risk, were properly considered by the jury before it ultimately concluded that the boat sold to Bailey was not defectively designed.

In cases involving strict liability for defective design, liability is determined by the product's defective condition; there is no need to prove that the defendant's conduct was negligent. Considerations such as the utility and risk of the product in question and the feasibility of safer alternatives are presented according to the facts as they are proved to be, not according to the defendant's perceptions. Thus, even though the defendant has exercised due care his product may be found defective. When the Baileys introduced evidence of the use of kill switches, Boatland was entitled to introduce rebuttal evidence of nonuse at the time of manufacture due to limitations imposed by the state of the art. Evidence offered under these circumstances is offered to rebut plaintiff's evidence that a safer alternative was feasible and is relevant to defectiveness. It was not offered to show that a custom existed or to infer the defendant's compliance therewith. We would be presented with a different question if the state of the art in 1973 with respect to kill switches had not been disputed and Boatland had attempted to avoid liability by offering proof that Bailey's boat complied with industry custom. . . .

Conclusion

For the reasons stated above the judgment of the court of civil appeals is reversed. The judgment rendered by the trial court, that the Baileys take nothing against Boatland, is affirmed.

POPE, J., concurring, in which BARROW, J., joins [opinion omitted].

On Rehearing

CAMPBELL, J., dissenting.

I dissent.

"State of the art" does not mean "the state of industry practice." "State of the art" means "state of industry knowledge." At the time of the manufacture of the boat in question, the device and concept of a circuit breaker, as is at issue in this case, was simple, mechanical, cheap, practical, possible, economically feasible and a concept seventy years old, which required no engineering or technical breakthrough. The concept was known by the industry. This fact removes it from "state of the art."

Boatland is a retail seller. It is not the manufacturer. From the adoption of strict liability in this case, and consideration of public policy, each entity involved in the chain of commercial distribution of a defective product has been subject to strict liability for injuries thereby caused, even though it is in no way responsible for the creation of a defective product or could not cure the defect. The remedy for a faultless retail seller is an action for indemnity against the manufacturer.

In products liability, the measure is the dangerously defective quality of the specific product in litigation. The focus is on the product, not the reasoning behind the manufacturer's option of design or the care exercised in making such decisions. Commercial availability or defectiveness as to Boatland is not the test. Defectiveness as to the product is the test. If commercial unavailability is not a defense or limitation on feasibility to the manufacturer, it cannot be a defense to the seller.

The manufacturer of the boat, Mr. Hudson, testified as follows as concerns the concept of a "kill switch." It is practically without dispute that this is one of the simplest mechanical devices and concepts known to man. Its function is, can be, and was performed by many and varied simple constructions. It is more a concept than an invention. The concept has been around most of this century. It is admittedly an easily incorporated concept. Was an invention required in order to incorporate a circuit breaker on a bass boat? Absolutely not! Did the manufacturer have to wait until George Horton invented his specific "Quick Kill" switch before it could incorporate a kill switch of some sort on its bass boats? Absolutely not! Mr. Hudson uses an even simpler electrical circuit breaker on his boats.

Mr. Hudson testified he could have made a kill switch himself, of his own, and of many possible designs, but simply did not do it. Why didn't he do it? He didn't think about it. He never had any safety engineer examine his boats. He hadn't heard of such, he puts them on now, but still thinks people won't use them.

Was the manufacturer faced with a limitation or state of the art due to commercial unavailability? No. If the manufacturer of this boat were the defendant in this case, would the majority hold under this evidence that the commercial unavailability of someone else's simple product is a limitation on the manufacturer's capability (feasibility) to incorporate a device performing the same safety function on its boat? Not if any semblance of strict product liability is to be preserved. . . .

What is this Court faced with in this case? Nothing more than a defendant seller attempting to avoid liability by offering proof that Bailey's boat complied with industry practice (which it did at that time) but not because of any limitations on manufacturing feasibility at that time. This is an industry practice case. The evidence does not involve "technological feasibility." The law of the majority opinion is that a simple device, not supplied by the manufacturer, is a defense in a strict liability suit, against a retailer, even though the industry practice was created by the manufacturing industry.

There is no dispute that commercially marketed "kill switches" for bass boats were unavailable to Boatland at the time it sold the boat. Horton's "Quick Kill" was unavailable. The important point is that there is no dispute that at the time of the manufacture of Mr. Bailey's boat, a circuit breaker, whether electrical or mechanical could have easily and cheaply been incorporated into the boat.

Evidence of commercial unavailability to this retail seller should not be admissible. If it is, the majority opinion has created a new and separate test for defectiveness for a retail seller in a strict liability case. . . .

I would hold that the trial court erred in permitting such evidence by Boatland to go to the jury, and would affirm the judgment of the Court of Civil Appeals. . . .

Restatement (Third) of Torts: Products Liability
(1998)

§2. CATEGORIES OF PRODUCT DEFECT

COMMENT:

d. Design defects: general considerations. . . . How the defendant's design compares with other, competing designs in actual use is relevant to the issue of whether the defendant's design is defective. Defendants often seek to defend their product designs on the ground that the designs conform to the "state of the art." The term "state of the art" has been variously defined to mean that the product design conforms to industry custom, that it reflects the safest and most advanced technology developed and in commercial use, or that it reflects technology at the cutting edge of scientific knowledge. The confusion brought about by these various definitions is unfortunate. This Section states that a design is defective if the product could have been made safer by the adoption of a reasonable alternative design. If such a design could have been practically adopted at time of sale and if the omission of such a design rendered the product not reasonably safe, the plaintiff establishes defect under Subsection (b). When a defendant demonstrates that its product design was the safest in use at the time of sale, it may be difficult for the plaintiff to prove that an alternative design could have been practically adopted. The defendant is thus allowed to introduce evidence with regard to industry practice that bears on whether an alternative design was practicable. Industry practice may also be relevant to whether the omission of an alternative design rendered the product not reasonably safe. While such evidence is admissible, it is not necessarily dispositive. If the plaintiff introduces expert testimony to establish that a reasonable alternative design could practically have been adopted, a trier of fact may conclude that the product was defective notwithstanding that such a design was not adopted by any manufacturer, or even considered for commercial use, at the time of sale.

The strong majority position is that state-of-the-art evidence is admissible in product design cases. See generally Gary C. Robb, A Practical Approach to Use of State of the Art Evidence in Strict Products Liability Cases, 77 Nw. U. L. Rev. 1 (1982). See also Potter v. Chicago Pneumatic Tool Co., 694 A.2d 1319, 1346 (Conn. 1997) (reprinted infra) ("the overwhelming majority of courts have held that, in design defect cases, state-of-the-art evidence is relevant to determining the adequacy of the product's design"); Sturm Ruger & Co., Inc. v. Day, 594 P.2d 38, 45 (Alaska 1979) ("While not, strictly speaking, a defense in products liability action, state of the art may be considered in determining whether a product is defective"), *cert. denied,* 454 U.S. 894 (1981). Compare Ky. Rev. Stat. §411.310(2) (Michie 1992) (authorizing presumption of no defect upon proof of manufacturer's adherence to state of the art in design, manufacturing methods, and testing) and Ariz. Rev. Stat. Ann. §12-683(1) (West 2003) (authorizing affirmative defense upon proof that product plans, manufacturing methods, inspection, testing, and labeling conformed with state of the art). For other states recognizing a state-of-the-art defense, see Iowa Code Ann. §668.12 (West 1998); N.J. Stat. Ann. §2A:58C-3(1) (West 2000); Ohio Rev. Code Ann. §2307.75(E) (Anderson 2001). Occasionally, a court may find itself entangled trying to sort out the parties' respective burdens of proof regarding state-of-the-art evidence. See, e.g., Cavanaugh v. Skil Corp., 751 A.2d 518 (N.J. 2000) (attempting to reconcile plaintiff's burden to prove reasonable alternative design with New Jersey statute allowing for state-of-the-art defense).

A minority of courts continue to take the position that strict liability leaves no place for a "state of the art" argument. See, e.g., Habecker v. Clark Equip. Co., 36 F.3d 278, 285 (3d Cir. 1994) (applying Pennsylvania law) (agreeing with plaintiff that state-of-the-art evidence is "unequivocally impermissible in a Pennsylvania products liability trial"); Murphy v. Chestnut, 464 N.E.2d 818 (Ill. App. Ct. 1984) (state-of-the-art not a valid defense to strict liability claim); Johnson v. Hannibal Mower Corp., 679 S.W.2d 884 (Mo. Ct. App. 1984) (evidence of compliance of lawnmower with standards of American National Standards Institute is inadmissible because compliance with state of the start is irrelevant to strict liability claim; that manufacturer had built the safest product possible under existing technology had no bearing on the claim).

A related, though distinct, issue is what role a manufacturer's compliance with industry standards should play in determining whether its product is defective. While state-of-the-art evidence may shield a manufacturer from liability altogether, compliance with industry norms is generally regarded as relevant but not dispositive on the issue of defect. Much of the confusion persists due to the courts' haphazard use of state-of-the-art terminology. Recall the discussion contained in the Products Liability Restatement §2, Comment *d,* supra. Nonetheless, some courts have been keen to draw a distinction between the two concepts. See, e.g., Cohen v. Winnebago 2000 WL 299459 (4th Cir. 2000) (applying South Carolina law) (recognizing the importance of properly delineating industry custom from technological feasibility when instructing the jury); Montgomery Ward & Co. v. Gregg, 554 N.E.2d 1145, 1156 (Ind. Ct. App. 1990) ("'state of the art' . . . is not a legal term of art meaning industry custom or practice"); Chown v. USM Corp., 297 N.W.2d 218, 221 (Iowa 1980) ("Custom refers to what was being done in the industry; state of the art refers to what feasibly could have been done"). We shall deal in a later section with whether a manufacturer's compliance with an applicable governmental regulation should render its product nondefective as a matter of law.

(b) Subsequent Remedial Measures

The question frequently arises whether a plaintiff should be permitted to introduce evidence of design changes adopted by the defendant subsequent either to distribution or accidental injury. Defendants often try to exclude such evidence on two grounds. First, defendants argue that the highly prejudicial nature of the evidence outweighs its probative value. Although the fact that such a change was made is admittedly relevant to the negligence issue, it is altogether too easy for jurors to jump blindly from the fact of post-sale design change to the conclusion of pre-sale fault. Alternatively, defendants contend that such evidence should be categorically excluded under the traditional rule in negligence cases barring evidence of subsequent remedial measures (Federal Rules of Evidence 407 and its state analogues). This rule is based primarily on the public policy concern that, were it not for the assurance that such evidence would be excluded from litigation, parties might refrain from making safety-related adjustments for fear that the evidence will be used against them.

For courts that purport to follow a true strict liability approach in design defect cases, the answer to the admissibility question is less clear. In Ault v. International Harvester Co., 528 P.2d 1148 (Cal. 1974) (en banc), the Supreme Court of California held that the rule barring evidence of subsequent remedial measures does not apply to a products liability action premised on a claim of strict liability. Since the rule by its terms applied only in cases of negligence or culpable conduct, the court reasoned that its extension to strict liability cases was unwarranted where "negligence or culpability is not a necessary ingredient." Furthermore, unlike traditional slip-and-fall negligence cases, the court stated that regarding large-scale manufacturers it was "manifestly unrealistic to suggest that such a producer will forego making improvements in its product, and risk innumerable additional lawsuits and the attendant adverse effects upon its public image, simply because evidence of adoption of such improvement may be admitted in an action. . . ." Id. at 1152.

The competing policy considerations on this issue received a thorough workout in an opinion authored by Judge Richard Posner. In Flaminio v. Honda Motor Co., Ltd., 733 F.2d 463 (7th Cir. 1984), the plaintiff was injured in a single-vehicle accident allegedly caused by vibration in the front end of the motorcycle he was driving. Judge Posner explained:

> The issue with respect to the allegation of defective design is whether the district court erred in excluding evidence (consisting of two blueprints) that, the plaintiffs say, shows that after the accident Honda, in an effort to reduce wobble, made the struts ("front forks") that connect the Gold Wing's handlebars to its front wheel two millimeters thicker. Rule 407 of the Federal Rules of Evidence makes evidence of subsequent remedial measures "not admissible to prove negligence or culpable conduct in connection with the event," but adds: "This rule does not require the exclusion of evidence of subsequent measures when offered for another purpose, such as proving ownership, control, or feasibility of precautionary measures, if controverted, or impeachment." Flaminio argues that the blueprints were admissible under the exceptions for "proving . . . feasibility of precautionary measures, if controverted," and for impeaching the defendants' evidence. But the first of these exceptions is inapplicable because the defendants did not deny the feasibility of precautionary measures against wobble. Their argument was that there is a tradeoff between wobble and "weave," and that in designing the model on which Flaminio was injured Japanese Honda had decided that weave was the greater danger because it occurs at high speeds and because the Gold Wing model — what motorcycle buffs call a "hog"— was designed for high speeds. The feasibility, as distinct from the net advantages, of reducing the danger of wobble was not in issue. As for the second exception, if the defendants had testified that they would never have thickened the struts on the Gold Wing the blueprints would have been impeaching. But the de-

fendants offered no such testimony. Although any evidence of subsequent remedial measures might be thought to contradict and so in a sense impeach a defendant's testimony that he was using due care at the time of the accident, if this counted as "impeachment" the exception would swallow the rule. . . .

[W]e agree with the majority view that the rule does apply to strict liability cases. We are not persuaded by the purely semantic argument to the contrary that since "culpable conduct" is not the issue in such a case—the defendant is liable, at least prima facie, even if he is not blameworthy in the sense of being willful or negligent, provided that he caused the plaintiff's injury—the rule is inapplicable by its own terms. Wisconsin law rejects this argument in holding that a defendant's blameworthiness must, under the state's comparative-negligence statute, be compared with the plaintiff's blameworthiness in strict liability cases, even though the defendant was not blameworthy in a negligence sense. A major purpose of Rule 407 is to promote safety by removing the disincentive to make repairs (or take other safety measures) after an accident that would exist if the accident victim could use those measures as evidence of the defendant's liability. One might think it not only immoral but reckless for an injurer, having been alerted by the accident to the existence of danger, not to take steps to correct the danger. But accidents are low-probability events. The probability of another accident may be much smaller than the probability that the victim of the accident that has already occurred will sue the injurer and, if permitted, will make devastating use at trial of any measures that the injurer may have taken since the accident to reduce the danger.

The analysis is not fundamentally affected by whether the basis of liability is the defendant's negligence or his product's defectiveness or inherent dangerousness. In either case, if evidence of subsequent remedial measures is admissible to prove liability, the incentive to take such measures will be reduced. Id. at 468-469.

Rule 407 has been amended, as follows, to exclude evidence of subsequent remedial measures in products liability cases regardless of whether plaintiff proceeds under negligence or strict liability.

FEDERAL RULES OF EVIDENCE

RULE 407 SUBSEQUENT REMEDIAL MEASURES

When, *after an injury or harm allegedly caused by an event,* measures are taken that, if taken previously, would have made the injury or harm less likely to occur, evidence of the subsequent measures is not admissible to prove negligence, culpable conduct, *a defect in a product, a defect in a product's design, or a need for a warning or instruction.* This rule does not require the exclusion of evidence of subsequent measures when offered for another purpose, such as proving ownership, control, or feasibility of precautionary measures, if controverted, or impeachment. (Emphasis added)

State courts have split sharply on the question posed in *Flaminio*. Some, following *Ault*'s lead, supra, hold that the subsequent repair rule does not apply to exclude evidence in strict liability actions. See, e.g., Forma Scientific, Inc. v. BioSera, 960 P.2d 108 (Colo. 1998); McFarland v. Bruno Mach. Corp., 626 N.E.2d 659 (Ohio 1994); Ford Motor Co. v. Fulkerson, 812 S.W.2d 119 (Ky. 1991); Sanderson v. Steve Snyder Enterprises, Inc., 491 A.2d 389 (Conn. 1985); Friedrichs v. Huebner, 329 N.W.2d 890 (Wis. 1983); Caldwell v. Yamaha Motor Co., 648 P.2d 519 (Wyo. 1982). Similar expressions can be found in state evidentiary schemes. See Tex. R. Civ. Evid. 407(a) ("nothing in this [subsequent repair] rule shall preclude admissibility in products liability cases based on strict liability"). Other courts, recognizing the distinction between negligence and strict liability to be artificial in design defect cases, apply the rule to bar evidence in strict liability actions as well. See, e.g., Duchess v. Langston Corp., 769 A.2d 1131 (Pa. 2001); Hyjek v. Anthony Indus., 944 P.2d 1036 (Wash. 1997); Cyr v. J.I. Case Co., 652 A.2d 685 (N.H. 1994); Krause v. American Aerolights, Inc., 762 P.2d 1011 (Or. 1988); Kallio v. Ford Motor Co., 407 N.W.2d 92 (Minn. 1987); Rix v. General Motors Corp., 723 P.2d 195 (Mont. 1986); Cover v. Cohen, 461 N.E.2d 864 (N.Y. 1984); Hallmark v. Allied Products Cor., 646 P.2d 319 (Ariz. 1982). See also Randolph L. Burns, Note, Subsequent Remedial Measures and Strict Products Liability: A New — Relevant — Answer to an Old Problem, 81 Va. L. Rev. 1141 (1995); Brent R. Johnson, Comment, The Uncertain Fate of Remedial Evidence: Victim of an Illogical Imposition of Federal Rule of Evidence 407, 20 Wm. Mitchell L. Rev. 191 (1994).

An interesting issue is whether a change in design made subsequent to sale but before plaintiff's injury is a "subsequent remedial measure." Much of the confusion stems from the ambiguous reference to an "event" as the triggering point for the rule's application. From a policy standpoint, one could argue that the sale, not the accident, is the important event. Certainly prejudice to the defendant derives from post-sale modifications; and regarding mass-produced and distributed products, post-sale modifications are likely to be post-accident also, regarding at least some victims, if not the actual plaintiff. Notwithstanding these considerations, the Iowa Supreme Court in Tucker v. Caterpillar, Inc., 564 N.W.2d 410 (Iowa 1997) held that evidence of a warning decal and manual issued after manufacture but before plaintiff's accident was not barred under Iowa's subsequent remedial measure rule. Holding that the term "event" referred to the accident or injury underlying the litigation, the Court reasoned that "public policy concerns about deterring safety improvements do not support exclusion of evidence of such measures taken *before* an accident." Id. at 413. But see General Motors Corp. v. Moseley, 447 S.E.2d 302 (Ga. Ct. App. 1994), *overruled on other grounds*, 496 S.E.2d 459 (1998) (considering long-term nature of planning and implementation of design change, fact that change preceded injury did not bar rule's application). Note that the amended Federal Rules of Evidence 407 has resolved the issue for the circuit courts by clarifying that the rule applies only after an alleged "injury or harm."

Evidence of post-accident modifications made by a third-party generally are not barred by the exclusionary rule. In Magnante v. Pettibone-Wood Mfg. Co., 228 Cal. Rptr. 420 (Ct. App. 1986), an intermediate California appellate court admitted evidence that a worker's employer had modified the design of a truss boom after an accident. The court held that even those courts that apply the "subsequent repair rule" to all products liability actions would permit evidence of changes made by a nonparty to the product. Admitting evidence of nonparty modification could not discourage manufacturers from making design changes to their products. See also Denolf v. Frank L. Jursik Co., 238 N.W.2d 1 (Mich. 1975); Hartman v. Opelika Mach. Welding Co., 414 So. 2d 1105 (Fla. App. 1982), *petition denied*, 426 So. 2d 27 (Fla. 1983); Ford Motor Co. v. Nuckolls, 894 S.W.2d 897 (Ark. 1995).

Since all courts permit a plaintiff to introduce subsequent remedial measures to rebut a defendant's contention that the suggested alternative design is not feasible, what is the big to-do all about? The only way that the defendant can keep the undesired evidence out of the case is to admit the feasibility of the plaintiff's alternative design. Thus, the plaintiff will get the crucial evidence before the jury in most instances, will he not? The answer may not be so clear-cut. Some courts, wary that the exception should not swallow up the rule, limit the concept of feasibility to technological capability alone. Thus, a defendant, while admitting feasibility in the technical sense, may be able to dispute the practicability of an alternative design in terms of added costs and offsetting risks without opening the door for plaintiff to introduce evidence of subsequent design changes. See, e.g., In re Joint E. Dist. and S. Dist. Asbestos Litig., 995 F.2d 343, 345 (2d Cir. 1993) ("'feasibility' is not an open sesame whose mere invocation parts Rule 407 and ushers in evidence of subsequent repairs and remedies"); Forma Scientific, Inc. v. BioSera, Inc., 960 P.2d 108 (Col. 1998) (Vollack, C.J., dissenting). For a decision truly grappling with the appropriate scope of the feasibility exception, see Duchess v. Langston, 769 A.2d 1131 (Pa. 2001).

Legislatures have found this a topic of great interest. A number of statutes have been passed circumscribing the use of subsequent remedial measures in products liability litigation. See, e.g., Ariz. Rev. Stat. Ann. §12-686 (West 2003); Colo. Rev. Stat. §13-21-404 (West 2002); Idaho Code §6-1406(1) (Michie 1998). See also MUPLA §107.

The Michigan statute is comprehensive. Mich. Comp. Laws. Ann. §600.2946(3) (West 2000) provides:

> With regard to the production of a product that is the subject of a product liability action, evidence of a philosophy, theory, knowledge, technique, or procedure that is learned, placed in use, or discontinued after the event resulting in the death of the person or injury to the person or property, which if learned, placed in use, or discontinued before the event would have made the event less likely to occur, is admissible only for the purpose of proving the feasibility of precautions, if controverted, or for impeachment.

(3) Manufacturers' Responsibility for Post-Sale Shifts in Public Attitudes Toward Risk

In an earlier discussion we noted that the time gap between the creation of a new product concept and the final trial of a product defect may be very long. It is not uncommon to encounter time gaps of 20 or 30, or more, years between the initial product marketing and the trial on the merits of a case. In the preceding sections we have considered how increases in risk information and technological know-how over time should be dealt with by the courts. But information is not the only thing that changes through time. Public attitudes toward risk can also change dramatically. On the one hand, the Nader safety revolution in the 1960s increased public sensitivity toward product-related risk in a marked fashion. On the other hand, the "insurance crisis" of the 1980s may have reduced expectations and produced a willingness to tolerate higher levels of risk.

These changing attitudes affect the outcomes in products liability cases in several ways. First, legal doctrine changes over time. For example, manufacturers who marketed products in the 1950s and 1960s did so under a regime of the "patent danger rule." The rule first came under heavy assault in the seventies, although academic criticism of it came somewhat earlier. What, then, of all the obviously dangerous (and therefore nondefective) products that were marketed during the heyday of the patent danger rule? Are they now to be deemed "not reasonably safe"? Note that the issue of prospective or retrospective overruling is not directly relevant. Even if the patent danger rule had been overruled prospectively (it wasn't), and the new doctrine was made to apply to all cases of injury that post-dated the date of the overruling decision, not much would be gained. Tort actions accrue at the time of injury. Thus, manufacturers may be stuck with millions of non-recallable, patently dangerous products that are still in use. When one adds to the overturning of the patent danger rule the judicial changes in recovery rules on such issues as delegability for installation of optional safety equipment, bystander liability, product alteration and misuse, contributory fault, recovery for mental distress, and the like, it becomes clear that manufacturers are being called upon to defend their products in very different legal environments than the ones that existed when the products were first marketed.

In the days of yore, prospective overruling gave would-be defendants a chance to limit their exposures by altering their behavior. And even retroactive overruling rarely affected anything more than a short period of time prior to the case that changed the rule. Usually, prior to a formal change in a rule, steady erosion signaled its ultimate demise so that surprise was rarely experienced. But the longevity of durable goods (especially productive machinery), coupled with the high number of units in use, confronted manufacturers who fully complied with legal mores at the time of manufacture with liabilities they could not anticipate and against which they could not effectively insure.

Even if a defendant should find itself being judged by a common law negligence standard in a case in which unfavorable rule changes do not apply, it still may be the case that a mid-1990s jury will be judging a 1972 or 1973 design decision that embodied a radically different attitude toward risk. Although courts rarely articulate this concern, they occasionally indicate that shifting public attitudes toward risk present problems. In Bruce v. Martin-Marietta Corp., 544 F.2d 442 (10th Cir. 1976) (applying Oklahoma law), a Martin 404 airplane, first sold in 1952, was chartered in 1970 by the Wichita State University football team. As the plane crashed into a mountain, seats in the passenger cabin broke loose from their floor attachments and blocked the exit. More than half the passengers were trapped in the airplane and died in the ensuing fire. Plaintiffs contended that the seats and seat fastenings were not designed or manufactured to withstand a crash. They submitted an affidavit from a recognized expert that airplane seats in common use on the date of the accident would have remained in place and would not have trapped the passengers in the burning aircraft. Thus, the design defect claim was based on a design in use more than seventeen years after the date of original sale of the aircraft. In upholding a summary judgment for the defendant, the Tenth Circuit said:

> [T]here is "general" agreement that to prove liability under §402A the plaintiff must show that the product was dangerous beyond the expectation of the ordinary customer. . . . A consumer would not expect a Model T to have the safety features which are incorporated in automobiles made today. The same expectation applies to airplanes. Plaintiffs have not shown that the ordinary consumer would expect a plane made in 1952 to have the safety features of one made in 1970. Id. at 447.

It is difficult to predict when a court will decide that the changing societal standards factor alone is sufficient to dictate a summary judgment or directed verdict for the defendant. This much is clear, however: as the gap between present expectations and past societal standards widens, judicial unease at allowing the case to reach the jury will increase. See, e.g., Hagans v. Oliver Mach. Co., 576 F.2d 97, 100-101, 104-105 (5th Cir. 1978) (applying Texas law); Ward v. Hobart Mfg. Co., 450 F.2d 1176, 1182-1185 (5th Cir. 1971) (applying Mississippi law). Juries have enough difficulty adjudicating foreseeability; to expect them to account for shifts in societal attitudes is unrealistic. For a discussion of this issue, see James A. Henderson, Jr., Coping with the Time Dimension in Products Liability, 69 Cal. L. Rev. 919, 923-924, 959-963 (1981); Gary T. Schwartz, New Products, Old Products, Evolving Law, Retroactive Law, 58 N.Y.U. L. Rev. 796 (1983).

Finally, we should be cautious before reaching the conclusion that what we are experiencing in products liability law is merely a reflection of greater public sensitivity to risk in general. What we may be witnessing is preoccupation with product-related risks by a public that blithely disregards other risks of equal or greater magnitude. The thesis that the risks selected by a society for attention and reduction are culturally determined and are often unrelated to the true magnitudes of the underlying problems is expressed in Mary Douglas & Aaron Wildavsky, Risk and Culture: An Essay on the Selection of Technical and Environmental Dangers (1982). Assuming the validity of the thesis that risks are chosen by society for political and sociological reasons, there emerges a greater reluctance to transpose upon the past modern risk-assessment models that have different risks at the top of their hit list. If changing political tastes of acceptable levels of risk are the inevitable by-products of cultural progression, then a manufacturer, with its point of production frozen in time, may face liability merely due to its inability to conform its past decision-making model to evolving societal norms. At bottom, that may be what is so offensive about an ex post facto law. It is no more tolerable when the newfound political judgment is clothed as a dollar verdict in a tort case.

c. **Should Reasonable Alternative Design Claims Be Submitted to Juries on Both Negligence and Strict Liability Grounds?**

Lecy v. Bayliner Marine Corporation
973 P.2d 1110 (Wash. Ct. App. 1999)

COX, J. . . .

In late September 1992, after chartering a motor yacht designed and manufactured by Bayliner, Karen and Henry Lecy and Marco and Pamela Bacich set off on a pleasure cruise from Anacortes to the San Juan Islands. Soon after entering navigable waters between two islands, the boat encountered some turbulence. The wind increased and the swells rose to between two and three feet in height. The couples gathered in the upper cabin. While there, Henry Lecy apparently fell against the port-side cabin door. Lecy and the door both went overboard. He drowned in spite of the rescue efforts of his companions.

Karen Lecy commenced a wrongful death action against Bayliner and others. She later amended her complaint to add a claim for negligent infliction of emotional distress. The Baciches commenced a separate action for negligent infliction of emotional distress against the same defendants. The actions were consolidated for trial.

Over Bayliner's objection, the trial court gave a special verdict form that included interrogatories and alternative answers for strict liability and negligence. Using that form, the jury found that the vessel's door system was not unreasonably dangerous either as to its design or its construction. But the jury then found that Bayliner was negligent in the design of that door system. Based on that finding, the jury further found that Bayliner's negligent design of the door system was the proximate cause of Henry Lecy's death and the emotional distress claims of the Bachiches and Karen Lecy. The jury assessed substantial damages for each of these claims. . . .

Bayliner contends that the trial court erred by denying its CR 50(b) motion for judgment notwithstanding the jury verdict. . . .

Bayliner . . . contends that it was entitled to judgment as a matter of law under federal maritime law because the jury's finding in Bayliner's favor on the strict liability claim precluded it, as a matter of law, from considering the negligent design claim. We agree. . . .

The threshold question that we must resolve in our analysis is what substantive law governs. The parties correctly conclude that the law of admiralty applies. Admiralty jurisdiction applies when (1) the claims arise from an event that occurred on navigable waters and (2) the activity has the potential to affect maritime commerce. Both prongs of this test are met here. The accident occurred on navigable waters. And the operation of a pleasure vessel on navigable waters bears a sufficient relation to maritime commerce to invoke admiralty jurisdiction. "With admiralty jurisdiction comes the application of substantive admiralty law."

The more difficult and crucial question is what substantive rule of admiralty governs. We first resolve that question and then proceed to apply that rule to this case.

Derived from both state and federal sources, "general maritime law is an amalgam of traditional common-law rules, modifications of those rules, and newly created rules." When there are no clear precedents in the law of admiralty, courts may "look to the law prevailing on the land." Courts should also be guided by the aim of maintaining uniformity in admiralty law. State law should be applied only where there is no governing federal statute or judicially created admiralty rule and where there is no likelihood of jeopardizing the uniformity of admiralty practice. In applying state law, courts should apply the general common law rather than the law of any particular state so as to further the goal of uniformity.

Substantive maritime law recognizes both strict liability and negligence in the area of product liability. But the parties here have not presented us with any maritime case that has addressed the precise question at issue here—whether a jury finding of no strict liability for design may be harmonized with a jury finding of negligent design. Our search reveals none. Thus, we turn to land-based federal and state cases and the Restatement (Third) of Torts for guidance.

At the time the parties argued the jury instructions, Bayliner objected to the wording of the special verdict form. In essence, Bayliner took the position that if the jury answered "no" to the interrogatory based on the strict liability for design defect, it should not be permitted to proceed to consider whether Bayliner had been negligent in the design of the door system. The trial court rejected the argument and gave the jury the special verdict form that allowed it to consider both theories, strict liability in design and negligent design.

At issue here is whether the special verdict form was proper in view of the jury's later answers to the interrogatories in that form. The relevant interrogatories and answers are set forth below:

QUESTION NO. 1: Was the door system for the port side of the pilot house of the vessel Checkmate unreasonably dangerous as designed by Bayliner?
. . . ANSWER: NO.
. . .
QUESTION NO. 6: Was the defendant negligent in the design of the door system in question?
. . . ANSWER: YES.

If the jury's answers to the special interrogatories that comprise a special verdict conflict, we attempt to harmonize the answers. But we cannot do so here.

Federal and state case law in other jurisdictions is generally in agreement that a jury's rejection of strict liability for design defect precludes a finding of negligent design. In *Lambert,* for instance, a California appellate court recently concluded that the jury's answers to interrogatories on a special verdict form were irreconcilable. The jury answered "no" to the question of whether the Blazer had a design defect, but answered "yes" to the question of whether General Motors was negligent in the design of the 1985 Blazer. The court concluded that the jury's finding of no design defect in the Blazer was fatally inconsistent with its conclusion that General Motors had negligently designed it. The court rejected Lambert's attempt to rescue the verdict by arguing that the jury may have found General Motors negligent for failing to test the vehicle or for failing to warn customers about its weak roof. In the absence of any defect, reasoned the court, these alleged omissions could not have made any difference. Testing cannot reveal a defect that does not exist, and a manufacturer cannot be negligent for failing to warn about a nonexistent defect.

In *Tipton,* the Sixth Circuit reached a similar result. There, by its answers to the interrogatories on a special verdict form, the jury found that the tire in question was not defective or unreasonably dangerous, but that Michelin had negligently designed or manufactured the tire. The court concluded that these answers were irreconcilable because both the strict liability and the negligence theory depended on a finding that the tire was defective. Thus, once the jury found that there was no defect in the tire, it was precluded from finding that Michelin had negligently designed or manufactured that tire. . . .

The Restatement (Third) of Torts lists cases that confirm this general trend. And the Fifth Circuit land-based cases, upon which Bayliner heavily relies, are expressly noted. The Restatement commentators also refer to the "mischief caused by dual instructions on both negligence and strict liability." The standard for product defect liability set forth in the Restatement is based on whether the product is "not reasonably safe" and whether the risk was foreseeable. Thus, reason the commentators, juries will necessarily consider the conduct of the manufacturer and do not need a separate negligence instruction to invite such consideration. . . .

Lecy and the Baciches rely on . . . Davis v. Globe Mach. Mfg. Corp. [684 P.2d 692 (Wash. 1984)]. There, Davis brought a products liability claim on the basis of both strict liability and negligence. The negligence claim was based on the manufacturer's alleged failure to warn. The trial court dismissed the negligence claim at the close of Davis' case. Davis appealed that dismissal. Globe argued that the issue was moot because the jury found the product reasonably safe under the strict liability test. On the strict liability claim, the jury responded "no" to the following interrogatory: "Did the defendant supply a product which was 'not reasonably safe' at the time it left defendant's control or fail to give an adequate warning necessary to make the use of the product reasonably safe?" The Supreme Court rejected Globe's argument, stating:

> Negligence and strict liability are not mutually exclusive [theories of recovery] because they differ in focus: *negligence focuses upon the conduct of the manufacturer while strict liability focuses upon the product.* . . .

But the court nonetheless concluded that the trial court properly dismissed the negligence claim because there was not sufficient evidence to support it.

Relying on the italicized statement above, Lecy and the Baciches argue that the jury verdict here can be reconciled under *Davis* because negligence focuses on the conduct of the manufacturer, while strict liability focuses on the product. But the record before us refutes this argument, and *Davis* is therefore distinguishable.

Here, the court gave the jury the standard instruction for strict liability for design defect. The focus of the instruction is on what makes a product not reasonably safe (or unreasonably dangerous) as designed. A product may be unreasonably dangerous. . . . if:

> at the time of manufacture, the likelihood that the product would cause the plaintiff's harm or similar harms, and the seriousness of those harms, outweighed the manufacturer's burden to design a product that would have prevented those harms and any adverse effect a practical, feasible alternative would have on the product's usefulness. . . .

Because the instruction on unreasonably dangerous design required the jury to engage in risk-utility balancing, it simply cannot be argued that this inquiry did not involve consideration of the manufacturer's conduct in designing the door system. Thus, the reliance on *Davis* for the proposition that strict liability and negligence do not overlap because the former is focused solely on the product while the latter is focused on the manufacturer's conduct is misplaced. Contrary to the contentions of Lecy and the Baciches, the jury here *did* consider the reasonableness of the manufacturer's conduct when it arrived at its conclusion that the door system was not unreasonably dangerous as designed.

Moreover, *Davis* cannot guide our decision here. While it states the uncontested proposition that strict liability and negligence are not mutually exclusive theories, it was not presented with the question—and thus did not decide—whether a finding of reasonably safe design precludes a finding of negligent design. . . .

In sum, we conclude that the reasoning of the case law from other jurisdictions and the commentary in the Restatement (Third) of Torts reflects the general common law approach to the question presented here. Applying this rule, we conclude that the jury's finding that the door system was not unreasonably dangerous as designed precludes it from finding that the door system was negligently designed.

We emphasize that our holding is limited to the situation where the jury finds a product not unreasonably dangerous *as designed,* but then purports to find that same product was negligently *designed.* We recognize that where, for instance, the jury is presented with a strict liability *design* defect claim and a negligent *manufacture* claim, a jury's rejection of strict liability may not preclude its finding of negligence. Because the two bases of liability are separate and do not necessarily overlap, the jury may properly reject strict liability, yet find negligence. . . .

We reverse the judgment and remand for a new trial.

Take a hard look at §2(b). Note that it sets forth a functional test for design defect. Risk-utility balancing is to be used to determine whether a reasonable alternative design was available. The Restatement makes no mention of whether the legal theory to support liability is strict liability, negligence or the implied warranty of merchantability. Any legal theory can be utilized as long as the plaintiff meets the requirements of §2(b). Since the test is the same regardless of which theory of liability the plaintiff pleads, it makes no sense for a court to submit a case to the jury on multiple theories. To do so invites inconsistent verdicts. A jury may find that the defendant was negligent but that its product was not defective. Think about it. How can one be negligent in manufacturing a nondefective product? You might say that it is possible that a defendant did not exercise reasonable care in thinking through the design options, but, even so, where's the beef? If the product as ultimately designed is not defective, then the negligence of the defendant is harmless. A strong majority agree with Lecy that a negligence/no defect verdict is inconsistent. In Garrett v. Hamilton Controls, Inc., 850 F.2d 253, 257 (5th Cir. 1998) (applying Texas law) the court hit the nail on the head:

> A manufacturer logically cannot be held liable for failing to exercise ordinary care when producing a product that is not defective because: (1) if a product is not unreasonably dangerous because of the way it was manufactured, it was not negligent to manufacture it that way and (2) even if the manufacturer was somehow negligent in the design or production of the product, that negligence cannot have caused the plaintiff's injury because the negligence did not render the product "unreasonably dangerous."

See also Golonka v. General Motors Corp., 65 P.3d 956, 965 (Ariz. Ct. App. 2003) ("When a plaintiff's claim for strict liability design and negligent design are factually identical, and the jury employs a risk/benefit analysis to determine that the manufacturer is not at fault for strict liability design, the jury cannot consistently find the product manufacturer at fault for negligent design"); Chestnut v. Ford Motor Co., 445 F.2d 967 (4th Cir. 1971) (to establish negligence, plaintiff must prove that the product was dangerously defective when it left the plaintiff's hands). A minority of courts have taken the position that a negligence/no defect verdict is not necessarily inconsistent. See, e.g., Trull v. Volkswagon of America, Inc. 320 F.3d 1 (1st Cir. 2002) (applying New Hampshire law); Livingston v. Isuzu Motors, Ltd., 910 F. Supp. 1473 (D. Mont. 1995); Greiten v. LaDow, 235 N.W.2d 677, 685 (Wis. 1975); Sharp ex. rel Gordon v. Case Corp., 595 N.W.2d 380, 388 (Wis. 1999).

The Restatement is indifferent as to whether the reasonable alternative design requirement should be clothed in negligence or strict liability language. It insists only that multiple theories not be used for the same functional test. Thus, a plaintiff could choose to argue either that the manufacturer acted negligently in failing to adopt a reasonable alternative design or the plaintiff might claim that the defendant was strictly liable for failing to adopt a reasonable alternative design. Though the issue of which theory should be utilized was of little moment to the Restaters, a recent study by two professors concludes that a plaintiff's choice of theory may have a significant impact on a jury. Professors Richard L. Cupp, Jr., and Danielle Polage undertook an empirical study of the impact of negligence v. strict liability instructions on mock jurors. Their results are reported in The Rhetoric of Strict Products Liability Versus Negligence: An Empirical Analysis, 77 N.Y.U. L. Rev. 874 (2002). The authors conclude that use of negligence terminology rather than strict liability was more likely to result in jurors' willingness to award any damages; and when awards of damages were made they were greater when negligence was the theory presented to them. Thus, a negligence instruction may improve the plaintiff's chances both in terms of imposing liability and receiving a higher damages award.

d. Can a Warning Substitute for a Reasonable Alternative Design?

At the outset of this chapter we discussed the rise and fall of the patent danger rule. We indicated that at the turn of the century courts had soundly rejected the notion that a manufacturer had no duty to adopt a reasonably safer design merely because a product's dangers were open and obvious. The Products Liability Restatement §3, Comment *g,* supra, is in full accord. Though the patent danger rule is dead, defendants often advocate an argument that is a first cousin to it. When a product is accompanied with stark and ominous warnings, defendants contend that the warnings should suffice and that there is no need to adopt a reasonable alternative design. Courts have not taken kindly to this argument.

Uniroyal Goodrich Tire Company v. Martinez
977 S.W.2d 328 (Tex. 1998)

PHILLIPS, Chief Justice, delivered the opinion of the Court, in which GONZALEZ, SPECTOR, ABBOTT and HANKINSON, Justices, join.

We must decide whether a manufacturer who knew of a safer alternative product design is liable in strict products liability for injuries caused by the use of its product that the user could have avoided by following the product's warnings. The court of appeals held that the mere fact that a product bears an adequate warning does not conclusively establish that the product is not defective. . . . Because we agree, we affirm the judgment of the court of appeals.

I

Roberto Martinez, together with his wife and children, sued Uniroyal Goodrich Tire Company ("Goodrich"), The Budd Company, and Ford Motor Company for personal injuries Martinez suffered when he was struck by an exploding 16" Goodrich tire that he was mounting on a 16.5" rim. Attached to the tire was a prominent warning label containing yellow and red highlights and a pictograph of a worker being thrown into the air by an exploding tire. The label stated conspicuously:

DANGER

NEVER MOUNT A 16" SIZE DIAMETER TIRE ON A 16.5" RIM. Mounting a 16" tire on a 16.5" rim can cause severe injury or death. While it is possible to pass a 16" diameter tire over the lip or flange of a 16.5" size diameter rim, it cannot position itself against the rim flange. If an attempt is made to seat the bead by inflating the tire, the tire bead will break with explosive force.

. . .

NEVER inflate a tire which is lying on the floor or other flat surface. Always use a tire mounting machine with a hold-down device or safety cage or bolt to vehicle axle.

NEVER inflate to seat beads without using an extension hose with gauge and clip-on chuck.

NEVER stand, lean or reach over the assembly during inflation.

. . .

Failure to comply with these safety precautions can cause the bead to break and the assembly to burst with sufficient force to cause serious injury or death.

Unfortunately, Martinez ignored every one of these warnings. While leaning over the assembly, he attempted to mount a 16" tire on a 16.5" rim without a tire mounting machine, a safety cage, or an extension hose. Martinez explained, however, that because he had removed a 16" tire from the 16.5" rim, he believed that he was mounting the new 16" tire on a 16" rim. Moreover, the evidence revealed that Martinez's employer failed to make an operable tire-mounting machine available to him at the time he was injured, and there was no evidence that the other safety devices mentioned in the warning were available.

In their suit, the Martinezes did not claim that the warnings were inadequate, but instead alleged that Goodrich, the manufacturer of the tire, Budd, the manufacturer of the rim, and Ford, the designer of the rim, were each negligent and strictly liable for designing and manufacturing a defective tire and rim. Budd and Ford settled with the Martinezes before trial, and the case proceeded solely against Goodrich.

At trial, the Martinezes claimed that the tire manufactured by Goodrich was defective because it failed to incorporate a safer alternative bead design that would have kept the tire from exploding. This defect, they asserted, was the producing cause of Martinez's injuries. Further, they alleged that Goodrich's failure to adopt this alternative bead design was negligence that proximately caused Martinez's injury.

The bead is the portion of the tire that holds the tire to the rim when inflated. A bead consists of rubber-encased steel wiring that encircles the tire a number of times. When the tire is placed inside the wheel rim and inflated, the bead is forced onto the bead-seating ledge of the rim and pressed against the lip of the rim, or the wheel flange. When the last portion of the bead is forced onto this ledge, the tire has "seated," and the air is properly sealed inside the tire. The bead holds the tire to the rim because the steel wire, unlike rubber, does not expand when the tire is inflating. The tire in this case was a 16" bias-ply light truck tire with a 0.037" gauge multi-strand weftless bead, or tape bead, manufactured in 1990. A tape bead consists of several strands of parallel unwoven steel wires circling the tire with each layer resting on top of the last, similar to tape wound on a roll. After a number of layers have been wound, the end of the bead is joined, or spliced, to the beginning of the same bead to form a continuous loop.

The Martinezes' expert, Alan Milner, a metallurgical engineer, testified that a tape bead is prone to break when the spliced portion of the bead is the last portion of the bead to seat. This is commonly called a hang-up. Milner testified that an alternative bead design, a 0.050" gauge single strand programmed bead, would have prevented Martinez's injuries because its strength and uniformity make it more resistant to breaking during a hang-up. Milner explained that the 0.050" single strand programmed bead is stronger because it is 0.013" thicker and that it is uniform because it is wound, or programmed, by a computer, eliminating the spliced portion of the bead that can cause the tire to explode during a hang-up. . . .

Milner explained that the computer technology required to manufacture the programmed bead was developed in 1972 and widely available by 1975. Milner testified that Goodyear began using a 0.051" gauge single strand programmed bead in its radial light truck tires in 1977, and that Yokohama began using a single strand programmed bead in its radial light truck tires in 1981. Milner also testified that General Tire began using a single strand programmed bead in its bias-ply light truck tires in 1982. Finally, Milner testified that Goodrich itself began using the single strand programmed bead in its 16" radial light truck tires in 1991. Based upon this evidence and his expert opinion, Milner testified that the tire manufactured by Goodrich with a tape bead was defective and unreasonably dangerous. Because Goodrich had also been sued in thirty-four other lawsuits alleging accidents caused by mismatching Goodrich tires, Milner asserted that Goodrich was grossly negligent in failing to adopt the 0.050" single strand programmed bead in its bias-ply 16" light truck tires.

Milner also testified that the rim designed by Ford and manufactured by Budd was defective because its size was not clearly marked on it and because it could have been redesigned to prevent a 16" tire from passing over its flange.

The jury found that Goodrich's conduct was the sole proximate cause of Martinez's injuries and that Goodrich was grossly negligent. Furthermore, the jury found that the tire manufactured by Goodrich was defective, while the wheel rim designed by Ford and manufactured by Budd was not defective. The jury allocated 100% of the producing cause of Martinez's injuries to the acts and omissions of Goodrich.

The court of appeals affirmed the award of actual damages, holding that there was legally sufficient evidence to support the finding of a design defect based upon its examination of the following factors: (1) the availability of safer design alternatives; (2) similar accidents involving the same product; (3) subsequent changes or modifications in design; (4) out-of-court experiments indicating Goodrich's knowledge of a design defect; and (5) expert testimony claiming a design defect. 928 S.W.2d at 70. The court rejected Goodrich's argument that Martinez's failure to heed the product's warnings was a complete defense to the product defect claim. However, the court of appeals reversed and rendered the award of punitive damages, holding that there was no evidence to support the jury's finding of gross negligence.

Only Goodrich applied to this Court for writ of error. As in the court of appeals, Goodrich's principal argument here is that no evidence supports the jury finding that the tire was defective because "the tire bore a warning which was unambiguous and conspicuously visible (and not claimed to be inadequate); the tire was safe for use if the warning was followed; and the cause of the accident was mounting and inflating a tire in direct contravention of those warnings.". . .

II

A

This Court has adopted the products liability standard set forth in section 402A of the Restatement (Second) of Torts. . . .

To prove a design defect, a claimant must establish, among other things, that the defendant could have provided a safer alternative design. *See Caterpillar,* 911 S.W.2d at 384 ("[I]f there are no safer alternatives, a product is not unreasonably dangerous as a matter of law."). Implicit in this holding is that the safer alternative design must be reasonable, i.e., that it can be implemented without destroying the utility of the product. *See id.* ("'Texas law does not require a manufacturer to destroy the utility of his product in order to make it safe.'"). . . .

The newly released Restatement (Third) of Torts: Products Liability carries forward this focus on reasonable alternative design. See Restatement (Third) of Torts: Products Liability. Section 2(b). . . .

To determine whether a reasonable alternative design exists, and if so whether its omission renders the product unreasonably dangerous (or in the words of the new Restatement, not reasonably safe), the finder of fact may weigh various factors bearing on the risk and utility of the product. [The court excepts Comment *f* from the Products Liability Restatement, supra.]

Goodrich urges this Court to depart from this standard by following certain language from Comment *j* of the Restatement (Second) of Torts. Comment *j* provides in part:

> Where warning is given, the seller may reasonably assume that it will be read and heeded; and a product bearing such a warning, which is safe for use if it is followed, is not in defective condition, nor is it unreasonably dangerous.

Restatement (Second) of Torts §402A cmt. *j* (1965). The new Restatement, however, expressly rejects the Comment *j* approach:

> Reasonable designs and instructions or warnings both play important roles in the production and distribution of reasonably safe products. In general, when a safer design can reasonably be implemented and risks can reasonably be designed out of a product, adoption of the safer design is required over a warning that leaves a significant residuum of such risks. For example, instructions and warnings may be ineffective because users of the product may not be adequately reached, may be likely to be inattentive, or may be insufficiently motivated to follow the instructions or heed the warnings. However, when an alternative design to avoid risks cannot reasonably be implemented, adequate instructions and warnings will normally be sufficient to render the product reasonably

safe. . . . *Warnings are not, however, a substitute for the provision of a reasonably safe design.*

Restatement (Third) of Torts: Products Liability §2 cmt. *l* (emphasis added). The Reporters' Notes in the new Restatement refer to Comment *j* as "unfortunate language" that "has elicited heavy criticism from a host of commentators." Restatement (Third) of Torts: Products Liability §2, Reporters' Note, cmt. *l* (citing Howard Latin, Good Warnings, Bad Products, and Cognitive Limitations, 41 U.C.L.A. L. Rev. 1193 (1994) (utilizing the work of cognitive theorists to demonstrate that warnings should only be used as a supplement to a design that already embodies reasonable safety and not as a substitute for it); Aaron D. Twerski, *et al.*, The Use and Abuse of Warnings in Products Liability: Design Defect Comes of Age, 61 Cornell L. Rev. 495, 506 (1976)). Similarly, this Court has indicated that the fact that a danger is open and obvious (and thus need not be warned against) does not preclude a finding of product defect when a safer, reasonable alternative design exists. . . . ("A number of courts are of the view that obvious risks are not design defects which must be remedied. (citations omitted). However, our Court has held that liability for a design defect may attach even if the defect is apparent.").

The drafters of the new Restatement provide the following illustration for why courts have overwhelmingly rejected Comment *j:*

ILLUSTRATION:
Jeremy's foot was severed when caught between the blade and compaction chamber of a garbage truck on which he was working. The injury occurred when he lost his balance while jumping on the back step of the garbage truck as it was moving from one stop to the next. The garbage truck, manufactured by XYZ Motor Co., has a warning in large red letters on both the left and right rear panels that reads "DANGER—DO NOT INSERT ANY OBJECT WHILE COMPACTION CHAMBER IS WORKING—KEEP HANDS AND FEET AWAY." The fact that adequate warning was given does not preclude Jeremy from seeking to establish a design defect under Subsection (b). The possibility that an employee might lose his balance and thus encounter the shear point was a risk that a warning could not eliminate and that might require a safety guard. Whether a design defect can be established is governed by Subsection (b).

Restatement (Third) of Torts: Products Liability §2 cmt. *l,* illus. 14. . . .

B

We do not hold, as the dissenting justices claim, that "a product is defective whenever it could be more safely designed without substantially impairing its utility," *Post* at 344, or that "warnings are irrelevant in determining whether a product is reasonably safe." *Post* at 345. Rather, as we have explained, we agree with the new Restatement that warnings and safer alternative designs are factors, among others, for the jury to consider in determining whether the product as designed is reasonably safe. *See* Restatement (Third) of Torts: Products Liability §2 cmt. *f.* While the dissenting justices say that they also agree with the Restatement's approach, they would, at least in this case, remove the balancing process from the jury. Instead, they would hold that Goodrich's warning rendered the tape bead design reasonably safe as a matter of law.

The dissenting justices first argue that Goodrich's warning was clear and that it could have been followed, and consequently Martinez was injured only by "[i]gnoring . . . his own good sense." *Post* at 343. Even if this were true, it is precisely because "it is not at all unusual for a person to fail to follow basic warnings and instructions," General Motors Corp. v. Saenz, 873 S.W.2d 353, 358 (Tex. 1993), that we have rejected the superseded Comment *j*. The dissent also notes that there have been few reported mismatch accidents involving tires with this particular warning label. While this is certainly relevant, and perhaps would persuade many juries, we cannot say that it conclusively establishes that the tire is reasonably safe when weighed against the other evidence. The jury heard firsthand how an accident can occur despite the warning label, and how a redesigned tire would have prevented that accident. The jury also heard evidence that Goodrich's competitors had incorporated the single strand programmed bead by the early 1980s, and that Goodrich itself adopted this design in 1991, a year after manufacturing the tire that injured Martinez. Under these circumstances, there is at least some evidence supporting the jury's finding of product defect. . . .

Because we conclude that there is some evidence to support the judgment of the court below on the theory of products liability, we need not consider Goodrich's claim that there is no evidence as to negligence. For the foregoing reasons, we affirm the judgment of the court of appeals.

HECHT, J., files a dissenting opinion, in which ENOCH and BAKER, JJ. join, and in which OWEN, J., joins in all but Part II. . . .

Comment *j* to Section 402A of the Restatement (Second) of Torts states: Where warning is given, the seller may reasonably assume that it will be read and heeded; and a product bearing such a warning, which is safe for use if it is followed, is not in defective condition, nor is it unreasonably dangerous.

We have followed the first clause of comment *j,* but only to the extent of holding that a plaintiff is entitled to a rebuttable presumption that had he been adequately warned of the dangers of a product, he would have avoided injury, despite the fact that experience teaches that "it is not at all unusual for a person to fail to follow basic warnings and instructions." The presumption is merely a procedural device to obviate the necessity of plaintiff's self-serving testimony that he would have heeded adequate warnings. In making the presumption rebuttable we recognized that the first clause is not always true. Further, we have never followed the second clause of comment *j,* and now the Restatement (Third) of Torts: Products Liability has withdrawn comment *j* altogether as "unfortunate language" that "has elicited heavy criticism from a host of commentators." The Court's firm rejection of comment *j,* which the Court has never adopted and the Restatement has now itself rejected, is perhaps beating a dead horse, but I agree that comment *j* does not correctly state what the law is or should be.

Since it is human nature to disregard instructions, a rule that any product is reasonably safe as long as it bears an adequate warning of the risks of its use is not feasible. Such behavior, however, does not warrant the opposite rule that warnings are irrelevant in determining whether a product is reasonably safe. I agree with the Court that comment *l* to Section 2 of the Restatement (Third) of Torts: Products Liability now has it about right: [The dissent quotes comment *l,* set forth in the majority opinion.]

I do not agree, however, that the Court correctly reads or follows comment *l.* Comment *l* limits but does not foreclose the role of warnings in making products reasonably safe, even when there is a safer alternative design. The Court stresses the last sentence of comment *l* and brushes past the first sentence. Taken as a whole, the comment says, correctly, I think, that a safer alternative design that eliminates a risk is required over a warning that leaves a significant residuum of risk because product users may not get the warning, may be inattentive, or may not be motivated to heed the warning. The illustration accompanying comment *l* is of a worker whose foot is severed by a garbage truck's blade and compaction chamber when he loses his balance jumping onto the back of the truck. A warning on the truck, "keep hands and feet away," does little to protect against a worker's foreseeable inadvertence or misstep in the usual discharge of his job. But the warning might well be adequate admonishment to the merely curious, even if the garbage truck could be designed to be safer, if the residuum of risk were insignificant. Even if the risk that a worker will lose his balance and slip is significant enough to warrant designing additional protections in the truck, the risk that someone will intentionally stick his hand in a place where it obviously may be hurt when he is effectively warned not to do so may not warrant design changes.

Section 2(b) of the Restatement (Third) of Torts: Products Liability states the applicable rule: [The court sets out §2(b).]

There are two components to this rule: the possibility of a safer, reasonable alternative design, *and* a product that is not reasonably safe without that design. Both are required. Even if a reasonable alternative design would make a product safer, the product is not defective unless the omission of the design makes the product not reasonably safe. The comparison is not between the two designs, but between the product alternatively designed and the product including any warning. Comment *f* to Section 2 explains: [The court excerpts from Comment *f*, supra.]

Given the ease with which injury can be avoided, there is no evidence that redesigning the bead wire will eliminate a "significant residuum of risk" in the tire as designed with the warning label. In fact, Martinez's own evidence is to the contrary. The record establishes that there has been only one other claimed injury caused by attempting to mount a 16" tire with a warning label on a 16.5" wheel. The record does not reflect whether that claim was ever proved. Thousands of 16" tires have been manufactured with warning labels; millions of 16.5" wheels have been manufactured without warning labels. Martinez's evidence (which should not have been admitted) shows thirty-four claims against Goodrich for injuries caused by mismatching unlabeled 16" tires on 16.5" wheels. There has been one other claim involving a labeled tire. The tire industry should not be compelled to redesign bead wires to make tires harder to explode — or pay damages for failing to do so — simply because one or perhaps two mechanics over the years failed to follow directions or their own good sense. . . .

The record in this case shows that Goodrich's tire including the warning label was not defectively designed as a matter of law. Even if that were not so, Goodrich is entitled to have its liability determined in a fair trial in which at least some responsibility for the accident is assigned to Martinez. . . . Because the Court denies Goodrich any relief, I respectfully dissent.

Having read the majority and dissent, on whose side do you come down? Note that both the majority and dissent embrace §2, Comment *l*. They differ only as to its application to the facts. What do you make of the dissent's argument that §2(b) requires proof of a reasonable alternative design *and* proof that the omission of the reasonable alternative design renders the product *not reasonably safe?* The dissent utilized the "not reasonably safe" requirement as the conceptual tool that allowed it, in light of the clear warnings provided with the product, to deny liability even though a safer alternative design was clearly available. Can you think of other reasons why the Restaters might have adopted a test for defect that required that both of these elements be established? If the safer alternative design suggested by plaintiff is reasonable, does it not necessarily follow that its omission renders the product not reasonably safe?

The view taken by the Restatement in §2, Comment *l* and adopted by the court in *Uniroyal* has its origin in Uloth v. City Tank Corp., 384 N.E.2d 1188 (Mass. 1978). The illustration of the employee who got his foot caught between the blade and the compaction chamber of a garbage truck set forth in *Uniroyal* is based on the *Uloth* fact pattern. For other cases adopting this view, see Rogers v. Ingersoll-Rand Co., 144 F.3d 841d (D.C. Cir. 1998) (warnings on a milling machine about the dangers that arise when machine is backing up does not shield the manufacturer from liability where defect in system prevented alarm from operating); Lewis v. American Cyanamid Co., 715 A.2d 967 (N.J. 1998) ("when considering plaintiff's reasonably foreseeable misuses, [the jury] must decide whether the [product's] design was defective despite the presence of warnings cautioning against such misuses"). See also Kampen v. American Isuzu Motors, 157 F.3d 306 (5th Cir. 1998) (applying Louisiana law) (approving Comment *l* but finding specific warning against misuse rendered the product use one that was not reasonably anticipated by the manufacturer); Leaf v. Goodyear Tire & Rubber Co., 590 N.W.2d 525 (Iowa 1999) (casting doubt as to propriety in design defect case of utilizing Comment *j* presumption that warning will be heeded when provided; Restatement §2 Comment *l* may be more appropriate governing standard); Eads v. R. D. Werner Co., 847 P.2d 1370 (Nev. 1993) (warning that a ladder can tip is not dispositive on the issue of defect when stronger side rails would have made the ladder more stable).

2. Risk-Utility Balancing Without Requiring a Reasonable Alternative Design

Vautour v. Body Masters Sports Industries, Inc.
784 A.2d 1178 (N.H. 2001)

DUGGAN, J.

The plaintiffs in this products liability action, David S. Vautour and Susan Vautour, appeal an order of the Superior Court (*Fitzgerald*, J.) granting a motion for directed verdict to the defendant, Body Masters Sports Industries, Inc. We reverse and remand.

Mr. Vautour was injured while using a leg press machine manufactured by the defendant. The leg press is designed to strengthen a weightlifter's leg muscles by allowing him or her to raise and lower a metal sled, which may be loaded with weights, along fixed carriage tracks. A manually engaged safety system allows weightlifters to adjust safety stops and to operate the machine while sitting in a fixed, inclined position. In this position, a weightlifter may perform either deep leg presses or calf raise exercises. With legs extended along the carriage track and the balls of the weightlifter's feet on the sled, a weightlifter performs calf raise exercises by rotating the ankles up and down so that the sled and weights move up and down.

The leg press has two sets of safety stops, the upper and the lower stops. The upper stops provide a place for the weightlifter to rest the weight after extending his or her legs and pushing up the sled. The lower stops prevent the sled and weights from landing in the weightlifter's lap if he or she loses control of the machine. When the upper stops of the machine are disengaged the lower stops are engaged. The warning label on the machine states, "Caution. Handles must be in locked position when doing calf exercises," thereby instructing weightlifters to engage the upper stops when performing calf raises.

Mr. Vautour's injury occurred while moving his feet down to do calf raises. Although he was aware of the machine's warning label, Mr. Vautour did not have the upper stops engaged at the time of his accident. As a result, the sled and his knees fell rapidly toward his chest, injuring his feet. Mr. Vautour brought suit against the defendant under the theories of strict liability, negligence, and breach of warranty. Mr. Vautour contends that the location of the safety stops "exposed users to an unreasonable risk of harm and that this design defect" caused his injuries.

At trial, Barry Bates, the plaintiffs' biomechanics expert, testified that the machine, as designed, is hazardous because it does not adapt well to a wide range of body sizes and weightlifters may perform calf raise exercises without the upper stops engaged. He testified that in his opinion the leg press was defective and dangerous to weightlifters "because of the location of the lower stops and the possibility that the weight carriage can drop onto the person, putting them beyond their normal performance range of motion." Bates proposed that the leg press should be designed with adjustable, rather than fixed stops. He testified that he had not designed a machine with adjustable stops and did not know of any manufacturer in the industry who made a machine using adjustable stops. He testified, however, that by using adjustable stops "anything that was used would be better" than the fixed stops to prevent injuries. Under cross-examination, Bates admitted that the adjustable stops would not reduce the risk of injury to a user if he or she failed to manually set the stops before operating the machine.

After the close of the plaintiffs' case in chief, the defendant moved for a directed verdict, or, in the alternative, for dismissal, on the ground that the plaintiffs had failed to introduce evidence sufficient to make out a prima facie case. After the plaintiffs withdrew their claim for breach of warranty, the superior court granted the defendant's motion for directed verdict on the strict liability and negligence claims, concluding that:

> The point at which safety stops could be placed along the sled carriage without interfering with the muscle-strengthening function of the machine, the point at which stops must be placed to ensure that users are reasonably safe from physical injury, and the degree of risk to which users might reasonably be exposed when engaging in such leg strengthening exercises are each factual questions which appear, by their nature, to require specialized knowledge in the areas of design engineering, physiognomy, bio-mechanics, and safety standards in the field of athletic training.

Because the average juror could not be expected to know about these topics and because the plaintiffs' expert failed to offer any testimony regarding the acceptable risk of injury, where the safety stops should be located, or how his proposed alternative design would prevent the type of injuries suffered by Mr. Vautour, the superior court concluded that the plaintiffs failed to introduce evidence sufficient to support their strict liability and negligence claims.

On appeal, the plaintiffs assert that they proved all of the essential elements of their strict liability claim and the superior court erred by requiring them to prove an alternative design as an additional element in the case. . . .

A product is defectively designed when it "is manufactured in conformity with the intended design but the design itself poses unreasonable dangers to consumers." Thibault v. Sears, Roebuck & Co., . . . 395 A.2d 843 (N.H. 1978). To prevail on a defective design products liability claim, a plaintiff must prove the following four elements: (1) the design of the product created a defective condition unreasonably dangerous to the user; (2) the condition existed when the product was sold by a seller in the business of selling such products; (3) the use of the product was reasonably foreseeable by the manufacturer; and (4) the condition caused injury to the user or the user's property. Chellman v. Saab-Scania AB, . . . 637 A.2d 148 (N.H. 1993).

To determine whether a product is unreasonably dangerous, we explained in Bellotte v. Zayre Corp., . . . 352 A.2d 723 (N.H. 1976), that a product "must be dangerous to an extent beyond that which would be contemplated by the ordinary consumer who purchases it, with the ordinary knowledge common to the community as to its characteristics." Id. In Price v. BIC Corp., . . . 702 A.2d 330 (N.H. 1997), we further explained that whether a product is unreasonably dangerous to an extent beyond that which would be contemplated by the ordinary consumer is determined by the jury using a risk-utility balancing test.

Under a risk-utility approach, a product is defective as designed "if the magnitude of the danger outweighs the utility of the product." W. Keeton *et al.,* Prosser and Keeton on the Law of Torts §99, at 699 (5th ed. 1984). We have articulated the risk-utility test as requiring a "multifaceted balancing process involving evaluation of many conflicting factors." *Thibault,* . . . 395 A.2d 843. In order to determine whether the risks outweigh the benefits of the product design, a jury must evaluate many possible factors including the usefulness and desirability of the product to the public as a whole, whether the risk of danger could have been reduced without significantly affecting either the product's effectiveness or manufacturing cost, and the presence and efficacy of a warning to avoid an unreasonable risk of harm from hidden dangers or from foreseeable uses. See *Price,* . . . 702 A.2d 330. "Reasonableness, forseeability, utility, and similar factors are questions of fact for the jury." *Thibault,* . . . 395 A.2d 843.

The defendant contends that the risk-utility test, as articulated in *Thibault,* implicitly requires a plaintiff to offer evidence of a reasonable alternative design. Because the jury is instructed to consider whether the risk of danger could have been reduced without significantly affecting the effectiveness of the product and the cost of manufacturing, the defendant contends that evidence of a reasonable alternative design is required. The defendant urges us to adopt the Restatement (Third) of Torts §2(b) (1998), which requires a plaintiff in a design defect case to prove that the risks of harm posed by the product could have been reduced or avoided by a reasonable alternative design. Restatement (Third) of Torts §2(b) provides that:

> [A product] . . . is defective in design when the foreseeable risks of harm posed by the product could have been reduced or avoided by the adoption of a reasonable alternative design by the seller or other distributor, or a predecessor in the commercial chain of distribution, and the omission of the alternative design renders the product not reasonably safe.

By requiring a plaintiff to present evidence of a safer alternative design, section 2(b) of the Restatement thus elevates the availability of a reasonable alternative design from merely "a factor to be considered in the risk-utility analysis to a requisite element of a cause of action for defective design." Hernandez v. Tokai Corp., 2 S.W.3d 251, 256 (Tex. 1999).

There has been considerable controversy surrounding the adoption of Restatement (Third) of Torts §2(b). *See, e.g.,* Note, Just What You'd Expect: Professor Henderson's Redesign of Products Liability, 111 Harv. L. Rev. 2366 (1998); Lavelle, Crashing Into Proof of A Reasonable Alternative Design: The Fallacy of The Restatement (Third) of Torts: Products Liability, 38 Duq. L. Rev. 1059 (2000); Schwartz, The Restatement, Third, Tort: Products Liability: A Model of Fairness and Balance, 10 Kan. J. L. & Pub. Pol'y 41 (2000); Vandall, The Restatement (Third) of Torts: Products Liability Section 2(B): The Reasonable Alternative Design Requirement, 61 Tenn. L. Rev. 1407 (1994). Most of the controversy stems from the concern that a reasonable alternative design requirement would impose an undue burden on plaintiffs because it places a "potentially insurmountable stumbling block in the way of those injured by badly designed products." Just What You'd Expect: Professor Henderson's Redesign of Products Liability, supra at 2373 (quotation omitted). Commentators have noted that for suits against manufacturers who produce highly complex products, the reasonable alternative design requirement will deter the complainant from filing suit because of the enormous costs involved in obtaining expert testimony. *See id.* Thus, because of the increased costs to plaintiffs of bringing actions based on defective product design, commentators fear that an alternative design requirement presents the possibility that substantial litigation expenses may effectively eliminate recourse, especially in cases in which the plaintiff has suffered little damage. *See id.;* see also Vandall, supra at 1425-26.

On a practical level, the Restatement's requirement of proof of an alternative design may be difficult for courts and juries to apply. To determine whether the manufacturer is liable for a design defect, the jury must currently decide whether the plaintiff has proven the four essential elements of a design defect case. *See* LeBlanc v. American Honda Motor Co., . . . 688 A.2d 556 (N.H. 1997). As part of this analysis, the jury must determine whether the design of the product created a defective condition unreasonably dangerous to the user. In order to prove this element under the Restatement, a plaintiff must meet the requirement of proving the "availability of a technologically feasible and practical alternative design that would have reduced or prevented the plaintiff's harm." Restatement (Third) of Torts §2 comment *f* at 24 (1998). The Restatement, however, contains far-reaching exceptions. According to the Restatement, the reasonable alternative design requirement does not apply when the product design is "manifestly unreasonable." *Id.* comment *e* at 21-22. Plaintiffs are additionally not required to produce expert testimony in cases in which the feasibility of a reasonable alternative design is obvious and understandable to laypersons. *See id.* comment *f* at 23. . . . Consequently, a requirement of proving a reasonable alternative design coupled with these broad exceptions will introduce even more complex issues for judges and juries to unravel.

A more important consideration is that while proof of an alternative design is relevant in a design defect case, it should be neither a controlling factor nor an essential element that must be proved in every case. As articulated in *Thibault*, the risk-utility test requires a jury to consider a number of factors when deciding whether a product is unreasonably dangerous. *See Thibault*, . . . 395 A.2d 843. This list is not meant to be exclusive, but merely illustrative. "Depending on the circumstances of each case, flexibility is necessary to decide which factors" may be relevant. Armentrout v. FMC Corp., 842 P.2d 175, 184 (Colo. 1992) (explaining in dictum that relevant factors cannot be confined to a single list which must always be applied regardless of circumstances). Thus, the rigid prerequisite of a reasonable alternative design places too much emphasis on one of many possible factors that could potentially affect the risk-utility analysis. *See* Bodymasters v. Wimberley, . . . 501 S.E.2d 556, 559 (Ga. Ct. App. 1998) (explaining that a risk-utility test requires the balancing of several factors, and no one factor alone is a prerequisite for bringing a claim). We are therefore satisfied that the risk-utility test as currently applied protects the interests of both consumers and manufacturers in design defect cases, and we decline to adopt section 2(b) of the Restatement. . . .

Here, the plaintiffs presented sufficient evidence that the leg press machine was unreasonably dangerous pursuant to the risk-utility balancing test. The plaintiffs' expert testified that the defendant's design was "dangerous to the user, from an injury perspective," and his proposed design was safer than the defendant's current design. Although he did not specify exactly where the safety stops should have been placed to prevent Mr. Vautour's injuries, he did testify that his design was mechanically feasible and, under similar circumstances, machines with such a design would be, overall, less dangerous. It was up to the jury to assess the weight to be given this testimony. . . . "Weighing of substantive evidence is the very essence of the jury's function. Consequently the trial judge has been granted little discretion to withdraw questions of substantive fact from a jury's consideration." . . . While certainly a reasonable jury could have found this evidence insufficient to establish that the leg press design was unreasonably dangerous, we cannot say that no reasonable jury could have found otherwise. Nor can we say, when viewing the evidence in the light most favorable to the plaintiffs, that the sole reasonable inference from this testimony is so overwhelmingly in favor of the defendant that no contrary verdict could stand. . . . Thus, we hold that the trial court erroneously granted the defendant's motion for directed verdict upon the plaintiffs' strict liability, design defect claim. Under New Hampshire law, the plaintiffs' evidence was sufficient to establish a *prima facie* case.

Reversed and remanded.

BROCK, C.J., and BRODERICK, J., sat for oral argument but did not take part in the final vote; NADEAU and DALIANIS, JJ., concurred.

We are puzzled. If the court is utilizing risk-utility balancing, how can it conclude that a reasonable alternative design is only one of several factors in deciding whether a product design is defective, and that even this need not be proven? Assume that there was no better place to locate the stops to avoid the risk of the weight carriage dropping and further assume that the defendant had adequately warned about the necessity of locking the upper stops. Would the court still have allowed a jury to find that this leg press machine to be unreasonably dangerous? Except in very rare instances (which will be discussed infra), courts have been loathe to find that products for which there are no alternative designs should be declared unreasonably dangerous per se. Furthermore, after trashing the RAD requirement, the court goes on to say that the plaintiff had presented evidence of a RAD in that he had suggested a better location for the stops. Accordingly, it was the function of the jury, not the judge, to decide whether the plaintiff's suggested alternative design would have made the leg press machine safer. The authors have responded to much of the criticism aimed at the RAD requirement in James A. Henderson, Jr. & Aaron D. Twerski, Achieving Consensus on Product Design, 83 Cornell L. Rev. 867 (1998) (article cites the scholarly articles that are supportive and critical of the RAD requirement).

3. *Product Category Liability*

The Products Liability Restatement confronts the question of whether liability ought ever to be imposed on a product category even though no alternative design is available. Section 2, Comments *d* and *e* speak to the issue:

Restatement (Third) of Torts: Products Liability
(1998)

§2. CATEGORIES OF PRODUCT DEFECT
. . .

COMMENT:
. . .

d. Design defects: general considerations. . . . The requirement in Subsection (b) that the plaintiff show a reasonable alternative design applies in most instances even though the plaintiff alleges that the category of product sold by the defendant is so dangerous that it should not have been marketed at all. See Comment *e*. Common and widely distributed products such as alcoholic beverages, firearms, and above-ground swimming pools may be found to be defective only upon proof of the requisite conditions in Subsection (a), (b), or (c). If such products are defectively manufactured or sold without reasonable warnings as to their danger when such warnings are appropriate, or if reasonable alternative designs could have been adopted, then liability under §§1 and 2 may attach. Absent proof of defect under those Sections, however, courts have not imposed liability for categories of products that are generally available and widely used and consumed, even if they pose substantial risks of harm. Instead, courts generally *e. Design defects: possibility of manifestly unreasonable design.* Several courts have suggested that the designs of some products are so manifestly unreasonable, in that they have low social utility and high degree of danger, that liability should attach even absent proof of a reasonable alternative design. In large part the problem is one of how the range of relevant alternative designs is described. For example, a toy gun that shoots hard rubber pellets with sufficient velocity to cause injury to children could be found to be defectively designed within the rule of Subsection (b). Toy guns unlikely to cause injury would constitute reasonable alternatives to the dangerous toy. Thus, toy guns that project ping-pong balls, soft gelatin pellets, or water might be found to be reasonable alternative designs to a toy gun that shoots hard pellets. However, if the realism of the hard-pellet gun, and thus its capacity to cause injury, is sufficiently important to those who purchase and use such products to justify the court's limiting consideration to toy guns that achieve realism by shooting hard pellets, then no reasonable alternative will, by hypothesis, be available. In that instance, the design feature that defines which alternatives are relevant — the realism of the hard-pellet gun and thus its capacity to injure — is precisely the feature on which the user places value and of which the plaintiff complains. If a court were to adopt this characterization of the product, and deem the capacity to cause injury an egregiously unacceptable quality in a toy for use by children, it could conclude that liability should attach without proof of a reasonable alternative design. The court would declare the product design to be defective and not reasonably safe because the extremely high degree of danger posed by its use or consumption so substantially outweighs its negligible social utility that no rational, reasonable person, fully aware of the relevant facts, would choose to use, or to allow children to use, the product.

O'Brien v. Muskin Corp.
463 A.2d 298 (N.J. 1983)

POLLOCK, J.

Plaintiff, Gary O'Brien, seeks to recover in strict liability for personal injuries sustained because defendant, Muskin Corporation, allegedly marketed a product, an above-ground swimming pool, that was defectively designed and bore an inadequate warning. In an unreported decision, the Appellate Division reversed the judgment for defendants and remanded the matter for trial. We granted certification, 91 N.J. 548, 453 A.2d 866 (1982), and now modify and affirm the judgment of the Appellate Division. . . .

O'Brien sued to recover damages for serious personal injuries sustained when he dove into a swimming pool at the home of Jean Henry, widow of Arthur Henry, now Jean Glass. . . . At the close of the plaintiff's case, the trial court determined that he had failed to prove a design defect in the pool. Accordingly, at the close of the entire case, the court refused to charge the jury on design defect. Instead, the court submitted the case to the jury solely on the adequacy of the warning.

In response to special interrogatories, . . . the jury found that O'Brien was guilty of contributory negligence, and allocated fault for the injury as 15% attributable to Muskin and 85% attributable to O'Brien. Thus, under New Jersey's comparative negligence statute, O'Brien was barred from recovery. See N.J.S.A. 2A:15-5.1. The trial occurred before our decision in Roman v. Mitchell, 82 N.J. 336, 413 A.2d 322 (1980), and the court did not give an "ultimate outcome" instruction; that is, the court failed to instruct the jury on the effect on plaintiff's recovery of its allocation of fault.

On appeal, the Appellate Division found that the trial court erred in removing from the jury the issue of design defect. Consequently, that court reversed the judgment against Muskin and remanded the matter for a new trial.

I

Muskin, a swimming pool manufacturer, made and distributed a line of above-ground pools. Typically, the pools consisted of a corrugated metal wall, which the purchaser placed into an oval frame assembled over a shallow bed of sand. This outer structure was then fitted with an embossed vinyl liner and filled with water.

In 1971, Arthur Henry bought a Muskin pool and assembled it in his backyard. The pool was a twenty-foot by twenty-four-foot model, with four-foot walls. An embossed vinyl liner fit within the outer structure and was filled with water to a depth of approximately three and one-half feet. At one point, the outer wall of the pool bore the logo of the manufacturer, and below it a decal that warned "DO NOT DIVE" in letters roughly one-half inch high.

On May 17, 1974, O'Brien, then twenty-three years old, arrived uninvited at the Henry home and dove into the pool. A fact issue exists whether O'Brien dove from the platform by the pool or from the roof of the adjacent eight-foot high garage. As his outstretched hands hit the vinyl-lined pool bottom, they slid apart, and O'Brien struck his head on the bottom of the pool, thereby sustaining his injuries.

In his complaint, O'Brien alleged that Muskin was strictly liable for his injuries because it had manufactured and marketed a defectively designed pool. In support of this contention, O'Brien cited the slippery quality of the pool liner and the lack of adequate warnings.

At trial, both parties produced experts who testified about the use of vinyl as a pool liner. One of the plaintiff's witnesses, an expert in the characteristics of vinyl, testified that wet vinyl was more than twice as slippery as rubber latex, which is used to line in-ground pools. The trial court, however, sustained an objection to the expert's opinion about alternative kinds of pool bottoms, specifically whether rubber latex was a feasible liner for above-ground pools. The expert admitted that he knew of no above-ground pool lined with a material other than vinyl, but plaintiff contended that vinyl should not be used in above-ground pools, even though no alternative material was available. A second expert testified that the slippery vinyl bottom and lack of adequate warnings rendered the pool unfit and unsafe for its foreseeable uses.

Muskin's expert testified that vinyl was not only an appropriate material to line an above-ground pool, but was the best material because it permitted the outstretched arms of the diver to glide when they hit the liner, thereby preventing the diver's head from striking the bottom of the pool. Thus, he concluded that in some situations, specifically those in which a diver executes a shallow dive, slipperiness operates as a safety feature. Another witness, Muskin's customer service manager, who was indirectly in charge of quality control, testified that the vinyl bottom could have been thicker and the embossing deeper. A fair inference could be drawn that deeper embossing would have rendered the pool bottom less slippery.

At the close of the entire case, the trial court instructed the jury on the elements of strict liability, both with respect to design defects and the failure to warn adequately. The court, however, then limited the jury's consideration to the adequacy of the warning. That is, the court took from the jury the issue whether manufacturing a pool with a vinyl liner constituted either a design or manufacturing defect.

[The court reviews the history of products liability law, observing that in design and warning cases, the critical question is the legal standard by which one measures defectiveness.]

Although the appropriate standard might be variously defined, one definition, based on a comparison of the utility of the product with the risk of injury that it poses to the public, has gained prominence. To the extent that "risk-utility analysis," as it is known, implicates the reasonableness of the manufacturer's conduct, strict liability law continues to manifest that part of its heritage attributable to the law of negligence. Risk-utility analysis is appropriate when the product may function satisfactorily under one set of circumstances, yet because of its design present undue risk of injury to the user in another situation. . . .

Although state-of-the-art evidence may be dispositive on the facts of a particular case, it does not constitute an absolute defense apart from risk-utility analysis. See Beshada v. Johns-Manville Products Corp., 90 N.J. 191, 202-05 & n.6, 447 A.2d 539 (1982). The ultimate burden of proving a defect is on the plaintiff, but the burden is on the defendant to prove that compliance with state-of-the-art, in conjunction with other relevant evidence, justifies placing a product on the market. Compliance with proof of state-of-the-art need not, as a matter of law, compel a judgment for a defendant. State-of-the-art evidence, together with other evidence relevant to risk-utility analysis, however, may support a judgment for a defendant. In brief, state-of-the-art evidence is relevant to, but not necessarily dispositive of, risk-utility analysis. That is, a product may embody the state-of-the-art and still fail to satisfy the risk-utility equation.

The assessment of the utility of a design involves the consideration of available alternatives. If no alternatives are available, recourse to a unique design is more defensible. The existence of a safer and equally efficacious design, however, diminishes the justification for using a challenged design.

The evaluation of the utility of a product also involves the relative need for that product; some products are essentials, while others are luxuries. A product that fills a critical need and can be designed in only one way should be viewed differently from a luxury item. Still other products, including some for which no alternative exists, are so dangerous and of such little use that under the risk-utility analysis, a manufacturer would bear the cost of liability of harm to others. That cost might dissuade a manufacturer from placing the product on the market, even if the product has been made as safely as possible. Indeed, plaintiff contends that above-ground pools with vinyl liners are such products and that manufacturers who market those pools should bear the cost of injuries they cause to foreseeable users.

A critical issue at trial was whether the design of the pool, calling for a vinyl bottom in a pool four feet deep, was defective. The trial court should have permitted the jury to consider whether, because of the dimensions of the pool and slipperiness of the bottom, the risks of injury so outweighed the utility of the product as to constitute a defect. In removing that issue from consideration by the jury, the trial court erred. To establish sufficient proof to compel submission of the issue to the jury for appropriate fact-finding under risk-utility analysis, it was not necessary for plaintiff to prove the existence of alternative, safer designs. Viewing the evidence in the light most favorable to plaintiff, even if there are no alternative methods of making bottoms for above-ground pools, the jury might have found that the risk posed by the pool outweighed its utility.

In a design-defect case, the plaintiff bears the burden of both going forward with the evidence and of persuasion that the product contained a defect. To establish a prima facie case, the plaintiff should adduce sufficient evidence on the risk-utility factors to establish a defect. With respect to above-ground swimming pools, for example, the plaintiff might seek to establish that pools are marketed primarily for recreational, not therapeutic purposes; that because of their design, including their configuration, inadequate warnings, and the use of vinyl liners, injury is likely; that, without impairing the usefulness of the pool or pricing it out of the market, warnings against diving could be made more prominent and a liner less dangerous. It may not be necessary for the plaintiff to introduce evidence on all those alternatives. Conversely, the plaintiff may wish to offer proof on other matters relevant to the risk-utility analysis. It is not a foregone conclusion that plaintiff ultimately will prevail on a risk-utility analysis, but he should have an opportunity to prove his case. . . .

In concluding, we find that, although the jury allocated fault between the parties, the allocation was based upon the consideration of the fault of Muskin without reference to the design defect. Perhaps the jury would have made a different allocation if, in addition to the inadequacy of the warning, it had considered also the alleged defect in the design of the pool.

All parties consented at trial to a dismissal of all claims against Kiddie City, on the assumption that it did not manufacture the vinyl liner and that it was merely a conduit between the manufacturer and the purchaser. That assumption was based on Muskin's acknowledgment throughout the pretrial proceedings that it made the vinyl liner. In the course of the trial, the purchaser testified that all parts of the pool, including the liner, arrived in Muskin boxes, but a Muskin witness testified, to everyone's surprise, that the liner was not a Muskin product. To avoid possible prejudice to Muskin and plaintiff, the Appellate Division vacated the dismissal of the claims as to Kiddie City. We believe the appropriate disposition is to reinstate the dismissal as to Kiddie City and to preclude Muskin from denying that it made the vinyl liner.

We modify and affirm the judgment of the Appellate Division reversing and remanding the matter for a new trial.

SCHREIBER, J., concurring and dissenting.

Until today, the existence of a defect was an essential element in strict product liability. This no longer is so. Indeed, the majority has transformed strict product liability into absolute liability and delegated the function of making that determination to a jury. I must dissent from that conclusion because the jury will not be cognizant of all the elements that should be considered in formulating a policy supporting absolute liability, because it is not satisfactory to have a jury make a value judgment with respect to a type or class of product, and because its judgment will not have precedential effect. . . .

My research has disclosed no case where liability was imposed, utilizing the risk-utility analysis, as a matter of law for an accident ascribable to a product in the absence of a defect (manufacturing flaw, available alternative, or inadequate warning) other than in the absolute liability context. . . .

There are occasions where the court has determined as a matter of law because of policy reasons that liability should be imposed even though there is no defect in the product. This is the absolute liability model. The typical example is fixing absolute liability when an ultrahazardous activity causes injury or damage. Liability is imposed irrespective of any wrongdoing by the defendant. In this situation the ultimate determination is that the industry should bear such costs, provided the jury has made the requisite findings on causation and damages.

Factors similar to those used in the risk-utility analysis for products liability are applied in the ultrahazardous activity case. The Restatement (Second) of Torts lists these elements:

§520. ABNORMALLY DANGEROUS ACTIVITIES

In determining whether an activity is abnormally dangerous, the following factors are to be considered:

(a) existence of a high degree of risk of some harm to the person, land or chattels of others;

(b) likelihood that the harm that results from it will be great;

(c) inability to eliminate the risk by the exercise of reasonable care;

(d) extent to which the activity is not a matter of common usage;

(e) inappropriateness of the activity to the place where it is carried on; and

(f) extent to which its value to the community is outweighed by its dangerous attributes.

It is conceivable that a court could decide that a manufacturer should have absolute liability for a defect-free product where as a matter of policy liability should be imposed. Suppose a manufacturer produced toy guns for children that emitted hard rubber pellets—an obviously dangerous situation. A court could reasonably conclude that the risks (despite warnings) outweighed the recreational value of the toy, that the manufacturer should bear the costs and that there should be absolute liability to a child injured by the toy.

The Restatement also cautions that whether an activity is an abnormally dangerous one so that it should be placed in the ultrahazardous category is to be settled by the court, not the jury. In its comment it states:

> The imposition of [absolute] liability, on the other hand, involves a characterization of the defendant's activity or enterprise itself, and a decision as to whether he is free to conduct it at all without becoming subject to liability for the harm that ensues even though he has used all reasonable care. This calls for a decision of the court; and it is no part of the province of the jury to decide whether an industrial enterprise upon which

the community's prosperity might depend is located in the wrong place or whether such an activity as blasting is to be permitted without liability in the center of a large city. [3 Restatement (Second) of Torts §520 comment *l*, at 43 (1965)]

It is important to note that the risk-utility analysis is *not* submitted to the jury for the purpose of determining absolute liability for a class or type of product. Dean Wade has explained that when a whole group or class or type of a product may be unsafe, "the policy issues become very important and the factors must be collected and carefully weighed. It is here that the court — whether trial or appellate — does consider these issues in deciding whether to submit the case to the jury." [Wade, On the Nature of Strict Tort Liability for Products, 44 Miss. L.J. 825, 838 (1973).]

When the case is submitted to the jury in strict liability, the jury must decide whether the product is defective and reasonably safe, not whether as a matter of policy the manufacturer should be absolutely liable. In determining questions of defectiveness and safety, *some* of the same risk-utility factors may be pertinent. However, reference to any one of the factors is to be made only when it is relevant and may be of assistance in deciding whether the product is defective and whether it is not reasonably safe. . . .

In Beshada v. Johns-Manville Prod. Corp., 90 N.J. 191, 447 A.2d 539 (1982), this Court held that a manufacturer was assumed to know of a dangerous condition at the time of manufacture, even though no one in the scientific community had knowledge of that danger. Despite that fact, the manufacturer was deemed to have had a duty to warn of that condition and to be responsible for not having done so. By denying the state of the art defense, and in effect a warning defense, the Court, relying substantially on "Risk Spreading" and "Accident Avoidance" — elements that would be submitted to a court and not a jury — sanctioned absolute liability. The Court thereby indicated that the industry should bear the costs of the hazards incident to the use of asbestos, even though there were no defects in the asbestos.

Now the Court goes one step further and decides that a jury may speculate that, though there is no manufacturing flaw, the duty to warn has been satisfied and the manufacturer could not possibly have designed the item in a safer manner, the manufacturer can be absolutely liable because the jury finds that the risk outweighs the product's usefulness. It is not appropriate to forsake uniformity of treatment of a class or type of product by permitting juries to decide these questions. Nor is it appropriate for a jury to make this value judgment in addition in resolving factual issues. Unless the jury is to consider the feasibility of spreading the loss and the intricacies of cost avoidance, see Guido Calabresi & Jon T. Hirschoff, "Toward a Test for Strict Liability in Torts," 81 Yale L.J. 1055 (1972), the jury will conduct its inquiry in the absence of evidence of all the elements that should properly be considered in adopting a policy of having the manufacturer spread the loss by setting the price to cover the costs of claims or insurance premiums.

The majority holds that the jury should have been permitted to decide whether the risks of above-ground swimming pools with vinyl bottoms exceed their usefulness despite adequate warnings and despite unavailability of any other design. The plaintiff had the burden of proving this proposition. Yet he adduced no evidence on many of the factors bearing on the risk-utility analysis. There was no evidence on the extent that these pools are used and enjoyed throughout the country; how many families obtain the recreational benefits of swimming and play during a summer; how many accidents occur in the same period of time; the nature of the injuries and how many result from diving. There was no evidence of the feasibility of risk spreading or of the availability of liability insurance or its cost. There was no evidence introduced to enable one to gauge the effect on the price of the product, with or without insurance. The liability exposures, particularly if today's decision is given retroactive effect, could be financially devastating.

These factors should be given some consideration when deciding the policy question of whether pool manufacturers and, in the final analysis, consumers should bear the costs of accidents arising out of the use of pools when no fault can be attributed to the manufacturer because of a flaw in the pool, availability of a better design, or inadequate warning. If this Court wishes to make absolute liability available in product cases and not leave such decisions to the Legislature, it should require that trial courts determine in the first instance as a matter of law what products should be subject to absolute liability. In that event the court would consider all relevant factors including those utilized in the risk-utility analysis.

The difference between absolute and strict liability is not one of semantics. Significantly different elements are evaluated by different entities with different standards of review. As used in this opinion, "strict liability" and "absolute liability" signify distinct and separate concepts. Strict liability is imposed where there is a defect in a product due to an individual product flaw, an improper design or an inadequate warning. Irrespective of strict liability, a manufacturer or other seller may nevertheless be liable in an appropriate case under *absolute* liability. Absolute liability is imposed where, on the basis of policy considerations including risk-spreading, it is determined that a manufacturer or other seller should bear the cost of injuries he causes to foreseeable users, regardless of the presence or absence of any defect. In some circumstances a manufacturer may be liable though a product is free from defects.

The majority's view of "strict liability" encompasses both strict liability and absolute liability. Although the majority and I adopt the same formulaic statement that strict liability is imposed only where there is a "defect," . . . the majority uses the term to include not only individual product flaw, improper design and inadequate warning cases, but also a fourth category of cases in which the jury decides that the risks outweigh the utility of the product. It follows from the majority's rationale that a jury may be permitted to find that there is a "defect" whenever there is an accident involving a product.

I join in the result, however. There was proof that the pool liner was slippery and that the vinyl bottom could have been thicker and the embossing deeper. As the majority states, a "fair inference could be drawn that deeper embossing would have rendered the pool bottom less slippery." The plaintiff's theory was that the dangerous condition was the extreme slipperiness of the bottom. Viewing the facts favorably from the plaintiff's frame of reference, I would agree that he had some proof that the pool was incorrectly designed and therefore was defective. This issue, together with causation, should have been submitted to the jury.

Other than as stated herein, I join in the majority's opinion and concur in the judgment reversing and remanding the matter for a new trial.

CLIFFORD, J., concurring in the result.

For affirmance as modified — WILENTZ, C.J., and CLIFFORD, HANDLER, POLLOCK and O'HERN, JJ. — 5.

Concurring and dissenting — SCHREIBER, J. — 1.

O'Brien has been effectively overruled by statute in New Jersey. It is clear that the drafters of the statute took dead aim at *O'Brien* when they provided that a product could not be found defective in design if "there was not a practical and technically feasible alternative design that would have prevented the harm without substantially impairing the reasonably anticipated or intended function of the product." N.J. Stat. Ann. §2A:58C-3(b)(1)-(3) (West 2000). The statute provides an exception from this provision when the product is (1) egregiously unsafe (2) one whose dangers are unknown to the reasonable consumer and (3) one that has little or no usefulness. The commentary to the statute gives an example of a dangerous toy gun as a product that would fit this exception. There is no doubt, however, that *O'Brien* on its facts is a dead letter. One other state has imposed liability based on a risk-utility analysis of the value of the product to society. In Halphen v. Johns-Manville Sales Corp., 484 So. 2d 110 (La. 1986) the court concluded that an asbestos manufacturer could be held to a strict liability standard for a product that fails to meet risk-utility norms because the dangers created by its use, even if unforeseen at the time of manufacture, outweigh its utility. Only if a product passed the risk-utility test so that its social value outweighed its risk was the plaintiff required to prove an alternative design. *Halphen,* like *O'Brien,* was overridden by statute. La. Rev. Stat. Ann. §9:2800.56(1) (West 1997). Notwithstanding such legislative reactions, one may still find a court considering category liability on occasion. See, e.g., Ruiz-Guzman v. Amvac Chemical Corp., 7 P.3d 795 (Wash. 2000) (entertaining the possibility that a pesticide may fail risk-utility balancing even absent proof of a RAD).

There was some concern in the early stages of SUV litigation that courts might adopt some form of category liability due to the SUV's generic rollover propensity. Although on occasion courts may appear to talk in terms of category liability, see, e.g., Bowserfield v. Suzuki Motor Corp., 111 F. Supp. 612, 619 (E.D. Pa. 2000) (assessing SUV's overall social utility as initial step in Pennsylvania's design defect jurisprudence), the vast majority of SUV cases are premised on the ability of auto manufacturers to adopt alternative designs allowing for enhanced stability and far-reduced rollover tendencies. See Ford Motor Co. v. Ammerman, 705 N.E.2d 539 (Ind. Ct. App. 1999) (upholding punitive damages award where plaintiff established design defect by showing manufacturer's rejection of safety alteration proposals intended to increase stability); Watkins v. Ford Motor Co., 190 F.3d 1213 (11th Cir. 1999) (applying Georgia law); Clay v. Ford Motor Co., 215 F.3d 663 (6th Cir. 2000) (applying Ohio law).

Putting aside the few sporadic attempts to jump-start product category liability, the case law has been close to unanimous in rejecting design defect liability when plaintiff has failed to proffer a reasonable alternative design. For cases involving firearms, see Perkins v. F.I.E. Corp., 762 F.2d 1250, 1273 (5th Cir. 1985) (applying Louisiana law); Hilberg ex rel. Hilberg v. F.W. Woolworth Co., 761 P.2d 236, 240 (Colo. Ct. App. 1988), overruled on other grounds, Casebolt v.

Cowan, 829 P.2d 352 (Colo. 1992); Riordan v. International Armament Corp. 477 N.E.2d 1293, 1298-1299 (Ill. App. Ct. 1985); Knott v. Liberty Jewelry & Loan Inc., 748 P.2d 661, 663-664 (Wash. Ct. App. 1988). For cases involving cigarettes, see Little v. Brown & Williamson Tobacco Corp., 243 F. Supp. 2d 480 (D.S.C. 2001); Neri v. R.J. Reynolds Tobacco Co., 2000 WL 33911224 (N.D.N.Y. 2000). Kotler v. American Tobacco Co. 731 F. Supp. 50, 52 (D. Mass. 1990), *aff'd*, 926 F.2d 1217 (1st Cir. 1990), judgment vacated, 112 S. Ct. 3019 (1992), on remand, 981 F.2d 7 (1st Cir. 1992) (applying Massachusetts law); Gianitsis v. American Brands, Inc., 685 F. Supp. 853, 856 (D.N.H. 1988) (applying New Hampshire law). For a case involving minitrail bikes, see Baughn v. Honda Motor Co., 727 P.2d 655, 660 (Wash. 1986) (en banc).

In McCarthy v. Olin Corp., 119 F.3d 148 (2d Cir. 1997) (applying New York law), a wrongful death action on behalf of victims who were killed in Colin Ferguson's highly publicized murderous shooting spree on the Long Island Railroad was brought against the manufacturer of the "Black Talon" bullets used by Ferguson. Black Talon ammunition incorporates a hollow point bullet that is designed to expand upon impact, exposing razor-sharp edges at a 90-degree angle to the bullet. The expansion dramatically increases the wounding power of the bullet. Plaintiffs argued that the bullets were defectively designed in that they caused more damage than would have been caused by an ordinary bullet. The claim was thus one for enhanced injury. See Chapter Three. The heart of plaintiffs' claim of design defect was that Black Talon bullets failed the risk-utility test, the governing test for defect in New York. In affirming the trial court's grant of defendant's motion to dismiss, the court said that "The purpose of the risk/utility analysis is to determine whether the risk of injury might have been reduced or avoided if the manufacturer had used a feasible alternative design. . . . However, the risk of injury to be balanced with the utility is a risk not intended as the primary function of the product. . . . There is no reason to search for an alternative safer design where the product's sole utility is to kill or maim. Accordingly we hold that appellants have failed to state a cause of action under New York strict products liability law." Id. at 155. In an interesting dissenting opinion, Judge Guido Calabresi suggested that Black Talon bullets might well fall under the exception set forth in §2, Comment *e* of the Restatement (Third) of Torts: Products Liability (1998) (see p.219, supra), Accord Downs v. R.T.S. Security, Inc., 670 So. 2d 434 (La. Ct. App. 1996).

Notwithstanding the overwhelming judicial rejection of product category liability, a debate rages in the law reviews as to its propriety. You will not be suprised that the authors side with the courts on this one. We present both sides of the story. Take your pick.

James A. Henderson, Jr. & Aaron D. Twerski, Closing the American Products Liability Frontier: The Rejection of Liability Without Defect
66 N.Y.U. L. Rev. 1263, 1298-1300, 1305-1306, 1316-1318 (1991)

Product-Category Liability: Some Initial Terminology

Before addressing the merits of the various product-category liability proposals, we should clarify certain issues of terminology that might seem confusing at first. Initially, one might argue that product-category liability would rest on a finding of defectiveness — the entire product category would be deemed defective either because it does not offer sufficient benefits to justify the injuries it causes or because it satisfies some other criterion. We prefer terminology that avoids reliance on defectiveness because we feel that legal terminology, whenever possible, should clarify what is happening in the litigation to which it refers. To stretch the term "defective" to include broad categories of products that are not defective in any traditional sense could mask the profound differences between this use of the term "defective" and its more traditional uses. Courts that have faced this issue appear to have sensed the possible confusion and have avoided using "defectiveness" terminology.

Of course, this first point regarding terminology also raises a point of substance: is risk-utility product-category liability really different from the liability traditionally imposed on product designs based on risk-utility balancing? If one were to think of every variation of product design as constituting a category unto itself — for example, if one thought of slightly longer-handled bicycles and slightly shorter-handled bicycles as constituting two separate categories — then the term "product-category liability" would apply to every instance in which a plaintiff attacked a product design as unreasonably dangerous, including all defective-design claims under traditional law. Thus, if a plaintiff injured while learning to ride a bicycle argued that the handlebars on the bicycle should have been slightly longer to increase side-to-side stability, she could be said to be attacking the *category* of "shorter-handled bicycles." And yet intuitively one knows that an attack on slightly shorter-handled bicycles is not categorical but marginal. The plaintiff is not attacking the category "bicycles" but rather a marginal variation within the category. In contrast, if the plaintiff were to argue that three wheels, arranged triangularly, are required to achieve adequate lateral stability, she would be making a categorical assault on bicycles. The essential difference between these two claims is what distinguishes product-category liability from traditional liability for defective design.

The variable that determines whether one is dealing with a product category or merely a marginal design variation within a category is the degree of substitutability of the alternative suggested by the plaintiff and the product as designed by the defendant. In traditional, intracategory design litigation, the alternative design suggested or implicated by the plaintiff is a relatively close substitute for the product as designed by the defendant. Bicycles with slightly longer handlebars are close substitutes for bicycles with slightly shorter handlebars. Presumably, if plaintiffs succeeded with longer-handle bar claims, the new alternative design would resemble so closely the older design as to be nearly a perfect substitute, thus effectively driving the former variation, which alone would carry the burden of tort liability, from the new bicycle market. A few bicycle design purists might be willing to pay a substantial premium for the older, shorter-handled but less stable design. But intuitively, it seems likely that this demand would be so small that it would not justify the continued mass production of the earlier design.

In contrast, when a plaintiff attacks a bicycle design on the ground that a two wheeled cycle is inherently unsafe, the next best alternative — a tricycle — is not a very close substitute. Although a far better substitute for a bicycle than many other products, a tricycle is a much less suitable substitute for a bicycle than was the two-wheeled cycle with slightly longer handle bars. Indeed, a tricycle is so poor a substitute for a bicycle that if a court held that three wheels were minimally required to produce a safe cycle, it would be imposing liability not for how the defendant designed the bicycle but for having designed and distributed any sort of bicycle in the first place. Drawing on terminology currently in use, the court could be said to condemn bicycles for the "unavoidably unsafe" aspect that defines two-wheeled transportation: lateral instability at low speeds. In other words, the court would be condemning the product for the very design feature—two-wheeledness—that not only rendered it more dangerous but also made it desirable to a majority of its users and consumers.

Problems of Implementation Presented by Product-Category Liability

. . . For the traditional process of adjudication to work rationally and properly, the parties must use applicable legal doctrine to focus their claims so that they may insist upon a favorable outcome as a matter of right. As Professor Fuller explained, some problems are polycentric in nature. They consist of elements that are connected to one another as are the strands of a spider's web, so that a decision with regard to any element affects the decisions with regard to all the others. Such problems are not suited to judicial resolution because neither side can move from element to element in an orderly sequence.

A certain degree of polycentricity inheres in defective product design cases generally. Yet courts are able to manage in these traditional contexts because plaintiffs typically propose alternative designs and ask the judiciary to focus on the relatively small, marginal differences between the defendant's design and the proposed alternative. With product-category liability, no comparison of marginal differences is necessary because the plaintiff is arguing that the entire product category, including all possible variations therein, should be subject to absolute liability. Quite literally, the question asked in product-category liability cases is: "taking all relevant considerations into account, is the product category in question appropriate for use and consumption in society?" Thus, the polycentricity that inheres in traditional design cases is magnified enormously.

That risk-utility-based product-category liability cases would be unadjudicable can be seen by considering how the parties would attempt to argue a typical claim. For example, in connection with a claim that small, cheap handguns are unreasonably dangerous and should be subject to strict liability, how small is small? How cheap is cheap? For what range of accidents and adverse outcomes are distributors to be liable? Are suicides by handguns to be compensable? How are the parties to obtain relevant data on the social costs associated with small handguns, especially if they cannot agree on the relevant parameters of the problem? Presumably small handguns serve useful as well as wasteful social purposes: people collect them as hobbyists and possess them for protection, deriving pleasure and senses of well-being. How can a court quantify those utilities?

To be answered rationally, the question whether handguns of a particular size and monetary price are "good for society" would require extended legislative or administrative hearings and investigations. Even if courts attacked these problems incrementally, on a case-by-case basis, it is unrealistic to hope that courts could adjudicate their ways to intelligent, consistent solutions. Bearing in mind the magnitude of the stakes involved—imposing absolute liability might tax small handguns off the market — it is hardly surprising that most courts have refused to get involved.

Explicit Attempts to Establish Product-Category Liability

. . . Many plaintiffs have asked the courts to adopt a theory of product-category liability. Notwithstanding the plaintiff's success in *O'Brien,* courts overwhelmingly have turned plaintiffs away as a matter of law, offering a variety of reasons. Most of the reasons mirror both the policy and implementation problems identified earlier in our discussion of the theoretical and practical problems that would flow from the adoption of product-category liability. Courts have said that risk-utility analysis should not apply to products whose dangers are so commonly known and which measure up to broad-based consumer expectations; that it would be extremely difficult to measure and monetize the psychic and emotional pleasure of owning handguns or smoking cigarettes; that product-category liability is a "radical doctrine which imprudently arrogates to the judicial process some very significant societal determinations;" that courts would have no way of preventing inconsistent jury verdicts for similar products; that the test is so expansive that sellers would face potential and unpredictable liability for almost any injury related to product use; that manufacturers would become insurers of their products; and that such highly political liability issues are best left to the legislature.

Several courts have noted that the list of products that would become subject to risk-utility attack is substantial. Alcohol, cigarettes, radar detectors, all-terrain vehicles, and high-speed automobiles are all products that arguably score high on the misery scale, and yet most are prominent fixtures in a free-market economy. Given the wide range of individual consumer behavior when making use of these products, judges understandably are loath to place the onus for injury on the manufacturer. Thus, one of the reasons that courts are hostile to the idea of product-category liability may be that they intuit that the list of product categories to which such an approach might apply is great and the implications for each product on the list enormous. Indeed, many judges appear to view the product-category liability derisively, describing it as "radical" and "delightfully nonsensical." [footnotes omitted].

The article called forth a response from Mark A. Geistfeld, Implementing Enterprise Liability: A Comment on Henderson and Twerski, 67 N.Y.U. L. Rev. 1157 (1992) and a rebuttal by Henderson and Twerski, The Unworkability of Court Made Enterprise Liability: A Reply to Geistfeld, 67 N.Y.U. L. Rev. 1174 (1992).

Ellen Wertheimer, The Smoke Gets in Their Eyes: Product Category Liability and Alternative Feasible Designs in the Third Restatement
61 Tenn. L. Rev. 1429 (1994)

. . . Professors Henderson and Twerski seem to equate product category liability with liability without defect. This is only true, of course, if the concept of defect is defined as necessarily including the failure to use an alternative feasible design. If defect is defined in terms of failed risk-utility tests, then the test of defectiveness does not require an alternative feasible design. Because it requires the application of a risk-utility test, this definition does not constitute liability without defect.

Treating liability in the absence of an alternative feasible design as synonymous with liability without defect also falls into the common trap of using the concepts of "danger" and "defect" interchangeably. These terms do not mean the same thing; "dangerousness" represents a factual characteristic of a product, while "defectiveness" is a legal conclusion about that product. A dangerous product is not necessarily defective, it is only defective if its costs outweigh its benefits. In short, liability depends upon whether a product is defective, not whether it is dangerous. The argument that the definition of defect must require proof of an alternative feasible design to avoid this problem is grounded on the mistaken idea that danger and defect are synonymous.

Dangerous products exist that clearly pass the risk-utility test and are therefore not defective; automobiles are one example. Although automobiles must meet certain safety standards, there is no way to eliminate all the risks that they pose. Yet no one could seriously argue that their dangers outweigh their utility. Although the safest automobile remains dangerous, automobiles are not defective because their benefits outweigh their remaining costs. An automobile manufacturer cannot be held liable simply because a car has proved generically dangerous; there must be more to show that the car was defective.

Interestingly, it is difficult to distinguish product category liability cases from other design defect cases in automobile litigation. For example, in Dreisonstok v. Volkswagenwerk, A.G., the plaintiff argued that the design of a Volkswagen minibus was defective when compared with the design of a passenger car. Plaintiff contended that the minibus design was defective because it did not embody the level of crashproofing possible for a passenger vehicle. This could be construed as either: (1) an argument that there was an alternative feasible design (passenger car) that should have been used instead, or (2) a challenge that minibuses as a product category are unavoidably unsafe and should not be manufactured at all. Given these two plausible interpretations, it is difficult to determine whether *Dreisonstok* was an alternative feasible design case or a product category liability case. The basic argument was that the minibus aspect of the design was defective, and that there was an alternative — the automobile. For plaintiff to prevail, however, requires the conclusion that minibuses are unavoidably unsafe because they are not cars.

Like cars, many drugs are dangerous without being defective because their dangers are outweighed by their utility. When the utility of a product outweighs its dangers, that product is not defective. No product is defective simply because it is dangerous.

My favorite example of a product which is dangerous, useless, and without alternative feasible design is the cigarette. If the Restatement (Third) requires proof of an alternative feasible design, cigarettes will be exempt from its coverage. Is this an appropriate result?

Lawsuits based on cigarette smoking have almost always been characterized as failure to warn cases. But a lawsuit against cigarette manufacturers for defective design need not involve failure to warn. In a lawsuit not brought on a failure to warn theory, the plaintiff would argue that cigarettes are defective under Section 402A because they fail the risk-utility test. Their defect lies in the fact that the dangers they embody outweigh any utility they might possess. Unfortunately, there is no alternative feasible design that would eliminate the dangers, but showing such an alternative feasible design was not required for liability under section 402A as originally written.

Current commentators reject the idea that cigarette manufacturers should be liable for their product. But they fail to make a convincing case for their position. On the contrary, a cigarette manufacturer's liability for its product would fulfill the purposes of strict products liability doctrine superbly.

Cigarettes cause untold injury and death, both to those who smoke and to those who are exposed to the smoke generated by others. This grotesque fact becomes even more appalling because manufacturers of cigarettes generate huge profits. The manufacturers, however, do not pay for the injuries their product causes. Strict products liability was designed to treat the injuries caused by products as a cost of doing business. Cigarette manufacturers thus receive a windfall because they collect profits on sales of their product, but do not pay its true costs. If cigarette manufacturers still turn a profit after properly being held liable for the true costs of their product, then presumably they will continue to make and sell cigarettes. If they do not continue to make a profit after paying the costs of their product, presumably they would halt production. Economists should rejoice in this result, because it represents the marketplace working to perfection. Products that make a profit will continue to be produced; those that do not make a profit, will not. If cigarette manufacturers are found liable for the injuries their product causes, they will raise their prices, and the costs will fall on smokers.

Strict products liability was designed to shift the costs of injuries caused by products from consumers to manufacturers and, through cost-spreading, to the consumers of a particular product. Exempting cigarette manufacturers from liability places the costs of injuries on nonsmokers and smokers alike, an utterly indefensible result. Indeed, society as a whole subsidizes cigarette production through health care costs and lost work days.

Product category liability challenges courts to struggle with evaluating the claimed costs and benefits of a product, but the task is not impossible. Indeed, courts frequently perform risk-utility tests, and there is no evidence that the absence of an alternative feasible design renders courts incapable of weighing the costs and benefits of a product. There are those who argue that allowing product category liability for cigarettes will open the floodgates to absolute liability. The response to this manifestly absurd assertion is, first, that plaintiffs must prove a product defective in order to recover for injuries it has caused, and second, that there is no other product currently available which, when used as intended, causes over 400,000 American deaths each year. Cigarettes are unique. [footnotes omitted]

Would Professor Wertheimer allow a jury to weigh the risk-utility of a minibus? Would it be irrational to conclude that the benefits of the minibus do not outweigh the rather substantial increased risk of harm to the driver and passengers when such vehicles are involved in collisions? And why should minibuses or automobiles, for that matter, not be made to pay the cost of accidents? Wouldn't the price of cars then reflect what she calls the "true costs" of the product?

Carl T. Bogus, War on the Common Law: The Struggle at the Center of Products Liability
60 Mo. L. Rev. 1, 30-34 (1995)

. . . "Product category liability," or "generic product risks," as it is sometimes called, refers to the situation that obtains when strict liability attaches to an entire class of products, regardless of how they have been designed, manufactured, or marketed. This occurs when a product generically fails a risk-utility test, that is, when a product remains unreasonably dangerous despite the best possible design, construction, and warnings to the consumer.

In the typical case, the plaintiff argues that the product lacked something that would have made it safer: a sanding machine should have been equipped with a guard; a boat or lawn mower should have had a deadman's switch; a nightgown should have been treated with a flame retardant; an automobile gas tank should have been lined with a nylon bladder. Although the focus is on the product rather than the manufacturer's conduct, there is nevertheless the idea of what the defendant did wrong — he sold a machine without a guard or a boat without a deadman's switch. He is morally culpable because he put a product into commerce knowing that it was unsafe in some fashion; if he was not aware of the unsafe characteristic, he must shoulder the responsibility for his ignorance. The deficiencies in the product and in defendant's conduct are flip sides of the same coin, and thus products liability is not divorced from traditional fault-based values.

When, however, a product is condemned generically, the court appears activist and doctrine seems detached from traditional values. It is one thing to say that a motorcycle is unreasonably dangerous unless it has crash bars or saddlebags to protect the rider in an accident, but it is quite another to say that motorcycles are unreasonably dangerous per se. Some would see such a decision as an attack on free choice, challenging the right of the individual to govern his own activity and "determine his own fate." This view may be expressed in the language of products liability law as follows: A product cannot be *unreasonably* dangerous if an individual, with full knowledge of the risks, has voluntarily elected to use it. In such a circumstance the individual has decided that, for him, the benefits of the product justify its risks.

To follow the motorcycle example, assume that nineteen-year-old John Doe buys his first motorcycle. The following week, while traveling on a highway at forty-five mph, he hits a small rock, loses control of the motorcycle and slams into a telephone poll at the side of the road. The accident leaves him paraplegic. He sues the motorcycle manufacturer, not because there was some defect in the workmanship or because the motorcycle could have been designed to be more stable after hitting small objects, but merely that motorcycles are unreasonably dangerous. He offers statistical data showing that motorcycle riders have a fatality rate about twenty-five times greater than that of automobile occupants. He argues that the costs that motorcycles impose on society-at-large exceed their benefits, and therefore strict liability applies. The manufacturer would assert the assumption of risk defense, which bars one from recovering after "voluntarily and unreasonably proceeding to encounter a known danger," and would almost certainly prevail. John Doe's lawsuit offends fundamental social mores — with freedom comes responsibility, and someone who has freely made a choice should not later be heard to complain about the consequences.

But what about those who have been injured without assuming the risks? If John Doe careened into a pedestrian instead of a telephone pole, should the pedestrian be able to bring a products liability action against the motorcycle manufacturer on a generic risk theory? Should the party paying John Doe's medical expenses be able to recover those costs from the manufacturer? In modern society, John Doe will almost never pay his own medical expenses. The costs will be borne by a private insurance company or a government program such as Medicare or Medicaid; if no third party is responsible, the medical provider will be forced to absorb most of the costs itself (and try to recoup them by charging other patients enough to cover the institution's free care and bad debt). This means the financial consequences of motorcycle riding are borne by everyone, not merely by motorcycle riders. . . . [footnotes omitted]

Do you foresee courts deciding that motorcycles flunk the great risk-utility test in the sky? Isn't the idea as radical as the courts have made it out to be?

The debate continues. Professor David Owen, after flirting with product category liability in David G. Owen, The Graying of Products Liability Law: Paths Taken and Untaken in the New Restatement, 61 Tenn. L. Rev. 1241, 1253-1257 (1994), now seems to clearly reject it. See David G. Owen, Defectiveness Redefined: Exploding the Myth of "Strict" Products Liability, 1996 U. Ill. L. Rev. 743, 774-775 (1996) ("Generally, the proper focal point for the risk-utility balance is the particular safety feature of the alternative design proposed by the plaintiff that would have prevented or reduced the plaintiff's harm. Ordinarily, therefore, what are relevant are the *incremental* ('marginal') risks and benefits of adopting the particular design safety feature proposed by the plaintiff — those (that would have been) incurred in *moving* from the manufacturer's actual design to the plaintiff's hypothetical alternative design."). Harvey M. Grossman, Categorical Liability: Why the Gates Should be Kept Closed, 36 S. Tex. L. Rev. 385 (1995). Also see Symposium on Generic Products Liability, 72 Chi.-Kent L. Rev. 1 et seq (1996).

Dawson v. Chrysler Corp.
630 F.2d 950 (3d Cir. 1980), *cert. denied,* 450 U.S. 959 (1981)

ADAMS, C.J.

This appeal from a jury verdict and entry of judgment in favor of the plaintiffs arises out of a New Jersey automobile accident in which a police officer was seriously injured. The legal questions in this diversity action, that are governed by New Jersey law, are relatively straight-forward. The public policy questions, however, which are beyond the competence of this Court to resolve and with which Congress ultimately must grapple, are complex and implicate national economic and social concerns. . . .

I. *Factual Background*

On September 7, 1974, Richard F. Dawson, while in the employ of the Pennsauken Police Department, was seriously injured as a result of an automobile accident that occurred in Pennsauken, New Jersey. As Dawson was driving on a rain-soaked highway, responding to a burglar alarm, he lost control of his patrol car — a 1974 Dodge Monaco. The car slid off the highway, over a curb, through a small sign, and into an unyielding steel pole that was fifteen inches in diameter. The car struck the pole in a backwards direction at a forty-five degree angle on the left side of the vehicle; the point of impact was the left rear wheel well. As a result of the force of the collision, the vehicle literally wrapped itself around the pole. The pole ripped through the body of the car and crushed Dawson between the seat and the "header" area of the roof, located just above the windshield. The so-called "secondary collision" of Dawson with the interior of the automobile dislocated Dawson's left hip and ruptured his fifth and sixth cervical vertebrae. As a result of the injuries, Dawson is now a quadriplegic. He has no control over his body from the neck down, and requires constant medical attention.

Dawson, his wife, and their son brought suit . . . against the Chrysler Corporation, the manufacturer of the vehicle in which Dawson was injured. . . . The plaintiffs' claims were based on theories of strict products liability and breach of implied warranty of fitness. They alleged that the patrol car was defective because it did not have a full, continuous steel frame extending through the door panels, and a cross-member running through the floor board between the posts located between the front and rear doors of the vehicle. Had the vehicle been so designed, the Dawsons alleged, it would have "bounced" off the pole following relatively slight penetration by the pole into the passenger space.

Expert testimony was introduced by the Dawsons to prove that the existing frame of the patrol car was unable to withstand side impacts at relatively low speed, and that the inadequacy of the frame permitted the pole to enter the passenger area and to injure Dawson. The same experts testified that the improvements in the design of the frame that the plaintiffs proposed were feasible and would have prevented Dawson from being injured as he was. According to plaintiffs' expert witnesses, a continuous frame and cross-member would have deflected the patrol car away from the pole after a minimal intrusion into the passenger area and, they declared, Dawson likely would have emerged from the accident with only a slight injury.

In response, Chrysler argued that it had no duty to produce a "crashproof" vehicle, and that, in any event, the patrol car was not defective. Expert testimony for Chrysler established that the design and construction of the 1974 Dodge Monaco complied with all federal vehicle safety standards, and that deformation of the body of the vehicle is desirable in most crashes because it absorbs the impact of the crash and decreases the rate of deceleration on the occupants of the vehicle. Thus, Chrysler's experts asserted that, for most types of automobile accidents, the design offered by the Dawsons would be less safe than the existing design. They also estimated that the steel parts that would be required in the model suggested by the Dawsons would have added between 200 and 250 pounds to the weight, and approximately $300 to the price of the vehicle. It was also established that the 1974 Dodge Monaco's unibody construction was stronger than comparable Ford and Chevrolet vehicles.

After all testimony had been introduced, Chrysler moved for a directed verdict, which the district judge denied. The jury thereupon returned a verdict in favor of the plaintiffs. In answers to a series of special interrogatories, the jurors concluded that (1) the body structure of the 1974 Dodge Monaco was defective and unreasonably dangerous; (2) Chrysler breached its implied warranty that the vehicle would be fit for use as a police car; (3) as a result of the defective design and the breach of warranty, Dawson sustained more severe injuries than he would have incurred had Chrysler used the alternative design proposed by Dawson's expert witnesses; (4) the defective design was the proximate cause of Dawson's enhanced injuries; and (5) Dawson's failure to use a seatbelt was not a proximate cause of his injuries. The jury awarded Mr. Dawson $2,064,863.19 for his expenses, disability, and pain and suffering, and granted Mrs. Dawson $60,000.00 for loss of consortium and loss of services. After the district court entered judgment, Chrysler moved for judgment notwithstanding the verdict or, alternatively for a new trial. The court denied both motions. The Dawsons then requested prejudgment interest of eight percent per annum of the damages award, accruing from the time suit was instituted to the date of the judgment. The trial judge granted the request in the amounts of $388,012.53 for Mr. Dawson and $11,274.72 for Mrs. Dawson.

On appeal, Chrysler raises the following contentions: (1) It owed no duty to the Dawsons to manufacture an automobile that would withstand the type of collision that occurred here. (2) The evidence presented by the Dawsons was insufficient to establish that the patrol car was defective and unreasonably dangerous or that Chrysler breached an implied warranty of fitness. (3) The evidence did not sufficiently establish that Dawson's injuries in fact were caused by the allegedly defective design.

We affirm.

II. Discussion

[The court concludes that strict liability applies, and that the defendant owed the plaintiff a duty to provide a reasonably crashworthy automobile. The court proceeds to the question of whether a jury could find for the plaintiff on the facts in this case.]

Chrysler maintains that, under these standards, the district court erred in submitting the case to the jury because the Dawsons failed, as a matter of law, to prove that the patrol car was defective. Specifically, it insists that the Dawsons did not present sufficient evidence from which the jury reasonably might infer that the alternative design that they proffered would be safer than the existing design, or that it would be cost effective, practical, or marketable. In short, Chrysler urges that the substitute design would be less socially beneficial than was the actual design of the patrol car. In support of its argument, Chrysler emphasizes that the design of the 1974 Dodge Monaco complied with all of the standards authorized by Congress in the National Traffic and Motor Vehicle Safety Act of 1966, Pub. L. 89-563, tit. I, §107, 80 Stat. 718, codified in 15 U.S.C. §1396 (1976), and set forth in accompanying regulations, 49 C.F.R. §571.1 (1979).

Compliance with the safety standards promulgated pursuant to the National Traffic and Motor Vehicle Safety Act, however, does not relieve Chrysler of liability in this action. For, in authorizing the Secretary of Transportation to enact these standards, Congress explicitly provided, "Compliance with any Federal motor vehicle safety standard issued under this subchapter does not exempt any person from any liability under common law." 15 U.S.C. §1397(c) (1976). Thus, consonant with this congressional directive, we must review Chrysler's appeal on the question of the existence of a defect under the common law of New Jersey that is set forth above.

Our examination of the record persuades us that the district court did not err in denying Chrysler's motion for judgment notwithstanding the verdict. The Dawsons demonstrated that the frame of the 1974 Dodge Monaco was noncontinuous — that is, it consisted of a front portion that extended from the front of the car to the middle of the front passenger seat, and a rear portion that ran from the middle of the rear passenger seat to the back end of the vehicle. Thus, there was a gap in the seventeen-inch side area of the frame between the front and rear seats. The plaintiffs also proved that, after colliding with the pole, the car slid along the left side portion of the rear frame until it reached the gap in the frame. At that point, the pole tore through the body of the vehicle into the passenger area and proceeded to push Dawson into the header area above the windshield.

Three experts — a design analyst, a mechanical engineer, and a biochemical engineer — also testified on behalf of the Dawsons. These witnesses had examined the patrol car and concluded that it was inadequate to withstand side impacts. They testified that there was an alternative design available which, had it been employed in the 1974 Monaco, would have prevented Dawson from sustaining serious injuries. The substitute design called for a continuous frame with an additional cross member running between the so-called B-posts — the vertical posts located at the side of the car between the front and rear seats. According to these witnesses, this design was known in the industry well before the accident and had been tested by a number of independent testing centers in 1969 and in 1973.

The mechanical engineer conducted a number of studies in order to ascertain the extent to which the alternative design would have withstood the crash. On the basis of these calculations, he testified that the pole would have penetrated only 9.9 inches into the passenger space, and thus would not have crushed Dawson. Instead, the engineer stated, the car would have deflected off the pole and back into the highway. Under these circumstances, according to the biochemical engineer, Dawson would have been able to "walk away from the accident" with but a bruised shoulder.

Also introduced by the Dawsons were reports of tests conducted for the United States Department of Transportation, which indicated that, in side collisions with a fixed pole at twenty-one miles per hour,[1] frame improvements similar to those proposed by the experts presented by the Dawsons reduced intrusion into the passenger area by fifty percent, from sixteen inches to eight inches. The study concluded that the improvements, "in conjunction with interior alterations, demonstrated a dramatic increase in occupant protection." There was no suggestion at trial that the alternative design recommended by the Dawsons would not comply with federal safety standards. On cross-examination, Chrysler's attorney did get the Dawsons' expert witnesses to acknowledge that the alternative design would add between 200 and 250 pounds to the vehicle and would cost an additional $300 per car. The Dawsons' experts also conceded that the heavier and more rigid an automobile, the less able it is to absorb energy upon impact with a fixed

---

1. Eyewitness as well as expert testimony was introduced to show that the speed of the car at the time of impact was between twenty-four and twenty-six miles per hour.

object, and therefore the major force of an accident might be transmitted to the passengers. Moreover, an expert for Chrysler testified that, even if the frame of the patrol car had been designed in conformity with the plaintiffs' proposals, Dawson would have sustained injuries equivalent to those he actually incurred. Chrysler's witness reasoned that Dawson was injured, not by the intrusion of the pole into the passenger space, but as a result of being thrown into the header area of the roof by the vehicle's initial contact with the pole — that is, prior to the impact of the pole against the driver's seat.

On the basis of the foregoing recitation of the evidence presented respectively by the Dawsons and by Chrysler, we conclude that the record is sufficient to sustain the jury's determination, in response to the interrogatory, that the design of the 1974 Monaco was defective. The jury was not required to ascertain that all of the factors enumerated by the New Jersey Supreme Court in [Cepeda v. Cumberland Engineering, Inc., 76 N.J. 152, 386 A.2d 816 (1978)] weighed in favor of the Dawsons in order to find the patrol car defective. Rather, it need only to have reasonably concluded, after balancing these factors, that, at the time Chrysler distributed the 1974 Monaco, the car was "not reasonably fit, suitable and safe for its intended or reasonably foreseeable purposes." [Suter v. San Angelo Foundry & Machine Co., 81 N.J. 150, 169, 406 A.2d 140, 149 (1979).] Moreover, our role in reviewing the record for purposes of determining whether a trial judge erred in denying a motion for a directed verdict or for judgment notwithstanding the verdict is necessarily a limited one. As we stated in [Huddell v. Levin, 537 F.2d 726 (3d Cir. 1976)], "'The Seventh Amendment bars appellate review of facts found by a jury in actions at common law. . . .'" 537 F.2d at 736 (quoting 9 C. Wright & A. Miller, Federal Practice and Procedure §2571, at 681 (1971)). Thus, we are admonished to review the record in this case in the light most favorable to the nonmoving party, the Dawsons, and to affirm the judgment of the district court denying the motions unless the record "is critically deficient of that minimum quantum of evidence from which a jury might reasonably afford relief." Denneny v. Siegel, 407 F.2d 433, 439 (3d Cir. 1969); accord, *Huddell*, 537 F.2d at 737. We hold that it is not. . . .

The remaining question in regard to the motion for judgment notwithstanding the verdict is whether the Dawsons presented sufficient evidence to permit the jury reasonably to conclude that the design defect was the proximate cause of Dawson's injuries. In this regard, Chrysler advances three arguments. First, it urges that the patrol car was substantially modified by Dawson's employer in such a way that the car, as sold by Chrysler, could not be said to have caused the injuries. Second, it maintains that Dawson's failure to wear a seat belt was, in fact, the proximate cause of his injuries.[2] Third, it claims that there was insufficient evidence that the defect caused Dawson to suffer more severe injuries than he would have incurred had the alternative design been employed — that is, had the patrol car not been defective.

Counsel for the Dawsons conceded that the patrol car had been modified by the addition of a tubular roll bar and a wire mesh screen that extended between

---

2. Dawson testified that, at the time of the accident, he was not wearing a seat belt, but that this was customary police practice in order to permit officers to enter and leave their vehicles as quickly as possible.

the front and rear passenger areas in order to separate the police officer from suspects. Dawsons' expert witnesses testified, however, that this alteration neither compromised the structural integrity of the vehicle, nor in any way contributed to Dawson's injuries. In contrast, the expert witnesses for Chrysler testified merely that they were not certain whether the modifications affected Dawson's injuries. Under these circumstances, the jury's implicit conclusion that the alterations were not the proximate cause of Dawson's injuries is supported by the evidence.

The jury specifically found in interrogatory five that Dawson's failure to wear his seatbelt was not a proximate cause of his injuries. Chrysler presented expert testimony that Dawson was injured when he "ramped" up the seat back into the roof of the car — that is, as he slid upwards out of his seat along the back rest — following the vehicle's initial impact with the pole. It argues therefore that, if Dawson had been wearing a seatbelt, he would not have been thrown out of the seat and would not have smashed into the roof of the car. Chrysler maintains that the jury's verdict is inconsistent with this testimony.

In *Huddell*, we noted in reviewing on appeal a question regarding causation that "the credibility of opinion evidence is for the fact-finder." Here, the Dawsons presented expert witnesses who contradicted Chrysler's theory of causation. Observing initially that the patrol car was moving backwards at a forty-five degree angle at the time of impact, the witnesses opined that the force of the collision must have pushed Dawson's back and left shoulder against the rear of the seat. Under these circumstances, they concluded, he did not "ramp" up the seat into the roof, but remained in the seat until the pole entered the passenger space, collided with the rear of the seat, and pushed both the seat and Dawson into the ceiling. In other words, had the pole been prevented from crushing up against the rear of the driver's seat, Dawson would not have been thrown into the ceiling. This testimony was corroborated by a third expert, who stated that the nature of Dawson's dislocated hip indicated that he was not thrown from the seat as Chrysler's witnesses maintained. The jurors reasonably could have found the testimony offered by the Dawsons' witnesses to be more persuasive than Chrysler's. Accordingly, Chrysler's contention that the jury's verdict is at odds with the evidence is without merit.

Chrysler's last argument regarding causation is that the plaintiffs failed to prove that Dawson's injuries were enhanced as a result of the design-defect in the patrol car. As with the other contentions, the record does not support this claim. The Dawsons presented expert testimony that the alternative design would have prevented the pole from intruding far enough into the passenger space to hit the front seat. And, as we have just observed, there was testimony that Dawson was not thrown into the ceiling of the car, but rather was crushed up against the roof as the pole forced the passenger seat into the roof. Had Dawson remained in his seat from gravity forces, and had the seat not been jammed against the roof, it is a reasonable inference that his cervical vertebrae would not have been ruptured. Indeed, the biochemical engineer who evaluated the accident and testified for the Dawsons concluded that, if the pole had not entered the patrol car and crushed Dawson, the officer would have suffered no more than a bruised shoulder. In view of this testimony, we cannot say that the jury's verdict on the question of proximate cause is unsupported by the record. . . .

author's dialogue 10

JIM: You know, Aaron, *Dawson* is included in this section on category liability against my better judgment. *Dawson* is an interesting case, but not because it raises the issue of category liability. If I were to apply a label to the problem that *Dawson* poses, I would say that it presents the problem of *seriatim* liability. Suppose that Chrysler designs a car like the Dodge Monaco with a frame with less rigidity. In a side collision the plaintiff suffers enhanced injury and a jury finds that the frame should have been more rigid. If Chrysler conforms to the wishes of the jury and designs its car with a more rigid frame it will face lawsuits from plaintiffs who suffer enhanced injury in head-on collisions. Occupants of a car that has a less rigid frame are better off in head-on collisions with a frame that is deformable and thus takes the energy of the crash rather than passing it on to passengers. So Chrysler switches to a rigid frame after the first case and the next jury nails Chrysler for not having a deformable, less rigid frame. Chrylser ends up liable either way. That is the problem that the *Dawson* court talks about. I don't see this being a category liability case. It's a problem with any reasonableness issue presented on similar facts in different cases to successive juries in a "*seriatim*" fashion.

AARON: I don't disagree with you that the *Dawson* court is concerned with what you call the *seriatim* problem. But I see the court embracing category liability as well. Remember that the plaintiff's alternative design was one that would add 200-250 pounds of steel to the Dodge Monaco. That's one heck of a lot of steel and costs an additional $300 per vehicle. You must admit that redesigning a small economy car so that it becomes a mid-size sedan does raise category liability problems. Now, I'm not sure at what point you cross the line between marginal change to mega change, but I suspect that 250 pounds of steel is getting close. The majority does talk about the fact that American cars are in competition with the small foreign car market and that auto manufacturers have been attempting to reduce auto size to get better gas mileage. No, Jim, *Dawson* legitimately raises the category liability question.

JIM: Look, Aaron, *Dawson* is still a far cry from *O'Brien*, in which the New Jersey court held that above-ground swimming pools as a class may be de-

III. Conclusion

Although we affirm the judgment of the district court, we do so with uneasiness regarding the consequences of our decision and of the decisions of other courts throughout the country in cases of this kind.

As we observed earlier, Congress, in enacting the National Traffic and Motor Vehicle Safety Act, provided that compliance with the Act does not exempt any person from liability under the common law of the state of injury. The effect of

clared defective. But even if *Dawson* does not raise the problem of category liability it may raise an enterprise liability problem that is a first-cousin to category liability. You know economists would look at the *seriatim* problem and say that it is just not a real issue. Auto manufacturers will learn from experience that whether they make the frame of a car more rigid or less rigid they will be found liable by juries. They will then simply adopt the version they think is more cost-effective, insure against the residual accident/liability costs of not doing it the other way, and add those insurance costs to the price of the car.

AARON: Isn't that inevitable in a system that is not governed solely by administrative regulation? As long as factfinders, be they judge or jury, will be deciding factually similar cases *seriatim* we will get some of what you refer to as enterprise liability in the form of inconsistent jury verdicts case to case.

JIM: I agree. But the rules shouldn't encourage such verdict patterns, and commentators shouldn't ignore the fact that they are problematic. And if you think that it's essentially harmless to encourage inconsistent verdicts case to case you must have skipped that material on enterprise liability we set out at the beginning of this chapter explaining why our legal system cannot make manufacturers insurers of last resort. It is always possible to conjure up some design fix that would have avoided or lessened a plaintiff's enhanced injury. Auto manufacturers thus become liable for making cars (not for making defective cars). A liability system that does not utilize a sensibly defined concept of defect as the linchpin will eventually self-destruct because of adverse selection and moral hazard problems. I thought we did a good job of explaining those concepts earlier in the text.

AARON: My memory is not half as bad as you think. The argument as to why enterprise liability cannot be insured against is good. I buy it. However, liability is not imposed in all cases where an auto crashes and a plaintiff suffers enhanced injuries. Liability is imposed only when a jury decides that a reasonable alternative design could have been adopted. Admittedly, juries can make contradictory findings and that is troubling. But as long as the reasonable alternative designs that juries are advocating call for marginal changes we will not seriously threaten insurability.

JIM: Which leaves us where we started. *Dawson* presents a *seriatim* problem, not a category liability problem.

---

this provision is that the states are free, not only to create various standards of liability for automobile manufacturers with respect to design and structure, but also to delegate to the triers of fact in civil cases arising out of automobile accidents the power to determine whether a particular product conforms to such standards. In the present situation, for example, the New Jersey Supreme Court has instituted a strict liability standard for cases involving defective products, has defined the term "defective product" to mean any such item that is not "reasonably fit, suitable and safe for its intended or reasonably foreseeable purposes," and has left to the jury the task of determining whether the product at issue measures up to this standard.

The result of such arrangement is that while the jury found Chrysler liable for not producing a rigid enough vehicular frame, a factfinder in another case might well hold the manufacturer liable for producing a frame that is too rigid. Yet, as pointed out at trial, in certain types of accidents — head-on collisions — it is desirable to have a car designed to collapse upon impact because the deformation would absorb much of the shock of the collision, and divert the force of deceleration away from the vehicle's passengers. In effect, this permits individual juries applying varying laws in different jurisdictions to set nationwide automobile safety standards and to impose on automobile manufacturers conflicting requirements. It would be difficult for members of the industry to alter their design and production behavior in response to jury verdicts in such cases, because their response might well be at variance with what some other jury decides is a defective design. Under these circumstances, the law imposes on the industry the responsibility of insuring vast numbers of persons involved in automobile accidents.

Equally serious is the impact on other national social and economic goals of the existing case-by-case system of establishing automobile safety requirements. As we have become more dependent on foreign sources of energy, and as the price of that energy has increased, the attention of the federal government has been drawn to a search to find alternative supplies and the means of conserving energy. More recently, the domestic automobile industry has been struggling to compete with foreign manufacturers which have stressed smaller, more fuel-efficient cars. Yet, during this same period, Congress has permitted a system of regulation by ad hoc adjudications under which a jury can hold an automobile manufacturer culpable for not producing a car that is considerably heavier, and likely to have less fuel efficiency.

In sum, this appeal has brought to our attention an important conflict that implicates broad national concerns. Although it is important that society devise a proper system for compensating those injured in automobile collisions, it is not at all clear that the present arrangement of permitting individual juries, under varying standards of liability, to impose this obligation on manufacturers is fair or efficient. Inasmuch as it was the Congress that designed this system, and because Congress is the body best suited to evaluate and, if appropriate, to change that system, we decline today to do anything in this regard except to bring the problem to the attention of the legislative branch.

Bound as we are to adjudicate this appeal according to the substantive law of New Jersey, and because we find no basis in that law to overturn the jury's verdict, the judgment of the district court will be affirmed.

In Chapter Three, we encountered cases dealing with claims that a plaintiff's injuries were enhanced because an auto had a manufacturing defect. *Dawson* raises the question of crashworthiness in its most common form. A huge body of case law deals with claims that autos were defectively designed and, as a result, either the driver or passengers suffered injuries that could have been avoided had a safer design been chosen. Crashworthiness litigation has become a subspecialty in the law of products liability. It is interesting to note that in the early days of products liability litigation, there was some controversy as to whether courts ought to recognize a cause of action for crashworthiness. An early case denying liability is Evans v. General Motors Corp., 359 F.2d 822 (7th Cir.) (applying Indiana law) *cert. denied,* 385 U.S. 836 (1966). But, beginning with Larsen v. General Motors Corp., 391 F.2d 495, 502 (8th Cir. 1968) (applying Minnesota law), crashworthiness liability was recognized as a theory of recovery when the court stated that a manufacturer had a duty to design an automobile "not only to provide a means of transportation, [but] to provide a safe means or as safe as is reasonably possible under the present state of the art." Since then, this genre of litigation has taken on tidal wave proportions. It is fair to say that today all states recognize crashworthiness liability.

Almost no aspect of automobile design has gone unchallenged. Cases have dealt with the design of door latches, Moisenko v. Volkswagenwerk Aktiengesellschaft, 1999 WL 1045075 (6th Cir. 1999) (applying Michigan law), fuel tanks, Gerow v. Mitch Crawford Holiday Motors, 987 S.W.2d 359 (Mo. Ct. App. 1999), roof strength, Hyundai Motor Co. v. Rodriguez, 995 S.W.2d 661 (Tex. 1999), seat belts, Griffin v. Kia Motors Corp., 843 So. 2d 336 (Fla. Dist. Ct. App. 2003), strength of pillars, Wright v. Louisiana Power & Light Co., 752 So. 2d 919 (La. Ct. App. 1999) and gas caps, Tomasovic v. American Honda Motor Co., 525 N.E.2d 1111 (Ill. Ct. App. 1988). Some of the cases call for moderate changes in the design of the car. However, as *Dawson* demonstrates, plaintiffs have not been shy to ask for some rather significant changes in automobile design. Whether the design alternative that serves as a predicate for liability in *Dawson* constitutes category liability is the subject of the following disagreement between the authors.

E. THE CONSUMER EXPECTATIONS STANDARD FOR DETERMINING DESIGN DEFECT

As the previous discussion has established, design review based on feasible alternative/risk-utility balancing seems close to (and most often identical with) negligence. This insight has not been lost on the commentators or the courts. Resisting wholesale reliance on risk-utility analysis, they argue that the economist's test for liability gives inadequate attention to many of the forces that shape consumer attitudes toward product-related risk. An early advocate of a test for liability that focuses on consumer expectations, rather than on risk-utility, is Professor Marshall Shapo. See A Representational Theory of Consumer Protection: Doctrine, Function and Legal Liability for Product Disappointment, 60 Va. L. Rev. 1109, 1370 (1974):

> Judgments of liability for consumer product disappointment should center initially and principally on the portrayal of the product which is made, caused to be made or permitted by the seller. This portrayal should be viewed in the context of the impression reasonably received by the consumer from representations or other communications made to him about the product by various means: through advertising, by the appearance of the product, and by the other ways in which the product projects an image on the mind of the consumer, including impressions created by widespread social agreement about the

product's function. This judgment should take into consideration the result objectively determinable to have been sought by the seller, and the seller's apparent motivation in making or permitting the representation or communication.

1. Consumer Expectations as a Sword to Impose Liability

Heaton v. Ford Motor Co.
435 P.2d 806 (Or. 1967)

GOODWIN, J.

The plaintiff appeals a judgment entered after an involuntary nonsuit in a products-liability case involving a wheel on a Ford 4-wheel-drive pickup truck. The principal question is whether the plaintiff produced sufficient evidence to support his allegation that the wheel was dangerously defective.

Plaintiff purchased the truck new in July 1963 to use for hunting and other cross-country purposes as well as for driving upon paved highways. He drove the truck some 7,000 miles without noticing anything unusual about its performance. Prior to the day of the accident the truck had rarely been off the pavement, and plaintiff swore that it had never been subjected to unusual stress of any kind. On the day of the accident, however, the truck, while moving on a "black-top" highway at normal speed, hit a rock which plaintiff described as about five or six inches in diameter. The truck continued uneventfully for about 35 miles, when it left the road and tipped over.

After the accident, the rim of the wheel was found to be separated from the "spider." Witnesses described the "spider" as the interior portion of the wheel which is attached to the vehicle by the lug nuts. The twelve rivets connecting the rim to the spider appeared to have been sheared off. The spider, according to one witness, showed signs of having been dragged along the ground. There was also a large dent in the rim and a five-inch cut in the inner tube at a spot within the tire that was adjacent to the dent in the rim. Only three of the rivets which had held the rim on the spider were found after the accident. . . .

In the type of case in which there is no evidence, direct or circumstantial, available to prove exactly what sort of manufacturing flaw existed, or exactly how the design was deficient, the plaintiff may nonetheless be able to establish his right to recover, by proving that the product did not perform in keeping with the reasonable expectations of the user. When it is shown that a product failed to meet the reasonable expectations of the user the inference is that there was some sort of defect, a precise definition of which is unnecessary. If the product failed under conditions concerning which an average consumer of that product could have fairly definite expectations, then the jury would have a basis for making an informed judgment upon the existence of a defect. The case at bar, however, is not such a case. . . .

The court's function is to decide whether the evidence furnishes a sufficient basis for the jury to make an informed decision. If the record permits, the jury determines whether the product performed as an ordinary consumer would have expected. In the case at bar the record furnishes no basis for a jury to do anything but speculate.

Where the performance failure occurs under conditions with which the average person has experience, the facts of the accident alone may constitute a sufficient basis for the jury to decide whether the expectations of an ordinary consumer of the product were met. High-speed collisions with large rocks are not so common, however, that the average person would know from personal experience what to expect under the circumstances. Nor does anything in the record cast any light upon this issue. The jury would therefore be unequipped, either by general background or by facts supplied in the record, to decide whether this wheel failed to perform as safely as an ordinary consumer would have expected. To allow the jury to decide purely on its own intuition how strong a truck wheel should be would convert the concept of strict liability into the absolute liability of an insurer.

The argument has been made that the question of the ordinary consumer's expectations should be treated for jury purposes in the same way that the question of reasonable conduct in a negligence case is treated. But in deciding in a negligence case what is reasonable conduct, the jury is deciding in a context of "right and wrong" how someone *should* have behaved. In making this decision they are presumed to know the relevant factors. If not, such information is provided, as in a medical malpractice case where there is expert testimony as to the proper standards.

In the defective-product area, courts have already decided how strong products *should* be: they should be strong enough to perform as the ordinary consumer expects. In deciding what the reasonable consumer expects, the jury is not permitted to decide how strong products should be, nor even what consumers should expect, for this would in effect be the same thing. The jury is supposed to determine the basically factual question of what reasonable consumers do expect from the product. Where the jury has no experiential basis for knowing this, the record must supply such a basis. In the absence of either common experience or evidence, any verdict would, in effect, be the jury's opinion of how strong the product *should* be. Such an opinion by the jury would be formed without the benefit of data concerning the cost or feasibility of designing and building stronger products. Without reference to relevant factual data, the jury has no special qualifications for deciding what is reasonable. . . .

While the matter was never presented to the trial court, and thus requires no extended discussion in this appeal, the plaintiff has referred in this court to certain advertising published by the defendant, to reinforce the plaintiff's claim that a consumer would have expected the wheel in question to be engineered and manufactured in such a manner as to withstand the kind of force applied to it in this case. The plaintiff does not contend that the advertising constituted misrepresentation under Restatement (Second) of Torts §402B, but rather that the advertising in general tends to create expectations of strength and durability under Section 402A. A general impression of durability, however, does not help a customer to form an expectation about the breaking point of a wheel. A "rugged" Ford truck could be expected to negotiate rough terrain, including five-or-six-inch rocks, at appropriate off-the-road speeds, but it does not follow that a user could expect the same thing at highway speeds. If such expectations do exist, the record should contain evidence to support the inference that they do.

Affirmed.

O'CONNELL, J. (dissenting).

. . . It is plaintiff's position that the theory of strict liability should be deemed applicable whenever a person is injured as a result of exposing himself to a hazard in reasonable reliance upon the capabilities of a product as represented by the seller. The gist of plaintiff's argument is summed up as follows:

> ... It is not unreasonable to suggest that the driver of a vehicle promoted as "solid," "rugged" and "built like a truck" will subject that vehicle and its passengers to hazards to which he would not subject a vehicle otherwise promoted. With specific reference to this case, it is not unreasonable to surmise that a driver of a vehicle so promoted who runs over a rock on the highway will not even consciously consider the possibility of stopping to check for damage because he takes it for granted that such an impact will not harm a vehicle which he has been conditioned to think of as "solid," "rugged," and "like a truck."

Plaintiff, then, is asking us to "take judicial notice of facts which form part of the common knowledge of people who possess average intelligence. . . ."

Apparently the majority opinion would hold that there was a failure of proof, irrespective of whether the question of strict liability is for the court or jury in a case of this kind. I disagree. If we had been presented with the same facts with the modification that plaintiff had struck a rock one inch in diameter rather than a five-inch rock, I am sure that the majority would have held that at least a jury question was made out. The beginning point of our reasoning would be that a manufacturer of automobiles must construct wheels of sufficient durability to withstand the impact of one-inch rocks, because one-inch rocks are not an uncommon obstacle on highways. A buyer could reasonably expect to have the wheel withstand such an impact and it would not be unreasonable for him to proceed on his journey after the impact. However, the buyer could not reasonably expect a wheel to remain safe after striking a rock two feet in diameter at seventy miles an hour. Somewhere along the continuum between one inch and two feet it will be necessary to draw a line. The line is drawn by deciding whether a manufacturer should be required to construct a wheel of such durability as to withstand the impact of a rock of the size in question. Whether the manufacturer has that duty in a particular case should depend, it seems to me, upon whether the manufacturer could reasonably foresee the likelihood that the hazard would be encountered by those using the product, and this would, of course, depend to some extent upon the representations made by the manufacturer with respect to the durability of the product.

The manufacturer's conduct must be measured against a standard of reasonableness, a standard similar to that employed in determining whether a defendant is negligent. Here, however, we do not measure defendant's conduct in terms of fault but simply upon the basis of its foreseeability. A jury is just as well equipped to judge the reasonableness of defendant's conduct on this score as it is when the inquiry is made as to defendant's negligence. The members of the jury draw upon their experiences and observations and set up some kind of a standard as a measure against which to appraise the defendant's conduct in the particular case. They would be justified in concluding that the wheel in this case was unreasonably dangerous according to the test stated in Restatement (Second) of Torts §402A, p.352 (1965), requiring a finding that "[t]he article sold must be dangerous to an extent beyond that which would be contemplated by the ordinary consumer who purchases it, with the ordinary knowledge common to the community as to its characteristics."

The majority apparently would require some evidence of what this community standard is. How is this to be done? Certainly this is not the type of question which calls for the testimony of an expert witness. Are we to call lay witnesses to testify what "would be contemplated by the ordinary consumer"? If that is required in the present case, it would be equally necessary in an ordinary negligence case to inform the jury of the community standard on such questions as the reasonableness of conduct in driving a car with respect to speed, lookout and control.

But we submit these questions of the reasonableness of defendant's conduct to the jury and, subject to the right of the court to decide as a matter of law that the standard was or was not met, we are willing to trust the jury's judgment as to the community standard and to appraise the defendant's conduct in light of it.

I believe that the question of defendant's liability is kept from the jury in the present case not because there is a lack of evidence upon which to sustain a verdict for plaintiff, but because the majority of the court, finding the imposition of strict liability a severe burden upon the seller, attempts to limit that burden by distorting the concept of the jury's function.

SLOAN, J., joins in this dissent.

Professor Douglas A. Kysar proposes a thoughtful variation of the consumer expectations test based on what consumers actually expect rather than on what they have a right to expect. In an article entitled The Expectations of Consumers, 103 Colum. L. Rev. 1700, 1763 (2003), he argues:

> A great deal of human judgment and decisionmaking research focuses on the manner in which individuals perceive and process information regarding risks. As it turns out, the notion of "risk" for most individuals is not a purely actuarial concept involving probabilistic estimates of harm. Rather, according to proponents of the "psychometric paradigm" view of risk perception, risk is a complex, textured assessment of numerous variables that surround a given environmental, health, or safety hazard. In addition to the likelihood and severity of a harm, individuals also appear to care about a variety of qualitative attributes, such as whether a risk is voluntarily confronted by the victim, whether its potential harm is equitably distributed among the population, whether it poses a particularly dreaded form of death or illness, whether it threatens future generations, and whether the perceived source of the risk is believed to be a trustworthy actor. Such factors do not appear within the basic model of cost-benefit analysis, which tends to abstract away from qualitative characteristics in order to provide a uniform basis for assessing a wide range of health and safety risks. . . .
>
> The risk perception literature therefore suggests a possible independent role for consumer expectations analysis in products liability. Just as lay reactions to risk depart from those of experts, consumer expectations of product safety can be expected to depart from the standards that would be derived under a risk-utility test. Importantly, many of these departures cannot easily be dismissed as irrationalities that should be ignored in favor of more narrow instrumentalist balancing. Rather, . . . many aspects of consumer beliefs and behavior can be said to represent a "rival rationality" that is wider in scope and richer in detail than the stark logic of risk-utility analysis. . . .
>
> To be sure, application of the consumer expectations doctrine must not consist of the type of largely unguided, formless judgment that commentators to date have associated with it. Rather, juries should be charged with the task of determining specifically, as a factual matter, what level of safety the ordinary consumer does expect, taking into account the type of factors that cognitive psychologists and other observers of human judgment and decisionmaking have identified as pertinent to public understanding and beliefs

about risk. Expert testimony therefore should be admissible for those aspects of a product's design, manufacture, or marketing that raise issues relating to lay risk perception. More specifically, to survive a summary judgment motion, plaintiffs must demonstrate the existence of a triable question of fact concerning the extent to which consumer risk perceptions and safety expectations of the product in question differ in legitimate and significant ways from the standards derived under risk-utility analysis. In this manner, despite the longstanding complaint of products liability scholars that consumer expectations fail to provide a coherent and workable basis for design defect liability, and despite the failure of courts generally to articulate such a basis, the doctrine will provide an important complement to the spare instrumentalist balancing of risk-utility analysis.

The authors of this casebook offer a brief response in the same issue of the Columbia Law Review.

Professor Kysar uses a hypothetical to illustrate an important difference between his approach and the Products Liability Restatement. He posits two airbag designs, *A* and *B*. Design *A* saves 3,000 persons from death over a certain number of miles driven, but kills 100 persons who would have survived in the absence of the device. Airbag *B* also saves 3,000 persons and kills only 90. The 100 persons killed by airbag *A* are more or less equally divided between males and females; of the 90 persons killed by airbag *B,* a majority are females. (Kysar never explains how this could happen, but one can infer that it is a function of the physical size of the victims.) *P,* a female, was riding in the right front seat of an automobile manufactured by *M* and equipped with airbag *B.* The airbag deployed in a minor accident, as it was designed to do, and killed *P. P*'s death would not have occurred in the absence of an airbag. *P*'s representative brings a wrongful death action against *M,* asserting that *M* should have adopted design *A,* which, compared with design *B,* would have improved *P*'s chances of survival. An expert testifies, based on opinion polls, that a majority of consumers in the jurisdiction prefer design *A,* because of its gender neutrality, over design *B,* even though design *A* kills more people. Kysar suggests that, under his approach, *P*'s representative should recover from *M.* He also implies that *P*'s representative might lose as a matter of law under §2(b) of the Restatement. Is Kysar's assessment of the plaintiff's chances under the Restatement accurate? If so, which outcome in the action against *M* is preferable on these facts?

Potter v. Chicago Pneumatic Tool Company
694 A.2d 1319 (Conn. 1997)

KATZ, Associate Justice.

This appeal arises from a products liability action brought by the plaintiffs against the defendants, Chicago Pneumatic Tool Company (Chicago Pneumatic), Stanley Works and Dresser Industries, Inc. (Dresser). The plaintiffs claim that they were injured in the course of their employment as shipyard workers at the General Dynamics Corporation Electric Boat facility (Electric Boat) in Groton as a result of using pneumatic hand tools manufactured by the defendants. Specifically, the plaintiffs allege that the tools were defectively designed because they exposed the plaintiffs to excessive vibration, and because the defendants failed to provide adequate warnings with respect to the potential danger presented by excessive vibration.

The defendants appeal from the judgment rendered on jury verdicts in favor of the plaintiffs, claiming [that] the interrogatories and accompanying instructions submitted to the jury were fundamentally prejudicial to the defendants [and that] the trial court should have rendered judgment for the defendants nothwithstanding the verdicts because (a) there was insufficient evidence that the tools were defective in that the plaintiffs had presented no evidence of a feasible alternative design. . . .

The trial record reveals the following facts, which are undisputed for purposes of this appeal. The plaintiffs were employed at Electric Boat as "grinders," positions which required use of pneumatic hand tools to smooth welds and metal surfaces. In the course of their employment, the plaintiffs used various pneumatic hand tools, including chipping and grinding tools, which were manufactured and sold by the defendants. The plaintiff's use of the defendants' tools at Electric Boat spanned approximately twenty-five years, from the mid-1960s until 1987. The plaintiffs suffer from permanent vascular neurological impairment of their hands, which has caused blanching of their fingers, pain, numbness, tingling, reduction of grip strength, intolerance of cold and clumsiness from restricted blood flow. As a result, the plaintiffs have been unable to continue their employment as grinders and their performance of other activities has been restricted. The plaintiffs' symptoms are consistent with a diagnosis of hand arm vibration syndrome. Expert testimony confirmed that exposure to vibration is a significant contributing factor to the development of hand arm vibration syndrome, and that a clear relationship exists between the level of vibration exposure and the risk of developing the syndrome.

In addition to these undisputed facts, the following evidence, taken in favor of the jury's verdict, was presented. Ronald Guarneri, an industrial hygienist at Electric Boat, testified that he had conducted extensive testing of tools used at the shipyard in order to identify occupational hazards. This testing revealed that a large number of the defendants' tools violated the limits for vibration exposure established by the American National Standards Institute (institute), and exceeded the threshold limit promulgated by the American Conference of Governmental and Industrial Hygienists (conference).

Richard Alexander, a mechanical engineering professor at Texas A & M University, testified that because machinery vibration has harmful effects on machines and on people, engineers routinely research ways to reduce or to eliminate the amount of vibration that a machine produces when operated. Alexander discussed various methods available to control vibration, including isolation (the use of springs or mass to isolate vibration), dampening (adding weights to dampen vibrational effects), and balancing (adding weights to counterbalance machine imbalances that cause vibration). Alexander testified that each of these methods has been available to manufacturers for at least thirty-five years.

Alexander also stated that, in 1983, he had been engaged by another pneumatic tool manufacturer to perform testing of methods by which to reduce the level of vibration in its three horsepower vertical grinder. The vertical grinder had a live handle, which contained hardware for the air power, and a dead handle, which vibrated significantly more than the live handle because it weighed less. Alexander modified the design by inserting rubber isolation mounts between the handles and the housing, and by adding an aluminum rod to the dead handle to match the weight of the two handles. As a result of these modifications, which were published in 1987, Alexander achieved a threefold reduction in vibration levels. . . .

After a six week trial, the trial court rendered judgment on jury verdicts in favor of the plaintiffs. Finding that the defendants' tools had been defectively designed so as to render them unreasonably dangerous, the jury awarded the plaintiffs compensatory damages. The jury also concluded that the manufacturers had provided inadequate warnings. Because the plaintiffs failed to prove that adequate warnings would have prevented their injuries, the jury did not award damages on that claim. . . .

We first address the defendants' argument that the trial court improperly failed to render judgment for the defendants notwithstanding the verdicts because there was insufficient evidence for the jury to have found that the tools had been defectively designed. Specifically, the defendants claim that, in order to establish a prima facie design defect case, the plaintiffs were required to prove that there was a feasible alternative design available at the time that the defendants put their tools into the stream of commerce. We disagree.

[The court's summary of the history of strict products liability is omitted.]

Although courts have widely accepted the concept of strict tort liability, some of the specifics of strict tort liability remain in question. In particular, courts have sharply disagreed over the appropriate definition of defectiveness in design cases. As the Alaska Supreme Court has stated: "Design defects present the most perplexing problems in the field of strict products liability because there is no readily ascertainable external measure of defectiveness. While manufacturing flaws can be evaluated against the intended design of the product, no such objective standard exists in the design defect context." Caterpillar Tractor Co. v. Beck, 593 P.2d 871, 880 (Alaska 1979).

Section 402A imposes liability only for those defective products that are "unreasonably dangerous" to "the ordinary consumer who purchases it, with the ordinary knowledge common to the community as to its characteristics." 2 Restatement (Second), supra §402A, comment (i). Under this formulation, known as the "consumer expectation" test, a manufacturer is strictly liable for any condition not contemplated by the ultimate consumer that will be unreasonably dangerous to the consumer. . . .

Other jurisdictions apply only a risk-utility test in determining whether a manufacturer is liable for a design defect. . . .

This court has long held that in order to prevail in a design defect claim, "[t]he plaintiff must prove that the product is unreasonably dangerous." Id. We have derived our definition of "unreasonably dangerous" from comment (i) to §402A, which provides that "the article sold must be dangerous to an extent beyond that which would be contemplated by the ordinary consumer who purchases it, with the ordinary knowledge common to the community as to its characteristics." 2 Restatement (Second), supra, §402A, comment (i). This "consumer expectation" standard is now well established in Connecticut strict products liability decisions.

The defendants propose that it is time for this court to abandon the consumer expectation standard and adopt the requirement that the plaintiff must prove the existence of a reasonable alternative design in order to prevail on a design defect claim. We decline to accept the defendants' invitation.

In support of their position, the defendants point to the second tentative draft of the Restatement (Third) of Torts: Products Liability (1995) (Draft Restatement

[Third]), which provides that, as part of a plaintiff's prima facie case, the plaintiff must establish the availability of a reasonable alternative design. Specifically, §2(b) of the Draft Restatement (Third) provides: "[A] product is defective in design when the foreseeable risks of harm posed by the product could have been reduced or avoided by the adoption of a reasonable alternative design by the seller or other distributor, or a predecessor in the commercial chain of distribution, and the omission of the alternative design renders the product not reasonably safe." The reporters to the Draft Restatement (Third) state that "[v]ery substantial authority supports the proposition that [the] plaintiff must establish a reasonable alternative design in order for a product to be adjudged defective in design." Draft Restatement (Third), supra, §2, reporters' note to comment (c), p.50.

We point out that this provision of the Draft Restatement (Third) has been a source of substantial controversy among commentators. See, e.g., John F. Vargo, "The Emperor's New Clothes: The American Law Institute Adorns a 'New Cloth' for Section 402A Products Liability Design Defects—A Survey of the States Reveals a Different Weave," 26 U.Mem. L. Rev. 493, 501 (1996) (challenging reporters' claim that Draft Restatement (Third)'s reasonable alternative design requirement constitutes "consensus" among jurisdictions). . . .

In our view, the feasible alternative design requirement imposes an undue burden on plaintiffs that might preclude otherwise valid claims from jury consideration. Such a rule would require plaintiffs to retain an expert witness even in cases in which lay jurors can infer a design defect from circumstantial evidence. Connecticut courts, however, have consistently stated that a jury may, under appropriate circumstances, infer a defect from the evidence without the necessity of expert testimony. . . .

Moreover, in some instances, a product may be in a defective condition unreasonably dangerous to the user even though no feasible alternative design is available. In such instances, the manufacturers may be strictly liable for a design defect notwithstanding the fact that there are no safer alternative designs in existence. See, e.g., O'Brien v. Muskin Corp. 94 N.J. 169, 184, 463 A.2d 298 (1983) ("other products, including some for which no alternative exists, are so dangerous and of such little use that . . . a manufacturer would bear the cost of liability of harm to others"). . . .

Although today we continue to adhere to our long-standing rule that a product's defectiveness is to be determined by the expectations of an ordinary consumer, we nevertheless recognize that there may be instances involving complex product designs in which an ordinary consumer may not be able to form expectations of safety. In such cases, a consumer's expectations may be viewed in light of various factors that balance the utility of the product's design with the magnitude of its risks. We find persuasive the reasoning of those jurisdictions that have modified their formulation of the consumer expectation test by incorporating risk-utility factors into the ordinary consumer expectation analysis. Thus, the modified consumer expectation test provides the jury with the product's risks and utility and then inquires whether a reasonable consumer would consider the product unreasonably dangerous. As the Supreme Court of Washington stated in Seattle-First National Bank v. Tabert, supra, at 154, 542 P.2d 774, "[i]n determining the reasonable expectations of the ordinary consumer, a number of factors must be considered. The relative cost of the product, the gravity of the potential harm from the claimed defect and the cost and feasibility of eliminating or minimizing the risk may be relevant in a particular case. In other instances the nature of the product or the nature of the claimed defect may make other factors relevant to the issue." Accordingly, under this modified formulation, the consumer expectation test would establish the product's risks and utility, and the inquiry would then be whether a reasonable consumer would consider the product design unreasonably dangerous.

In our view, the relevant factors that a jury may consider include, but are not limited to, the usefulness of the product, the likelihood and severity of the danger posed by the design, the feasibility of an alternative design, the financial cost of an improved design, the ability to reduce the product's danger without impairing its usefulness or making it too expensive, and the feasibility of spreading the loss by increasing the product's price. The availability of a feasible alternative design is a factor that the plaintiff may, rather than must, prove in order to establish that a product's risks outweigh its utility.

Furthermore, we emphasize that our adoption of a risk-utility balancing component to our consumer expectation test does not signal a retreat from strict tort liability. In weighing a product's risks against its utility, the focus of the jury should be on the product itself, and not on the conduct of the manufacturer.

Although today we adopt a modified formulation of the consumer expectation test, we emphasize that we do not require a plaintiff to present evidence relating to the product's risks and utility in every case. As the California Court of Appeals has stated: "There are certain kinds of accidents—even where fairly complex machinery is involved—[that] are so bizarre that the average juror, upon hearing the particulars, might reasonably think: 'Whatever the user may have expected from that contraption, it certainly wasn't that.'" Akers v. Kelley Co., 173 Cal. App.3d 633, 651, 219 Cal. Rptr. 513 (1985). Accordingly, the ordinary consumer expectation test is appropriate when the everyday experience of the particular product's users permits the inference that the product did not meet minimum safety expectations. See Soule v. General Motors Corp., 8 Cal.4th 548, 567, 882 P.2d 298, 34 Cal. Rptr.2d 607 (1994).

Conversely, the jury should engage in the risk-utility balancing required by our modified consumer expectation test when the particular facts do not reasonably permit the inference that the product did not meet the safety expectations of the ordinary consumer. Furthermore, instructions based on the ordinary consumer expectation test would not be appropriate when, as a matter of law, there is insufficient evidence to support a jury verdict under that test. In such circumstances, the jury should be instructed solely on the modified consumer expectation test we have articulated today.

With these principles in mind, we now consider whether, in the present case, the trial court properly instructed the jury with respect to the definition of design defect for the purposes of strict tort liability. The trial court instructed the jury that a manufacturer may be strictly liable if the plaintiffs prove, among other elements, that the product in question was in a defective condition, unreasonably dangerous to the ultimate user. The court further instructed the jury that, in determining whether the tools were unreasonably dangerous, it may draw its conclusions based on the reasonable expectations of an ordinary user of the defendants' tools. Because there was sufficient evidence as a matter of law to support the determination that the tools were unreasonably dangerous based on the ordinary consumer expectation test, we conclude that this instruction was appropriately given to the jury....

BERDON, J., concurring.

I write separately with respect to part I of the court's opinion regarding the test for determining whether a manufacturer is liable for a design defect. I would not depart from our long-standing rule that the consumer expectation test must be employed — that is, the product "must be dangerous to an extent beyond that which would be contemplated by the ordinary consumer who purchases it, with the ordinary knowledge common to the community as to its characteristics." 2 Restatement (Second), Torts, §402A, comment (i) (1965). Although the court today agrees that this test is to be applied to cases such as the present case, it adopts, by way of dicta, another test for "complex product designs."

I am concerned about the court adopting a risk-utility test for complex product designs — that is, a test where the trier of fact considers "the product's risks and utility and then inquires whether a reasonable consumer would consider the product unreasonably dangerous." Adopting such a test in a factual vacuum without the predicate facts to address its full implications can lead us down a dangerous path. More importantly, adopting such a risk-utility test for "complex product designs" sounds dangerously close to requiring proof of the existence of "a reasonable alternative design," a standard of proof that the court properly rejects today.

Finally because the court insists on addressing this issue that is not before us, I would at least sort out the burden of proof for the risk-utility test by adopting "a presumption that danger outweighs utility if the product fails under circumstances when the ordinary purchaser or user would not have so expected." W. Prosser & W. Keeton, Torts (5th ed. 1984) §99, p.702. Adoption of this presumption would lessen the concern that the risk-utility test undermines one of the reasons that strict tort liability was adopted — "the difficulty of discovering evidence necessary to show that danger outweighs benefits." Id.

One question under the consumer expectations test is whether the court is concerned with the expectations of a reasonable person or with the actual expectations of the plaintiff. The Supreme Court of California has made it clear that "the jury considers the expectations of a hypothetical reasonable consumer, rather than those of the particular plaintiff in the case." Campbell v. General Motors Corp., 649 P.2d 224, 233 n.6 (Cal. 1982). See also Wheeler v. HO Sports, Inc., 232 F.3d 754 (10th Cir. 2000) (applying Oklahoma law) (plaintiff unable to show that specialized life vest failed consumer expectations; professional surfers who constituted "ordinary consumers" would not expect vest to function as ordinary life preserver).

Several courts have rejected the Products Liability Restatement and have embraced the consumer expectations test. See, e.g., Delaney v. Deere & Co., 999 P.2d 930, 946 (Kan. 2000) ("Kansas has adopted the consumer expectations test . . . as the standard for design defect"); Green v. Smith & Co., 629 N.W.2d 727, 741 (Wis. 2001) ("Wisconsin strict products liability law applies the consumer-contemplation test and only the consumer-contemplation test in all strict products liability cases"); Rahmig v. Mosley Machinery Co., Inc., 412 N.W.2d 56 (Neb. 1987) (pre-Products Liability Restatement case adopting the consumer-contemplation test and rejecting the need for plaintiff to establish a safer design). Other courts, while expressing allegiance to the consumer expectations test, stop short of a full endorsement. See, e.g., Dart v. Wiebe Mfg., Inc., 709 P.2d 876 (Ariz. 1985) (consumer expectations test is adequate for manufacturing defect but will only "sometimes work well" in design cases as consumer will very often not know what to expect); Warner v. Fruehauf Trailer Co. v. Boston, 654 A.2d 1272, 1276 (D.C. App. 1995) ("In general, the plaintiff must 'show the risks, costs and benefits of the product in question and alternative designs,'" but the court implies in a footnote that consumer expectations test may be appropriate in some cases); McCathern v. Toyota Motor Co., 23 P.3d 320, 331 (Or. 2001) (court held that Oregon statute mandates application of the consumer expectations test but held that where average consumer would not know what to expect then court may have to resort to risk-utility balancing).

The consumer expectations test has a core of academic supporters as well. See, e.g., F. Patrick Hubbard, Reasonable Human Expectations: A Normative Model for Imposing Strict Liability for Defective Products, 29 Mercer L. Rev. 465 (1978); Marshall S. Shapo, A Representational Theory of Consumer Protection: Doctrine, Function and Legal Liability for Product Disappointment, 60 Va. L. Rev. 1109 (1974); Jerry J. Phillips, Consumer Expectations, 53 S. Cal. L. Rev. 1047 (2002).

Comment g to §2(b) of the Products Liability Restatement rejects the consumer expectations test as a stand-alone test for design defect:

> *g. Consumer expectations: general considerations.* Under Subsection (b), consumer expectations do not constitute an independent standard for judging the defectiveness of product designs. Courts frequently rely, in part, on consumer expectations when discussing liability based on other theories of liability. Some courts, for example, use the term "reasonable consumer expectations" as an equivalent of "proof of a reasonable, safer design alternative," since reasonable consumers have a right to expect product designs that conform to the reasonableness standard in Subsection (b). Other courts, allowing an inference of defect to be drawn when the incident is of a kind that ordinarily would occur as a result of product defect, observe that products that fail when put to their manifestly intended use disappoint reasonable consumer expectations. See §3. However, consumer expectations do not play a determinative role in determining defectiveness. . . . Consumer expectations, standing alone, do not take into account whether the proposed alternative design could be implemented at reasonable cost, or whether an alternative design would provide greater overall safety. Nevertheless, consumer expectations about product performance and the dangers attendant to product use affect how risks are perceived and relate to foreseeability and frequency of the risks of harm, both of which are relevant under Subsection (b). . . . Such expectations are often influenced by how products are portrayed and marketed and can have a significant impact on consumer behavior. Thus, although consumer expectations do not constitute an independent standard for judging the defectiveness of product designs, they may substantially influence or even be ultimately determinative on risk-utility balancing in judging whether the omission of a proposed alternative design renders the product not reasonably safe. . . .

Early rejection of the consumer expectations test can be found in Turner v. General Motors Corp., 584 S.W.2d 844 (Tex. 1979). The plaintiff in that case suffered serious injuries when his 1969 Chevrolet Impala sedan overturned as he swerved to avoid a collision with a truck. The car rolled over once and the roof caved in at the driver's corner when it hit the ground. Although his seat belt was buckled, the plaintiff suffered a crushed vertebra, resulting in paralysis. The plaintiff alleged that the roof structure of the car was inadequately designed to withstand a rollover collision. The court in *Turner* used the occasion to indicate its dissatisfaction with the consumer expectations test. It reiterated the criticism that consumer expectations would hardly be anything more than the personal experiences of the jurors. See also Bilotta v. Kelley Co., 346 N.W.2d 616 (Minn. 1984). Wright v. Brooke Group, Ltd., 652 N.W.2d 159 (Iowa 2002). For an exhaustive compilation of authority, see Reporters' Note to §2 of the Products Liability Restatement.

The consumer expectations test has drawn fire from respected academic commentators. Professor Page Keeton, for example, argues that:

> It is quite clear that to the extent that a maker knows, or in the exercise of ordinary care should know, of a risk or hazard that users may not discover or appreciate, liability results for breach of the duty to disclose what a reasonable person would disclose. This ground of liability protects users and consumers to a considerable extent from harm resulting from unappreciated dangers. It is submitted, however, that an inquiry as to whether the danger in fact of the design outweighed the benefits of the design would better protect users and consumers, without placing an undue burden on manufacturers and suppliers. The court's primary justification for the retention of the contemplation test is the ease with which the plaintiff can establish a design defect under this test by circumstantial evidence. If a claimant proves that a product fails under circumstances the ordinary purchaser or user would not have expected, a case has been made. That is clearly so, but the question is, should it be so? I think not. If the court would permit the defendant to show under a risk-utility analysis by way of rebuttal that it would not be feasible, then the position would be supportable. [Keeton, Products Liability — Design Hazards and the Meaning of Defect, 10 Cumb. L. Rev. 293, 310 (1979).]

A similar note is sounded by Professor Mary J. Davis in Design Defect Liability: In Search of a Standard of Responsibility, 39 Wayne L. Rev. 1217, 1236-1237 (1993):

> Perhaps the most important criticism of the consumer expectations test as it relates to design defects is the impossibility of the task it requires: to define just what an ordinary consumer expects of the technical design characteristics of a product. While it can be assumed that consumers expect a certain level of safety, how is that level defined when it comes to specific design criteria? For example, what do consumers expect of the structural soundness of one type of metal as opposed to another with slightly different characteristics that, if used, would require changes in still other aspects of the design? If the ordinary consumer can be said reasonably to expect a product to be "strong," how strong is strong? Is a general impression of strength or quality sufficient when it comes to technical design features? If so, how is that impression measurable against the actual condition of the design feature in question? These difficult questions led many courts to reject the consumer expectations test as the sole test for defective design.

Also see David G. Owen, M. Stuart Madden, & Mary J. Davis, Madden & Owen on Products Liability §8.3 (3d ed. 2000) (sharply criticizing consumer expectation test and noting that it has been abandoned by most modern courts).

PROBLEM FIFTEEN

Sophie Wydler, a junior executive at the New California Savings Bank, was crossing the street while returning to her office from a lunch break when a truck driven by Walter Sandhaus ran her down. Wydler brought suit against Sandhaus for negligent driving and against International Harvester (IH) for defectively designing the IH Model 404 that Sandhaus was driving at the time. The complaint alleged that the design of the truck prevented the driver from seeing pedestrian traffic immediately in front and to the right of the truck, and that the front-end profile of the vehicle should have been lowered to eliminate the blind spot. The case went to trial and experts on both sides testified regarding the benefits and disadvantages of the Model 404 design and those of the alternative design suggested by the plaintiff. Defendant's expert argued that the plaintiff's suggested alternative design would have required lowering the engine by at least three inches. Lowering the engine could not be accomplished without positioning the engine in close proximity to the gas tank. In that position, the high temperature from the heat of the engine would pose an unacceptable fire hazard. The gas tank could be repositioned, but only at the cost of creating other risks of accidental injury. The IH expert opined that drivers of heavy commercial trucks are experts who are well aware of the visibility problems that attend driving such large vehicles and know that their only way to compensate for the lack of visibility is by driving slowly with greater vigilance.

After the completion of the testimony, the court asked the parties to submit requests for instructions. The attorney representing the plaintiff submitted the following instruction to deal with the question of the defective design of the truck:

> A product is dangerously defective when it is in a condition unreasonably dangerous to the user. Unreasonably dangerous in this context means dangerous to an extent beyond that which would be contemplated by the ordinary purchaser of this type of product in the community. In considering the expectations of an ordinary purchaser, you may consider the expectations of anyone who may reasonably be expected to be affected by the product, such as a pedestrian.

You are an associate with the law firm representing International Harvester. The senior partner handling the case asks you to draft a memorandum opposing plaintiff's requested instruction. He also wants you to suggest an alternative instruction that would be less prejudicial to the defendant and yet acceptable to the court. He wants you to support your alternative instruction with a memorandum. The Supreme Court of New California, the state in which all the events occurred, has cited with approval the decision of the Oregon court in Heaton v. Ford Motor Co., supra.

THE UNIFORM COMMERCIAL CODE AND THE CONSUMER EXPECTATIONS TEST

In Chapter One we noted that in the early days of products liability law, strict liability actions for manufacturing defects were brought under Article 2 of the Uniform Commercial Code. Under the Code, every sale of goods is accompanied by an implied warranty of merchantability that the goods "are fit for the ordinary purposes for which such goods are used." The Code test for defect worked well for manufacturing defects. However, when plaintiffs sought to use the Code definition for defect in design cases involving personal injury, the question arose as to whether the risk-utility test for defect was to be engrafted into the Code or whether the Code mandated a consumer-expectations test. Most courts utilized whatever test for defect they used in a case brought in tort as the test for defect under the Code. One court, however, made it clear that if a plaintiff brings an action in implied warranty under Article 2, the case would be covered under the consumer expectation test. In *Denny v. Ford Motor Co.*, 662 N.E.2d 730 (N.Y. 1995), the plaintiff, Nancy Denny, was severely injured when the Ford Bronco II (a utility vehicle designed for use on off-road and rugged terrain) she was driving rolled over. The rollover accident occurred when Denny slammed on her brakes in an effort to avoid a deer that had walked directly into her motor vehicle's path. She sued Ford, asserting claims of negligence, strict products liability, and breach of the implied warranty of merchantability.

Plaintiffs introduced evidence to show that small utility vehicles, like the Bronco, present a significantly higher risk of rollover accidents than do ordinary passenger automobiles. Ford countered that the design features of which plaintiff complained were necessary to the vehicle's off-road capabilities. The trial judge instructed the jury on both strict products liability and the implied warranty of merchantability. On the former, the jury was instructed on risk-utility balancing and to find for plaintiff only if the Bronco was not reasonably safe. On the latter, they were given a consumer expectations charge. Ford objected to the two charges, contending that the standard for design defect is the same whether the action is brought under tort or the Uniform Commercial Code. Interestingly, the jury found for the defendant under risk-utility standards, i.e., the Bronco was "reasonably safe," but found for the plaintiff on the grounds that the Bronco fell below consumer expectations. The case was originally tried in federal district court and went up on appeal to the Second Circuit. The Circuit certified to the New York Court of Appeals the question as to whether the standard for design defect under the Uniform Commercial Code was identical to or different from the risk-utility standard which governs New York products liability law.

The New York Court of Appeals decided that the implied warranty of merchantability of the U.C.C. embodied a "consumer expectations" test that the court was not at liberty to disregard. The court observed:

> . . . As long as that legislative source of authority [the U.C.C.] exists, we are not free to merge the warranty cause of action with its tort-based sibling regardless of whether, as a matter of policy, the contract-based warranty claim may fairly be regarded as a historical relic that no longer has any independent substantive value. Rather, we must construe and apply this separate remedy in a manner that remains consistent with its *current* roots in contract law. . . . Id. at 736.

The Products Liability Restatement proposes a single test for defect whether the action is brought in tort or is based on the implied warranty of merchantability. It also decries the practice of submitting to a jury two identical claims with different doctrinal labels. Section 2, Comment *n* states:

> *n. Relationship of definitions of defect to traditional doctrinal categories.* The rules in this Section and in other provisions of this Chapter 1 define the bases of tort liability for harm caused by product defects existing at time of sale or other distribution. The rules are stated functionally rather than in terms of traditional doctrinal categories. Claims based on product defect at the time of sale or other distribution must meet the

requisites set forth in Subsections (a), (b) or (c), or the other provisions in this Chapter. As long as these requisites are met, doctrinal tort categories such as negligence or strict liability may be utilized in bringing the claim.

Similarly, a product defect claim satisfying the requisites of Subsections (a), (b) or (c), or other provisions in this Chapter, may be brought under the implied warranty of merchantability provisions of the Uniform Commercial Code. It is recognized that some courts have adopted a consumer expectations definition for design and failure-to-warn defects in implied warranty cases involving harm to persons or property. This Restatement contemplates that a well-coordinated body of law governing liability for harm to persons or property arising out of the sale of defective products requires a consistent definition of defect, and that the definition properly should come from tort law, whether the claim carries a tort label or one of implied warranty of merchantability.

A recently proposed change in Article 2 of the Uniform Commercial Code appears to agree with the Products Liability Restatement. In May 2003, the National Conference of Commissioner of Uniform State Laws and the American Law Institute approved a new version of Article 2 to be submitted to the states for approval. The official commentary to §2-314(2)(c) contains the following language:

> Suppose that an unmerchantable lawn mower causes personal injury to the buyer, who is operating the mower. Without more, the buyer can sue the seller for breach of the implied warranty of merchantability and recover for injury to person "proximately resulting" from the breach. Section 2-715(2)(b).
>
> This opportunity does not resolve the tension between warranty law and tort law where goods cause personal injury or property damage. The primary source of that tension arises from disagreement over whether the concept of defect in tort and the concept of merchantability in Article 2 are coextensive where personal injuries are involved, *i.e.,* if goods are merchantable under warranty law can they still be defective under tort law, and if goods are not defective under tort law can they be unmerchantable under warranty law? The answer to both questions should be no, and the tension between merchantability in warranty and defect in tort where personal injury or property damage is involved should be resolved as follows:
>
>> When recovery is sought for injury to person or property, whether goods are merchantable is to be determined by applicable state products liability law. When, however, a claim for injury to person or property is based on an implied warranty of fitness under Section 2-315 or an express warranty under Section 2-313 or an obligation arising under Section 2-313A or 2-313B, this Article determines whether an implied warranty of fitness or an express warranty was made and breached, as well as what damages are recoverable under Section 2-715.
>
> To illustrate, suppose that the seller makes a representation about the safety of a lawnmower that becomes part of the basis of the buyer's bargain. The buyer is injured when the gas tank cracks and a fire breaks out. If the lawnmower without the representation is not defective under applicable tort law, it is not unmerchantable under this section. On the other hand, if the lawnmower did not conform to the representation about safety, the seller made and breached an express warranty and the buyer may sue under Article 2.

Under the revised Article 2, no state should feel bound to apply a contract-like consumer expectations test in a products liability personal injury or property damage case. It is free to apply its tort law if its sees fit to do so. Presumably, under the new Article 2, New York would no longer be bound to the "historical relic" of warranty law and would apply a risk-utility test in a design defect case.

2. Consumer Expectations as a Shield Against Liability

Halliday v. Sturm, Ruger & Co., Inc.
792 A.2d 1145 (Md. 2002)

WILNAT, Judge.

This case arises from the tragic death of Jordan Garris. In June, 1999, Jordan shot himself while playing with his father's handgun. Jordan's mother, petitioner here, seeks to hold the manufacturer of the handgun, respondent Sturm, Ruger & Co. (Sturm Ruger), liable for Jordan's death. The Circuit Court for Baltimore City, by granting respondent's motion for summary judgment, found no liability. A divided Court of Special Appeals affirmed. Halliday v. Sturm, Ruger & Co., . . . 770 A.2d 1072 (2001). We shall do likewise.

Background

The handgun in question is a Ruger P89 semi-automatic pistol. To fire the gun, one must place a loaded magazine into it, pull the slide at the top of the gun as far to the rear as possible and then release it, ensure that a safety lever is in the "fire" position, and then pull the trigger. Even when loaded, the gun will not fire unless the trigger is pulled with the safety lever in the "fire" position.

Jordan's father, Clifton Garris, purchased the gun in March, 1999, from On Target, Inc., a retail firearms store. With the purchase of the gun came an instruction manual, the offer of a free safety course, which Garris declined, a pamphlet entitled "Youth Handgun Safety Act Notice" published by the Federal Bureau of Alcohol, Tobacco and Firearms, a lock box in which to store the gun and the magazine, and a padlock for the box. . . .

The instruction manual provided multiple warnings and instructions regarding the storage and use of the gun. On the cover of the manual, and embossed on the barrel of the gun itself, was an admonition to read the manual before using the gun. Among other warnings and instructions in the manual is a highlighted box entitled "WARNING — STORAGE" in which, in red letters, is the statement "Firearms should always be stored securely and unloaded, away from children and careless adults" and the statement, in capital letters, "STORE SECURELY AND UNLOADED." In the part on "THE BASIC RULES OF SAFE FIREARMS HANDLING," which itself is in red capital letters, is a section headed, in red capital letters, "FIREARMS SHOULD BE UNLOADED WHEN NOT IN USE," and in that section is the warning:

> "Firearms and ammunition should be securely locked in racks or cabinets when not in use. Ammunition should be safely stored separate from firearms. Store your firearms out of sight of visitors and children. It is the gun owner's responsibility to be certain that

children and persons unfamiliar with firearms cannot gain access to firearms, ammunition, or components."

Garris signed an acknowledgment that the On Target salesperson explained the instruction manual, the safety lever, and the action of the gun. The Youth Handgun Safety Act Notice warned Garris, in highlighted letters, that the misuse of handguns was a leading contributor to juvenile violence and fatalities and that "safely storing and securing firearms away from children will help prevent the unlawful possession of handguns by juveniles, stop accidents, and save lives."

Garris disregarded virtually every one of these warnings and opportunities. He did not store either the gun or the magazine in the lock box but rather placed the gun under his mattress and kept the loaded magazine on a bookshelf in the same room, so that it was visible and accessible to Jordan. Jordan found the handgun under his father's mattress. He also found the loaded magazine. From watching television, the child knew how to load the magazine into the gun, and he did so. While playing with the gun, he apparently pulled the slide and thereby placed a bullet into the chamber. Either the safety lever was in the "fire" position already or Jordan moved it there. He then pulled the trigger, shot himself in the head, and died two days later. . . .

He was three years old.

Petitioner alleged that the gun was defective and unreasonably dangerous because its design "failed to incorporate reasonable devices to prevent its use by young children," in particular "one or more of the following: a grip safety, a heavy trigger-pull, a child-resistant manual safety, a built-in lock, a trigger lock, and/or personalized gun technology that would have substantially reduced the likelihood that a child could fire the gun. . . ." Citing data released by the Centers for Disease Control and Prevention to the effect that 1,641 children under ten were accidentally killed by handguns between 1979 and 1996, petitioner averred in her complaint that "it was foreseeable that the gun would be found and handled by a young child, and that it would be fired by a young child, with resulting foreseeable grievous or fatal injury to the child and/or others." Petitioner contended that the handgun industry was aware of the problem of young children finding and injuring themselves with handguns and, in the 1880's [sic 1980's], had developed a childproof grip safety, but that Sturm Ruger manufactured the gun without that, or any other, childproof device.

Sturm Ruger responded to the complaint with a motion to dismiss or, in the alternative, for summary judgment, the latter based on the assertions that (1) as a matter of law, the gun was not in a defective condition or unreasonably dangerous, and (2) it was used in a manner that was contrary to the clearly worded instructions and warnings that accompanied the product when sold, and was therefore *mis*used. Attached to a memorandum that accompanied the motion were copies of the instruction manual, the Youth Handgun Safety Act Notice, an affidavit from the On Target salesman attesting, among other things, to his recommendation that Garris purchase a trigger lock, and a picture of the lock box. Sturm Ruger argued that the gun did not malfunction but rather performed exactly as it was designed to function, and that the accident occurred because of Garris's failure to heed clear warnings.

In response, petitioner argued that it is "inconsistent with the proper function of a gun to design it so that it can be fired by young children." The lack of child-resistant features, she claimed, made the gun foreseeably dangerous to small children, and, "because firing by small children is not one of the proper functions of a gun, a gun fired by a small child has not performed properly." She urged that Garris's failure to heed the warnings and keep the gun securely locked was not a defense to liability because that also was foreseeable. . . . Also attached was an affidavit from Stephen Teret, a professor at the Johns Hopkins School of Hygiene and Public Health, who recounted statistics dealing with accidental gun-related deaths of children and evidence that a substantial number of gun owners, including those with children in the home, store their guns in an unsafe manner. Based on this data, Teret offered the opinion in his affidavit that reliance by Sturm Ruger on the instruction manual and the provision of a lock box was inadequate to protect children from the risk of unintended gun death.

The essence of petitioner's case was that, when dealing with design defects in a strict liability claim, the court should apply a "risk-utility" analysis in lieu of a "consumer expectation" test and hold that the gun in question failed that preferred test because (1) the risk of excluding child safety features outweighs the utility of that exclusion, and (2) alternative safer designs could have been adopted economically. She argued to the Circuit Court that "the central thing that Sturm Ruger did wrong in designing this gun . . . is to sell a gun a three year old could shoot." The court rejected that argument, holding instead that, under Maryland law, the risk-utility test applied only when the product malfunctioned and that the gun in question did not malfunction. . . .

The core of the intermediate appellate court's ultimate conclusion was the holding of this Court in Kelley v. R.G. Industries, Inc., . . . 497 A.2d 1143 (1985), that the risk-utility test did not apply to a product, including a gun, that did not malfunction and its own determination that the gun in this case operated exactly as it was supposed to operate and therefore did not malfunction. . . . Two judges on the nine-judge *en banc* panel dissented. They concluded that the consumer expectation test that we applied in *Kelley* was no longer Maryland law, that the alleged design defect should be considered under a risk-utility analysis, and that, under that analysis, there was a triable issue.

Discussion

The principal issue presented here is whether, in examining whether a product in general, or a handgun in particular, is defective for purposes of a strict liability action, this Court should continue to apply the "consumer expectation" test, as urged by Sturm Ruger, or should adopt instead a version of the "risk-utility" analysis, as requested by petitioner. It would be helpful, therefore, at the outset, to define these two standards.

The consumer expectation test emanates from §402A of the Restatement (Second) of Torts which, under certain circumstances, makes the seller of a product that is in a "defective condition unreasonably dangerous" to the consumer liable for the physical harm caused to the consumer by that product. The test defines what is meant by the terms "defective condition" and "unreasonably dangerous." Comment g to §402A defines "defective condition" as a "condition not contemplated by the ultimate consumer, which will be unreasonably dangerous to him." Comment *i,* in speaking to the term "unreasonably dangerous," states that the article must be dangerous "to an extent beyond that which would be contemplated by the ordinary consumer who purchases it, with the ordinary knowledge common to the community as to its characteristics." Thus, Prosser and Keeton explain that, under the consumer expectation or contemplation test set forth in §402A, a product is defectively dangerous "if it is dangerous to an extent beyond that which would be contemplated by the ordinary consumer who purchased it with the ordinary knowledge common to the community as to the product's characteristics." W. Page Keeton et al., Prosser and Keeton on The Law of Torts, §99, at 698 (5th ed. 1984).

The "risk-utility" test, which has been applied principally to alleged defects in the *design* of a product, regards a product as defective and unreasonably dangerous, for strict liability purposes, if the danger presented by the product outweighs its utility. Where this test is applied, the issue usually becomes whether a safer alternative design was feasible, for, if so, that would likely alter the balance by reducing the extent of the danger. Indeed, §2 of the Restatement (Third) of Torts: Product Liability, . . . adopts this test for design defect cases. . . .

This Court first adopted the concept of strict liability, as articulated in Restatement (Second) of Torts §402A, in Phipps v. General Motors Corp., 363 A.2d 955 (1976). Paraphrasing the language in that section, we said that, to recover in an action for strict liability,

> "it must be established that (1) the product was in a defective condition at the time that it left the possession or control of the seller, (2) that it was unreasonably dangerous to the user or consumer, (3) that the defect was a cause of the injuries, and (4) that the product was expected to and did reach the consumer without substantial change in its condition."

Id. at 344, 363 A.2d at 955. . . .

Phipps involved an alleged design defect in an automobile — latent defects in the accelerator mechanism, the carburetor and its components, and the motor mounts — that caused the accelerator to stick and the car to be driven off the road. We observed that, when dealing with an alleged error in the *manufacturing* process, there was less difficulty in applying the consumer expectation test, but that when "the alleged defect is the result of the design process so that the product causing injury was in a condition intended by the manufacturer, the test has proved more difficult to apply." Id. . . . 363 A.2d at 959. That difficulty, we added, had caused some commentators to suggest that the theory of strict liability articulated in §402A was not really applicable to design defects and that a design defect case still required "a weighing of the utility of risk inherent in the design against the magnitude of the risk," which was a test generally affiliated with negligence actions. Id. . . . 363 A.2d at 959. . . .

Although we applied the consumer expectation test set forth in §402A to the situation before us in *Phipps,* that language certainly left open whether there were other conditions in which, in a design defect case, a risk-utility analysis might be appropriate, and, indeed, we also stated in *Phipps* that "in some circumstances the question of whether a particular design is defective may depend upon a balancing of the utility of the design and other factors against the magnitude of that risk." Id. . . . 363 A.2d at 961. With that opening, the Court of Special Appeals and the U.S. Court of Appeals for the Fourth Circuit alluded to or applied such an analysis in a number of design defect cases, usually involving the absence of some form of safety device that would, allegedly, have made a potentially dangerous product less so. See, for example, Banks v. Iron Hustler Corp., . . . 475

A.2d 1243 (1984) (failure to provide shield on conveyor belt to guard against contact with "nip" points where belt came into contact with rollers); Troja v. Black & Decker Mfg. Co., . . . 101, 488 A.2d 516 (1985) (absence of safeguard to prevent radial arm saw from operating when guide fence removed); Valk Manufacturing v. Rangaswamy, . . . 537 A.2d 622 (1988) (protruding hitch in snowplow); Singleton v. International Harvester Co., 685 F.2d 112, 115 (4th Cir. 1981) (holding that, under *Phipps,* design defects were to be treated as negligence rather than under strict liability principles).

We revisited the issue of which test to apply in *Kelley,* supra 304 Md. 124, 497 A.2d 1143, in connection with handguns. The plaintiff there was injured when he was shot during a robbery attempt. He sued the gun manufacturer, claiming, among other things, that the gun was "abnormally dangerous." Responding to questions certified to us by the U.S. District Court, we opined on whether (1) the manufacturer of a handgun, in general, was liable under any strict liability theory to a person injured as a result of the criminal use of its product, and (2) the manufacturer of a particular category of small, cheap handgun, sometimes referred to as "Saturday Night Specials," which were regularly used in criminal activity, was strictly liable to a person injured by such a handgun during the course of a crime. In answering the first question, we cited *Phipps* for the proposition that "in determining whether a product is defective, in its design or manufacture, Maryland cases have generally applied the 'consumer expectation' test," id. . . . 497 A.2d at 1148, and we concluded that "[a] handgun manufacturer or marketer could not be held liable under this theory." Id. 497 A.2d at 1148. We explained:

> "[A] handgun is not defective merely because it is capable of being used during criminal activity to inflict harm. A consumer would expect a handgun to be dangerous, by its very nature, and to have the capacity to fire a bullet with deadly force. Kelley confuses a product's *normal function,* which may well be dangerous, with a defect in a product's design or construction."

Id. (emphasis in original). . . .

On that premise, we concluded that, "regardless of the standard used to determine whether a product is 'defective' under §402A, a handgun which functions as intended and as expected is not 'defective' within the meaning of that section," noting that "this has been the consistent conclusion in other jurisdictions which have confronted the issue." Id. That conclusion, in turn, led to the ultimate holding that, under existing strict liability principles, as applied in Maryland, a handgun manufacturer or marketer was generally not liable for gunshot injuries resulting from a criminal's use of the product.

Having so concluded, we took note that the common law was dynamic and could be changed, suggesting the prospect of adopting new theories that might create liability, but we pointed out that "we have consistently recognized that common law principles should not be changed contrary to the public policy of the State set forth by the General Assembly." Id. . . , 497 A.2d at 1151. We looked, then, to the handgun laws then in force, which allowed persons to own and possess handguns and, under certain circumstances, to carry them. From that, we concluded that "to impose strict liability upon the manufacturers or marketers of handguns for gunshot injuries resulting from the misuse of handguns by others, would be contrary to Maryland public policy as set forth by the Legislature." Id. . . , 497 A.2d at 1153.

Our response to the second question posed was different. We determined that there was a "limited category of handguns which clearly is not sanctioned as a matter of public policy" and that to impose strict liability upon the manufacturers and marketers of those handguns, which we denoted as "Saturday Night Specials," would *not* be contrary to the public policy set by the General Assembly. Id. Those kinds of guns, characterized by short barrels, low weight, easy concealability, cheap quality, inaccuracy, and unreliability, rendered them particularly attractive for criminal use but virtually useless for any legitimate purpose. Id . . . , 497 A.2d 1143, at 1153-54. After surveying both Federal and State legislation, we determined that those types of guns really were in a separate category, that their use for criminal purposes was entirely foreseeable by their manufacturers and marketers, and that holding such manufacturers and marketers strictly liable for injuries to innocent persons from the criminal misuse of those guns would be consistent with public policy. Whether a particular gun fell within that limited category, we said, was an issue of fact for a trial court to determine.

In Simpson v. Standard Container Co., 527 A.2d 1337 (1987), the Court of Special Appeals properly followed our pronouncements in *Kelley*. The case involved a gasoline can that, despite clear warnings to the contrary, the buyer stored, full of gasoline, in his basement, where a four-year-old child found and opened it, causing the gasoline to spill, ignite, and severely burn the child. The action against the manufacturer alleged that the can was defective because it was designed without a childproof cap, and the argument was presented that liability should attach under a risk-utility analysis because (1) the danger of a child spilling gasoline and igniting a fire was foreseeable, (2) a container equipped with a childproof cap was available in the industry at nominal cost, and (3) the product was defective because the risk outweighed the utility of the container without the cap. Affirming the dismissal of the action, the intermediate appellate court correctly noted that "to determine whether a product is defective in its design, Maryland cases have generally used the 'consumer expectation' test." Id. . . . 527 A.2d at 1340. . . .

In a string of other cases, however, the Court of Special Appeals continued to apply the risk-utility test in design defect cases involving the lack of a safety device, sometimes, unfortunately, by misconstruing, side-stepping, or ignoring what we said in *Kelley*.

Petitioner raises four questions in her brief but really presents five propositions. First, she urges that we depart from *Kelley,* abandon the consumer expectation test, and adopt the risk-utility test in strict liability actions based on design defects, as the Court of Special Appeals has done, as a number of other States have done, and as the Restatement (Third) of Torts: Product Liability has done. Second, she asks either that, in applying that test, we do not require that a product malfunction as a prerequisite or that we regard the use of the gun by a three-year-old as a malfunction. Third, she requests that we not carve out an exception to the risk-utility test for handguns. Fourth, she contends that, because Garris's conduct in leaving the gun and the magazine accessible to Jordan was foreseeable, it did not constitute a misuse of the product, and, finally, she argues that the warnings contained in the instruction manual do not suffice to shield Sturm Ruger from liability.

There has been a great deal of ferment regarding these issues, both in Maryland and elsewhere. Some of the debate is grounded in theory — whether, on the one hand, a consumer expectation test is either relevant or workable in a design defect situation, especially when the product is inherently dangerous, or, on the other, whether a departure from the consumer expectation test necessarily reintroduces negligence concepts, by focusing on the manufacturer's conduct rather than the product itself, and thus becomes inconsistent with the notion and function of strict liability.

That debate has a practical significance. The concept of strict liability, especially as formulated in §402A of Restatement (Second), was regarded as an important pro-consumer advance; relieving persons injured by products from the requirement of proving negligence on the part of manufacturers or others in the distribution chain and focusing, instead, on the product itself, made it easier to obtain a recovery for a defectively designed or manufactured product. Substitution of a risk-utility analysis, however, especially as formulated in the Restatement (Third), has attracted considerable criticism and has been viewed by many as a retrogression, as returning to negligence concepts and placing a very difficult burden on plaintiffs. . . . (citation omitted)

To some extent, the debate over where the country is on this issue depends on how one counts and categorizes—whether intermediate appellate court decisions are regarded as definitive, how to deal with decisions based on statutes, how to deal with situations where one test is used for one type of case but not another, and whether the author is correctly reading the cases. There is also the overlay of §§3 and 4 of Restatement (Third), which may excuse the plaintiff from having to establish a reasonable alternative design when a defect may be inferred through a form of *res ipsa loquitur* analysis (§3) or where the product fails to comply with a product safety statute or regulation (§4).

The courts still seem to be split with respect to gun cases. Some follow the approach of *Kelley,* apply the consumer expectation test, and hold that a manufacturer may not be held liable for design defect on a risk-utility analysis unless the gun malfunctions. In some States, Texas and California among them, that approach is governed by statute. . . . Others have, as petitioner urges, adopted a risk-utility analysis without regard to malfunction and held gun manufacturers liable, even when the gun operates precisely as intended, for failure to attach an available safety feature that might have precluded the gun from firing. We have discerned no significant shift or coalescence of views in this regard since our decision in *Kelley.*

The one arena in which *Kelley,* itself, and the question of gun safety in general, has produced the most significant and relevant debate has been the Maryland General Assembly. Immediately on the heels of *Kelley,* bills representing nearly opposite viewpoints were introduced into the Legislature—one, SB 151 (1986), would have directly overturned the second part of *Kelley* and expressly precluded liability on the part of manufacturers and merchants of "Saturday Night Specials" for injuries caused by another's use of such a weapon, and another, SB 98 (1986), would have made it a misdemeanor to sell a "Saturday Night Special." Both failed.

In 1988, the Legislature adopted a different approach. By 1988 Md. Laws, ch. 533, it (1) created a Handgun Roster Board within the Department of Public Safety and Correctional Services and charged that Board with creating a Handgun Roster—a listing of the kinds of handguns that could lawfully be sold in Maryland, (2) established certain standards for the Board to consider in determining whether to include a particular handgun on the Roster, including ease of concealment, accuracy of the weapon, quality of materials and manufacture, reli-

> **author's dialogue 11**
>
> **JIM:** Do you believe *Halliday*?
>
> **AARON:** Of course, I believe it. It's right there for you to read.
>
> **JIM:** Oh, come on, Aaron. Why did the court in *Halliday* have to adopt the consumer expectations test in order to deny recovery? It could have adopted the language in §2, Comment *g* of the Restatement that says that "although consumer expectations do not constitute an independent standard for judging the defectiveness of product designs, they may substantially influence or even be *ultimately determinative* on risk-utility balancing in judging whether the omission of a proposed alternative design renders the product defective."
>
> **AARON:** I'm glad you mentioned that language from the Restatement. I never really understood what those words meant. If I'm not mistaken, that language came from the members during floor discussion at the Annual Meeting. We thought it would not cause mischief so we agreed to it. Now you're telling me that it has real meaning.
>
> **JIM:** You're showing your age, Aaron. When we talked after the meeting and I objected to the language at the time, you said it could be interpreted to mean that in some cases consumer expectations so overwhelm the case that they resolve the risk-utility issue as a matter of law. Like there is an elephant in the living room. Sometimes you can't ignore the elephant.
>
> **AARON:** Now that you mention it, I do recall saying something like that. But if I said it, I still don't see how it works in practice. In *Halliday* plaintiff sug-

ability as to safety, and utility for legitimate sporting activities, self-protection, and law enforcement, and (3) prohibited the manufacture and sale in Maryland of any handgun not listed on the Roster. The law also added two provisions dealing with civil liability. It provided that a person "may not be held strictly liable for damages of any kind resulting from injuries to another person sustained as a result of the criminal use of a firearm by a third person," absent evidence of a conspiracy between the two, but added that "this section may not be construed to otherwise negate, limit, or modify the doctrine of negligence or strict liability relating to abnormally dangerous products or activities and defective products."

The clear thrust of this law was to overturn the second part of *Kelley* and preclude strict liability actions based on the criminal use of handguns but to attempt to control the distribution and sale of handguns that were particularly dangerous or that had no legitimate utility through the device of the Handgun Roster. It would appear that the Legislature adopted some form of risk-utility analysis in establishing the standards for the Roster Board to consider in deciding whether to include particular kinds of handguns on the Roster. . . .

Conclusion

It is clear that, under the consumer expectation test that we applied in *Kelley*, no cause of action had been stated in this case. There was no malfunction of the gested some very sensible alternative designs that would have prevented hundreds of accidental shootings of children every year. How does the consumer expectations test (elephant or no elephant) respond to that argument?

JIM: I'll have to think about that. But let me make a prediction. The Maryland court used the consumer expectation test in *Halliday* as a shield to protect against liability. What will they do when they face a run-of-the-mill design defect case and have to decide whether the plaintiff can use the test as a sword to win a case without proving a reasonable alternative design? They will rue the day that they turned their back on reasonable alternative design.

AARON: I agree. But now I'll make a prediction of my own. Maryland courts will end up saying that consumers have a right to expect reasonably designed products and will end up turning their consumer expectations test into a risk-utility test. They have too many risk-utility cases in their published decisions. It's a shame that they felt pressured by a gun case to give voice to the consumer expectations test. The legislative history in Maryland is full of initiatives telling the courts that they don't want them fooling around with guns under standard products liability law. The Maryland court could simply have said that it wasn't going to face the reasonable alternative design issue in this case because the legislature did not want standard products law to govern guns. They came very close to actually saying that.

JIM: You know, Aaron, this may be one of those times when you are right.

---

gun; regrettably, it worked exactly as it was designed and intended to work and as any ordinary consumer would have expected it to work. The gun is a lawful weapon and was lawfully sold. What caused this tragedy was the carelessness of Jordan's father in leaving the weapon and the magazine in places where the child was able to find them, in contravention not only of common sense but of multiple warnings given to him at the time of purchase.

We are asked to modify *Kelley* in various ways that would permit an action to proceed against the manufacturer of the weapon. We are asked to modify the common law to impose liability on gun manufacturers who have failed to incorporate into their products one or another kind of device that would make the weapon childproof, quite apart from the inclusion of other safety devices, clear warnings regarding the storage of the weapon, and the offer of a lock box in which to store it. Although, as we noted, some courts have done that, there is no consensus in that regard. We were asked in *Kelley* to extend and create new theories of liability, which we declined to do, noting that "we have consistently recognized that common law principles should not be changed contrary to the public policy of the State set forth by the General Assembly of Maryland." . . . (citations omitted)

That caution is especially appropriate here. Given the controversy that continues to surround the risk-utility standard articulated for design defect cases in §2 of the Restatement (Third), we are reluctant at this point to cast aside our existing jurisprudence in favor of such an approach on any broad, general basis. Nor is there a need to do so in this case, which deals with more specific issues that have been presented on several occasions to the General Assembly and have been considered and debated in that arena. So far, the Legislature has chosen not to place these burdens on gun manufacturers but has attempted to deal with the problem in other ways. We shall respect that policy choice.

JUDGMENT OF COURT OF SPECIAL APPEALS AFFIRMED, WITH COSTS.

Although most of the advocates for the consumer expectations test see it as more favorable to plaintiffs, a leading treatise notes that "courts have used the consumer expectations test most frequently to *deny* recovery to plaintiffs in cases involving obvious design hazards." D. Owens, M. Madden and M. Davis, Madden and Owens on Products Liability §8.3 (3d ed. 2000).

In Sperry-New Holland v. Prestage, 617 So. 2d 248, 254 (Miss. 1993), the court acknowledged that it was abandoning the consumer expectations test because "for a plaintiff to recover, the defect in a product which causes his injuries must not be one which the plaintiff, as an ordinary consumer, would know to be unreasonably dangerous to him. In other words, if the plaintiff, applying the knowledge of an ordinary consumer, sees a danger and can appreciate the danger, then he cannot recover for any injury resulting from the appreciated danger." Examples of this phenomenon creating questionable results abound. In Kelly v. Rival Manufacturing Co., 704 F. Supp. 1039 (W.D. Okla. 1989), parents of an 11-month-old child brought suit against a crock-pot manufacturer after the pot, partially filled with heated beans, fell upon the child as he was in his walker and caused serious burns to his body. The plaintiff alleged a host of design defects in the crock-pot and suggested alternative designs which would have prevented injuries to children from this kind of utensil, which retains its heat long after electricity is shut off and the pot is unplugged. The court refused to consider the design claims, saying:

> In manufacturers' products liability actions involving minor plaintiffs, the question of whether a product is unreasonably dangerous is not premised on the viewpoint of the minor child, but rather based upon the contemplation of the parent consumer who purchased the product. Id. at 1043.

Also see, Brown v. Sears Roebuck & Co., 328 F.3d 1274 (10th Cir. 2003) (applying Utah law) (summary judgment for defendant proper where plaintiff did not establish that danger of lawn tractor's operation in reverse not appreciated by ordinary consumer; plaintiff barred from proving reasonable alternative design that would have prevented injuries).

Interestingly, legislation in several states has given new life to the §402A Comment *i* "consumer expectations" test as a defense to a design defect claim. Though the legislation is not the equivalent of the "patent danger" rule, it does negate liability for dangers which are commonly known and are inherent to the product. N.J. Rev. Stat. §2A:58C-3 (West 2000) is illustrative:

In any product liability action against a manufacturer or seller for harm allegedly caused by a product that was designed in a defective manner, the manufacturer or seller shall not be liable if: . . .

(2) the characteristics of the product are known to the ordinary consumer or user, and the harm was caused by an unsafe aspect of the product that is an inherent characteristic of the product and that would be recognized by the ordinary person who uses or consumes the product with the ordinary knowledge common to the class of persons for whom the product is intended, except that this paragraph shall not apply to industrial machinery or other equipment used in the workplace and it is not intended to apply to dangers posed by products such as machinery or equipment that can feasibly be eliminated without impairing the usefulness of the product. . . .

Also see Ohio Rev. Code Ann. §2307.75(E) (Anderson 2001).

F. THE TWO-PRONG STANDARD FOR DETERMINING DESIGN DEFECT

Soule v. General Motors Corporation
882 P.2d 298 (Cal. 1994)

BAXTER, J.

Plaintiff's ankles were badly injured when her General Motors (GM) car collided with another vehicle. She sued GM, asserting that defects in her automobile allowed its left front wheel to break free, collapse rearward, and smash the floorboard into her feet. GM denied any defect and claimed that the force of the collision itself was the sole cause of the injuries. Expert witnesses debated the issues at length. Plaintiff prevailed at trial, and the Court of Appeal affirmed the judgment. We granted review to resolve . . . [whether] a product's design [may] be found defective on grounds that the product's performance fell below the safety expectations of the ordinary consumer . . . if the question of how safely the product should have performed cannot be answered by the common experience of its users . . .

Facts

On the early afternoon of January 16, 1984, plaintiff was driving her 1982 Camaro in the southbound center lane of Bolsa Chica Road, an arterial street in Westminster. There was a slight drizzle, the roadway was damp, and apparently plaintiff was not wearing her seat belt. A 1972 Datsun, approaching northbound, suddenly skidded into the path of plaintiff's car. The Datsun's left rear quarter struck plaintiff's Camaro in an area near the left front wheel. Estimates of the vehicles' combined closing speeds on impact vary from 30 to 70 miles per hour. The collision bent the Camaro's frame adjacent to the wheel and tore loose the bracket that attached the wheel assembly (specifically, the lower control arm) to the frame. As a result, the wheel collapsed rearward and inward. The wheel hit the underside of the "toe pan"—the slanted floorboard area beneath the pedals—

causing the toe pan to crumple, or "deform," upward into the passenger compartment. Plaintiff received a fractured rib and relatively minor scalp and knee injuries. Her most severe injuries were fractures of both ankles, and the more serious of these was the compound compression fracture of her left ankle. This injury never healed properly. In order to relieve plaintiff's pain, an orthopedic surgeon fused the joint. As a permanent result, plaintiff cannot flex her left ankle. She walks with considerable difficulty, and her condition is expected to deteriorate.

After the accident, the Camaro was acquired by a salvage dealer, Noah Hipolito. Soon thereafter, plaintiff's son, Jeffrey Bishop, and her original attorney, Richard Hawkins, each inspected and photographed the car and its damaged floorboard area. The failed bracket assembly was retrieved. However, Hipolito later discarded the damaged toe pan, repaired the Camaro, and resold it. Thus, except for the bracket assembly, no part of the vehicle was retained as evidence.

Plaintiff sued GM for her ankle injuries, asserting a theory of strict tort liability for a defective product. She claimed the severe trauma to her ankles was not a natural consequence of the accident, but occurred when the collapse of the Camaro's wheel caused the toe pan to crush violently upward against her feet. Plaintiff attributed the wheel collapse to a manufacturing defect, the substandard quality of the weld attaching the lower control arm bracket to the frame. She also claimed that the placement of the bracket, and the configuration of the frame, were defective designs because they did not limit the wheel's rearward travel in the event the bracket should fail.

The available physical and circumstantial evidence left room for debate about the exact angle and force of the impact and the extent to which the toe pan had actually deformed. The issues of defect and causation were addressed through numerous experts produced by both sides in such areas as biomechanics, metallurgy, orthopedics, design engineering, and crash-test simulation.

Plaintiff submitted the results of crash tests, and also asserted the similarity of another real-world collision involving a 1987 Camaro driven by Dana Carr. According to plaintiff's experts, these examples indicated that Camaro accidents of similar direction and force do not generally produce wheel bracket assembly failure, extensive toe pan deformation, or severe ankle injuries such as those plaintiff had experienced. These experts opined that without the deformation of the toe pan in plaintiff's car, her accident could not have produced enough force to fracture her ankles.

A metallurgist testifying on plaintiff's behalf examined the failed bracket from her car. He concluded that its weld was particularly weak because of excess "porosity" caused by improper welding techniques. Plaintiff's experts also emphasized the alternative frame and bracket design used by the Ford Mustang of comparable model years. They asserted that the Mustang's design, unlike the Camaro's, provided protection against unlimited rearward travel of the wheel should a bracket assembly give way.

GM's metallurgist disputed the claims of excessive weakness or porosity in the bracket weld. Expert witnesses for GM also countered the assertions of defective design. GM asserted that the Camaro's bracket was overdesigned to withstand forces in excess of all expected uses. According to expert testimony adduced by GM, the Mustang's alternative frame and bracket configuration did not fit the Ca-

The Two-Prong Standard for Determining Design Defect

maro's overall design goals and was not distinctly safer for all collision stresses to which the vehicle might be subjected. Indeed, one witness noted, at least one more recent Ford product had adopted the Camaro's design. . . .

The court instructed the jury that a manufacturer is liable for "enhanced" injuries caused by a manufacturing or design defect in its product while the product is being used in a foreseeable way. Over GM's objection, the court gave the standard design defect instruction without modification. . . . This instruction advised that a product is defective in design "if it fails to perform as safely as an ordinary consumer would expect when used in an intended *or* reasonably foreseeable manner or if there is a risk of danger inherent in the design which outweighs the benefit of the design." (italics added.)

The jury was also told that in order to establish liability for a design defect under the "ordinary consumer expectations" standard, plaintiff must show (1) the manufacturer's product failed to perform as safely as an ordinary consumer would expect, (2) the defect existed when the product left the manufacturer's possession, (3) the defect was a "legal cause" of plaintiff's "enhanced injury," and (4) the product was used in a reasonably foreseeable manner. . . .

In a series of special findings, the jury determined that the Camaro contained a defect (of unspecified nature) which was a "legal cause" of plaintiff's "enhanced injury." . . . Plaintiff received an award of $1.65 million.

GM appealed. Among other things, it argued that the trial court erred by instructing on ordinary consumer expectations in a complex design-defect case, and by failing to give GM's special instruction on causation.

Following one line of authority, the Court of Appeal concluded that a jury may rely on expert assistance to determine what level of safe performance an ordinary consumer would expect under particular circumstances. Hence, the Court of Appeal ruled, there was no error in use of the ordinary consumer expectations standard for design defect in this case. . . .

Discussion

1. Test for Design Defect

A manufacturer, distributor, or retailer is liable in tort if a defect in the manufacture or design of its product causes injury while the product is being used in a reasonably foreseeable way. Because traffic accidents are foreseeable, vehicle manufacturers must consider collision safety when they design and build their products. Thus, whatever the cause of an accident, a vehicle's producer is liable for specific collision injuries that would not have occurred but for a manufacturing or design defect in the vehicle. . . .

In Barker v. Lull Engineering Co., supra, 573 P.2d 443 (*Barker*), the operator of a high-lift loader sued its manufacturer for injuries he received when the loader toppled during a lift on sloping ground. The operator alleged various *design* defects which made the loader unsafe to use on a slope. [T]he court instructed that the operator could recover only if a defect in the loader's design made the machine "'unreasonably dangerous for its intended use.'" [citation omitted] The operator appealed the defense verdict, citing the "unreasonably dangerous" instruction as prejudicial error.

The manufacturer responded that even if the "unreasonably dangerous" test was inappropriate for manufacturing defects, . . . it should be retained for design defects. . . .

The *Barker* court disagreed. It reasoned as follows: Our [earlier decisions] sought to avoid the danger that a jury would *deny* recovery, as the Restatement had intended, "so long as the product did not fall below the ordinary consumer's expectations as to [its] safety. . . ." (*Barker,* supra, fn. omitted.) This danger was particularly acute in design defect cases, where a manufacturer might argue that because the item which caused injury was identical to others of the same product line, it must necessarily have satisfied ordinary consumer expectations. . . .

Despite these difficulties, *Barker* explained, it is possible to define a design defect, and the expectations of the ordinary consumer are relevant to that issue. At a minimum, said *Barker,* a product *is* defective in design if it *does* fail to perform as safely as an ordinary consumer would expect. This principle, *Barker* asserted, acknowledges the relationship between strict tort liability for a defective product and the common law doctrine of warranty, which holds that a product's presence on the market includes an implied representation "'that it [will] safely do the jobs for which it was built.'" . . . "Under this [minimum] standard," *Barker* observed, "an injured plaintiff will frequently be able to demonstrate the defectiveness of the product *by resort to circumstantial evidence, even when the accident itself precludes identification of the specific defect at fault.* [Citations.]" [citations omitted, italics added]

However, *Barker* asserted, the Restatement had erred in proposing that a violation of ordinary consumer expectations was *necessary* for recovery on this ground. "As Professor Wade has pointed out, . . . the expectations of the ordinary consumer cannot be viewed as the exclusive yardstick for evaluating design defectiveness because '[i]n many situations . . . *the consumer would not know what to expect,* because he would have *no idea* how safe the product could be made.'" (573 P.2d 443, quoting Wade, On the Nature of Strict Tort Liability for Products (1973) 44 Miss. L.J. 825, 829, italics added.)

Thus, *Barker* concluded, "a product may be found defective in design, even if it satisfies ordinary consumer expectations, if through hindsight the jury determines that the product's design embodies 'excessive preventable danger,' or, in other words, if the jury finds that the risk of danger inherent in the challenged design outweighs the benefits of such design. [Citations.]" . . . *Barker* held that under this latter standard, "a jury may consider, among other relevant factors, the gravity of the danger posed by the challenged design, the likelihood that such danger would occur, the mechanical feasibility of a safer alternative design, the financial cost of an improved design, and the adverse consequences to the product and to the consumer that would result from an alternative design. [Citations.]" (Id. at p. 431.) *Barker* also made clear that when the ultimate issue of design defect calls for a careful assessment of feasibility, practicality, risk, and benefit, the case should not be resolved simply on the basis of ordinary consumer expectations. As *Barker* observed, "past design defect decisions demonstrate that, as a practical matter, in many instances it is simply impossible to eliminate the balancing or weighing of competing considerations in determining whether a product is defectively designed or not. . . ."

An example, *Barker* noted, was the "crashworthiness" issue presented in Self v. General Motors Corp., supra. The debate there was whether the explosion of a vehicle's fuel tank in an accident was due to a defect in design. This, in turn, entailed concerns about whether placement of the tank in a position less vulnerable to rear end collisions, even if technically feasible, "would have created a greater risk of injury in other, more common situations." (*Barker,* supra) Because this complex weighing of risks, benefits, and practical alternatives is "implicit" in so many design-defect determinations, *Barker* concluded, "an instruction which appears to preclude such a weighing process under all circumstances may mislead the jury." (Id.). . . .

Campbell v. General Motors Corp., (1982) 649 P.2d 224 (*Campbell*) provided additional strong hints about the proper use of the ordinary consumer expectations prong of *Barker.* Plaintiff Campbell, a bus passenger, was thrown from her seat and injured during a sharp turn. She sued GM, the manufacturer of the bus, alleging that the vehicle was defectively designed because there was no "grab bar" within easy reach of her seat. Campbell presented no expert testimony, but she submitted photographs of the interior of the bus, showing where safety bars and handles were located in relation to the seat she had occupied. At the conclusion of her case in chief, GM moved for nonsuit, arguing that her evidence of design defect and proximate cause was not sufficient. The trial court granted the motion, but we reversed. We emphasized that in order to establish a design defect under *Barker*'s ordinary consumer expectations test, it was enough for Campbell to show "the objective conditions of the product" so that the jurors could employ "[their] own sense of whether the product meets ordinary expectations as to its safety under the circumstances presented by the evidence. Since public transportation is a matter of common experience, no expert testimony was required to enable the jury to reach a decision on this part of the *Barker* inquiry." (*Campbell,* supra)

"Indeed, it is difficult to conceive what testimony an 'expert' could provide. The thrust of the first *Barker* test is that the product must meet the safety expectations of the general public as represented by the ordinary consumer, not the industry or a government agency. '[O]ne can hardly imagine what credentials a witness must possess before he can be certified as an expert on the issue of *ordinary* consumer expectations.'" (*Campbell,* supra, 32 Cal. 3d at pp. 126-127, 184 Cal. Rptr. 891, 649 P.2d 224, quoting Schwartz, Foreword: Understanding Products Liability (1979) 67 Cal. L. Rev. 435, 480, italics added.)

Had we ended our discussion at this point, it would have been clear that a product violates ordinary consumer expectations only when the circumstances arouse such reasonable expectations based on common experience of the product's users. However, dictum in the next paragraph of *Campbell* injected ambiguity. We said, "The quantum of proof necessary to establish a prima facie case . . . under the first [i.e., ordinary consumer expectations] prong of *Barker* cannot be reduced to an easy formula. However, *if* the product is one within the common experience of ordinary consumers" (italics added), it will generally be enough for the injured plaintiff to show the circumstances of the accident and "the objective features of the product which are relevant to an evaluation of its safety. . . ." One might infer from this passage that the ordinary consumer expectations prong of *Barker* is not limited to product performance "within the common experience" of the product's ordinary consumers. . . .

In *Barker,* we offered two alternative ways to prove a design defect, each appropriate to its own circumstances. The purposes, behaviors, and dangers of certain products are commonly understood by those who ordinarily use them. By the same token, the ordinary users or consumers of a product may have reasonable, widely accepted minimum expectations about the circumstances under which it should perform safely. Consumers govern their own conduct by these expectations, and products on the market should conform to them.

In some cases, therefore, "ordinary knowledge . . . as to . . . [the product's] characteristics" (Rest. 2d Torts, supra, §402A, com. *i.*, p. 352) may permit an inference that the product did not perform as safely as it should. *If* the facts permit such a conclusion, and *if* the failure resulted from the product's design, a finding of defect is warranted without any further proof. The manufacturer may not defend a claim that a product's design failed to perform as safely as its ordinary consumers would expect by presenting expert evidence of the design's relative risks and benefits.[3]

However, as we noted in *Barker,* a complex product, even when it is being used as intended, may often cause injury in a way that does not engage its ordinary consumers' reasonable minimum assumptions about safe performance. For example, the ordinary consumer of an automobile simply has "no idea" how it should perform in all foreseeable situations, or how safe it should be made against all foreseeable hazards. (*Barker,* supra)

An injured person is not foreclosed from proving a defect in the product's design simply because he cannot show that the reasonable minimum safety expectations of its ordinary consumers were violated. Under *Barker*'s alternative test, a product is still defective if its design embodies "excessive preventable danger" . . . that is, unless "the benefits of the . . . design outweigh the risk of danger inherent in such design" (id.). But this determination involves technical issues of feasibility, cost, practicality, risk, and benefit (id., at p. 431, 143 Cal. Rptr. 225, 573 P.2d 443) which are "impossible" to avoid. . . . In such cases, the jury *must* consider the manufacturer's evidence of competing design considerations . . . and the issue of design defect cannot fairly be resolved by standardless reference to the "expectations" of an "ordinary consumer."

As we have seen, the consumer expectations test is reserved for cases in which the *everyday experience* of the product's users permits a conclusion that the product's design violated *minimum* safety assumptions, and is thus defective *regardless of expert opinion about the merits of the design.* It follows that where the minimum safety of a product is within the common knowledge of lay jurors, expert witnesses may not be used to demonstrate what an ordinary consumer would or should expect. Use of expert testimony for that purpose would invade the jury's function (see Evid. Code, §801, subd. (a)), and would invite circumvention of the rule that the risks and benefits of a challenged design must be carefully balanced whenever the issue of design defect goes beyond the common experience of the product's users.[4]

---

3. For example, the ordinary consumers of modern automobiles may and do expect that such vehicles will be designed so as not to explode while idling at stoplights, experience sudden steering or brake failure as they leave the dealership, or roll over and catch fire in two-mile-per-hour collisions. If the plaintiff in a product liability action proved that a vehicle's design produced such a result, the jury could find forthwith that the car failed to perform as safely as its ordinary consumers would expect, and was therefore defective.

4. Plaintiff insists that manufacturers should be forced to design their products to meet the "objective" safety demands of a "hypothetical" reasonable consumer who is fully informed about what he or she

By the same token, the jury may not be left free to find a violation of ordinary consumer expectations whenever it chooses. Unless the facts actually permit an inference that the product's performance did not meet the minimum safety expectations of its ordinary users, the jury must engage in the balancing of risks and benefits required by the second prong of *Barker*.

Accordingly, as *Barker* indicated, instructions are misleading and incorrect if they allow a jury to avoid this risk-benefit analysis in a case where it is required. Instructions based on the ordinary consumer expectations prong of *Barker* are not appropriate where, as a matter of law, the evidence would not support a jury verdict on that theory. Whenever that is so, the jury must be instructed solely on the alternative risk-benefit theory of design defect announced in *Barker*.[5]

GM suggests that the consumer expectations test is improper whenever "crashworthiness," a complex product, or technical questions of causation are at issue. Because the variety of potential product injuries is infinite, the line cannot be drawn as clearly as GM proposes. But the fundamental distinction is not impossible to define. The crucial question in each individual case is whether the circumstances of the product's failure permit an inference that the product's design performed below the legitimate, commonly accepted minimum safety assumptions of its ordinary consumers.[6]

GM argues at length that the consumer expectations test is an "unworkable, amorphous, fleeting standard" which should be entirely abolished as a basis for design defect. In GM's view, the test is deficient and unfair in several respects. First, it defies definition. Second, it focuses not on the objective condition of products, but on the subjective, unstable, and often unreasonable opinions of consumers. Third, it ignores the reality that ordinary consumers know little about how safe the complex products they use can or should be made. Fourth, it invites the jury to isolate the particular consumer, component, accident, and injury before it instead of considering whether the whole product fairly accommodates the competing expectations of all consumers in all situations (see Daly v. General Motors Corp., supra). Fifth, it eliminates the careful balancing of risks and benefits which is essential to any design issue. . . .

We fully understand the dangers of improper use of the consumer expectations test. However, we cannot accept GM's insinuation that ordinary consumers lack any legitimate expectations about the minimum safety of the products they use. In particular circumstances, a product's design may perform so unsafely that the defect

---

should expect. Hence, plaintiff reasons, the jury may receive expert advice on "reasonable" safety expectations for the product. However, this function is better served by the risk-benefit prong of *Barker*. There, juries receive expert advice, apply clear guidelines, and decide accordingly whether the product's design is an acceptable compromise of competing considerations. . . .

5. Plaintiff urges that any limitation on use of the consumer expectations test contravenes *Greenman's* purpose to aid hapless consumers. But we have consistently held that manufacturers are not insurers of their products; they are liable in tort only when "defects" in their products cause injury. (E.g., Daly v. General Motors Corp. (1978) 20 Cal.3d 725, 733, 144 Cal. Rptr. 380, 575 P.2d 1162; *Cronin*, supra, 8 Cal.3d 121, 133.) *Barker* properly articulated that a product's design is "defective" only if it violates the "ordinary" consumer's safety expectations, or if the manufacturer cannot show the design's benefits outweigh its risks. . . .

6. Contrary to GM's suggestion, ordinary consumer expectations are not irrelevant simply because expert testimony is required to prove that the product failed as marketed, or that a condition of the product as marketed was a "substantial," and therefore "legal," cause of injury. We simply hold that the consumer expectations test is appropriate only when the jury, fully appraised of the circumstances of the accident or injury, may conclude that the product's design failed to perform as safely as its ordinary consumers would expect.

is apparent to the common reason, experience, and understanding of its ordinary consumers. In such cases, a lay jury is competent to make that determination. . . .

Applying our conclusions to the facts of this case, however, we agree that the instant jury should not have been instructed on ordinary consumer expectations. Plaintiff's theory of design defect was one of technical and mechanical detail. It sought to examine the precise behavior of several obscure components of her car under the complex circumstances of a particular accident. The collision's exact speed, angle, and point of impact were disputed. It seems settled, however, that plaintiff's Camaro received a substantial oblique blow near the left front wheel, and that the adjacent frame members and bracket assembly absorbed considerable inertial force.

An ordinary consumer of automobiles cannot reasonably expect that a car's frame, suspension, or interior will be designed to remain intact in any and all accidents. Nor would ordinary experience and understanding inform such a consumer how safely an automobile's design should perform under the esoteric circumstances of the collision at issue here. Indeed, both parties assumed that quite complicated design considerations were at issue, and that expert testimony was necessary to illuminate these matters. Therefore, injection of ordinary consumer expectations into the design defect equation was improper.

We are equally persuaded, however, that the error was harmless, because it is not reasonably probable defendant would have obtained a more favorable result in its absence. . . .

Here there were no instructions which specifically remedied the erroneous placement of the consumer expectations alternative before the jury. Moreover, plaintiff's counsel briefly reminded the jury that the instructions allowed it to find a design defect under either the consumer expectations or risk-benefit tests. However, the consumer expectations theory was never emphasized at any point. As previously noted, the case was tried on the assumption that the alleged design defect was a matter of technical debate. Virtually all the evidence and argument on design defect focused on expert evaluation of the strengths, shortcomings, risks, and benefits of the challenged design, as compared with a competitor's approach. . . .

Under these circumstances, we find it highly unlikely that a reasonable jury took that path. We see no reasonable probability that the jury disregarded the voluminous evidence on the risks and benefits of the Camaro's design, and instead rested its verdict on its independent assessment of what an ordinary consumer would expect. Accordingly, we conclude, the error in presenting that theory to the jury provides no basis for disturbing the trial judgment.[8]

[Discussion of other issues omitted.]

---

8. In a separate argument, raised for the first time in GM's brief on the merits, both GM and the Council urge us to reconsider *Barker's* holding — embodied in the standard instruction received by this jury — that under the risk-benefit test, the manufacturer has the burden of proving that the utility of the challenged design outweighs its dangers. (*Barker,* supra. . . .) We explained in *Barker* that placement of the risk-benefit burden on the manufacturer is appropriate because the considerations which influenced the design of its product are "peculiarly within . . . [its] knowledge." (Id. . . .) Furthermore, we observed, the "fundamental policies" of *Greenman* dictate that a manufacturer who seeks to escape design defect liability on risk benefit grounds "should bear the burden of persuading the trier of fact that its product should not be judged defective. . . ." (Id. . . .)

GM argues that *Barker* unfairly requires the manufacturer to "prove a negative" — i.e., the absence of

Conclusion

The trial court erred when it instructed on the consumer expectations test for design defect.... However, [the] error [did not cause] actual prejudice. Accordingly, the judgment of the Court of Appeal, upholding the trial court judgment in favor of plaintiff, is affirmed.

KENNARD, GEORGE, WERDEGAR and BOREN, JJ., concur.

[Concurring opinions omitted]

As the court in *Soule* noted, *Barker* refused to adopt the "unreasonably dangerous" test for defect because it feared that the Comment *i* (consumer expectations) interpretation of "unreasonably dangerous" would tag along with it. To impose liability only for dangers that are beyond the contemplation of the ordinary consumer might give new life to the patent danger rule. As explained earlier, the patent danger rule declares that any design-related hazard that is, or should be, obvious to a reasonable product user cannot be the basis of a valid claim of defective design. *Barker* made it clear that, in California at least, no formulation of defect that could lead courts to reimpose the patent danger rule was acceptable.

One might imagine that the *Barker-Soule* two-prong test for defect resolves the problem by explicitly allowing the consumer expectations test to serve as a sword but not as a shield against liability. But experience teaches otherwise.

Thus, for example, in Todd v. Societe Bic, 21 F.3d 1402 (7th Cir. 1994), the court, in applying Illinois law, which follows a test identical to *Barker-Soule,* denied an infant plaintiff recovery based on adult consumer expectations. In that case, a two-year-old was killed by a fire started by a four-year-old who ignited a Bic lighter. The plaintiff alleged a design defect in Bic lighters in that they were not designed with child-resistant features. The court, in affirming the district court's grant of summary judgment to defendant, held that "children are not ordinary consumers under the consumer contemplation test. Unlike ordinary consumers, children lack knowledge common to the community regarding consumer products. This lack of knowledge makes children particularly unfit subjects for any test meant to measure consumer expectations." Id. at 1408. The court then went on to decide whether under the risk-utility prong of the Illinois rule there might be liability. Plaintiff had suggested alternative designs (which Bic had, in fact, adopted in later models) that could have prevented injury. The court concluded, "No Illinois court has applied the risk-utility test to a simple but obviously dangerous product." Id. at 1411. It is sometimes difficult for a court to rid itself of the notion that a product may still fail risk-utility balancing once it finds that consumer expectations were unambiguously met.

---

a safer alternative design. The Council suggests our "peculiar knowledge" rationale is unrealistic under liberal modern discovery rules. We are not persuaded. *Barker* allows the evaluation of competing designs, but it does not require proof that the challenged design is the safest possible alternative. The manufacturer need only show that given the inherent complexities of design, the benefits of its chosen design outweigh the dangers. Moreover, modern discovery practice neither redresses the inherent technical imbalance between manufacturer and consumer nor dictates that the injured consumer should bear the primary burden of evaluating a design developed and chosen by the manufacturer. GM and the Council fail to convince us that *Barker* was incorrectly decided in this respect.

Developments post-*Soule* in California raise the question of whether the consumer expectations test will be read as narrowly as *Soule* suggests. In Bresnahan v. Chrysler Corp., 38 Cal. Rptr. 2d 446 (Ct. App. 1995), plaintiff was driving her 1988 Chrysler LeBaron when she was rear-ended at low speed by another car. When the collision occurred, the LeBaron's passive restraint air bag inflated, forcing plaintiff's left arm and hand upward. Her hand struck the LeBaron's overarching windshield, cracking it, and her elbow impacted the windshield's side pillar. Plaintiff suffered a fractured elbow, requiring extensive treatment.

Plaintiff decided to try the case solely on the consumer expectations test and sought to exclude all evidence with regard to risk-utility factors. Defendant countered that under *Soule* a case dealing with the crashworthiness characteristics of an automobile could proceed only under the risk-utility theory. The trial court sided with the defendant. The court reversed on appeal, saying:

> We believe that, on the showing before us, an ordinary consumer would be capable of forming an expectation, one way or the other, about whether the design of the highly publicized and by now commonplace product of an air bag-equipped automobile satisfied minimal safety expectations in causing that result (assuming that it was the cause). Plaintiff's theory here does not pose the consumer unawareness that attended the design defect claim in *Soule*. In contrast to *Soule's* complex and murky situation regarding the crashworthiness of wheel brackets and frames, ordinary experience may well advise a consumer what measure of safety to expect from her car's side windshield assembly and air bag in a minor rear-end collision.
>
> . . . [C]hrysler cannot disqualify the consumer expectations test on the basis of asserted governmental conclusions that the benefits of air bags in high-speed collisions outweigh and justify the risk of injuries such as occurred here. Risk-benefit weighing is not a formal part of, nor may it serve as a "defense" to, the consumer expectations test. (*Soule,* supra, 8 Cal. 4th at p.566.) Chrysler's implicit suggestion that the favorableness to it of the risk-benefit test requires its use begs the question. [Id. at 451-52.]

Is the gist of this decision that plaintiff should recover even if Chrysler could establish that an alternate design would provide less overall safety than that provided by the design that caused the plaintiff's injury?

In a later case, Pruitt v. General Motors Corp., 86 Cal. Rptr. 2d 4 (Ct. App. 1999), on facts similar to *Bresnahan*—an air bag deployed in a low-impact collision, fracturing plaintiff's jaw—the trial court refused to give a consumer expectations design-defect instruction and the jury returned a verdict for the defendant. The court of appeals affirmed the judgment:

For other indications that California reads the consumer expectations test narrowly, see Snyder v. Ortho-McNeil Pharmaceuticals, 2002 WL 1161208 (Cal. Ct. App. 2002) (consumer expectations test unsuitable for medical devices); Morson v. Superior Court, 109 Cal. Rptr. 2d 343 (Ct. App. 2001) (consumer expectations test not appropriate to decide whether design of latex gloves is defective); McCabe v. American Honda Motor Co., 123 Cal. Rptr. 2d 303, n.7, (Ct. App. 2002) (consumer expectations test invisages an inquiry similar to that employed in res ipsa loquitur cases). But see Arnold v. Dow Chemical Co., 110 Cal. Rptr. 2d 722 (Ct. App. 2001) (insecticide "within the ordinary experience and understanding of the consumer").

In *Barker,* the California court held that in order to foster the purposes behind the strict products liability doctrine, it was necessary to alter the traditional burden of proof. The court said:

> **authors' dialogue 12**
>
> **JIM:** Aaron, after all the fireworks, what's your take on the role that the consumer expectations test plays in design defect litigation?
>
> **AARON:** Except for Wisconsin and Kansas — two states that are true believers — I believe that most of the cases that allow for liability under the consumer expectations test are cases that would be covered by Section 3 of the Products Liability Restatement which supports an inference of defect when the incident that caused the harm was of a kind that ordinarily occurs as a result of product defect. So my short answer is that I don't think that the consumer expectations test plays much of a role in design litigation.
>
> **JIM:** But aren't more cases getting to juries on a consumer expectations instruction than would reach under risk utility? Courts are giving it more play than you think.
>
> **AARON:** Look at the cases that go to juries with both a risk-utility and consumer expectations instruction. Invariably the plaintiff has presented evidence of a reasonable alternative design. What courts are doing is allowing cases to go to a jury on dual instructions, thus giving the plaintiff two bites at the apple. Whether that is fair or not, we can debate. But, in any event, plaintiff has offered sufficient evidence of a reasonable alternative design so that the court is not prepared to direct a verdict for the defendant on that issue.
>
> **JIM:** But what if a jury comes back with a verdict for the defendant on risk-utility and for the plaintiff on consumer expectations? You can't say that consumer expectations is just window dressing.
>
> **AARON:** I have two responses. First, those cases are few and far between. Now and then it happens. The *Denny* case in New York is an example. But there are not many other examples out there. Second, courts are prepared to allow a looser jury standard once they are convinced that a practical alternative was probably available. Would courts be so free-wheeling with the consumer expectations instruction if they knew that a reasonable alternative design was not in the picture? I think not.
>
> **JIM:** The problem with your thesis is that you can't prove it. How is anyone to know what lurks in the minds of judges? But if I get you right, the consumer expectations test allows a jury that may be scared off by a risk-utility instruction as being too technical to do risk-utility justice but under a less rigid standard. That's interesting.

Because most of the evidentiary matters which may be relevant to the determination of the adequacy of a product's design under the "risk-benefit" standard — e.g., the feasibility and cost of alternative designs — are similar to issues typically presented in a negligent design case and involve technical matters peculiarly within the knowledge of the manufacturer, we conclude that once the plaintiff makes a prima facie showing that the injury was proximately caused by the product's design, the burden should appropriately shift to the defendant to prove, in light of the relevant factors, that the product is not defective. 573 P.2d at 455.

Though urged by defendants to reexamine this position in *Soule,* the court refused to do so. *Soule,* supra, n.8.

Several other jurisdictions have adopted the *Barker* two-step test for liability. See, e.g., Acoba v. General Tire Co., 986 P.2d 288 (Haw. 1999); Caterpillar Tractor Co. v. Beck, 593 P.2d 871 (Alaska 1979); Hansen v. Baxter Healthcare Corp., 764 N.E.2d 35 (Ill. 2002); Jackson v. General Motors Corp. 60 S.W.3d 800 (Tenn. 2001); Knitz v. Minster Mach. Co., 432 N.E.2d 814 (Ohio 1982), *cert. denied,* 459 U.S. 857. However, it appears that only California, Alaska and Illinois have coupled the two-step liability test with a shift to defendant of the burden of proof on the risk-utility issue.

PROBLEM SIXTEEN

Jack Sittner was seriously injured when a three-wheel all-terrain vehicle manufactured by ATV Inc. overturned when he was driving the ATV on his one-acre lawn. Sittner has sued ATV Inc. claiming that the design of the ATV was defective. At trial, he is prepared to introduce expert testimony that ATV Inc. could have adopted a mechanical suspension system and that such a design could have been adopted at reasonable cost. In deposing ATV's expert, Dr. Roger Cart, Sittner's attorney learns that Cart has developed statistics that compare the annual injury and fatality rates (adjusted for hours of participation) for ATVs with a host of other activities and products. He is prepared to testify that the risk of death in SCUBA diving is four times greater than ATV riding, and the risk of death is two and one-half times greater in football; deaths involving passenger cars are slightly greater and deaths arising from motorcycling are substantially greater.

Sittner's attorney has filed a motion in limine to exclude Dr. Cart's comparative risk assessment. New California has adopted the *Barker-Soule* two-prong tests for defect. Plaintiff, however, retains the burden of proof on either of the tests. You are the trial judge faced with the decision of whether to grant the plaintiff's motion to exclude the comparative statistics. Would you exclude the testimony as to: (1) the consumer expectations test? (2) the risk-utility test? Or would you allow Dr. Cart to testify as to either or both of the issues?

G. IDIOSYNCRATIC STANDARDS FOR DETERMINING DESIGN DEFECT

If there is yet insufficient confusion, the student must take into account the work product of several courts who have decided to go it alone. Consider, for example, the decision of the Pennsylvania Supreme Court in Azzarello v. Black Bros. Co., Inc., 391 A.2d 1020 (Pa. 1978), in which the court held that it was for the court, not the jury, to decide whether a product was "unreasonably dangerous." As guidance for trial courts, the court propounded the following questions:

Should an ill-conceived design which exposes the user to the risk of harm entitle one injured by the product to recover? Should adequate warnings of the dangerous propensities of an article insulate one who suffers injuries from those propensities? When does the utility of a product outweigh the unavoidable danger it may pose? These are questions of law and their resolution depends upon society policy. . . . It is a judicial function to decide whether, under plaintiff's averment of the facts, recovery would be justified; and only after this judicial determination is made is the cause submitted to the jury to determine whether the facts of the case support the averments of the complaint. [Id. at 1026.]

The court then held that a jury should be told that "a manufacturer is effectively the guarantor of his product's safety." Id. The court went on to explain:

For the term guarantor to have any meaning in this context the supplier must at least provide a product which is designed to make it safe for the intended use. Under this standard, in this type case, the jury may find a defect where the product left the supplier's control lacking any element necessary to make it safe for its intended use or possessing any feature that renders it unsafe for the intended use. [Id. at 1027.]

Azzarello has been treated harshly by most commentators. See Sheila Birnbaum, Unmasking the Test for Design Defect: From Negligence [to Warranty] to Strict Liability to Negligence, 33 Vand. L. Rev. 593, 636-639 (1980); James A. Henderson, Jr., Products Liability: Controversial New Decision on Design Defects, 2 Corp. L. Rev. 246, 248 (1979); Comment, Returning the "Balance" to Design Defect Litigation in Pennsylvania: A Critique of Azzarello v. Black Bros. Co., Inc., 89 Dick. L. Rev. 149 (1984); Note, Restatement (Second) of Torts—Section 402A—Uncertain Standards of Responsibility in Design Defect Cases—After *Azzarello,* Will Manufacturers Be Absolutely Liable in Pennsylvania?, 24 Vill. L. Rev. 1035, 1050 (1979). For a more charitable reading of *Azzarello,* see Ellen Wertheimer, *Azzarello* Agonistes: Bucking the Strict Products Liability Tide, 66 Temp. L. Rev. 419 (1993).

Though the jury instructions mandated by *Azzarello* appear to allow juries almost untrammeled discretion, trial courts in Pennsylvania take very seriously the admonition in *Azzarello* that they must first decide as a matter of law whether, as a matter of societal policy, the case should go to the jury. As it turns out, Pennsylvania courts look to whether the plaintiff has provided credible evidence of a reasonable alternative design. In the absence of such proof they have rather consistently granted defense motions for summary judgment or directed verdict. See, e.g., Fitzpatrick v. Madonna, 623 A.2d 322 (Pa. Super. Ct. 1993) (in wrongful death action alleging defective design of outboard motor, court reversed jury finding for plaintiff for failure to establish a reasonable alternative design); Fritchey v. Rhone-Poulenc, Inc., 1996 WL 240009 (E.D. Pa. 1996), (defendant's motion for directed verdict granted absent plaintiff's ability to demonstrate that RAD of colorless chemical would have averted accident without compromising product's utility), *aff'd,* 106 F.3d 385 (3d Cir. 1996); Wallace v. Tesco Engineering Inc., CCH Prod. Liability Rptr. ¶14.523 (E.D. Pa. 1996) (directed verdict granted to defendant where employee who slipped due to assembly line oil spillage failed to proffer safer alternative design); Kupetz v. Deere and Co., 644 A.2d 1213, 1218 (Pa. Super. Ct. 1994) (among the facts a plaintiff must demonstrate in a crashworthiness case "[is] that the design of the vehicle was defective and that when the design was made, an alternative, safer design, practicable under the circumstances, existed"). One writer is convinced that the Pennsylvania cases are consistent with the Third Restatement's definition of design defect. See John M. Thomas, Defining "Design Defect" in Pennsylvania: Reconciling Azzarello and the Restatement (Third) of Torts, 71 Temp. L. Rev. 217 (1998). In Phillips v. Cricket Lighters, 2003 WL 22860315, the Pennsylvania Supreme Court split 3-3 as to whether it should continue its allegiance to *Azzarello* or whether it should formally adopt the Products Liability Restatement test for design defect.

In short, one must be careful when drawing conclusions about the law from jury instructions. The latter come into play once a court has made fundamental decisions as to whether the plaintiff has made out a prima facie case. A court may have a stringent test for defect and a loosely worded jury instruction once it has decided that liability may be appropriate.

The most recent addition to the constellation of theories is that of public nuisance. In actions brought against gun manufacturers, several courts have denied motions of summary judgment made by defendants claiming that the marketing and distribution of firearms unreasonably interferes with the health and safety of the citizens of various cities. See, e.g., Cincinnati v. Berretta U.S.A. Corp., 768 N.E.2d 1136 (Ohio 2002); City of Chicago v. Berretta U.S.A. Corp., 785 N.E.2d 16 (Ill. App. Ct. 2002); James v. Arms Technologies, Inc., 820 A.2d 27 (N.J. Sup. Ct. 2003).

Which is it to be? Feasible Alternative Design? Consumer Expectations? Risk-Utility-Based Category Liability? Nuisance? All of the above?

H. SPECIAL DUTY PROBLEMS IN DESIGN LITIGATION

Having examined the potential standards for prosecuting a design defect case, it is now beneficial to examine a set of issues that raise the question of whether the law may decide that for well-defined policy reasons, the issue of design defect should not be decided by the courts but rather should be deferred to other decision-makers. Such a deferral may result in a finding of no liability for defective design or in a finding that the violation of a standard already set in stone and beyond debate renders a product defective in design. For lack of a better word, we borrow from the duty terminology of the law of torts as a label to describe the issues we consider in this section.

1. Whether and to What Extent Should Courts Defer to Markets?

Linegar v. Armour of America, Inc.
909 F.2d 1150 (8th Cir. 1990)

BOWMAN, Circuit Judge.

. . . Armour of America, Inc. (Armour) appeals a judgment based on a jury verdict in favor of the widow and children of Jimmy Linegar, a Missouri State Highway Patrol trooper who was killed in the line of duty. The jury found that the bullet-resistant vest manufactured by Armour and worn by Linegar at the time of the murder was defectively designed, and it awarded his family $1.5 million in damages. We reverse.

On April 15, 1985, as part of a routine traffic check, Linegar stopped a van with Nevada license plates near Branson, Missouri. The van's driver produced an Oregon operator's license bearing the name Matthew Mark Samuels. Linegar ascertained from the Patrol dispatcher that the name was an alias for David Tate, for whom there was an outstanding warrant on a weapons charge. Linegar did not believe the driver matched the description the dispatcher gave him for Tate, so he decided to investigate further.

A fellow trooper, Allen Hines, who was working the spot check with Linegar, then approached the passenger's side of the van while Linegar approached the driver's side. After a moment of questioning, Linegar asked the driver to step out of the van. The driver, who was in fact David Tate, brandished an automatic weapon and fired at the troopers first from inside and then from outside the van. By the time Tate stopped firing, Hines had been wounded by three shots and Linegar, whose body had been penetrated by six bullets, lay dead or dying. None of the shots that hit the contour-style, concealable protective vest Linegar was wearing — there were five such shots — penetrated the vest or caused injury. The wounds Linegar suffered all were caused by shots that struck parts of his body not protected by the vest.

The Missouri State Highway Patrol issued the vest to Linegar when he joined the Patrol in 1981. The vest was one of a lot of various sizes of the same style vest the Patrol purchased in 1979 directly from Armour. The contour style was one of several different styles then on the market. It provided more protection to the sides of the body than the style featuring rectangular panels in front and back, but not as much protection as a wrap-around style. The front and back panels of the contour vest, held together with Velcro closures under the arms, did not meet at the sides of the wearer's body, leaving an area along the sides of the body under the arms exposed when the vest was worn. This feature of the vest was obvious to the Patrol when it selected this vest as standard issue for its troopers and could only have been obvious to any trooper who chose to wear it. The bullet that proved fatal to Linegar entered between his seventh and eighth ribs, approximately three-and-one-fourth inches down from his armpit, and pierced his heart.

The theory upon which Linegar's widow and children sought and won recovery from Armour was strict liability in tort based on a design defect in the vest. . . .

The parties agree that Missouri substantive law controls in this diversity case. Under Missouri products liability law, plaintiff potentially had available to her three theories of recovery: negligence, strict liability, and breach of warranty. . . .

To recover under a theory of strict liability in tort for defective design, Missouri law requires that a party prove the following elements:

(1) [the] defendant sold the product in the course of its business;
(2) the product was then in a defective condition unreasonably dangerous when put to a reasonably anticipated use;
(3) the product was used in a manner reasonably anticipated;
(4) [the] plaintiff was damaged as a direct result of such defective condition as existed when the product was sold. . . .

While there is some dispute between the parties over various of the elements, we predicate our reversal on the dearth of plaintiff's evidence of element (2). We conclude that, as a matter of law, the contour vest Trooper Linegar was wearing when he was murdered was not defective and unreasonably dangerous.

Under the Missouri law of strict liability in tort for defective design, before a plaintiff can recover from the seller or manufacturer he must show that "the design renders the product unreasonably dangerous." *Nesselrode v. Executive Beechcraft, Inc.*, 707 S.W.2d 371, 377 (Mo. 1986) (en banc). Ordinarily, that will be a jury question, and "the concept of unreasonable danger, which is determinative of whether a product is defective in a design case, is presented to the jury as an ultimate issue without further definition," id. at 378, as it was here. In this case, however, there was simply no evidence that the vest's design made it unreasonably dangerous, and the District Court should have declared that, as a matter of law, the vest was not defective, and directed a verdict or granted judgment for Armour notwithstanding the verdict. *See* Racer v. Utterman, 629 S.W.2d 387, 394 (Mo. Ct. App. 1981) ("Unless a court can say as a matter of law that the product is not unreasonably dangerous the question is one for the jury."), *cert. denied,* 459 U.S. 803, 103 S. Ct. 26, 74 L. Ed. 2d 42 (1982).

The Missouri cases leave the meaning of the phrase "unreasonably dangerous" largely a matter of common sense, the court's or the jury's. The Missouri Supreme Court has stated, however, that a product is defectively designed if it "creates an unreasonable risk of danger to the consumer or user when put to normal use." *Nesselrode,* 707 S.W.2d at 375. Among the factors to be considered are "the conditions and circumstances that will foreseeably attend the use of the product." Jarrell v. Fort Worth Steel & Mfg. Co., 666 S.W.2d 828, 836 (Mo. Ct. App. 1984). The conditions under which a bullet-resistant vest will be called upon to perform its intended function most assuredly will be dangerous, indeed life-threatening, and Armour surely knew that. It defies logic, however, to suggest that Armour reasonably should have anticipated that anyone would wear its vest for protection of areas of the body that the vest obviously did not cover. . . .

The judgment of the District Court is reversed. The District Court shall enter a final judgment in favor of *Armour.*

We have no difficulty in concluding as a matter of law that the product at issue here was neither defective nor unreasonably dangerous. Trooper Linegar's protective vest performed precisely as expected and stopped all of the bullets that hit it. No part of the vest nor any malfunction of the vest caused Linegar's injuries. *See Richardson,* 741 S.W.2d at 754 ("The cases uniformly hold that the doctrine of strict liability under the doctrine of 402A is not applicable unless there is some malfunction due to an improper or inadequate design or defect in manufacturing."). The vest was designed to prevent the penetration of bullets where there was coverage, and it did so; the amount of coverage was the buyer's choice. The Missouri Highway Patrol could have chosen to buy, and Armour could have sold the Patrol, a vest with more coverage; no one contests that. But it is not the place of courts or juries to set specifications as to the parts of the body a bullet-resistant garment must cover. A manufacturer is not obliged to market only one version of a product, that being the very safest design possible. If that were so, automobile manufacturers could not offer consumers sports cars, convertibles, jeeps, or compact cars. All boaters would have to buy full life vests instead of choosing a ski belt or even a flotation cushion. Personal safety devices, in particular, require personal choices, and it is beyond the province of courts and juries to act as legislators and preordain those choices.

In this case, there obviously were trade-offs to be made. A contour vest like the one here in question permits the wearer more flexibility and mobility and allows better heat dissipation and sweat evaporation, and thus is more likely to be worn than a more confining vest. It is less expensive than styles of vests providing more complete coverage. If manufacturers like Armour are threatened with economically devastating litigation if they market any vest style except that offering maximum coverage, they may decide, since one can always argue that more coverage is possible, to get out of the business altogether. Or they may continue to market the vest style that, according to the latest lawsuit, affords the "best" coverage. Officers who find the "safest" style confining or uncomfortable will either wear it at risk to their mobility or opt not to wear it at all. *See* Transcript Vol. II at 333 (testimony of Missouri Highway Patrol Trooper Don Phillips that he continued to wear the Armour contour-style vest with his summer uniform, even though the Patrol had issued him a wrap-around vest). Law enforcement agencies trying to work within the confines of a budget may be forced to purchase fewer vests or none at all. How "safe" are those possibilities? "The core concern in strict tort liability law is safety." *Nesselrode,* 707 S.W.2d at 375. We are firmly convinced that to allow this verdict to stand would run counter to the law's purpose of promoting the development of safe and useful products, and would have an especially pernicious effect on the development and marketing of equipment designed to make the always-dangerous work of law enforcement officers a little safer.

The death of Jimmy Linegar by the hand of a depraved killer was a tragic event. We keenly feel the loss that this young trooper's family has suffered, and our sympathies go out to them. But we cannot allow recovery from a blameless defendant on the basis of sympathy for the plaintiffs. To hold Armour liable for Linegar's death would cast it in the role of insurer for anyone shot while wearing an Armour vest, regardless of whether any shots penetrated the vest. That a manufacturer may be cast in such a role has been soundly rejected by courts applying Missouri law. . . .

The judgment of the District Court is reversed. The District Court shall enter a final judgment in favor of Armour.

Scarangella v. Thomas Built Buses, Inc.
717 N.E.2d 679 (N.Y. 1999)

LEVINE, J.

A school bus being operated in reverse by a co-employee struck and severely injured plaintiff Concetta Scarangella, a school bus driver for third-party defendant Huntington Coach Corp., Inc. The accident occurred in Huntington's bus parking yard on September 26, 1988. The vehicle was one of ten new school buses that defendant Thomas Built Buses, Inc., sold Huntington in 1988. At that time, Thomas offered buyers as an optional safety feature a back-up alarm that would automatically sound when a driver shifted the bus into reverse gear, but Huntington chose not to purchase this optional equipment.

After plaintiff and her husband commenced this action for negligence, breach of warranty and products liability, Thomas made a motion to preclude plaintiff from submitting to the jury her claim that the lack of a back-up alarm was a design defect. In support of its motion, Thomas submitted a memorandum of law and excerpts from the deposition of Huntington's President and Chief Operating Officer, Kevin Clifford.

According to Clifford's deposition testimony, Huntington owned and operated 190 school buses and had 300 employees. Clifford had worked for the company for over 30 years and had been a president of the New York State School Bus Owners Association. Clifford explained that he was aware that the backup alarms were available but made a considered decision not to purchase them. He opted against the alarm because "it screams" when a bus is put in reverse gear, and he intended to park the buses at a bus yard in the middle of a residential neighborhood where his company had been experiencing problems with neighbors concerning noise pollution. When the buses were being parked in the bus yard, there "had to be a tremendous amount of backing up," and Clifford believed it was unnecessary to equip all 100 buses in the lot with the "screaming" alarms. Instead, Clifford instructed the drivers to be cautious and to use the bus's ordinary horn before backing up.

In response to Thomas's motion, plaintiff proffered no specific evidence. She based her design defect claim entirely on the proposition that, because a school bus driver always has a substantial blind spot when operating the vehicle in reverse, a school bus must invariably be equipped with an automatically engaged back-up alarm. Supreme Court concluded that there was no triable issue of fact on this design defect claim. It thus granted defendant's motion to preclude plaintiff from presenting any evidence on the issue to the jury.

Plaintiff proceeded to trial on the theory that the bus was defectively designed because it did not have proper mirrors. At the conclusion of plaintiff's case, the Trial Judge directed a verdict for defendant and dismissed the complaint. The Appellate Division affirmed. . . .

A defectively designed product "'is one which, at the time it leaves the seller's hands, is in a condition not reasonably contemplated by the ultimate consumer and is unreasonably dangerous for its intended use; that is one whose utility does not outweigh the danger inherent in its introduction into the stream of commerce'" (Voss v. Black & Decker Mfg. Co., 450 N.E.2d 204). A manufacturer can be held liable for selling a defectively designed product because the manufacturer "is in the superior position to discover any design defects and alter the design before making the product available to the public". . . .

In Voss, we identified seven non-exclusive factors to be considered in balancing the risks created by the product's design against its utility and cost. . . . As relevant here, these include the likelihood that the product will cause injury, the ability of the plaintiff to have avoided injury, the degree of awareness of the product's dangers which reasonably can be attributed to the plaintiff, the usefulness of the product to the consumer as designed as compared to a safer design and the functional and monetary cost of using the alternative design. . . . An additional pertinent factor that may be taken into account is "the likely effects of [liability for failure to adopt] the alternative design on . . . the range of consumer choice among products" (Restatement [Third] of Products Liability §2, comment *f*). Where a court, after considering the relevant facts and risk-utility factors, determines that the plaintiff has failed to make out a prima facie case of a design defect, the claim should not be submitted to the jury. . . .

Biss v. Tenneco, Inc. . . ., 409 N.Y.S.2d 874, *lv denied* . . ., 416 N.Y.S.2d 1025, and Rainbow v. Albert Elia Bldg. Co. . . . 436 N.Y.S.2d 480, *affd,* 449 N.Y.S.2d 967) applied New York's design defect jurisprudence to fact patterns in which the buyer of a product elected not to purchase an optional safety device to accompany it. Biss held that a manufacturer of a loader vehicle could not be found liable for negligent design where an employee of the purchaser was injured due to the absence of an optional roll-over protection structure the purchaser chose not to have included when the vehicle was acquired. The opinion reasoned that "defendants had fulfilled their duty to exercise reasonable skill and care in designing the product as a matter of law when they advised the purchaser that an appropriate safety structure . . . was available. . . . If knowledge of available safety options is brought home to the purchaser, the duty to exercise reasonable care in selecting those appropriate to the intended use rests upon him. He is the party in the best position to exercise an intelligent judgment to make the trade-off between cost and function, and it is he who should bear the responsibility if the decision on optional safety equipment presents an unreasonable risk to users" (Biss v. Tenneco, Inc., supra. . . .)

In Rainbow, plaintiff claimed that a motorcycle without an optional safety feature, side crash bars, was unreasonably dangerous. The plaintiff was "an experienced motorcyclist [who] . . . had been a successful motorcycle racer for many years [and] . . . had removed crash bars mounted on a previously owned motorcycle". . . . The court dismissed plaintiff's complaint, holding that the buyer "was in the best position to exercise an intelligent judgment in making the trade-off between cost and function and thus to decide whether crash bars were reasonably necessary on his motorcycle for his purposes" (id.).

In contrast, in Rosado v. Proctor & Schwartz, Inc. . . . 494 N.Y.S.2d 851 . . . a manufacturer who sold a textile machine with completely exposed massive gears, chains and pulleys, with no safety disconnect switches, could not escape responsibility for a user's injury by inserting boilerplate language in its sales contract that required the buyer to install any necessary safety devices. In contrast to the instant case, the manufacturer there did not give the buyer the choice of a machine that was already equipped with the safety equipment. We held that "where, as here, the manufacturer is in the best position to know the dangers inherent in its product, and the dangers do not vary depending on jobsite, it is also in the best position to determine what safety devices should be employed. . . . To allow a manufacturer . . . which sells a product . . . with no safety devices, to shift the ultimate duty of care to others through boilerplate language in a sales contract, would erode the economic incentive manufacturers have to maintain safety and give sanction to the marketing of dangerous, stripped down, machines". . . .

We can thus distill some governing principles for cases where a plaintiff claims that a product without an optional safety feature is defectively designed because the equipment was not standard. The product is not defective where the evidence and reasonable inferences therefrom show that: (1) the buyer is thoroughly knowledgeable regarding the product and its use and is actually aware that the safety feature is available; (2) there exist normal circumstances of use in which the product is not unreasonably dangerous without the optional equipment; and (3) the buyer is in a position, given the range of uses of the product, to balance the benefits and the risks of not having the safety device in the specifically contemplated circumstances of the buyer's use of the product. In such a case, the buyer, not the manufacturer, is in the superior position to make the risk-utility assessment, and a well-considered decision by the buyer to dispense with the optional safety equipment will excuse the manufacturer from liability. When the factors are not present, there is no justification for departure from the accepted rationale imposing strict liability upon the manufacturer because it "is in the superior position to discover any design defects." . . .

Applying the foregoing principles, plaintiff failed to make a prima facie showing that the lack of a back-up alarm on the bus that injured her was a design defect. First, Huntington was a highly knowledgeable consumer. Huntington and its management had owned and operated school buses serving a number of school districts for decades and certainly were aware that a bus driver had a blind spot when a bus was operated in reverse. It is also undisputed that when it purchased the bus, Huntington knew that the back-up alarm was available. The product was in the exact condition contemplated and selected by Huntington at the time of purchase.

Second, the uncontradicted evidence showed that, in the actual circumstances of the operation of the buses in reverse by Huntington, the risk of harm from the absence of a back-up alarm was not substantial. In his pre-trial deposition, Huntington's president indicated that the only significant incidence of operating buses in reverse was in positioning buses in and backing them out of the yard. Plaintiff submitted no evidence regarding Huntington buses backing up under any other circumstances, e.g., while transporting children to and from school or outside the parking yard. Indeed, at the trial plaintiff herself testified that, because of the blind spot, Huntington drivers were instructed as part of their training not to operate buses in reverse except in the yard. Drivers were also instructed to exercise caution and sound their regular horns when backing up.

Thus, the individuals at risk from the absence of back-up alarm equipment on Huntington buses were almost exclusively its drivers and other employees at its parking yard. It was readily inferable from the only evidence submitted on the motion that these persons at risk, including plaintiff, were fully aware of a bus driver's blind spot in backing up a bus and the resultant hazard, and could be expected to exercise special care whenever positioned in proximity to the rear of any bus that was idling or moving in reverse in the yard. Again, plaintiff made no factual showing to the contrary that school children, other pedestrians or occupants of other vehicles were exposed to any hazards of the operation of Huntington buses in reverse, without back-up alarms.

Third, Huntington was in a position to balance the benefits and the dangers of not having the safety device, given the contemplated use of the bus. After weighing the risks against the costs, Huntington made a considered decision not to buy the backup alarm. Only Huntington knew how it would instruct and train its drivers and when and how the buses would be operated in reverse. Huntington and not Thomas was in a position to assess the efficacy of alternative safety measures in its operational rules and training of drivers. The buyer had the ability to understand and weigh the significance of costs associated with noise pollution and neighborhood relations, given the particular suburban location of the parking lot, against the anticipated, foreseeable risks of operating buses in a parking lot without a back-up alarm device or safeguard.

As shown above, plaintiff was confronted with proof that brought this case within the Biss-Rainbow three-factor analysis of the sophisticated consumer's knowledge of the safety feature, the existence of reasonably safe circumstances of normal use and the superior vantage point of the buyer in risk-utility balancing with respect to its own individualized use of the product. Plaintiff failed to submit, in opposition to the preclusion motion, any proof negating any of these three factors. Indeed, she failed to make out a prima facie case with evidence regarding other relevant considerations generally applicable in design defect cases, e.g., the ability of the plaintiff to have avoided injury, the plaintiff's degree of awareness of the potential danger, the cost of the back-up alarm or the effect of liability on the range of consumer choice (see Restatement [Third] of Products Liability, op. cit., §2, comment *f,* illustrations 9 and 10). Thus, plaintiff created no triable issues for the jury in connection with her claim that the absence of a back-up alarm was a design defect, and preclusion was warranted here.

Accordingly, the order of the Appellate Division should be affirmed, with costs.

In the vast majority of cases alleging design defect, courts do not defer to the market even when consumers are fully aware of the dangers associated with the risks attendant to the use of the product. If a reasonable alternative design is available that would protect the consumer, failure to adopt such an alternative design may be found to render a product not reasonably safe. You will recall that merely because a product's dangers are open and obvious does not shield a product seller from liability. Nor can sellers purge themselves from liability by offering extensive warnings of product-related risks. Risk-utility balancing requires that reasonable designs be adopted to avoid risks even though consumers decide to purchase the product with full knowledge of the attendant dangers.

One cannot simply ring the bell of "consumer choice" and expect the courts to defer to the market. What, then, is so special about *Linegar* and *Scarangella?* In both cases plausible reasonable alternative designs were offered by the plaintiff that would have avoided the plaintiffs' injuries. And in both cases the appellate court said that there was no liability as a matter of law because the court wanted to maximize consumer choice. There is no easy answer as to when paternalism ends and consumer choice takes over. Perhaps we may invoke Justice Stewart's definition of obscenity "I can't define it but I know it when I see it." At some point in the continuum, the role of consumer choice is of such a magnitude that it cannot be ignored. To a significant degree the hostility of courts to category liability stems from their unwillingness to deny consumers the right to purchase products that would otherwise become unavailable if we were to tax through tort law all injuries arising from their use. Consider the following illustration taken from the Products Liability Restatement §2, comment *f:*

> ILLUSTRATION:
> 9. John was driving a compact automobile manufactured by the ABC Auto Company when he lost control and collided with a tree. John suffered serious injuries. John brings a products-liability claim against ABC, arguing that the design of his car is defective in that it does not offer the same level of crashworthiness as does a full-size automobile. John's experts admit that reducing the size of an automobile unavoidably increases the risk of injuries to occupants in collisions. John can identify no specific feature of the ABC automobile that could have been designed differently so as to be safer without increasing its size and substantially reducing its desirable characteristics of lower cost and lower fuel economy. John has not established a defect within the meaning of Subsection

(b) [the section requiring a reasonable alternative design]. Although ABC's design is less safe than larger vehicles, the only way to make it safer, on John's own proof, is to make it larger, and the costs of doing that are unacceptably great. Moreover, eliminating smaller automobiles from the market would unduly restrict the range of consumer choice among automobile designs. Thus, the ABC design is not, by reason of its being smaller than other automobiles, "not reasonably safe." Given that the risks and benefits associated with relative automobile size are generally known, decisions regarding which sizes to purchase and use should be left to purchasers and users in the market.

However, when courts detect that consumers are vulnerable because their choices are limited or impaired, they will roll out paternalism to provide the necessary protection. Thus, when employees are required to work on machines without reasonably available safety features that should protect them from their own inadvertence, inattention or even rank stupidity, courts may impose liability no matter how clearly visible the danger. See, e.g., Jurado v. Western Gear Works, 619 A.2d 1312 (N.J. 1993) (failure to install guard at nip point of collating machine); Micallef v. Miehle Co., 348 N.E.2d 571 (N.Y. 1976) (plaintiff injured when he sought to remove a blemish from a high speed press while in operation; injury could have been avoided by a guard that would have prevented employee's hand from getting caught between the cylinder and the ink-form roller). Note that the fact that the plaintiff is an employee does not guarantee that the court will not play the duty card to deny liability. In both *Linegar* and *Scarangella* the plaintiffs were employees for whom the employer chose the less safe alternative. So we once again pose the question: How does one differentiate *Linegar* and *Scarangella* from the huge body of case law that imposes liability on a manufacturer for failing to adopt safer alternative designs that would prevent harm to employees from even the most obvious of dangers?

2. *Whether and to What Extent Should Courts Defer to Safety Statutes or Administrative Regulations?*

In discussing the extent to which products liability law should defer to statute or administrative regulation in setting the standard for defective design, we put to one side the question of federal preemption. When a court finds that design regulations mandated by federal administrative agencies or federal statute are intended to preempt all state common law standard setting, then federal supremacy nullifies any attempt to set design standards more demanding than those adopted by Congress or the agencies. Federal preemption will be dealt with at length in Chapter Seven. In this section we will assume no federal preemption but instead will inquire as to whether courts should, as a matter of good sense, defer to administrative regulation in deciding whether to direct a verdict for the plaintiff (if the defendant violated an administrative regulation) or for the defendant (if the defendant complied with an administrative regulation).

When courts adopt state or federal product safety regulations as the governing standard for product safety, the task of making difficult design choices is transferred to governmental bodies with expertise in the designated area. Most of the regulations relevant to products liability emanate from federal administrative agencies such as the National Highway Traffic Safety Administration (NHTSA), the Food and Drug Administration (FDA), Consumer Product Safety Commission (CPSC) and the Environmental Protective Agency (EPA).

By far the most common plea made to courts is that they adopt a safety regulation as the governing common law standard for design. We thus now examine under what circumstances courts are likely to adopt the state or federal standard as their own and remove from the finder of fact the issue of what standard should govern design.

Restatement (Third) of Torts: Products Liability
(1998)

§4. NONCOMPLIANCE AND COMPLIANCE WITH
PRODUCT SAFETY STATUTES OR REGULATIONS

In connection with liability for defective design or inadequate instructions or warnings:

(a) a product's noncompliance with an applicable product safety statute or administrative regulation renders the product defective with respect to the risks sought to be reduced by the statute or regulation; and

(b) a product's compliance with an applicable product safety statute or administrative regulation is properly considered in determining whether the product is defective with respect to the risks sought to be reduced by the statute or regulation, but such compliance does not preclude as a matter of law a finding of product defect.

COMMENT:

. . .

d. Noncompliance with product safety statute or administrative regulation. . . . In contrast to Subsection (a), the parallel common-law rule governing noncompliance with safety statutes or regulations in negligence actions not involving product liability claims recognizes that noncompliance with an applicable safety statute or regulation does not constitute failure to use due care when the defendant establishes a justification or excuse for the violation. For example, if noncompliance with an administrative regulation under conditions of emergency or temporary impossibility would not constitute a violation in a direct enforcement proceeding, noncompliance alone does not prove negligence. In connection with the adequacy of product designs and warnings, however, design and marketing decisions are made before distribution to users and consumers. The product seller therefore has the option of deferring sale until statutory or regulatory compliance is achieved. Consequently, justification or excuse of the sort anticipated in connection with negligence claims generally does not apply in connection with failure to comply with statutes or regulations governing product design or warnings.

e. Compliance with product safety or administrative regulation. . . . , Subsection (b) addresses the effects of compliance with a federal statute or regulation to be nonpreemptive. It addresses the question, under state law, of the effect that compliance with product safety statutes or regulations — federal or state — should have on the issue of product defectiveness. Subsection (b) reflects the traditional view that the standards set by most product safety statutes or regulations generally are only minimum standards. Thus, most product safety statutes or reg-

> **authors' dialogue 13**
>
> **AARON:** Jim, why has there been so much resistance to compliance with administrative regulation as a defense? We have some pretty good federal administrative agencies. The FDA, NHTSA, and the EPA. They do a decent job. Probably as good as the courts do. And we would save all the wear and tear of trying to develop standards on a case by case basis.
>
> **JIM:** Sometimes yes and sometimes no. You remember way back when in the 1980s, before we became partners we used to run into each other in legislative hearings in Washington. Every year there was another industry sponsored bill. I don't know if you recall but one such bill would have made administrative regulation binding on the courts if the administrative standard was issued from an agency that was adjudged to be competent.
>
> **AARON:** Ah, those were the good old days. If my memory serves me right that's when you got the reputation among plaintiffs' lawyers as being somewhere to the right of Atilla the Hun.
>
> **JIM:** Hey, that's not fair. I never testified in favor of provisions that I thought were unfairly loaded on the side of industry. In any event you're not one to talk. It's like the pot calling the kettle black. But back to the subject, that bill went nowhere. Agency representatives told the congressional committee that the last thing they needed was for courts to pass on the competence of what their agencies were doing.
>
> **AARON:** Okay, that was a nutty idea. But what about the statutes creating a

ulations establish a floor of safety below which product sellers fall only at their peril, but they leave open the question of whether a higher standard of product safety should be applied. This is the general rule, applicable in most cases.

Occasionally, after reviewing relevant circumstances, a court may properly conclude that a particular product safety standard set by statute or regulation adequately serves the objectives of tort law and therefore that the product that complies with the standard is not defective as a matter of law. Such a conclusion may be appropriate when the safety statute or regulation was promulgated recently, thus supplying currency to the standard therein established; when the specific standard addresses the very issue of product design or warning presented in the case before the court; and when the court is confident that the deliberative process by which the safety standard was established was full, fair, and thorough and reflected substantial expertise. Conversely, when the deliberative process that led to the safety standard with which the defendant's product complies was tainted by the supplying of false information to, or the withholding of necessary and valid information from, the agency that promulgated the standard or certified or approved the product, compliance with regulation is entitled to little or no weight.

rebuttable presumption that a product that meets agency standards is not defective? That isn't crazy.

JIM: It's not crazy. But it's nearly worthless. It leaves plaintiffs where they were before, with the burden of coming forward with a reasonable alternative design. The only thing that will work is something with teeth. For example, requiring plaintiff to prove defect by clear and convincing evidence if the product meets relevant federal standards.

AARON: That kind of proposal is DOA. Either it doesn't really add anything or, if it does, it puts too much power in the hands of federal agencies whose policies and standards change based on which party controls the White House. What might work is the two step process that our good friend Hans Linde, the former Chief Justice of the Supreme Court of Oregon, once suggested in Wilson v. Piper Aircraft [579 P.2d 1287 (Or. 1978)]. First, courts should determine that the administrative agency utilizes the same legal standard for regulation as the courts use in deciding whether a product is defective. Second, courts should examine whether, in fact, the agency utilizing the standard did a thorough job of applying the standard in the specific instance.

JIM: It's an interesting idea. But like Michaelangelo's horse, it won't fly. Can you imagine a court hearing evidence concerning how an agency standard was developed? We would be subpoenaing half the bureaucrats in Washington to testify in the fifty states. Who would run the federal government?

AARON: Not a half-bad idea. They would probably do less damage if they were away from their desks testifying in products liability cases in Boise, Idaho.

Section 4(a) reflects the common law rule that violation of statute is negligence per se. In a similar fashion, violation of statute or administrative regulation constitutes defect per se. See, e.g., Harned v. Dura Corp., 665 P.2d 5, 12-13 (Alaska 1983); Toole v. Richardson-Merrell, Inc. 60 Cal. Rptr. 398, 409 (Ct. App. 1967). See generally, Malcolm Wheeler, The Use of Criminal Statutes to Regulate Product Safety, 13 J. Legal Stud. 593 (1984).

A more difficult question is whether a court should treat a manufacturer's compliance with a governmental regulation as conclusive that a product design is nondefective as a matter of law. The general rule is reflected in Restatement §4(b). See, e.g., Soproni v. Polygon Apartment Partners, 971 P.2d 500, 505 (Wash. 1999); Beatty v. Trailmaster Products, Inc., 625 A.2d 1005, 1014 (Md. 1993); Sours v. General Motors Corp., 717 F.2d 1511, 1517 (6th Cir. 1983) (applying Ohio law). Manufacturers have lobbied state legislative bodies and the United States Congress to require courts to give governmental regulation preclusive effect. Several states treat compliance with statute as a presumption of nondefectiveness. See, e.g., Utah Code Ann. §78-15-6(3) (2002); Kan. Stat. Ann. §60-3304 (1994); Colo. Rev. Stat. §13-21-403 (West 2002). The overwhelming majority of states follow the position set forth in §4(b).

However, decisions have indicated a judicial unwillingness to apply these presumptions with any bite. Even where the presumption is found to apply, plaintiffs may be able to survive motions for summary judgment with evidence that would otherwise create a prima facie case. See, e.g., McClain v. Chem-Lube Corp., 759 N.E.2d 1096 (Ind. App. Ct. 2001) (summary judgment for defendant chemical manufacturer improper without consideration of plaintiff's designated rebuttal evidence that product was unreasonably dangerous); Rogers ex rel. Rogers v. Cosco, Inc., 737 N.E.2d 1158 (Ind. App. Ct. 2000) (trial court required to consider plaintiff's evidence attempting to rebut presumption of manufacturer's compliance with Federal Motor Vehicle Safety Standards); Berg v. Jensen, 1997 WL 308857, *4 (N.D. Ill. 1997) (applying Illinois law) (finding that Illinois' statute allows a plaintiff to rebut presumption "with a variety of evidence and leaves the determinations regarding the effect of the evidence to the court or the jury without mandating a specific outcome").

The question remains, however, whether there are conditions under which a common law court will adopt the governmental design standard not only as a minimum standard but as the appropriate standard for design defect litigation. Section 4, Comment *e* of the Products Liability Restatement, set forth above, suggests that in some cases a court should treat compliance with a statute as dispositive on the issue of design defect even absent a presumption statute. Some courts concur. See, e.g., Lorenz v. Celotex Corp., 896 F.2d 148 (5th Cir.) (applying Texas law), *reh'g denied*, 901 F.2d 1110 (5th Cir. 1990) (compliance with safety regulation constitutes strong and substantial evidence of lack of defect); Ramirez v. Plough, Inc., 863 P.2d 167, 176, (Cal. 1993) ("Lacking the procedure and the resources to conduct the relevant inquiries, we conclude that the prudent course is to adopt for tort purposes the existing legislative and administrative standard of care on this issue."); Dentson v. Eddins & Lee Bus Sales, 491 So. 2d 942, 944 (Ala. 1986) ("[I]n this context, involving school transportation, an area traditionally reserved for the legislature, we find that the legislature's pronouncement is conclusive: a school bus in Alabama may not be found defective . . . because it is not equipped with passenger seat belts."); Jones v. Hittle Services, Inc., 549 P.2d 1303, 1390 (Kan. 1976) (stating in dictum, "Compliance is evidence of due care and that the conforming product is not defective, and may be conclusive in the absence of a showing of special circumstances."). See also Ashley W. Warren, Compliance with Governmental Regulatory Standards: Is It Enough to Immunize a Defendant from Tort Liability?, 49 Baylor L. Rev. 763 (1997), Richard Ausness, The Case for a "Strong" Regulatory Compliance Defense, 55 Md. L. Rev. 1210 (1996).

3. Beyond the Pale: High Profile No-Duty Cases

In the previous sections we examined certain cases in which the courts decided not to impose a duty on a manufacturer to make a product reasonably safe. The decision to allow the market to choose between two types of bullet-proof vests is properly viewed as a duty issue. Although an argument can be mounted that the vest with less protection is reasonably safe, the better way to view the case is that the court preferred to allow consumer choice to determine the desirable level of safety. The decision to give consumer choice primacy is a policy decision that is best given effect under the rubric of duty. We will encounter more duty rules of this genre in the ensuing chapters. They are part and parcel of the law of products liability.

On occasion we run into a no-duty rule that is very broad in its scope. Unlike the no-duty rules described earlier that are carved out with a scalpel, these no-duty rules have all the subtlety of a meat ax. They pronounce to the world that a court is unwilling to enter the thicket of a certain class of litigation.

Hamilton v. Beretta U.S.A. Corp.
750 N.E.2d 1055 (N.Y. 2001)

WESLEY, J.

In January 1995 plaintiffs — relatives of people killed by handguns — sued 49 handgun manufacturers in Federal court alleging negligent marketing, design defect, ultra-hazardous activity and fraud. A number of defendants jointly moved for summary judgment. The United States District Court for the Eastern District of New York (Weinstein, J.), dismissed the product liability and fraud causes of action, but retained plaintiffs' negligent marketing claim (*see,* Hamilton v Accu-Tek, 935 F. Supp. 1307, 1315). Other parties intervened, including plaintiff Stephen Fox, who was shot by a friend and permanently disabled. The gun was never found; the shooter had no recollection of how he obtained it. Other evidence, however, indicated that he had purchased the gun out of the trunk of a car from a seller who said it came from the "south." Eventually, seven plaintiffs went to trial against 25 of the manufacturers.

Plaintiffs asserted that defendants distributed their products negligently so as to create and bolster an illegal, underground market in handguns, one that furnished weapons to minors and criminals involved in the shootings that precipitated this lawsuit. Because only one of the guns was recovered, plaintiffs were permitted over defense objections to proceed on a market share theory of liability against all the manufacturers, asserting that they were severally liable for failing to implement safe marketing and distribution procedures, and that this failure sent a high volume of guns into the underground market.

After a four-week trial, the jury returned a special verdict finding 15 of the 25 defendants failed to use reasonable care in the distribution of their guns. Of those 15, nine were found to have proximately caused the deaths of the decedents of two plaintiffs, but no damages were awarded. The jury awarded damages against three defendants — American Arms, Beretta U.S.A. and Taurus International Manufacturing — upon a finding that they proximately caused the injuries suffered by Fox and his mother (in the amounts of $3.95 million and $50,000, respectively). Liability was apportioned among each of the three defendants according to their share of the national handgun market: for American Arms, 0.23% ($9,000); for Beretta, 6.03% ($241,000); and for Taurus, 6.80% ($272,000).

Defendants unsuccessfully moved for judgment as a matter of law pursuant to Federal Rules of Civil Procedure rule 50(b). The District Court articulated several theories for imposing a duty on defendants "to take reasonable steps available at the point of . . . sale to primary distributors to reduce the possibility that these instruments will fall into the hands of those likely to misuse them" (Hamilton v Accu-Tek, 62 F. Supp. 2d 802, 825). The court noted that defendants, as with all manufacturers, had the unique ability to detect and guard against any foreseeable risks associated with their products, and that ability created a special "protective relationship" between the manufacturers and potential victims of gun violence (id., at 821). It further pointed out that the relationship of handgun manufacturers with their downstream distributors and retailers gave them the authority and ability to control the latter's conduct for the protection of prospective crime victims. Relying on Hymowitz v Eli Lilly & Co. (73 NY2d 487, *cert denied* 493 US 944), the District Court held that apportionment of liability among defendants on a market share basis was appropriate and that plaintiffs need not connect Fox's shooting to the negligence of a particular manufacturer.

On appeal, the Second Circuit certified the following questions to us:

"(1) Whether the defendants owed plaintiffs a duty to exercise reasonable care in the marketing and distribution of the handguns they manufacture?

"(2) Whether liability in this case may be apportioned on a market share basis, and if so, how?"

We accepted certification and now answer both questions in the negative.

Parties' Arguments

Plaintiffs argue that defendant-manufacturers have a duty to exercise reasonable care in the marketing and distribution of their guns based upon four factors: (1) defendants' ability to exercise control over the marketing and distribution of their guns, (2) defendants' general knowledge that large numbers of their guns enter the illegal market and are used in crime, (3) New York's policy of strict regulation of firearms and (4) the uniquely lethal nature of defendants' products.

According to plaintiffs, handguns move into the underground market in New York through several well-known and documented means including straw purchases (a friend, relative or accomplice acts as purchaser of the weapon for another), sales at gun shows, misuse of Federal firearms licenses and sales by non-stocking dealers (i.e., those operating informal businesses without a retail storefront). Plaintiffs further assert that gun manufacturers have oversaturated markets in states with weak gun control laws (primarily in the Southeast), knowing those "excess guns" will make their way into the hands of criminals in states with stricter laws such as New York, thus "profiting" from indiscriminate sales in weak gun states. Plaintiffs contend that defendants control their distributors' conduct with respect to pricing, advertising and display, yet refuse to institute practices such as requiring distribution contracts that limit sales to stocking gun dealers, training salespeople in safe sales practices (including how to recognize straw purchasers), establishing electronic monitoring of their products, limiting the number of distributors, limiting multiple purchases and franchising their retail outlets.

Defendants counter that they do not owe a duty to members of the public to protect them from the criminal acquisition and misuse of their handguns. Defendants assert that such a duty—potentially exposing them to limitless liability—should not be imposed on them for acts and omissions of numerous and remote third parties over which they have no control. Further, they contend that, in light of the comprehensive statutory and regulatory scheme governing the distribution and sale of firearms, any fundamental changes in the industry should be left to the appropriate legislative and regulatory bodies.

The Duty Equation

The threshold question in any negligence action is: does defendant owe a legally recognized duty of care to plaintiff? Courts traditionally "fix the duty point by balancing factors, including the reasonable expectations of parties and society generally, the proliferation of claims, the likelihood of unlimited or insurer-like liability, disproportionate risk and reparation allocation, and public policies affecting the expansion or limitation of new channels of liability" (Palka v Servicemaster Mgt. Servs. Corp., 83 NY2d 579, 586). Thus, in determining whether a duty exists, "courts must be mindful of the precedential, and consequential, future effects of their rulings, and 'limit the legal consequences of wrongs to a controllable degree'" (Lauer v City of New York, 95 NY2d 95, 100 [quoting *Tobin v Grossman,* 24 NY2d 609, 619]).

Foreseeability alone does not define duty—it merely determines the scope of the duty once it is determined to exist (*see,* Eiseman v State of New York, 70 NY2d 175, 187). The injured party must show that a defendant owed not merely a general duty to society but a specific duty to him or her, for "[w]ithout a duty running directly to the injured person there can be no liability in damages, however careless the conduct or foreseeable the harm" (*Lauer,* supra, at 100). That is required in order to avoid subjecting an actor "to limitless liability to an indeterminate class of persons conceivably injured by any negligence in that act" (*Eiseman,* supra, at 188). Moreover, any extension of the scope of duty must be tailored to reflect accurately the extent that its social benefits outweigh its costs.

The District Court imposed a duty on gun manufacturers "to take reasonable steps available at the point of . . . sale to primary distributors to reduce the possibility that these instruments will fall into the hands of those likely to misuse them" (Hamilton v. Accu-Tek, supra, 62 F. Supp. 2d, at 825). We have been cautious, however, in extending liability to defendants for their failure to control the conduct of others. "A defendant generally has no duty to control the conduct of third persons so as to prevent them from harming others, even where as a practical matter defendant can exercise such control" (D'Amico v. Christie, 71 NY2d 76, 88). This judicial resistance to the expansion of duty grows out of practical concerns both about potentially limitless liability and about the unfairness of imposing liability for the acts of another.

A duty may arise, however, where there is a relationship either between defendant and a third-person tortfeasor that encompasses defendant's actual control of the third person's actions, or between defendant and plaintiff that requires defendant to protect plaintiff from the conduct of others. Examples of these relationships include master and servant, parent and child, and common carriers and their passengers.

The key in each is that the defendant's relationship with either the tortfeasor or the plaintiff places the defendant in the best position to protect against the risk of harm. In addition, the specter of limitless liability is not present because the class of potential plaintiffs to whom the duty is owed is circumscribed by the relationship. We have, for instance, recognized that landowners have a duty to protect tenants. patrons or invitees from foreseeable harm caused by the criminal conduct of others while they are on the premises. However, this duty does not extend beyond that limited class of plaintiffs to members of the community at large (*see,* Waters v New York City Hous. Auth., 69 N.Y.2d, 225, 228-231). In *Waters,* for example, we held that the owner of a housing project who failed to keep the building's door locks in good repair did not owe a duty to a passerby to protect her from being dragged off the street into the building and assaulted. The Court concluded that imposing such a duty on landowners would do little to minimize crime, and the social benefits to be gained did "not warrant the extension of the landowner's duty to maintain secure premises to the millions of individuals who use the sidewalks of New York City each day and are thereby exposed to the dangers of street crime" (id., at 230).

Similar rationale is relevant here. The pool of possible plaintiffs is very large — potentially, any of the thousands of victims of gun violence. Further, the connection between defendants, the criminal wrongdoers and plaintiffs is remote, running through several links in a chain consisting of at least the manufacturer, the federally licensed distributor or wholesaler, and the first retailer. The chain most often includes numerous subsequent legal purchasers or even a thief. Such broad liability, potentially encompassing all gunshot crime victims, should not be imposed without a more tangible showing that defendants were a direct link in the causal chain that resulted in plaintiffs' injuries, and that defendants were realistically in a position to prevent the wrongs. Giving plaintiffs' evidence the benefit of every favorable inference, they have not shown that the gun used to harm plaintiff Fox came from a source amenable to the exercise of any duty of care that plaintiffs would impose upon defendant manufacturers. . . .

In sum, analysis of this State's longstanding precedents demonstrates that defendants — given the evidence presented here — did not owe plaintiffs the duty they claim; we therefore answer the first certified question in the negative.

Market Share Liability

The Second Circuit has asked us also to determine if our market share liability jurisprudence is applicable to this case. Having concluded that these defendant-manufacturers did not owe the claimed duty to these plaintiffs, we arguably need not reach the market share issue. However, because of its particularly significant role in this case, it seems prudent to answer the second question.

Market share liability provides an exception to the general rule that in common-law negligence actions, a plaintiff must prove that the defendant's conduct was a cause-in-fact of the injury. This Court first examined and adopted the market share theory of liability in Hymowitz v Eli Lilly & Co. (73 NY2d 487, supra). In *Hymowitz,* we held that plaintiffs injured by the drug DES were not required to prove which defendant manufactured the drug that injured them but instead, every manufacturer would be held responsible for every plaintiff's injury based on its share of the DES market. Market share liability was necessary in *Hymowitz* because DES was a fungible product and identification of the actual manufacturer that caused the injury to a particular plaintiff was impossible. The Court carefully noted that the DES situation was unique. Key to our decision were the facts that (1) the manufacturers acted in a parallel manner to produce an identical, generically marketed product; (2) the manifestations of injury were far removed from the time of ingestion of the product; and (3) the Legislature made a clear policy decision to revive these time-barred DES claims.

Circumstances here are markedly different. Unlike DES, guns are not identical, fungible products. Significantly, it is often possible to identify the caliber and manufacturer of the handgun that caused injury to a particular plaintiff. Even more importantly — given the negligent marketing theory on which plaintiffs tried this case — plaintiffs have never asserted that the manufacturers' marketing techniques were uniform. Each manufacturer engaged in different marketing activities that allegedly contributed to the illegal handgun market in different ways and to different extents. Plaintiffs made no attempt to establish the relative fault of each manufacturer, but instead sought to hold them all liable based simply on market share.

In *Hymowitz,* each manufacturer engaged in tortious conduct parallel to that of all other manufacturers, creating the same risk to the public at large by manufacturing the same defective product. Market share was an accurate reflection of the risk they posed. Here, the distribution and sale of every gun is not equally negligent, nor does it involve a defective product. Defendants engaged in widely-varied conduct creating varied risks. Thus, a manufacturer's share of the national handgun market does not necessarily correspond to the amount of risk created by its alleged tortious conduct. No case has applied the market share theory of liability to such varied conduct and wisely so. . . .

This case challenges us to rethink traditional notions of duty, liability and causation. Tort law is ever changing; it is a reflection of the complexity and vitality of daily life. Although plaintiffs have presented us with a novel theory — negligent marketing of a potentially lethal yet legal product, based upon the acts not of one manufacturer, but of an industry — we are unconvinced that, on the record before us, the duty plaintiffs wish to impose is either reasonable or circumscribed. Nor does the market share theory of liability accurately measure defendants' conduct. Whether, in a different case, a duty may arise remains a question for the future.

Accordingly, both certified questions should be answered in the negative.

On the subject of negligent marketing as a basis for manufacturers' liability, the Products Liability Restatement contains the following paragraph from Comment *n* to Section 2:

> Finally, negligence retains its vitality as an independent theory of recovery for a wide range of product-related, harm-causing behavior not involving defects at time of sale. This Restatement includes several such topics in later Chapters, including post-sale failure to warn (see §10); post-sale failure to recall (see §11); and a successor's liability for its own failure to warn (see §13). Other topics are covered in the Restatement, Second, of Torts. Thus, for example, negligent entrustment is treated in §390. Liability for negligent service, maintenance, or repair, or negligent overpromotion of a product is governed by the rules set forth in §§291 et seq.

Note that two causation issues played a role in the *Hamilton* court's no-duty decision: (1) whether the defendants' alleged negligence in marketing was the but-for cause of the harm to plaintiffs and (2) whether causation could be placed at the doorstep of any given defendant-manufacturer of guns. For a discussion of the role that causation played in the no-duty ruling of the court, see Aaron D. Twerski and Anthony J. Sebok, Liability Without Cause? Further Ruminations on Cause-in-Fact as Applied to Handgun Liability, 32 Conn. L. Rev. 1379 (2000).

The terrorist attack on the World Trade Center on September 11, 2001, brought about wrongful death, personal injury, and property claims for damages running into billions of dollars. Numbered among the defendants were the airlines, the Port Authority of New York and New Jersey, and World Trade Center. Our focus in the ensuing discussion will be the claims brought against Boeing, the manufacturer of the airplanes that were highjacked and used by the suicide bombers at the Pentagon and in Pennsylvania.

In re September 11 Litigation
2003 WL 22077747 (S.D.NY)

ALVIN K HELLERSTEIN, U.S. District Judge . . .
[Discussion of claims against defendants other than Boeing is omitted]

Some of those who were injured and the successors of those who died in the Pentagon, in American Airlines flight 77 which crashed into the Pentagon, and in United Air Lines flight 93 which crashed into the Shanksville, Pennsylvania field, claim the right to recover against Boeing, the manufacturer of the two "757" jets flown by United and American. Plaintiffs allege that Boeing manufactured inadequate and defective cockpit doors, and thus made it possible for the hijackers to invade the cockpits and take over the aircraft. Boeing moves to dismiss the lawsuits.

I hold that plaintiffs have alleged legally sufficient claims for relief under the laws applicable to the claims, Virginia and Pennsylvania, respectively. I therefore deny the motion except for certain claims, as discussed below.

Thus far, three individual complaints have been filed with respect to the flight 77 crash. They charge Boeing with strict tort liability and negligent design based on an unreasonably dangerous design of the cockpit doors. *See* Edwards v. American Airlines, Inc., No. 02 Civ. 9234 (brought on behalf of a decedent who was a passenger on flight 77); Powell v. Argenbright Security, Inc., No. 02 Civ. 10160 (brought on behalf of a decedent who died while working at the Pentagon); Gallop v. Argenbright Security, Inc., No. 03 Civ. 1016 (plaintiffs injured at the Pentagon site).

The plaintiffs' First Amended Flight 77 Master Liability Complaint contains three counts applicable to Boeing. Count Six alleges strict tort liability for an unreasonably dangerous design of the cockpit doors. Count Seven alleges that Boeing breached its duty of care by failing to design the cockpit doors and accompanying locks in a manner that would prevent hijackers and/or passengers from accessing the cockpit. Count Eight alleges that Boeing violated its express or implied warranty that the aircraft structure and frame, with respect to the cockpit doors, were fit for the purposes for which they were designed, intended and used. . . .

Boeing moves to dismiss both the claims of negligent design and breach of warranty, arguing that it did not owe a duty to prevent the use of the plane as a weapon, and that the independent and supervening acts of the terrorists, not Boeing's acts, caused the injuries of the plaintiffs. A plaintiff, to state a claim of negligence, must allege the existence of a legal duty, violation of that duty, and

Special Duty Problems in Design Litigation

proximate causation which results in injury. Marshall v. Winston, 389 S.E.2d 902, 904 (Va. 1990). In order to state a claim of breach of warranty, plaintiff may invoke the Virginia law of an implied warranty of merchantability, which guarantees that a product "was reasonably safe for its intended use when it was placed in the stream of commerce." Turner v. Manning, Maxwell & Moore, Inc., 217 S.E.2d 863, 868-69 (Va. 1975). . . .

The existence of duty in the products liability context is a question of law. "[T]he purpose of making the finding of a legal duty as a prerequisite to a finding of negligence, or breach of implied warranty, in products liability is to avoid the extension of liability for every conceivably foreseeable accident, without regard to common sense or good policy." *Jeld-Wen,* 501 S.E.2d at 396 (citations omitted). Legal duty may extend to a user of the product, as well as to its purchaser. *See Morgen Indus.,* 471 S.E.2d at 492.

While the existence of duty is a question of law, whether a product is unreasonably dangerous is generally a question of fact, id., as is the question whether the misuse was reasonably foreseeable, Slone v. General Motors Corp., 457 S.E.2d 51, 54 (Va. 1995). Courts have emphasized that these determinations require careful examination of the record. *Compare Slone,* 457 S.E.2d at 54 (ruling in favor of reasonable foreseeability), *with Jeld-Wen,* 501 S.E.2d at 397 (ruling against reasonable foreseeability). In Slone v. General Motors Corp., the court held that plaintiff could proceed with a claim against a truck manufacturer. 457 S.E.2d at 54. While the plaintiff was dumping a load of gravel using the truck with a dump bed attached, the vehicle flipped backwards, crushing the truck cab and injuring the plaintiff. The court ruled that the plaintiff adequately had alleged both an unreasonably dangerous condition and a reasonably foreseeable misuse, by claiming that the design of the truck cab provided inadequate roof support and that the possibility of rollover was reasonably foreseeable by the truck manufacturer. *See id.* However, in *Jeld-Wen,* 501 S.E.2d at 396-97, the court examined a claim brought when a child, who had gently touched a screen window that had a defective latch, fell through the open window when the screen fell out. The court distinguished the foreseeability of the screen being dislodged by the child's touch and the foreseeability of the child's losing his balance and falling through the open window. The court held that since the screen was not intended to support a child's body weight and prevent the child from falling through the window, the screen manufacturer could not reasonably foresee its misuse in the manner claimed.

Boeing argues that its design of the cockpit was not unreasonably dangerous in relation to reasonably foreseeable risks, and that the risk of death to passengers and ground victims caused by a terrorist hijacking was not reasonably foreseeable. The record at this point does not support Boeing's argument. There have been many efforts by terrorists to hijack airplanes, and too many have been successful. The practice of terrorists to blow themselves up in order to kill as many people as possible has also been prevalent. Although there have been no incidents before the ones of September 11, 2001 where terrorists combined both an airplane hijacking and a suicidal explosion, I am not able to say that the risk of crashes was not reasonably foreseeable to an airplane manufacturer. Plaintiffs have alleged that it was reasonably foreseeable that a failure to design a secure cockpit could contribute to a breaking and entering into, and a take-over of, a cockpit by hijackers or other unauthorized individuals, substantially increasing the risk of injury and death to people and damage to property. I hold that the allegation is sufficient to establish Boeing's duty. . . .

Boeing next argues that its design of the cockpit doors on its "757" passenger aircraft, even if held to constitute an "unreasonably dangerous condition," was not the proximate cause of plaintiffs' injuries. Boeing argues that the criminal acts of the terrorists in hijacking the airplanes and using the airplanes as weapons of mass destruction constituted an "efficient intervening cause" which broke the "natural and continuous sequence" of events flowing from Boeing's allegedly inadequate design. *See* Sugarland Run Homeowners Ass'n v. Halfmann, 535 S.E.2d 469, 472 (Va. 2000) (a "proximate cause of an event is that 'act or omission which, in natural and continuous sequence, unbroken by an efficient intervening cause, produces the event, and without which that event would not have occurred,'" quoting Beale v. Jones, 171 S.E.2d 851, 853 (Va. 1970)). Plaintiffs have the burden to prove proximate cause and, generally, the issue is a question of fact to be resolved by a jury. *Sugarland,* 535 S.E.2d at 472. However, when reasonable people cannot differ, the issue becomes a question of law for the court. Id.

The record at this point does not support Boeing's argument that the invasion and take-over of the cockpit by the terrorists must, as a matter of law, be held to constitute an "efficient intervening act" that breaks the "natural and continuous sequence" flowing from Boeing's allegedly inadequate design. Plaintiffs allege that Boeing should have designed its cockpit door to prevent hijackers from invading the cockpit, that acts of terrorism, including hijackings of airplanes, were reasonably foreseeable, and that the lives of passengers, crew and ground victims would be imminently in danger from such hijackings. Virginia law does not require Boeing to have foreseen precisely how the injuries suffered on September 11, 2001 would be caused, as long as Boeing could reasonably have foreseen that "some injury" from its negligence "might probably result." *See* Blondel v. Hays, 403 S.E.2d 340, 344 (Va. 1991) ("[A] reasonably prudent [person] ought under the circumstances to have foreseen that some injury might probably result from that negligence"). Given the critical nature of the cockpit area, and the inherent danger of crash when a plane is in flight, one cannot say that Boeing could not reasonably have foreseen the risk flowing from an inadequately constructed cockpit door. . . .

[T]he danger that a plane could crash if unauthorized individuals invaded and took over the cockpit was the very risk that Boeing should reasonably have foreseen. "Privacy" within a cockpit means very little if the door intended to provide security is not designed to keep out potential intruders.

[In] Gaines-Tabb v. ICI Explosives USA, Inc., 160 F.3d 613 (10th Cir. 1998), . . . the courts of appeals . . . addressed the question of causation and held that defendants' actions or inactions were not the "legal proximate cause" of the injuries suffered by the victims of the 1993 World Trade Center and 1995 Oklahoma City bombings. They ruled that the manufacturers of the fertilizer products utilized in the attacks, having made lawful and economically and socially useful fertilizer products, did not have to anticipate that criminals would misappropriate ingredients, mix them with others, and make bombs to bring down a building. The bomb-making by the terrorists were found to be superseding and intervening events and were not natural or probable consequences of any design defect in defendants' products. *See Arcadian Corp.,* 189 F.3d at 318; *Gaines-Tabb,* 160 F.3d at 621.

In re Korean Air Lines Disaster of September 1, 1983, No. 83-3442, 1985 U.S. Dist. LEXIS 17211 (D.D.C. 1985), involved lawsuits by the legal successors of passengers who died when Korean Airlines passenger flight 007 was shot down by Russian fighter planes. The passenger plane had flown off course and over a sensitive military zone in Russia. Russian fighter pilots intercepted the plane and, instead of following international protocol for causing the plane to return to international routes over the high seas or to land at a selected landing field, shot it down. Plaintiffs sued Boeing, the manufacturer of the airplane, alleging that a product defect in its navigation systems caused it to fly off course and over Soviet territory, and that Boeing's improper and unsafe design was therefore the proximate cause of plaintiffs' damages. The court dismissed the complaint, holding that Boeing could not foresee that the Soviet Union would destroy an intruding aircraft in violation of international conventions, and had no ability to guard against such conduct. *See id.* at *17-20. The court held, consequently, that Boeing did not owe a duty to passengers with respect to such risks, and that the actions of the Russian pilots were independent and supervening causes that broke the chain of causation.

These three cases do not offer Boeing much support in its motion. In each, the acts of the third-parties were held to be superseding causes because they were not reasonably foreseeable to the product manufacturer. In *Gaines-Tabb* and *Arcadian,* the courts of appeals held that the fertilizer manufacturers could not reasonably foresee that terrorists would mix their products with other ingredients to create explosives to cause buildings to collapse and occupants to be killed. In *KAL,* the court held that the manufacturer of airplane navigational systems could not reasonably foresee that a passenger aircraft that strayed off course would be shot down by hostile military forces in violation of international conventions. In the cases before me, however, plaintiffs allege that Boeing could reasonably have foreseen that terrorists would try to invade the cockpits of airplanes, and that easy success on their part, because cockpit doors were not designed to prevent easy opening, would be imminently dangerous to passengers, crew and ground victims. Plaintiffs' allegations that duty and proximate cause existed cannot be dismissed as a matter of law on the basis of the record now before me.

[The court found that the case could not be dismissed under Pennsylvania law for reasons similar to those set forth above under Virginia law.]

Do you agree with Judge Hellerstein? Has he stretched duty well beyond sensible bounds? If you get past the duty issue is there any way to stop the steamroller against Boeing?

I. RELYING ON EXPERT TESTIMONY TO PROVE DESIGN DEFECT: *DAUBERT* REVISITED

Earlier in this chapter we set forth case law concerning the evidentiary burden plaintiffs bear in making out a prima facie case where proof of a reasonable alternative design is required. We noted that some courts have set a fairly exacting standard by thoroughly examining evidence regarding such matters as cost, efficiency and safety of a proposed alternative design. Additionally, the ghost of *Daubert* may haunt a plaintiff trying to establish an alternative design. Defendants often argue that expert testimony regarding a proposed alternative design should not be admitted since such testimony may fail to meet the four-pronged test set forth in *Daubert*. If plaintiff cannot get expert testimony on reasonable alternative design before the jury, the case for design defect is for all practical purposes dead. Indeed, one of the major complaints of the plaintiff's bar against the reasonable alternative design standard is that, unlike the amorphous consumer expectations standard (in which plaintiff need only provide soft evidence as to what a reasonable consumer might expect), plaintiff's feet are held to the fire. The alternative design standard for recovery requires that plaintiff provide credible expert testimony that can be the subject of a *Daubert* challenge in most cases.

For the most part plaintiffs have been able to beat back *Daubert* challenges to expert testimony. See, e.g., Sand Hill Energy, Inc. v. Ford Motor Co., 83 S.W.3d 483 (Ky. 2002), *judgment vacated on other grounds,* 123 S.Ct. 2072 (2003) (majority reinstated judgment for plaintiff where plaintiff introduced competent expert testimony of an alternative gear-shifting design that would have prevented car from slipping into reverse); Clark v. Chrysler Corp. 310 F.3d 461 (6th Cir. 2002) (applying Kentucky law) (judgment against defendant manufacturer affirmed; expert satisfied *Daubert* standards in establishing a reasonable alternative design of door-latch systems); Lauzon v. Senco Products, 270 F.3d 681 (8th Cir. 2001) (applying Minnesota law) (overturning grant of summary judgment for pneumatic nail-gun manufacturer; exclusion of expert testimony was an abuse of trial court's discretion where expert had sufficient experience, education, and knowledge to proffer alternative design).

The Products Liability Restatement in §2, Comment *f* takes the position that plaintiff should not be saddled with the responsibility of producing a prototype in order to prove a reasonable alternative design. Instead, qualified expert testimony that the proffered alternative design could have been practically adopted should suffice. See, e.g., Martin v. Michelin N. Am., 92 F. Supp. 2d 745, 759-60 (E.D. Tenn. 2000) (holding that, under §2(b), Comment *f,* "plaintiff was not required to produce a prototype tire in order to make out a prima facie case. [Q]ualified expert testimony on the subject suffices"); Leaf v. Goodyear Tire & Rubber Co., 590 N.W.2d 525, 535 (Iowa 1999) (relying on §2(b), Comment *f* in "not requiring the plaintiff to produce a prototype in order to make out a prima facie case"); Gen. Motors Corp. v. Sanchez, 997 S.W.2d 584, 592 (Tex. 1999) (holding that "plaintiffs did not have to build and test an automobile transmission to prove a safer alternative design. A design need only prove 'capable of being developed'" under §2(b), Comment *f*).

Courts are quite willing, however, to find plaintiff's expert testimony inadmissible under *Daubert* when such testimony is weak and without foundation. See, e.g., Rypkema v. Time Mfg. Co., 263 F. Supp. 2d 687, 2003 WL 21203407 (S.D.N.Y. 2003) (summary judgment for defendant manufacturer of aerial lift bucket granted in the absence of competent testimony of reasonable alternative design; expert report bereft of engineering methodology, lacking scientific basis for conclusions, and opposed by equally qualified expert); Dhillon v. Crown Controls Corp., 269 F.3d 865 (7th Cir. 2001) (applying Illinois law) (summary judgment for defendant upheld due to plaintiff's inability to present competent expert testimony that alternative forklift design proposed was tested and would actually have been safer). There is little question that *Daubert* challenges are a fact of life any time plaintiff presents expert testimony of a reasonable alternative design. Even in states that follow the consumer expectations test, plaintiffs very often introduce evidence of a reasonable alternative design to help convince the jury on the issue of defect. If the judge is not satisfied with the competence of the expert opinion, the court will refuse to allow the testimony even though the evidence of alternative design may be crucial to the plaintiff's prima facie case. Thus, *Daubert* may be cause for concern for a plaintiff trying to hold a manufacturer liable for defective design in any jurisdiction.

J. SPECIAL PROBLEMS OF MISUSE, ALTERATION, AND MODIFICATION

In this Section we shall attempt to straighten out the mess that courts and legislatures have created in product design cases by treating the issues of product use (foreseeable and unforeseeable), misuse, abuse, alteration, and modification as affirmative defenses. The issues need to be clarified once and for all. They are not difficult to understand, and absolutely nothing is gained by continuing to treat them as separate sources of concern.

Much of the confusion up until now stems from the fact that the manufacturer's duty to adopt reasonable product designs includes the duty to foresee and guard against a certain amount of foolish behavior on the part of users and consumers. That was one of the points emphasized at the beginning of this chapter, when we first embarked on our study of liability for defective product designs. Thus, whenever a court decides as a matter of law that a design resulting in injury is not defective, it is possible to talk in terms of the user's "misuse" of the product. However, we would prefer instead to stick with the traditional, tried-and-true terminology from first-year torts. On the liability side, every design case presents three basic issues: (1) duty/breach; (2) proximate causation; and (3) contributory fault. We advise the student, when confronted with a design case, to work through each of these issues, resolving the first before going on to the second, and the second before the third. The behavior of the user or consumer will be relevant in connection with all three, but in different ways.

In connection with the duty/breach issue, there is general agreement that the burden is on the plaintiff to make his case. Thus, for example, in Newman v. Utility Trailer and Equip. Co., 564 P.2d 674, 676-677 (Or. 1977) (en banc), the court properly observed:

It is obvious that trial courts are experiencing difficulty in distinguishing foreseeability of use from foreseeability of the risk of harm. Before a manufacturer or other seller is strictly liable for injury inflicted by a product, the product must have been put to a foreseeable use. As an example: if a shovel is used to prop open a heavy door, but, because of the way the shovel was designed, it is inadequate to the task and the door swings shut and crushes the user's hand, no responsibility for the injury results by reason of the shovel's not being designed to prop open doors since it was not reasonably foreseeable by the manufacturer or seller that it would be so used.

More recently, in Jurado v. Western Gear Works, 619 A.2d 1312, 1318 (N.J. 1993), the New Jersey Supreme Court expressed similar sentiments:

> To the extent that misuse relates to the duty to design a safe product, a manufacturer has a duty to make sure that its manufactured products placed into the stream of commerce are suitably safe when properly used for their intended or reasonably foreseeable purposes. . . . When someone is injured while using a product for an unforeseeable purpose or in an unforeseeable manner, the misuse sheds no light on whether the product is defective, because a manufacturer is not under a duty to protect against unforeseeable misuses. . . .

See also Ferguson v. Winkler & Co., 79 F.3d 1221 (D.C. Cir. 1996), *cert. denied,* 117 S.Ct. 360 (1996).

With respect to the second issue, proximate cause, most believe the burden is also on the plaintiff. Hughes v. Magic Chef, Inc., 288 N.W.2d 542 (Iowa 1980) so holds. But the issue is not free from controversy. Ellsworth v. Sherrie Lingerie, Inc., 495 A.2d 348 (Md. 1985) agrees with *Hughes* and sets forth both the cases supporting the view that misuse should be considered in deciding whether plaintiff has made out a prima facie case and those holding that misuse is an affirmative defense. With respect to the third issue, contributory fault, everyone agrees that the defendant bears the burden of making out the affirmative defense.

The important point here is that misuse, abuse, alteration, and modification are not discrete problems and should be analyzed under one of the three legitimate issues described above. Having said that, one further point remains. Despite our admonitions, many courts, commentators, and legislatures insist on talking as though misuse, et al., have lives of their own. Our advice? When treating these concepts as independently significant helps your client, do not look a gift horse in the mouth. On the other hand, when giving "misuse" independent significance hurts your client, scream "let's get back to the basics!" at the top of your lungs.

With regard to proximate cause in design defect cases, we note that it will be rare that a defendant will be entitled to a directed verdict on the grounds that product misuse, alteration, or modification were outside the scope of foreseeable risk. Since safety features are there to protect against a broad range of foolish and even reckless use, it will be for the jury to determine whether or not user conduct was foreseeable. But a recent Alabama case teaches us that even when design defect and cause-in-fact can be established, the conduct of product users may be so outrageous that a court will use proximate cause to cut off a manufacturer's liability.

Morguson v. 3M Co.
857 So. 2d 796 (Ala. 2003)

HOUSTON, Justice.

Sara Morguson ("Morguson"), as executrix of the estate of Douglas W. Morguson, deceased, filed a wrongful-death action against Druid City Hospital ("DCH"), Phillip Smith ("Smith"), 3M Company f/k/a Minnesota Mining & Manufacturing Company ("3M"), and Baxter Healthcare Corporation n/k/a Edward Lifesciences Corporation ("Baxter") arising out of the death of her husband, Douglas Morguson (hereinafter sometimes referred to as the "decedent"). Morguson, DCH, and Smith entered into a pro tanto settlement for $975,000. Thereafter, the trial court granted 3M's and Baxter's (the remaining defendants) motions for a summary judgment. Morguson appealed. We affirm.

I. Facts

Mr. Morguson was admitted to DCH to undergo quintuple coronary artery bypass graft and cardiopulmonary bypass surgery, commonly known as "bypass surgery." Because this is open-heart surgery, it requires the use of a heart-lung machine and related equipment; the machine and equipment together are known as a perfusion system and the perfusion system is operated by a medical technician known as a perfusionist. Essentially, the perfusion system consists of a series of pumps and tubes that act as the patient's heart and lungs while the heart is stopped during surgery. The pumps transport blood and medications through the tubes to and from various other pumps, as well as to and from the patient. The pumps used during Mr. Morguson's surgery were manufactured by 3M; the tubes were manufactured by Baxter.

Only one part of the perfusion system is at issue in this case: the left ventricular pump and the left vent tubing. The left ventricular pump operates the left ventricular vent to decompress the heart. The left vent tubing is inserted into the open end of the cannula, a small tube the surgeon places into the left ventricle of the heart. The opposite end of the left vent tubing is connected to a reservoir by the perfusionist. The middle section of the left vent tubing is looped through the inside of the left vent pump. The pump is marked with arrows indicating the direction the blood should flow through the tubing.

The left vent tubing contains a one-way safety valve, a safety device that, when the tube is inserted in the patient, is located approximately 12 inches from the heart. The one-way safety valve ensures that blood and air in the vent tubing flow only away from the heart; it prevents the flow of any blood or air back to the heart. Arrows on the one-way safety valve indicate the direction in which the blood should flow.

Dr. Ferguson was the cardiothoracic surgeon performing Mr. Morguson's bypass surgery, and Smith, a DCH employee, was the assigned perfusionist. Before the surgery, Smith, whose primary responsibility was to operate the heart-lung machine, assembled the perfusion system. In assembling the perfusion system, Smith failed to loop the left vent tubing through the left vent pump correctly; instead, Smith assembled it so that the direction of blood flow through the left vent tubing was toward Mr. Morguson's heart rather than away from it. Pursuant to DCH protocol, after Smith assembled the perfusion system, he was required to perform a "pre-bypass safety checklist" in preparation for Mr. Morguson's surgery. As part of this checklist, Smith was required to determine whether the direction of the vent tubing was correct. Despite this requirement, Smith did not check the tubing direction in the pumps, and he falsified the safety checklist to indicate that he had.

Shortly after Mr. Morguson's surgery began, Dr. Ferguson detected a problem; blood was not coming out of Mr. Morguson's heart and through the left vent tubing even though the left vent pump was on. Dr. Ferguson told Smith to figure out what was causing the problem. Without checking, Smith informed Dr. Ferguson that the tubing direction was correct; it was not.

Based on Smith's falsely reporting that the left vent tubing was installed so that the blood flow was in the correct direction, Dr. Ferguson reasoned that the one-way safety valve was defective and decided to remove it. The left vent pump was stopped and the left vent tubing was disconnected. Because the one-way safety valve was built into the tubing, its removal required the surgical team to cut out that part of the tubing containing the valve and then splice the tubing. After the one-way safety valve had been removed, the left vent tubing was reconnected and the left vent pump was restarted. At this point, air was pumped into Mr. Morguson's heart; he died 20 days after the surgery.

Dr. Brian Frist, one of Morguson's medical experts, theorized as to the cause of death. According to Dr. Frist, after air was introduced into Mr. Morguson's heart, it migrated through his vascular system and into his brain, creating an air embolus. Once inside the brain, the embolus caused a blockage of the brain's vascular structure. This blockage caused a lack of oxygenated blood to provide nutrients and to remove waste. The brain matter in the area affected by the blockage was unable to perform its function with regard to other bodily functions, such as respiration. The malfunctioning brain led to generalized organ system failure and to Mr. Morguson's death 20 days after the surgery. . . .

Morguson alleged that 3M and Baxter were liable for the decedent's death under the Alabama Extended Manufacturer's Liability Doctrine ("AEMLD") because, she argues, the perfusion pump, which was manufactured by 3M, and the left vent tubing, which was manufactured by Baxter, were defective. Specifically, Morguson alleged that the pump and the tubing were unreasonably dangerous because the designs of both were defective. . . . Both 3M and Baxter moved for a summary judgment, and the trial court granted those motions. This appeal involves only the product-liability claims Morguson asserted against 3M and Baxter. . . .

The plaintiff has the burden of presenting substantial evidence of proximate cause. Hicks v. Vulcan Eng'g Co., 749 So. 2d 417, 424 (Ala. 1999). "Proximate cause is an act or omission that in a natural and continuous sequence, unbroken by any new and independent causes, produces an injury or harm and without which the injury or harm would not occur.". . .

II. Issues on Appeal

. . . Morguson argues that 3M and Baxter failed to prove that an intervening or superseding cause occurred that absolved them from liability. . . . Morguson [also] argues that she proffered evidence establishing the existence of safer, practical, alternative designs of the perfusion pump and vent tubing. . . .

Morguson argues that the errors, omissions, and misrepresentations made by Smith and Dr. Ferguson during the decedent's surgery were not independent and superseding causes that broke the causal chain between the allegedly defective left vent pump and left vent tubing and the decedent's death. We disagree.

It is Morguson's burden to present substantial evidence creating a genuine issue of material fact as to whether the left vent pump and left vent tubing were defective and unreasonably dangerous when the products were sold and whether their defective condition was the proximate cause of the decedent's death. See *Kirk*, 650 So. 2d at 866. The cornerstone of proximate cause is foreseeability. . . . In the present case, the actions taken by Smith and the surgical team during the surgery were not foreseeable by 3M and Baxter.

In assembling the perfusion system before Mr. Morguson's surgery, Smith improperly threaded the left vent tubing through the left vent pump, despite the fact that the inflow and outflow ports of the pumps are marked with arrows indicating the correct directional flow. This improper threading caused the flow through the vent tubing to be directed toward Mr. Morguson's heart, rather than away from it. Smith then failed to follow DCH protocol by not verifying the vent tubing direction during the pre-bypass safety checklist; rather than confirm that the perfusion system was set up correctly Smith falsified the checklist to indicate that he had. Next, after Dr. Ferguson noticed that blood was not flowing out of Mr. Morguson's heart and asked Smith to check the left vent pump and the left vent tubing, Smith again misrepresented that they were set up correctly. Finally, the surgical staff removed the one-way safety valve in the left vent tubing. All of Morguson's experts agree that had the one-way safety valve been in place, air could not have gone to Mr. Morguson's heart.

It may have been foreseeable that a perfusionist would improperly assemble the perfusion system (which is precisely why the pre-bypass safety checklist exists). However, it is clearly not foreseeable 1) that the perfusionist would not check the vent tubing direction during the pre-bypass safety checklist; 2) that the perfusionist would falsify the safety checklist to state that he had checked the direction of the vent tubing; 3) that the perfusionist would lie to the surgeon about having checked the direction of the vent tubing after being asked directly to do so; and 4) that the surgical team would cut the one-way safety valve out of the vent tubing. . . .

Therefore, we hold that the trial court's summary judgment on this issue was correct because the actions of Smith and the surgical team were not foreseeable and the removal of the one-way safety valve amounted to an intervening and superseding cause that broke any causal chain between the manufacture of the perfusion system and Mr. Morguson's death. . . .

[Another issue] Morguson raises is that the perfusion pump and the vent tubing were defectively designed. Morguson contends that her expert witnesses proffered alternative designs of the perfusion pump and vent tubing that would have prevented Mr. Morguson's death by eliminating the danger of human error. However, we previously stated that 3M and Baxter were relieved from liability because the actions of Smith and the surgical team, which were unforeseeable, . . . amounted to an intervening and superseding cause that broke the causal chain. Therefore, this issue is without merit. . . .

In conclusion, we hold that Morguson failed to present substantial evidence to rebut 3M's and Baxter's showing that there were no genuine issues of material facts and that 3M and Baxter were entitled to judgments as a matter of law as to Morguson's claims. Accordingly, the summary judgments for 3M and Baxter are affirmed.

AFFIRMED.

The plaintiff in *Morguson* contended that her experts were prepared to proffer a reasonable alternative design of a perfusion pump that would have prevented Mr. Morguson's death by eliminating the danger of human error. Admittedly, the human error in this case was egregious — perhaps even willful — but why should that make a difference? Under traditional tort law, where a defendant creates a hazard that is then triggered by an intentional act of a third party, the issue of proximate cause is almost always for the jury to decide. Consider, for example, Britton v. Wooten, 817 S.W.2d 443 (Ky. 1991), in which trash, negligently allowed to accumulate next to a building, ignited from an unknown source. The court concluded:

> In the present case whether the spark ignited in the trash accumulated next to the building was ignited negligently, or even criminally, or if it was truly accidental, is not the critical issue. The issue is whether the movant can prove that the respondent caused or permitted trash to accumulate next to its building in a negligent manner which caused or contributed to the spread of the fire and the destruction of the lessor's building. If so, the source of the spark that ignited the fire is not a superseding cause under any reasonable application of modern tort law. [Id. at 451.]

In one case, Jurado v. Western Gear Works, 619 A.2d 1312 (N.J. 1993) the court suggested that in some design defect cases a finding of defective design might preclude any argument that the defect was not the proximate cause of the injury. In that case plaintiff, an employee, working in the vicinity of a high speed printing press slipped and fell. When he extended his right hand to break his fall his hand came in contact with the running machine at its nip point causing serious personal injury. The plaintiff's expert testified that there should have been a guard around the nip point to prevent accidents of this type. The court opined:

> In some situations, however, the issue of proximate cause is predetermined by the finding that the product is defective solely because of the manufacturer's failure to protect against a foreseeable misuse. As Professor Aaron D. Twerski explains:
>
>> If a court determines that a design defect exists [solely] because the manufacturer has failed to include [] safety devices, there is no proximate cause question of any moment left to consider. The very reason for declaring the design defective was to prevent this kind of foreseeable misuse. Proximate cause could not, in such a case, present an obstacle on the grounds of misuse. To do so would negate the very reason for declaring the design defective in the first instance.
>>
>> [The Many Faces of Misuse: An Inquiry Into the Emerging Doctrine of Comparative Causation, 29 Mercer L. Rev. 403, 421 (1978).]
>
> In sum, when misuse is an issue in a design-defect case, the jury should first determine whether the plaintiff used the product for an objectively foreseeable purpose. If the jury finds that the plaintiff's purpose was not foreseeable, the defendant did not breach any duty owed to the plaintiff. If, however, the jury finds that the plaintiff's purpose was foreseeable, it must then decide whether the product was defective. . . .

If the jury finds that the product is defective, it must then decide whether the misuse proximately caused the injury. In cases in which the product is defective solely because of a foreseeable misuse, the determination of defect predetermines the issue of proximate cause. In other cases, however, where a product is defective for reasons other than the particular misuse, the jury must separately determine proximate cause. Id. 619 A. 2d at 1319.

One class of cases in which courts have refused to impose liability (either on proximate cause or no-duty grounds) involves alteration or modification of safe products. The New York Court of Appeals faces this issue in Robinson v. Reed-Prentice Div. of Package Machinery Co., 403 N.E.2d 440 (N.Y. 1980). In that case an employee of Plastic Jewel Parts Co. suffered severe injuries when his hand was caught between the molds of a plastic molding machine. The plaintiff sued Reed-Prentice, the manufacturer of the machine. Reed-Prentice had sold the machine to the plaintiff's employer with a safety gate in place that would have prevented injury to employees. However, the machine as sold to Jewel did not comport with the buyer's production needs. The Court of Appeals summarized the record as follows:

Plastic Jewel purchased the machine in order to mold beads directly onto a nylon cord. The cord was stored in spools at the back of the machine and fed through the mold where the beads were molded around it. After each molding cycle, the beads were pulled out of the mold and the nylon cord was reset in the mold for the next cycle. To allow the beads to be molded on a continuous line, Plastic Jewel determined that it was necessary to cut a hole of approximately 6 by 14 inches in the Plexiglas portion of the safety gate. The machine, as designed, contracted for and delivered, made no provision for such an aperture. At the end of each cycle, the now corded beads would be pulled through the opening in the gate, the nylon cord would be restrung, and the next cycle would be started by opening and then closing the safety gate without breaking the continuous line of beads. While modification of the safety gate served Plastic Jewel's production needs, it also destroyed the practical utility of the safety features incorporated into the design of the machine for it permitted access into the molding area while the interlocking circuits were completed. Although the record is unclear on this point, plaintiff's hand somehow went through the opening cut into the safety gate and was drawn into the molding area while the interlocks were engaged. The machine went through the molding cycle, causing plaintiff serious injury.

The record contains evidence that Reed-Prentice knew, or should have known, the particular safety gate designed for the machine made it impossible to manufacture beads on strings. During the period immediately prior to the purchase of the machine, Reed-Prentice representatives visited the Plastic Jewel plant and observed two identical machines with holes cut in the Plexiglas portion of their safety gates. At that meeting, Plastic Jewel's plant manager discussed the problem with a Reed-Prentice salesman and asked whether a safety gate compatible with its product needs could be designed. Moreover, a letter sent by Reed-Prentice to Plastic Jewel establishes that the manufacturer knew precisely what its customer was doing to the safety gate and refused to modify its design. However, the letter pointed out that the purchaser had "completely flaunted the safeties built into this machine by removing part of the safety window," and that it had not "held up your end of the purchase when you use the machine differently from its design" and the manufacturer stated "[a]s concerns changes, we will make none in our safety setup or design of safety gates." At trial, plaintiff's expert indicated that there were two modifications to the safety gate which could have been made that would have made it possible to mold beads on a string without rendering the machine unreasonably dangerous. Neither of these modifications were made, or even contemplated, by Reed-Prentice. [Id. at 477-478.]

In absolving the manufacturer from liability as a matter of law, the court said:

> The manufacturer's duty, however, does not extend to designing a product that is impossible to abuse or one whose safety features may not be circumvented. A manufacturer need not incorporate safety features into its product so as to guarantee that no harm will come to every user no matter how careless or even reckless. Nor must he trace his product through every link in the chain of distribution to insure that users will not adapt the product to suit their own unique purposes. The duty of a manufacturer, therefore, is not an open-ended one. It extends to the design and manufacture of a finished product which is safe at the time of sale. Material alterations at the hands of a third party which work a substantial change in the condition in which the product was sold by destroying the functional utility of a key safety feature, however foreseeable that modification may have been, are not within the ambit of a manufacturer's responsibility. Acceptance of plaintiff's concept of duty would expand the scope of a manufacturer's duty beyond all reasonable bounds and would be tantamount to imposing absolute liability on manufacturers for all product-related injuries. [Id. at 444.]

It is not clear why the manufacturer who had full knowledge that its product was being used by employees in a dangerous fashion did not have a duty to supply the needed safety device. Judge Fuchsberg had this to say in dissent:

> Plastic Jewel had made frequent but unavailing entreaties of the manufacturer and its sales and service personnel seeking some modification of the machine that would eliminate the need for piercing the safety gate. As expert testimony revealed, the machine could easily have been made safe for the anticipated use by either of at least two simple modifications. One, at a cost of only $200, would be the installation of "dual hand controls," which would cause the machine to stop unless both of the operator's hands were safely occupied pressing buttons spaced widely apart. The second, at a cost of $400 to $500, would, by conversion of the horizontal gate to a vertical one, allow for the extrusion of the product without a dangerously wide aperture.
>
> This array of facts proved the allegations that Reed-Prentice had been negligent "in selling and distributing a machine which [it] knew or should have known to be dangerous, defective and unsafe" as well as "in failing to affix proper and adequate warnings of the dangers." The law of negligence therefore required no extension to permit a finding of liability. . . . [Id. at 445.]

In Lopez v. Precision Papers Inc., 484 N.Y.S.2d 585 (App. Div. 1985), *aff'd,* 492 N.E.2d 1214 (N.Y. 1986), plaintiff was rendered a paraplegic due to an injury he suffered when a large roll of paper fell from a wooden pallet on a forklift machine he was operating within a warehouse. Plaintiff alleged that the forklift was defectively designed because (a) relied on a non-welded, easily removable safety canopy; and (b) it lacked a gauge that would have indicated the weight of the load being raised or its attendant hazards to the vehicle and the driver. The trial court, citing *Robinson,* held that the manufacturer should not be liable due to the fact that the removable overhead safety canopy had been removed by the plaintiff's employer. On appeal, the intermediate court reversed, holding:

> In *Robinson,* the modification was so substantial that it permanently destroyed the functional utility of a safety gate. Under no view of the facts could one conclude that that

modification was intended either for versatility of functioning or for ease of cleaning. We believe that *Robinson* represents a sensible limitation on the scope of manufacturer liability lest a manufacturer be made an insurer against all injuries that might arise from the use or misuse of a product.

The facts here simply do not approach those of *Robinson*. . . . Because of the ease with which the overhead guard could be removed and the forklift's added versatility when operated without the guard, there is a legitimate jury question as to the scope of the forklift's intended purpose. . . . In short, the jury must ascertain whether in light of these factors, the manufacturer, given its resources and expertise, breached its duty by placing a product on the market that is not reasonably safe. [Id. at 587.]

Courts continue to apply *Robinson* to shield manufacturers in cases dealing with product alterations, but note that *Lopez* provides an exception to the rule where a manufacturer purposely designs a product to permit use without safety features. See Patino v. Lockformer Co., 757 N.Y.S.2d 107 (N.Y. App. Div. 2003) (affirming summary judgment for defendant manufacturer of roll forming machine because the machine was originally equipped with many inter-connected safeguards, which were later removed by a third party); 755 N.Y.S.2d 798 (N.Y. App. Div. 2003) (holding that trial court erred in denying defendant manufacturer's motion for summary judgment where no evidence was produced showing that altered bench grinder was designed to permit use without factory installed safeguards.).

CHAPTER FIVE
Liability for Failure to Warn

This chapter focuses on the issues presented when a products liability plaintiff claims that the defendant, or a predecessor of the defendant in the chain of distribution, failed to adequately instruct or warn of product-related risks. Instructions and warnings serve two functions. They reduce risks of harm by helping users and consumers to behave more carefully; and they enable users and consumers to make informed decisions regarding whether to encounter risks that cannot be eliminated by careful use and consumption. Regarding what might be termed the "risk-reduction" function, adequate warnings allow product users and consumers to use and consume more carefully than if they remained ignorant of hidden product risks. (In some cases, persons other than product users and consumers are in positions to reduce the relevant risks.) Thus, in connection with this risk-reduction function, the cases and problems in this chapter assume that the addressees of warnings have opportunities to alter their modes of product use and consumption to reduce risks of injury. This chapter also considers instances in which this assumption is not warranted—instances in which the only risk-avoidance method open to the user and consumer is the decision not to use the product in the first instance. In those "informed choice" cases, which typically involve consumables such as prescription drugs and cosmetics, once the choice to use or consume is made, the user or consumer can do little or nothing to reduce the risk of injury.

In connection with the cases to be considered in this chapter, a distinction may be drawn between instructions and warnings. Instructions tell product users what they should do to reduce the risks of injury. "Wear insulated gloves to protect your hands." Warnings describe risks that would not otherwise be obvious to persons of average intelligence and experience. "Caution! The top of this product becomes very hot!" Often, product suppliers will be required to provide both sorts of information. Sometimes only the warning is necessary, as when what to do about it is obvious. Less frequently, only instructions are required, as when the risk is obvious but an effective risk-avoidance technique is not.

Another factor to bear in mind is the role of doctrine. As these materials will make clear, failure-to-warn products liability cases have been brought under both negligence and strict liability. Negligence focuses on the conduct of the defendant, while strict liability focuses on the defective product irrespective of the conduct of the defendant. Courts have faced considerable difficulty in applying this theoretical distinction to failure-to-warn actions. It is relatively simple to talk about a hairline crack in a soda bottle as a product defect, separate and apart from the conduct of the defendant. However, "failure to warn" implies that someone "failed" to do something he was supposed to do. This characterization translates easily into the language of negligence. It is harder to fit "failure to warn" under the rubric of strict liability. For example, in Hauenstein v. Loctite Corp., 347 N.W.2d 272, 274 (Minn. 1984), the court noted that in a failure-to-warn action brought against the manufacturer, "if the failure to warn is not negligent, the product is not 'defective' and there is no strict liability."

One more preliminary observation remains. Some judges (and commentators) succumb to the temptation to assume that instructions and warnings are, so to speak, "free." That is, they take the view that while modifying a design to make it safer may (and usually does) have serious cost implications, the costs of adding a few words of warning are almost nil. In some cases this assumption is obviously false; if a manual of instructions and warnings is required, such a manual costs money to prepare and distribute. But if all that is missing is a simple "This product can explode and injure you if you drop it" in an existing manual of instructions and warnings, the marginal monetary costs of doing so seem to approach zero. On that view, no appreciable risk would seem too small not to be warned against, given the very low monetary costs of doing so. Are there not other, nonmonetary costs associated with warning about all risks, however small? Think about this question as you consider the materials that follow.

A. THE BASIC DUTY TO WARN AT TIME OF SALE

When we speak of "the basic duty," we refer to those circumstances in which the central issue is whether or not some instruction or warning should have been forthcoming. Thus, in the cases and problems in this section, the defendants typically have said little or nothing whatsoever about the relevant risks, and argue that they owed no duty to speak up at all. A subsequent section will address the question of what must be warned about, and by what means, once a duty to warn is found to exist.

1. The General Rule

Restatement (Third) of Torts: Products Liability
(1998)

§2. CATEGORIES OF PRODUCT DEFECT

A product is defective when, at the time of sale or distribution, it contains a manufacturing defect, is defective in design, or is defective because of inadequate instructions or warnings. A product: . . .

(c) is defective because of inadequate instructions or warnings when the foreseeable risks of harm posed by the product could have been reduced or avoided by the provision of reasonable instructions or warnings by the seller or other distributor, or a predecessor in the commercial chain of distribution, and the omission of the instructions or warnings renders the product not reasonably safe.

COMMENT:

i. Inadequate instructions or warnings. Commercial product sellers must provide reasonable instructions and warnings about risks of injury posed by products. Instructions inform persons how to use and consume products safely. Warnings alert users and consumers to the existence and nature of product risks so that they can prevent harm either by appropriate conduct during use or consumption or by choosing not to use or consume. In most instances the instructions and warnings will originate with the manufacturer, but sellers down the chain of distribution must warn when doing so is feasible and reasonably necessary. In any event, sellers down the chain are liable if the instructions and warnings provided by predecessors in the chain are inadequate. See Comment *o*. Under prevailing rules concerning allocation of burdens of proof, plaintiff must prove that adequate instructions or warnings were not provided. Subsection (c) adopts a reasonableness test for judging the adequacy of product instructions and warnings. It thus parallels Subsection (b), which adopts a similar standard for judging the safety of product designs. . . .

Section 1 of the Products Liability Restatement subjects all sellers and other commercial distributors of products to liability for harm caused by product defects. (See pp.55-56, supra.) Thus, all commercial actors who come within the boundaries of "sellers or other distributors" owe duties to warn of nonobvious product risks. (For treatments of boundary issues see p.45, et seq., supra.) The interesting basic duty questions arise in connection with commercial actors who fall close to the boundaries. For example, suppose that a homeowner has a problem with a washer/drier and calls a repairman. While working on the problem, the repairman notices something dangerously defective with the appliance having nothing to do with the problem he was called to repair. If he says nothing, is he liable for harm subsequently caused by the defect? Observe that the issue presented does not turn on whether the repairer is considered to be a seller of the washer/drier. Clearly, he is not. But repairers owe duties of reasonable care. The issue is one of basic policy—should repairers owe duties to warn of dangers that they have not been called upon to fix? Generally, courts have answered that question in the negative. See, e.g., Seo v. All-Makes Overhead Doors, 119 Cal. Rptr. 2d 160 (Cal. Ct. App. 2002) (no duty on the part of a repairer of remote-controlled gate to correct or warn of defects unrelated to repair). But see Thompson v. F. B. Cross & Sons, Inc., 798 A.2d 1036 (Del. 2000) (summary judgment inappropriate where issue of fact exists as to whether contractor working on machine merely replaced existing system or whether contractor's choice of components and reconfiguration constituted a design change).

A related question is whether nonmanufacturing sellers—wholesalers and retailers—owe duties to warn of the dangers their products create. Clearly they are strictly liable as commercial sellers of products when the manufacturers fail to warn. But do they owe independent duties to warn even if the manufacturers' warnings are adequate? The Louisiana Court of Appeal adopted the majority view that such sellers owe independent duties to warn only if they actually know of the risks and know them to be hidden from the purchaser. See Hopper v. Crown, 555 So. 2d 46 (La. App. 1989). In Cohen v. Steve's Ice Cream, 737 F. Supp. 8 (D.C. Mass. 1990), a bulk seller of flammable extract manufactured by another company was held not liable to an employee of the ice cream company to which the defendant had sold the extract in 55-gallon drums. The ice cream company had repackaged the extract in smaller containers, one of which leaked and caused a fire. The plaintiff's employer, not the bulk seller, was responsible for the plaintiff's injuries.

In Breidenstein v. Ludlow Corp., 498 N.Y.S.2d 639 (N.Y. App. Div. 1986), the court reversed a plaintiff's judgment against the casual seller of a used mill machine. (Casual sellers, you will recall from Chapter One, are not strictly liable as product sellers.)

> The court erred in failing to grant summary judgment to defendant dismissing plaintiff's negligence claim against it. From approximately 1965 to 1976 defendant was the owner of a mill machine manufactured by Thropp Corporation. When used by defendant, it was equipped with a safety device subjected to weekly inspection. It was dismantled and sold "as is" to Eemco Machines, Inc., who reconstructed it according to the specifications of Plaslok Corporation. Plaintiff, an employee of Plaslok, was allegedly injured while operating the machine. Plaintiff contended that defendant was negligent in failing to warn Eemco of the danger of using the machine without the safety device in use during its period of ownership. That argument is without merit. We find as a matter of law that defendant, a casual seller, cannot be held liable given the sale and shipment of only certain parts of the dismantled machine and the modification by Eemco, which involved the entire rebuilding of the machine. Id. at 639.

2. No Duty to Warn of Obvious, Generally Known Risks

The general rule regarding obvious, generally known risks is set forth in the following Comment and Illustration to §2(c) of the Products Liability Restatement:

> **J. Warnings: obvious and generally known risks.** In general, a product seller is not subject to liability for failing to warn or instruct regarding risks and risk-avoidance measures that should be obvious to, or generally known by, foreseeable product users. When a risk is obvious or generally known, the prospective addressee of a warning will or should already know of its existence. Warning of an obvious or generally known risk in most instances will not provide an effective additional measure of safety. Furthermore, warnings that deal with obvious or generally known risks may be ignored by users and consumers and may diminish the significance of warnings about non-obvious, not-generally-known risks. Thus, requiring warnings of obvious or generally known risks could reduce the efficacy of warnings generally. When reasonable minds may differ as to whether the risk was obvious or generally known, the issue is to be decided by the trier of fact. The obviousness of risk may bear on the issue of design defect rather than failure to warn.
>
> ILLUSTRATION:
>
> 12. XYZ Ladder Co. manufactures kitchen step ladders for home use. Sid used an XYZ ladder to post a sign above the door of his home office, unaware that his five-year-old son was playing in the office. While Sid was standing on the ladder, his son suddenly open the door, which struck the ladder. Sid fell off the ladder and suffered a fractured hip. There were no warnings on the ladder, nor in the instruction booklet that came with it, not to use the ladder in front of an unlocked door. The danger should be obvious to foreseeable product users. No reasonable trier of fact would find XYZ liable for failing to warn about it and the court should rule for XYZ as a matter of law.

Jamieson v. Woodward & Lothrop
247 F.2d 23 (D.C. Cir.), *cert. denied,* 355 U.S. 855 (1957)

PRETTYMAN, Cir. J.

Appellant, Mrs. Marguerite Jamieson, bought . . . an elastic exerciser manufactured by Helena Rubinstein, Inc., which she had seen advertised in a magazine. She bought by brand name, "Lithe-Line," and no special instructions as to use were given her by the vendor's salesperson. While she was using the exerciser she suffered a sudden unconsciousness, and although she testified she did not know what happened it appears to be a reasonable inference that the exerciser slipped and struck her in the eye. She sued . . . Helena Rubinstein, Inc., for negligence. The defendant answered. . . . The District Court, on the basis of the complaint, the answers, the deposition, and the exhibits, granted summary judgment for the defendant. This appeal followed. . . .

The court is divided in its view of the judgment in favor of the manufacturer, Helena Rubinstein, Inc. A majority agree with the District Court, and so the judgment will be affirmed.

The theory of the plaintiff as to the manufacturer, as set forth in her complaint, was that the exerciser was inherently dangerous and that the manufacturer had failed to warn or otherwise protect her against such danger. In answer to an interrogation she said that when the solid rubber rope is subjected to stress, as in an exercise, great potential striking power is created; that the rope "can depart from the instep" in the course of an exercise; and that no safety or protective device was provided and no warning given.

The exerciser in question was an ordinary rubber rope, about the thickness of a large lead pencil, about forty inches long, with loops on the ends. It had no imperfections or defects whatsoever and no added gadgets. It never broke or went awry. It was a simple elastic exerciser. With the rope came a set of "Instructions." These consisted of a series of eight silhouette sketches of exercises to be done with the rope, with a summary description of each exercise. There were no instructions as to how to operate the device; there was no device to operate, the article in question being merely a rubber rope. In appearance it resembled a child's skipping rope.

In the course of her program Mrs. Jamieson began one of the most normal and natural of exercises. She lay down on the floor, put the rope under her feet, held on to the handles, and, with knees stiff, raised her feet straight up, intending then to lower them and so, alternately raising and lowering them, to give her body muscles a workout. Apparently the rope slipped off the soles of her feet and hit her in the eye. She suffered a serious injury.

The unfortunate event was an accident, we think,—an event so natural that responsibility for it is by common consent not ascribed to fault. Of course one is truly sorry for the unfortunate victim of a chance accident, but the premise of pecuniary liability for tort is not the fact of injury but is negligence. . . .

There are on the market vast numbers of products as to which the law holds the manufacturer to a duty to warn of foreseeable dangers or to provide safeguards against such dangers. But there are also on the market vast numbers of potentially dangerous products as to which the manufacturer owes no duty of warning or other protection. The law does not require that an article be accident-proof or incapable of doing harm. It would be totally unreasonable to require that a manufacturer warn or protect against every injury which may ensue from mishap in the use of his product. Almost every physical object can be inherently dangerous or potentially dangerous in a sense. A lead pencil can stab a man to the heart or puncture his jugular vein, and due to that potentiality it is an "inherently dangerous" object; but, if a person accidentally slips and falls on a pencil-point in his pocket, the manufacturer of the pencil is not liable for the injury. He has no obligation . . . to issue a warning with its sale. A tack, a hammer, a pane of glass, a chair, a rug, a rubber band, and myriads of other objects are truly "inherently dangerous," because they might slip. They cause accidents and injury even more often, we expect, than do rubber exercisers. But the doctrines fashioned by the law for inherently dangerous objects do not encompass these things. A hammer is not . . . defective . . . because it may hurt the user if it slips. A manufacturer cannot manufacture a knife that will not cut or a hammer that will not mash a thumb or a stove that will not burn a finger. The law does not require him to warn of such common dangers. On the other end of the spectrum of practicalities, a manufacturer . . . might be liable for failure to provide . . . an emphatic warning to users of an electric power saw, but he would not be liable if he failed so to provide in respect to a kitchen knife.

If a hand slips in a normal operation with a non-defective device, a knife will cut and a lighted stove will burn and an automobile will crash into a tree; but no authority holds that manufacturers must warn of such contingencies. All this is firmly established commercial law and custom. We doubt that any book of instructions given with a car warns that, if a user accidentally steps on the accelerator instead of on the brake, he may be hurt; nevertheless, so far as we are able to ascertain, no case has yet held the manufacturer liable under such circumstances. . . .

Neither an exact definition of liabilities nor a precise delineation of the boundaries is necessary in the present case. It seems clear under all or any of the cases or text authorities that, where a manufactured article is a simple thing of universally known characteristics, not a device with parts or mechanism, the only danger being not latent but obvious to any possible user, if the article does not break or go awry, but injury occurs through a mishap in normal use, the article reacting in its normal and foreseeable manner, the manufacturer is not liable for negligence. If a man drops an iron dumbbell on his foot the manufacturer is not liable.

The case at bar falls within the category just described. The only "dangerous condition" was that a rubber rope is elastic and when stretched will, when released, return to its original length with some degree of force. Small boys know that fact and fashion slingshots upon the principle. Surely every adult knows that, if an elastic band, whether it be an office rubber band or a rubber rope exerciser, is stretched and one's hold on it slips, the elastic snaps back. There was no duty on the manufacturer to warn of that simple fact.

The "Instructions" given with this rope were simply an illustrated text depicting various exercises which might be performed with it. They were affirmative. No mechanism was involved. There were no instructions as to how to operate the device; there was no "operation" of a "device"; the only action was to stretch the rope and then relax the tension. The instructions showed in silhouette eight exercises to be done with the rope. They were the time-honored routine known to every high school gym class, a modern rendition of the old-time "Daily Dozen." The one Mrs. Jamieson was doing was described thus:

TUMMY FLATTENER
Lie on back. Place hands in loops of Lithe-Line. Place feet in middle; pull legs up and lower to ground.

While she was executing this simple maneuver the rope slipped off her feet. The "instructions" did not say that, if the rope, while stretched, slipped out of her hand or off her foot, it might hit her in the eyes, the nose, the mouth, or the ear, thereby possibly causing a detached retina, a chipped septum, a split lip which might become fatally infected, or a ruptured eardrum resulting in permanent deafness. But we are of clear opinion that the manufacturer cannot be held negligent for failing to give such instructions.

The reasonably foreseeable injury from a mishap with this rope was not great — a cut lip, bloody nose, or black eye, at the most. This lady's injury, a detachment of the retina in one eye, is not the sort of thing reasonably anticipated from the snapback of a rubber elastic of this sort. At the same time it is obvious that any injury to an eye may have dire consequences. So may a cut finger or a broken wrist. But we do not find in the authorities a doctrine that, if the injury ordinarily foreseen is relatively minor and so need not be warned against, a manufacturer must nevertheless warn against any dire unusual consequence which, also obviously, may ensue. Quite to the contrary it is well established that a manufacturer is not liable, unless serious bodily harm is reasonably foreseeable. Of course, so far as foreseeability is concerned, not only may the usual be foreseen, but the unusual may often be foreseen as a remote possibility. A manufacturer may foresee as a remote possibility that a metal decoration on a jewelry box may scratch one and cause an infection; the heel of a lady's shoe may break at an inopportune moment, causing serious injury; or that a stickpin may stab a man to the heart. Yet for these remote eventualities the law imposes no liability on the manufacturer. "Reasonably foreseeable" in the rule here applicable does not encompass the far reaches of pessimistic imagination. . . .

Since the rope in the case at bar was without defect or accessory gadgets and did not break or fail in any manner, no fault, and surely no negligence, can be ascribed to the manufacturer merely because it slipped off the lady's foot while in perfectly normal use. It would be erroneous to hold that the manufacturer may be liable for damages if he fails to warn users that a rope such as this might slip off a foot or out of a hand. When all the discussion of involved legal principles has been concluded, the case remains as simple as it was in the beginning: A lady was doing a simple exercise with a simple rubber rope, and it slipped off her foot and hit her in the eye. That is the whole of it. And the question is equally simple: Was the manufacturer therefore negligent? We think it was not. To hold otherwise would go beyond any reasonable dictates of justice in fixing the liabilities of manufacturers of products sold on the market.

Affirmed.

WASHINGTON, Cir. J. (dissenting), with whom EDGERTON, C.J., and BAZELON and FAHY, Cir. JJ., join.

I would reverse as to defendant Rubinstein.

Mrs. Jamieson bought the Lithe-Line, manufactured and marketed by this defendant, for the purpose of reducing her abdomen. Instructions for its use were packed in the container with the Lithe-Line. On the afternoon of the day the device was delivered to her home in nearby Virginia, plaintiff said, she read the instructions through, did two of the exercises there described and recommended "to get the feel of the rubber hose," and then proceeded to the "Tummy Flattener" exercise, the particular exercise "that was supposed to reduce" the abdomen. She followed the recommended procedure contained in the instruction booklet and, while so doing, the Lithe-Line slipped off her feet and struck her across the eyes, knocking her unconscious and causing a detached retina and permanent partial loss of vision in the left eye. The injury occurred while she was performing the exercise exactly as the manufacturer had directed and recommended, without any deviation from the instructions and without fault on her part, so far as the record before us shows. Her suit is based, not on the theory that the manufacturer put on the market an exerciser in itself inherently dangerous, as the majority appears to believe, but on the premise that the exerciser *when used as directed* by the manufacturer became dangerous and that the manufacturer owed a duty to warn . . . her against such danger. In other words, her theory is that the use of the Lithe-Line in the Tummy Flattener exercise as directed by the manufacturer created an unreasonable risk of injury which gave rise to a duty toward users of the device. That theory of liability finds abundant support not only in the decisions of the Virginia courts, which govern here, but also in the general law of negligence. . . .

The majority states that "Any article may slip in use." If that premise is accepted, it must follow that the manufacturer could and should have foreseen that the Line might slip while being used in the Tummy Flattener exercise. From the directions for the exercise in question—and the accompanying drawing—it would appear that if the Line slips, the user's face will usually be in the path of the recoil. While injury of the type here involved and other serious injuries, as for example a broken nose or broken teeth, are perhaps less likely than a facial bruise, a black eye, a bloody nose, or a cut lip, all were within the range of possibility and all can reasonably be regarded as sufficiently serious to impose a duty on the manufacturer to take reasonable steps to reduce the danger. It would be a rare woman indeed who would willingly use an exerciser which, without fault on her part, could give her a black eye or a cut lip or any facial injury. . . .

The Lithe-Line was marketed for a particular class of persons—overweight women who desired to reduce or "streamline" parts of their body. It was not marketed for individuals who could be expected to have any special training or experience. The tendency of expanded rubber to contract to its original length, when released, is undoubtedly commonly known and was known by Mrs. Jamieson, according to her deposition. But the fact that she understood this hardly justifies the legal conclusion that she or any other user of the Lithe-Line would understand, without some tests, training or experience, that rubber of the type and consistency used in the Lithe-Line, when stretched in the Tummy Flattener exercise as directed, would or could recoil and strike the face of the user, with the impact alleged to have occurred. . . .

. . . [R]easonable minds could differ as to whether the manufacturer could justifiably expect that prospective users would remain fully aware of the danger after reading his advertising claims, even assuming for purposes of argument that

The Basic Duty to Warn at Time of Sale

they might otherwise be reasonably expected to recognize and appreciate it. The leaflet of instructions furnished with the Lithe-Line stated inter alia:

> Lithe-Line — easily the best turn done to the body beautiful since the curve was invented. For, given enough of this ingenious little elastic rope it is possible for *any* body to prune the hips, sleek the legs, carve the waistline. . . . And do it pleasantly! As a cat does it — with the same grace-giving movements. . . . You'll have great fun, besides, pulling and stretching, bending and twisting. . . . A real workout is yours, too, against the tenacity of the Lithe-Line. You'll marvel at the supple way your body responds with new lines of rhythm and beauty as you stretch yourself into shape and gain the grace and poise that you've coveted all your life!

The atmosphere created by such statements, especially the representation that it is possible for "*any* body" to reduce with it, directed at weight-conscious women such as the plaintiff, can reasonably be expected to dispel any suspicion of danger and to "lull the user . . . into a false sense of security," and this "might also reasonably have been foreseen by the defendant." . . .

So here, I would hold that it is for the jury to say, after hearing evidence, whether there was a duty to warn or otherwise protect plaintiff from the danger. . . . At the present stage, a jury could reasonably find that women purchasing the Lithe-Line for purposes of reducing would be warranted in assuming that an exercise, prescribed without any qualification by a well-known and reputable manufacturer such as the defendant, could be performed with the device issued by that manufacturer without injury, and that a duty to warn or otherwise protect existed.

Thus, I must disagree strongly with the majority view. I think that the evidence adduced thus far — the device itself plus the directions and the plaintiff's testimony on deposition that she was injured as she used the device precisely as directed — indicate at the very least that there may be liability and that the plaintiff is entitled to an opportunity to present her evidence. This is not to say, of course, that if evidence were received the plaintiff would necessarily prevail. It would be a question for the trier of fact on all the evidence to resolve the factual issues bearing on the manufacturer's alleged negligence and the affirmative defenses, if any, which might be pleaded. . . .

Whether or not the application of the "no duty to warn of obvious dangers" rule to the particular facts in *Jamieson* was correct, the rule itself is solidly embedded in the caselaw. See, e.g., Felle v. W. W. Grainger, Inc., 755 N.Y.S.2d 535 (N.Y. App. Div. 2003) (manufacturer had no duty to warn of open and obvious nature of the risk taken by plaintiff, who had seven years of experience operating a grinder and thus should have appreciated the danger of placing his face in proximity to a rapidly rotating and completely unguarded sanding wheel); Roland v. Daimler-Chrysler Corp., 33 S.W.3d 468 (Tex. App. 2001) (holding that manufacturer of pickup truck had no duty to warn of danger of ejection posed by riding in open bed); Hutton v. Globe Hoist Co., 158 F. Supp. 2d 371 (S.D.N.Y. 2001) (finding that the danger of car falling from hydraulic lift in auto repair shop is obvious as a matter of law and that knowing to run in the direction opposite the fall is even more obvious); Brewer v. Harley Davidson, Inc., 172 F.3d

62 (10th Cir. 1999) (A motorcycle manufacturer has no duty to warn users that leg protectors could be installed to prevent injury in the event of collision; the danger was open and obvious and required no warning); Weiner v. American Honda Motor Co. 718 A.2d 305 (Pa. Super. Ct. 1998) (auto manufacturer has no duty to warn of the open and obvious danger that a 180-pound industrial gas canister placed in a hatchback's cargo compartment unrestrained would catapult forward during a head on collision and injure plaintiff sitting in the front seat).

When reasonable persons can differ as to the obviousness of the danger, the issue is for the trier of fact. *See,* e.g., Stanley v. Aeroquip Corp., 181 F.3d 103 (6th Cir. 1999); Osontoski v. Wal-Mart Stores, Inc., 143 F.3d 1027 (6th Cir. 1998); Lagano v. Chrysler Corp., 141 F.3d 1151 (2d Cir. 1998). See also, Restatement (Third) of Torts: Products Liability §2, cmt. *j* (1998), supra.

A relevant factor in determining the obviousness of the risk is the expertise of the class of users for whom the product is intended. In Antcliff v. State Employees Credit Union, 327 N.W.2d 814 (Mich. 1982), the plaintiff was seriously and permanently injured when the support system of a powered scaffold on which he was standing unexpectedly gave way and fell to the ground. Plaintiff's safety line apparently failed, and he fell with the scaffold. Plaintiff and a co-worker personally designed the support system and rigged the scaffold. The scaffold was manufactured and sold by the defendant to the plaintiff's employer. The plaintiff claimed that the defendant failed to provide warnings and instructions concerning how the scaffold should be set up, and that such failure caused the accident. The Michigan high court affirmed the lower court's denial of this claim as a matter of law, concluding:

> [P]laintiff and his co-worker were both journeyman painters. In view of their knowledge and experience as riggers, we feel constrained to charge them with full appreciation of the danger of inadequately supporting the scaffold on which they worked. As a result, the circumstances here (a non-defective product lacking in dangerous propensities and a known or obvious product-connected danger) do not support application of the policy which would require [the defendant] to provide instructions for the safe rigging of its product.
>
> Moreover, the contrary conclusion would lead to demonstrably unfair and unintended results. There are countless skilled operations, such as the rigging of scaffolding, which involve otherwise non-dangerous products in potentially dangerous situations. A manufacturer of such a product should be able to presume mastery of the basic operation. The more so when, as here, the manufacturer affirmatively and successfully limits the market of its product to professionals. In such a case, the manufacturer should not be burdened with the often difficult task of providing instructions on how to properly perform the basic operation. [Id. at 821.]

In *Antcliff,* the court held that the defendant owed no duty to warn plaintiff's class of users, because that class of users was knowledgeable about the relevant risks. A related question is presented when it is not so clear that the class of users knew of the risks, but it is clear that the individual plaintiff knew. Should such a case be dealt with under the heading of "duty," as in *Antcliff* or under some other heading, such as "proximate causation," or "assumption of the risk"? The New York appellate court in *Felle,* noted supra, blurred the distinction. In Burke v. Spartanics, 252 F.3d 131 (2d Cir. 2001), the Second Circuit affirmed the district court's judgment on a jury verdict in favor the defendant manufacturer, because failure to warn could not have been the cause of plaintiff's injury where the plaintiff was sufficiently aware of the dangers posed by a metal shearing machine. In Raimbeault v. Takeuchi, 772 A.2d 1056 (R.I. 2001), The Supreme Court of Rhode Island spoke instead in terms of "assumption of the risk" to arrive at a similar result. In affirming judgment for the defendant, the court noted that ample testimony from the plaintiff at trial, which showed that plaintiff had five years of experience with the excavator that caused his injuries, indicated his awareness of the risks involved in using an earth-mover with a rotating cab on an embankment. Cf. Moran v. Eastern Equipment Sales, Inc., 818 N.E.3d 848 (Conn. App. Ct. 2003) (whether plaintiff was sophisticated user was for the jury; the plaintiff's actual level of sophistication was less important to question of defendant's duty to warn than whether defendant had reason to anticipate that users would appreciate the dangers).

One group of cases in which the obviousness of the risks has been the subject of controversy involves alcoholic beverages. The general rule is that the risks of excessive drinking are obvious. Thus, in Russell v. Bishop, Prod. Liab. Rep. (CCH) ¶10,849 (Tenn. Ct. App. 1986), the appellate court affirmed the trial court's granting of defendant's motion for summary judgment. The parents of a young woman killed in an automobile accident sued the manufacturer of a bottle of whiskey that the drunken driver of the other vehicle had consumed prior to the accident. The plaintiff argued that the defendant should have included, on the label attached to the whiskey bottle, a warning against drinking too much and driving while intoxicated. Plaintiffs' expert, the county director of traffic safety, testified in an affidavit that such a warning, in the form of a chart correlating alcohol consumption with body weight, was feasible and had proven effective in programs designed to rehabilitate persons convicted of drunk driving. The appellate court concluded:

> This Court is not unmindful of the tragic consequences of drinking and driving, nor unsympathetic to the plight of the Plaintiffs. We hold simply that under the common law of this State as enunciated to date, no cause of action arises against the distiller, and if a change is to be made in regard thereto it should not be by this Court, but the highest judicial authority in the State. [Id. at 29,407.]

See also Brown Forman Corp. v. Brune, 893 S.W.2d 640 (Tex. App. 1994) (no duty to warn of the dangers of rapidly consuming a large quantity of tequila); Maguire v. Pabst Brewing Co., 387 N.W.2d 565 (Iowa 1986) (no duty to warn of the dangers of drinking beer prior to driving automobile).

But there have been exceptions. In Hon v. Stroh Brewery Co., 835 F.2d 510 (3d Cir. 1987), the plaintiff's husband died from pancreatitis at the age of 26. Medical experts supported the plaintiff's claim that relatively moderate consumption of beer distributed by the defendant — two or three cans per night on an average of four nights a week for a period of six years — caused his fatal disease. The district court granted summary judgment for the defendant, relying on the general rule that the risks of drinking alcohol are widely known. The court of appeals reversed, concluding (Id. at 514):

> [The medical] affidavits provide evidence tending to show that beer in the quantity and manner [decedent] consumed it can have fatal consequences. Nothing in the record sug-

gests that [decedent] was aware of this fact, however. Moreover [one medical] affidavit tends to show that the general public is unaware that consumption at this level and in this manner can have any serious adverse effects. There is no evidence in the record that the public appreciates any hazard that may be associated with this kind of consumption.

Did this case involve risk reduction, informed choice, or both?

A more startling exception to the general rule that risks of drinking alcohol are obvious was made in McGuire v. Joseph E. Seagram & Sons, Inc., 790 S.W.2d 842 (Tex. App. 1990). The plaintiffs were chronic alcoholics who sought damages from several distillers for "certain diseases, bodily injury, financial ruin, mental anguish and loss of consortium caused by the addictive drug, alcohol." They alleged that the defendants failed to communicate to consumers twenty-four separate items of information relating to alcoholic beverages. Notwithstanding the defendants' argument that the dangers of long-term overconsumption of alcohol were well known, the intermediate appellate court held that given the "vastly increasing complexities in relationships between and among human beings, (coupled with entire new fields of scientific knowledge and empirical wisdom)" (790 S.W.2d at 852), there was reason to reexamine the law and to "implant correlative duties." Although the Texas Supreme Court reversed and held that knowledge of the dangers of overconsumption of alcohol is widespread (814 S.W.2d 385) (Tex. 1991), the intermediate court decision is a stark example of a court turning its back on the traditional rule.

The Federal Alcoholic Beverage Labelling Act of 1988, 27 U.S.C.A. §215 (West Supp. 1996), contains the following provisions:

> Section 215. On and after the expiration of the 12-month period following the date of enactment of this title, it shall be unlawful for any person to manufacture, import, or bottle for sale or distribution in the United States any alcoholic beverage unless the container of such beverage bears the following statement:
>
>> **GOVERNMENT WARNING:** (1) According to the Surgeon General, women should not drink alcoholic beverages during pregnancy because of the risk of birth defects. (2) Consumption of alcoholic beverages impairs your ability to drive a car or operate machinery, and may cause health problems.
>
> Section 216. No statement relating to alcoholic beverages and health, other than the statement required by section 215, shall be required under State law to be placed on any container of an alcoholic beverage, or on any box, carton, or other package, irrespective of the material from which made, that contains such a container.

What effect should this statute have on claims such as the one in *Hon,* supra, that accrue after the effective date of the statute?

For general treatments of the basic duty to instruct or warn, see generally Hardy C. Dillard & Harris Hart, II, Products Liability: Directions for Use and Duty to Warn, 41 Va. L. Rev. 145 (1955); Michael S. Jacobs, Toward a Process-Based Approach to Failure to Warn, 71 N.C. L. Rev. 121 (1992); James A. Henderson, Jr. & Aaron D. Twerski, Doctrinal Collapse in Products Liability: The Empty Shell of Failure to Warn, 65 N.Y.U. L. Rev. 265 (1990); W. Page Keeton, Products Liability—Inadequacy of Information, 48 Tex. L. Rev. 398 (1970); John A. Kidwell, Duty to Warn: A Description of the Model of Decision, 53 Tex. L. Rev. 1375 (1975); James B. Sales, The Duty to Warn and Instruct for Safe Use in Strict Liability, 13 St. Mary's L.J. 521 (1982); Victor E. Schwartz

& Russell W. Driver, Warnings in the Workplace: The Need for a Synthesis of Law and Communication Theory, 52 U. Cin. L. Rev. 38 (1983); Stephen M. Bressler, Note, The Warning Claim in an Arizona Products Liability Action: Limitations on the Duty to Warn, 25 Ariz. L. Rev. 395 (1983).

PROBLEM SEVENTEEN

A senior partner in the law firm in which you are an associate has asked for input in a products case he is handling on behalf of Starbrite Pools, Inc., a major manufacturer of above-ground swimming pools. The plaintiff is Jack Parent, age nineteen, who broke his neck in a diving accident nine months ago in one of Starbrite's pools. The complaint is lengthy and complicated, and contains a number of different claims. The partner wants your assistance in connection with the failure-to-warn claim. The plaintiff alleges that nine months ago he was visiting the home of neighbors, Ed and Alice Bancroft, who had invited him and his younger sisters over for an afternoon swim in their backyard swimming pool. The Bancrofts had bought the pool four years earlier from a Starbrite retail outlet, and had paid Starbrite personnel to set up the pool in their backyard. The pool was oval-shaped, 12 feet by 24 feet, and uniformly four feet in depth. Ed Bancroft had built a sturdy wooden deck level with the top of the side of the pool closest to the house, on which the Bancrofts had placed law furniture. The vinyl liner of the pool indicated, in four-inch contrasting lettering facing inwards just below the top of the side of the pool and just above the water level, that the water was three and one-half feet deep. The lettering read "3½ feet deep" and ran, at one-foot intervals, around the entire inner circumference of the pool.

The plaintiff and his family had just moved into the neighborhood, and had never used the pool before that day. When he and his sisters arrived at the Bancroft's house dressed in their bathing suits, they went immediately to the pool area, walked up steps to the poolside wooden deck, and took off their shoes and outer garments preparatory to going swimming. His two sisters entered the pool by sitting on the decking at the edge and sliding feet first into the water. Jack dove head-first into the water, struck his head on the unyielding pool bottom, and broke his neck. He was rendered a quadriplegic, a permanent condition.

The complaint claims that Starbrite should have warned swimmers not to dive into the pool and that doing so would likely lead to severe and permanent injury, including quadriplegia. The complaint does not allege specifically what Starbrite should have said, or how it should have said it to people using the pool. It simply asserts that the failure to provide any warning at all rendered the pool defective and that the failure-to-warn defect proximately caused the plaintiff's injuries.

The partner explains that the lawyers representing the plaintiff are experienced trial lawyers and will argue effectively for their client. It appears that they have lined up an expert witness, a qualified cognitive psychologist, whom the partner has seen in action before. She will testify that an adequate warning in this case could have served as a "prompt," reminding swimmers such as Jack Parent of the danger of diving that, while understood abstractly, tend to get suppressed from consciousness in the excitement of the moment. Also, the expert will almost certainly rely on the "optimism bias" in her testimony—a built-in tendency for otherwise rational people to assume that "it can't happen to me." Vivid, even shocking, warnings can bring reality home to such actors, penetrating and offsetting the otherwise potentially disastrous effects of this cognitive bias.

The partner wants your "take" on the plaintiff's failure-to-warn claim. In responding to his query, you are to assume that the high court of your state recognizes §2(c) and Comment *j* of the Products Liability Restatement, supra, as accurate statements of the relevant law. Should the plaintiff be required to propose specifically what the warning should have been? Can we fashion an argument that any feasible warning would not have made a difference? How can we counter, or exclude entirely, plaintiff's expert? Do you think the plaintiff will reach the jury with his failure-to-warn claim?

TO SPEAK OR NOT TO SPEAK; OR, "DIGGING YOUR OWN GRAVE WITH THE BEST OF INTENTIONS"

Imagine that you are general counsel to a medium-size manufacturer of a product whose risks are pretty obvious to the average user but arguably are not obvious to a subset of foreseeable (though by no means typical) users who are less than normally intelligent, attentive, or experienced. The question is whether you will advise the manufacturer to warn the minority of unintelligent, inattentive, and inexperienced users, assuming that the warning could be attached to the product and would likely reach those users. Or rather, the question is what considerations you should weigh in deciding what is the best advice to render. The marketing people tell you they don't like warnings. "Most of our users don't need them, and they hurt our product-image," they insist. But if the savings in liability would be significant, the CEO indicates that he will use them. How would you set about to assess the value to the company of going ahead and warning about fairly obvious risks?

The purpose of this note is to raise the possibility that supplying a warning in such a context might increase, rather than decrease, the company's exposure to liability. Without any warning, you will be able to argue on behalf of the client that the risk is obvious and no reasonable person would seriously consider warning of it. You may lose the argument, but at least it can be made with a straight face. But once some kind of warning is provided, the "no duty" argument is more difficult to make — the warning itself works as an admission by the company, in effect, that an underlying duty to warn was owed. You may still argue that the warning was sufficient, of course. But the question of whether an admitted duty to warn was breached sounds like a question of fact for the jury. Thus, you might actually increase your overall exposure to liability by warning rather than choosing not to warn. And if you try to make the warning against low-level risks strong enough to be impervious to attack, the gripes of the marketing people will be (even if they were not before) well grounded.

A case presenting the possibility of a manufacturer incurring such self-inflicted wounds is May v. Dafoe, 611 P.2d 1275, review denied, 93 Wash.2d 1030 (1980). An incubator manufacturer went ahead and warned its users (medical personnel) against administering too-high concentrations of oxygen to premature infants (too much oxygen can cause blindness), even though it insisted that it owed no duty to warn doctors about the current state of medical research. The plaintiff argued that the doctor who administered oxygen to the injured infant misunderstood, and assumed that if lower concentrations were used, the duration of use did not matter. In fact, duration mattered as much as concentration, and the baby was blinded. The court of appeals affirmed a directed verdict for the defendant-manufacturer, reiterating the view that manufacturers owe no duty to warn doctors about the current state of medical research, but only about the design, engineering, and functional dangers associated with their products.

The defendant in *May* escaped the fate of having dug its own grave. But should it have escaped? And will the next such defendant be so fortunate, regardless of the merits of the plaintiff's case?

PROBLEM EIGHTEEN

The vice president in charge of marketing for a medium-sized television antenna manufacturer in your area seeks your advice concerning the instructions and/or warnings that should accompany his company's products. More particularly, he is concerned with what he refers to as a "rash of incidents" in recent months involving injuries and deaths caused when persons (typically unskilled "do-it-yourselfers") allow the antennae to come in contact with uninsulated power lines while installing the antennae on rooftops and other high places. A few of these accidents have involved his own products; a greater number have involved products manufactured and distributed by others. "You would think that the risks were obvious," he says. "But something must be breaking down. Should we include in our packaging, for the first time, warnings about the risks of power lines? No one else does it. But should we be the first?" Making reasonable assumptions where necessary, advise him on this matter.

3. No Duty to Warn of Unknowable Risks

Anderson v. Owens-Corning Fiberglas Corp.
810 P.2d 549 (Cal. 1991)

PANELLI, J.

Defendants are or were manufacturers of products containing asbestos. Plaintiff Carl Anderson filed suit in 1984, alleging that he contracted asbestosis and other lung ailments through exposure to asbestos and asbestos products (i.e., preformed blocks, cloth and cloth tape, cement, and floor tiles) while working as an electrician at the Long Beach Naval Shipyard from 1941 to 1976. Plaintiff allegedly encountered asbestos while working in the vicinity of others who were removing and installing insulation products aboard ships. . . .

Plaintiff's amended complaint alleged a cause of action in strict liability for the manufacture and distribution of "asbestos, and other products containing said substance . . . which caused injury to users and consumers, including plaintiff." . . . Plaintiff alleged that defendants marketed their products with specific prior knowledge, from scientific studies and medical data, that there was a high risk of injury and death from exposure to asbestos or asbestos-containing products; that defendants knew consumers and members of the general public had no knowledge of the potentially injurious nature of asbestos; and that defendants failed to warn users of the risk of danger. Defendants' pleadings raised the state-of-the-art defense, i.e., that even those at the vanguard of scientific knowledge at the time the products were sold could not have known that asbestos was dangerous to users in the concentrations associated with defendants' products.

Plaintiff moved before trial to prevent defendants from presenting state-of-the-art evidence. . . . The trial court granted the motion. . . . The defendants then moved to prevent plaintiff from proceeding on the failure-to-warn theory. . . . In response to the court's request for an offer of proof on the alleged failure to warn, plaintiff referred to catalogs and other literature depicting workers without respirators or protective devices and offered to prove that, until the mid-1960's, defendants had given no warnings of the dangers associated with asbestos, that various warnings given by some of the defendants after 1965 were inadequate, and, finally, that defendants removed the products from the market entirely in the early 1970's. Defendants argued in turn that the state of the art, i.e., what was scientifically knowable in the period 1943-1974, was their obvious and only defense to any cause of action for failure to warn, and that, in view of the court's decision to exclude state-of-the-art evidence, fairness dictated that plaintiff be precluded from proceeding on that theory. With no statement of reasons, the trial court granted defendants' motion. . . . After a four-week trial, the jury returned a verdict for defendants. . . .

Plaintiff moved for a new trial, asserting that the court erred in precluding proof of liability on a failure-to-warn theory. . . . The court granted the motion. . . . Plaintiff . . . urged that knowledge or knowability, and thus state-of-the-art evidence, was irrelevant in strict liability for failure to warn. . . . The trial court agreed.

The Court of Appeals, in a two-to-one decision, upheld the order granting a new trial on both grounds. The appellate court added that, "in strict liability asbestos cases, including those prosecuted on a failure to warn theory, state of the art evidence is not admissible since it focuses on the reasonableness of the defendant's conduct, which is irrelevant in strict liability." The dissenting justice urged that the majority had imposed "absolute liability," contrary to the tenets of the strict liability doctrine, and that the manufacturers' right to a fair trial included the right to litigate all relevant issues, including the state of the art of scientific knowledge at the relevant time. We granted review. . . .

Failure to Warn Theory of Strict Liability

. . . In Cavers v. Cushman Motor Sales, Inc. (1979) 95 Cal. App. 3d 338, 157 Cal. Rptr. 142, the first case in which failure to warn was the sole theory of liability, the appellate court approved the instruction that a golf cart, otherwise properly manufactured, could be defective if no warning was given of the cart's propensity to tip over when turning and if the absence of the warning rendered the product substantially dangerous to the user. *Cavers* was principally concerned with the propriety of the term "substantially dangerous" and concluded that it is necessary to weigh the degree of danger involved when determining whether a warning defect exists. . . .

[Early] cases did not address the specific factual question whether or not the manufacturer or distributor knew or should have known of the risks involved in the products, either because the nature of the product or the risk involved made such a discussion unnecessary or because the plaintiff limited the action to risks about which the manufacturer/distributor obviously knew or should have known. Moreover, the appellate courts in these same cases did not discuss knowledge or knowability as a component of the failure to warn theory of strict liability. However, a knowledge or knowability component clearly was included as an implicit condition of strict liability. In that regard, California was in accord with authorities in a majority of other states.

Only when the danger to be warned against was "unknowable" did the knowledge component of the failure-to-warn theory come into focus. Such cases made it apparent that eliminating the knowledge component had the effect of turning strict liability into absolute liability. . . .

[The court reviews other California Court of Appeals decisions.]

In sum, the foregoing review of the decisions of the Courts of Appeal persuades us that California is well settled into the majority view that knowledge, actual or constructive, is a requisite for strict liability for failure to warn and that [our earlier decision], if not directly, at least by implication, reaffirms that position.

However, even if we are implying too much from the language in [our earlier decision,] the fact remains that we are now squarely faced with the issue of knowledge and knowability in strict liability for failure to warn in other than the drug context. Whatever the ambiguity of [our earlier decision,] we hereby adopt the requirement as propounded by the Restatement Second of Torts and acknowledged by the lower courts of this state and the majority of jurisdictions, that knowledge or knowability is a component of strict liability for failure to warn.

One of the guiding principles of the strict liability doctrine was to relieve a plaintiff of the evidentiary burdens inherent in a negligence cause of action. . . . Indeed, it was the limitations of negligence theories that prompted the development and expansion of the doctrine. The proponents of the minority rule, including the Court of Appeals in this case, argue that the knowability requirement, and admission of state-of-the-art evidence, improperly infuse negligence concepts into strict liability cases by directing the trier of fact's attention to the conduct of the manufacturer or distributor rather than to the condition of the product. Similar claims have been made as to other aspects of strict liability, sometimes resulting in limitations on the doctrine and sometimes not. . . .

[The court discusses earlier decisions not involving failure to warn.]

As these cases illustrate, the strict liability doctrine has incorporated some well-settled rules from the law of negligence and has survived judicial challenges asserting that such incorporation violates the fundamental principles of the doctrine. It may also be true that the "warning defect" theory is "rooted in negligence" to a greater extent than are the manufacturing- or design-defect theories. The "warning defect" relates to a failure extraneous to the product itself. Thus, while a manufacturing or design defect can be evaluated without reference to the conduct of the manufacturer . . . the giving of a warning cannot. The latter necessarily requires the communicating of something to someone. How can one warn of something that is unknowable? If every product that has no warning were defective per se and for that reason subject to strict liability, the mere fact of injury by an unlabelled product would automatically permit recovery. That is not, and has never been, the purpose and goal of the failure-to-warn theory of strict liability. Further, if a warning automatically precluded liability in every case, a manufacturer or distributor could easily escape liability with overly broad, and thus practically useless, warnings. . . .

We therefore reject the contention that every reference to a feature shared with theories of negligence can serve to defeat limitations on the doctrine of strict liability. Furthermore, despite its roots in negligence, failure to warn in strict liability differs markedly from failure to warn in the negligence context. Negligence law in a failure-to-warn case requires a plaintiff to prove that a manufacturer or distributor did not warn of a particular risk for reasons which fell below the acceptable standard of care, i.e., what a reasonably prudent manufacturer would have known and warned about. Strict liability is not concerned with the standard of due care or the reasonableness of a manufacturer's conduct. The rules of strict liability require a plaintiff to prove only that the defendant did not adequately warn of a particular risk that was known or knowable in light of the generally recognized and prevailing best scientific and medical knowledge available at the time of manufacture and distribution. Thus, in strict liability, as opposed to negligence, the reasonableness of the defendant's failure to warn is immaterial.

Stated another way, a reasonably prudent manufacturer might reasonably decide that the risk of harm was such as not to require a warning as, for example, if the manufacturer's own testing showed a result contrary to that of others in the scientific community. Such a manufacturer might escape liability under negligence principles. In contrast, under strict liability principles the manufacturer has no such leeway; the manufacturer is liable if it failed to give warning of dangers that were known to the scientific community at the time it manufactured or distributed the product. Whatever may be reasonable from the point of view of the manufacturer, the user of the product must be given the option either to refrain from using the product at all or to use it in such a way as to minimize the degree of danger. Davis v. Wyeth Laboratories, Inc. (9th Cir. 1968) 399 F.2d 121, 129-130, described the need to warn in order to provide "true choice": "When, in a particular case, the risk qualitatively (e.g., of death or major disability) as well as quantitatively, on balance with the end sought to be achieved, is such as to call for a true choice judgment, medical or personal, the warning must be given. [Fn. omitted.]" . . . Thus, the fact that a manufacturer acted as a reasonably prudent manufacturer in deciding not to warn, while perhaps absolving the manufacturer of liability under the negligence theory, will not preclude liability under strict liability principles if the trier of fact concludes that, based on the information scientifically available to the manufacturer, the manufacturer's failure to warn rendered the product unsafe to its users.

The foregoing examination of the failure-to-warn theory of strict liability in California compels the conclusion that knowability is relevant to imposition of liability under that theory. Our conclusion not only accords with precedent but also with the considerations of policy that underlie the doctrine of strict liability.

We recognize that an important goal of strict liability is to spread the risks and costs of injury to those most able to bear them. However, it was never the intention of the drafters of the doctrine to make the manufacturer or distributor the insurer of the safety of their products. It was never their intention to impose absolute liability.

Conclusion

Therefore, in answer to the question raised in our order granting review, a defendant in a strict products liability action based upon an alleged failure to warn of a risk of harm may present evidence of the state of the art, i.e., evidence that the particular risk was neither known nor knowable by the application of scientific knowledge available at the time of manufacture and/or distribution. The judgment of the Court of Appeal is affirmed with directions that the matter be remanded to the trial court for proceedings in accord with our decision herein.

LUCAS, C.J., and KENNARD, ARABIAN and BAXTER, JJ., concur. . . .

MOSK, J., concurring and dissenting.

In my view the trial court properly granted a new trial and the Court of Appeal, in a thoughtful analysis of the law, correctly affirmed the order. I thus concur in the result.

I must express my apprehension, however, that we are once again retreating from "[t]he pure concepts of products liability so pridefully fashioned and nurtured by this court." (Daly v. General Motors Corp. (1978) 20 Cal. 3d 725, 757, 144 Cal. Rptr. 380, 575 P.2d 1162 (dis. opn. by Mosk, J.).) . . .

The majority distinguish failure-to-warn strict liability claims from negligence claims on the ground that strict liability is not concerned with a standard of due care or the reasonableness of a manufacturer's conduct. This is generally accurate. However in practice this is often a distinction without a substantial difference. Under either theory, imposition of liability is conditioned on the defendant's actual or constructive knowledge of the risk. Recovery will be allowed only if the defendant has such knowledge yet fails to warn. . . .

We should consider the possibility of holding that failure-to-warn actions lie solely on a negligence theory. "[A]lthough mixing negligence and strict liability concepts is often a game of semantics, the game has more than semantic impact — it breeds confusion and inevitably, bad law." (Henderson & Twerski, Doctrinal Collapse in Products Liability: The Empty Shell of Failure to Warn, 65 N.Y.U. L. Rev. at p.278.) If, however, the majority are not ready to take that step, I would still use this opportunity to enunciate a bright-line rule to apply in failure-to-warn strict liability actions.

Here plaintiff alleged, among other claims, that defendants marketed their products "with specific prior knowledge" of the high risks of injury and death from their use. If plaintiff can establish at the new trial that defendants had actual knowledge, then state of the art evidence — or what everyone else was doing at the time — would be irrelevant and the trial court could properly exclude it. Actual knowledge may often be difficult to prove, but it is not impossible with adequately probing discovery. Defendants, of course, can produce evidence that they had no such prior actual knowledge.

On the other hand, if plaintiff is only able to show, by medical and scientific data or other means, that defendants should have known of the risks inherent in their products, then contrary medical and scientific data and state of the art evidence would be admissible if offered by defendants.

Thus I would draw a clear distinction in failure-to-warn cases between evidence that the defendants had actual knowledge of the dangers and evidence that the defendants should have known of the dangers.

With the foregoing rule in mind, the parties should proceed to the new trial ordered by the trial court and upheld by the Court of Appeal. Thus I would affirm the judgment of the Court of Appeal.

In Carlin v. Superior Court, 920 P.2d 1347 (Cal. 1996) the Supreme Court of California faced the question of whether *Anderson* requires the application of strict liability in a case against a prescription drug manufacturer for its alleged failure to warn physicians of the risks associated with its drug. The defendant urged that the strict-liability approach outlined in *Anderson,* even if liability for unknowable risks were not part of it, would expose drug manufacturers to crushing liability that would inhibit new-drug development. The Supreme Court rejected defendant's argument and, with three separate dissenting opinions, held that *Anderson* required strict liability in that context as well as all others.

For an interesting analysis of the actual differences it makes whether courts use strict liability or negligence rhetoric see Richard L. Cupp & Danielle Polage, The Rhetoric of Strict Products Liability Versus Negligence: An Empirical Analysis, 77 N.Y.U. L. Rev. 874 (2002), already referred to in Chapter Four in the context of design litigation. The authors observe that in defective design and warning cases, courts and commentators are increasingly questioning the substantive distinction between negligence and strict liability causes of action. They point out that the Restatement (Third) of Torts: Products Liability adopts a risk/utility analysis that reflects a trend among jurisdictions and draws from principles of reasonableness for both negligence or strict liability claims. The authors conducted an empirical study of mock jurors and found that jurors hearing the case under negligence language were more likely to find the defendant liable and award more in damages than the strict liability jurors. The study found no obvious advantages to plaintiffs from using strict liability language, challenging the notion that strict liability is generally a pro-plaintiff doctrine under courts' increasingly dominant approaches to design and warning cases.

The leading decision allowing triers of fact to find defendants liable for failing to warn of risks that were scientifically unknowable at the time the defendant distributed the product is Beshada v. Johns-Manville Products Corp., 447 A.2d 539 (N.J. 1982). The court concluded that imposing such liability was consistent with the "liability without fault" aspects of strict liability. It would also help to achieve the major goals of strict liability: risk spreading, accident avoidance, and simplification of proof at trial. Regarding the accident avoidance goal, the court observed that "[b]y imposing on manufacturers the costs of failure to discover hazards, we create an incentive for them to invest more actively in safety research." Id. at 548.

The New Jersey Supreme Court addressed the question of whether the holding in *Beshada* applied in prescription drug cases and held that it did not. See Feldman v. Lederle Laboratories, 479 A.2d 374 (N.J. 1984). The court first concluded that strict liability applied to drug manufacturers, and then proceeded to the question of whether or not *Beshada* applied:

> If *Beshada* were deemed to hold generally or in all cases, particularly with respect to a situation like the present one involving drugs vital to health, that in a warning context knowledge of the unknowable is irrelevant in determining the applicability of strict liability, we would not agree. Many commentators have criticized this aspect of the *Beshada* reasoning and the public policies on which it is based. The rationale of *Beshada* is not applicable to this case. We do not overrule *Beshada,* but restrict *Beshada* to the circumstances giving rise to its holding. We note, in passing, that, although not argued and determined in *Beshada,* there were or may have been data and other information generally available, aside from scientific knowledge, that arguably could have alerted the manufacturer at an early stage in the distribution of its product to the dangers associated with its use.
>
> In strict liability warning cases, unlike negligence cases, however, the defendant should properly bear the burden of proving that the information was not reasonably available or obtainable and that it therefore lacked actual or constructive knowledge of the defect. The defendant is in a superior position to know the technological material or data in the particular field or specialty. The defendant is the expert, often performing self-testing. It is the defendant that injected the product in the stream of commerce for its economic gain. As a matter of policy the burden of proving the status of knowledge in the field at the time of distribution is properly placed on the defendant. [Id. at 454-456, 479 A.2d at 387-388.]

As the excerpt from *Feldman,* above, indicates, most courts and commentators have rejected the proposition that product sellers should be strictly liable for harm caused by risks that were unknowable and unforeseeable at the time of sale. Comment *m* to §2 of the Restatement (Third) of Torts: Products Liability (1998) reflects the clear majority position on this issue.

> *m. Reasonably foreseeable uses and risks in design and warning claims.* Subsections (b) [design] and (c) [warnings] impose liability only when the product is put to uses that it is reasonable to expect a seller or distributor to foresee. Product sellers and distributors are not required to foresee and take precautions against every conceivable mode of use and abuse to which their products might be put. Increasing the costs of designing and marketing products in order to avoid the consequences of unreasonable modes of use is not required.
>
> In cases involving a claim of design defect in a mechanical product, forseeability of risk is rarely an issue as a practical matter. Once the plaintiff establishes that the product was put to a reasonably foreseeable use, physical risks of injury are generally known or reasonably knowable by experts in the field. It is not unfair to charge a manufacturer with knowledge of such generally known or knowable risks.
>
> The issue of foreseeability of risk of harm is more complex in the case of products such as prescription drugs, medical devices, and toxic chemicals. Risks attendant to use and consumption of these products may, indeed, be unforeseeable at the time of sale. Unforeseeable risks arising from foreseeable product use or consumption by definition cannot specifically be warned against. Thus, in connection with a claim of inadequate design, instruction, or warning, plaintiff should bear the burden of establishing that the risk in question was known or should have been known to the relevant manufacturing community. The harms that result from unforeseeable risks — for example, in the human body's reaction to a new drug, medical device, or chemical — are not a basis of liabil-

ity. Of course, a seller bears responsibility to perform reasonable testing prior to marketing a product and to discover risks and risk-avoidance measures that such testing would reveal. A seller is charged with knowledge of what reasonable testing would reveal. If testing is not undertaken, or is performed in an inadequate manner, and this failure results in a defect that causes harm, the seller is subject to liability for harm caused by such defect.

ILLUSTRATION:

15. ABC Adhesives Inc. manufactures a chemical adhesive for use in laying ceramic tile. Recently it has become known that prolonged use of its ceramic adhesive over many years by diabetics can cause severe aggravation of the diabetic condition. Diabetics who have been using the ABC adhesive and have suffered serious aggravation of their condition bring an action against ABC for failing to warn about the risks of prolonged product use. However, it cannot be established that, at the time ABC's product was distributed, special risks to diabetics were reasonably foreseeable or that reasonable testing of the product would have led to the discovery of the risks. ABC is not liable since the risks attendant to such product use were not reasonably foreseeable.

For support of the position taken in comment *m,* see, e.g., Vassallo v. Baxter Healthcare Corp., 696 N.E.2d 909, 923 (Mass. 1998) (overruling previous Massachusetts case law that imposed liability in failure to warn cases based on a "hindsight approach" and adopting the principles of the Products Liability Restatement in recognition of the "clear judicial trend" that defendant will not be held liable for failure to warn about risks that "were not reasonably foreseeable at the time of sale or could not have been discovered by way of reasonable testing prior to marketing the product."). Also see Fibreboard Corp. v. Fenton, 845 P.2d 1168 (Colo. 1993) (en banc), *reh'g denied* ("We agree with the petitioners that state-of-the-art evidence is properly admissible to establish that a product is not defective and unreasonably dangerous because of failure-to-warn. A manufacturer cannot warn of dangers that were not known to it or knowable in light of the generally recognized and prevailing scientific and technical knowledge available at the time of manufacture and distribution.); Payne v. Soft Sheen Prod., Inc., 486 A.2d 712, 721 (D.C. 1985); Woodill v. Parke Davis & Co., 402 N.E.2d 194, 198 (Ill. 1980) ("We perceive that requiring a plaintiff to plead and prove that the defendant manufacturer knew or should have known of the danger that caused the injury, and that the defendant manufacturer failed to warn plaintiff of that danger, is a reasonable requirement, and one which focuses on the nature of the product and the adequacy of the warning, rather than on the conduct of the manufacturer."). But see Sternhagen v. Dow Co., 935 P.2d 1139, 1142-46 (Mont. 1997) (rejecting a "state of the art" defense to failure-to-warn causes of action as contrary to strict products liability, despite recognition of the principles of the Restatement (Third) of Torts: Products Liability, and instead applying "imputation of knowledge doctrine" whereby the manufacturer is deemed to have knowledge of a "product's undiscovered or undiscoverable dangers" as "more consistent with existing Montana law" because such doctrine "reinforces" the courts' "commitment to provide maximum protection for consumers, while still assuring 'an appropriate limitation to a manufacturer's liability'"); Durden v. Hydro Flam Corp., 983 P.2d 943, at 952 (Mont. 1999) (following *Sternhagen* and continuing to reject "state of the art defense" in strict products liability action because to adopt it would inject negligence principles into strict liability law).

The overwhelming majority of commentators have argued against imputing time-of-trial knowledge to a product seller. See generally Patricia M. Danzon,

Tort Reform and the Role of Government in Private Insurance Markets, 13 J. Legal Stud. 3 (1984); James A. Henderson, Jr., Coping with the Time Dimension in Products Liability, 69 Calif. L. Rev. 919 (1981); Alan Schwartz, Products Liability, Corporate Structure, and Bankruptcy: Toxic Substances and the Remote Risk Relationship, 14 J. Legal Stud. 689 (1985); John W. Wade, On the Effect in Product Liability of Knowledge Unavailable Prior to Marketing, 58 N.Y.U. L. Rev. 734 (1983); Ellen Wertheimer, Unknowable Dangers and the Death of Strict Products Liability: The Empire Strikes Back, 60 U. of Cin. L. Rev. 1183 (1992) (arguing against the majority rule and finding that the overwhelming majority of cases refuse to impute time-of-trial knowledge to a manufacturer).

LIABILITY INSURANCE AND LONG-TAIL, UNKNOWABLE RISKS

Beshada and the asbestos liability litigation of which it is part present two important issues involving liability insurance. First, can manufacturers adequately insure against risks that are unknown at the time the products are distributed? Second, regarding liability insurance actually in place (whether or not it is adequate), as of what time does the plaintiff's "bodily injury" (the insured-against event) occur for purposes of determining which of several insurance policies covers the liability in question?

Regarding the first of these issues, a number of commentators have argued that manufacturers cannot, by hypothesis, insure against risks no one knows exist. As a consequence, when liability is later imposed strictly, based on hindsight, all they can do is charge the losses against earnings or capital, or go out of business. Either way, inefficiencies result. See generally Patricia M. Danzon, Tort Reform and the Role of Government in Private Insurance Markets, 13 J. Legal Stud. 517 (1984); Alan Schwartz, Products Liability, Corporate Structure and Bankruptcy: Toxic Substances and the Remote Risk Relationship, 14 J. Legal Stud. 689 (1985). Of course, this begs the question of whether efficiency ought to be an overriding consideration. For an argument that fairness reasons do not support hindsight-based strict liability, see generally James A. Henderson, Jr., Coping with the Time Dimension in Products Liability, 69 Calif. L. Rev. 919 (1981). For a contrary perspective, see Joseph A. Page, Generic Product Risks: The Case against Comment *k* and for Strict Liability, 58 N.Y.U. L. Rev. 853 (1983).

Regarding the issue of which liability policy should cover a risk that took 20 or 30 years (from first distribution to full manifestation of plaintiff's injury) to materialize, courts have disagreed. The problem in these cases stems from the fact that typically a number of different insurers wrote liability coverage over the relevant period, and the policy language is ambiguous. Some courts have held that insurers who wrote liability coverage during the period of the plaintiff's exposure should be "on the risk." See, e.g., Insurance Co. of N. Am. v. Forty-Eight Insulations, Inc., 633 F.2d 1212 (6th Cir. 1980), *cert. denied*, 454 U.S. 1109 (1981). Other courts have held that it should be insurers under policies in effect when the plaintiff first manifests his injury. See, e.g., Eagle-Picher Industries, Inc. v. Liberty Mutual Insurance Co., 682 F.2d 12 (6th Cir. 1982), *cert. denied*, 460 U.S. 1028 (1983). And still others have held that insurers at both points in time are liable under their policies. See, e.g., Keene Corp. v. Insurance Co. of N. Am., 667 F.2d 1034 (D.C. Cir. 1981), *cert. denied*, 455 U.S. 1007 (1982).

Apart from the question of whether to hold product sellers liable for harm caused by risks that are unknown and unknowable at the time of sale, the *Anderson* decision raises the question of how to conceptualize the failure-to-warn claim for purposes of allowing the plaintiff to plead and argue separate negligence and strict liability counts on the same facts in the same case. Consider the following decision.

Olson v. Prosoco, Inc.
522 N.W.2d 284 (Iowa 1994)

SNELL, Justice.

I. Facts

David Olson is a bricklayer foreman employed by Seedorf Masonry Company (Seedorf). Late on the afternoon of December 15, 1988, Olson spotted a fifteen gallon drum of mortar cleaner sitting on the ground. To prevent the cleaner drum from freezing to the ground, he picked it up and moved it onto a nearby pallet. When Olson dropped the drum on the pallet, the bung closure popped out of the drum, splashing hydrochloric acid based cleaner into his right eye. Despite extensive medical care, Olson eventually lost sight in his right eye. In April 1991 doctors fitted Olson with an artificial eye.

The mortar cleaner, called "Sure Klean 600," is manufactured and packaged by Prosoco. The fifteen gallon drum into which Prosoco packages the cleaner is manufactured by Delta Drum Corporation (Delta Drum). The bung closures used in the fifteen gallon drums are manufactured by Rieke Corporation (Rieke). Olson initially named Rieke and Delta Drum in this lawsuit. Rieke and Delta Drum settled their cases with Olson. Olson sued Prosoco under several theories of strict liability and negligence. Prosoco requested a state-of-the-art defense jury instruction with regard to Olson's strict liability and negligence theories. The jury found Prosoco one-hundred percent at fault for Olson's injuries under both theories.

II. Strict Liability and Negligence Claims . . .

Prosoco contends the submission of instructions on both strict liability and negligence theories was duplicative and confusing, resulting in prejudicial error. . . .

Olson contends the submission of a strict liability instruction does not preclude liability based on a negligence theory. He stresses that our decision in *Hillrichs* was limited strictly to the facts of that case and claims that in the case at bar the strict liability and negligence instructions submitted do not depend on the same elements of proof. . . .

Generally, there are two competing views regarding the failure to warn/strict liability question. The first is that there is little, if any, difference between strict liability and negligence in failure to warn cases. Opposing this view are cases that apply varying forms of a strict liability analysis in failure to warn cases. Some jurisdictions impose strict liability by imputing knowledge of a product's propensity to injure as it did to a defendant-manufacturer, and then asking the jury: With such knowledge would the defendant have been negligent in selling the product without a warning?

Other jurisdictions apply strict liability by requiring plaintiffs to prove defendants knew or should have known of the danger. . . . A different analysis is made in some cases to distinguish strict liability from negligence concepts in failure to warn cases on the ground that in negligence the focus is on the defendant's conduct, while in strict liability, the focus is on the condition of the product.

After reviewing the authorities and comments on the failure to warn question, we believe any posited distinction between strict liability and negligence principles is illusory. We fail to see any distinction between negligence and strict liability in the analyses of those jurisdictions injecting a knowledge requirement into their strict liability/failure to warn equation. The standard applied by these "strict liability" jurisdictions is exactly the same in practice as holding defendants to an expert standard of care under a negligence theory. The burden on plaintiffs is the same. They must prove a defendant knew or should have known of potential risks associated with the use of its product, yet failed to provide adequate directions or warnings to users. With regard to those jurisdictions imputing to defendants knowledge of its product's propensity to injure as it did, we have refused in the past to impose a duty upon manufacturers to warn of unknowable dangers.

We also find the product/conduct distinction made by several jurisdictions to justify maintaining a strict liability/failure to warn theory of little practical significance. See, e.g., Anderson, 281 Cal. Rptr. at 537, 810 P.2d at 558. According to courts taking stock in this distinction, under a strict liability theory the focus is on the unreasonably dangerous condition of the product. In contrast, these courts hold the question in negligence cases is whether the defendant's conduct breached a duty to exercise reasonable care. In practice, the courts basing the application of a strict liability theory on this distinction cannot help but slip back into the type of analyses virtually identical to those employed in negligence cases. Inevitably the conduct of the defendant in a failure to warn case becomes the issue. . . .

Maintaining the distinction to justify submission of failure to warn claims under both strict liability and negligence theories is a vain effort. We hold it was error to submit instructions regarding Prosoco's failure to warn under both negligence and strict liability theories. . . . Both instructions essentially required the jury to determine whether Prosoco negligently failed to warn users of the dangers in moving or using Sure Klean 600 in fifteen gallon containers.

We believe that the correct submission of instructions regarding a failure to warn claim for damages is under a theory of negligence and the claim should not be submitted as a theory of strict liability. In testing the defendant's liability for negligence in failing to warn, the defendant should be held to the standard of care of an expert in its field. The relevant inquiry therefore is whether the reasonable manufacturer knew or should have known of the danger, in light of the generally recognized and prevailing best scientific knowledge, yet failed to provide adequate warning to users or consumers. . . .

In reviewing the instructions given on the theory of negligence, we find that the claim of failure to warn as submitted substantially invoked this standard. Special verdict form No. 1 found Prosoco one-hundred percent liable on the claim of negligence. Also submitted by a special verdict form was the claim of strict liability under which the jury found Prosoco one-hundred percent at fault.

We have reversed and remanded cases where a general verdict of liability resulted from the submission of two theories, one of which contained an error in the instructions. . . . In these situations, we were unable to determine that the verdict resulted from a theory that was free of error. . . . However, in the case at bar, the special verdicts are sufficiently insulated from each other to stand on their own. We do not believe the error in submitting a failure to warn instruction as part of the strict liability claim had any prejudicial effect on the jury's consideration of the same issue contained in the negligence claim. . . .

We have considered all of the arguments and issues raised by Prosoco in this appeal. No reversible error has occurred. The judgment entered by the trial court is affirmed.

Affirmed.

4. Informed Choice Warnings

The terminology of "informed choice" bothers some people. (See Authors' Dialogue 14, infra.) Obviously, a product user or consumer's threshold decision not to use or consume the product in the first instance has risk-reduction implications, but these materials reserve the phrase "risk reduction warnings" for situations in which adequately informed users and consumers can "have their cake and eat it too"—situations in which, when adequate instructions and warnings are given, they can go ahead and derive the benefits from use or consumption and yet reduce or avoid the risks of which the instructions and warnings inform them. In contrast, the phrase "informed choice" connotes an "eat the cake or don't eat it" situation. As with all legal distinctions, this one gives way under pressure. Even in a classic case of the product user being able to use the product more safely thanks to clear warnings, the user may also decide to reduce his level of usage to reduce the residual risks of injury. And even when the warning says "One out of one million people who take this drug become blind as a result," the consumer who chooses to go ahead and take it can be on the lookout for early symptoms that might reduce the severity of his injury if he turns out (inescapably, once he decides to consume) to be one of the unlucky few. But products liability mavens have come to recognize that informed choice deserves to be distinguished from risk reduction.

The earliest case recognizing a products liability informed choice cause of action is Davis v. Wyeth Laboratories, Inc., 399 F.2d 121 (9th Cir. 1968). In that case, the defendant manufacturer sold polio vaccine without warning of the risk that one person in a million would contract polio from taking the vaccine. The court held that the manufacturer had a duty to warn the consumer of the risks involved and that the failure to meet this duty rendered the drug "unfit" and "unreasonably dangerous" within the meaning of §402A. The court stated:

> In such cases, then the drug is fit and its danger is reasonable only if the balance is struck in favor of its use. Where the risk is otherwise known to the consumer, no problem is presented, since a choice is available. Where not known, however, the drug can properly be marketed only in such fashion as to permit the striking of the balance; that is, by full disclosure of the existence and extent of the risk involved. . . .
>
> There will, of course, be cases where the personal risk, although existent and known, is so trifling in comparison with the advantage to be gained as to be de minimis. Ap-

The Basic Duty to Warn at Time of Sale

pellee so characterizes this case. It would approach the problem from a purely statistical point of view; less than one out of a million is just not unreasonable. This approach we reject. When, in a particular case, the risk qualitatively (e.g., of death or major disability) as well as quantitatively, on balance with the end sought to be achieved, is such as to call for a true choice judgment, medical or professional, the warning must be given. 399 F.2d at 129-30.

The informed choice theory was extended beyond prescription drugs to impose liability against asbestos manufacturers in favor of industrial insulation workers who suffered asbestosis and mesothelioma after exposure over a 30-year period to insulation products containing asbestos. In Borel v. Fiberboard Paper Products Corp., 493 F.2d 1076 (5th Cir. 1973) *cert. denied,* 419 U.S. 869 (1974) the court held that under §402A "a seller has a responsibility to inform users and consumers of dangers which the seller either knows or should know at the time the product is sold. The requirement that the danger be reasonably foreseeable, or scientifically discoverable, is an important limitation of the seller's liability." The court acknowledged that the "requirement of foreseeability coincides with the standard of due care in negligence cases in that a seller must exercise reasonable care and foresight to discover a danger in his product and to warn users and consumers of that danger."

The court went on to note that the utility of insulation products containing asbestos may outweigh the known foreseeable risk to insulation workers and thus justify their marketing. But it reasoned that the failure to give adequate warnings may render the products unreasonably dangerous. The court said:

> The rationale for this rule is that the user or consumer is entitled to make his own choice as to whether the product's utility or benefits justify exposing himself to the risk of harm. Thus, a true choice situation arises, and a duty to warn attaches, whenever a reasonable man would want to be informed of the risk in order to decide whether to expose himself to it. Id. at 1089.

Comment *i* to §2 of the Products Liability Restatement agrees with the thrust of these cases. It provides:

> *i. Inadequate instructions or warnings* . . .
> In addition to alerting users and consumers to the existence and nature of product risks so that they can, by appropriate conduct during use or consumption, reduce the risk of harm, warnings also may be needed to inform users and consumers of nonobvious and not generally known risks that unavoidably inhere in using or consuming the product. Such warnings allow the user or consumer to avoid the risk warned against by making an informed decision not to purchase or use the product at all and hence not to encounter the risk. In this context, warnings must be provided for inherent risks that reasonably foreseeable product users and consumers would reasonably deem material or significant in deciding whether to use or consume the product. Whether or not many persons would, when warned, nonetheless decide to use or consume the product, warnings are required to protect the interests of those reasonably foreseeable users or consumers who would, based on their own reasonable assessments of the risks and benefits, decline product use or consumption. When such warnings are necessary, their omission renders the product not reasonably safe at time of sale. Notwithstanding the defective condition of the product in the absence of adequate warnings, if a particular user or consumer would have decided to use or consume even if warned, the lack of warnings is not a legal cause of that plaintiff's harm. Judicial decisions supporting the duty to

provide warnings for informed decisionmaking have arisen almost exclusively with regard to those toxic agents and pharmaceutical products with respect to which courts have recognized a distinctive need to provide risk information so that recipients of the information can decide whether they wish to purchase or utilize the product. . . .

In Watkins v. Ford Motor Co., 190 F.3d 1213 (11th Cir. 1999), the plaintiff claimed that the defendant failed adequately to warn of the risks of rollover in a Ford Bronco II. Ford argued that no driver could have prevented the emergency situation that led to the rollover that injured the plaintiff. Quoting Comment *i,* supra, the court held that a warning might have led the plaintiff not to take the risk in the first instance. Id. at 1219. See also McArdle v. Navistar International Corp., 762 N.E.2d 137 (Ind. Ct. App. 2002) (reversing summary judgment for defendant where passenger claims that he would not have ridden in automobile at all if warnings regarding station wagon buckling following rear-impact collision had been given).

PROBLEM NINETEEN

You just received the following memorandum from a partner in the law firm in which you are an associate:

Memorandum

To: Associate
From: Barb Fischel
Subject: Applicability of strict liability in *Borel*-type cases

I am working on a case in which our client, Jeffrey Polsby, is dying from liver cancer that we maintain was caused by his exposure to chemical solvents at his workplace over a period of 17 years. We claim that the defendant solvent manufacturer failed adequately to warn our client of the cancer risks associated with long-term exposure to its product. The case is fairly close to *Borel* on its facts, and I think we will reach the jury on our failure-to-warn count against the manufacturer.

One aspect of the case bothers me, however, and I would like your reactions to it. Our case on behalf of Mr. Polsby is weaker than *Borel* in one respect — the manufacturer in our case did supply the employer with warning signs which the employer posted in the shop where Polsby worked. The signs told the workers that continued exposure to the solvent could cause serious liver damage, and instructed them to wear latex gloves while using the solvent and to avoid direct contact with the skin. We insist that the warnings were inadequate (no mention of cancer, foreseeable that workers would ignore signs when no symptoms had appeared after years of exposure, etc.), but we could lose on this issue. What bothers me is why the manufacturer should get off the hook even if the warnings are found to be adequate.

Our investigation into the background data reveals that approximately one out of 20,000 or so workers will develop liver cancer (a greater-than-normal cancer rate) from long-term exposure (eight years or longer) to the solvent, notwithstanding efforts to avoid direct contact. Suppose that the manufacturer had spelled that fact out in grisly detail in its warnings: "You have a one in 20,000 chance of getting liver cancer if you choose to continue to work with this product, compared with a one in 200,000 chance in the general population not exposed to the product. Thus, your chances of getting liver cancer, while still remote, will be ten times greater than would otherwise be the case if you were not exposed to this product." Let us assume that such a warning, posted on the worker's first day of exposure to the solvent, would meet the test set forth in Borel v. Fibreboard. My question is why that should get the manufacturer off the liability hook. Imagine that the worker had gone into a new car dealership and bought a new automobile. If a sign were posted on the windshield: "Warning! There is a 1/20,000 chance that this vehicle contains a latent defect that will cause a harmful accident!" would that get the manufacturer off the hook if a defect caused a harmful accident? Of course not — Henningsen v. Bloomfield Motors taught us that much before I went to law school. So why should a "1/20,000 warning" about liver cancer be treated differently?

Putting the question a little differently, if *Henningsen* teaches us that consumers are not in a position to understand and act intelligently in reaction to warnings about remote risks of defect-caused injury, why should the manufacturer in our chemical solvent case be allowed to escape liability on that basis? If you think there is something to my argument that *Borel's* reliance on the idea of "consumer choice" is misplaced, then I am inclined to want to include it in my trial brief, in case we can't sell the judge and jury on our view of the facts.

Respond to the partner's memorandum.

Now for an eye-opener. In the following case, Judge Guido Calabresi has taken this informed choice theory and moved it into an entirely new sphere.

Liriano v. Hobart Corp.
170 F.3d 264 (2d Cir. 1999)

CALABRESI, Circuit Judge:

In Liriano v. Hobart Corp., 132 F.3d 124 (2d Cir. 1998) ("Liriano I"), we certified to the New York Court of Appeals the question of whether a manufacturer can be liable under a failure-to-warn theory in a case in which the substantial modification defense would preclude liability under a design defect theory. We also certified the question of whether, if failure-to-warn liability could exist, it would nonetheless be unavailable as a matter of law on the facts of the present case. The New York Court of Appeals answered the first question in the affirmative and declined to answer the second. See Liriano v. Hobart Corp., 700 N.E.2d 303 (1998) ("Liriano II"). Consequently, we now address the second question ourselves, and we find it to be a close one. Viewing the facts, as we must, in the light most favorable to the plaintiff, we resolve that question in the negative. We also find that all other claims the appellants have raised on appeal lack merit. We therefore affirm the decision of the district court granting judgment and damages for the plaintiff. . . .

Background

[The following recitation of the facts is taken from "Liriano I."]

Luis Liriano, a seventeen-year-old employee in the meat department at Super Associated grocery store ("Super"), was injured on the job in September 1993 when he was feeding meat into a commercial meat grinder whose safety guard had been removed. His hand was caught in the "worm" that grinds the meat; as a result, his right hand and lower forearm were amputated.

The meat grinder was manufactured and sold in 1961 by Hobart Corporation ("Hobart"). At the time of the sale, it had an affixed safety guard that prevented the user's hands from coming into contact with the feeding tube and the grinding "worm." No warnings were placed on the machine or otherwise given to indicate that it was dangerous to operate the machine without the safety guard in place. Subsequently, Hobart became aware that a significant number of purchasers of its meat grinders had removed the safety guards. And in 1962, Hobart began issuing warnings on its meat grinders concerning removal of the safety guard.

There is no dispute that, when Super acquired the grinder, the safety guard was intact. It is also not contested that, at the time of Liriano's accident, the safety guard had been removed. There is likewise no doubt that Hobart actually knew, before the accident, that removals of this sort were occurring and that use of the machine without the safety guard was highly dangerous. And Super does not question that the removal of the guard took place while the grinder was in its possession.

Liriano sued Hobart under several theories, including failure to warn. Hobart brought a third-party claim against Super. The United States District Court . . . dismissed all of Liriano's claims except the one based on failure to warn, and the jury returned a verdict for Liriano on that claim. It attributed five percent of the liability to Hobart and ninety-five percent to Super. The district court then held a partial retrial limited to the issue of whether and to what extent Liriano was responsible for his own injury. On that retrial, the jury assigned Liriano one-third of the fault. . . .

Hobart and Super appealed, arguing (1) that as a matter of law, there was no duty to warn, and (2) that even if there had been a duty to warn, the evidence presented was not sufficient to allow the failure-to-warn claim to reach the jury. . . . We certified questions (1) and (2) to the New York Court of Appeals. That Court answered question (1) in Liriano's favor, saying that there can indeed be a duty to warn in a case like this one. The Court of Appeals, however, declined to answer question (2). . . .

Discussion

A. Sufficiency of the Evidence

Hobart makes two arguments challenging the sufficiency of the evidence. The first concerns the obviousness of the danger that Liriano faced, and the second impugns the causal relationship between Hobart's negligence and Liriano's injury.

Each of these arguments implicates issues long debated in the law of torts. With respect to the asserted clarity of the danger, the question is when a danger is so obvious that a court can determine, as a matter of law, that no additional warning is required. With respect to causation, the issue is whether a jury may infer that a defendant's particular negligence was the cause-in-fact of a plaintiff's actual injury from the general fact that negligence like the defendant's tends to cause injuries like the plaintiff's. . . .

(1) Obviousness

The courts of New York have several times . . . ruled that judges should be very wary of taking the issue of liability away from juries, even in situations where the relevant dangers might seem obvious, and especially when the cases in question turn on particularized facts. See, e.g., . . . Cabri v. Long Island R.R. Co., 306 N.Y. 765, 118 N.E.2d 475 (1954) (holding that the danger of crossing railroad tracks is not so obvious as to prevent the issue of contributory negligence from reaching the jury). . . .

But the . . . tendency of the New York Court of Appeals to permit issues of obviousness to go to the jury do not fully dispose of the question before us. . . . And it is not surprising that there have been situations in which New York state courts have deemed dangers to be sufficiently clear so that warnings were, as a matter of law, not necessary. See, e.g., Dickerson v. George J. Meyer Mfg., . . . 669 N.Y.S.2d 1001, 1002 (4th Dep't 1998) (holding that there is no duty to warn of the danger of closely examining the mechanical workings of a machine while the machine is operating); Pigliavento v. Tyler Equip. Corp., . . . 669 N.Y.S.2d 747, 749 (3d Dep't 1998) (holding that there is no duty to warn of the danger of falling from an unguarded platform on a concrete mixer truck); Carvis v. Mele, . . . 521 N.Y.S.2d 260, 261 (2d Dep't 1987) (holding that there is no duty to warn of the danger of diving headfirst into an above-ground swimming pool only four feet deep).

If the question before us were, therefore, simply whether meat grinders are sufficiently known to be dangerous so that manufacturers would be justified in believing that further warnings were not needed, we might be in doubt. On one hand, . . . most New Yorkers would probably appreciate the danger of meat grinders [without warning]. Any additional warning might seem superfluous. On the other hand, Liriano was only seventeen years old at the time of his injury and had only recently immigrated to the United States. He had been on the job at Super for only one week. He had never been given instructions about how to use the meat grinder, and he had used the meat grinder only two or three times. And, as Judge Scheindlin noted, the mechanism that injured Liriano would not have been visible to someone who was operating the grinder. It could be argued that such a combination of facts was not so unlikely that a court should say, as a matter of law, that the defendant could not have foreseen them or, if aware of them, need not have guarded against them by issuing a warning. That argument would draw strength from the Court of Appeals' direction that the question of whether a warning was needed must be asked in terms of the information available to the injured party rather than the injured party's employer, 700 N.E.2d at 308, and its added comment that "in cases where reasonable minds might disagree as to the extent of the plaintiff's knowledge of the hazard, the question is one for the jury." Id.

Nevertheless, it remains the fact that meat grinders are widely known to be dangerous. Given that the position of the New York courts on the specific question before us is anything but obvious, we might well be of two minds as to whether a failure to warn that meat grinders are dangerous would be enough to raise a jury issue.

But to state the issue that way would be to misunderstand the complex functions of warnings. As two distinguished torts scholars have pointed out, a warning can do more that exhort its audience to be careful. It can also affect what activities the people warned choose to engage in. See James A. Henderson, Jr., and Aaron D. Twerski, Doctrinal Collapse in Products Liability: The Empty Shell of Failure to Warn, 65 N.Y.U. L. Rev. 265, 285 (1990). And where the function of a warning is to assist the reader in making choices, the value of the warning can lie as much in making known the existence of alternatives as in communicating the fact that a particular choice is dangerous. It follows that the duty to warn is not necessarily obviated merely because a danger is clear.

To be more concrete, a warning can convey at least two types of messages. One states that a particular place, object, or activity is dangerous. Another explains that people need not risk the danger posed by such a place, object, or activity in order to achieve the purpose for which they might have taken that risk. Thus, a highway sign that says "Danger—Steep Grade" says less than a sign that says "Steep Grade Ahead—Follow Suggested Detour to Avoid Dangerous Areas."

If the hills or mountains responsible for the steep grade are plainly visible, the first sign merely states what a reasonable person would know without having to be warned. The second sign tells drivers what they might not have otherwise known: that there is another road that is flatter and less hazardous. A driver who believes the road through the mountainous area to be the only way to reach her destination might well choose to drive on that road despite the steep grades, but a driver who knows herself to have an alternative might not, even though her understanding of the risks posed by the steep grade is exactly the same as those of the first driver. Accordingly, a certain level of obviousness as to the grade of a road might, in principle, eliminate the reason for posting a sign of the first variety. But no matter how patently steep the road, the second kind of sign might still have a beneficial effect. As a result, the duty to post a sign of the second variety may persist even when the danger of the road is obvious and a sign of the first type would not be warranted.

One who grinds meat, like one who drives on a steep road, can benefit not only from being told that his activity is dangerous, but from being told of a safer way. As we have said, one can argue about whether the risk involved in grinding meat is sufficiently obvious that a responsible person would fail to warn of that risk, believing reasonably that it would convey no helpful information. But if it is also the case—as it is—that the risk posed by meat grinders can feasibly be reduced by attaching a safety guard, we have a different question. Given that attaching guards is feasible, does reasonable care require that meat workers be informed that they need not accept the risks of using unguarded grinders? Even if most ordinary users may—as a matter of law—know of the risk of using a guardless meat grinder, it does not follow that a sufficient number of them will — as a matter of law — also know that protective guards are available, that using them is a realistic possibility, and that they may ask that such guards be used. It is precisely these last pieces of information that a reasonable manufacturer may have a duty to convey even if the danger of using a grinder were itself deemed obvious.

Consequently, the instant case does not require us to decide the difficult question of whether New York would consider the risk posed by meat grinders to be obvious as a matter of law. A jury could reasonably find that there exist people who are employed as meat grinders and who do not know (a) that it is feasible to reduce the risk with safety guards, (b) that such guards are made available with the grinders, and (c) that the grinders should be used only with the guards. Moreover, a jury can also reasonably find that there are enough such people, and that warning them is sufficiently inexpensive, that a reasonable manufacturer would inform them that safety guards exist and that the grinder is meant to be used only with such guards. Thus, even if New York would consider the danger of meat grinders to be obvious as a matter of law, that obviousness does not substitute for the warning that a jury could, and indeed did, find that Hobart had a duty to provide. It follows that we cannot say, as a matter of law, that Hobart had no duty to warn Liriano in the present case. We therefore decline to adopt appellants' argument that the issue of negligence was for the court only and that the jury was not entitled, on the evidence, to return a verdict for Liriano.

(2) Causation

On rebriefing following the Court of Appeals decision, Hobart has made another argument as to why the jury should not have been allowed to find for the plaintiff. In this argument, Hobart raises the issue of causation. It maintains that Liriano "failed to present any evidence that Hobart's failure to place a warning [on the machine] was causally related to his injury." Whether or not there had been a warning, Hobart says, Liriano might well have operated the machine as he did and suffered the injuries that he suffered. Liriano introduced no evidence, Hobart notes, suggesting either that he would have refused to grind meat had the machine borne a warning or that a warning would have persuaded Super not to direct its employees to use the grinder without the safety attachment.

Hobart's argument about causation follows logically from the notion that its duty to warn in this case merely required Hobart to inform Liriano that a guard was available and that he should not use an unguarded grinder. The contention is tightly reasoned, but it rests on a false premise. It assumes that the burden was on Liriano to introduce additional evidence showing that the failure to warn was a but-for cause of his injury, even after he had shown that Hobart's wrong greatly increased the likelihood of the harm that occurred. But Liriano does not bear that burden. When a defendant's negligent act is deemed wrongful precisely because it has a strong propensity to cause the type of injury that ensued, that very causal tendency is evidence enough to establish a *prima facie* case of cause-in-fact. The burden then shifts to the defendant to come forward with evidence that its negligence was *not* such a but-for cause. . . .

The district court did not err. We affirm its decision in all respects.

authors' dialogue 14

JIM: I don't like this "informed choice" terminology.

AARON: Why not? I think it's, well, informative.

JIM: I agree it captures the "threshold decision to use or consume" aspects of these cases, but that bit of clarity comes at a high price. "Informed choice" sounds too much like "informed consent" from medical malpractice.

AARON: What's wrong with that? The two situations are quite analogous, I think.

JIM: No, they're not. Informed consent in malpractice conjures notions of the patient consenting to physical contacts that would otherwise constitute highly offensive invasions of the patient's personal dignity. It has the feel of battery law about it. Personal sovereignty is at issue.

AARON: You're talking ancient history, Jim. In medical malpractice informed consent in most states no longer involves battery. It's now part of the law of negligence, much less personal.

JIM: Reasonableness may be the test for what a doctor must tell the patient, but from there on it has the look and feel of battery. If the doc doesn't get informed consent, the doc is strictly liable for bad outcomes. But let's not rehash malpractice law. In the products setting, the personal invasion implications of "informed choice" can led to remarkably wrong-headed conclusions.

AARON: Give us an example. You're losing me.

JIM: *Liriano* is the poster-child. When Judge Calabresi invokes the idea of informed choice on behalf of the young worker, he transforms the case into an invasion of the plaintiff's personal dignity. All of a sudden, instead of being concerned with whether a warning would've saved the kid's arm, it becomes a matter of punishing the manufacturer for not having treated him with sufficient respect to tell him that an alternative – the safety guard – was theoretically available. Even if the kid couldn't do anything about it, the manufacturer became implicated in the employer's exploitation of immigrant laborers.

AARON: Even if your diagnosis is accurate, I'm not sure that's so bad in that case. By keeping the manufacturer on the hook, even by using the "pixie dust" of informed choice, almost all of the liability ended up, via contribution, where it belonged – in the employer's lap.

JIM: Your last point is some comfort. But using informed choice that way is bound to cause mischief down the road, don't you agree?

AARON: Let me think about it before I make an informed decision whether to use or consume your conclusions.

For a holding directly contrary to *Liriano,* see Chaney v. Hobart International, Inc., 54 F. Supp. 2d 677 (E.D. La. 1999). On facts almost identical to *Liriano* the court granted defendant's motion for summary judgment on plaintiff's claim that adequate warning was not provided about the dangers of using the meat grinder without a feed pan in place.

> As dangerous as the meat grinder may have been without a feed pan guard, it was clearly "not dangerous to an extent beyond that which would be contemplated by the ordinary consumer." The possibility of injury is glaring.

For a thoughtful analysis of *Liriano* and the informed-choice approach to duty to warn, see Robert G. Knaier, Note, An Informed-Choice Duty to Instruct? Liriano, Burke, and the Practical Limits of Subtle Jurisprudence, 88 Cornell L. Rev. 814 (2003), in which the author argues that *Liriano* recognized a subtle, but coherent, duty to warn. He cautions, however, that *Liriano* threatens to undermine practical limitations on liability by enabling nearly every well-plead failure to warn claim to reach the jury. For a sharp critique of *Liriano,* see Hildy Bowbeer and David S. Killorian, Liriano v. Hobart Corporation: Obvious Dangers, The Duty to Warn of Safe Alternatives and the Heeding Presumption, 65 Brook. L. Rev. 717 (1999).

B. WHO MUST WARN WHOM?

Persons v. Salomon North America, Inc.
265 Cal. Rptr. 773 (Cal. Ct. App. 1990)

SCOTLAND, J.

Plaintiff brought this action to recover damages for personal injuries sustained in a skiing accident. Before trial, plaintiff entered into a sliding scale settlement agreement with The Cornice Ski and Sport, Inc. ("Cornice"), where she rented skis equipped with Salomon 444 ski bindings; settled with United Merchandising, doing business as Big 5 Sporting Goods, where she purchased her ski boots; dismissed her action against defendant Mammoth Mountain Ski Area, Inc., where she skied on the date of her accident, and dismissed her action against defendant Edison Brothers Stores, Inc., the successor in interest to United Sporting Goods, where she previously had purchased skis and ski bindings. The case was tried before a jury against the only remaining defendant, Salomon North America, Inc. ("Salomon"), the distributor and wholly owned subsidiary of the manufacturer of the bindings which Cornice affixed to the rental skis.

At trial, uncontradicted evidence established that the Salomon 444 bindings were incompatible with plaintiff's untreated thermoplastic boots. Thus, when plaintiff fell while skiing, the bindings did not release and her left knee was injured. Salomon was aware of the conflict between its bindings and thermoplastic boots. Although Salomon did not warn plaintiff that the bindings should not be used with her ski boots unless the boots were lubricated, evidence was presented from which the jury could find that Salomon had warned Cornice about the incompatibility and had given Cornice instructions on how to recognize and treat thermoplastic boots to avoid the problem.

The trial court denied plaintiff's motion for partial directed verdict, and the jury returned special verdicts in Salomon's favor.

Although not clearly delineating her primary claim of error, plaintiff appears to contend that the trial court erred in denying her motion for a partial directed verdict. Plaintiff argues that Salomon is strictly liable as a matter of law because it had a duty to warn plaintiff, the ultimate user of the bindings, about the aforesaid danger and failed to do so. We disagree. . . .

In determining the propriety of the trial court's ruling, we must consider the scope of Salomon's duty to warn of the danger posed by the incompatibility between its 444 bindings and untreated thermoplastic boots. On appeal, as she did in the trial court, plaintiff contends that Salomon had a duty, as a matter of law, to directly inform plaintiff, the ultimate user. Salomon retorts that its duty was fulfilled by the warning it gave Cornice. Salomon argues that it is impossible to directly warn those who rent bindings distributed by Salomon, thus defendant was entitled to rely on Cornice to pass Salomon's warning on to individuals to whom the ski shop rented skis equipped with Salomon 444 bindings. . . .

Strict liability generally focuses on the product to determine whether it is defective rather than on the actions of its manufacturer. This concept is readily applied in design or manufacturing cases where the defect is inherent in the product. However, in failure to warn cases where the product is both flawlessly designed and manufactured, the defect is not inherent in the product; rather, the product is rendered defective because of the actions of the manufacturer in failing to adequately warn of the dangerous propensities of its product. . . .

Thus, courts have recognized that the test for failure to warn under strict liability contains a standard of reasonableness. Factors such as "the normal expectations of the consumer as to how the product will perform, degrees of simplicity or complication in the operation or use of the product, the nature and magnitude of the danger to which the user is exposed, the likelihood of injury, and the feasibility and beneficial effect of including a warning" must be considered to determine whether a warning is necessary.

Another circumstance which should be considered is the reliability of a third party, e.g., a business intermediary, to convey the warning to the ultimate user. This factor is contained in Comment *n* to section 388 of the Restatement Second of Torts. Although Comment *n* relates to a product liability cause of action for negligent failure to warn where the manufacturer alerted only the intermediate distributors, we conclude that its factors also should apply to failure to warn under strict liability. . . .

With these general principles in mind, we first look to the feasibility of Salomon providing an effective warning directly to the ultimate consumer. Although there are few instances in today's marketplace where a product is delivered directly to the consumer from the factory which manufactured it, "[m]any . . . articles can be made to carry their own message to the understanding of those who are likely to use them by the form in which they are put out, by the container in which they are supplied or by a label or other device, indicating with a substantial sufficiency this dangerous character." (Rest. 2d Torts, §388, Comment *n*, p.310.) On the other hand, courts have recognized that the manufacturers and distributors of certain products may have no effective way to convey product warnings to the ultimate consumer. . . .

Considering the evidence adduced at trial, we perceive no practical method in which Salomon can provide an effective warning directly to the consumer who rents Salomon bindings from a ski shop. Plaintiff does not suggest that Salomon should have put a warning on or in the product container. Such a warning would be ineffective because the renter doesn't see the product container. The ski shop removes the bindings from their containers and affixes the bindings to skis which the shop rents to its customers. Rather, plaintiff argues that Salomon could have put a decal on its bindings stating, "Warning: Do not use with incompatible thermal plastic [sic] boots."

Plaintiff's suggestion ignores the testimony of her own expert. The thrust of that evidence is that Salomon failed to sufficiently warn Cornice of the danger because defendant's technical manuals did not contain adequate instructions on how to identify thermoplastic boots. The expert never asserted that Salomon should have notified plaintiff of the danger. To the contrary, it is clear from her expert's testimony that a statement affixed to the bindings simply warning plaintiff not to use them with incompatible thermoplastic ski boots would have been wholly ineffectual. Plaintiff's expert acknowledged that consumers would have difficulty distinguishing a thermoplastic boot from a hard plastic boot. In fact, the expert testified that even he "would have trouble walking into a ski store and arbitrarily seeing which boots are [thermoplastic] and which were not." Accordingly, a sufficient warning necessarily must include detailed instructions on how to identify thermoplastic boots. Since it took pages of trial transcript to set forth the methods of identifying thermoplastic boots, it takes little imagination to recognize that putting such an extensive warning directly on the minimal surface of the binding is not feasible.

The evidence establishes another reason why a warning on the binding is unworkable — it would have no beneficial effect for consumers who have no technical expertise. . . . According to plaintiff's expert, in order to identify a thermoplastic boot he would perform a "calibrated release check," a technical test requiring the use of a special measuring device. In the expert's view, using a fingernail test to determine the softness of the boot material and checking to see if the boot is stamped with a DIN marking (an industry standard relating to the characteristics of the boot) are not necessarily conclusive tests for identifying a thermoplastic boot. This evidence supports the opinion of defendant's expert who testified that a warning to the ultimate consumer would not have been helpful, because a typical user has insufficient knowledge and expertise to recognize thermoplastic boots and benefit from the warning. In fact, plaintiff's husband acknowledged that he and plaintiff did not know her boots were thermoplastic and relied on Cornice to provide appropriate equipment with proper safety adjustments.

In this respect, we see a parallel between this case and Stevens v. Cessna Aircraft Company, supra, 115 Cal. App. 3d 431, 170 Cal. Rptr. 925, a wrongful death action arising out of an airplane crash. In *Stevens,* the plaintiff claimed that Cessna was strictly liable because it failed to warn passengers about the load capacity of the plane it manufactured. Summary judgment was granted in favor of Cessna. Affirming, the appellate court noted: "The simple warning notice for the passenger compartment suggested by plaintiff would not be effective. Whether the plane can fly safely with a given total weight of passengers depends upon too many additional factors for a passenger to make an informed and intelligent judgment from such a notice . . . [T]he passenger necessarily depends upon the skill and judgment of the pilot to determine the load capacity of the airplane in light of the flying conditions to be encountered. Plaintiff's argument implies logically that numerous other bits of information should be posted in the passenger compartment to enable the passengers to second-guess the pilot on a myriad of flying decisions. It would be impossible ultimately to provide meaningful information to the passenger, and in the long run a rule requiring the manufacturer to provide such information directly to the passenger would not be in the interests of passenger safety." (Id., at pp.433-434, 170 Cal. Rptr. 925.)

Similarly, the evidence in this case sufficiently established that a direct warning to plaintiff would have been ineffective, and thus unnecessary, because of the ultimate user's lack of ability to make an informed judgment from such notice and the fact that the skier necessarily relies on the knowledge and technical expertise of the ski shop in selecting rental skis and bindings and making proper adjustments to set the bindings at an appropriate release level based on the skier's height, weight and skiing ability.

When a manufacturer or distributor has no effective way to convey a product warning to the ultimate consumer, the manufacturer should be permitted to rely on downstream suppliers to provide the warning. "Modern life would be intolerable unless one were permitted to rely to a certain extent on others doing what they normally do, particularly if it is their duty to do so." (Rest. 2d Torts, §388, Comment *n,* p.308.)

Here, Cornice was in the business of renting skis and bindings. It had an independent duty to exercise reasonable care in supplying this equipment and was itself subject to strict liability for failure to warn its customers of the dangerous propensities of articles it rented. . . .

The evidence establishes that Salomon 444 bindings do not pose a danger unless used with nonstandard or untreated thermoplastic boots. Once it has distributed its bindings to rental shops such as Cornice, Salomon has no practical way, other than warning and educating the rental shops of the danger, to control its product to see that the bindings are not used with untreated thermoplastic boots. Moreover, issuance of an effective warning depends upon proper identification of the skier's boot. Salomon cannot be expected to know the identity of the ultimate user of its rental bindings much less the type of boot the consumer is using. However, the ski shop technician has direct contact with each customer and has the ability, applying Salomon's technical manual and seminar training, to identify a customer's boot, assess its compatibility with Salomon bindings, lubricate the boot if necessary and set a safe release level.

Having provided a warning to Salomon dealers, defendant had a reasonable basis to believe Cornice would pass along the product warning and was justified in relying upon Cornice to perform its independent duty to warn as required by law. . . .

The judgment is affirmed.

BLEASE, Acting P.J., and MARLER, J., concur.

Who Must Warn Whom?

In Gonzalez v. Volvo of America Corp., 752 F.2d 295 (7th Cir. 1985), plaintiffs were injured when their Volvo station wagon ran off the road and overturned while pulling a U-Haul trailer. The plaintiffs claimed that a mismatch of the trailer hitch and the bumper caused the accident, and that defendant Volvo should have warned them about the risks. The court found for defendant Volvo as a matter of law:

> We acknowledge that Section 402A imposed upon Volvo a duty to provide plaintiffs with a reasonably safe station wagon. In our opinion, however, this duty did not extend to a requirement to warn them that a particular trailer hitch was unsafe to use, particularly when it was installed as appropriate by a company engaged in the business of renting trailers. The intervention of a professional such as U-Haul is the rule and not the exception when consumers rent trailer hitches. It was the duty of such professionals and not the duty of defendant-appellant to select an appropriate hitch for plaintiffs. Stated otherwise, the station wagon which defendant Volvo furnished to plaintiffs was not dangerous beyond the expectations of ordinary consumers. Ordinary consumers consult trailer lessors such as U-Haul when renting trailer hitches, a necessary addition if the trailer is to be utilized. It is the advice of such third parties, and not the warnings of automobile manufacturers upon which ordinary consumers do, and should be entitled to, rely. [Id. at 300.]

Courts differ regarding whether manufacturers of component parts owe a duty to warn ultimate users of risks associated with the products in which their components are foreseeably incorporated. The general subject of component manufacturers' liability is taken up in Section A of Chapter Nine, infra. But it is useful in this "who/whom" context to consider the question of the component manufacturer's duty to warn ultimate users and consumers. Thus, in Maake v. Ross Operating Valve Co., 717 P.2d 923 (Ariz. 1985), the court recognized such a duty. Defendant manufactured palm buttons and pneumatic valves that had been installed in a 60-year-old power press. Plaintiff suffered injury when the press cycled unexpectedly. Defendant had placed no warning, aimed at operators, on the safety devices that such cycling might occur. The court held that a jury might find defendant liable for failure to warn. More often than not courts deny a duty to warn ultimate users. Thus, in Frazier v. Materials Transportation Company, 609 F. Supp. 933 (W.D. Pa. 1985), the plaintiff was injured when he jumped from a hydraulic meat dumping machine. He had been standing on the machine while cleaning it. After raising himself by activating the lift, he found he could not reach the stop button. Fearful of being dumped into a large meat grinder below the dumping machine, he jumped to the floor below and suffered injuries. The plaintiff joined the manufacturer of switches that activated a circuit to show the position of the dumping machine, the manufacturer of the hydraulic mechanism, and the assembler of the machine, alleging that all should have warned him of the dangers of riding the machine, including the difficulties of stopping it. The court ruled for the component part manufacturers as a matter of law, concluding:

> We reject these contentions. Suppliers of component parts, no matter how small or insignificant, should not be held to inquire into their ultimate use and foresee all possible applications in order to satisfy a duty to warn of potential danger associated with the finished product. [Id. at 935.]

Whether a bulk supplier has a duty to warn all foreseeable users of the risks associated with a product's use also implicates a "who/whom" problem. In Hoffman v. Houghton Chemical Corp., 751 N.E.2d 848 (Mass. 2001), the Supreme Judicial Court of Massachusetts affirmed judgment in favor of the defendant, a bulk supplier of toluene, a highly volatile and flammable chemical allegedly involved in an explosion that killed two workers and injured several others at an ink plant. The court adopted the "bulk supplier doctrine" as an affirmative defense in products liability actions, reasoning that the nature of bulk products requires separate consideration and that the bulk suppliers should be able to rely on the intermediary's own obligation to provide safety measures for its end users. The court justified its holding as follows:

> Under the bulk supplier doctrine, the bulk supplier is by no means absolved of its duty either to supply adequate warnings to the intermediary or to ensure that its reliance on the intermediary is reasonable, but it is permitted to discharge its duty to warn in a practical and responsible way that equitably balances the realities of its business with the need for consumer safety. Id. at 857.

Prescription drugs present interesting variations on the "Who Must Warn Whom?" theme. We defer treatment of prescription drug cases until Section B of Chapter Nine, infra. But it is difficult to talk intelligently about the "Who/Whom?" question without anticipating some of the issues raised in prescription drug cases. Thus, in most instances the manufacturer of a prescription drug must supply relevant warnings to the prescribing physician rather than to the patient. The physician is the person who makes the risk-benefit calculus and recommends which drug be taken; the patient's role is essentially passive. But some courts are beginning to extend duties to warn patients directly. See, e.g., Perez v. Wyeth Laboratories, 734 A.2d 1245 (N.J. 1999). And courts have even extended drug manufacturers' duties to warn medical personnel other than the prescribing physicians when the circumstances warrant. For example, in Holley v. Burroughs Wellcome Co., 330 S.E.2d 228 (N.C. App. 1985), the plaintiff suffered severe and irreversible brain damage as a result of the improper administration of general anesthesia. The plaintiff contended that the manufacturers of the anesthesia and a muscle relaxant, which in combination led to the plaintiff's injury, failed to warn of the relevant risks. The defendants argued that the anesthesiologist who prescribed and administered the anesthesia admitted that he knew of the risks independently, and thus any failure to warn was not, as a matter of law, the proximate cause of the plaintiff's injury. The court rejected the defendants' argument on two grounds. First, the prescribing doctor's self-serving and unimpeachable testimony (he had settled the malpractice action against himself, and presumably wanted to appear well-informed in the products liability action) could not be allowed to defeat the plaintiff's cause of action as a matter of law. And second, even if it did serve to negate the claim based on defendants' failure to warn the doctor, the plaintiff still could succeed with his claim that the defendants also should have warned the doctor's assistant, a nurse anesthetist, who was otherwise ignorant of the relevant risks and who could have acted on adequate warnings to prevent the plaintiff's injury.

This underlying theme of the manufacturer's duty to warn including a duty to warn any and all persons who are in a position to act effectively on the information is captured in Comment *i* to §2(c) of the Products Liability Restatement:

Depending on the circumstances, Subsection (c) may require that instructions and warnings be given not only to purchasers, users, and consumers, but also to others who a reasonable seller should know will be in a position to reduce or avoid the risk of harm. There is no general rule as to whether one supplying a product for the use of others through an intermediary has a duty to warn the ultimate product user directly or may rely on the intermediary to relay warnings. The standard is one of reasonableness in the circumstances. Among the factors to be considered are the gravity of the risks posed by the product, the likelihood that the intermediary will convey the information to the ultimate user, and the feasibility and effectiveness of giving a warning directly to the user. Thus, when the purchaser of machinery is the owner of a workplace who provides the machinery to employees for their use, and there is reason to doubt that the employer will pass warnings on to employees, the seller is required to reach the employees directly with necessary instructions and warnings if doing so is reasonably feasible.

C. THE SUFFICIENCY OF THE DEFENDANT'S WARNING

Obviously, the question of whether the warnings accompanying the product are adequate blurs over into the question raised in Section A, supra, concerning the extent of the defendant seller's duty to warn. All of the cases in this Section C could, for example, be said to raise the issue of whether the defendant owed a duty to provide more specific, or more forceful, warnings. No great mischief is done when the concepts of duty and sufficiency are mingled together in this way. But strictly speaking, the two issues raise the separate issues of duty, on the one hand, and breach, on the other. Why would a defendant prefer to talk in "duty" terms? Could it have something to do with the tradition that holds that questions of duty are questions of law, for the judge, and questions of breach are questions of fact, for the jury? In any event, when the manufacturer supplies warnings with the product that causes harm, the defendant usually concedes the basic duty issue and argues that the instructions and warnings provided were adequate. The defendant in such a case is theoretically free to argue that no duty was owed in the first instance, but the fact that a warning was actually given usually makes the "no duty whatever" argument more difficult.

Tesmer v. Rich Ladder Co.
380 N.W.2d 203 (Minn. Ct. App. 1986)

CRIPPEN, J.

The jury returned verdicts of $759,350 for appellant David Tesmer and $115,000 for appellant Suzanne Tesmer in this negligence and products liability case. The trial court granted judgment notwithstanding the verdict (JNOV), and the Tesmers appeal.

Facts

Suzanne Tesmer purchased a ladder made by respondent R. D. Werner Co. as a gift for her husband, David Tesmer. The ladder is a 36-foot aluminum extension ladder that weighs approximately 85 pounds. David Tesmer used the ladder to paint the exterior of appellants' home. He used the ladder for three to four weeks without incident. On June 5, 1977 he was working at a height of approximately 24 feet. He fell to the ground, sustaining severe injuries. He is totally and permanently disabled. Appellants introduced evidence that the ladder had slipped backwards and out from underneath David Tesmer when he fell. After the fall the ladder came to rest perpendicular to the wall of the house. White paint was splattered on the base of the house where David Tesmer fell. He testified that the ladder slid out backwards from underneath him.

Appellants' evidence indicates that the angle formed by the ladder and the ground was too acute. In other words, the base of the ladder was set too far out from the house. Appellants' expert testified that an angle of 75½ degrees is critical for proper and safe use of the ladder. If the ladder is set up at too acute an angle, there is a risk that the bottom of the ladder will slip backwards. If the ladder and the ground form too wide an angle there is a risk of the top tipping away from the building. Appellants' expert further testified that the ladder industry knows of these risks and knows ordinary users tend to set up extension ladders at too acute an angle. He testified that the ladder had been set up at 68-69 degrees at the time of the accident. One neighbor testified that the ladder was at a "bad angle." Another neighbor testified that it was at a "dangerous" angle of approximately 60 degrees. The ladder had an instruction label that included the following instructions for setting up the ladder:

> Set up single or extension ladders at 75½ degrees by placing the bottom ¼ of the length being used out from the vertical resting point.

David Tesmer testified that he read some, but not all, of the instructions, and understood that the directions addressed safe use of the ladder. He testified he did not understand what the "75½ degrees" meant. Appellants' expert testified that the instruction label is inadequate because it does not identify the risk of the ladder slipping, it does not identify the "vertical resting point," it does not identify the "length being used," and because it does not motivate the user to follow the instructions given. He submitted his own version of adequate instructions.

David Tesmer's testimony about the ladder's angle conflicted somewhat with the reports of his neighbors. He testified that he thought he was using the ladder in a safe manner, and that the ladder was set up at an angle of 70-72 degrees at the time of the accident. . . .

The jury delivered its special verdict that the ladder was labeled with inadequate warnings and instructions for safe use, [and that] the inadequate labeling directly caused the accident. . . .

Werner moved for JNOV or a new trial, or in the alternative a remittitur. The trial court granted judgment for the defendant based on a conclusion about evidence on the cause of the plaintiff's injury.

Issue

Was it error to grant judgment notwithstanding the verdict?

Analysis

. . . The trial court correctly accepted the jury's finding of negligence. The Tesmers introduced evidence from which the jury could conclude that the manufacturer's instructions were inadequate. The Tesmers' expert deemed the instructions inadequate because they did not identify the risk of the ladder slipping, they did not identify the "vertical resting point," they did not identify "the length being used," and they did not motivate the user to follow the instructions. Appellants introduced evidence that David Tesmer did not understand the instructions. David Tesmer testified that he read the instructions, but did not understand what the "75½ degrees" meant.

The critical question is whether there was a reasonable basis for the jury's finding that this negligence directly caused the accident.

The trial court held that the defects in the . . . instructions did not directly cause the accident. The court stated that "[p]laintiffs also introduced evidence, and claim, that David Tesmer actually set the ladder up at the proper angle as set forth on the label. . . . If he complied with the instructions concerning the safe operation of the ladder, it is obvious that the defective labeling was not the direct cause of the accident." In the course of proving absence of any fault on his part, David Tesmer did testify that he set up the ladder with care, was conscientious about following the instructions for using the ladder, and thought he was using the ladder in a safe manner. However, this does not compel the conclusion that he did in fact set up the ladder at the proper angle of 75½ degrees.

The jury's finding of direct cause was justified for several reasons. First, evidence from lay witnesses indicated that the ladder was set up at an angle deviating substantially from 75½ degrees. One neighbor testified that the ladder was at a "bad angle," and another neighbor observed that it was at a "dangerous" angle of 60 degrees. Additionally, appellants' expert opined that the ladder was at 68-69 degrees. This is a reasonable basis for the jury's conclusion that the ladder was set up at an unsafe angle.

Second, evidence supported sufficiently the inference that if the ladder slipped out from underneath David Tesmer, it must have been set up with too acute an angle between the legs of the ladder and the ground. It was shown that when ladders are set up at too acute an angle, there is a risk that they will slip. David Tesmer testified that the ladder slid out from underneath him. Circumstantial evidence supported his testimony. After the fall the ladder came to rest with the top of the ladder next to the house and the ladder perpendicular to the wall of the house. White paint was splattered on the base of the house where David Tesmer fell.

Third, and most importantly, we conclude that there was no equally probable theory explaining David Tesmer's fall. . . . Here the evidence supports the Tesmers' theory more than other theories, even those devised by speculation. The evidence supports the inferences accepted by the jury, that the ladder was set up at an unsafe angle due to defective instructions and that therefore the ladder slid out from underneath David Tesmer, such that he fell and was injured.

It is conceivable that David Tesmer fell because he reached too far to one side while painting and lost his balance. It is also conceivable that he fell because he stood on the top rung of the ladder. However, these explanations of the cause of the accident are not equally supported by the evidence. The evidence indicates that David Tesmer was a cautious painter. Nor does the record show that these actions would have caused the ladder to slide out from underneath the user. . . .

Decision

Testimony supported the jury's finding that respondent's negligence and defective product directly caused appellant's injuries. The verdict cannot be overturned. Reversed.

The Eleventh Circuit ruled on the adequacy of a warning supplied with a cordless telephone. The handset of the phone had a switch that, in the "standby" position, allowed the phone to ring. To talk on the phone, the user had to push the switch to the "talk" position. The use of the phone, including the switch, was explained in the instruction manual, which the plaintiff said she read: "CAUTION—LOUD RING. Move switch to talk position before holding receiver to ear." The first time plaintiff answered the phone after it was installed, she forgot to push the switch to "talk." As she put the receiver to her ear, it rang again and permanently impaired her hearing. The district court granted summary judgment for the defendant-manufacturer. The court of appeals reversed and sent the case back for trial on the sufficiency of the warning. See Watson v. Uniden Corp. of America, 775 F.2d 1514 (11th Cir. 1985). Might this have been a design case "in disguise?"

In Mattis v. Carlon Electrical Products, 296 F.3d 856 (8th Cir. 2002), a twenty-five year old apprentice electrician read the safety warnings on the label of a can of glue before using the product. He opened and closed the can at least ten to twelve times throughout the workday. The plaintiff worked one more day, using the cement, before he was admitted to the hospital and diagnosed with reactive airways dysfunction syndrome (RADS). The court of appeals affirmed judgment in favor of the plaintiff, stating that "although the label stated 'vapor harmful,' this warning was followed by the statements, 'may irritate eyes and skin' and 'vapors may cause flash fires.' The label does not make it clear that *inhalation* of the vapors is harmful." Id. at 861.

In Benjamin v. Wal-Mart Stores, Inc., 61 P.3d 257 (Ore. Ct. App. 2002), the Oregon intermediate appellate court affirmed a verdict and judgment for the plaintiff in a case involving the asphyxiation death of the plaintiff's father. The father died while sleeping in a closed tent heated by a propane space heater. A decal on the heater read in part: "WARNING: FOR OUTDOOR USE ONLY. Never use inside house, camper, tent, vehicle or other unventilated or enclosed areas." The plaintiff introduced expert testimony that the warning was inadequate because it failed to state that the heater reduces oxygen and produces carbon monoxide and that the user should not operate the heater while sleeping. The expert further testified that the warning was "too vague," the lettering too small, and the black and white coloring inadequate. The court reasoned that "although the warning told the user not to operate the heater in a tent or any other unventilated or enclosed area, it did not convey the 'consequences'—that is, the 'nature and the extent of the danger'—of doing so." 61 P.3d at 266 (quoting Schmeiser v. Trus Joist, 540 P.2d 998, 1004 (Ore. 1975); Anderson v. Klix Chemical, 472 P.2d 806, 810 (Ore. 1970)). See also, Mattis v. Harrell Co., Inc. 828 So. 2d 248 (Ala. 2002) (reversing summary judgment for defendants based on an expert's statement that the warning on a piece of farm machinery was inadequate because it failed to identify the risk and likelihood of injury associated with attempting to open the hydraulic-cylinder latch manually and failed to state the consequences of not following the instruction).

Comment *i* to §2(c) of the Products Liability Restatement supplies the following summary of how courts should approach the task of evaluating the sufficiency of product warnings:

> In evaluating the adequacy of product warnings and instructions, courts must be sensitive to many factors. It is impossible to identify anything approaching a perfect level of detail that should be communicated in product disclosures. For example, educated or experienced product users and consumers may benefit from inclusion of more information about the full spectrum of product risks, whereas less-educated or unskilled users may benefit from more concise warnings and instructions stressing only the most crucial risks and safe-handling practices. In some contexts, products intended for special categories of users, such as children, may require more vivid and unambiguous warnings. In some cases, excessive detail may detract from the ability of typical users and consumers to focus on the important aspects of the warnings, whereas in others reasonably full disclosure will be necessary to enable informed, efficient choices by product users. Product warnings and instructions can rarely communicate all potentially relevant information, and the ability of a plaintiff to imagine a hypothetical better warning in the aftermath of an accident does not establish that the warning actually accompanying the product was inadequate. No easy guideline exists for courts to adopt in assessing the adequacy of product warnings and instructions. In making their assessments, courts must focus on various factors, such as content and comprehensibility, intensity of expression, and the characteristics of expected user groups. . . .

PROBLEM TWENTY

A senior partner in the litigation department of the law firm in which you are an associate has sought your help in a case recently brought to her. The clients, Mr. and Mrs. Ronald Kritzik and their daughter Kathy, want to bring an action in tort based on injuries suffered by Kathy after she began to wear contact lenses. The clients have related the following events: Kathy, an attractive 16-year-old girl, had been pestering her parents for months to let her get contact lenses to replace her glasses. Early last December, they arranged for an appointment with Dr. Richard Quell, a local optometrist, who advertised his services in the Yellow Pages and in the local newspaper. They told Kathy that the contact lenses were to be her Christmas present.

Dr. Quell examined Kathy and decided that because she suffered from astigmatism, she would be better off with hard contact lenses than with the more popular soft lenses. Hard lenses provide a kind of "encasement" that prevents the distortion in vision that can sometimes occur with soft lenses. Dr. Quell fitted Kathy with the lenses in the early afternoon of December 24. She felt comfortable wearing her new lenses, and was delighted by the improvement in her looks once rid of what she considered rather ugly-looking glasses. Dr. Quell told Kathy that for the first week she was to wear her lenses for no more than four hours per day. He told her that more than four hours' use could cause "real trouble." After fitting Kathy with the lenses, Dr. Quell had her sit in the waiting room for 15 minutes. He then examined Kathy once again and found that the fit was excellent. As Kathy was leaving, Dr. Quell said, "Remember, Kathy — no more than four hours a day. You don't want to hurt those pretty eyes of yours."

That same evening, Kathy went to a Christmas Eve party. Four hours had already passed but she was feeling "great." She hardly felt that she was wearing the lenses. The party lasted until 2:00 A.M. and Kathy did not remove the lenses until 4:00 A.M., when she went to bed. According to Kathy, at no time up to that point did her eyes bother her in any way. When she awoke at 10:00 A.M. on Christmas morning, she felt a burning sensation in both eyes. Mrs. Kritzik called Dr. Quell and told him what had happened. He saw Kathy immediately. Fifteen hours of continuous wear had caused ulcerated corneas. When Dr. Quell discovered the ulcerations, he was furious. "Kathy," he said, "why didn't you listen to directions? Twice I told you to remove the lenses after four hours." Kathy, somewhat ashamed of herself, replied, "I guess that I thought it was just doctor talk. My eyes weren't irritated or tearing or anything." Then she thought for a few seconds and with a half-smile remarked, "You know, when I left for the party at eight and I thought to myself, should I take the lenses out like you said, I had this crazy thought. 'What the heck, I already broke curfew; que será, será.'" Dr. Quell shook his head in disbelief. "Kathy, overwearing hard lenses for three or four hours isn't likely to cause trouble. But every hour after that, the lenses eat away at the cornea. I hope to God this is reversible." The next several weeks were hell. The pain resulting from the ulcerated corneas was excruciating. Although the ulcers eventually healed, residual scarring may permanently affect her vision.

The lenses worn by Kathy were manufactured by Seenco, Inc. They came with an instruction booklet entitled "How to Care for Your Contact Lenses." Kathy had read the booklet carefully when she got her lenses. A box in the booklet, outlined in bright red, contained the following message:

> Instructions for wearing these lenses will be given to you by your physician or optometrist. Failure to follow the instructions carefully may result in irritation to the eyes and could cause serious complications, including impairment of vision.

The senior partner is concerned that the case may be too "thin" and may be dismissed on a motion for summary judgment or a motion for direct verdict. She has asked you to assess the likelihood of getting to a jury. You are to assume that all relevant events took place in New California. Indicate any further information that should be obtained.

It will be recalled from Chapter Four that the reasonable alternative design standard in design litigation lends itself to a fairly robust motions practice, in which judges are able to play a meaningful role in deciding which design claims should, and which should not, reach the jury. Indeed, that is one of the reasons that plaintiff's lawyers favor the consumer expectations test for defective design — the vagueness of the expectations test sends almost all design claims, at least the ones that do not involve obvious risks, to the jury. In connection with failure to warn, it is more difficult for courts to rule as a matter of law on plaintiffs' claims even if they adopt the Restatement's standard for warnings defects. Perhaps that is what the drafters of Comment *i* to §2 of the Products Liability

Restatement meant when they observed that, while the liability standard for warnings in Subsection (c) is formulated in essentially identical terms as the standard for defective designs in Subsection (b), (see p.37, supra, for a side-by-side comparison), "the defectiveness concept is more difficult to apply in the warnings context." One question is whether the judge's instructions to the jury really matter in affecting outcomes. Consider the following decision.

Lewis v. Sea Ray Boats, Inc.
65 P.3d 245 (Nev. 2003)

BEFORE THE COURT EN BANC.
By the Court, MAUPIN, J.:

Leo Gasse was killed and Robin Lewis catastrophically injured due to carbon monoxide poisoning during an overnight outing in a Sea Ray pleasure boat at the Lake Mead National Recreation Area. Lewis, along with Gasse's heirs, Teresa Rae Webb and Tricia Marie Gasse, brought suit against Sea Ray Boats, Inc., alleging that Sea Ray is strictly liable in tort in connection with the incident. A jury returned a verdict in favor of Sea Ray, finding that the boat was not a defective or unreasonably dangerous product. This appeal followed.

Appellants' primary contention centers on the district court's failure to adopt appellants' proffered instructions on their theory of liability; that warnings concerning the risk of carbon monoxide migration secondary to use of the boat's air conditioning system were inadequate. Because we conclude that appellants were entitled to more specific instructions with regard to the warnings issue, we reverse the district court's judgment and remand this matter for a new trial.

Facts

In May 1991, Leo Gasse and Jimmy Paxson purchased a used Sea Ray pleasure boat from a Las Vegas area Sea Ray dealership. In addition to gasoline propulsion engines, the boat contained a small gasoline generator, which powered the boat's accessories, including the air conditioner.

On May 29, 1993, during a weekend cruise on Lake Mead, Gasse and Lewis "side-tied" the boat to a beach and went to sleep in the boat's cabin, leaving the gasoline generator running to power the air conditioner. The next morning, Anthony Caro, Jr., a friend who was staying at the beach, knocked on the cabin door and received no response. He returned later that afternoon, boarded the boat, and found Gasse dead and Lewis barely breathing. Mr. Caro testified that the engines were not running when he first checked on the couple and when he returned.

Subsequent investigation confirmed that the generator, rather than the engines, was the source of the carbon monoxide, a tasteless odorless gas. This proposition was bolstered by other trial testimony that, had engine exhaust been the source, the couple may have been able to detect the problem because of the distinctive odor of exhaust fumes.

Two warnings regarding carbon monoxide poisoning accompanied the sale of this type of boat in 1981, one written by ONAN, the generator manufacturer,[1] and the other by the National Marine Manufacturers' Association (NMMA).[2] Sea Ray provided boat purchasers with an assortment of other manuals, none of which are relevant to this case. Both warnings primarily addressed the danger of carbon monoxide exposure from engine exhaust.

When Gasse and Paxson purchased the boat, the Sea Ray dealership service manager, George Schenk, and the salesman, Curt Snouffer, warned of the danger of exhaust fumes and carbon monoxide, and the necessity of ventilating the boat to remove hazardous fumes. Schenk and Snouffer demonstrated this process by opening a window and the hatch to allow for flow-through ventilation, and explained the need to have the rear door remain open when running the main propulsion engines. Lastly, Schenk indicated that idling the engine with the front hatch closed could cause accumulations of carbon monoxide.

Appellants theorized that a process described as "migrating carbon monoxide" caused the accident. The process occurs when carbon monoxide, although safely exhausted from the boat's gasoline generator into the open air, is blown back into the boat by wind, entering the passenger cabin through small openings. Sea Ray's expert agreed with this theory of causation, but noted that such a phenomenon is quite rare and for carbon monoxide to accumulate to dangerous levels, passenger cabin ventilation must have been obstructed.

Sea Ray's expert testified regarding the safety of sleeping with the air conditioner running. He admitted that although boaters will often sleep with the air conditioner running unless warned not to do so, certain precautions should be taken. These include: (1) posting a watch, since in 1981, the year the boat was manufactured, no carbon monoxide detection devices were available; (2) anchoring the boat from the bow rather than the side, so that any wind currents would blow away from the stern; or (3) creating flow-through ventilation before going to sleep. The expert conceded that Sea Ray's manual contained no such instructions or warnings, but stressed that no incidents of this type resulting in death had ever been reported in connection with the particular pleasure boat model involved in this case. Sea Ray's expert also voiced his opinion that the warnings given were adequate with regard to carbon monoxide exposure, and that the risk of "migrating" carbon monoxide from on-board generators was not a known hazard when the boat was originally purchased in 1981.

---

1. The warning states: WARNING! ENGINE EXHAUST GAS (CARBON MONOXIDE) IS DEADLY!

   Carbon monoxide is an odorless, colorless gas formed by incomplete combustion of hydrocarbon fuels. Carbon Monoxide is a dangerous gas that can cause unconsciousness and is potentially lethal.

   Some of the symptoms or signs of carbon monoxide inhalation are: Dizziness; Vomiting; Intense Headache; Muscular Twitching; Weakness and Throbbing in Temples; and Sleepiness

   If you experience any of the above symptoms, get out into fresh air immediately. The best protection against carbon monoxide inhalation is a regular inspection of the complete exhaust system. If you notice a change in the sound or appearance of the exhaust system, shut the unit down immediately and have it inspected and repaired at once by a competent mechanic.

2. The warning states:

   WARNING: Use care in running the engine continuously when the boat is closed up in bad weather, particularly when the boat is not in motion. Exhaust fumes and carbon monoxide may accumulate in the passenger areas, so be alert to any indication that exhaust fumes are present, and ventilate accordingly.

The Sufficiency of the Defendant's Warning

Sea Ray's expert additionally relied upon a Nevada Department of Wildlife booklet found on the boat after the incident. The booklet discussed the hazards of exhaust fumes, warned that carbon monoxide itself is tasteless and odorless, that plenty of air flow should be maintained because exhaust fumes can blow back into a boat when running downwind, and that adequate ventilation was required when using catalytic heaters for warmth.

The warnings that are the subject of this appeal specifically addressed the danger of carbon monoxide exposure from exhaust fumes, generally addressed dangers attendant to carbon monoxide exposure, and only inferentially addressed dangers in connection with generator fumes. All of this is important because, as noted, the discrete odor from engine exhaust would arguably alert the passengers to the presence of noxious fumes, while emissions from the generator probably would not.

Appellants submitted a proposed jury instruction regarding legal requirements for an "adequate warning" based on Pavlides v. Galveston Yacht Basin, Inc., a Fifth Circuit case applying a three-factor test under Texas law for determining whether a product warning was adequate. The proposed instruction read as follows:

> A warning must (1) be designed so it can reasonably be expected to catch the attention of the consumer; (2) be comprehensible and give a fair indication of the specific risks involved with the product; and (3) be of an intensity justified by the magnitude of the risk.

The district court rejected this proposed instruction and instead gave the following two instructions:

> First:
> Although you are to consider only the evidence in the case in reaching a verdict, you must bring to the consideration of the evidence your everyday common sense and judgment as reasonable men and women. Thus, you are not limited solely to what you see and hear as the witnesses testify. You may draw reasonable inferences from the evidence which you feel are justified in the light of common experience, keeping in mind that such inferences should not be based on speculation or guess.
> Second:
> The question of whether or not a given warning is legally sufficient depends upon the language used and the impression that such language is calculated to make upon the mind of the average user of the product. . . .

During deliberations, the jury sent a note to the trial judge, requesting a definition of an "adequate warning." Appellants proposed an instruction taken from a products liability treatise to the district court.[6] The district court rejected this instruction, as well as again rejecting appellants' proposed *Pavlides* instruction. Consequently, the district court simply reread the two instructions it had previously given on the issue to the jury.

---

6. The instruction defining "adequate warning" offered by appellants stated:

> To be adequate a necessary warning by its size, location, and intensity of language or symbol, must be calculated to impress upon a reasonably prudent user of the product the nature and extent of the hazard involved. The language used must be direct and should, where applicable, describe the method of safe use.

After the trial judge reread the instructions, the jury foreman informed the judge that the reading did not assist the jury in its deliberations. The district court again sought a definition of "adequate warning" from the parties. Appellants reoffered the treatise definition, arguing that it was essentially consistent with Nevada case authority. The district court again rejected the treatise definition, and refused to instruct the jury further, despite the confusion. Soon after the rereading of the jury instructions, one juror was replaced during deliberations for unspecified reasons. Shortly thereafter, the jury returned a verdict in favor of Sea Ray. This appeal followed.

Discussion

Respondent contends that warning instructions in cases such as this one should be generally worded and that the adequacy of warnings should be left to the common sense of the finder of facts. Appellants contend that the district court erred by not instructing the jury with their more specific definition of "adequate warning." We agree with appellants. . . .

In the instant matter, the purchasers of the boat were comprehensively warned about the dangers of carbon monoxide poisoning from exhaust fumes, fumes characterized by a distinctive odor. Here, however, the injuries sustained by Gasse and Lewis were not caused by exhaust fumes; they were caused by odorless and tasteless carbon monoxide fumes from the generator that powered the boat's air conditioner. Whether the warnings described above, which generally addressed dangers and symptoms of carbon monoxide poisoning and specifically addressed carbon monoxide exposure secondary to engine exhaust and running the heater, sufficiently apprised Gasse and his co-owner of carbon monoxide poisoning from use of the air conditioner remained the primary issue of fact throughout the trial below. Thus, the text of the "warnings" instruction became critical to the jury's fact-finding mission.

Here, the district court's "warnings" instructions provided very little in the way of guidance, other than to generally state that whether a warning is legally sufficient depends upon the "impression" that the warnings language "is calculated to make upon the mind of the average user of the product," and that the jury should use its common sense in resolving the issue. This instruction was not sufficient to assist the jury in resolving the liability issues based upon Sea Ray's alleged failure to warn. First, in [earlier decisions,] we refused to exonerate products manufacturers as a matter of law from strict tort liability based upon general warnings language. Second, these instructions left lay jurors, persons in much the same position as the users of the product at issue, to search their imaginations to test the adequacy of the warnings. Third, given that experts testified in this case to the nature and quality of the warnings that were given and their supposed behavioral impact, the jurors were entitled to more specific guidance as to the law governing the duty to warn in connection with consumer products.

We therefore embrace the rule of law stated in the *Pavlides* instructions offered by appellants below, and hold that Nevada trial courts should advise juries that warnings in the context of products liability claims must be (1) designed to reasonably catch the consumer's attention, (2) that the language be comprehensible and give a fair indication of the specific risks attendant to use of the product, and (3) that warnings be of sufficient intensity justified by the magnitude of the risk.

The district court's failure to instruct the jury as suggested by appellants mandates reversal for a new trial.

James A. Henderson, Jr. & Aaron D. Twerski, Doctrinal Collapse in Products Liability: The Empty Shell of Failure to Warn
65 N.Y.U. L. Rev. 265, 292-294 (1990)

We use the phrase "preliminary risk-utility screening" to refer to a court's initial assessment of the relative proximity or remoteness of a product-related risk, measured by the probability of injury that a reasonable defendant would have perceived at the time she acted. To understand how this preliminary screening process affects judicial decisionmaking in failure-to-warn cases, we will first consider in the defective-design context how it helps courts decide which cases should not reach the jury. This comparison is important because it highlights the potential ability of preliminary screening to serve as an independent test of the validity of plaintiffs' failure-to-warn claims.

When a judge's initial assessment of a design claim reveals that, at the time the defendant acted, the risk of plaintiff's injury was quite remote, a distinctive train of logic is set in motion. The judge knows that design changes have risk-utility implications extending beyond the category of user and consumer represented by the plaintiff. Any design change will have to be weighed against the possible increased cost it will impose on the manufacturer, and against the new potential risks it will pose for the consumer. Design changes, in other words, come in "chunks," and the chunks tend to come in minimum sizes. The risk of injury, therefore, must exceed some instinctive, judicially-measured threshold of significance before a costly design change is evaluated under full-blown risk-utility balancing.

While every design change suggested by an injured plaintiff need not require a complete product overhaul, even the smallest chunk of alternative design entails at least some degree of modification. An analogy to writing and editing a paper helps to illustrate this point. Introducing a new idea toward the end of a nearly-completed paper will almost inevitably require revisions at various earlier stages in order to maintain the argument and logic of the piece. When the benefits to be gained by making this late addition are minimal, the writer may intuitively decide that it is simply not worth the effort to add the new section if doing so would require reorganizing and rewriting significant portions of the paper. Likewise, in design litigation, judges frequently determine at the outset that an improved design which might have protected the plaintiff would nonetheless require such costly and elaborate alterations that the change simply does not merit a more careful analysis under full-blown risk-utility balancing. Judges can, and often do, wait to intervene until more substantial risk-utility data are before them, much as an editor might wait to abandon a proposed addition to a text until she had carefully reviewed the entire piece. But when the relevant risks are remote, those data (which, after all, are costly to obtain) may not be required in order to reach, at the outset of the analysis, a principled decision not to impose the change.

In contrast to suggested alternatives in design cases, suggested alternatives in failure-to-warn cases appear to be easily compartmentalized. Like additional memory chips which are used to expand the capacity of a computer, warnings would seem to be added easily without requiring adjustments to the rest of the machine. When a risk is perceived in the context of an alternative design, it can be addressed only by a design change which unavoidably affects other related risks and utilities and thereby generates a not insignificant minimum threshold of avoidance costs. But when a risk is perceived in the context of failure to warn, a tailor-made remedy seems to be automatically available, precisely limited to the category of users and consumers represented by the plaintiff. The plaintiff argues that the manufacturer should share the information, however remote the risks it describes, with users and consumers.[1] The relative remoteness of the risk may create problems for the failure-to-warn plaintiff when the court reaches the full-blown risk-utility stage of the analysis—eliminating remote risks cannot justify much in the way of avoidance costs. The remoteness of the risk may also create problems with causation—would telling the plaintiff about a remote risk have done any good? We will address those problems in subsequent discussions. But at the preliminary screening stage, the remoteness of the perceived risk will rarely provide the court in a failure-to-warn case with an independent means of taking the plaintiff's claim from the jury. This difficulty will occur because the plaintiff who claims that the manufacturer failed to warn, unlike the plaintiff claiming defective design, will be able to tailor his suggested alternative course of conduct precisely to the facts of his case in terms that have no immediately obvious consequences for other aspects of production, marketing, and distribution. All the defendant must do, contends the plaintiff, is add slightly to his warnings. On its face, the failure-to-warn claim is so modestly self-contained that, even when the risk is remote, it nevertheless fails to trigger the preliminary risk-utility screening which courts give to design-defect claims because the apparent unobtrusiveness of the plaintiff's request automatically counterbalances the remoteness of the risk. Thus, the relative unlikelihood of injury viewed ex ante loses its independent capacity to serve as a basis for taking the failure-to-warn case from the jury.

Occasionally, courts explicitly recognize that, contrary to loose talk in other opinions, warnings are not free. An example is Cotton v. Buckeye Gas Products Co., 840 F.2d 935 (D.C. Cir. 1988), in which plaintiff was injured when a fire broke out due to mishandled gas cylinders. The plaintiff claimed that the defendant should have provided more adequate warnings of the risks associated with leaving the valves open on used but not empty cylinders. At trial the court granted defendant's motion for J.N.O.V. after a verdict was returned for the plain-

---

1. In addition to arguments based on cost, plaintiffs frequently succeed at trial in characterizing risks previously considered unknowable as "knowable from the outset" by a reasonable observer. Simply stated, it is extremely difficult for a court to dismiss as a matter of law, a failure-to-warn claim on remoteness grounds when the plaintiff has introduced evidence that the risk actually materialized in the form of the plaintiff's injury. Because the product did, in fact, cause the injury, a court is sorely tempted to permit the inference to be drawn that a reasonable product distributor should have foreseen the risk of injury and should have warned against it. Thus the plaintiff will argue that at least some additional information was obtainable and should have been shared with him in the form of a warning, even if information sufficient to justify massive redesign or withholding of the product from the market was not.

tiff. The court of appeals held that additional warnings were not required because the warnings given were adequate. The employer had sufficient knowledge of the relevant risks, and the plaintiff would not have heeded them anyway. The opinion contains the following observations:

> Failure-to-warn cases have the curious property that when the episode is examined in hindsight, it appears as though addition of warnings keyed to a particular accident would be virtually cost free. What could be simpler than for the manufacturer to add the few simple items noted above [what the plaintiff claimed should have been said in addition to what was said]. The primary cost is, in fact, the increase in time and effort required for the user to grasp the message. The inclusion of each extra item dilutes the punch of every other item. Given short attention spans, items crowd each other out; they get lost in fine print. Here in fact Buckeye responded to the information-cost problem with a dual approach: a brief message on the canisters themselves and a more detailed one in the . . . pamphlet delivered to [the employer] and posted on the bulletin board at the construction site where [the plaintiff] was employed.
>
> Plaintiff's analysis completely disregards the problem of information costs. He asserts that "it would have been neither difficult nor costly for Buckeye to have purchased or created for attachment to its propane cylinders a clearer, more explicit label, such as the alternatives introduced at trial, warning of propane's dangers and instructing how to avoid them." But he offers no reason to suppose that any alternative package of warnings was preferable. He discounts altogether the warnings in the pamphlet, without even considering what the canister warning would look like if Buckeye had supplemented that not only with the special items he is personally interested in — in hindsight — but also with all other equally valuable items (i. e., "equally" in terms of the scope and probability of the danger likely to be averted and the incremental impact of the information on user conduct). If every foreseeable possibility must be covered, "the list of foolish practices warned against would be so long, it would fill a volume." Unlike plaintiff, we must review the record in light of these obvious information costs. (840 F.2d at 937-938).

The court goes on to review the actual warning given compared with the warning proposed by the plaintiff, and concludes that the warning was adequate as a matter of law.

In Hood v. Ryobi North America, 17 F. Supp. 2d 448 (D. Md. 1998), plaintiff was injured when a saw blade detached from a saw from which he had removed the guards contrary to multiple warnings not to do so. The court granted defendant's motion for summary judgment, dismissing plaintiff's argument that the warnings were inadequate because they failed to give notice that removal of guards could cause the blade to fly through the air. The Fourth Circuit affirmed, concluding that there is no need for an "encyclopedic" warning providing a significant level of detail, or to specify the exact nature of the injury to be expected. 181 F.3d 608, 610 (4th Cir. 1999). In another blade-guard case, Burt v. Makita USA, Inc., 212 F. Supp. 2d 893 (N.D. Ind. 2002), a worker was hit in the eye by an incompletely installed guard. A co-worker had started to install the guard, but left the area to get additional tools. During the co-worker's absence, the plaintiff attempted to use the saw. The court granted summary judgment for the defendants, noting that under Indiana law, the defendants had no duty to warn of an unforeseeable use of the product.

Broussard v. Continental Oil Co.
433 So. 2d 354 (La. App.), *cert. denied*, 440 So. 2d 726 (La. 1983)

STOKER, J.

This is a personal injury suit by Mildredge T. Broussard against Black & Decker (U.S.), Inc. and The Home Insurance Company. Plaintiff-appellant (Broussard) was badly burned in an explosion of natural gas sparked by a Black & Decker hand drill. Broussard was using the drill while working at a Continental Oil Company (Conoco) plant at Grand Chenier, Louisiana. . . .

The verdict of the jury at trial was that Black & Decker was not at fault for failure to adequately warn in connection with the accident. . . .

Background Facts

Plaintiff was directly employed by Crain Brothers Construction Company, and the trial court found he was the statutory employee of Conoco. On the day of the accident, plaintiff and four other men, including Sanders Miller, were in the process of building a sump box enclosure at the end of a natural gas vent line (pipe) at the Grand Chenier plant. Plaintiff was a carpenter's helper and Miller was a carpenter. Upon arriving at the site, both men noticed that natural gas could be heard and smelled coming from the vent line. Miller immediately notified Conoco's relief plant foreman about the escaping gas and asked if it could be shut off. The foreman refused to do so because the whole plant would have had to be shut down to prevent the gas from being vented at the location of the sump box. After Miller requested a shut down a second time, the foreman talked to Mr. Leeman, another Conoco employee and the plant supervisor. Miller was again told nothing could be done.

Miller testified that he recognized the danger of working around the flammable natural gas. The workers took what precautions they could to minimize the risk of igniting the natural gas fumes. Cigarettes, cigarette lighters and matches were left in the work vehicles. The vehicles were parked some distance away from the site. A gasoline powered electricity generator was placed at the end of two 50-foot extension cords. Miller warned the plaintiff to be careful not to cause a spark while hammering, especially when the fumes were heavy.

The explosion occurred as plaintiff was standing inside a plywood box loosely held together and being constructed as a concrete form. He was positioned inside the form to drill holes in its sides through which rods were to be inserted. It is not seriously contested that sparks from the drill plaintiff was using ignited the natural gas fumes coming from the vent line. Such sparks are normally emitted from this and similar type drills when the "brushes" inside the armature of the drill contact and slide along the inside surface of the rapidly spinning cylinder in which the brushes sit. There is no evidence, nor is the issue before this Court, that the design which allows the creation and emission of these sparks constitutes a design defect. Rather, the issues relate to the failure to warn on the part of the defendant manufacturer of the hazard of explosion.

Both the plaintiff Broussard and Sanders Miller testified that they were unaware at the time of the accident that sparks from electrical power drills could ignite gaseous atmospheres. Allen Nunez, the relief foreman, likewise testified that neither he nor anyone at the Conoco plant knew of the potential of explo-

The Sufficiency of the Defendant's Warning

sion in a like situation before the accident occurred. However, a warning that would have informed the users of the drill of the precise cause and effect encountered appears in [item 18 in] the owner's manual. Black & Decker claim that a copy of this manual is placed in every box containing one of their drills as it leaves the manufacturer's control. . . .

Did Black & Decker Fail to Provide Adequate Warning?

With reference to adequacy of warning of the danger from the emission of sparks, Black & Decker contends item eighteen in the owner's manual was sufficient. Plaintiff Broussard contends that it was not. Broussard contends that Black & Decker was guilty of fault in not putting the warning on the drill itself. Item eighteen reads as follows:

> 18. DO NOT OPERATE portable electric tools in gaseous or explosive atmospheres. Motors in these tools normally spark, and the sparks might ignite fumes.

The warning set forth in these words is adequate; the question is whether it was sufficient to put it in the owner's manual or whether it was unreasonable under the circumstances not to put this warning on the drill itself. . . . [T]here was a warning on the drill which read, "CAUTION: For Safe Operation See Owner's Manual."

We are confronted here with the application of absolute liability of a manufacturer. The product, the drill, does not contain a defect in the ordinary sense of design or manufacturing defect, but ordinary use of the drill is dangerous under the factual circumstances which were present in this case, i.e., use in the presence of natural gas fumes. Unreasonable risk is a requirement of strict liability just as it is in negligence.

The judicial process involved in deciding whether a risk is unreasonable in strict liability is similar to that employed in determining whether a risk is unreasonable in a traditional negligence problem and in deciding the scope of duty or legal cause under the duty risk analysis. . . .

In approaching our decision in this case we accept at face value the assertions of Broussard and Sanders Miller that they were unaware that the drill in question would emit sparks when in operation. . . .

The questions before us are:

1. Was adequate warning given through the general caution on Black & Decker's drill directing users to consult the owner's manual for safe operation?
2. If the general warning was not adequate, was it unreasonable for Black & Decker not to place on the drill itself the warning contained in item 18 of its safety rules contained in the owner's manual?

These questions must be tested together as they rest on the same practical considerations.

Plaintiff's own expert witness unwittingly pointed up the difficulty in putting warnings on the drill itself. This expert demonstrated the use of warnings through symbols as opposed to words. The expert devised a series of symbols of his own creation based on international symbols which he suggested could have been placed on the drill itself. The symbols purportedly represent ten of the eighteen warnings Black & Decker set forth in the owner's manual. . . .

While we think the use of symbols as suggested by plaintiff's expert merits no consideration, we note that the expert deemed at least ten of the warnings represented by the symbols were worthy of being noted on the drill. The fact that numerous risks other than sparking explosions or fires merit notice is a significant factor. The suggested use of symbols is also significant because the reason for it is the recognition that the space on the drill is not large enough to contain extensive warnings and cautions in words. This factor will be discussed later, but at this point we will state our opinion relative to the efficacy [of] symbols in lieu of words. . . .

We think counsel for plaintiff recognized lack of merit in the suggested use of symbols. On plaintiff's behalf Exhibit P-17 was introduced in evidence. On the side of this exhibit a label measuring approximately 2⅝ inches by 1¼ inches was affixed on which the following words were typed:

SAFETY RULES
- Don't abuse cord
- Wear proper apparel
- Don't use in damp areas
- Use proper extension cords outdoors
- Don't touch metal parts when drilling near any electrical wiring
- Remove tightening key
- Unplug to change bits
- Use safety glasses
- Avoid gaseous areas
- Secure work

SEE MANUAL FOR COMPLETE TEXTS

The whole of the above quoted material is typed in small letter characters in a slantwise or diagonal fashion on the label in order to fit. It will be noted that the only reference to the risk of igniting gas from emission of sparks is contained in the three words, "Avoid gaseous areas."

We are not impressed with plaintiff's Exhibit P-17. The most important failing of the exhibit is that the mere words, "Avoid gaseous areas" does not meet the test of [adequacy] because it does not explain or point out the precise risk of injury posed by use in gaseous areas. Moreover, this exhibit graphically illustrates the problem of attempting to put multiple warnings on a hand drill of the size and nature involved.

Defendant considers that more than ten warnings should be given. Nevertheless, if only ten are selected, deficiencies in any scheme for putting them all on the drill become apparent. As a practical matter, the effect of putting at least ten warnings on the drill would decrease the effectiveness of all of the warnings. A consumer would have a tendency to read none of the warnings if the surface of the drill became cluttered with the warnings. Unless we should elevate the one hazard of sparking to premier importance above all others, we fear that an effort to tell all about each hazard is not practical either from the point of view of availability of space or of effectiveness. We decline to say that one risk is more worthy of warning than another.

With the merits and demerits of the arguments urged by the parties in mind, we now decide whether Black & Decker exposed plaintiff to unreasonable risk. . . . We conclude that defendant acted reasonably toward plaintiff and all persons who might use its hand drill. In view of the numerous risks which a manufacturer of a hand drill must explicitly describe, the most practical and effective thing which the manufacturer could do is to direct the user to the owner's manual as Black & Decker did.

For the reasons we have given we hold that the jury's finding of no fault on the part of Black & Decker was correct. . . .

Decree

For the reasons assigned, the judgment of the trial court is affirmed. All costs of this appeal are to be paid by plaintiff.

Affirmed.

In Williams v. Super Trucks, Inc. (La. Ct. App. 2003), the Louisiana intermediate appellate court affirmed a verdict for defendant in a case in which a truck axle snapped in half due to heat having been applied during repair of the axle's bearings. Although the truck's manual warned against the use of heat to replace the vehicle's wheel bearings, the plaintiff argued that the warning was inadequate as a matter of law because it should have been provided on the axle itself. The court, however, upheld the jury's verdict, in light of testimony that warnings on the axle would not have been readable given the corrosion and wear on vehicle axles and that such warnings could, themselves, contribute to the axle's weakening.

One problem that recurs in these warnings cases involves the difficulties of getting warnings to persons who do not read, or at least do not read English. Thus, in Hubbard-Hall Chemical Co. v. Silverman, 340 F.2d 402 (1st Cir. 1965), the court of appeals affirmed a judgment in favor of the representatives of two farm laborers who were killed by exposure to poisonous insecticide. The labels on the bags of insecticide bore extensive (and, for literate users, presumably adequate) warnings in English, but neither of the decedents could read English. Even though the label containing the warnings had been approved by the United States Department of Agriculture, the court below was warranted in imposing liability for the defendant's failure to use the traditional skull-and-crossbones symbol to communicate the danger to the decedents.

Another version of this problem arose in Campos v. Firestone Tire & Rubber Co., 485 A.2d 305 (N.J. 1984). Plaintiff was born and raised in Portugal, and did not read English. He was injured while installing a new truck tire on a three-piece rim assembly manufactured by defendant. An adequate warning in English was supplied and prominently posted at the workplace. Plaintiff's expert argued that defendant should have produced a graphic or symbolic warning against inserting one's hand in the assembly during tire inflation — a sign containing a picture of a hand inside the assembly, with a red diagonal line through it, similar to international road signs. The high court concluded that a jury could find that defendant breached its duty to warn, and remanded the case for a new trial. However, in Torres-Rios v. LPS Laboratories, 152 F.3d 11 (1st Cir. 1998), a prominent display of a flame symbol on a drum containing flammable electrical contact cleaner was held to be an adequate warning as a matter of law in the absence of federal requirements to provide warnings in English, even though the product was sold in Puerto Rico where the dominant language is Spanish.

On the subject of foreign language warnings see generally S. Mark Mitchell, Note, A Manufacturer's Duty to Warn in a Modern Day Tower of Babel, 29 Ga. J. Int'l & Comp. L. 573 (2001).

D. POST-SALE WARNINGS

Although the time-of-sale duty to warn is long-established, the product seller's post-sale duty to warn is of more recent vintage. Consider §10 of the Products Liability Restatement:

§10. LIABILITY OF COMMERCIAL PRODUCT SELLER OR DISTRIBUTOR FOR HARM CAUSED BY POST-SALE FAILURE TO WARN

(a) One engaged in the business of selling or otherwise distributing products is subject to liability for harm to persons or property caused by the seller's failure to provide a warning after the time of sale or distribution of a product if a reasonable person in the seller's position would provide such a warning.

(b) A reasonable person in the seller's position would provide a warning after the time of sale if:

(1) the seller knows or reasonably should know that the product poses a substantial risk of harm to persons or property; and

(2) those to whom a warning might be provided can be identified and can reasonably be assumed to be unaware of the risk of harm; and

(3) a warning can be effectively communicated to and acted on by those to whom a warning might be provided; and

(4) the risk of harm is sufficiently great to justify the burden of providing a warning.

COMMENT:

a. Rationale. Judicial recognition of the seller's duty to warn of a product-related risk after the time of sale, whether or not the product is defective at the time of original sale within the meaning of other Sections of this Restatement, is relatively new. Nonetheless, a growing body of decisional and statutory law imposes such a duty. Courts recognize that warnings about risks discovered after sale are sometimes necessary to prevent significant harm to persons and property. Nevertheless, an unbounded post-sale duty to warn would impose unacceptable burdens on product sellers. The costs of identifying and communicating with product users years after sale are often daunting. Furthermore, as product designs are developed and improved over time, many risks are reduced or avoided by subsequent design changes. If every post-sale improvement in a product design were to give rise to a duty to warn users of the risks of continuing to use the existing design, the burden on product sellers would be unacceptably great.

As with all rules that raise the question whether a duty exists, courts must make the threshold decisions that, in particular cases, triers of fact could reasonably find that product sellers can practically and effectively discharge such an obligation and that the risks of harm are sufficiently great to justify what is typically a substantial post-sale undertaking. In deciding whether a claim based on breach of a post-sale duty to warn should reach the trier of fact, the court must determine whether the requirements in Subsection (b)(1) through (4) are supported by proof. The legal standard is whether a reasonable person would provide a post-sale warning. In light of the serious potential for overburdening sellers in this regard, the court should carefully examine the circumstances for and against imposing a duty to provide a post-sale warning in a particular case. . . .

j. Distinguishing post-sale failures to warn from defects existing at the time of sale. When a product is defective at the time of sale liability can be established without reference to a post-sale duty to warn. A seller who discovers after sale that its product was defective at the time of sale within the meaning of this Restatement cannot generally absolve itself of liability by issuing a post-sale warning. As long as the original defect is causally related to the harm suffered by the plaintiff, a prima facie case under this Restatement can be established notwithstanding reasonable post-sale efforts to warn. Of course, even when a product is defective at the time of sale a seller may have an independent obligation to issue a post-sale warning based on the rule stated in this Section. Thus, a plaintiff may seek recovery based on both a time-of-sale defect and a post-sale failure to warn. . . .

Lovick v. Wil-Rich
588 N.W.2d 688 (Iowa 1999)

CADY, Justice.

The manufacturer of a farm cultivator appeals from a judgment entered by the district court in favor of the product user in this product liability action. We conclude the district court failed to fully instruct the jury on the negligence claim based upon a post-sale duty to warn, and this incomplete instruction constituted prejudicial error. We affirm in part, reverse in part, and remand for a new trial.

I. Background Facts and Proceedings.

On May 20, 1993, Leo Lovick set out to cultivate a field preparatory to spring planting. He was an experienced farmer. The land was owned by Paul Rotgers and Lovick was using his cultivator.

Lovick pulled the cultivator to the field with a tractor. The wings of the cultivator were in the upright, vertical position to accommodate its transportation. Once in the field, Lovick attempted to unfold or lower the wings into position to begin cultivation.

The wings of the cultivator folded and unfolded by the operation of two hydraulic cylinders, which also held the wings in its vertical position. Additionally, the wings were secured in the upright position by a metal pin manually inserted under each wing, near the rear of the implement. The pins were designed to hold the wing in the vertical position in the event of hydraulic or mechanical failure.

Lovick positioned himself under the left wing of the cultivator to remove the first pin. The wing immediately fell when the pin was removed. Lovick was severely injured. Later investigation revealed the wing fell when Lovick removed the pin because the linkage attaching the cylinder to the wing had broken. Consequently, the pin was the only device holding the wing in its upright position at the time it was removed.

Wil-Rich first introduced the vertical fold model cultivator into the market in 1971. Since that time it has manufactured approximately 35,000 units. The cultivator which injured Lovick was manufactured and sold by Wil-Rich in 1981. Rotgers purchased the cultivator in "the late 80's." He was at least the second owner. The cultivator contained a warning sign which cautioned the operator to remove the pin prior to lowering the wings. Wil-Rich placed the warning on the cultivator because it believed hydraulic pressure against the wing pins could break the hydraulic cylinder. The operator's manual further warned against going under the wings to remove the pins.

In 1983, Wil-Rich received a report that a wing of one of its cultivators had fallen and injured the operator. Since that time, it received eight other such reports. In 1988, Wil-Rich began to affix a warning label to the cultivators it manufactured to caution operators of the danger of going under the wing to remove the pin. Wil-Rich added this warning in response to the reports of operators injured by a falling cultivator wing, as well as changes in engineering standards.

In 1994, Wil-Rich began a campaign to notify current owners of its cultivators of the danger of falling wings. It also made a backup safety-latch kit available for installation on the wings.

Lovick instituted a strict liability and negligence action against Wil-Rich. He sought compensatory and punitive damages. At trial, Lovick successfully introduced evidence that Deere & Company, a competitor of Wil-Rich, instituted a safety program in 1983 for its similarly designed cultivator after learning of instances of the wing falling on the operator. The Deere & Company program included efforts to locate the cultivator owners, and equip the existing cultivators with a wing safety latch and an upgraded warning label. Lovick also introduced evidence of the nine other accidents involving the wing of a Wil-Rich cultivator falling on an operator.

Wil-Rich investigated the prior accidents as the information became available. It also became aware of the Deere & Company post-sale warning program in 1987, but did not institute its post-sale warning program prior to 1994 essentially due to the practical difficulties of identifying and locating the owners and users of previously sold cultivators.

The trial court submitted the case to the jury on the strict liability theory of defective design and the negligence claim of breach of a post-sale duty to warn. It also submitted punitive damages on the negligence claim. The jury returned a verdict in the amount of $2,057,000. The verdict included $500,000 in punitive damages and $400,000 in loss of consortium to Lovick's wife. . . .

III. *Post-Sale Duty to Warn.*

We first address the issue of whether the trial court erred in instructing the jury on the duty of Wil-Rich to warn. Wil-Rich claimed it had no duty to warn following the sale. It further claimed the instruction given by the district court was too vague to permit the jury to understand the scope of the duty or to properly determine whether it was breached.

A. Existence of Duty....

The body of law we have developed concerning a manufacturer's duty to warn has been predicated on warning of inadequacies at the time of manufacture and sale. A growing number of jurisdictions, however, have now expanded this duty to require warnings after the sale when the product later reveals a defect not known at the time of sale. See 3, American Law of Products Liability §32:79 (3d ed. 1998). . . .

Iowa unceremoniously joined this growing trend in 1986 when our legislature enacted the products liability state-of-the-art defense statute. In establishing the state-of-the-art defense in products liability actions, our legislature added:

> Nothing contained in this section shall diminish the duty of an assembler, designer, supplier of specifications, distributor, manufacturer or seller to warn concerning subsequently acquired knowledge of a defect or dangerous condition that would render the product unreasonably dangerous for its foreseeable use or diminish the liability for failure to so warn.

Iowa Code §668.12 (1987). Although no statutory or judicial post-sale duty to warn had been recognized in Iowa prior to the statute, section 668.12 clearly established our legislature's understanding of the duty. We previously recognized this statutory post-sale duty, but have not had the occasion to begin to consider its specific application or parameters. This case presents such an occasion.

The district court recognized the existence of a post-sale duty to warn but only submitted a general reasonableness standard of care instruction to the jury. Wil-Rich claims the instruction was legally insufficient because the duty to warn is not absolute and the instruction did not identify the important factors to consider in determining whether the duty would be breached in a particular case. It requested an instruction which told the jury it was required to give a warning if it knew the cultivator posed a substantial risk of harm, the operator could be identified and would be unaware of the harm, a warning could be effectively communicated and acted upon, and the risk of harm was great enough to justify imposing a duty.

We acknowledge a post-sale duty to warn is compatible with the traditional point-of-sale duty to warn. See Frumer & Friedman, 1 Products Liability §2.22(2) (1991). It serves the same underlying purpose to reduce the chance of injury by equalizing the asymmetry of information between the parties. It is understandable that our legislature wanted to join the growing list of jurisdictions which recognize this post-sale duty. Yet, there are some distinctions which are important to recognize in considering the scope and nature of the post-sale duty.

Foremost, the burden of a manufacturer to warn product users can radically change after the sale has occurred and the manufacturer no longer has control over the product. Warning labels can be easily placed on products the manufacturer still controls. However, once the product is sold, a variety of circumstances can impede, if not make impossible, the ability of a manufacturer to warn users. Thus, while the rationale for post-sale and point-of-sale duties to warn are nearly identical, the parameters of those duties must be separately identified.

Most states which have considered the parameters of the post-sale duty to warn have developed various factors to guide its implementation. The American Law Institute recently distilled some of these factors from these decisions in the adoption of the post-sale duty to warn in the Restatement (Third) of Torts: Products Liability §10 (1998). The Restatement uses the reasonable person test to determine liability for the failure to warn following the sale, and articulates four factors to guide the determination of the reasonableness of the seller's conduct.

[The opinion sets out the text of §10, supra.]

We agree negligence is the appropriate theory to resolve post-sale failure to warn product liability claims. This theory of recovery is consistent with our approach to our prior cases involving the duty to warn at the point of sale. See Olson v. Prosoco, Inc., 522 N.W.2d 284, 288-90 (Iowa 1994). It recognizes the analytical merger of strict liability and negligence in determining liability for failure to warn, and we perceive no reason to resurrect the former distinction in post-sale failure to warn claims. The fighting question is whether it is necessary to articulate the various factors to consider in analyzing the reasonableness of a manufacturer's conduct once it acquires knowledge of a defect in a product following the sale.

B. Post-Sale Warning Jury Instruction. . . .

Although we recognize a post-sale duty to warn, we have identified potential circumstances faced by manufacturers after the sale of a product not present prior to the sale. The jury instruction given in this case, however, failed to inform the jury of these circumstances, or how they might impact the reasonableness of a manufacturer's conduct. Instead, the jury was told that if Wil-Rich subsequently learned its product is defective and unreasonably dangerous, it had a duty to warn those it knows or reasonably should know will be affected by the use of the product. This is essentially the same standard applied to a point-of-sale warning claim. We believe this standard is insufficient to guide the jury.

The duty to warn analysis at the point-of-sale essentially focuses on the foreseeability of a defective product. This standard does not, however, identify the special burdens which may exist for manufacturers to discharge this duty. Thus, if used in a post-sale case, it restricts the jury's considerations to the danger of the product and the manufacturer's foreseeability of the danger. It excludes numerous critical factors identified by the Restatement. The jury is not told to consider the manufacturer's ability to identify users, the likelihood the risk of harm is unknown, the ability to effectively communicate a warning, and any other burden in providing a warning compared to the risk of harm. These factors are critical to understanding the reasonableness of the conduct.

We believe the post-sale failure to warn instruction must be more specific than the point of sale failure to warn instruction and inform the jury to consider those factors which make it burdensome or impractical for a manufacturer to provide a warning in determining the reasonableness of its conduct. It is prejudicial error to fail to do so. Accordingly, we adopt the Restatement (Third) of Torts: Products Liability §10, including the need to articulate the relevant factors to consider in determining the reasonableness of providing a warning after the sale.

We recognize the comments to the Restatement refer to the need for the court to consider the four factors in deciding whether a post-sale breach of duty to warn claim should reach the jury. See Restatement (Third) of Torts: Products Liability §10 cmt. *a*. Clearly, the particular circumstances of a case may permit a trial court to utilize the factors to determine as a matter of law no duty existed.

Normally, however, the jury determines whether a warning of a product danger should have been given. Thus, if the trial court finds sufficient proof to impose a duty, the Restatement factors must be further utilized so the jury can understand the extent of the duty and properly perform its function in deciding the reasonableness of the conduct.

Our decision today confirms the existence of a post-sale duty for manufacturers to warn when it is reasonable to do so. The trial court may determine no duty existed in a particular case as a matter of law. Otherwise, the trial court should instruct the jury to determine whether it was reasonable to provide a warning by using the four Restatement factors.

We recognize the Restatement approach gives rise to other issues, but they are not before us at this time. We hold trial courts must incorporate the Restatement factors in instructing the jury on the duty to warn following the sale. . . .

V. Conclusion

[The Court affirmed the judgment for compensatory damages in favor of the plaintiff based on a claim that the cultivator was defectively designed. The Court's discussion of design defect is omitted from the opinion. Plaintiff's claim for punitive damages was predicated on the negligent post-sale failure to warn claim. Since the court concluded that the instruction on post-sale failure to warn was erroneous, it reversed the finding of punitive damages and ordered a new trial on post-sale failure to warn and punitive damages.]

AFFIRMED IN PART, REVERSED IN PART, AND REMANDED FOR NEW TRIAL

Did the Iowa court correctly apply the Restatement test? Does the Restatement enumerate factors to be taken into consideration before imposing a post-sale duty to warn? Or does it mandate that no such duty will be recognized unless all of the factors are present?

Judicial support for the post-sale duty to warn is strong. See, e.g., Thongchoom v. Graco Children's Products, Inc., 71 P.3d 214 (Wash. Ct. App. 2003); Savage v. Scripto-Tokai Corp., 2003 WL 21283807 (D. Conn. 2003); Myers v. Hearth Technologies, Inc., 621 N.W.2d 787 (Minn. Ct. App. 2001); Hiner v. Deer & Co., 161 F. Supp. 2d 1279 (D. Kan. 2001); Crowston v. Goodyear Tire & Rubber Co., 521 N.W.2d 401 (N.D. 1994). But there are some holdouts. See, e.g., Smith v. Daimlerchrysler Corp., 2002 WL 31814534 (Del. Super. Ct. 2002); McLennan v. American Eurocopter Corp., 245 F.3d 403 (5th Cir. 2001); Modelski v. Navistar, 707 N.E.239 (Ill. App. Ct. 1999); Boatmen's Trust Co. v. St. Paul Fire & Marine Ins. Co., 995 F. Supp. 956 (E.D. Ark. 1998). Other courts, like Pennsylvania, impose a post-sale duty to warn only if the product was defective from the time of manufacture and the manufacturer had notice of the defect. DeSantis v. Frick Co., 745 A.2d 624 (Pa. Super. Ct. 2000), appeal granted, 785 A.2d 89 (Pa. 2000), appeal dismissed as improvidently granted, 778 A.2d 619 (Pa. 2001).

An interesting application of the post-sale duty to warn is in the context of products plaintiffs' efforts to circumvent statutes of repose. Many jurisdictions have enacted time bars to tort liability that begin to run at the time of original sale by the last member of the vertical chain of product distribution. In contrast to statutes of limitations, which run from the time the plaintiff knows or has reason to know he has been injured by the product, and thus always give the diligent plaintiff time to file a claim, statutes of repose can bar claims before the plaintiff even suffers injury. The harshness of statutes of repose has led some plaintiffs to argue that, in addition to whatever defects may have existed at the time of original sale, claims for which are barred by an applicable statute of repose, the defendant manufacturer also breached a post-sale duty to warn, claims for which are not time-barred because the period of repose has not yet run. Were courts to recognize such post-sale warning claims indiscriminately, statutes of repose could be circumvented in every instance involving original design or warning defects. On the other hand, for courts automatically to hold such post-sale warnings claims to be time-barred after the running of the period of repose would undermine the manufacturer's incentives to provide timely warnings. Outcomes depend, of course, on the wording of the repose statute involved in a particular case. When the defect existed at the time of original sale, courts tend to hold that the claim based on the post-sale duty merges with the claim based on original defect, and is therefore time-barred. See, e.g., Land v. Yamaha Motor Corp., 272 F.3d 514 (7th Cir. 2001) (applying Indiana law). But when the post-sale duty is based on new information that became available after the time of original sale, the post-sale breach is deemed to be independent of the original defect and the failure to warn claim is not time-barred. See, e.g., Hunter v. Werner Co., 574 S.E.2d 426 (Ga. Ct. App. 2002).

For a useful in-depth treatment of manufacturers' post-sale duties to warn see generally M. Stuart Madden, Modern Post-Sale Warnings and Other Obligations, 27 Wm. Mitchell L. Rev. 33 (2000). For a critique of applying statutes of repose to post-sale failure to warn claims, see Frank E. Kulbaski III, Statutes of Repose and the Post-Sale Duty to Warn: Time for a New Interpretation, 32 Conn. L. Rev. 1027 (2000).

An obligation somewhat related to the post-sale duty to warn is the duty to recall. Much like the post-sale duty to warn, this duty entails an informational component in that recall notice certainly may warn users of the dangers posed by a given product. However, beyond this, the duty to recall also encompasses a duty to retrieve the product and physically correct some feature of the recalled product or, if correction is not feasible, to remove the product from the stream of commerce. Generally the duty to recall is fairly circumscribed. As the Restatement (Third) of Torts: Products Liability §11 explains, courts have refused to recognize a common law duty to recall products. As the Restatement notes, a duty to recall arises only when a governmental directive issued pursuant to a statute or administrative regulation specifically requires that a product seller or distributor recall a product line or when a seller or distributor voluntarily undertakes to recall a product. In the latter case, the seller or distributor may be liable if it fails to exercise a reasonable degree of care. As Comment *a.* of the Restatement asserts, a duty to recall imposes significant burdens on manufacturers, and as such, imposition of such a duty should be left to government agencies that have the data-gathering capacity to best determine when the benefits of a recall justify its burdens.

The admissibility of recall letters to prove a product's defective design at time of sale relates inextricably to the issue of subsequent remedial measures previously discussed. See Chapter Four, p.195, supra. As noted earlier, state courts are split as to the appropriate scope of the rule in products liability actions. Those courts that apply the subsequent remedial measures rule explicitly to all products liability actions based on defective design would certainly consider barring recall evidence under the rule as well. See, e.g., In re Air Crash Disaster at Sioux City, 1991 WL 279282 (N.D. Ill. 1991) ("Judge Posner's analysis in *Flaminio* [that Rule 407 applies equally to strict products liability and negligence actions] applies fully to the 'identical' arguments plaintiffs offer in support of excluding recall letters from the scope of Rule 407"); Giglio v. Saab-Scania of America, Inc., 1992 WL 329557 (E.D. La. 1992) (excluding evidence of recall campaign, finding that "there can be little doubt that a recall campaign is a measure 'taken which, if taken previously, would have made the event less likely to occur'").

E. SPECIAL PROBLEMS WITH PROXIMATE CAUSE

1. Would the Plaintiff Have Heeded an Adequate Warning?

The issue of but-for-the-defect, pursued in Section C of Chapter Three, supra, is especially difficult in the context of failure to warn. Under every approach taken in every jurisdiction, the plaintiff must show that the defendant's failure to warn was the proximate cause of the plaintiff's injury. To do that, the plaintiff must show that if an adequate instruction or warning had been given, the addressee (typically the product user or consumer) would have acted differently in a manner that would have reduced or avoided the plaintiff's injury. For example, in Gray v. Cannon, 807 So. 2d 924 (La. Ct. App. 2002), an automobile passenger was injured in an accident allegedly caused by a tire blow-out. The plaintiff claimed, inter alia., that the manufacturer should have warned the driver not to drive on tires with low air pressure. The tire in question had a slow leak that caused it to overheat and fail catastrophically. In affirming summary judgment for the tire manufacturer, the court noted that the tires "seemed fine" to the parties involved in the accident. Thus, any failure to warn against driving on an underinflated tire was not a cause of the plaintiffs' harm: "an absence of warnings, unless it is coupled with the knowledge that *would have* called the warnings into play, was not 'reasonably connected' to the accident caused by the tire's eventual rupture." Id. at 929. The "what if" inquiries that the causation issue presents in failure-to-warn cases are among the most difficult that courts confront.

The intermediate appellate court of Washington confronted these difficulties in Ayers v. Johnson & Johnson Baby Products Co., 797 P.2d 527 (Wash. Ct. App. 1990), involving a 15-month-old toddler who aspirated (breathed in) baby oil and suffered irreversible brain injury. The trial court set aside a $2,500,000 verdict in favor of the child and his family, in part on the ground that a more adequate warning by the defendant would not have done any good. The family had kept the baby oil on a high shelf along with other products they did not want the toddler to reach. The child's teen-aged sister had transferred some of the oil into a small bottle which she kept in her purse to use after high school gym class. On the day of the accident the sister inadvertently left her purse on the floor in their home. The toddler found the purse, opened the small bottle and began to drink its contents. At that moment the child's mother entered the room, discovered the child drinking the contents, and yelled at him to stop. Responding reflexively, the boy gasped and inhaled the oil into his lungs, where it prevented his lungs from functioning properly. When the mother discovered he had been drinking baby oil her concerns were alleviated and she took no further steps to check for difficulties. Hours later, she discovered the child had suffered brain damage from oxygen deprivation.

The plaintiffs claimed that Johnson & Johnson should have warned of the risks of aspiration and the very great harm that could result if aspiration should occur. In reversing the JNOV entered below, the appellate court reasoned:

> Family members testified that house rules required that anything known to be dangerous be kept high out of reach of the twin baby boys. Mrs. Ayers testified that she was a label reader and that had she known of the risks of aspiration, everyone else in the family would have known also. Laurie Ayers, who left the purse containing the baby oil on the floor, testified that Mrs. Ayers told all the family members to keep items known to be dangerous away from the boys. Laurie said that, never having been told of any risks associated with baby oil, she thought it was "no big deal" when she left her purse on the floor because there was nothing in it that could be harmful.
>
> Mr. Ayers also testified that products known to be dangerous were kept up on a top shelf out of reach. He testified further that had the product carried a warning of the risks, they would not have had it in the house.
>
> An appropriate inference from all this is that because the product was without a warning, the family members did not know it was dangerous and so did not treat it as such. The family members' testimony shows that they did not know of the particular harm that could result from aspirating mineral oil. . . . (797 P.2d at 291-292).

One judge dissented in *Ayers* on the ground that but-for causation had not been established. The Supreme Court of Washington, sitting en banc, unanimously affirmed the decision of the Court of Appeals, in an opinion closely tracking that of the intermediate court. Ayers v. Johnson & Johnson Baby Products Co., 818 P.2d 1337 (Wash. 1991).

The susceptability of infants to suffer injury at the hands of apparently innocuous household products knows no bounds. Thus, in Fraust v. Swift & Co., 610 F. Supp. 711 (W.D. Pa. 1985), the district court denied the defendant's motion for summary judgment, ruling that the mother of a 16-month-old infant might not have known of the risk of feeding him a peanut butter sandwich. The child choked on the peanut butter and suffered severe brain damage. A jury might find that the defendant-manufacturer breached its duty to warn of hidden dangers and that the breach proximately caused the injuries. And in Emery v. Federated Foods, Inc., 863 P.2d 426 (Mont. 1993), a two-and-one-half-year-old toddler choked on a marshmallow in the kitchen of his home, suffering brain injuries. The Supreme Court of Montana reversed summary judgment for the defendant, holding that genuine issues of fact were presented regarding whether a warning should have been given that young children might choke on marshmallows and, if warnings had been given, the child's mother would have been able to prevent the injury. The dissent took a different view: "The net result of the majority opinion may well be that warnings must be placed on nearly every food item available to the public if the provider is to avoid litigation for a claim of products liability — an interesting challenge for the providers of edible items." Id. at 434.

Obviously, the but-for causation issue looms large in these "child ingestion" cases. Even if warnings had been given, would the warnings have made any difference? As in *Ayers,* supra, the parents swear on a Bible, no doubt sincerely, that "If we had only known, we would have saved our baby!" But if all foods came with warnings in big red letters: "Babies may choke on this and suffer brain damage," would parents keep *everything* in the house locked away where older siblings could not get them and give them to the toddlers?

In response to the obvious difficulties of trying to answer the but-for questions in these cases, courts began to hold that when a product is sold without a warning, a rebuttable presumption arises that the consumer would have read any warning provided by the manufacturer and acted so as to minimize the risks. In an influential early decision, the Texas high court affirmed an alternative holding of the trial court giving the plaintiff a new trial on what, without a presumption, would have been very weak evidence of causation. See Jacobs v. Technical Chemical Co., 480 S.W.2d 602 (Tex. 1972). The court explained:

> It has been suggested that the law should supply the presumption that an adequate warning would have been read. "Where warning is given, the seller may reasonably assume that it will be read and heeded." Restatement (Second) of Torts §402A, Comment *j* (1965). Such a presumption works in favor of the manufacturer when an adequate warning is present. Where there is no warning, as in this case, however, the presumption that the user would have read an adequate warning works in favor of the plaintiff user. In other words, the presumption is that Jacobs would have read an adequate warning. The presumption may, however, be rebutted if the manufacturer comes forward with contrary evidence that the presumed fact did not exist. Depending upon the individual facts, this may be accomplished by the manufacturer's producing evidence that the user was blind, illiterate, intoxicated at the time of the use, irresponsible or lax in judgment or by some other circumstance tending to show that the improper use was or would have been made regardless of the warning. Id. at 606.

In the decade after *Jacobs,* other courts followed suit. See, e.g., Reyes v. Wyeth Labs., 498 F.2d 1264 (5th Cir.), *cert. denied,* 419 U.S. 1096 (1974); Nissen Trampoline Co. v. Terre Haute First National Bank, 332 N.E.2d 820 (Ind. Ct. App. 1975), *rev'd on other grounds,* 358 N.E.2d 974 (Ind. 1977); Cunningham v. Charles Pfizer & Co., Inc., 532 P.2d 1377 (Okla. 1974).

The trend in favor of applying a heeding presumption in warnings cases has been substantial. See, e.g., Tenbarge v. Ames Taping Tool Systems Inc., 190 F.3d 862 (8th Cir. 1999) (applying Missouri law) (manufacturer of dry wall taping gun, who provided no warning of repetitive stress injury, was subject to a rebuttable presumption that had a warning been given it would have been heeded). In 1998, the Third Circuit predicted that Pennsylvania would adopt a heeding presumption in failure to warn cases. Pavlik v. Lane Limited/Tobacco Exporters International, 135 F.3d 876, 883 (3d Cir. 1998). Although Pennsylvania's high court has not yet decided this issue, the lower courts have indeed adopted a heeding presumption in two asbestos-related cases. See, e.g., Lonasco v. A-Best Products

Co., 757 A.2d 367 (Pa. Super. Ct. 2000); Coward v. Owens-Corning Fiberglas Corp., 729 A.2d 614 (Pa. Super. Ct. 1999).

Other courts continue to place the traditional burden on the plaintiff to establish causation in failure to warn cases. See, e.g., Wilson v. Bradlees of New England, 250 F.2d 10 (1st Cir. 2001) (refusing to recognize the heeding presumption in suit based on diversity jurisdiction where New Hampshire has not adopted the "read and heed" presumption). Riley v. American Honda Motor Co., 856 P.2d 196 (Mont. 1993) (a heeding presumption is unwarranted since warnings often go unread and even when read are ignored); Hiner v. Bridgestone/Firestone, Inc., 978 P.2d 505 (Wash. 1999) (failure to warn that installation of snow tires on front wheels only can cause poor mishandling was not cause-in-fact of accident since plaintiff had not examined tires for any warnings imprinted on the tire and had not read the instruction manual).

How much evidence should be sufficient to rebut the presumption that, if a warning had been given, the plaintiff would have heeded it? And what happens to the presumption when the defendant introduces sufficient rebuttal evidence?

Golonka v. General Motors Corp.
65 P.3d 956 (Ariz. Ct. App. 2003)

TIMMER, Presiding Judge.

Factual and Procedural History

On April 17, 1997, Ruth Golonka pulled her 1987 GM Sierra truck in front of her neighbor's curb to load chairs into the truck bed. She attempted to shift her transmission into "park" but, according to GM, mis-shifted to a position between "park" and "reverse." Before exiting the truck, Mrs. Golonka did not turn off the engine, remove the key, or set the parking brake. Mrs. Golonka walked to the rear of the truck and dropped the tailgate to load the chairs. The truck then shifted into "reverse" and backed over Mrs. Golonka, killing her.

Mrs. Golonka's husband and children ("Plaintiffs") brought this wrongful death lawsuit against GM based on theories of strict product liability (defective transmission design and an information defect) and negligence (transmission design and failure to warn). Plaintiffs sought both compensatory and punitive damages.

At the conclusion of the subsequent jury trial, GM moved for judgment as a matter of law ("JMOL") on the non-design aspects of each claim, arguing that Plaintiffs had failed to present evidence that any information defect or failure to warn caused Mrs. Golonka's death. GM also moved for a JMOL on Plaintiffs' request for punitive damages. The court denied both motions. . . .

The jurors found GM at fault on the negligence claim and assigned 40% of fault to Mrs. Golonka and the remaining 60% to GM. The jurors also found GM at fault on the products liability claim alleging an information defect and assigned 50% of fault to Mrs. Golonka and the remaining 50% to GM. But the jurors found GM not at fault on the products liability claim alleging defective design. The jury awarded compensatory and punitive damages to Plaintiffs. After the trial court denied GM's renewed motion for JMOL and its motion for new trial, this appeal followed. . . .

Discussion

GM argues that the trial court erred by (1) denying GM's motion for JMOL because Plaintiffs failed to prove that any information defect or failure to warn regarding mis-shifts caused Mrs. Golonka's death and (2) denying GM's motion for new trial because a jury instruction incorrectly imposed a burden on GM to disprove that Mrs. Golonka would have heeded any warning about mis-shifts. . . .

B. Denial of JMOL on Failure-to-Warn Claims

GM argues that the trial court erred by denying the motion for JMOL on the failure-to-warn claims because Plaintiffs did not prove that any deficiency in GM's warnings caused Mrs. Golonka's death. To prove causation, Plaintiffs were required to present evidence that if GM had issued a proper warning, Mrs. Golonka would have taken precautions to avoid the accident. Gosewisch v. Am. Honda Motor Co., 153 Ariz. 400, 403, 737 P.2d 376, 379 (1987) (superseded by A.R.S. §12-683 (1992) with respect to affirmative defenses). Although causation is ordinarily a question of fact for the jury, GM contends that because no properly admitted evidence demonstrated that Mrs. Golonka would have heeded a different or better warning about mis-shifts, the court should have granted a JMOL in favor of GM on the warnings claims. Plaintiffs counter that they satisfied their burden of proof by introducing admissible evidence that Mrs. Golonka would have heeded a proper warning, and the trial court therefore properly denied the motion for JMOL.

GM contends that we should follow the supreme court's decision in *Gosewisch,* which affirmed the trial court's refusal to give a warnings instruction in a products liability case because the plaintiff had failed to introduce any evidence that the alleged defective warning had caused plaintiff's injury. But unlike the situation in *Gosewisch,* Plaintiffs in this case introduced causation evidence.

GM engineer Robert Lange testified that an audible warning of mis-shifts was feasible in the 1970s and could have been installed in GM vehicles from that time forward. Plaintiffs also provided the jury with GM engineer Roger McCarthy's testimony in a similar case that a person would react with "surprise and shock" and "investigate" the first time he or she heard an audible warning or saw flashing lights triggered by a mis-shift, although that person might ignore such warnings if repeated multiple times. Plaintiffs' expert witness, Dr. Mark Sanders, opined that an audible warning of a mis-shift would be "very effective."

Reasonable persons could infer from this evidence that an audible warning system would have alerted Mrs. Golonka to a mis-shift before she walked behind the truck and dropped its tailgate, and that the warning would have caused her to take action to prevent the accident.

Plaintiffs also introduced evidence that GM could have issued better warnings in its owner's manual, or by sending warning letters or on-product labels to customers. According to Dr. Sanders, a warning label about mis-shifts affixed to the visor or steering column, or a separate warning letter, "would have definitely increased the probability that [Mrs. Golonka] would have taken appropriate action."

This evidence supported a conclusion that a different or better written warning would have prevented Mrs. Golonka's death.

Finally, Plaintiffs introduced evidence that Mrs. Golonka had read portions of the owner's manual for the 1987 Sierra truck, had heeded the truck's "service vehicle soon" light when activated, and had heeded safety warnings for other products. The jury could have reasonably inferred from this evidence that Mrs. Golonka was safety conscious and would have heeded a better warning about mis-shifts. . . .

Plaintiffs introduced sufficient evidence of causation to submit the warnings claims to the jury. Consequently, the trial court did not err by denying GM's motion for JMOL.

C. Jury Instruction on Heeding Presumption

GM next argues that the trial court erred by instructing the jury on the so-called "heeding presumption." We will reverse on this basis only if the instruction was both erroneous and prejudicial to GM's substantial rights.

The "heeding presumption" is a rebuttable presumption used in a strict liability information defect case to allow the fact-finder to presume that the person injured by product use would have heeded an adequate warning, if given. The presumption is useful to plaintiffs in such cases, as it might otherwise be difficult to demonstrate how an injured or deceased person would have reacted to a given warning. Coffman v. Keene Corp., 133 N.J. 581, 628 A.2d 710, 719 (1993) (recognizing heeding presumption eases difficulty of showing absence of warning was substantial factor in causing injury).

The trial court instructed the jury on the heeding presumption as follows:

> Where a warning is given, a seller may reasonably assume that it will be read and heeded. If you find the warning is adequate, then your verdict must be for Defendant on this claim. However, if you find the warning to be inadequate, then you must start with the presumption that an adequate warning would have been read and heeded. In those circumstances, the Defendant then has the burden of proving that it is more probably true than not that an adequate warning would not have been read or would not have been heeded. You may consider all the evidence presented in this case to make that determination. If you find the Defendant has proved that an adequate warning would not have been read or heeded, then your verdict must be for Defendant on this claim. If you find that Defendant has not proved that an adequate warning would not have been read or heeded, then you may return a verdict for Plaintiff on this claim if you find that Plaintiff has proved the other elements of this claim.

GM contends the court erred in giving this instruction because (1) the heeding presumption is not utilized in Arizona, (2) even if the presumption is utilized, it is inapplicable in this case, and (3) the instruction incorrectly shifted the burden of persuasion to GM concerning causation. We address each contention in turn.

1. The Heeding Presumption in Arizona

In Dole Food, 188 Ariz. at 305-06, 935 P.2d at 883-84, this court recognized and applied the heeding presumption to reverse entry of summary judgment in a strict liability information defect case. The court described the presumption as springing from comment *j* to Restatement (Second) §402A. [See excerpt from *Ja-*

cobs, supra.] Because comment *j* has been highly criticized by commentators and was ultimately dropped from the Restatement (Third) of Torts, GM argues that the heeding presumption is no longer viable in Arizona. See Restatement (Third) §2, Reporters' Note, cmt. *l* (characterizing comment *j* as containing "unfortunate language" that "has elicited heavy criticism from a host of commentators").

GM overlooks the fact, however, that courts have adopted the heeding presumption without reference to comment *j.* In Sheehan v. Pima County, 135 Ariz. 235, 238, 660 P.2d 486, 489 (App.1982), the court described the heeding presumption as a presumption of due care "founded on a law of nature and has for its motives the fear of pain, maiming and death." While this foundation for the heeding presumption may be shaky in light of the increasing number of warnings in our society that are routinely ignored, sound public policy and procedural convenience reasons exist for use of the presumption.

In light of the difficulty of demonstrating how an injured or deceased person would have reacted to a particular warning, manufacturers who issue products with inadequate safety warnings could escape any consequence, thereby decreasing the incentive for manufacturers to adequately warn consumers of dangers inherent in product use. By easing the burden of proving causation, "[t]he use of the heeding presumption provides a powerful incentive for manufacturers to abide by their duty to provide adequate warnings." Coffman, 628 A.2d at 718.

Additionally, use of the heeding presumption is often procedurally desirable. Specifically, the presumption assists plaintiffs in proving causation in cases in which the injured person has either died or has become incapacitated, and evidence of how that person would have reacted to an adequate warning is therefore limited or unavailable. . . .

In summary, use of the heeding presumption in strict liability failure-to-warn cases furthers Arizona's policy of protecting the public from defective and unreasonably dangerous products. The presumption is also procedurally desirable to ensure that legitimate claims of information defect are fairly addressed. For these reasons, the heeding presumption is viable in Arizona.

2. *Applicability of Heeding Presumption in this Case*

GM next argues that even assuming the viability of the heeding presumption in Arizona, the trial court erred in instructing the jury on it because the presumption dissipated in the face of evidence supporting a finding that Mrs. Golonka would not have heeded an adequate warning about mis-shifts.

To resolve the [issue,] we examine the operation of presumptions used in civil cases in Arizona. Thereafter, we decide how the heeding presumption operates and whether the court correctly instructed the jury on the presumption in this case.

In 1938, the Arizona Supreme Court adopted the "bursting bubble" theory of presumptions championed by Harvard Law Professor James B. Thayer. See Seiler v. Whiting, 52 Ariz. 542, 547-48, 84 P.2d 452, 454-55 (1938). Under this theory, the existence of the presumed fact is assumed unless the party against whom the presumption operates meets the burden of production or proof imposed by the presumption. In such cases, even if the fact-finder might disbelieve the rebuttal evidence, the "bubble is burst," and the existence or non-existence of the presumed fact must be determined as if the presumption had never operated in the case. The trial court rather than the jury determines whether the party opposing the presumed fact has presented sufficient evidence to destroy the presumption. If the presumption is rebutted, the court should not refer to the presumption in jury instructions, although the jury may still draw reasonable inferences from the facts originally giving rise to the presumption. . . .

Arizona courts generally hold that a presumption is a procedural device that shifts the burden of producing contrary evidence to the party opposing the presumed fact but leaves the burden of persuasion on the proponent of the evidence. However, . . . some presumptions shift to the party opposing the presumption the burden to persuade the court of the non-existence of the presumed fact. The courts in these cases do not explain why some presumptions shift the burden of persuasion rather than the burden of production, and we do not discern a common thread among the cases for doing so. . . . Consequently, we do not attempt to divine specific reasons underlying the burden-shifting effects of all presumptions. Instead, we adhere to the generally held view that a presumption serves to shift the burden of producing evidence, unless the substantive common law or legislative enactment giving rise to the presumption compels a conclusion that the presumption shifts the burden of persuasion to the party opposing the presumed fact.

Following the general rule, we [hold] that the heeding presumption shifts the burden of production rather than the burden of persuasion. Plaintiffs contended at oral argument that the inherent difficulties of proving that an information defect caused a product-related injury, coupled with the public's desire to encourage manufacturers to provide adequate warnings, create a public policy reason for deciding that the heeding presumption shifts the burden of persuasion. We disagree. Although presumably aware of such difficulties, our supreme court has nevertheless held that the plaintiff in a strict products liability case based on information defect bears the burden of proving that the manufacturer's failure to issue an adequate warning proximately caused the injury at issue. Gosewisch, 153 Ariz. at 403, 737 P.2d at 379. The court further recognized that the heeding presumption, without deciding its viability, merely reduces, not eliminates, that burden.

Based on the foregoing, the heeding presumption serves to shift the burden of production to the manufacturer. The manufacturer meets this burden by introducing evidence that would permit reasonable minds to conclude that the injured party would not have heeded an adequate warning. The court determines whether the manufacturer has rebutted the presumption and, if so, the presumption is destroyed, the existence or non-existence of the presumed fact must be determined as if the presumption had never operated in the case, and the jury is never told of the presumption. However, the jury may still draw reasonable inferences from the facts originally giving rise to the presumption. We now decide whether the trial court in this case properly applied the heeding presumption.

GM introduced competent evidence to rebut the heeding presumption. The owner's manual for Mrs. Golonka's truck cautioned that before the driver leaves the vehicle, "to reduce the risk of personal injury as a result of vehicle movement," the driver should apply the parking brake, shift to park, shut off the engine, and remove the key. Despite this warning, Mrs. Golonka apparently did not set the parking brake, turn off the engine, or remove the key immediately prior to the accident. Mrs. Golonka also apparently ignored a buzzer that activated when she opened her door with the key still in the ignition. According to expert testimony elicited by GM, had Mrs. Golonka followed these steps, she would have prevented the accident.

Evidence that Mrs. Golonka ignored safety warnings that related to the accident would have allowed reasonable minds to conclude that she would have similarly ignored adequate warnings about mis-shifts. The court therefore erred by instructing the jury on the presumption rather than finding that the presumption had spent its force. Although we do not lightly overturn a jury's verdict, we are compelled to do so here because the erroneous jury instruction creates substantial doubt that the jurors were properly guided in their deliberations. The success of Plaintiffs' information defect claim depended in significant part on their ability to prove that Mrs. Golonka would have heeded an adequate warning about mis-shifts, which in turn would have prevented her death. The evidence on this point was greatly disputed and vehemently argued to the jury by both Plaintiffs and GM. The jury's resolution of this disputed issue of fact may well have turned on who bore the burden of proving the fact. Thus, the court's instruction, which mistakenly shifted the burden to GM, prejudiced GM's substantial rights and requires a new trial on Plaintiffs' negligent failure-to-warn claim and their strict liability information defect claim. . . .

Conclusion

For the foregoing reasons, we hold that the jury necessarily found GM at fault only for negligent failure to warn and strict liability information defect. The trial court correctly denied GM's motion for JMOL on these claims. . . . However, although the court properly recognized the viability of the heeding presumption in Arizona, the court improperly instructed the jury on this presumption. Because this error prejudiced GM's substantial rights, we reverse and remand for a new trial on Plaintiffs' claims for negligent failure to warn and strict liability information defect.

2. *When the Defendant's Failure to Warn Causes Plaintiff to Suffer Harm from Another Product*

Powell v. Standard Brands Paint Co.
212 Cal. Rptr. 395 (Cal. Ct. App. 1985)

SIMS, J.

Plaintiffs Bruce Powell and Dale Mereness appeal from a summary judgment granted in favor of defendant Standard Brands Paint Company (Standard Brands) in an action for personal injuries. We affirm.

Factual and Procedural Background

As relevant to this appeal, the complaint prepared by plaintiffs' attorneys stated that defendant Standard Brands and other defendants were the suppliers or manufacturers "of certain equipment and cleaning solvents, specifically being, but not limited to a buffer and/or thinner referred to herein." The complaint further alleged that Standard Brands and other defendants "negligently and carelessly op-

authors' dialogue 15

AARON: I really don't like the heeding presumption. It's an embarrassment.

JIM: Don't mince words, Aaron; tell me how you really feel.

AARON: Failure to warn claims are difficult enough for defendants. It's essentially a rhetorical tort. Unlike design, there's no technology involved. All the plaintiff needs to do is cook up a story with his lawyer about something that wasn't obvious that they should have told him, and he's getting to the jury. Informed choice makes it even easier. "Many people wouldn't have cared, but I do — I'm special." But-for causation is, or was, the defendant's only hope. "Even if we should have told you, it wouldn't have made any difference, for crying out loud." But now many states put the burden on defendant to prove it wouldn't have mattered. Every warnings claim has clear sailing to the jury.

JIM: You are exaggerating, of course. But I get your point. Don't you at least agree that when the person who should have been warned is dead, or otherwise unavailable to testify, there should be a presumption?

AARON: Yes, but we don't need a formal presumption. Circumstantial proof and common sense should be enough in those cases to avoid unfairness to the plaintiff. But an across-the-board presumption is overkill. The *Ayers* case (p.379, supra) is a good example of what I'm talking about. Even if Johnson & Johnson had told that family all about the dangers of aspiration of baby oil, the same thing would've happened. The dissent was clearly right in that case.

JIM: I'm glad you mentioned *Ayers.* I read the majority as saying that when a tragedy like that occurs once in a blue moon, the manufacturer should pay on almost an "enterprise liability" basis. For me, the subtext was the court's willingness to suspend the normal rules to allow the one-family-in-a-million to receive no-fault insurance coverage, in effect, for their loss. It's an "echo of enterprise liability," if you will.

AARON: And you approve of such lawlessness? You, of all people?

JIM: Let's just say I understand it. It doesn't upset me that much.

AARON: Well, I don't approve one bit. Even if *Ayers* is understandable (where did you get that "subtext" jargon?), in most cases the heeding presumption works unfairly against the manufacturer. In any other area of the law it would be laughed out of court.

JIM: My hunch is that when a products plaintiff tries to rely on the presumption in a case where common sense suggests that a warning wouldn't have made any difference, the court will take the case from the jury on causation grounds.

AARON: But in the "old days," that was easy because the court could say that the plaintiff had not carried the burden of production on but-for causation. But once the burden is on the defendant, via the heeding presumption, what's the court going to say?

JIM: Reasonable minds can't differ? Let me think about it.

erated, controlled, warned, supplied, maintained, managed, designed, manufactured, or modified said buffer and/or thinner which proximately caused the injuries and damages to plaintiff as herein described." Paragraph X of the complaint pleaded in pertinent part, "That on or about June 10, 1982, . . . *while plaintiff was stripping a tile floor with said* buffer and *thinner,* an explosion occurred due to the negligence of the defendants, and each of them, proximately causing the hereinafter described injuries and damages to plaintiff." (Italics added.)

As relevant here, plaintiff sought recovery for damages on theories of negligence and strict liability.

In moving for summary judgment, Standard Brands competently showed that plaintiffs commenced work on June 9, 1982, using lacquer thinner supplied by Standard Brands to remove sealer from ceramic tile. They worked without incident throughout the evening until they had used up the Standard Brands lacquer thinner. However, plaintiffs were unable to finish the job on June 9. The following day, June 10, plaintiffs' employer ordered two five-gallon containers of lacquer thinner from codefendant Harris Automotive (Harris). This lacquer thinner was manufactured by codefendant Grow Chemical Coatings Company (Grow).[10] Working in an area approximately 25-50 feet from where they had worked the previous evening, plaintiffs commenced pouring the Grow lacquer thinner on the tile floor and buffing the thinner with the electric buffer. During this operation, an explosion occurred, seriously injuring both plaintiffs and giving rise to the instant lawsuit.

Plaintiffs relied primarily on the declaration of plaintiff Powell. Powell declared that the lacquer thinner purchased from Standard Brands contained neither warnings nor safety instructions and that "Had anyone at Standard Brands advised us of the dangerous nature of lacquer thinner or of its highly flammable characteristics, I would not have used it on the job and would not have been using it at the time of my injury."

The trial court granted the motion and plaintiffs appeal from the summary judgment entered in favor of Standard Brands.

Discussion . . .

As best we understand it, plaintiffs assert on appeal that Standard Brands owed them a duty to warn them of the dangerous properties of its lacquer thinner, that it breached its duty to warn, and that its failure to warn was a legal proximate cause of the injuries suffered by plaintiffs. To our knowledge, no reported decision has held a manufacturer liable for its failure to warn of risks of using its product, where it is shown that the immediate efficient cause of injury is a product manufactured by someone else. Unfortunately, in addressing the merits of plaintiffs' important and novel contention, we find the meagre brief filed by plaintiffs' attorneys of little assistance. Needless to say, however, we believe our own research has produced a correct result. . . .

---

10. The declarations submitted on the motion for summary judgment do not indicate whether the Grow thinner contained warnings. . . . Plaintiffs' complaint alleged that defendants Grow and Harris wrongfully failed to warn of risks of their product. The burden was on defendant Standard Brands to refute those pleaded allegations by competent evidence. It did not do so. For present purposes, we must assume the unchallenged allegations of the complaint control and that the Grow lacquer thinner contained inadequate warnings.

Standard Brands has not refuted plaintiffs' pleaded assertions that said defendant owed plaintiffs a duty to warn of risks of *its* product and that it breached its duty. However, the evidence is undisputed that the immediate efficient cause of plaintiffs' injuries was the explosion of a product manufactured not by Standard Brands but rather by Grow. The question posed is whether Standard Brands' failure to warn was a legal proximate cause of plaintiffs' injuries. We conclude, in the circumstances of this case, it was not. . . .

Where a defendant has committed a wrongful act, and where a third person also commits a later wrongful act, and both are alleged to have caused plaintiff's injuries, the courts have asked whether the subsequent act of the third party was a superseding cause that served to break the requisite chain of causation between defendant's wrongful act and the injury. Whether the act of the third person is a superseding cause depends in part on whether it (and plaintiff's injury) was reasonably foreseeable.

On the undisputed facts tendered in this case, we conclude the explosion of Grow's product, and plaintiffs' consequent injuries, were not reasonably foreseeable consequences of Standard Brands' failure to warn as a matter of law. We explain.

Although there appears to be some uncertainty about the knowledge required of a manufacturer to justify liability for failure to warn of *its* product it is clear the manufacturer's duty is restricted to warnings based on the characteristics of *the manufacturer's own product.* Understandably, the law does not require a manufacturer to study and analyze the products of others and to warn users of risks of those products. A manufacturer's decision to supply warnings, and the nature of any warnings, are therefore necessarily based upon and tailored to the risks of use of the manufacturer's own product. Thus, even where the manufacturer erroneously omits warnings, the most the manufacturer could reasonably foresee is that consumers might be subject to the risks of the manufacturer's own product, since those are the only risks he is required to know.

From the foregoing, it follows that if plaintiff's theory of liability (asserted on appeal) has any validity, it would be limited to situations where the risks of use of the product immediately causing injury are identical to the risks of use of the product previously used with inadequate warnings. No other risks are reasonably foreseeable. As a practical matter, a contrary conclusion would require each manufacturer to ascertain the risks of products manufactured by others within an industry and to warn of the highest risks a consumer might encounter. Such a requirement would place on each manufacturer an untoward duty and would penalize inventive manufacturers whose products are, in fact, of lower risk than other products in the industry.

We therefore believe the theory of liability now asserted by plaintiffs would require at a minimum that: (a) the product immediately causing injury (product B) was subject to the same generic description as the product previously used with inadequate warnings (product A), e.g., "lawnmower," "electric drill," "aspirin," etc.; (b) product B was generally used for the same purposes as product A by consumers; (c) product B's warnings were inadequate; and (d) *product B had risks of use identical to those of product A.* This theory of liability gains credence to the extent a generically identical product (with presumably identical risks of use) is made by a limited number of manufacturers in an industry, and there is an industry-wide practice of omitting warnings on the product. In such a situation, each manufacturer has reason to know that the risks of use associated with its product are the same as the risks of the other products and that a consumer will receive no adequate warnings from the other products.

In this case we need not decide whether a manufacturer who fails to warn of its product may be held liable for injuries immediately caused by the use of a product with the same generic description and identical risks of use, because it is clear plaintiffs' attorneys never pleaded facts necessary to support that legal theory, nor anything remotely resembling it, in the trial court. . . .

The complaint prepared by plaintiffs' attorneys did not plead that Standard Brands' absence of warnings caused plaintiffs to use a generically identical product, nor a product with the same risks of use, nor even a substantially similar product, without knowledge of its dangers. Indeed, the complaint pleads no relationship of similarity whatsoever between the Standard Brands and the Grow products. Rather, the complaint prepared by plaintiffs' attorneys states plaintiffs were using Standard Brands' product when an explosion occurred. The complaint tendered a theory that the Standard Brands product was the immediate efficient cause of injury, i.e., plaintiffs were using it when it exploded. That pleading was the one defendant had to encounter on its motion for summary judgment. Standard Brands showed, contrary to plaintiffs' pleading, plaintiffs were not using its product at the time of explosion. Standard Brands therefore refuted the only theory of causation pleaded by plaintiffs' attorneys. There was no other viable theory of causation pleaded, and the trial court had no duty to invent one. . . .

We conclude, on the facts pleaded and adjudicated on the motion for summary judgment, it was not reasonably foreseeable as a matter of law that Standard Brands' failure to warn of risks of its product would cause plaintiffs to suffer injuries while using the product of another. In the circumstances, the explosion of Grow's product was an intervening and superceding cause of injury to plaintiffs. Consequently, Standard Brands' failure to warn was not a proximate cause of plaintiffs' injuries as a matter of law. Standard Brands' motion for summary judgment was properly granted.

The judgment is affirmed.

Courts often treat this question under the "duty/breach" heading. See, e.g., Block v. Wyeth, Inc., 2003 WL 203067 (N.D. Tex. 2003), in which the plaintiff was injured by a generic drug. The plaintiff sued the manufacturer of the patented form of the same drug, alleging that the manufacturer of the generic drug, identical to the patented drug, had copied the patented drug's warnings verbatim, and that such warnings were inadequate. The district court granted defendant Wyeth's motion to dismiss, concluding: "Block invites this Court to extend Texas tort law into new and uncharted territory. This Court believes the Texas Supreme Court would decline such an invitation and must therefore do likewise." Id. at 3.

Powell and *Block* absolve a manufacturer from liability for failing to warn when the plaintiff was injured by a look-alike product emanating from another manufacturer. Earlier in this chapter, in connection with our discussion of Persons v. Salomon North America, Inc., we confronted a related but different issue: whether a seller or manufacturer has a duty to warn of dangers arising when its product is combined with another manufacturer's product, causing injury, and where neither product is, by itself, defective. A majority have recognized such a duty. See, e.g., Scheman-Gonzales v. Saber Manuf. Co., 2002 Fla. App. LEXIS 4620 (2002) (duty to warn of mismatch of tire and rim); Rastelli v. Goodyear Tire & Rubber Co., 591 N.E.2d 222, 225-26 (N.Y. 1992) (acknowledging that where the combination of one sound product with another sound product creates a dangerous condition, the manufacturer of each product has a duty to warn). But see Firestone Steel Products Co. v. Barajas, 927 S.W.2d 608, 614 (Tex. 1996) (holding that a "manufacturer generally does not have a duty to warn or instruct about another manufacturer's products").

3. Did the Plaintiff Suffer the Sort of Harm that an Adequate Warning Would Have Aimed at Preventing?

This is the failure-to-warn version of the "result within the risk" proximate cause issue presented in Section D of Chapter Three, supra. In the authors' experience, it can be a "sleeper" issue, often obscured by the more vivid but-for issues in the sorts addressed in the preceding subsections. That is, the natural tendency is to focus on whether an adequate warning would have made any difference. This can be a difficult question to answer, as the heeding presumption cases bear witness. But when it is clear that a better warning would have prevented injury, it is tempting to conclude that the defendant's failure to warn has proximately caused the plaintiff's harm. Consider the following Problem.

PROBLEM TWENTY-ONE

The facts in Problem Twenty, supra, involving injury to Kathy Kritzik's eyes from wearing contact lenses for too long a period, are incorporated herein by reference.

The Kritziks have learned, since the episode with the contact lenses, that women who take birth control pills and women who go through pregnancy are subject to changes in the cornea. Continual daily use of contact lenses without correction for such changes may cause distortion of the cornea, a condition that corrects itself in several months when the lenses are no longer used. Women who take the pill should have their eyes checked more frequently than others to assure that such distortion does not take place. Unbeknownst to either Dr. Quell or Kathy's parents, Kathy had been taking birth control pills during the months preceding last Christmas. Neither Dr. Quell nor the Seenco booklet indicated to Kathy that contact lenses should be monitored more carefully for women who are taking birth control pills. Kathy insists that she would not have asked her parents for contact lenses had she been told of the possibility of corneal distortion connected with her taking birth control pills. "I didn't want my folks to know about my taking the pill," she explains.

The senior partner handling the case is concerned that the element of proximate cause may be too weak and that the case may be dismissed on a motion for summary judgment or a motion for directed verdict. She has asked you to assess the likelihood of getting to a jury. You are to assume that all relevant events took place in New California. Indicate any further information that should be obtained. Assume that Ayers v. Johnson & Johnson, supra, is a decision of the New California Supreme Court.

F. OTHER FORMS OF DEFECTIVE MARKETING

Failures to instruct or warn constitute by far the lion's share of defective marketing cases, but not all of them. Occasionally, a product whose risks are quite obvious and more than offset by corresponding benefits from normal use finds its way into the hands of a user who is predictably incapable of handling the product safely. (It might be said that such cases present a "mismatch" of product and user.) Sometimes the issue presented in such a case involves the design of the product itself. In other cases, the design of the packaging has been found defective because it did not adequately resist the efforts of a young child to open the package and consume its harmful contents.

The sorts of "mismatch" cases of interest here are those in which defendant's marketing techniques appear inadequate in trying to prevent the mismatch from occurring — where, for example, inherently and unavoidably dangerous products, designed for adult use, are marketed directly to children, or are marketed to adults without adequate reminders to keep the products out of the hands of children. The latter type of case, of course, may be subsumed under the "failure to instruct or warn" umbrella. But the former cannot so comfortably be characterized, and constitutes a separate category of defective marketing cases.

A case involving this sort of mismatch is Salvi v. Montgomery Ward & Co., Inc., 489 N.E.2d 394 (Ill. App. Ct. 1986), in which the plaintiff alleged that the defendant/manufacturer had defectively designed the safety on its BB gun and that the defendant/retailer had negligently sold the gun to the plaintiff's brother, then 14 years of age, whose carelessness eventually led to the plaintiff's being shot in the eye. The trial court sent both claims to the jury, which returned a verdict in favor of the manufacturer and against the retailer in the amount of $570,000. The container in which the BB gun was packaged warned that it should not be allowed in the possession of a child under the age of 16 without adult supervision. The accident occurred while the plaintiff's brother was cleaning the gun. Notwithstanding the fact that an Illinois statute set the age of 13 as the age below which it was criminal to sell an air gun to a minor, and the fact that the plaintiff's brother was over 15 years of age when the accident occurred, the court of appeals affirmed the verdict against the retailer. Referring to such cases as involving "negligent entrustment" of dangerous instrumentalities, other courts have reached the same result on similar facts. See, e.g., Moning v. Alfono, 254 N.W.2d 759 (Mich. 1977) (young plaintiff struck in eye with missile from slingshot sold by defendant to 11-year-old user).

In some "mismatch" cases, plaintiffs claim that defendants not only negligently allowed the product mismatch to occur, but that they negligently encouraged it by targeting the mismatched group. In Merrill v. Navegar, 89 Cal. Rptr. 2d 146 (Cal. Ct. App. 1999) *rev'd* 28 P.3d 116 (Cal. 2001), the trial court granted summary judgment for a defendant gun manufacturer at trial. The plaintiffs claimed that the manufacturer negligently advertised its product in such a way as to increase their appeal to criminals by, for example, publicizing its product's nonglare finish, combat slash, threaded barrel suitable for silencers, flash muzzles and extension, and "excellent resistance to fingerprints." The plaintiffs argued that this marketing in turn caused a fatal shooting. The intermediate court found that the defendant owed the public a duty not to create unreasonable risks by advertising firearms so as to appeal to persons with criminal purposes. On appeal, the Supreme Court of California reversed because the plaintiffs had produced no evidence showing that the perpetrator of the fatal shooting had been influenced by defendant's advertisement, or that the perpetrator had even seen the advertisement.

Another category of defective marketing cases involve advertisements that encourage consumers to use a product in unsafe and gratuitously dangerous ways. Jamieson v. Woodward & Lothrop, supra, involving the elastic exerciser that injured the plaintiff's eye, might have been (but was not) viewed by the court as a "negligent advertising" case. One decision that comes very close to recognizing such a basis for liability is Leichtamer v. American Motors Corp., 424 N.E.2d 568 (Ohio 1981). The plaintiffs were injured when they drove a Jeep Model CJ-7 off the top of a ridge, flying almost 50 feet through the air and landing upside down near the bottom of the slope 25 feet below. The plaintiffs argued that the defendant-manufacturer's advertising induced such user behavior, and that the roll bars should therefore have been able to withstand the great forces put upon them:

> Cited as exemplary of this "intentional incitement of unlawful conduct" was the sound track employed in the Jeep television commercials: "My Jeep CJ is the toughest rig around"; "That's Jeep guts — Guts to take you where only the toughest dares to go"; "Jeep guts — will take you places you have never been before"; "CJ-5 — will give the young couples the ride of their lives on the dunes and gutsy ground steering"; "All right, which one of you guys is going to climb that big old hill with me? I mean you guys aren't yellow, are you? Is it a steep hill? Yeah, little lady, you could say it's a steep hill. Let's try it. The King of the Hill, is about to discover the new Jeep CJ-7"; "That Jeep four-wheel drive is tough enough to go anywhere." . . . The television commercials relied upon by the Court of Appeals demonstrated an off-the-road use. The commercials are relevant to the foreseeable use of the vehicle and the unreasonable danger of the product when used as intended. [Id. at 471, 424 N.E.2d at 579.]

In some negligent marketing cases, particularly in the area of prescription drugs, plaintiffs claim that their use of a product and resulting harm was caused by the distorting effects of the defendant's "overpromotion" of its product. One of the clearest examples of a court grounding its decision on the defendant's negligent "overpromotion" of a product is Stevens v. Parke, Davis & Co., 507 P.2d 653 (Cal. 1973), in which the plaintiff recovered a substantial judgment based on the defendant's having induced her physician to negligently prescribe a dangerous drug that the physician knew full well was dangerous. The court concluded:

> We are satisfied from a review of the evidence . . . that the jury could reasonably find that [the doctor's] negligent prescription of Chloromycetin for Mrs. Stevens was a foreseeable consequence of the extensive advertising and promotional campaign planned and carried out by the manufacturer. The record reveals in abundant detail that Parke, Davis made every effort, employing both direct and subliminal advertising, to allay the fears

of the medical profession which were raised by knowledge of the drug's dangers. It cannot be said, therefore, that [the doctor's] prescription of the drug despite his awareness of its dangers was anything other than the foreseeable consequence — indeed, the desired result — of Parke, Davis' over-promotion. 507 P.2d at 664.

Decades later, one court revisiting the issue of "overpromotion" in a prescription drug case cited *Stevens* for the proposition that "an adequate warning to the [medical] profession may be eroded or even nullified by overpromotion of the drug through a vigorous sales program which may have the effect of persuading the prescribing doctor to disregard the warnings given." Motus v. Pfizer, Inc., 196 F. Supp. 2d 984, 998 (C.D. Cal. 2001). However, as is often the case in negligent advertising cases (see also *Merrill,* supra), the court granted the defendant's motion for summary judgment because the plaintiff had failed to produce evidence showing that the defendant's marketing had persuaded, or even reached, the prescribing doctor.

For further discussion of negligent marketing cases not involving failure to warn or instruct, see Richard C. Ausness, Will More Aggressive Marketing Practices Lead to Greater Tort Liability for Prescription Drug Manufacturers?, 37 Wake Forest L. Rev. 97 (2002), Jean M. Eggen & John G. Culhane, Gun Torts: Defining a Cause of Action for Victims in Suits Against Gun Manufacturers, 81 N.C. L. Rev. 115 (2002), Patrick Cohoon, An Answer to the Question Why the Time Has Come to Abrogate the Learned Intermediary Rule in the Case of Direct-to-Consumer Advertising of Prescription Drugs, 42 S. Tex. L. Rev. 1333 (2001).

CHAPTER SIX
Express Warranty and Misrepresentation

A. EXPRESS WARRANTY

Centuries ago, a body of law developed in England to regulate commercial dealings among merchants. The substance of this specialized "law merchant" drew heavily from the customs of the marketplace and reflected a shared desire to give effect to commercial agreements and to uphold the reasonable expectations of participants when deals broke down. Among the features of this complex body of law were "warranties"—obligations imposed by law on sellers of goods requiring them to stand behind the quality of their goods and to make buyers whole when the quality fell short of promised performance levels or reasonable expectations.

Given its practical significance, and the accompanying need for a uniform and predictable set of rules, the law merchant gradually came to be codified by statute. In the United States, the first great statute governing sales warranties was the Uniform Sales Act, which controlled commercial practices dealing with the sale of goods. Beginning in 1954, state legislatures replaced the Sales Act and other commercial law statutes with the Uniform Commercial Code (U.C.C., Code), Article 2 of which governs sale-of-goods transactions. Today, the law of commercial sales warranties in this country is governed largely by the U.C.C.

At about the same time that state legislatures began adopting the Code, state courts were engaged in developing the common law of products liability. Generally, under the Code's express warranty provision, a consumer may be able to recover for injuries suffered when a product fails to live up to a seller's *promises* regarding the quality, character, or performance of a good even if the buyer cannot prove that the *product* was defectively manufactured or designed, or marketed with insufficient warnings.

1. What Is Warranted

Breach of an express warranty occurs when goods fail to conform to a promise made by the seller to the buyer regarding their character or their capacity to perform. Most express warranty claims arise from statements made in three contexts: (1) statements (written or oral) made by a seller to a buyer at or before the time of sale; (2) statements packaged with the goods at the time of sale; and (3) statements directed to the public at large, such as through advertising.

U.C.C. §2-313 sets forth the rules that determine how a warranty may be created.

UNIFORM COMMERCIAL CODE

§2-313. EXPRESS WARRANTIES BY AFFIRMATION, PROMISE, DESCRIPTION, SAMPLE

(1) Express warranties by the seller are created as follows:

(a) Any affirmation of fact or promise made by the seller to the buyer which relates to the goods and becomes part of the basis of the bargain creates an express warranty that the goods shall conform to the affirmation or promise.

(b) Any description of the goods which is made part of the basis of the bargain creates an express warranty that the goods shall conform to the description.

(c) Any sample or model which is made part of the basis of the bargain creates an express warranty that the whole of the goods shall conform to the sample or model.

(2) It is not necessary to the creation of an express warranty that the seller use formal words such as "warrant" or "guarantee" or that he have a specific intention to make a warranty, but an affirmation merely of the value of the goods or a statement purporting to be merely the seller's opinion or commendation of the goods does not create a warranty.

OFFICIAL COMMENT...

3. The present section deals with affirmations of fact by the seller, descriptions of the goods or exhibitions of samples, exactly as any other part of a negotiation which ends in a contract is dealt with. No specific intention to make a warranty is necessary if any of these factors is made part of the basis of the bargain. In actual practice affirmations of fact made by the seller about the goods during a bargain are regarded as part of the description of those goods; hence no particular reliance on such statements need be shown in order to weave them into the fabric of the agreement. Rather, any fact which is to take such affirmations, once made, out of the agreement requires clear affirmative proof. The issue normally is one of fact....

8. Concerning affirmations of value or a seller's opinion or commendation under subsection (2), the basic question remains the same: What statements of the seller have in the circumstances and in objective judgment become part of the basis of the bargain? As indicated above, all of the statements of the seller do so unless good reason is shown to the contrary....

Baxter v. Ford Motor Co.
12 P.2d 409 (Wash. 1932)

HERMAN, J.

During the month of May, 1930, plaintiff purchased a model A Ford town sedan from defendant St. John Motors, a Ford dealer, who had acquired the automobile in question by purchase from defendant Ford Motor Company. Plaintiff claims that representations were made to him by both defendants that the windshield of the automobile was made of non-shatterable glass which would not break, fly, or shatter. October 12, 1930, while plaintiff was driving the automobile through Snoqualmie Pass, a pebble from a passing car struck the windshield of the car in question, causing small pieces of glass to fly into plaintiff's left eye, resulting in the loss thereof. Plaintiff brought this action for damages for the loss of his left eye and for injuries to the sight of his right eye. The case came to trial, and, at the conclusion of plaintiff's testimony, the court took the case from the jury and entered judgement for both defendants. From that judgement, plaintiff appeals.

The principal question in this case is whether the trial court erred in refusing to admit in evidence, as against respondent Ford Motor Company, the catalogues and printed matter furnished by that respondent to respondent St. John Motors to be distributed for sales assistance. Contained in such printed matter were statements which appellant maintains constituted representations or warranties with reference to the nature of the glass used in the windshield of the car purchased by appellant. A typical statement, as it appears in appellant's exhibit for identification No. 1, is here set forth:

> Triplex Shatter-Proof Glass Windshield. All of the new Ford cars have a Triplex shatterproof glass windshield — so made that it will not fly or shatter under the hardest impact. This is an important safety factor because it eliminates the dangers of flying glass — the cause of most of the injuries in automobile accidents. In these days of crowded, heavy traffic, the use of this Triplex glass is an absolute necessity. Its extra margin of safety is something that every motorist should look for in the purchase of a car — especially where there are women and children. . . .

Respondent Ford Motor Company contends that there can be no implied or express warranty without privity of contract, and warranties as to personal property do not attach themselves to, and run with, the article sold. . . .

In the case at bar, the automobile was represented by the manufacturer as having a windshield of non-shatterable glass "so made that it will not fly or shatter under the hardest impact." An ordinary person would be unable to discover by the usual and customary examination of the automobile whether glass which would not fly or shatter was used in the windshield. In that respect, the purchaser was in a position similar to that of the consumer of a wrongly labeled drug, who has bought the same from a retailer, and who has relied upon the manufacturer's representation that the label correctly set forth the contents of the container. For many years, it has been held that, under such circumstances, the manufacturer is liable to the consumer, even though the consumer purchased from a third person the commodity causing the damage. Thomas v. Winchester, 6 N.Y. 397, 57 Am. Dec. 455.

The rule in such cases does not rest upon contractual obligations, but rather on the principle that the original act of delivering an article is wrong, when, because of the lack of those qualities which the manufacturer represented it as having, the absence of which could not be readily detected by the consumer, the article is not safe for the purposes for which the consumer would ordinarily use it. . . .

Since the rule of caveat emptor was first formulated, vast changes have taken place in the economic structures of the English speaking peoples. Methods of doing business have undergone a great transition. Radio, bill boards and the products of the printing press have become the means of creating a large part of the demand that causes goods to depart from factories to the ultimate consumer. It would be unjust to recognize a rule that would permit manufacturers of goods to create a demand for their products by representing that they possess qualities which they, in fact, do not possess; and then, because there is no privity of contract existing between the consumer and the manufacturer, deny the consumer the right to recover if damages result from the absence of those qualities, when such absence is not readily noticeable. . . .

[Reversed and remanded.]

On retrial, Ford Motor Co. sought to introduce expert testimony that no auto manufacturer produced a better windshield at the time. The trial judge excluded the testimony and the appellate court affirmed. 35 P.2d 1090 (Wash. 1934). Why wasn't the expert testimony allowed in? *b/c it is irrelevant to the Q of express warranty. This Expert testimony would only speak to reasonable alternative design.*

PROBLEM TWENTY-TWO

Sarah Goldenberg, a lovely six-year-old girl, suffered from a severe and relatively rare form of asthma. Any number of conditions, including shifts in temperament such as anger or excitement in anticipation of a coming event, could trigger an asthma attack. Many foods were on Sarah's forbidden list. The foods to which Sarah was most allergic were milk and milk products. Although Sarah had a sweet tooth and loved chocolate, she knew that eating a chocolate bar was out of the question. Even the chocolate bars labeled "non-dairy" often contained slight traces of milk sufficient to trigger a severe allergic reaction, but in amounts so minute that they need not be reported on the label.

In light of Sarah's condition, the only chocolate bars that her parents would permit her to eat were kosher chocolate bars that were labeled "non-dairy." According to kosher dietary law, it is impermissible to eat dairy and meat derivative foods at the same time. Thus, kosher rabbinical supervision assures that even slight traces of dairy products are not present in chocolate that is labeled "kosher non-dairy." The Goldenbergs do not observe these dietary laws, but know that the strictness of the rabbinical supervision is the best assurance available to them that the candy Sarah eats contains no milk derivatives whatsoever.

Last fall, during a family get-together, Sarah's grandmother bought and gave to Sarah a kosher-certified non-dairy chocolate bar. The label of the bar read "kosher non-dairy." Apparently, the batch of bars from which that bar came included a different emulsifier that was similar, but not precisely identical, to the emulsifier normally used. The rabbi performing the kosher supervision of ingredients did not pick up on the substitution, and thus was unaware that the particular batch contained a slight trace of milk powder. The problem was subsequently corrected, but not before the batch of chocolate bars containing the traces of milk powder reached the market and one bar was given to Sarah.

After consuming the chocolate bar, Sarah reacted violently to the trace of milk powder. Rushed to the emergency room of the nearest hospital, she died shortly after arrival. Sarah's parents consulted an attorney about bringing an action against Tasty Kosher Chocolates Inc., the manufacturer of the chocolate bar that triggered her fatal asthmatic attack. The Goldenbergs' attorney filed suit based on breach of express warranty.

You represent Tasty Kosher Chocolates Inc. In preparing your defense of this case, you consulted a rabbinic authority seeking to discover the religious ramifications that attend a consumer's innocent consumption of a non-kosher product. The rabbi tells you that if a purchaser relies on a competent rabbinic supervisor who certifies a product as kosher, then there is no moral culpability if the product turns out to be non-kosher. Nonetheless, the rabbi said, "It is unsettling to have eaten non-kosher food." You are about to file a motion for summary judgment. Making reasonable assumptions of fact where necessary, draft a memorandum in support of the motion.

2. Basis of the Bargain—The Reliance Controversy

Under the Uniform Sales Act, a plaintiff was required to prove her reliance on a seller's promise in order to state a claim for breach of an express warranty. The Act provided:

> Any affirmation of fact or any promise by the seller relating to the goods is an express warranty if the natural tendency of such affirmation or promise is to induce the buyer to purchase the goods, *and if the buyer purchases the goods relying thereon.* (emphasis added)

Under the Sales Act, regardless of how egregious a manufacturer's broken promise appeared, courts were unwilling to countenance a breach of express warranty claim absent a showing of reliance. For example, in McCully v. Fuller Brush Co., 415 P.2d 7 (Wash. 1966), plaintiff, while doing extensive cleaning, suffered permanent skin damage after immersing her bare hands in the defendant's household cleaning solution. Despite the undisputed evidence that several of the product's ingredients were well-known skin irritants, the product was labeled as being "Kind to Your Hands." The court held that plaintiff could not proceed under an express warranty theory where her evidence "f[ell] short of establishing the essential element of reliance." Id. at 11.

With the element of reliance drawing heavy fire from courts and academics, the U.C.C. did away with the term and replaced it instead with the nebulous "basis of the bargain" test. Whether this change was intended to preserve, modify, or displace altogether the element of reliance remained unclear.

Cipollone v. Liggett Group, Inc.
893 F.2d 541 (3d Cir. 1990)

BECKER, Circuit Judge.

This appeal is from a final judgment in a protracted products liability case in which the plaintiff, Antonio Cipollone, seeks to hold Liggett Group, Inc., Lorillard, Inc., and Philip Morris, Inc., three of the leading firms in the tobacco industry, liable for the death from lung cancer of his wife, Rose Cipollone, who smoked cigarettes from 1942 until her death in 1984. . . .

Rose Cipollone was born in 1925 and began to smoke in 1942. She smoked Chesterfield brand cigarettes, manufactured by Liggett, until 1955. In her deposition, introduced into evidence at the trial, she stated that she smoked the Chesterfield brand to be "glamorous," to "imitate" the "pretty girls and movie stars" depicted in Chesterfield advertisements, and because the advertisements stated that Chesterfield cigarettes were "mild." Mrs. Cipollone stated that she understood the description of Chesterfield cigarettes as "mild" to mean that the cigarettes were safe.

Mrs. Cipollone also testified that she was an avid reader of a variety of magazines, frequently listened to the radio, and often watched television during the years that she smoked the Chesterfield brand. Although she could not specifically remember which Chesterfield advertisements she saw or heard during those years, Chesterfield advertisements appeared continuously in those media during that period. Several of these advertisements were introduced into evidence. The following copy appeared commonly in Chesterfield magazine advertisements during the year 1952:

> PLAY SAFE Smoke Chesterfield.
> NOSE, THROAT, and Accessory Organs not Adversely Affected by Smoking Chesterfields. First such report ever published about any cigarette. A responsible consulting organization has reported the results of a continuing study by a competent medical specialist and his staff on the effects of smoking Chesterfield cigarettes. A group of people from various walks of life was organized to smoke only Chesterfields. For six months this group of men and women smoked their normal amount of Chesterfields—10 to 40 a day. 45% of the group have smoked Chesterfields continually from one to thirty years for an average of 10 years each. At the beginning and at the end of the six-months period each smoker was given a thorough examination, including X-ray pictures, by the medical specialist and his assistants. The examination covered the sinuses as well as the nose, ears and throat. The medical specialist, after a thorough examination of every member of the group, stated: "It is my opinion that the ears, nose, throat and accessory organs of all participating subjects examined by me were not adversely affected in the six-month period by smoking the cigarettes provided."

5 J.A. 21, 22 (c. 1952). The defendants stipulated that Mrs. Cipollone had seen many of these advertisements. . . .

In 1955, Mrs. Cipollone stopped smoking Chesterfield cigarettes and began to smoke L & M filter cigarettes, also made by Liggett. In response to a question as to why she switched to the L & M brand, Mrs. Cipollone stated that "[w]ell, they were talking about the filter tip, that it was milder and a miracle it would keep the stuff inside a trap, whatever." When asked why she desired the filter tip, she testified that "it was the new thing and I figured, well, go along[, and that] it was better [because t]he bad stuff would stay in the filter then." When asked whether concern about the "bad stuff" was due to a concern about her health, she stated "[n]ot really. . . . It was the trend. Everybody was smoking the filter cigarettes and I changed, too."

She also stated that although she could not remember any specific advertisements, she did "recall the ads and . . . remember the tips [and] the messages of a filter, a safer, something to that effect. . . . That it would filter the nicotine and the tar and the tobacco[, and t]hat it would be a cleaner and fresher smoke." Mrs. Cipollone also stated that she "recall[ed] seeing an ad that said doctors recommend you smoke . . . I think it was L & M's. . . . [T]hrough advertising, I was led to assume that they were safe and they wouldn't harm me. . . . There was lots of advertising. There was advertising everywhere. There was advertising in magazines, on billboards, in newspapers.". . .

Mr. Cipollone brought his express warranty claim under U.C.C. §2-313(1), which provides:

> (1) Express warranties by the seller are created as follows:
> (a) Any affirmation of fact or promise made by the seller to the buyer which relates to the goods and becomes *part of the basis of the bargain* creates an express warranty that the goods shall conform to the affirmation or promise.
> (b) Any description of the goods which is made *part of the* basis of the bargain creates an express warranty that the goods shall conform to the description.

N.J.S.A. §12A:2-313(1) (emphases added). With respect to this issue, the district court gave the following instructions to the jury:

> [P]laintiff must prove . . . that Liggett, prior to 1966, made one or more of the statements claimed by the plaintiff and that such statements were affirmations of fact or promises by Liggett . . . [and] that such statements were part of the basis of the bargain between Liggett and consumers like Rose Cipollone. . . .
>
> The law does not require plaintiff to show that Rose Cipollone specifically relied on Liggett's warranties.
>
> Ordinarily a guarantee or promise in an advertisement or other description of the goods becomes part of the basis of the bargain if it would naturally induce the purchase of the product and no particular reliance by the buyer on such statement needs to be shown. However, if the evidence establishes that the claimed statement cannot fairly be viewed as entering into the bargain, that is, that the statement would not naturally induce the purchase of a product, then no express warranty has been created.

4 J.A. at 232-34.

Liggett contends that this interpretation of "part of the basis of the bargain" is flawed because the jury should also have been instructed that Mrs. Cipollone's nonreliance on the advertisements would preclude those advertisements from becoming "part of the basis of the bargain." Liggett argues that the express warranty verdict must therefore be set aside. Although our interpretation of the precise meaning of "reliance" differs somewhat from Liggett's, we agree.[1]

A.

Authority on the question whether reliance is a necessary element of section 2-313 is divided. Although a few courts have held that reliance is not a neces-

---

1. Initially, we emphasize that a representation made by a seller is not an express warranty if it is made in such a manner that both the seller and the buyer should understand to be a representation upon which the buyer will not rely. "[A]ll descriptions by merchants must be read against the applicable trade usages. . . ." N.J.S.A. §12A:2-313 U.C.C. Comment 5. A representation made in a manner that is generally recognized not to be a basis upon which purchasers make a decision to purchase goods cannot be a warranty when read against "applicable trade usages." This requirement is in accord with the traditional common law "puffing" exception in the law of contracts. See H. Hunter, Modern Law of Contracts: Breach and Remedies ¶4.02[3], at 4-7 to 4-8 (1986 & Supp. 1989). But Liggett has not contended, and we do not think it could, that its advertisements to consumers are generally recognized as not forming the basis upon which cigarette purchasing decisions are made. If such were the case, Liggett would not have spent millions of dollars on advertising.

sary element of section 2-313, the more common view has been that it is, and that either a buyer must prove reliance in order to recover on an express warranty or the seller must be permitted to rebut a presumption of reliance in order to preclude recovery. Some treatise writers support this interpretation. No New Jersey court or panel of this court has squarely addressed the question.

The history of section 2-313(1)(a), although informative, fails to give a clear answer as to whether reliance is required. Section 2-313(1)(a) is an adaptation of section 12 of the Uniform Sales Act. A comparison of the two sections reveals that they are substantially the same except for the replacement of section 12's express reliance requirement with section 2-313(1)(a)'s basis of the bargain requirement. The district court reasoned that the omission of the word "reliance" from section 2-313(1)(a), in light of section 12's use of that word, implied that reliance was no longer an element of express warranties. See 693 F. Supp. at 213. Liggett contends that "if U.C.C. §2-313 wrought the radical change in New Jersey warranty law that the trial court has read into it," then "[o]ne would think that the New Jersey Study Comments would have at least made reference to it." Liggett Br. at 19. We note in this regard that the New Jersey Study Comment One to section 12A:2-313 states that "[t]his section of the Code is comparable to section 12 of the Sales Act (N.J.S.A. 46:30-18), except that it characterized the warranties of sample and description as express warranties." There is no reference to the reliance issue.

Liggett argues that reliance must have some place in the "basis of the bargain" determination. Thus, even if reliance should be assumed, based on what "would reasonably induce the purchase of a product," a defendant must have an opportunity to prove nonreliance. This position finds some support in the U.C.C. comments. U.C.C. Official Comment 3 states:

> In actual practice affirmations of fact made by the seller about the goods during a bargain are regarded as part of the description of those goods; hence no particular reliance on such statements need be shown in order to weave them into the fabric of the agreement. Rather, *any fact which is to take such affirmations, once made, out of the agreement requires clear affirmative proof.* The issue normally is one of fact. [Emphasis added.]

Moreover, comment 8 states that "all of the statements of the seller [become part of the basis of the bargain] *unless good reason is shown to the contrary.*" (Emphasis added.) The plain language of these comments supports Liggett's position, at least to the extent it indicates that a defendant must be given some opportunity to show that the seller's statements were not meant to be part of the basis of the bargain.

A final argument in support of a reliance requirement is found in the amicus brief. Without a reliance requirement, one runs the risk of draining the term "basis of the bargain" of all meaning, because the buyer's subjective state of mind becomes completely irrelevant. The district court instructed the jury that a statement could be considered part of the basis of the bargain if it "would naturally induce the purchase of the products." This instruction is completely objective and would permit a buyer to sue for breach of express warranty even if the seller's warranties were advertisements made in another state or country, and even if the buyer did not hear of the claims in these advertisements until the day that she walked into an attorney's office to bring suit for personal injury. It strains the

Express Warranty

language to say that a statement is part of the "basis" of the buyer's "bargain," when that buyer had no knowledge of the statement's existence.

The above arguments notwithstanding, it is possible to read the "basis of the bargain" requirement as requiring some subjective inducement of the buyer, without requiring a reliance finding. Requiring that the buyer *rely* on an advertisement, whether by imposing this burden initially on the buyer bringing suit, or by allowing the seller to rebut a presumption of reliance, puts a heavy burden on the buyer — a burden that is arguably inconsistent with the U.C.C. as a whole, with other comments to section 2-313 in particular, and with several commentators' suggestions in this area.

The reliance requirement does not comport well with U.C.C. Official Comment 7 to section 2-313. Comment 7 states that "[i]f language is used after the closing of the deal . . . the warranty becomes a modification, and need not be supported by consideration if it is otherwise reasonable and in order. . . ." N.J.S.A. §12A:2-313 U.C.C. Comment 7. If a post-closing promise — on which, by definition, a seller cannot rely in deciding to make a purchase — can create a warranty, then it is difficult to see why a pre-closing promise can create a warranty only if relied upon.

Additionally, a reliance requirement seems inconsistent with U.C.C. Official Comment 4 to section 2-313. Comment 4 states that "the whole purpose of the law of warranty is to determine what it is that the seller has in essence agreed to sell." N.J.S.A. §12A:2-313 U.C.C. Comment 4. Reliance is irrelevant to what a seller agrees to sell.

In light of these seemingly inconsistent mandates on the reliance question, some might argue that it is foolish to try to reconcile what is patently inconsistent. We reject this suggestion however, because we find it feasible to reconcile the competing arguments, and we believe that the New Jersey Supreme Court would want us to try. We believe that the most reasonable construction of section 2-313 is neither Liggett's reliance theory, which fails to explain how reliance can be relevant to "what a seller agreed to sell," or the district court's purely objective theory, which fails to explain how an advertisement that a buyer never even saw becomes part of the "basis of the bargain." Instead, we believe that the New Jersey Supreme Court would hold that a plaintiff effectuates the "basis of the bargain" requirement of section 2-313 by proving that she read, heard, saw or knew of the advertisement containing the affirmation of fact or promise. Such proof will suffice "to weave" the affirmation of fact or promise "into the fabric of the agreement," U.C.C. Comment 3, and thus make it part of the basis of the bargain. We hold that once the buyer has become aware of the affirmation of fact or promise, the statements are presumed to be part of the "basis of the bargain" unless the defendant, by "clear affirmative proof," shows that the buyer knew that the affirmation of fact or promise was untrue. We believe that by allowing a defendant to come forward with proof that the plaintiff did not believe in the warranty,[2] we are reconciling, as the New Jersey Supreme Court would want us to,

---

2. If the defendant proves that the buyer did not believe in the warranty, the plaintiff should then be given the opportunity to show that the buyer nonetheless relied on the warranty. It is possible to disbelieve, but still rely on, the existence of a warranty. In this sense, the buyer can "buy" a lawsuit. Thus, if the buyer disbelieved the warranty, but could prove that she was relying on it when she bought the product, she could return the product for stipulated damages — for example, a refund — or economic damages — the difference between "the value of the goods accepted and the value the goods would have had

the U.C.C. comments, the U.C.C. case law, and traditional contract principles, which serve as the background rules to the U.C.C.

As indicated above, Comment 4 and Comment 7, as well as the largely dominant objective theory of contracts, militate in favor of an interpretation of express warranty that ignores the buyer's subjective state of mind. Under the extreme version of this theory apparently adopted by the district court, all the buyer should have to show is what the seller agreed to sell. In other words, an express warranty would be created when a seller makes statements to the public at large that would induce a reasonable buyer to purchase the product, even if the actual buyer never heard those statements. We find this result untenable, however. First, as mentioned above, this interpretation drains all substantive meaning from the phrase "basis of the bargain," and would allow a seller to collect even if that seller was unaware of the warranty until she walked into her attorney's office to file suit. Second, this interpretation is difficult, if not impossible, to square with other comments to the U.C.C. As discussed above, Comment 3 states that "no particular reliance on such statements need be shown. . . . Rather, any fact which is to take such affirmations, once made, out of the agreement requires clear affirmative proof." Comment 8 states that "all of the statements of the seller [become part of the basis of the bargain] unless good reason is shown to the contrary." Clearly, both Comment 3 and Comment 8 envision some mechanism for overcoming the presumption that the seller's statements, even if heard by the actual buyer, are a basis of the bargain. Much of the case law supports this "belief" principle. A statement in the bill of sale that the goods are new does not constitute an express warranty when both the buyer and the seller knew that the statement was false. See Coffee v. Ulysses Irrigation Pipe Co., 501 F. Supp. 239 (N.D. Tex. 1980). When a buyer has operated trucks before and knows that they need repairs, he cannot sue in express warranty on the seller's statement that the trucks were in good condition. See Janssen v. Hook, 1 Ill. App. 3d 318, 272 N.E.2d 385 (1971). "The same representations that could have constituted an express warranty early in the series of transactions might not have qualified as an express warranty in a later transaction if the buyer had acquired independent knowledge as to the fact asserted." Royal Business Machines v. Lorraine Corp., 633 F.2d 34, 44 (7th Cir. 1980). See also Overstreet v. Norden Laboratories, Inc., 669 F.2d 1286, 1291 (6th Cir. 1982) ("[A] statement known to be incorrect cannot be an inducement to enter a bargain."); Wendt v. Beardmore Suburban Chevrolet, Inc., 219 Neb. 775, 782, 366 N.W.2d 424, 429 (1985) (Car dealer's statements were not a basis of the bargain when plaintiff suspected that the car had been in an accident and had his mechanic inspect it.).

Although these cases reject, to a certain extent, one traditional contract principle, that terms should be construed objectively, they embrace another traditional contract principle, that of looking at the intention of the parties in light of the surrounding circumstances. See 3 R. Anderson, Uniform Commercial Code §2-313:36, at 29 (1983 & Supp. 1987). The relevant intent is that the statement be

---

if they had been warranted," U.C.C. §2-714. Such a buyer could not recover consequential damages, however. She would be barred by both U.C.C. §2-715 ("[I]f [the injured person] discover[s] the defect prior to his use, the injury would not proximately result from the breach of warranty."), and traditional contract principles, under which a buyer has a duty to mitigate damages and cannot recover for damages that she "could have avoided without undue risk, expense or humiliation," Restatement (Second) of Contracts §350(1) (1965). . . .

part of the basis of the bargain, and that, "as in the case of any contract term, is a question of the intent of the parties." Id. at 30.[3]

B.

Applying our interpretation of section 2-313 to the case at bar, we conclude that the district court's jury instructions were erroneous for two reasons. First, they did not require the plaintiff to prove that Mrs. Cipollone had read, seen, or heard the advertisements at issue. Second, they did not permit the defendant to prove that although Mrs. Cipollone had read, seen, or heard the advertisements, she did not believe the safety assurances contained therein. We must therefore reverse and remand for a new trial on this issue. . . .

Do you understand footnote 3? Aren't the chances pretty good that any instruction a trial judge might give pursuant to this opinion will be found to be in error?

Cipollone is representative of the confusion engendered by the "basis of the bargain" terminology. Some courts have interpreted the phrase synonymously with the old reliance requirement. See, e.g., American Tobacco Co. v. Grinnel, 951 S.W.2d 420, 436 (Tex. 1997) ("'Basis of the bargain' loosely reflects the common-law express warranty requirement of reliance"); Phillips v. Ripley & Fletcher Co., 541 A.2d 946, 950 (Me. 1988) (holding that comments to Maine's version of U.C.C. §2-314 "meant to continue the uniform sales act requirement that the purchaser must show reliance on the affirmation in order to make out a cause of action for breach of a[n express] warranty"). Others hold that the enactment of U.C.C. §2-314 eliminated the need to prove reliance. See, e.g., Torres v. Northwest Eng'g Co., 949 P.2d 1004, 1027 (Haw. Ct. App. 1997) (finding it illogical for U.C.C. drafters to purposefully abandon Uniform Sales Act's reliance test and yet preserve reliance as required element in breach of express warranty claim); Lutz Farms v. Asgrow Seed Co., 948 F.2d 638, 645 (10th Cir. 1991) (applying Colorado law) ("it appears that the majority of jurisdictions that have addressed the issue have found it unnecessary to require reliance from the buyer before a statement by the seller can be considered an express warranty"). For an exhaustive treatment of the issue, see generally Steven Z. Hodaszy, Express Warranties Under the Uniform Commercial Code: Is There a Reliance Requirement?, 66 N.Y.U. L. Rev. 468 (1991). See also Robert S. Adler, The Last Best Argument for Eliminating Reliance from Express Warranties: Real World Consumers Don't Read Warranties, 45 S.C. L. Rev. 429 (1994); John E. Murray, Jr., The Revision of Article 2: Romancing the Prism, 35 Wm. & Mary L. Rev. 1447 (1994); Sid-

---

3. Although we have emphasized the relevance of a buyer's *belief,* our construction of section 2-313 can be read as simply fleshing out the more commonly discussed *reliance* requirement with a framework of shifting presumptions and burdens of proof. Thus, in the context of advertisements claimed to be warranties, a plaintiff buyer must first prove that she saw the advertisements. This raises a (rebuttable) presumption of belief, which in turn raises an irrebuttable presumption of reliance. Next, a defendant seller may rebut the presumption of reliance, but only by proving that the plaintiff disbelieved the advertisement. Successfully proving disbelief creates a new rebuttable presumption of nonreliance. Finally, the plaintiff may rebut this presumption by proving reliance directly. Whether our holding is read as imposing a "belief" requirement or a "reliance" requirement thus is probably just a question of semantics, not substance.

ney Kwestel, Freedom from Reliance: A Contract Approach to Express Warranty, 26 Suffolk U. L. Rev. 959 (1992).

Cipollone dealt with an express warranty allegedly created by a seller's statements made via advertising and the media. What if a manufacturer's promises or affirmations are not directed to the public at large, but are contained instead in documents accompanying the sale of a product?

Yarusso v. International Sport Marketing, Inc.
1999 WL 463531 (Del. Super. Ct. April 1, 1999)

DEL PESCO, Judge. . . .

The relevant facts are as follows. Brian Yarusso ("Yarusso") was rendered quadriplegic as the result of an accident which occurred on October 20, 1991. The accident occurred while Yarusso was driving his off-road motorcycle (specifically designed for off road use in that it lacked certain things such as a horn, lights, and other features which are required for on road use, and it was lighter in weight) at a motocross track located off Church Road in Newark, Delaware. He was riding alone when he began, but after awhile, another motocross rider arrived and the two raced one another. Yarusso was injured when his bike, traveling over a series of moguls, hit one of the moguls in such a way that he was catapulted over the handlebars of his bike. He landed on his head, flipped over and eventually came to rest, face down in the dirt. At the time of the accident Yarusso was wearing a full array of safety equipment, including a Moto-5 helmet (the "helmet") manufactured by defendant, Bell Sports, Inc. ("Bell"). Plaintiff seeks damages for enhanced injuries claiming that a defect in the design of the helmet caused the enhanced injuries. Plaintiff also claims that certain [warranties] were breached.

The jury found no negligence but specifically found, in separate interrogatories, that the defendant breached an express . . . warranty and that the breach was a proximate cause of enhanced injuries. . . .

[I]n view of the evidence, in particular the testimony of Sundahl [a senior engineer at Bell], it is easy to see the basis for the jury's conclusion that a warranty was breached. Sundahl testified that the language in the owner's manual was "wrong." The owner's manual said that the "Moto-5 is designed to absorb the force of a blow first by spreading it over as wide an area of the outer shell as possible, and by crushing the non-resilient inner liner." There was a factual issue as to whether the inner liner crushed. The jury apparently concluded that it did not. A breach of warranty was established. The next question was proximate cause. The plaintiff's expert, Stalnaker, testified that if there had been crush of the liner it would have absorbed a sufficient amount of the force of the fall to reduce it to a point where the plaintiff's anatomy could have tolerated it, without injury. The verdict was not against the weight of the evidence.

The Warranty Claims

The evidence indicates that at the time plaintiff purchased the helmet he received an owner's manual for the helmet. . . .

Express Warranty 409

The second page of the owners manual contains the language which plaintiff contends constitutes express warranties. On the second page there are four title headings — Introduction, Helmet Performance, Proper Fit, and Retention System. Each is in bold type and underlined similar to the Limited Warranty on the first page.

Under the heading "Introduction" the following language appears:

> Your new Moto-5 helmet is another in the long line of innovative off-road helmets from Bell. It has been designed and developed by Bell to meet the needs of today's off-road enthusiasts. The materials used in its construction have been carefully chosen by Bell for their performance characteristics, durability and the comfort of the wearer. It has been carefully built, almost entirely by hand, and each critical component has been inspected numerous times during the manufacturing process. *The primary function of a helmet is to reduce the harmful effects of a blow to the head.* However, it is important to recognize that the wearing of a helmet is not an assurance of absolute protection. NO HELMET CAN PROTECT THE WEARER AGAINST ALL FORESEEABLE IMPACTS. To get the most out of your new helmet, it is important that you understand how to use it and care for it properly. READ THIS MANUAL THOROUGHLY BEFORE USING YOUR NEW HELMET. (Underlining added)

Directly below the "introduction" heading is the "Helmet Performance" heading under which the following language appears:

> *The Moto-5 is designed to absorb the force of a blow first by spreading it over as wide an area of the outer shell as possible, and second by the crushing of the non-resilient inner liner.* Damage to the helmet after an impact is not a sign of any defect in the helmet design or construction. It is exactly what the helmet is designed to do.
>
> See the section in this manual on Repair and Inspection Services for instructions on what to do if your helmet is subjected to a severe impact.

Concerning the purchase of the helmet plaintiff testified:

Q. . . . Do you remember buying this helmet?
A. Yes.
Q. Why did you buy this helmet?
A. I bought that helmet — I looked. I, basically, whenever I buy something, its [sic] something I've done for a fairly long time, I believe you get what you pay for. And, I mean, with tools I've bought over the years for my profession, I always try to buy the best and I look into whatever is the best out there and I try to buy whatever is the best. And after talking with several guys that I rode with, I went to Honda East Yamaha, which is where I bought all the parts for my bike, and after talking to the guys that work with that equipment, they all suggested the Bell Moto-5 because it was the top-of-the-line helmet, the best protector. . . . I read some literature on it and I purchased it knowing all that.
Q. Okay. And you got with the helmet a copy of the owner's manual, P106?
A. Yes.
Q. Did you read it?
A. Yes, I did.
Q. Did you believe it?
A. I did believe it.

Q. What it said?
A. Yeah, I believed it.
Q. Why did you wear a helmet?
A. I wore a helmet because I wanted to protect myself, I wanted to be safe, and I wanted to avoid from injuring my head or my neck, and that was my understanding of what helmets were supposed to do, and I just wanted to be safe.

A. Creation of Express Warranty

The plaintiff contends that express warranties were created through Bell with the following language in the owner's manual: "The Moto-5 is designed to absorb the force of a blow first by spreading it over as wide an area of the outer shell as possible, and second by crushing of the non-resilient inner liner" and "[t]he primary function of a helmet is to reduce the harmful effects of a blow to the head."

Defendant contends that the statements were not a basis of the bargain since the plaintiff had not read and could not have relied on the representations in the owner's manual when he bought the helmet.

Express warranties arise by a seller's affirmation of fact or promise, description of the goods, or a sample or model. To create an express warranty, the representation must become a part of the "basis of the bargain." Proof of reliance is not necessary to create to create [sic] an express warranty. Any affirmation of fact or promise by the seller is presumed to be a part of the basis of the bargain, and the burden is on the manufacturer to show, by clear proof, that the parties did not intend their bargain to include these affirmations.

The affirmations and descriptions in the manual prepared by the manufacturer are part of what the seller has agreed to sell and became part of the basis of the bargain. In addition, the plaintiff testified that he had read the manual, was aware of the statements about the helmet and expected it to be true. Under these facts, the Court concludes that a jury could justifiably find that an express warranty had been made, that the express warranty was part of the basis for the bargain, and that the plaintiff relied on the warranty. . . .

For the reasons set forth herein, the defendants motions for judgment as a matter of law or new trial are *denied*.

It is so ordered.

Does it make sense to impose liability on Bell even though Yarusso did not read the owner's manual until after he had bought the helmet? How could statements contained in the owner's manual form "part of the basis of the bargain" under U.C.C. §2-313 if Yarusso did not know about them when purchasing the product?

The conceptual problems raised by treating statements made in non-traditional bargaining settings under a one-size-fits-all express warranty provision are not lost on commentators. Professor James J. White, a preeminent commercial law scholar, argues in Freeing the Tortious Soul of Express Warranty Law, 72 Tul. L. Rev. 2089 (1998) that much of the analytical quagmire attending warranty claims results from the unhappy marriage of tort and contract principles. Observing that not all warranty claims are the same, Professor White calls for a revision to U.C.C. §2-313 that would "unbundle" the heretofore interwoven strands of express warranty liability depending on whether they are based on traditional contract notions, tort principles, or something different altogether. Under such a scheme, written or oral assurances made before or concurrently with a sales transaction would be governed by traditional contract principles. Post-sale statements accompanying the sale of goods, by virtue of being reduced to writing and anticipated by both the seller and buyer, would be enforceable by statute as though part of the contract for sale. Finally, liability for statements directed to the public at large, due to the "irrepressible minimum" of tort buried inside such claims, would require an unabashed showing of reliance as a prerequisite for recovery.

In May of 2003, the National Conference on Commissioners on Uniform State Laws (NCCUSL) and the American Law Institute (ALI), the two institutions responsible for preparing and approving the U.C.C., announced they had completed a revision of U.C.C. Article 2. See Uniform Commercial Code Proposed Amendments to Article 2. Sales (Proposed Final Draft, April 18, 2003). Regarding express warranties, the revised U.C.C. adopts Professor White's tripartite framework. Leaving the main text of §2-313 mostly unchanged, the drafters have added the following sections:

UNIFORM COMMERCIAL CODE
(PROPOSED AMENDMENTS TO ARTICLE 2)

§2-313A. OBLIGATION TO REMOTE PURCHASER CREATED BY RECORD PACKAGED WITH OR ACCOMPANYING GOODS.

. . . (3) If in a record packaged with or accompanying the goods the seller makes an affirmation of fact or promise that relates to the goods, provides a description that relates to the goods, or makes a remedial promise, and the seller reasonably expects the record to be, and the record is, furnished to the remote purchaser, the seller has an obligation to the remote purchaser that:

(a) the goods will conform to the affirmation of fact, promise or description unless a reasonable person in the position of the remote purchaser would not believe that the affirmation of fact, promise or description created an obligation. . . .

PRELIMINARY OFFICIAL COMMENT

1. Sections 2-313A and 2-313B are new, and they follow case law and practice in extending a seller's obligations regarding new goods to remote purchasers. Section 2-313A deals with what are commonly called "pass through warranties." The usual transaction in which this obligation arises is when a manufacturer sells goods in a package to a retailer and include [sic] in the package a record that sets forth the obligations that the manufacturer is willing to undertake in favor of the final party in the distributive chain, who is the person that buys or leases the goods from the retailer. . . .

No direct contract exists between the seller and the remote purchaser, and thus the seller's obligation under this section is not referred to as an "express warranty." Use of "obligation" rather than "express warranty" avoids any inference that the part of the basis of the bargain as would be required to create an express warranty under Section 2-313. . . .

§2-313B. OBLIGATION TO REMOTE PURCHASER CREATED BY COMMUNICATION TO THE PUBLIC

. . . (3) If in an advertisement or a similar communication to the public a seller makes an affirmation of fact or promise that relates to the goods, provides a description that relates to the goods, or makes a remedial promise, and the remote purchaser enters into a transaction of purchase with knowledge of and with the expectation that the goods will conform to the affirmations of fact, promise, or description, or that the seller will perform the remedial promise, the seller has an obligation to the remote purchaser that:

    (a) the goods will conform to the affirmations of fact, promise or description unless a reasonable person in the position of the remote purchaser would not believe that the affirmation of fact, promise or description created an obligation. . . .

PRELIMINARY OFFICIAL COMMENT

1. . . . This section deals with obligations to a remote purchaser created by advertising or a similar communication to the public. The normal situation where this obligation will arise is when a manufacturer engages in an advertising campaign directed towards all or part of the market for its product and will make statements that if made to an immediate buyer would amount to an express warranty or remedial promise under Section 2-313. . . .

3. This section provides an additional test for enforceability not found in Section 2-313A. For the obligation to be created the remote purchaser must, at the time of purchase, have knowledge of the affirmation of fact, promise, description or remedial promise and must also have an expectation that the goods will conform or that the seller will comply. This test is entirely subjective, while the reasonable person test in subsection (3)(a) is objective in nature. Both tests must be met.

Note that the drafters make clear their intention to remove §§213A and 213B from the scope of the "basis of the bargain" test, which remains intact in §2-313. The reliance element has been eliminated entirely with respect to "pass-through" statements included in the package, but reliance has returned in full force regarding statements directed to the public at large. How these provisions will play out remains to be seen. Considering that it took roughly a decade for the enactment of the current U.C.C., it will be quite a while before courts have their say on the matter. See D. Owen, M. Madden & M. Davis, Madden & Owen on Products Liability, §4:24 (3d ed. 2000). The journey to ratification may be a bumpy one. Already some industry representatives are taking issue with the prospect of broad liability under the pass-through warranty provision of §213A and may be prepared to do battle in state legislatures to block its enactment.

NOTE: THE IMPLIED WARRANTY OF FITNESS FOR PARTICULAR PURPOSE

Another type of warranty that depends on firm expectations as to product quality is the implied warranty of fitness for particular purpose, U.C.C. §2-315. This warranty arises whenever the buyer relies on the seller's expertise in selecting a product to perform a particular purpose communicated by the buyer to the seller. Section 2-315 of the Uniform Commercial Code describes the warranty:

> Where the seller at the time of contracting has reason to know any particular purpose for which the goods are required and that the buyer is relying on the seller's skill or judgment to select or furnish suitable goods, there is . . . an implied warranty that the goods shall be fit for such purpose.

A significant difference between this type of implied warranty and an express warranty is that in connection with the latter, the seller does the talking, whereas in the former, the buyer does the talking. Thus, a warranty of fitness for particular purpose could be likened to an implied-in-fact promise by the seller that the goods will meet the buyer's unusual, but communicated, requirements. See, e.g., Catania v. Brown, 231 A.2d 668 (Conn. Cir. Ct. 1967); Controltek, Inc. v. Kwikee Enters., Inc., 585 P.2d 670 (Or. 1978); J. White & R. Summers, The Law Under the Uniform Commercial Code §9-10 (4th ed. 1995).

B. MISREPRESENTATION

The tort of misrepresentation developed at common law in actions for fraud and deceit. To sustain a cause of action, the plaintiff had to establish that the defendant intended to mislead the plaintiff. In Webster v. L. Romano Eng'g Corp., 34 P.2d 428, 430 (Wash. 1934), a case involving a claim to recover for pecuniary loss, the court summarized the elements of an action in fraud:

> But what is fraud? . . . We have . . . recognized certain essential elements that enter into its composition. These are: (1) A representation of an existing fact; (2) its materiality; (3) its falsity; (4) the speaker's knowledge of its falsity or ignorance of its truth; (5) his intent that it should be acted on by the person to whom it is made; (6) ignorance of its falsity on the part of the person to whom it is made; (7) the latter's reliance on the truth of the representation; (8) his right to rely upon it; (9) his consequent damage.

See also Pace v. Parrish, 247 P.2d 273, 274-275 (Utah 1952).

Restatement (Second) of Torts
(1965)

§310. CONSCIOUS MISREPRESENTATION INVOLVING RISK OF PHYSICAL HARM

An actor who makes a misrepresentation is subject to liability to another for physical harm which results from an act done by the other or a third person in reliance upon the truth of the representation, if the actor

(a) intends his statement to induce or should realize that it is likely to induce action by the other, or a third person, which involves an unreasonable risk of physical harm to the other, and

414   6. Express Warranty and Misrepresentation

> (b) knows
>> (i) that the statement is false, or
>> (ii) that he has not the knowledge which he professes.

§311. NEGLIGENT MISREPRESENTATION INVOLVING RISK OF PHYSICAL HARM

(1) One who negligently gives false information to another is subject to liability for physical harm caused by action taken by the other in reasonable reliance upon such information, where such harm results
> (a) to the other, or
> (b) to such third persons as the actor should expect to be put in peril by the action taken.

(2) Such negligence may consist of failure to exercise reasonable care
> (a) in ascertaining the accuracy of the information, or
> (b) in the manner in which it is communicated.

In products liability litigation, misrepresentation overlaps with express warranty and implied warranty of fitness for a particular purpose on the contract side, and with failure-to-warn on the tort side. Although for the most part these other doctrines cover the cases adequately, the tort of misrepresentation may be a useful weapon in a plaintiff's arsenal for several reasons. First, one need not be a party to a sales transaction to be held liable for misleading another into using a product in a way that causes injury or loss. It is more difficult to fit such product-related conduct by non-suppliers into the other contract or tort categories. Second, although tortious failure-to-warn doctrine may be adequate to cover personal injury or property losses, it may not be available to recover economic loss damages, and warranty actions may be difficult to establish since the seller may have cleverly worded his formal representations with regard to the performance capability of the product. The action for intentional misrepresentation may fill the gap. Third, one must not forget that the contractual remedies may allow for more limited damages, be subject to more restrictive statutes of limitation, or be open to attack on such grounds as the parol evidence rule. And finally, the tort of misrepresentation may trigger remedies for malevolent conduct. It is, of course, possible to make the allegation of intentional or wanton misconduct in the context of a failure-to-warn case. Nonetheless, misrepresentation may more effectively characterize the true nature of the proceedings.

The Restatement sections set out above do not consider whether a faultless defendant should be strictly liable in tort for harm caused by false representations. Now that the privity requirement has been all but eliminated in express warranty cases involving personal injury or property damage, products liability plaintiffs have less occasion to make use of tort claims based on innocent misrepresentations. In any event, the Restatement (Second) of Torts includes a special rule imposing privity-free strict liability for innocent misrepresentations made by commercial product sellers:

§402B. MISREPRESENTATION BY SELLER OF CHATTELS TO CONSUMER

One engaged in the business of selling chattels who, by advertising, labels, or otherwise, makes to the public a misrepresentation of a material fact concerning the character or quality of a chattel sold by him is subject to liability for physical harm to a consumer of the chattel caused by justifiable reliance upon the misrepresentation, even though

(a) it is not made fraudulently or negligently, and

(b) the consumer has not bought the chattel from or entered into any contractual relation with the seller.

Crocker v. Winthrop Laboratories
514 S.W.2d 429 (Tex. 1974)

REAVLEY, J.

Glenn E. Crocker became addicted to a new drug produced by Winthrop Laboratories and known as "talwin" which had been previously thought to be nonaddictive. When he was in a weakened condition and his tolerance to drugs very low because of a period of detoxification, Crocker obtained an injection of a narcotic and died soon thereafter. His widow and representative, Clarissa Crocker, brought this action for damages due to his suffering while alive as well as for his wrongful death. She recovered judgment against Winthrop Laboratories in the trial court. The Court of Civil Appeals reversed and rendered judgment for the drug company, holding that while some of the facts found by the jury (including the positive misrepresentation by the drug company that talwin was non-addictive) would warrant the recovery, the additional finding that the drug company could not reasonably have foreseen Crocker's addiction (because of his unusual susceptibility and the state of medical knowledge when the drug was marketed), constituted a complete defense. We hold that the latter finding does not bar the recovery, and we affirm the judgment of the trial court.

In July of 1967 Glenn Crocker suffered a double hernia, as well as frostbite of two fingers, while working as a carpenter in a cold storage vault. He was then 49 years old and was not a user of drugs or alcohol. His hernia was successfully repaired. The circulation of blood in his fingers, however, was not restored. Skin grafts were done on the fingers in October, but it was necessary to amputate part of his thumb in November and part of his middle finger the following January (1968). Prior to November 23, 1967, when Dr. Mario Palafox amputated part of his thumb, the several doctors who had treated him had prescribed both demerol (a narcotic) and talwin for relief of pain without observing any cause to believe him to be then addicted to any drug. Crocker told Dr. Palafox that he liked the relief he received from talwin, and Dr. Palafox responded that this was fortunate because talwin had no addicting side effect.

Crocker did develop an addiction to talwin, however, and was able to obtain prescriptions from several doctors as well as to cross the Mexican border to Juarez and acquire the same drug without a prescription under the name of "sosigon." He was hospitalized on June 3, 1968 by a psychiatrist, Dr. J. Edward Stern, for a process of detoxification (to remove the toxic agents in his body) and treatment of his drug dependency. After six days in the hospital being withdrawn from talwin as well as all narcotics, and at a time when his tolerance for potent drugs was very low, Crocker walked out of the hospital and went to his home. Because of his agitated condition and the threats he made against his wife, he was finally successful in having her call Dr. Eugene Engel who, on June 10, 1968, came to the Crocker home and gave Mr. Crocker an injection of demerol. Crocker went to his bed for the last time.

Winthrop Laboratories first put talwin on the market in July of 1967 after extensive testing and approval by the Federal Drug Administration. The descriptive material on the new drug circulated by Winthrop Laboratories in 1967 gives no warning of the possibilities of addiction. There is a heading of a paragraph in the product information of the 1967 edition of Physicians' Desk Reference Book which reads: "Absence of addiction liability." This might be considered misleading, but in view of the evidence of verbal assurances as to the properties of talwin by the drug company's representative, there is no need to deal further with the printed materials. Dr. Palafox, a prominent orthopedic surgeon in El Paso, allowed Crocker to have liberal use of talwin and assured him that it was non-addictive because of the assurance by a representative of the drug company who had detailed the doctor on the nature of the drug. There had been an extended and specific conversation between the drug company representative and Dr. Palafox about talwin, and Dr. Palafox was told that talwin was as harmless as aspirin and could be given as long as desired. Dr. Palafox testified that the representative of the defendant insisted that talwin could have no addicting effect.

Subsequent experience has proved that talwin is an extremely useful drug for the relief of pain but that it cannot be regarded as non-addictive. Doctors Palafox and Stern had seen other patients dependent upon talwin. Dr. Arthur S. Keats, chairman of the Department of Anesthesiology at Baylor School of Medicine in Houston, who did original work on the drug and who testified during this trial on the call of the drug company, agreed with the attorney for Mrs. Crocker that "there are a tremendous number of people that do develop a talwin addiction."

Dr. Palafox was of the opinion that if he had not been assured of the non-addictive character of talwin, he could probably have avoided addiction or dependence by Crocker upon any drug.

Plaintiff's medical testimony depicted the addiction to talwin as a producing cause of the death of Crocker when taken together with the chain of events including the detoxification process and the injection of Demerol.

The findings of the jury included the following:

1. That the defendant failed to advise the public during the year 1967 that its drug talwin could cause physical dependence.
2. That the failure of the defendant to advise the public that the drug talwin could cause physical dependence made such drug unreasonably dangerous as marketed in 1967. The jury was instructed that a drug is unreasonably dangerous "if under all the circumstances under which it is marketed, it subjected the Plaintiff to an unreasonable risk of harm even though the manufacturer did not know and could not know of the risk involved."
3. That the defendant drug company represented to the medical profession during the year 1967 that its drug talwin would not cause physical dependence.
4. That such representation was relied upon by Dr. Mario Palafox in prescribing talwin for the deceased.
5. That the deceased became physically dependent upon the drug talwin.
6. That the physical dependence of Crocker on the drug talwin was a producing cause of his death.

These findings, without more, would justify a recovery by the plaintiff under the rules of both sections 402A and 402B of the Restatement, Torts, Second. . . .

The carefully written opinion of the Court of Civil Appeals has correctly foreseen that we would apply Section 402B of the Restatement and that the judgment for plaintiff should be affirmed depending upon the effect to be given the findings of the jury in response to special issues 9 and 10. Those findings were as follows:

9. That Crocker's addiction or dependency upon talwin was an abreaction. Abreaction was defined as "an unusual reaction resulting from a person's unusual susceptibility to the product or intended effect of the product in question; that is, such person's reaction is different in the presence of the drug in question from that in the usual person. An abreaction is one in which an unusual result is produced by a known or theoretical mechanism of action. An abreaction is one which could not have been reasonably foreseen in an appreciable class or number of potential users prior to the time Glenn E. Crocker became addicted or dependent on talwin."
10. That at the time Crocker was taking talwin under doctors' prescriptions, the state of medical knowledge was such that Winthrop Laboratories could not have reasonably foreseen, in the exercise of ordinary care, that talwin would cause an addiction in an appreciable number of persons.

[The court concludes that the mere fact that the potentially endangered users were few in number should not preclude liability for failure to warn, but that the defendant cannot be held for failing to warn of risks not known or reasonably knowable at the time of sale.]

Liability of Winthrop Laboratories will be predicated upon the finding of misrepresentation that the drug would not cause physical dependence, a fact conceded by the attorney for the company in his jury argument, and upon the findings of reliance and causation. Whatever the danger and state of medical knowledge, and however rare the susceptibility of the user, when the drug company positively and specifically represents its product to be free and safe from all dangers of addiction, and when the treating physician relies upon that representation, the drug company is liable when the representation proves to be false and harm results. . . .

Judgment affirmed.

Most cases dealing with representations about product performance are covered under the express warranty provisions of U.C.C. §2-313. However, courts occasionally couch their decisions in both tortious misrepresentation as well as express warranty terminology. See, e.g., Hauter v. Zogarts, 534 P.2d 377 (Cal. 1975) (holding that plaintiff entitled to recover under theory of misrepresentation or breach of express warranty for injury resulting from false assurances regarding safety of golf-ball training unit); Klages v. General Ordnance Equip. Corp., 367 A.2d 304 (Pa. Super. Ct. 1976) (jury allowed to find defendant liable under either misrepresentation or breach of express warranty for false claims characterizing mace spray as having ability to "instantly stop and subdue entire groups"); Williams v. Dow Chemical Co., 255 F. Supp. 2d 219 (S.D.N.Y. 2003) (granting summary judgment to defendant as to both express warranty and misrepresentation claims absent plaintiffs' showing of reliance on defendant pesticide manufacturer's allegedly false portrayal of product safety conveyed through pamphlets and informational material). In such cases, the semantic difference between the two theories may have an impact. "Misrepresentation" sounds more ominous and more tort-like than the bland terminology of "express warranty." Misrepresentation carries negative connotations to both judge and jury even when based in strict liability. For example, in the context of a misrepresentation claim, it is far easier to argue to a jury that the defendant's statements were "lies" (even if the defendant was not a liar). It is more difficult to attach such emotion-laden language to a breach of contract claim.

The American Law Institute attached the following caveat to §402B: "The Institute expresses no opinion as to whether the rule stated in this section may apply . . . where the representation is not made to the public, but to an individual. . . ." Clearly, §§310 and 311 of the Restatement (Second) set forth earlier, apply to representations made to individuals. (Indeed, those sections apply generally to representations made *by* individuals—even individuals not in the business of selling products.) Though the issue raised in the caveat to §402B is rarely addressed, there may be occasional indications that the section applies only to public misrepresentations. See, e.g., Lewis & Lambert Metal Contractors, Inc. v. Jackson, 914 S.W.2d 584 (Tex. App. 1994) (holding that "Section 402B . . . does not apply to private misrepresentations").

According to its terms, §402B supports recovery only for "physical harm." As a later chapter will make clear, many courts have refused to allow recovery for pure economic losses under tort claims of negligence or strict liability. Would a court today allow recovery under §402B (strict liability for innocent misrepresentation) for pure economic loss absent a showing of physical harm? In Ritter v. Custom Chemicides, Inc., 912 S.W.2d 128 (Tenn. 1995), the Supreme Court of Tennessee answered this question in the negative. Recovery for pure economic loss is allowed, however, when the plaintiff can prove either intentional or negligent misrepresentation. See, e.g., Jarmco v. Polygard, Inc., 668 So. 2d 300 (Fla. Dist. Ct. App. 1996).

Restatement (Third) of Torts: Products Liability
(1998)

§9. LIABILITY OF COMMERCIAL PRODUCT SELLER OR DISTRIBUTOR FOR HARM CAUSED BY MISREPRESENTATION

One engaged in the business of selling or otherwise distributing products who, in connection with the sale of a product, makes a fraudulent, negligent, or innocent misrepresentation of material fact concerning the product is subject to liability for harm to persons or property caused by the misrepresentation.

COMMENT:

a. Liability for fraudulent or negligent misrepresentation. The rules in the Restatement, Second, of Torts, governing liability for fraudulent and negligent misrepresentation are contained in §§310 and 311. Case law has followed these Sections. Although these Sections do not explicitly apply to commercial product sellers, they admit of such application. Given the availability to plaintiffs of the rule under §402B of the Restatement, Second, of Torts, subjecting product sellers to strict liability even in the absence of fraud or negligence, (see Comment b), there can be no doubt that product sellers are subject to liability for fraudulent or negligent misrepresentation. By hypothesis, given the rule stated in §402B, a plaintiff who proves that the misrepresentation that caused harm was made fraudulently or negligently should have a remedy.

b. Liability for innocent misrepresentation. The rules governing liability for innocent product misrepresentation are stated in Restatement, Second, of Torts §402B. Case law has followed that Section. Section 402B contains two caveats. The first caveat leaves open the question whether a seller should be liable under §402B for an innocent misrepresentation that is made to an individual and not to the public at large. This question remains open. Case law on the subject of liability for innocent misrepresentation has dealt exclusively with public misrepresentations. The second caveat to §402B leaves open the question whether a seller should be liable for an innocent misrepresentation where harm to persons or property is caused to one who is not a consumer of the product. Case law has not resolved the issue of whether an innocent misrepresentation may, in the absence of a product defect, be a basis of liability to a nonconsumer who suffers harm as a result of reliance by an intermediary.

In Miller v. Pfizer Inc., 196 F. Supp. 2d 1095 (D. Kan. 2002) plaintiff argued that §9 of the Products Liability Restatement disposes of the reliance requirement for claims for misrepresentation. In that case, parents of a child who committed suicide while being treated with Zoloft, a widely used anti-depressant, argued that Pfizer was liable for misrepresentation because it had "gone to great lengths to reassure doctors that the violence and suicide problems they have heard about, mainly with its chief . . . competitor Prozac, would not occur with Zoloft." Id. at 1119. In response to defendant's claim that plaintiff could not prevail on a claim of misrepresentation absent evidence demonstrating that the prescribing physician had relied on the defendant's alleged misrepresentations, plaintiff contended that it was unnecessary under §9 to prove reliance on a product's misrepresentation. Rejecting plaintiff's argument, the court held that §9, in stating that the alleged harm must be "caused by the misrepresentation," does indeed require proof of a plaintiff's reliance on a product's misrepresentation. The district court cited to a prior decision by the Kansas Supreme Court that held that "[t]he reliance element of misrepresentation serves the function of causation in fact; that the misrepresentation causes someone to act or refrain from acting." Id. at 1120. Accord Labelle v. Phillip Morris Inc., 243 F. Supp. 2d 508 (D. S.Car. 2001) (applying Pennsylvania law) (summary judgment for defendant granted due to plaintiff's inability to show decedent's reliance on defendants' statements regarding the safety of smoking).

Courts appear to be split as to the kind of evidence necessary to establish the element of reliance on a claim of misrepresentation. In Williams v. Phillip Morris, Inc., 48 P.3d 824 (Or. Ct. App.), *rev. denied,* 61 P.3d 938 (2002) plaintiff alleged that tobacco companies had engaged in decades-long conduct of deceptive advertising designed to lull consumers into the belief that cigarettes were not dangerous to one's health. Defendant claimed that there was insufficient evidence showing that plaintiff's decedent had relied on any misrepresentations it may have made. In upholding the jury's verdict in plaintiff's favor, the court said:

> There is evidence that Williams received the message that defendant intended to communicate and that the message affected his decision to continue smoking and not to make more serious efforts to overcome his addiction to cigarettes. Williams read the *Oregonian,* other newspapers and magazines, and watched television, all of which were media through which defendant conveyed its message. The evidence includes examples of newspaper stories describing the dangers of tobacco that also contain statements from industry spokespersons insisting that the dangers were not proved and at times attacking the validity of the research suggesting harmful effects. Industry newspaper advertisements conveyed the same message. For instance, in an article published in the *Oregonian* in 1991, an industry spokesman said that the dangers were not proven and argued that the money that the CTR spent on research showed how open-minded the industry was. [Id. at 834-835.]

The court pointed to specific evidence showing that Williams had, in fact, relied on the assurances of the tobacco companies that its cigarettes were safe. It is not clear from the opinion, however, whether the evidence regarding public statements conveyed through advertising and the media set forth in the language above would suffice to establish reliance on its own. However, in White v. R.J. Reynolds Tobacco Co., 109 F. Supp. 2d 424 (D. Md. 2000), the court made it clear that a plaintiff could not establish reliance based on his exposure to alleged misrepresentations by the tobacco companies regarding the safety of smoking conveyed via publications and electronic media. The court said it would not presume reliance due merely to the fact that "[the plaintiff's decedent had] read the newspaper and magazines, watched television and listened to the radio where these misrepresentations were made. . . . The Court will not presume anything of the kind, because such a presumption would be nothing but speculation." Id. at 429.

The *White* court also addressed the issue of whether representations made to and relied upon by third parties could support an action for misrepresentation when the plaintiff herself did not rely on such representations. The issue was left as a caveat to §402B and was not resolved in the Products Liability Restatement §9. The court in *White* had this to say in response to plaintiff's claim that the manufacturer should be liable for making allegedly false representations to government officials, physicians, and teachers who then passed on the misinformation to the plaintiff:

> Plaintiffs' argument fails because, under Maryland law, there is no fraudulent misrepresentation cause of action for statements made to third parties. . . . Even if there were such a cause of action, it would fail because plaintiffs do not have evidence (or even allegations) of reliance by those third persons allegedly deceived. Even in cases that have held that a defendant may be liable for an injury to a consumer for misrepresentations to someone else (*e.g.,* a person buys a product that is then used by her guest or child, who is injured by the product), the plaintiff must prove that the purchaser herself brought the product in reliance on the manufacturers' representations. *See* Restatement, Second, of Torts §402B cmt. *j.* [Id. at 430.]

For general discussions of the role of misrepresentation in products liability, see David G. Owen, The Highly Blameworthy Manufacturer: Implications For

authors' dialogue 16

JIM: What's your reaction to the newly revised Article 2 of the Uniform Commercial Code?

AARON: That's a tall order. What section of Article 2 worries you?

JIM: I'm concerned about the section that imposes a reliance requirement on claims of public advertising.

AARON: Jim, I can't believe that you think that one should be held liable for express warranty without reliance. Reliance is the surrogate for causation.

JIM: No, no, you're reading me wrong. Of course there should be a reliance requirement. What concerns me is that we have two almost identical causes of action — misrepresentation and express warranty — and I'm not sure that the reliance requirement is the same for each action. I'm concerned that we are going to get in the same mess that we got into when the Code recognized a cause of action for the implied warranty of merchantability and then the courts imposed strict liability in torts. To this day some courts have had a devil of a time deciding whether they are one in the same or different. We agonized over the dual theories in the Restatement and said that they are functionally equivalent.

AARON: I understand your concern. But, if anything, the revised Article 2-313B brings the U.C.C. closer to the common law of misrepresentation by doing away with the "basis of the bargain" jargon and requiring that the buyer have purchased the goods with the "knowledge of and with the expectation that the goods will conform" with the warranty. The new U.C.C. section also provides another out. If a "reasonable person in the position of the remote purchaser" would not believe the warranty, then there is no liability. This a pretty good section.

JIM: I still worry, Aaron. In the tobacco misrepresentation cases courts have only paid lip service to the reliance requirements. Some courts have intimated that it is enough that plaintiff read the publications that contained the advertisements. A lot of smokers may never have seen the ads and if they saw them they may not have believed them.

AARON: You're right, Jim. But what do you want from the drafters of the Code? They can't stop common-law courts from making up an alternate cause of action with less stringent requirements for recovery. That's the curse of a common-law court system that treats legislation with contempt. The Code folks have got it right. We can only hope that the Code will influence the courts to treat misrepresentation in a similar fashion.

JIM: I agree. The U.C.C. could not realistically have sought to preempt other common law claims predicated on a different theory. Such a proposal would have been D.O.A. in the states. Misrepresentation is a tort that covers conduct other than the sale of products. I'm just sick and tired of multiple causes of action for the same basic underlying conduct. I wish that courts would stop the nonsense.

Rules of Liability and Defense in Products Liability Actions, 10 Ind. L. Rev. 769 (1977); Jerry J. Phillips, Product Misrepresentation and the Doctrine of Causation, 2 Hofstra L. Rev. 561 (1974); Marshall S. Shapo, A Representational Theory of Consumer Protection: Doctrine, Function and Legal Liability for Product Disappointment, 60 Va. L. Rev. 1109 (1974).

NOTE: REPRESENTATIONS AS THE MOOD MUSIC FOR DETERMINING PRODUCT DEFECT UNDER EXISTING LAW

The most significant source of product representations is Madison Avenue. Indeed, one of the authors has argued to his classes for years on end that much of products liability reflects the inability of American engineering to match the claims made for products by advertisers. However, it is no easy matter to establish that an advertising claim constitutes an express warranty. The question of which kinds of statements are puffing and constitute only "the seller's opinion or commendation of the goods," and which cross over the line and constitute a warranty has baffled the courts for decades. The legal staffs of the corporate giants take the trouble (in most instances) to see to it that advertisements remain on the right side of the line, if only by a hairsbreadth.

Should the plaintiff include in a traditional products liability case based on defect a plausible, although not likely winnable, express warranty claim based on advertising? We think the answer is clearly yes. The simple fact is that even if the express warranty claim cannot stand on its own, it is highly relevant to the overall issue of product safety. How a product is portrayed to the public is an important factor in determining how it will be used and what liberties consumers will take with it. Courts should be wary of allowing an inherently weak design case to be bolstered by an equally weak failure-to-warn claim. Here we ask whether it is right to bolster a weak design case with representational claims that may be unable to survive on their own. We think this raises a different question. Plaintiffs have every right and incentive to press the express warranty claim as aggressively as possible. First, they may convince a court or a jury of its inherent merits. Second, in the event they do not, the issue of product portrayal is justifiably in the case on the overarching issue of product safety. See Products Liability Restatement §2, Comments *f* and *g*.

It is difficult to support a thesis such as we have just set forth with case authority. But now and then you strike it lucky. In Hill v. Searle Laboratories, 884 F.2d 1064, 1070 (8th Cir. 1989), the plaintiff suffered injury when an IUD perforated her uterus and became partially embedded in her small bowel. A significant issue in the case was whether an IUD was an "unavoidably unsafe" drug in which case the seller would be exempt from strict liability. In a wonderfully confused opinion, the court denied the special drug exemption to IUDs for a host of reasons. One important factor was that "IUD manufacturers, through mass advertising and merchandising practices, generated a general sense of product quality, making it difficult for consumers to fully understand the risks involved with the use of an IUD." Id. at 1070. The court linked the representational background of the case to the underlying cause of action, suggesting that although neither might stand alone, both might stand together.

CHAPTER SEVEN
Federal Preemption

The most potent defense to a products liability claim based on either failure to warn or defective design is that the federal government has preempted the right of state courts and legislatures to independently set standards for warning or design. This defense should be distinguished from the defense under state law of compliance with statute. As we have noted earlier, most states treat compliance with a relevant regulation or statute as a circumstance that a factfinder may take into consideration in deciding whether a product is defective, but that does not bar a finding of product defect. When, however, a court finds federal preemption, the supremacy clause of the United States Constitution mandates that the federal standard govern the litigation. If the defendant has complied with that federal standard, the plaintiff cannot press her state law claim.

For almost a century the United States Supreme Court has recognized three circumstances that warrant federal preemption. In English v. Gen. Elec. Co., 496 U.S. 72, 78-79 (1990), the court reiterated this preemption trilogy:

> First, Congress can define explicitly the extent to which its enactments preempt state law. . . . Preemption fundamentally is a question of congressional intent, . . . and when Congress has made its intent known through explicit statutory language, the courts' task is an easy one.
>
> Second, in the absence of explicit statutory language, state law is preempted where it regulates conduct in a field that Congress intended the Federal Government to occupy exclusively. Such an intent may be inferred from a "scheme of federal regulation . . . so pervasive as to make reasonable the inference that Congress left no room for the States to supplement it," or where an Act of Congress "touch[es] a field in which the federal interest is so dominant that the federal system will be assumed to preclude enforcement of state laws on the same subject." . . . "Where . . . the field which Congress is said to have pre-empted" includes areas that have "been traditionally occupied by the States," congressional intent to supersede state laws must be "'clear and manifest.'" . . .
>
> Finally, state law is preempted to the extent that it actually conflicts with federal law. Thus, the Court has found preemption where it is impossible for a private party to comply with both state and federal requirements, . . . or where state law "stands as an obstacle to the accomplishment and execution of the full purposes and objectives of Congress."

The problem in the preemption area has been trying to predict whether the Supreme Court will decide that a given statute or administrative law rule fits into one of the three pigeon holes described above. Any given Supreme Court preemption decision can make sense on its own bottom. But reading them together is a maddening experience. One senses that a Ouija board would be of greater assistance than access to the most learned constitutional scholar in attempting to predict how the Supreme Court will rule in a pending case. Although the Supreme Court bears considerable responsibility for the reigning confusion, in some areas Congress has also been a culprit. Congress has enacted several statutory schemes giving administrative agencies rulemaking power to set certain regulatory standards and declaring its intent, in an explicit preemption clause, that states should not establish conflicting regulations. At the same time, Congress has stated in so-called saving clauses that compliance with a federal safety standard does not exempt any person from liability under a state's common law. Trying to read preemption and saving clauses together has been no easy task. Congress quite clearly has sought to placate both industry and consumers by speaking out of both sides of its mouth. And in the event that no one should understand how both can work in tandem, that job is left to the United States Supreme Court, which does not have to face the wrath of political constituencies.

A. FEDERAL PREEMPTION OF WARNING CLAIMS

The United States Supreme Court's involvement in federal products liability preemption was triggered when plaintiffs brought suit against cigarette companies for failing to adequately warn about the dangers associated with smoking. Since the passage of the Federal Cigarette Labeling and Advertising Act of 1965, 15 U.S.C. §§1331-1340 (1982 and Supp. II 1984) (hereinafter the Cigarette Act), which became effective January 1, 1966, most courts had ruled in favor of federal preemption — that is, they ruled against the recognition of a state-imposed common law duty to warn of the dangers of cigarettes. The relevant portion of the Cigarette Act provides that "No requirement or prohibition based on smoking and health shall be imposed under state law with respect to the advertising or promotion of any cigarettes the packages of which are labeled in conformity with the provisions of this chapter." Id. §1334(b). In Cipollone v. Liggett Group, Inc., 893 F.2d 541 (3d Cir. 1990), *cert. granted*, 1991 U.S. 1793 (U.S. 1991), the Third Circuit upheld its earlier determination that the Cigarette Act impliedly preempts those state law damage claims that "necessarily [depend] on the assertion that a party bear the duty to provide a warning to consumers in addition to the warning Congress has required on cigarette packages." Id. at 552.

Several federal courts of appeals followed *Cipollone*'s lead. See, e.g., Palmer v. Liggett Group, 825 F.2d 620 (1st Cir. 1987); Pennington v. Visitron Corp., 876 F.2d 414 (5th Cir. 1989); Roysdon v. R. J. Reynolds Tobacco Co., 849 F.2d 230 (6th Cir. 1987). However, some state courts disagreed with the decision. In Dewey v. R. J. Reynolds Tobacco Co., 577 A.2d 1239 (N.J. 1990), the Supreme Court of New Jersey held that, although plaintiff's decedent had not smoked defendant's cigarettes until 11 years after the passage of the Cigarette Act, the Act neither expressly nor impliedly preempted plaintiff's failure to warn claim. The time had come for the United States Supreme Court to resolve this thorny preemption problem. In the case that follows the Court found that at least some common law claims were expressly preempted by Congress.

Cipollone v. Liggett Group, Inc.
505 U.S. 504, 112 S. Ct. 2608, 120 L. Ed. 2d 407 (1992)

Justice STEVENS delivered the opinion of the Court, except as to Parts V and VI.

"WARNING: THE SURGEON GENERAL HAS DETERMINED THAT CIGARETTE SMOKING IS DANGEROUS TO YOUR HEALTH." A federal statute enacted in 1969 requires that warning (or a variation thereof) to appear in a conspicuous place on every package of cigarettes sold in the United States. The questions presented to us by this case are whether that statute, or its 1965 predecessor which required a less alarming label, pre-empted petitioner's common-law claims against respondent cigarette manufacturers.

Petitioner is the son of Rose Cipollone, who began smoking in 1942 and who died of lung cancer in 1984. He claims that respondents are responsible for Rose Cipollone's death because they breached express warranties contained in their advertising, because they failed to warn consumers about the hazards of smoking, because they fraudulently misrepresented those hazards to consumers, and because they conspired to deprive the public of medical and scientific information about smoking. The Court of Appeals held that petitioner's state-law claims were pre-empted by federal statutes, 893 F.2d 541 (CA3 1990), and other courts have agreed with that analysis. The highest court of the State of New Jersey, however, has held that the federal statutes did not pre-empt similar common-law claims. Because of the manifest importance of the issue, we granted certiorari to resolve the conflict, 499 U.S. 935, 111 S. Ct. 1386, 113 L. Ed. 2d 443 (1991). We now reverse in part and affirm in part.

I

On August 1, 1983, Rose Cipollone and her husband filed a complaint invoking the diversity jurisdiction of the Federal District Court. Their complaint alleged that Rose Cipollone developed lung cancer because she smoked cigarettes manufactured and sold by the three respondents. After her death in 1984, her husband filed an amended complaint. After trial, he also died; their son, executor of both estates, now maintains this action.

Petitioner's . . . amended complaint alleges several different bases of recovery, relying on theories of strict liability, negligence, express warranty, and intentional tort. These claims, all based on New Jersey law, divide into five categories. The "design defect claims" allege that respondents' cigarettes were defective because respondents failed to use a safer alternative design for their products and because the social value of their product was outweighed by the dangers it created. [Citations to the trial record and other sources are here, and hereafter, omitted.] The "failure to warn claims" allege both that the product was "defective as a result of [respondents'] failure to provide adequate warnings of the health consequences of cigarette smoking" and that respondents "were negligent in the manner [that] they tested, researched, sold, promoted and advertised" their cigarettes. The "express warranty claims" allege that respondents had "expressly warranted that smoking the cigarettes which they manufactured and sold did not present any significant health consequences." The "fraudulent misrepresentation claims" allege that respondents had willfully, "through their advertising, attempted to neutralize the [federally mandated] warnin[g]" labels and that they had possessed, but had "ignored and failed to act upon" medical, and scientific data indicating that "cigarettes were hazardous to the health of consumers." Finally, the "conspiracy to defraud claims" allege that respondents conspired to deprive the public of such medical and scientific data.

As one of their defenses, respondents contended that the Federal Cigarette Labeling and Advertising Act, enacted in 1965, and its successor, the Public Health Cigarette Smoking Act of 1969, protected them from any liability based on their conduct after 1965. In a pretrial ruling, the District Court concluded that the federal statutes were intended to establish a uniform warning that would prevail throughout the country and that would protect cigarette manufacturers from being "subjected to varying requirements from state to state," but that the statutes did not pre-empt common-law actions. Accordingly, the court granted a motion to strike the pre-emption defense entirely.

The Court of Appeals accepted an interlocutory appeal . . . and reversed. The court rejected respondents' contention that the federal Acts expressly pre-empted common-law actions, but accepted their contention that such actions would conflict with federal law. Relying on the statement of purpose in the statutes, the court concluded that Congress' "carefully drawn balance between the purposes of warning the public of the hazards of cigarette smoking and protecting the interests of national economy" would be upset by state-law damages actions based on noncompliance with "warning, advertisement, and promotion obligations other than those prescribed in the [federal] Act." . . . The court did not, however, identify the specific claims asserted by petitioner that were pre-empted by the Act.

This Court denied a petition for certiorari and the case returned to the District Court for trial. Complying with the Court of Appeals' mandate, the District Court held that the failure-to-warn, express-warranty, fraudulent-misrepresentation, and conspiracy-to-defraud claims were barred to the extent that they relied on respondents' advertising, promotional, and public relations activities after January 1, 1966 (the effective date of the 1965 Act). The court also ruled that while the design defect claims were not pre-empted by federal law, those claims were barred on other grounds. Following extensive discovery and a 4-month trial, the jury answered a series of special interrogatories and awarded $400,000 in damages to Rose Cipollone's husband. In brief, it rejected all of the fraudulent misrepresentation and conspiracy claims, but found that respondent Liggett had breached its duty to warn and its express warranties before 1966. It found, however, that Rose Cipollone had voluntarily and unreasonably encounter[ed] a known danger by smoking cigarettes and that 80% of the responsibility for her injuries was attributable to her. For that reason, no damages were awarded to her estate. However, the jury awarded damages to compensate her husband for losses caused by respondents' breach of express warranty.

On cross-appeals from the final judgment, the Court of Appeals affirmed the District Court's pre-emption rulings but remanded for a new trial on several issues not relevant to our decision. We granted the petition for certiorari to consider the pre-emptive effect of the federal statutes.

II

Although physicians had suspected a link between smoking and illness for centuries, the first medical studies of that connection did not appear until the 1920's.

The ensuing decades saw a wide range of epidemiologic and laboratory studies on the health hazards of smoking. Thus, by the time the Surgeon General convened an advisory committee to examine the issue in 1962, there were more than 7,000 publications examining the relationship between smoking and health.

In July 1965, Congress enacted the federal cigarette labeling and advertising act.

Section 2 of the Act declares the statute's two purposes: (1) adequately informing the public that cigarette smoking may be hazardous to health, and (2) protecting the national economy from the burden imposed by diverse, nonuniform, and confusing cigarette labeling and advertising regulations. In furtherance of the first purpose, §4 of the Act made it unlawful to sell or distribute any cigarettes in the United States unless the package bore a conspicuous label stating: "CAUTION: CIGARETTE SMOKING MAY BE HAZARDOUS TO YOUR HEALTH." In furtherance of the second purpose, §5, captioned "Preemption," provided in part:

> "(a) No statement relating to smoking and health, other than the statement required by section 4 of this Act, shall be required on any cigarette package.
> "(b) No statement relating to smoking and health shall be required in the advertising of any cigarettes the packages of which are labeled in conformity with the provisions of this Act."

Although the Act took effect January 1, 1966, §10 of the Act provided that its provisions affecting the regulation of advertising would terminate on July 1, 1969.

As that termination date approached, federal authorities prepared to issue further regulations on cigarette advertising. The FTC announced the reinstitution of its 1964 proceedings concerning a warning requirement for cigarette advertisements. The Federal Communications Commission (FCC) announced that it would consider "a proposed rule which would ban the broadcast of cigarette commercials by radio and television stations." State authorities also prepared to take actions regulating cigarette advertisements.

It was in this context that Congress enacted the Public Health Cigarette Smoking Act of 1969 (1969 Act or Act), which amended the 1965 Act in several ways. First, the 1969 Act strengthened the warning label, in part by requiring a statement that cigarette smoking "is dangerous" rather than that it "may be hazardous." Second, the 1969 Act banned cigarette advertising in "any medium of electronic communication subject to [FCC] jurisdiction." Third, and related, the 1969 Act modified the pre-emption provision by replacing the original §5(b) with a provision that reads:

> "(b) No requirement or prohibition based on smoking and health shall be imposed under State law with respect to the advertising or promotion of any cigarettes the packages of which are labeled in conformity with the provisions of this Act."

Although the Act also directed the FTC not to "take any action before July 1, 1971, with respect to its pending trade regulation rule proceeding relating to cigarette advertising, the narrowing of the pre-emption provision to prohibit only restrictions imposed under State law" cleared the way for the FTC to extend the warning-label requirement to print advertisements for cigarettes. The FTC did so in 1972.

III

Article VI of the Constitution provides that the laws of the United States "shall be the supreme Law of the Land; . . . any Thing in the Constitution or Laws of any state to the Contrary notwithstanding." Art. VI, cl. 2. Thus, since our decision in M'Culloch v. Maryland, 17 U.S. (4 Wheat.) 316, 427, 4 L. Ed. 579 (1819), it has been settled that state law that conflicts with federal law is without effect. Consideration of issues arising under the Supremacy Clause "start[s] with the assumption that the historic police powers of the States [are] not to be superseded by . . . Federal Act unless that [is] the clear and manifest purpose of Congress." Accordingly, "'[t]he purpose of Congress is the ultimate touchstone'" of pre-emption analysis.

Congress' intent may be explicitly stated in the statute's language or implicitly contained in its structure and purpose. In the absence of an express congressional command, state law is pre-empted if that law actually conflicts with federal law, or if federal law so thoroughly occupies a legislative field "'as to make reasonable the inference that Congress left no room for the States to supplement it.'"

The Court of Appeals was not persuaded that the pre-emption provision in the 1969 Act encompassed state common-law claims. It was also not persuaded that the labeling obligation imposed by both the 1965 and 1969 Acts revealed a congressional intent to exert exclusive federal control over every aspect of the relationship between cigarettes and health. Nevertheless, reading the statute as a whole in the light of the statement of purpose in §2, and considering the potential regulatory effect of state common-law actions on the federal interest in uniformity, the Court of Appeals concluded that Congress had impliedly pre-empted petitioner's claims challenging the adequacy of the warnings on labels or in advertising or the propriety of respondents' advertising and promotional activities.

In our opinion, the pre-emptive scope of the 1965 Act and the 1969 Act is governed entirely by the express language in §5 of each Act. When Congress has considered the issue of pre-emption and has included in the enacted legislation a provision explicitly addressing that issue, and when that provision provides a "reliable indicium of congressional intent with respect to state authority," Malone v. White Motor Corp., 435 U.S., at 505, 98 S. Ct., at 1190, "there is no need to infer congressional intent to pre-empt state laws from the substantive provisions" of the legislation. Such reasoning is a variant of the familiar principle of expression unius est exclusio alterius: Congress' enactment of a provision defining the pre-emptive reach of a statute implies that matters beyond that reach are not pre-empted. In this case, the other provisions of the 1965 and 1969 Acts offer no cause to look beyond §5 of each Act. Therefore, we need only identify the domain expressly pre-empted by each of those sections. As the 1965 and 1969 provisions differ substantially, we consider each in turn.

IV

In the 1965 pre-emption provision regarding advertising (§5(b)), Congress spoke precisely and narrowly: "No statement relating to smoking and health shall be required in the advertising of [properly labeled] cigarettes." Section 5(a) used the same phrase ("No statement relating to smoking and health") with regard to cigarette labeling. As §5(a) made clear, that phrase referred to the sort of warning provided for in §4, which set forth verbatim the warning Congress determined to be appropriate. Thus, on their face, these provisions merely prohibited state and federal rulemaking bodies from mandating particular cautionary statements on cigarette labels (§5(a)) or in cigarette advertisements (§5(b)).

Beyond the precise words of these provisions, this reading is appropriate for several reasons. First, as discussed above, we must construe these provisions in light of the presumption against the pre-emption of state police power regulations. This presumption reinforces the appropriateness of a narrow reading of §5. Second, the warning required in §4 does not by its own effect foreclose additional obligations imposed under state law. That Congress requires a particular warning label does not automatically pre-empt a regulatory field. Third, there is no general, inherent conflict between federal pre-emption of state warning requirements and the continued vitality of state common-law damages actions. For example, in the Comprehensive Smokeless Tobacco Health Education Act of 1986, Congress expressly pre-empted state or local imposition of a "statement relating to the use of smokeless tobacco products and health" but, at the same time, preserved state-law damages actions based on those products. All of these considerations indicate that §5 is best read as having superseded only positive enactments by legislatures or administrative agencies that mandate particular warning labels.

This reading comports with the 1965 Act's statement of purpose, which expressed an intent to avoid "diverse, nonuniform, and confusing cigarette labeling and advertising regulations with respect to any relationship between smoking and health." Read against the backdrop of regulatory activity undertaken by state legislatures and federal agencies in response to the Surgeon General's report, the term "regulation" most naturally refers to positive enactments by those bodies, not to common-law damages actions.

The regulatory context of the 1965 Act also supports such a reading. As noted above, a warning requirement promulgated by the FTC and other requirements under consideration by the States were the catalyst for passage of the 1965 Act. These regulatory actions animated the passage of §5, which reflected Congress' efforts to prevent "a multiplicity of State and local regulations pertaining to labeling of cigarette packages," and to "preemp[t] all Federal, State, and local authorities from requiring any statement relating to smoking and health in the advertising of cigarettes."[1]

For these reasons, we conclude that §5 of the 1965 Act only pre-empted state and federal rulemaking bodies from mandating particular cautionary statements and did not pre-empt state-law damages actions.[2]

---

1. Justice Scalia takes issue with our narrow reading of the phrase "No statement." His criticism, however, relies solely on an interpretation of those two words, artificially severed from both textual and legislative context. As demonstrated above, the phrase "No statement." in §5(b) refers to the similar phrase in §5(a), which refers in turn to §4, which itself sets forth a particular statement. This context, combined with the regulatory setting in which Congress acted, establishes that a narrow reading of the phrase "No statement." is appropriate.

2. This interpretation of the 1965 Act appears to be consistent with respondents' contemporaneous understanding of the Act. Although respondents have participated in a great deal of litigation relating to cigarette use beginning in the 1950's, it appears that this case is the first in which they have raised §5 as a pre-emption defense.

V

Compared to its predecessor in the 1965 Act, the plain language of the preemption provision in the 1969 Act is much broader. First, the later Act bars not simply "statement[s]" but rather "requirement[s] or prohibition[s] . . . imposed under State law." Second, the later Act reaches beyond statements "in the advertising" to obligations "with respect to the advertising or promotion" of cigarettes.

Notwithstanding these substantial differences in language, both petitioner and respondents contend that the 1969 Act did not materially alter the pre-emptive scope of federal law. Their primary support for this contention is a sentence in a Committee Report which states that the 1969 amendment "clarified" the 1965 version of §5(b). We reject the parties' reading as incompatible with the language and origins of the amendments. As we noted in another context, "[i]nferences from legislative history cannot rest on so slender a reed. Moreover, the views of a subsequent Congress form a hazardous basis for inferring the intent of an earlier one." The 1969 Act worked substantial changes in the law: rewriting the label warning, banning broadcast advertising, and allowing the FTC to regulate print advertising. In the context of such revisions and in light of the substantial changes in wording, we cannot accept the parties' claim that the 1969 Act did not alter the reach of §5(b).

Petitioner next contends that §5(b), however broadened by the 1969 Act, does not pre-empt common-law actions. He offers two theories for limiting the reach of the amended §5(b). First, he argues that common-law damages actions do not impose "requirement[s] or prohibition[s]" and that Congress intended only to trump state statute[s], injunction[s], or executive pronouncement[s]. We disagree; such an analysis is at odds both with the plain words of the 1969 Act and with the general understanding of common-law damages actions. The phrase "[n]o requirement or prohibition" sweeps broadly and suggests no distinction between positive enactments and common law; to the contrary, those words easily encompass obligations that take the form of common-law rules. As we noted in another context, "[state] regulation can be as effectively exerted through an award of damages as through some form of preventive relief. The obligation to pay compensation can be, indeed is designed to be, a potent method of governing conduct and controlling policy.

Although portions of the legislative history of the 1969 Act suggest that Congress was primarily concerned with positive enactments by States and localities, see S. Rep. No. 91-566, p.12, the language of the Act plainly reaches beyond such enactments. We must give effect to this plain language unless there is good reason to believe Congress intended the language to have some more restrictive meaning. In this case there is no "good reason to believe" that Congress meant less than what it said; indeed, in light of the narrowness of the 1965 Act, there is "good reason to believe" that Congress meant precisely what it said in amending that Act.

Moreover, common-law damages actions of the sort raised by petitioner are premised on the existence of a legal duty, and it is difficult to say that such actions do not impose "requirements or prohibitions." It is in this way that the 1969 version of §5(b) differs from its predecessor: Whereas the common law would not normally require a vendor to use any specific statement on its packages or in its advertisements, it is the essence of the common law to enforce duties that are either affirmative requirements or negative prohibitions. We therefore reject petitioner's argument that the phrase "requirement or prohibition" limits the 1969 Act's pre-emptive scope to positive enactments by legislatures and agencies.

Petitioner's second argument for excluding common-law rules from the reach of §5(b) hinges on the phrase "imposed under State law." This argument fails as well. At least since Erie R. Co. v. Tompkins, 304 U.S. 64, 58 S. Ct. 817, 82 L. Ed. 1188 (1938), we have recognized the phrase "state law" to include common law as well as statutes and regulations. Indeed just last Term, the Court stated that the phrase "'all other law, including State and municipal law'" "does not admit of [a] distinction . . . between positive enactments and common-law rules of liability." Although the presumption against pre-emption might give good reason to construe the phrase "state law" in a pre-emption provision more narrowly than an identical phrase in another context, in this case such a construction is not appropriate. As explained above, the 1965 version of §5 was precise and narrow on its face; the obviously broader language of the 1969 version extended that section's pre-emptive reach. Moreover, while the version of the 1969 Act passed by the Senate pre-empted "any State statute or regulation with respect to . . . advertising or promotion," the Conference Committee replaced this language with "State law with respect to advertising or promotion." In such a situation, §5(b)'s pre-emption of "state law" cannot fairly be limited to positive enactments.

That the pre-emptive scope of §5(b) cannot be limited to positive enactments does not mean that that section pre-empts all common-law claims. For example, as respondents concede, §5(b) does not generally pre-empt "state-law obligations to avoid marketing cigarettes with manufacturing defects or to use a demonstrably safer alternative design for cigarettes." For purposes of §5(b), the common law is not of a piece.

Nor does the statute indicate that any familiar subdivision of common-law claims is or is not pre-empted. We therefore cannot follow petitioner's passing suggestion that §5(b) pre-empts liability for omissions but not for acts, or that §5(b) pre-empts liability for unintentional torts but not for intentional torts. Instead we must fairly but — in light of the strong presumption against pre-emption — narrowly construe the precise language of §5(b) and we must look to each of petitioner's common-law claims to determine whether it is in fact pre-empted. The central inquiry in each case is straightforward: we ask whether the legal duty that is the predicate of the common-law damages action constitutes a "requirement or prohibition based on smoking and health . . . imposed under State law with respect to . . . advertising or promotion," giving that clause a fair but narrow reading. As discussed below, each phrase within that clause limits the universe of common-law claims pre-empted by the statute.

We consider each category of damages actions in turn. In doing so, we express no opinion on whether these actions are viable claims as a matter of state law; we assume, arguendo, that they are.

Failure to Warn

To establish liability for a failure to warn, petitioner must show that "a warning is necessary to make a product . . . reasonably safe, suitable and fit for its intended use," that respondents failed to provide such a warning, and that that failure was a proximate cause of petitioner's injury. In this case, petitioner offered two closely related theories concerning the failure to warn: first, that respondents "were negligent in the manner [that] they tested, researched, sold, promoted, and advertised" their cigarettes; and second, that respondents failed to provide "adequate warnings of the health consequences of cigarette smoking."

Petitioner's claims are pre-empted to the extent that they rely on a state-law "requirement or prohibition . . . with respect to . . . advertising or promotion." Thus, insofar as claims under either failure-to-warn theory require a showing that respondents' post-1969 advertising or promotions should have included additional, or more clearly stated, warnings, those claims are pre-empted. The Act does not, however, pre-empt petitioner's claims that rely solely on respondents' testing or research practices or other actions unrelated to advertising or promotion.

Breach of Express Warranty

. . . Petitioner's evidence of an express warranty consists largely of statements made in respondents' advertising. Applying the Court of Appeals' ruling that Congress pre-empted "damage[s] actions . . . that challenge . . . the propriety of a party's actions with respect to the advertising and promotion of cigarettes," the District Court ruled that this claim "inevitably brings into question [respondents'] advertising and promotional activities, and is therefore pre-empted" after 1965. As demonstrated above, however, the 1969 Act does not sweep so broadly: The appropriate inquiry is not whether a claim challenges the "propriety" of advertising and promotion, but whether the claim would require the imposition under state law of a requirement or prohibition based on smoking and health with respect to advertising or promotion.

A manufacturer's liability for breach of an express warranty derives from, and is measured by, the terms of that warranty. Accordingly, the "requirement[s]" imposed by an express warranty claim are not "imposed under State law," but rather imposed by the warrantor. If, for example, a manufacturer expressly promised to pay a smoker's medical bills if she contracted emphysema, the duty to honor that promise could not fairly be said to be "imposed under state law," but rather is best understood as undertaken by the manufacturer itself. While the general duty not to breach warranties arises under state law, the particular "requirement . . . based on smoking and health . . . with respect to the advertising or promotion [of] cigarettes" in an express warranty claim arises from the manufacturer's statements in its advertisements. In short, a common-law remedy for a contractual commitment voluntarily undertaken should not be regarded as a "requirement . . . imposed under State law" within the meaning of §5(b).[3]

That the terms of the warranty may have been set forth in advertisements rather than in separate documents is irrelevant to the pre-emption issue (though possibly not to the state law issue of whether the alleged warranty is valid and enforceable) because, although the breach of warranty claim is made "with respect . . . to advertising," it does not rest on a duty imposed under state law.

---

3. Justice Scalia contends that because the general duty to honor express warranties arises under state law, every express warranty obligation is a "requirement . . . imposed under State law," and that, therefore, the Act pre-empts petitioner's express warranty claim. Justice Scalia might be correct if the Act pre-empted "liability" imposed under state law; but instead the Act expressly pre-empts only a "requirement or prohibition" imposed under state law. That a "contract has no legal force apart from the [state] law that acknowledges its binding character," Norfolk & Western R. Co. v. Train Dispatchers, 499 U.S. 117, 130, 111 S. Ct. 1156, 1164, 113 L. Ed. 2d 95 (1991), does not mean that every contractual provision is "imposed under State law." To the contrary, common understanding dictates that a contractual requirement, although only enforceable under state law, is not "imposed" by the State, but rather is "imposed" by the contracting party upon itself.

Accordingly, to the extent that petitioner has a viable claim for breach of express warranties made by respondents, that claim is not pre-empted by the 1969 Act.

Fraudulent Misrepresentation

Petitioner alleges two theories of fraudulent misrepresentation. First, petitioner alleges that respondents, through their advertising, neutralized the effect of federally mandated warning labels. Such a claim is predicated on a state-law prohibition against statements in advertising and promotional materials that tend to minimize the health hazards associated with smoking. Such a prohibition, however, is merely the converse of a state-law requirement that warnings be included in advertising and promotional materials. Section 5(b) of the 1969 Act pre-empts both requirements and prohibitions; it therefore supersedes petitioner's first fraudulent misrepresentation theory.

Regulators have long recognized the relationship between prohibitions on advertising that downplays the dangers of smoking and requirements for warnings in advertisements. For example, the FTC, in promulgating its initial trade regulation rule in 1964, criticized advertising that "associated cigarette smoking with such positive attributes as contentment, glamour, romance, youth, happiness . . . at the same time suggesting that smoking is an activity at least consistent with physical health and well-being." The Commission concluded:

> "To avoid giving a false impression that smoking [is] innocuous, the cigarette manufacturer who represents the alleged pleasures or satisfactions of cigarette smoking in his advertising must also disclose the serious risks to life that smoking involves."

Longstanding regulations of the Food and Drug Administration express a similar understanding of the relationship between required warnings and advertising that "negates or disclaims" those warnings: "A hazardous substance shall not be deemed to have met [federal labeling] requirements if there appears in or on the label . . . statements, designs, or other graphic material that in any manner negates or disclaims [the required warning]." In this light it seems quite clear that petitioner's first theory of fraudulent misrepresentation is inextricably related to petitioner's first failure-to-warn theory, a theory that we have already concluded is largely pre-empted by §5(b).

Petitioner's second theory, as construed by the District Court, alleges intentional fraud and misrepresentation both by "false representation of a material fact [and by] conceal[ment of] a material fact." The predicate of this claim is a state-law duty not to make false statements of material fact or to conceal such facts. Our pre-emption analysis requires us to determine whether such a duty is the sort of requirement or prohibition proscribed by §5(b).

Section 5(b) pre-empts only the imposition of state-law obligations "with respect to the advertising or promotion" of cigarettes. Petitioner's claims that respondents concealed material facts are therefore not pre-empted insofar as those claims rely on a state-law duty to disclose such facts through channels of communication other than advertising or promotion. Thus, for example, if state law obliged respondents to disclose material facts about smoking and health to an administrative agency, §5(b) would not pre-empt a state-law claim based on a failure to fulfill that obligation.

Moreover, petitioner's fraudulent misrepresentation claims that do arise with respect to advertising and promotions (most notably claims based on allegedly false statements of material fact made in advertisements) are not pre-empted by §5(b). Such claims are predicated not on a duty "based on smoking and health" but rather on a more general obligation, the duty not to deceive. This understanding of fraud by intentional misstatement is appropriate for several reasons. First, in the 1969 Act, Congress offered no sign that it wished to insulate cigarette manufacturers from longstanding rules governing fraud. To the contrary, both the 1965 and the 1969 Acts explicitly reserved the FTC's authority to identify and punish deceptive advertising practices — an authority that the FTC had long exercised and continues to exercise. This indicates that Congress intended the phrase "relating to smoking and health" (which was essentially unchanged by the 1969 Act) to be construed narrowly, so as not to proscribe the regulation of deceptive advertising.

Moreover, this reading of "based on smoking and health" is wholly consistent with the purposes of the 1969 Act. State-law prohibitions on false statements of material fact do not create "diverse, nonuniform, and confusing" standards. Unlike state-law obligations concerning the warning necessary to render a product "reasonably safe," state-law proscriptions on intentional fraud rely only on a single, uniform standard: falsity. Thus, we conclude that the phrase "based on smoking and health" fairly but narrowly construed does not encompass the more general duty not to make fraudulent statements. Accordingly, petitioner's claim based on allegedly fraudulent statements made in respondents' advertisements is not pre-empted by §5(b) of the 1969 Act.[4]

For a thorough discussion of post-*Cipollone* preemption decisions, see M. Stuart Madden, Federal Preemption of Inconsistent State Safety Obligations, 21 Pace L. Rev. 103 (2000). One author argues that *Cipollone* does not preempt post-1969 failure to warn claims on the cigarette package itself. Michael D. Green, Cipollone Revisited: A Not So Little Secret About the Scope of Cigarette Preemption, 82 Iowa L. Rev. 1257 (1997). For a critique on the Supreme Court's preemption jurisprudence in the field of products liability, see Mary J. Davis, The Supreme Court and Our Culture of Irresponsibility, 31 Wake Forest L. Rev. 1075 (1996) (excoriating the Supreme Court for fostering institutional irresponsibility with its expansive interpretation of federal preemption that frees major defendants from common-law tort liability).

Taking their cue from the *Cipollone* decision, plaintiffs in cigarette litigation have based their post-1969 claims against tobacco companies not on failure to warn but on misrepresentation, express warranty, and violations of consumer protection statutes. See, e.g., Wright v. Brooke Group Ltd., 114 F. Supp. 2d 797, 824-25, 828 (N.D. Iowa 2000) (fraudulent concealment of the addictive nature of cigarettes in channels other than advertising and claims of fraudulent misrepre-

---

4. Both Justice Blackmun and Justice Scalia challenge the level of generality employed in our analysis. Justice Blackmun contends that, as a matter of consistency, we should construe failure-to-warn claims not as based on smoking and health, but rather as based on the broader duty "to inform consumers of known risks." Justice Scalia contends that, again as a matter of consistency, we should construe fraudulent misrepresentation claims not as based on a general duty not to deceive, but rather as "based on smoking and health." Admittedly, each of these positions has some conceptual attraction. However, our ambition here is not theoretical elegance, but rather a fair understanding of congressional purpose.

sentation and express warranty are not preempted); Williams v. Phillip Morris, Inc., 48 P.3d 824 (Or. Ct. App. 2002) (affirmative misrepresentations of the safety of cigarettes are not preempted); Castano v. American Tobacco Co., 870 F. Supp. 1425, 1431-1432 (E.D. La. 1994) (claims of fraud, deceit, and violation of consumer fraud statutes held not preempted). Some of the Castano claims were held to be proper for class certification, 100 F.R.D. 544 (E.D. La. 1995). In a landmark opinion, Castano v. American Tobacco Co., 84 F.3d 734 (5th Cir. 1996), the Fifth Circuit reversed, but not on preemption grounds. Describing the case as "what may be the largest class action ever attempted in federal court," id. at 736, and labeling it "humongous," id. at 743, the opinion of the court of appeals concludes:

> We have once before stated that "traditional ways of proceeding reflect far more than habit. They reflect the very culture of the jury trial. . . ." In re Fibreboard Corp., 893 F.2d 706, 711 (5th Cir. 1990). The collective wisdom of individual juries is necessary before this court commits the fate of an entire industry or, indeed, the fate of a class of millions, to a single jury. For the foregoing reasons, we reverse and remand with instructions that the district court dismiss the class complaint. [Id. at 752.]

NOTE: DRUGS AND PESTICIDES: PREEMPTION OR NOT?

In two other areas courts have struggled with the question of whether federal regulations preempt common law failure to warn claims. Drug and pesticide manufacturers have sought to convince courts that warning claims against them are either expressly or impliedly preempted. Drug manufacturers have generally been unsuccessful in arguing that warnings that meet with the approval of the Food and Drug Administration (FDA) should bar product liability claims concerning the adequacy of the warnings needed to alert physicians (or patients) to the risks associated with taking the drug. See, e.g., Feldman v. Lederle Laboratories, 479 A.2d 374, 389-391 (N.J. 1984) (claim that failure to warn that tetracycline can cause tooth discoloration is not preempted because there is nothing preventing a drug manufacturer from warning of risks without first receiving FDA approval); MacDonald v. Ortho Pharmaceutical Corp., 475 N.E.2d 65, 70 (Mass. 1985) (claim that warnings accompanying birth control pills were inadequate were not preempted by compliance with FDA labeling requirements since "[t]he regulatory history of the FDA requirements belies any objective to cloak them with preemptive effect"); Bell v. Lollar, 791 N.E.2d 849 (Ind. Ct. App. 2003) (review of authority holding that FDA regulations are minimum standards and do not preempt common law claims; court finds generic drug manufacturers subject to the same labeling requirements as non-generic drug producers for failing to add to the warnings of the listed generic drug since generics should not be granted greater protection than pioneer non-generic drugs). But see Hurley v. Lederle Laboratories, 863 F.2d 1173, 1179 (5th Cir. 1998) (court in dictum notes that when a drug company has provided all necessary and available information to the FDA on which to base a warning, then FDA approval of warning preempts product liability failure to warn claim).

Pesticide manufacturers have had more success in pressing their preemption claims. The Federal Insecticide, Fungicide, and Rodenticide Act, U.S.C.A. §§136-136y (hereinafter FIFRA) provides, in relevant part, that "[a state regulating the

> **authors' dialogue 17**
>
> **JIM:** Aaron, students tell me that they don't understand the kinds of fraud actions that are not federally preempted. Do you find the *Cipollone* decision puzzling on that score? I think I'm okay with the Court's exposition.
>
> **AARON:** Well, you are a better man than I am. The Court sets forth two kinds of fraud that are not preempted. One is pretty straightforward. What the court calls "false misrepresentation of material fact" is the classic common law fraud cause of action. It is the "fraudulent concealment of material fact" that is somewhat baffling.
>
> **JIM:** Well, the Court does say that fraudulent concealment claims escape preemption only "insofar as those claims rely on a state-law duty to disclose such facts through channels of communication other than advertising and promotion." The example the Court gives is that if state law required tobacco companies to disclose material facts about smoking and health to an administrative agency, then a common law claim predicated on such a failure to disclose is not preempted.
>
> **AARON:** I honestly don't know what they are saying and what's worse, I don't understand why they are saying it. First, I doubt that such reporting requirements exist for any state agency. If the FDA doesn't require such reporting, I'll bet that state agencies don't demand it. More important, if I read the Court right, the reasons that the Court has exempted intentional fraud from preemption is that the Court believes that Congress did not seek to protect

sale or use of a federally registered pesticide] shall not impose or continue in effect any requirements for labeling or packaging in addition to or different from those required under this subchapter." Id. §136v(a) and (b). Although the language seems to indicate a congressional intent to preempt state regulation of pesticide labeling, in a leading pre-*Cipollone* case, Ferebee v. Chevron Chemical Co., 736 F.2d 1529 (D.C. Cir. 1984), *cert. denied,* 469 U.S. 1062, the court held that FIFRA did not preempt state common law tort suits based on inadequate labeling. In the context of a discussion of differing state and federal objectives, particularly with respect to compensation, the court concluded: "The fact that EPA has determined that Chevron's label is adequate *for purposes of FIFRA* does not compel a jury to find that the label is also adequate *for purposes of state tort law* as well." Id. at 1540.

Post-*Cipollone* decisions have found the preemption language of FIFRA to be analogous to that of the Cigarette Labeling Act and have held common law claims based on failure to warn to be expressly preempted. See, e.g., Papas v. Upjohn Co. 985 F.2d 516 (11th Cir. 1993) (failure to warn about the dangers of the pesticide, Zoecon, expressly preempted by FIFRA); National Bank of Commerce of El Dorado, Arkansas v. Dow Chemical Co., 165 F.3d 602 (8th Cir. 1999) (state law product liability claims alleging that inadequate labeling on roach pesticide caused child's birth defect expressly preempted by FIFRA); Netland v. Hess & Clark, 284 F.3d 895 (8th Cir. 2002) (plaintiff's failure to warn claim that repetitive spraying of Bovinal on his house caused him to suffer from tobacco companies from fraud. Well, why would they want to protect tobacco companies from intentional fraudulent concealment? What difference does it make that the concealment was to a state agency or to consumers in the market place? If state law allows a cause of action for fraudulent concealment, so be it. Why was it necessary to limit the fraudulent concealment to cases outside of "advertising or promotion?" I really don't get it.

JIM: I may be wrong, Aaron, but here is my take on it. Fraudulent concealment can be either negligent or intentional. Negligent concealment of material facts is nothing more than a fancy way of saying that the defendant is liable for failure to warn. The heart of *Cipollone* is that negligent failure to warn cases are preempted. I think that the Court did not want to get into the distinction between negligent failure to warn and intentional failure to warn. Almost every negligent failure to warn case can be framed as an intentional failure to warn. Instead of saying "You should have known about the danger," we now simply allege that you actually "knew about the danger" and failed to tell me. Unless the Court found some way to limit the intentional concealment cause of action, it would swallow the classic failure to warn preemption. So they allow fraudulent concealment only outside advertising or promotion, activities in which negligent failures to warn arise.

AARON: Holy Toledo. You have a rich imagination, Jim. Where do you see any of this in the Court's opinion? And if that is what they are saying, they are off the chart. We make the distinction between negligence and intentional tort all the time. I said it before and I'll say it again—I just don't get it.

---

aplastic anemia expressly preempted by FIFRA); Dow Agrosciences v. Bastes, 332 F.3d 323 (5th Cir. 2003) (claim that herbicide marketed to control the growth of weeds in peanuts stunted the growth of and otherwise damaged farmers' peanut crops preempted by FIFRA; court rejected argument that claims regarding product effectiveness are not within the scope of FIFRA preemption). The cited cases make it clear, though, that claims based on defective design or manufacturing defects are not preempted.

B. FEDERAL PREEMPTION OF DESIGN DEFECT CLAIMS

The Supreme Court has not limited the preemption doctrine to failure to warn claims. Defendants have importuned the Court to find that the presence of federal regulations should prohibit plaintiffs from pursuing common law claims of design defect.

In Freightliner Corp. v. Myrick, 514 U.S. 280 (1995), plaintiffs who were injured or killed in collisions with trucks and trailers brought suit against the manufacturers, contending that their vehicles' lack of an antilock braking system (ABS) rendered them defective in design. The defendants countered with the argument that the design claims were federally preempted because the National

Highway and Traffic Safety Administration (NHTSA) had issued regulations requiring an ABS for tractor-trailers. The regulation, however, was suspended by the Ninth Circuit Court of Appeals' finding that the regulation (Standard 121) was neither "reasonable nor practicable at the time it was put into effect." See Pacaar, Inc. v. NHTSA, 573 F.2d 632, 640 (9th Cir. 1978), *cert. denied,* 439 U.S. 862 (1978). The contention of the defendant in *Myrick* was that the "absence of regulation itself constituted regulation." 514 U.S. at 286. The Court rejected the argument out of hand, noting that the very language of the Act applied to preempt state law only "[w]henever a Federal motor vehicle safety standard . . . is in effect" with respect to "the same aspect of performance" regulated by a state standard. In a footnote, the Court said that it need not reach the issue whether the preemption clause trumps only state statutes and regulations or whether it bars common law claims as well. The absence of any governing federal standard in the case was dispositive.

In Medtronic, Inc. v. Lohr, 518 U.S. 470 (1996), plaintiff, who suffered from heart disease, had a Medtronic pacemaker implanted in her heart. In December of 1990, the pacemaker failed, resulting in a "complete heart block" that required emergency surgery. Plaintiff alleged that the pacemaker was defectively manufactured and designed. The defendant moved for summary judgment, claiming that allowing a common law court to decide the adequacy of the pacemaker design ran afoul of 21 U.S.C §360k(a) of the Medical Device Act (MDA), which provides:

§360K. STATE AND LOCAL REQUIREMENTS RESPECTING DEVICES

(a) General rule

Except as provided in subsection (b) of this section, no State or political subdivision of a State may establish or continue in effect with respect to a device intended for human use any requirement . . .

(1) which is different from, or in addition to, any requirement applicable under this chapter to the device, and

(2) which relates to the safety or effectiveness of the device or to any other matter included in a requirement applicable to the device under this chapter.

The FDA has interpreted this preemption provision in these terms:

> State or local requirements are preempted only when the [FDA] has established specific counterpart regulations or there are other specific requirements applicable to a particular device under the Act, thereby making any existing divergent sate or local requirements applicable to the device different from or in addition to, the specific [FDA] requirements.

Medtronic argued that any common law cause of action is a "requirement" that alters incentives and imposes duties "different from, or in addition to" the generic federal standards that the FDA has promulgated in response to the MDA. Justice Stevens, writing for the plurality, was skeptical that the MDA intended to preempt common law actions for defective design and the Court ultimately found the contention that the MDA preempted a design defect claim for the Medtronic pacemaker to be specious.

The Court noted that the MDA provides different standards of adminstrative review for medical devices. Class III medical devices undergo a rigorous premarket approval (PMA). Congress, however, allowed for "grandfathering" of

Class III medical devices that were on the market at the time the MDA was passed in 1976 that exempted them from the PMA process. The Act also provided that medical devices that were "substantially equivalent" to preexisting devices did not require PMA. The simple reality was that the Medtronic pacemaker never underwent significant federal oversight. The FDA treated it as a clone or a close relative to a preexisting device that was allowed on the market without a PMA. Under these facts the Court found that preemption was unwarranted.

The Court, however, did not address whether common law tort actions would be preempted where a medical device was subject to a PMA. Though the plurality left this question open, it appears that five members of the Court would have found preemption in such a case.

At least one court has held that the FDA's PMA of a medical device does not preempt state tort claims. See Goodlin v. Medtronic, Inc., 167 F.3d 1367 (11th Cir. 1999) (holding that state claims for negligent design and strict products liability were not preempted by the MDA in light of the Supreme Court's admonition that congressional intent is "the ultimate touchstone" in a preemption case and because of the court's inability to discern the imposition of a "specific federal requirement"). But see Kemp v. Medotronic, Inc., 231 F.3d 216 (6th Cir. 2000) (disagreeing with the 11th Circuit in finding that FDA approval of a medical device that has undergone the full PMA process preempts common law claim of design defect). For an interesting analysis of the preemption issue, see Robert B. Leflar and Robert S. Adler, The Preemption Pentad; Federal Preemption of Products Liability Claims After Medtronic, 64 Tenn. L. Rev. 691 (1997).

Far and away the most important design preemption case emanated from the controversy as to whether auto manufacturers who complied with National Highway and Traffic and Safety Administration (NHTSA) regulations regarding the installation of air bags could be subject to common law tort claims. Today air bags are mandatory equipment on all new cars. But, as the following case makes clear, there was a period of time when NHTSA allowed auto manufacturers the right to "phase in" air bags so long as they chose to install other approved passive restraint devices that would protect drivers and passengers in the event of a collision. Courts split sharply as to whether NHTSA regulations preempted common law design defect actions for cars manufactured in the "phase in" era that were not equipped with air bags. In a highly contentious decision, the Court found in favor of federal preemption.

Geier v. American Honda Motor Company, Inc.
529 U.S. 861 (2000)

BREYER, J., delivered the opinion of the Court, in which REHNQUIST, C.J., and O'CONNOR, SCALIA, and KENNEDY, JJ., joined. STEVENS, J., filed a dissenting opinion, in which SOUTER, THOMAS, and GINSBURG, JJ., joined, *post,* p.1928.

Justice BREYER delivered the opinion of the Court.

This case focuses on the 1984 version of a Federal Motor Vehicle Safety Standard promulgated by the Department of Transportation under the authority of the National Traffic and Motor Vehicle Safety Act of 1966, 80 Stat. 718, 15 U.S.C. §1381 *et seq.* (1988 ed.). The standard, FMVSS 208, required auto manufacturers to equip some but not all of their 1987 vehicles with passive restraints. We ask whether the Act pre-empts a state common-law tort action in which the plaintiff claims that the defendant auto manufacturer, who was in compliance with the standard, should nonetheless have equipped a 1987 automobile with airbags. We conclude that the Act, taken together with FMVSS 208, pre-empts the lawsuit.

I

In 1992, petitioner Alexis Geier, driving a 1987 Honda Accord, collided with a tree and was seriously injured. The car was equipped with manual shoulder and lap belts which Geier had buckled up at the time. The car was not equipped with airbags or other passive restraint devices.

Geier and her parents, also petitioners, sued the car's manufacturer, American Honda Motor Company, Inc., and its affiliates (hereinafter American Honda), under District of Columbia tort law. They claimed, among other things, that American Honda had designed its car negligently and defectively because it lacked a driver's side airbag. The District Court dismissed the lawsuit. The court noted that FMVSS 208 gave car manufacturers a choice as to whether to install airbags. And the court concluded that petitioners' lawsuit, because it sought to establish a different safety standard — *i.e.,* an airbag requirement — was expressly pre-empted by a provision of the Act which pre-empts "any safety standard" that is not identical to a federal safety standard applicable to the same aspect of performance, 15 U.S.C. §1392(d) (1988 ed.). . . .

The Court of Appeals agreed with the District Court's conclusion but on somewhat different reasoning. It had doubts, given the existence of the Act's "saving" clause, 15 U.S.C. §1397(k) (1988 ed.), that petitioners' lawsuit involved the potential creation of the kind of "safety standard" to which the Safety Act's express pre-emption provision refers. But it declined to resolve that question because it found that petitioners' state-law tort claims posed an obstacle to the accomplishment of FMVSS 208's objectives. For that reason, it found that those claims conflicted with FMVSS 208, and that, under ordinary pre-emption principles, the Act consequently pre-empted the lawsuit. The Court of Appeals thus affirmed the District Court's dismissal.

Several state courts have held to the contrary, namely, that neither the Act's express pre-emption nor FMVSS 208 pre-empts a "no airbag" tort suit. See, *e.g.,* Drattel v. Toyota Motor Corp., . . . 699 N.E.2d 376, 379-386, (N.Y. 1998); Minton v. Honda of America Mfg., Inc., . . . 684 N.E.2d 648, 655-661 (Ohio 1997); Munroe v. Galati, . . . 938 P.2d 1114, 1116-1120 (Ariz. 1997); Wilson v. Pleasant, 660 N.E.2d 327, 330-339 (Ind. 1995); Tebbetts v. Ford Motor Co., . . . 665 A.2d 345, 347-348 (N.H. 1995). All of the Federal Circuit Courts that have considered the question, however, have found pre-emption. One rested its conclusion on the Act's express pre-emption provision. See, *e.g.,* Harris v. Ford Motor Co., 110 F.3d 1410, 1413-1415 (C.A.9 1997). Others, such as the Court of Appeals below, have instead found pre-emption under ordinary pre-emption principles by virtue of the conflict such suits pose to FMVSS 208's objectives, and thus to the Act itself. See, *e.g.,* Montag v. Honda Motor Co., 75 F.3d 1414, 1417 (C.A.10 1996); Pokorny v. Ford Motor Co., 902 F.2d 1116, 1121-1125 (C.A.3 1990); Taylor v. General Motors Corp., 875 F.2d 816, 825-827 (C.A.11 1989); Wood v. General Motors Corp., 865 F.2d 395, 412-414 (C.A.1 1988). We granted certiorari to resolve these differences. We now hold that this kind of "no airbag" lawsuit conflicts with the objectives of FMVSS 208, a standard authorized by the Act, and is therefore pre-empted by the Act.

In reaching our conclusion, we consider three subsidiary questions. First, does the Act's express pre-emption provision pre-empt this lawsuit? We think not. Second, do ordinary pre-emption principles nonetheless apply? We hold that they do. Third, does this lawsuit actually conflict with FMVSS 208, hence with the Act itself? We hold that it does.

II

We first ask whether the Safety Act's express pre-emption provision pre-empts this tort action. The provision reads as follows:

"Whenever a Federal motor vehicle safety standard established under this subchapter is in effect, no State or political subdivision of a State shall have any authority either to establish, or to continue in effect, with respect to any motor vehicle or item of motor vehicle equipment[,] any safety standard applicable to the same aspect of performance of such vehicle or item of equipment which is not identical to the Federal standard." 15 U.S.C. §1392(d) (1988 ed.).

American Honda points out that a majority of this Court has said that a somewhat similar statutory provision in a different federal statute—a provision that uses the word "requirements"—may well expressly pre-empt similar tort actions. See, *e.g.,* Medtronic, Inc. v. Lohr, 518 U.S. 470, 502-504 . . . (1996) (plurality opinion). . . . Petitioners reply that this statute speaks of pre-empting a state-law "safety *standard,*" not a "requirement," and that a tort action does not involve a safety *standard.* Hence, they conclude, the express pre-emption provision does not apply.

We need not determine the precise significance of the use of the word "standard," rather than "requirement," however, for the Act contains another provision, which resolves the disagreement. That provision, a "saving" clause, says that "[c]ompliance with" a federal safety standard "does not exempt any person from any liability under common law." 15 U.S.C. §1397(k) (1988 ed.). The saving clause assumes that there are some significant number of common-law liability cases to save. And a reading of the express pre-emption provision that excludes common-law tort actions gives actual meaning to the saving clause's literal language, while leaving adequate room for state tort law to operate—for example, where federal law creates only a floor, *i.e.,* a minimum safety standard. See, *e.g.,* Brief for United States as *Amicus Curiae* 21 (explaining that common-law claim that a vehicle is defectively designed because it lacks antilock brakes would not be pre-empted by 49 C.F.R. §571.105 (1999), a safety standard establishing minimum requirements for brake performance). Without the saving clause, a broad reading of the express pre-emption provision arguably might pre-empt those actions, for, as we have just mentioned, it is possible to read the pre-emption provision, standing alone, as applying to standards imposed in common-law tort actions, as well as standards contained in state legislation or regulations. And if so, it would pre-empt all nonidentical state standards established in tort actions covering the same aspect of performance as an applicable federal standard, even if the federal standard merely established a minimum standard. On that broad reading of the pre-emption clause little, if any, potential "liability at common law" would remain. And few, if any, state tort actions would remain for the saving clause to save. We have found no convincing indication that Congress wanted to pre-empt, not only state statutes and regulations, but also common-law tort actions, in such circumstances. Hence the broad reading cannot be correct. The language of the pre-emption provision permits a narrow reading that excludes common-law actions. Given the presence of the saving clause, we conclude that the pre-emption clause must be so read.

III

We have just said that the saving clause *at least* removes tort actions from the scope of the express pre-emption clause. Does it do more? In particular, does it foreclose or limit the operation of ordinary pre-emption principles insofar as those principles instruct us to read statutes as pre-empting state laws (including common-law rules) that "actually conflict" with the statute or federal standards promulgated thereunder?. . . .

Nothing in the language of the saving clause suggests an intent to save state-law tort actions that conflict with federal regulations. The words "[c]ompliance" and "does not exempt," 15 U.S.C. §1397(k) (1988 ed.), sound as if they simply bar a special kind of defense, namely, a defense that compliance with a federal standard automatically exempts a defendant from state law, whether the Federal Government meant that standard to be an absolute requirement or only a minimum one. See Restatement (Third) of Torts: Products Liability §4(b), Comment *e* (1997) (distinguishing between state-law compliance defense and a federal claim of pre-emption). It is difficult to understand why Congress would have insisted on a compliance-with-federal-regulation precondition to the provision's applicability had it wished the Act to "save" all state-law tort actions, regardless of their potential threat to the objectives of federal safety standards promulgated under that Act. Nor does our interpretation conflict with the purpose of the saving provision, say by rendering it ineffectual. As we have previously explained, the saving provision still makes clear that the express pre-emption provision does not of its own force pre-empt common-law tort actions. And it thereby preserves those actions that seek to establish greater safety than the minimum safety achieved by a federal regulation intended to provide a floor.

Moreover, this Court has repeatedly "decline[d] to give broad effect to saving clauses where doing so would upset the careful regulatory scheme established by federal law." United States v. Locke, ante, at 106-107, 120 S. Ct. 1135; see American Telephone & Telegraph Co. v. Central Office Telephone, Inc., 524 U.S. 214, 227-228, . . . (1998) (*AT&T*); Texas & Pacific R. Co. v. Abilene Cotton Oil Co., 204 U.S. 426, 446, . . . (1907). We find this concern applicable in the present case. And we conclude that the saving clause foresees — it does not foreclose — the possibility that a federal safety standard will pre-empt a state common-law tort action with which it conflicts. . . .

IV

The basic question, then, is whether a common-law "no airbag" action like the one before us actually conflicts with FMVSS 208. We hold that it does.

In petitioners' and the dissent's view, FMVSS 208 sets a minimum airbag standard. As far as FMVSS 208 is concerned, the more airbags, and the sooner, the better. But that was not the Secretary's view. The Department of Transportation's (DOT's) comments, which accompanied the promulgation of FMVSS 208, make clear that the standard deliberately provided the manufacturer with a range of choices among different passive restraint devices. Those choices would bring about a mix of different devices introduced gradually over time; and FMVSS 208 would thereby lower costs, overcome technical safety problems, encourage technological development, and win widespread consumer acceptance — all of which would promote FMVSS 208's safety objectives. See generally 49 Fed. Reg. 28962 (1984).

A

The history of FMVSS 208 helps explain why and how DOT sought these objectives. . . . In 1967, DOT, understanding that seatbelts would save many lives, required manufacturers to install manual seat belts in all automobiles. 32 Fed. Reg. 2408, 2415. It became apparent, however, that most occupants simply would not buckle up their belts. Ibid. See 34 Fed. Reg. 11148 (1969). DOT then began to investigate the feasibility of requiring "passive restraints," such as airbags and automatic seatbelts. Ibid. In 1970, it amended FMVSS 208 to include some passive protection requirements, 35 Fed. Reg. 16927, while making clear that airbags were one of several "equally acceptable" devices and that it neither "'favored' [n]or expected the introduction of airbag systems." Ibid. In 1971, it added an express provision permitting compliance through the use of nondetachable passive belts, 36 Fed. Reg. 12858, 12859 and in 1972, it mandated full passive protection for all front seat occupants for vehicles manufactured after August 15, 1975. . . .

B

Read in light of this history, DOT's own contemporaneous explanation of FMVSS 208 makes clear that the 1984 version of FMVSS 208 reflected the following significant considerations. First, buckled up seatbelts are a vital ingredient of automobile safety. Id., at 29003; *State Farm,* 463 U.S. at 52 . . . ("We start with the accepted ground that if used, seatbelts unquestionably would save many thousands of lives and would prevent tens of thousands of crippling injuries"). Second, despite the enormous and unnecessary risks that a passenger runs by not buckling up manual lap and shoulder belts, more than 80% of front seat passengers would leave their manual seatbelts unbuckled. 49 Fed. Reg. 28983 (1984) (estimating that only 12.5% of front seat passengers buckled up manual belts). Third, airbags could make up for the dangers caused by unbuckled manual belts, but they could not make up for them entirely. Id., at 28986 (concluding that, although an airbag plus a lap and shoulder belt was the most "effective" system, airbags alone were *less* effective than buckled up manual lap and shoulder belts).

Fourth, passive restraint systems had their own disadvantages, for example, the dangers associated with, intrusiveness of, and corresponding public dislike for, nondetachable automatic belts. Id., at 28992-28993. Fifth, airbags brought with them their own special risks to safety, such as the risk of danger to out-of-position occupants (usually children) in small cars. Id., at 28992, 29001; see also 65 Fed. Reg. 30680, 30681-30682 (2000) (finding 158 confirmed airbag-induced fatalities as of April 2000, and amending rule to add new requirements, test procedures, and injury criteria to ensure that "future air bags be designed to create less risk of serious airbag-induced injuries than current air bags, particularly for small women and young children"); U.S. Dept. of Transportation, National Highway Traffic Safety Administration, National Accident Sampling System Crashworthiness Data System 1991-1993, p.viii (Aug. 1995) (finding that airbags caused approximately 54,000 injuries between 1991 and 1993).

Sixth, airbags were expected to be significantly more expensive than other passive restraint devices, raising the average cost of a vehicle price $320 for full frontal airbags over the cost of a car with manual lap and shoulder seatbelts (and potentially much more if production volumes were low). 49 Fed. Reg. 28990 (1984). And the agency worried that the high replacement cost—estimated to be $800—could lead car owners to refuse to replace them after deployment. Id., at 28990, 29000-29001; see also id., at 28990 (estimating total investment costs for mandatory airbag requirement at $1.3 billion compared to $500 million for automatic seatbelts). Seventh, the public, for reasons of cost, fear, or physical intrusiveness, might resist installation or use of any of the then-available passive restraint devices, id., at 28987-28989—a particular concern with respect to airbags, id., at 29001 (noting that "[a]irbags engendered the largest quantity of, and most vociferously worded, comments").

FMVSS 208 reflected these considerations in several ways. Most importantly, that standard deliberately sought variety—a mix of several different passive restraint systems. It did so by setting a performance requirement for passive restraint devices and allowing manufacturers to choose among different passive restraint mechanisms, such as airbags, automatic belts, or other passive restraint technologies to satisfy that requirement. Id., at 28996. And DOT explained why FMVSS 208 sought the mix of devices that it expected its performance standard to produce. Id. at 28997. DOT wrote that it had *rejected* a proposed FMVSS 208 "all airbag" standard because of safety concerns (perceived or real) associated with airbags, which concerns threatened a "backlash" more easily overcome "if airbags" were "not the only way of complying." Id., at 29001. It added that a mix of devices would help develop data on comparative effectiveness, would allow the industry time to overcome the safety problems and the high production costs associated with airbags, and would facilitate the development of alternative, cheaper, and safer passive restraint systems. Id., at 29001-29002. And it would thereby build public confidence, id., at 29001-29002, necessary to avoid another interlock-type fiasco.

The 1984 FMVSS 208 standard also deliberately sought a *gradual* phase-in of passive restraints. Id., at 28999-29000. It required the manufacturers to equip only 10% of their car fleet manufactured after September 1, 1986, with passive restraints. Id., at 28999. It then increased the percentage in three annual stages, up to 100% of the new car fleet for cars manufactured after September 1, 1989. Ibid. And it explained that the phased-in requirement would allow more time for manufacturers to develop airbags or other, better, safer passive restraint systems. It would help develop information about the comparative effectiveness of different systems, would lead to a mix in which airbags and other nonseatbelt passive restraint systems played a more prominent role than would otherwise result, and would promote public acceptance. Id., at 29000-29001.

Of course, as the dissent points out, post, at 19-20, FMVSS 208 did not guarantee the mix by setting a ceiling for each different passive restraint device. In fact, it provided a form of extra credit for airbag installation (and other nonbelt passive restraint devices) under which each airbag-installed vehicle counted as 1.5 vehicles for purposes of meeting FMVSS 208's passive restraint requirement. 49 C.F.R. §571.208, S4.1.3.4(a)(1) (1999); 49 Fed. Reg. 29000 (1984). But why should DOT have bothered to impose an airbag ceiling when the practical threat to the mix it desired arose from the likelihood that manufacturers would install, not too many airbags too quickly, but too few or none at all? After all, only a few years earlier, Secretary Dole's predecessor had discovered that manufacturers intended to meet the then-current passive restraint requirement almost entirely (more than 99%) through the installation of more affordable automatic belt systems. 46 Fed. Reg. 53421 (1981); *State Farm,* 463 U.S. at 38. The extra credit, as DOT explained, was designed to "encourage manufacturers to equip *at least some* of their cars with airbags." 49 Fed. Reg. 29001 (1984) (emphasis added) (responding to comment that failure to mandate airbags might mean the "end of . . . airbag technology"); see also id., at 29000 (explaining that the extra credit for airbags "should promote the development of what may be better alternatives to automatic belts *than would otherwise be developed*" (emphasis added)). The credit provision *reinforces* the point that FMVSS 208 sought a gradually developing mix of passive restraint devices; it does not show the contrary.

Finally FMVSS 208's passive restraint requirement was conditional. DOT believed that ordinary manual lap and shoulder belts would produce about the same amount of safety as passive restraints, and at significantly lower costs — *if only auto occupants would buckle up.* See id., at 28997-28998. Thus, FMVSS 208 provided for rescission of its passive restraint requirement if, by September 1, 1989, two-thirds of the States had laws in place that, like those of many other nations, required auto occupants to buckle up (and which met other requirements specified in the standard). Id., at 28963, 28993-28994, 28997-28999. The Secretary wrote that "coverage of a large percentage of the American people by seat-belt laws that are enforced would largely negate the incremental increase in safety to be expected from an automatic protection requirement." Id., at 28997. In the end, two-thirds of the States did not enact mandatory buckle-up laws, and the passive restraint requirement remained in effect.

In sum, as DOT now tells us through the Solicitor General, the 1984 version of FMVSS 208 "embodies the Secretary's policy judgment that safety would best be promoted if manufacturers installed *alternative* protection systems in their fleets rather than one particular system in every car." Brief for United States as *Amicus Curiae* 25; see 49 Fed. Reg. 28997 (1984). Petitioners' tort suit claims that the manufacturers of the 1987 Honda Accord "had a duty to design, manufacture, distribute and sell a motor vehicle with an effective and safe passive restraint system, including, but not limited to, airbags." App. 3 (Complaint, ¶11).

In effect, petitioners' tort action depends upon its claim that manufacturers had a duty to install an airbag when they manufactured the 1987 Honda Accord. Such a state law — *i.e.,* a rule of state tort law imposing such a duty — by its terms would have required manufacturers of all similar cars to install airbags rather than other passive restraint systems, such as automatic belts or passive interiors. It thereby would have presented an obstacle to the variety and mix of devices that the federal regulation sought. It would have required all manufacturers to have installed airbags in respect to the entire District-of-Columbia-related portion of their 1987 new car fleet, even though FMVSS 208 at that time required only that 10% of a manufacturer's nationwide fleet be equipped with any passive restraint device at all. It thereby also would have stood as an obstacle to the gradual passive restraint phase-in that the federal regulation deliberately imposed. In addition, it could have made less likely the adoption of a state mandatory buckle-up law. Because the rule of law for which petitioners contend would have stood "as an obstacle to the accomplishment and execution of" the important means-related federal objectives that we have just discussed, it is pre-empted. . . .

One final point: We place some weight upon DOT's interpretation of FMVSS 208's objectives and its conclusion, as set forth in the Government's brief, that a tort suit such as this one would "'stan[d] as an obstacle to the accomplishment and execution'" of those objectives. Brief for United States as *Amicus Curiae* 25-26 (quoting *Hines,* at 67, 61 S. Ct. 399). Congress has delegated to DOT authority to implement the statute; the subject matter is technical; and the relevant history and background are complex and extensive. The agency is likely to have a thorough understanding of its own regulation and its objectives and is "uniquely qualified" to comprehend the likely impact of state requirements. . . .

[T]he language of FMVSS 208 and the contemporaneous 1984 DOT explanation is clear enough — even without giving DOT's own view special weight. FMVSS 208 sought a gradually developing mix of alternative passive restraint devices for safety-related reasons. The rule of state tort law for which petitioners argue would stand as an "obstacle" to the accomplishment of that objective. And the statute foresees the application of ordinary principles of pre-emption in cases of actual conflict. Hence, the tort action is pre-empted.

The judgment of the Court of Appeals is affirmed.

It is so ordered.

Justice STEVENS, with whom Justice SOUTER, Justice THOMAS, and Justice GINSBURG join, dissenting.

Airbag technology has been available to automobile manufacturers for over 30 years. There is now general agreement on the proposition "that, to be safe, a car must have an airbag.". . . Indeed, current federal law imposes that requirement on all automobile manufacturers. See 49 U.S.C. §30127; 49 C.F.R. §571.208, S4.1.5.3 (1998). The question raised by petitioner's common-law tort action is whether that proposition was sufficiently obvious when Honda's 1987 Accord was manufactured to make the failure to install such a safety feature actionable under theories of negligence or defective design. The Court holds that an interim regulation motivated by the Secretary of Transportation's desire to foster gradual development of a variety of passive restraint devices deprives state courts of jurisdiction to answer that question. I respectfully dissent from that holding, and especially from the Court's unprecedented extension of the doctrine of pre-emption. As a preface to an explanation of my understanding of the statute and the regulation, these preliminary observations seem appropriate.

"This is a case about federalism," Coleman v. Thompson, 501 U.S. 722, 726 . . ., 115 L. Ed. 2d 640 (1991), that is, about respect for "the constitutional role of the States as sovereign entities." Alden v. Maine, 527 U.S. 706, 713, . . . (1999). It raises important questions concerning the way in which the Federal Government may exercise its undoubted power to oust state courts of their traditional jurisdiction over common-law tort actions. The rule the Court enforces today was not enacted by Congress and is not to be found in the text of any

Executive Order or regulation. It has a unique origin: It is the product of the Court's interpretation of the final commentary accompanying an interim administrative regulation and the history of airbag regulation generally. Like many other judge-made rules, its contours are not precisely defined. I believe, however, that it is fair to state that if it had been expressly adopted by the Secretary of Transportation, it would have read as follows:

> "No state court shall entertain a common-law tort action based on a claim that an automobile was negligently or defectively designed because it was not equipped with an airbag;
>
> "Provided, however, that this rule shall not apply to cars manufactured before September 1, 1986, or after such time as the Secretary may require the installation of airbags in all new cars; and
>
> "Provided further, that this rule shall not preclude a claim by a driver who was not wearing her seatbelt that an automobile was negligently or defectively designed because it was not equipped with any passive restraint whatsoever, or a claim that an automobile with particular design features was negligently or defectively designed because it was equipped with one type of passive restraint instead of another."

Perhaps such a rule would be a wise component of a legislative reform of our tort system. I express no opinion about that possibility. It is, however, quite clear to me that Congress neither enacted any such rule itself nor authorized the Secretary of Transportation to do so. It is equally clear to me that the objectives that the Secretary intended to achieve through the adoption of Federal Motor Vehicle Safety Standard 208 would not be frustrated one whit by allowing state courts to determine whether in 1987 the life-saving advantages of airbags had become sufficiently obvious that their omission might constitute a design defect in some new cars. Finally, I submit that the Court is quite wrong to characterize its rejection of the presumption against pre-emption, and its reliance on history and regulatory commentary rather than either statutory or regulatory text, as "ordinary experience-proved principles of conflict preemption." . . .

III

When a state statute, administrative rule, or common-law cause of action conflicts with a federal statute, it is axiomatic that the state law is without effect. U.S. Const., Art. VI, cl. 2; Cipollone v. Liggett Group, Inc., 505 U.S. 504, 516 . . . (1992). On the other hand, it is equally clear that the Supremacy Clause does not give unelected federal judges *carte blanche* to use federal law as a means of imposing their own ideas of tort reform on the States. Because of the role of States as separate sovereigns in our federal system, we have long presumed that state laws — particularly those, such as the provision of tort remedies to compensate for personal injuries, that are within the scope of the States' historic police powers — are not to be pre-empted by a federal statute unless it is the clear and manifest purpose of Congress to do so. Medtronic, Inc. v. Lohr, 518 U.S. 470, 485. . . .

IV

Even though the Safety Act does not expressly pre-empt common-law claims, Honda contends that Standard 208 — of its own force — implicitly pre-empts the claims in this case. . . .

Honda argues, and the Court now agrees, that the risk of liability presented by common-law claims that vehicles without airbags are negligently and defectively designed would frustrate the policy decision that the Secretary made in promulgating Standard 208. This decision, in their view, was that safety—including a desire to encourage "public acceptance of the airbag technology and experimentation with better passive restraint systems"—would best be promoted through gradual implementation of a passive restraint requirement making airbags only one of a variety of systems that a manufacturer could install in order to comply, rather than through a requirement mandating the use of one particular system in every vehicle. In its brief supporting Honda, the United States agreed with this submission. It argued that if the manufacturers had known in 1984 that they might later be held liable for failure to install airbags, that risk "would likely have led them to install airbags in all cars," thereby frustrating the Secretary's safety goals and interfering with the methods designed to achieve them. Brief for United States as *Amicus Curiae* 25.

There are at least three flaws in this argument that provide sufficient grounds for rejecting it. First, the entire argument is based on an unrealistic factual predicate. Whatever the risk of liability on a no-airbag claim may have been prior to the promulgation of the 1984 version of Standard 208, that risk did not lead any manufacturer to install airbags in even a substantial portion of its cars. If there had been a realistic likelihood that the risk of tort liability would have that consequence, there would have been no need for Standard 208. The promulgation of that standard certainly did not *increase* the pre-existing risk of liability. Even if the standard did not create a previously unavailable pre-emption defense, it likely *reduced* the manufacturers' risk of liability by enabling them to point to the regulation and their compliance therewith as evidence tending to negate charges of negligent and defective design. See Part II, supra. Given that the pre-1984 risk of liability did not lead to widespread airbag installation, this reduced risk of liability was hardly likely to compel manufacturers to install airbags in all cars—or even to compel them to comply with Standard 208 during the phase-in period by installing airbags exclusively.

Second, even if the manufacturers' assessment of their risk of liability ultimately proved to be wrong, the purposes of Standard 208 would not be frustrated. In light of the inevitable time interval between the eventual filing of a tort action alleging that the failure to install an airbag is a design defect and the possible resolution of such a claim against a manufacturer, as well as the additional interval between such a resolution (if any) and manufacturers' "compliance with the state law duty in question," . . . by modifying their designs to avoid such liability in the future, it is obvious that the phase-in period would have ended long before its purposes could have been frustrated by the specter of tort liability. Thus, even without preemption, the public would have been given the time that the Secretary deemed necessary to gradually adjust to the increasing use of airbag technology and allay their unfounded concerns about it. Moreover, even if any no-airbag suits were ultimately resolved against manufacturers, the resulting incentive to modify their designs would have been quite different from a decision by the Secretary to mandate the use of airbags in every vehicle. For example, if the extra credit provided for the use of nonbelt passive restraint technologies during the phase-in period had (as the Secretary hoped) ultimately encouraged manufacturers to develop a nonbelt system more effective than the airbag, manufacturers held liable for failing to install passive restraints would have been free to respond by modifying their designs to include such a system *instead of* an airbag. It seems clear, therefore, that any potential tort liability would not frustrate the Secretary's desire to encourage both experimentation with better passive restraint systems and public acceptance of airbags.

Third, despite its acknowledgement that the saving clause "preserves those actions that seek to establish greater safety than the minimum safety achieved by a federal regulation intended to provide a floor," . . . the Court completely ignores the important fact that by definition all of the standards established under the Safety Act—like the British regulations that governed the number and capacity of lifeboats aboard the *Titanic*—impose minimum, rather than fixed or maximum, requirements. 15 U.S.C. §1391(2); see Norfolk Southern R. Co. v. Shanklin, ante at 359, 120 S. Ct. 1467 (2000) (BREYER, J., concurring) ("[F]ederal *minimum* safety standards should not pre-empt a state tort action"); Hillsborough County v. Automated Medical Laboratories, Inc., 471 U.S. 707, 721, . . . (1985). The phase-in program authorized by Standard 208 thus set minimum percentage requirements for the installation of passive restraints, increasing in annual stages of 10, 25, 40, and 100%. Those requirements were not ceilings, and it is obvious that the Secretary favored a more rapid increase. The possibility that exposure to potential tort liability might accelerate the rate of increase would actually further the only goal explicitly mentioned in the standard itself: reducing the number of deaths and severity of injuries of vehicle occupants. Had gradualism been independently important as a method of achieving the Secretary's safety goals, presumably the Secretary would have put a ceiling as well as a floor on each annual increase in the required percentage of new passive restraint installations. For similar reasons, it is evident that variety was not a matter of independent importance to the Secretary. Although the standard allowed manufacturers to comply with the minimum percentage requirements by installing passive restraint systems other than airbags (such as automatic seatbelts), it encouraged them to install airbags and other nonbelt systems that might be developed in the future. The Secretary did not act to ensure the use of a variety of passive restraints by placing ceilings on the number of airbags that could be used in complying with the minimum requirements. Moreover, even if variety and gradualism had been independently important to the Secretary, there is nothing in the standard, the accompanying commentary, or the history of airbag regulation to support the notion that the Secretary intended to advance those purposes at all costs, without regard to the detrimental consequences that pre-emption of tort liability could have for the achievement of her avowed purpose of reducing vehicular injuries. . . .

V

For these reasons, it is evident that Honda has not crossed the high threshold established by our decisions regarding pre-emption of state laws that allegedly frustrate federal purposes: it has not demonstrated that allowing a common-law no-airbag claim to go forward would impose an obligation on manufacturers that directly and irreconcilably contradicts any primary objective that the Secretary set forth with clarity in Standard 208. Gade v. National Solid Wastes Management Assn., 505 U.S. at 110 . . . (KENNEDY, J., concurring in part and concurring in judgment); *id.* at 111 . . . ("A freewheeling judicial inquiry into whether [state law] is in tension with federal objectives would undercut the principle that it is Congress [and federal agencies,] rather than the courts[,] that pre-empt state law"). Furthermore, it is important to note that the text of Standard 208 (which the Court does not even bother to quote in its opinion), unlike the regulation we reviewed in Fidelity Fed. Sav. & Loan Assn. v. De la Cuesta, 458 U.S. at 158 . . . does not contain any expression of an intent to displace state law. Given our repeated emphasis on the importance of the presumption against pre-emption, see, *e.g.*, CSX Transp., Inc. v. Easterwood, 507 U.S. at 663-664 . . . ; Rice v. Santa Fe Elevator Corp., 331 U.S. 218, 230, . . . (1947), this silence lends additional support to the conclusion that the continuation of whatever common-law liability may exist in a case like this poses no danger of frustrating any of the Secretary's primary purposes in promulgating Standard 208. See Hillsborough County v. Automated Medical Laboratories, Inc., 471 U.S. at 721 . . . ; Silkwood v. Kerr-McGee Corp., 464 U.S. at 251 . . . ("It is difficult to believe that [the Secretary] would, without comment, remove all means of judicial recourse for those injured by illegal conduct"). . . .

. . .

Because neither the text of the statute nor the text of the regulation contains any indication of an intent to pre-empt petitioners' cause of action, and because I cannot agree with the Court's unprecedented use of inferences from regulatory history and commentary as a basis for implied pre-emption, I am convinced that Honda has not overcome the presumption against pre-emption in this case. I therefore respectfully dissent.

In the aftermath of *Geier,* several commentators expressed concern that the Court had effectively abandoned the traditional presumption against preemption, resulting in an unwarranted extension of the doctrine. See Mary J. Davis, Unmasking the Presumption in Favor of Preemption, 53 S.C. L. Rev. 967, 1008-1012 (2002) (characterizing Geier as a "seismic shift" in the Court's preemption analysis that improperly drifts away from any meaningful assessment of congressional intent); Susan Reaker-Jordan, A Study in Judicial Sleight of Hand: Did Geier v. American Honda Motor Co. Eradicate the Presumption Against Preemption?, 17 B.Y.U. J. Pub. L. 1 (2002) (criticizing the Court for muddying up its preemption jurisprudence and for enabling the preemption doctrine to more easily trump state law). Also see The Supreme Court 1999 Term: Leading Cases, Federal Preemption of State Law, 114 Harv. L. Rev. 339 (2000) (reading Geier as "signal[ing] the Court's subtle drift away from the presumption against pre-emption in favor of a more functional federal law preference rule").

Geier settled the air bag issue, and more. Courts post-*Geier* have found that as long as an auto manufacturer chose one of the approved passive restraint devices, no common law design defect claim could be brought on the ground that one of the approved devices was superior to the other. See, e.g., Carrasquilla v. Mazda Motor Corp., 166 F. Supp. 2d 169 (M.D. Pa. 2001) (finding that auto manufacturer's choice to incorporate shoulder/lap belts approved by FMVSS 208 preempts any claim of design defect for vehicle's passenger restraint system). Nor could a claim be premised on the grounds that an auto manufacturer should have added to the approved options. See Hernandez-Gomez v. Volkswagen of America, 32 P.3d 424 (Ariz. App. Ct. 2991) (holding that NHTSA approval of passive restraint system adopted by manufacturer preempts claim that additional safety devices should have been implemented); James v. Mazda Motor Corp., 222 F.3d 1323 (11th Cir. 2000) (same). Outside the air bag issue, the preemptive effect of NHTSA regulations may not be as forceful. See, e.g., Harris v. Great Dane Trailers, Inc., 234 F.3d 398, 401 (8th Cir. 2000) (finding that NHTSA regulations concerning the reflective tape on a trailer are only minimum standards that do not preempt common law claims).

The authors read *Geier* as a very limited case that is not likely to alter the Court's general hostility to preemption. The air bag controversy was a hot political issue for many years. NHTSA, for the reasons proffered by the Court, sought to fashion a political compromise to govern the "phase in" period. It is not likely that a case bearing all the hallmarks of *Geier* will present itself in the near future.

Further evidence that defendants will face considerable resistance in establishing that common law design defect claims are preempted by federal regulations comes from the United States Supreme Court's recent decision in Sprietsong v. Mercury Marine, 537 U.S. 51 (2002). Plaintiff's decedent was killed when his boat overturned and he was thrown from the boat and struck by the propeller. Plaintiff brought an action against the boat manufacturer claiming that the boat was defectively designed in that the motor was not protected by a propeller guard. Defendant argued that such common law design claims were preempted by the Federal Boat and Safety Act of 1971 (FBSA). Under the Act, the Secretary of Transportation is authorized to establish regulations for recreational vessels and mandate the installation of safety equipment. In 1986, after a lengthy study, the Secretary decided not to take regulatory action with regard to propeller guards. Among the reasons proffered was that present technology was such that feasible propeller guards might produce blunt trauma injuries by collision with the guard. The Court limited *Geier* to its special facts and was unwilling to find that in the FBSA, which had both an expression preemption and saving clause, preempted common law claims. The Court refused to give preemptive effect to the decision of the Secretary of Transportation not to regulate propeller guards. The decision not to regulate at the federal level did not militate against a state setting its own standards either through statutory regulation or via state common law actions for defective design. In short, the Court post-*Geier* was back to business as usual.

CHAPTER EIGHT
Affirmative Defenses

A. CONDUCT-BASED DEFENSES

1. Background Principles

a. Introduction

The question of what share of responsibility should be borne by a plaintiff who contributes to his own injury has troubled the courts in nonproducts tort litigation. The problem is even more acute in products liability cases. Unlike the usual tort case where the parties are complete strangers to each other prior to the injury-causing accident, in the products case the defendant provides the user with a defective product that becomes the instrumentality of harm. The conceptual difficulties stem from the fact that the possibility of user misconduct must be taken into account in the original design and manufacturing decisions—if a pattern of user misconduct is foreseeable, the manufacturer may have a duty to exercise due care to protect against it. Given the manufacturer's heightened responsibility, it will likely be difficult to assess the user's proper share of the overall liability when a claim is litigated. Consider, for example, a drill press with a defective safety guard at the point of operation. When the failure of the safety guard to function properly is a cause of injury to the user, is it fair to bar the plaintiff or reduce his recovery as a result of his negligent conduct that also contributed to the accident? If the very reason for installing an effective safety guard is to prevent injuries to users who negligently or inadvertently place their hands at the danger point, does it make sense to cut back on the initial assessment that the injury is best avoided by the manufacturer?

Another consideration must be weighed in the balance in deciding whether it is appropriate to apply contributory fault principles to products liability cases. As we noted in Chapter Four, consumer expectations play a role in establishing how safe a product ought to be. Madison Avenue has blurred the once-clear line of demarcation between express warranty and the implied warranty of merchantability. To some extent, a consumer's interaction with a product is a function of a highly sophisticated marketing processes. It ill behooves a manufacturer who has encouraged various forms of risky user behavior to argue that the consumer failed to follow societal norms for careful product use.

On the other hand, to free the user from all responsibility when interacting with a defective product seems equally unwise. A defective product will often signal to the user that something is wrong. Should a user be free to disregard such danger signals? And what of user conduct that would be deemed negligent irrespective of the product's defectiveness? Should product prices reflect accident costs that, in truth, are only marginally related to product defects?

b. Contributory Negligence

During the period in which the operative theory for recovery for defective products was based in negligence, contributory negligence and assumption of the risk operated as a total bar to plaintiff's recovery in most jurisdictions. The earliest contributory negligence case is generally considered to be Butterfield v. Forrester, 11 East. 60, 103 Eng. Rep. 926 (K.B. 1809), in which the plaintiff rode his horse at a high rate of speed into a pole the defendant had left in the road. Lord Ellenborough, speaking for the court, declared:

> A party is not to cast himself upon an obstruction which has been made by the fault of another, and avail himself of it, if he do not himself use common and ordinary caution to be in the right. . . One person being in fault will not dispense of another's using ordinary care for himself.

The doctrine was soon introduced to America in Smith v. Smith, 19 Mass. (2 Pick.) 621 (1824), and was thereafter rapidly adopted by other American courts.

Section 463 of the Restatement (Second) of Torts defines contributory negligence as "conduct on the part of the plaintiff which falls below the standard to which he should conform for his own protection, and which is a legally contributing cause co-operating with the negligence of the defendant in bringing about the plaintiff's harm." Section 464 sets the appropriate standard of conduct as that "of a reasonable man under like circumstances." This parallels the reasonable person standard of care for the protection of others.

With the introduction of strict products liability, courts felt free to reexamine the appropriateness of contributory fault as a complete defense. Again, the Restatement (Second) of Torts §402A was influential in setting the tone. Comment *n* provides:

> *n. Contributory negligence.* Since the liability with which this Section deals is not based upon negligence of the seller, but is strict liability, the rule applied to strict liability cases applies. Contributory negligence of the plaintiff is not a defense when such negligence consists merely in a failure to discover the defect in the product, or to guard against the possibility of its existence. On the other hand the form of contributory negligence which consists in voluntarily and unreasonably proceeding to encounter a known danger, and commonly passes under the name of assumption of risk, is a defense under this Section as in other cases of strict liability. If the user or consumer discovers the defect and is aware of the danger, and nevertheless proceeds unreasonably to make use of the product and is injured by it, he is barred from recovery.

The Restatement (Second) of Torts §402A was written in 1964, when the overwhelming majority rule was that contributory negligence served as a total defense to negligence. Since then comparative fault has swept the country. Contributory fault remains as a total bar to recovery (even in nonproducts liability cases) in five jurisdictions: Alabama, Maryland, North Carolina, Virginia, and the District

Conduct-Based Defenses

of Columbia. A few of the jurisdictions that continue to apply contributory fault have created exceptions to the rule. For example, Virginia utilizes comparative fault for actions involving railroad employees involved in interstate commerce and for cases in which statutory railroad signals are given, but otherwise maintains contributory fault as a complete bar. Given the fact that the majority of jurisdictions have adopted some form of comparative fault, the real question is not whether contributory negligence should serve as a total bar to a products liability claim, but whether comparative negligence should operate as a partial defense in that context. This problem will be dealt with in the following section.

c. Comparative Fault

Before taking sides on the question of applying comparative fault to various kinds of user conduct in products liability cases, it will be useful to identify the different strains that make up the cacophony known generically as "comparative fault" or "comparative negligence." It should be noted that even before the advent of the products liability revolution, contributory negligence as a complete bar to a claimant's recovery had come under heavy attack. See, e.g., Fleming James, Contributory Negligence, 62 Yale L.J. 691 (1953); Robert Leflar, The Declining Defense of Contributory Negligence, 1 Ark. L. Rev. 1 (1946). Dissatisfaction with the all-or-nothing quality of contributory negligence led to the adoption of comparative negligence systems under which the plaintiff's fault served to reduce but not necessarily eliminate recovery.

The comparative negligence concept is not new. It was first recognized in admiralty law (see Mole & Wilson, A Study of Comparative Negligence, 17 Cornell L.Q. 333 (1932)), and its origins have been traced to ancient Roman and medieval sea law (see Turk, Comparative Negligence on the March, 28 Chi.-Kent L. Rev. 189 (1950)). The first state to enact a general comparative negligence statute was Mississippi, in 1910. Miss. Code Ann. §1454 (Cum. Supp. 1985). The Federal Employers Liability Act, enacted in 1906, also incorporated the principle. 45 U.S.C.A. §53 (1982).

Comparative negligence has been adopted in American jurisdictions in various forms. The Reporters' Note to §7 of the Restatement (Third) of Torts: Apportionment of Liability (2000) describes the various forms of comparative responsibility as follows:

> Under a modified system, the plaintiff is barred from recovery if the factfinder assigns the plaintiff a percentage of responsibility equal to or above 50 percent or 51 percent. If the factfinder assigns the plaintiff a percentage of responsibility below that percentage, the plaintiff's recovery is reduced by the percentage the factfinder assigns to the plaintiff. Under a pure system, the plaintiff's recovery is always reduced by the percentage of responsibility the factfinder assigns to the plaintiff, regardless of its magnitude. The plaintiff is never barred from recovery merely because of the percentage of responsibility the factfinder assigns to the plaintiff. This [Restatement] adopts pure comparative responsibility. A court should use modified comparative responsibility only when a statute requires it to do so. . . .

Currently, twelve jurisdictions utilize pure comparative fault. (Alaska, Arizona, California, Florida, Kentucky, Louisiana, Mississippi, Missouri, New Mexico,

New York, Rhode Island, and Washington.) Eleven jurisdictions have adopted a modified comparative responsibility system that bars plaintiff from recovering if his percentage of negligence is found to be 50 percent or more. (Arkansas, Colorado, Georgia, Idaho, Kansas, Maine, Nebraska, North Dakota, Tennessee, Utah, and West Virginia.) Twenty-one jurisdictions utilize a modified comparative responsibility system with a 51 percent bar. (Connecticut, Delaware, Hawaii, Illinois, Indiana, Iowa, Massachusetts, Minnesota, Montana, Nevada, New Hampshire, New Jersey, Ohio, Oklahoma, Oregon, Pennsylvania, South Carolina, Texas, Vermont, Wisconsin, and Wyoming.)

Although most jurisdictions have elected to adopt either a pure or modified form of comparative responsibility, two other forms of comparative responsibility systems deserve mention. South Dakota allows a plaintiff to recover only if his negligence is slight in comparison to the gross negligence of a defendant. Michigan has adopted a unique form of comparative responsibility. Under Michigan Law, if a plaintiff's percentage of fault is greater than the aggregate fault of the defendant(s), the court reduces economic damages by the percentage of comparative fault and the plaintiff will not be allowed to recover noneconomic damages. When the plaintiff's percentage of fault is less than the aggregate fault of the defendant(s), the court will reduce the plaintiff's recovery for both economic and noneconomic loss. Thus, Michigan seems to have created a hybrid system of comparative responsibility utilizing aspects of both pure and modified comparative responsibility. See Mich. Comp. Laws Ann. §600.2959.

(1) Multiple Defendants

When a plaintiff's negligence is greater than that of any single defendant but less than that of the aggregate of all defendants, does he recover? Under pure comparative fault, of course, no such problem arises. However, jurisdictions that follow the modified forms of comparative negligence disagree sharply on this question. Three different approaches to the problem are outlined below.

(a) Unit Rule

The plaintiff's negligence is compared to the combined negligence of all the defendants. If the plaintiff's conduct has not reached the 50 or 51 percent cut-off, he may recover even if the negligence of each individual defendant is less than that of plaintiff. See, e.g., Wong v. Hawaiian Scenic Tours, Ltd., 642 P.2d 930 (Haw. 1982); N.J. Stat. Ann. §2A:15-5.1 (West 2000); Colo. Rev. Stat. §13-21-111 (2002); Elder v. Orluck, 515 A.2d 517 (Pa. 1986). In Beaudoin v. Texaco, Inc., 653 F. Supp 512 (D.N.D. 1987), the court found that the plaintiff's negligence should be compared with the combined negligence of both defendants, including that of the employer who was immune from suit.

(b) Modified Unit Rule

A defendant who is less negligent than the plaintiff is liable only for his individual percentage of the total damage. All defendants who are more negligent than plaintiff are jointly and severally liable. See Or. Rev. Stat. §18.485 (1995); Texas Civ. Prac. & Rem. Code Ann. §33.013 (West 1997). But see Ind. Stat. Ann. §34-4-33-5(b)(4) (Michie 1998).

(c) Individual Rule

The plaintiff may not recover against any individual defendant whose negligence is equal to or less than the negligence of the plaintiff. See, e.g., Idaho Code §6-801 (1998), as construed in Odenwalt v. Zaring, 624 P.2d 383 (1980); Minn. Stat. Ann. Chap. 604.01 (West 2000); Erickson v. Whirlpool Corp., 731 F. Supp 1426 (D. Minn. 1990); Wis. Stat. Ann. §895-045 (Supp. 1994).

(2) Assumption of the Risk and Last Clear Chance

Since assumption of the risk and last clear chance have traditionally allocated the entire loss to either the plaintiff or the defendant, many courts and legislatures confronting the issue have abolished the doctrine after adopting comparative negligence. With respect to assumption of the risk, however, further qualification is in order. The courts in a number of jurisdictions have correctly perceived that "assumption of risk" has been used to describe the situation where the defendant simply has no duty to the plaintiff or has not breached the duty to act reasonably (see Andren v. White-Rodgers Co., infra).

(3) Superseding Cause

Several courts have now decided that superseding cause no longer has a role to play in tort litigation. Though the adoption of comparative fault hastened the death of superseding cause, the doctrine was *in extemis* even before comparative fault came on the scene. Few will mourn its passing.

Barry v. Quality Steel Products, Inc., et al.
820 A.2d 258 (Conn. 2003)

NORCOTT, J.

The dispositive issue in this appeal involves the viability of the doctrine of superseding cause. The plaintiffs, Neil Barry, Diana Barry, Bernard Cohade and Lynn Cohade, appeal from the judgment of the trial court in favor of the named defendant, Quality Steel Products, Inc. (Quality Steel), and the defendant Ring's End, Inc. (Ring's End). On appeal, the plaintiffs claim that the trial court improperly instructed the jury on the doctrine of superseding cause because: (1) the alleged negligence of the plaintiffs' employer, DeLuca Construction Company (DeLuca), was not outside the scope of the original risk posed by the defendants' defective product; and (2) any negligence by DeLuca was not the sole proximate cause of the plaintiffs' injuries. The defendants claim that the trial court properly instructed the jury on the doctrine of superseding cause because the jury could consider the combined negligence of the plaintiffs, their coworker and DeLuca as a superseding cause of the plaintiffs' accident. As we explain herein, we conclude that the doctrine of superseding cause, as applied in the present case, no longer plays a useful role in our common law of proximate cause. Accordingly, we reverse the judgment of the trial court in favor of the defendants and order a new trial. . . .

The jury reasonably could have found the following facts. The plaintiffs were employed as carpenters by DeLuca. On February 26, 1998, the plaintiffs were putting shingles on the roof of the New Canaan Nature Center when the platform staging on which they were working collapsed, causing the plaintiffs to fall to the ground and sustain severe injuries. Immediately prior to the collapse, the plaintiffs were working on a wooden plank attached to the roof by roof brackets designed and manufactured by Quality Steel and purchased from Ring's End.

The roof brackets were used as part of a structure that created a platform on which the plaintiffs could work. To install the brackets, the plaintiffs nailed them to the roof through three slots on the bracket. After the brackets were attached to the roof, a plank was placed on top of the brackets, which then provided a surface on which the plaintiffs could stand in order to shingle the roof. Although there had been additional pipe scaffolding located around the perimeter of the roof prior to the time the plaintiffs fell, it was taken down before the plaintiffs' accident.

After working on the planks for several hours in the morning, the plaintiffs returned to the planking after lunch and began shingling the roof on the right side of the building. Shortly after the plaintiffs returned to work on the roof, the planking suddenly fell out from under them and they fell to the ground. Almost immediately after the plaintiffs fell, Gene Marini, the general superintendent at DeLuca, discovered one of the roof brackets used by the plaintiffs in a distorted condition on the ground near where they fell.

Quality Steel's instruction label on the roof brackets suggests that the user attach the brackets to the roof using sixteenpenny nails.[1] The defendants introduced evidence that some of the brackets were installed by another DeLuca employee, Nate Manizza, using eightpenny nails. The plaintiffs both testified that when they installed roof brackets they used larger, twelvepenny nails. Neither the plaintiffs nor Manizza could remember if they had installed the specific brackets that had collapsed causing the plaintiffs to fall. Cohade testified, however, that he saw Manizza installing the brackets in the general area where the plaintiffs fell. There was also testimony from both the plaintiffs' and the defendants' experts that the use of a twelvepenny nail would be sufficient to hold the bracket to the roof and would not be causative of the collapse of the planking that occurred in this case.

The defendants also introduced evidence, through expert testimony, that DeLuca had violated the federal Occupational Safety and Health Administration (OSHA) regulations by failing to provide additional fall protection for the plaintiffs while they were working on the New Canaan Nature Center roof. The plaintiffs offered, and the jury reasonably could have found, however, that OSHA, in its investigation of the plaintiffs' accident, did not find any violations of roofing standards at the project site and that the roof brackets were an acceptable method of providing fall protection.

---

1. The penny reference indicates the size of a nail. The plaintiffs' expert witness, Karl Puttlitz, a metallurgist, explained during his testimony: "As you increase in penny size, the dimensions [of the shaft and the nail itself] increase incrementally. . . ."

The jury also reasonably could have found that the roof bracket designed and manufactured by Quality Steel and used by the plaintiffs before the platform collapsed was undersized in comparison to the manufacturing specifications. Specifically, both the plaintiffs' and the defendants' experts testified that the platform arm of the roof bracket was thinner than required by Quality Steel's own specifications. Additionally, the jury, through their special interrogatories, found that Quality Steel's product was defective and unreasonably dangerous at the time it was manufactured and sold by the defendants, and that the defective condition of the product was a proximate cause of the plaintiffs' accident. . . .

I

The plaintiffs claim that the trial court improperly instructed the jury on the doctrine of superseding cause because: (1) the plaintiffs' injuries were not outside the scope of the risk created by the defendants' misconduct in manufacturing and selling a defective product; and (2) any negligence on the part of DeLuca was not the sole proximate cause of the plaintiffs' injuries. The defendants claim, in response, that the combined negligence of the plaintiffs, DeLuca and Manizza, constituted sufficient evidence of a superseding cause, thereby exonerating the defendants from the plaintiffs' product liability claim. We need not consider the propriety of the trial court's instructions on the doctrine of superseding cause because we conclude that the doctrine should be abandoned in a case such as the present one.

We begin our analysis with an examination of the relationship among proximate cause, concurrent cause and superseding cause. "Proximate cause results from a sequence of events unbroken by a superseding cause, so that its causal viability continued until the moment of injury or at least until the advent of the immediate injurious force." Coburn v. Lenox Homes, Inc., . . . 441 A.2d 620 (1982). "[T]he test of proximate cause is whether the defendant's conduct is a substantial factor in bringing about the plaintiff's injuries." Paige v. St. Andrew's Roman Catholic Church Corp., . . . 734 A.2d 85 (1999). A concurrent cause is one that is "contemporaneous and coexistent with the defendant's wrongful conduct and actively cooperates with the defendant's conduct to bring about the injury." Wagner v. Clark Equipment Co., 700 A.2d 38 (1997). Finally, "[a] superseding cause is an act of a third person or other force which by its intervention prevents the actor from being liable for harm to another which his antecedent negligence is a substantial factor in bringing about." (Internal quotation marks omitted.) Id., at 179.

"The function of the doctrine of superseding cause is not to serve as an independent basis of liability, regardless of the conduct of a third party whose negligent conduct may have contributed to the plaintiff's loss. The function of the doctrine is to define the circumstances under which responsibility *may be shifted entirely* from the shoulders of one person, who is determined to be negligent, to the shoulders of another person, who may also be determined to be negligent, or to some other force." (Emphasis added; internal quotation marks omitted.) Id. "Thus, the doctrine of superseding cause serves as a device by which one admittedly negligent party can, by identifying another's superseding conduct, exonerate himself from liability by shifting the causation element entirely elsewhere." . . .

Id. If a third person's negligence is found to be the superseding cause of the plaintiff's injuries, that negligence, rather than the negligence of the party attempting to invoke the doctrine of superseding cause, is said to be the sole proximate cause of the injury. . . .

The circumstances under which a defendant's liability for negligence shifts entirely to the superseding conduct of a third person has been well defined in our case law. "Even if a plaintiff's injuries are in fact caused by a defendant's negligence, a superseding cause may break that causal connection if it so entirely supersedes the operation of the defendant's negligence that it alone, without his negligence contributing thereto in any degree, produces the injury; or it must be the non-concurring culpable act of a human being who is legally responsible for such act. . . . If a defendant's negligence was a substantial factor in producing the plaintiff's injuries, the defendant would not be relieved from liability for those injuries even though another force concurred to produce them." . . . Wagner v. Clark Equipment Co., 700 A.2d 38.

In the present case, the jury's interrogatories reveal two possible sources of a superseding cause. The first possible superseding cause of the plaintiffs' injuries was DeLuca's failure to provide additional fall protection for the plaintiffs. The second possible superseding cause was Manizza's use of eightpenny nails to attach the roof brackets to the roof.

We take this opportunity to clarify our approach to the doctrine of superseding cause and its continuing validity in our tort jurisprudence. As will be discussed in further detail later in this opinion, we conclude that the doctrine of superseding cause no longer serves a useful purpose in our jurisprudence when a defendant claims that a subsequent negligent act by a third party cuts off its own liability for the plaintiff's injuries. We conclude that under those circumstances, superseding cause instructions serve to complicate what is fundamentally a proximate cause analysis. Specifically, we conclude that, because our statutes allow for apportionment among negligent defendants; . . . and because Connecticut is a comparative negligence jurisdiction; . . . the simpler and less confusing approach to cases, such as the present one, where the jury must determine which, among many, causes contributed to the plaintiffs' injury, is to couch the analysis in proximate cause rather than allowing the defendants to raise a defense of superseding cause.

We first note that, although nearly every treatise involving the law of torts acknowledges the existence of the doctrine of superseding cause, it is defined differently by various scholars. For example, one treatise notes that the problem of superseding cause is not primarily one of causation but, rather, "one of policy as to imposing legal responsibility." W. Prosser & W. Keeton, Torts (5th Ed. 1984) §44, p.301. Additionally, other treatises support the view that the doctrine of superseding cause is merely a more complicated analysis of whether the defendant's actions were the proximate cause of the plaintiff's injuries. For example, one treatise states: "[Superseding] cause is merely proximate cause flowing from a source not connected with the party sought to be charged. While the term may have some descriptive value, unduly elaborate discussion of [superseding] cause as such tends to becloud rather than clarify the relatively simple idea of causal connection. When it is determined that a defendant is relieved of liability by reason of [superseding] cause, it would appear to mean simply that the negligent conduct of someone else — and not that of the defendant — is the proximate cause *of the event."* (Emphasis added.) 1 T. Shearman & A. Redfield, Negligence (Rev. Ed. 1941) §37, pp.99-100.

Under this latter approach, the fact finder need only determine whether the allegedly negligent conduct of any actor was a proximate cause, specifically, whether the conduct was a substantial factor in contributing to the plaintiff's injuries. If such conduct is found to be a proximate cause of the plaintiff's foreseeable injury, each actor will pay his or her proportionate share pursuant to our apportionment statute, regardless of whether another's conduct also contributed to the plaintiff's injury. Put differently, the term superseding cause merely describes more fully the concept of proximate cause when there is more than one alleged act of negligence, and is not functionally distinct from the determination of whether an act is a proximate cause of the injury suffered by the plaintiff. We find this latter approach, that the doctrine of superseding cause is, in essence, a determination regarding proximate cause or causes, persuasive and hereby adopt it in our case law.

Thus, the doctrine of superseding cause no longer serves a useful purpose in our negligence jurisprudence. Historically, the doctrine reflects the courts' attempt to limit the defendants' liability to foreseeable and reasonable bounds. See W. Prosser & W. Keeton, supra, §44, p.302. In this regard, the doctrine of superseding cause involves a question of policy and foreseeability regarding the actions for which a court will hold a defendant accountable. This aspect of superseding cause is already incorporated in our law regarding proximate causation. As some commentators have noted, however, the doctrine was also shaped in response to the harshness of contributory negligence and joint and several liability. See T. Christlieb, "Why Superseding Cause Analysis Should Be Abandoned," 72 Tex. L. Rev. 161, 165-66 (1993). Under this reasoning, in order to avoid what some courts determined was an undue burden on the plaintiff under contributory negligence regimes, courts developed certain ameliorative doctrines, which identified some aspect of the defendant's negligent act that served as a basis for shifting the plaintiff's negligence to the defendant so that the plaintiff could recover for his losses. Id., at 165. Thus, the courts sometimes labeled a defendant's negligence as an intervening act that cut off any contributory negligence of the plaintiff, which, had it not been superseded by the defendant's negligence, would have constituted a total bar to recovery. Id.

We conclude that this aspect of the doctrine of superseding cause has no place in our modern system of comparative fault and apportionment. We agree with the author of the previously cited note that it is inconsistent to conclude simultaneously that all negligent parties should pay in proportion to their fault, . . . but that one negligent party does not have to pay its share because its negligence was somehow "superseded" by a subsequent negligent act. . . . We also find persuasive the author's criticism of the Restatement (Second) method; see 2 Restatement (Second), Torts §§442 through 453, pp.467-91 (1965); which looks to the nature of the subsequent negligent act to determine whether it somehow supersedes the previous act. T. Christlieb, supra, 72 Tex. L. Rev. at 184. This approach gives undue prominence to the temporal order of the allegedly negligent acts. As the author aptly notes, causal contributions do not operate in neat temporal sequences; rather, most events, such as the events giving rise to the plaintiff's injury in the present case, result from a convergence of many conditions. Id., at 185. The Restatement (Second) approach, then, has the potential of misleading the fact finder regarding the determination of whether each allegedly tortious act is a proximate cause of the plaintiff's injury by placing too much emphasis on the timing of the acts.

Moreover, it is no longer necessary to utilize doctrines that aid fact finders in making policy decisions regarding how to assign liability among various defendants and the plaintiff because those decisions already are inherent in our modern scheme of comparative negligence and apportionment. Thus, under the approach we adopt herein, the question to be answered by the fact finder is whether the various actors' allegedly negligent conduct was a cause in fact and a proximate cause of the plaintiff's injury in light of all the relevant circumstances. If found to be both, each actor will be liable for his or her proportionate share of the plaintiff's damages.

At least two other states also have addressed the issue of whether the doctrine of superseding cause continues to play a useful role in their negligence jurisprudence after the advent of comparative fault and apportionment regimes. Because these cases illustrate aspects of the approach we adopt here today, we discuss them in detail.

[The court discusses Torres v. El Paso Electric Co., 732, 987 P.2d 386 (1999), and Control Techniques, Inc. v. Johnson, 762 N.E.2d 104 (Ind. 2002).]

We find these two cases persuasive and conclude that the rationale supporting the abandonment of the doctrine of superseding cause outweighs any of the doctrine's remaining usefulness in our modern system of torts. Specifically, as the New Mexico Supreme Court determined, we believe that the instruction on superseding cause complicates what is essentially a proximate cause analysis and risks jury confusion. The doctrine also no longer serves a useful purpose in our tort jurisprudence, especially considering our system of comparative negligence and apportionment, where defendants are responsible solely for their proportionate share of the injury suffered by the plaintiff. Thus, it is no longer appropriate to give an instruction of the doctrine of superseding cause in cases involving multiple acts of negligence. Instead, under the approach we adopt herein, if the defendant was both the cause in fact and a proximate cause of the plaintiff's injury, the defendant will be liable for his or her proportionate share of the damages, notwithstanding other acts of negligence that also may have contributed to the plaintiff's injury.

This analysis leads to the conclusion that the doctrine of superseding cause should not have been presented to the jury in the present case. Upon retrial, therefore, the fact finder must determine if the defendants' manufacture and sale of a defective product was a cause in fact and a proximate cause of the plaintiffs' injuries, without reference to the doctrine of superseding cause. . . .

[Reversed and remanded.]

2. *Application of Comparative Fault in Products Liability*

It does not follow from the adoption of comparative fault as a general matter that it should be applied in products liability cases. One must first decide whether it is appropriate (or even possible) to compare a product defect with the plaintiff's fault. The Products Liability Restatement takes a strong position on this matter favoring the application of comparative fault in products liability cases.

Restatement (Third) of Torts: Products Liability
(1998)

§17. APPORTIONMENT OF RESPONSIBILITY BETWEEN OR AMONG PLAINTIFF, SELLERS, AND DISTRIBUTORS OF DEFECTIVE PRODUCTS, AND OTHERS

(a) A plaintiff's recovery of damages for harm caused by a product defect may be reduced if the conduct of the plaintiff combines with the product defect to cause the harm and the plaintiff's conduct fails to conform to generally applicable rules establishing appropriate standards of care.

(b) The manner and extent of the reduction under Subsection (a) and the apportionment of plaintiff's recovery among multiple defendants are governed by generally applicable rules apportioning responsibility.

a. Can Fault and Defect Be Compared?

(1) Manufacturing Defects: Comparing Apples and Oranges

Early on in the products liability era, the United States Court of Appeals for the Third Circuit struggled with the question of whether one could compare fault with defect. Other courts have followed in its footsteps. In Murray v. Fairbanks Morse, 610 F.2d 149 (3d Cir. 1079), plaintiff was injured while installing an electrical control housed in a one-and-a-half-ton unit onto a platform. The manufacturer of the unit had attached two iron cross members to the open bottom of the unit. A cherry picker lifted the unit over the platform and sought to align it with pre-drilled holes so that it could be fastened with bolts. The holes were not perfectly aligned so plaintiff chose to use a crow bar to rock the heavy unit into alignment. The accident occurred when plaintiff put his weight on one of the cross members. It gave way and plaintiff fell ten feet onto a concrete floor incurring severe injury to his spine. Plaintiff claimed that the control panel was defective because it had only been tack-welded to the unit. Defendant contended that plaintiff's method of installation was highly dangerous. The jury awarded the plaintiff $2 million but found the plaintiff to be 5 percent at fault. The trial court reduced plaintiff's damages accordingly.

Since defendant was held strictly liable for the defective weld, the court was faced with the question of how it could compare product defect (no fault) with plaintiff conduct (fault). The court reasoned as follows:

> The substitution of the term fault for defect, however, would not appear to aid the trier of fact in apportioning damages between the defect and the *conduct* of the plaintiff. The key conceptual distinction between strict products liability theory and negligence is that the plaintiff need not prove fault conduct on the part of the defendant in order to recover. The jury is not asked to determine if the defendant deviated from a standard of care in producing his product. There is no proven faulty conduct of the defendant to compare with the faulty conduct of the plaintiff in order to apportion the responsibility for an accident. . . . A comparison of the two is therefore inappropriate. . . .
>
> In apportioning damages we are really asking how much of the injury was caused by the defect in the product versus how much was caused by the plaintiff's own actions.

We agree with the Ninth Circuit when it noted that comparative causation "is a conceptually more precise term than 'comparative fault' since fault alone without causation does not subject one to liability." Pan-Alaska Fisheries, Inc. v. Marine Construction & Design Co., 565 F.2d 1129, 1139 (9th Cir. 1977). The appropriate label for the quality of the act is insignificant. . . . Thus, the underlying task in each case is to analyze and compare the causal conduct of each party regardless of its label. Although fault, in the sense of the defendant's product or the plaintiff's failure to meet a standard of care, must exist before a comparison takes place, the comparison itself must focus on the role each played in bringing about the particular injury. . . .

Did the *Murray* court resolve the problem of how to compare plaintiff conduct with product defect? How does one compare causation? If a semi-trailer with defective brakes collides with a negligently driven Volkswagen bug, does the semi-trailer bear more casual responsibility for the accident? Isn't comparative causation simply nonsense? See Aaron D. Twerski, The Many Faces of Misuse: An Inquiry into the Emerging Doctrine of Comparative Causation, 29 Mercer L. Rev. 403 (1978).

(2) Generic Defects: Comparing Fault Under Risk-Utility Balancing

The difficulties a court may have in comparing fault when faced with a manufacturing defect claim would seem to melt away when the claim is based on defective design or failure to warn. In manufacturing defect cases the defendant need not be at fault. The defendant may have used the best quality control extant and still be liable. In design and failure to warn cases, where defect is determined by risk-utility balancing, one can easily compare the negligence of the defendant-manufacturer in making a bad risk-utility decision with the negligent conduct of the plaintiff. Courts occasionally note the difference between manufacturing and design defect cases when applying comparative fault principles. See Webb v. Navistar International Transportation Corp., infra. However, most courts just go their merry way applying comparative fault to all forms of product defect.

b. Should Fault and Defect Be Compared?

(1) Are Products Liability Cases Different?

Webb v. Navistar Int'l 1994 Transportation Corp.
692 A.2d 343 (Vt. 1997)

DOOLEY, J. . . .

I.

On November 13, 1985, at approximately 9:30 P.M., Bruce Webb learned that some of his cows might be out of the pasture. He and his father got out their tractor, a 1978 Model 464 farm tractor manufactured by Navistar, and they proceeded down Route 207 with Bruce Webb standing on the draw bar and his father driving. En route, the tractor was struck in the rear by a car driven by an allegedly intoxicated operator. As a result of the accident, Bruce Webb suffered serious injuries to his legs.

Plaintiffs filed suit against Navistar, the driver of the car, and others. The complaint alleged negligence, breach of warranty, and strict products liability. Claims against all defendants other than Navistar were ultimately dismissed, and the case proceeded to trial against Navistar solely on the products liability claim. Plaintiffs argued that the tractor was defectively designed because (1) it allowed operation of a white field light at highway speeds without provision for separate red tail lights, and (2) it failed to provide a safe passenger location so that Bruce Webb could have ridden on the tractor without exposure to injury. They contended further that defendant failed to provide adequate warnings of these dangers.

The case was tried, and the trial court directed a verdict in defendant's favor on both claims. On appeal, we affirmed the directed verdict regarding defendant's failure to provide a safe passenger location, but reversed as to whether the design of the field light was defective and whether the manufacturer's warning on its use was inadequate. . . .

The second trial focused on the lighting system of the tractor. The Model 464 tractor has a red taillight, two amber lights with road flashers, two red rear reflectors, a reflective slow-moving-vehicle triangle and a white field light mounted on the left rear bumper. A cautionary decal on the left front fender directs operators to use the flashing amber lights at all times when on public roads. The light system is designed so that when the flashing amber lights are in use, the red taillight activates and the white field light does not work. At the time of the accident, the flashing amber lights and the taillight did not work, and the reflectors were missing. In addition, by riding on the draw bar, Webb blocked the view of the reflective triangle. The cautionary decal also warned against riding the tractor unless a seat or platform is provided and instructed the operator to "[k]eep others off."

The owner's manual for the tractor also provides warnings and instructions. On pages 3 and 4, the manual sets forth rules for safe operation of the tractor. Here, the manual warns: "No riders allowed." It also contains an instruction not to use the white field light on the highway on page 55, under the heading CAUTION!

Webb testified that while travelling on the highway he employed both the headlights and the rear field light on the rationale that more light was better than less light. He indicated that it had not occurred to him that operating the tractor on the highway at night with the rear field light on was a hazard. The operator of the automobile that collided with the tractor testified that he believed the white field light mounted on the left rear bumper was the headlight of an approaching "one-eyed" car.

Plaintiffs tried the case on two theories: (1) that the lighting system was defective because it allowed the tractor to be operated on highways with the field light illuminated, and (2) that defendant failed to adequately warn consumers of the known risk of using the field light while operating the tractor on the highway. The jury returned a verdict in favor of plaintiffs on liability, and the parties stipulated to damages. Defendant appeals, arguing that the evidence was insufficient to support the verdict and that the court erred by failing to instruct the jury that it may apportion liability between the parties. We have the benefit of briefs of amicus parties on both sides of the comparative liability issue.

II.

Defendant argues that the evidence was insufficient for the jury to find that its tractor was defective, that its warnings were inadequate, and that either the defective tractor or the inadequate warnings proximately caused Webb's injuries. . . .

The jury could reasonably conclude that the danger of operating the tractor on a highway at night with the field light illuminated was not a danger obvious to the ordinary consumer, and plaintiffs presented evidence of a safety device that could have been installed by defendant to prevent such use. . . . Moreover, the question of whether a manufacturer provided adequate warnings about foreseeable dangers is a question of fact properly left to the jury. . . .

III.

I do not believe, however, that the judgment in this case can be affirmed. I agree with defendant that comparative liability principles are applicable in strict products liability actions and should have been charged to the jury in this case. Because the split in the Court reserves the details of implementing comparative principles for another day, I state only the reasons we adopt a comparative causation rule. . . .

Justifications for reducing plaintiffs' burden [in strict products liability] rest upon two public policies. First, strict liability protects the consumer, see Restatement (Second) of Torts §402A cmt. *c* (consumer entitled to maximum protection), by creating an incentive for manufacturers to produce safe products. . . . Second, strict products liability is justified on the ground that manufacturers are in the best position to spread the cost of injury resulting from defective products by passing it on to consumers as a cost of doing business . . . see . . . Restatement (Second) of Torts §402A cmt. *c* (public policy demands that burden of accidental injuries caused by products be placed on those who market them who may treat as cost of production against which liability insurance may be obtained).

Under the Restatement (Second) formulation of products liability, defenses are limited. Assumption of risk is a complete bar to recovery. "If the user or consumer discovers the defect and is aware of the danger, and nevertheless proceeds unreasonably to make use of the product and is injured by it, [the user or consumer] is barred from recovery." Restatement (Second) of Torts §402A cmt. *n*. Product misuse has traditionally been a bar to recovery as well. Id. §402A cmt. *h;* see, e.g., Kennedy v. City of Sawyer, 618 P.2d 788, 796 (Kan. 1980) (assumption of risk and product misuse traditionally barred all recovery for strict products liability claims); Smith v. Smith, 278 N.W.2d 155, 161 (S.D. 1979) (recovery barred where consumer assumes risk or misuses product). On the other hand, the Restatement (Second) provides that negligence that "consists merely in a failure to discover the defect in the product, or to guard against the possibility of its existence" is not a defense at all. Restatement (Second) of Torts §402A cmt. *n*.

Conduct-Based Defenses

The Restatement (Second) does not address the issue of shared responsibility and does not address the effect of the user's negligence beyond the limited circumstances described in comment *n* to §402A. If we view these omissions as intentional, and we choose to follow §402A, we are left with the harsh "all-or-nothing" approach of negligence actions prior to the adoption of our comparative negligence statute. . . .

The overwhelming majority of states have rejected the "all or nothing" rule, either by rejecting the limits of §402A or by supplementing its provisions, and have applied principles of comparative liability in strict products liability actions [citing authority].[3] The United States District Court for the District of Vermont has endorsed this approach and predicted we will do so also. See Smith v. Goodyear Tire & Rubber Co., 600 F. Supp. 1561, 1568 (D. Vt. 1985).

In addition, the tentative draft of the Restatement (Third) of Torts provides for apportioning liability between the plaintiff and the manufacturer or seller. See Restatement (Third) of Torts: Products Liability §7 (Tentative Draft No. 1, 1994). Similarly, the Uniform Comparative Fault Act §1 provides that a claimant's contributory fault proportionately reduces compensatory damages in strict products liability actions. 12 U.L.A. 127 (1996). Many commentators maintain that adopting comparative liability principles in strict products liability actions is the fairest approach. See, e.g., . . . D. Noel, Defective Products: Abnormal Use, Contributory Negligence, and Assumption of Risk, 25 Vand. L. Rev. 93, 117-18 (1972) (contributory negligence should diminish plaintiff's damages); V. Schwartz, Strict Liability and Comparative Negligence, 42 Tenn. L. Rev. 171, 179-81 (1974) (comparative principles should apply in strict products liability); J. Wade, On the Nature of Strict Tort Liability for Products, 44 Miss. L.J. 825, 850 (1973) (same).

The primary reason that courts adopt comparative liability principles in strict products liability actions is "because it is fair to do so." . . . Adopting comparative liability principles "will accomplish a fairer and more equitable result" because the plaintiff's award is reduced by an amount equal to the degree to which the plaintiff is responsible for the accident. . . . Most courts reject the framework that places the burden of loss on one party where two parties contributed to causing the injury. . . . Comparative liability principles also further fairness by preventing a negligent plaintiff from recovering as much as a plaintiff who has taken all reasonable precautions. . . .

Moreover, there is no reason to impose the cost of a plaintiff's negligence upon the manufacturer to spread among other consumers of the product . . . see also Restatement (Third) of Torts: Products Liability §7 cmt. *a* (Tentative Draft No. 1, 1994) (unfair to impose costs of substandard plaintiff conduct on manufacturers, who will be impelled to pass on costs to all consumers, including those who use and consume product safely). The instant case is illustrative. Here, plaintiff stood on the draw bar of the tractor while it traveled down a public road. Although he understood the importance of the warning against such action, he chose to disregard the warning. As a result, he blocked the view of the reflective

---

3. In addition, some states have adopted comparative principles in strict products liability actions by statute. See, e.g., Ark. Code Ann. §16-64-122 (Michie 1987 & Supp. 1995); Colo. Rev. Stat. §13-21-406 (1987); Minn. Stat. Ann. §604.01 (West 1988 & Supp. 1997); Miss. Code Ann. §11-7-15 (1972); Mo. Ann. Stat. §537.765 (Vernon 1988); N.Y. Civ. Prac. L. & R. §1411 (McKinney 1976); Utah Code Ann. §§78-27-37, -38 (1996); Wash. Rev. Code Ann. §§4.22.005.015 (West 1988).

triangle and the single amber flashing light that may have been operable. Moreover, he failed to maintain the reflectors and the other flashing light. If the jury may reduce plaintiff's recovery to the extent that his injuries were caused by his negligence, defendant is not held liable for the cost of injuries attributed to plaintiff's negligence and does not pass this cost on to those farmers who heed the warnings posted on their tractors. Strict products liability was intended to spread the cost of injuries resulting from defective products; it was never intended to spread the cost of injuries resulting from user negligence. . . .

Apportioning liability more effectively spreads recoveries from manufacturers for selling defective products than the "all or nothing" framework. Under the "all or nothing" framework, some plaintiffs receive windfalls because they collect damages for injuries caused by their own negligence in addition to damages for injuries caused by the product defect. On the other hand, some plaintiffs receive nothing because the court or jury has determined that their negligence constitutes misuse, assumption of risk or an intervening cause, concepts often difficult to distinguish. . . . Applying principles of comparative liability will reduce the total damages awarded to some plaintiffs but will also extend recoveries to some plaintiffs formerly barred from any recovery; thus, recoveries will be more equitably distributed among plaintiffs.

A minority of courts have rejected comparative liability principles in the context of strict products liability actions and continue to impose the "all or nothing" framework set forth in the Restatement (Second) of Torts §402A. See, e.g., Bowling v. Heil Co., . . . 511 N.E.2d 373, 380 [Ohio 1987] (finding no rationale to persuade it that comparative fault principles should apply to products liability actions); *Kimco Dev. Corp.,* 637 A.2d at 606 [Pa. 1993] (declining to extend negligence concepts to strict products liability area). . . .

We draw two reasons from those decisions for retaining the "all or nothing" rule. First, several courts have suggested that it is too confusing to inject negligence concepts into strict liability actions, see, e.g., *Kimco Dev. Corp.,* 637 A.2d at 606 (conceptual confusion would ensue should negligence and strict liability concepts be commingled), and that juries will be unable to compare a defective product with a plaintiff's negligent conduct to apportion liability. . . .

Most courts have rejected this concern as semantic and theoretical. "We are convinced that in merging the two principles what may be lost in symmetry is more than gained in fundamental fairness," *Daly,* . . . 575 P.2d at 1172 [Cal. 1978], and "fairness and equity are more important than conceptual and semantic consistency." *Kaneko,* 654 P.2d at 352 [Haw. 1982]. Further, apportioning liability will be less difficult for juries than the current framework, which requires juries to distinguish between defenses that courts and scholars are often unable to differentiate. As the Supreme Court of Texas noted, assumed risk and unforeseeable misuse are nothing more than extreme variants of contributory negligence. See *Duncan,* 665 S.W.2d at 423 [Tex. 1984]. And the line between contributory negligence—resulting in total recovery—and assumed risk or misuse—resulting in no recovery—is difficult to draw. . . . There is no need to draw shadowy lines between misuse, assumption of risk and contributory negligence, however, if all defenses may constitute a basis for apportioning liability. . . .

Second, the "all or nothing" courts maintain that comparative principles would undermine the purposes of imposing strict liability on manufacturers because this approach reduces the incentive to produce safe products and fails to allocate the risk for loss from injury to manufacturers who are in a better position to absorb it. See *Kimco Dev. Corp.*, 637 A.2d at 606-07. On the contrary, applying principles of comparative liability in strict products liability actions is completely consistent with the purposes of imposing strict liability on manufacturers. Indeed, it will have no effect on the principal purpose of adopting this doctrine; the plaintiff is still relieved from proving negligence of the manufacturer or privity of contract with it. . . .

Nor is it clear that adopting comparative principles will significantly reduce the incentive to produce safe products. . . . Recoveries may be reduced in some cases, but more plaintiffs will recover if assumption of the risk and product misuse are no longer total bars to recovery. Overall, the cost of a defect may be the same under either approach.

Courts rejecting comparative liability assume that the primary purpose in strict products liability actions is to spread the cost of injury. Because manufacturers are in a better position than plaintiffs to spread this cost, they reason that it is inconsistent with strict products liability to reduce recoveries in proportion to plaintiff negligence. . . . If spreading the cost of all injuries were the goal, then apportioning liability between the parties would be adverse to the goal. We note, however, that the purpose has been to spread the cost of injuries resulting from *defective products*. The issue here is whether to spread the cost of injuries resulting from *user negligence* in addition to that resulting from a defect. No rationale to support such risk allocation has been presented. Strict liability is not absolute liability; manufacturers are not insurers of user safety. . . .

On balance the reasons to adopt comparative principles greatly outweigh the reasons to reject this approach. The comparative approach is fairer to all parties, and properly implemented, will not reduce the incentive to produce safe products.

IV.

. . . I reach this conclusion as part of the development of the common law of products liability in this state and not because of the Vermont comparative negligence statute, 12 V.S.A. §1036. The statute applies only to "an action . . . to recover damages for *negligence*." (Emphasis added.) We must presume that the Legislature intended the plain meaning of the statutory language. . . . The wording covers actions based on negligence, but not on strict liability. The majority of courts confronting this question have reached the same conclusion. . . .

Even though the comparative negligence statute does not apply, we could construct a comparable causation rule that would mirror its terms. In this case, the main significance of such a rule is that plaintiffs could not recover if the causal effect of the negligence of Bruce Webb was greater than the causal effect of the liability of defendant. Using this test, Justice Morse would hold that, as a matter of law, a majority of plaintiffs' damages were caused by the negligence of Bruce Webb so that plaintiffs cannot recover at all.

I do not subscribe to the "half-or-nothing" framework of [the comparative negligence statute] for products liability cases. The rule is inconsistent with the policy of ensuring that manufacturers bear the cost of casting defective products into the market. The manufacturer must remain responsible for damages resulting from the defect, regardless of the extent to which other factors contributed to the injuries. . . .

The dissent characterizes the adoption of comparative causation as a major step toward abolishing the doctrine of strict products liability. I find this conclusion to be greatly exaggerated. I doubt that a balanced and properly designed rule on comparative causation will significantly reduce the incentive for manufacturers to produce safe products; indeed, it may increase the incentive. . . .

If comparative principles ever apply in a strict liability case, they should apply here. The jury could find that a number of Bruce Webb's actions or omissions reflected lack of due care for his safety. Some of these actions or omissions do not involve the condition of the tractor and are not related to plaintiffs' liability theory. For example, irrespective of what lighting was available or in use, the jury could find that Bruce Webb was negligent in riding on the draw bar and covering up a reflector and an amber light while the tractor was being operated on a highway. On remand, I would allow at least that determination.

Reversed and remanded.

MORSE, Justice, concurring.

I agree with Justice Dooley that principles of comparative fault should apply to some products liability claims. We disagree, however, on the basis for comparative fault. Justice Dooley believes we should reverse and remand this case for a third trial because the trial judge failed to instruct the jury on comparative causation. I would reverse because on the facts no reasonable juror could find Bruce Webb less than fifty-one percent responsible for the accident, and thus, under 12 V.S.A. §1036 (comparative negligence), judgment would have been entered for defendant.

No matter how the claim is labeled, the 402A claim here is essentially a negligence claim that defendant did not design the tractor carefully enough or warn plaintiff reasonably of the dangers. In any products liability design/warning case, ever since the doctrine was first formulated, the plaintiff has been required to prove that the product was negligently designed or negligently warned. Accordingly, it follows that 12 V.S.A. §1036, our comparative negligence statute, should control. Section 1036 provides in part:

> Contributory negligence shall not bar recovery *in an action* by any plaintiff, or his legal representative, *to recover damages for negligence* resulting in death, personal injury or property damage, if the negligence was not greater than the causal total negligence of the defendant or defendants, but the damage shall be diminished by general verdict in proportion to the amount of negligence attributed to the plaintiff. (Emphasis added.)

The plain language of the statute indicates that it applies in an action to recover damages for negligence. Because plaintiffs' defective design/warning claim is a negligence claim, §1036 must therefore apply. Other courts have similarly applied their comparative negligence statutes to such claims. . . .

If there were such a thing as true "strict liability" whereby a manufacturer is liable for injury no matter how carefully the product is designed and warned for safety, I would agree the comparative negligence statute should not apply. (I have not as yet come across such a cause of action in the product design/warning field). When a product is defective in the sense it did not turn out as it was intended in the manufacturing process, the manufacturer should be strictly liable for proximate resulting harm. But that is not this case.

Under §1036, recovery is barred if a plaintiff's total negligence is greater than the negligence of the defendant. Applying §1036 in this case, I would reverse the jury verdict and enter judgment for defendant because the evidence showed as a matter of law that Bruce Webb's negligence was greater than the negligence of defendant due to defective design or inadequate warnings. Neither the lighting system of the tractor nor the allegedly inadequate warning against use of the field light on a public road was a significant cause of the accident. Rather, Webb failed to maintain the flashing lights, and consequently, could not mind the warning decal on the tractor to "use flashing warning lights at all times on public roads." Had the flashing lights worked and been turned on as instructed by the warning, the field light would not have operated. Any deficiency in the lighting system of the tractor was exceedingly minor when compared with plaintiff's failure to keep the flashing lights in working order. Moreover, plaintiff aggravated the situation further by riding on the draw bar and blocking view of the reflective slow-moving-vehicle triangle and the single flashing amber light that may have been working. A reasonable juror would have to conclude that the major fault and cause for the accident was attributable to plaintiff.

Accordingly, I would reverse. . . .

JOHNSON, Justice, dissenting. . . .

I.

Justice Dooley and Justice Morse would hold, under varying circumstances, that when a plaintiff alleges injury caused by a defective product, the defendant that produced or distributed the product can reduce or eliminate its liability for damages by showing that the plaintiff's negligent conduct was a contributing cause of the injury. I believe that such a holding would take a major step toward abolition of the doctrine of strict products liability by undermining the principal purpose of the doctrine — to promote the manufacture and distribution of safe products. I see no justification in law, policy, or the facts of this case to extend the doctrine of comparative fault to strict products liability actions.[4]

Notwithstanding assertions to the contrary in Justice Dooley's opinion, my position is followed by a significant number of jurisdiction. 1 A. Best, Comparative Negligence: Law and Practice §9.20[6], at 41-42 (1996) (significant number of jurisdictions continue to reject or limit application of comparative negligence in strict products liability actions); Annotation, Applicability of Comparative Negligence Doctrine to Actions Based on Strict Liability in Tort, 9 A.L.R.4th 633, 638-41 (1981) (reviewing cases in which courts have refused to compare fault); see, e.g., Kinard v. Coats Co., . . . 553 P.2d 835, 837 (Colo. Ct. App. 1976) (better-reasoned position is that comparative negligence has no application to products liability actions); Lippard v. Houdaille Indus., Inc., 715 S.W.2d 491, 493 (Mo. 1986) (en banc) (refusing to apply comparative fault principles to products liability actions); Bowling v. Heil Co., . . . 511 N.E.2d 373, 380 (Ohio 1987) (better-reasoned decisions are those that have declined to inject plaintiff's negligence into law of products liability); Kimco Dev. Corp. v. Michael D's Carpet

---

4. For the reasons stated by Justice Dooley, I oppose Justice Morse's position, which would unabashedly return strict products liability actions to the realm of negligence law, at least with respect to warning/design cases.

Outlets, . . . 637 A.2d 603, 605-06 (Pa. 1993) (agreeing with cited jurisdictions refusing to extend negligence concepts to products liability actions).

Further, although a majority of jurisdiction compare fault in products liability actions, that majority is hopelessly divided on when and what to compare and how to implement the comparison. See M. Roszkowski & R. Prentice, Reconciling Comparative Negligence and Strict Liability: A Public Policy Analysis, 33 St. Louis U. L.J. 19, 40-47 (1988) (discussing various approaches taken by jurisdictions that compare fault in products liability actions). Some courts compare any and every type of contributory negligence, other courts compare only contributory negligence that rises to the level of assumption of risk or unforeseeable misuse, and still others compare all types of contributory negligence except when the negligence can be labeled as a failure to discover or guard against the risk posed by the defective product. . . .

III.

The principal argument for comparing plaintiffs' negligence in products liability actions is couched in terms of fairness. It is fairer to compare, so the argument goes, because the comparison avoids imposing upon manufacturers and careful consumers the costs caused by negligent consumers. But the real issue is whether a higher value should be placed on the deterrence of product defects than is placed on laying the correct amount of blame on the particular actors involved in an accident that was statistically predictable. . . .

Some courts have reasoned that comparing negligence does not greatly affect the incentive to produce safe products because a manufacturer's liability is reduced only to the extent that the trier of fact finds that the user's conduct contributed to the injury, and manufacturers are not able to predict in any given case whether contributory negligence will reduce the plaintiff's judgment. . . . This reasoning does not hold up under scrutiny.

Although manufacturers may not be able to anticipate careless behavior in any given case, they know with virtual certainty that a product will cause a calculable number of accidents, and they will often be able to predict the extent of plaintiffs' negligence by evaluating accidents on a statistical basis. H. Latin, The Preliminary Draft of a Proposed Restatement (Third) of Torts: Products Liability —Letter, 15 J. Prod. & Tox. Liab. 169, 179 (1993); D. Sobelsohn, Comparing Fault, 60 Ind. L.J. 413, 438 (1985). From their calculations, manufacturers can approximate the total liability exposure that those accidents will create, and will then incur increased production costs for safety features only when it makes economic sense to do so. In this way, "the effect of reductions in liability costs as a result of comparative apportionment can make a major difference on the manufacturer's marginal investments in safety." Latin, supra, at 179.

To the extent that product liability would be reduced by comparing plaintiffs' negligence, the incentive to produce safe products would also be reduced. . . . M. Davis, Individual and Institutional Responsibility: A Vision for Comparative Fault in Products Liability, 39 Vill. L. Rev. 281, 344 (1994) (if manufacturers need only compensate those injured during careful use, losses resulting from defective product will never be fully considered in evaluating needed investment in safety). For example, if a particular feature of a product results in accidents costing $1 million, and redesign of the product to eliminate the dangerous feature would cost $900,000, the manufacturer would not have any incentive to redesign the product if the manufacturer could predict that a certain percentage of consumers would negligently contribute to their injuries while using the product, thereby making it cheaper for the manufacturer to pay tort claims rather than redesign the defective product. . . .

We can be certain that, based on statistical accident data and marketing analyses, manufacturers make conscious, calculated choices regarding the safety of their products, choices that are affected by legal principles. If the law provides an economic incentive for a manufacturer to add safety features to a particular product, thousands of people may be spared injury. If, on the other hand, reduced tort damages from comparing plaintiffs' negligence convinces a manufacturer that it would not make economic sense to add safety features to its product, many consumers, including careful ones, may later be injured by the defective product. Assuming that they are able to fend off a defendant's claims of comparative negligence, those careful consumers may obtain full monetary damages, but at the expense of their health or even their lives. This is *not* a fair result. . . .

But there is another important reason why I am persuaded that it is unfair to use comparative principles in strict liability cases. The victim's negligence may be the result of a moment's inattention to some detail, carelessness in a time of crisis, or miscalculation as to the danger involved in using a product a certain way. These types of ordinary negligence, to which all of us fall prey at times, cannot be regarded as equivalent to the manufacturer's responsibility to design safe products and warn the public of dangers that accompany use of their products. . . .

This is where the superficial appeal to fairness falls apart. As a general proposition, we can all agree that each person should bear responsibility for his or her own conduct. It is for this reason that comparative negligence has been accepted as fair in other contexts. But the doctrine of comparative negligence arose in cases where the fault of the parties was of a similar order — carelessness versus carelessness. In strict products liability cases, however, we have fault of very different kinds. The garden-variety carelessness that may contribute to an injury in the use of a product is simply not of the same magnitude as the design, manufacture and release into commerce of a dangerously defective product or a product whose dangers are hidden by inadequate warnings. It is *not* fair, therefore, to treat the two as equivalent. . . .

Plaintiffs who voluntarily assume a known risk should, in my judgment, be barred from recovery. Limiting the assumption-of-risk defense tends to penalize legitimate commercial interests unfairly rather than promote fairness to consumers. Justice Dooley's opinion proclaims that comparing conduct amounting to a voluntary assumption of a known risk benefits consumers, but it undermines the doctrine of strict liability, which provides a powerful incentive for manufacturers and vendors to create and purvey only those products that are safe for everyone. In short, the majority imagines a problem negatively affecting consumers and then creates a cure far worse than the "problem" it seeks to rectify.

Second, while it may not always be easy to distinguish assumption of risk from ordinary contributory negligence, the subjective component of assumption of risk makes the defense qualitatively distinct from other forms of contributory negligence . . . (plaintiff must voluntarily encounter risk despite being subjectively aware of existence of risk and appreciating extent of danger; many courts distinguish assumption of risk from contributory negligence on point that only assumption of risk involves application of subjective standard to plaintiff's conduct); see also Zahrte v. Sturm, Ruger & Co., . . . 661 P.2d 17, 18 (Mont. 1983) (subjective element of assumption of risk makes it distinct from contributory negligence). . . .

In sum, (1) manufacturers have the opportunity to make calculated, informed choices concerning product safety; (2) economic factors and legal principles drive their decisions; (3) those decisions can affect the health and safety of thousands or even millions of people; and (4) enterprises can more easily absorb and equitably pass on to the public the costs of defective products as part of doing business. On the other hand, (1) consumers lack the expertise and information about products possessed by manufacturers; (2) liability law provides no incentive for them to be more careful; (3) their contributory negligence is foreseeable, such that its costs can be equitably spread among all product users; and (4) most importantly, their negligence is simply not equivalent in kind to the act of designing and manufacturing a defective product. For these reasons, there is nothing unfair about imposing full liability on a manufacturer who places in the stream of commerce a defective product that is a proximate cause of the plaintiff's injuries, even if the plaintiff's negligence contributed to those injuries. Products should be designed to protect not only ideal consumers, but also careless, illiterate, ignorant, and inattentive ones as well. . . .

I would affirm the judgment below. I am authorized to say that Justice Gibson joins in my opinion.

Having read *Webb,* how do you come out on the question of reducing plaintiff's recovery based on comparative fault? The dissent's protestation notwithstanding, the overwhelming majority of courts apply comparative fault to products liability claims. Two Restatement projects have endorsed this view. See Restatement of Torts (Third): Products Liability §17 (1998) set forth supra; Restatement of Torts (Third): Apportionment of Liability §1, comment *b.*

The dissent is correct in pointing out that some courts refuse to apply comparative fault when the plaintiff's only negligence consists in not discovering the defect. See *Murray,* supra. See also Star Furniture Co. v. Pulaski Furniture Co., 297 S.E.2d 854, 862 (W.Va. 1982). And some courts will only apply comparative fault when the plaintiff's conduct amounts to assumption of risk. See, e.g., Suter v. San Angelo Foundry & Mach. Co., 406 A.2d 140 (N.J. 1979). But these carve-outs are a distinct minority view. Well over 20 states mandate the application of comparative fault to products liability actions and allow for no exceptions to the rule. See, e.g., Huffman v. Caterpillar Tractor Co., 908 F.2d 1470 (10th Cir. 1990) (applying Colorado law) (holding that the Colorado comparative fault statute covers all forms of culpable conduct); N.Y. C.P.L.R. §1411 (McKinney 1976). Both the Products Liability Restatement and the Apportionment Restatement set forth, supra, take the position that courts ought not to be called upon to make fine distinctions among various types of plaintiff conduct as a matter of law. Instead, juries should weigh all forms of plaintiff conduct in deciding how much fault to apportion to the parties.

The issues of misuse and product alteration by the plaintiff have given rise to an inordinate amount of confusion. It's high time this mess gets straightened out. Product misuse and alteration may manifest themselves at three different stages of a products liability case. First, if an injury is caused by the kind of product misuse that cannot reasonably be designed against, then the product is simply not defective. A buzzsaw cannot be rendered reasonably safe for purposes of cutting a child's hair. See, e.g., Jurado v. Western Gear Works, 619 A.2d 1312 (N.J. 1993). In the second category of cases, the product is defective, but the factfinder must evaluate whether the use to which the product was being put was so unreasonable or unforeseeable that the plaintiff has not met his burden of showing proximate cause. In these cases, the issue should be whether the plaintiff has established a prima facie case. See, e.g., Smith ex rel. Smith v. Bryco Arms, 33 P.3d 638 (N.M. Ct. App. 2001) (reversing trial court's grant of summary judgment for defendant gun manufacturer on grounds of proximate cause; fact issue existed as to whether teenage boy's misuse of firearm in deliberately pulling trigger when gun aimed at friend's head was reasonably foreseeable by manufacturer); White v. Caterpillar, Inc., 867 P.2d 100, 107-108 (Colo. Ct. App. 1993) (upholding misuse instruction where the misuse rather than the defect caused the injury; however, the court noted that misuse is not an absolute bar if the consumer's misuse could have been reasonably anticipated by the manufacturer); Gibbs v. The O'Malley Lumber Company, 868 P.2d 355 (Ct. App. Ariz. 1994); Smith v. Louis Berkman Company, 894 F. Supp. 1084, 1091 (W.D. Ky. 1995).

In the third category of misuse, the plaintiff's misuse or modification of the product contributes — along with the defect in the defendant's product — to causing the harm. Usually, these cases get submitted for comparative fault allocation, resulting in a reduction of damages. In Jimenez v. Sears, Roebuck and Company, 904 P.2d 861 (Ariz. 1995), the plaintiff bought an electric disc grinder, read the manual, checked to see if the machine was working properly, and proceeded to use the tool. After 45 minutes, the disc shattered, injuring Jimenez. Jimenez was familiar with the type of tool and disregarded a suggestion in the manual to wear a leather apron. The defendant alleged that the plaintiff also must have turned the safety guard away from him during the tool's operation. The court held that, under Arizona's comparative fault statute, misuse was an apportionable contributing cause rather than a bar to recovery when it was a concurrent cause of the plaintiff's harm. See also Barnard v. Saturn Corp., 790 N.E.2d 1023 (Ind. Ct. App. 2003) (holding that plaintiff's misuse of car jack should be taken into account under principles of comparative fault rather than serving as a complete bar to recovery); States v. R.D. Werner Co., 799 P.2d 427 (Colo. Ct. App. 1990); Standard Havens Products, Inc. v. Benitez, 648 So. 2d 1192, 1197 (Fla. 1994) ("product misuse reduces a plaintiff's recovery in proportion to his or her own comparative fault").

A considerable body of literature has grown up around the subject of comparative fault and its applicability to products litigation. See, e.g., Note, The Aftermath of Owens and Whitehead — Products Liability and Comparative Fault in Tennessee — How Deep Does the Relationship Run?, 32 U. Mem. L. Rev. 443 (2002); Mary J. Davis, Individual and Institutional Responsibility: A Vision for

Comparative Fault in Products Liability, 39 Vill. L. Rev. 281 (1994); Dix Noel, Defective Products: Abnormal Use, Contributory Negligence, and Assumption of Risk, 25 Vand. L. Rev. 93, 117-18 (1972) (contributory negligence should diminish plaintiff's damages).

SOCIAL CONTROL OF PRODUCT-RELATED ACCIDENTS: THE SEAT BELT DEFENSE AND GOVERNMENTAL CONTROL OF DRIVERS' BEHAVIOR

As of 2003, a large majority of states have passed Mandatory Seat Belt Use Laws (MULS). The seat belt defense has become a serious topic of debate in recent years. Auto manufacturers contend that even if they have contributed to causing the plaintiff's injury by supplying a defective vehicle, the plaintiff has co-authored the injury by failing to buckle up. The issue has been covered by statute in many jurisdictions. The seat belt statutes break down into three categories:

(1) *Failure to wear a seat belt may not be used to reduce recovery.* Illinois specifically provides that "failure to wear a seat belt shall not be considered evidence of negligence, shall not limit the liability of an insurer, and shall not diminish any recovery for damages arising out of . . . operation of a motor vehicle." 625 ILCS 5/12-603.1 (1996). Similar statutes have been enacted in Arkansas, Connecticut, Georgia, Louisiana, Massachusetts, Minnesota, New Mexico, Pennsylvania, Tennessee, Utah, Virginia, and West Virginia.

(2) *Failure to wear a seat belt may be used to reduce recovery.* The New York statute provides that failure to wear a seat belt may be introduced into evidence in order to reduce recovery. N.Y. Veh. & Traf. Law 1229-c (McKinney 2002). In Colorado, reduction is limited to awards for pain and suffering and is not used to limit recovery of economic loss and medical payments. Colo. Rev. Stat. 42-4-437(7). Also see Waterson v. General Motors Corp., 544 A.2d 537 (N.J. 1988) (reducing plaintiff recovery for failure to wear a seat belt).

(3) *Reduction is permitted, with a cap.* Iowa, Michigan, Missouri, and Oregon allow for reduction of damages based on the failure to wear a seat belt, but cap the reduction. Iowa Code §321.445 (1997) (5 percent); Mich. Comp. Laws §257.710e(4) (5 percent); Missouri Statutes §307.178 (1994) (1 percent); Or. Rev. Stat. §18.590 (2001) (5 percent). It may be hardly worth the cost of hiring an expert to testify that the failure to wear the seat belt aggravated the injury to reduce recovery by such minimal percentages.

However, the Restatement (Third) of Torts: Apportionment of Liability (2000) takes a radically different position from that of the majority. The Restatement says that the factfinder should consider the plaintiff's conduct in failing to wear a seat belt when assigning percentages of responsibility.

See generally Victor E. Schwartz, Comparative Negligence §§4-6 (b) (3d ed. 1994); Arthur Best, Comparative Negligence: Law and Practice §4.40 (1) (rep. Vol. 1996); Comparative Negligence Manual 3d §14:1 (1995 & Supp. 2002).

*(2) The Crashworthiness Imbroglio: Should Fault
Be Compared with Enhanced Injury?*

D'Amario v. Ford Motor Company
806 So. 2d 424 (Fla. 2001)

PER CURIAM.

We have for review the decision in Ford Motor Co. v. D'Amario, 732 So. 2d 1143 (Fla. 2d DCA 1999), . . . on the issue of whether principles of comparative fault apply in a crashworthiness case. We hold that principles of comparative fault concerning apportionment of fault as to the cause of the underlying crash will not ordinarily apply in crashworthiness or enhanced injury cases.[2] Because the manufacturer alleged to be responsible for a defective product that results in a second accident and injury ordinarily may not be held liable for the injuries caused by the initial accident, the fault of the manufacturer may not be compared or apportioned with the fault of the driver of the vehicle who allegedly caused the initial crash.

Secondary Injury Cases

[The case before us involves a lawsuit] premised on the crashworthiness doctrine. Such cases, which are also often referred to as "secondary collision" or "enhanced injury" cases, involve both an initial accident and a subsequent or secondary collision caused by an alleged defective condition created by a manufacturer, which is unrelated to the cause of the initial accident but which causes additional and distinct injuries beyond those suffered in the primary collision. One court has explained that the damages sought in such cases "are not for injuries sustained in the original collision but for those sustained in the second impact where some design defect caused an exacerbated injury which would not have otherwise occurred as a result of the original collision." Meekins v. Ford Motor Co., 699 A.2d 339, 341 (Del. Super. Ct. 1997).

[The court noted that Florida had in past decisions held that an auto manufacturer has a duty to design its cars so that they are reasonably crashworthy.]

In [the case at bar], Clifford Harris, a minor, was injured when the car in which he was riding as a passenger collided with a tree and then burst into flames. The car was driven by a friend of Harris who was allegedly intoxicated and speeding at the time of the accident. As described in the opinion below:

> A witness to the crash circled the car twice and noticed a fire in the engine area. Some minutes later, the fire spread and an explosion occurred, engulfing the car in flames. Harris was severely injured, losing three limbs and suffering burns to much of his body.

---

2. We say ordinarily because we recognize that in some cases a valid issue may exist as to whether the plaintiff's negligence contributed to the cause of the *enhanced injuries*. In that case, the automobile manufacturer should be permitted to assert that plaintiff's negligence was a legal cause of the enhanced injuries.

Harris, and his mother, Karen D'Amario, sued Ford alleging that a defective relay switch in the automobile caused Harris's injuries. The plaintiffs did not seek damages against Ford for the injuries to Harris caused by the initial collision with the tree. Rather, they sought damages for the injuries caused by the alleged defective relay switch only. Ford asserted as an affirmative defense that the injuries were proximately caused by the negligence of a third party. . . .

Prior to jury selection, the plaintiffs moved to exclude evidence about the driver's alcohol consumption on the day of the accident and the trial court ruled that evidence of the driver's alcohol consumption would be excluded. The court reasoned that the acts leading up to the collision were not at issue, rather, the issue as to Ford's liability concerned events occurring after the initial collision with the tree. However, at trial, Ford moved to amend its affirmative defenses to include an allegation that Harris's injuries were caused by the fault of a third party, and proffered evidence of the driver's intoxication and excessive speed. The trial court granted Ford's request and held that an apportionment defense was available and evidence of the driver's actions in causing the initial accident could be admitted in support of such defense. In the face of such ruling, the parties stipulated to the jury that the negligent and excessive speed of the driver caused the initial accident and that at the time the driver had a blood alcohol level of .14 percent.

Following deliberations, the jury returned a verdict for the defense, finding that Ford was not a legal cause of the injuries to Harris. Because the jury found for the defense, it did not reach the question on the interrogatory verdict form as to the driver's comparative negligence. D'Amario subsequently moved for a new trial, alleging that the court erred in permitting evidence of the driver's intoxication to go to the jury. . . .

Analysis

Comparative Fault in Crashworthiness Cases

As noted above, although we recognized the crashworthiness doctrine . . . some time ago, the issue of whether principles of comparative fault apply in enhanced injury cases is one of first impression for this Court. . . .

The Majority View

Outside of Florida, courts have wrestled with the comparative fault issue and have adopted conflicting views. Under what has been characterized by Whitehead v. Toyota Motor Corp., 897 S.W.2d 684 (Tenn. 1995), as the "majority view," the fault of the plaintiff or a third party in causing the initial accident is recognized as a defense to a crashworthiness case against a product manufacturer. This line of cases reasons that the fault of the person causing the accident that created the circumstances in which the second accident occurred should be compared with the role of the automobile manufacturer's negligence in designing a defective product in assessing total responsibility for the claimant's injuries. See Montag v. Honda Motor Co., 75 F.3d 1414, 1419 (10th Cir. 1996) (interpreting Colorado law); Keltner v. Ford Motor Co., 748 F.2d 1265, 1267 (8th Cir. 1984) (applying

Arkansas law); Hinkamp v. American Motors Corp., 735 F. Supp. 176, 178 (E.D.N.C. 1989), *aff'd,* 900 F.2d 252 (4th Cir. 1990); General Motors Corp. v. Farnsworth, 965 P.2d 1209, 1218 (Alaska 1998) (holding it was error not to instruct jury on plaintiff's comparative fault in a strict liability action against manufacturer based on defective seatbelt and not to allocate fault to third person who may have caused the accident). . . .

In Meekins v. Ford Motor Co., [699 A.2d 339 (Del. Super. Ct. 1997),] a Delaware trial judge set out a comprehensive analysis discussing the arguments on both sides of the issue, before ultimately concluding that principles of comparative fault should apply in enhanced injury cases. First, the court reasoned that while some cases may present a clear factual delineation between primary injuries and secondary injuries, whereby the driver's comparative fault should be excluded from consideration, most cases do not. The court stated that there are usually several acts of negligence involved, all of which may have been a cause of the plaintiff's injuries, and "it would be difficult and confusing to instruct a jury that it should not consider the cause of the collision but only the cause of the enhanced injuries." 699 A.2d at 345. Second, the court was concerned that a rule excluding consideration of the plaintiff driver's fault in causing an accident would logically extend to prevent the plaintiff from suing a negligent third party who caused the accident, and thereby run counter to well-established principles of tort law:

> Another logical hurdle inherent in plaintiff's position is this. If a plaintiff negligently crashes his vehicle into a tree and suffers an enhanced injury because of a design defect in his car, plaintiff says that the manufacturer is liable for the enhanced injury regardless of the plaintiff's negligence in causing the collision. But what if a plaintiff collides with another vehicle and the driver of that vehicle is negligent? Assume also that the enhanced injuries caused to the plaintiff by a design defect in his car are clearly identifiable. Under ordinary rules of proximate cause the other driver would have potential liability for all of the plaintiff's injuries, but logically, following the enhanced injury theory of the plaintiff, only the manufacturer should have the liability because the other driver's conduct in causing the initial collision would not have caused the injury absent the design defect. Thus, carrying the theory to its logical conclusion, plaintiff should have no recovery against the other driver for his negligence in causing the collision. This result would run counter to well settled principles of tort law.

Id. Finally, the court noted that the rule concerning proximate causation should be no different in enhanced injury cases than that applied in ordinary negligence cases. It reasoned that "[t]he existence of other proximate causes of an injury does not relieve a plaintiff driver under Delaware's comparative negligence statute from responsibility for his own conduct which proximately caused him injury. . . . Public policy seeks to deter not only manufacturers from producing a defective product but to encourage those who use the product to do so in a responsible manner." Id. at 345-46. Thus, the court concluded that "[i]t is obvious that the negligence of a plaintiff who causes the initial collision is one of the proximate causes of all of the injuries he sustained, whether limited to those the original collision would have produced or including those enhanced by a defective product in the second collision." Id. at 346.

The Minority View

In contrast to the approach of the "majority" view, the "minority" view, rejecting the application of comparative fault principles, focuses on the underlying rationale for imposing liability against automobile manufacturers for secondary injuries caused by a design defect. The federal district court in Jimenez v. Chrysler Corp., 74 F. Supp. 2d 548 (D.S.C. 1999) . . . explained the essential rationale of the minority view:

> The crashworthiness doctrine imposes liability on automobile manufacturers for design defects that enhance, rather than cause, injuries. The doctrine applies if a design defect, not causally connected to the collision, results in injuries greater than those that would have resulted were there no design defect. The issue for purposes of a crashworthiness case, therefore, is enhancement of injuries, not the precipitating cause of the collision.

74 F. Supp. 2d at 565 (citations omitted). The district court in *Jimenez* pointed out that the rule of damages in crashworthiness cases also effectively acts to apportion fault and responsibility between the first and second collisions and their respective causes:

> First of all, such a rule intrinsically dovetails with the crashworthiness doctrine: Because a collision is presumed, and enhanced injury is foreseeable as a result of the design defect, the triggering factor of the accident is simply irrelevant. Secondly, *the concept of "enhanced injury" effectively apportions fault and damages on a comparative basis; defendant is liable only for the increased injury caused by its own conduct, not for the injury resulting from the crash itself.* Further, the alleged negligence causing the collision is legally remote from, and thus not the legal cause of, the enhanced injury caused by a defective part that was supposed to be designed to protect in case of a collision.

Id. at 566 (emphasis added). Under this reasoning, concerns about fairness in apportioning responsibility for damages based upon fault in crashworthiness cases are satisfied by the limitation of liability of a manufacturer to only those damages caused by the defective product.

Hence, the primary reason offered by courts excluding evidence of the driver's fault in causing an accident is that the accident-causing fault is not relevant to whether an automobile manufacturer designed a defective product, and, further, that such evidence, if admitted, may be unduly prejudicial to the plaintiff. See Cota v. Harley Davidson, . . . 684 P.2d 888, 895-96 (Ariz. Ct. App. 1984) (holding that evidence of the plaintiff's intoxication and conduct in causing the initial accident was not relevant in a crashworthiness case against a motorcycle manufacturer based on a design defect in the motorcycle's gas tank system) . . . cf. Green v. General Motors Corp., . . . 709 A.2d 205, 212-13 (N.J. Ct. App. Div. 1998) (holding that plaintiff's excessive speed was not relevant to issue of defective design but was relevant to issue of proximate cause of injuries).

Consistent with this approach, the Iowa Supreme Court has held that evidence of the plaintiff's intoxication and excessive speed is not admissible in a crashworthiness case against a vehicle manufacturer. In Reed v. Chrysler Corp., 494 N.W.2d 224 (Iowa 1992), the court explained:

> The theory, which presupposes the occurrence of accidents precipitated for myriad reasons, focuses alone on the enhancement of resulting injuries. The rule does not pretend

that the design defect had anything to do with causing the accident. It is enough if the design defect increased the damages. So any participation by the plaintiff in bringing the accident about is quite beside the point.

494 N.W.2d at 230. . . .

Florida Law

The automobile manufacturers urge us to adopt the "majority" view and contend that Florida statutory and case law requires juries to apportion fault among all persons who contributed to the resulting injuries and that enhanced-injury cases do not constitute an exception to this well-established rule. They cite section 768.81(3), Fla. Stat. (1997), which provides for the entry of "judgment against each party liable on the basis of such party's percentage of fault" and this Court's interpretation of the statute in Fabre v. Marin, 623 So. 2d 1182 (Fla. 1993).

In *Fabre* this Court concluded "that section 768.81 was enacted to replace joint and several liability with a system that requires each party to pay for noneconomic damages only in proportion to the percentage of fault by which that defendant contributed to the accident." Id. at 1185. We interpreted the term "party" to include all persons who contributed to the accident "regardless of whether they have been or could have been joined as defendants." Id. However, it is not entirely clear that our holding in *Fabre* resolves the question presented today since *Fabre* involved a simple automobile accident involving joint and *concurrent* tortfeasors, and did not involve successive tortfeasors or enhanced or secondary injuries allegedly stemming from a manufacturing or design defect.

On the other hand, the estate and D'Amario contend that our statutory and case law support the minority view. They rely on Florida case law dealing with successor tortfeasors and analogous circumstances. After considering the majority and minority views discussed above, we conclude that the minority view is more consistent with the principles of tort law and comparative fault as presently developed in Florida.

[The court's discussion of an initial tortfeasor's liability for injuries sustained by a plaintiff for subsequent malpractice that enhances the original injury is omitted.]

[U]nlike automobile accidents involving damages solely arising from the collision itself, a defendant's liability in a crashworthiness case is predicated upon the existence of a distinct and second injury caused by a defective product, and assumes the plaintiff to be in the condition to which he is rendered after the first accident. No claim is asserted, however, to hold the defendant liable for that condition. Thus, crashworthiness cases involve separate and distinct injuries — those caused by the initial collision, and those subsequently caused by a second collision arising from a defective product. . . .

Hence, a primary collision, by whatever cause, is presumed to have occurred in crashworthiness cases, and it is further presumed that a manufacturer, . . . may not be held responsible for the injuries caused by the primary collision. Further, only the cause of the enhanced injury is at issue in crashworthiness cases such as those at issue here because the only damages sought are those caused by the defective products. Thus the focus in such cases against a manufacturer is not on the conduct that gave rise to the initial accident, but rather, on the conduct that allegedly caused the enhanced or secondary injuries. It will always be conceded in such cases that the fault of others was completely responsible for the happening of the first accident. . . .

We agree that to automatically compare the fault of the driver in causing the accident with the fault of the automobile manufacturer for the subsequent enhanced injury would be, as Reichert explains, to confuse two different causes—the cause of the accident and the cause of the enhanced injury. See Reichert, Limitations on Manufacturer Liability in Second Collision Actions, supra, at 117-18. The essential point is that under the crashworthiness doctrine, . . . the initial collision and its separate cause is always presumed, and the cause of the initial collision is simply not at issue in the determination of the cause of the second collision. Instead, any analysis concerning the causal connection of the second collision to the separately claimed damages depends solely upon whether a defect existed and gave rise to the enhanced injuries suffered by the plaintiff. . . .

No Liability for Initial Accident

We are not unmindful of the concerns that a manufacturer not end up improperly being held liable for damages caused by the initial collision. Of course, we must remember that in crashworthiness cases the plaintiff not only has the burden of proving the existence of a defect and its causal relationship to her injuries, but she must also prove the existence of additional or enhanced injuries caused by the defect. In this regard, we are impressed with the reasoning of the federal district court in *Jimenez* that the proper application of the crashworthiness doctrine is also consistent with comparative fault principles. The major concern of those courts following the majority rule is in seeing that successive tortfeasors only be held liable for the damages they cause, and not be held liable for damages caused by the initial tortfeasor. We agree with this concern, but see no reason why it cannot be properly addressed, as in *Jimenez,* by a recognition of the crashworthiness doctrine's legal rationale limiting a manufacturer's liability only to those damages caused by the defect. . . .

Conclusion

In sum, we hold that principles of comparative fault involving the causes of the first collision do not generally apply in crashworthiness cases. Such a rule, we believe, recognizes the important distinction between fault in causing the accident and fault in causing additional or enhanced injuries as a result of a product defect, a distinction that defines and limits a manufacturer's liability in crashworthiness cases. In such cases, the automobile manufacturer is solely responsible for the enhanced injuries to the extent the plaintiff demonstrates the existence of a defective condition and that the defect proximately caused the enhanced injuries. Thus, an automobile manufacturer who allegedly designed a defective product may not be held liable for damages caused by the initial collision and may not apportion its fault with the fault of the driver of the vehicle who caused the initial accident.

We believe this rule will ensure both fairness in the apportionment of damages and that the jury will not be unduly confused about the issues in the case, especially in cases like those before us today [involving] drinking and driving. Because the initial collision is presumed in crashworthiness cases, the jury's focus in such cases should be on whether a defect existed and whether such defect proximately caused the enhanced injuries. Unfortunately, . . . the jur[y's] focus was shifted to the conduct of the intoxicated drive[r] who caused the initial acciden[t]. In light of the confusion caused by the introduction of accident-causing fault and the improper focus placed on the non-party drive[r's] intoxication . . . , we conclude that . . . D'Amario [is] entitled to a new trial.

Accordingly, we quash the Second District's decision in *D'Amario*. . . .

It is so ordered. . . .

The Products Liability Restatement disagrees with *D'Amario* on both of its holdings. First, §16, comment *f* allows for the reduction of plaintiff's recovery in crashworthness cases based on the plaintiff's share of fault in causing the accident. It does, however, recognize that a jury may legitimately consider the manufacturer's obligation to protect persons in circumstances in which they are unable to protect themselves when apportioning fault between the parties. Second, §16(d) takes the position that the defendant whose conduct caused the accident and the auto manufacturer who is responsible for the enhanced injuries are joint tortfeasors whose respective fault must be apportioned according to the relevant statute governing joint and several liability. Thus, in a state that limits recovery against a joint tortfeasor based on each defendant's percentage of fault, an auto manufacturer's fault would be limited to the fault assessed against it by the jury. See §16, Illustration 8.

Do you understand how *D'Amario* reached the conclusion that the negligent driver who caused the accident is not the proximate cause of the enhanced injuries? Isn't it foreseeable to a drunken driver who causes an accident that the auto he collides with might be defectively designed? Think of the following hypothetical: The defendant drunken driver, possessing wealth equal to that of Donald Trump, collides with a Yugo. Plaintiff, a passenger in the Yugo, suffers enhanced injuries due to a design defect in the Yugo. Plaintiff sues Yugo for enhanced injuries but discovers that Yugo has gone bankrupt. Is there any court in the world that would let the wealthy drunken driver off the hook on the grounds that his negligent conduct was not a proximate cause of the plaintiff's enhanced injuries? What the devil could the court mean by saying that the driver's conduct was not a proximate cause of the plaintiff's second-collision injuries? Why was it necessary for the court to hinge its reasoning on proximate cause?

Finally, does it follow that a state that refuses to reduce a *plaintiff's* verdict based on her comparative fault in a crashworthness case must necessarily find that apportionment of fault between *defendants* (e.g., a drunken driver and an auto manufacturer) is not allowed for enhanced injuries?

(3) Should Plaintiff's Fault Be Compared with Defendant's Breach of Express Warranty?

In the precomparative fault era when contributory negligence was a complete bar, courts were reluctant to recognize contributory negligence as a defense to an express warranty action. In Bahlman v. Hudson Motor Co., 288 N.W.2d 309 (Mich. 1939), plaintiff purchased an auto relying on the representation that the roof was rugged and because it was made from a single sheet of steel. Plaintiff was injured when, due to his negligence, the car turned over and his head was lacerated by a jagged edge of the roof. The representations that the roof was rugged and made from a single sheet of steel were false. The court held that the auto manufacturer's representations were not limited to non-negligent accidents only and thus refused to recognize contributory negligence as a defense. Now that comparative negligence has removed the threat of plaintiff fault operating as a total bar, courts appear willing to entertain comparative fault as a defense to personal injury actions based on express warranty. The Restatement (Third) of Torts: Apportionment of Liability §1(b) endorses the across-the-board applicability of comparative fault to all tort actions regardless of the theory on which the cause of action is predicated. Recent cases are in accord. See Torres v. Northwest Eng'g Co., 949 P.2d 1004 (Hawaii 1997) (holding that pure comparative fault principles apply to reduce plaintiff's recovery in express warranty actions); Lougbridge v. Goodyear Tire & Rubber Co., 207 F. Supp. 2d 1187 (D. Colo. 2002) (applying Colorado's comparative fault statute to an express warranty claim based on the statute's plain language covering any action brought "as a result of injury to persons or property").

(4) No Duty/Primary Assumption of Risk: Reintroducing Plaintiff's Conduct as a Total Bar

One form of contributory fault — assumption of risk — may still operate as a total bar to a plaintiff's products liability claim. You will remember from first-year torts that many courts draw a distinction between what they call "primary assumption of the risk," which operates as a no-duty rule negating liability entirely, and "secondary assumption of the risk," which is merely a form of contributory fault and only reduces the plaintiff's damages. At some level the no-duty analysis is clearly appropriate. For example, if a person asks a neighbor to borrow the family car and the neighbor responds, "You're welcome to use it but you should know that the brakes are dangerous," liability should not be imposed on the neighbor when the brakes fail and the borrower is injured. The owner of the car has fulfilled his responsibility to the borrower by disclosing the risk. Whether the borrower acted voluntarily or under the compulsion of personal need is of no moment. The car owner has no duty to rescue the borrower from the implications of his own choice to use the car and take his chances. In such a case the car owner should bear no liability, and comparative negligence should play no role. Similarly, a baseball park will generally not be held liable for injuries suffered by a fan sitting outside of the screened-in portion of the field. The risks of fast-moving foul balls are well known and the costs (both monetary and nonmonetary) attendant to screening the entire ball field are high. A court would be justified in holding as a matter of law that the owner of the ball field did not breach a duty to spectators. Akins v. Glens Falls City School District, 424 N.E.2d 531 (N.Y. 1981).

When contributory negligence and assumption of the risk were total bars it mattered little whether the terminology used to describe the "no-recovery" result was no duty, no breach, assumption of the risk, or even "the XYZ syndrome." Now that courts and legislatures have assimilated contributory negligence and assumption of the risk into comparative negligence, the nomenclature matters a great deal. Characterizing the case as one in which there is "no duty" will absolve the defendant from liability, whereas labeling it as an affirmative defense may well mean that the plaintiff will recover a reduced verdict. See Turcotte v. Fell, 502 N.E.2d 964, 967 (N.Y. 1986).

Whether a given fact pattern is weighty enough to trigger a no-duty analysis is not self-evident. Consider the following decision.

Andren v. White-Rodgers Co.
465 N.W.2d 102 (Minn. App. 1991)

SHORT, Judge.

This products liability action arises from a liquid propane gas explosion in Robert Andren's cabin. On appeal from a grant of summary judgment, Andren argues the trial court erred in deciding his lighting of a cigarette in a basement filled with gas was a legal bar to recovery. We disagree and affirm.

Andren owned a lake cabin which was heated by liquid propane (LP) gas. A line ran from an LP tank outside the cabin to a space heater in the basement. Andren bought the space heater in used condition in 1982 and installed it himself. The heater operated for several winters without problems.

In January of 1985, Andren went to check on the cabin. When he entered the basement, he noticed the smell of LP gas. After turning on the basement light, Andren discovered the smell of gas grew stronger as he walked further into the basement. Believing the pilot light on the heater had blown out, Andren sent his daughter upstairs to find matches to use to light the heater later. Andren then tried to open the basement windows to air out the room.

Because the basement windows were jammed shut, Andren decided to get a screwdriver from his car to pry them open. Before Andren left the basement, he stopped just inside the door and lit a cigarette. The LP gas exploded and the basement began to burn. Andren's hands, face and head were severely burned.

Although Andren had no formal training regarding LP gas appliances, he had installed over 100 LP gas heaters. Andren had also used LP gas appliances all of his life. He knew LP gas was dangerous and could explode if exposed to a spark or an open flame. Andren specifically knew not to smoke or to light a match when the smell of LP gas was in the air.

Andren claims a defective regulator in the gas heater allowed LP gas to leak into the basement. He sued the manufacturer, White-Rodgers Company, and the retailer, Sears, Roebuck & Co., alleging strict liability, breach of warranty and negligence. The manufacturer brought Flexan Corporation into the lawsuit by alleging it provided the defective regulator part. The manufacturer moved for summary judgment and agreed, for purposes of the motion, the valve in the LP gas heater was defective. The trial court granted summary judgment against Andren and held Andren's claims were barred because he primarily assumed the risk of injury. . . .

The only issue before this court is whether primary assumption of the risk can be a bar to recovery in a products liability case. . . .

Minnesota law recognizes two types of assumption of the risk. . . .

Primary assumption of the risk arises:

Where parties have voluntarily entered a relationship in which plaintiff assumes well-known, incidental risks. As to those risks, the defendant has no duty to protect the plaintiff and, thus, if the plaintiff's injury arises from an incidental risk, the defendant is not negligent.

Olson v. Hansen, 299 Minn. 39, 44, 216 N.W.2d 124, 127 (1974). Conversely, secondary assumption of the risk "is a type of contributory negligence where the plaintiff voluntarily encounters a known and appreciated hazard created by the defendant without relieving the defendant of his duty of care with respect to such hazard." Armstrong v. Mailand, 284 N.W.2d 343, 349 (Minn. 1979). The elements of both primary and secondary assumption of the risk are whether a person had (a) knowledge of the risk; (b) an appreciation of the risk; and (c) a choice to avoid the risk but voluntarily chose to chance the risk. . . .

The manifestations of acceptance and consent dictate whether primary or secondary assumption of the risk is applicable in a given case. . . .

The wisdom and reasonableness of the plaintiff's actions are not factors in the determination. . . .

The doctrine of primary assumption of the risk defines the limits of a defendant's duty to the plaintiff. . . .

By voluntarily entering into a situation where the defendant's negligence is obvious, the plaintiff accepts and consents to it and agrees "to undertake to look out for himself and relieve the defendant of the duty." W. Keeton, D. Dobbs, R. Keeton & D. Owen, Prosser and Keeton on Torts, §68, at 485 (5th ed. 1984). . . .

Andren argues the trial court erred by granting summary judgment for respondents because primary assumption of the risk does not apply in products liability cases. We disagree. In *Armstrong,* the supreme court applied the doctrine of primary assumption of the risk to a products liability claim. See *Armstrong,* 284 N.W.2d at 352. The supreme court stated that the public policies underlying strict liability actions did not require the plaintiff's conduct to be removed from consideration when the court assessed liability. . . .

Thus, primary assumption of the risk is applicable in a products liability action involving a defective product. See also Wagner v. Firestone Tire & Rubber Co., 890 F.2d 652, 657 (3d Cir. 1989) (assumption of risk is a complete defense in design defect cases); Rolfes v. International Harvester Co., 817 F.2d 471, 474 (8th Cir. 1987) (Iowa law provides that assumption of the risk is a defense in a defective product case); Restatement (Second) of Torts §402A, comment *n* (1965).

The abolition of the latent-patent danger rule does not preclude the application of primary assumption of the risk to a products liability action. The latent-patent danger rule absolves a manufacturer from liability for injuries caused by a defective product when the danger is obvious. Holm v. Sponco Mfg., Inc., 324 N.W.2d 207, 210 (Minn. 1982). Conversely, primary assumption of the risk relieves a defendant of liability when the plaintiff knows and appreciates a danger, yet voluntarily chooses to chance the risk. . . .

Thus, primary assumption of the risk involves subjective and volitional elements which are beyond the scope of the latent-patent danger rule.

The three elements of both primary and secondary assumption of the risk are present in this case. First, Andren demonstrated his knowledge of the risk by testifying he knew LP gas was dangerous and was specifically aware that lighting a cigarette in a room filled with LP gas would cause an explosion. Second, the record shows appellant appreciated the risk because he recognized the smell of LP gas in the basement, and knew he should not light a cigarette while he was in the basement. Finally, the evidence is clear Andren had a choice to avoid the danger by not smoking, yet he voluntarily chose to light the cigarette.

Andren's lighting of a cigarette in a gas-filled room was a voluntary acceptance of a known danger. See *Armstrong,* 284 N.W.2d at 351. The volitional act constituted consent to relieve respondents of their duty to protect Andren from harm. That Andren lighted the cigarette without considering its consequences makes his act no less volitional, . . . because it is clear a reasonable person in his position must have understood the danger. . . .

In essence, respondents were relieved of their duty to protect Andren because Andren was in an equal position to protect himself. . . .

Further, the smell of gas in this case alerted Andren to the need to use extreme caution in the basement. In any products liability case, the plaintiff must establish a causal relationship between the defect and the injury. . . .

Here, the issue of causation did not require jury determination where the obvious danger of Andren's activities eliminates the alleged defective valve as the substantial cause of the accident. See Balder v. Haley, 399 N.W.2d 77, 82 (Minn. 1987) (no need to submit causation to jury because it was clear that failure to warn had no causal relationship to plaintiff's injury). Under these circumstances, the trial court properly granted summary judgment for respondents.

Andren primarily assumed the risk of an explosion when he lit a cigarette in a room filled with LP gas, thereby barring his products liability claim against respondents. Further, as there was no jury question on the causal relationship between the product defect and Andren's injury, the trial court properly granted summary judgment for respondents.

Affirmed.

NORTON, J. (dissenting).

I respectfully dissent. Contrary to the majority's opinion, I do not believe that the doctrine of primary assumption of risk applies to this case. I would remand this case for a jury to decide the negligence of all parties. . . .

Primary assumption of the risk is inapplicable in the present case because Andren never agreed to relieve defendants of their duty to protect him. I do not agree that consent to release defendants from their duty can be implied from Andren's act of lighting a cigarette. He would never have consented to self combustion. Absent a manifestation of consent, Andren's act embodied secondary, not primary, assumption of the risk. As secondary assumption of the risk is a form of contributory negligence, . . . I would remand this case to a jury for an apportionment of fault. . . .

Isn't the dissent absolutely right? The plaintiff scores high on the stupidity scale, but it is hard to believe that he was suicidal. Courts continue to struggle with the line drawn between true assumption of the risk and comparative fault. In Sanchez v. Hillerich, 128 Cal. Rptr. 2d 529 (2002), plaintiff, a college baseball pitcher, sued the manufacturer of a bat for serious injuries sustained when struck by a line drive off the bat of a hitter. The bat used by the hitter was a newly designed hollow aluminum alloy bat with a pressurized air bladder which substantially increased the speed at which the ball leaves the surface of the bat. The defendant sought summary judgment on the grounds that the plaintiff's claim was barred by primary assumption of risk. Defendant argued that being hit by a line drive is one of the inherent risks of the sport. The court denied summary judgment and found that it was for a jury to determine whether the special nature of the bat increased the inherent risks normally attributable to baseball and whether the plaintiff subjectively knew and appreciated the nature of the increased risk.

Blankenship v. CRT Tree, 2002 WL 31195215 (Ohio App. Ct. 2002), indicates that the behavior of a plaintiff can be so outrageous that the courts will employ primary assumption of the risk as a total bar. Plaintiff, an employee of CRT (a tree cutting business) gave into the entrities of a fellow employee who operated a hydraulic crane to engage in bungee bouncing. Unlike bungee jumping where one jumps off a high structure while wearing a harness that is attached to a bungee cord, in "bungee bouncing" the person is attached with a bungee cord to a crane. When the operator takes up and lets out the cable of the crane, it creates a bouncing motion for the participant. Plaintiff fell from a height of 105 feet while bungee bouncing and suffered serious injury. He sued a host of defendants including the crane manufacturer alleging that the crane was defective due to a lack of safety precautions, warnings, and instructions.

The trial court granted defendant's motion for summary judgment. On appeal the court held that the plaintiff was barred from recovery by primary assumption of the risk. The court said that the dangers attendant to bungee bouncing from such an elevated height are well known. The activity is so fraught with high danger that defendant owed no duty to a plaintiff who voluntarily engaged in such activity.

PROBLEM TWENTY-THREE

Maryanne Hammond woke her husband, Jim, at 3:00 A.M. one Tuesday morning three weeks ago. Maryanne was seven months pregnant and her bag of waters had just ruptured. While examining herself Maryanne noticed that the umbilical cord was visible. From what she had learned at her childbirth classes she knew she had a "prolapsed cord," and that unless she got to the hospital immediately, the baby would be in serious jeopardy. Jim dressed quickly and went outside to start the car. As fate would have it, his car would not start. Jim quickly ran to his next-door neighbor and rang the bell repeatedly. Trish Devaney staggered to the door and found Jim frantic. Jim told Trish that he had to have her car to take his wife to the hospital.

Trish Devaney owned a new Chevy Chevette that had about 10,500 miles on it. She immediately agreed to let Jim have the car. When Trish handed Jim the keys she told him to drive carefully. "Jim," she said, "the steering has not felt right. I don't know what's wrong. I got a recall letter from GM about defects in the steering column. I haven't had the time to take the car in to check it out." Jim responded, "Steering is the least of my problems now."

Jim was wrong. On the way to the hospital, while making a sharp left turn, the steering mechanism failed and Jim lost control of the car. Jim was seriously injured. Maryanne lost the baby and suffered severe internal injuries. (The baby was born alive, but survived for only a short period.) Jim had not wanted to worry Maryanne on their way to the hospital, and had not said anything to her about the car having steering problems.

Assuming that Andren v. White-Rodgers Co., supra, was recently cited with approval by the Supreme Court of New California, do Jim and Maryanne have causes of action against General Motors, either on their own behalf or as representatives of their deceased child?

B. NON-CONDUCT-BASED DEFENSES

1. *Time-Based Defenses*

Statutes of limitations give voice to policies that override the normal desire of the law to compensate an injured plaintiff at the expense of the defendant who has manufactured a defective product that caused a plaintiff's harm. The two policies most often offered in support of time bars are: (1) memories become cloudy and less reliable, witnesses die, and documentary evidence is lost (see, e.g., Order of Railroad Telegraphers v. Railway Express Agency, 321 U.S. 342, 348-349; Davis v. Munie, 85 N.E. 943, 944 (Ill. 1908)); and (2) the time bar signals to the defendant that his time for final repose has arrived and that he can close his books on the event in question (see, e.g., M'Cluny v. Silliman, 28 U.S. (3 Pet.) 270, 277 (1830); Developments in the Law — Statutes of Limitations, 63 Harv. L. Rev. 1177, 1185 (1950)).

Products liability cases have been subjected to two different types of time bars: "open ended" and "fixed period."

a. Open-Ended Time Bars

The normal tort statute of limitations begins to run when the cause of action accrues — at the time of injury to the plaintiff. Time bars for tort claims differ from state to state. Some are as short as one year, others as long as six years from the time of injury. The vast majority of jurisdictions bar actions after two or three years have passed. These statutes of limitations provide little in the way of repose to manufacturers. The injury may not occur until 40 years after the sale to the initial purchaser. The one- to six-year period after injury assumes that evidence regarding the injury to the plaintiff will not be stale; but to the extent that proof of defect is intertwined with questions as to how the product was used over the years, a time bar that is activated by injury to the plaintiff provides little protection against much stale and unreliable evidence that will be brought to bear on proof of defect.

Depending on the jurisdiction, the statute of limitations starts to run in a prod-

> **authors' dialogue 18**
>
> **JIM:** Aaron, I know that you have long favored an independent role for assumption of the risk, separate and apart from the no-duty formulation. My own view is that there is no reason to keep assumption of the risk around. In cases where primary assumption of the risk should bar the plaintiff's claim, a no-duty analysis can do the job.
>
> **AARON:** You know, Jim, I have come around to your way of thinking. In fact, I have begun to consider the possibility that, at least in products cases, even your no-duty analysis should not bar a plaintiff from recovery. We ought simply to compare the conduct of the plaintiff with the defendant's defect and apportion fault under comparative negligence or comparative responsibility.
>
> **JIM:** Goodness, Aaron. You have made a one-hundred-and-eighty-degree change in your thinking. What prompts you to take the position that primary assumption of the risk or no-duty should play no role in products liability cases?
>
> **AARON:** Hear me out, Jim. Think of your classic cases of primary assumption of risk — the passenger who voluntarily gets into the car with a drunk driver or a friend who borrows a car after being told that the car's steering mechanism is broken. In both cases those doctrines would deny plaintiff any recovery — the relationship between the plaintiff and the defendant is such that it is sensible to say that the plaintiff has relieved the defendant of the normal obligations that they would otherwise owe each other. In the products context, however, the defendant manufactures a defective product. Does it make sense to say that the plaintiff by her conduct relieves the defendant of obligations to her with regard to the defect? If the plaintiff were to say to the drunken driver "I want to ride with you but I insist that you drink two cups of coffee," defendant may respond by saying "Get lost. You take me as I am. If not, you can walk to your destination." In the products case, however, there is no discourse, no options offered. The user may have choices other than being forced to use the product in its dangerous state, but I do not see the user relieving the defendant of its responsibility for making a defective product.
>
> **JIM:** Oh, no, Aaron. There are cases of primary assumption of the risk that operate similarly with respect to products. For example, if I leave a box of

ucts liability action when some or all of the following factors are established: (1) plaintiff knows or reasonably should know of the injury; (2) plaintiff knows or reasonably should know of the causal connection between the injury and the harmful product; and (3) plaintiff knows or reasonably should know of a particular defendant's identity.

dangerous firecrackers out in the park and mark them with a sign saying "Danger — Explosive Fireworks," I may be liable to a child who plays with the fireworks and gets hurt, but if you, an adult, come along and say "I want to play with the fireworks, I'll take my chances" you should be barred by primary assumption of the risk.

AARON: Jim, the trouble with you is that you are hooked on hypotheticals. As a general rule, the primary assumption of risk cases are relational and fairness demands that a defendant who clearly identifies the risk and gives the plaintiff the option not to assume it should not be held liable. Products are just different. The user is sort of stuck with the product. She must forgo using something she paid for and choose another option because the defendant screwed up and made a defective product.

JIM: What about a third party who did not pay for the product and decides to use the product with full knowledge of the risk?

AARON: There you go again with your hypotheticals. But let me answer you. Getting rid of the no-duty rule will simplify things without changing many outcomes. Even without the no-duty analysis, the plaintiff will likely be totally barred and, if not, her recovery will be dramatically reduced. In cases that would otherwise fall within the rubric of no-duty/primary assumption of the risk, plaintiffs are likely to be denied recovery because the defect is not the proximate cause of the harm. As we move into the range of no-duty cases, courts and/or juries are likely to find that the intervening willful conduct breaks the chain of proximate cause. And even if plaintiff surmounts that hurdle, in two-thirds of the states she must confront modified comparative fault. A plaintiff whose assumption of the risk is so clear that a court would free defendant of liability on no-duty grounds is not likely to be treated with mercy by a jury. They would almost certainly find her fault to be more than 50 percent, thus barring her completely. The only problem left is that some jurisdictions have pure comparative fault. In some cases, a plaintiff might recover 10 or 20 percent of the total verdict. Big deal. That's a small price to pay for simplicity. All products liability cases should go to juries on comparative fault.

JIM: I can't believe what you just said. You have not only abandoned assumption of risk, but you now take the position that clear no-duty cases should go to juries. I just think you're wrong. It is the function of courts to make the call in clear no-duty cases.

---

(1) Knowledge of Injury as a Trigger

The general rule in most jurisdictions is that the statute of limitations is not triggered until a plaintiff, exercising due diligence, knows or reasonably should know of his injury. In Wyatt v. A-Best Company, Inc., 910 S.W.2d 851, 853

(Tenn. 1995), the court held that workers exposed to asbestos did not have sufficient knowledge of their injuries when they were informed by form letter that the results of union-conducted x-ray tests indicated the "possibility of an asbestos related disease." Rather, the letter "triggered a duty on plaintiffs' parts to determine, with due diligence, whether they, in fact, had an asbestos-related disease," but "did not commence the running of the statute of limitations." Id. at 856. See also Cowgill v. Raymark Industries, 780 F.2d 324 (3d Cir. 1985). But see Blanco v. American Telephone and Telegraph Company, 646 N.Y.S.2d 99 (App. Div. 1996), which held that a plaintiff who suffered repetitive stress injuries as a result of continuous typing on a computer keyboard was barred by the statute of limitations which began running from the onset of the use of the keyboard. Thus, knowledge of injury was not a prerequisite to the running of the statute.

Whether the knowledge of one disease triggers the statute of limitations for other diseases is a matter of some dispute. See, e.g., Wilson v. Johns-Manville Sales Corp., 684 F.2d 111 (D.C. Cir. 1982) (holding that the statute of limitations in a case when terminal mesothelioma succeeded mild asbestosis did not begin to run on the second, different, disease until that disease's manifestation. Parks v. A.P. Green Indus., Inc., 754 N.E.2d 1052, 1058 (Ind. Ct. App. 2001) (plaintiff's suit for asbestosis did not trigger the statute of limitations for lung cancer since they are separate diseases). Accord Martinez-Ferrer v. Richardson-Merrell, Inc., 164 Cal. Rptr. 591 (Cal. Ct. App. 1980); Pierce v. Johns-Manville Sales Corp., 464 A.2d 1020 (Md. 1983); Carroll v. Owens-Corning Fiberglas Corp., 37 S.W.3d 699, 703 (Ky. 2000). For a thorough discussion of this issue in relation to the asbestos litigation, see James A. Henderson, Jr. & Aaron D. Twerski, Asbestos Litigation Gone Mad: Exposure-Based Recovery for Increased Risk, Mental Distress, and Medical Monitoring, 53 S.C. L. Rev. 815 (2002).

(2) Knowledge of the Causal Connection Between the Injury and the Product as a Trigger

In some jurisdictions the statute of limitations will not run until the plaintiff is aware of the causal connection between his injury and the harmful product. See, e.g., Shea v. Kueffel & Esser of New Jersey, 668 F. Supp. 41 (D. Mass. 1986), *aff'd,* 823 F.2d 543 (1987); Raymond v. Eli Lilly & Co., 371 A.2d 170 (N.H. 1977). In Vispisiano v. Ashland Chemical Co., 527 A.2d 66 (N.J. 1987), plaintiff, a worker in a toxic chemical plant, sustained personal injuries as a result of exposure to dangerous chemicals at the workplace. The court held that the worker, exercising reasonable diligence and intelligence, did not discover the causal connection between his health problems and the chemicals until a doctor actually diagnosed the connection, in spite of the fact that the plaintiff admitted that he had earlier suspected that the chemicals were to blame. The court held that the plaintiff was reasonable in relying on an earlier medical diagnosis that attributed his condition to stress or diet, and that his intuitions should not be held against him. *Vispisiano* was extended in Wanner v. Philip Carey Manufacturing Company, 580 A.2d 734 (N.J. Super. Ct. App. Div. 1989). In that case the court held that a plaintiff who contracted pleural asbestosis was not put on notice of his illness by virtue of his doctor informing him that his pulmonary examination showed "some scarring" and "some decrement" since an average person could not be expected to appreciate the nature of such an illness based on the tone of the doctor's report.

In Lee v. Wolfson, 265 F. Supp. 2d 14 (D.D.C. 2003), plaintiff brought suit against Daimler Chrysler Corporation (DCC) in 2002 to recover damages for injuries sustained in 1988 when a Jeep Wrangler rolled down the ramp of a parking garage and struck her as she was exiting her car. Plaintiff initially brought suit against the owner of the Jeep and the parking garage but later added DCC as a defendant after the National Highway Traffic Safety Administration issued a public recall of the Jeep to repair a design defect in the brake system that allowed the parking brake to self-release without warning. Defendant DCC argued that the plaintiff's claims were time barred. The plaintiff claimed that the discovery rule applied and due to the latency of the design defect, she was unaware she had a cause of action against DCC until the public recall occurred. The court denied DCC's motion to dismiss on the grounds that the question of whether the plaintiff was diligent in discovering the connection between the defective brakes and her injuries was one of fact for the jury.

Not all courts massage the facts pertaining to the critical moment of notice into a such a plaintiff-friendly mold. In Mine Safety Appliances Co. v. Stiles, 756 P.2d 288 (Alaska 1988), the plaintiff received serious head injuries when a 58-pound metal hole cover fell 16 feet onto his head. The plaintiff brought an action against the manufacturer of the safety helmet he was wearing at the time. The action was brought after expiration of the period of the statute of limitations, but the plaintiff claimed that he had not discovered the alleged defect in the helmet until six years later. The plaintiff appears to have argued that, when struck by such a heavy object falling from such a height, reasonable people would attribute the injuries to an act of God, or the like. But the court concluded that the plaintiff should have been more diligent:

> The simple fact is that although Stiles had knowledge of enough facts to prompt a reasonable person to investigate shortly after the accident, Stiles did nothing to investigate his claim within the two-year period [following the accident.] We hold that the statute of limitations began to run as soon as Stiles regained his competency shortly after the accident. [Id. at 292.]

Similarly, in Cochran v. GAF Corporation, 666 A.2d 245 (Pa. 1995), plaintiff was diagnosed with adenocarcinoma, but the doctors did not attribute the cause to any product. Plaintiff simply assumed that his disease was caused by his smoking one-and-a-half packs of cigarettes a day. Four years later doctors pinned the disease on plaintiff's exposure to asbestos. The court held that plaintiff's mistaken assumption did not toll the statute of limitations because he was put on inquiry at the time of the initial diagnosis and should have found out the cause; his failure to do so was lack of due diligence as a matter of law.

(3) Knowledge of the Defendant's Identity as a Trigger

Some jurisdictions toll the statute of limitations until plaintiff knows the specific identity of the defendant who caused the harm. In Lawhon v. L.B.J. Institutional Supply, Inc., 765 P.2d 1003 (Ariz. Ct. App. 1988), a customer in a restaurant died from consuming a sulphite product sprinkled on vegetables to keep them fresh. The plaintiff was a chronic asthmatic who presumably knew of his affliction and was aware of what had happened to him, as were the persons accompanying him. The court held that the action was not time-barred, even though it was beyond the statutory period following the injury, because the victim was required to know not only that an injury had occurred and what caused it, but also the specific identity of the responsible party. Because the plaintiff did not know who supplied the sulphite, the statute of limitations did not commence to run at the time of injury. See also Orear v. Int'l. Paint Co., 796 P.2d 759 (Wash. Ct. App. 1990) (shipyard worker's suit against manufacturer of defective epoxy paints was not time-barred since a cause of action could not accrue until the plaintiff had actual or imputed knowledge of the defendant's identity). But see, Apgar v. Lederle Laboratories, 588 A.2d 380 (N.J. 1991). Plaintiff bought a products liability action against drug manufacturer 25 years after she ingested certain drugs she claimed were defective. The plaintiff argued that she did not violate the statute of limitations because she did not know the identity of the defendants until two years before the filing of her complaint. The Court dismissed the plaintiff's complaint reasoning she could have brought suit naming "John Doe" as a defendant if the identity of the wrongdoer was unknown.

b. Fixed-Period Time Bars

A fixed-period time bar selects an event that the defendant can control or reasonably predict as the trigger that commences the running of the time period. Typically the triggering event is sale by the manufacturer or the time when the product was first purchased for use. After a fixed time period (ranging from 4 to 12 years), a plaintiff is totally barred from bringing his action. These statutes accomplish repose at the expense of considerable unfairness to injured claimants. It should be noted that U.C.C. §2-725 belongs to this category of repose statutes. It provides:

> (1) An action for breach of any contract for sale must be commenced within four years after the cause of action has accrued. By the original agreement the parties may reduce the period of limitation to not less than one year but may not extend it.
> (2) A cause of action accrues when the breach occurs, regardless of the aggrieved party's lack of knowledge of the breach. A breach of warranty occurs when tender of delivery is made, except that where a warranty explicitly extends to future performance of the goods and discovery of the breach must await the time of such performance the cause of action accrues when the breach is or should have been discovered.

The applicability of the U.C.C. statute of limitations to personal injury actions has been a matter of substantial debate in the courts. Many courts will allow the plaintiff to choose between the tort or U.C.C. statute of limitations, whichever is longer. See, e.g., Redfield v. Mead Johnson & Co., 512 P.2d 776 (Or. 1973). In any event, the U.C.C. four-year-from-time-of-sale cutoff generally bars only plaintiff's U.C.C. action for breach of warranty and does not bar the tort suit. See, e.g., Victorson v. Bock Laundry Machine Co., 335 N.E.2d 275 (N.Y. 1975).

To close the open loop of the injury-triggering device, many states have enacted products liability repose statutes. The Oregon statute, Or. Rev. Stat. §30.905 (2003), is illustrative:

STATUTE OF LIMITATIONS FOR PRODUCT LIABILITY CIVIL ACTIONS

(1) Except as provided in ORS 30.907 and 30.908 (1) to (4), a product liability civil action may not be brought for any death, personal injury or property damage that is caused by a product and that occurs more than eight years after the date on which the product was first purchased for use or consumption.

(2) Except as provided in ORS 30.907 and 30.908(1) to (4), a product liability civil action for personal injury or property damage must be commenced not later than the earlier of:

(a) Two years after the date on which the plaintiff discovers, or reasonably should have discovered, the personal injury or property damage and the causal relationship between the injury or damage and the product, or the causal relationship between the injury or damage and the conduct of the defendant; or

(b) Ten years after the date on which the product was first purchased for use or consumption . . .

Plaintiffs can occasionally circumvent statutes of repose by insisting on literal readings of such statutes. In Barber Greene Co. v. Urbantes, 517 So. 2d 768 (Fla. Ct. App. 1988), a 12-year statute of repose governing products liability actions was held not to apply when the products in question were leased rather than sold. Given the equation of leasing and selling elsewhere in products liability law, the distinction in this case at first blush makes no sense. However, the statute reads as follows:

Actions for products liability . . . must be begun within the period prescribed in the chapter, . . . but in any event within 12 years after the date of delivery of the completed product to its original purchaser. . . .

Based on the statutory language, the court held that the statute did not apply to a lease situation.

An interesting problem arises when plaintiffs try to bypass the statutory time period by bringing an action for breach of a post-sale duty to warn. This issue is explored in depth in Frank E. Kulbaski III, Statutes of Repose and the Post-Sale Duty to Warn: Time for a New Interpretation, 32 Conn. L. Rev. 1027 (2000).

Repose statutes have been subjected to sharp attack under state constitutional provisions. Most courts have found them to be constitutional. They have, however, been overturned in several jurisdictions, see infra.

PROBLEM TWENTY-FOUR

Margaret O'Reilly purchased a new Buick Skylark from Darien Motors in September, five years ago. The following July, she was driving the Skylark on the Meadowlane Parkway that runs between Midwood and Santa Anna in New California. She was traveling 75 m.p.h. in a 50 m.p.h. zone when she lost control of her steering. Her car collided with a cement embankment and turned over. O'Reilly was seriously injured as a result of the accident. She considered whether to see a lawyer about bringing an action against General Motors, but she thought that she had lost control of the car due to her speeding. She decided that there was no chance of success and dismissed the lawsuit from her mind.

In September of last year, O'Reilly received a registered recall letter from General Motors. The letter stated that General Motors had been experiencing difficulties with steering mechanisms in Buick Skylarks of the model year she had purchased. Apparently the problem stemmed from a bad batch of steel that had been used on Buick Skylark steering shafts that were manufactured during a certain week. All cars that had serial numbers ending with the letters "AOH" had steering shafts made of steel from the suspect batch. O'Reilly had purchased an AOH car. The letter instructed O'Reilly to bring the car to any local Buick dealer for replacement of the steering mechanism.

When O'Reilly received the recall letter she immediately called you to inquire about proceeding with a lawsuit against General Motors. You told O'Reilly that there might well be statute of limitations problems in this case. However, you explained that without the allegedly defective steering column it would be impossible to establish defect. O'Reilly responded that, strange as it might seem, the car was available for examination. Apparently the New California Safety Council sets up public exhibits in all the major cities to demonstrate the evils of speeding. O'Reilly said that they called her about two months after the accident to ask her for the crushed vehicle to use as an exhibit. She agreed. "The car is in the Midwood Town Square for you to see."

After exploring the matter with those responsible for maintaining the exhibit, you arranged for the vehicle to be dismantled for an examination by an engineer. The report has just arrived at your office. The expert's unequivocal opinion is that the break in the steering column resulted from a fatigue crack rather than from impact. In short, the expert is confident that the steering mechanism failed prior to impact and was a substantial cause of O'Reilly's loss of control of her car.

Now you have a statute of limitations problem. Can you overcome the argument that O'Reilly's case is barred by New California's two-year statute of limitations, which governs all tort actions?

NOTE: CONSTITUTIONALITY OF STATUTES OF REPOSE

Plaintiffs unhappy with summary dismissal of their actions under repose statutes that bar them even before the injury occurs, have challenged their constitutionality under various provisions of state constitutional law. See, e.g., Berry v. Beech Aircraft Corp., 717 P.2d 670 (Utah 1985) (constitutional challenge based on "open courts" provision of the state constitution). Other courts have challenged repose statutes on the grounds that they are arbitrary and unfair. In Lankford v. Sullivan, Long & Hagerty, 416 So. 2d 996 (Ala. 1982), the Alabama Supreme Court held unconstitutional a repose statute that required that a products liability action "must be brought within ten years after the manufactured product is first put to use." It found that it was unlikely that the repose statute would resolve the problems allegedly caused by the "long tail" permitted by an injury-accrual statute. The court then commented:

> The statute, by tying the period to date of use, as opposed to the accrual date of the cause of action, would permit a purchaser of a defective product to sue for injuries re-

ceived nine years and eleven months after the first use, whereas it would bar the action of a purchaser who was injured by the same defective product ten years and one month after he first used the product.

Another arbitrary aspect of the statute, which might more properly be classified as a due process problem, is that it does not provide for an extension of the limitation period for someone injured shortly before the expiration period. Suppose a person was injured on the last day of the ten-year period; presumably he would have to file suit that very day or else be barred by the statute. Thus the limitation period effected by the statute ranges from one day to one year, depending upon when the injury occurs. This is clearly arbitrary. The statute has no savings clause to provide for those injuries occurring near the expiration of the ten-year period. [Id. at 1003.]

The New Hampshire court in Heath v. Sears, Roebuck & Co., 464 A.2d 288 (N.H. 1983), waxed even more eloquent in its decision striking down that state's repose statute:

> The unreasonableness inherent in a statute which eliminates a plaintiff's cause of action before the wrong may reasonably be discovered was noted by Judge Frank [who] condemned the "Alice in Wonderland" effect of such a result:
>
>> Except in topsy-turvy land, you can't die before you are conceived, or be divorced before you marry, or harvest a crop never planted, or burn down a house never built, or miss a train running on a non-existent railroad. For substantially similar reasons, it has always heretofore been accepted, as a sort of logical "axiom," that a statute of limitations does not begin to run against a cause of action before that cause of action exists, i.e., before a judicial remedy is available to a plaintiff.
>
> [Id. at 295-296, quoting from Dincher v. Marlin Firearms Co., 198 F.2d 821, 823 (2d Cir. 1952).]

Ohio has added a new wrinkle to the equation, basing a holding of unconstitutionality on the right to a remedy guaranteed under the state's constitution. In a series of cases, the high court invalidated various parts of Ohio's tort, products, and medical malpractice statutes of repose. In Burgess v. Eli Lilly and Company, 609 N.E.2d 140, 142 (Ohio 1993), the court invalidated a provision whereby the statute began to run for victims of DES exposure as soon as they knew or should have known that they had an injury that "may be related to [DES] exposure," saying: "There is more than a semantic difference between knowing that one has a DES-caused injury and knowing that one *may* have such an injury. A degree of certainty is missing. Knowledge of the possibility that an injury may be related to a specific cause simply does not reach the constitutionally mandated threshold granting every person a remedy in due course of law for an injury done." Ohio again struck down a general tort statute of repose on right-to-remedy-grounds in Brennaman v. R.M.I. Company, 639 N.E.2d 425 (Ohio 1994). Also see Hazine v. Montgomery Elevator Company, 861 P.2d 625 (Ariz. 1993) (holding that the Arizona repose statute violates the state's constitutional provision guaranteeing that a right of action to recover damages for injuries may not be abrogated); Dickie v. Farmers Union Oil Company, 611 N.W.2d 168 (N.D. 2000) (holding that the North Dakota repose statute creates an unconstitutional classification in violation of the equal protection clause of the North Dakota constitution).

But other courts are not as sympathetic to the constitutional challenges. See McIntosh v. Melroe Co., 729 N.E.2d 972, 973 (Ind. 2000) (holding that Indiana's statute of repose that runs from the time of a product's initial delivery "is a permissible legislative decision to limit the liability of manufacturers of goods over ten years old and does not violate [constitutional guarantees]"); Pullum v. Cincinnati, Inc., 476 So. 2d 657, 659 (Fla. 1985) (upholding a Florida statute under an equal protection attack; "holding that . . . [t]he legislature, in enacting this statute of repose, reasonably decided that perpetual liability places an undue burden on manufacturers, and it decided that twelve years from the date of sale is a reasonable time for exposure to liability for manufacturing of a product"); Radke v. H.C. Davis Sons' Mfg. Co., 486 N.W.2d 204 (Neb. 1992) (holding that manufacturers have a right to immunity after a statute of repose has run). For a thorough discussion of the constitutional issues, see Stephen J. Werber, The Constitutional Dimension of a National Products Liability Statute of Repose, 40 Vill. L. Rev. 985 (1995) (includes Appendix listing all states with statutes of repose and the constitutional status). Also see Jerry J. Phillips, An Analysis of Proposed Reform of Products Liability Statutes of Limitations, 56 N.C.U. L. Rev. 663 (1978), and Francis E. McGovern, The Variety, Policy and Constitutionality of Product Liability Statutes of Repose, 30 Am. U. L. Rev. 579 (1981). If these relatively moderate procedural initiatives to limit liability cannot be successfully implemented, manufacturers are likely to push for more draconian changes in substantive law. Although such changes could cause greater retrenchment of the rights of claimants, they are, ironically, likely to be treated with greater deference by the courts. Precisely because they would be substantive and addressed directly to the hard issues, they would be less vulnerable to constitutional challenge.

2. Contract-Based Defenses

In Chapter Nine we will examine whether disclaimers or other contractual limitations on liability will be allowed to blunt causes of actions that are tort based. The student is reminded that contractual arrangements between parties in the distributive chain (e.g., "hold-harmless" clauses or indemnification agreements) are likely to be accorded considerable respect.

3. Worker Compensation Barriers

In Chapter Two we examined the interplay between the worker compensation and products liability compensation systems. Although a few courts have recognized limited exceptions to the immunity of the worker compensation system (e.g., dual capacity, intentional tort, limited contribution), for the most part the products liability compensation system bears the full brunt of defect-related accidents that take place in the workplace environment.

4. Governmental Immunity

A full treatment of governmental immunity is beyond the scope of this text. See generally W. Prosser & P. Keeton, The Law of Torts §131 (5th ed. 1984). Suffice

Non-Conduct-Based Defenses

it to say that in most jurisdictions governmental entities can today be sued for ordinary operational negligence. Where such suits are maintainable, governmental entities are potential defendants in product-related cases. An injury caused by the combined negligence of a governmental entity (in misusing a product) and a product manufacturer (who sold a defective product) should expose the governmental entity to the same liability that would be imposed on a private party.

A significant class of cases has emerged where government negligence has combined with product defect to cause harm in a military setting. In a series of cases the courts have immunized the military from tort liability for injury to members of the armed forces who are injured by governmental negligence in the course of their duties. The leading case is Feres v. United States, 340 U.S. 135 (1950), which held that it would be wrong to subject the military to ordinary tort liability rules; to do so would affect military discipline and subject the military to the myriad tort laws of the 50 states. The Court also held that service-related benefits programs provide military personnel with adequate protection. *Feres* was reaffirmed in United States v. Johnson, 481 U.S. 681, 107 S. Ct. 2063 (1987). The doctrine has been further extended to shield the military from collateral actions for contribution and indemnification. See Stencel Aero Engineering Corp. v. United States, 431 U.S. 666 (1977); In re "Agent Orange" Product Liability Litigation, 603 F. Supp. 239 (E.D. N.Y. 1985). The doctrine outlined above is referred to as the *Feres-Stencel* doctrine.

The practical effect of the *Feres-Stencil* doctrine is that when a defective product causes injury and the military's negligence is a concurrent cause of the harm, the product manufacturer is liable for all the damages suffered by the plaintiff in all states that impose joint and several liability. Suppliers of goods to be used by the military have been most unhappy with this situation. (See the discussion of joint and several liability, supra, pp.67-70.) They, in turn, have sought refuge in a doctrine that has become known as the government contractor defense.

5. *Government Contractor Defense*

When a manufacturer has designed a product for the military in accordance with federal government specifications, the government contractor defense may shield it from liability. Boyle v. United Technologies Corp., 487 U.S. 500 (1988) set the standard for determining when the defense applies. In that case, David Boyle, a Marine helicopter copilot, was killed after his military helicopter crashed off the Virginia coast. Though Boyle survived the initial crash, he was unable to extricate himself from the cockpit and drowned as a result. Plaintiff, representing his deceased son, brought an action against the manufacturer of the helicopter alleging, inter alia, that its cockpit's emergency escape system was defectively designed. In assessing whether the helicopter manufacturer could raise the government contractor defense, the Court set forth the following three-pronged test:

> Liability for design defects in military equipment cannot be imposed, pursuant to state law, when (1) the United States approved reasonably precise specifications; (2) the equipment conformed to those specifications; and (3) the supplier warned the United States about the dangers in the use of the equipment that were known to the supplier but not to the United States. [Id. at 512.]

The Court went on to explain the policies served by these criteria:

> The first two of these conditions assure that the suit is within the area where the policy of the [government's] "discretionary function" would be frustrated — i.e., they assure that the design feature in question was considered by a Government officer, and not merely by the contractor itself. The third condition is necessary because, in its absence, the displacement of state tort law would create some incentive for the manufacturer to withhold knowledge of risks, since conveying that knowledge might disrupt the contract but withholding it would produce no liability. We adopt this provision lest our effort to protect discretionary functions perversely impede them by cutting off information highly relevant to the discretionary decision. [Id.]

Courts have had occasion to speak to *Boyle*'s precise parameters. There is a consensus that manufacturing defect claims are, for the most part, outside the scope of the government contracted defense. The method of manufacture is generally left to the manufacturer and is not the subject of negotiation with the government. See, e.g., Torrington Co. v. Stutzman, 46 S.W.3d 829, 847 (Tex. 2000) (stating that courts have traditionally refrained from applying the defense to manufacturing defects since they are deviations from an intended design that "cannot be considered the product of an exercise of discretion"). If, however, the government would specify how a product should be manufactured, then the government contractor defense might well apply. See Snell v. Bell Helicopter Texron, Inc., 107 F.3d 744, 748 (9th Cir. 1997).

Most courts hold that the defense applies to bar failure to warn as well as design defect claims. Thus, if (1) the government exercised its discretion in approving the warnings, (2) the contractor provided warnings that conformed to the approved warnings, and (3) the contractor warned the government of the dangers in the product's use about which the contractor knew but the government did not, then the adequacy of the warning on the product is not subject to a common-law products liability claim. See, e.g., Densberger v. United Tech. Corp., 297 F.3d 66, 75 (2d Cir. 2002) (interpreting *Boyle* to mean that "ultimate product users cannot sue the contractor for failure to warn if the government controlled which warnings the contractor was allowed to provide"); Emory v. McDonnell Douglas Corp., 148 F.3d 347, 349-50 (4th Cir. 1998) (noting that "many circuits" including the Second, Fifth, Sixth, Seventh, and Ninth have recognized application of the defense in failure to warn cases).

In terms of *Boyle*'s "reasonably precise specifications" requirement, courts have generally found that mere "rubber stamp approval" by the government of a manufacturer's specifications is insufficient to trigger the defense. See Tate v. Boeing Helicopters, 55 F.3d 1150, 1154 (6th Cir. 1995) (holding that the defense cannot be maintained "when the government merely accepts, without any substantive review or evaluation, decisions made by a government contractor"; the policy of protecting the government's discretionary function cannot be served in such a case "because the government made no judgment as to the [product's] particular feature"). As to whether the government contractor defense applies to both nonmilitary and military equipment, "district courts have taken positions on both sides of the question." Yeroshefsky v. Unisys Corp., 962 F. Supp. 710, 717 (D. Md. 1997).

For further treatment of the issue, see Cantu & Young, The Government Contractor Defense: Breaking the *Boyle* Barrier, 62 Alb. L. Rev. 403 (1998); Seidelson, The Government Contractor Defense and the Negligent Contractor: the Devil Made Me Do It, 7 Widener J. Pub. L. 259 (1998); Beh, The Government Contractor Defense: When Do Government Interests Justify Excusing a Manufacturer's Liability for Defective Products?, 28 Seton Hall L. Rev. 430 (1997); Hedrick, the New Single Process Initiative Threatens to Erode the *Boyle* Military Contractor Defense, 24 Transp. L.J. 129 (1997); Cass and Gillette, The Government Contractor Defense: Contractual Allocation of Public Risk, 77 Va. L. Rev. 257 (1991); Green and Matasar, The Supreme Court and the Products Liability Crisis: Lessons from *Boyle*'s Government Contractor Defense, 63 S. Cal. L. Rev. 637 (1990).

PART III
Special Problem Areas

CHAPTER NINE
Special Products and Product Markets

A. COMPONENT PARTS AND RAW MATERIALS

Comment *b* to §19 of the Products Liability Restatement, enlarging on the definition of "product," contains the general rule governing component parts: "Component parts are products, whether sold or distributed separately or assembled with other component parts. An assemblage of component parts is also, itself, a product. Raw materials are products, whether manufactured, such as sheet metal; processed, such as lumber; or gathered and sold or distributed in raw condition, such as unwashed gravel and farm produce." As sellers of products, sellers of component parts and raw materials are liable in tort for harm caused by product defects. If that were all there were to the story of component parts, the subject could hardly be deemed special enough to warrant separate treatment in a section of its own. Consider the following materials.

Zaza v. Marquess & Nell, Inc.
675 A.2d 620 (N.J. 1996)

This appeal presents the question of whether . . . a component part fabricator that builds a system component in accordance with the specifications of the owner, which component is not dangerous until it is integrated into the larger system, can be held strictly liable to an injured employee for the failure of the owner, installer-assembler, and training consultant to install safety devices and provide warnings. The Appellate Division[, reversing summary judgment for defendant,] found that such a fabricator could be held strictly liable. We now reverse.

I

On January 28, 1990, plaintiff Gerardo Zaza, an employee of Maxwell House Coffee (Maxwell House), a division of General Foods Manufacturing Corporation, discovered a clog in a quench tank located in the Hoboken plant. While working to repair the quench tank, hot molten water and carbon within the quench tank overflowed and landed on plaintiff's back, arms and upper extremities, causing second degree burns over twenty-one percent of plaintiff's body.

The quench tank is an integral part of a large, complex manufacturing process — the Maxwell House trecar-carbon regeneration system — which is used to produce decaffeinated coffee beans. The system contains a multiple hearth furnace, a quench tank, and numerous pipes, watering screws, scrubbers and fans. All of those parts must be fully integrated and assembled in order to create a properly working trecar-carbon regeneration system. It is a two-fold system. In the top portion of the system, the ultimate coffee product is made, and a byproduct (carbon) is reclaimed in the lower portion. The quench tank is located in the lower portion where the carbon regeneration process takes place. After the basic coffee product has been made in the top portion, the carbon, which has been heated in the multiple hearth furnace to 1700 degrees Fahrenheit, leaves the furnace through a large tube and enters the quench tank. At the same time the molten carbon enters the quench tank, cool water is pumped into the quench tank at the rate of twenty-two gallons per minute. The superheated carbon-water mixture moves through the quench tank for approximately thirty minutes, then exits the tank through two pipelines, and finally comes to rest in separate storage tanks where it is kept for future processing.

The initial designs for the quench tank were prepared by Maxwell House and were submitted to the engineering firm of Marquess and Nell, Inc., (Marquess) who prepared the final design plans. Marquess contracted with defendant International Sheet Metal & Plate Mfg., Inc. (International) for a fabricated quench-tank. Maxwell House hired Brennan Company, Inc. (Brennan) to assemble and integrate the trecar-carbon regeneration system. Calgon Carbon Company (Calgon) was hired to prepare training materials on how to operate the system and to educate Maxwell House employees in the use of the trecar-carbon regeneration system. William J. Merz, an engineer employed by Calgon, conducted a training session for Maxwell House employees on how to use the trecar-carbon regeneration system, including the quench tank. Plaintiff attended the training session.

The specifications on which defendant bid for the quench tank did not require that the fabricator prepare or install any safety devices. Rather, the specifications called for the fabricator to cut holes for the safety devices. The quench tank fabricated by defendant is best described as a stainless steel tank with holes in it. The tank also contains six flanges, which are devices used to hold pipes in place. The quench tank was sold to Maxwell for $7,400. When it was delivered to Maxwell House, professional installers had to connect water ingress piping, carbon extrusion piping and water discharge piping before it could be made operational.

The final plans and specifications for the trecar-carbon regeneration system incorporated three safety devices designed to avoid an overflow of the molten fluid out of the quench tank. These safety devices were to be installed by Maxwell House and Brennan. The devices included a spectacle shut-off valve, a high-level fluid sensor, and an overflow pipe. The spectacle shut-off valve was designed to stop the flow of the molten carbon from leaving the hearth furnace and entering the quench tank whenever personnel were working on the quench tank or associated piping. It was supposed to be located in the chute between the hearth furnace and the quench tank. The high-level fluid sensor was designed to trigger an alarm and light whenever the fluid level in the quench tank reached a dangerous level. The overflow pipe was to be located eight inches below the top of the quench tank and was designed to divert the fluids within the quench tank through a piping system to another location away from the user if the fluids reached a high level within the tank. It is uncontroverted that the installation of the overflow pipe would have prevented the quench tank from pouring out its molten contents on plaintiff.

Although all three safety devices were included in the design plans prepared by Marquess, none was actually in operation at the time plaintiff sustained his injuries. Brennan, the installer, claims that its function was to install and integrate the quench tank into the system based on the plans provided to it by Maxwell House, that Maxwell House decided to omit the safety devices recommended by Marquess, and that Maxwell House approved the installation. Maxwell House's decision to omit the safety devices appears to have been deliberate. Although the spectacle shut-off valve was on site and available when the tank was being installed, Maxwell House chose not to install it. When an engineer informed Maxwell House of the omission, the company chose to disregard the advice. . . .

II

We first focus on whether a fabricator, who produces a non-defective component part for an integrated manufacturing system in accordance with the designs and specifications of the owner, has a legal duty to ensure that the owner and installer-assembler properly integrate the component into the system. . . .

IV

Plaintiff contends that International had a non-delegable duty to see that Maxwell House and its team of hired professional assemblers properly integrated the quench tank into the trecar-carbon regeneration system. But the cases cited by plaintiff involved either suits against manufacturers of finished products or rebuilders of machinery. It was within the power of the defendants in those cases to install safety devices. In contrast, the fabricator of a component part that is not inherently dangerous has no control over whether the purchaser properly installs the component part into the final system.

Where a finished product is the result of work by more than one party, a court must examine at what stage installation of safety devices is feasible and practicable. In many jurisdictions, responsibility for installing a safety device is determined by reference to three criteria: (1) the trade custom indicating the party that normally would install the safety device; (2) the relative expertise of the parties, looking to which party is best acquainted with the design problems and safety techniques in question; and (3) practicality, focusing on the stage at which installation of the device is most feasible. See, e.g., Verge v. Ford Motor Co., 581 F.2d 384 (3d Cir. 1978) . . .

V

In its recent draft, the American Law Institute (A.L.I.) concluded that a component part manufacturer generally is not liable unless the component itself is defective or the component provider substantially participated in the design of the final product.

[I]t would be unjust, impractical, and inefficient to impose liability solely on the ground that the manufacturer of the integrated product utilizes the component in a manner that renders the integrated product defective. To hold a component supplier to the same liability as the seller of the integrated product would require the component seller to scrutinize another's product with respect to which the component seller has no role in developing. This would impose substantial costs on the component seller, who would have to develop sufficient sophistication to review the decisions of the business entity that already has assumed responsibility with regard to the integrated product.

[Restatement (Third) of Torts §10 cmt. *a* (Tentative Draft No. 3, 1996) (hereinafter Restatement, Tentative Draft).]

The majority of courts from other jurisdictions have held that a manufacturer of a component part, which is not dangerous until it is integrated by the owner into a larger system, cannot be held strictly liable to an injured employee for the failure of the owner and/or assembler to install safety devices, so long as the specifications provided are not so obviously dangerous that it would be unreasonable to follow them. For example, in Jordan v. Whiting Corp., 49 Mich. App. 481, 212 N.W.2d 324 (1973), *rev'd* in part on other grounds, 396 Mich. 145, 240 N.W.2d 468 (1976), a plaintiff brought suit against the manufacturer of component parts used in a crane. The plaintiff alleged that the assembled crane was defectively designed. However, the component parts were not in and of themselves defective. The trial court granted a directed verdict to the component part manufacturer and the verdict was affirmed on appeal. The appellate court stated:

> The obligation that generates the duty to avoid injury to another which is reasonably foreseeable does not — at least yet — extend to the anticipation of how manufactured components not in and of themselves dangerous or defective can become potentially dangerous dependent upon the nature of their integration into a unit designed, assembled, installed, and sold by another. [*Jordan*, supra, 212 N.W.2d at 328.] . . .

Plaintiff does not allege any manufacturing defect in the quench tank itself. The quench tank was not in and of itself dangerous or defective. It was a sheet metal tank with holes in it. Specifically, plaintiff's expert alleged that "the design of the Quench tank was improper in not including an overflow pipe and/or an automatic shutoff when the superheated carbon-water mixture reached a certain level in the Quench tank." . . .

[I]t was not feasible, practical, or reasonable for defendant, a sheet metal fabricator with no prior experience in the assembly and installation of trecar-carbon regeneration systems, to attach the safety devices to the quench tank. The safety devices could not have been incorporated into the quench tank at its factory. The shut-off valve was not located in or on the quench tank, but rather in the chute between the hearth furnace and the tank. Similarly, installation of the overflow line required that the tank be first installed in Maxwell House's plant. Further, defendant lacked the expertise required to attach the safety devices and to integrate the tank into the trecar-carbon regeneration system — a system that was actually composed of separate "systems" interfacing with one another.

Furthermore the work performed by Maxwell House and its assemblers in order to integrate the quench tank into the trecar-carbon regeneration system constituted a substantial change to the quench tank. Before it became part of the complex trecar-regeneration system, the quench tank was merely an isolated unoperative component. It was not until it was installed as part of the regeneration system that it became a functional, operative product.

As stated previously, the critical issue in design-defect cases is the reasonableness of the manufacturer in marketing that design. International acted in a reasonably prudent manner in fabricating the quench tank and in delivering it to Maxwell House without incorporating the safety devices. It was not feasible or practical for defendant to attach the safety devices to the tank. International manufactured the quench tank in strict accordance with the specifications provided by Maxwell House, a knowledgeable and experienced purchaser and user. International was not the designer, manufacturer, or installer of the trecar-carbon regeneration system.

International is in the business of welding sheet metal to form tanks and other objects. It is a small family-run business located in a one-story cinder block building, that employs fifteen people, many of whom are family members. International was not expected to, and did not have, the experience or the ability to integrate and assemble all the complex parts of the total trecar-carbon regeneration system. That system was so complex that even Maxwell House, a large company skilled for years in the making of coffee, did not have enough expertise to install and assemble the system. Maxwell House found it necessary to hire Brennan, an outside company, to assemble and integrate the trecar-carbon regeneration system. Maxwell House also found it necessary to hire Calgon to prepare training manuals for its employees in the use of the trecar-carbon regeneration system and to instruct its employees on how to operate the system.

The design plans provided that the safety devices would be provided by others. International acted reasonably in relying on Maxwell House and its experienced assemblers, two entities with superior knowledge of the trecar-carbon regeneration system, to properly install the tank into the complicated system. Defendant had no control over the quench tank once it was sold and no control over the final assembly of the system. Maxwell House retained complete control over the design of the regeneration system and the quench tank's installation into the system.

It was not defendant's failure to attach the safety devices in the quench tank that caused plaintiff's injury. Defendant did exactly what it was paid $7,400 to do; its sole obligation was to produce a component part that was safe and satisfactory according to the specifications provided by Maxwell House. It did that. Under those circumstances, we find that International is not strictly liable for its failure to install the safety devices on the quench tank.

VII

Plaintiff also asserts that International had a duty to warn of the dangers of operating the quench tank without safety devices. . . .

The majority of jurisdictions also hold that a supplier of a component part that does not contain a latent defect has no duty to warn the subsequent assembler of any danger that may arise after the components are assembled. Mitchell v. Sky Climber Inc., 396 Mass. 629, 487 N.E.2d 1374, 1376 (1986); see Frazier v. Materials Transp. Co., 609 F. Supp. 933 (W.D. Pa. 1985); . . . For example, in . . . [Munger v. Herder Mfg. Corp., 456 N.Y.S.2d 271 (1982)], an employee of the Scott Paper Company was injured when the arm of a tension roll assembly in a paper machine fell upon him. The injured employee sued the four corporations that manufactured various components of the paper machine. The plaintiff argued that each of the component part manufacturers had a duty to foresee and warn employees that Scott might not post appropriate warnings. The court disagreed, holding that in the absence of any proof that the component designs were defective or that the parts were wrongfully manufactured, no public policy can be served by imposing liability on a manufacturer of specialized parts of a highly technical machine, particularly when, as here, the parts were created in accordance with the design, plans and specifications of the owner and assembler of the unit. Id. 456 N.Y.S.2d at 273. . . .

The prevailing view is that a manufacturer of a component part, not dangerous in and of itself, does not have a duty to warn an employee of the immediate purchaser of the component where the immediate purchaser is aware of the need to attach safety devices. Restatement, Tentative Draft §10 cmt. *b*. For example, in Crossfield v. Quality Control Equipment Co., 1 F.3d 701, 704 (8th Cir. 1993), the court held that, under Missouri law, the supplier of a non-defective chain for use in a machine that malfunctioned did not have a duty to warn. The court stated:

> To impose responsibility on the supplier of the chain in the context of the larger defectively designed machine system would simply extend liability too far. This would mean that suppliers would be required to hire machine design experts to scrutinize machine systems that the supplier had no role in developing. Suppliers would be forced to provide modifications and attach warnings on machines that they never designed nor manufactured. Mere suppliers cannot be expected to guarantee the safety of other manufacturers' machinery. [Ibid.]

Similarly, in Lesnefsky v. Fischer & Porter Co., 527 F. Supp. 951 (E.D. Pa. 1981), the court held that a manufacturer of a control panel for a brewery cooker was not liable for injuries sustained by an employee of the brewery where it appeared that the control panel was manufactured according to the brewery's specifications, the brewery had superior knowledge about the operations of such equipment, and the brewery maintained complete control over the installation of the equipment. The plaintiff, an employee of the brewery, was injured when boiling water spilled out of an access port on the cooker. Id. at 953. The cooker was operated by a control panel manufactured by the defendant pursuant to the specifications provided by the brewery. Ibid. The plaintiff argued that the defendant was liable for not designing a temperature override control or a shut-off valve and because the defendant had a duty to warn the user of the inherent risks involved in operating the cooker without such safety devices. Ibid. The component part manufacturer alleged that it was not liable since it did not design, manufacture or install the steam valve or hatch cover, the parts which caused the plaintiff's injuries. Ibid. The court agreed, stating that the component part was not defective and there was no evidence that the part was so obviously dangerous that the manufacturer had an obligation to warn the ultimate user of the risk, or to refuse to manufacture the panel without making modifications. The court also noted that the manufacturer lacked the expertise required to recognize risks which might arise in the operation of the control panel in the brewery. Id. at 954. . . .

Holding defendant liable would impose on a component part fabricator, whose products were built in accordance with the designer's specifications and whose part when it left defendant's plant was not defective, the duty to investigate whether the use of its nondefective product would be made dangerous by the integration of that product into the complex system designed and installed by experts. Component fabricators would become insurers for the mistakes and failures of the owners and installers to follow their own plans. Defendant would have to retain an expert to determine whether each and every integrated manufacturing system that incorporates one of its sheet metal products is reasonably safe for its intended use. In Bond v. E.I. DuPont De Nemours & Co., 868 P.2d 1114, 1120 (Colo. App. 1993), the court in holding that a seller of Teflon integrated by the manufacturer in a prosthesis had no duty to warn observed: "there is little social utility in placing the burden on a manufacturer of component parts or supplier of raw materials against injuries caused by the final product when the component parts or raw materials themselves were not unreasonably dangerous." See also Kealoha v. E.I. DuPont de Nemours & Co., 844 F. Supp. 590, 594 (D. Hawaii 1994) ("Permitting plaintiffs to maintain a suit against the bulk suppier of inherently safe raw materials would lead to absurd consequences: there would be no end to potential liability if every manufacturer of nuts, bolts and screws could be held liable when this hardware was used in a defective product."). . . .

It would serve no useful purpose to hold defendant strictly liable to plaintiff for the failure of Maxwell House and its installer-assembler, Brennan, to install the safety devices or for its failure and the failure of its trainer, Calgon, to adequately warn plaintiff. Holding defendant liable would result in an unreasonable expansion of the products liability law. "In the developing steps towards higher consumer and user protection through higher trade morality and responsibility, the law should view trade relations realistically rather than mythically." Schipper v. Levitt and Sons, Inc., 44 N.J. 70, 99, 207 A.2d 314 (1965).

Accordingly, we reverse the judgment of the Appellate Division and grant summary judgment in favor of defendant International.

[Dissenting opinion omitted].

The court in *Zaza* refers to Restatement (Third) of Torts: Products Liability §10, Tentative Draft No. 3, 1996. In the final draft of the Restatement that section was slightly modified and renumbered:

Restatement (Third) of Torts: Products Liability
(1998)

§5. **LIABILITY OF COMMERCIAL SELLER OR DISTRIBUTOR OF PRODUCT COMPONENTS FOR HARM CAUSED BY PRODUCTS INTO WHICH COMPONENTS ARE INTEGRATED**

One engaged in the business of selling or otherwise distributing product components who sells or distributes a component is subject to liability for harm to persons or property caused by a product into which the component is integrated if:

(a) the component is defective in itself, as defined in this Chapter, and the defect causes the harm; or

(b)(1) the seller or distributor of the component substantially participates in the integration of the component into the design of the product; and

(2) the integration of the component causes the product to be defective, as defined in this Chapter, and

(3) the defect in the product causes the harm.

The case law strongly supports the Restatement's position. In In re Temporomandibular Joint (TMJ) Implants Products Liability Litigation. 97 F.3d 1050 (8th Cir. 1996), applying Minnesota law, the court of appeals affirmed summary judgment for a manufacturer of Teflon film incorporated into joint implants. The court reasoned that the failure of the Teflon product was not due to a flaw in the component part itself but because the implant manufacturer had made an "erroneous decision to incorporate what turned out to be an unsuitable material into its implants." Id. at 1157. Thus, the film manufacturer could not be held strictly liable for implant failure. See Id. at 1056-57. The court further explained that

> making suppliers of inherently safe raw materials and component parts pay for the mistakes of the finished product manufacturer would not only be unfair, but it also would impose an intolerable burden on the business world, especially where, as here, the raw material or component part . . . accounts for only a few cents worth of the cost of the entire finished product. . . . [Id.]

The court noted, however, that a supplier of component parts could be held strictly liable for product failure if "the parts it supplies were specially designed for a particular use. . . ." Id. at 1056 n.8. (citing Fleck v. KDI Sylvan Pools. Inc., 981 F.2d 107,118 (3d Cir. 1992)). Also see Port Authority of New York & New Jersey v. Arcadian Corp., 189 F.3d 305 (3d Cir. 1999) (relying on *Zaza* and affirming dismissal of design defect claim against fertilizer manufacturer under both New Jersey and New York law where terrorists had incorporated defendant's fertilizer into explosive devices detonated under the World Trade Center); In re Silicone Gel Breast Implants Product Liability Lit., 996 F. Supp. 1110 (N.D. Ala. 1997) (relying on Restatement (Third) of Torts: Products Liability §5 and granting summary judgment to silicone manufacturer which supplied material for silicone gel breast implants that caused injuries under both the sophisticated bulk purchaser and component sellers doctrines); Cimino v. Raymark Indus., 151 F.3d 297 (5th Cir. 1998) (relying on Restatement (Third) of Torts: Products Liability §5 and holding that manufacturer's asbestos was not "defective in itself" pursuant to Restatement §2, and that manufacturer of asbestos, which sold it for incorporation into fiberboard insulation but did not substantially participate in the integration of asbestos into fiberboard, was not liable for design defect or failure to warn in personal injury and wrongful death action). For a congressional attempt to limit the liability of suppliers of raw materials and component parts that are sold to medical implant manufacturers, see Biomaterials Access Assurance Act, Pub. L. No. 105-230 (1998). For an article employing a "cheapest cost avoider" approach determining the liability of component manufacturers, see David A. Fischer, Product Liability: A Commentary on the Liability of Suppliers of Component Parts and Raw Materials, 53 S.C. L. Rev. 1137 (2002). For an excellent review of the authority, see Edward M. Mansfield, Reflections on Current Limits

authors' dialogue 19

AARON: Remember how we were going to handle component parts in the Restatement when we started?

JIM: I sure do. We were simply going to state the obvious — that component parts are products, in their own right. And we followed through on our plan. The third sentence in Comment *b* to §19 says that "Component parts are products, whether sold or distributed separately or assembled with other component parts." And Comment *b* also says that raw materials are products, whether manufactured, processed, or simply gathered and sold in their natural state. But we didn't see any need for a separate section on the subject of component parts.

AARON: Well, how did the subject get onto our radar screen to wind up in §5? I seem to recall that one of our advisers urged us to look into it. John Frank, a lawyer from Phoenix, I think.

JIM: You're right, except John wasn't an adviser. He's a member of the A.L.I. Council, the governing body that screens and supervises all the Restatement work of the Institute.

AARON: Whatever. I just remember that he was the one who told us it was a "hot" topic and we ought to look into it. At first, I don't think we understood what he was talking about. Of course if a defective component gets incorporated into a product, it makes the product defective, also. Who needs a special section to make that clear? But we went ahead and read some cases and realized that it was at least arguable that the manufacturer of a nondefective component should be liable when the component's inclusion in an integrated product makes the integrated product defective. That was the aspect that we hadn't understood earlier.

JIM: Remember the *Cronin* decision in California, in Chapter One? (See p.33, supra.) Defective bread racks in a bakery truck collapsed and harmed the plaintiff in a minor fender bender. Remember how the plaintiff joined General Motors, the manufacturer of the truck chassis, along with Olson, the company who assembled the bread truck? When we discussed *Cronin* in class, we couldn't figure any way, except searching for deep pockets, that GM could be liable for the failure of the bread racks. Maybe there was evidence that GM was actively involved in the truck assembly.

AARON: But that wouldn't be enough under §5 unless GM's chassis somehow contributed to making the bread racks weaker.

JIM: You're right. No wonder the plaintiff agreed to dismissing GM from the *Cronin* case prior to trial. (See p.34, n.3.)

on Component and Raw Material Supplier Liability and the Proposed Third Restatement, 84 Chi.-Kent L. Rev. 22 (1995). For a dissenting view, see Mark M. Hager, Don't Say I Didn't Warn You Even Though I Didn't: Why the Pro-Defendant Consensus on Warning Law Is Wrong, 61 Tenn. L. Rev. 1125 (1994).

B. PRESCRIPTION DRUGS AND MEDICAL DEVICES

Liability for harm caused by prescription drugs and medical devices is generally predicated on the failure of the manufacturer to adequately warn the prescribing physician of risks associated with the use of the product. Manufacturers and other distributors are liable for manufacturing defects, but most cases involve failure to warn. Less often, though with increasing frequency, plaintiffs claim that the manufacturer should have warned them directly. Even less often, plaintiff's claim that a prescription drug was defectively designed.

1. Liability Based on Failure to Warn

a. Warning the Health Care Provider

Any analysis of liability for prescription drugs must begin with the following comment to §402A of the Restatement of Torts (Second).

Restatement (Second) of Torts
(1965)

§402A. SPECIAL LIABILITY OF SELLER OF PRODUCT FOR PHYSICAL HARM TO USER OR CONSUMER

COMMENT

k. Unavoidably unsafe products. There are some products which, in the present state of human knowledge, are quite incapable of being made safe for their intended and ordinary use. These are especially common in the field of drugs. An outstanding example is the vaccine for the Pasteur treatment of rabies, which not uncommonly leads to very serious and damaging consequences when it is injected. Since the disease itself invariably leads to a dreadful death, both the marketing and the use of the vaccine are fully justified, notwithstanding the unavoidable high degree of risk which they involve. Such a product, properly prepared, and accompanied by proper directions and warning, is not defective, nor is it *unreasonably* dangerous. The same is true of many other drugs, vaccines, and the like, many of which for this very reason cannot legally be sold except to physicians, or under the prescription of a physician. It is also true in particular of many new or experimental drugs as to which, because of lack of time and opportunity for sufficient medical experience, there can be no assurance of safety, or perhaps even of purity of ingredients, but such experience as there is justifies the marketing and use of the drug notwithstanding a medically recognizable risk. The seller of such products, again with the qualification that they are properly prepared and marketed, and proper warning is given, where the situation calls for it, is not to be held to strict liability for unfortunate consequences attending their use, merely because he has undertaken to supply the public with an apparently useful and desirable product, attended with a known but apparently reasonable risk.

In the several decades following promulgation of §402A by the American Law Institute, Comment *k* was interpreted by courts to limit the duty of drug manufacturers to providing adequate warnings to learned intermediaries—the physicians who prescribe drugs and who make sure that the right drugs reach the right patients. Under the so-called "learned intermediary rule," manufacturers need not warn patients directly, nor will courts review the reasonableness of prescription drug designs. The learned intermediary rule retains its vitality in the vast majority of courts. See, e.g., Talley v. Danek Medical, Inc., 179 F.3d 154 (4th Cir. 1999) (a spinal implant manufacturer satisfied its duty to warn by providing adequate warnings about the implant to an injured recipient's physician); Martin v. Hacker, 628 N.E.2d 1308 (N.Y. 1993) (finding warnings sufficient to convey the suicidal effects of Reserpine to a reasonably prudent physician). Several courts have followed the rationale of the learned intermediary rule and applied the doctrine to cases involving prescription medical devices. See, e.g., Vaccariello v. Smith & Nephew Richards, Inc., 763 N.E.2d 160 (Ohio 2002) (pedicle screw); Ellis v. C.R. Bard, Inc., 311 F.3d 1272 (11th Cir. 2002) (Morphine-drip pump). The Products Liability Restatement sets out the traditional learned intermediary rule in this way:

Restatement (Third) of Torts: Products Liability
(1998)

§6. Liability of Commercial Seller or Distributor for Harm Caused by Defective Prescription Drugs and Medical Devices

(a) A manufacturer of a prescription drug or medical device who sells or otherwise distributes a defective drug or medical device is subject to liability for harm to persons caused by the defect. A prescription drug or medical device is one that may be legally sold or otherwise distributed only pursuant to a health-care provider's prescription.

(b) For purposes of liability under Subsection (a), a prescription drug or medical device is defective if at the time of sale or other distribution the drug or medical device:

. . .

(3) is not reasonably safe due to inadequate instructions or warnings as defined in Subsection (d).

. . .

(d) A prescription drug or medical device is not reasonably safe due to inadequate instructions or warnings if reasonable instructions or warnings regarding foreseeable risks of harm are not provided to:

(1) prescribing and other health-care providers who are in a position to reduce the risks of harm in accordance with the instructions or warnings. . . .

COMMENT:

. . .

b. Rationale. The obligation of a manufacturer to warn about risks attendant to the use of drugs and medical devices that may be sold only pursuant to a health-care provider's prescription traditionally has required warnings directed to health-care providers and not to patients. The rationale supporting this "learned intermediary" rule is that only health-care professionals are in a position to understand the significance of the risks involved and to assess the relative advantages and disadvantages of a given form of prescription-based therapy. The duty then devolves on the health-care provider to supply to the patient such information as is deemed appropriate under the circumstances so that the patient can make an informed choice as to therapy. Subsection (d)(1) retains the "learned intermediary" rule. . . .

d. Manufacturers' liability for failure adequately to instruct or warn prescribing and other health-care providers. Failure to instruct or warn is a major basis of liability for manufacturers of prescription drugs and medical devices. When prescribing health-care providers are adequately informed of the relevant benefits and risks associated with various prescription drugs and medical devices, they can reach appropriate decisions regarding which drug or device is best for specific patients. Sometimes a warning serves to inform health-care providers of unavoidable risks that inhere in the drug and medical device. By definition, such a warning would not aid the health-care provider in reducing the risk of injury to the patient by taking precautions in how the drug is administered or the medical device is used. However, warnings of unavoidable risks allow the health-care provider, and thereby the patient, to make an informed choice whether to utilize the drug or medical device. Beyond informing prescribing health-care providers, a drug or device manufacturer may have a duty under the law of negligence to use reasonable measures to supply instructions or warnings to nonprescribing health-care providers who are in positions to act on such information so as to reduce or prevent injury to patients.

Sterling Drug, Inc. v. Yarrow
408 F.2d 978 (8th Cir. 1969)

BECKER, C.D.J.

[The plaintiff, a South Dakota housewife, brought an action against Sterling Drug, Inc., claiming that her vision had been permanently damaged by the use of "Aralen," a prescription drug manufactured and sold by the defendant for use in the treatment of rheumatoid arthritis and other diseases. The plaintiff claimed that Sterling had been negligent in testing, manufacturing, and marketing the drug, and in failing to warn the public, the plaintiff, her physician, and retail druggists of the potential dangers from use of the drug. Sitting without a jury, the trial judge found that the defendant had negligently failed to warn the plaintiff's prescribing physician, and entered judgment for $180,000. The plaintiff had begun using Aralen in 1958, when her physician, Dr. Olson, had been introduced to Aralen by one of Sterling's traveling salesmen or "detail men." The plaintiff used the drug on a daily basis until October 19, 1964, when it was discontinued on the advice of Dr. Olson at the time of a complete physical examination. The physical examination was made at the suggestion of the plaintiff's ophthalmologist, who had observed a deterioration of the plaintiff's vision and suspected that it might be caused by the medications she was taking. At no time up to and including October 19, 1964, had Dr. Olson read or heard of any warnings concerning irreversible vision loss (chloroquine retinopathy) caused by taking Aralen, except from the plaintiff's ophthalmologist. Nevertheless, he discontinued the plaintiff's medication on October 19, 1964. A follow-up examination in January, 1965, revealed a marked deterioration in the plaintiff's condition.

The opinion outlines the advancements in knowledge of the side effects of chloroquine phosphate (marketed by the appellant under the registered trademark name "Aralen") prior to October 19, 1964. Beginning in 1957, reports in various medical journals indicated that the drug was causing, or might be causing, side effects of the sort suffered by the plaintiff. The opinion continues:]

The evidence strongly supports the findings of the trial court that appellant usually communicates its product information to physicians prescribing its products:

(1) by "detail men," who are specially trained field representatives engaged in selling and promoting the use of its products by personal calls in which oral presentations are made and literature and samples delivered,
(2) by listings of drugs in an annually published advertising medium known as Physicians' Desk Reference,
(3) by "product cards" which are mailed and distributed by detail men to physicians and are available at medical conventions and hospital exhibits, and
(4) by special letters mailed to physicians.

The evidence summarized in part hereinabove also strongly supports the finding of the trial court that, beginning in 1957, medical publications suggested some connection between retinal eye changes and chloroquine; that from the medical publications this connection became increasingly evident by the year 1959 and reasonably apparent in the year 1962; that in 1961 reports that the retinal changes associated with the drug were irreversible began to appear.

These publications were received currently and read carefully by the medical librarians in the medical department of appellant, which also supplied information to physicians and medical information and instruction to detail men trained under the auspices of the Department of Sales Promotion of appellant.

Nevertheless, the detail men who made regular personal calls on prescribing physicians and customers were never, in the relevant period, instructed to invite attention of the physicians and customers to the reported dangers of irreversible retinal damage from prolonged use of the drug by patients. The warnings of side effects in general, and of retinal damage in particular, when given by appellant were limited to the product cards, the Physicians' Desk Reference and to the "Dear Doctor" letter dated February 1963, discussed hereinafter.

The record shows that appellant was contemporaneously aware of the reports, summarized above, that chloroquine phosphate caused irreversible retinal damage in a substantial percentage of those using the recommended dosage for rheumatoid arthritis for extended periods of time. The evidence supports the findings of fact of the trial court concerning the limited nature of warnings given by appellant to those prescribing the drug. These findings of fact are not clearly erroneous within the meaning of Rule 52(a) F.R. Civ. P.

On this record of the medical reports summarized above, the trial court would have been warranted in holding that the warnings on the product cards and in the Physicians' Desk Reference concerning irreversible retinal damage did not always, in the relevant period, represent the full state of the reported medical knowledge in respect to the percentage of patients affected, the irreversibility of the retinal damage and the toxicity of the recommended drug in affected cases. (This is mentioned because appellant contends that the judgment below should be reversed outright on the ground that a submissible case of failure to warn was not made on any theory.)

Dr. Foley, appellant's Medical Director and Vice-President, testified that in August 1962, because of appearance of additional reports of side effects of chloroquine, that he, and other members of appellant's staff, felt that appellant should add additional information in the literature on the drug. To do so (he testified) appellant's staff consulted with the Food and Drug Administration until January 1963, finally developing the letter, the "Dear Doctor" letter. In the meantime, no special warning was given physicians. During this period appellant's staff was unwilling to accept the accuracy of the percentages of affected patients reported in the medical literature, and questioned the figures. Finally in January 1963, through its advertising department, appellant contracted with a mailing service, specializing in mailings to the medical profession, for the mailing of the "Dear Doctor" letter to all physicians and hospital personnel in the United States. Some 248,000 copies of the letter were reproduced, were mailed in envelopes addressed by addressograph plates and sent by first class mail. The letter read as follows:

IMPORTANT DRUG PRECAUTIONS
Dear Doctor:
The recent experience of various investigators has shown that Aralen® (brand of chloroquine), used alone or as an adjunct to other drugs and therapeutic measures, may be very helpful in the management of patients with lupus erythematosus or rheumatoid arthritis. Although many physicians have found that the incidence of serious side effects is lower than that encountered with other potent agents that are often employed in such patients, certain ocular complications have sometimes been reported during prolonged daily administration of chloroquine. Therefore, when chloroquine or any other antimalarial compound is to be given for long periods, it is essential that measures be taken to avoid or minimize these complications.

Thus initial and periodic (trimonthly) ophthalmologic examinations (including expert slit-lamp, fundus and visual field studies) should be performed. The initial examination will reveal if any visual abnormalities, either coincidental or due to the disease, are present and will establish a base line for further assessment of the patient's vision. Should corneal changes occur (which are thought to be reversible and which sometimes even fade on continuance of treatment), the advantages of withdrawing the drug must be weighed in each case against the therapeutic benefits that may accrue from continuation of treatment (sometimes a severe relapse follows withdrawal). If visual disturbances occur — which are not fully explainable by difficulties of accommodation or corneal opacities — and particularly if there is any suggestion of visual field restriction or retinal change, administration of the drug should be stopped immediately and the patient closely observed for possible progression.

We should like to request your cooperation in reporting to Winthrop Laboratories or to the Food and Drug Administration any patients in your own practice who have developed impairment of vision or retinal change during or subsequent to the administration of chloroquine.

A reference card of a convenient size for filing is enclosed. It contains information on the various indications for Aralen (including lupus erythematosus, rheumatoid arthritis, malaria and amebiasis), dosage, side effects and precautions.

>Very truly yours,
>WINTHROP LABORATORIES
>/s/ E.J. Foley
>E. J. Foley, M.D.
>Vice President
>Medical Director

Dr. Justus B. Rice, who retired in 1960, formerly Director of the Department of Medical Research of appellant, called by appellant as an expert witness for appellant, testified in part as follows:

Q. Now, let me ask you this first, doctor: in view of the seriousness of the situation, why wasn't [sic] these letters sent out by registered mail or certified mail?
A. I have no idea. This all happened after I left, and was not in my department.
Q. I realize that, but you had been with this company for how many years?
A. Since 1937; about 23 years.
Q. And had been a vice president of it?
A. That's right.
Q. And let me ask you this: based on your experience, wasn't there one way to make sure that every doctor had the information, and that was to instruct your detail men to call on every doctor?
A. I don't know whether that would have done it or not.
Q. But that would have been a way of having a personal contact, wouldn't it?
A. It might have.
Q. Yes. And a personal contact, then, would be something that we could show here in court, couldn't we?
A. I don't know how you'd show it.
Q. Well, after all is said and done, I'll put it this way: you're here, Dr. Rice, and I'm here?
A. Yes.
Q. Now if five years later or ten years later, one of us says that he wasn't here, don't you think it's easy to prove with the people that are here in this courtroom?
A. Yes, that's a case.

Appellant called as an expert on practices in the drug industry Dr. George Hazel, Vice President of Medical Affairs of Abbott Laboratories, which did not supply chloroquine phosphate. Dr. Hazel undertook to testify, without objection, as an expert on the actions and alleged omissions of appellant under industry custom. On cross-examination this witness testified as follows:

Q. Well, doctor, don't you agree that that ought to be up to the physician to determine whether or not he wants to continue giving a drug to a patient, where there's going to be serious side effects?
A. It is up to the physician.
Q. And if it's up to the physician, then isn't it imperative that the manufacturer of that drug see that the physician who is prescribing the medicine has full knowl-

edge, of these serious side effects, so that he can weigh and make his own determination?

A. *I think the drug manufacturer makes what he and for the most part the medical profession and the official control agencies of the drug industry feel is the best method of acquainting the physician with these dangers.* The degree to which the drug manufacturer should try to teach the doctor therapy and all about drugs is debated. Some of the people in academic medicine feel that the drug industry should have little part in this. The drug industry operates under certain legal requirements and what are generally considered moral responsibilities. (emphasis added)

Q. I don't think you've answered my question, and I'll ask it again. I believe you can answer it yes or no, doctor. I don't want to belabor the point, but don't you agree with me that it is the duty of the manufacturer of a drug, when it has knowledge that serious side effects have occurred, to see that the physicians that's prescribing such a drug are given notice of these serious side effects, and of the possibility that their patients may suffer such serious side effects from the continued use of that drug; don't you believe that that's the duty of the drug company?

A. I think that is a duty of the drug company, and it has been done. . . .

The direct and circumstantial evidence amply supports a finding that, prior to October 19, 1964, Dr. Olson was not aware of the dangers of irreversible retinal damage from prolonged use of the drug. There was ample direct evidence from Dr. Olson, and opinion evidence from qualified professional witnesses, to support the findings that Dr. Olson (and other general practitioners) receive so much literature on drugs that it is impossible to read all of it; that Dr. Olson relied on detail men, medical conventions, medical journals and conversations with other doctors for information on drugs he was prescribing; that Dr. Olson was inundated with literature and product cards of various manufacturers; that a change in literature and an additional letter were insufficient to present new information to Dr. Olson; that detail men visit physicians at frequent intervals and could give an effective warning which would affirmatively notify the doctor of the dangerous side effects of chloroquine phosphate on the retina. These findings of fact were not clearly erroneous. . . .

Appellant contends that in this case the trial court adopted an erroneous view that the law required appellant to warn of dangers of the use of Aralen by the most effective method; that, therefore, the ultimate determination of the fact that appellant breached a duty to warn by the most effective method (by detail men) was induced by application of an erroneous legal standard, a standard higher than the admitted duty to make reasonable efforts to warn. Amicus curiae [Pharmaceutical Manufacturers Association] supports appellant by a post-trial extra-record affidavit on the number of detail men on the detail force of 136 companies producing 90% of the output of prescription drugs in the United States. Amicus curiae argues that "the trial court has, in effect, asserted that a drug manufacturer should personally notify, by use of detail men, each of the nation's 248,000 physicians of new warning information on a prescription drug"; that this is an unreasonable duty.

This extra-record information is not all judicially noticeable, but will be assumed to be true for the purposes of this appeal, since it does not require reversal of the trial court.

We hold that appellant and amicus curiae have misconstrued the memorandum opinion of the trial court, and have taken out of context a portion of the memorandum dealing with the trial court's reasoning in the fact finding process of applying the standard of reasonableness. The trial court clearly applied, recognized and expressly enunciated the undisputed standard of a duty to make reasonable efforts to warn the medical profession of the side effects of the drug. . . .

This does not mean that every physician in the United States must have been given an immediate warning by a personal messenger. But it does mean that the trial court was justified in finding that it was unreasonable to fail to instruct the detail men, at least, to warn the physicians on whom they regularly called of the dangers of which appellant had learned, or in the exercise of reasonable care should have known. In none of the arguments of appellant, and of amicus curiae, and in none of the expert testimony offered by appellant is there an explanation of the reason the available detail men were not instructed to give such warnings in the course of their regular calls. . . .

The "Dear Doctor" letter could have been reasonably found to be lacking in emphasis, timeliness and attention inviting qualities. A reasoning mind could find that appellant's warning actions were unduly delayed, reluctant and lacking in a sense of urgency, and therefore unreasonable under the circumstances. While a warning in February 1963 in an attention inviting letter would probably have been timely in this case if promptly received and heeded by appellee's physician, it could be inferred that a reasonably earlier warning, with greater intensity could well have reached appellee's physician directly, or indirectly through other professional channels such as conversations with other doctors and discussions at conventions. The delay in issuance of the "Dear Doctor" letter from August 1962 to February 1963, its wording, and the manner of its circulation could be found unreasonable considering the magnitude of the risk involved. The trier of the fact could reasonably conclude that the urgency of the circumstances reasonably required more than the relatively slow action and relative lack of emphasis employed in composing and circulating the "Dear Doctor" letter. The longer the warning was delayed the greater the risk became. Further Dr. Rice, former Director of Medical Research of appellant, offered as an expert witness, could give no explanation of the failure to send the letter by registered or certified mail. . . .

None of the assignments of error are supported by the record in this case. . . .

The judgment of the trial court is affirmed.

The court in *Yarrow* applied a negligence test in determining the defendant's legal responsibility for failing to warn. Would the same test be applied today, in this era of "strict liability?" We addressed this question of the doctrinal basis of failure-to-warn liability in Chapter Five, in the broader context of nonprescription products. The New York Court of Appeals affirmed negligence as the doctrine-of-choice in prescription drug, failure-to-warn cases in Martin v. Hacker, 628 N.E.2d 1308 (N.Y. 1993). The Supreme Court of California applied strict liability in Carlin v. Superior Court 920 P.2d 1347 (Cal. 1996), discussed in the text following *Anderson* in Chapter Five, Section A.4., supra. For a thorough discussion of the competing public policy concerns implicated by prescription pharmaceutical liability, see M. Stuart Madden, The Enduring Paradox of Products Liability Law Relating to Prescription Pharmaceuticals, 21 Pace L. Rev. 313 (2001).

Some courts have extended the duty of manufacturers of prescription drugs to warn nonpatients other than prescribing physicians. Thus, in Hoffman v. Sterling Drug, Inc., 485 F.2d 132 (3d Cir. 1973) (applying Pennsylvania law), another Aralen case, the court stood ready to impose liability upon the defendant for having failed adequately to warn treating, as well as prescribing, physicians of the dangers inherent in its product. See also, Stahl v. Novartis Pharmaceuticals Corp., 283 F.3d 254 (5th Cir. 2002). And you may recall the holding in Holley v. Burroughs Wellcome Co., mentioned earlier in Chapter Five in connection with the "Who must warn whom?" issue, that the manufacturer of a muscle relaxant owed a duty to warn not only the attending anesthetist but also his assistant.

b. Warning the Patient Directly

An intriguing question is whether drug manufacturers must warn patients directly. A leading case is Reyes v. Wyeth Laboratories, Inc., 498 F.2d 1264 (5th Cir.), *cert. denied,* 419 U.S. 1096 (1974), in which the manufacturer of an oral polio vaccine was held liable for having failed directly to warn the plaintiff, who contracted polio from vaccine taken at a free public health clinic. See also Cunningham v. Charles Pfizer & Co., Inc., 532 P.2d 1377 (Okla. 1974), in which the Supreme Court of Oklahoma held that a drug manufacturer could be held strictly liable under §402A for having failed to warn a child's parents of the risks of contracting polio from the defendant's polio vaccine. The vaccine was administered in a mass immunization program, and the defendant had warned the medical society sponsoring the program. See generally Marc A. Franklin & Joseph E. Mais, Jr., Tort Law and Mass Immunization, 65 Cal. L. Rev. 754 (1977).

In light of the fact that federal law mandates that patients be given warning about the risks associated with taking birth control pills, plaintiffs have sought to abrogate the traditional rule that warnings to the doctor are sufficient. They have been largely unsuccessful. Where the warnings to the physician were more elaborate than those given to the patient and the patient suffered a side effect not listed in the direct warning to the patient, courts have still relied on the learned intermediary rule to deny recovery on the grounds that notwithstanding the federal mandate to warn, a drug manufacturer has no common law duty to warn the patient directly. See Martin v. Ortho Pharmaceutical Corp., 661 N.E.2d 352 (Ill. 1996); West v. Searle & Co., 806 S.W.2d 608 (Ark. 1991) (oral contraceptives). Skill v. Martinez, 91 F.R.D. 498 (D.N.J. 1981), *aff'd,* 677 F.2d 368 (3d Cir. 1982) (oral contraceptives). See also Odom v. G.D. Searle & Co., 979 F.2d 1001 (4th Cir. 1992) (intrauterine devices); Terhune v. A.H. Robins Co., 577 P.2d 975 (Wash. 1978) (intrauterine device). But see Lukaszewicz v. Ortho Pharm. Corp., 510 F. Supp. 961 (D. Wis. 1981) (denying an oral contraceptive manufacturer's motion to dismiss because federal regulations require manufacturers to warn the patient as well as the physician).

In cases in which courts hold drug companies to warn consumers directly, the question of the adequacy of warnings presents problems usually not encountered when warnings are directed only at learned intermediaries. Thus, in MacDonald v. Ortho Pharmaceutical Corp., 475 N.E.2d 65 (Mass.), *cert. denied,* 106 S. Ct. 250 (1985), the plaintiffs claimed that the warnings contained on the pill-dispenser label and in a booklet that a young mother received along with defendant's oral contraceptive pills were inadequate, resulting in massive injuries to her from a pill-induced stroke. As required by the then-effective regulations promulgated by the United States Food and Drug Administration (FDA), the pill dispenser she received was labeled with a warning that "oral contraceptives are powerful and effective drugs which can cause side effects in some users and should not be used at all by some women," and that "[t]he most serious known side effect is abnormal blood clotting which can be fatal." Id. at 66. The warning also referred MacDonald to a booklet which she obtained from her gynecologist, and which was distributed by Ortho pursuant to FDA requirements.

The defendant's booklet contained the following information:

> Blood clots occasionally form in the blood vessels of the legs and the pelvis of apparently healthy people and may threaten life if the clots break loose and then lodge in the lung or if they form in other vital organs, such as the brain. It has been estimated that about one woman in 2,000 on the pill each year suffers a blood clotting disorder severe enough to require hospitalization. The estimated death rate from abnormal blood clotting in healthy women under 35 not taking the pill is 1 in 500,000, whereas for the same group taking the pill it is 1 in 66,000. For healthy women over 35 not taking the pill, the rate is 1 in 200,000 compared to 1 in 25,000 for pill users. Blood clots are about three times more likely to develop in women over the age of 34. For these reasons it is important that women who have had blood clots in the legs, lungs or brain not use oral contraceptives. Anyone using the pill who has severe leg or chest pains, coughs up blood, has difficulty breathing, sudden severe headache or vomiting, dizziness or fainting, disturbances of vision or speech, weakness or numbness of an arm or leg, should call her doctor immediately and stop taking the pill. Id. at 66-67, n.4.

The jury returned a verdict for plaintiffs, and the trial court entered j.n.o.v. for defendant on the ground that the defendant owed no duty to warn the patient directly.

On appeal, the Supreme Judicial Court held that the defendant owed the patient in this case a duty to warn her of the dangers inherent in her using the pill. The court then turned to an issue not reached below — the adequacy of the defendant's warnings:

> Ortho argues that reasonable minds could not differ as to whether MacDonald was adequately informed of the risk of the injury she sustained by Ortho's warning that the oral contraceptives could cause "abnormal blood clotting which can be fatal" and further warning of the incremental likelihood of hospitalization or death due to blood clotting in "vital organs, such as the brain." We disagree. . . . We cannot say that this jury's decision that the warning was inadequate is so unreasonable as to require the opposite conclusion as a matter of law. The jury may well have concluded, in light of their common experience and MacDonald's testimony, that the absence of a reference to "stroke" in the warning unduly minimized the warning's impact or failed to make the nature of the risk reasonably comprehensible to the average consumer. Similarly, the jury may

have concluded that there are fates worse than death, such as the permanent disablement suffered by MacDonald, and that the mention of the risk of death did not, therefore, suffice to apprise an average consumer of the material risks of oral contraceptive use. Id. at 71.

A vigorous dissent argued against recognizing a duty on the part of prescription drug manufacturers to warn patients directly. Following *MacDonald,* Massachusetts courts have limited the manufacturers' duty to warn patients directly to oral contraceptives. For example, in Linnen v. A.H. Robins Co., 2000 WL 89379 (Mass. Super. Ct. 1999), the court held that the drug manufacturer had no duty to warn the patient directly about the risks associated with diet pills. The court disagreed with the plaintiff's argument that the peculiar characteristics of oral contraceptives also applied to diet drugs, finding that the prescription of fen-phen constituted an "ordinary interaction between a doctor and patient." Id. at 3.

With the advent of commercial advertising of prescription drugs in newspapers, magazines, and television, it was only a matter of time before a plaintiff would argue that for drugs marketed directly to patients that adequate warnings of risks associated with the use of such drugs be communicated directly to them. The first salvo was fired in New Jersey to the ears of a very receptive court.

Perez v. Wyeth Laboratories Inc.
734 A.2d 1245 (N.J. 1999)

O'HERN, J.

Our medical-legal jurisprudence is based on images of health care that no longer exist. At an earlier time, medical advice was received in the doctor's office from a physician who most likely made house calls if needed. The patient usually paid a small sum of money to the doctor. Neighborhood pharmacists compounded prescribed medicines. Without being pejorative, it is safe to say that the prevailing attitude of law and medicine was that the "doctor knows best."

Pharmaceutical manufacturers never advertised their products to patients, but rather directed all sales efforts at physicians. In this comforting setting, the law created an exception to the traditional duty of manufacturers to warn consumers directly of risks associated with the product as long as they warned health-care providers of those risks.

For good or ill, that has all changed. Medical services are in large measure provided by managed care organizations. Medicines are purchased in the pharmacy department of supermarkets and often paid for by third-party providers. Drug manufacturers now directly advertise products to consumers on the radio, television, the Internet, billboards on public transportation, and in magazines. For example, a recent magazine advertisement for a seasonal allergy medicine in which a person is standing in a pastoral field filled with grass and goldenrod, attests that to "TAKE [THE PRODUCT]" is to "TAKE CLEAR CONTROL." Another recent ad features a former presidential candidate, encouraging the consumer to "take a little courage" to speak with "your physician." The first ad features major side effects, encourages the reader to "talk to your doctor," and lists a brief summary of risks and contraindications on the opposite page. The second ad provides a phone number and the name of the pharmaceutical company, but does not provide the name of the drug.

The question in this case, broadly stated, is whether our law should follow these changes in the marketplace or reflect the images of the past. We believe that when mass marketing of prescription drugs seeks to influence a patient's choice of a drug, a pharmaceutical manufacturer that makes direct claims to consumers for the efficacy of its product should not be unqualifiedly relieved of a duty to provide proper warnings of the dangers or side effects of the product.

I. *The Norplant System (Norplant)*

This appeal concerns Norplant, a Food and Drug Administration (FDA)-approved, reversible contraceptive that prevents pregnancy for up to five years. The Norplant contraceptive employs six thin, flexible, closed capsules that contain a synthetic hormone, levonorgestrel. The capsules are implanted under the skin of a woman's upper arm during an in-office surgical procedure characterized by the manufacturer as minor. A low, continuous dosage of the hormone diffuses through the capsule walls and into the bloodstream. Although the capsules are not usually visible under the skin, the outline of the fan-like pattern can be felt under the skin. Removal occurs during an in-office procedure, similar to the insertion process. . . .

According to plaintiffs, Wyeth began a massive advertising campaign for Norplant in 1991, which it directed at women rather than at their doctors. Wyeth advertised on television and in women's magazines such as Glamour, Mademoiselle and Cosmopolitan. According to plaintiffs, none of the advertisements warned of any inherent danger posed by Norplant; rather, all praised its simplicity and convenience. None warned of side effects including pain and permanent scarring attendant to removal of the implants. Wyeth also sent a letter to physicians advising them that it was about to launch a national advertising program in magazines that the physicians' patients may read.

Plaintiffs cite several studies published in medical journals that have found Norplant removal to be difficult and painful. One study found that thirty-three percent of women had removal difficulty and forty percent experienced pain. Another study found that fifty-two percent of physicians reported complications during removal. Medical journals have catalogued the need for advanced medical technicians in addition to general surgeons for Norplant removal. Plaintiffs assert that none of this information was provided to consumers.

In 1995, plaintiffs began to file lawsuits in several New Jersey counties claiming injuries that resulted from their use of Norplant. Plaintiffs' principal claim alleged that Wyeth, distributors of Norplant in the United States, failed to warn adequately about side effects associated with the contraceptive. Side effects complained of by plaintiffs included weight gain, headaches, dizziness, nausea, diarrhea, acne, vomiting, fatigue, facial hair growth, numbness in the arms and legs, irregular menstruation, hair loss, leg cramps, anxiety and nervousness, vision problems, anemia, mood swings and depression, high blood pressure, and removal complications that resulted in scarring.

Class action certification was denied. All New Jersey Norplant cases were consolidated in Middlesex County. Eventually, twenty-five New Jersey Norplant cases involving approximately fifty Norplant users were pending in the Superior Court in Middlesex County.

After a case management conference, plaintiffs' counsel sought a determination of whether the learned intermediary doctrine applied. Pursuant to that conference, five bellwether plaintiffs were selected to challenge defendant's motion for summary judgment concerning the learned intermediary doctrine. The trial court dismissed plaintiffs' complaints, concluding that even when a manufacturer advertises directly to the public, and a woman is influenced by the advertising campaign, "a physician is not simply relegated to the role of prescribing the drug according to the woman's wishes." Consequently, the court held that the learned intermediary doctrine applied. Ibid. According to the court, the physician retains the duty to weigh the benefits and risks associated with a drug before deciding whether the drug is appropriate for the patient. . . .

Plaintiffs appealed. . . . The Appellate Division affirmed the trial court's grant of summary judgment in favor of defendants and its determination that the learned intermediary doctrine applied. . . .

We granted plaintiffs' petition for certification. 156 N.J. 410 (1998). . . .

III. Direct-to-Consumer Advertising

It is paradoxical that so pedestrian a concern as male-pattern baldness should have signaled the beginning of direct-to-consumer marketing of prescription drugs. Upjohn Company became the first drug manufacturer to advertise directly to consumers when it advertised for Rogaine, a hair-loss treatment. Jon D. Hanson & Douglas A. Kysar, Taking Behavioralism Seriously: Some Evidence of Market Manipulation, 112 Harv. L. Rev. 1420, 1456 (1999). The ad targeted male consumers by posing the question, "Can an emerging bald spot . . . damage your ability to get along with others, influence your chance of obtaining a job or date or even interfere with your job performance?" Ibid. (footnotes omitted). A related ad featured an attractive woman asserting suggestively, "I know that a man who can afford Rogaine is a man who can afford me." Ibid. (footnote omitted).

Advertising for Rogaine was the tip of the iceberg. Since drug manufacturers began marketing directly to consumers for products such as prescription drugs in the 1980s, "almost all pharmaceutical companies have engaged in this direct marketing practice." . . .

Pressure on consumers is an integral part of drug manufacturers' marketing strategy. From 1995 to 1996, drug companies increased advertising directed to consumers by ninety percent. . . . "John F. Kamp, senior vice president of the American Association of Advertising Agencies, said that prescription drug companies spent $1.3 billion on print and broadcast advertising aimed at consumers last year, up from $843 million in 1997. . . ." Robert Pear, Drug Companies Getting F.D.A. Reprimands for False or Misleading Advertising, N.Y. Times, Mar. 28, 1999, at 28. . . .

> The American Medical Association (AMA) has long maintained a policy in opposition to product-specific prescription ads aimed at consumers. A 1992 study by the Annals of Internal Medicine reports that a peer review of 109 prescription ads found 92 per cent of the advertisements lacking in some manner.

The difficulties that accompany this [type of advertising] practice are manifest. "The marketing gimmick used by the drug manufacturer often provides the consumer with a diluted variation of the risks associated with the drug product." Even without such manipulation, [t]elevision spots lasting 30 or 60 seconds are not conducive to 'fair balance' [in presentation of risks]." Given such constraints, pharmaceutical ads often contain warnings of a general nature. However, "[r]esearch indicates that general warnings (for example, see your doctor) in [direct-to-consumer] advertisements do not give the consumer a sufficient understanding of the risks inherent in product use." Consumers often interpret such warnings as a "general reassurance" that their condition can be treated, rather than as a requirement that "specific vigilance" is needed to protect them from product risks.

[Hanson & Kysar, supra, 112 Harv. L. Rev. at 1456.]

IV. How Has the Law Responded to These Changes?

A. The new Restatement (Third) of Torts has left the issue to "developing case law."

Parallel to the developments in drug marketing, the American Law Institute was in the process of adopting the Restatement (Third) of Torts: Products Liability (1997). The comment to Section 6 explains that subsection (d)(1) sets forth the traditional rule of the learned intermediary that drug and medical device manufacturers are liable for failing to warn of a drug's risks only when the manufacturer fails to warn the health-care provider of risks attendant to a specific drug. Restatement, supra, §6(d) comment *a*. That same comment also notes that subsection (d)(2) reflects decisional law and provides limited exceptions to the traditional rule by requiring manufacturers to warn patients in certain circumstances. Ibid. Because situations may exist when the health-care provider assumes a "much-diminished role as an evaluator or decisionmaker," it is appropriate to impose a duty on the manufacturer to warn the patient directly. Id. at §6d comment *b*. Despite the early effort to provide an exception to the doctrine in the case of direct marketing of pharmaceuticals to consumers, the drafters left the resolution of that issue to "developing case law." Id. at §6d comment *e*. One commentator described the Restatement's approach as a "tepid endorsement" of the learned intermediary doctrine. Charles J. Walsh et al., The Learned Intermediary Doctrine: The Correct Prescription for Drug Labeling, 48 Rutgers L. Rev. 821, 869 (1994). Thus, under the new Restatement, "warnings may have to be provided to a health-care provider or even to the patient," depending on the circumstances. William A. Dreier, The Restatement (Third) of Torts: Products Liability and the New Jersey Law—Not Quite Perfect Together, 50 Rutgers L.J. 2059, 2097 (1998). . . .

B. The New Jersey Products Liability Act does not legislate the boundaries of the learned intermediary doctrine.

As noted, the New Jersey Products Liability Act provides:

An adequate product warning or instruction is one that a reasonably prudent person in the same or similar circumstances would have provided with respect to the danger and that communicates adequate information on the dangers and safe use of the product, taking into account the characteristics of, and the ordinary knowledge common to, the persons by whom the product is intended to be used, or in the case of prescription drugs, taking into account the characteristics of, and the ordinary knowledge common to, the prescribing physician. If the warning or instruction given in connection with a drug or device or food or food additive has been approved or prescribed by the federal Food and Drug Administration under the "Federal Food, Drug, and Cosmetic Act," 52 Stat. 1040, 21 U.S.C. §301 et seq, ... a rebuttable presumption shall arise that the warning or instruction is adequate. . . .

[N.J.S.A. 2A:58C-4.]

The Senate Judiciary Committee Statement that accompanied L. 1987, c. 197 recites: "The subsection contains a general definition of an adequate warning and a special definition for warnings that accompany prescription drugs, since, in the case of prescription drugs, the warning is owed to the physician." See N.J.S.A. 2A:58C-1 (providing the Committee Statement) (emphasis added). At oral argument, counsel for Wyeth was candid to acknowledge that he could not "point to a sentence in the statute" that would make the learned intermediary doctrine applicable to the manufacturers' direct marketing of drugs, but rather relied on the Committee Statement. Although the statute provides a physician-based standard for determining the adequacy of the warning due to a physician, the statute does not legislate the boundaries of the doctrine. . . .

C. Direct advertising of drugs to consumers alters the calculus of the learned intermediary doctrine. . . .

A . . . recent review summarized the theoretical bases for the [learned intermediary] doctrine as based on four considerations.

> First, courts do not wish to intrude upon the doctor-patient relationship. From this perspective, warnings that contradict information supplied by the physician will undermine the patient's trust in the physician's judgment. Second, physicians may be in a superior position to convey meaningful information to their patients, as they must do to satisfy their duty to secure informed consent. Third, drug manufacturers lack effective means to communicate directly with patients, making it necessary to rely on physicians to convey the relevant information. Unlike [over the counter products], pharmacists usually dispense prescription drugs from bulk containers rather than as unit-of-use packages in which the manufacturer may have enclosed labeling. Finally, because of the complexity of risk information about prescription drugs, comprehension problems would complicate any effort by manufacturers to translate physician labeling for lay patients. For this reason, even critics of the rule do not suggest that pharmaceutical companies should provide warnings only to patients and have no tort duty to warn physicians. [Lars Noah, Advertising Prescription Drugs to Consumers: Assessing the Regulatory and Liability Issues, 32 Ga. L. Rev. 141, 157-159 (1992).]

Consumer-directed advertising of pharmaceuticals . . . belies each of the premises on which the learned intermediary doctrine rests.

> First, the fact that manufacturers are advertising their drugs and devices to consumers suggests that consumers are active participants in their health care decisions, invalidat-

ing the concept that it is the doctor, not the patient, who decides whether a drug or device should be used. Second, it is illogical that requiring manufacturers to provide direct warnings to a consumer will undermine the patient-physician relationship, when, by its very nature, consumer-directed advertising encroaches on that relationship by encouraging consumers to ask for advertised products by name. Finally, consumer-directed advertising rebuts the notion that prescription drugs and devices and their potential adverse effects are too complex to be effectively communicated to lay consumers. Because the FDA requires that prescription drug and device advertising carry warnings, the consumer may reasonably presume that the advertiser guarantees the adequacy of its warnings. Thus, the common law duty to warn the ultimate consumer should apply. [Susan A. Casey, Comment, Laying an Old Doctrine to Rest: Challenging the Wisdom of the Learned Intermediary Doctrine, 19 Wm. Mitchell L. Rev. 931, 956 (1993) (footnotes omitted).] . . .

Obviously, the learned intermediary doctrine applies when its predicates are present. "In New Jersey, as elsewhere, we accept the proposition that a pharmaceutical manufacturer generally discharges its duty to warn the ultimate users of prescription drugs by supplying physicians with information about the drug's dangerous propensities." Had Wyeth done just that, simply supplied the physician with information about the product, and not advertised directly to the patients, plaintiffs would have no claim against Wyeth based on an independent duty to warn patients. The question is whether the absence of an independent duty to warn patients gives the manufacturer the right to misrepresent to the public the product's safety.

D. Prescription drug manufacturers that market their products directly to consumers should be subject to claims by consumers if their advertising fails to provide an adequate warning of the product's dangerous propensities.

In reaching the conclusion that the learned intermediary doctrine does not apply to the direct marketing of drugs to consumers, we must necessarily consider that when prescription drugs are marketed and labeled in accordance with FDA specifications, the pharmaceutical manufacturers should not have to confront "state tort liability premised on theories of design defect or warning inadequacy." Note, A Question of Competence: The Judicial Role in the Regulation of Pharmaceuticals, 103 Harv. L. Rev. 773, 773 (1990). We draw much of this summary concerning the specifics of FDA pharmaceutical regulation from the brief of amicus curiae, the Pharmaceutical Research and Manufacturers of America. Because such regulations may change from day-to-day, our commentary concerning the current regulations may soon become moot.

The FDA is authorized to regulate advertisements for prescription drugs pursuant to 21 U.S.C.A. Section 352(n) of the Food, Drug and Cosmetic Act, 21 U.S.C.A. Sections 301-397. Advertisements subject to Section 352(n) include "advertisements in published journals, magazines, other periodicals, and newspapers, and advertisements broadcast through media such as radio, television, and telephone communication systems." 21 C.F.R. §202.1(l)(1). . . .

Section 352(n) of the Act contains the "brief summary requirement," which is a misnomer considering that the summary is anything but brief. Accordingly, all advertisements must include a description of "side effects, contraindications, and effectiveness as shall be required in regulations. . . ." 21 U.S.C.A. §352(n)(3). The regulations addressing prescription drugs also require that the brief summary provide "all the risk-related information in a product's approved package labeling," which is usually a package insert or product package insert. 62 Fed. Reg. 43,171 (Aug. 12, 1997) (citing 21 C.F.R. §202.1(e)(1) and (e)(3)(iii)). As noted by amicus curiae, the FDA "[r]egulations are exhaustive, addressing issues as broad as the requirement that ads be fairly balanced (21 C.F.R. §202.1(e)(6)) and as narrow as how graphs must be labeled (21 C.F.R. §202.1(e)(7)(iv)) and the type size used to set forth a medicine's established name (21 C.F.R. §202.1(b)(2))."

In August 1997, the FDA released a Draft Guidance, which specifically addresses consumer-directed broadcast advertisements such as radio, television and telephone communications. 21 Fed. Reg. 43, 172 (Aug. 12, 1997). Broadcast advertisements must contain a "major statement" of the major risks of the drug. Ibid. Instead of presenting a brief summary with the broadcast, which is not as feasible as in the print media, the Guidance proposes an alternative requirement known as the "adequate provision" requirement. Ibid. That provision provides that the manufacturer "may make adequate provision for the dissemination of the approved package labeling in connection with the broadcast presentation (§202.1(e)(1))." Ibid. The Guidance explains that four components must be present to meet the "adequate provision" requirement in broadcasts — a toll-free number that provides information concerning where consumers might find information about package labeling; an alternative mechanism for obtaining package labeling information for consumers who do not have access to technology such as the Internet; a statement directing consumers to pharmacists and/or physicians; and an Internet web-page address. See Guidance for Industry: Consumer-Directed Broadcast Advertisements. Within two years of the release of the Guidance, the FDA "intends to evaluate the effects of the guidance. . . ." 62 Fed. Reg 43,172. These FDA actions indicate that the agency views direct-to-consumer advertising as a means of providing consumers with improved access to important information about prescription drugs.

FDA regulations are pertinent in determining the nature and extent of any duty of care that should be imposed on pharmaceutical manufacturers with respect to direct-to-consumer advertising. Presently, any duty to warn physicians about prescription drug dangers is presumptively met by compliance with federal labeling. See N.J.S.A. 2C:58-4. That presumption is not absolute. Nevertheless, FDA regulations serve as compelling evidence that a manufacturer satisfied its duty to warn the physician about potentially harmful side effects of its product.

We believe that in the area of direct-to-consumer advertising of pharmaceuticals, the same rebuttable presumption should apply when a manufacturer complies with FDA advertising, labeling and warning requirements. That approach harmonizes the manufacturer's duty to doctors and to the public when it chooses to directly advertise its products, and simultaneously recognizes the public interest in informing patients about new pharmaceutical developments. Moreover, a rebuttable presumption that the duty to consumers is met by compliance with FDA regulations helps to ensure that manufacturers are not made guarantors against remotely possible, but not scientifically-verifiable, side-effects of prescription drugs, a result that could have a "significant anti-utilitarian effect." Michael D. Green,

Statutory Compliance and Tort Liability: Examining the Strongest Case, 30 U. Mich. J.L. Ref. 461, 466-67 (1997) (noting that over deterrence in drug advertising context could impede and delay manufacturers from research and development of new and effective drugs, force beneficial drugs from market, lead to shortages in supplies and suppliers of pharmaceuticals, and create unnecessary administrative costs).

We believe that this standard is fair and balanced. For all practical purposes, absent deliberate concealment or nondisclosure of after-acquired knowledge of harmful effects, compliance with FDA standards should be virtually dispositive of such claims. By definition, the advertising will have been "fairly balanced." This presumptive effect is in accordance with legislative intent that we discern from the punitive damages provision of the Products Liability Act. See L. 1987, c. 142, §5(c). That provision prohibits, in the case of the sale of pharmaceutical products, an award of punitive damages if there has been compliance with FDA labeling and pre-marketing requirements, impliedly reserving compensatory damages for those rare cases when the presumption is overcome. N.J.S.A. 2A: 58C-5(c).

V

The final issues in this case concern proximate cause, that is, whether misinformation actually affected these patients and, if so, whether the intervention of the physician (without whom the product may not reach the patient) breaks the chain of causation. . . .

Although the physician writes the prescription, the physician's role in deciding which prescription drug is selected has been altered. With the arrival of direct-to-consumer advertising, patients now enter physician's offices with "preconceived expectations about treatment because of information obtained from DTC [direct-to-consumer] advertisements." Tamar V. Terzian, Direct-to-Consumer Prescription Drug Advertising, 25 Am. J.L. & Med. 149, 157 (1999). Consequently,

> [p]hysicians may relent to patient pressure, even if it is not in the best interest of the patient. In fact, physicians state that they are increasingly asked and pressured by their patients to prescribe drugs that the patient has seen advertised. For example, the diet drug combinations known as fen-phen was prescribed despite little hard scientific evidence of its potential side-effects. Physicians are under attack for prescribing the pills too often and too readily to inappropriate patients. Physicians argue that it is not their fault; rather, they claim pushy patients, prodded by DTC advertisements, pressed, wheedled, begged and berated them for quick treatments. This scenario comes at a time when physicians cannot afford to lose patients, because their income is already strained by managed care cost cutting. Physicians complain that it is impossible to compete with pharmaceutical companies' massive advertising budgets, and resign themselves to the fact that if consumers make enough noise, they will eventually relent to patient pressure.
>
> [Id. at 157-58 (footnotes omitted).]

We disagree that these "ads change the physician into 'simply a functionary, filling out prescriptions[,]'" but we must examine whether the changed relationship affects the finding of proximate cause. . . .

As a matter of policy . . . , we could hold that even if deceptive advertising were a substantial contributing factor influencing a patient's choice of a medicine, the intervening role of the physician should insulate the manufacturer who has engaged in deceptive trade practices. In other contexts, we have not insulated manufacturers when another might have given better warning. Freund v. Cellofilm Properties, Inc., 87 N.J. 229, 245, 432 A.2d 925 (1981). . . .

The superseding cause rationale is appealing because it is based on the familiar tort concept that a tortfeasor is liable only for the injuries that he or she proximately causes. Despite its appeal, one problem with using the causation rationale is the inherent difficulty of establishing causation in failure-to-warn cases as compared with other product liability claims. In a typical defective design case, a plaintiff points to the existence of a viable alternative design and asserts that the manufacturer's failure to use that design proximately caused the plaintiff's injury. Failure-to-warn claims, however, entail a different sort of showing. A plaintiff suing under a failure-to-warn theory must presumably establish that she would have heeded an adequate warning if one were given. Due to the individualized nature of the inquiry into what warning would have caused the plaintiff to alter her behavior, Professors Henderson and Twerski suggest that predicting how additional information would have affected any given individual may be well nigh impossible.

On balance, we believe that the patient's interest in reliable information predominates over a policy interest that would insulate manufacturers. "Products liability law is based on concepts of fairness, feasibility, practicality and functional responsibility. We have always stressed the public's interest in motivating individuals and commercial entities to invest in safety to protect workers." Zaza v. Marquess and Ness, Inc., 144 N.J. 34, 64, 675 A.2d 620 (1996). Within bounds, that policy extends to consumers of pharmaceuticals.

Obviously, the physician is almost always the essential link between the patient and the pharmaceutical. Most ads for drugs caution the patient to consult with a physician. Because of that essential link, under the learned intermediary rule drug manufacturers were found not liable even if they did not provide an adequate warning to those physicians who eventually prescribed a drug, to inform them of the risk.

> Courts have differed in their application of the learned intermediary doctrine in cases in which the defendant claimed that the prescribing physician knew of the risk that the manufacturer did not warn about. Some courts have applied a presumption that the physician would not have prescribed the product if an adequate warning had been given. The defendant may then rebut the presumption with evidence that the physician's decision would not have been affected by such a warning. Other courts have refused to create such a presumption, and have required the plaintiff to prove that an adequate warning would actually have changed the physician's decision. The courts have also differed in the quantum of proof a defendant must establish to show that the physician would have prescribed the drug even if the manufacturer had warned of the risk. . . . [Richard J. Heafey & Don M. Kennedy, Products Liability: Winning Strategies and the User, §10.03 (1999).]

However, we must consider as well a case in which a diabetic patient might have been influenced by advertising to request a drug from a physician without being warned by the manufacturer or the physician of the special dangers posed to a diabetic taking the drug. If an overburdened physician does not inquire whether the patient is a diabetic, the question remains whether the manufacturer should be relieved entirely of responsibility. In the case of direct marketing of drugs, we believe that neither the physician nor the manufacturer should be entirely relieved of their respective duties to warn. Pharmaceutical manufacturers may seek contribution, indemnity or exoneration because of the physician's deficient role in prescribing that drug. In each case, a jury must resolve the close questions of whether a breach of duty has been a proximate cause of harm, and how that causative harm, if found, may be apportioned among culpable defendants. In our experience, jurors are extremely skilled at sorting out the justly and legally responsible parties. . . .

The judgment of the Appellate Division is reversed and the matter is remanded to the Law Division for further proceedings.

[Dissenting opinion of POLLACK, J. is omitted.]

In In Re Norplant Contraceptive Products Liability Litigation, 215 F. Supp. 2d 795 (D.C.E.D. Tex. 2002), multiple plaintiffs sued a prescription contraceptive device manufacturer, alleging failure to warn consumers and prescribing physicians about the device's dangerous side effects. The district court denied summary judgment in favor of the manufacturer as to the consumers who had the device implanted in New Jersey under the *Perez* direct-to-consumer advertising exception, but granted summary judgment as to the consumers from states that do not recognize a duty to warn patients directly. The court rejected the direct-to-consumer advertising exception and found that the 26 side effects listed on the manufacturer's warning to physicians satisfied its duty to warn under the learned intermediary doctrine. See also Presto v. Sandoz, 487 S.E.2d 70 (Ga. Ct. App. 1997) (rejecting plaintiff's claim that drug manufacturer who provided an antipsychotic medication brochure to parents owed a duty to warn them directly; brochure advised consultation with physician).

The possibility of a direct-to-consumer advertising exception to the learned intermediary doctrine has generated a great deal of discussion among scholars and commentators. For arguments against such an exception, see Richard J. Ausness, Will More Aggressive Marketing Practices Lead to Greater Tort Liability for Prescription Drug Manufacturers?, 37 Wake Forest L. Rev. 97 (2002) (arguing that industry self-regulation or governmental regulation would better serve consumers than potentially open-ended tort liability); Lars Noah, Advertising Prescription Drugs to Consumers: Assessing the Regulatory and Liability Issues, 32 Ga. L. Rev. 141 (1997); Michael C. Allen, Medicine Goes Madison Avenue: An Evaluation of the Effect of Direct-To-Consumer Pharmaceutical Advertising on the Learned Intermediary Doctrine, 20 Campbell L. Rev. 113 (1997). For arguments in favor of an exception, see Patrick Cohoon, Comment, An Answer to the Question Why the Time Has Come to Abrogate the Learned Intermediary Rule in the Case of Direct to Consumer Advertising of Prescription Drugs, 42 S. Tex. L. Rev. 1333 (2001); Bradford B. Lear, The Learned Intermediary Doctrine in the Age of Direct Consumer Advertising, 65 Mo. L. Rev. 1101 (2000). Even in New Jersey, where *Perez* recognizes a duty to warn patients directly, one commentator argues that "despite the apparently pro-plaintiff language of the Perez opinion, the New Jersey Supreme Court has announced a rather conservative rule." William A. Drier, Direct-To-Consumer Advertising Liability: An Empty Gift to Plaintiffs, 30 Seton Hall L. Rev. 806, 808 (2000).

Subsection (d)(2) of §6 of the Products Liability Restatement recognizes a duty to warn patients directly "when the manufacturer knows or has reason to know that health-care providers will not be in a position to reduce the risks of harm in accordance with the instructions or warnings [given to them.]" Comment *e* to §6 addresses the issue:

> *e. Direct warnings to patients.* Warnings and instructions with regard to drugs or medical devices that can be sold legally only pursuant to a prescription are, under the learned intermediary" rule, directed to health-care providers. Subsection (d)(2) recognizes that direct warnings and instructions to patients are warranted for drugs that are dispensed or administered to patients without the personal intervention or evaluation of a health-care provider. An example is the administration of a vaccine in clinics where mass inoculations are performed. In many such programs, health-care providers are not in a position to evaluate the risks attendant upon use of the drug or device or to relate them to patients. When a manufacturer supplies prescription drugs for distribution to patients in this type of unsupervised environment, if a direct warning to patients is feasible and can be effective, the law requires measures to that effect.
>
> Although the learned intermediary rule is generally accepted and a drug manufacturer fulfills its legal obligation to warn by providing adequate warnings to the health-care provider, arguments have been advanced that in two other areas courts should consider imposing tort liability on drug manufacturers that fail to provide direct warnings to consumers. In the first, governmental regulatory agencies have mandated that patients be informed of risks attendant to the use of a drug. A noted example is the FDA requirement that birth control pills be sold to patients accompanied by a patient package insert. In the second, manufacturers have advertised a prescription drug and its indicated use in the mass media. Governmental regulations require that, when drugs are so advertised, they must be accompanied by appropriate information concerning risk so as to provide balanced advertising. The question in both instances is whether adequate warnings to the appropriate health-care provider should insulate the manufacturer from tort liability.
>
> Those who assert the need for adequate warnings directly to consumers contend that manufacturers that communicate directly with consumers should not escape liability simply because the decision to prescribe the drug was made by the health-care provider. Proponents of the learned intermediary rule argue that, notwithstanding direct communications to the consumer, drugs cannot be dispensed unless a health-care provider makes an individualized decision that a drug is appropriate for a particular patient, and that it is for the health-care provider to decide which risks are relevant to the particular patient. The Institute leaves to developing case law whether exceptions to the learned intermediary rule in these or other situations should be recognized. . . .

2. *Liability for Defective Drug Designs*

Brown v. Superior Court (Abbott Laboratories)
751 P.2d 470 (Cal. 1988)

MOSK, J.

In current litigation several significant issues have arisen relating to the liability of manufacturers of prescription drugs for injuries caused by their products. Our first and broadest inquiry is whether such a manufacturer may be held strictly liable for a product that is defective in design . . .

authors' dialogue 20

JIM: I'm not sure the Products Restatement does enough with the subject of drug companies warning patients directly. I recall that our early drafts included a provision recognizing such a duty when drug manufacturers advised directly to consumers. We had a few cases and thought that that was the direction the law would take.

AARON: Yeah. But a majority of our advisers urged us not to push things. Especially the members who were judges, who argued that we should leave it to the courts to work out sensible solutions. "Handle it in a comment," they advised. "Leave the black letter flexible on the issue."

JIM: You know better than I that we didn't put issues to a formal vote with the advisers. But I remember the discussions you're talking about. The judges made a persuasive case for going easy in the black letter. Especially coming from the judges, the argument carried weight. They had no substantive stake—simply an institutional commitment to reaching the right position.

AARON: That touches on the question of the proper role of the Reporters and the Institute regarding developing areas of the law. We felt an obligation to reflect not only existing case law, but also the Institute's sense of what rules were reasonable and where the law was headed.

JIM: The hardest aspect of §6 in that regard was §6(c), dealing with prescription drug design liability. We saw a trend in favor of exposure to liability, but had to pull a coherent rule together from what was available. It certainly has been a controversial topic among scholars.

AARON: When we get to the drug design materials in the book, the students can judge for themselves if what we did makes sense. Time will tell.

A. Strict Liability in General

The doctrine of strict liability had its genesis in a concurring opinion by Justice Roger Traynor in Escola v. Coca Cola Bottling Co. (1944) 24 Cal. 2d 453, 461, 150 P.2d 436. He suggested that a manufacturer should be absolutely liable if, in placing a product on the market, it knew the product was to be used without inspection, and it proved to have a defect that caused injury. The policy considerations underlying this suggestion were that the manufacturer, unlike the public, can anticipate or guard against the recurrence of hazards, that the cost of injury may be an overwhelming misfortune to the person injured whereas the manufacturer can insure against the risk and distribute the cost among the consuming public, and that it is in the public interest to discourage the marketing of defective products. This court unanimously adopted Justice Traynor's concept in Greenman v. Yuba Power Products, Inc. (1963) 59 Cal. 2d 57, 62, holding a manufacturer strictly liable in tort and using the formulation of the doctrine set forth in *Escola*.

Strict liability differs from negligence in that it eliminates the necessity for the injured party to prove that the manufacturer of the product which caused injury was negligent. It focuses not on the conduct of the manufacturer but on the product itself, and holds the manufacturer liable if the product was defective . . .

This court refined and explained application of the principle in Cronin v. J.B.E. Olson Corp. (1972) 8 Cal. 3d 121, and Barker v. Lull Engineering Co. (1978), 20 Cal. 3d 413 (hereafter *Barker*). In *Cronin,* we rejected the requirement of section 402A that the defect in a product must be "unreasonably dangerous" to the consumer in order to invoke strict liability, holding that the requirement "rings of negligence" (8 Cal. 3d at p.132) and that the showing of a defect which proximately caused injury is sufficient to justify application of the doctrine.

Barker defined the term "design defect" in the context of strict liability. In that case the plaintiff was injured while operating a piece of heavy construction equipment, and claimed that a safety device called an "outrigger" would have prevented the accident. We held that the defendant could be held liable for a defect in design.

Barker identified three types of product defects. (20 Cal. 3d at p.428.) First, there may be a flaw in the manufacturing process, resulting in a product that differs from the manufacturer's intended result. The archetypal example of such a defect was involved in *Escola,* supra, 24 Cal. 2d 453, where a Coca Cola bottle exploded. Such a manufacturing defect did not exist in the heavy equipment that caused the injury in *Barker,* and is not alleged in the present case.

Second, there are products which are "perfectly" manufactured but are unsafe because of the absence of a safety device, i.e., a defect in design. This was the defect alleged in *Barker*. It held that a product is defectively designed if it failed to perform as safely as an ordinary consumer would expect when used as intended or in a manner reasonably foreseeable, or if, on balance, the risk of danger inherent in the challenged design outweighs the benefits of the design. (20 Cal. 3d at p.430) Plaintiff asserts this test should be applied in the present case because DES contained a design defect.

The third type of defect identified in *Barker* is a product that is dangerous because it lacks adequate warnings or instructions. According to plaintiff, defendants here failed to warn of the dangers inherent in the use of DES. We are concerned, therefore, with the second and third types of defects described in *Barker.*

B. *Strict Liability and Prescription Drugs*

Even before *Greenman* was decided, the members of the American Law Institute, in considering whether to adopt a rule of strict liability, pondered whether the manufacturer of a prescription drug should be subject to the doctrine. (38 ALI Proc. 19, 90-92, 98 (1961).) During a rather confusing discussion of a draft of what was to become section 402A, a member of the institute proposed that drugs should be exempted from strict liability on the ground that it would be "against the public interest" to apply the doctrine to such products because of "the very serious tendency to stifle medical research and testing." Dean Prosser, who was the reporter for the Restatement Second of Torts, responded that the problem was a real one, and that he had it in mind in drafting section 402A. A motion to exempt prescription drugs from the section was defeated on the suggestion of Dean Prosser that the problem could be dealt with in the comments to the section. However, a motion to state the exemption in a comment was also defeated. (38 ALI Proc. 19, 90-98, supra.) At the next meeting of the institute in 1962, section 402A was approved together with comment k thereto. (41 ALI Proc. 227, 244 (1962).)

The comment provides that the producer of a properly manufactured prescription drug may be held liable for injuries caused by the product only if it was not accompanied by a warning of dangers that the manufacturer knew or should have known about. . . .

Comment k has been analyzed and criticized by numerous commentators. While there is some disagreement as to its scope and meaning, there is a general consensus that, although it purports to explain the strict liability doctrine, in fact the principle it states is based on negligence. (E.g., Schwartz, Unavoidably Unsafe Products (1985) 42 Wash. & Lee L. Rev. 1139, 1141; McClellan, Drug Induced Injury (1978) 25 Wayne L. Rev. 1, 2.) That is, comment k would impose liability on a drug manufacturer only if it failed to warn of a defect of which it either knew or should have known. This concept focuses not on a deficiency in the product — the hallmark of strict liability — but on the fault of the producer in failing to warn of the dangers inherent in the use of its product that were either known or knowable — an idea which "rings of negligence," in the words of *Cronin*, supra, 8 Cal. 3d 121, 132.

Comment k has been adopted in the overwhelming majority of jurisdictions that have considered the matter.

We are aware of only one decision that has applied the doctrine of strict liability to prescription drugs. (Brochu v. Ortho Pharmaceutical Corp. (1st Cir. 1981) 642 F.2d 652, 654-657.) Most cases have embraced the rule of comment k without detailed analysis of its language. A few, notably Kearl v. Lederle Laboratories, 172 Cal. App. 3d 812 [,218 Cal. Rptr. 453 (1985)] (hereafter *Kearl*), have conditioned application of the exemption stated therein on a finding that the drug involved is in fact "unavoidably dangerous," reasoning that the comment was intended to exempt only such drugs from strict liability. . . .

We appear, then, to have three distinct choices:

(1) to hold that the manufacturer of a prescription drug is strictly liable for a defect in its product because it was defectively designed, as that term is defined in *Barker,* or because of a failure to warn of its dangerous propensities even though such dangers were neither known nor scientifically knowable at the time of distribution;
(2) to determine that liability attaches only if a manufacturer fails to warn of dangerous propensities of which it was or should have been aware, in conformity with comment k; or
(3) to decide, like *Kearl* and Toner v. Lederle Laboratories, supra, 732 P.2d 297, 303-309, that strict liability for design defects should apply to prescription drugs unless the particular drug which caused injury is found to be "unavoidably dangerous."

We shall conclude that

(1) a drug manufacturer's liability for a defectively designed drug should not be measured by the standards of strict liability;

(2) because of the public interest in the development, availability, and reasonable price of drugs, the appropriate test for determining responsibility is the test stated in comment *k;* and

(3) for these same reasons of policy, we disapprove of the holding of *Kearl* that only those prescription drugs found to be "unavoidably dangerous" should be measured by the comment *k* standard and that strict liability should apply to drugs that do not meet the description.

1. Design Defect

Barker, as we have seen, set forth two alternative tests to measure a design defect: first, whether the product performed as safely as the ordinary consumer would expect when used in an intended and reasonably foreseeable manner, and second, whether, on balance, the benefits of the challenged design outweighed the risk of danger inherent in the design. In making the latter determination, the jury may consider these factors: "the gravity of the danger posed by the challenged design, the likelihood that such danger would occur, the mechanical feasibility of a safer alternative design, the financial cost of an improved design, and the adverse consequences to the product and to the consumer that would result from an alternative design." (20 Cal. 3d at p.431.)

Defendants assert that neither of these tests is applicable to a prescription drug like DES. As to the "consumer expectation" standard, they claim, the "consumer" is not the plaintiff but the physician who prescribes the drug, and it is to him that the manufacturer's warnings are directed. A physician appreciates the fact that all prescription drugs involve inherent risks, known and unknown, and he does not expect that the drug is without such risks. We agree that the "consumer expectation" aspect of the *Barker* test is inappropriate to prescription drugs. While the "ordinary consumer" may have a reasonable expectation that a product such as a machine he purchases will operate safely when used as intended, a patient's expectations regarding the effects of such a drug are those related to him by his physician, to whom the manufacturer directs the warnings regarding the drug's properties. The manufacturer cannot be held liable if it has provided appropriate warnings and the doctor fails in his duty to transmit these warnings to the patient or if the patient relies on inaccurate information from others regarding side effects of the drug.

The second test, which calls for the balancing of risks and benefits, is inapposite to prescription drugs, according to defendants, because it contemplates that a safer alternative design is feasible. While the defective equipment in *Barker* and other cases involving mechanical devices might be "redesigned" by the addition of safety devices, there is no possibility for an alternative design of a drug like DES, which is a scientific constant compounded in accordance with a required formula. (See *Sindell,* 26 Cal. 3d at p.605.)

We agree with defendants that *Barker* contemplates a safer alternative design if possible, but we seriously doubt their claim that a drug like DES cannot be "redesigned" to make it safer. For example, plaintiff might be able to demonstrate at trial that a particular component of DES rendered it unsafe as a miscarriage preventative and that removal of that component would not have affected the efficacy of the drug. Even if the resulting product, without the damaging component, would bear a name other than DES, it would do no violence to semantics to view it as a "redesign" of DES.

Or plaintiff might be able to prove that other, less harmful drugs were available to prevent miscarriage; the benefit of such alternate drugs could be weighed against the advantages of DES in making the risk/benefit analysis of *Barker*. As the Court of Appeal observed, defendants' attempt to confine the issue to whether there is an "alternative design" for DES poses the problem in an "unreasonably narrow" fashion. (See Comment, The Failure to Warn Defect (1983), 17 U.S.F. L. Rev. 743, 755-762.). . . .

It is indisputable, as plaintiff contends, that the risk of injury from such drugs is unavoidable, that a consumer may be helpless to protect himself from serious harm caused by them, and that, like other products, the cost of insuring against strict liability can be passed on by the producer to the consumer who buys the item. Moreover, as we observe below, in some cases additional testing of drugs before they are marketed might reveal dangerous side effects, resulting in a safer product.

But there is an important distinction between prescription drugs and other products such as construction machinery . . . the producers of which were held strictly liable. In the latter cases, the product is used to make work easier or to provide pleasure, while in the former it may be necessary to alleviate pain and suffering or to sustain life. Moreover, unlike other important medical products (wheelchairs, for example), harm to some users from prescription drugs is unavoidable. Because of these distinctions, the broader public interest in the availability of drugs at an affordable price must be considered in deciding the appropriate standard of liability for injuries resulting from their use.

Perhaps a drug might be made safer if it was withheld from the market until scientific skill and knowledge advanced to the point at which additional dangerous side effects would be revealed. But in most cases such a delay in marketing new drugs — added to the delay required to obtain approval for release of the product from the Food and Drug Administration — would not serve the public welfare. Public policy favors the development and marketing of beneficial new drugs, even though some risks, perhaps serious ones, might accompany their introduction, because drugs can save lives and reduce pain and suffering.

If drug manufacturers were subject to strict liability, they might be reluctant to undertake research programs to develop some pharmaceuticals that would prove beneficial or to distribute others that are available to be marketed, because of the fear of large adverse monetary judgments. Further, the additional expense of insuring against such liability — assuming insurance would be available — and of research programs to reveal possible dangers not detectable by available scientific methods could place the cost of medication beyond the reach of those who need it most. . . .

The possibility that the cost of insurance and of defending against lawsuits will diminish the availability and increase the price of pharmaceuticals is far from theoretical. Defendants cite a host of examples of products which have greatly increased in price or have been withdrawn or withheld from the market because of the fear that their products would be held liable for large judgments.

For example, according to defendant E.R. Squibb & Sons, Inc., Bendectin, the only antinauseant drug available for pregnant women, was withdrawn from sale in 1983 because the cost of insurance almost equalled the entire income from sale of the drug. Before it was withdrawn, the price of Bendectin increased by over 300%. (132 Chemical Week (June 12, 1983) p.14.)

Drug manufacturers refused to supply a newly discovered vaccine for influenza on the ground that mass inoculation would subject them to enormous liability. The government therefore assumed the risk of lawsuits resulting from injuries caused by the vaccine. (Franklin & Mais, Mass Immunization Programs (1977) 65 Cal. L. Rev. 754, 769 et seq.; Feldman v. Lederle Laboratories (1983) 460 A.2d 203, 209.) One producer of diphtheria-tetanus-pertussis vaccine withdrew from the market, giving as its reason "extreme liability exposure, cost of litigation and difficulty of continuing to obtain adequate insurance." (Hearing Before Subcom. on Health and the Environment of House Com. on Energy and Commerce on Vaccine Injury Compensation, 98th Cong., 2nd Sess. (Sept. 10, 1984) p.295.) There are only two manufacturers of the vaccine remaining in the market, and the cost of each dose rose a hundredfold from 11 cents in 1982 to $11.40 in 1986, $8 of which was for an insurance reserve. The price increase roughly paralleled an increase in the number of lawsuits from one in 1978 to 219 in 1985. (232 Science (June 13, 1986) p.1,339.) Finally, a manufacturer was unable to market a new drug for the treatment of vision problems because it could not obtain adequate liability insurance at a reasonable cost. (N.Y. Times (Oct. 14, 1986) p.10.)

There is no doubt that, from the public's standpoint, these are unfortunate consequences. And they occurred even though almost all jurisdictions follow the negligence standard of comment k. It is not unreasonable to conclude in these circumstances that the imposition of a harsher test for liability would not further the public interest in the development and availability of these important products.

We decline to hold, therefore, that a drug manufacturer's liability for injuries caused by the defective design of a prescription drug should be measured by the standard set forth in *Barker*.

2. Failure to Warn

For these same reasons of policy, we reject plaintiff's assertion that a drug manufacturer should be held strictly liable for failure to warn of risks inherent in a drug even though it neither knew nor could have known by the application of scientific knowledge available at the time of distribution that the drug could produce the undesirable side effects suffered by the plaintiff. . . .

3. The *Kearl* Test

One further question remains in this aspect of the case. Comment k, as we have seen, provides that the maker of an "unavoidably unsafe" product is not liable for injuries resulting from its use if the product is "properly prepared, and accompanied by proper directions and warning." With the few exceptions noted above, the courts which have adopted comment k have viewed all prescription drugs as coming within its scope.

Kearl suggested that not all drugs are "unavoidably dangerous" so as to merit the protection of the negligence standard of comment k, and it devised a test to separate those which meet that description from those which do not. It held that the question whether a drug should be exempt from strict liability as "unavoidably dangerous" presents a mixed question of law and fact which should be decided on the basis of evidence to be taken by the trial judge out of the presence of the jury. The judge should determine, after hearing the evidence,

(1) whether, when distributed, the product was intended to confer an exceptionally important benefit that made its availability highly desirable;
(2) whether the then-existing risk posed by the product was both "substantial" and "unavoidable"; and
(3) whether the interest in availability (again measured as of the time of distribution) outweighs the interest in promoting enhanced accountability through strict liability design defect review.

If these questions are answered in the affirmative the liability of the manufacturer is tested by the standard of comment *k;* otherwise, strict liability is the applicable test.

The Court of Appeal in the present case refused to adopt this approach on the ground that it required the trial judge to decide questions of fact which were ordinarily left to the jury, and that it presented the specter of inconsistent verdicts in various trial courts: in one case the question of liability for injuries caused by a specific drug would be tested by a negligence standard, while in another, involving the same drug, the judge might conclude that strict liability was the appropriate test.

We acknowledge that there is some appeal in the basic premise of *Kearl.* It seems unjust to grant the same protection from liability to those who gave us thalidomide as to the producers of penicillin. If some method could be devised to confine the benefit of the comment *k* negligence standard to those drugs that have proved useful to mankind while denying the privilege to those that are clearly harmful, it would deserve serious consideration. But we know of no means by which this can be accomplished without substantially impairing the public interest in the development and marketing of new drugs, because the harm to this interest arises in the very process of attempting to make the distinction. . . .

Kearl gives the manufacturer a chance to avoid strict liability. But the eligibility of each drug for favorable treatment must be tested at a trial, with its attendant litigation costs, and the drug must survive two risk/benefit challenges, first by the judge and then by the jury. In order to vindicate the public's interest in the availability and affordability of prescription drugs, a manufacturer must have a greater assurance that his products will not be measured by a strict liability standard than is provided by the test stated in *Kearl.* Therefore, we disapprove the portion of *Kearl* which holds that comment *k* should not be applied to a prescription drug unless the trial court first determines that the drug is "unavoidably dangerous."

In conclusion, and in accord with almost all our sister states that have considered the issue, we hold that a manufacturer is not strictly liable for injuries caused by a prescription drug so long as the drug was properly prepared and accompanied by warnings of its dangerous propensities that were either known or reasonably scientifically knowable at the time of distribution. . . .

The judgment of the Court of Appeal is affirmed.

California intermediate appellate courts have held that *Brown* applies to implanted medical devices as well as drugs. See, e.g., Artiglio v. Superior Court, 27 Cal. Rptr. 2d 589 (Cal. Ct. App. 1994) (breast implant); Hufft v. Horowitz, 5 Cal. Rptr. 2d 377 (Cal. Ct. App. 1992) (inflatable penile prosthesis). But *Brown* does not apply to latex surgical gloves. See Morson v. Superior Court, 109 Cal. Rptr. 2d 343 (Cal. Ct. App. 2001) (noting that prescriptions from an intermediary medical professional are not required to obtain latex gloves). Washington and Utah follow California's approach. See Young v. Key Pharms., 922 P.2d 59 (Wash. 1996); Grundberg v. Upjohn Co., 813 P.2d 89 (Utah 1991).

In the jurisdictions that have adopted comment *k*, most apply it on a case-by-case basis as an affirmative defense. In Ortho Pharmaceutical Corp. v. Heath, 722 P.2d 410 (Colo. 1986), overruled on other grounds, Armentrout v. FMC Corp., 842 P.2d 175 (Colo. 1992), the court found that it was possible to make out a design defect case against a drug manufacturer based on risk-utility balancing "without regard to the availability of warnings." It did, however, allow the jury to hear evidence as to whether the drug in question was an "unavoidably unsafe product" within the meaning of Restatement of Torts (Second) §402A, Comment *k*.

In Tobin v. Astra Pharmaceutical Products, Inc., 993 F.2d 528 (6th Cir.), *cert. denied* sub nom., 114 S. Ct. 304 (1993), the court of appeals affirmed a verdict and judgment in favor of a young woman who had taken a prescription drug during pregnancy, allegedly causing cardiac failure and necessitating a heart transplant. The drug in question was designed to prolong pregnancy and prevent premature delivery, but it also posed serious risks of potentially fatal reactions in patients with plaintiff's presenting conditions. At the close of trial, the jury found that the drug provided no benefits to any class of patients and created such serious risks that it was defective in design. The court of appeals concluded, "We find that there was sufficient evidence before the jury to conclude that a prudent manufacturer knowing all the risks would not market [the drug]." Id. at 540.

Restatement (Third) of Torts: Products Liability
(1998)

§6. LIABILITY OF COMMERCIAL SELLER OR DISTRIBUTOR FOR HARM CAUSED BY DEFECTIVE PRESCRIPTION DRUGS AND MEDICAL DEVICES

(a) A manufacturer of a prescription drug or medical device who sells or otherwise distributes a defective drug or medical device is subject to liability for harm to persons caused by the defect. . . .

(b) For purposes of liability under Subsection (a), a prescription drug or medical device is defective if at the time of sale or other distribution the drug or medical device:

(2) is not reasonably safe due to defective design as defined in Subsection (c) . . .

(c) A prescription drug or medical device is not reasonably safe due to defective design if the foreseeable risks of harm posed by the drug or medical device are sufficiently great in relation to its foreseeable therapeutic benefits that reasonable health-care providers, knowing of such foreseeable risks and therapeutic benefits, would not prescribe the drug or medical device for any class of patients. . . .

COMMENT:

b. Rationale. . . . The traditional refusal by courts to impose tort liability for defective designs of prescription drugs and medical devices is based on the fact that a prescription drug or medical device entails a unique set of risks and benefits. What may be harmful to one patient may be beneficial to another. Under Subsection (c) a drug is defectively designed only when it provides no net benefit to any class of patients. Courts have concluded that as long as a drug or medical device provides net benefits to some persons under some circumstances, the drug or device manufacturer should be required to instruct and warn healthcare providers of the foreseeable risks and benefits. Courts have also recognized that the regulatory system governing prescription drugs is a legitimate mechanism for setting the standards for drug design. In part, this deference reflects concerns over the possible negative effects of judicially imposed liability on the cost and availability of valuable medical technology. This deference also rests on two further assumptions: first, that prescribing health-care providers, when adequately informed by drug manufacturers, are able to assure that the right drugs and medical devices reach the right patients; and second, that governmental regulatory agencies adequately review new prescription drugs and devices, keeping unreasonably dangerous designs off the market.

Nevertheless, unqualified deference to these regulatory mechanisms is considered by a growing number of courts to be unjustified. An approved prescription drug or medical device can present significant risks without corresponding advantages. At the same time, manufacturers must have ample discretion to develop useful drugs and devices without subjecting their design decisions to the ordinary test applicable to products generally under §2(b). Accordingly, Subsection (c) imposes a more rigorous test for defect than does §2(b), which does not apply to prescription drugs and medical devices. The requirement for establishing defective design of a prescription drug or medical device under Subsection (c) is that the drug or device have so little merit compared with its risks that reasonable health-care providers, possessing knowledge of risks that were known or reasonably should have been known, would not have prescribed the drug or device for any class of patients. Thus, a prescription drug or medical device that has usefulness to any class of patients is not defective in design even if it is harmful to other patients. Because of the special nature of prescription drugs and medical devices, the determination of whether such products are not reasonably safe is to be made under Subsections (c) and (d) rather than under §§2(b) and 2(c). . . .

f. Manufacturers' liability for defectively designed prescription drugs and medical devices. Subsection (c) reflects the judgment that, as long as a given drug or device provides net benefits for a class of patients, it should be available to them, accompanied by appropriate warnings and instructions. Learned intermediaries must generally be relied upon to see that the right drugs and devices reach the right patients. However, when a drug or device provides net benefits to no class of patients — when reasonable, informed health-care providers would not prescribe it to any class of patients — then the design of the product is defective and the manufacturer should be subject to liability for harm caused.

A prescription drug or device manufacturer defeats a plaintiff's design claim by establishing one or more contexts in which its product would be prescribed by reasonable, informed health-care providers. That some individual providers do, in fact, prescribe defendant's product does not in itself suffice to defeat the plaintiff's claim. Evidence regarding the actual conduct of health-care providers, while relevant and admissible, is not necessarily controlling. The issue is whether, objectively viewed, reasonable providers, knowing of the foreseeable risks and benefits of the drug or medical device, would prescribe it for any class of patients. Given this very demanding objective standard, liability is likely to be imposed only under unusual circumstances. The court has the responsibility to determine when the plaintiff has introduced sufficient evidence so that reasonable persons could conclude that plaintiff has met this demanding standard.

ILLUSTRATION:

1. ABC Pharmaceuticals manufactures and distributes D, a prescription drug intended to prolong pregnancy and thus to reduce the risks associated with premature birth. Patricia, six months pregnant with a history of irregular heart beats, was given D during a hospital stay in connection with her pregnancy. As a result, she suffered heart failure and required open-heart surgery. In Patricia's action against ABC, her expert testifies that, notwithstanding FDA approval of D five years prior to Patricia's taking the drug, credible studies published two years prior to Patricia's taking the drug concluded that D does not prolong pregnancy for any class of patients. Notwithstanding a finding by the trier of fact that ABC gave adequate warnings to the prescribing physician regarding the serious risks of heart failure in patients with a history of irregular heart beats, the trier of fact can find that reasonably informed health-care providers would not prescribe D for any class of patients, thus rendering ABC subject to liability.

James A. Henderson, Jr. & Aaron D. Twerski, Drug Designs *Are* Different
111 Yale L.J. 151 (2001)

In an essay published in this Journal entitled Is There a Design Defect in the Restatement (Third) of Torts: Products Liability?, 109 Yale L.J. 1087 (2000) George Conk criticizes the American Law Institute and the Reporters of the new Restatement for immunizing prescription drug manufacturers from liability for defective design. In doing so, he joins other commentators who have been critical of this aspect of the new Restatement, upon which we served as Reporters. Because Conk claims to have history on his side, and because this most recent criticism may prove to be disproportionately influential, we offer a response both to him and to other critics.

Conk praises the general product-design standard adopted by the Restatement, which predicates liability for almost all nonprescription products upon proof that a reasonable alternative design could have been adopted that would have avoided or reduced harm to the plaintiff. However, he criticizes the Restatement's provisions relating to defective drug design for not applying the same "reasonable alternative" standard. (The Restatement deems a drug defective in design only if it would not be prescribed for any class of patients.) In his view, the Restatement test for defective drug design would protect prescription drug manufacturers from liability even if a plaintiff could show that an alternatively designed drug would have avoided unnecessary risk. Conk argues that during the late 1970s and early 1980s, the absence of a reasonable alternative design standard for prescription drugs allowed distributors of blood to escape liability for supplying blood products contaminated with the hepatitis C virus and that the Restatement test would condone such noxious results in the future. Claiming this regrettable history as support for his position, Conk urges that the defectiveness of prescription drug designs should be determined by the same standard as is generally applicable to nonprescription products.

Our critics have misread the prescription drug design provision of the new Restatement. It does not immunize prescription drug manufacturers for defective design. Plaintiffs may establish defectiveness by showing that safer alternative drugs were available on the market that reasonable health care providers would have prescribed in place of a defendant's drug for all classes of patients. . . .

II. Conk's Critique Contains Significant Errors

. . .

A. Contrary to Conk's Reading, the New Restatement Does Allow Courts to Consider Already-Marketed Alternatives in Assessing a Drug Design's Defectiveness

Conk reads the prescription drug design provision in section 6(c) to prevent plaintiffs from establishing defect by showing that a safer alternative to a defendant's drug was available. We emphatically disagree with Conk's insistence that section 6(c) does not allow any alleged RAD to be considered by the court in determining whether a prescription product's design is defective. The key to understanding the meaning of section 6(c) on this point lies in its explicit reliance on the construct of whether "reasonable health-care providers" would knowingly "prescribe the drug or medical device for any class of patients." Obviously, such a reasonable provider should consider available alternative drugs in deciding which drug, if any, to prescribe. Indeed, that may be said to be the essence of the healer's craft—assessing and comparing all available courses of medical treatment. Conk's suggestion that the new Restatement requires the hypothetical prescribing physician to focus exclusively on the risks and benefits of a given drug in isolation, wearing blinders that prevent consideration of other readily available drugs, attributes a meaning to section 6(c) that would require that physician to violate her Hippocratic oath.

Admittedly, section 6(c)'s description of the risks of harm that would support a finding of defectiveness as "great in relation to [the drug's] therapeutic benefits" might lead, at first blush, to Conk's conclusion. That is, this language might suggest that the drug is to be judged on its own bottom, in isolation from all other possible alternatives. And comment *f* appears to reinforce this reading with its first sentence: "Subsection (c) reflects the judgment that, as long as a given drug or device provides net benefits for a class of patients, it should be available to them. . . ." But the admittedly ambiguous phrase "provides net benefits" must, in fairness, be read to refer to "net benefits in light of available alternatives." This reading is made clear by the second sentence in comment *f*: "Learned intermediaries must generally be relied upon to see that the right drugs and devices reach the right patients." This second sentence conjures the appropriate image of responsible prescribing physicians deciding what is best for their patients among available alternatives — not the distorted image that Conk reads into section 6(c) of a health-care provider acting with blinders firmly in place.

Our reading of section 6(c) is bolstered by the reality that, if Conk's contrary reading were correct — if the design standard under section 6(c) were whether, judged in isolation, a given drug benefitted any class of patients — then there would be no reason to couch the standard in terms of what a reasonable physician would do for her patients. Section 6(c) could just as easily have said "a prescription drug or medical device is defective if, on balance, it benefits no class of patients." In fact, section 6(c) must have been intended to allow reasonable alternatives to be considered by the hypothetical prescribing physicians, because the blinders Conk reads into section 6(c), by forcing those physicians needlessly to harm many of their hypothetical patients, would otherwise constitute a gratuitous insult to the medical profession. . . .

It follows from the foregoing exposition of the meaning of section 6(c) that it does allow plaintiffs to condemn as defective prescription product designs based on proof of a RAD. Conk's criticism of section 6(c) for ruling out any such proof is, therefore, in error. But inasmuch as section 6(c) does not impose the same RAD-based standard as does the general design defect provision in section 2(b), his criticism retains vitality and deserves further consideration. Section 6(c)'s version of RAD departs from section 2(b) in two important respects. The first relates to the sources upon which plaintiffs may rely. Under section 6(c), plaintiffs relying on a RAD are limited to alternative drugs or medical devices actually approved by the FDA, marketed by manufacturers, and available to be prescribed by health-care providers at the time the plaintiff's physician prescribed the defendant's drug. In contrast, if section 2(b) applied to prescription products, plaintiffs would be able, in appropriate cases, to prove that the defendant could have and should have developed and marketed a safer alternative, even if none had actually been developed.

The second important difference between the Restatement's treatments of defective product design generally and defective prescription drug design in particular relates not to the sources of the potential RADs from which plaintiffs may draw, but to the analytical power wielded by the RAD once its availability has been established. Under the general design standard in section 2(b), a RAD that provides an overall increase in safety may condemn a defendant's design as defective even if the defendant's design would clearly and rationally be preferred by one or more classes of users or consumers. Under the rule in section 2(b), if the omission of the RAD renders a defendant's product not reasonably safe, the welfare of those classes of consumers who benefit from the defendant's design are sacrificed to the greater welfare of the greater number of consumers who are exposed to unreasonable risk by the same design. In contrast, a RAD under section 6(c) condemns a given drug as defectively designed only if the RAD provides a net benefit to all classes of users. Under the prescription drug design provision, disadvantaging one or more classes of patients by denying them a particular drug or medical device is never warranted simply because such denial might benefit an even larger number of patients for whom the drug or service might be misprescribed. This difference, like the earlier-described difference relating to the proper sources of RAD upon which plaintiffs may rely, matters a great deal to critics such as George Conk who insist that the RAD-based standard in section 2(b) should apply to all products, including prescription drugs and medical devices. . . .

III. Responding More Broadly to Critics: The New Restatement Has Clearly Got It Right

A. The *Restatement* Is Correct in Not Allowing Plaintiffs to Argue that a Drug Manufacturer Should Have Developed a Safer Alternative Drug

The new Restatement's refusal to consider not-yet-approved alternative drugs in assessing the defendant's drug design does not rest on judicial deference to the FDA's expertise. As noted earlier, if two FDA-approved drugs are equally efficacious and one presents greater risk of harm, FDA approval does not insulate the manufacturer of the more dangerous drug from liability. Nor does the fact that the warnings accompanying a drug meet FDA guidelines insulate the drug manufacturer from liability for failure to warn. Finally, section 6(c) does not defer to the FDA when the approved drug would not be prescribed by reasonable medical providers to any class of patients. In that circumstance, section 6(c) tacitly admits that the FDA occasionally makes mistakes by approving worthless drugs that no competent provider would prescribe for any class of patients. Section 6(c)'s refusal to consider not-yet-approved drugs does not rest on unshakeable confidence in the FDA.

Why, then, does the rule in section 6(c) of the Restatement refuse to hold liable a manufacturer for not developing a safer alternative drug that would have prevented the plaintiff's injury? Such refusal rests not on deference to the FDA but on an understandable reluctance to allow courts to determine whether a proposed alternative drug would have received FDA approval. Development by a manufacturer of a safer alternative drug does not, by itself, help anyone. For physicians to prescribe such a safer drug, it must reach the market. To reach the market, a prescription drug must be approved by the FDA. Thus, the question of whether a new alternative drug should have been developed by the defendant must be recast as whether the proposed alternative drug would have won FDA approval in time to help the plaintiff. No court can answer that question without seeking, in some manner, to replicate the FDA approval process. A brief description of the FDA approval process reveals why courts could never hope successfully to undertake such an inquiry. . . .

[The FDA approval process lasts anywhere from 7 to 12 years and involves animal testing and years of controlled testing on humans. No court could through litigation replicate the FDA process and be able to predict that an alternative drug design would attain FDA approval and actually reach the consumer market.]

B. The *Restatement* Properly Rejects an Aggregative, All-Patients-Considered Approach to Defective Drug Design

This Section compares the merits of the new Restatement's narrower "benefits any class of patients" approach and the broader "reasonableness under all the circumstances" approach championed by our critics. Once not-yet-approved alternative drugs are eliminated from judicial consideration, as the preceding Section makes clear they must be, the important difference between the approach in the new Restatement and the approach urged by our critics relates to the question of whose welfare should be taken into account in determining defectiveness. Section 6(c) of the Restatement considers only the welfare of patients who are helped by a defendant's prescription drug, refusing to deem a drug defective in design if it benefits any class of patients. In contrast, critics of the Restatement advocate an aggregative approach in which the defectiveness of a prescription drug's design is determined by considering the drug's potential impact on all patients for whom it might, properly or improperly, be prescribed. Under the latter approach, the court weighs the risks of injury to some patients caused by misprescription and detrimental consumption of the drug against the potential benefits to other patients from proper prescription and beneficial consumption. Even if a drug would benefit a significant number of people, the drug is defective in design if those for whom the drug is improperly prescribed by negligent physicians suffer, in the aggregate, greater harm. The welfare of all patients is taken into account under the proposed approach, not just the welfare of those helped by a drug's proper prescription and consumption.

The all-patients-considered approach based on aggregate consumer welfare is functionally equivalent to the approach taken in section 2(b) of the new Restatement in connection with most nonprescription products. In nonprescription contexts, aggregation of consumer interests — weighing potential risks to some consumers against potential benefits to others — represents a necessary compromise. If the products liability system could somehow refrain from deeming an inherently dangerous product defective in design when sold to and used by persons cautious enough to avoid accidents, while deeming the same product defective when sold to and used by accident-prone individuals, the liability system would presumably prefer to implement such a pattern of differential defectiveness and liability. But such differentiation is not possible for nonprescription products, which are available to everyone on the open market. It follows that aggregation of consumer interests is necessary; a product design is deemed defective or not defective taking into account all potential users and consumers. Under this aggregative approach, cautious users and consumers must pay for designed-in safety features that they do not need, a wasteful investment in care justified only because less cautious users and consumers who need the safety features benefit to a greater extent. . . .

The new Restatement relies on this mechanism of differential product distribution — medical prescription on a selective basis by licensed physicians — to justify its rule in section 6(c) that a drug design is not defective (and thus deserves to be marketed with adequate warnings) as long as at least one class of patients derives benefit, in light of all other available drugs and drug-related therapies, from its use. By rejecting this rule and treating prescription product designs the same as all other product designs, our critics reveal their lack of confidence in the capacity of learned intermediaries to see that the right drugs reach the right patients. If the assumptions supporting judicial reliance on the mechanism of differential distribution via medical prescription were to erode too far — if most physicians arranged to be judgment-proof and joined in epidemics of misprescription — the critics' insistence that drug designs be treated the same as all other product designs might be persuasive. But we see no reason on the evidence before us to conclude that significant erosion has occurred. Indeed, we anticipate that the coming era of electronic information transmittal and retrieval will reinforce the continued efficacy of judicial reliance on learned intermediaries to maximize consumer welfare derived from having a wide array of prescription drugs available to health care providers and their patients. . . .

IV. Conclusion

Our response to Conk and other critics should be clear enough. Drug designs are different, after all. The new Restatement allows courts to consider safer, FDA-approved drugs already on the market in determining the defectiveness of a prescription drug's design. But the new Restatement does not allow a plaintiff to assert that the defendant manufacturer could have developed and marketed a safer prescription drug in time to have avoided plaintiffs' injuries. To allow such claims would ask of courts more than they could responsibly deliver. Moreover, the new Restatement does not allow plaintiffs to demonstrate defectiveness by showing that a drug that provides benefits, when properly prescribed for one or more classes of patients, causes greater detriment when improperly prescribed for other classes of patients. Assuming that the manufacturer has given the necessary warnings and has not overpromoted the drug, misprescription should be solely the negligent physician's responsibility. To deny one group of patients a beneficial drug merely because adequately-warned physicians may misprescribe the same drug for another group of patients would be unfair and inefficient, and the new Restatement will have none of it.

As revealed in this Essay, the Restatement's treatment of defective prescription products has become a lightning rod for criticism. Most observers are in general agreement that the guidelines set forth a half-century ago in section 402A, comment k of the Restatement (Second) are unintelligible and that the cases seeking to interpret that section are confusing. In connection with section 6(c) of the Restatement (Third), we plead guilty to the charge that we did not restate existing case law. One could hardly be expected to restate gibberish. Instead, we opted for a fresh look at the question of design liability for prescription products and utilized the case law to illuminate the underlying issues in this difficult area. Some cases did get it right, and we drew on them for support. We do not, as our critics argue, defer blindly to FDA expertise. We do, however, question the institutional competence of courts to decide whether safer drugs could have received FDA approval and been brought to market in time to have helped any given patient. Finally, we reject outright the idea that drugs that well serve a class of patients should be declared defective either because physicians may negligently misprescribe the drugs or because patients who are fully warned of the relevant risks choose to accept those risks in order to improve the aesthetic quality of their lives. Our critics wonder why the ALI approved the drug design section of the new Restatement without objection or serious debate. We believe that it was so readily accepted because it made good common sense. It still does.

George W. Conk, The True Test: Alternative Safer Designs for Drugs and Medical Devices in a Patent-Constrained Market
49 UCLA L. Rev. 737 (2002)

I. The "True Meaning" According to the Scribes of the Products Liability Restatement's Section 6(c) on Prescription Drug and Device Design Liability — Making Meaning Plain

The "retired reporters" of the American Law Institute's (ALI's) Products Liability Restatement, Professors James Henderson and Aaron Twerski, . . . have offered a rebuttal to my critique of the prescription drug and medical device design defect rule promulgated in section 6(c) of the new Restatement. My essay . . . criticized the ALI rule that excludes prescription drugs and medical devices from the Products Liability Restatement's general measure of product design defect — the reasonable alternative design test. The rule's identical treatment of medical devices is itself the object of substantial criticism.

The retirees now offer in mitigation a previously unrecognized exception to the special rule proposed in the Products Liability Restatement regarding liability for defective design of prescription drugs and medical devices — section 6(c). The reporters now construe the blackletter rule to permit a finding that a drug is defective if comparison with another drug, already approved by the Food and Drug Administration (FDA) and available as part of the existing formulary, shows the challenged drug to be unreasonably dangerous for all classes of users. The reporters presumably would extend the new, broader construction to medical devices as well.

The interpretation offered is surprising. The reporters concede that their "phraseology" may have been "ambiguous," and that the comments and illustrations following the blackletter statement may be unillustrative. But the logic of the rule and the reporters' note, they say, show that the "true meaning," their new, expansive construction of the rule, was lying there waiting to be discovered all along. . . .

III. The Patent Monopoly and the Need for the Alternative Safer Design Test for Prescription Drugs and Medical Devices

The reporters would limit the alternative designs by which a product can be tested for defect to competing FDA-approved products. That is a particularly constrained approach in the case of patented prescription drugs. Successful drugs are commonly monopolized for two decades by the patent holder. The competing producer must either engage in protracted, burdensome litigation to declare invalid the patent underlying the innovator's drug, design a substantially different and superior drug, or stay out of the market.

The prospect of designing a new, improved version of an existing drug encounters not only the potentially high cost of development. The would-be competitor also faces the threat of litigation by pharmaceutical companies seeking to preserve their patent monopoly by either patenting new formulations or methods of use for the old product, or by employing the doctrine of equivalents to block the marketing of a revised version of the drug developed by another.

The doctrine of equivalents, a judicial construction, creates a zone of protection around a patent, extending protection beyond literal copying. The doctrine permits the patentee to go beyond the patent's written claims and grants to the patent monopolist the right to bar the use or sale of "equivalents" that "perform substantially the same function in substantially the same way to obtain the same result even though they differ in name, form, or shape." Despite the doctrine's tumultuous life, the U.S. Supreme Court recently confirmed its vitality, noting that there is "significant disagreement within the Court of Appeals for the Federal Circuit." While warning that a patent holder cannot recapture what it surrendered by claim amendment during the prosecution phase, the court explained the "essential inquiry" as: "Does the accused product or process contain elements identical or equivalent to each claimed element of the patented invention?" If it does, then the challenged product infringes on the patent even though it differs in form, name, or shape. . . .

VII. Medical Devices—The Final, Fatal Flaw in Section 6(c)

In trying to divine the "true meaning" of section 6(c), as the reporters say they have now done, it is instructive to consider the inclusion of devices in the section. The reporters, for reasons unexpressed, have carved in black letter an abhorrence of design defect liability against both pharmaceutical and medical device manufacturers. They would insulate both from ordinary principles of liability, so long as the device or drug is dispensed only by prescription or can be used only by a licensed person. Because no one but a physician could decide to implant a coronary stent or insert an intrauterine device (IUD), those devices are presumably subject to section 6(c).

Medical devices are often mechanical devices. Other than to note that devices, like drugs, are subject to FDA premarket review, the reporters have not attempted to explain why they should be excluded from ordinary principles of liability. Among the early medical device product liability cases were those involving women injured by the Dalkon Shield IUD. The litigation proceeded on design defect theories, such as that the tailstring of the IUD caused a wicking effect and transmitted bacteria. Due to their massive number, the cases presented management challenges, but no conceptual hurdles, for courts. If a practical and feasible alternative existed for such a design, whether in a change of material or in a competing, safer product, conventional products liability law proved adequate to handle the problems. Despite the medical nature of the products, no special rules were needed. Yet even under the newly construed section 6(c), such plaintiffs would be hobbled by the need to show that another, safer product was already on the market. Identification of the flaw and reasonably mature demonstration that there was a safer alternative design would not meet section 6(c)'s requirements, even with the gloss the reporters have now added.

Yet, if the product had the same defect and risk of harm, but it were a tampon, section 6(c) would present no obstacle, because it is a nonprescription product. Tampon cases have been handled successfully under the conventional approaches to product design defects. The anomalies, which would result from even the broad construction of section 6(c), show the rule to be fatally flawed as a guide to consistent and coherent adjudication of design defects in medical products.

The reporters say little on the issue of medical devices because, except for the FDA approval requirement, none of the rationales they employ in defense of their broad construction of section 6(b) apply to devices. As observed in the piece the reporters seek to refute, the amendment of a tentative draft of the Products Liability Restatement to include devices with prescription drugs was an unremarked-upon element on the floor of the ALI's annual meetings that addressed the section. But subsequent scholarship illuminates the failings of the rule for medical devices. . . .

Conclusion

. . .

It is important that courts not shrink from the task of judging the reasonableness of drug and medical device designs. Tort system review and compensation for failure to act reasonably to develop safe designs is particularly important. The broad play allowed to patents to "encompass foreseeable variations, not just of a claim element, but of a patent claim — also leads to higher costs. Society at large would bear the latter costs in the form of virtual foreclosure of competitive activity within the penumbra of each issued patent claim." The patent system's limits on competitive development of safer and more effective designs makes the tort system's functions of deterrence and compensation of particular importance in regard to the designs of drugs and medical devices.

The reporters' saving construction of section 6(c)'s "net benefit for any class of patients" rule (that drugs can be found defective only by comparison with other FDA-approved products on the market), though welcome, fails to save the blackletter rule. Section 6(c) fails to provide adequate guidance to courts. The rule is patently inadequate for devices and in the illustrated cases is also inadequate for analysis of drug design defects. Further, as technology matures the rule will have even less justification and will eventually be seen as an unjustified protective shield for two favored industries. The broad trend among courts to evaluate both drug and medical device design defect claims on a case-by-case basis is fundamentally correct. Therefore, the reporters' unabashed refusal to "restate" the case law was a mistake. The reporters are correct that the Restatements should not only summarize the experience of the past, but also should draw lessons from it for the future. To fail to do both would turn the Restatements into a mere catalog, which would ill-serve the future. A Restatement's blackletter law should both map the past and provide a flexible guide to the uncharted. In the case of section 6(c), the reporters drew the wrong lesson from the past (that case-by-case analysis of drug design defect claims is "inappropriate"), thus providing a flawed rule for the future (that courts are incompetent to review both drugs and devices for design defects).

A much richer guide for courts' analysis of liability for defective design of products lies in the alternative safer design test of section 2(b), the Restatement of the Law (Third) Torts: Products Liability. Restatements are written on paper, not chiseled in stone. They can be changed — and this one should be changed.

The Supreme Court of Nebraska was the first state high court to confront the question of whether to adopt §6(c). In Freeman v. Hoffman-LaRoche Inc., 618 N.W.2d 827 (Neb. 2000), the plaintiff alleged she developed numerous health problems from taking her prescription acne treatment medication. The court declined to adopt §6(c), viewing it as "too strict of a rule under which recovery from strict liability would be nearly impossible." Id. at 840. Instead, plaintiffs are required to plead the consumer expectations test and the defendant raise comment *k* as an affirmative defense. Id. Citing *Freeman,* the Georgia Court of Appeals in Bryant v. Hoffman-LaRoche Inc., 585 S.E.2d 723 (Ga. App. 2003), adopted a risk-utility approach to prescription drug design, allowing the defendant drug company to raise comment *k* by way of an affirmative defense. Although the majority refuses to adopt §6(c)'s "no reasonable provider" approach, Presiding Judge Andrews concurred specially to note that he would adopt §6(c), finding that "the different treatment accorded prescription drugs under §6(c) is a practical adjustment from the §2 general risk-utility that is appropriate to the unique nature of the products." Id. at 34. Several federal courts have also discussed §6. See, e.g., Taylor v. Danek Med., Inc., 1998 U.S. Dist. LEXIS 20265 (E.D. Pa. 1998) (predicting that the Supreme Court of Pennsylvania will eventually adopt §6(c)).

3. Pharmacists' Liability for Prescription Products

Pharmacists have frequently been afforded special protection by courts in products liability actions. Consider the limited circumstances under which the Products Liability Restatement imposes liability on retail sellers of prescription drugs:

Restatement (Third) of Torts: Products Liability
(1998)

§6. LIABILITY OF COMMERCIAL SELLER OR DISTRIBUTOR FOR HARM CAUSED BY DEFECTIVE PRESCRIPTION DRUGS AND MEDICAL DEVICES

. . .

(e) A retail seller or other distributor of a prescription drug or medical device is subject to liability for harm caused by the drug or device if:

(1) at the time of sale or other distribution the drug or medical device contains a manufacturing defect as defined in §2(a); or

(2) at or before the time of sale or other distribution of the drug or medical device the retail seller or other distributor fails to exercise reasonable care and such failure causes harm to persons.

COMMENT:

h. Liability of retail seller of prescription drugs and medical devices for defective designs and defects due to inadequate instructions or warnings. The rule governing most products imposes liability on wholesalers and retailers for selling a defectively designed product, or one without adequate instructions or warnings, even though they have exercised reasonable care in marketing the product. See §1, Comment *e,* and §2, Comment *o.* Courts have refused to apply this general rule to nonmanufacturing retail sellers of prescription drugs and medical devices and, instead, have adopted the rule state in Subsection (e). That rule subjects retailers to liability only if the product contains a manufacturing defect or if the retailer fails to exercise reasonable care in connection with distribution of the drug or medical device. In so limiting the liability of intermediary parties, courts have held that they should be permitted to rely on the special expertise of manufacturers, prescribing and treating health-care providers, and governmental regulatory agencies. They have also emphasized the needs of medical patients to have ready access to prescription drugs at reasonable prices.

Observe that retailers of prescription drugs and medical devices are strictly liable under §6(e) for harm caused by manufacturing defects and, otherwise, only if they are proven to have been negligent. The leading case applying a negligence standard to pharmacists for harm caused by generic risks is Murphy v. E.R. Squibb & Sons, Inc., 221 Cal. Rptr. 447 (Cal. 1985) (finding that, although pharmacists fill a hybrid role as service providers and products sellers, defendant pharmacists were primarily service providers and immune from strict liability). In Parker v. St. Vincent Hospital, 919 P.2d 1104 (N.M. 1996) the high court followed the majority in including hospitals in the "only-if-negligent" role, citing §6(e) with approval. See also San Diego Hospital Association v. Superior Court, 35 Cal. Rptr. 2d 489 (Cal. App. 1994).

Traditionally, pharmacists are not held strictly liable for injuries as long as a prescription is accurately filled. See, e.g., Morgan v. Wal-Mart Stores, Inc., 30 S.W.3d 455 (Tex. Ct. App. 2000); Johnson v. Walgreen, Co., 675 So. 2d 1036 (Fla. Dist. Ct. App. 1996). Pharmacists may also have a duty to be alert for obvious errors on the face of the prescription. See, e.g., McKee v. American Home Products Corp., 782 P.2d 1045 (Wash. 1989); Horner v. Spalitto, 1 S.W.3d 519 (Mo. Ct. App. 1999) (holding that pharmacist owed a higher standard of care than accurately filling a prescription when prescription called for three times the normal dosage). Courts often rely on the learned intermediary doctrine in finding that patients are expected to rely upon their physicians, not their pharmacists, for warnings. As the *McKee* court reasoned, "[r]equiring the pharmacist to warn of potential risks associated with a drug would interject the pharmacist into the physician-patient relationship and interfere with ongoing treatment." Id. at 712.

However, courts are finding the learned intermediary doctrine less persuasive as pharmacists take on greater responsibilities than merely measuring and dispensing prescriptions, and pharmacists have been found liable for failure to warn drug users under special circumstances. For example, courts may find that pharmacies willfully undertake a duty to warn customers of the dangers associated with the drugs they sell. In Cottam v. CVS Pharmacy, 764 N.E.2d 814 (Mass. Sup. Ct. 2002), the defendant pharmacy had voluntarily distributed a list of potential side effects associated with a certain prescription drug. The pharmacy did not represent that the list was exhaustive. Nonetheless, in affirming judgment on a verdict finding the defendant to have been negligent, the appellate court found that when a pharmacy undertakes to warn customers of some potential side effects of a drug, it undertakes to warn of all known side effects. See also Baker v. Arbor Drug, 544 N.W.2d 727 (Mich. Ct. App. 1996) (finding that a pharmacy undertakes a duty to warn where it advertises the efficacy of its drug interaction computer database in protecting consumers). But see Kasin v. Osco Drug, Inc., 728 N.E.2d 77 (Ill. App. Ct. 2000).

Several courts have gone further in imposing a duty to warn on pharmacies. In Happel v. Wal-Mart Stores, Inc., 766 N.E.2d 1118 (Ill. 2002), the trial court granted the defendant pharmacy's motion for summary judgment. In affirming the intermediate court's reversal of summary judgment, the Supreme Court of Illinois imposed a duty to warn on the part of the pharmacy where it had been informed of the plaintiff's known allergies and knew that filling her prescription was certain to cause an allergic reaction. Given this knowledge, a duty to warn was found to be reasonable. In Lasley v. Shrake's Country Club Pharmacy, 880 P.2d 1129 (Ariz. Ct. App. 1994), the defendant pharmacy had filled the plaintiff's prescriptions for nearly 30 years. The plaintiff, who eventually required in-patient hospitalization and treatment for addiction, alleged that the pharmacy was negligent for failing to warn customers of the drugs' dangerous propensities and failing to keep track of customers' dependency on the drugs. The court held that the pharmacy owed a duty of reasonable care to its customers, and remanded the case for a jury determination of whether that duty was breached.

On the more general subject of the liability of manufacturers of prescription drugs, see generally Aaron Arnold, Note, Rethinking Design Defect Law, Should Arizona Adopt the Restatement (Third) of Torts: Products Liability, 45 Ariz. L. Rev. 173 (2003); R. Paul Asbury, Comment, Pharmacist Liability: The Doors of Litigation are Opening, 40 Santa Clara L. Rev. 907 (2000); R. Paul Asbury, Comment, Pharmacist Liability: The Doors of Litigation are Opening, 40 Santa Clara L. Rev. 907 (2000); James E. Britain, Product Honesty Is the Best Policy: A Comparison of Doctors and Manufacturers' Duty to Disclose Drug Risks and the Importance of Consumer Expectations in Determining Product Defect, 79 Nw. U. L. Rev. 342 (1984); Richard L. Cupp, Jr., The Continuing Search for Proper Perspective: Whose Reasonableness Should Be At Issue in a Product Design Defect Analysis? Seventh Annual Health Law Symposium Proving Product Defect After the Restatement (Third) of Torts: Products Liability, 30 Seton Hall L. Rev. 233 (1999); Richard L. Cupp, Jr., Rethinking Conscious Design Liability for Prescription Drugs: The Restatement (Third) Standard Versus a Negligence Approach, 63 Geo. Wash. L. Rev. 76 (1994); Katrina Fox, Note, A Weighty Issue: Will Pharmacists Survive the Fen-Phen Feeding Frenzy? Kohl v. American Home Products Corporation and a Pharmacists' Duty to Warn of the Dangers of Prescription Drugs, 2001 B.Y.U. L. Rev. 1349 (2001); Michael D. Green, Safety as an Element of Pharmaceutical Quality: The Respective Roles of Regulation and Tort Law, 42 St. Louis U. L.J. 163 (1998); James A. Henderson, Jr., Prescription Drug Design Liability Under the Proposed Restatement (Third) of Torts: A Reporter's Perspective, 48 Rutgers L. Rev. 471 (1996); Steven W. Huang, The Omnibus Reconciliation Act of 1990: Redefining Pharmacists' Legal Responsibilities, 24 Am. J.L. & Med. 417 (1998); Richard A. Merrill, Compensation for Prescription Drug Injuries, 59 Va. L. Rev. 1 (1973); George C. Pratt & Fred W. Parnon, Diagnosis of a Legal Headache: Liability for Unforeseeable Defects in Drugs, 53 St. John's L. Rev. 517 (1979); David S. Torborg, Comment, Design Defect Liability and Prescription Drugs: Who's In Charge?, 59 Ohio St. L.J. 633 (1998); Teresa Moran Schwartz, Prescription Products and the Proposed Restatement (Third), 61 Tenn. L. Rev. 1357 (1994); Michael J. Wagner & Laura L. Peterson, The New Restatement (Third) of Torts: Shelter from the Product Liability Storm for Pharmaceutical Companies and Medical Device Manufacturers?, 53 Food & Drug L.J. 225 (1998).

C. USED PRODUCTS

1. The Tort Rules Governing Liability

Crandell v. Larkin and Jones Appliance Co.
334 N.W.2d 31 (S.D. 1983)

DUNN, J.

This is an appeal from a judgment entered by the trial court granting a motion to dismiss a products liability action against a commercial seller of used products. We reverse and remand.

On February 4, 1978, Gloria (Mrs. A. L.) Crandell (appellant) purchased a used Coronado clothes dryer from Larkin and Jones Appliance Company, Inc. (appellee). The dryer, which was displayed on appellee's sales floor, had a tag affixed to it which described the machine as "Larkin and Jones Quality Reconditioned Unit" which was "Tag-Tested" and "Guaranteed." In addition to these written representations, the salesman assured appellant that the dryer carried a ninety-day guarantee for "workmanship, parts and labor." Appellant purchased the dryer because of the guarantee and the $100 price tag. Appellee apparently delivered and installed the dryer that same day.

Late in the afternoon of February 18, 1978, appellant asked her son to put a blanket in the dryer to dry. Fifteen to twenty minutes later appellant noticed smoke coming through the furnace vents in her bedroom. Appellant ran to the utility room in the basement and saw the room was full of smoke, apparently coming from the dryer. Appellant opened the dryer door with wet towels because flames were coming out the front. Appellant's attempts to smother the flames in the drum with the wet towels was unsuccessful. Appellant then called the fire department. By the time of their arrival, the fire had spread to other areas of the utility room and had also caused significant smoke damage throughout appellant's home. Total damages to appellant's property as a result of the fire were in excess of $25,000.

Several days prior to the fire, appellant noticed the dryer had apparently overheated a load of clothing. To compensate for this, appellant put the heat selector dial on a lower setting and continued to use the dryer. According to appellant, the thought of a fire did not even occur to her.

Fire department personnel testified the sole ignition source of the fire was inside the dryer. Other expert testimony established that the fire originated in the dryer when the blanket being dried became so hot that it ignited.

None of the theories for recovery which were presented to the trial court were accepted. Appellant now appeals, contending the trial court erred in not finding appellee strictly liable and in not finding that appellee breached express and implied warranties. We address each contention in turn.

We adopted the strict liability theory, as set forth in Restatement (Second) of Torts: §402A, in Engberg v. Ford Motor Company, 87 S.D. 196, 205 N.W.2d 104 (1973), and thereby created a new cause of action in tort. Restatement (Second) of Torts §402A neither expressly includes nor excludes commercial sellers of used products from its coverage. Rather, its coverage applies to "one who sells any product." We have not determined whether the strict liability doctrine should be broadened to cover the commercial sale of used products. We now undertake that inquiry.

Courts and commentators disagree as to whether strict liability should apply to a commercial seller of used products. Courts rejecting strict liability for used products have primarily dealt with fact patterns which did not involve guarantees or reconditioned, rebuilt, or recapped products. In Rix v. Reeves, 23 Ariz. App. 243, 245, 532 P.2d 185, 187 (1975), a case involving the sale of a used wheel, the court specifically limited its holding when it stated: "By used products we do not refer to products rebuilt by a manufacturer, nor do we mean to imply that there is never any liability when used products are sold."

More recently the Oregon Supreme Court in Tillman v. Vance Equipment Co., 286 Or. 747, 596 P.2d 1299 (1979), came to the same conclusion in a case involving the sale of a used crane "as is" which was inspected and approved by the purchaser. There, the court was reluctant to hold every commercial used-goods dealer responsible for injuries caused by defects in its goods. The court stated:

> We conclude that holding every dealer in used goods responsible regardless of fault for injuries caused by defects in his goods would not only affect the prices of used goods; it would work a significant change in the very nature of used goods markets. Those markets, generally speaking, operate on the apparent understanding that the seller, even though he is in the business of selling such goods, makes no particular representation about their quality simply by offering them for sale. *If a buyer wants some assurance of quality, he typically either bargains for it in the specific transaction or seeks out a dealer who routinely offers it* (by, for example, providing a guarantee, limiting his stock of goods to those of a particular quality, advertising that his used goods are specially selected, or in some other fashion). The flexibility of this kind of market appears to serve legitimate interests of buyers as well as sellers.
>
> We are of the opinion that the sale of a used product, *without more,* may not be found to generate the kind of expectations of safety that the courts have held are justifiably created by the introduction of a new product into the stream of commerce. 286 Or. at 755-56, 596 P.2d at 1303-04 (emphasis added, footnote omitted).

We agree with the rationale provided by these courts to the extent it applies to the broad commercial used-product market. We believe, however, that those used-product merchants who rebuild or recondition goods are subject to the strict liability doctrine. The application of strict liability to sellers of used products, who rebuild or recondition those products, helps to protect the reasonable expectations of consumers.

Appellant alleges the trial court erred in finding that recovery was precluded under strict liability because it was not established that the defect caused the accident. . . .

At trial, appellant presented two expert witnesses to testify as to the existence of a defect and the cause of the fire. Both witnesses were professors of electrical engineering at the South Dakota School of Mines and Technology in Rapid

City, South Dakota. The witnesses examined the dryer after the fire and prepared a report documenting their findings. That report and their testimony concluded that the clothes dryer was defective. They found that contact points on the thermostats were pitted and in a very deteriorated condition. The witnesses believed that the two thermostats malfunctioned, thereby allowing the heat element to rise to temperatures high enough to cause the blanket to ignite. This evidence, coupled with the knowledge that a properly functioning dryer would not start a blanket on fire, leads us to conclude the dryer was defective. As one of the experts noted: "I don't know how I could reach a conclusion other than the dryer is defective if the thing (blanket) you put in it catches fire."

As to causation, we can find no credible evidence to support the trial court's position that causation was not established. Here, it is undisputed that appellant did not tamper with or misuse the dryer prior to the fire. Expert testimony established that the dryer was defective and identified the exact components, the thermostats, that failed to function properly allowing the temperature inside the drum to reach temperatures high enough to cause a fire. In our view, this evidence goes well beyond the preponderance requirement in establishing causation.

Finally, we look to the requirement that the defect existed when the product was in appellee's hands. Contrary to appellee's assertion, it was not necessary to show appellee created the defect, but only that the defect existed when the product was distributed by and under appellee's control. Evidence produced at trial provides sufficient circumstantial evidence to meet this requirement. First, and most obvious, the fire occurred within two weeks of leaving appellee's hands. Second, one of the experts testified that in his opinion one of the thermostats became inoperative quite some time prior to the fire. In his opinion, the back-up thermostat eventually became so worn that it too failed to function properly. Finally, it was established at trial that the wrong type of thermostats were in the dryer at the time of sale. According to the expert testimony, this improper equipment also contributed to the fire's inception. We believe this evidence establishes the existence of a defect while the product was in the hands of appellee.

All this aside, however, appellee would have us believe that strict liability is negated in this case because appellant assumed the risk by continuing to use the machine after it overheated on one occasion. At the close of trial, appellee moved to amend its pleadings to allege the defense of assumption of the risk. The trial court in its memorandum opinion and findings of fact and conclusions of law specifically excluded the use of this defense theory. Lacking a notice of review, we must conclude this issue is not preserved for appeal. Even if the trial court had approved the use of the assumption of the risk defense, however, there was no credible evidence to support such a defense theory. While appellant acknowledged the dryer on one occasion dried her clothing so that they were "abnormally hot," she simply turned the heat selector to a lower setting. We do not find this an abnormal reaction and cannot imagine that a reasonable person, by so reacting, would thereby assume the risk of a fire starting in the dryer. . . .

For all the reasons set forth above, we reverse the judgment of the trial court and remand this case for entry of a judgment awarding damages in accordance with the stipulation agreed to by the parties.

All the Justices concur.

Restatement (Third) of Torts: Products Liability
(1998)

§8. LIABILITY OF COMMERCIAL SELLER OR DISTRIBUTOR OF DEFECTIVE USED PRODUCTS

One engaged in the business of selling or otherwise distributing used products who sells or distributes a defective used product is subject to liability for harm to persons or property caused by the defect if the defect:

(a) arises from the seller's failure to exercise reasonable care; or

(b) is a manufacturing defect under §2(a) or a defect that may be inferred under §3 and the seller's marketing of the product would cause a reasonable person in the position of the buyer to expect the used product to present no greater risk of defect than if the product were new; or

(c) is a defect under §2 or §3 in a used product remanufactured by the seller or a predecessor in the commercial chain of distribution of the used product; or

(d) arises from a used product's noncompliance under §4 with a product safety statute or regulation applicable to the used product.

A used product is a product that, prior to the time of sale or other distribution referred to in this Section, is commercially sold or otherwise distributed to a buyer not in the commercial chain of distribution and used for some period of time.

NOTE: TORT AND CONTRACT— SOMETHING OLD, SOMETHING NEW

The controversy that swirls around the issue of whether strict liability ought to apply to used products reveals a strange ambivalence that pervades the entire field of products liability. We have already seen that the vast majority of courts have placed products liability firmly within the scope of tort law. Only a small minority draw the doctrinal basis for strict liability from the Uniform Commercial Code. Try as we may, however, it is impossible to totally divorce products liability law from contract law. The fact remains that the buyer of a product is not a stranger to the transaction. The buyer purchases the product for value. Expectations with regard to quality and performance of a product are at least partially, and often significantly, a function of price and other terms. Putting aside express warranties, one has different expectations when purchasing a Rolls Royce than when purchasing a Yugo. To be sure, tort law has triumphed on one important issue: When a new product fails to meet a manufacturer's own standard for product quality it is considered defective. Both the Rolls Royce and the Yugo must be free of manufacturing defects.

When we turn to used products, it is much more difficult to disregard contract norms. First, used products markets tend to be almost perfect. One can, for example, purchase a used car for $100 to $30,000. It is clear that expectations change along the price spectrum. But pinpointing what consumer expectations are at any given price is no easy task. Second, it is far from certain that a commercial seller of used products is in a better position than the buyer to discover latent manufacturing defects or weaknesses that arise from extended product use. Third, there is a real possibility that the imposition of strict liability on commercial sellers of used goods will drive the prices of such products so high that consumers will prefer to buy used products on a private and individual basis from classified advertisements in local newspapers. Since strict liability does not apply to private noncommercial sales, such private sales would not reflect a strict liability price hike. On the other hand, private sellers also lack the resources to make any kind of sophisticated inspection of the products they sell. It would be difficult to make out a case of negligence against a noncommercial seller. The net effect of imposing strict liability on commercial sellers might be to drive purchasers of used goods to buy from less responsible, noncommercial sellers who do not have the expertise to undertake "reasonable inspection." More rather than fewer dangerous used products will reenter the stream of commerce.[1]

Notwithstanding the foregoing arguments, a substantial number of courts do impose strict liability for the sale of used products. Thus, in Frey v. Harley Davidson Motor Co., Inc. 734 A.2d 1 (Pa. App. 1999) the defendant sold a used motorcycle, the jumper wire of which had been severed, causing the headlight not to function and thereby reducing the cycle's visibility. The court held that strict liability was appropriate, emphasizing that defendant was a large dealer who specialized in high-end resales. The public had a right to expect that the seller's used vehicles would meet the manufacturer's specifications. See also Nelson v. Nelson Hardware, Inc. 467 N.W.2d 518 (Wis. 1991); Gonzalez v. Rutherford Corp., 881 F. Supp. 829 (E.D. N.Y. 1995); Thompson v. Rockford Machine Tool Co., 744 P.2d 357 (Wash. Ct. App. 1987); Ferragamo v. Massachusetts Bay Transportation Authority, 481 N.E.2d 477 (Mass. 1985); Jordan v. Sunnyslope Appliance Propane & Plumbing Supplies Co., 660 P.2d 1236 (Ariz. App. 1983); Turner v. International Harvester Co., 336 A.2d 62 (N.J. Super. Ct. App. Div. 1975); Hovenden v. Tenbush, 529 S.W.2d 302 (Tex. Ct. Civ. App. 1975). Not surprisingly, these cases place heavy emphasis on the ability of the commercial used product seller to spread the risk. The opposing view denying liability is well set forth in Peterson v. Idaho First National Bank, 791 P.2d 1303, 1306 (Idaho 1990). See also Peterson v. Superior Court. 899 P.2d 905, 914-916 (Cal. 1995); Tillman v. Vance Equipment Co., 596 P.2d 1299 (Or. 1979). The Supreme Court of Oklahoma followed *Tillman* in refusing to apply strict liability doctrine to the seller of a used shuttle bus. Allenberg v. Bentley Hedges Travel Serv., Inc., 22 P.3d 223 (Okla. 2001). In so doing, the court noted that the policy considerations supporting strict liability for manufacturers and distributors of new products did not support liability for sellers of used products. Id. at 230. In Pacific National Insurance Co. v. Gormsen Appliance Co., 284 Cal. Rptr. 78 (Cal. Ct. App. 1991), the court extended the rejection of strict liability to lessors of used products.

A few courts, like *Crandell,* attempt to straddle the line. In a somewhat narrower opinion than *Crandell,* the New Jersey Supreme Court held that strict liability applies to defective repairs or replacement of parts performed by a dealer who sells used products. Realmuto v. Straub Motors. 322 A.2d 440 (N.J. 1974).

---

1. For a full exposition of this thesis see James A. Henderson, Jr., Extending the Boundaries of Strict Products Liability: Implications of the Theory of the Second Best, 128 Pa. L. Rev. 1036 (1980). See also Nelson by Hibbard v. Nelson Hardware, Inc., 467 N.W.2d 518, 529-530 (Wis. 1991).

See also Stillie v. AM International, Inc., 841 F. Supp. 370 (D. Kan. 1993); Wynia v. Richard-Ewing Equipment Company, Inc., 17 F.3d 1084 (8th Cir. 1994) (applying South Dakota law and finding that *Crandell* is still the governing rule in South Dakota); Peterson v. Lou Bachrodt Chevrolet Co., 329 N.E.2d 785 (Ill. 1975). See generally Derrick Williams, Second Hand Jurisprudence in Need of Legislative Repair: The Application of Strict Liability to Commercial Sellers of Used Goods, 9 Tex. Wes. L. Rev. 255 (2003) (arguing that judicial policy-consideration approach to determining whether sellers of used products should be subject to strict liability will lead to injustice in an area of law better governed by legislative action); William L. Humes, Note, Application of Strict Liability in Tort to the Retailers of Used Products: A Proposal, 16 Okla. City U. L. Rev. 373 (1991) (discussing policy considerations of imposing strict liability on used product sellers).

2. The Role of Disclaimers in Determining Liability for Used Products

We have set forth the controversy concerning the imposition of strict liability against used product sellers. We have yet to focus on a very practical question. Many, if not most, used product sales are accompanied by disclaimers. The sellers usually sell the products "as is." Should disclaimers between the seller and buyer be honored to negate liability to the buyer or third parties injured by the used product? Your first reaction might well be—have you lost your marbles? The subject under discussion is liability for harm caused by defective products. And everyone knows that disclaimers are not worth the paper they are written on. Well, not so fast. There is a story to be told. At the end of the story you will have to decide whether disclaimers should be given some effect with regard to the sale of used products. But, for starters, why are disclaimers not effective to protect a seller from liability arising from the sale of a new product?

To understand the ins and outs of disclaimers we have no alternative but to set forth several sections of the U.C.C. and the comments thereto.

UNIFORM COMMERCIAL CODE

§2-316. EXCLUSION OR MODIFICATION OF WARRANTIES

(1) Words or conduct relevant to the creation of an express warranty and words or conduct tending to negate or limit warranty shall be construed wherever reasonable as consistent with each other; but subject to the provisions of this Article on parol or extrinsic evidence (Section 2-202) negation or limitation is inoperative to the extent that such construction is unreasonable.

(2) Subject to subsection (3), to exclude or modify the implied warranty of merchantability or any part of it the language must mention merchantability and in case of a writing must be conspicuous, and to exclude or modify any implied warranty of fitness the exclusion must be by a writing and conspicuous. Language to exclude all implied warranties of fitness is sufficient if it states, for example, that "There are no warranties which extend beyond the description on the face hereof."

(3) Notwithstanding subsection (2)

(a) unless the circumstances indicate otherwise, all implied warranties are excluded by expressions like "as is," "with all faults" or other language which in common understanding calls the buyer's attention to the exclusion of warranties and makes plain that there is no implied warranty; and

(b) when the buyer before entering into the contract has examined the goods or the sample or model as fully as he desired or has refused to examine the goods there is no implied warranty with regard to defects which an examination ought in the circumstances to have revealed to him; and

(c) an implied warranty can also be excluded or modified by course of dealing or course of performance or usage of trade.

(4) Remedies for breach of warranty can be limited in accordance with the provisions of this Article on liquidation or limitation of damages and on contractual modification of remedy (Sections 2-718 and 2-719).

OFFICIAL COMMENT

1. This section is designed principally to deal with those frequent clauses in sales contracts which seek to exclude "all warranties, express or implied." It seeks to protect a buyer from unexpected and unbargained language of disclaimer by denying effect to such language when inconsistent with language of express warranty and permitting the exclusion of implied warranties only by conspicuous language or other circumstances which protect the buyer from surprise. . . . This Article treats the limitation or avoidance of consequential damages as a matter of limiting remedies for breach, separate from the matter of creation of liability under a warranty. If no warranty exists, there is of course no problem of limiting remedies for breach of warranty. Under subsection (4) the question of limitation of remedy is governed by the sections referred to rather than by this section. . . .

§2-302. Unconscionable Contract or Clause

(1) If the court as a matter of law finds the contract or any clause of the contract to have been unconscionable at the time it was made the court may refuse to enforce the contract, or it may enforce the remainder of the contract without the unconscionable clause, or it may so limit the application of any unconscionable clause as to avoid any unconscionable result.

(2) When it is claimed or appears to the court that the contract or any clause thereof may be unconscionable the parties shall be afforded a reasonable opportunity to present evidence as to its commercial setting, purpose and effect to aid the court in making the determination.

OFFICIAL COMMENT

1. This section is intended to make it possible for the courts to police explicitly against the contracts or clauses which they find to be unconscionable. In the past such policing has been accomplished by adverse construction of language, by manipulation of the rules of offer and acceptance or by determinations that the clause is contrary to public policy or to the dominant purpose of the contract. . . . The principle is one of the prevention of oppression and unfair surprise (Cf. Campbell Soup Co. v. Wentz, 172 F.2d 80 (3d Cir. 1948)) and not of disturbance of allocation of risks because of superior bargaining power. . . .

§2-719. CONTRACTUAL MODIFICATION OR LIMITATION OF REMEDY

(1) Subject to the provisions of subsections (2) and (3) of this section and of the preceding section on liquidation and limitation of damages,

   (a) the agreement may provide for remedies in addition to or in substitution for those provided in this Article and may limit or alter the measure of damages recoverable under this Article, as by limiting the buyer's remedies to return of the goods and repayment of the price or to repair and replacement of non-conforming goods or parts; and

   (b) resort to a remedy as provided is optional unless the remedy is expressly agreed to be exclusive, in which case it is the sole remedy.

(2) Where circumstances cause an exclusive or limited remedy to fail of its essential purpose, remedy may be had as provided in this Act.

(3) Consequential damages may be limited or excluded unless the limitation or exclusion is unconscionable. Limitation of consequential damages for injury to the person in the case of consumer goods is prima facie unconscionable but limitation of damages where the loss is commercial is not.

OFFICIAL COMMENT

3. Subsection (3) recognizes the validity of clauses limiting or excluding consequential damages but makes it clear that they may not operate in an unconscionable manner. Actually such terms are merely an allocation of unknown or undeterminable risks. The seller in all cases is free to disclaim warranties in the manner provided in Section 2-316.

What gives? Are disclaimers unconscionable or not? Read carefully §2-316, comment 1 and §2-719, comment 3. Got it? How does U.C.C. §2-302 fit into this picture? If after chewing these sections over you believe that disclaimers of strict liability are ok under the Code, you have some allies. In Ford Motor Co. v. Moulton, 511 S.W.2d 690, 693 (Tenn.), *cert. denied,* 419 U.S. 870 (1974), the Tennessee Supreme Court upheld the validity of a disclaimer even though the claim was for personal injuries arising from a defective steering column. *Moulton is* apparently still in force in Tennessee. See McCullough v. General Motors Corp., 577 F. Supp. 41 (W.D. Tenn. 1982).

But most courts disagree. Starting with Henningsen v. Bloomfield Motors Co., 161 A.2d 69 (N.J. 1960), discussed in Chapter One, supra, tort courts have been decidedly hostile toward disclaimers. In striking down the disclaimer of the implied warranty of merchantability which was part of the standard automobile sale agreement, the *Henningsen* court waxed eloquent:

> The gross inequality of bargaining position occupied by the consumer in the automobile industry is thus apparent. There is no competition among the car makers in the area of the express warranty. Where can the buyer go to negotiate for better protection? Such control and limitation of his remedies are inimical to the public welfare and, at the very least, call for great care by the courts to avoid injustice through application of strict common-law principles of freedom of contract. Because there is no competition among the motor vehicle manufacturers with respect to the scope of protection guaranteed to the buyer, there is no incentive on their part to stimulate good will in that field of pub-

lic relations. Thus, there is lacking a factor existing in more competitive fields, one which tends to guarantee the safe construction of the article sold. Since all competitors operate in the same way, the urge to be careful is not so pressing. . . .

Public policy at a given time finds expression in the Constitution, the statutory law and in judicial decisions. In the area of sale of goods, the legislative will has imposed an implied warranty of merchantability as a general incident of sale of an automobile by description. The warranty does not depend upon the affirmative intention of the parties. It is a child of the law; it annexes itself to the contract because of the very nature of the transaction. . . . True, the Sales Act authorizes agreements between buyer and seller qualifying the warranty obligations. But quite obviously the Legislature contemplated lawful stipulations (which are determined by the circumstances of a particular case) arrived at freely by parties of relatively equal bargaining strength. The lawmakers did not authorize the automobile manufacturer to use its grossly disproportionate bargaining power to relieve itself from liability and to impose on the ordinary buyer, who in effect has no real freedom of choice, the grave danger of injury to himself and others that attends the sale of such a dangerous instrumentality as a defectively made automobile. In the framework of this case, illuminated as it is by the facts and the many decisions noted, we are of the opinion that Chrysler's attempted disclaimer of an implied warranty of merchantability and of the obligations arising therefrom is so inimical to the public good as to compel an adjudication of its invalidity . . . , 161 A.2d at 87-95.

Strong stuff. Would you feel any different if auto companies or other competitors engaged in a warranty war? Shouldn't you be given the option of purchasing a car with or without a disclaimer, thus enjoying the benefit of a discounted price if you seek to buy the product sans the warranty? Is the *Henningsen* reasoning consistent with §2-302?

In any event, the law is quite clear. Professors White and Summers have it right when they conclude "that whenever a consumer's blood is spilled, even wild horses could not stop a sympathetic court from plowing through the most artfully drafted and conspicuously printed disclaimer clause in order to grant relief." Handbook on the Law of the Uniform Commercial Code 485 (4th ed. 1994). See also Ford Motor Co. v. Tritt, 430 S.W.2d 778 (Ark. 1968); Walsh v. Ford Motor Co., 298 N.Y.S.2d 538 (1969); Tuttle v. Kelley-Springfield Tire Co., 585 P.2d 1116 (Okla. 1978).

Restatement (Third) of Torts: Products Liability
(1998)

§18. DISCLAIMERS, LIMITATIONS, WAIVERS, AND OTHER CONTRACTUAL EXCULPATIONS AS DEFENSES TO PRODUCTS LIABILITY CLAIMS FOR HARM TO PERSONS

Disclaimers and limitations of remedies by product sellers or other distributors, waivers by product purchasers, and other similar contractual exculpations, oral or written, do not bar or reduce otherwise valid products liability claims against sellers or other distributors of new products for harm to persons.

If you are quite ready to bury disclaimers in personal injury products liability cases altogether, consider the role of disclaimers in used products cases. Assume that a court decides to apply strict liability to used products. Now further assume that the seller has clearly disclaimed liability by selling the product "as is." Should persons injured by the used product have a cause of action against the commercial used product seller? Cf. §8 of the Products Liability Restatement, supra.

Before jumping to conclusions, it is worth taking a moment to consider how courts treat warnings in products liability cases. Both disclaimers and warnings are communications from the seller to the buyer about the product. Warnings have a rather good reputation in products liability law. Manufacturers who are honest and straightforward about a product's performance capabilities are, in general, treated with considerable solicitude. Disclaimers for new products, as noted earlier, have gotten a very bad rap. Why is that?

Warnings convey specific information to a buyer about avoiding risk in using the product. In some cases warnings inform the consumer that there is a basic nonreducible risk that cannot be avoided. In either event, with an eye to a specific set of harms, the consumer is told the limitations of the product. It is a real-world communication, the kind of information that would be conveyed by a good friend or a neighbor. Disclaimers are made of different stuff. They might be taken as a communication by the seller to the buyer that the seller has little confidence in his wares and that the buyer should lower his expectations for product performance. But with new products that just isn't the case. The disclaimer is a legal artifice created by the law of contracts for the seller to walk away from any problems that may arise with regard to the product. Where consumer expectations remain high, notwithstanding the disclaimer, courts are not willing to let lawyer's talk deprive consumers of their legitimate expectations.

But aren't used-product disclaimers somewhat different? When a commercial used-product seller markets a three-year-old product "as is," the seller may be telling the buyer that the product has been subject to significant wear and tear and the buyer ought to have drastically reduced expectations for it. The analogy to a pure no-duty argument in tort is compelling. The disclaimer in this context may be more than a legal artifice. Admittedly, the seller is not in a position to specifically warn about the problems that may arise. The seller does not, in fact, know when and how they may surface. But the communication is not merely lawyer's talk. The seller is, so to speak, rubbing the buyer's nose into the realities of the sale, telling the buyer that he must be on full alert. "It's your baby, not mine."

Having made the distinction, we note its shortcomings. Some used products bear hefty price tags. A two-year-old Cadillac or Lexus may sell for more than many other new cars do. Doesn't price reflect expectations? On the other hand, once the expectations are something less than perfect, should we not allow contract a fairly free hand in working out the equities between the buyer and seller?

This story has a satisfactory ending. Most courts recognize disclaimers for used-product sales. See, e.g., Harber v. Altec Industries Inc. 812 F. Supp. 954 (W.D. Mo.), *aff'd,* 5 F.3d 339 (8th Cir. 1993); LaRosa v. Superior Court, 176 Cal. Rptr. 224 (Cal. Ct. App. 1981) (strict liability inapplicable against seller of used punch press sold "as is" when press malfunctioned and caused personal injuries to plaintiff); Tillman v. Vance Equipment Company, 596 P.2d 1299 (Or. 1979) (strict liability inapplicable in personal injury action against seller of used crane sold "as is" where defect existed at time of manufacture). But some disagree. See, e.g., Gonzalez v. Rutherford Corp., 881 F. Supp. 829 (E.D. N.Y. 1995).

The authors struggled with the issue in drafting §8 of the Products Liability Restatement. Liability for manufacturing defects in used products depends on whether a reasonable person would "expect the used product to present no greater risk of defect than if the product were new." However, rather than giving a disclaimer conclusive effect and thus barring claims for personal injury, comment k to §8 takes the position that a disclaimer is a factor which may bear on the reasonable buyer's expectations as to whether the product presents no greater risk of defect than if it were new. An earlier draft had given conclusive effect to disclaimers for used products, but that position was rejected by the ALI membership.

PROBLEM TWENTY-FIVE

Your client, American Alarm Systems Inc. (AAS), manufactures and markets smoke alarms nationally. It advertises its products in trade journals as well as in popular magazines. Recently, AAS sold 1,000 of its Jiffy Smoke Alarm units to General Merchandise, Inc. In the contract of sale, AAS specifically disclaimed all express warranties and the implied warranty of merchantability. In a separate clause AAS agreed to replace any defective smoke alarm and specifically disclaimed any liability for personal injury or other consequential damages. General Merchandise sold 200 of the Jiffy Smoke Alarms to Home Safe, Inc., a large retailer of home safety systems (locks, burglar alarms, smoke alarms, etc.) in Los Alamos, New California. General Merchandise's sale contract with Home Safe was identical to that which AAS had made with General Merchandise.

When the units arrived at Home Safe, they were offered for sale for $35 each. Two units were removed from the boxes and placed on a display shelf. Two months later, after most of the units had been sold, Home Safe put the two display units on special sale for $15. The sign next to the units read "Display Models $35." The $35 was crossed out and $15 was written under it. The sign also said "Before You Take the Unit Home, Test It on Our Smoke Alarm Tester."

Jack Resnick had just moved into a new office and warehouse complex out of which he ran a computer sales and service business. Over the years, Resnick had cultivated several lucrative accounts for which he did data processing. He sold both hardware and software in addition to servicing these data processing accounts. Resnick was always in the market for a bargain. When he saw the two Jiffy Smoke Alarms on sale for $15 at the Home Safe store, he took them off the shelf and tested them on the testing machine. They seemed to be operating properly. He purchased both units and took them to his new place of business, where he installed one in the warehouse and one in the storeroom where he kept the computer discs for the data processing accounts.

On December 4, Resnick was working late in the outer office adjacent to the disc storeroom and a short walk from the warehouse. Around 8:30 P.M. he smelled smoke. He dashed into the warehouse and found it filled with smoke. The alarm was ringing. He ran back into the office to call the fire department, and then ran into the storeroom in which the computer discs were stored, seeking to save as many as he could. The alarm in the storeroom was not ringing, although the storeroom was filled with smoke. He pulled as many of the discs as possible from the storeroom, but finally was forced by the heat and smoke to leave the building. When the fire department came they found him standing across the

authors' dialogue 21

JIM: I remember that we alternated responsibility for drafting the used products Section. You came up with the first draft, which applied Sections 1 and 2 to used products, judging them as though they were new at the time of sale by the commercial used product seller. At the same time, the seller could disclaim liability in whole or part even for personal injuries. Our idea was that the standard for judging the defectiveness of a used product was so fact sensitive — how old was the product, what condition was it in, and the like — that it was best to let the parties work it out via contract. We had caselaw that seemed to back us up, although it was admittedly ambiguous. We had a neat, clean draft that we thought got the job done by deferring the important decisions to the used product market.

AARON: And then the advisers came down on us like a ton of bricks. They just would not accept the idea that disclaimers should be given dispositive effect. They agreed that the cases showed that the terms of the sales contract, including disclaimer language, should affect the seller's liability, pro and con. But they insisted that courts should determine defectiveness, not the parties. I got so upset with their dismissive attitude, I asked you to take over the next draft.

JIM: And I didn't do much better. I got us all bogged down in trying to occupy the middle ground with a complicated structure that even I had a hard time understanding. The advisers didn't like that much better than our first draft. So we took various drafts to the next three Annual Meetings and had lengthy debates that led to redrafts on top of redrafts.

AARON: I remember at the last Annual Meeting of the Institute at which our project was scheduled to be considered, when we were looking to get final approval, we asked the President, Charlie Wright,[2] to announce on our behalf that the membership could approve §8 or reject it, but that we had been through 14 or 15 drafts over a three-year period and we were not going to try our hand again. We thought §8 was a good proposal and faithful to the cases. But we were burned out on the subject of used products liability.

JIM: And then the membership approved §8 without further discussion. Go figure.

---

2. Charles Alan Wright, a world-renowned legal academic at the University of Texas for more than 45 years, was President of the American Law Institute during the Products Liability Restatement project. He died in 2000, after the Products Restatement had been published.

---

street, complaining of sharp pains in his chest. He was taken to the hospital, where doctors found serious lung damage from the smoke inhalation.

Resnick's ill-fated attempt to save the computer discs proved to be useless. Most of the discs were destroyed by the heat and smoke. The cost of reproducing the data stored on the destroyed discs will be well over $250,000. In addition, the computer hardware losses exceed $550,000. Some, but not all, of the hardware losses are covered by fire insurance.

Resnick's major factual premise—that the smoke alarm in the storeroom did not sound—will be difficult to refute. It should have sounded well before Resnick smelled smoke. Had it sounded, the noise given off would have been loud enough that Resnick would have certainly heard it, even if he had been sleeping at the time. The alarm in the warehouse appears to have been too far away for Resnick to hear until he entered the warehouse building. The Jiffy Smoke Alarm in the storeroom was substantially destroyed in the fire; it reveals nothing about why it failed to work. AAS is concerned about its potential liability in this case. It is also interested in your opinion as to whether it can recoup potential losses from others in the distributive chain.

Based upon the Code sections and comments reproduced supra, prepare a memorandum outlining the legal position of AAS.

D. FOOD, NONPRESCRIPTION DRUGS, AND COSMETICS

1. Food Products

It may seem obvious that one engaged in the business of selling or otherwise distributing food products that contain manufacturing, design, or instructional defects can be found strictly liable for resulting harm. Yet, in food cases, it is often unclear whether a harm-causing ingredient constitutes a product defect or not. Consider the California Supreme Court's decision in Mix v. Ingersoll Candy Co., 59 P.2d 144 (Cal. 1936), in which the court directed a verdict for a restaurateur for injuries sustained by a customer who had swallowed a fragment of a chicken bone contained in a chicken pie. Did the presence of the bone in the chicken pie constitute a defect? The court explained, "Bones which are natural to the type of meat served cannot legitimately be called a foreign substance and a consumer who eats meat dishes ought to anticipate and be on his guard against the presence of such bones." Id. The court in *Mix* adopted what came to be known as the "foreign-natural" test for determining whether a harm-causing ingredient contained in food constitutes a defect. A strong majority of courts today rely on the concept of "consumer expectations" instead of the "foreign-natural" test to decide such manufacturing defect cases. While the naturalness or foreignness of a harmful object will be a relevant consideration in determining reasonable expectations, it will not be controlling. See, e.g., Jackson v. Nestle-Beich, Inc., 589 N.E.2d 547 (Ill. 1992). In that case a plaintiff broke his tooth on a pecan shell imbedded in a chocolate covered pecan candy; the Supreme Court affirmed the reversal of summary judgment for the defendant, holding that the foreign-natural test, which would operate as a complete bar on these facts, should not be applied. See also Mitchell v. BBB Servs. Co., Inc., 2003 WL 1923519 (Ga. Ct. App. 2003) (applying the consumer expectations standard in reversing summary judgment for defendant based on the foreign-natural test to bone in hamburger meat); Clime v. Dewey Beach Enterprises, 831 F. Supp. 341 (D. Del. 1993); but see Harris-Teeter, Inc. v. Burroughs, 399 S.E.2d 801 (Va. 1991) (applying foreign-natural test); Mitchell v. TGI Friday's, 748 N.E.2d 89 (Ohio Ct. App. 2000) (employing both tests).

Restatement (Third) of Torts: Products Liability
(1998)

§7. LIABILITY OF COMMERCIAL SELLER OR DISTRIBUTOR FOR HARM CAUSED BY DEFECTIVE FOOD PRODUCTS

One engaged in the business of selling or otherwise distributing food products who sells or distributes a food product that is defective under §2, §3, or §4 is subject to liability for harm to persons or property caused by the defect. Under §2(a), a harm-causing ingredient of the food product constitutes a defect if a reasonable consumer would not expect the food product to contain that ingredient.

COMMENT:

a. General applicability of §§2, 3, and 4 to food products. Except for the special problems identified in Comment *b,* liability for harm caused by defects in commercially distributed food products are determined under the same rules generally applicable to non-food products. A food product may contain a manufacturing defect under §2(a), as when a can of peas contains a pebble; may be defectively designed under §2(b), as when the recipe for potato chips contains a dangerous chemical preservative; or may be sold without adequate warnings under §2(c), as when the seller fails to inform consumers that the dye applied to the skins of oranges contains a well-known allergen. Section 3 may allow a plaintiff to reach the trier of fact when, unable to identify the specific defect, the plaintiff becomes violently ill immediately after consuming the defendant's food product and other causes are sufficiently eliminated. And §4 may apply when a commercially distributed food product fails to conform to applicable safety statutes or administrative regulations.

b. The special problem under §2(a). When a plaintiff suffers harm due to the presence in food of foreign matter clearly not intended by the product seller, such as a pebble in a can of peas or the pre-sale spoilage of a jar of mayonnaise, the claim is readily treated under §2(a), which deals with harm caused by manufacturing defects. Food product cases, however, sometimes present unique difficulties when it is unclear whether the ingredient that caused the plaintiff's harm is an unanticipated adulteration or is an inherent aspect of the product. For example, is a one-inch chicken bone in a chicken enchilada, or a fish bone in fish chowder, a manufacturing defect or, instead, an inherent aspect of the product? The analytical problem stems from the circumstance that food products in many instances do not have specific product designs that may be used as a basis for determining whether the offending product ingredient constitutes a departure from design, and is thus a manufacturing defect. Food recipes vary over time, within the same restaurant or other commercial food-preparation facility, from facility to facility, and from locale to locale.

Faced with this indeterminacy, some courts have attempted to rely on a distinction between "foreign" and "natural" characteristics of food products to determine liability. Under that distinction, liability attaches only if the alleged adulteration is foreign rather than natural to the product. Most courts have found this approach inadequate, however. Although a one-inch chicken bone may in some sense be "natural" to a chicken enchilada, depending on the context in which consumption takes place, the bone may still be unexpected by the reasonable consumer, who will not be able to avoid injury, thus rendering the product not reasonably safe. The majority view is that, in this circumstance of uncertainty, the issue of whether a food product containing a dangerous but arguably natural component is defective under §2(a) is to be determined by reference to reasonable consumer expectations within the relevant context of consumption. A consumer expectations test in this context relies upon culturally defined, widely shared standards that food products ought to meet. Although consumer expectations are not adequate to supply a standard for defect in other contexts, assessments of what consumers have a right to expect in various commercial food preparations are sufficiently well-formed that judges and triers of fact can sensibly resolve whether liability should be imposed using this standard.

California, the originator of the foreign-natural test in Mix v. Ingersoll Candy Co., supra, has revisited the issue in a lengthy and prolix opinion. In Mexicali Rose v. Superior Court, 822 P.2d 1292 (Cal. 1992), the court held that:

> The strict foreign-natural test . . . should be rejected as the exclusive test for determining liability when a substance natural to food injures a restaurant patron. We conclude instead that in deciding the liability of a restauranteur for injuries caused by harmful substances in food, the proper tests to be used by the trier of facts are as follows:
>
> If the injury-producing substance is natural to the preparation of the food served, it can be said that it was reasonably expected by its very nature and the food cannot be determined unfit or defective. A plaintiff in such a case has no cause of action in strict liability or implied warranty. If however, the presence of the natural substance is due to a restauranteur's failure to exercise due care in food preparation, the injured patron may sue under a negligence theory.
>
> If the injury-causing substance is foreign to the food served then the injured patron may also state a cause of action in implied warranty and strict liability, and the trier of fact will determine whether the substance (i) could be reasonably expected by the average consumer and (ii) rendered the food unfit or defective.

Id. at 1303. Dissenting opinions found that the court's decision was badly out of harmony with the vast majority of authority throughout the country, and argued that there was no good reason for not simply applying a consumer expectation test to both foreign and natural substances. See id. at 1304-1316.

In Livingston v. Marie Callenders, Inc., 72 Cal. App. 4th 830 (1999), the court held that it was for the jury to decide whether a restaurant should have warned a customer, who suffered an allergic reaction, that a bowl of vegetable soup contained monosodium glutamate. The test was whether a consumer would reasonably expect the soup to contain such an ingredient and, if not, whether the restaurant knew or should have known of the presence in the soup of that ingredient. For an exploration of the surprisingly sparse case law dealing with products liability and food allergies, see Jonathan Bridges, Note, Suing for Peanuts, 75 N.D. L. Rev. 1269 (2000).

Law review commentators have been unanimous in preferring the "reasonable consumer expectation" test over the "foreign-natural" test for food-related defects. See, e.g., Stacy L. Mojica, Note, Breach of Implied Warranty: Has the Foreign/Natural Test Lost Its Bite?, 20 Mem. St. U. L. Rev. 377 (1990); Michael I. Spak, Bone of Contention: The Foreign-Natural Test and the Implied Warranty of Merchantability for Food Products, 12 J.L. & Com. 23 (1992). Section 7 of the new Restatement (Third) of Torts: Products Liability adopts the consumer expectations standard for food products. See generally David G. Owen, Manufacturing Defects, 53 S.C. L. Rev. 851 (2002) (tracing the historical development of food defect liability in some detail and exploring the transition from the foreign-natural test to the consumer expectations standard).

One interesting area of food-related products liability that is still developing deals with the purveyors of fast food. A few self-described "victims" have brought actions against fast food providers seeking to recover for their fast-food-related ill health under such theories as failure to warn, breach of implied warranty, and misrepresentation. Thus far, however, these lawsuits have proven unsuccessful. See, e.g., Pelman v. McDonald's Corp., 237 F. Supp. 2d 512 (S.D.N.Y. 2003) (finding no duty to warn of well-known fast food effects on health). See also Franklin E. Crawford, Note, Fit for Its Ordinary Purpose? Tobacco, Fast Food, and the Implied Warranty of Merchantability, Ohio St. L. Rev. (2002) (arguing that courts may one day find that fast food sellers purvey unmerchantable products under the U.C.C.).

Consider the following critique of §7 by Professor Katherine VanTassel, in Adding Biotech Foods to the Tort System, Western Mass. Law Tribune, August 2003:

> The increasing presence of genetically modified [GM] food on the shelves of grocery stores is a concern to many consumers as well as presenting novel issues for the legal system. One of those issues is the standard that should be applied in lawsuits against the food industry claiming such products are defective. A major milestone in the area of products liability was reached when the American Law Institute adopted the Restatement [Third] of Torts: Products Liability [1998] ["Restatement Third"]. Reflecting current trends in the case law, the Restatement Third soundly rejected the use of the highly subjective and arbitrary "reasonable consumer expectation test" for determining whether a product design is defective and replaced it with an objective, easily applied test which provides greater uniformity and predictability for both industry and consumers.
>
> Unfortunately, the Restatement Third retained "consumer expectations" as the test for analyzing liability for harm from food products, arguably including GM food, a choice that is short-sighted in light of our need to establish a global food supply necessary to feed a growing world population. . . .
>
> [R]egretfully, the Restatement Third retains the "consumer expectation test" in addressing both whether a food product contains a manufacturing defect and whether it is defectively designed. . . .
>
> [The Restatement's rationale for judging food product designs based on consumer expectations is] without merit when dealing with GM food. First, GM food clearly has a design like any other manufactured product. Second, while consumers may have well-informed, culturally defined and widely shared standards when it comes to some foods, they certainly do not when it comes to GM foods. The technology is simply too new. Moreover, there is no requirement that GM food be labeled as such. A recent survey conducted by the University of Richmond revealed that 62 percent of those surveyed said that they had not eaten any genetically modified foods, and very few of those surveyed

were aware that more than sixty percent of the packaged foods sold in U.S. supermarkets contain bio-engineered ingredients.

Thus, [the Restatement's] rationale for treating food products differently from all other products [does not] hold water. [R]egardless of the validity of the Restatement Third's rationales, considerations germane to developing a global food supply mandate the rejection of the consumer expectation test and the adoption of the same standard for evaluating harm from food products that is used for all other products. . . .

In this fashion, juries can weigh the benefits of a GM food product against its risks in a reasoned fashion to weed out those which are not beneficial to society.

What is your "take" on this critique of §7? On §7, itself? Does the Restatement contradict itself by relying on consumer expectations in §7 but rejecting them as the standard for defective designs generally in §2(b)?

2. *Nonprescription Drugs and Cosmetics*

Because nonprescription drugs and cosmetics do not fall within the complex scheme of FDA regulation applied to prescription drugs and medical devices, one might expect them to be subject to a products liability regime similar to the system applicable to nonprescription products generally. The surprise comes when one discovers that nonprescription drugs and cosmetics are subjected to a specific set of liability rules all their own. Thus, in Kaempfe v. Lehn & Fink Products, 249 N.Y.S.2d 840 (N.Y. App. Div. 1964), *aff'd,* 231 N.E.2d 294 (N.Y. 1967), the plaintiff sought to recover for injuries suffered from the application of a spray-on deodorant. The product contained aluminum sulfate, which caused the plaintiff to suffer her first, and fairly severe, allergic reaction. The deodorant contained no manufacturing defect, and the label on the can stated that the deodorant contained aluminum sulfate. The label also stated that the deodorant was "safe for normal skin." No warning was given that the deodorant might cause allergic reactions in sensitive users.

The trial court submitted plaintiff's failure-to-warn claim to the jury, which returned its verdict for the plaintiff. On appeal, the court reversed and ordered judgment for the defendant. Stressing that only one in 150,000 users of the product would suffer such a reaction, the appellate court concluded (249 N.Y.S.2d at 846-847):

> In light of the foregoing, the plaintiff, as the basis for imposing upon defendant a special duty of warning, was bound at the very least to show (1) that she was one of a substantial number or of an identifiable class of persons who were allergic to the defendant's product, and (2) that defendant knew, or with reasonable diligence should have known of the existence of such number or class of persons. There was, however, a failure of proof as to both of these requirements. Furthermore, it does not appear that a special warning here would have been effective for any purpose. . . .
>
> The statement that the product contained a particular sulphate was adequate to warn any and all persons who knew that they had an allergy with respect to the same. As to those persons, an additional express warning not to use the product would serve no purpose. Specific words of caution would be meaningless as to those, such as the plaintiff, who did not know of their allergy to the particular sulphate. The plaintiff's prior use of deodorants containing the particular ingredient did not yield any manifestations of sensitivity and she expected none when she applied the defendant's product. So, it is difficult

to see that a special warning in general terms of danger to the infinitesimal few with an allergy would be of any help or have persuaded plaintiff here from the purchase and use of defendant's merchandise. Under the circumstances, the special warning would have been wholly ineffective. And the defendant should not be held negligent in failing to give a warning which would have served no purpose.

In Daley v. McNeil Consumer Prods. Co., 164 F. Supp. 2d 367 (S.D.N.Y. 2001), the plaintiff sued the manufacturer of Lactaid for failure to warn after the plaintiff allegedly suffered an allergic reaction from consuming the product to aid in her digestion of milk. In granting the defendant's motion for summary judgment with respect to the plaintiff's failure to warn claim, the court cited *Kaempfe,* supra, noting that there is no duty to warn of potential reactions unless a product contains an ingredient "to which a substantial number of the population are allergic." 164 F. Supp. 2d at 374.

Comment *j* to §402A, Restatement (Second) of Torts (1965) embraces the rule in *Kaempfe.* Decisions also appear to adopt the *Kaempfe* approach to the question of manufacturer's duty to warn of remote risks of allergic reactions, and impose a "substantial number" or "appreciable number" limitation. Thus, in Thomas v. Amway Corp., 488 A.2d 716 (R.I. 1985), the plaintiff suffered severe allergic reactions from using the defendant's liquid soap. The plaintiff claimed that the defendant failed to warn users of the possibility of an allergic reaction. The trial judge excluded from evidence a letter from the defendant to the plaintiff telling her that a small number of other users had made similar complaints, and directed a verdict for the defendant. On appeal, the Supreme Court of Rhode Island affirmed. Although the letter should have been admitted as relevant to the issues of causation and notice to defendant, the error was harmless because the plaintiff failed to prove "that there was something in [the soap] which caused her rash." Id. at 722. The court also observed that the plaintiff "has merely shown that the use of the product resulted in injury." Ibid. Can these statements be reconciled? Is the court imposing a "substantial number" limitation without coming out and saying so?

In Presbrey v. Gillette Co., 435 N.E.2d 513 (Ill. App. Ct. 1982), the court was more explicit about the basis for reversing the judgment below for the plaintiff:

> It is clear that use of the Gillette Right Guard Extra Strength Anti-Perspirant ("Extra Strength") caused an injurious reaction to the plaintiff. We conclude, however, that the evidence has failed to show that Gillette's "Extra Strength" contained an ingredient to which a substantial number of the population is allergic. The Aluminum Zirconyl Hydroxychloride Complex in "Extra Strength" is not a primary irritant. There is nothing in the pre-marketing testing by Gillette to show that the product contained any ingredient which was injurious to a number of people. There was unimpeached testimony that the zirconium complex in the "Extra Strength" is not a known sensitizer. . . . Evidence that the product's ingredients were not known sensitizers or irritants in itself was sufficient to overcome any otherwise applicable presumption of plaintiff's "normality" and once Gillette carried the burden of going forward with this evidence, the jury could not infer that the product could permanently sensitize "normal" users from plaintiff's testimony that he had not manifested sensitivity before using defendant's product. [435 N.E.2d at 520-521.]

For a critique of the "appreciable number" limitation, see David A. Fischer, Products Liability — The Meaning of Defect, 39 Mo. L. Rev. 339, 354-355 (1974).

For treatments of the broader issues raised in this section, see generally Page Keeton, Products Liability — Drugs and Cosmetics, 25 Vand. L. Rev. 131 (1972); Michael D. Schattman, A Cause of Action for the Allergic Consumer, 8 Hous. L. Rev. 827 (1971); David F. Pursel, Note, The Allergic Plaintiff — Formulating a Cause of Action in Oklahoma, 30 Okla. L. Rev. 439 (1977).

Two more recent treatments shed further light on allergic reaction liability. In Carol Rogerson & Michael J. Trebilcock, Products Liability and the Allergic Consumer: A Study in Problems of Framing an Efficient Liability Regime, 36 U. Toronto L.J. 52 (1986), the authors argue that there are several paradigms for allergic reactions which should be treated differently to achieve efficient outcomes. See also James A. Henderson, Jr., Process Norms in Products Litigation: Liability for Allergic Reactions, 51 U. Pitt. L. Rev. 761 (1990), in which the author concludes that although sudden, unexpected allergic reactions affect victims in much the same ways as do manufacturing defects, the traditional approach of limited liability is appropriate because courts could not cope institutionally with a more robust liability system for allergic reaction injuries.

The Products Liability Restatement addresses these issues in a Comment to §2(c), the basic failure-to-warn provision:

> *k. Warnings: adverse allergic or idiosyncratic reactions.* Cases of adverse allergic or idiosyncratic reactions involve a special subset of products that may be defective because of inadequate warnings. Many of these cases involve nonprescription drugs and cosmetics. However, virtually any tangible product can contain an ingredient to which some persons may be allergic. Thus, food, nonprescription drugs, toiletries, paint, solvents, building materials, clothing, and furniture have all been involved in litigation to which this Comment is relevant. . . .
>
> The general rule in cases involving allergic reactions is that a warning is required when the harm-causing ingredient is one to which a substantial number of persons are allergic. The degree of substantiality is not precisely quantifiable. Clearly the plaintiff in most cases must show that the allergic predisposition is not unique to the plaintiff. In determining whether the plaintiff has carried the burden in this regard, however, the court may properly consider the severity of the plaintiff's harm. The more severe the harm, the more justified is a conclusion that the number of persons at risk need not be large to be considered "substantial" so as to require a warning. Essentially, this reflects the same risk-utility balancing undertaken in warnings cases generally. But courts explicitly impose the requirement of substantiality in cases involving adverse allergic reactions.
>
> The ingredient that causes the allergic reaction must be one whose danger or whose presence in the product is not generally known to consumers. When both the presence of an allergenic ingredient in the product and the risks presented by such ingredient are widely known, instructions and warnings about that danger are unnecessary. When the presence of the allergenic ingredient would not be anticipated by a reasonable user or consumer, warnings concerning its presence are required. Similarly, when the presence of the ingredient is generally known to consumers, but its dangers are not, a warning must be given.
>
> Finally, as required in Subsection (c), warnings concerning risks of allergic reactions that are not reasonably foreseeable at the time of sale need not be provided. . . .
>
> ILLUSTRATION:
> 13. XYZ produces an over-the-counter nonprescription medicine containing aspirin, a well-known allergen to which a substantial minority of persons are sensitive. XYZ may reasonably assume that those who are allergic to aspirin are aware of their allergy or

that, if they are not aware, warnings of possible allergic reactions would not be heeded. Thus, it is necessary to warn only of the fact that the medicine contains aspirin.

In 1997, Congress enacted the Food and Drug Administration Modernization Act 111 Stat. 2296 (1997). This broad legislation contains a provision preempting state regulation of nonprescription drug warnings, 21 USCS §379 (West 2003). Under this statute, state and local governments are precluded from creating warning requirements for nonprescription drugs different that those mandated by federal regulation. Although §379(e) states that "[nothing] in this section shall be construed to modify or otherwise affect any action or the liability of any person under the product liability law of any state," at least one court has interpreted the Act to preempt failure to warn claims. See Green v. BDI Pharmaceuticals, 803 So. 2d 68 (La. Ct. App. 2001). In *Green,* the plaintiffs brought action against the manufacturer of an over-the-counter stimulant alleging that the manufacturer failed to warn of the addictive propensities of its product, which contained epinephrine. The trial court granted the manufacturer's motion for summary judgment, and the appellate court affirmed. The court found that the manufacturer had included all federally required warnings on its label for products containing epinephrine and that the manufacturer should prevail as a matter of law because §379 was intended to preempt state law. The court neglects to discuss §379(e), which appears to insulate products liability actions from the effects of the statute. It is unclear whether other courts will also find that federal law has preempted failure to warn claims regarding nonprescription drugs.

CHAPTER TEN
Special Elements of the Plaintiff's Recovery

A. RECOVERY OF COMPENSATORY DAMAGES

Successful plaintiffs in tort and products liability actions can, generally, recover damages for personal injury, including: (1) reasonably necessary medical expenses, both past and future; (2) lost earnings, both past and future, with the latter being conceptualized as "recovery for impairment of earning capacity"; and (3) intangible elements such as physical pain and suffering and mental upset. Under the collateral source rule, recoveries are not reduced by amounts plaintiffs receive from sources such as health insurance and worker compensation. In the past three decades, state legislatures have placed significant limitations on some of these aspects of compensatory damages.

1. Limitations on Noneconomic Damage Awards

Since 1975, many state legislatures have addressed the open-ended nature of awards for pain and suffering by enacting flat caps that limit the maximum amount of recovery for noneconomic loss. Some of these caps apply only to malpractice cases. See, e.g., Cal. Civ. Code §3333.2 (West 1997) ($250,000); Va. Code Ann. §8.01-581.15 (LexisNexis Supp. 2003) ($1.5 million, increased by annual increments to $2 million in 2008); W. Va. Code Ann. §55-7B-8 (LexisNexis Supp. 2003) ($500,000 for certain permanent disabilities or wrongful death, otherwise $250,000; amounts adjusted annually according to the Consumer Price Index (CPI)). Some states have passed general caps that apply to products liability cases as well. See, e.g., Alaska Stat. §09.17.020 (LexisNexis 2002) (generally, the greater of $400,000 or life expectancy in years times $8,000 but, in an action for personal injury, the greater of $1,000,000 or life expectancy in years times $25,000); Colo. Rev. Stat. §13-21-102.5(3)(a) (2002) ($500,000 if justified by clear and convincing evidence, otherwise $250,000; amounts adjusted annually according to the CPI); Idaho Code §6-1603 (LexisNexis Supp. 2003) ($250,000, adjusted annually according to the CPI); 735 Ill. Comp. Stat. Ann. 5/2-1115.1 (LexisNexis Supp. 2003) ($500,000, adjusted annually according to the CPI); Kan. Stat. Ann. §60-19a01 (1994) ($250,000); Md. Code Ann., Courts & Judicial Proceedings §11-108(b) (LexisNexis 2002) ($500,000, increased by $15,000 each year beginning in 1995).

These statutory limitations on recovery of noneconomic damages have been subject to constitutional attack under various provisions of state constitutions. In Smith v. Department of Ins., 507 So. 2d 1080 (Fla. 1987), the Supreme Court of Florida overturned a provision of the state's 1986 Tort Reform & Insurance Act in holding that the $450,000 cap on pain and suffering damages in tort actions violated the state constitution's right-of-access-to-court provision. Several other state courts have found these limitations unconstitutional as well. See, e.g., Knowles v. United States, 544 N.W.2d 183 (S.D. 1996); Brannigan v. Usitalo, 587 A.2d 1232 (N.H. 1991); Sofie v. Fibreboard Corp., 771 P.2d 711 (Wash. 1989); Lucas v. United States, 757 S.W.2d 687 (Tex. 1988). However, many courts have upheld the limitations as constitutionally sound. See, e.g., Adams v. Children's Mercy Hospital, 832 S.W.2d 898 (Mo. 1992), *cert. denied,* 506 U.S. 991 (1992); Murphy v. Edmonds, 601 A.2d 102 (Md. 1992); Butler v. Flint Goodrich Hospital of Dillard University, 607 So. 2d 517 (La. 1992); Samsel v. Wheeler Transport Services, 789 P.2d 541 (Kan. 1990) (good review of authority); Fein v. Permanente Medical Group, 695 P.2d 665 (Cal. 1985); Franklin v. Mazda Motor Corp., 704 F. Supp. 1325 (D. Md. 1989). In order to assure that legislation setting caps for noneconomic damages should not be declared unconstitutional, Texas recently amended its constitution to explicitly grant the legislature authority to set limits on noneconomic damage awards. Tex. Const. Art. 3, §66 (2003). For a critique of the legislative initiatives seeking to limit noneconomic damages, see Jonathan Hoffman, By the Course of the Law: The Origins for the Open Courts Clause of State Constitutions, 74 Or. L. Rev. 1279 (1995).

2. *Modifications of the Collateral Source Rule*

At common law, injured plaintiffs could receive benefits from both tort and collateral sources. "Where a plaintiff is compensated for his injuries by some source independent of the tortfeasor — insurance, for example — . . . plaintiff is still permitted to make a full recovery against the tortfeasor himself, even though this gives the plaintiff a double recovery or even a recovery for losses he never had at all." D.B. Dobbs, Remedies 581 (1973). Approximately half the states have either abolished or modified the collateral source rule. Colorado, for example, reduces a plaintiff's damage award according to the amount a plaintiff has received or will receive from any individual, corporation, insurance company, or related fund. Colo. Rev. Stat. Ann. §13-21-111.6 (2002). See also, Ky. Rev. Stat. Ann. §411.188 (Michie 1992) (permitting the admission of collateral source payments and subrogation rights into evidence in any civil action to recover damages). Some states will allow for the reduction of damage awards by collateral sources only in actions for medical malpractice. See, e.g., Me. Rev. Stat. Ann. tit. 24 §2906 (West 2000); Mass. Ann. Laws ch. 231, §60G (Lexis 2000). States differ considerably, but it appears that double recovery from collateral sources may be on the way out.

3. Reforms Allowing Periodic Payment of Damages

At least 20 states provide that courts may order periodic payment of damages rather than lump sum awards. Once again differences among the various statutory schemes are substantial. In New York, for example, in an action to recover damages for personal injury, injury to property or wrongful death, the court must provide for periodic payment installments if the award of future damages exceeds $250,000. N.Y. Civ. Prac. L. & R. §5041(e) (McKinney Supp. 1991). In Washington, unlike New York, a provision for periodic payments will be made upon the request of a party in a personal injury or property damage action where a verdict or award for future damages is at least $100,000. Wash. Rev. Code Ann. §4.56.260 (West 1991). In Alaska, the court will allow periodic payments only at the plaintiff's request. Alaska Stat. §09.17.040 (1995). In Alabama, state law allows periodic payments in medical liability judgments over $100,000. Ala. Code §6-5-486 (1993). In Colorado, awards for future damages over $150,000 must be made by periodic payments and the trial judge may order periodic payments in awards for future damages of $150,000 or less. Colo. Rev. Stat. §13-64-203 (1995). When a claimant who is awarded periodic payments for future damages dies prior to the termination date of such payments, some states reduce the remaining sum to present value and pay that amount to the claimant's estate in a lump sum. See, e.g., Fla. Stat. Ann. §768.78(1)(b) (West Supp. 2003); Wash. Rev. Code Ann. §4.56.260 (West 1988). New York, however, does not allow for a reduction to present value; rather, upon the death of the plaintiff (judgment creditor), the liability for future installments not yet due terminates unless the parties explicitly agreed otherwise. See, e.g., N.Y. Civ. Prac. L. & R. §§5035 and 5045 (McKinney 1992).

B. RECOVERY FOR PURE EMOTIONAL UPSET

Tort law generally has had more than its share of difficulties in deciding whether to permit recovery for pure emotional upset not caused by physical harm. Products liability cases have increased the problem exponentially. Unlike garden-variety mental distress cases that involve a small number of victims and injury-triggering events within a limited period of time, products cases can affect untold numbers of victims whose injuries may play out over decades.

Before tackling the problems arising from products cases, it is necessary briefly to review the state of the law generally with regard to recovery in tort for emotional upset. Beginning with State Rubbish Collectors Association v. Siliznoff, 240 P.2d 282 (Cal. 1952), most jurisdictions have recognized a cause of action for the intentional infliction of severe emotional distress not caused by physical harm. See, e.g., Harris v. Jones, 380 A.2d 611, 613, n.1 (Md. 1977) (listing 37 states that have recognized a cause of action for intentional infliction of emotional distress); Eckenrode v. Life of America Insurance Co., 470 F.2d 1 (7th Cir. 1972); George v. Jordan Marsh Co., 268 N.E.2d 915 (Mass. 1971).

The cause of action for negligent infliction of emotional distress has had a more checkered history. Most courts have attempted to screen negligent distress claims by attaching some kind of objective filter to limit liability. One such approach is to require that plaintiffs demonstrate physical harm resulting from their mental distress in order to bring suit. See, e.g., Sullivan v. Boston Gas Co., 605 N.E.2d 805 (Mass. 1993); Brown v. Matthews Mortuary, Inc., 801 P.2d 37, 44-45 (Idaho 1990). In terms of mental distress claims by bystanders who witness a relative being injured by a tortious act, many courts have required that plaintiff's witnessing of the traumatic event be in the so-called "zone of danger." See, e.g., Asavo v. Cardinal Glennon Memorial Hospital, 799 S.W.2d 595 (Mo. 1995); Bovsun v. Sanperi, 461 N.E.2d 843 (N.Y. 1984). Other courts have been more lenient in accommodating plaintiffs' emotional distress claims. See, e.g., Corgan v. Muehling, 574 N.E.2d 602 (Ill. 1991) (allowing recovery for mental distress to bystander not in zone of danger); Dillon v. Legg, 441 P.2d 912 (Cal. 1968) (rejecting "zone of danger" test and allowing recovery for bystanders). In Thing v. LaChusa, 771 P.2d 814 (Cal. 1989), though, the Supreme Court of California held that contemporary viewing of the accident was an absolute prerequisite for bystander recovery. For the most part, these restrictions are well entrenched in most jurisdictions and there does not appear to be a groundswell to adopt more liberal approaches.

The rise of products liability litigation did not significantly disturb the judiciary's traditional approach to mental distress claims. In fact, the standard product-related mental distress cases often did not differ analytically from the one-on-one negligent mental distress cases. For instance, in Walker v. Clark Equip. Co., 320 N.W.2d 561 (Iowa 1982), the Supreme Court of Iowa recognized plaintiff's right to recover for her distress over watching an allegedly defective forklift crush her brother. In that case, there was little reason to distinguish the role of the manufacturer of the defective product from that of the negligent automobile driver responsible for inflicting mental distress on a sibling-bystander. So long as the plaintiff was entitled to recover for the mental anguish caused by a defendant's negligence, it mattered little whether the horrific sight resulted from products or non-product-related misconduct. See also Wallace v. Parks Corp., 629 N.Y.S.2d 570 (1995) (distinguishing between compensable and non-compensable products liability mental distress claims based on traditional zone-of-danger-test). Some courts, however, are not as quick to engraft traditional mental distress analyses onto products liability claims. See, e.g., Speed Products Eng'g, 654 N.E.2d 1365 (Ill. 1995) (holding that bystander/witness to his wife's gory death could not recover for his own emotional distress in a strict products liability action, notwithstanding Illinois precedent allowing such recovery in claims based on negligence).

When a product defect causes only property damage, recovery for consequential emotional upset is likely to be denied. For example, in White Consolidated Industries, Inc. v. Wilkerson, 1999 WL 236498 (Ala. 1999), a defect in a window air conditioner caused a fire that burned down the plaintiffs' home. Recovery for plaintiffs' mental anguish over watching the fire was denied as a matter of law.

Some products liability cases involve plaintiffs who were more than mere bystanders. The following New York decision presents a particularly vivid example.

Kennedy v. McKesson Co.
448 N.E.2d (N.Y. 1983)

MEYER, J.

A complaint which alleges that plaintiff, a dentist, delivered to defendants for repair an anesthetic machine he had purchased from them, that defendants were negligent in replacing the color-coded decals on the machine with the result that, intending to administer oxygen to a patient, plaintiff in fact administered nitrous oxide, causing the death of the patient, that as a result plaintiff's mental condition was such that he was unable to carry on his professional work and because of the damage to his reputation was obliged to withdraw from practice states a valid cause of action permitting recovery by plaintiff for such pecuniary loss as may be proved but not permitting recovery for the emotional injury claimed to have resulted. The order of the Appellate Division (88 A.D.2d 785, 451 N.Y.S.2d 530) should, therefore, be modified, with costs to the appellant, to reinstate so much of the complaint as seeks to recover damages for other than emotional injuries and, as so modified, affirmed.

I

The complaint, the sufficiency of which is the subject of this appeal, alleges the following facts: Plaintiff is a dental surgeon. Defendant Hradil is an employee of defendant Norton-Starr, Inc. Norton is a distributor of products of defendant McKesson Company. Plaintiff bought through Hradil a McKesson anesthetic machine. In September, 1976, he arranged through Hradil and Norton for the overhaul and adjustment of the machine. When the machine was returned the color-coded identification decals for the oxygen and nitrous oxide connections had been reversed and defendants had failed to install, or inform plaintiff that they could install, connectors of different sizes for the oxygen and nitrous oxide which would have prevented improper connection of the machine. On December 10, 1976, plaintiff removed four wisdom teeth from the mouth of a patient and upon completion of the extraction adjusted the machine to administer 100% oxygen to the patient. In fact the patient received 100% nitrous oxide as a result of which she died. A civil action against plaintiff for damages for wrongful death of the patient resulted, and there was a criminal investigation all of which resulted in plaintiff's mental ill health, damaged his reputation, and caused him permanently to withdraw from practice.

Defendants moved to dismiss the complaint for failure to state a cause of action. Supreme Court held that defendants having breached a duty owed to plaintiff, he was entitled to recover for emotional harm as well as for any pecuniary loss sustained. The Appellate Division reversed and dismissed the complaint holding that no cause of action was stated when emotional harm results indirectly through the reaction of the plaintiff to injury negligently caused to another.

II

Dismissal of the complaint was clearly erroneous, for Becker v. Schwartz, 46 N.Y.2d 401, 413, 413 N.Y.S.2d 895, 386 N.E.2d 807 and Johnson v. State of

New York, 37 N.Y.2d 378, 383, 372 N.Y.S.2d 638, 334 N.E.2d 590 both recognized that a plaintiff who states a cause of action in his own right predicated upon a breach of duty flowing from defendant to plaintiff may recover the pecuniary expenses he has borne as a result of that breach.

The more difficult question is whether damages for emotional injury are recoverable. Examination of our decisions involving recovery for emotional harm reveals three distinct lines of cases. The first recognizes that when there is a duty owed by defendant to plaintiff, breach of that duty resulting directly in emotional harm is compensable even though no physical injury occurred. That principle had its beginning in Ferrara v. Galluchio, 5 N.Y.2d 16, 176 N.Y.S.2d 996, 152 N.E.2d 249. That was a malpractice action in which plaintiff recovered from defendant, a specialist in X-ray therapy, for radiodermatitis caused by excessive radiation, the sum of $25,000, which included $15,000 for mental anguish arising from cancerphobia induced by a dermatologist's advice to plaintiff that she should be checked every six months because of the possibility that cancer might develop. We held (at p.21, 176 N.Y.S.2d 996, 152 N.E.2d 249) that "[f]reedom from mental disturbance is now a protected interest in this State" and that the evidence presented a sufficient guarantee of germaneness to permit the jury to pass upon the claim. It was extended in Battalla v. State of New York, 10 N.Y.2d 237, 219 N.Y.S.2d 34, 176 N.E.2d 729 [failure properly to lock ski-lift belt], Johnson v. State of New York, 37 N.Y.2d 378, 372 N.Y.S.2d 638, 334 N.E.2d 590, supra [false information that plaintiff's mother had died] and Lando v. State of New York, 39 N.Y.2d 803, 385 N.Y.S.2d 759, 351 N.E.2d 426 [failure for 11 days to recover plaintiff's daughter's body] to allow recovery for emotional injury by a plaintiff to whom a direct duty was owed, even though unlike plaintiff Ferrara, plaintiffs Battalla, Johnson and Lando incurred no physical injury. At least under the circumstances of those cases, we held, the sophistication of the medical profession and the likelihood of genuine and serious mental distress arising from the circumstances of the case warranted allowing the jury to weed out spurious claims, though there was no contemporaneous physical harm to provide an index of reliability.

The second group of cases has its genesis in Tobin v. Grossman, 24 N.Y.2d 609, 301 N.Y.S.2d 554, 249 N.E.2d 419. The issue there was whether the operator of a motor vehicle who caused injury to plaintiff's two-year-old son owed a duty also to plaintiff on the basis of which she could recover for her injuries due to shock and fear for her child even though she did not view the accident. After extended discussion of foreseeability of the injury, proliferation of claims, fraudulent claims, inconsistency of the zone of danger rule, unlimited liability, unduly burdensome liability, and the difficulty of circumscribing the area of liability, we declined to recognize the claimed duty because "there appears to be no rational way to limit the scope of liability" other than drawing arbitrary distinctions (24 N.Y.2d, at p.618, 301 N.Y.S.2d 554, 249 N.E.2d 419), and "[t]here are too many factors and each too relative to permit creation of only a limited scope of liability or duty" (supra, at p.619, 301 N.Y.S.2d 554, 249 N.E.2d 419). Similar cases are Lafferty v. Manhasset Med. Center Hosp., 54 N.Y.2d 277, 445 N.Y.S.2d 111, 429 N.E.2d 789 dismissing an action by a daughter-in-law who witnessed a negligent blood transfusion of her mother-in-law and participated in the ensuing efforts to save the mother-in-law, and Vaccaro v. Squibb Corp., 52

N.Y.2d 809, 436 N.Y.S.2d 871, 418 N.E.2d 386 dismissing a complaint by the mother of a child born with severe birth defects as the claimed result of the mother's ingestion of a drug, which alleged no physical injury to the mother.

The third branch of the emotional injury decisions involves the violation of a duty to plaintiff which results in physical injury to a third person but only financial or emotional harm or both to the plaintiff. Progenitor in that line is Howard v. Lecher, 42 N.Y.2d 109, 397 N.Y.S.2d 363, 366 N.E.2d 64, in which recovery was sought for the emotional (but not financial, see, supra, 397 N.Y.S.2d 363, 366 N.E.2d 64) injury to the parents of a two-year-old child afflicted with Tay-Sachs disease whom they had had to watch degenerate and die. We held that a complaint which alleged defendant obstetrician's awareness of plaintiffs' eastern European lineage and consequent susceptibility of their offspring to the disease and his failure to take or evaluate a history or to cause proper tests to be made, failed to state a cause of action. Notwithstanding the presence in *Howard* of a duty of the doctor to the parents absent in *Tobin* (supra), we denied recovery on the policy reasoning of *Tobin*. Becker v. Schwartz and Park v. Chessin, 46 N.Y.2d 401, 413 N.Y.S.2d 895, 386 N.E.2d 807, involved claims on behalf of the parents of children born with Down's Syndrome and polycystic kidney disease resulting from claimed similar malpractice of the obstetrician involved. Though we upheld the parents' claim for pecuniary damages resulting from the duty flowing from defendants to them, we refused to permit recovery for psychic or emotional harm because, as in *Howard,* to do so would have "inevitably led to the drawing of artificial and arbitrary boundaries" (46 N.Y.2d, at pp.413-414, 413 N.Y.S.2d 895, 386 N.E.2d 807, quoting from Howard v. Lecher, 42 N.Y.2d, at p.113, 397 N.Y.S.2d 363, 366 N.E.2d 64).

The rule to be distilled from those cases is that there is no duty to protect from emotional injury a bystander to whom there is otherwise owed no duty, and, even as to a participant to whom a duty is owed, such injury is compensable only when a direct, rather than a consequential, result of the breach. The fear and upset induced by being left suspended high above the ground on an insecure ski lift is compensable, but that which results from the death of a patient under the circumstances described in the instant complaint is not. It will not do to argue as did the dissenters below that the injury here was inflicted directly upon plaintiff and the death of the patient was only an unintended result of defendant's breach of duty. The duty in *Howard* and in *Becker* (supra) was as direct and the resulting deaths as unintended as in the present case.

Nor is it an answer to suggest as do the dissenters here that plaintiff seeks recovery not because he observed the patient die but because he was, as a result of defendant's negligence, the very instrument of her death, and that *Becker* can be distinguished by reason of its reference to the mitigating joy of parenting a child "that even an abnormality cannot fully dampen" (46 N.Y.2d, at pp.414-415, 413 N.Y.S.2d 895, 386 N.E.2d 807). The mothers, if not the fathers, involved in *Howard* (supra) and *Becker* were equally, though more painfully because over a much longer period, the cause of death of their infants, and the speculativeness of damage was only one among many of the policy factors considered in *Tobin* in the search for a "rational practical boundary for liability" (24 N.Y.2d, at p.618, 301 N.Y.S.2d 554, 249 N.E.2d 419). Moreover, the dissent's repeated reference to liability to more than one person (at pp.508, 509, 462 N.Y.S.2d 425, 426, 448

N.E.2d 1336, 1337) misconceives the court's holding in this case, which is simply that recovery for breach of duty includes damages for emotional injury only to the extent that that injury results directly rather than consequentially. Thus, had defendant's breach resulted in gases escaping from the machine and ruining a family manuscript or portrait, plaintiff's recovery would be limited to the value of the physical item; recovery of the sentimental or emotional loss consequent upon its destruction would not be permitted (Lake v. Dye, 232 N.Y. 209, 214, 133 N.E. 448; Furlan v. Rayan Photo Works, 171 Misc. 839, 12 N.Y.S.2d 921; Twersky v. Pennsylvania R.R. Co., 152 Misc. 300, 273 N.Y.S. 328; Valentino v. Nasio Studio, 136 Misc. 826).

If the distinction thus drawn appears overfine that is the inevitable result of the fact that the drawing of any line necessarily differentiates between close cases. But to extend the rule as plaintiff argues and as would the dissenters here and below would be not only to ignore stare decisis but also to face Trial Judges and juries with a distinction extremely difficult, if not impossible, to articulate or conceptualize. It would, moreover, be anomalous, allowing recovery for emotional injury by the dentist but denying such recovery to members of the patient's family.

For the foregoing reasons, the order of the Appellate Division should be modified, with costs to appellant, to reinstate so much of the complaint as seeks to recover damages for other than emotional injuries and, as so modified, affirmed.

JASEN, J. (dissenting in part).

I am compelled to dissent because I believe the complaint in this action alleges a valid cause of action not only for pecuniary loss resulting from loss of professional reputation, but also alleges a valid cause of action for emotional injury suffered by a person to whom the defendants owed a duty which lies despite any separate liability that defendants would have to another person also injured by their negligence.

This case is before us on the basis of the defendants' motions to dismiss for failure to state a cause of action. We are thus obligated to give the complaint a liberal construction, assuming the allegations to be true. (Underpinning & Foundation Constructors v. Chase Manhattan Bank, N.A., 46 N.Y.2d 459, 386 N.Y.S.2d 1319, 414 N.E.2d 298; Cohn v. Lionel Corp., 21 N.Y.2d 559, 289 N.Y.S.2d 404, 236 N.E.2d 634.) The threshold question before this court, I believe, is whether or not the necessary elements of a tort have been pleaded — that is, whether facts sufficient to conclude that the defendants owed the plaintiff a duty and they breached that duty, resulting in a foreseeable injury to the plaintiff — are alleged. Assuming that all the necessary elements of a cause of action sounding in tort have been alleged in the complaint, the motion to dismiss must be denied unless the injury plaintiff seeks to recover for is not recognized in this State.

The majority, by allowing the plaintiff to pursue his cause of action for injury to his reputation and the resultant pecuniary loss apparently agrees that the defendants owed the plaintiff a duty which according to the allegations in the complaint was breached. Since the same factual allegations support the cause of action for emotional distress, the plaintiff should also be allowed to continue to pursue that cause of action unless recovery for nonphysical injury is barred by public policy. I can only conclude that the implication of the majority's holding is that a cause of action alleging an injury of emotional distress is no longer cognizable under New York law, at least in those cases where the defendant is also liable to another person for physical injury caused by the same negligent acts.

My disagreement with the majority's conclusion is twofold. In the first instance, I find it logically inconsistent to say that the plaintiff can recover for one type of injury flowing from the breach of a duty owed him, but that he cannot recover for a different type of injury flowing from that same breach. The majority, despite this logical inconsistency, concludes that this result is mandated by this State's policy, as expressed in previous opinions of this court, which limits the scope of duty when three people are involved in a situation causing injury. I do not agree that the precedent of this court or the policy embodied in those decisions does mandate such a result. Indeed, a deference to both policy and stare decisis requires that plaintiff's cause of action for emotional injury not be dismissed.

To my mind, this case is more properly aligned with Battalla v. State of New York, 10 N.Y.2d 237, 219 N.Y.S.2d 34, 176 N.E.2d 729 and its progeny than the line of cases coming under the rationale and policy of Tobin v. Grossman, 24 N.Y.2d 609, 301 N.Y.S.2d 554, 249 N.E.2d 419. The first line of cases recognized liability for emotional injury as a result of the defendant's breach of its duty to the plaintiff. The second line of cases limits liability so that third parties cannot recover for emotional injuries resulting from observing the physical injury sustained by another person as a result of the defendant's breach of the duty owed that other person. This case, I believe, is readily distinguishable from the second line of cases so that this plaintiff should be allowed to pursue his remedy under Battalla v. State of New York (supra). Furthermore, I see no basis for concluding that a third line of cases has developed which arguably bars one plaintiff from recovering for his emotional injuries merely because the tortfeasor is also liable for physical injuries sustained by a third person even when the defendant has breached its duty to both persons.

In Vitolo v. Dow Corning Corp., 634 N.Y.S.2d 362 (N.Y. 1995), a New York trial court considered motions to dismiss the complaint in a case brought by a surgeon who had implanted silicone breast prostheses, manufactured by the defendant, in over 1,800 women between 1978 and 1991. In January 1992, the FDA banned further such use of the silicone implants. Plaintiff alleged that use of the defective implants had adversely affected his business by subjecting him to numerous lawsuits, damaging his professional reputation and significantly distracting him from his occupation by requiring him to testify in pending litigation. Plaintiff additionally sought recovery for the accompanying emotional strain he was forced to bear. The defendant relied on Kennedy v. McKesson Co., supra, in moving to dismiss the plaintiff's claims against the breast implant manufacturer. The plaintiff sought to distinguish *Kennedy* on the ground that the defendant in that case provided a service, whereas here the defendant in this case was a product manufacturer. The trial court, citing *Kennedy,* granted defendant's motion to dismiss in connection with all claims except those based on alleged damage to plaintiff's professional practice and reputation.

C. RECOVERY FOR PURE ECONOMIC LOSS

It is axiomatic that a defendant is generally held liable for all harms to persons or property proximately caused by a product defect. Economic losses flowing from harm to persons or property, such as lost earning capacity or lost rental values, are typically recoverable under tort. "Pure economic loss," on the other hand, is a court's shorthand reference to the situation in which the plaintiff suffers economic loss that does not flow from harm to persons or property, such as economic loss caused by a product failing to operate properly (e.g., a faulty fuse causing an assembly line to halt production for several hours). The question here is whether the rules determining recovery for this type of pure economic loss should be governed by contract rather than tort principles.

Pure economic loss has traditionally been recoverable in contract actions, including products actions based on breach of warranty. Almost from the outset of judicial recognition of strict tort liability, courts have been besieged by plaintiffs seeking to recover for pure economic loss on the basis of tort rather than only on the basis of breach of warranty. Bearing in mind that the Uniform Commercial Code permits the recovery of consequential damages when a warranty has been breached, why have plaintiffs in pure economic loss cases pressed tort actions? In most cases, plaintiffs are seeking to escape from (1) the Code statute of limitations that runs from the time of delivery of the product, (2) the Code provisions that permit disclaimer of warranties or limitation of remedies, or (3) the privity of contract requirement that immunizes non-privity defendants from liability. These impediments can be avoided if the case sounds in tort; they will remain as good defenses if the case sounds in warranty.

Tort statutes of limitations typically begin to run from the time of injury or from the time that a reasonable person should have discovered such injury. Thus, if the plaintiff can convince a court to "tortify" the claim, an action that would otherwise be time-barred under U.C.C. §2-725(1) (four years from tender of delivery) may still be very much alive. Similarly, tortifying a claim may aid a plaintiff in escaping contractual disclaimers and limitations on liability. Courts have generally been hostile to disclaimers and limitation of remedies in cases that sound in tort. Finally, privity of contract remains an obstacle in many states for cases that do not have a personal injury component.

The case law and much of the literature on pure economic loss are distressingly difficult to follow. Rather than focusing on the appropriateness of applying the Code rule or the tort rule to a given fact pattern and articulating the policy grounds for so doing, the discussion seems to concern itself with the typology of the injury and/or the injury-producing event. Is the loss more tort-like or contractual in nature? It often seems that courts are seeking to determine whether, in the world of Platonic forms, the case will be relegated to the room that houses tort cases or the one that houses contract claims. Consider the following decision from the United States Supreme Court.

East River Steamship Corp. v. Transamerica Delaval, Inc.
476 U.S. 858 (1986)

BLACKMUN, J., delivered the opinion of the Court.

In this admiralty case, we must decide whether a cause of action in tort is stated when a defective product purchased in a commercial transaction malfunctions, injuring only the product itself and causing purely economic loss. The case requires us to consider preliminarily whether admiralty law, which already recognizes a general theory of liability for negligence, also incorporates principles of products liability, including strict liability. Then, charting a course between products liability and contract law, we must determine whether injury to a product itself is the kind of harm that should be protected by products liability or left entirely to the law of contracts.

I

In 1969, Seatrain Shipbuilding Corp. (Shipbuilding), a wholly owned subsidiary of Seatrain Lines, Inc. (Seatrain), announced it would build the four oil-transporting supertankers in issue — the T.T. Stuyvesant, T.T. Williamsburgh, T.T. Brooklyn, and T.T. Bay Ridge. Each tanker was constructed pursuant to a contract in which a separate wholly owned subsidiary of Seatrain engaged Shipbuilding. Shipbuilding in turn contracted with respondent, now known as Transamerica Delaval, Inc. (Delaval), to design, manufacture, and supervise the installation of turbines (costing $1.4 million each, see App. 163) that would be the main propulsion units for the 225,000-ton, $125 million, ibid., supertankers. When each ship was completed, its title was transferred from the contracting subsidiary to a trust company (as trustee for an owner), which in turn chartered the ship to one of the petitioners, also subsidiaries of Seatrain. Queensway Tankers, Inc., chartered the Stuyvesant; Kingsway Tankers, Inc., chartered the Williamsburgh; East River Steamship Corp. chartered the Brooklyn; and Richmond Tankers, Inc., chartered the Bay Ridge. Each petitioner operated under a bareboat charter, by which it took full control of the ship for 20 or 22 years as though it owned it, with the obligation afterwards to return the ship to the real owner. Each charterer assumed responsibility for the cost of any repairs to the ships.

The Stuyvesant sailed on its maiden voyage in late July 1977. On December 11 of that year, as the ship was about to enter the Port of Valdez, Alaska, steam began to escape from the casing of the high-pressure turbine. That problem was temporarily resolved by repairs, but before long, while the ship was encountering a severe storm in the Gulf of Alaska, the high-pressure turbine malfunctioned. The ship, though lacking its normal power, was able to continue on its journey to Panama and then San Francisco. In January 1978, an examination of the high-pressure turbine revealed that the first-stage steam-reversing ring virtually had disintegrated and had caused additional damage to other parts of the turbine. The damaged part was replaced with a part from the Bay Ridge, which was then under construction. In April 1978, the ship again was repaired, this time with a part from the Brooklyn. Finally, in August, the ship was permanently and satisfactorily repaired with a ring newly designed and manufactured by Delaval.

The Brooklyn and the Williamsburgh were put into service in late 1973 and late 1974, respectively. In 1978, as a result of the Stuyvesant's problems, they were inspected while in port. Those inspections revealed similar turbine damage. Temporary repairs were made, and newly designed parts were installed as permanent repairs that summer. . . .

II

The charterers' second amended complaint, filed in the United States District Court for the District of New Jersey, invokes admiralty jurisdiction. It contains five counts alleging tortious conduct on the part of respondent Delaval and seeks $3.03 million in damages, App. 73, for the cost of repairing the ships and for income lost while the ships were out of service. The first four counts, read liberally, allege that Delaval is strictly liable for the design defects in the high-pressure turbines of the Stuyvesant, the Williamsburgh, the Brooklyn, and the Bay Ridge, respectively. The fifth count alleges that Delaval, as part of the manufacturing process, negligently supervised the installation of the astern guardian valve on the Bay Ridge. The initial complaint also had listed Seatrain and Shipbuilding as plaintiffs and had alleged breach of contract and warranty as well as tort claims. But after Delaval interposed a statute of limitations defense, the complaint was amended and the charterers alone brought the suit in tort. The nonrenewed claims were dismissed with prejudice by the District Court. Delaval then moved for summary judgment, contending that the charterers' actions were not cognizable in tort.

The District Court granted summary judgment for Delaval, and the Court of Appeals for the Third Circuit, sitting en banc, affirmed. East River S.S. Corp. v. Delaval Turbine, Inc., 752 F.2d 903 (1985). The Court of Appeals held that damage solely to a defective product is actionable in tort if the defect creates an unreasonable risk of harm to persons or property other than the product itself, and harm materializes. Disappointments over the product's quality, on the other hand, are protected by warranty law. Id., at 908, 909-910. The charterers were dissatisfied with product quality: the defects involved gradual and unnoticed deterioration of the turbines' component parts, and the only risk created was that the turbines would operate at a lower capacity. Id., at 909. See Pennsylvania Glass Sand Corp. v. Caterpillar Tractor Co., 652 F.2d 1165, 1169-1170 (CA3 1981). Therefore, neither the negligence nor the strict liability claims were cognizable.

Judge Garth concurred on "grounds somewhat different," 752 F.2d, at 910, and Judge Becker, joined by Judge Higginbotham, concurred in part and dissented in part. Id., at 913. Although Judge Garth agreed with the majority's analysis on the merits, he found no strict liability claim presented because the charterers had failed to allege unreasonable danger or demonstrable injury.

Judge Becker largely agreed with the majority's approach, but would permit recovery for a "near miss," where the risk existed but no calamity occurred. He felt that the first count, concerning the Stuyvesant, stated a cause of action in tort. The exposure of the ship to a severe storm when the ship was unable to operate at full power due to the defective part created an unreasonable risk of harm.

We granted certiorari to resolve a conflict among the Courts of Appeals sitting in admiralty. . . .

III...

B...

When torts have occurred on navigable waters within the United States, the Court has imposed an additional requirement of a "maritime nexus"—that the wrong must bear "a significant relationship to traditional maritime activity." See Executive Jet Aviation, Inc. v. City of Cleveland, 409 U.S. 249, 268, 93 S. Ct. 493, 504, 34 L. Ed. 2d 454 (1972); Foremost Ins. Co. v. Richardson, 457 U.S. 668, 102 S. Ct. 2654, 73 L. Ed. 2d 300 (1982). We need not reach the question whether a maritime nexus also must be established when a tort occurs on the high seas. Were there such a requirement, it clearly was met here, for these ships were engaged in maritime commerce, a primary concern of admiralty law. . . .

C...

The Courts of Appeals sitting in admiralty overwhelmingly have adopted concepts of products liability, based both on negligence, Sieracki v. Seas Shipping Co., 149 F.2d 98, 99-100 (CA3 1945), *aff'd* on other grounds, 328 U.S. 85, 66 S. Ct. 872, 90 L. Ed. 1099 (1946), and on strict liability, Pan-Alaska Fisheries, Inc. v. Marine Constr. & Design Co., 565 F.2d 1129, 1135 (CA9 1977) (adopting Restatement (Second) of Torts §402A (1965)). Indeed, the Court of Appeals for the Third Circuit previously had stated that the question whether principles of strict products liability are part of maritime law "is no longer seriously contested." Ocean Barge Transport Co. v. Hess Oil Virgin Islands Corp., 726 F.2d 121, 123 (CA3 1984) (citing cases).

We join the Courts of Appeals in recognizing products liability, including strict liability, as part of the general maritime law. This Court's precedents relating to injuries of maritime workers long have pointed in that direction. . . . Our incorporation of products liability into maritime law, however, is only the threshold determination to the main issue in this case.

IV

Products liability grew out of a public policy judgment that people need more protection from dangerous products than is afforded by the law of warranty. See Seely v. White Motor Co., 63 Cal. 2d 9, 15, 45 Cal. Rptr. 17, 21, 403 P.2d 145, 149 (1965). It is clear, however, that if this development were allowed to progress too far, contract law would drown in a sea of tort. See G. Gilmore, The Death of Contract 87-94 (1974). We must determine whether a commercial product injuring itself is the kind of harm against which public policy requires manufacturers to protect, independent of any contractual obligation.

A

The paradigmatic products-liability action is one where a product "reasonably certain to place life and limb in peril," distributed without reinspection, causes bodily injury. See, e.g., MacPherson v. Buick Motor Co., 217 N.Y. 382, 389, 111 N.E. 1050, 1051, 1053 (1916). The manufacturer is liable whether or not it is negligent because "public policy demands that responsibility be fixed wherever it will most effectively reduce the hazards to life and health inherent in defective products that reach the market." Escola v. Coca Cola Bottling Co., 24 Cal. 2d, at 462, 150 P.2d, at 441 (concurring opinion).

For similar reasons of safety, the manufacturer's duty of care was broadened to include protection against property damage. See Marsh Wood Products Co. v. Babcock & Wilcox Co., 207 Wis. 209, 226, 240 N.W. 392, 399 (1932); Genesee County Patrons Fire Relief Assn. v. L. Sonneborn Sons, Inc., 263 N.Y. 463, 469-473, 189 N.E. 551, 553-555 (1934). Such damage is considered so akin to personal injury that the two are treated alike. See Seely v. White Motor Co., 63 Cal. 2d, at 19, 45 Cal. Rptr., at 24, 403 P.2d, at 152.

In the traditional "property damage" cases, the defective product damages other property. In this case, there was no damage to "other" property. Rather, the first, second, and third counts allege that each supertanker's defectively designed turbine components damaged only the turbine itself. Since each turbine was supplied by Delaval as an integrated package, see App. 162-163, each is properly regarded as a single unit. "Since all but the very simplest of machines have component parts, [a contrary] holding would require a finding of 'property damage' in virtually every case where a product damages itself. Such a holding would eliminate the distinction between warranty and strict products liability." Northern Power & Engineering Corp. v. Caterpillar Tractor Co., 623 P.2d 324, 330 (Alaska 1981). The fifth count also alleges injury to the product itself. Before the high-pressure and low-pressure turbines could become an operational propulsion system, they were connected to piping and valves under the supervision of Delaval personnel. See App. 78, 162-163, 181. Delaval's supervisory obligations were part of its manufacturing agreement. The fifth count thus can best be read to allege that Delaval's negligent manufacture of the propulsion system — by allowing the installation in reverse of the astern guardian valve — damaged the propulsion system. Cf. Lewis v. Timco, Inc., 736 F.2d 163, 165-166 (CA5 1984). Obviously, damage to a product itself has certain attributes of a products-liability claim. But the injury suffered — the failure of the product to function properly — is the essence of a warranty action, through which a contracting party can seek to recoup the benefit of its bargain.

B

The intriguing question whether injury to a product itself may be brought in tort has spawned a variety of answers. At one end of the spectrum, the case that created the majority land-based approach, Seely v. White Motor Co., 63 Cal. 2d 9, 45 Cal. Rptr. 17, 403 P.2d 145 (1965) (defective truck), held that preserving a proper role for the law of warranty precludes imposing tort liability if a defective product causes purely monetary harm. See also Jones & Laughlin Steel Corp. v. Johns-Manville Sales Corp., 626 F.2d 280, 287 and n.13 (CA3 1980) (citing cases).

At the other end of the spectrum is the minority land-based approach, whose progenitor, Santor v. A and M Karagheusian, Inc., 44 N.J. 52, 66-67, 207 A.2d 305, 312-313 (1965) (marred carpeting), held that a manufacturer's duty to make nondefective products encompassed injury to the product itself, whether or not the defect created an unreasonable risk of harm. See also LaCrosse v. Schubert, 72 Wis. 2d 38, 44-45, 240 N.W.2d 124, 127-128 (1976). The courts adopting this approach, including the majority of the Courts of Appeals sitting in admiralty that have considered the issue, e.g., Emerson G.M. Diesel, Inc. v. Alaskan Enterprise, 732 F.2d 1468 (CA9 1984), find that the safety and insurance rationales behind strict liability apply equally where the losses are purely economic. These courts reject the Seely approach because they find it arbitrary that economic losses are recoverable if a plaintiff suffers bodily injury or property damage, but not if a product injures itself. They also find no inherent difference between economic loss and personal injury or property damage, because all are proximately caused by the defendant's conduct. Further, they believe recovery for economic loss would not lead to unlimited liability because they think a manufacturer can predict and insure against product failure. See Emerson G.M. Diesel, Inc. v. Alaskan Enterprise, 732 F.2d, at 1474.

Between the two poles fall a number of cases that would permit a products-liability action under certain circumstances when a product injures only itself. These cases attempt to differentiate between "the disappointed users . . . and the endangered ones," Russell v. Ford Motor Co., 281 Or. 587, 595, 575 P.2d 1383, 1387 (1978), and permit only the latter to sue in tort. The determination has been said to turn on the nature of the defect, the type of risk, and the manner in which the injury arose. See Pennsylvania Glass Sand Corp. v. Caterpillar Tractor Co., 652 F.2d 1165, 1173 (CA3 1981) (relied on by the Court of Appeals in this case). The Alaska Supreme Court allows a tort action if the defective product creates a situation potentially dangerous to persons or other property, and loss occurs as a proximate result of that danger and under dangerous circumstances. Northern Power & Engineering Corp. v. Caterpillar Tractor Co., 623 P.2d 324, 329 (1981).

We find the intermediate and minority land-based positions unsatisfactory. The intermediate positions, which essentially turn on the degree of risk, are too indeterminate to enable manufacturers easily to structure their business behavior. Nor do we find persuasive a distinction that rests on the manner in which the product is injured. We realize that the damage may be qualitative, occurring through gradual deterioration or internal breakage. Or it may be calamitous. Compare Morrow v. New Moon Homes, Inc., 548 P.2d 279 (Alaska 1976), with Cloud v. Kit Mfg. Co., 563 P.2d 248, 251 (Alaska 1977). But either way, since by definition no person or other property is damaged, the resulting loss is purely economic. Even when the harm to the product itself occurs through an abrupt, accident-like event, the resulting loss due to repair costs, decreased value, and lost profits is essentially the failure of the purchaser to receive the benefit of its bargain—traditionally the core concern of contract law. See E. Farnsworth, Contracts §12.8, pp.839-840 (1982).

We also decline to adopt the minority land-based view espoused by Santor and Emerson. Such cases raise legitimate questions about the theories behind restricting products liability, but we believe that the countervailing arguments are more powerful. The minority view fails to account for the need to keep products liability and contract law in separate spheres and to maintain a realistic limitation on damages.

C

Exercising traditional discretion in admiralty, see Pope & Talbot, Inc. v. Hawn, 346 U.S. 406, 409, 74 S. Ct. 202, 204, 98 L. Ed. 143 (1953), we adopt an approach similar to Seely and hold that a manufacturer in a commercial relationship has no duty under either a negligence or strict products-liability theory to prevent a product from injuring itself.

> The distinction that the law has drawn between tort recovery for physical injuries and warranty recovery for economic loss is not arbitrary and does not rest on the 'luck' of one plaintiff in having an accident causing physical injury. The distinction rests, rather, on an understanding of the nature of the responsibility a manufacturer must undertake in distributing his products. Seely v. White Motor Co., 63 Cal. 2d, at 18, 45 Cal. Rptr., at 23, 403 P.2d, at 151.

When a product injures only itself the reasons for imposing a tort duty are weak and those for leaving the party to its contractual remedies are strong.

The tort concern with safety is reduced when an injury is only to the product itself. When a person is injured, the "cost of an injury and the loss of time or health may be an overwhelming misfortune," and one the person is not prepared to meet. Escola v. Coca Cola Bottling Co., 24 Cal. 2d, at 462, 150 P.2d, at 441 (concurring opinion). In contrast, when a product injures itself, the commercial user stands to lose the value of the product, risks the displeasure of its customers who find that the product does not meet their needs, or, as in this case, experiences increased costs in performing a service. Losses like these can be insured. Society need not presume that a customer needs special protection. The increased cost to the public that would result from holding a manufacturer liable in tort for injury to the product itself is not justified. Cf. United States v. Carroll Towing Co., 159 F.2d 169, 173 (CA2 1947).

Damage to a product itself is most naturally understood as a warranty claim. Such damage means simply that the product has not met the customer's expectations, or, in other words, that the customer has received "insufficient product value." See J. White and R. Summers, Uniform Commercial Code 406 (2d ed. 1980). The maintenance of product value and quality is precisely the purpose of express and implied warranties. See U.C.C. §2-313 (express warranty), §2-314 (implied warranty of merchantability), and §2-315 (warranty of fitness for a particular purpose). Therefore, a claim of a nonworking product can be brought as a breach-of-warranty action. Or, if the customer prefers, it can reject the product or revoke its acceptance and sue for breach of contract. See U.C.C. §§2-601, 2-608, 2-612.

Contract law, and the law of warranty in particular, is well suited to commercial controversies of the sort involved in this case because the parties may set the terms of their own agreements. The manufacturer can restrict its liability, within limits, by disclaiming warranties or limiting remedies. See U.C.C. §§2-316, 2-719. In exchange, the purchaser pays less for the product. Since a commercial situation generally does not involve large disparities in bargaining power, cf. Henningsen v. Bloomfield Motors, Inc., 32 N.J. 358, 161 A.2d 69 (1960), we see no reason to intrude into the parties' allocation of the risk.

While giving recognition to the manufacturer's bargain, warranty law sufficiently protects the purchaser by allowing it to obtain the benefit of its bargain. See J. White and R. Summers, supra, ch. 10. The expectation damages available in warranty for purely economic loss give a plaintiff the full benefit of its bargain by compensating for forgone business opportunities. See Fuller and Perdue, The Reliance Interest in Contract Damages: 1, 46 Yale L.J. 52, 60-63 (1936); R. Posner, Economic Analysis of Law §4.8 (3d ed. 1986). Recovery on a warranty theory would give the charterers their repair costs and lost profits, and would place them in the position they would have been in had the turbines functioned properly. See Hawkins v. McGee, 84 N.H. 114, 146 A. 641 (1929). Thus, both the nature of the injury and the resulting damages indicate it is more natural to think of injury to a product itself in terms of warranty.

A warranty action also has a built-in limitation on liability, whereas a tort action could subject the manufacturer to damages of an indefinite amount. The limitation in a contract action comes from the agreement of the parties and the requirement that consequential damages, such as lost profits, be a foreseeable result of the breach. See Hadley v. Baxendale, 9 Ex. 341, 156 Eng. Rep. 145 (1854). In a warranty action where the loss is purely economic, the limitation derives from the requirements of foreseeability and of privity, which is still generally enforced for such claims in a commercial setting. See U.C.C. §2-715; J. White and R. Summers, Uniform Commercial Code 389, 396, 406-410 (2d ed. 1980).

In products-liability law, where there is a duty to the public generally, foreseeability is an inadequate brake. Cf. Petitions of Kinsman Transit Co., 388 F.2d 821 (CA2 1968). See also Perlman, Interference with Contract and Other Economic Expectancies: A Clash of Tort and Contract Doctrine, 49 U. Chi. L. Rev. 61, 71-72 (1982). Permitting recovery for all foreseeable claims for purely economic loss could make a manufacturer liable for vast sums. It would be difficult for a manufacturer to take into account the expectations of persons downstream who may encounter its product. In this case, for example, if the charterers — already one step removed from the transaction — were permitted to recover their economic losses, then the companies that subchartered the ships might claim their economic losses from the delays, and the charterers' customers also might claim their economic losses, and so on. "The law does not spread its protection so far." Robins Dry Dock & Repair Co. v. Flint, 275 U.S. 303, 309, 48 S. Ct. 134, 135, 72 L. Ed. 290 (1927).

And to the extent that courts try to limit purely economic damages in tort, they do so by relying on a far murkier line, one that negates the charterers' contention that permitting such recovery under a products-liability theory enables admiralty courts to avoid difficult linedrawing. Cf. Ultramares Corp. v. Touche, 255 N.Y. 170, 174 N.E. 441 (1931); State ex rel. Guste v. M/V Testbank, 752 F.2d 1019, 1046-1052 (CA5 1985) (en banc) (dissenting opinion), *cert. pending,* No. 84-1808. . . .

D . . .

Thus, whether stated in negligence or strict liability, no products-liability claim lies in admiralty when the only injury claimed is economic loss. [Affirmed.]

In Saratoga Fishing Co. v. J.M. Martinac & Co., 520 U.S. 875 (1997), the Supreme Court clarified what constitutes injury to the "product itself" under *East River,* as well as how recovery would be affected if the party seeking damages is not the initial purchaser of the product. In that case, an individual purchased a boat from the defendant-manufacturer and subsequently added certain equipment to the boat. The individual then sold the boat to the plaintiff. Sometime thereafter the boat sank due to an engine-room fire that resulted from a defectively designed hydraulic system supplied to the defendant-manufacturer by a component supplier. Characterizing the additional equipment as "other property" rather than the "product itself," the Supreme Court held that the plaintiff could recover for the physical damage to the equipment added by the initial purchaser explaining that:

> When a Manufacturer places an item in the stream of commerce by selling it to an Initial User, that item is the "product itself" under *East River*. Items added to the product by the Initial User are therefore "other property," and the Initial User's sale of the product to a Subsequent User does not change these characterizations. [Id. at 1786.]

The Court justified its holding on several grounds. For one, the Court reasoned that to hold the manufacturer liable for damage to the equipment added by the initial purchaser only when the initial purchaser still possessed the product "makes the scope of a manufacturer's liability turn on what seems . . . a fortuity." Id. at 1787. Moreover, the Court noted that subsequent purchasers are not as able as initial purchasers to adjust the risks of harm by contractual agreement, and it is likely more difficult for initial purchasers (consumers) to offer a warranty to subsequent purchasers on used products. Id. Finally, the Court did not agree with the respondents' contention that its holding would expose manufacturers to too great a potential of tort liability. The Court explained that "a host of other tort principles, such as foreseeability, proximate cause, and the 'economic loss' doctrine already do . . . limit liability in important ways." Id. In fact, earlier in the opinion the Court stated that preventing subsequent purchasers from recovering for damage to equipment added by initial purchasers would create a "tort damage immunity beyond that set by any relevant precedent." Id. at 1787.

The Products Liability Restatement adopts the economic loss rule set forth in *East River* and *Saratoga Fishing*.

Restatement (Third) of Torts: Products Liability
(1998)

§21. Definition of "Harm to Persons or Property": Recovery for Economic Loss

For purposes of the Restatement, harm to persons or property includes economic loss if caused by harm to:
  (a) the plaintiff's person; or
  (b) the person of another when harm to the other interferes with an interest of the plaintiff protected by tort law; or
  (c) the plaintiff's property other than the defective product itself.

COMMENT:

e. Harm to the plaintiff's property other than the defective product itself. A defective product that causes harm to property other than the defective product itself is governed by the rules of this Restatement. What constitutes harm to other property rather than harm to the product itself may be difficult to determine. A product that nondangerously fails to function due to a product defect has clearly caused harm only to itself. A product that fails to function and causes harm to surrounding property has clearly caused harm to other property. However, when a component part of a machine or a system destroys the rest of the machine or system, the characterization process becomes more difficult. When the product or system is deemed to be an integrated whole, courts treat such damage as harm to the product itself. When so characterized, the damage is excluded from the coverage of this Restatement. A contrary holding would require a finding of property damage in virtually every case in which a product harms itself and would prevent contractual rules from serving their legitimate function in governing commercial transactions.

Not all courts agree with *East River* and the Products Liability Restatement. Consider the following case emanating from the California Supreme Court.

Jimenez v. The Superior Court
58 P.3d 450 (Cal. 2002)

KENNARD, J.

In California, a manufacturer, distributor, or retailer of a defective product is strictly liable in tort for any resulting harm to a person *or* to property other than the product itself. This case presents two issues: (1) Can a manufacturer of windows installed in a mass-produced home during its construction ever be strictly liable in tort for harm resulting from defects in those windows? (2) If so, is that manufacturer strictly liable in tort for resulting physical damage to other parts of the house in which the windows have been installed? We answer "yes" to both questions.

Facts and Proceedings

In 1988, developer McMillin Scripps II completed the Galleria and Renaissance housing developments in the Scripps Ranch area of San Diego. Viking Industries, Inc. (Viking) manufactured the windows in the Galleria development; T.M. Cobb (Cobb) manufactured the windows in the Renaissance development.

Plaintiffs Filipina and Nestor Jimenez, owners of one of the Galleria homes, brought this action against window manufacturers Viking and Cobb, and also against two companies (Medallion Industries, Inc., and Minnoch Supply Co.) that had supplied and installed the windows. On behalf of themselves and all homeowners in the Galleria and Renaissance developments, plaintiffs asserted that defendants had "designed, developed, manufactured, produced, supplied and placed into the stream of commerce" defective windows installed in the Galleria and Renaissance homes, and that the defects caused property damage. They alleged strict liability and negligence causes of action.

Window manufacturer Cobb moved for summary adjudication of the strict liability cause of action. Cobb argued that the manufacturer of a product installed in a mass-produced home, unless it has ownership or control over the housing development, cannot be held strictly liable to a homeowner for a defective or dangerous condition in the home. In response, plaintiffs conceded that Cobb did not own or control the Renaissance housing development, but they argued that manufacturers of component parts of mass-produced houses are strictly liable for damages caused by those component parts, including damage to other parts of the houses in which they are installed. Plaintiffs asserted that the allegedly defective windows installed in their home had damaged the "stucco, insulation, framing, drywall, paint, wall coverings, floor coverings, baseboards, and other parts of the home."

The trial court granted window manufacturer Cobb's motion for summary adjudication. The parties later stipulated, and the trial court ordered, that the ruling also applied to window manufacturer Viking. Plaintiffs petitioned the Court of Appeal for a writ of mandate.

The Court of Appeal issued a writ directing the trial court to vacate its order granting the defense motion for summary adjudication. It held that the doctrine of strict products liability applied to manufacturers of defective component parts installed in mass-produced homes, and that this strict liability extended to injuries to other parts of the house in which the defective component was installed. We granted the petitions for review of defendant window manufacturers Cobb and Viking. . . .

[The court's general discussion regarding the liability of component part manufacturers is omitted. The court held that manufacturers of component parts are subject to strict liability in tort when their defective products cause harm.]

The Economic Loss Rule

Two years after our 1963 decision in *Greenman* . . . , 377 P.2d 897, which held that manufacturers are strictly liable in tort for injuries that their defective products cause to consumers, we decided Seely v. White Motor Co., (1965) 403 P.2d 145 (*Seely*). In that case, the plaintiff purchased a truck for use in his business, but he discovered that the truck bounced violently, preventing normal use of the truck for his business. Eventually the truck overturned when its brakes failed. The plaintiff then sued the truck manufacturer to recover the cost of repairing the damage to the truck caused by the accident, the amount he had paid on the purchase price, and business profits he lost because of the truck's bouncing problem. . . . The action was tried to the court, which found that the bouncing problem was a defect in the truck for which the manufacturer was responsible under its written warranty, but that this problem had not caused the accident in which the truck overturned. . . . The court awarded the plaintiff damages for breach of warranty, consisting of the amount paid on the purchase price of the truck and lost business profits attributable to the bouncing problem. (Ibid.)

The truck manufacturer appealed, and we affirmed the judgment. We rejected a contention that strict products liability had entirely superseded the law governing product warranties. We explained: "The distinction that the law has drawn between tort recovery for physical injuries and warranty recovery for economic loss is not arbitrary and does not rest on the 'luck' of one plaintiff in having an accident causing physical injury. The distinction rests, rather, on an understanding of the nature of the responsibility a manufacturer must undertake in distributing his products." . . . We concluded that the nature of this responsibility meant that a manufacturer could appropriately be held liable for physical injuries (including both personal injury and damage to property other than the product itself), regardless of the terms of any warranty. . . . But the manufacturer could not be held liable for "the level of performance of his products in the consumer's business unless he agrees that the product was designed to meet the consumer's demands." . . .

This reasoning ultimately outlined the framework of our economic loss rule, which the United States Supreme Court later adopted in large part for purposes of tort liability under admiralty jurisdiction. (See East River S.S. Corp. v. Transamerica Delaval (1986) 476 U.S. 858, . . . (*East River*).) As we stressed in *Seely,* recovery under the doctrine of strict liability is limited solely to "physical harm to person or property." . . . Damages available under strict products liability do not include economic loss, which includes "'damages for inadequate value, costs of repair and replacement of the defective product or consequent loss of profits — without any claim of personal injury or damages to other property. . . .'"

Most recently, in Aas v. Superior Court (2000) . . . 12 P.3d 1125, we applied the economic loss rule in a negligence action by homeowners against the developer, contractor, and subcontractors who built their dwellings. In *Aas,* the plaintiffs alleged that their homes suffered from many construction defects, but they conceded that many of the defects had caused no bodily injury or property damage. The trial court barred them from introducing evidence of the defects that had caused no injury to persons or property. We upheld the trial court's ruling. We explained that under the economic loss rule, "appreciable, nonspeculative, present injury is an essential element of a tort cause of action." . . . "Construction defects that have not ripened into property damage, or at least into involuntary out-of-pocket losses," we held, "do not comfortably fit the definition of '"appreciable harm"' — an essential element of a negligence claim." . . .[1]

(2) In summary, the economic loss rule allows a plaintiff to recover in strict products liability in tort when a product defect causes damage to "other property," that is, property *other than the product itself.* The law of contractual warranty governs damage to the product itself. . . .

To apply the economic loss rule, we must first determine what the product at issue is. Only then do we find out whether the injury is to the product itself (for which recovery is barred by the economic loss rule) or to property other than the defective product (for which plaintiffs may recover in tort). Defendant window manufacturers argue that here the "product" is the entire house in which their windows were installed, and that the damage caused to other parts of the house by the allegedly defective windows is damage to the product itself within the economic loss rule, thus precluding application of strict liability. We disagree.

California decisional law has long recognized that the economic loss rule does not necessarily bar recovery in tort for damage that a defective product (e.g., a window) causes to other portions of a larger product (e.g., a house) into which the former has been incorporated. In Aas v. Superior Court, supra . . . , we observed that "the concept of recoverable physical injury or property damage" had over time "expanded to include damage to one part of a product caused by another, defective part." The list of examples we gave (ibid.) included Stearman v. Centex Homes (2000) . . . 92 Cal. Rptr. 2d 761, in which the Court of Appeal affirmed a judgment making a builder strictly liable in tort for damages that a defective foundation caused to the interior and exterior of a home. *Aas* also cited with approval the part of Casey v. Overhead Door Corp., . . . Cal. Rptr. 2d 603,

---

1. In the wake of our decision in Aas v. Superior Court, supra, 24 Cal. 4th 627, the Legislature established a limited new cause of action for certain specified housing defects. (Stats. 2002, ch. 722, §3 [enacting new Civ. Code, §895 et seq., eff. Jan. 1, 2003].)

in which the Court of Appeal affirmed a nonsuit for the defendant on a tort claim for defective windows only because the plaintiffs had failed to prove that the windows damaged other property. The nonsuit would not have been proper, the Court of Appeal explained, had the plaintiffs been able to support their assertion that the windows had "caused damage to the drywall and framing and resulted in insect infestation and damage to personal property." . . . Defendants' argument here that the house is the relevant product for purposes of applying the economic loss rule is inconsistent with these and other decisions recognizing that the duty of a product manufacturer to prevent property damage does not necessarily end when the product is incorporated into a larger product.

Applying this principle to the facts before us here, we conclude that the manufacturer of a defective window installed in a mass-produced home may be held strictly liable in tort for damage that the window's defect causes to other parts of the home in which it is installed. . . .

Conclusion and Disposition

This court assumed a leading role in holding manufacturers, distributors, and retailers of defective products strictly liable for physical injuries resulting from the defects. We imposed this strict liability to assure just compensation to innocent victims, to give all those in the distributive chain an incentive to improve product safety and performance, and to promote equitable spreading and apportionment of the losses resulting from physical injuries as a cost of doing business. These policy considerations support the conclusions we reach here: to impose strict liability on the manufacturers of windows installed in mass-produced homes for physical injuries caused by defects in those windows, and to include within the scope of this strict liability damage to other parts of the houses in which these defective windows are installed.

The judgment of the Court of Appeal is affirmed. . . .

Concurring Opinion by KENNARD, J.

The majority opinion, which I authored, holds that the economic loss rule does not bar recovery for damages that defective windows cause to other components of mass-produced homes in which they are installed. . . . It does not hold, however, that the economic loss rule can never bar recovery for damages that one part or element of a finished product causes to other parts or elements of the same finished product. I write separately to express and explain my view that the crucial inquiry for applying the economic loss rule in this context is whether the component part has been so integrated into the overall unit that it has lost its separate identity.

The economic loss rule limits tort recovery under strict products liability to damages for physical harm to a person or to property other than the defective product itself. . . . To apply the economic loss rule, therefore, one must first determine what the product at issue is. Only then can one determine whether the injury is to the product itself (and therefore subject to the economic loss rule) or to property other than the defective product (and thus subject to strict products liability in tort). Here, defendant window manufacturers have argued that the "product" is the entire house in which their windows were installed, and that the damage caused to other parts of the house by the allegedly defective windows is damage to the product itself within the economic loss rule, thus precluding application of strict liability. For the reasons that follow, I conclude that the windows may be regarded as a distinct product for purposes of the economic loss rule.

The manufacturer of a component part may be strictly liable in tort for physical injuries caused by defects in the component. As the Restatement Third of Torts recognizes: "One engaged in the business of selling or otherwise distributing product components who sells or distributes a component is subject to liability for harm to persons or property caused by a product into which the component is integrated if: (a) the component is defective in itself . . . and the defect causes the harm. . . ." (Rest. 3d Torts, Products Liability, §5.) A comment in the Restatement Third of Torts addresses the issue of a component causing damage to the product of which it is a part. It says: "When a component part of a machine or a system destroys the rest of the machine or system, the characterization process becomes more difficult. When the product or system is deemed to be an integrated whole, courts treat such damage as harm to the product itself. When so characterized, the damage is excluded from the coverage of this Restatement. A contrary holding would require a finding of property damage in virtually every case in which a product harms itself and would prevent contractual rules from serving their legitimate function in governing commercial transactions." (Rest. 3d Torts, Products Liability, §21, com. *e,* pp.295-296.) Under the Restatement view, in other words, the manufacturer of component will not be strictly liable in tort for injury to other parts of the unit in which it is installed if the component has been so integrated into the overall unit that it has lost its separate identity.

Instructive here is the United States Supreme Court's decision in East River S.S. Corp. v. Transamerica Delaval (1986) 476 U.S. 858. . . . There, companies that chartered oil-transporting supertankers brought an action under maritime law seeking to hold a turbine manufacturer strictly liable in tort for income losses and repair costs resulting when a defective part of the supertankers' turbines damaged other parts of the turbines. (Id. at pp.859-860.) Adopting an economic loss rule similar to the one this court had articulated in Seely v. White Motor Co. . . . , the high court held that "a manufacturer in a commercial relationship has no duty under either a negligence or strict products-liability theory to prevent a product from injuring itself." . . . The court determined that the defective part of the turbine had been so integrated into the turbine that it lost its separate identity, and thus the manufacturer was not strictly liable in tort for injury that the component part caused to the turbine. The court reasoned that "each turbine was supplied by [the turbine designer, manufacturer, and installer] as an integrated package [and] each is properly regarded as a single unit." . . . Thus, the high court in *East River* determined, consistent with the Restatement Third of Torts, Products Liability, that the defective part had been so integrated into the turbine that it could not be regarded as a separate product.

Thereafter, the United States Supreme Court in Saratoga Fishing Co. v. J.M. Martinac & Co. (1997) 520 U.S. 875, . . . addressed a related, yet distinguishable, issue in the context of equipment added to a ship *after* it had been originally built and outfitted. In *Saratoga,* the court considered whether a skiff, a net, and various spare parts added to a ship after its original sale were "other property"—that is, property other than the ship itself—so as to allow a second purchaser of the ship to recover in tort from the manufacturer for the loss of these items when the ship caught fire and sank. . . . The court allowed recovery because the extra equipment was "other property." The court noted that the ship as originally outfitted, without the extra equipment, was the product that was "placed in the stream of commerce by the manufacturer and its distributors." . . . The high court's decision is consistent with the view that a nonintegrated component may be a separate product for purposes of strict products liability law. The extra equipment at issue in *Saratoga* had not been so integrated into the ship that it lost its separate identity.

I would adopt for California the interpretation of the economic loss rule articulated in these two decisions of the United States Supreme Court and in the Restatement Third of Torts, discussed above. Under this interpretation, in determining whether a component manufacturer is strictly liable in tort for harm that its defective product causes to a larger object of which it is a component, the pertinent inquiry is whether the component has been so integrated into the larger unit as to have lost its separate identity. If so, strict liability is improper. But if the component retains its separate identity, so that it may be readily separated from the overall unit, the component manufacturer may be strictly liable for damages to the larger unit.

Windows are not so integrated into houses as to lose their separate identity. Windows can be readily removed from houses and replaced with other windows. A window that has been removed from one house can then be installed in another house. For this reason, I conclude that a window manufacturer is strictly liable in tort for damages that defects in its windows cause to other parts of the homes, such as stucco, insulation, framing, drywall, and baseboards. . . .

Most courts have bought into the view of the Products Liability Restatement and deny recovery when the defective component causes damage to the product into which it is integrated. The Supreme Court of Wisconsin explicitly approved §21, supra, in State Farm Mutual Automobile Ins. Co. v. Ford Motor Co., 592 N.W.2d 201 (Wis. 1999). A defective ignition switch in a 4 × 4 truck caused a fire that destroyed the truck. No other losses were caused. The court denied the plaintiff's tort claim for the value of the truck as a matter of law. Also see Progressive Ins. Co. v. General Motors Corp., 749 N.E.2d 484 (Ind. 2001) (no tort recovery for economic loss resulting from defective wiring, fuel lines, and transmission lines that sparked fire in and damaged automobiles); Steinter v. Ford Motor Co., 606 N.W.2d 783 (N.D. 2002) (same); Northwest Arkansas Masonry Inc. v. Summit Specialty Products, Inc., 31 P.3d 982 (Kan. App. 2002) (defect in masonry cement that did not properly harden could not serve as grounds for products liability action; the economic loss rule barred action in tort); Sherman v. Sea Ray Boats, Inc., 649 N.W.2d 783 (Mich. App. 2002) (latent decay in the wood of a boat constituted damage to the "product itself" and could not support a products liability against the manufacturer).

Some courts reject *East River* and allow recovery for damage to the product itself when such damage is brought about by a sudden and highly dangerous occurrence that endangers the consumer. See, e.g., American Fire & Casualty Co. v. Ford Motor Co., 588 N.W.2d 437 (Iowa 1999) (truck caught fire causing damage to the truck and its contents; court held that economic loss rule applies only to a product that disappoints consumer expectations and does not apply to a defective product that endangers others).

Plaintiffs have argued that the economic loss rule should be limited to commercial transaction but consumers who have suffered economic loss should be allowed to bring product liability actions. Courts have not been hospitable to their entrities. See, e.g., Progressive Ins. Co. v. General Motors Corp., supra; Sherman v. Sea Ray Boats, Inc., supra.

One class of cases remain a puzzlement. Owners of buildings that have incurred significant costs when required by law to undertake asbestos rebatement have been successful in getting courts to allow them to bring actions in tort for their economic loss. Had the plaintiffs been limited to their U.C.C. warranty actions, they would have been time-barred. Typically, asbestos was installed several decades before a suit was brought, well beyond the four years from tender of delivery provided by UCC 2-725(1). Under tort law the statute of limitations does not generally begin to run until discovery of the injury. Courts have held that asbestos insulation integrated into the building is damage to other property; see, e.g., Board of Education of City of Chicago v. A. C. and S., Inc., 546 N.E.2d 580 (Ill. 1989); City of Greenville v. W.R. Grace & Co., 827 F.2d 975 (4th Cir. 1987). Also see Richard G. Ausness, Tort Liability for Asbestos Removal Costs, 73 Or. L. Rev. 505 (1994). It is almost impossible to reconcile the finding that damaged caused by asbestos fully integrated into a building constitutes damage to "other property" with *East River* and its progeny.

Furthermore, the asbestos cases remain problematic in that they allow recovery for damages before any injury has become manifest. Asbestos is only dangerous when it becomes friable. Abatement anticipates that at some time in the future asbestos may crumble and the fibers then released would cause lung cancer. In non-asbestos cases courts have refused to allow recovery in tort even if the product may become dangerous in the future. See, e.g., In re Bridgestone/Firestone, Inc., 288 F.3d 1012, 1016-1017 (7th Cir. 2002) (no tort action for tires that are more prone to blowout in the future); In re General Motors type III Door Latch Lit v. General Motors Corp., 2001 WL 103434 (N.D. Ill. 2002) (no recovery in tort for defective door latches that have yet to cause injury). Accord. Ziegelmann v. Dailmer Chrysler Corp., 649 N.W.2d 556 (N.D. 2002).

Burgler alarm and fire alarm cases have caused courts to confront the economic loss question in nontraditional settings. In Lobianco v. Property Protection, Inc., 437 A.2d 417 (Pa. 1981), plaintiff sued for the value of jewelry stolen from her home when a burglar alarm system installed by the defendant failed to work. Although the alarm system malfunctioned within the 90-day warranty period, the court refused recovery under the contract because it specifically limited damages to repairs and excluded recovery for loss or damages to possessions, persons, or property. Plaintiff then sought to avoid the contract by couching her cause of action in strict tort liability. The trial court dismissed this claim as well on the ground that the alarm system was "not dangerous and did not cause any physical harm to [plaintiff] or her property." The appellate court spurned the trial court's rationale:

> Suppose that the burglar, or burglars, who took appellant's jewelry had broken the mirror on her dressing table. If we were to accept the lower court's reasoning, and construe

"physical harm" as requiring appellant to prove damage to her property, we should conclude that the mirror had suffered physical harm but the jewelry had not. This conclusion would be artificial; it would make the outcome of the case depend on happenstance, with no reference to the reason Section 402A was adopted. [Id. at 422.]

Nonetheless, the court dismissed the strict tort liability claim, finding that the purposes supporting strict liability would not be served by applying §402A to this case:

. . . Homeowners are not "otherwise defenseless victims" of burglar alarm manufacturers in the same sense that a buyer of an automobile, for example, may be the victim of the automobile manufacturer. If the property is valuable, the homeowner may insure it. To apply Section 402A to the present case would in practical effect excuse the homeowner from having to insure the property and would shift the risk of its loss to the burglar alarm manufacturer. This would represent a less, not more, equitable allocation of the risk. The homeowner, not the manufacturer, knows what property is in the home, and its value; the manufacturer does not. Even if the manufacturer were to find out what property was in the home before installing the burglar alarm system, the homeowner could, and probably would, add other property, without notice to the manufacturer. As between the homeowner and the manufacturer, the manufacturer is more "defenseless" than the homeowner. If the homeowner buys a silver service or a stereo system, at least he can get insurance against its loss; but the manufacturer cannot, for it will not know that the service or stereo has been put in the home. Thus it may not be said that "'the risk of injury can be insured by the manufacturer and distributed among the public as a cost of doing business.'" [Id. at 424-425, quoting Ray v. Alad Corp., 560 P.2d 3 (Cal. 1977), quoting from *Escola*, supra p.12.]

A plaintiff who suffered substantial losses when his jewelry store was burglarized sued the alarm manufacturer for the failure of its system to function properly at the central station where it was supposed to signal security personnel. Even though the burglars caused physical damage to the premises (in addition to stealing the jewels), the court characterized the case as one for economic loss and thus dismissed claims for both negligence and strict liability due to the defective alarm equipment. Arell's Fine Jewelers, Inc. v. Honeywell, Inc., 566 N.Y.S.2d 505 (App. Div. 4th Dept. 1991).

In Butler v. Pittway Corp., 770 F.2d 7 (2d Cir. 1985) a homeowner sought to recover for damage caused when two smoke alarms failed to go off in time to warn the owner of a fire. Plaintiff sued for the damage that would have been avoided had the alarms sounded. The district court held that the damage was economic loss that could not be recovered under strict tort liability. The Second Circuit reversed. The Court of Appeals found that a smoke alarm that did not go off at the proper time was an unreasonably dangerous product and that the damage suffered constituted "property damage" within the meaning of §402A. Similarly, in Laaperi v. Sears, Roebuck & Co., Inc., 787 F.2d 726 (1st Cir. 1986), the First Circuit affirmed a judgment in excess of $1 million against the seller of a smoke detector for failing to warn the buyer that in the event that a fire resulted from a short circuit, the alarm, which was powered by electrical current, might not function. Three youngsters were killed and one was injured when the alarm failed to sound. It was plaintiff's contention that, had he been warned about this danger, he would have purchased a battery-powered smoke detector as a back-up or taken some other precaution, such as wiring the detector to a circuit of its own, in order to better protect his family in the event of an electrical fire. Can all these cases be reconciled? Should they be? See generally Swartz, Swartz & Cantor, Smoke-Detector Litigation, 22 Trial 30 (November 1986).

For helpful treatments of the economic loss issue see Robert L. Rabin, Tort Recovery for Negligently Inflicted Economic Loss: A Reassessment, 37 Stan. L. Rev. 1513 (1985); Gary T. Schwartz, Economic Loss in American Tort Law: The Examples of J'Aire and of Products Liability, 23 San Diego L. Rev. 37 (1986); Note, The Recovery of Economic Loss Damages in Tort: Pennsylvania Law and "Social Adjustment," 31 U. Pitt. L. Rev. 213 (1989); Harvey S. Perlman, Interference With Contract and Other Economic Expectations: A Clash of Tort and Contract Doctrine, 49 U. Chi. L. Rev. 61 (1982); William K. Jones, Product Defect Causing Commercial Loss: The Ascendency of Contract Over Tort, 44 U. Miami L. Rev. 731 (1990).

PROBLEM TWENTY-SIX

The owners of The King's Table, a popular restaurant maintaining a thriving business in Ithaca, New California, suddenly discovered the presence of polychlorinated biphenyl, or PCB (a toxic chemical which is a known carcinogen), in the basement of their building. The PCB originated in lubricating oil that had clogged gas meters. In order to alleviate the problem, the Consolidated Electric Company (ConEl), who had sold the gas to the restaurant and was responsible for maintaining the gas meters, sent an environmental clean-up team to The King's Table. The members of the clean-up team were dressed in protective clothing and gas masks, and looked like spacemen from Mars. The local newspapers photographed the scene and local television stations covered the event. Marie Witkins, a longtime tenant who lived on the second floor above the restaurant, had contracted cancer shortly before the time of the incident. After learning of the PCB in the basement, Witkins sued ConEl for causing her disease. Apparently as a result of the adverse publicity surrounding the entire episode, business at The King's Table has fallen off sharply. Customers have been scared away from the premises by the PCB risk and the attendant fear of cancer. Although the restaurant will survive the episode, the losses in revenues and goodwill are substantial.

The standard contract between ConEl and its customers, in effect in this case, limits liability to direct losses and disclaims liability for consequential losses. King's Table, Inc., which owns and operates the restaurant, is a closely held family corporation. Lloyd Rangsten, president and majority stockholder, has contacted a senior partner of the law firm in which you are an associate about bringing an action against ConEl. The partner called you in this morning and told you that she has strong reservations about whether the complaint can withstand attack. She is desirous of bringing an action if there is even a respectable chance that the case can go forward. Lloyd Rangsten is a long-time friend whom the partner wants to help. She says "Look, even if there is only a 5 percent chance of success I want to pursue it. ConEl may be afraid of another tort action and may be willing to settle to avoid the negative publicity. Lloyd is in bad financial shape and even a $20,000-$30,000 settlement would be meaningful. Find me a hook."

Considering the preceding cases and materials, determine whether there is a plausible cause of action on behalf of Lloyd Rangsten and the other King's Table stockholders against ConEl, and what course of action you would recommend in any event.

C. Wolfram, Modern Legal Ethics*
594-596 (1986)

The "warm zeal" with which a lawyer is to urge a client's interests is part of the very model of an advocate. But professional rules and substantive law impress limits on a lawyer's zeal. To what extent must a lawyer decline to take steps in litigation for a client that are not warranted by the facts or existing law? May a lawyer, for example, file an action against a defendant solely to gain the advantage of the nuisance value of a settlement for some portion of the defendant's anticipated defense costs? Reciprocally, may a lawyer assert a defense if it is legally insupportable but when the plaintiff's travels on the road to ultimate success will require an extended period of time during which the defendant will have the interest-free use of the money sought? Those and similar questions ask whether, and to what extent, a lawyer should serve as a filter of clients' desires to take aggressive moves in litigation.

The lawyer codes have consistently reflected the position that not every client wish to litigate should be furthered by a lawyer. Following 1908 Canon 30, the 1969 code, in DR 7-102(A)(1), provides that a lawyer shall not take action in behalf of a client "when he knows or it is obvious that such action would serve merely to harass or maliciously injure another." Further, under DR 7-102(A)(1) a lawyer is not to assert a claim or defense "unwarranted under existing law" unless it is supported by a good-faith argument for the alternation of existing law. In 1983 Model Rule 3.1 these separate statements are collapsed into a single standard that limits a lawyer to actions or other steps in litigation that are "not frivolous," a standard that explicitly includes actions based on a good-faith argument to alter existing law. Probably in recognition of the attention currently being given to limiting discovery abuses, a separate provision, MR 3.4(d), specifically provides that a lawyer should not make "frivolous" discovery requests or fail to make "reasonably diligent" efforts to comply with proper discovery requests by another party.

Those professional standards can very likely do little to restrain advocates from taking steps that, based on other calculations, seem in the best interests of clients. Judicial statements can be found requiring lawyers to question clients closely about doubtful claims, to refuse to assist clients in groundless litigation, and to withdraw if not satisfied that a client's position has merit. But discipline is rarely imposed for violations of the anti-harassment rules and then mainly for moves in litigation that sometimes seem more psychopathic than nasty, that in-

---

*Reprinted from C. Wolfram, Modern Legal Ethics (1986) with permission of the West Publishing Company.

volve patently fraudulent schemes, or that arise in limited areas in which courts express a special concern for lawyer forthrightness.

The approach of the common law, essentially, was to leave a party oppressed by bad-faith litigation to the costly solace of victory and, possibly, to limited tort remedies such as that for malicious abuse of civil process. Asserted fears of chilling litigant access to the courts have thus far prevented much effective relief from such tort-based concepts. Courts also possess a traditional power to enjoin litigation but only in the rare case of extremely vexing and repeated frivolous suits.

The professional standards and the common-law reticence about harassment in litigation have been largely overtaken by recent developments in other arenas, particularly involving fee-shifting for bad-faith litigation. It has become apparent, as complaints about abusive litigation have been heard recently on all sides, that the state of affairs permitted by existing professional and tort regulation is not tolerable. One response has been the judicial development and extension of the doctrine empowering courts to require a party, or the party's lawyer, to pay the legal fees of an adversary oppressed by bad-faith litigation. Another has been the assertion by courts of the power to screen papers and positions of litigants and, on the motion of an aggrieved party or at the court's own behest, to impose sanctions, including fee awards, against a party who engages in harassing or otherwise inappropriate litigation. The sanctions available in those and similar contexts include, in addition, damages, cost sanctions, dismissal or default, and similar preclusion orders against the client.

Note that, as Professor Wolfram observes, not only plaintiffs' lawyers but also defendants' lawyers can be liable for overzealous litigation. A lawyer can also act unreasonably in refusing to pursue a case. Professor Underwood reviews cases in which attorneys were found liable for malpractice for failing to do adequate research before advising that a claim was not likely to be successful and for failing to advise potential clients of an approaching expiration of the statute of limitations. See generally Underwood, Taking and Pursuing a Case: Some Observations Regarding "Legal Ethics" and Attorney Accountability, 74 Ky. L.J. 173 (1985-1986).

D. SPECIAL PROBLEMS IN TOXIC TORTS LITIGATION

1. Increased Risk of Future Injury

The advent of toxic torts litigation presented significant complications for plaintiffs in seeking adequate redress for their injuries. Unlike the standard tort case in which a plaintiff suffers an immediately cognizable injury, exposure to toxic substances often introduces latent risks that may or may not manifest themselves later into potentially fatal or debilitating diseases. The litigation against the manufacturers of asbestos is paradigmatic. Though exposure to asbestos fibers unquestionably enhances a plaintiff's chance of contracting cancer or mesothelioma, the overall possibility of contracting such diseases is remote. Even where a plaintiff suffers from asbestosis, a condition that impairs respiratory functions, the possibility of developing cancer or mesothelioma is relatively small.

In the past, plaintiffs seeking recovery for asbestos-related injuries were placed in a pincers. On the one hand, plaintiffs were pressed by the firmly embedded "single action rule" of torts. This rule, in order to avoid repetitive litigation, required plaintiffs to consolidate all of their claims for damages against a certain defendant in a single action. Claims for injuries that were not addressed in the litigation were subsequently barred. Plaintiffs who came down with pleural thickening or asbestosis were therefore required to seek recovery for all future harms that might arise. But when they attempted to do so they were faced with the argument that they could not establish that such future harms were probable to eventuate. On the other hand, if they waited until they developed cancer or mesothelioma, they were told that the statute of limitations had began to run at the onset of pleural thickening or asbestosis. Plaintiffs were thus caught between the Scylla of bringing a timely, yet not fully ripe claim for damages and the Charybdis of bringing a fully matured, yet possibly time-barred action.

Not surprisingly, plaintiffs sought some creative avenues to seek adequate compensation. One such approach was to seek redress for the increased risk of harm a plaintiff faced as a result of exposure to a defendant's toxic substances even though the plaintiff did not currently suffer from a disease or illness. Though courts struggled for a way to allow plaintiffs to recover in full, they were unnerved by the prospect of chipping away at the core principle of tort law that a plaintiff suffer a cognizable injury as a precondition to bringing suit. Consider how the New Jersey Supreme Court handled the challenge in the following case.

Mauro v. Raymark Industries, Inc.
116 N.J. 126, 561 A.2d 257 (1989)

STEIN, J.

I

Plaintiffs, Roger Mauro (hereinafter plaintiff) and Lois Mauro, his wife, instituted this action against several manufacturers of asbestos products based on injuries allegedly sustained as a result of inhalation of asbestos fibers in the course of Mauro's employment at Ancora State Psychiatric Hospital. Mauro testified that he was employed as a repairman and later as a plumber-steam fitter. From 1964 until the mid-to-late 1970s he used or was exposed to materials containing asbestos manufactured by defendants, including pipe covering and asbestos cement. The exposure occurred when he was ripping out old insulation material and installing new insulation. He testified that defendants' products contained no warnings.

In 1981 plaintiff and his co-workers participated in tests conducted by the New Jersey Department of Health to determine the prevalence of asbestos-related disease among plumbers and steam fitters in state institutions. Plaintiff was informed by Dr. Peter Gann, the department's Chief of Occupational Medicine, that although the results of his physical examination and lung function test were "normal," he had bilateral thickening of both chest walls and calcification of the diaphragm. Dr. Gann's letter informing plaintiff of his condition stated: "[Y]our exposure to asbestos has been significant and there is some evidence that this exposure may increase the risk of development of lung cancer." . . .

In its charge to the jury at the conclusion of the trial, the trial court rejected Mauro's claim for enhanced risk of developing cancer. . . .

However, the court permitted the jury to consider Mauro's claim for damages caused by emotional distress relating to his fear of developing cancer, provided the jury found that Mauro sustained an asbestos-related injury. The court also permitted the jury to consider Mauro's claim for damages caused by his present medical condition, as well as the cost of future medical surveillance. . . .

The Appellate Division affirmed. . . .

II

It is important to recognize at the outset that the rule of law advocated by plaintiffs, i.e., that tort victims should have a present cause of action for a significant but unquantified enhanced risk of future injury, represents a significant departure from traditional, prevailing legal principles. . . .

The long-standing rule in New Jersey is that prospective damages are not recoverable unless they are reasonably probable to occur. The rationale for adopting this standard was explained by Justice Francis, then sitting in the Appellate Division, in Budden v. Goldstein, 43 N.J. Super. 340, 346-47, 128 A.2d 730 (1957):

> In the admeasurement of damages, it is well known that no recovery can be allowed for possible future consequences of an injury inflicted by a wrongdoer. In order for suggested future results to be includible as an element of damage, it must appear that they are reasonably certain or reasonably probable to follow. . . . [M]any of the authorities throughout the country use the expression "reasonably certain" or "reasonable certainty" as the test and consider "reasonably probable" or "reasonable probability" inadequate and erroneous; others accept the latter statement. Our cases do not seem to have dealt specifically with the question of whether the two have the same significance in relation to quantum of proof, and so may be used interchangeably. It seems to us that in a resolution of the conflicting interests involved, reasonable probability is the just yardstick to be applied. Basically, our view comes down to this: a consequence of an injury which is possible, which may possibly ensue, is a risk which the injured person must bear because the law cannot be administered so as to do reasonably efficient justice if conjecture and speculation are to be used as a measure of damages. On the other hand, a consequence which stands on the plane of reasonable probability, although it is not certain to occur, may be considered in the evaluation of the damage claim against the defendant. In this way, to the extent that men can achieve justice through general rules, a just balance of the warring interests is accomplished.

Although most of the courts that have addressed claims for enhanced-risk damages in toxic-tort cases have applied the general rule requiring proof that the threatened injury be probable, commentators on the subject have generally encouraged recognition of an enhanced-risk cause of action in such cases even if the threat of contingent harm is less than probable, or is unquantified.

[D]efendants asserted at oral argument that plaintiff's claim premised on enhanced risk of disease had been fully adjudicated by submission to the jury of the claims for medical surveillance and emotional distress, contending that there were no other components of the enhanced-risk cause of action. Defendants' argument misconceives the essential nature of a claim predicated on enhanced risk of disease. Simply stated, it is a claim for damages based on a prospective injury, conceptually analogous to the claim of a personal-injury plaintiff with a damaged knee to recover damages for the prospective onset of an arthritic condition that may result from the knee injury. Under our case law, the personal-injury plaintiff conceivably could claim medical-surveillance damages and emotional-distress damages on the basis that the knee injury might cause arthritis, but could not recover damages for the prospective arthritic condition—the "enhanced risk" of arthritis—unless its occurrence was established as a matter of reasonable medical probability. Thus, the fact that Mauro's claims for medical surveillance and emotional distress, attributable to his enhanced risk of cancer, were submitted to the jury does not exhaust his claim for damages based on the prospective occurrence of cancer—the "enhanced risk" of cancer. The question before us is whether that component of the claim should have been submitted to the jury in the absence of evidence establishing the future occurrence of cancer as a reasonable medical probability. We hold that the prospective-cancer component of plaintiff's enhanced-risk claim was properly withheld from the jury.

We first observe that the decided cases throughout the country that have considered the question, both in the context of asbestos litigation and claims based on exposure to other toxic chemicals, are almost uniform in their conclusion that in order to recover damages, plaintiff must prove that the prospective disease is at least reasonably probable to occur.

Although the weight of authority compellingly argues against recognition of an enhanced-risk-of-cancer claim by a plaintiff with an asbestos-related injury absent proof that satisfies the standard of reasonable medical probability, our analysis would be incomplete without consideration of policy arguments that oppose the general rule. Foremost among these is the concern that deferral of the prospective-injury claim may preclude any recovery when the disease eventually occurs because of the substantial difficulties inherent in attempting to prove causation in toxic-tort cases. If the enhanced-risk claim is deferred, a plaintiff asserting the claim when the second injury occurs will inevitably confront the defense that the injury did not result from exposure to toxic chemicals but was "the product of intervening events or causes."

Recognition of a claim for significantly enhanced risk of disease would also enhance the tort-law's capacity to deter the improper use of toxic chemicals and substances, thereby addressing the contention that tort law cannot deter polluters who view the cost of proper use or disposal as exceeding the risk of tort liability.

The rule of reasonable medical probability is also challenged as an artificial, all-or-nothing standard that rejects future-injury claims supported by substantial evidence that barely falls short of the required quantum of proof. . . . Can I really put the terms "reasonable probability" and "greatly increased probability" on a scale and expect to see a decided tip in one direction or the other? The scientific reports indicate a 40 to 45 percent chance of contracting cancer among asbestos workers. It will be for the jury to determine whether the future onset of cancer is probable based on the proofs presented by the plaintiffs and subject to cross-examination by the defendants. . . . The court in [an earlier case] appeared to adopt the reasonable-probability standard, but permitted the jury to determine whether the proofs were sufficient to meet it.

Other considerations weigh in favor of limiting recognition of enhanced-risk claims to those that prove to a reasonable medical probability the likelihood of future injury. Those claims that fail to meet this standard, if presented to juries, would require damage awards for diseases that are prospective, speculative, and less than likely to occur. The more speculative the proof of future disease, the more difficult would be the juries' burden of calculating fair compensation. Inevitably, damage awards would be rendered for diseases that will never occur, exacting a societal cost in the form of higher insurance premiums and higher product costs.

The vast number of asbestos-related claims now pending in state and federal courts throughout the country is a matter of public record. The formidable burden of litigating such claims would be significantly greater if a substantial percentage of these cases also involved disposition of damage claims for the relatively unquantified enhanced risk of future disease.

Equally persuasive to this Court, however, is the availability of a future opportunity to assert such claims if and when the disease occurs, combined with the present availability of medical surveillance and emotional distress damages in appropriate cases. In our view, removal of the statute-of-limitations and single-controversy doctrines as a bar to the institution of suit when the disease for which plaintiff is at risk ultimately occurs enhances the quality of the remedy that tort law can provide in such cases. If the disease never occurs, presumably there will be no claim and no recovery. If it does occur, the resultant litigation will involve a tangible claim for present injury, rather than a speculative claim for future injury. Hence, juries will be better able to award damages in an amount that fairly reflects the nature and severity of the plaintiff's injury. . . .

By adapting the statute-of-limitations and the single-controversy doctrines to the realities of toxic-tort cases, we have ameliorated the potential unfairness of applying the reasonable-probability standard to this type of litigation. Moreover, our case law affords toxic-tort plaintiffs the right to receive full compensation for any provable diminution of bodily health, accommodating all damage claims attributable to present injury and deferring compensation only for disease not yet incurred and not reasonably probable to occur. Recognition of present claims for medical surveillance and emotional distress realistically addresses significant aspects of the present injuries sustained by toxic-tort plaintiffs, and serves as an added deterrent to polluters and others responsible for the wrongful use of toxic chemicals. In our view, these developments in New Jersey law affecting toxic-tort plaintiffs argue persuasively against modification of the reasonable-probability standard in such cases. We therefore will not disturb the trial court's refusal to submit to the jury plaintiff's damage claim based on his enhanced risk of cancer.

Judgment affirmed.

Mauro is representative of a long line of cases that have accommodated toxic tort plaintiffs by eliminating the single-controversy doctrine. In the overwhelming majority of jurisdictions, plaintiffs need no longer fear that a subsequent action for the development of a more serious disease will be barred by a previous suit. So long as each are distinct injuries, a plaintiff will be allowed to seek recovery as illnesses manifest themselves. See, e.g., Sopha v. Owens-Corning Fiberglas Corp., 601 N.W.2d 627, 642 (Wis. 1999) ("The diagnosis of a malignant asbestos-related condition creates a new cause of action" distinct from the initial development of a non-malignant asbestos-related condition); Carroll v. Owens-Corning Fiberglass Corp., 37 S.W.3d 609 (Ky. 2000) (holding that cancer and asbestosis are separate diseases that trigger the running of statutes of limitations relative to their discovery). See generally James A. Henderson, Jr. & Aaron D. Twerski, Asbestos Litigation Gone Mad: Exposure-Based Recovery for Increased Risk, Mental Distress, and Medical Monitoring, 53 S.C. L. Rev. 815, 821 n.22 (2002) (listing authority).

The *Mauro* decision, however, is more controversial in allowing recovery for emotional distress and medical monitoring costs. As will be seen in the ensuing sections, these issues are the subject of contentious debate among courts and academics regarding their proper place in toxic torts litigation. These arguments often go to the heart of traditional no-duty analyses and implicate broader policy questions over the proper regulatory function of courts in an increasingly environmental-conscious society.

2. Recovery for Emotional Upset

A new and revitalized strain of emotional distress claims arose from the flood of toxic torts cases that swamped judicial dockets. Plaintiffs, unable to demonstrate any physical injury arising from their exposure to hazardous substances and barred from recovering for increased risks, sought to develop a cause of action that would allow them to recover without having to wait until they developed cancer or mesothelioma. Most courts have not taken kindly to their entreaties.

Metro-North Commuter R.R. Co. v. Buckley
521 U.S. 424 (1997)

Justice BREYER, delivered the opinion of the Court.

The basic question in this case is whether a railroad worker negligently exposed to a carcinogen (here, asbestos) but without symptoms of any disease can recover under the Federal Employers' Liability Act (FELA or Act), . . . for negligently inflicted emotional distress. We conclude that the worker before us here cannot recover unless, and until, he manifests symptoms of a disease. . . .

I

Respondent, Michael Buckley, works as a pipefitter for Metro-North, a railroad. For three years (1985-1988) his job exposed him to asbestos for about one hour per working day. During that time Buckley would remove insulation from pipes, often covering himself with insulation dust that contained asbestos. Since 1987, when he attended an "asbestos awareness" class, Buckley has feared that he would develop cancer — and with some cause, for his two expert witnesses testified that, even after taking account of his now-discarded 15-year habit of smoking up to a pack of cigarettes per day, the exposure created an *added* risk of death due to cancer, or to other asbestos-related diseases of either 1% to 5% (in the view of one of plaintiff's experts), or 1% to 3% (in the view of another). Since 1989, Buckley has received periodic medical check-ups for cancer and asbestosis. So far, those check-ups have not revealed any evidence of cancer or any other asbestos-related disease.

Buckley sued Metro-North under the FELA, a statute that permits a railroad worker to recover for an "injury . . . resulting . . . from" his employer's "negligence." 45 U.S.C. §51. He sought damages for his emotional distress and to cover the cost of future medical check-ups. His employer conceded negligence, but it did not concede that Buckley had actually suffered emotional distress, and it argued that the FELA did not permit a worker like Buckley, who had suffered no physical harm, to recover for injuries of either sort. After hearing Buckley's case, the District Court dismissed the action. The court found that Buckley did not "offer sufficient evidence to allow a jury to find that he suffered a real emotional injury." . . . And, in any event, Buckley suffered no "physical impact;" hence any emotional injury fell outside the limited set of circumstances in which, according to this Court, the FELA permits recovery. Id., at 620; see Consolidated Rail Corporation v. Gottshall, 512 U.S. 532. . . .

Buckley appealed, and the Second Circuit reversed. 79 F.3d 1337 (1996). Buckley's evidence, it said, showed that his contact with the insulation dust (containing asbestos) was "massive, lengthy, and tangible," id., at 1345, and that the contact "would cause fear in a reasonable person," id., at 1344. Under these circumstances, the court held, the contact was what this Court in *Gottshall* had called a "physical impact"—a "physical impact" that, when present, permits a FELA plaintiff to recover for accompanying emotional distress. The Second Circuit also found in certain of Buckley's workplace statements sufficient expression of worry to permit sending his emotional distress claim to a jury. . . .

II

The critical question before us in respect to Buckley's "emotional distress" claim is whether the physical contact with insulation dust that accompanied his emotional distress amounts to a "physical impact" as this Court used that term in *Gottshall.* In *Gottshall,* an emotional distress case, the Court interpreted the word "injury" in FELA §1, a provision that makes "[e]very common carrier by railroad . . . liable in damages to any person suffering injury while . . . employed" by the carrier if the "injury" results from carrier "negligence." . . .

The Court stated that "common-law principles," where not rejected in the text of the statute, "are entitled to great weight" in interpreting the Act, and that those principles "play a significant role" in determining whether, or when, an employee can recover damages for "negligent infliction of emotional distress." . . .

[I]t recognized that the common law of torts does not permit recovery for negligently inflicted emotional distress *unless* the distress falls within certain specific categories that amount to recovery-permitting exceptions. The law, for example, does permit recovery for emotional distress where that distress accompanies a physical injury. . . . The Court then held that FELA §1, mirroring the law of many States, sometimes permitted recovery "for damages for negligent infliction of emotional distress," . . . and, in particular, it does so where a plaintiff seeking such damages satisfies the common law's "zone of danger" test. It defined that test by stating that the law permits "recovery for emotional injury" by

> "those plaintiffs who *sustain a physical impact* as a result of a defendant's negligent conduct, or who are placed in immediate risk of physical harm by that conduct." Id., at 547-548 . . . (emphasis added).

The case before us, as we have said, focuses on the italicized words "physical impact." The Second Circuit interpreted those words as including a simple physical contact with a substance that might cause a disease at a future time, so long as the contact was of a kind that would "cause fear in a reasonable person." . . . In our view, however, the "physical impact" to which *Gottshall* referred does not include a simple physical contact with a substance that might cause a disease at a substantially later time — where that substance, or related circumstance, threatens no harm other than that disease-related risk.

First, *Gottshall* cited many state cases in support of its adoption of the "zone of danger" test quoted above. And in each case where recovery for emotional distress was permitted, the case involved a threatened physical contact that caused, or might have caused, immediate traumatic harm. [Citing authority.]

Second, *Gottshall*'s language, read in light of this precedent, seems similarly limited. 512 U.S. at 555 . . . ("zone of danger test . . . is consistent with FELA's central focus on physical perils"). . . .

Taken together, language and cited precedent indicate that the words "physical impact" do not encompass every form of "physical contact." And, in particular, they do not include a contact that amounts to no more than an exposure — an exposure, such as that before us, to a substance that poses some future risk of disease and which contact causes emotional distress only because the worker learns that he may become ill after a substantial period of time.

Third, common-law precedent does not favor the plaintiff. Common law courts do permit a plaintiff who suffers from a disease to recover for related negligently caused emotional distress, . . . and some courts permit a plaintiff who exhibits a physical symptom of exposure to recover. . . . But with only a few exceptions, common law courts have denied recovery to those who, like Buckley, are disease and symptom free. [Citing authority.]

Fourth, the general policy reasons to which *Gottshall* referred — in its explanation of why common law courts have restricted recovery for emotional harm to cases falling within rather narrowly defined categories — militate against an expansive definition of "physical impact" here. Those reasons include: (a) special "difficulty for judges and juries" in separating valid, important claims from those that are invalid or "trivial," *Gottshall,* 512 U.S. at 557 . . . (b) a threat of "unlimited and unpredictable liability," ibid.; and (c) the "potential for a flood" of comparatively unimportant, or "trivial," claims, ibid.

To separate meritorious and important claims from invalid or trivial claims does not seem easier here than in other cases in which a plaintiff might seek recovery for typical negligently caused emotional distress. The facts before us illustrate the problem. The District Court, when concluding that Buckley had failed to present "sufficient evidence to allow a jury to find . . . a real emotional injury," pointed out that, apart from Buckley's own testimony, there was virtually no evidence of distress. . . . Indeed, Buckley continued to work with insulating material "even though . . . he could have transferred" elsewhere, he "continued to smoke cigarettes" despite doctors' warnings, and his doctor did not refer him "either to a psychologist or to a social worker." . . . The Court of Appeals reversed because it found certain objective corroborating evidence, namely "workers' complaints to supervisors and investigative bodies." 79 F.3d at 1346. Both kinds of "objective" evidence — the confirming and disconfirming evidence — seem only indirectly related to the question at issue, the existence and seriousness of Buckley's claimed emotional distress. Yet, given the difficulty of separating valid from invalid emotional injury claims, the evidence before us may typify the kind of evidence to which parties and the courts would have to look.

The Court in *Gottshall* made a similar point:

> "Testing for the 'genuineness' of an injury alone . . . would be bound to lead to haphazard results. Judges would be forced to make highly subjective determinations concerning the authenticity of claims for emotional injury, which are far less susceptible to objective medical proof than are their physical counterparts. To the extent the genuineness test could limit potential liability, it could do so only inconsistently." 512 U.S. at 552. . . .

More important, the physical contact at issue here — a simple (though extensive) contact with a carcinogenic substance — does not seem to offer much help in separating valid from invalid emotional distress claims. That is because contacts, even extensive contacts, with serious carcinogens are common. See e.g., Nicholson, Perkel & Selikoff, Occupational Exposure to Asbestos: Population at Risk and Projected Mortality — 1980-2030, 3 Am. J. Indust. Med. 259 (1982) (estimating that 21 million Americans have been exposed to work-related asbestos); U.S. Dept. of Health and Human Services, 1 Seventh Annual Report on Carcinogens 71 (1994) (3 million workers exposed to benzene, a majority of Americans exposed outside the workplace); Pirkle, et al., Exposure of the U.S. Population to Environmental Tobacco Smoke, 275 JAMA 1233, 1237 (1996) (reporting that 43% of American children lived in a home with at least one smoker, and 37% of adult nonsmokers lived in a home with at least one smoker or reported environmental tobacco smoke at work). They may occur without causing serious emotional distress, but sometimes they do cause distress, and reasonably so, for cancer is both an unusually threatening and unusually frightening disease. See Statistical Abstract of United States 94 (1996) (23.5 percent of Americans who died in 1994 died of cancer); American Cancer Society, Cancer Facts & Figures — 1997, p.1 (half of all men and one third of all women will develop cancer). The relevant problem, however, remains one of evaluating a claimed emotional reaction to an *increased* risk of dying. An external circumstance — exposure — makes some emotional distress more likely. But how can one determine from the external circumstance of exposure whether, or when, a claimed strong emotional reaction to an *increased* mortality risk (say from 23% to 28%) is reasonable and genuine, rather than overstated — particularly when the relevant statistics themselves are controversial and uncertain (as is usually the case), and particularly since neither those exposed nor judges or juries are experts in statistics? The evaluation problem seems a serious one.

The large number of those exposed and the uncertainties that may surround recovery also suggest what *Gottshall* called the problem of "unlimited and unpredictable liability." Does such liability mean, for example, that the costs associated with a rule of liability would become so great that, given the nature of the harm, it would seem unreasonable to require the public to pay the higher prices that may result? Cf. Priest, The Current Insurance Crisis and Modern Tort Law, 96 Yale L.J. 1521, 1585-1587 (1987). The same characteristics further suggest what *Gottshall* called the problem of a "flood" of cases that, if not "trivial," are comparatively less important. In a world of limited resources, would a rule permitting immediate large-scale recoveries for widespread emotional distress caused by fear of future disease diminish the likelihood of recovery by those who later suffer from the disease? Cf. J. Weinstein, Individual Justice in Mass Tort Litigation 10-11, 141 (1995); Schuck, The Worst Should Go First: Deferral Registries in Asbestos Litigation, 15 Harv. J. L. & Pub. Pol'y 541 (1992).

We do not raise these questions to answer them (for we do not have the answers), but rather to show that general policy concerns of a kind that have led common law courts to deny recovery for certain classes of negligently caused harms are present in this case as well. That being so, we cannot find in *Gottshall*'s underlying rationale any basis for departing from *Gottshall*'s language and precedent or from the current common-law consensus. That is to say, we cannot find in *Gottshall*'s language, cited precedent, other common law-precedent, or related concerns of policy, a legal basis for adopting the emotional-distress recovery rule adopted by the Court of Appeals.

Buckley raises several important arguments in reply. He points out, for example, that common law courts do permit recovery for emotional distress where a plaintiff has physical symptoms; and he argues that his evidence of exposure and enhanced mortality risk is as strong a proof as an accompanying physical symptom that his emotional distress is genuine.

This argument, however, while important, overlooks the fact that the common law in this area does not examine the genuineness of emotional harm case by case. Rather, it has developed recovery-permitting categories the contours of which more distantly reflect this, and other, abstract general policy concerns. The point of such categorization is to deny courts the authority to undertake a case by case examination. The common law permits emotional-distress recovery for that category of plaintiffs who suffer from a disease (or exhibit a physical symptom), for example, thereby finding a special effort to evaluate emotional symptoms warranted in that category of cases—perhaps from a desire to make a physically injured victim whole or because the parties are likely to be in court in any event. In other cases, however, falling outside the special recovery-permitting categories, it has reached a different conclusion. The relevant question here concerns the validity of a rule that seeks to redefine such a category. It would not be easy to redefine "physical impact" in terms of a rule that turned on, say, the "massive, lengthy, [or] tangible" nature of a contact that amounted to an exposure, whether to contaminated water, or to germ-laden air, or to carcinogen-containing substances, such as insulation dust containing asbestos. But, in any event, for the reasons we have stated . . . we cannot find that the common law has done so. . . .

Finally, Buckley argues that the "humanitarian" nature of the FELA warrants a holding in his favor. We do not doubt that, the FELA's purpose militates in favor of recovery for a serious and negligently caused emotional harm. Cf. *Gottshall,* 512 U.S. at 550, 114 S. Ct., at 2407-2408. But just as courts must interpret that law to take proper account of the harms suffered by a sympathetic individual plaintiff, so they must consider the general impact, on workers as well as employers, of the general liability rules they would thereby create. Here the relevant question concerns not simply recovery in an individual case, but the consequences and effects of *a rule of law that would permit that recovery*. And if the common law concludes that a legal rule permitting recovery here, from a tort law perspective, and despite benefits in *some* individual cases, would on balance cause more harm than good, and if we find that judgment reasonable, we cannot find that conclusion inconsistent with the FELA's humanitarian purpose.

[The Court went on in Part III to consider and ultimately reject Buckley's contention that a lump sum recovery for medical monitoring costs was sustainable even absent exhibitions of symptoms or disease.]

IV

For the reasons stated, we reverse the determination of the Second Circuit, and we remand the case for further proceedings consistent with this opinion.

It is so ordered.

[Justice GINSBURG's concurrence in the judgment in part and dissent in part is omitted.]

Though *Metro-North* held that mere exposure to asbestos was not an "injury" within the meaning of the FELA, the Court did not address what type of physical impact *could* substantiate an award for emotional upset. At least a partial answer to the question was provided by the Court in Norfolk & Western Railway Co. v. Ayers, 123 S. Ct. 1210 (2003). The action was nearly identical to the one brought in *Metro-North*. Plaintiffs, exposed to asbestos fibers, brought an action under the FELA seeking compensation for their fear of developing cancer. However, unlike the plaintiff in *Metro-North* who had merely been exposed to asbestos, the plaintiffs in Ayers had actually contracted asbestosis. The majority relied heavily on this difference in sustaining plaintiffs' recovery for emotional upset, recalling that *Metro-North* "sharply distinguished exposure-only plaintiffs from 'plaintiffs who suffer from a disease,' and stated, unambiguously, that '[t]he common law permits emotional distress for [the latter] category.'"

The dissent, authored by Justice Kennedy, criticized the majority opinion for ignoring the realities of the asbestos litigation. Taking note of the FELA's purpose to provide adequate compensation for injured federal employees, the dissent argued that it would be inequitable to parcel out to the plaintiffs substantial monetary relief from a finite and dwindling pool of assets required to satisfy the claims of all potential claimants. Moreover, to allow recovery for the fear of contracting cancer based on the development of asbestosis would be to sanction damages based on little more than speculation:

> The majority . . . would permit recovery because "[t]here is an undisputed relationship between exposure to asbestos sufficient to cause asbestosis, and asbestos-related cancer."
> . . . To state that some relationship exists without examining whether the relationship is enough to support recovery, however, ignores the central issue in this case. There is a fundamental premise in this case — conceded, as I understand it, by all parties — and it is this: There is no demonstrated causal link between asbestosis and cancer. . . . The

incidence of asbestosis correlates with the less-frequent incidence of cancer among exposed workers, . . . but this does not suffice. Correlation is not causation. Absent causation, it is difficult to conceive why asbestosis is any more than marginally more suitable a predicate for recovering for fear of cancer than the fact of mere exposure. This correlation the Court relies upon does not establish a direct link between asbestosis and asbestosis-related cancer, and it does not suffice under common-law precedents as a predicate condition for recovery of damages based upon fear. [*Ayers,* 123 S. Ct. at 1231-1232.]

As *Ayers* demonstrates, courts are often called upon to perform some rather difficult line-drawing in determining what constitutes the principle "injury" to which parasitic mental distress claims may attach. In cases involving asbestos, some courts have extended the boundary beyond asbestosis to include other asbestos-induced physiological changes in the lungs. See, e.g., Herber v. Johns-Manville Corp., 785 F.2d 79 (3d Cir. 1986) (applying New Jersey law) (pleural thickening sufficient impact to warrant recovery for emotional distress damages); McCleary v. Armstrong World Indus., Inc., 913 F.2d 257 (5th Cir. 1990) (applying Texas law) (pleural fibrosis). A majority of courts maintain more stringent standards and will not allow recovery for asymptomatic pleural thickening. See, e.g., Simmons v. Pacor, 674 A.2d 232-237 (Pa. 1996) ("asymptomatic pleural thickening is not a compensable injury which gives rise to cause of action"). For an example of a court employing a similar analysis in relation to a mental distress claim for the fear of contracting AIDS, see Johnson v. Am. Nat'l Red Cross, 578 S.E.2d 106 (Ga. 2003) (holding that plaintiff must demonstrate actual exposure to an infectious agent in order to recover damages for emotional upset).

3. *Medical Monitoring*

We have seen that courts have generally been reluctant to grant plaintiffs recovery for latent harms that have not matured into cognizable physical injuries. A strong majority have thus rejected claims for increased risk of harm or for mental distress arising from fear of developing cancer when the plaintiff is asymptomatic. Plaintiffs have, however, succeeded in many jurisdictions in pressing their claim for the costs of medically monitoring their conditions after exposure to highly toxic substances. One of the first cases to recognize a cause of action for medical monitoring was In re Paoli Railroad Yard PCB Litigation, 916 F.2d 829 (3d Cir. 1990) (applying Pennsylvania law) (*Paoli I*). In that case, plaintiff railroad workers who were exposed to polychlorinated biphenyls (PCBs) brought an action against a litany of defendants involved either in the manufacture of PCBs or the operation of the railroad yard. Framing the issue as "not whether it is reasonably probable that plaintiffs will suffer harm in the future, but rather whether medical monitoring is, to a reasonable degree of medical certainty, necessary in order to diagnose properly the warning signs of disease," id. at 851, the court articulated several policy reasons for allowing plaintiffs to recover the costs of medical monitoring. Many courts have followed in *Paoli I*'s footsteps since then. See generally Thomas M. Goutman, Medical Monitoring: How Bad Science Makes Bad Law, 39-55 (2001) (listing states that recognize medical monitoring claims). The following case from the supreme court of West Virginia is representative of the majority view in its reasoning and conclusions.

Bower v. Westinghouse Elec. Corp.
522 S.E.2d 424 (W. Va. 1999)

McGRAW, J.

This case comes to the Court on certified question from the United States District Court for the Northern District of West Virginia, and asks us to resolve the question of whether this jurisdiction recognizes a common-law cause of action for recovery of anticipated medical monitoring costs in circumstances where the plaintiffs have been tortiously exposed to toxic substances, but do not presently exhibit symptoms of any resulting disease. We conclude that West Virginia law supports such a claim for relief.

I.
Background

Plaintiffs . . . allege that they were exposed to toxic substances as a result of defendants maintaining a cullet pile containing debris from the manufacture of light bulbs. The pile covers approximately two acres and is 42 feet deep at certain points. It is uncontested that tests performed in 1994 identified the presence of 30 potentially deleterious substances. None of the plaintiffs presently exhibit symptoms of any disease related to the alleged exposure.

Plaintiffs have asserted the following causes of action against defendants: (1) negligent maintenance and operation of the refuse pile; (2) nuisance; (3) trespass; (4) negligent infliction of emotional distress; and (5) intentional disregard for the health and safety of plaintiffs. As relief, the complaint seeks, inter alia, consequential damages in the form of medical monitoring costs.

Defendant North American Philips Corporation ("Philips") removed the case to the District Court pursuant to 28 U.S.C §1332 (1994 & Supp. 1996) (diversity of citizenship). Philips and its codefendant, CBS Corporation (formerly Westinghouse Electric Corporation) ("CBS"), subsequently moved to dismiss plaintiffs' claim for medical monitoring under Fed. R. Civ. P. 12(b)(6) or, in the alternative, Fed. R. Civ. P. 56. In support of their motion, defendants cited Ball v. Joy Mfg. Co., 755 F. Supp. 1344, 1370-72 (S.D. W. Va. 1990),[2] . . . and asserted

---

2. Federal courts interpreting West Virginia law have previously held that there is no basis for a claim of medical monitoring absent an accompanying physical injury. In *Ball*, the United States District Court for the Southern District of West Virginia ruled that the plaintiffs in that case could not pursue a medical monitoring claim because they had not otherwise proven an "actionable injury" under state law. The court framed its analysis by stating that "the law of West Virginia allows a plaintiff to recover the cost of reasonable and necessary future medical and hospital services where the evidence establishes that such future expenses are reasonably certain to be incurred as a result of an injury of the plaintiff which was proximately caused by the defendant's actions." . . .

In affirming *Ball*, the Fourth Circuit Court of Appeals went further and, in effect, construed our holding in *Jordan* to require proof of physical injury as a condition precedent to recovery of future medical expenses:

> A claim for medical surveillance costs is simply a claim for future damages. Plaintiff correctly points out that the law of West Virginia allows the recovery of the reasonable value of future medical expenses necessitated by the defendant's wrong. . . . However, such relief is only available where a plaintiff has sustained a physical injury that was proximately caused by the defendant. . . . Federal courts continue to apply *Ball* to reject medical monitoring claims arising under West Virginia law. . . .

As will be explained anon, the *Bell* decisions do not accurately reflect West Virginia law.

that "West Virginia law does not recognize an independent cause of action for medical monitoring." Plaintiffs responded by arguing that *Ball* no longer accurately reflects West Virginia law, an assertion they supported by citing to this Court's recent holding in Marlin v. Bill Rich Constr., Inc., . . . 482 S.E.2d 620 (W. Va. 1996), where we concluded that a plaintiff is not required to prove a present physical injury in the context of asserting a claim for negligent infliction of emotional distress. Alternatively, plaintiffs sought to certify to this Court the question of whether medical monitoring damages are a proper form of relief under West Virginia law. The District Court granted the latter motion, and we subsequently agreed to accept the certified question.

Reformulation of Certified Question

The District Court has requested that we define West Virginia law with respect to the following question:

> In a case of negligent infliction of emotional distress absent physical injury, may a party assert a claim for expenses related to future medical monitoring necessitated solely by fear of contracting a disease from exposure to toxic chemicals?

Taken literally, this question asks whether a plaintiff who suffers emotional distress without physical injury can obtain consequential damages in the form of future costs associated with diagnosing maladies precipitated "solely by the fear of contracting a disease." We do not think that the District Court intended to pose such a narrow question. Rather, as stated elsewhere in the certification order, the court is clearly asking the broader question of "whether West Virginia law permits an independent cause of action to recover future medical monitoring costs absent physical injury." . . .

The pleadings in this case indicate that plaintiffs are seeking, inter alia, compensation for the cost of future medical testing aimed at diagnosing potential ailments caused by the alleged toxic exposure. While plaintiffs have couched their argument in favor of recognizing such a claim in terms of recent refinements in our law governing causes of action for negligent infliction of emotional distress, it is clear that the question posed by the District Court is aimed at revisiting the issue that first arose in Ball v. Joy Manufacturing — namely, whether West Virginia law recognizes a cause of action for future medical monitoring absent a present physical injury. Consequently, based upon our interpretation of the underlying legal controversy, and with due consideration of the language and concepts originally employed by the District Court, we reformulate the question as follows:

> Whether, under West Virginia law, a plaintiff who does not allege a present physical injury can assert a claim for the recovery of future medical monitoring costs where such damages are the proximate result of defendant's tortious conduct? . . .

IV.
Discussion

Defendants argue that West Virginia law precludes the award of future medical monitoring expenses absent evidence of a present physical injury. In the alternative, they urge the Court to impose certain requirements on claims for medical monitoring so as to reasonably narrow the universe of potential plaintiffs. We reject the former argument, but take the considered suggestions of the parties into account in formulating a standard governing medical monitoring claims.

A. Recognizing a Claim for Medical Monitoring

A claim for medical monitoring seeks to recover the anticipated costs of long-term diagnostic testing necessary to detect latent diseases that may develop as a result of tortious exposure to toxic substances. Over the past decade, a growing number of courts have recognized this cause of action as a well-grounded extension of traditional common-law tort principles. Since the landmark decision in Askey v. Occidental Chemical Corp., . . . 477 N.Y.S.2d 242 (1984), appellate courts in at least six other states have permitted claims for medical monitoring. Likewise, a growing number of federal courts sitting in diversity have interpreted state law to permit such claims. What these decisions uniformly acknowledge is that significant economic harm may be inflicted on those exposed to toxic substances, notwithstanding the fact that the physical harm resulting from such exposure is often latent. See In re Paoli R.R. Yard PCB Litig., 916 F.2d 829, 852 (3d Cir. 1990) [hereinafter "Paoli I"], ...

As the Fourth Circuit correctly surmised, a claim for medical monitoring is essentially "a claim for future damages." Ball v. Joy Tech., Inc., 958 F.2d 36, 39 (4th Cir. 1991).

Consequently, we resort to elementary principles of tort law to determine whether medical monitoring is a proper subject of compensatory damages.

Since before the turn of the century, this jurisdiction sanctioned the recovery of future medical expenses where a plaintiff could prove with reasonable certainty that such costs would be incurred as a proximate consequence of a defendant's tortious conduct. . . . In . . . Jordan v. Bero, . . . 210 S.E.2d 618, (W. Va. 1974), we stated that "[t]o warrant recovery for future medical expenses, the proper measure of damages is . . . the reasonable value of medical services as will probably be necessarily incurred by reason of the permanent effects of a party's injuries." . . . Although *Jordan* and cases dealing with similar subject matter sometimes speak in terms of compensating a plaintiff for the anticipated cost of treating a "permanent injury," we have never held that lasting physical harm is an absolute prerequisite for recovery of future medical expenses. Indeed, we have never before dealt with a case such as this where the plaintiff sought future medical expenses with respect to a latent disease.

We now reject the contention that a claim for future medical expenses must rest upon the existence of present physical harm. The "injury" that underlies a claim for medical monitoring — just as with any other cause of action sounding in tort — is "the invasion of any legally protected interest." Restatement (Second) of Torts §7(1) (1964). As one of the first courts to grapple with this subject observed:

> It is difficult to dispute that an individual has an interest in avoiding expensive diagnostic examinations just as he or she has an interest in avoiding physical injury. When a defendant negligently invades this interest, the injury to which is neither speculative nor resistant to proof, it is elementary that the defendant should make the plaintiff whole by paying for the examinations.

Friends for All Children, Inc. v. Lockheed Aircraft Corp., . . . 746 F.2d 816, 826 (D.C. Cir. 1984) (footnote omitted). "Although the physical manifestations of an injury may not appear for years, the reality is that many of those exposed have suffered some legal detriment; the exposure itself and the concomitant need for medical testing constitute the injury." Hansen v. Mountain Fuel Supply, 858 P.2d 970, 977 (Utah 1993) (citations omitted). A number of courts have employed similar logic to sustain claims for medical monitoring costs. . . .

The court in *Friends for All Children* gave the following often-quoted hypothetical to illustrate the soundness of permitting recovery for necessary diagnostic testing even in the absence of physical injury:

> Jones is knocked down by a motorbike which Smith is riding through a red light. Jones lands on his head with some force. Understandably shaken, Jones enters a hospital where doctors recommend that he undergo a battery of tests to determine whether he has suffered any internal head injuries. The tests prove negative, but Jones sues Smith solely for what turns out to be the substantial cost of the diagnostic examinations.
>
> 746 F.2d 825. In such circumstances it is clear that even in the absence of physical injury Jones ought to be able to recover the cost for the variety of diagnostic examinations proximately caused by Smith's negligent action. . . . The motorbike rider, through his negligence, caused the plaintiff, in the opinion of medical experts, to need specific medical services — a cost that is neither inconsequential nor of a kind the community generally accepts as a part of the wear and tear of daily life. Under these principles of tort law, the motorbiker should pay.

Id. Thus, it logically follows that a plaintiff asserting a claim for medical monitoring costs is not required to prove present physical harm resulting from tortious exposure to toxic substances.

Nor is the plaintiff required to demonstrate the probable likelihood that a serious disease will result from the exposure. As the Third Circuit indicated in *Paoli I,* "the appropriate inquiry is not whether it is reasonably probable that plaintiffs will suffer [physical] harm in the future, but rather whether medical monitoring is, to a reasonable degree of medical certainty, necessary in order to diagnose properly the warning signs of disease." 916 F.2d at 851. See also 2 Dan B. Dobbs, *Law of Remedies* §8.1(3), at 380 n.30 (2d ed. 1993) ("diagnosis expenses — medical monitoring — may be both reasonable and reasonably certain to occur in the future, even if the disease it is intended to diagnose is not reasonably certain to occur").

The California Supreme Court in *Potter* detailed a number of policy considerations that favor recognizing a right to recover medical monitoring costs:

> First, there is an important public health interest in fostering access to medical testing for individuals whose exposure to toxic chemicals creates an enhanced risk of disease, particularly in light of the value of early diagnosis and treatment for many cancer patients. . . . Second, there is a deterrence value in recognizing medical surveillance claims — "allowing plaintiffs to recover the cost of this care deters irresponsible discharge of toxic chemicals by defendants. . . ." Third, "the availability of a substantial remedy before the consequences of the plaintiffs' exposure are manifest may also have the beneficial effect of preventing or mitigating serious future illnesses and thus reduce the overall costs to the responsible parties." . . . In this regard, the early detection of cancer may improve the prospects for cure, treatment, prolongation of life and minimization of pain and disability. Finally, societal notions of fairness and elemental jus-

tice are better served by allowing recovery of medical monitoring costs. That is, it would be inequitable for an individual wrongfully exposed to dangerous toxins, but unable to prove that cancer or disease is likely, to have to pay the expense of medical monitoring when such intervention is clearly reasonable and necessary. . . .

This Court is in agreement with these statements.

We therefore align this jurisdiction with those that have considered the issue, and conclude that a cause of action exists under West Virginia law for the recovery of medical monitoring costs, where it can be proven that such expenses are necessary and reasonably certain to be incurred as a proximate result of a defendant's tortious conduct. The certified question, as reformulated, is therefore answered in the affirmative.

B. Elements of a Claim for Medical Monitoring

Having determined that a claim for recovery of future medical monitoring costs is cognizable under West Virginia law, we are compelled to define the elements necessary to sustain such a claim.

We have consistently held that the "future effect of an injury must be proven with reasonable certainty in order to permit a jury to award an injured party future damages." . . . This flows from the more general rule that "'proof of damages . . . cannot be sustained by mere speculation or conjecture.'" . . . Thus, as the Court stated in . . . *Jordan,* "proof of future medical expenses is insufficient as a matter of law in the absence of any evidence as to the necessity and cost of such future medical expenses."

The various state and federal courts addressing this issue have moved toward relative consensus on the elements necessary to establish a claim for medical monitoring. The New Jersey Supreme Court was the first to attempt to forge a standard. In *Ayers,* the court stated that

> the cost of medical surveillance is a compensable item of damages where the proofs demonstrate, through reliable expert testimony predicated upon the significance and extent of the exposure to chemicals, the toxicity of the chemicals, the seriousness of the diseases for which individuals are at risk, the relative increase in the chance of onset of disease in those exposed, and the value of early diagnosis, that such surveillance to monitor the effect of exposure to toxic chemicals is reasonable and necessary.

106 N.J. at 606, ... The Third Circuit Court of Appeals followed shortly thereafter with the adoption of a four-element standard in *Paoli I.*[8] This was later

---

8. The four-factor test stated in *Paoli I* is as follows:

1. Plaintiff was significantly exposed to a proven hazardous substance through the negligent action of the defendant.
2. As a proximate result of exposure, plaintiff suffers a significantly increased risk of contracting a serious latent disease.
3. That increased risk makes periodic diagnostic medical examinations reasonably necessary.
4. Monitoring and testing procedures exist which make the early detection and treatment of the disease possible and beneficial.

Paoli I, 916 F.2d at 852.

modified in light of the Utah Supreme Court's holding in *Hansen,* by adding the requirement that the monitoring regime must be "'different than the one that would have been prescribed in the absence of the particular exposure.'" In re Paoli R.R. Yard PCB Litig., 35 F.3d 717, 789 (3d Cir. 1994) [hereinafter *Paoli II*]. . . .

With the significant divergence of eliminating the requirement that diagnostic monitoring must be tied to the existence of a proven treatment protocol, we substantially adopt the *Paoli* test. Thus, in order to sustain a claim for medical monitoring expenses under West Virginia law, the plaintiff must prove that (1) he or she has been significantly exposed; (2) to a proven hazardous substance; (3) through the tortious conduct of the defendant; (4) as a proximate result of the exposure, plaintiff has suffered an increased risk of contracting a serious latent disease relative to the general population; (5) the increased risk of disease makes it reasonably necessary for the plaintiff to undergo periodic diagnostic medical examinations different from what would be prescribed in the absence of the exposure; and (6) monitoring procedures exist that make the early detection of a disease possible. We will briefly discuss these elements in turn.

1. Significant Exposure. Before liability can attach with respect to the cost of medical monitoring, the plaintiff must first be exposed to a hazardous substance. . . .

2. Proven Hazardous Substance. The plaintiff must present scientific evidence demonstrating a probable link between exposure to a particular compound and human disease.

3. Tortious Conduct. Liability for medical monitoring is predicated upon the defendant being at fault in exposing the plaintiff to a particular hazardous substance. Fault is established through application of existing theories of tort liability. "Recognition that a defendant's conduct has created the need for future medical monitoring does not create a new tort. It is simply a compensable item of damage when liability is established under traditional theories of recovery." . . . This is not to say that a plaintiff may not, as a matter of pleading, assert a separate cause of action based upon medical monitoring; rather, it means that underlying liability must be established based upon a recognized tort — e.g., negligence, strict liability, trespass, intentional conduct, etc.

4. Increased Risk. Again, the plaintiff is not required to show that a particular disease is certain or even likely to occur as a result of exposure. . . . All that must be demonstrated is that the plaintiff has a significantly increased risk of contracting a particular disease relative to what would be the case in the absence of exposure. Importantly, "no particular level of quantification is necessary to satisfy this requirement." . . .

5. Necessity of Diagnostic Testing. Diagnostic testing must be "reasonably necessary" in the sense that it must be something that a qualified physician would prescribe based upon the demonstrated exposure to a particular toxic agent. This Court is not entirely in accord with the statement in *Hansen* to the effect that if a reasonable physician would not prescribe . . . [medical monitoring] for a particular plaintiff because the benefits of monitoring would be outweighed by the costs, which may include, among other things, the burdensome frequency of the monitoring procedure, its excessive price, or its risk of harm to the patient, then recovery would not be allowed.

858 P.2d at 980; see also *Paoli II,* 35 F.3d at 788. While there obviously must be some reasonable medical basis for undergoing diagnostic monitoring, factors such as financial cost and the frequency of testing should not be given significant weight. Moreover, the requirement that diagnostic testing must be medically advisable does not necessarily preclude the situation where such a determination is based, at least in part, upon the subjective desires of a plaintiff for information concerning the state of his or her health.

  6. *Existence of Monitoring Procedures.* Medical monitoring must be available in order to be a necessary, compensable item of damages. "If no such test exists, then periodic monitoring is of no assistance and the cost of such monitoring is not available." *Bourgeois,* 716 So. 2d at 361. In the event diagnostic testing later becomes available, then a plaintiff will have the right at such later time to demonstrate the effectiveness of the test, and be compensated for utilizing it, so long as all the other elements of the cause of action are satisfied. . . .
  We agree with the Pennsylvania Supreme Court that a plaintiff should not be required to show that a treatment currently exists for the disease that is the subject of medical monitoring. *Redland,* . . . 696 A.2d at 146 n.8. In this age of rapidly advancing medical science, we are hesitant to impose such a static requirement. In *Bourgeois,* Chief Justice Calogero gave a poignant justification for permitting recovering even in instances where there is no proven treatment:

One thing that . . . a plaintiff might gain [even in the absence of available treatment] is certainty as to his fate, whatever it might be. If a plaintiff has been placed at an increased risk for a latent disease through exposure to a hazardous substance, absent medical monitoring, he must live each day with the uncertainty of whether the disease is present in his body. If, however, he is able to take advantage of medical monitoring and the monitoring detects no evidence of disease, then, at least for the time being, the plaintiff can receive the comfort of peace of mind. Moreover, even if medical monitoring did detect evidence of an irreversible and untreatable disease, the plaintiff might still achieve some peace of mind through this knowledge by getting his financial affairs in order, making lifestyle changes, and, even perhaps, making peace with estranged loved ones or with his religion. Certainly, those options should be available to the innocent plaintiff who finds himself at an increased risk for a serious latent disease through no fault of his own.

  As a final matter, defendant CBS and several *amici curiae* argue that plaintiffs should only be compensated for medical monitoring costs through the establishment of a court-administered fund, to the exclusion of lump-sum damage awards. While there are situations where utilization of such funds may be beneficial, see *Ayers,* . . . 525 A.2d at 314 ("the use of a court-supervised fund to administer medical-surveillance payments *in mass exposure cases* . . . is a highly appropriate exercise of the Court's equitable powers") (emphasis added), we do not presently see a need to constrain the discretion of the trial courts to fashion appropriate remedies in cases such as these.

V.

Conclusion

We answer the question posed by the District Court, as reformulated, in the affirmative, and conclude that West Virginia law recognizes a cause of action for future medical monitoring costs where such necessary expenses are incurred as a proximate result of a defendant's tortious acts. Having answered the certified question, this case is dismissed from the docket of this Court.

Certified question answered; case dismissed.

MAYNARD, Justice, dissenting:

I dissent in this case because I believe that West Virginia law does not permit an independent cause of action to recover future medical monitoring costs absent physical injury, and this Court has no authority to create such a cause of action. . . .

The . . . most troubling aspect of this decision is the majority's violation of the constitutional separation of powers doctrine by usurping the Legislature's authority to enact laws. . . . We reiterated more recently that the creation, augmentation, repeal or abolishment of complete causes of action is a legislative power. . . . Up until approximately the last twenty-five years, the Court respected that fact. This decision shows just how far this Court has moved from its constitutional underpinnings and its proper role.

Finally, even if this Court did have the power to create causes of action, I would not agree with the one created by this decision. The majority rejects the fundamental 200 year old tort law principle that a plaintiff may not recover damages unless he or she has a present injury, and replaces it with the speculative and amorphous showing of "increased risk." The majority admits that "the plaintiff is not required to show that a particular disease is certain or even likely to occur as a result of exposure" (citation omitted). Because of this decision, plaintiffs will now be compensated when there is no injury, thus providing a windfall for plaintiffs. As one commentator has recently suggested, lawyers can now advertise, "Don't wait until you're hurt, call now."[1] In fact, the practical effect of this decision is to make almost every West Virginian a potential plaintiff in a medical monitoring cause of action. Those who work in heavy industries such as coal, oil, gas, timber, steel, and chemicals as well as those who work in older office buildings, or handle ink in newspaper offices, or launder the linens in hotels have, no doubt, come into contact with hazardous substances. Now all of these people may be able to collect money as victorious plaintiffs without any showing of injury at all.

We recently stated, "[t]he one area, above all, where a court should exercise caution is when it is deciding its own power." . . . The majority exercised no

---

1. Victor Schwartz, Some lawyers ask, Why wait for injury: Sue now!!, USA TODAY, July 15, 1999, at 17A.

caution whatsoever in this case. Consequently, it exceeded its legitimate powers and usurped the function of the Legislature. As a result, its holding here is not only judge-made law, it is bad law. For these reasons, I respectfully dissent.

Not all courts agree with *Bower*'s conclusion. There is a significant rearguard movement questioning the wisdom of awarding medical monitoring costs where plaintiffs have not suffered a cognizable physical injury. Some of the more powerful arguments against recognizing an action for medical monitoring costs were laid out in the Supreme Court's decision in *Metro-North*, infra. Specifically, the Court had grave reservations that:

> [T]ens of millions of individuals may have suffered exposure to substances that might justify some form of substance-exposure-related medical monitoring . . . And that fact, along with uncertainty as to the amount of liability, could threaten both a 'flood' of less important cases (potentially absorbing resources better left available to those more seriously harmed . . .) and the systemic harms that can accompany "unlimited and unpredictable liability." [Id. at 442.]

More recently, the Kentucky Supreme Court rejected an action for medical monitoring in Wood v. Wyeth-Ayerst Laboratories, 82 S.W.3d 849 (Ky. 2002). Plaintiff, a "Fen-Phen" diet drug consumer, sought recovery for the costs of monitoring against the highly publicized and acknowledged risks of heart valve abnormalities linked to the use of the drug. After weighing the arguments on both sides, the court found the analysis in *Metro-North* persuasive and was unwilling to depart from a long line of precedent holding that a plaintiff suffer physical injury as a prerequisite to the accrual of an action. Id. at 853. Accord Badillo v. Am. Brands, Inc., 16 P.3d 435 (Nev. 2001); Hinton v. Monsanto Co., 813 So. 2d 827 (Ala. 2001). See also In re Berg Litigation, 293 F.3d 1127 (9th Cir. 2002) (finding that plaintiffs not entitled to recover under Price-Anderson Act for medical monitoring costs associated with the risk of contracting cancer as a result of exposure to nuclear radiation absent plaintiffs' showing of present physical injury).

Professors Henderson and Twerski, in their article Asbestos Litigation Gone Mad: Exposure-Based Recovery for Increased Risk, Mental Distress, and Medical Monitoring, 53 S.C. L. Rev. 815 (2002), offer a rejoinder to the oft-repeated policy arguments underlying *Bower* and its ilk:

> But if the social benefits derived from court-sanctioned medical monitoring are questionable to the point of being dubious, the serious negative impacts of such liability on the business firms involved cannot be doubted. Given that negligently distributed or discharged toxins can be perceived to lie around every corner in the modern industrialized world, and their effects on risk levels are at best speculative, the potential tort claims involved are inherently limitless and endless. When courts require plaintiffs to prove that they have been, or are likely to become, physically injured as a result of exposures to asbestos or other toxic substances, defendants' potential liabilities are contained within natural boundaries. In contrast, in the medical monitoring context, there are no such natural boundaries. . . .

authors' dialogue 22

JIM: Do you see any way to fix the asbestos mess short of intervention by Congress?

AARON: I doubt it. As long as state courts are willing to award mental distress damages and medical monitoring for anyone ever exposed to asbestos, we will continue throwing company after company into bankruptcy. Asbestos plaintiffs have begun targeting anyone and everyone that had any connection with asbestos as potential defendants. Almost all of the asbestos manufacturers are already in bankruptcy. Now automobile manufacturers and other users of asbestos are being sued on the grounds that they should have known about the dangers of asbestos and should not have used them in their products. For example, brake linings in trucks and cars contained small amounts of asbestos. Employees of garages and auto repair shops now claim that they were exposed to asbestos and are entitled to either mental distress damages or medical monitoring. It's just never-ending.

JIM: Hold it, Aaron. You are overstating the problem. Very few courts allow mental distress damages for exposure to asbestos. There must be some physical manifestation of asbestos-related injury in the body of the plaintiff. *Metro-North* is really the law in most all states on this issue.

AARON: OK. But what about asymptomatic pleural thickening? Some states allow recovery for mental distress even though the likelihood of anyone contracting asbestosis or mesothelioma is very remote. And what about asbestosis? *Ayers* allowed recovery for mental distress because the plaintiff feared that he would contract cancer or mesothelioma. There are enough asbestosis cases to break the bank.

JIM: I agree with you that asymptomatic pleural thickening should not support an action for mental distress, but why wasn't the court right in *Ayers*? Asbestosis is a serious disease and fear of developing cancer or mesothelioma is not stretched.

AARON: The problem is that asbestosis is a label that doctors can easily place on even the most minor of changes in lung pathology. If it becomes the key to recovery, doctors can easily conform the facts to the pleadings without violating their Hippocratic oath. It is all in the eyes of the beholder.

JIM: I give up. The only way to clean up the asbestos mess is through congressional action. Asbestos is unique. We can't and shouldn't mess up traditional tort law principles to deal with a once-in-a-century problem.

Another inescapable implication of the inherent vagueness and open-endedness of medical monitoring litigation is that the courts will face, in the long run, an overwhelming flood of litigation in this area. . . . The West Virginia Supreme Court may believe that it "did justice" in *Bower* by adopting an ostensibly sensible rule of liability with which lower courts will be able to render medical monitoring decisions that are fair, rational, and manageable. But surely *Bower* has unwittingly brought upon the West

Virginia judiciary the potential for a plague of future litigation of questionable substantive benefit with which it is institutionally incapable of dealing. . . .

Finally, it must be understood that judicial recognition of claims for preinjury medical surveillance threatens the conceptual integrity of the American common law of torts. When one reflects objectively on what is happening in jurisdictions like West Virginia, at the conceptual level these medical monitoring claims combine elements of failure to rescue and pure economic loss. In effect, the plaintiffs in these cases want to force the defendants to pay the purely economic costs of rescuing them from a medical predicament. In both of these areas of the common law of torts, courts have traditionally proceeded with great caution, perceiving correctly that, however superficially appealing plaintiffs' claims may appear in the short run, the open-endedness of robust liability regimes would prove highly problematic in the long run. . . . [Id. at 844-46.]

Putting to one side the wisdom of allowing recovery for medical monitoring, the West Virginia court left open the question of whether medical monitoring costs should be paid to plaintiffs who actually avail themselves of the services or whether the cost of medical monitoring should be paid to plaintiffs in a lump sum. The difficulty with lump-sum payments is that they may be utilized for vacations to Florida rather than for the purposes for which they were awarded. A fair number of courts demand that courts monitor the payment for services actually rendered. See, e.g., Potter v. Firestone Fire & Rubber Co., 863 P.2d 795, 824 n.23 (Cal. 1993); Hansen v. Mountain Fuel Supply Co., 858 P.2d 970, 981 (Utah 1993); Redland Soccer Club, Inc. v. Dept. of the Army, 696 A.2d 137, 196 n.9 (Pa. 1997). Also see In re: St. Jude Medical Inc. Silzone Heart Valves Prod. Liab. Litigation, 2003 WL/589527 (Minn. 2003) (class certification granted because plaintiff was seeking relief for actual medical monitoring rather than lump sum damages).

For further scholarship on the issue, see Andrew R. Klein, 64 Brook. L. Rev. 1 (2002); Mark Geistfeld, The Analytics of Duty: Medical Monitoring and Related Forms of Economic Loss, 88 Va. L. Rev. 1921 (2002); John C. P. Goldberg & Benjamin C. Zipursky, Unrealized Torts, 88 Va. L. Rev. 1625 (2002); Victor E. Schwartz et al., Medical Monitoring—Should Tort Law Say Yes?, 34 Wake Forest L. Rev. 1057 (1999); and George W.C. McCarter, Medical Sue-Veillance: A History and Critique of the Medical Monitoring Remedy In Toxic Tort Litigation, 45 Rutgers L. Rev. 227 (1993).

E. RECOVERY OF PUNITIVE DAMAGES

1. Standard Limitations Imposed by the States

Wangen v. Ford Motor Co.
294 N.W.2d 437 (Wis. 1980)

ABRAHAMSON, J.

The central question on appeal is whether punitive damages are recoverable in a product liability suit based on negligence or strict liability in tort (sometimes referred to as strict products liability). We conclude that they are recoverable. [Ford moved to dismiss all causes of action for punitive damages, but the trial court denied Ford's motion. The court of appeals, in an unpublished decision, upheld the trial court's ruling that punitive damages were available in products liability cases "given a satisfactory evidentiary basis." However, the court of appeals distinguished between causes of action brought in strict liability and causes brought in negligence, holding that punitive damages are not recoverable in a products liability action predicated on negligence.]

I

This appeal involves two lawsuits which were commenced against Ford Motor Company and others as a result of an automobile accident on July 1, 1975 involving a 1967 Ford Mustang. The cases were consolidated and are before us at the pleading stage; all facts set forth are derived from the pleadings.

The occupants of the 1967 Ford Mustang involved in the accident were Robin DuVall, the driver, Terri Wangen, her sister, Kip Wangen, her brother, and Christopher DuVall, her son. Robin DuVall stopped her 1967 Ford Mustang at an intersection to make a left turn, and a car driven by Patrick J. Hawley ran into the rear end of the Mustang. The DuVall Mustang was pushed into the opposite lane of travel where it collided with a car driven by Thomas J. Curran. The Mustang's fuel tank ruptured, a fire ensued, and all occupants of the Mustang sustained severe injuries. Christopher DuVall and Kip Wangen died as a result of their injuries. . . . The claim for compensatory damages against Ford is based on Ford's alleged negligence in the design, manufacture, assembly, sale and distribution of the 1967 Mustang and on Ford's strict liability in tort arising out of the sale of the 1967 Mustang in a defective condition unreasonably dangerous to users.

The allegations in support of recovery of punitive damages from Ford Motor Company are that Ford knew that the fuel tanks on this and other 1967 Mustangs were dangerously defective before and after the manufacture of the car in question; that corrective design changes were made in models manufactured after this particular model but prior to the date of the instant accident; that Ford failed to warn users of the car of the potential danger both after the danger became apparent and after Ford had changed the design to reduce the danger; that Ford failed to recall, repair or modify the defective vehicles after the defect became apparent in order to avoid the expense of those procedures and to prevent potential lost sales caused by adverse publicity; and that Ford's conduct in failing to warn, repair or recall the known defective vehicles constituted intentional, deliberate, reckless, willful, wanton, gross, callous, malicious and fraudulent disregard for the safety of users of Ford's product. . . .

II . . .

A

Ford Motor Company asserts that punitive damages are recoverable only in actions based on intentional, personal torts, and are not recoverable in product liability actions which are grounded in negligence or strict liability. Ford argues that the concept of punitive damages is antithetical to the theories of negligence and strict liability because punitive damages are based on the defendant's intentional conduct. Ford's argument is premised on two assumptions: that intentional conduct is the only conduct justifying punitive damages and that the same facts which justify compensatory damages must be sufficient to justify punitive damages. This court has never adopted this view of punitive damages. . . .

This court has rested its analysis of punitive damages not on the classification of the underlying tort justifying compensatory damages but on the nature of the wrongdoer's conduct. Although the usual aggravating circumstances required for the recovery of punitive damages are often found as substantive elements of the tort itself, this court has said a claim for punitive damages may be supported by proof of aggravating circumstances beyond those supporting compensatory damages. . . .

If there is tortious conduct supporting a claim for compensatory damages, we can find no logical or conceptual difficulty in allowing a claim for punitive damages in a negligence or strict liability action if the plaintiff is able to establish the elements of "outrageous" conduct justifying punitive damages. . . .

C

Ford maintains that punitive damages are unnecessary in product liability cases to effect punishment and deterrence, which are the objectives of imposing punitive damages in the traditional tort action and that our outlawing punitive damages in all products liability cases is in the public interest because the recovery of punitive damages would cause economically and socially undesirable consequences.

1

Ford does not assert that there are no valid policy grounds for awarding punitive damages. Ford does not urge the complete abolition of punitive damages in all tort cases. Ford merely asserts that the accepted justifications for punitive damages, namely, punishment and deterrence, have no application in the product liability context.

In light of the history of punitive damages in Wisconsin, it is understandable why Ford is not urging the abolition of punitive damages in all tort cases. . . .

[The court reviews Wisconsin cases imposing punitive damages.]

In light of this court's repeated reaffirmation of the concept of punitive damages as a civil deterrent to "outrageous" behavior, and because apparently some businesses have found it in their interests to operate with reckless disregard to consumer safety, this court cannot, in good conscience, prohibit punitive damages in all product liability cases unless there is a strong showing that such prohibition is in the public interest. . . .

2

Ford asserts that in product liability cases compensatory damages operate as a substantial punishment and deterrence against the manufacture and distribution of unreasonably safe products and the punitive damages are not necessary. Ford contends that product liability cases differ in nature from the traditional punitive damage tort case in which generally only one plaintiff is involved and in which compensatory damages are relatively small. In product liability cases there are potentially many plaintiffs who will recover compensatory damages. Ford maintains that there has been a substantial increase in the number of product liability cases brought and the amount of damages awarded; that Ford is exposed to multiple, substantial compensatory damage awards; and that the cost of paying products liability claims and buying products liability insurance has become a significant cost of doing business.

The counterargument, which is frequently made to Ford's argument and which we find persuasive, is that the need for punitive damage may be particularly appropriate in a product liability case because mere compensatory damages might be insufficient to deter the defendant from further wrongdoing. Some may think it cheaper to pay damages or a forfeiture than to change a business practice. In Funk v. Kerbaugh, 222 Pa. 18, 70 A. 953, 954 (1908), the defendant wilfully carried out blasting in such a way as to damage buildings belonging to the plaintiff "because it was cheaper to pay damages . . . than to do work in a different way." The possibility of the manufacturer paying out more than compensatory damages might very well deter those who would consciously engage in wrongful practices and who would set aside a certain amount of money to compensate the injured consumer. Punishment of manufacturers guilty of intentional or reckless breaches of their obligation by imposing punitive damages might diminish the profitability of misconduct and any unfair competitive advantages such manufacturers might otherwise have. . . .

Ford also argues that punitive damages in a product liability case, unlike in the traditional punitive damage tort case, would not serve the purposes of punishment and deterrence because the public, not the manufacturer, would pay the damages through higher prices for goods. We recognize, as did the court of appeals, an inconsistency between the concept of punitive damages as a deterrent and the possibility that punitive damages can be passed on to consumers as a cost of production. This court adopted strict liability in tort in product liability cases partly because "the seller is in the paramount position to distribute the costs of the risks created by the defective product he is selling. He may pass the cost on to the consumer via increased prices." Dippel v. Sciano, 37 Wis. 2d 443, 450, 155 N.W.2d 55, 58 (1967). Manufacturers are, however, not always able to pass on to their customers all costs, including multiple punitive damage awards. Ford's contention was ably refuted by the circuit court for Eau Claire county, the Honorable Thomas H. Barland, Circuit Judge, in Barager v. Ford Motor Co. (Memorandum Decision dated September 15, 1977, in circuit court case No. 76 CV 215), on appeal to this court, case No. 77-274. The *Barager* case, like the instant case, presents the issue whether punitive damages can be claimed in a product liability case. Judge Barland stated:

> Finally, Ford argues that even if punitive damages were awarded against it, it would not be punished because it would merely pass on the cost of doing business. That argument flies in the face of all the statements in Ford's annual reports and quarterly statements regarding competitive pricing. It does not follow under economic logic that a punitive damage award will be passed on in whole or in part as a cost of doing business. It may or may not, depending upon Ford's price standing in relation to its competitors and its

own financial condition. It could mean lower profits for Ford. It could result in stockholder complaints about a lower profit margin because of punitive damage awards for unsafe cars, thereby spurring Ford on to exercise more care in the safe design of its automobiles. It could result in a greater scrutiny by Ford's management of its auto design from the safety standpoint. All of these changes, with the exception of lower profits or higher costs, if they were to take place, would benefit the public as a whole. . . .

3 . . .

Ford argues that if the punitive damages are not passed on to the consumer the innocent shareholder bears the burden. But the loss of investment and the decline in value of investments are risks which investors knowingly undertake, and investors should not enjoy ill-gotten gains. There is a public interest in encouraging shareholders and corporate management to exercise closer control over the operations of the entity, and the imposition of punitive damages may serve this interest.

Ford argues that as a practical matter there will be a limit to the amount of punitive damages a manufacturer can pay and to the number of times a manufacturer will be — or should be — punished for the same product. Thus the injured parties who win the race to the courthouse reap "the bonanza of punitive damages." The later plaintiffs may receive little or no punitive damages. Ford further asserts that punitive damages are a windfall to the injured party and, if they are to be awarded, they should be awarded to the public. Although Ford's arguments have a certain equitable ring to them, we should not be sidetracked by them. Ford would solve the inequity of awarding punitive damages to some plaintiffs by having this court eliminate all punitive damages and by having us allow the wrongdoer to go unpunished. The supposed unfairness Ford attributes to punitive damages ignores the effort and money required of the early plaintiffs to uncover and prove the misconduct. Later plaintiffs will often be able to use the information gathered by the first plaintiffs and benefit from the early favorable verdicts and settlements. The "windfall criterion" overlooks that the payment of punitive damages to the injured party is justifiable as a practical matter, because such damages do serve to compensate the injured party for uncompensated expenses, e.g., attorneys' fees and litigation expenses, and that the windfall motivates reluctant plaintiffs to go forward with their claims. If punitive damages were to be paid to the public treasury, fewer wrongdoers would be punished because the injured would have no inducement to spend the extra time and expense to prove a claim for punitive damages once an action had been brought. The basic question in determining whether punitive damages should be outlawed in product liability cases is not whether some injured party is going to make a profit but whether punitive damages will punish and deter, objectives which are in the public interest.

Ford views its strongest argument as the one that most concerned Judge Friendly in [Roginsky v. Richardson-Merrell, Inc., 378 F.2d 832 (2d Cir. 1967),] namely that large claims for punitive damages in multiple product liability cases cannot be administered fairly to avoid ruinous results to the defendant for a single defect appearing in many products. Judge Friendly saw no way to impose an "effective ceiling on punitive awards in hundreds of suits in different courts [which] may result in an aggregate which, when piled on large compensatory damages, could reach catastrophic amounts." *Roginsky,* supra, 378 F.2d 832, 839. . . .

We are persuaded that the problems Ford raises as to punitive damages, especially the problem of controlling multiple awards, can be minimized in this state in the litigation process. We are persuaded that punitive damages may play a vital role in product liability cases and that the role must be shaped, as is the role of all damages awards, to fit the context in which the particular case arises. Judicial controls exist in this state for determining whether the imposition of punitive damages is appropriate in the particular case and for determining the amount of the punitive damages award which will serve the punishment and deterrent objectives of punitive damages without inflicting a penalty on a defendant disproportionate to the defendant's wrong and contrary to the public interest. We believe the judicial controls, which we describe below, will provide for fair administration of punitive damage awards in this state.

4

In Wisconsin the trial judge initially determines whether the evidence establishes a proper case for the allowance of punitive damages and for the submission of the issue to the jury. . . .

[The court next concludes that the plaintiff should be required to prove that the wrongdoer's conduct was "outrageous" to a reasonable certainty by evidence that is clear, satisfactory, and convincing. Also, the judge should review the jury award for possible excessiveness.]

D

Having decided that punitive damages are recoverable in a product liability case where there is a showing of malice, vindictiveness, ill-will, or wanton, willful or reckless disregard of plaintiff's rights, we now turn to the plaintiff's complaint to determine if it pleads facts sufficient to support a claim for punitive damages. . . .

On the basis of the facts pleaded and reasonable inferences therefrom the complaint alleges that Ford knew of the defects in the design of the gas tank and filler neck and in the lack of barrier between the gas tank and passenger compartment in the 1967 Mustang and of the fire hazard associated with the design because of tests run by Ford as early as 1964; that for years before this accident Ford knew that these defects were causing serious burn injuries to occupants of these and similar cars; that years before the accident involved in the instant case Ford knew how to correct these defects in ways that would have prevented the plaintiffs' burns, but Ford intentionally concealed this knowledge from the government and the public; that despite this knowledge Ford deliberately chose not to recall its 1967 Mustangs and not to disclose the defects to the public by the issuance of warnings because Ford wanted to avoid paying the costs of recall and repair and wanted to avoid the accompanying bad publicity; and that Ford's conduct was intentional, reckless, willful, wanton, gross and fraudulent. These facts, if proved by the plaintiff, portray conduct which is willful and wanton and in reckless disregard of the plaintiff's rights. We conclude that the complaint alleges facts sufficient to state a claim for punitive damages in a product liability action predicated on negligence or strict liability. . . .

Decision of the court of appeals affirmed in part and reversed in part; order of the circuit court affirmed in part and reversed in part; and cause remanded to the circuit court.

COFFEY, Justice (dissenting).

I dissent because the majority has extended application of the concept of punitive damages, established by this court's prior case law. . . .

I agree that the question of whether to abolish punitive damages is not for this court to decide, as it has been a part of our law for so long. However, I also believe that this court should not extend the recovery of punitive damages to any class of cases other than those in which they have been historically permitted. . . .

The majority has unwisely usurped the legislative function in this case, and, for the above reasons, I must dissent. Let us allow our democracy to function in the manner the framers of our constitution intended. Let each of the three branches of government operate independent of one another. Let no branch usurp or invade the province or responsibility of another. Let not the majority further roil the already turbulent waters of products liability by riding a "new wave" of social, economic and political improvement. If social welfare experimentation is to be conducted, it should be done by the legislature. The implications for the free enterprise system, and therefore the structure of our economy, are too disturbing to leave a decision of this magnitude to five jurists.

Many courts are quite insistent that the behavior of the defendant be truly egregious before imposing primitive damages. Thus in Robert Ford v. GACS Inc., 265 F.3d 670 (8th Cir. 2001) GACS, manufacturer of a ratchet system for securing cars to automobile transporters, was held not to have acted with "wantonness or bad motive" by continuing to manufacture a product despite knowledge of some injuries. The court found that: (1) "the fact that [GACS] worked to design a safer system belies the level of reckless indifference or conscious disregard for the safety of others necessary to support an award of punitive damages" even though GACS chose not to market the safer design; (2) a 10 percent chance that an individual driver would be injured by the system in a single year did not establish that the manufacturer was aware that the system was "unreasonably dangerous;" (3) GACS's decision to continue marketing the device because its major customer had approved only that type of device was motivated by considerations of utility and not by bad faith.

Similarly, in Bonnette v. Conoco Inc., 837 So. 2d 1219 (La. 2003), a refinery that knowingly sold asbestos contaminated dirt to contractors for use in a residential development, was not "wanton and reckless" in failing to inform anyone that the dirt was contaminated because the refinery did not violate any state environmental regulations. Since the particular type of construction was not regulated by the state environmental protection agency (the "DEQ"), the refinery had not violated any environmental regulations by failing to warn that the dirt was contaminated. Furthermore, the refinery's actions after plaintiffs discovered the contamination were "in excess" of what the DEQ "would have required of them." The court held that the refinery's conduct did not satisfy the statutory "wanton and reckless conduct" standard necessary to impose punitive damages stemming from the handling of toxic substances:

> Although the actions of [the defendant,] including his failure to take any steps to inform anyone of the presence of asbestos on the site, leave much to be desired, it is clear that [defendant's] actions were not in violation of any DEQ regulation. Because [defendant] acted in compliance with DEQ regulations in effect during the events at issue, we cannot say that defendant's conduct was highly unreasonable or that it involved an extreme departure from ordinary care.

States have utilized a wide range of other techniques to rein in punitive damages. Thirty-two states have legislation regulating punitive damage. Of those 32, 24 states require plaintiffs to meet a heightened burden of proof to be entitled to punitive damages. Most states require "clear and convincing evidence" of wrongdoing and Colorado requires proof equivalent to the criminal standard: "beyond a reasonable doubt." See Colo. Rev. Stat. §13-25-127(2) (2002). In addition, at least eight states and the District of Columbia have imposed the "clear and convincing" evidence standard by judicial decision.[1] However, the Supreme Court of Kentucky invalidated a statute imposing the "clear and convincing" standard because it substantially altered a common law right.[2]

Seventeen states have enacted statutes that limit the dollar amount of punitive damage awards, either by imposing an absolute cap on punitive damages or by limiting punitive damages to some multiple of compensatory damages.[3] Nebraska,

---

1. See, Victor E. Schwartz, Mark A. Behrens, & Joseph P. Mastrosimone, Reining in Punitive Damages "Run Wild:" Proposals for Reform by Courts and Legislatures, 65 Brook. L. Rev. 1003, 1013 n.53 (1999) (listing cases: Linthicum v. Nationwide Life Ins. Co., 723 P.2d 675 (Ariz. 1986); Jonathan Woodner Co. v. Breeden, 665 A.2d 929 (D.C. App. 1995); Masaki v. General Motors Corp., 780 P.2d 566 (Haw. 1989); Travelers Indem. Co. v. Armstrong, 442 N.E.2d 349 (Ind. 1982); Tuttle v. Raymond, 494 A.2d 1353 (Me. 1985); Owens-Illinois v. Zenobia, 601 A.2d 633 (Md. 1992); Rodriguez v. Suzuki Motor Corp., 936 S.W.2d 104 (Mo. 1996); Hodges v. S.C. Toof & Co., 833 S.W.2d 896 (Tenn. 1992); Wangen v. Ford Motor Co., 294 N.W.2d 437 (Wis. 1980)).

2. Williams v. Wilson, 972 S.W.2d 260 (Ky. 1998) (the "clear and convincing" evidence standard substantially alters a common law right, which pre-dates the Kentucky constitution, to recover punitive damages stemming from personal injury. The Kentucky doctrine of "jural rights" prohibits the legislature from interfering with common law rights of recovery in actions stemming from personal injury or death.).

3. Ala. Code §§6-11-20, 6-11-21 (1993 & Supp. 2003) (in physical injury cases, the greater of three times the award of compensatory damages or $1.5 million); Alaska Stat. §09.17.020 (LexisNexis 2002) (amended by 2003 Alaska Sess. Laws 85; generally, the greater of three times the award of compensatory damages or $500,000); Civil Justice Reform Act, 2003 Ark. Acts 649 (the greater of $250,000 or three times the award of compensatory damages, but not greater than $1,000,000); Colo. Rev. Stat. §13-21-102(1)(a) (2002) (punitive damages may not exceed compensatory damages); Fla. Stat. Ann. §768.73 (West Supp. 2003) (generally, the greater of $500,000 or three times the amount of compensatory damages); Ga. Code Ann. §51-12-5.1 (2000) ($250,000); Idaho Code §6-1604 (Michie Supp. 2003) (the greater of $250,000 or three times the amount of compensatory damages); Ind. Code Ann. §34-51-3-4 (LexisNexis 1998) (the greater of $50,000 or three times the compensatory damages); Kan. Stat. Ann. §60-3701 (1998) (the lesser of the gross annual income of the defendant or $5 million, except that if the court finds that the profitability of the defendant's conduct outweighs the punitive damages, it shall award one and one-half times the amount of profit which defendant gained or is expected to gain); Miss. Code Ann. §11-1-65 (West Supp. 2003) (between $20 million and 4% of the defendant's net worth as determined by a sliding scale in the statute); Nev. Rev. Stat. Ann. §42.005 (LexisNexis 2002); N.J. Stat. Ann. §2A:15-5.14 (West 2000) (generally, the greater of $350,000 or five times the compensatory damages); N.C. Gen. Stat. §1D-1 (2001) et seq. (the greater of $250,000 or three times the compensatory damages); N.D. Cent. Code §32-03.2-11 (Supp. 2001) (amended by 2003 N.D. Laws 48; the greater of $250,000 or two times the compensatory damages); Okla. Stat. Ann. tit. 23, §9.1 (West Supp. 2003) (reckless conduct: the greater of $100,000 or the amount of compensatory damages; intentional conduct: the greater of $500,000

Massachusetts, New Hampshire, and Washington do not recognize punitive damages as a common law remedy. Louisiana awards punitive damages by statute only and in limited circumstances. In at least one state, Georgia, punitive damages arising out of a products liability suit are exempt from the statutory cap. Ga. Code Ann. §51-12-5.1(e)(1) (2000).

At least six states require a percentage of punitive damages to be contributed to a state administered fund.[4] One federal district court, McBride v. Gen. Motors Corp., 737 F. Supp. 1563 (M.D. Ga. 1990), has found that fund contribution statutes violate the federal constitution on a number of grounds including equal protection. Some state courts that have addressed the same issue have disagreed.[5]

At least five states have enacted statutes that exempt drug manufacturers or sellers from liability for punitive damages if the drug that caused injury was labeled, manufactured, marketed, and distributed in compliance with F.D.A. regulations.[6]

Three states, Connecticut, Kansas, and Ohio, require the court to determine the amount of punitive damages after a jury's finding that punitive damages are appropriate. A number of states have provisions for a separate proceeding to determine the amount of punitive damages to be awarded.[7]

The subject of punitive damages has attracted considerable scholarly commentary. See generally David G. Owen, A Punitive Damages Overview: Functions, Problems and Reform, 39 Vill. L. Rev. 363 (1994) (reviewing the policy for punitive damages, the problems posed by punitive damages, and the most common proposals for punitive damage reforms); Victor E. Schwartz et al., Reining in Punitive Damages "Run Wild:" Proposals for Reform by Courts and Legislatures, 65 Brook. L. Rev. 1003 (1999) (arguing that excessive punitive damages awards pose a major problem in many states); Michael L. Rustad & Thomas H. Koenig, Taming the Tort Monster: The American Civil Justice System as a Battleground of Social Theory, 68 Brook. L. Rev. 1 (2002) (contending that the need for tort reform is overblown; reviewing the history of punitive damages and concluding that "[t]ort retrenchment is jeopardizing the social role of tort law in protecting the public from corporate and individual misbehavior"); M. Stuart

---

or twice the amount of compensatory damages); Tex. Civ. Prac. & Rem. Code Ann. §41 (Vernon 1997) et seq. (amended by 2003 Tex. Sess. Law Serv. 204; generally, the greater of two times the amount of compensatory damages plus punitive damages not to exceed $750,000 or $200,000); Va. Code Ann. §8.01-38.1 (Michie 2000) ($350,000).

4. See Alaska Stat. §09.17.020(j) (LexisNexis 2002) (50% of punitive damage award must be paid to state fund); Ga. Code Ann. §51-12-5.1(2) (2000) (75% of punitive damage award must be paid to state fund); Ind. Code Ann. §34-51-3-6(b) (LexisNexis 1998) (75% of punitive damage award must be paid to a state fund); Iowa Code Ann. §668A.1 (West 1998) (75% of punitive damage award must be paid to a state fund if the conduct that harmed the plaintiff was not intentional); Mo. Ann. Stat. §537.675(3) (West Supp. 2003) (50% of punitive damage award must be paid to state fund); Utah Code Ann. §78-18-1(3)(a) (2002) (50% of punitive damage awarded in excess of $20,000 must be paid to state fund).

5. See, e.g., State v. Mosely, 436 S.E.2d 632, 263 Ga. 680 (1993); Mack Trucks Inc. v. Conckle, 263 Ga. 539, 436 S.E.2d 635 (1993) (both holding that the Georgia statute does not violate either the state or federal constitutions). See also Cheatham v. Pohle, 789 N.E.2d 467 (Ind. 2003) (upholding the Indiana state fund statute); Evans ex rel. Kutch v. State, 56 P.3d 1046 (Alaska 2002) (upholding the Alaska state fund statute).

6. Ariz. Rev. Stat. Ann. §12-701 (West 2003); Mich. Comp. Laws. Ann. §600.2946 (West 1999); Ohio Rev. Code Ann. §2307.80(C) (Anderson 2001); N.J. Stat. Ann. §2A:58C-5 (West 2000); Utah Code Ann. §78-18-2 (2002).

7. See, e.g., Minn. Stat. Ann. §549.20(4) (West 2000); Mont. Code Ann. §27-1-221(7)(a) (2001); Nev. Rev. Stat. Ann. §42.005(3) (LexisNexis 2002); N.J. Stat. Ann. §2A:15-5.13 (West 2000) (defendant may request bifurcated trial on damages).

Madden, Renegade Conduct and Punitive Damages in Tort, 53 S.C. L. Rev. 1175 (2002) (efforts of state legislatures and the U.S. Supreme Court have been successful in creating a fair and rational place for punitive damages); Cass Sunstein et al., Punitive Damages: How Juries Decide (2002) (findings originally published in Cass Sunstein et al., Deliberating About Dollars: The Severity Shift, 100 Colum. L. Rev. 139 (2002)), reviewed by Neal R. Feigenson, Can Tort Juries Punish Competently?, 78 Chi.-Kent L. Rev. 239 (2003). Utilizing the findings of mock juror and jury experiments, Professor Sunstein found that jurors award arbitrary and unpredictable punitive damage judgments because of systematic biases and a lack of clear guidance as to how moral judgments should be translated into dollar awards. He concludes that, overall, jurors tend to award punitive damages more frequently and in higher amounts than the law should allow. Without taking issue with the study's empirical findings, Feigenson criticizes the author's conclusion: that jury verdicts on punitive damages are unjust because they tend to overcompensate plaintiffs. Feigenson argues that punitive damages serve an important retributive role in society, which lay jurors are as capable of enforcing as experts.

2. *Federal Constitutional Control of Punitive Damages*

State Farm Mutual Automobile Ins. Co. v. Campbell
123 S. Ct. 1513 (2003)

Justice KENNEDY delivered the opinion of the Court.

We address once again the measure of punishment, by means of punitive damages, a State may impose upon a defendant in a civil case. The question is whether, in the circumstances we shall recount, an award of $145 million in punitive damages, where full compensatory damages are $1 million, is excessive and in violation of the Due Process Clause of the Fourteenth Amendment to the Constitution of the United States.

I

In 1981, Curtis Campbell (Campbell) was driving with his wife, Inez Preece Campbell, in Cache County, Utah. He decided to pass six vans traveling ahead of them on a two-lane highway. Todd Ospital was driving a small car approaching from the opposite direction. To avoid a head-on collision with Campbell, who by then was driving on the wrong side of the highway and toward oncoming traffic, Ospital swerved onto the shoulder, lost control of his automobile, and collided with a vehicle driven by Robert G. Slusher. Ospital was killed, and Slusher was rendered permanently disabled. The Campbells escaped unscathed. . . .

In the ensuing wrongful death and tort action, Campbell insisted he was not at fault. Early investigations did support differing conclusions as to who caused the accident, but "consensus was reached early on by the investigators and witnesses that Mr. Campbell's unsafe pass had indeed caused the crash." . . . Campbell's insurance company, petitioner State Farm Mutual Automobile Insurance Company (State Farm), nonetheless decided to contest liability and declined offers by Slusher and Ospital's estate (Ospital) to settle the claims for the policy limit of $50,000 ($25,000 per claimant). State Farm also ignored the advice of one of its own investigators and took the case to trial, assuring the Campbells that "their assets were safe, that they had no liability for the accident, that [State Farm] would represent their interests, and that they did not need to procure separate counsel." . . . To the contrary, a jury determined that Campbell was 100 percent at fault, and a judgment was returned for $185,849, far more than the amount offered in settlement.

At first State Farm refused to cover the $135,849 in excess liability. Its counsel made this clear to the Campbells: "'You may want to put for sale signs on your property to get things moving.'" . . . Nor was State Farm willing to post a supersedeas bond to allow Campbell to appeal the judgment against him. Campbell obtained his own counsel to appeal the verdict. During the pendency of the appeal, in late 1984, Slusher, Ospital, and the Campbells reached an agreement whereby Slusher and Ospital agreed not to seek satisfaction of their claims against the Campbells. In exchange the Campbells agreed to pursue a bad faith action against State Farm and to be represented by Slusher's and Ospital's attorneys. The Campbells also agreed that Slusher and Ospital would have a right to play a part in all major decisions concerning the bad faith action. No settlement could be concluded without Slusher's and Ospital's approval, and Slusher and Ospital would receive 90 percent of any verdict against State Farm.

In 1989, the Utah Supreme Court denied Campbell's appeal in the wrongful death and tort actions. . . . State Farm then paid the entire judgment, including the amounts in excess of the policy limits. The Campbells nonetheless filed a complaint against State Farm alleging bad faith, fraud, and intentional infliction of emotional distress. The trial court initially granted State Farm's motion for summary judgment because State Farm had paid the excess verdict, but that ruling was reversed on appeal. . . . On remand State Farm moved *in limine* to exclude evidence of alleged conduct that occurred in unrelated cases outside of Utah, but the trial court denied the motion. At State Farm's request the trial court bifurcated the trial into two phases conducted before different juries. In the first phase the jury determined that State Farm's decision not to settle was unreasonable because there was a substantial likelihood of an excess verdict.

Before the second phase of the action against State Farm we decided BMW of North America, Inc. v. Gore, 517 U.S. 559, L. Ed. 2d 809 (1996), and refused to sustain a $2 million punitive damages award which accompanied a verdict of only $4,000 in compensatory damages. Based on that decision, State Farm again moved for the exclusion of evidence of dissimilar out-of-state conduct. . . . The trial court denied State Farm's motion. . . .

The second phase addressed State Farm's liability for fraud and intentional infliction of emotional distress, as well as compensatory and punitive damages. The Utah Supreme Court aptly characterized this phase of the trial:

> "State Farm argued during phase II that its decision to take the case to trial was an 'honest mistake' that did not warrant punitive damages. In contrast, the Campbells introduced evidence that State Farm's decision to take the case to trial was a result of a national scheme to meet corporate fiscal goals by capping payouts on claims company wide. This scheme was referred to as State Farm's 'Performance, Planning and Review,' or PP & R, policy. To prove the existence of this scheme, the trial court allowed the Campbells to introduce extensive expert testimony regarding fraudulent practices by State

Farm in its nation-wide operations. Although State Farm moved prior to phase II of the trial for the exclusion of such evidence and continued to object to it at trial, the trial court ruled that such evidence was admissible to determine whether State Farm's conduct in the Campbell case was indeed intentional and sufficiently egregious to warrant punitive damages." . . .

Evidence pertaining to the PP&R policy concerned State Farm's business practices for over 20 years in numerous States. Most of these practices bore no relation to third-party automobile insurance claims, the type of claim underlying the Campbells' complaint against the company. The jury awarded the Campbells $2.6 million in compensatory damages and $145 million in punitive damages, which the trial court reduced to $1 million and $25 million respectively. Both parties appealed.

The Utah Supreme Court sought to apply the three guideposts we identified in *Gore,* supra, . . . and it reinstated the $145 million punitive damages award. Relying in large part on the extensive evidence concerning the PP&R policy, the court concluded State Farm's conduct was reprehensible. The court also relied upon State Farm's "massive wealth" and on testimony indicating that "State Farm's actions, because of their clandestine nature, will be punished at most in one out of every 50,000 cases as a matter of statistical probability," . . . and concluded that the ratio between punitive and compensatory damages was not unwarranted. Finally, the court noted that the punitive damages award was not excessive when compared to various civil and criminal penalties State Farm could have faced, including $10,000 for each act of fraud, the suspension of its license to conduct business in Utah, the disgorgement of profits, and imprisonment. . . . We granted certiorari. . . .

II

We recognized in Cooper Industries, Inc. v. Leatherman Tool Group, Inc., 532 U.S. 424, . . . that in our judicial system compensatory and punitive damages, although usually awarded at the same time by the same decisionmaker, serve different purposes. . . . Compensatory damages "are intended to redress the concrete loss that the plaintiff has suffered by reason of the defendant's wrongful conduct." . . . (citing Restatement (Second) of Torts §903, pp.453-454 (1979)). By contrast, punitive damages serve a broader function; they are aimed at deterrence and retribution. *Cooper Industries,* supra. . . .

While States possess discretion over the imposition of punitive damages, it is well established that there are procedural and substantive constitutional limitations on these awards. . . . The reason is that "elementary notions of fairness enshrined in our constitutional jurisprudence dictate that a person receive fair notice not only of the conduct that will subject him to punishment, but also of the severity of the penalty that a State may impose." . . . To the extent an award is grossly excessive, it furthers no legitimate purpose and constitutes an arbitrary deprivation of property. . . .

Although these awards serve the same purposes as criminal penalties, defendants subjected to punitive damages in civil cases have not been accorded the protections applicable in a criminal proceeding. This increases our concerns over the imprecise manner in which punitive damages systems are administered. We have admonished that "punitive damages pose an acute danger of arbitrary deprivation of property. Jury instructions typically leave the jury with wide discretion in choosing amounts, and the presentation of evidence of a defendant's net worth creates the potential that juries will use their verdicts to express biases against big businesses, particularly those without strong local presences." . . .

In light of these concerns, in *Gore* supra, . . . we instructed courts reviewing punitive damages to consider three guideposts: (1) the degree of reprehensibility of the defendant's misconduct; (2) the disparity between the actual or potential harm suffered by the plaintiff and the punitive damages award; and (3) the difference between the punitive damages awarded by the jury and the civil penalties authorized or imposed in comparable cases. . . . We reiterated the importance of these three guideposts in *Cooper Industries* and mandated appellate courts to conduct *de novo* review of a trial court's application of them to the jury's award. . . . Exacting appellate review ensures that an award of punitive damages is based upon an "'application of law, rather than a decisionmaker's caprice.'". . .

III

Under the principles outlined in BMW of North America, Inc. v. Gore, this case is neither close nor difficult. It was error to reinstate the jury's $145 million punitive damages award. We address each guidepost of *Gore* in some detail.

A

"The most important indicium of the reasonableness of a punitive damages award is the degree of reprehensibility of the defendant's conduct." . . . We have instructed courts to determine the reprehensibility of a defendant by considering whether: the harm caused was physical as opposed to economic; the tortious conduct evinced an indifference to or a reckless disregard of the health or safety of others; the target of the conduct had financial vulnerability; the conduct involved repeated actions or was an isolated incident; and the harm was the result of intentional malice, trickery, or deceit, or mere accident. . . . The existence of any one of these factors weighing in favor of a plaintiff may not be sufficient to sustain a punitive damages award; and the absence of all of them renders any award suspect. It should be presumed a plaintiff has been made whole for his injuries by compensatory damages, so punitive damages should only be awarded if the defendant's culpability, after having paid compensatory damages, is so reprehensible as to warrant the imposition of further sanctions to achieve punishment or deterrence. . . .

Applying these factors in the instant case, we must acknowledge that State Farm's handling of the claims against the Campbells merits no praise. The trial court found that State Farm's employees altered the company's records to make Campbell appear less culpable. State Farm disregarded the overwhelming likelihood of liability and the near-certain probability that, by taking the case to trial, a judgment in excess of the policy limits would be awarded. State Farm amplified the harm by at first assuring the Campbells their assets would be safe from any verdict and by later telling them, postjudgment, to put a for-sale sign on their house. While we do not suggest there was error in awarding punitive damages based upon State Farm's conduct toward the Campbells, a more modest punishment for this reprehensible conduct could have satisfied the State's legitimate objectives, and the Utah courts should have gone no further.

This case, instead, was used as a platform to expose, and punish, the perceived deficiencies of State Farm's operations throughout the country. The Utah Supreme Court's opinion makes explicit that State Farm was being condemned for its nationwide policies rather than for the conduct direct toward the Campbells. 65 P.3d at 1143 ("The Campbells introduced evidence that State Farm's decision to take the case to trial was a result of a national scheme to meet corporate fiscal goals by capping payouts on claims company wide"). This was, as well, an explicit rationale of the trial court's decision in approving the award, though reduced from $145 million to $25 million. . . . ("[T]he Campbells demonstrated, through the testimony of State Farm employees who had worked outside of Utah, and through expert testimony, that this pattern of claims adjustment under the PP&R program was not a local anomaly, but was a consistent, nationwide feature of State Farm's business operations, orchestrated from the highest levels of corporate management").

The Campbells contend that State Farm has only itself to blame for the reliance upon dissimilar and out-of-state conduct evidence. The record does not support this contention. From their opening statements onward the Campbells framed this case as a chance to rebuke State Farm for its nationwide activities. . . . ("You're going to hear evidence that even the insurance commission in Utah and around the country are unwilling or inept at protecting people against abuses"); . . . ("[T]his is a very important case. . . . It transcends the Campbell file. It involves a nationwide practice. And you, here, are going to be evaluating and assessing, and hopefully requiring State Farm to stand accountable for what it's doing across the country, which is the purpose of punitive damages"). This was a position maintained throughout the litigation. In opposing State Farm's motion to exclude such evidence under *Gore,* the Campbells' counsel convinced the trial court that there was no limitation on the scope of evidence that could be considered under our precedents. . . .

A State cannot punish a defendant for conduct that may have been lawful where it occurred. . . . Nor, as a general rule, does a State have a legitimate concern in imposing punitive damages to punish a defendant for unlawful acts committed outside of the State's jurisdiction. Any proper adjudication of conduct that occurred outside Utah to other persons would require their inclusion, and, to those parties, the Utah courts, in the usual case, would need to apply the laws of their relevant jurisdiction. Phillips Petroleum Co. v. Shutts, 472 U.S. 797. . . .

Here, the Campbells do not dispute that much of the out-of-state conduct was lawful where it occurred. They argue, however, that such evidence was not the primary basis for the punitive damages award and was relevant to the extent it demonstrated, in a general sense, State Farm's motive against its insured. Brief for Respondents 46-47 ("Even if the practices described by State Farm were not malum in se or malum prohibitum, they became relevant to punitive damages to the extent they were used as tools to implement State Farm's wrongful PP&R policy"). This argument misses the mark. Lawful out-of-state conduct may be probative when it demonstrates the deliberateness and culpability of the defendant's action in the State where it is tortious, but that conduct must have a nexus to the specific harm suffered by the plaintiff. A jury must be instructed, furthermore, that it may not use evidence of out-of-state conduct to punish a defendant for action that was lawful in the jurisdiction where it occurred. . . .

For a more fundamental reason, however, the Utah courts erred in relying upon this and other evidence: The courts awarded punitive damages to punish and deter conduct that bore no relation to the Campbells' harm. A defendant's dissimilar acts, independent from the acts upon which liability was premised, may not serve as the basis for punitive damages. A defendant should be punished for the conduct that harmed the plaintiff, not for being an unsavory individual or business. Due process does not permit courts, in the calculation of punitive damages, to adjudicate the merits of other parties' hypothetical claims against a defendant under the guise of the reprehensibility analysis, but we have no doubt the Utah Supreme Court did that here. . . . Punishment on these bases creates the possibility of multiple punitive damages awards for the same conduct; for in the usual case nonparties are not bound by the judgment some other plaintiff obtains. . . .

The Campbells have identified scant evidence of repeated misconduct of the sort that injured them. Nor does our review of the Utah courts' decisions convince us that State Farm was only punished for its actions toward the Campbells. Although evidence of other acts need not be identical to have relevance in the calculation of punitive damages, the Utah court erred here because evidence pertaining to claims that had nothing to do with a third-party lawsuit was introduced at length. Other evidence concerning reprehensibility was even more tangential. For example, the Utah Supreme Court criticized State Farm's investigation into the personal life of one of its employees and, in a broader approach, the manner in which State Farm's policies corrupted its employees. . . . The Campbells attempt to justify the courts' reliance upon this unrelated testimony on the theory that each dollar of profit made by underpaying a third-party claimant is the same as a dollar made by underpaying a first-party one. . . . For the reasons already stated, this argument is unconvincing. The reprehensibility guidepost does not permit courts to expand the scope of the case so that a defendant may be punished for any malfeasance, which in this case extended for a 20-year period. In this case, because the Campbells have shown no conduct by State Farm similar to that which harmed them, the conduct that harmed them is the only conduct relevant to the reprehensibility analysis.

B

Turning to the second *Gore* guidepost, we have been reluctant to identify concrete constitutional limits on the ratio between harm, or potential harm, to the plaintiff and the punitive damages award. *Gore,* supra, at 582, 116 S. Ct. 1589 ("[W]e have consistently rejected the notion that the constitutional line is marked by a simple mathematical formula, even one that compares actual *and potential* damages to the punitive award"); . . . . We decline again to impose a bright-line ratio which a punitive damages award cannot exceed. Our jurisprudence and the principles it has now established demonstrate, however, that, in practice, few awards exceeding a single-digit ratio between punitive and compensatory damages, to a significant degree, will satisfy due process. In *Haslip,* in upholding a punitive damages award, we concluded that an award of more than four times the amount of compensatory damages might be close to the line of constitutional impropriety. 499 U.S., at 23-24. . . . We cited that 4-to-1 ratio again in *Gore.*

517 U.S., at 581. . . . The Court further referenced a long legislative history, dating back over 700 years and going forward to today, providing for sanctions of double, treble, or quadruple damages to deter and punish. . . . While these ratios are not binding, they are instructive. They demonstrate what should be obvious: Single-digit multipliers are more likely to comport with due process, while still achieving the State's goals of deterrence and retribution, than awards with ratios in range of 500 to 1, . . . or, in this case, of 145 to 1.

Nonetheless, because there are no rigid benchmarks that a punitive damages award may not surpass, ratios greater than those we have previously upheld may comport with due process where "a particularly egregious act has resulted in only a small amount of economic damages." . . . The converse is also true, however. When compensatory damages are substantial, then a lesser ratio, perhaps only equal to compensatory damages, can reach the outermost limit of the due process guarantee. The precise award in any case, of course, must be based upon the facts and circumstances of the defendant's conduct and the harm to the plaintiff.

In sum, courts must ensure that the measure of punishment is both reasonable and proportionate to the amount of harm to the plaintiff and to the general damages recovered. In the context of this case, we have no doubt that there is a presumption against an award that has a 145-to-1 ratio. The compensatory award in this case was substantial; the Campbells were awarded $1 million for a year and a half of emotional distress. This was complete compensation. The harm arose from a transaction in the economic realm, not from some physical assault or trauma; there were no physical injuries; and State Farm paid the excess verdict before the complaint was filed, so the Campbells suffered only minor economic injuries for the 18-month period in which State Farm refused to resolve the claim against them. The compensatory damages for the injury suffered here, moreover, likely were based on a component which was duplicated in the punitive award. Much of the distress was caused by the outrage and humiliation the Campbells suffered at the actions of their insurer; and it is a major role of punitive damages to condemn such conduct. Compensatory damages, however, already contain this punitive element. . . .

The Utah Supreme Court sought to justify the massive award by pointing to State Farm's purported failure to report a prior $100 million punitive damages award in Texas to its corporate headquarters; the fact that State Farm's policies have affected numerous Utah consumers; the fact that State Farm will only be punished in one out of every 50,000 cases as a matter of statistical probability; and State Farm's enormous wealth. . . . Since the Supreme Court of Utah discussed the Texas award when applying the ratio guidepost, we discuss it here. The Texas award, however, should have been analyzed in the context of the reprehensibility guidepost only. The failure of the company to report the Texas award is out-of-state conduct that, if the conduct were similar, might have had some bearing on the degree of reprehensibility, subject to the limitations we have described. Here, it was dissimilar, and of such marginal relevance that it should have been accorded little or no weight. The award was rendered in a first-party lawsuit; no judgment was entered in the case; and it was later settled for a fraction of the verdict. With respect to the Utah Supreme Court's second justification, the Campbells' inability to direct us to testimony demonstrating harm to the people of Utah (other than those directly involved in this case) indicates that the adverse effect on the State's general population was in fact minor.

The remaining premises for the Utah Supreme Court's decision bear no relation to the award's reasonableness or proportionality to the harm. They are, rather, arguments that seek to defend a departure from well-established constraints on punitive damages. While States enjoy considerable discretion in deducing when punitive damages are warranted, each award must comport with the principles set forth in *Gore*. Here the argument that State Farm will be punished in only the rare case, coupled with reference to its assets (which, of course, are what other insured parties in Utah and other States must rely upon for payment of claims) had little to do with the actual harm sustained by the Campbells. The wealth of a defendant cannot justify an otherwise unconstitutional punitive damages award. . . . ("[Wealth] provides an open-ended basis for inflating awards when the defendant is wealthy. . . . That does not make its use unlawful or inappropriate; it simply means that this factor cannot make up for the failure of other factors, such as 'reprehensibility,' to constrain significantly an award that purports to punish a defendant's conduct"). The principles set forth in *Gore* must be implemented with care, to ensure both reasonableness and proportionality.

C

The third guidepost in *Gore* is the disparity between the punitive damages award and the "civil penalties authorized or imposed in comparable cases." . . . We note that, in the past, we have also looked to criminal penalties that could be imposed. . . . The existence of a criminal penalty does have bearing on the seriousness with which a State views the wrongful action. When used to determine the dollar amount of the award, however, the criminal penalty has less utility. Great care must be taken to avoid use of the civil process to assess criminal penalties that can be imposed only after the heightened protections of a criminal trial have been observed, including, of course, its higher standards of proof. Punitive damages are not a substitute for the criminal process, and the remote possibility of a criminal sanction does not automatically sustain a punitive damages award.

Here, we need not dwell long on this guidepost. The most relevant civil sanction under Utah state law for the wrong done to the Campbells appears to be a $10,000 fine for an act of fraud. . . . an amount dwarfed by the $145 million punitive damages award. The Supreme Court of Utah speculated about the loss of State Farm's business license, the disgorgement of profits, and possible imprisonment, but here again its references were to the broad fraudulent scheme drawn from evidence of out-of-state and dissimilar conduct. This analysis was insufficient to justify the award.

IV

An application of the *Gore* guideposts to the facts of this case, especially in light of the substantial compensatory damages awarded (a portion of which contained a punitive element), likely would justify a punitive damages award at or near the amount of compensatory damages. The punitive award of $145 million, therefore, was neither reasonable nor proportionate to the wrong committed, and it was an irrational and arbitrary deprivation of the property of the defendant. The proper calculation of punitive damages under the principles we have discussed should be resolved, in the first instance, by the Utah courts.

The judgment of the Utah Supreme Court is reversed, and the case is remanded for proceedings not inconsistent with this opinion.

It is so ordered.

[The dissenting opinion by Justices SCALIA and THOMAS are omitted.]

[Justice GINSBURG (dissenting) reviews the evidence of State Farm's conduct and finds it to be outrageous.]

The Court dismisses the evidence describing and documenting State Farm's PP&R policy and practices as essentially irrelevant, bearing "no relation to the Campbells' harm." . . . It is hardly apparent why that should be so. What is infirm about the Campbells' theory that their experience with State Farm exemplifies and reflects an overarching underpayment scheme, one that caused "repeated misconduct of the sort that injured them," . . . ? The Court's silence on that score is revealing: Once one recognizes that the Campbells did show "conduct by State Farm similar to that which harmed them," . . . it becomes impossible to shrink the reprehensibility analysis to this sole case, or to maintain, at odds with the determination of the trial court, . . . that "the adverse effect on the State's general population was in fact minor," ante, at 1525.

Evidence of out-of-state conduct, the Court acknowledges, may be "probative [even if the conduct is lawful in the state where it occurred] when it demonstrates the deliberateness and culpability of the defendant's action in the State where it is tortious. . . . "Other acts" evidence concerning practices both in and out of State was introduced in this case to show just such "deliberateness" and "culpability." The evidence was admissible, the trial court ruled: (1) to document State Farm's "reprehensible" PP&R program; and (2) to "rebut [State Farm's] assertion that [its] actions toward the Campbells were inadvertent errors or mistakes in judgment." . . . Viewed in this light, there surely was "a nexus" . . . between much of the "other acts" evidence and "the specific harm suffered by [the Campbells]." . . .

When the Court first ventured to override state-court punitive damages awards, it did so moderately. The Court recalled that "in our federal system, States necessarily have considerable flexibility in determining the level of punitive damages that they will allow in different classes of cases and in any particular case." *Gore,* 517 U.S., at 568 . . . Today's decision exhibits no such respect and restraint. No longer content to accord state-court judgments "a strong presumption of validity." . . . the Court announces that "few awards exceeding a single-digit ratio between punitive and compensatory damages, to a significant degree, will satisfy due process." . . . Moreover, the Court adds, when compensatory damages are substantial, doubling those damages "can reach the outermost limit of the due process guarantee." . . . In a legislative scheme or a state high court's design to cap punitive damages, the handiwork in setting single-digit and 1-to-1 benchmarks could hardly be questioned; in a judicial decree imposed on the States by this Court under the banner of substantive due process, the numerical controls today's decision installs seem to me boldly out of order.

. . .

I remain of the view that this Court has no warrant to reform state law governing awards of punitive damages. . . . Even if I were prepared to accept the flexible guides prescribed in *Gore,* I would not join the Court's swift conversion of those guides into instructions that begin to resemble marching orders. For the reasons stated, I would leave the judgment of the Utah Supreme Court undisturbed. . . .

The authors offer the following reactions to *State Farm:*

(1) We believe that the court was frustrated with its attempts at jawboning courts into controlling punitive damages. After more than a decade of cajoling, the court decided that only firm legislative-like guidelines would work. Justice Ginsburg is right that the majority has engaged in outright legislation.

(2) The court did not resolve the question of what kind of multiples would be appropriate in a case of punitive damages where a defendant's reckless and wanton conduct causes personal injury or death. That is presumably an open question. However, two points lead us to believe that the Court will not countenance large multiples even in personal injury cases. First, the damages to the plaintiff in *State Farm* were not purely economic loss. Plaintiff was suing for pain and suffering, humiliation, etc. Although the threat was not to life and limb, the case involves damages that are akin to personal injury damages. Second, the Court's dictum that when "compensatory damages are substantial" than a one-to-one ratio may reach the limits of due process is a powerful statement. Admittedly, the Court notes immediately after making this statement that the damages did not arise "from some physical assault or trauma." Nonetheless, where substantial compensatory damages are awarded, it is hard to see this Court allowing multiples over single digits. We will have to wait and see. But, our guess is that even in personal injury cases the threat of multiples over ten are likely to be found unconstitutional.

Several courts have sharply reduced punitive damages claims in personal injury cases in light of *State Farm.* See, e.g., Henley v. Philip Morris, Inc., 2003 WL 22211589 (Cal. App. 2003) (reduced punitive damage award from $25 million to $9 million. Since compensatory damages were $1.5 million, the court reduced the ratio from 17-1 to 6-1 to conform with *State Mutual*); Bocci v. Rey Pharmaceuticals, Inc., 76 P.3d 669 (Or. App. 2003) (court reduced punitive damage from a ratio of 45-1 to a ratio of 7-1: compensatory damage award was $500,000.00).

(3) The statement by the Court that "[t]he wealth of the defendant cannot justify an otherwise unconstitutional punitive damages award" deserves careful consideration. The Court makes it clear that wealth may be taken into account in setting the amount of punitives but that it cannot serve as a surrogate for the reprehensibility necessary to justify punitives.

(4) The refusal of the Court to take into account defendant's out of state lawful conduct may have a profound effect on product liability cases. It is not clear that a finding of design defect in one state would be found to be so in another state. Standards for design defect differ (e.g., risk-utility, consumer expectations). Jury instructions differ. If a product is defective in state A and not in state B, the fact that a jury finds the defendant's conduct to be reckless need not be determinative under *State Farm.* A defendant's conduct may be noxious but if the product is not defective in another state there would be no liability on which to predicate punitive damages.

The subject of a constitutional control of punitive damages has engaged the

authors' dialogue 23

AARON: *State Farm* has to be the most important constitutional law decision affecting tort law in the history of the United States Supreme Court. What brought about such a radical intrusion into the traditional right of state courts to decide tort-related issues?

JIM: I'm not sure that *State Farm* wins the all-time prize. Some of the federal preemption decisions wiped out state common-law causes of action entirely. But, I won't quibble with you that *State Farm* is a knockout case. My take is that the court saw punitive awards playing an unacceptably large role in tort litigation. Whether they were right or not is debatable. My colleague Ted Eisenberg did a study on actual punitive damage awards and found that punitives rarely exceeded the amount awarded in compensatories.

AARON: I actually heard Ted's presentation. It was impressive. But, my resollection is that Ted did not take into account the influence of potential punitive damages on settlements. Punitives have an *in terrorem* effect on defendants. Nobody is willing to bet the house as long as there is a real possibility that punitive damages will be huge and unrestricted. Over the last year I have read about jury awards of punitive damages running into the hundreds of millions of dollars that have been upheld by the trial judge. And in one recent cigarette case a trial judge let stand a jury award in excess of $4 billion. Admittedly these awards will almost certainly be drastically cut back after appellate review. But the noise gets to be awfully loud. The perception that punitive damages are out of line was just too widespread.

JIM: You may be right. But there are still a lot of unanswered questions about the scope of *State Farm.* Punitives may still play a significant role in tort litigation. First, nobody knows the answer as to whether *State Farm* will govern cases where a plaintiff suffered serious personal injury. Second, and even more important in the products liability context, *State Farm* does not address the issue of repetitive punitive damages against a manufacturer for a single design or failure to warn error. Hundreds, even thousands, of plaintiffs may bring individual lawsuits and each seek punitive damages.

AARON: You may be technically correct. But I see the handwriting on the wall. The Supreme Court wrote a decision telling the world that it would no longer countenance business as usual with regard to punitives. Lower courts have begun responding by cutting back sharply on punitive damage awards even in personal injury cases. Sometime in the next two or three years the Supreme Court will take a personal injury punitive damage case and they may well choose to review a case where other courts have awarded punitives and we will get clarity on these issues. When it is all said and done, punitive damages will continue to play a role in our tort system but the appearance of a free-for-all will be gone.

interest of scholars. For pre-*State Farm* articles, see generally John Calvin Jeffries, Jr., A Comment on the Constitutionality of Punitive Damages, 72 Va. L. Rev. 139 (1986); Dorsey D. Ellis, Punitive Damages, Due Process, and the Jury, 40 Ala. L. Rev. 975 (1989); Allan Howard Scheiner, Judicial Assessment of Punitive Damages, the Seventh Amendment, and the Politics of Jury Power, 91 Colum. L. Rev. 142 (1991); Bruce J. Ennis, Punitive Damages and the U.S. Constitution, 25 Tort & Ins. L.J. 587 (1990). We expect that *State Farm* will spawn a new body of scholarly literature in the ensuing years. For an interesting post-*State Farm* article, see Catherine M. Sharkey, Punitive Damages as Societal Damages, 113 Yale L.J. 347 (2003) (arguing for the recognition of societal compensatory damages for redress of third party and societal harm).

PART IV
Institutional Perspectives

CHAPTER ELEVEN

Special Features Reflecting the Fact That Most Products Defendants Are Corporations

A. THE GENERAL RULE OF LIMITED SHAREHOLDER LIABILITY (AND EXCEPTIONS THERETO)

In most of the cases and problems in this book, the defendants against whom products liability claims are brought are corporations. Legally, for most purposes, that fact is of no consequence. As a practical matter, of course, jurors are probably less sympathetic with corporate (compared with individual) defendants. But from a legal standpoint the corporation is treated in most contexts as a person no different from a flesh-and-blood individual. The materials in this chapter focus on features of our products liability system that more formally reflect the fact that most products liability defendants are corporations.

The general rule is that shareholders are not personally liable for the debts of the corporation, including debts generated by products liability judgments. See generally Model Business Corp. Act §6.22 (1984). This limited liability rule presents the possibility that corporations will over-engage, from a broader social perspective, in risky activities because the gains to be derived by investors from a successful venture more than outweigh the investors' exposure to the risk of losing their shares in the equity should the corporation incur tort liabilities (net of insurance) that exceed its available assets. As we shall see, courts sometimes "pierce the veil" of limited liability and allow creditors to reach the shareholders individually. Given the presence of the risk of over-engagement in risky activities, generally referred to as the "moral hazard" problem (see the note on the effects of liability insurance at the end of Chapter One), why should not the veil be pierced in every instance? Why, in other words, should the general rule be one of limited liability?

In seeking answers to these questions, some commentators have emphasized the necessity for a limited liability rule to attract relatively wealthy individuals to invest in widely held corporations. See Henry G. Manne, Our Two Corporation Systems: Law and Economics, 53 Va. L. Rev. 259 (1967) (the seminal article). Others emphasize that the limited liability rule is necessary for the existence of an organized securities market. See Paul Halpern, Michael Trebilcock, & Stuart

Turnbull, An Economic Analysis of Limited Liability in Corporation Law, 30 U. Toronto L.J. 117 (1980) (without limited liability, different investors would place different values on identical shares, depending on the investors' individual levels of wealth).

Professors Easterbrook and Fischel provide a number of rationales for the general rule of limited liability. See Frank M. Easterbrook & Daniel R. Fischel, Limited Liability and the Corporation, 52 U. Chi. L. Rev. 89 (1985). Building on Manne's earlier work, they develop two sets of reasons that justify the rule from an economic efficiency perspective: (1) limited liability decreases the need for investors to monitor both corporate managers (upon whose conduct corporate liability hinges) and fellow shareholders (upon whose solvency their own liabilities would hinge under a limitless liability regime); and (2) the limited liability rule shifts the risks of losses-above-net-value from the shareholders (who are relatively inefficient risk bearers) to the creditors (who are relatively more efficient risk bearers), thus reducing the firm's costs of capital. The first set of reasons borrows heavily from theories of the firm;[1] the second resembles the reasons developed in Chapter Two for shifting (via strict products liability) residual accident losses from accident victims to product sellers.[2]

Notwithstanding nearly unanimous support among courts, commentators, and other policymakers for the general rule of limited shareholder liability, some writers question whether the better general rule, from the standpoint of allocative efficiency and fairness, would be unlimited shareholder liability. In Henry Hansmann & Reinier Kraakman, Toward Unlimited Shareholder Liability for Corporate Torts, 100 Yale L.J. 1879 (1991), the authors challenge the traditional assumption that unlimited shareholder liability would either unduly burden capital markets or shift tort losses above net value of the firm to less efficient risk bearers. Regarding the likely effects of unlimited liability on capital markets (that is, the possibility that unlimited liability would discourage many investors, especially wealthy investors, from buying shares in corporations), the authors rely heavily on moving from the traditional joint-and-several liability rule to a several liability, "pro rata liability only," rule. Under their proposed approach, each shareholder's potential liability for above-net-worth tort losses would be in proportion to the percentage of outstanding shares the shareholder owned at the time share-

---

1. Most of us, most of the time, think of corporations and other complex institutions as if they were single, integrated personalities. We assume, when we are not concentrating on the implications of our assumption, a congruence between "the firm" and those within the firm who manage it. "The Theory of Firm" looks inside this "black box" assumption and seeks to understand what goes on within the firm in response to signals, including tort liability signals from the outside. Often, a firm's response will be different from what one might have imagined, and may even be counterproductive from the "black box" perspective, because that particular response serves to further the career plans of managers within the firm. See generally Brudney, Corporate Governance, Agency Costs and Rhetoric of Contract, 85 Colum. L. Rev. 1403 (1985); Fama, Agency Problems and the Theory of the Firm, 881 Pol. Econ. 288 (1980); Jensen & Meckling, Theory of the Firm: Managerial Behavior, Agency Costs and Ownership Structure, 3 J. Fin. Econ. 305 (1976).

2. Observe that this "risk-shifting" rationale highlights the fundamental conflict in this chapter. Corporation law reflects the view that creditors — including, presumably, tort creditors — are more efficient riskbearers than are shareholders of corporations that sell products. Tort law reflects the view that tort creditors — including victims of defective products — are less efficient risk-bearers than are corporations that sell products. Corporation law seeks via limited liability to promote the production of goods and services; tort law seeks via threats of liability to constrain production.

holder liability attached. Liability would attach at the earliest of three moments: (1) when the tort claims in question were filed; (2) when management first became aware that, with high probability, tort claims would be filed; or (3) when the corporation dissolved without leaving a contractual successor. The second question of who, between tort plaintiffs and shareholders, represents the cheaper risk bearers the authors believe to be a question for tort law, not corporation law, to answer. They submit that under the current regime of limited liability, almost by hypothesis, corporations lack adequate incentives to invest in care or keep their levels of investment in risky activities anywhere near optimal. The truth is that, under current law in mass-tort settings, tort victims subsidize investors. This subsidy is believed necessary to induce investors to invest; the authors argue to the contrary. Space does not permit us even to sketch the authors' arguments. Suffice it to say that their biggest problems lie in implementation more than pure theory. How, for example, will the wealthier, more substantial investors monitor corporate management to achieve optimal levels of care and engagement in risky activity? What would prevent shareholders who have purchased shares after the timing event for liability (see above) from capturing control and dissipating the corporation's assets, thus increasing the older, liable-in-tort shareholders' exposures to liability? How are courts to prevent corporations from turning to debt rather than equity as a primary means of capitalizing their enterprises? These and a number of other problems would have to be solved. But if they could be solved, the authors claim that unlimited shareholder liability would be the appropriate rule.

Toward the end of the article, under the heading, "Shareholder Liability as a Problem of Tort Law," the authors conclude (100 Yale L.J. at 1918-1919):

> . . . There may be good reasons for retreating somewhat from recent expansions of enterprise liability, although this remains a debatable issue. But, even so, limited liability is an extremely crude check on the courts; it restricts liability excessively in some cases and not enough in others, and it motivates shareholders and corporations to behave opportunistically. If the scope of enterprise liability needs to be narrowed, the appropriate reform is not to invite firms to opt out of the tort system by exploiting limited liability. Rather, one should craft liability rules and damage measures that impose costs upon corporations and their shareholders only to the extent that these actors appear to be the cheapest cost avoiders and/or insurers. Indeed, there is already evidence that the courts have recently, on their own, begun taking a more conservative approach to enterprise liability.
>
> Moreover, precisely the opposite argument seems equally plausible: with unlimited liability, courts would be forced to consider the appropriate scope of enterprise liability more thoughtfully, in the full awareness that limited liability would not automatically constrain any tendency toward excessive liability. Courts could not award generous damages under the illusion that only corporations, and not individuals, would bear the resulting costs. Rather, they could not escape the fact that tort liability large enough to bankrupt a publicly-held corporation would also impose direct costs upon thousands of individual shareholders.
>
> We do not want to exaggerate our faith in tort law as a means of controlling behavior. It is a very rough and costly mechanism. But it usefully discourages the most severe forms of opportunistic cost externalization. Moreover, if any class of actors is likely to respond rationally to the deterrence incentives created by tort law, it is corporations and their shareholders. Similarly, if tort law is to have any role in shifting risks to low-cost insurers, then using it to shift risks to the equity market makes sense. Con-

sequently, allowing corporations to avoid tort liability through the simple device of limited liability seems, at the very least, highly suspect.

Hansmann and Kraakman's proposal stirred a lively debate among corporate law scholars. See, e.g., Janet C. Alexander, Unlimited Shareholder Liability Through a Procedural Lens, 106 Harv. L. Rev. 387 (1992); Joseph A. Grundfest, The Limited Future of Unlimited Liability: A Capital Markets Perspective, 102 Yale L.J. 387 (1992); Henry Hansmann & Reinier Kraakman, Do the Capital Markets Compel Limited Liability? A Response to Professor Grundfest, 102 Yale L.J. 427 (1992); Reinier Kraakman, A Procedural Focus on Unlimited Shareholder Liability, 106 Harv. L. Rev. 446 (1992); David W. Leebron, Limited Liability, Tort Victims, and Creditors, 91 Colum. L. Rev. 1565 (1991); Robert B. Thompson, Unpacking Limited Liability: Direct and Vicarious Liability of Corporate Participants for Torts of the Enterprise, 47 Vand. L. Rev. 1 (1994).

Notwithstanding arguments in support of a general rule of unlimited liability, the limited shareholder liability remains the consensus position.

In the relatively rare instances in which courts have pierced the corporate veil and allowed creditors to reach individual shareholders, they have emphasized factors such as the relatively small number of shareholders (the closeness of the corporation) and the relative inadequacy of the capitalization in relation to the risks of loss to nonshareholders (the thinness of the capitalization). See, e.g., Menton v. Cavaney, 364 P.2d 473 (Cal. 1961); Walkovszky v. Carlton, 223 N.E.2d 6 (N.Y. 1966).

Another factor that may bear on courts' willingness to pierce the corporate veil is that in some cases the shareholder in question is, itself, a parent corporation of the primarily-liable subsidiary. In William P. Hackney & Tracey G. Bensen, Shareholder Liability for Inadequate Capital, 43 U. Pitt. L. Rev. 837, 873 (1982), the authors conclude that the courts are generally more willing to allow creditors to reach the assets of corporate, rather than noncorporate, shareholders. However, empirically, this may not be the case. See Robert B. Thompson, Piercing the Veil Within Corporate Groups: Corporate Shareholders as Mere Investors, 13 Conn. J. Int'l L. 379 (1999) (finding that courts pierce the veil more often to get to an individual who is a shareholder than to reach another corporation who is a shareholder). In any event, consider the following products liability decision.

Nelson v. International Paint Co., Inc.
734 F.2d 1084 (5th Cir. 1984)

RANDALL, Cir. J.:

In this Texas diversity case, plaintiffs-appellants Alfred and Vida Nelson appeal from a summary judgment rendered against them in their products liability suit against International Paint Company, Inc., defendant-appellee, a New Jersey corporation. Finding that there is no genuine issue as to any material fact, we affirm the district court's grant of summary judgment.

I. Factual and Procedural Background

Alfred Nelson was injured on June 30, 1978, when he inhaled toxic fumes while painting over a weld at a construction site in Kodiak, Alaska. Nelson alleges that his injury was caused by [defective] paint.

At the time that he was injured, Nelson was using a marine anti-fouling paint known as "Inter-Trop Red 50." The label on the paint can Nelson was using carried the name "International Paint Company, Inc.," and listed addresses for the company in New York, New Orleans, and San Francisco. Also present on the label was the trademark "International Paint Company."

Shortly after his injury, Nelson returned home to Texas, where he employed Texas counsel to file a products liability action against the manufacturer of the paint. The Texas counsel contacted an Alaska attorney, and arranged for him to sue the manufacturer and distributor of the paint in the courts of that state. That attorney left Alaska before the suit was filed, but an associate in his firm brought suit in Alaska state court in April, 1980, naming among the defendants International Paint Company, Inc. ("IPCO"), and International Paint Co. (California), Inc. ("CALCO"), IPCO's wholly-owned subsidiary, which is headquartered in San Francisco. However, because of Nelson's ill-health, and their concern that the new Alaska counsel was inexperienced, the Nelsons directed that a voluntary non-suit be taken in the Alaska court.

The Nelsons then filed suit against IPCO in the court below on May 15, 1980. They sought damages on the basis of strict liability in tort and breach of implied warranty. . . .

Through IPCO's answer to an interrogatory on June 16, 1981, the Nelsons' Texas counsel learned that Inter-Trop Red 50 was manufactured not by IPCO, but by CALCO.[5] The Nelsons added CALCO as a party-defendant, but CALCO moved to dismiss the complaint against it for lack of personal jurisdiction. The Nelsons opposed the motion, arguing that the court had jurisdiction over CALCO because CALCO was so closely integrated with IPCO that the business conducted in Texas by IPCO could be imputed to CALCO for purposes of jurisdiction. The district court found that IPCO and CALCO were sufficiently separate entities that the Nelsons could not obtain personal jurisdiction over CALCO in Texas. The court then ordered the Nelsons' claim against CALCO transferred to the United States District Court for the Northern District of California. The Nelsons did not appeal that order.

After the Nelsons' action against CALCO was transferred to California, CALCO moved to dismiss because the statute of limitations had run. The district court there granted the motion, holding that California law applied to the action, and that the state's one-year statute of limitations barred suit against CALCO. The Nelsons appealed, but the Ninth Circuit affirmed. Nelson v. International Paint Co., 716 F.2d 640 (9th Cir. 1983).

Meanwhile, in Texas, IPCO moved for summary judgment, contending that it did not design, manufacture, or market the paint that caused Nelson's injuries, and thus that it could not be held liable for Nelson's injuries. The district court granted IPCO's motion for summary judgment, and the Nelsons now appeal.

II. Issues on Appeal

The Nelsons raise several issues on appeal: first, they contend that the evidence shows that there is a genuine issue of fact as to whether IPCO developed

---

5. IPCO did, however, manufacture the same product under the name "1609 Supertrop." CALCO's "Inter-Trop Red 50" was marketed more for the everyday consumer, while IPCO's "1609 Supertrop" was aimed primarily at large commercial and industrial customers.

the formula; second, they contend that because IPCO's name was on the paint can label, it is liable as the manufacturer under the Restatement (Second) of Torts §400; third, they argue that because the IPCO label caused them to sue IPCO rather than CALCO, IPCO should be estopped from denying liability for CALCO's acts; and, finally, they assert that there is a genuine fact issue whether IPCO can be held liable as the "alter ego" of CALCO. We consider each one of their arguments in turn, mindful that "[w]e must view the evidence in the light most favorable to the opposing party, resolving all reasonable doubts concerning the facts in [its] favor. . . ." Miles v. American Telephone & Telegraph Co., 703 F.2d 193, 194 (5th Cir. 1983).

[Discussion of the first issue is omitted.]

B. IPCO's Liability Under the Restatement (Second) of Torts §400

The Nelsons contend next that, despite the district court's finding to the contrary, there was evidence that IPCO was aware that CALCO was labeling Inter-Trop Red 50 as an IPCO product. They argue that such knowledge is relevant because, under their reading of Texas law, IPCO can be held strictly liable for Nelson's injuries as the manufacturer of Inter-Trop Red 50 if IPCO allowed CALCO to sell Inter-Trop Red 50 under IPCO's name, despite the fact that IPCO did not design, manufacture, or sell the paint. Because we do not believe that, under Texas law, IPCO can be held liable on the ground that the Nelsons assert, it is unnecessary for us to decide whether the Nelsons introduced any evidence indicating that IPCO knew that CALCO was selling Inter-Trop Red 50 as an IPCO product.[6]

The Nelsons assert that if IPCO allowed CALCO to put out Inter-Trop Red 50 as an IPCO product, IPCO faces liability under the Restatement (Second) of Torts §400 (1966), which provides that:

> One who put out as his own product a chattel manufactured by another is subject to the same liability as though he were its manufacturer.

The rationale underlying this section of the Restatement is apparent: For example, if Sears markets a blender as a "Sears" product, it leads consumers to believe that Sears is responsible for and stands behind the product. Accordingly, because Sears has induced such reliance on the part of consumers, Sears will be held liable as the manufacturer of the blender, even if it entrusted another company with the responsibility for manufacturing a safe and reliable blender that Sears will sell as its own.[7] . . .

---

6. The district court found that IPCO had no knowledge that CALCO was using IPCO's name on Inter-Trop Red 50. The Nelsons contend that Grant Johnson, an IPCO vice-president and chief operating officer of CALCO, testified that he was aware that CALCO was using IPCO labels on its products. IPCO asserts that Johnson's deposition testimony cannot be so construed; instead, IPCO contends that Johnson spoke merely of the fact that he was aware that the two companies used the same artwork to save costs. IPCO also points out that the label for Inter-Trop Red 50 registered with the Environmental Protection Agency read "International Paint Co. [California] Inc.," and that it had no knowledge that CALCO was using an unregistered label.

7. The Restatement (Second) of Torts §400 Comment *d* explains that: The rule stated in this Section applies only where the actor puts out the chattel as his own product. The actor puts out a chattel as his own product in two types of cases. The first is where the actor appears to be the manufacturer of the chattel. The second is where the chattel appears to have been made particularly for the actor. In the first type of case the actor frequently causes the chattel to be used in reliance upon his care in making it; in the second, he frequently causes the chattel to be used in reliance upon a belief that he has required it

In [earlier] cases, the defendant was held liable because it distributed another's defective product under its own name. Here, however, we are presented with a situation where a distributor has marketed a product not under its name, but another's. Nevertheless, the Nelsons contend that if IPCO allowed CALCO to put out Inter-Trop Red 50 under IPCO's name, IPCO should be vicariously liable under section 400, despite the fact that IPCO did not manufacture or market the can of paint that injured Nelson.

The Texas courts have expressly rejected this interpretation of section 400. In Stanford v. Dairy Queen Products of Texas, 623 S.W.2d 797 (Tex. App. 1981), the plaintiffs, a husband and wife, alleged that the wife became ill after eating an "unwholesome" cheeseburger sold at a Dairy Queen restaurant in Burnet County, Texas. They brought suit against three defendants, one of whom was Dairy Queen Products of Texas, a partnership.[8] Dairy Queen Products possessed exclusive authority in Texas over the use of the registered trade name "Dairy Queen." Its business consisted of authorizing others to use the "Dairy Queen" name in the operation of restaurants throughout the state, including the one where the wife suffered injury. The partnership also had the responsibility for maintaining the value of the "Dairy Queen" trade name by, inter alia, conducting periodic inspections of the restaurants and conducting advertising campaigns.

The plaintiffs brought suit against Dairy Queen Products and the other two defendants in Travis County, where the plaintiffs resided. Because Dairy Queen Products' principal place of business was in Bexar County, it interposed a plea of privilege because the general venue rule in Texas at that time provided that Texas residents could be sued only in the county of their domicile. Although the plaintiffs opposed a transfer of venue, the trial court sustained Dairy Queen Products' plea. On appeal, the plaintiffs argued that some of the enumerated exceptions to the general venue rule allowed them to sue Dairy Queen Products outside of Bexar County. One such exception that the plaintiffs relied on was that Dairy Queen Products could be sued in Travis County if it was the manufacturer of the product that caused the wife's injuries.[9] The plaintiffs argued that because Dairy Queen Products allowed the restaurant owner to use the Dairy Queen name

---

to be made properly for him and that the actor's reputation is an assurance to the user of the quality of the product. On the other hand, where it is clear that the actor's only connection with the chattel is that of a distributor of it (for example, as a wholesale or retail seller), he does not put it out as his own product and the rule stated in this section is inapplicable. Thus, one puts out a chattel as his own product when he puts it out under his name or affixes to it his trade name or trademark. When such identification is referred to on the label as an indication of the quality or wholesomeness of the chattel, there is an added emphasis that the user can rely upon the reputation of the persons so identified. . . .

8. The other two defendants named were the owner of the land and the building housing the Dairy Queen restaurant, and the lessee of the property who owned and operated the restaurant. The plaintiffs alleged that the defendants (1) breached a warranty of fitness of consumer goods manufactured by the defendants; (2) were strictly liable for selling defective food; (3) negligently dispensed tainted food; and (4) were liable under Tex. Bus. & Com. Code Ann. §§17.46 & 17.50 (Vernon Supp. 1983) (deceptive trade practices).

9. At that time, Tex. Rev. Civ. Stat. Ann. art. 1995, §31 (Vernon 1964 & Supp. 1982) (repealed), provided:

> Breach of warranty by a manufacturer.—Suits for breach of warranty by a manufacturer of consumer goods may be brought in any county where the cause of action or a part thereof accrued, or in any county where such manufacturer may have an agency or representative, or in the county in which the principal office of such company may be situated, or in the county where the plaintiff or plaintiffs reside.

Subdivision 31 has subsequently been recodified at Tex. Rev. Civ. Stat. Ann. art. 1995 §3 (c) (Vernon Supp. 1983).

on the restaurant's products, Dairy Queen could be held liable as the manufacturer of those products under the Restatement (Second) of Torts §400. 623 S.W.2d at 797. The court disagreed:

> The record establishes as a matter of law that a restaurant employee in the Burnet, Texas "Dairy Queen" was the literal "manufacturer" of the sandwich in the sense of actually assembling the various ingredients of the sandwich, processing them and preparing the sandwich from its various ingredients. Moreover, appellee was not the actual "vendor" of the sandwich to which §400 of the Restatement imputes the actual manufacturer's liability. In this case, the Burnet, Texas restaurant employee or employees were the literal manufacturer and the literal vendor. Reliance upon the Restatement is therefore misplaced. 623 S.W.2d at 805. . . .

Thus, even if the Nelsons could show at trial that IPCO knew that CALCO was distributing Inter-Trop Red 50 under the IPCO label, the Texas courts have made it clear that no cause of action can lie against IPCO as the "manufacturer" under section 400 of the Restatement.

C. Estoppel

The Nelsons contend also that if IPCO knew that CALCO was using IPCO labels, IPCO should be estopped from denying liability because the mislabeling caused the Nelsons to sue the wrong party. The Nelsons contend that because the label of the paint that allegedly caused Nelson's injuries carried IPCO's name, they brought suit in Texas only against IPCO, and that by the time they discovered that CALCO was the manufacturer of the paint, the statute of limitations had run against CALCO. Thus, they argue that IPCO should face liability for CALCO's acts.

Again, we do not believe that whether IPCO knew that CALCO was using IPCO's name is material here because the Nelsons failed to adduce any evidence that they detrimentally relied on the fact that IPCO's name was the only one on the label. Although the label did not carry CALCO's name, it listed CALCO's San Francisco address. The Nelsons' original lawsuit named CALCO as a defendant and alleged that CALCO manufactured and distributed Inter-Trop Red 50. Presumably the Nelsons' Alaska counsel discovered that CALCO manufactured Inter-Trop Red 50 from the fact that CALCO's address was on the label of the paint can in question. That the Nelsons named CALCO in their original complaint demonstrates that they did not detrimentally rely on the fact that only IPCO's name was on the label.

Because the Nelsons dismissed the suit before either IPCO or CALCO could answer, neither party misled the Nelsons as to who manufactured the paint that caused Nelson's injuries. However, the Nelsons were aware that CALCO existed and may have manufactured Inter-Trop Red 50, and the failure of Texas counsel to name CALCO as a defendant in the Texas suit cannot redound in the Nelsons' favor. Moreover, once the present action was brought, discovery was had and IPCO never misrepresented to the Nelsons or their attorney that it was the manufacturer of Inter-Trop Red 50.

D. CALCO as the Alter Ego of IPCO

Finally, the Nelsons assert that CALCO was simply an agent or conduit through which IPCO did its business, so that whether they sued IPCO or

CALCO, both are, in essence, the same. However, we find that the material facts with regard to this issue are undisputed, and that there is no basis for regarding CALCO as the alter ego of IPCO.

As a threshold matter, the Nelsons contend that the question whether a subsidiary is the alter ego of its parent is, in all cases, one for the jury. We disagree. Our past decisions make clear that, in the lack of sufficient evidence to place the alter ego issue in dispute, a corporate defendant may be entitled to summary judgment.

Under Texas law, the question whether a parent corporation can be held responsible for a subsidiary's acts rests in large part on whether the plaintiff seeks to hold the parent liable for a tort or contract claim. In a tort case, such as this, the Texas courts have been willing to hold a parent liable for a subsidiary's acts where the parent has so dominated the subsidiary that the subsidiary is found to be a mere agent or conduit through which the parent conducts its business. Of particular significance in most tort cases is whether the subsidiary is undercapitalized, because tort claimants usually have not voluntarily dealt with the subsidiary, and the question is whether a parent should be able to transfer a risk of loss or injury to members of the general public in the name of a subsidiary that may be marginally financed. . . .

Such a consideration is not at issue here. The present suit lies against the parent itself, not its subsidiary. Furthermore, the Nelsons do not even suggest that CALCO, or even IPCO for that matter, is undercapitalized. Nor is there any evidence in the record to that effect. Nonetheless, the Nelsons assert that CALCO was operated merely as an agent of IPCO, and that IPCO is therefore liable for CALCO's acts.

For example, the Nelsons assert that CALCO should be regarded as IPCO's alter ego because some of CALCO's directors sit on IPCO's board. Also relevant, they contend, is that IPCO owns 100% of CALCO's stock. Yet in [Gentry v. Credit Plan Corp., 528 S.W.2d 571 (Tex. 1975)], the Texas Supreme Court held that a "subsidiary corporation will not be regarded as the alter ego of its parent merely because of stock ownership, a duplication of some or all of the directors or officers, or an exercise of the control that stock ownership gives to stockholders." 528 S.W.2d at 573.

The factors relevant to determining whether a subsidiary will be held to be the alter ego of its parent, and thus impute liability to the parent, were recently discussed in . . . a case similar to the instant one. In [that case,] the plaintiffs were injured when a tire on the pickup truck in which they were traveling blew out and caused the truck to turn over. Although the tire carried the "Goodyear" trademark, it was not manufactured by Goodyear, but rather by its wholly-owned French subsidiary. Although Goodyear denied that it had designed, manufactured, or sold the tire, the plaintiffs sought to hold Goodyear liable on the ground that its French subsidiary was merely a conduit through which Goodyear carried on its business of manufacturing and selling tires under the Goodyear trademark.

The court listed the following factors as relevant to determining whether a subsidiary is a mere agent of the parent:

> [W]hether the two file consolidated income tax returns; whether operating capital is financed by the parent or borrowed from other sources; the extent to which separate books and accounts are kept; whether they both have common departments of business; whether they have separate meetings of shareholders and directors; [and] whether the

officer or director of the one corporation is permitted to determine the policies of the other. . . . 652 S.W.2d at 609.

[In the earlier case] the jury found that Goodyear's French subsidiary was not Goodyear's alter ego, and the jury's finding was upheld on appeal.

In the present case, the material facts are not in dispute. IPCO and CALCO do not file consolidated income tax returns. IPCO does not provide CALCO's operating capital, and CALCO has never borrowed money from IPCO (or anyone else, for that matter). CALCO keeps its financial records separate from those of IPCO's, and each corporation has its own account managers, treasurers and controllers. Each maintains its own headquarters. They have separate Board of Directors meetings. There are no mutual employees and they share no ownership of property. They each have their own distribution systems and sales force, and they each manage and maintain their own factories, as well as secure their own raw materials. Nor do IPCO and CALCO have the same operating officers. Although Grant Johnson, CALCO's chief operating officer, is an executive vice-president of IPCO, Johnson's position with IPCO appears to be in title only, since IPCO has never employed or paid Johnson, and Johnson is not involved in the operations of IPCO.

The Nelsons note that CALCO does not maintain its own research and development facilities, but rather uses IPCO's. However, CALCO pays IPCO for the research and development information it receives, just as it would pay any other company for that service. Similarly, although IPCO and CALCO jointly advertise some of their products, each corporation pays its proportionate share of costs. Although both IPCO and CALCO sell products under the "International Paint Company" trademark, the two are operated as separate companies and are represented as such.

In sum, the Nelsons have satisfied none of the criteria found to be indicative of an agency relationship between the parent and the subsidiary. The evidence makes clear that IPCO and CALCO are distinct entities, and that the district court correctly granted IPCO summary judgment on this issue. . . .

In Fletcher v. Atex, Inc., 68 F.3d 1451 (2d Cir. 1995), issues similar to those in *Nelson* were resolved in similar fashion. The plaintiff brought an action against Eastman Kodak Company and its wholly-owned subsidiary, Atex, Inc., alleging repetitive stress injuries resulting from plaintiff's use of a personal computer keyboard manufactured by Atex. The plaintiff argued that Kodak was liable as the parent on grounds similar to those advanced in *Nelson*. Applying New York law, the district court granted summary judgment in favor of Kodak. The court of appeals affirmed, citing *Nelson* and reaching essentially the same conclusions on the claims that Atex was the alter ego of Kodak and that Kodak was an apparent manufacturer under §400 of the Restatement (Second) of Torts. Regarding a concert-of-action allegation, the court of appeals concluded (68 F.3d at 1464-1466):

> The plaintiffs' final theory of liability is that Kodak acted in tortious concert with Atex in designing and marketing the allegedly defective keyboards. The plaintiffs present alternative arguments for Kodak's liability under the so-called concerted action doctrine. First, they argue that "the evidence of Kodak's direct participation in the marketing of the defective keyboard equipment" raises an issue of material fact regarding Kodak's act-

ing in concert with Atex. In the alternative, they argue that Kodak could be liable under a separate theory of concerted action under which liability may be premised upon "concerted action by substantial assistance." . . .

Under the first theory of concerted action, New York law "provides for joint and several liability on the part of all defendants having an understanding, express or tacit, to participate in a common plan or design to commit a tortious act." Rastelli v. Goodyear Tire & Rubber Co., 79 N.Y.2d 289, 295, 582 N.Y.S.2d 373, 375, 591 N.E.2d 222, 224 (1992). . . . The documents offered by the plaintiffs do not suggest any "agreement" between Kodak and Atex to act "jointly and tortiously." They merely refer to general statements about the "merger" between Atex and Kodak and the "marriage" between the two companies.

Furthermore, none of the evidence demonstrates that Kodak's actions were tortious. The fact that Kodak prepared guidelines for its employees to use in relation to their own computer workstations does not constitute tortious conduct with regard to the keyboards developed and sold by Atex. There is no allegation that Kodak's internal guidelines were ever used in conjunction with the design or manufacture of the Atex keyboards. . . .

In their second argument, the plaintiffs contend that even if there was no agreement between the parties to act tortiously, Kodak may be liable under the concerted action theory by providing "substantial assistance or encouragement" to Atex in furtherance of its tortious conduct. A "substantial assistance" claim based on §876 of the Restatement (Second) of Torts requires evidence that (1) the defendant knows that the other's conduct constitutes a breach of duty and (2) the defendant gives substantial assistance or encouragement to the other's conduct. Restatement (Second) of Torts §876(b).

We find that, viewed in the light most favorable to the plaintiffs, Kodak's general awareness of the hazards of repetitive stress injuries and the Kodak laboratory's evaluation of the Atex keyboards in 1990 are insufficient to raise a question of material fact regarding Kodak's knowledge of or substantial assistance in Atex's allegedly tortious conduct. Kodak's knowledge about repetitive stress injuries generally cannot be construed as knowledge of the alleged defective design of the Atex keyboard or Atex's alleged failure to warn keyboard users of the hazards of repetitive stress injuries. Furthermore, the plaintiffs have offered no evidence to contradict the defendant's assertions that Kodak's one-time evaluation of the keyboards in 1990 occurred years after the keyboards in question were designed and distributed. Finally, the plaintiffs present no evidence to suggest that Kodak was involved — either before or after the 1990 evaluation — in the decision to include warnings about repetitive stress disorders or user guidelines with Atex keyboards. Thus, we find that summary judgment on this claim was also appropriate.

PROBLEM TWENTY-SEVEN

Rona and Peter Godalfo called your office recently to discuss a products liability matter. The initial call was made by Rona, who seemed agitated and asked to see you as soon as possible. Rona identified herself as an officer of Safe Level Locks, Inc. (SLL). You have done legal planning for a friend of hers, and the friend suggested she call you. When Rona and Peter came in to see you it became clear that they have a products liability corporate problem that has taken on domestic relations overtones. The following story unfolded. Rona and Peter started a small business in 1985. Peter holds numerous patents for various kinds of commercial and residential locks. Rona has strong managerial capabilities. Their marriage brought together these skills and they parlayed them into a successful business. They have net assets worth over $2 million, primarily in stock in SLL, a closely held corporation. SLL owns a building on a two-acre lot in upstate New California, and employs about 20 workers. Both Rona and Peter draw substantial salaries from SLL. Their combined annual incomes exceed $150,000.

Peter has something of the mad genius in him. Two years ago he developed and patented a lock that he hopes to market to nuclear power plants. The lock is highly sophisticated, responding to electronic signals. Without seeking advice of counsel, the Godalfos formed a new corporation, High Tech Extension, Inc. (HTE), to manufacture and market these new electronic locks.

Rona has been reading the business literature and is afraid that Peter's tomfoolery will end up putting them into bankruptcy. The SLL products produced by the other company are very low-risk items. Even if an SLL lock does not work properly, very little can go wrong that will result in injury to persons or property. On the other hand, HTE locks could lead to disaster should they fail to operate. Furthermore, improper maintenance of an HTE lock could cause the lock to fail. Rona contends that more than 15 years of hard work and financial success could go up in smoke if an HTE lock should fail and cause a disastrous accident. Peter argues that the HTE locks are terrific new products that enhance safety. "We can make a fortune and help a lot of people," he insists. Rona wants out of HTE and Peter insists on staying in. Peter contends that he has created a separate corporation — and that should be enough.

As you probe into the facts in your questioning, you discover that SLL and HTE use the same employees and the same workplace to manufacture their respective locks. Salaries to employees are prorated based on the gross receipts of the two corporations. Thus, employees are paid biweekly from a check issued by SLL. The books, however, reflect a payment of 25 percent from HTE to SLL. Both companies maintain separate products liability insurance policies, with the same carrier, for $2 million each, with a $250,000 deductible. Two weeks ago, the insurance company notified the Godalfos that it will require them to insure both companies under one policy, with a substantial increase in premium and an increase in the deductible to $500,000. Rona called the agent, who explained that the carrier is concerned that both corporations could be liable for any losses caused by defective HTE locks. The agent's statement upset Rona deeply, and led her to call your office.

Rona insists that she will walk away from the business (and the marriage) unless SLL is protected from products liability that could wipe it out because of an HTE accident. She wants to know whether you can assure her that SLL can be insulated from HTE liability. Peter has his back against the wall. He knows he must provide Rona her assurance or close down HTE. They ask you to prepare a memorandum telling them how to accomplish the goal of insulating SLL.

Assume that Nelson v. International Paint, supra, is the law of New California and that the material that follows *Nelson* accurately reflects the majority view in the United States. Prepare a memorandum advising the Godalfos as to whether they can protect SLL, and, if so, what steps they should take to accomplish that objective.

In their article excerpted supra, Professors Easterbrook and Fischel develop and critique at least four other ways of reducing the temptations for corporate managers to over-engage their firms in risky activities. Referring to "the problem of moral hazard," the authors consider: (1) minimum capital requirements; (2) mandatory liability insurance requirements; (3) personal liability imposed directly on the managers themselves; and (4) direct administrative regulation of especially risky activities, such as the construction and operation of nuclear power plants (52 U. Chi. L. Rev. at 114-117).

The third of these suggestions has received much attention in the law journals in past years. Some writers believe that such penalties are unnecessary — that, with reasonable monitoring of managerial behavior, adequate levels of corporate compliance with societal norms can be achieved. See, e.g., K. Elzinga & W. Breit, The Antitrust Penalties: A Study in Law and Economics 115, 134-135 (1976). Other observers, less confident in relatively conservative measures, have suggested a variety of penalties (typically criminal in nature) aimed at managers individually. See, e.g., John C. Coffee, "No Soul to Damn, No Body to Kick": An Unscandalized Inquiry into the Problem of Corporate Punishment, 79 Mich. L. Rev. 386 (1981).

The possibility of criminal sanctions being imposed on products manufacturers was brought closer to home when, on September 13, 1978, the Grand Jury for Elkhart County, Indiana, returned an indictment charging Ford Motor Company with recklessly designing and manufacturing a 1973 Pinto automobile in which three teenage girls were incinerated when their automobile's gas tank exploded after a rear-end collision. That case provided a point of departure for Malcolm Wheeler in his article, The Use of Criminal Statutes to Regulate Product Safety, 13 J. Legal Stud. 593 (1984). The author concludes:

> In recent years, legislatures and, to a lesser extent, prosecutors have increasingly resorted to criminal sanctions against manufacturers to regulate the risk associated with defective products. Deterrence is the only commonly advanced penal purpose that might, even in theory, be furthered by the new trend. This article has shown the existence of substantial, and perhaps excessive, deterrence of manufacturers by social institutions now in place: existing market forces, private tort actions, and civil regulatory systems. Any desirable additional deterrence can best be obtained by making minor modifications to those systems. Enormous resources must be committed to any extensive system of criminal control. There is no reason to believe that this game is worth the candle. [Id. at 618.]

One interesting aspect of this question is the extent to which penalties aimed at managers individually may induce firms to supply managers with some form or other of indemnity against manager-directed liabilities. Professor Kraakman explores this possibility in Corporate Liability Strategies and the Costs of Legal Controls, 93 Yale L.J. 857 (1984):

> The continuum from enterprise to gatekeeper [manager] liability imposes increasingly burdensome compliance costs on firms, costs that grow in tandem with the difficulty of deterring low-visibility offenses. On the one hand, the legal risks of the firm's individual participants grow more onerous as we expand the scope of absolute personal liability and the range of participants at risk. On the other hand, broadening the scope of liability and limiting opportunities for risk shifting increases the would-be offender's costs of coordinating illegal activity and "bonds" the firm's compliance more securely.
>
> These observations, however, only begin the investigation of the relationship between penalties and organizational structure. The operation of particular systems of gatekeeper liability remains to be explored, as does the difficult issue of when gatekeeper liability

is a sensible enforcement tool at all. Although gatekeeper liability is the most intrusive and most costly of the liability strategies, it may nonetheless rank below other kinds of regulatory response to chronic noncompliance on both dimensions. The next step beyond conscripting gatekeepers is, after all, to impose upon the firm specialized public monitors who are legally empowered to report wrongdoing or veto it on the spot. Thus, while gatekeeper liability is more draconian than simpler modes of dual liability, it is less intrusive than at least some forms of on-site inspection or reporting. [Id. at 897.]

Professor Lynn LoPucki concludes that it will be increasingly possible in the future for enterprises to "judgment-proof" themselves from tort liability. See Lynn M. LoPucki, The Death of Liability, 106 Yale L.J. 1 (1996). Among the strategies that will accomplish this objective are what he describes as "ownership strategies." The parent-subsidiary structure, reflected in the preceding materials, will play an important role. In addition, and of even greater potential, is asset securitization. LoPucki explains (106 Yale L.J. at 23-28):

Asset securitization is the issuance of securities representing the ownership of designated assets. In the prototypical asset-securitization transaction, the asset is the accounts receivable of a business. As part of the asset-securitization transaction, the debtor creates a "bankruptcy remote vehicle," a separate legal entity, and "sells" the accounts to it. The bankruptcy remote entity obtains the money to buy the assets through a public or private offering of its own securities. The debtor may continue to service the accounts under contract with the bankruptcy remote entity, processing payments, dunning customers who fail to pay, and filing lawsuits against some of them. All that necessarily changes is that the debtor no longer owns the accounts.

Asset securitization is by far the most rapidly growing segment of the U.S. credit markets. Financial historians have traced asset securitization back more than a century, but the boom in asset securitization began in the 1970s with the U.S. government's efforts to encourage the development of secondary mortgage markets. Once the technique proved successful, it quickly spread to student-loan-backed securities, credit-card-receivable-backed securities and other sectors of finance. From 1990 to 1993, the percentage of all consumer debt that is securitized grew from 10.5% to 15.5%. By 1988, securitized credit obligation issuers accounted for about 15.7% of total net borrowing by financial sectors of the U.S. credit markets; by the second quarter of 1993, they accounted for 38.8%. It had been predicted that by 1997, 80% or more of all new capitalization might be securitized — a prediction that may not be far wrong.

Asset securitization is both a substitute for borrowing and a powerful new strategy for judgment proofing. Like the parent-subsidiary strategy, the asset-securitization strategy puts ownership of the company's valuable assets in an entity separate from the one that is at risk for liability. The advantage of the asset-securitization strategy over the parent-subsidiary strategy is virtual elimination of the risk that the courts will disregard the entity that holds the assets. Though the bankruptcy remote vehicle is created pursuant to the debtor's plan, it is not only separately incorporated but is at all times controlled by arms-length investors. The terms of the transaction between the debtor and the bankruptcy remote vehicle have real economic consequences for both. What is perhaps more important, by the time the issues are litigated, the bankruptcy remote vehicle may be publicly held, with hundreds or thousands of innocent investors. Considering that even the most provocative division of a company into separate asset-holding and liability-incurring entities — one with one hundred percent congruity of ownership — is likely to be honored by the courts, its seems unlikely that the courts will consolidate the bankruptcy remote vehicles created in asset securitizations, which typically have no congruity of ownership with the debtor. . . .

Through asset securitization, a company potentially could divest itself of all of its assets, yet continue to use all of those assets in the continued operation of its business. To grasp the enormous potential, assume that, through a series of asset securitizations, Exxon Corporation disposes of all of its assets. As the cash from these transactions becomes available, Exxon distributes the cash to its shareholders in the form of dividends, leaving the company with neither assets nor liabilities. (I will refer to this judgment-proof Exxon as "Zero-Asset Exxon.") Because Exxon contracts to continue use of each asset even as it sells it, the operations of Zero-Asset Exxon remain exactly as they were when it was a multi-billion dollar company. But as a result of the asset securitization transactions and the distribution of the proceeds, Zero-Asset Exxon is now judgment proof. . . .

Asset securitization may be the silver bullet capable of killing liability. In the few skirmishes in which asset securitization structures have been challenged in bankruptcy, they have been upheld. Though the effect ultimately may be to defeat liability interests, this outcome should not be surprising. Liability is in disrepute. Asset securitization, by contrast, is widely regarded as an engine of the U.S. economy. . . .

Having identified the various judgment-proofing strategies, the author acknowledges that regulators are certain to make efforts to constrain such behavior and thereby rescue the liability system. One method of constraining judgment-proofing strategies would be for regulators to condition the right to do business in this country on a demonstration of financial responsibility. Regarding this possibility LoPucki observes (106 Yale L.J. at 88-89):

Whatever the method of enforcement, if the system [of imposing financial responsibility] worked, it would bar persons not wealthy enough to demonstrate financial responsibility . . . from engaging in liability-generating economic activity. . . . This frames a central tension in the struggle over liability: Americans do not want judgment-proof businesses to be able to operate, but neither do they want to exclude persons of moderate means from participation in the economy. The system currently accommodates that conflict by permitting persons who cannot demonstrate financial responsibility to participate in all but a few industries [such as banking and insurance] and excusing nonpayment of liabilities when they exceed the debtor's ability to pay.

To limit participation in the economy to those who could prove financial responsibility adequate for the role they chose would drastically reduce economic opportunity for all but the wealthiest segment of society. Not only would the reduction injure those barred from businesses and occupations because they could not demonstrate financial responsibility, but their absence would also reduce competition in the businesses and occupations that they could not enter. Economic activity would slow, prices would increase, and the gap between rich and poor would widen.

If an economy-wide requirement of financial responsibility were adopted, there would be strong pressures to relax the standards for persons of modest means. The issue would be how to separate the wealthy from the not-so-wealthy so that the system could favor the latter. But that brings the inquiry full circle. The liability system, as currently conceived, *is* a system for determining "what wealth particular judgment creditors should be able to reach." The problem is that the system's schemes for making that determination have consistently been defeated by strategy. What we need, and currently do not have, are meaningful definitions of a "wealthy person" and of that person's "wealth."

LoPucki's conclusion is as provocative as his analysis (106 Yale L.J. at 90):

. . . Judgment proofing need not spread to every industry to kill the liability system. Once substantial numbers of large companies judgment-proof substantial portions of their operations, the inequity of the system will be apparent. The system will force businesses that expose themselves to liability to pay large judgments for liability, but will be unable to reach those who resist. Such glaring inequity will lead to action. Unless the resistors can be brought under control, it is likely that the system will be dismantled.

Strategies by which the system can attempt to postpone liability's day of reckoning are plentiful. But they are drastic measures that would require traumatic change. Ultimately, nearly all are vulnerable to counter strategies. General financial responsibility requirements could provide a long term solution, but only at a political cost that the system may be unwilling to pay. Given a choice between having to be financially responsible to participate in the economy and the death of liability, the American people may well choose the latter.

Professor James J. White responds to LoPucki's analysis in Corporate Judgment Proofing: A Response to Lynn M. LoPucki's The Death of Liability, 107 Yale L.J. 1363 (1998). White reads LoPucki as addressing the potential for judgment proofing by publicly traded companies. He begins his critique by relying on basic economic theory (107 Yale L.J. at 1369):

> The poker metaphor [used by LoPucki — that judgment proof firms are like poker players who play without putting chips in the pot —] reveals the problem with the hypothesis. No one will allow a person to play poker unless that person puts chips in the pot and thereby commits himself to pay if he loses. In the hypothetical leveraged corporation, the creditors who are asked to put up $90 million of the chips will understand that their chips stand behind only $10 million of capital and will appreciate that they will lose $90 million if the business fails. Understanding that they are being made to take the risks that are traditionally assigned to the equity holders, but appreciating that they will not enjoy the gains of equity holders, the lenders will either refuse to make the loan or insist upon a share of the gains that looks much like the payment that would have to be made to an equity holder. Put another way, the lenders to such a highly leveraged business will behave like equity holders and will insist upon the control and payment that normally goes to equity holders, even though they are technically creditors. The changes wrought by the contract creditors (bringing about the end of a business or diminishing its leverage) will also protect the involuntary creditors.

White then turns to empirical data drawn from Standard & Poor's Compustat database that show that the trends predicted by LoPucki are not in place. For example, White points out that ratios of secured debt to assets and assets to liabilities have remained constant from 1981 through 1995. He concludes (107 Yale L.J. at 1412):

> The specter of widespread judgment proofing by commercial firms is mere fantasy. The data from the Compustat database show that public companies grant much more modest levels of security than would be necessary to render themselves judgment proof. The same data show that most companies have free assets that greatly exceed their liabilities and that their asset-to-liability ratios have changed only modestly over the last fifteen years. The data also show that these public companies carry substantial amounts of liability insurance — apparently the same or greater insurance coverage than fifteen years ago. While these data do not disprove the possibility of judgment proofing by an occasional company, they refute the proposition that judgment proofing is widespread among American commercial firms.
>
> The many barriers to judgment proofing discussed in Part III suggest that the absence of judgment proofing is unlikely to change. Among the barriers is the resistance of contract creditors, which redounds not only to their benefit but also to the benefit of in-

voluntary creditors such as tort claimants. Many laws, such as workers' compensation laws, stand directly in the way, and a close examination of a subsidiary's legal and economic relation to its parent shows that this theoretical avenue to judgment proofing is difficult and abstract.

Although my data are taken exclusively from public companies, I believe that data from private companies would be no different. Almost all of the barriers in Part III to judgment proofing apply equally to public and private firms. And even if the judgment-proofing devices identified by Professor LoPucki were used more frequently by private than by public firms, their use would present a substantially smaller social problem, for a company's liability-producing capacity is proportional to its size. In addition, contract creditors and other guardians of corporate solvency may be even more watchful of private than of public companies.

In summary, corporate judgment proofing is not a significant social problem today, and it is unlikely to become one. Liability lives.

Professor LoPucki's reply to White's critique appears in Lynn LoPucki, Virtual Judgment Proofing: A Rejoinder, 107 Yale L.J. 1413 (1998). In addition to accusing White of artificially construing his Death of Liability piece as applicable only to publicly traded companies and quarreling with White's methodology, LoPucki introduces the idea of "virtual companies" (107 Yale L.J. at 1433-34):

The computerization of contracting is driven by forces much larger than the desire to avoid liability. For years, analysts have been predicting the advent of virtual companies — companies that literally consist of nothing but a web of contractual relationships. Instead of setting up its own data processing, "customer service, telemarketing, billing and collection, purchasing, employee training, accounting, publishing, legal administration and so on," the virtual company will "outsource" these functions — that is, contract with others to provide them:

Let's take, for an example, an airline. A handful of strategists put their heads together to decide where to fly and what to charge. As with many airlines these days, they lease their aircraft and hire flight and ground crews on contract. But then they hit the networks to find vendors for just about all other operations — passenger reservations, baggage tracking, accounting, aircraft loading, weather monitoring, route planning and seat-revenue maximizing. Almost overnight, they're flying.

Because the virtual company does not own the resources it commandeers, it is born judgment proof. Even if it is highly profitable, a liberal dividend policy will keep it judgment proof without running afoul of the law.

Alternatively, a virtual company can take on the role of a company that owns things, but does not do things. Sara Lee was recently hailed by the *Wall Street Journal* as the first virtual company. Sara Lee plans to outsource the manufacturing of its products and become merely a distributor. To accomplish that, the company is selling its manufacturing operations. That move alone will not relieve Sara Lee of liability for its products. But it would be only a short step further for Sara Lee to contract for the sale and distribution of its products by others. Sara Lee's sole assets would then be the trademarks and contract rights. The new Restatement (Third) of Torts makes clear that such a company would not be liable to purchasers of products bearing the company's trademark provided that the company did not participate substantially in the design, manufacture, or distribution of the product. The no-name subcontractors who manufactured and distributed for Sara Lee could judgment proof themselves to the limit of the law, without concern for public relations. They would be invisible to Sara Lee's customers in the ordinary operation of the business, just as was the franchisee in Mobil Oil v. Bransford. They would emerge from the shadows only to show their empty pockets in litigation. Neither Sara Lee nor its subcontractors would have to pay products liability claims.

The specter of judgment proofing and the specter of the virtual company are one and the same, and the specter is advancing. White's rallying cry, "Liability lives," remains accurate. But for how long?

For further developments in the ongoing judgment proofing debate, see Steven L. Schwarcz, The Inherent Irrationality of Judgment Proofing, 52 Stan. L. Rev. 1 (1999) (arguing that arm's-length transactions will not be lucrative for judgment proofing purposes because of tax, public image, and liability considerations that will be accounted for in contracts and further arguing that non-arm's-length transactions can be overcome by traditional legal doctrine); Lynn M. LoPucki, The Irrefutable Logic of Judgment Proofing, 52 Stan. L. Rev. 55 (1999) (refuting Schwarcz's argument, point by point). For an innovative solution to the judgment proofing problem, see Nina A. Mendelson, A Control-Based Approach to Shareholder Liability for Corporate Torts, 102 Colum L. Rev. 1203 (2002) (proposing a "control-based" approach that would discriminate among shareholders to selectively pierce the corporate veil).

B. A SPECIAL EXTENSION OF LIABILITY: SUCCESSOR CORPORATIONS

Martin v. Abbott Laboratories
102 Wash. 2d 581, 689 P.2d 368 (1984) (en banc)

[This case was also discussed in Chapter Three, dealing with causation. The underlying substantive issue is whether pharmaceutical companies should be liable for harm allegedly caused by DES, a prescription drug manufactured and sold by the defendants. One subsidiary issue, of primary importance here, is whether Stanlabs Pharmaceutical Company, which purchased all of the assets of Stanley Drug Products, Inc., can be held liable for harm allegedly caused by drugs manufactured and sold by Stanley before the sale of Stanley's assets to Stanlab. The portions of the majority and dissenting opinions dealing with this issue are reproduced herein.]

DORE, J. . . .

The Martins contend that the trial court erred in granting summary judgment in favor of Stanlabs Pharmaceutical Company for acts of Stanley Drug Products, Inc. Traditionally, a corporation purchasing the assets of another corporation does not, by reason of the purchase of assets, become liable for the debts and liabilities of the selling corporation. The courts have recognized, however, that the traditional rule allows a transferring corporation, under certain circumstances, to effectively avoid its obligations to the detriment of *creditors* and minority *shareholders*. Thus, Washington has recognized four narrow exceptions to the traditional rule: (1) the purchaser expressly or impliedly agrees to assume liability; (2) the purchase is a de facto merger or consolidation; (3) the purchaser is a mere continuation of the seller; or (4) the transfer of assets is for the fraudulent purpose of escaping liability. In any of these four circumstances, the court will

A Special Extension of Liability: Successor Corporations

find that the acquiring entity is a successor to the liabilities and obligations of the selling corporation.

Recently, however, courts have come to recognize that the traditional rule of nonliability, with its four exceptions, was developed solely on corporate law principles to protect the rights of commercial creditors and dissenting shareholders following corporate acquisitions. These traditional rules of successor liability fail to address the particular circumstances of a products liability claimant.

> Although the common law exceptions protect commercial creditors, they frequently leave the products liability plaintiff without a remedy. Since an acquiring corporation will generally purchase the transferor's assets for consideration adequate to avoid those known liabilities that the traditional rule seeks to protect (i.e., traditional debts and obligations), the traditional rule looks to the transferor as the source of recovery. If, however, the transferor has dissolved, and if more than two years have elapsed from the time of dissolution, the injured plaintiff is left without a remedy. Thus, while the traditional rules of corporate law satisfy the needs of traditional creditors whose claims arise before or soon after the predecessor's dissolution, those rules provide no adequate remedy for the typical products liability plaintiff whose claims frequently arise years after the product's purchase.
>
> The failure of the traditional rules of successor liability to meet the needs of the products liability plaintiff results from the rule's limited purpose. The rule's purpose is to protect persons having obligations against a business entity. Although a products liability plaintiff falls into that class of person, the traditional rule was fashioned to meet the needs of only those claimants whose claims were clearly identifiable at the time of the transfer. Fashioned long before the advent of the modern products liability doctrine, the traditional rule did not anticipate the social policies underlying the new doctrine. Consequently, the application of the traditional rule frustrates the policies of modern products liability. (Footnotes omitted.) Casenote, Successor Liability in Washington, 6 U. Puget Sound L. Rev. 323, 331-33 (1983).

In an effort to make the traditional corporate approach more responsive to products liability law, several courts have broadened the "mere continuation" exception in order to expand corporate successor liability in certain situations. See [Turner v. Bituminous Casualty Co., 397 Mich. 406, 422-431, 244 N.W.2d 873 (1976)]; Cyr v. B. Offen & Co., Inc., 501 F.2d 1145, 1152-54 (1st Cir. 1974).

The "mere continuation" exception was first expanded by a federal court applying New Hampshire law in Cyr v. B. Offen & Co., Inc., supra, 501 F.2d at 1152-54. In *Cyr*, two printing press employees were seriously injured in 1969 by the drying ovens of a machine manufactured in 1959 by B. Offen & Company, a sole proprietorship. In 1963, a group of employees of the original manufacturer had formed the defendant corporation, B. Offen & Company, Inc., and had purchased for cash the drying system of the presses from the executor of the estate of the sole proprietor. The contract of sale between the successor corporation and the predecessor's estate provided for the purchase of the predecessor's good will, contract and service obligations, and the continued operation of the predecessor's business without substantial change. The contract expressly disclaimed successor corporation liability for costs incurred by the torts of the predecessor. The court held that there was sufficient justification for a jury to treat the successor corporation as the mere continuation of its predecessor for the purposes of imposing tort liability for injuries caused by defective products. It found that the successor corporation continued to produce the same product, through the same employees, in the same physical plant, and under the same supervision as its predecessor, and that by use of essentially the same name held itself out to the world as the same enterprise.

The *Cyr* court justified its holding on the public policy considerations underlying strict products liability. It recognized that the successor corporation, not being the original manufacturer, is not the specific legal entity that placed the defective product in the stream of commerce or made implied representations as to its safety. Nonetheless, there were several other policy justifications for imposing strict products liability on the successor. The first was, in essence, the risk-spreading approach:

> The very existence of strict liability for manufacturers implies a basic judgment that the hazards of predicting and insuring for risk from defective products are better borne by the manufacturer than by the consumer. The manufacturer's successor, carrying over the experience and expertise of the manufacturer, is likewise in a better position than the consumer to gauge the risks and the costs of meeting them. The successor knows the product, is as able to calculate the risk of defects as the predecessor, is in position to insure therefor and reflect such cost in sale negotiations, and is the only entity capable of improving the quality of the product. *Cyr* at 1154.
>
> The court also reasoned that the successor corporation, having reaped the benefits of continuing its predecessor's product line, exploiting its accumulated good will and enjoying the patronage of its established customers, should be made to bear some of the burdens of continuity, namely, liability for injuries caused by its defective products. . . .

Rather than expand a rule designed for other purposes, the California Supreme Court developed an exception for successor liability specifically designed to deal with products liability claims. Ray v. Alad Corp., 19 Cal. 3d 22, 560 P.2d 3, 136 Cal. Rptr. 574 (1977).

In *Ray,* the manufacturer of a defective ladder had sold its assets for cash and dissolved prior to the products liability claim. A new and separately owned corporation acquired the plant, equipment, inventory, trade name, personnel, customer lists, and goodwill of the manufacturer, and continued the same line of business under the same corporate name. There was no intervening manufacturing hiatus during or after the sales transaction. The court recognized that if it applied the traditional successor liability rules, the victim would be without a remedy because the predecessor had received adequate consideration for its assets, distributed the consideration to its shareholders, and dissolved before the plaintiff's claim arose. The court determined that none of the four stated exceptions to the general rule of nonliability under the traditional corporate law approach was a sufficient basis for imposing liability on the purchasing corporation. Nevertheless, the court determined that a departure from that traditional approach was called for by the policies underlying strict tort liability for injuries caused by defective products. Rather than adopt the expanded "mere continuation" exception to the corporate law approach as developed in *Cyr* . . . the *Ray* court abandoned the traditional analysis. It developed instead the following formulation, which has since come to be known as the "product line" approach to successor corporation liability for injuries caused by defective products:

> We . . . conclude that a party which acquires a manufacturing business and continues the output of its line of products under the circumstances here presented assumes strict

tort liability for defects in units of the same product line previously manufactured and distributed by the entity from which the business was acquired. *Ray,* at 34, 560 P.2d 3, 136 Cal. Rptr. 574.

The *Ray* court formulated this successor liability test based on the underlying strict products liability policies of compensation of injured victims and the allocation of product defect causing injury costs throughout society.

> [C]onsiderations favoring continued protection for injured users of defective products . . . include (1) the nonavailability to plaintiff of any adequate remedy against [the transferor] as a result of [their] liquidation prior to plaintiff's injury, (2) the availability to [the transferee] of the knowledge necessary for gauging the risks of injury from previously manufactured [units] together with the opportunity to provide for meeting the cost arising from those risks by spreading it among current purchasers of the product line and (3) the fact that the good will transferred to and enjoyed by [the transferee] could not have been enjoyed by [the transferor] without the burden of liability for defects in [units] sold under its aegis. *Ray,* at 25, 560 P.2d 3, 136 Cal. Rptr. 574.

The court's duty under the *Ray* rule is (1) to determine whether the transferee has acquired substantially all the transferor's assets, leaving no more than a mere corporate shell; (2) to determine whether the transferee is holding itself out to the general public as a continuation of the transferor by producing the same product line under a similar name; and (3) to determine whether the transferee is benefiting from the goodwill of the transferor. . . .

We now find it appropriate to adopt the *Ray* "product-line" criteria for successor liability in products liability actions. . . .

While both the product-line exception and the expanded mere continuation exception are founded on the same principles, we find it appropriate to retain the traditional corporate exceptions for their intended purposes and adopt the product-line exception specifically formulated for product liability claims.

This narrowly drawn rule strikes a fair balance among the competing considerations of products liability and corporate acquisitions. Imposition of liability is properly based on the successor's receipt of the benefit from the predecessor's product line. The benefit of being able to take over a going concern manufacturing a specific product line is necessarily burdened with potential products liability linked to the product line. This standard allows the parties to a transfer to consider potential products liability and in fairness to the competing considerations still leaves some claimants uncompensated and some forms of transfer immune.

In the case at bar, the same factors discussed by this court in [Meisel v. M & N Modern Hydraulic Press Co., 97 Wash. 2d 403, 645 P.2d 689 (1982),] preclude the grant of summary judgment to Stanlabs Pharmaceutical Company. All reasonable inferences must be resolved against the movant and considered in the light most favorable to the nonmoving party. Specifically, this court must assume, for summary judgment purposes, that the Martins have no other remedy than that against Stanlabs Pharmaceutical Company. The affidavits, depositions, and admissions show that Stanlabs Pharmaceutical Company purchased substantially all of the assets of Stanley Drug Products, Inc., including all going concern value, customers lists, and the name Stanley Drug Products, Inc. Further, issues of fact remain concerning Stanlabs Pharmaceutical Company's continuation of Stanley

Drug Products, Inc.'s tabletizing and distribution of DES, the similarity of Stanlabs Pharmaceutical Company's and Stanley Drug Products, Inc.'s names and product lines, the use by Stanlabs Pharmaceutical Company of containers bearing Stanley Drug Products, Inc.'s name after Stanlabs Pharmaceutical Company succeeded to its assets, and Stanlabs Pharmaceutical Company's assumption of Stanley Drug Products, Inc.'s goodwill.

Here, only Stanlabs Pharmaceutical Company moved for summary judgment. Given the trial court's apparent application of an incorrect legal standard — one that does not take into account our adoption of the *Ray* criteria — and given the facts recited above which arguably support a finding of successor liability, we hold that the trial court erred in granting Stanlabs Pharmaceutical Company's motion for summary judgment. . . .

We remand to the trial court to proceed in accordance with the provisions of this opinion.

PEARSON, J. (concurring in part, dissenting in part).

I concur with the majority except with respect to the imposition of strict liability on Stanlabs Pharmaceutical Company because of its status as successor corporation to Stanley Drug Products, Inc. It is my belief that the traditional rule of nonliability for successor corporations should not be abandoned in favor of the product line rule of Ray v. Alad Corp., 19 Cal. 3d 22, 560 P.2d 3, 136 Cal. Rptr. 574 (1977). I realize that the majority's adoption of the *Ray* rule is consistent with dicta appearing in Meisel v. M & N Modern Hydraulic Press Co., 97 Wash. 2d 403, 645 P.2d 689 (1982). In *Meisel* we noted, in a unanimous opinion, that the *Ray* rule "may well be salutary, and it would not be inconsistent with this court's prior holdings to adopt it." *Meisel,* at 408 n.1, 645 P.2d 689. However, upon further reflection, I am now convinced that the *Ray* product line rule is inconsistent with several major policy considerations underlying the imposition of strict liability. These policy considerations are ignored by the majority.

I

Initially, I note that in the 7 years since *Ray* was decided only two other jurisdictions have adopted the product line rule. See Ramirez v. Amsted Indus., Inc., 86 N.J. 332, 431 A.2d 811 (1981); Dawejko v. Jorgensen Steel Co., 290 Pa. Super. 15, 434 A.2d 106 (1981). The majority of jurisdictions which have addressed the question of whether to impose strict liability on a successor corporation have expressly rejected the *Ray* approach.

II . . .

It is readily apparent that the purpose of strict liability . . . is in no way furthered by holding a successor corporation liable for defects in its predecessor's products merely because the successor manufactures the same type of product as did the predecessor. The successor is outside the original producing and marketing chain. The successor did not make the product, nor did it place the product into the channels of trade. In short, the successor had nothing to do with the creation of the risk presented by the defective product. Moreover, since the successor was never in a position to eliminate the risk, a major purpose of strict liability in modifying the manufacturer's behavior is also lost. . . .

III

I turn now to examine the points of justification offered in support of the *Ray* rule.

The first justification offered by the courts which have adopted *Ray* is that the plaintiff has lost his remedy against the dissolved predecessor and can only sue the successor; there is no one else to look to. It seems to me, however, that this is merely a statement of the problem rather than a justification for any particular solution to the problem. . . .

The second justification offered in support of the *Ray* approach is that the successor corporation is better able to gauge the risks of liability, insure against those risks, and spread the cost among the consuming public, than is the injured plaintiff. Simply stated, the successor should be liable because it can afford it.

I fear that this rationale is illusory. I question whether the successor may, realistically, be able to obtain open-ended products liability insurance to cover accidents resulting from defects in the predecessor's product. Recent studies indicate that many manufacturers, especially smaller companies, have great difficulty obtaining products liability insurance even for their *own* products, and find it impossible to cover the cost by raising prices because they have to compete with larger manufacturers who can keep the price down. . . .

The final justification offered for the *Ray* rule is that, because the successor enjoys the good will of the predecessor, the successor should bear the corresponding burden of liability for the predecessor's products which created that good will. The problem with this benefit/burden rationale is that the benefit, in terms of good will stemming from an established trade name or product, has been considered and negotiated during the acquisition of the predecessor corporation. The successor, then, has already paid once for its predecessor's good will. To require the successor to assume liability for its predecessor's defective products on the basis of acquired good will would be, in effect, requiring the successor to pay twice for that good will. This hardly seems equitable, especially when one considers that it is the predecessor, and not the successor, which has benefited most directly from this intangible good will. The predecessor has received the profits from the sale of the product which created the good will, in addition to receiving the profit from the sale as an asset of the good will itself. It is true that the successor does benefit in a remote way from the good will purchased from the predecessor. However, the revelation of past production failures injures that good will and deprives the successor of the benefit it has purchased. Thus, the successor has lost the benefit of its bargain. Imposing strict liability upon a successor corporation because that corporation is supposedly enjoying the benefits of its predecessor's good will is illogical where those benefits no longer remain. Yet that is what the majority does by adopting the product line exception to the general rule of successor nonliability. . . .

I would affirm the trial court's grant of summary judgment to Stanlabs Pharmaceutical Company.

As indicated in the opinions in *Martin*, several states, including Washington, have adopted the product-line extension of successor liability. Several others have imposed liability based on a continuation of the predecessor's business enterprise even when there was no stock transfer or a common identity of corporate directors. See, e.g., Andrews v. John E. Smith's Sons, Co., 369 So. 2d 781 (Ala. 1979); Turner v. Bituminous Casualty Co., 244 N.W.2d 873 (Mich. 1976). In Foster v. Cone-Blanchard Machine Co., 597 N.W.2d 506 (Mich. 1999), the Michigan Supreme Court refused to apply *Turner* against a successor when the predecessor (in *Foster,* an "intermediate successor,") continued as an active corporation after the transfer-of-assets transaction. The availability of the predecessor, the court reasoned, eliminated the need to impose successor liability.

An overwhelming majority of courts have rejected both the product-line and continuation of business enterprise rules in favor of the four traditional bases of successor liability outlined at the outset of the majority opinion in *Martin*. See, e.g., Florom v. Elliott Mfg., 867 F.2d 570 (10th Cir. 1989) (applying Colorado law); Sorenson v. Allied Products Corp., 706 N.E.2d 1097 (Ind. App. 1999); Pancratz v. Monsanto Co., 547 N.W.2d 198 (Iowa 1996); Nissen Corp. v. Miller, 594 A.2d 564 (Md. 1991); Costello v. Unipress Corp., No. C6-95-2341, 1996 WL 106215 (Minn. Ct. App. Mar. 12, 1996); Welco Industries, Inc. v. Applied Companies, 617 N.E.2d 1129 (Ohio 1993); Downtowner, Inc. v. Acrometal Products, Inc., 347 N.W.2d 118 (N.D. 1984); Harris v. T. I., Inc., 413 S.E.2d 605 (Va. 1992); Jordan v. Ravenswood Aluminum Corp., 455 S.E.2d 561 (W. Va. 1995); Fish v. Amsted Industries, Inc., 376 N.W.2d 820 (Wis. 1985).

The Restatement (Third) of Torts: Products Liability §12 (1998) adopts the majority position on the issue of successor liability.

In some products liability cases, successor liability is employed in tandem with veil piercing directed to shareholders. For example, in Patin v. Thoroughbred Power Boats, Inc. 294 F.3d 640 (5th Cir. 2002) the husband and wife owners of a boat manufacturing corporation formed a new corporation to continue their operations following fears of liability. The court allowed plaintiffs injured by a predecessor's boat to sue the successor corporation because it was found to be a "mere continuation" of its predecessor. In reaching this conclusion, the court noted that the successor was wholly owned by the same shareholders, located at the same address, used the same assets and had the same directors. In further allowing the plaintiff to pierce the corporate veil and sue the shareholders directly, the court noted that the second corporation was a "mere instrumentality" of the shareholders and that it had been formed for an improper purpose — to escape liability.

The law review literature on the successor liability question is extensive. See, e.g., Michael D. Green, Successor Liability: The Superiority of Statutory Reform to Protect Product Liability Claimants, 72 Cornell L. Rev. 17 (1986); David Morris Phillips, Products Liability of Successor Corporations: A Corporate and Commercial Law Perspective, 11 Hofstra L. Rev. 249 (1982); Jerry J. Phillips, Product Line Continuity and Successor Corporation Liability, 58 N.Y.U. L. Rev. 906 (1983); Mark J. Roe, Mergers, Acquisitions, and Tort: A Comment on the Problem of Successor Corporation Liability, 70 Va. L. Rev. 1559 (1984); Carol A. Rogala, Nontraditional Successor Product Liability: Should Society Be Forced to Pay the Cost?, 68 U. Det. L.J. 37 (1990); George I. Wallach, Products Liability: A Remedy in Search of a Defendant — The Effect of a Sale of Assets and Subsequent Dissolution on Product Dissatisfaction Claims, 41 Mo. L. Rev. 321 (1976); Note, Assumption of Products Liability in Corporate Acquisitions, 55 B.U. L. Rev. 86 (1975); Note, Expanding the Products Liability of Successor Corporations, 27 Hastings L.J. 1305 (1976); Note, Postdissolution Product Claims and the Emerging Rule of Successor Liability, 64 Va. L. Rev. 861 (1978); Comment, Successor Liability: The Debate Over the Continuity of Enterprise Exception in Ohio Is Really No Debate at All, 21 Ohio N. L. Rev. 297 (1994).

CHAPTER TWELVE
Adjusting the Liability System to the Demands of a National Economy

A. THE PATCHWORK QUILT OF EXISTING STATE LAW

Tort law in the United States is predominantly state common law with an overlay of state legislation. Each of the sovereign states has been free to fashion its liability rules to suit its own taste. The resulting differences are significant. The majority of jurisdictions that have adopted comparative fault have retained some form of joint and several tort liability. As of 1999, some 46 states have adopted comparative fault. (See Chapter Eight, Section A.) They remain, however, hopelessly divided as to whether a pure or modified system of fault comparison should be applied. With regard to products liability, most (but not all) will permit fault comparison to take place.

A majority of states have modified the common law joint tortfeasor doctrine and now limit a defendant's liability to its percentage of fault. Variations among the 35 states that have implemented such reform are quite substantial. (See Chapter Two, Section A.) Every state has a worker compensation system. But whether the worker compensation carrier is entitled to recover from the manufacturer on a subrogation lien remains a matter of sharp division among the states. (See Chapter Two, Section A.) And the list goes on.

Legislative activity at the state level has, until recently, been sporadic and piecemeal. Some states have passed fairly comprehensive products liability reform. See, e.g., Idaho Code §§6-1401 et seq. (Supp. 1999); Ind. Code Ann. §§34-6-2.29 et seq. (West Supp. 1998); Ky. Rev. Stat. Ann. §§411.300 et seq. (Banks-Baldwin 1994); Tex. Civ. Prac. & Rem. Code Ann. §§82.001 et seq. (Vernon 1997); Wash. Rev. Code Ann. §§7.72.010 et seq. (West Supp. 1992). Given the legislative activity in response to the products liability crisis since 1980, however, the total work-product throughout the country has been substantial. The following is a list of subjects that have been addressed by state legislation:

(1) production defect
(2) design defect
(3) failure to warn
(4) express warranty
(5) product misuse
(6) product alteration

(7) contributory fault
(8) assumption of risk
(9) unavoidably dangerous products
(10) inherently dangerous products
(11) obvious dangers
(12) technological feasibility
(13) liability of wholesalers and retailers
(14) joint and several liability
(15) statutes of limitations
(16) statutes of repose
(17) worker compensation
(18) punitive damages
(19) subsequent remedial measures as evidence of defect
(20) economic loss arising from product liability claims
(21) mitigation of damages for failure to wear a seat belt
(22) periodic payment of damages
(23) caps on damages
(24) collateral source recovery
(25) frivolous law suits
(26) contingent fees
(27) limitation on municipal liability

The list is imposing. By 2004, most American jurisdictions had passed legislation in direct response to what sponsors of such measures call "the torts crisis." Most of the legislation seeks to provide some measure of protection to defendants who claim to be hard-hit by the far-reaching decisions of common law courts. Whether the widely perceived crisis is real or not is unclear. One empirical analysis concludes that there is no crisis. See Deborah Jones Merritt and Kathryn Ann Barry, Is the Tort System in Crisis? New Empirical Evidence, 60 Ohio St. L.J. 315 (1999).

In any event, the country has been experiencing a legislative "torts revolution," the likes of which have not been seen in the history of the republic. If anyone ever doubted the vitality of federalism and the ability of states to focus attention on a perceived national problem and seek out innovative solutions, developments in the eighties and nineties demonstrate that state legislatures are alive and well. To be sure, with so much activity in the works, some proposed legislation is unduly restrictive, some neanderthal, and some downright silly. Nonetheless, state legislatures seem intent on providing some check on the discretion of courts in developing the common law of torts and products liability. As they do, they add further complexity to the patchwork quilt. As one travels from one state to another, an abridged Martindale-Hubbell summary may soon become as useful as a road map.

The dynamic federalism described above is not without its downside. Interstate competition can lead to undesirable results. States may adopt rules of law not because they perceive them to be correct or just but to protect parochial interests. It is rare that courts articulate this theme, but in Blankenship v. General Motors Corp., 406 S.E.2d 781, 786 (W. Va. 1991), Justice Neely of the West Virginia Supreme Court made a public confession to this effect:

[T]he manufacturers and amicus have strong arguments. Nonetheless, West Virginia is a small rural state with .66 percent of the population of the United States. Although some members of this Court have reservations about the wisdom of many aspects of tort law, as a court we are utterly powerless to make the *overall* tort system for cases arising in interstate commerce more rational: Nothing that we do will have any impact whatsoever on the set of economic trade-offs that occur in the *national* economy. And, ironically, trying unilaterally to make the American tort system more rational through being uniquely responsible in West Virginia will only punish our residents severely without, in any regard, improving the system for anyone else. . . .

The defendant before us, General Motors, is the largest producer of automobiles in the world. In light of the fact that all of our sister states have adopted a cause of action for lack of crashworthiness, General Motors is *already* collecting a product liability premium every time it sells a car anywhere in the world, including West Virginia. West Virginians, then, are already paying the product liability insurance premium when they buy a General Motors car, so this Court would be both foolish and irresponsible if we held that while West Virginians must pay the premiums, West Virginians can't collect the insurance after they're injured. . . .

Our conclusion today to adopt the rule most favorable to the plaintiff in crashworthiness cases is based upon the same actuarial considerations that have prompted us finally to adopt the doctrine of crashworthinesss — namely, that we are *already* paying for full coverage. Indeed, in some world other than the one in which we live, where this Court were called upon to make national policy, we might very well take a meat ax to some current product liability rules. Therefore, we do not claim that our adoption of rules liberal to plaintiffs comports, necessarily, with some Platonic ideal of perfect justice. Rather, for a tiny state incapable of controlling the direction of the national law in terms of appropriate trade-offs among employment, research, development, and compensation for the injured users of products, the adoption of rules liberal to plaintiffs is simple self-defense. . . .

B. UNIFORM LAWS APPROACH

In 1976, the United States Department of Commerce chaired an 18-month interagency study on the topic of products liability. Its final report, issued in November 1977, recommended that a uniform product liability law be prepared. In early 1979, a "Draft Uniform Product Liability Law" was published in the Federal Register for public comment. 44 Fed. Reg. 2996. A final version of the uniform act was promulgated later in 1979 under the name of "Model Uniform Product Liability Act" and is now generally known by its acronym, MUPLA. See 44 Fed. Reg. 62,714 (1979).

MUPLA explicitly identifies the problems that brought it into existence. Section 101, entitled "Findings," proclaims:

(A) Sharply rising product liability insurance premiums have created serious problems in commerce resulting in:

(1) Increased prices of consumer and industrial products;

(2) Disincentives for innovation and for the development of high-risk but potentially beneficial products;

(3) An increase in the number of product sellers attempting to do business without product liability insurance coverage, thus jeopardizing both their continued existence and the availability of compensation to injured persons; and

(4) Legislative initiatives enacted in a crisis atmosphere that may, as a result, unreasonably curtail the rights of product liability claimants.

(B) One cause of these problems is that product liability law is fraught with uncertainty and sometimes reflects an imbalanced consideration of the interests it affects. The rules vary from jurisdiction to jurisdiction and are subject to rapid and substantial change. These facts militate against predictability of litigation outcome.

(C) Insurers have cited this uncertainty and imbalance as justifications for setting rates and premiums that, in fact, may not reflect actual product risk or liability losses.

(D) Product liability insurance rates are set on the basis of countrywide, rather than individual state, experience. Insurers utilize countrywide experience because a product manufactured in one state can readily cause injury in any one of the other states, the District of Columbia, or the Commonwealth of Puerto Rico. One ramification of this practice is that there is little an individual state can do to solve the problems caused by product liability.

(E) Uncertainty in product liability law and litigation outcome has added to litigation costs and may put an additional strain on the judicial system.

(F) Recently enacted state product liability legislation has widened existing disparities in the law. . . .

Although MUPLA emphasizes the need for certainty and uniformity so that insurers may be able to set rates with greater confidence in their predictions as to ultimate exposure, clearly the act seeks substantive changes that favor the business community. It is important to note that MUPLA was not proposed by the Department of Commerce as a federal products liability bill. It was offered as a model for voluntary use by the states. To date, several states have borrowed some of its provisions. However, not a single state has enacted it in whole or even in significant part. And there does not appear to be even a remote chance that widespread adoption will ever take place. Unlike the Uniform Commercial Code, which was built upon a broad consensus of the business and banking communities, the important sectors of the body politic disagree over what rules should govern products liability. Consumer groups, labor unions, and the trial bar see the world from very different perspectives than do manufacturers. Given the diverse political make-ups of the various states, even moderate, middle-of-the-road reform will almost certainly not take place at the state level in a way that will promote uniformity. The atmosphere is too charged and the voices too strident for a national consensus to develop and manifest itself.

Even if MUPLA will not lead to uniform state law, it has become an important source of secondary authority. Courts often cite the MUPLA provisions in resolving common law questions. It is viewed by some as a Restatement, or better yet, "Prestatement" of the law of products liability. Students should become familiar with both the text and the accompanying analysis. Professor Victor Schwartz, who was in charge of the effort, sought to balance the competing views of consumer groups and the business community. MUPLA helped crystallize the issues for both bench and bar. If it did not bring about uniform resolution of the problems, it certainly helped to bring about a uniform understanding of the critical issues in products litigation.

C. THE NEW RESTATEMENT (THIRD) OF TORTS: PRODUCTS LIABILITY

Reference has been made throughout this casebook to the American Law Institute's Restatement (Third) of Torts: Products Liability (1998). To the extent the Restatement gains acceptance by American courts, it will promote uniformity among the states.

D. FEDERAL LEGISLATIVE SOLUTIONS

1. Substantive Law Reform

With 50-plus state legislatures going their own ways and demonstrating no inclination to adopt MUPLA, and with 50-plus state court systems possessing their own doctrinal biases, the quest for a uniform solution to the so-called "products liability crisis" has turned to Congress. Beginning in 1979, bills have been introduced each year (in either the House or the Senate) to "federalize" and thus (hopefully) to render uniform much of present-day products liability law. Some of these proposals have been modest and directed toward a limited number of issues; others have attempted to regulate all aspects of products litigation. Nonetheless, most of the proposals have not sought radical restructuring of the tort system, contenting themselves with offering corrections of present-day products liability law.

The saga of the efforts to pass federal products liability legislation is too long to tell in a few short pages. Suffice it to say that legislation embodying manufacturers' wish lists is a thing of the past. In the past several years the legislative agenda has been more modest.

In 1996, proponents of federal legislative reform came close to success. Both houses of Congress passed the "Common Sense Product Liability Legal Reform Act of 1996." The most noteworthy aspects of the legislation:

(1) Eliminated strict liability against non-manufacturing sellers (i.e., wholesalers and retailers) unless the manufacturer is not subject to jurisdiction or the court determines that the manufacturer would be unable to satisfy a judgment against it.

(2) Established a total bar in a products liability action if plaintiff was under the influence of alcohol or drugs at the time of accident and the alcohol or drugs are found to be more than 50 percent responsible for the accident.

(3) Reduced plaintiff's recovery by the percentage of responsibility allocated to non-intended misuses or alterations of products that proximately cause the plaintiff's harm.

(4) Established a two-year statute of limitations running from the time plaintiff should have discovered the harm and its cause; set in place a 15-year statute of repose for durable goods.

(5) Adopted a maximum $250,000 cap for punitive damages subject to judicial enlargement based on a host of factors. Any party may request bifurcation of trial on compensatory and punitive damages.
(6) Eliminated joint and several liability for non-economic loss.
(7) Reduced damages against a product manufacturer by the amount of worker's compensation benefit paid to the employee in cases where the employer is found by clear and convincing evidence to have contributed to plaintiff's harm. The Act also eliminates the employer subrogation lien in those cases.
(8) Provided significant immunity to sellers of biomaterials that are sold as raw material or components for use in medical implants.

In April 1996, President Clinton vetoed the legislation. He expressed his dislike for provisions of the bill dealing with curtailment of joint and several liability and those capping punitive damage awards.

2. Insurance Availability: The Risk Retention Act

At about the same time that Congress began considering substantive law reform for products liability, it also sought to deal with restrictive state insurance regulations that were preventing businesses from pooling their products liability risks. In order to facilitate the formation of products liability risk-retention groups, the Risk Retention Act preempted state law to the extent necessary to provide federal authority for interstate operation of such groups. 15 U.S.C. §§3901 et seq. (1981). It was hoped that the presence of these alternatives in the marketplace would provide businesses whose favorable claims experience had not been reflected in their premium rates with an opportunity to reduce their insurance costs via collective self-insurance.

The Risk Retention Act of 1986, P.L. 99-563, amended the Risk Retention Act of 1981 to permit groups other than product manufacturers to purchase liability insurance utilizing risk retention groups. By permitting discrete groups that have favorable claims records to self-insure, Congress was hoping, once again, that by broadening the insurance market it could help the liability crisis. Under the 1986 Act, organizations such as associations, businesses, profit and not-for-profit corporations, professional corporations and partnerships, churches, hospitals, schools, universities, and state and local governments and their agencies would be permitted to form risk retention groups to cover risks specifically related to their operations. Since risk retention groups often operate outside the confines of state insurance law, the Act provides that notice to that effect must be given to all purchasers of risk retention insurance.

E. ARE JUDICIAL SOLUTIONS VIABLE?

While legislative battles rage in the halls of Congress, courts must hear and decide cases brought before them. They have not been able to close their eyes to the truly national character of American products liability litigation. Although no one has easy answers, it is comforting to observe that courts are struggling toward solutions.

1. Federal Common Law

In re "Agent Orange" Product Liability Litigation
635 F.2d 987 (2d Cir. 1980), *cert. denied,* 102 S. Ct. 980 (1981)

KEARSE, Cir. J.

This appeal presents the question whether claims asserted by veterans of the United States armed forces against companies which supplied the United States government with chemicals that are alleged to have been contaminated and to have injured the veterans and their families, are governed by federal common law. Defendants-appellants Diamond Shamrock Corporation, Monsanto Company, Thompson-Hayward Chemical Company, Hercules Incorporated and the Dow Chemical Company were the manufacturers of various herbicides including "Agent Orange" (hereinafter collectively referred to as "Agent Orange") for use by the military as defoliants in the Vietnam War. The plaintiffs, veterans of that war and their families, allege that they have sustained various physical injuries by reason of the veterans' exposure to Agent Orange. Plaintiffs seek redress of those injuries under federal common law, and have invoked the "federal question" jurisdiction of the district court. 28 U.S.C. §1331(a) (1976). Defendants contest the existence of a federal common law cause of action, and moved below to dismiss for lack of subject matter jurisdiction. The United States District Court for the Eastern District of New York, George C. Pratt, Judge, denied their motion. . . .

We agree with defendants that there is no federal common law right of action under the circumstances of this litigation. Accordingly, we reverse.

I

A. The Third Amended Complaint

The basic thrust of the Complaint is relatively simple: defendants manufactured a "phenoxy herbicide," Agent Orange, for use by the military in Vietnam. The herbicide was allegedly contaminated with certain toxic organic chemicals, including 2,3,7,8-tetrachlorodibenzo-p-dioxin ("dioxin"), which plaintiffs describe as "one of the most toxic substances ever developed by man." The plaintiff veterans assert that they were exposed to Agent Orange, and thus to the dioxin it contained, while serving in Vietnam. They claim to have sustained various physical injuries, or to be "at risk" of such injuries, by reason of that exposure. Plaintiffs seek relief on a number of theories, including strict product liability, negligence, and breach of warranty.

What marks these proceedings as somewhat extraordinary are the size of the plaintiff class and the scope of the relief that is sought. Plaintiffs purport to represent the 2.4 million veterans who served as combat soldiers in Southeast Asia from 1962 through 1971, as well as most of the families or survivors of those veterans. Fifteen plaintiff subclasses are identified; many of these subclasses consist of persons who are "at risk" of, but have yet to sustain, various physical injuries. . . .

Defendants deny that there is any causal connection between exposure to Agent Orange and the injuries that plaintiffs claim to have sustained, and vigorously contest the propriety of the various remedial measures that plaintiffs seek to impose on them. This case, however, is still at the pleading stage, and for purposes of deciding the jurisdictional question before us, plaintiffs' factual allegations must be accepted as true.

B. The Decision of the District Court

Plaintiffs argue that federal common law should be applied to their claims principally because of the unique federal nature of the relationship between the soldier and his government, relying chiefly on United States v. Standard Oil Co., 332 U.S. 301, 305 67 S. Ct. 1604, 1606, 91 L. Ed. 2067 (1947) ("Perhaps no relation between the Government and a citizen is more distinctively federal in character than that between it and members of its armed forces."). They contend that this interest brings the case within the doctrine of Clearfield Trust Co. v. United States, 318 U.S. 363, 366, 63 S. Ct. 573, 574, 87 L. Ed. 838 (1943), which held that, in order to ensure uniformity and certainty, "[t]he rights and duties of the United States on commercial paper which it issues are governed by federal rather than local law." Plaintiffs argue that the government similarly has an interest in having all of its veterans compensated by government contractors who manufactured or marketed Agent Orange, and that application of the respective states' laws would impede recovery on a uniform basis.

The district court rejected the contention that *Clearfield Trust* stated the controlling principle, recognizing that the United States, a party to *Clearfield Trust,* is not party to the plaintiffs' claims here. Rather, the court recognized that since the present action involves only private parties, the federal common law issue is controlled by the principles set forth in Miree v. DeKalb County, 433 U.S. 25, 97 S. Ct. 2490, 53 L. Ed. 2d 557 (1977), and Wallis v. Pan American Petroleum Corp., 384 U.S. 63, 86 S. Ct. 1301, 16 L. Ed. 2d 369 (1966). After reviewing the latter decisions, the district court applied a three-factor test to determine whether federal common law governs plaintiffs' claims:

> (1) the existence of a substantial federal interest in the outcome of a litigation; (2) the effect on this federal interest should state law be applied; and (3) the effect on state interests should state law be displaced by federal common law.

With respect to the first factor, the district court recognized two principal federal interests that may be affected by the present lawsuits: the federal government's interest in its relations with members of the armed forces, and its interest in its relations with suppliers of war materiel. As to the government's interest in the welfare of its veterans, the court stated that:

> Soldiers serving in the armed forces are government charges, entitled to government protection. Torts committed by war contractors against soldiers in action constitute "harms inflicted" on the soldiers and "interference" with the relationship between soldiers and the government. Such harms and interferences implicate federal interests identified in [United States v. Standard Oil, supra].

. . . Finally, the court reasoned that because of the large number of veterans claiming injury, and the large potential liability of the five defendants, the foregoing federal interests were "substantial" for purposes of the federal common law analysis:

> The estimated number of involved veterans ranges from thousands to millions, and the estimated potential liability of the five war contractors ranges from millions to billions of dollars. As the number of veterans and the size of the claims against the war contractors increase so the federal interest in this litigation expands.

As to the government's interest in its relations with its military suppliers — the court referred to a number of "speculative" ways in which lawsuits such as the present ones might adversely affect that interest, pointing out that in response to any increase in their potential liability, military suppliers might raise their prices, attach conditions to the use of their products, or stop dealing with the government altogether. The court concluded that

> government relations with war contractors might well be drastically altered by changes in the rules governing liability of war contractors to soldiers for injuries caused by inherently "dangerous" war materials.

Turning to the second part of its test, the court found that the federal interest it had identified would be adversely affected if the issues in these lawsuits were adjudicated under state law:

> Application of varying state laws would burden federal interests by creating uncertainty as to the rights of both veterans and war contractors. It would also be unfair in that essentially similar claims, involving veterans and war contractors identically situated in all relevant respects, would be treated differently under different state laws.

Finally, as to the third part of its test, the court determined that application of federal common law would not have any significant adverse impact on state interests. While noting that "[t]ort claims are traditionally matters for state law, which has developed comprehensive substantive and procedural rules to govern them," the court distinguished the instant tort actions, finding that

> state law has not considered the complex question of a war contractor's liability to soldiers injured by toxic chemicals subject to federal regulation while engaged in combat and serving abroad.

The court concluded:

> Because state law is no more or less developed as to such claims than federal common law, application of federal common law thereto would not significantly displace state law.

Having found substantial federal interests that would be adversely affected by application of state law to the instant claims, and having determined that there were no substantial state interests in having state law applied, the district court ruled that plaintiffs had stated valid causes of action under the federal common law. The court therefore held that it had subject matter jurisdiction over the case, and denied defendants' motion to dismiss. This appeal followed.

II

Both plaintiffs and defendants accept the three-part test that the district court applied to the federal common law issue, and for purposes of discussion we accept that framework. But, focusing our consideration chiefly on the first factor of the test, i.e., "the existence of a substantial federal interest in the outcome of the litigation," we disagree with the district court's analysis and conclude that the court gave insufficient weight to the Supreme Court's repeated admonition that

> [i]n deciding whether rules of federal common law should be fashioned, normally the guiding principle is that a *significant conflict between some federal policy or interest and the use of state law in the premises must first be specifically shown.* . . .

Wallis v. Pan American Petroleum Corp., supra, 384 U.S. at 68, 86 S. Ct. at 1304, quoted with emphasis in Miree v. DeKalb County, supra, 433 U.S. at 31, 97 S. Ct. at 2494. Principally we reject the district court's conclusion that there is an identifiable federal policy at stake in this litigation that warrants the creation of federal common law rules.

In considering plaintiffs' contentions, it is essential to delineate precisely the relation of the United States to the claims here at issue. These claims are brought by former servicemen and their families against private manufacturers; they are not asserted by or against the United States, and they do not directly implicate the rights and duties of the United States. They are thus unlike the claims in United States v. Standard Oil Co., supra, in which the government brought suit to recover for its payments to a soldier injured as a result of the defendant's negligence, and Clearfield Trust Co. v. United States, supra, in which the government brought suit to enforce its rights in commercial paper issued by it. In each of those cases the government was a party seeking to enforce its own asserted rights, and analysis reveals two federal concerns which are inherent in such cases. First, the government has an interest in having uniform rules govern its rights and obligations. Second, the government has a substantive interest in the contents of those uniform rules. The first interest prizes uniformity for its own sake and is content-neutral; it does not dictate the substance of the federal common law rule to be applied. Thus, in United States v. Standard Oil Co., supra, the Court applied federal common law, recognizing the government's interest in uniformity, but refused to impose the liability argued for by the United States as the substance of that law.

The present litigation is fundamentally different from *Standard Oil* and *Clearfield Trust* with respect to both uniformity interest and substantive interest in the content of the rules to be applied. Since this litigation is between private parties and no substantial rights or duties of the government hinge on its outcome, there is no federal interest in uniformity for its own sake. See e.g., Miree v. DeKalb County, supra, 433 U.S. at 28, 97 S. Ct. at 2493. The fact that application of state law may produce a variety of results is of no moment. It is in the nature of a federal system that different states will apply different rules of law, based on their individual perceptions of what is in the best interests of their citizens. That alone is not grounds in private litigation for judicially creating an overriding federal law. . . .

The second fundamental difference between the present litigation and the

Clearfield Trust type of case is that in the latter, the government's substantive interest in the litigation is essentially monothetic, in that it is concerned only with preserving the federal fisc, whereas here the government has two interests; and here the two interests have been placed in sharp contrast with one another. Thus, the government has an interest in the welfare of its veterans; they have given of themselves in the most fundamental way possible in the national interest. But the government also has an interest in the suppliers of its materiel; imposition, for example, of strict liability as contended for by plaintiffs would affect the government's ability to procure materiel without the exaction of significantly higher prices, or the attachment of onerous conditions, or the demand of indemnification or the like. As plaintiffs' counsel has observed, "this litigation will have a direct and lasting impact on the relationship between the federal government and war contractors . . . and between the federal government and veterans." (Letter dated October 21, 1980, V. J. Yannacone, Jr. to A. D. Fusaro.) It is obvious that the government is interested. But unlike a simple uniformity interest, neither the government's interest in its veterans nor its interest in its suppliers is content-neutral. Each interest will be furthered only if the federal rule of law to be applied favors that particular group.

The extent to which either group *should* be favored, and its welfare deemed "paramount" . . . is preeminently a policy determination of the sort reserved in the first instance for Congress. The welfare of veterans and that of military suppliers are clearly federal concerns which Congress should appropriately consider in setting policy for the governance of the nation, and it is properly left to Congress in the first instance to strike the balance between the conflicting interests of the veterans and the contractors, and thereby identify federal policy. Although Congress has turned its attention to the Agent Orange problem, it has not determined what the federal policy is with respect to the reconciliation of these two competing interests. . . .

We conclude that in the present case, while the federal government has obvious interests in the welfare of the parties to the litigation, its interest in the *outcome* of the litigation, i.e., in how the parties' welfares should be balanced, is as yet undetermined.[1] The teaching of *Wallis* and *Miree* is that before federal common law rules should be fashioned, the use of state law must pose a threat to an "identifiable" federal policy. Wallis v. Pan American Petroleum Corp., supra, 384 U.S. at 68, 86 S. Ct. at 1304; Miree v. DeKalb County, supra, 433 U.S. at 31-33, 97 S. Ct. at 2494, 2495. In the present litigation the federal policy is not yet identifiable. We conclude, therefore, that the district court erred in ruling that plaintiffs' claims were governed by federal common law. The order denying defendants' motion to dismiss for lack of subject matter jurisdiction is accordingly.

Reversed.

[The dissenting opinion of Chief Judge Feinberg is omitted.]

---

1. The large number of veterans claimed in the class does not reveal the content of a federal policy reconciling the competing interests, any more than does the possibility that the defendant companies would have to be liquidated to pay the claims of the class.

Scholarly commentary has been critical of the Second Circuit and has lined up behind the dissent authored by Chief Judge Feinberg. See, e.g., Aaron D. Twerski, With Liberty & Justice for All: An Essay on Agent Orange and Choice of Law, 52 Brooklyn L. Rev. 341, 347-350 (1986); Susan J. Stabile, Note, Tort Remedies for Servicemen Injured by Military Equipment: A Case for Federal Common Law, 55 N.Y.U. L. Rev. 606, 623 (1980).

In Jackson v. Johns-Manville Sales Corp., 750 F.2d 1314 (5th Cir. 1985), *cert. denied*, 106 S. Ct. 3339 (1986), plaintiff contracted asbestosis as a result of exposure to asbestos manufactured by the defendant. He sought to recover damages for mental anguish arising from his fear of later contracting cancer (cancerphobia). He also sought to recover punitive damages. The defendant argued that the number of pending and future claims made it certain that the awarding of such damages would deplete its resources and assure that it would be unable to pay compensatory damages to future claimants. This would then set up a conflict between claimants across state lines as to rights to recover from limited resources. The defendant argued that such an interstate conflict demanded the application of federal common law.

The majority acknowledged the logic of the defendant's argument but declined to apply federal common law, relying heavily on the Second Circuit opinion in the *Agent Orange* case, supra.

It is a sign of the times that five dissenting judges were prepared to abandon *Erie* on these special facts and adopt federal common law. The dissenters responded to the argument of the majority that the problem required a federal legislative solution:

> The majority says, and we agree, that legislation would be the preferred solution to the dilemma of providing an adequate scheme for the proper distribution of compensation. But Congress has failed to enact any of the asbestos compensation bills proposed to date. Courts enjoy no comparable ability to refuse to decide cases brought before them. We must decide Jackson's claims. But it is not just Jackson's rights which are at stake. Literally, the rights of tens of thousands of claimants in cases presently being litigated depend on what we do. Untold thousands more who have not yet manifested the symptoms of the insidious diseases that can result from asbestos fibre inhalation also depend upon our decision. We cannot wait to see if the impasse in Congress ultimately will be broken by lawmaking.
>
> The Supreme Court, as the only institution other than Congress capable of imposing the uniformity necessary to resolve this problem in a just manner, should be afforded the chance to deal with the singular problem presented by these cases. That Court has the power to formulate federal common law which will ensure equitable compensation for all claimants. Its ability to address the controlling issues with a single voice is not only necessary for just resolution of pending litigation; it is even more important to expeditious and equitable settlement of claims. A uniform set of rules would not only protect the rights of individual claimants and the effective functioning of the judicial system, but would also aid the efforts of the asbestos companies and their insurers to develop an effective procedure for resolving these disputes on a rational basis without resorting to the courts. . . . [Id. at 1331-1333.]

For a subsequent history of the case dealing with issues of recovery for cancerphobia, see Jackson v. Johns-Manville Sales Corp., 781 F.2d 394 (5th Cir. 1986). For a treatment of the broader area of federal common law, see generally

Martha A. Field, Sources of Law: The Scope of Federal Common Law, 99 Harv. L. Rev. 881 (1986).

2. Federal Preemption of State Law

By interpreting federal regulations to preempt state law, federal courts strive for national uniformity in products liability law. As you will recall from Chapter Seven, courts addressing this issue in the context of failure to warn and defective design have not applied the doctrine consistently to different subject areas. Preemption can be express, though most statutes do not specifically so provide. In cases where the statutory language is less straightforward, defendants argue that a court may find implied preemption in two ways: (a) Congress intended to occupy the field in a given area so completely that no room is left for the states to supplement federal regulation; or (b) state law may be in direct conflict with federal regulation on some specific matter, so that the manufacturer cannot reasonably be expected to comply with both. For an argument in favor of giving greater consideration to state sovereignty where federal preemption is asserted as a defense to products liability claims, see Stacey Allen Carroll, Note, Federal Preemption of State Products Liability Claims: Adding Clarity and Respect for State Sovereignty to the Analysis of Federal Preemption Defenses, 36 Ga. L. Rev. 797 (2002).

3. National Management of Mass Tort Litigation

Mass tort litigation has grabbed the national spotlight. The scope of these mass tort actions is breathtaking. That one court might dispose of thousands of cases arising from 50-plus jurisdictions in one fell swoop speaks volumes about the national character of this genre of litigation. The subject of mass tort is beyond the scope of this casebook. Several casebooks are devoted to treatments of the subject. See Gerald W. Boston and M. Stuart Madden, Law of Environmental and Toxic Torts (2d ed. 2001); Linda S. Mullenix, Mass Tort Litigation (1996). Two law review symposia contain helpful treatments by scholars and practitioners analyzing the benefits and detriments attending mass tort litigation. See Symposium, Mass Torts: Serving Up Just Desserts, 80 Cornell L. Rev. 811 (1995); Symposium, National Mass Tort Conference, 73 Tex. L. Rev. 1523 (1995). The American Law Institute completed an exhaustive study of the subject. See Complex Litigation: Statutory Recommendations and Analysis (1994).

Many mass tort actions have involved so-called "toxic torts." Products such as asbestos, bendectin, silicone breast implants, DES, HIV-tainted blood, and cigarettes have all been proposed as appropriate for class-action treatment. After a history of early hostility to class treatment of mass torts, the courts began to warm to the idea. In Jenkins v. Raymark Industries, Inc., 782 F.2d 468, 473 (5th Cir. 1986), the court upheld the certification of an asbestos class action, saying:

> Courts have usually avoided class actions in the mass accident or tort setting. Because of differences between individual plaintiffs on issues of liability and defenses of liability, as well as damages, it has been feared that separate trials would overshadow the

common disposition for the class. The courts are now being forced to rethink the alternatives and priorities by the current volume of litigation and more frequent mass disasters.

However, several years later, the same court turned thumbs down on an attempt to certify a new asbestos class action in In re Fibreboard Corp., 893 F.2d 706, 712 (5th Cir. 1990), holding that:

> [Too many disparities exist] among the various plaintiffs for their common concerns to predominate. The plaintiffs suffer from different diseases, some of which are more likely to have been caused by asbestos than others. The plaintiffs were exposed to asbestos in various manners and to varying degrees. The plaintiffs' lifestyles differed in material respects. To create the requisite commonality for trial, the discrete components of the class members' claims and the asbestos manufacturers' defenses must be submerged.

Several decisions have signaled that courts are troubled by the "rush to class certification." Two United States Supreme Court decisions have refused to certify a nationwide class for the purpose of settling mass tort actions. See Amchem Prods. Inc. v. Windsor, 117 S. Ct. 2231 (1997); Ortiz v. Fibreboard Corp., 119 S. Ct. 2295 (1999).

In re Rhone-Poulenc Rorer, Inc., 51 F.3d 1293, 1296-1300 (7th Cir. 1995), *cert. denied,* 116 S. Ct. 184 (1995), Judge Richard Posner minced no words in his opinion decertifying a class action brought on behalf of hemophiliacs who received HIV-contaminated blood. The case was predicated on the negligence of pharmaceutical companies for inadequately testing and screening blood donors in the early 1980s. Posner decried the premature certification of the class by the district court. He noted that the defendant had won 12 of the 13 cases had been litigated in various courts around the country and Posner questioned the wisdom of:

> [F]orcing these defendants to stake their companies on the outcome of a single jury trial, or be forced by fear of the risk of bankruptcy to settle even if they have no legal liability, when it is entirely feasible to allow a final, authoritative determination of their liability for the colossal misfortune that has befallen the hemophiliac population to emerge from a decentralized process of multiple trials, involving different juries, and different standards of liability, in different jurisdictions; and when, in addition, the preliminary indications are that the defendants are not liable for the grievous harm that has befallen the members of the class. . . .
> One jury, consisting of six persons (the standard federal civil jury nowadays consists of six regular jurors and two alternates), will hold the fate of an industry in the palm of its hand. This jury, jury number fourteen, may disagree with twelve of the previous thirteen juries — and hurl the industry into bankruptcy. That kind of thing can happen in our system of civil justice (it is not likely to happen, because the industry is likely to settle — whether or not it really is liable) without violating anyone's legal rights. But it need not be tolerated when the alternative exists of submitting an issue to multiple juries constituting in the aggregate a much larger and more diverse sample of decisionmakers. . . .

Judge Posner went on to note that plaintiffs from 50 different jurisdictions would have their cases tried under a single, all-purpose negligence instruction. He argued that such an "Esperanto"-like instruction would be inconsistent with the law in many jurisdictions. For example, many jurisdictions would allow drug companies in a case such as this to plead conformance to medical custom as an absolute defense to the action. Judge Posner was also concerned that creating a class for the trial of the negligence issue alone and sending the case back for trial for individual plaintiffs on issues such as comparative fault and proximate cause would raise serious constitutional questions as to whether a defendant's Seventh Amendment right to jury trial had been violated.

Judge Posner's reasoning was given great weight in the Fifth Circuit's decision to decertify a class action brought on behalf of cigarette smokers alleging that tobacco companies fraudulently failed to inform them that nicotine is addictive and manipulated the nicotine levels of cigarettes to get and keep smokers addicted. Plaintiffs sought a host of remedies including damages for emotional distress, a fund for medical monitoring, damages for economic loss, and punitive damages. The Court in Castano v. American Tobacco Co., 84 F.3d 734 (5th Cir. 1996), addressed all of the issues discussed by Judge Posner in the *Rhone-Poulenc* case and found that they were equally relevant (if not even more aggravated) in the cigarette litigation. The first cigarette smokers' case to be certified as a class action proceeded though the first two phases of trial, resulting in a jury verdict in favor of the class, before the class was decertified. Liggett Group Inc. v. Engle, 2003 WL 21180319 (Fla. Dist. Ct. App.). The court noted that, "even though there is a common nucleus of facts concerning the defendants' conduct, this case presents a multitude of individualized issues which make it particularly unsuitable for class treatment." Id. at 8. But see Davis v. American Home Products, 844 So. 2d 242 (La. Ct. App. 2003) (finding evidence sufficient to satisfy commonality, adequacy of representation, and numerosity requirements in plaintiffs' strict liability action against the manufacturer of the Norplant implant contraceptive device).

Class decertification in these cases has left the status of class actions in mass tort cases very much up in the air. For an assessment from a judge's perspective, see Helen E. Freedman, Product Liability Issues in Mass Torts—View From the Bench, 15 Touro L. Rev. 685 (1999). See also Victor E. Schwartz, Mark A. Behrens & Leah Lorber, Federal Courts Should Decide Interstate Class Actions: A Call for Federal Class Action Diversity Jurisdiction Reform, 37 Harv. J. on Legis. 483 (2000). Whatever future lies in store for class actions, the federal courts have in place procedures for consolidation of both discovery and trial of mass tort actions. See generally 15 Charles Alan Wright, Arthur R. Miller, & Edward H. Cooper, Federal Practice and Procedure, §3861 et seq. (1986).

F. AREAS OF SPECIAL FEDERAL COMPETENCE

1. *The Federal Bankruptcy System*

Anyone who reads the newspapers cannot help but be aware that it has become almost fashionable for a large corporation, besieged by thousands of products liability claims that threaten its capacity to meet its obligations, to file for reorganization and discharge in federal bankruptcy court. Our purpose here is not to turn you into a bankruptcy expert, but you must know something about the subject if you are to be a competent products liability expert. One question you should carry into these materials is this: Given the limited liability rule considered in the preceding chapter dealing with the corporate aspects of products liability, of what utility is a discharge in bankruptcy to a corporate products liability defendant? Consider the following excerpt.

Note, The Manville Bankruptcy: Treating Mass Tort Claims in Chapter 11 Proceedings
96 Harv. L. Rev. 1121, 1121-1131 (1983)

The reorganization petition filed in federal bankruptcy court by the Manville Corporation on August 26, 1982, placed a major challenge before the new federal bankruptcy system, which the Supreme Court had recently shaken with its decision in Northern Pipeline Construction Co. v. Marathon Pipe Line Co.[2] Whereas Congress had foreseen the issues raised by the *Northern Pipeline* case when it passed the Bankruptcy Reform Act of 1978 (BRA), it did not anticipate that a healthy and solvent corporation[3] might seek refuge from potentially massive but speculative tort liability in the BRA's chapter 11 reorganization provisions. Although Manville and UNR Industries[4] are the first such apparently healthy corporations to file chapter 11 petitions in the face of massive tort claims, manufacturers in a variety of industries that face similar liability could follow suit.

The *Manville* filing presents a stark contrast to the traditional reorganization case, in which the debtor knows the identities of its creditors and the amount of its debts. In such cases, the debtor seeks the aid of the court only in restructuring its finances and satisfying its existing creditors to the greatest extent possible. The most extraordinary aspects of the *Manville* case are that the majority of Manville's creditors are unknown and that the majority of the debts on which Manville bases its claims of prospective insolvency are contingent and unliquidated. Manville thus appears to be attempting to use the bankruptcy power largely as a tool to limit the aggregate size of its current and future liabilities. If successful, Manville's strategy will have a profound effect on all asbestos-related tort litigation; Manville is the nation's largest asbestos manufacturer and the "deepest pocket" among the codefendants in the many asbestos-related suits.

The Bankruptcy Reform Act of 1978 reaffirms bankruptcy courts' broad equitable and statutory powers to deal flexibly with unorthodox bankruptcy petitions

---

2. 102 S. Ct. 2858 (1982). The Supreme Court held unconstitutional the new bankruptcy system created by the Bankruptcy Reform Act of 1978 (BRA), Pub. L. No. 95-598, 92 Stat. 2549 (codified at 11 U.S.C., in scattered sections of 28 U.S.C., and in scattered sections of other titles (Supp. V. 1981)). The basis of the Court's holding was that, although the bankruptcy courts were established under article I of the Constitution, they were empowered by the BRA to adjudicate matters of private rights over which only article III courts are to have jurisdiction. 102 S. Ct. at 2879-80.

3. Manville's financial statements at the time of its chapter 11 filing showed a net worth (total shareholders' equity) of $1.2 billion. Consolidated Balance Sheet Filed with Chapter 11 Petition, In re Johns-Manville Corp., Nos. 82B 11,656 to 82B 11,676 (Bankr. S.D.N.Y. filed Aug. 26, 1982).

4. UNR Industries (Unarco), a codefendant in most of the asbestos-related litigation, is a smaller corporation that produced asbestos only until 1962. UNR was actually the first asbestos manufacturer to file a chapter 11 petition. See In re UNR Indus., Nos. 82-B-9841 to 82-B-9851 (Bankr. N.D. Ill. filed July 29, 1982). Yet another asbestos manufacturer, Amatex Corporation joined UNR and Manville on November 1, 1982. In re Amatex Corp., No. 82-05,220K (Bankr. E.D. Pa. filed Nov. 1, 1982).

by means ranging from dismissal to extraordinary relief. The new Bankruptcy Code has been interpreted to confer the traditional equitable power to dismiss petitions filed in bad faith, even though the Code does not explicitly impose a good faith requirement. The "bad faith" doctrine that was developed at common law has been held to be incorporated into the Bankruptcy Code through section 1112(b), which permits bankruptcy courts to dismiss a petition "for cause," whether or not such cause is among the nine explicitly enumerated in section 1112(b).

Typically, reorganization cases dismissed for bad faith have been of four types: those in which there is no reasonable chance of successful rehabilitation, those that attempt to work a fraud on the court, those filed to settle internal disputes of a business entity, and those in which the conduct of the debtor clearly indicates that its sole intent is to hinder or delay its creditors. Manville's filing does not necessarily fit within any of these categories. First, the strength of Manville's ongoing operations leaves no doubt that a successful reorganization is feasible. Second, although some asbestos claimants have alleged that Manville has attempted to defraud the court by placing assets in newly created subsidiaries beyond the court's reach, those allegations remain unproven; in any event, proof of such a segregation of assets would more likely result in the bankruptcy judge's taking control of the segregated assets than in the dismissal of the entire case. Third, Manville's filing is clearly motivated by external problems with creditors rather than by internal squabbles. Finally, although the tort claimants argue that hindrance and delay are indeed Manville's primary motives, courts have generally been reluctant to find such a motive except in the most extreme cases, those in which it appears that delay is the *sole* reason for the filing.

These four categories are illustrative rather than exclusive; that Manville may not fit neatly within any of them does not mean that its petition may not be dismissed. The underlying inquiry, as in all instances of alleged bad faith reorganization petitions, is whether the debtor "seeks to abuse the bankruptcy law by employing it for a purpose for which it was not intended to be used." The Bankruptcy Code, however, does not lend itself easily to such an inquiry, it embodies many varied purposes — protecting jobs, ensuring a fresh start for debtors, ensuring equitable treatment for creditors — designed to benefit debtors and creditors alike.

Manville can argue that filing a chapter 11 petition at such an early date is entirely consistent with the basic policy of the Bankruptcy Code that encourages debtors to file petitions before their financial position deteriorates to the point at which rehabilitation is no longer feasible, even if that point would be reached before actual insolvency. Not only may creditors file involuntary petitions when debtors have waited too long without filing voluntary petitions, but moreover both section 1112(b) of the Code and the case law warn debtors that a petition will be dismissed when there is little or no likelihood of successful rehabilitation.

Nonetheless, the absence of a requirement of insolvency as a prerequisite for filing a chapter 11 petition should not be interpreted to mean that financial condition is not a relevant consideration when evaluating the good faith of such a petition. Moving along a continuum from balance sheet and equitable insolvency[5]

---

5. There are two distinct types of insolvency: balance sheet insolvency (liabilities exceed assets) and equitable insolvency (inability to pay debts as they come due). The Bankruptcy Code defines "insolvency"

toward perfect financial health, one eventually reaches a point of relative financial soundness at which application of the bankruptcy laws could not have been contemplated by Congress. Unfortunately, Congress has never identified the point at which the invocation of the bankruptcy power ceases to be legitimate. Such line-drawing was left to the courts, to be accomplished by applying equitable principles and the policies of the Code to individual cases. In general, the inquiry should focus on whether the debtor is more likely than not to reach either balance sheet or equitable insolvency in the foreseeable future.

In the *Manville* case, the court's inquiry should involve a careful scrutiny of the company's present financial condition, projected earnings, and projected asbestos-related liability. The asbestos claimants should be given an opportunity to challenge the findings of the medical study of projected asbestosis occurrence that Manville commissioned as well as Manville's assessment of its financial condition. If the creditors succeed in showing that Manville is more likely than not to remain solvent for the foreseeable future, the reorganization petition should be dismissed as an attempted misuse of the bankruptcy power. If, however, the creditors are unable to show that Manville's projections of future financial ruin are inaccurate, immediate filing would appear necessary to further two basic policies of the Bankruptcy Code — the protection of future claimants and the protection of jobs. Dismissal of Manville's chapter 11 petition and a return to the status quo would deplete the company's assets and thus prejudice future asbestos claimants unable to execute their judgments fully. Further, to meet its future liabilities, Manville might be forced to liquidate in full or in part and thereby to eliminate a large number of jobs.

If the *Manville* bankruptcy court determines that the reorganization should proceed, its major task will be disposing of the overwhelming number of tort claims within its jurisdiction. The liquidation of contingent claims is governed by the estimation provision of the Bankruptcy Code, section 502(c). The term "estimation" is misleading insofar as it suggests a mere guess or a lack of procedure; estimation in bankruptcy can be a full adjudication. Normally, the process of estimating individual claims is carried out before the bankruptcy judge. The unusual nature of the *Manville* case, however, may permit the bankruptcy court to read section 502(c) in a way that would allow it to lift the automatic stay on outside litigation and leave the estimation of individual asbestos claims to other courts, as long as the bankruptcy court estimated Manville's total asbestos-related liability, placed a limit on that liability, and established a compensation fund[6] for recovery by present and future asbestos claimants.

Under this reading, the bankruptcy court would estimate Manville's total liability by statistical means. It could employ epidemiological studies to determine the future incidence of asbestos-related disease, and then study the data from the 3500 claims against Manville that have already reached judgment or settlement

---

in balance sheet terms for general purposes, 11 U.S.C. §101(26) (Supp. V 1981), whereas it adopts the equity test for the filing of involuntary petitions, id. §303(h)(1); see S. Rep. No. 989 at 25, 34, reprinted in 1978 U.S. Code Cong. & Ad. News at 5811, 5820; H.R. Rep. No. 595 at 312, 323, reprinted in 1978 U.S. Code Cong. & Ad. News at 6269, 6280.

6. The size of the fund would necessarily be fixed to assure Manville of an upper limit on its liability. The absence of such a ceiling would render the bankruptcy proceeding pointless: it would deny the debtor the "fresh start" so vital to reorganizations . . . and would violate the "feasibility" requirement of 11 U.S.C. §1129(a) (11) (Supp. V 1981) by reexposing the debtor to the massive liability that drove it into bankruptcy in the first place.

to determine the average cost of each claim. The estimation of Manville's aggregate liability, a process entirely distinct from the estimation of individual claims, would not directly determine the recovery rights of any individual.

A compensation fund could then be created from Manville's future available assets and revenues. By comparing the size of the fund to Manville's total estimated tort liability, the court could determine the percentage of each asbestos judgment that could be paid from the fund. Plaintiffs winning judgments in other courts would execute their judgments in the bankruptcy court, from which they would receive payment on a pro rata basis to ensure that funds be conserved to compensate all future claimants proportionally. If after several years the court discovered that its estimate of Manville's aggregate liability had been inaccurate, it could readjust the percentage of each claim to be paid out of the fund.[7]

For further discussion of the issues presented in these cases, see generally Mark J. Roe, Corporate Strategic Reaction to Mass Tort, 72 Va. L. Rev. 1 (1986); Mark J. Roe, Bankruptcy and Mass Tort, 84 Colum. L. Rev. 846-850 (1984).

Difficulties continue to plague the Manville bankruptcy. In July 1990 the following problem arose. Under the agreement reached in bankruptcy court Manville set up an independent trust that would settle all pending and future asbestos claims.

In 1988 the company turned over $2.5 billion in assets to the trust. Only $675 million was cash from Manville and its insurers. Manville also agreed to pay the trust $75 million a year starting in August 1991 and continuing through 2014. The company would also pay 20 percent of its annual profits from 1992 until all of the claims are paid.

The trust has received some additional money from Manville and its insurers since 1988, for a total of $958 million in cash. As of March 1990, it had spent most of the cash settling more than 22,000 cases at an average of $42,000 each. At that rate, the trust would need $7.5 billion to cover more than 130,000 remaining claims, future claims, and administrative costs. When the trust was set up, organizers predicted an average settlement of $25,000.

Judge Jack B. Weinstein of the U.S. District Court for the Eastern District of New York called the situation "a judicial emergency" and ordered a complete restructuring and refinancing of the trust. He told the trust to replace its first-come-first-served method of paying victims with a system that would give priority to the most seriously ill.

As a result of the potential bankruptcy of the trust, a Settlement Agreement was entered into between asbestos plaintiffs and the trust. The "Settlement" is reported at 120 Bank. Rptr. 668 (E.D.N.Y. 1990). The class settlement was approved by Judge Weinstein, 129 Bank. Rptr. 710 (S. & E.D. 1991). It provides for the protection of future claimants by limiting recovery to present claimants and establishes two categories of plaintiffs to be treated differently according to the seriousness of their injuries. The settlement encourages resolution of claims by use of the claims-resolution process set forth and creates strong disincentives for those seeking classical litigation within the court system. The lengthy opin-

---

7. Some would argue that such a system would be unfair, because an adjustment in the percentage of each claim that would be paid from the fund would result in unequal treatment of the claimants; later claimants would receive proportionally more or less compensation than would earlier claimants. This sort of inequality, however, is far more desirable than the alternative, which is to ignore the future claimants and to take the risk that, within the fixed fund, there will be no assets at all to compensate them.

ion by Judge Weinstein contains an exhaustive discussion of the asbestos saga and discusses the problems that plagued the administration of the trust. It is well worth reading. For those who remain skeptical about the ability of the judiciary to manage and administer mass tort compensation, the Manville story should strengthen their resolve that there must be a better way.

In 1994, Congress essentially confirmed the *Manville* approach and adopted it for other asbestos-related bankruptcies. See Bankruptcy Code §524 (g), (h).

Still not settled is the issue of how to determine what kinds of claims are cognizable at the time of the bankruptcy determination. While the Code offers a very broad definition of "claim," there remains disagreement as to how the definition is to be applied. Courts have adopted three different tests for which potential claims can be recognized in the bankruptcy confirmation proceeding. The three tests were delineated in Epstein v. Official Committee of Unsecured Creditors of Estate of Piper Aircraft Corp., 58 F.3d 1573 (11th Cir. 1995). Epstein, who represented the future claimants against the aircraft manufacturer, appealed a ruling that future claimants who could not be identified at the time of the filing for bankruptcy were not properly considered claimants and could not get a piece of the set-aside monies if they subsequently sued the bankrupt Piper. The court rejected outright the "accrued state law claim test," which disallows any participation if a state law-based cause of action has not accrued, as too narrow. The second test, called the "conduct test," was advocated by appellant Epstein. This test confers a right of payment based on when the conduct, such as manufacture or sale, occurred. Under this test, persons who in the future are injured while flying in defective planes manufactured by Piper prior to petition can recover from the bankruptcy fund. Appellant argued that the policies that gave rise to the Code's creation supported the conduct test. The court acknowledged that the Code was created with an eye toward subsuming many outstanding issues under the province of the bankruptcy court, and granting broad equity powers to handle such matters. But it found that the conduct test could be applied too broadly in some circumstances. Accordingly, it found that the prepetition relationship test was the proper one. The prepetition relationship test limits participation to individuals who have a relationship with the debtor pior to the petition filing date. Relationships are defined to include "contact, exposure, impact, or privity, between the claimant and the debtor's product." Id. 58 F.3d at 1577. The court did, however, broaden the time period during which plaintiffs could come in under the wire by holding that relationships formed between the petition date and the confirmation date were covered, thus creating the new "Piper test."

The bankruptcy ploy for dealing with cases that threaten the financial viability of a company continues to grab national attention. Dow Corning filed for bankruptcy in 1995 after being inundated with lawsuits for its silicone-gel implants. Potential claimants were given a deadline of early 1997 to be included in the bankruptcy fund.

2. *Admiralty*

Article III, §2, of the United States Constitution provides that "[t]he judicial power shall extend to all cases of admiralty and maritime jurisdiction." A plaintiff in a products liability action that has an important maritime nexus may thus have a choice to proceed in a regular tort action or to bring suit under federal maritime law. The leading case setting forth the requisites for invoking federal maritime jurisdiction is Executive Jet Aviation, Inc. v. City of Cleveland, 93 S. Ct. 493 (1972). In that case, plaintiff's plane lost power from ingesting seagulls into its engines while taking off from defendant's airport. The plane crashed and sank in the navigable waters of Lake Erie. The court said:

> [W]e conclude that the mere fact that the alleged wrong "occurs" or "is located" on or over navigable waters . . . is not of itself sufficient to turn an airplane negligence case into a "maritime tort." It is far more consistent with the history and purpose of admiralty to require also that the wrong bear a significant relationship to traditional maritime activity. We hold that unless such a relationship exists, claims arising from airplane accidents are not cognizable in admiralty in the absence of legislation to the contrary. Id. at 268.

See also Foremost Insurance Co. v. Richardson, 102 S. Ct. 2654 (1982).

It may be to the plaintiff's advantage to style the case in admiralty. In White v. Johns-Manville Corp., 662 F.2d 234 (4th Cir. 1981), *cert. denied,* 102 S. Ct. 1037 (1982), plaintiff brought suit against an asbestos manufacturer but found that the accrual date under state tort law began to run from his last exposure to the defendant's product. The Fourth Circuit found that "the installation of the asbestos products has a direct effect on marine navigation and commerce," and that the asbestos products used by shipyard workers were "designed, advertised and marketed as maritime asbestos products" Id. at 239, 240; it therefore subjected the defendant asbestos manufacturers to federal admiralty jurisdiction. Under maritime law the equitable doctrine of laches governed and the claims were not automatically time barred. The Fourth Circuit has since recanted and joined the other circuits in denying maritime jurisdiction to the asbestos claims. Oman v. Johns-Manville Corp., 764 F.2d 224 (4th Cir.), *cert. denied* sub nom. Oman v. H.K. Porter Co., 106 S. Ct. 351 (1985).

However, it seems that the Supreme Court is not at all averse to torts taking place in navigable waters where there is an effect on traditional maritime activities generally coming under federal maritime jurisdiction. In Jerome B. Grubart, Inc. v. Great Lakes Dredge & Dock Co., 115 S. Ct. 1043 (1995), the Court reiterated the test promulgated in *Executive Jet* and clarified in Sisson v. Ruby, 110 S. Ct. 2892 (1990). The Court explained: "Although we agree with petitioners that these cases do not say that every tort involving a vessel on navigable waters falls within the scope of admiralty jurisdiction no matter what, they do show that ordinarily that will be." 115 S. Ct. at 1053. The Court made clear that only one potential tortfeasor need be engaged in marine activities, and pointed out that in *Sisson,* supra, a defective washer/dryer was one cause of the accident, but the fact that washer/dryer manufacture is not a marine activity did not prevent federal jurisdiction from attaching.

The Supreme Court of Nevada applied the *Grubart* test in Lewis v. Sea Ray Boats, Inc., where a couple took a weekend cruise aboard a used boat purchased from the defendants. 65 P.3d 245 (Nev. 2003). After leaving the gasoline generator on overnight to power the air conditioner, one passenger died and the other was seriously injured by carbon monoxide poisoning. In reversing the district court's judgment in favor of the defendants on several grounds, the court concluded that while the "location" prong for determining whether the exercise of federal maritime jurisdiction was met, the "connection" prong was not because "the incident in question here had no potential for disruption of maritime commerce" on the reservoir where the accident occurred. 65 P.3d at 250, 251.

When the admiralty nexus is unmistakable, federal admiralty jurisdiction is regularly exercised. See, e.g., Sperry Rand Corp. v. Radio Corp. of America, 618 F.2d 319 (5th Cir. 1980) (products liability claim arising from damage to a vessel on navigable waters asserted by the manufacturer of a marine gyropilot steering system against manufacturer of electrical components that failed). It may also be to the plaintiff's advantage to apply the maritime pure comparative fault doctrine rather than more restrictive state law. Pan-Alaska Fisheries, Inc. v. Marine Construction & Design Co., 565 F.2d 1129 (9th Cir. 1977).

It has been observed that in admiralty, federal courts have access to an enclave wherein they may develop products liability doctrine unmolested by the restraints of *Erie*. See generally Paul S. Edelman, Products Liability in Maritime Law, 14 Forum 230 (1978); Raymond E. Dombroski, Jr., Comment, Maritime Products Liability: Tort and Contract Considerations Affecting Jurisdiction, 52 Temp. L.Q. 283 (1979); Joseph M. Costello, Forensic Issues in Admiralty and Products Liability, 62 Tul. L. Rev. 587 (1988). Perhaps the most famous example of this phenomenon is the decision of the United States Supreme Court in East River Steamship Corp. v. Transamerica Delaval Inc., 106 S. Ct. 2295 (1986). The Court's decision denying recovery under tort when there was no damage to persons or other property but only damage to the product itself has been highly influential on the development of state law on this topic.

CHAPTER THIRTEEN
International Perspectives on Products Liability

Although the developments in products liability law that most directly affect American firms involve claims brought in American courts based on events that have occurred within this country, American manufacturers and distributors cannot afford to ignore the international legal implications of their business activities. Transportation and communications technologies have intensified the interdependence of national economies and created a global marketplace. Moreover, our major trading partners have given increased attention to their own products liability laws. The first part of this chapter briefly describes the products liability systems of two of our principal economic competitors, the European Community and Japan; the second part raises the question of whether our liability system burdens American business firms with significant competitive disadvantages vis-à-vis their foreign rivals.

A. FOREIGN PRODUCTS LIABILITY LAW

Gary T. Schwartz, Product Liability and Medical Malpractice in Comparative Context, in The Liability Maze
36-51, 63-67, 70-75 (1991 Huber & Litan eds.) (Footnotes Omitted)[1]

[The author begins his analysis of European and Japanese products liability law by observing that those systems apply legal rules in manufacturing defect cases that approximate the strict liability of American law.]

. . . How do these legal systems deal with the manufacturer's possible liability for inadequate product design? One 1982 House of Lords case makes clear that English manufacturers can incur liability for negligent design. In a 1986 case the defendant, in assembling a specialized sports car, incorporated an engine marketed by the Ford Motor Company. That engine included a design feature that entailed a small risk of a carburetor fire. Although acknowledging that the chance

---

[1]. The authors believe that the chapter from which this text is excerpted is the best short summary of foreign products liability available. The heavily footnoted, longer version, and the book in which it appears, are recommended reading for all products liability mavens.

of a harmful incident was "quite . . . small," an English court perceived that the harm that could ensue from such an incident would be quite serious; accordingly, the court found the design inadequate. The court also rejected the defendant's claim that it had behaved reasonably in accepting an engine marketed and recommended by an industry leader like Ford. Rather, the court reasoned, the defendant, though apparently a small-scale concern, had an obligation to conduct its own engineering review of the adequacy of the Ford design. . . .

Claims of negligent design have clearly been permitted by German law; the plaintiff must identify a feasible alternative design that suggests that the manufacturer's chosen design poses an unreasonable risk of injury. French law likewise approves of the theory of negligent design. It is hard to figure out, however, what the criteria are for ascertaining negligence in these design cases; in particular, it is uncertain what emphasis French law places on "hidden" hazards in negligent design cases. Claims of negligent design are also viable under Japanese law. In one case involving a Mitsubishi automobile, a Japanese court ruled that since the manufacturer operates under a "high duty of care," it can be found negligent even if its design complies with both public regulation and industry practice; in this respect, Japanese law is in harmony with modern American legal norms. (French and German law also reject the defense of regulatory compliance.) In Japan the courts, in ruling that the approval of a drug by the Japanese equivalent of the Food and Drug Administration does not afford the drug manufacturer a tort defense, extend their aggressiveness by rejecting any doctrine of governmental immunity and hence holding the government liable along with the drug manufacturers on a joint-and-several basis. (To be sure, by calling for a sharing of liability between manufacturer and government, Japanese law reduces the liability the manufacturer would otherwise bear on its own.)

A manufacturer's negligent failure to warn has also produced liability under these countries' legal systems. In Japan drug manufacturers have been held responsible for side effects that they were evidently unaware of when they sold the drugs, but that they could have learned of had they done a more extensive job of premarketing testing. In France courts have been described as engaging in a "strict" and "stringent" review of the adequacy of product warnings. A 1983 case concerned an adhesive product sold in a package that contained warning labels identifying the product as "highly flammable"; despite these labels, the court found the manufacturer liable for a failure to provide explicit instructions on how to use the product safely. In Germany a 1972 case perceived that the warning obligations borne by drug manufacturers were "especially strict." In addition, German law has obliged the manufacturer to provide warnings about product hazards that relate to "the intended product use in its broadest sense"; accordingly, manufacturers, while not required to warn about clear instances of misuse, must nevertheless provide warnings that relate to a considerable range of "foreseeable misapplications." In this regard, German law has moved much of the way in the American direction. In one case a German court ruled that Honda (and its importer) had failed to warn existing owners of Honda motorcycles about the dangers of attaching to that motorcycle a windshield that another company had recently begun to market. By imposing on manufacturers (and importers) a duty to warn that continues long after the original product sale and by combining that duty with a requirement that manufacturers conduct tests on accessories produced by independent companies, this case in its own way goes further than any American failure-to-warn opinion. In England a leading failure-to-warn case is Wright

v. Dunlop Rubber Company. *Wright* can be interestingly compared with Borel v. Fibreboard Paper Products Corp., the 1973 American opinion that has provided the framework for American asbestos litigation. . . .

Recent Law Reform

The multinational law I have described is law that was largely in place by 1980. There are also recent law-reform efforts in Japan and Europe that need to be examined. . . . [For a summary of Japan's Product Liability Act of 1994, see excerpted article following this article.]

In January 1977 the Council of Europe's "Convention on Product Liability" was opened for signatures. In that year the Convention was signed by Belgium, France, Austria, and Luxembourg. However, no signatures have been obtained since 1977, largely because European countries were aware that the European Community (EC)[2] had begun working on the draft of a directive on product liability. Moreover, even the states that signed the Convention never went on to formally ratify it; for lack of the requisite number of ratifications, the Convention has never gone into effect. Meanwhile the EC Directive, after years of discussion, was finally adopted on July 25, 1985, and then "notified" on July 30, 1985. Such directives are not generally self-enforcing; the Product Liability Directive calls on all member states to adopt implementing legislation by July 30, 1988. England complied with its obligation by adopting a Consumer Protection Act in 1987. Germany approved its implementing statute in late 1989; the statute went into effect on January 1, 1990. Implementing legislation is currently under consideration in France.

What are the legal doctrines that the Directive endorses? Under article 1 of the Directive, "the producer shall be liable for damage caused by a defect in his product." Since there is no mention of negligence here, the producer's liability is implicitly strict liability. Of course, to say that a producer is strictly liable for a product "defect" is to spotlight the importance of the definition of "defect." According to article 6, "a product is defective when it does not provide the safety which a person is entitled to expect, taking all circumstances into account, including the presentation of the product." This is without doubt a weak definition. Indeed, it runs the risk of being viciously circular, since one is "entitled" to expect that level of safety which the law itself requires. Moreover, by requiring that "all circumstances [be taken] into account" in identifying defects, the Directive emphasizes how unstructured and open-ended its criterion of defect seems to be. The Directive's definition also makes no effort to take advantage of the American experience with the defect concept: it does not distinguish between manufacturing defects, design defects, and warning defects, nor does it establish criteria that would enable courts to identify any of those defects. The language of

---

2. The European Community (EC), established in 1957 by the Treaty of Rome, has twelve Member States: Belgium, Denmark, France, Germany, Greece, Ireland, Italy, Luxembourg, the Netherlands, Portugal, Spain, and the United Kingdom. The combined populations of these countries exceed 342 million, and the combined gross domestic products exceed $6,010 billion. The corresponding figures for the U.S. are 242 million and $4,435 billion, respectively. The EC consists of three subsidiary Communities: The European Economic Community, the European Atomic Energy Commission, and the European Coal and Steel Community. It can best be described as a common market on the path to complete economic and political union through the harmonization of national laws and policies. For an overview of the history and institutions of the EC, see The Economics of the European Community 11-39 (A.M. El-Agraa 2d ed. 1985).—EDS.

"the safety which a person is entitled to expect" seems to resemble the "ordinary consumer expectations" theme that once was popular in American product liability law. In America, however, that theme has declined in popularity, as judges and scholars have come to appreciate the nebulousness of the "consumer expectations" notion. American law, of course, refers to "consumer expectations," while the Directive refers to the expectations of "a person." Apparently, controversy is already raging within the Community about whether the article 6 concept of "a person" should be interpreted as including "producing persons" as well as "consumer persons."

The Directive makes clear that a product "shall not be considered defective for the *sole reason* that a better product is subsequently put into circulation" (emphasis added). This does not entail, however, the rejection of any pro-plaintiff position that an American court might adopt: the most that such a court might hold is that a later, better product is *some evidence* of the earlier product's defectiveness. The Directive also says that a manufacturer is not liable if "the defect is due to compliance . . . with mandatory regulations issued by the public authorities." This language falls short of establishing that compliance with regulations is a full defense. Rather, its point seems to be that a design that is *compelled* by public regulation cannot be regarded as defective and actionable. (Only if a design has been so compelled can it be said that the defect is "due to" the manufacturer's compliance with the regulation.) . . .

The issue on which the Directive withholds final judgment concerns the manufacturer's liability for product hazards that were not reasonably knowable at the time of original product sale. Recall that most American jurisdictions recognize a state-of-the-art limitation on liability, primarily in design and warning cases. What Americans talk about in "state-of-the-art" terms is what Europeans discuss in the language of "development risk." How to handle development risks was the most controversial issue the Community faced in preparing its Directive. In the Directive the EC Council of Ministers left this controversy unresolved. Under article 7(e) of the Directive, the producer bears no liability if the defect in the product could not have been "discovered" at the time the product was originally placed in circulation, on account of "the state of scientific and technical knowledge at the time." However, article 15.1(b) says that member states, in passing legislation to implement the Directive, have the option of dispensing with this "unknowability" defense. . . .

As for affirmative defenses in product liability cases, the Directive sets forth rules that do not much differ from those in effect in the United States. For example, disclaimers of liability are ineffective, and something like comparative negligence is the primary doctrinal response to issues of faulty behavior by the victim. In three other respects, however, the Directive comes across as distinctly conservative by American standards. The Directive, first of all, includes not only a conventional statute of limitations but also a statute of repose: all liabilities called for by the Directive are extinguished ten years after the date at which the product is put into circulation. . . .

The Directive's damage provisions can likewise be regarded as conservative. The Directive gives countries the option of incorporating a ceiling on liability for all damages resulting from a particular product line. . . .

The third conservative feature in the Directive is one that needs to be carefully described. Article 9 states that the Directive, standing alone, does not provide for the award of "non-material damage"—that is, damages for pain and suffering. Article 9 then goes on to say, however, that "this Article shall be without prejudice to national provisions relating to non-material damage." In pondering the meaning of article 9, one should consider article 13, which says that the Directive "shall not affect any rights which an injured person" has under his own nation's laws "at the moment when" the Directive was notified—July 30, 1985. This article is a key part of the Directive; under its auspices, for example, plaintiffs, by relying on negligence theories endorsed by their member states in 1985, can assert claims that otherwise would be wiped out by the Directive's statute of repose or precluded by the ceiling on liability the Directive authorizes. As for article 9, it can be interpreted as deriving its meaning from article 13; under this interpretation, the plaintiff, in order to collect pain-and-suffering damages, needs to invoke article 13 and assert a claim that relies on his member state's 1985 version of negligence law. . . .

Pattern of Litigation and Cost of Liability

What can be said . . . about the level of product litigation in the United States compared with the levels in other countries? A recent article by P.S. Atiyah compares liability in England and the United States. According to his calculations, the lawsuit-per-capita rate for all of tort law in the United States is about four times what it is in England; moreover, the per-capita cost of torts in this country is, in his estimate, perhaps ten times the English cost. His product liability numbers are even more one-sided: there are 70,000 product liability lawsuits in the United States annually, and only 200 in the United Kingdom. To be sure, the 350-to-1 ratio these numbers provide may be misleading. For one thing, as Atiyah makes clear, "claims" may lead to "lawsuits" more frequently in this country than they do in England; the American-English claims ratio might therefore be much less than the lawsuit ratio. Additionally, in England, as in the United States, there are large numbers of employees who have suffered disease on account of exposure to asbestos. In America tort suits resulting from these diseases are brought against manufacturers (since employers are shielded from tort liability by the exclusivity doctrine in workers' compensation). In England, however, an employee injured on the job not only has a workers' compensation-type claim (which he enforces against a government compensation fund) but also a possible tort action against his employer. Moreover, an English statute imposing on employers a near strict liability to keep job sites free of asbestos makes these tort actions against employers especially easy to win. Accordingly, asbestos victims in England usually sue their employers in tort and make no effort to bring much more complicated actions against product manufacturers. A high volume of asbestos litigation thus exists in England, but it focuses on employer defendants and so does not swell the number of product liability claims against manufacturers (as it does in the United States).

Because of factors such as these, the notion of a 350-to-1 American-English product liability relationship is not meaningful. Still, without a doubt product liability is thriving in the United States in a way that it is not in England. This point can be confirmed by two simple observations. As of 1988 no product liability verdict had ever been entered against a drug manufacturer; and until the 1986 specialty sports-car case described earlier, no auto manufacturer had ever been held liable under a theory of negligent design. Furthermore, there is reason to believe that the huge difference between the level of product liability in the United States and its level in England is matched by similar differences between the United States and other countries. John Fleming's 1982 article described the German strict liability drug statute enacted in 1976. Between 1976 and 1982 not a single claim had been filed under the statute. Five years later the liability costs that drug companies were incurring because of the statute equaled less than one-half of one percent of those companies' sales revenues. A Canadian product liability defense lawyer recently discussed one product that was widely distributed both in the United States and Canada. In the United States there were a thousand claims against the manufacturer because of that product; in Canada, only eight. One study of product liability in the Netherlands reported that in the past fifty years only five cases by injured consumers against the manufacturers of allegedly defective products resulted in published judicial opinions. The 1985 EC Directive has occasioned a spate of law review articles written (or coauthored) by European scholars. None of these articles suggest significant pre Directive differences in the litigation patterns from one member state to another, and several articles indicate that the litigation rate in the country under study is no more than a fraction of what the rate is perceived to be in the United States. . . .

. . . As far as Japan is concerned, it is often pointed out that the number of trials and lawsuits in Japan (both for personal injury and for other kinds of losses) is quite low. One explanation commonly offered for this is that the Japanese legal system is costly and inefficient in a way that discourages the presenting of claims. A second common explanation is that Japanese cultural attitudes inhibit victims from even considering bringing lawsuits. However, a recent article coauthored by Mark Ramseyer, which focuses on auto accidents in Japan, offers a different description. Although Ramseyer agrees that the number of Japanese auto accident cases that are finally tried in court is low, he thinks the legal system functions effectively — providing parties with such clear signals on the likely judicial results that the parties can (and do) settle claims for appropriate values without coming near the courthouse. Claims centers set up by liability insurance companies often facilitate these settlements. A small number of auto accident trials in Japan is thus compatible with a large number of claims and appropriate resolutions.

Ramseyer's account of the auto accident situation in Japan seems convincing. His evidence, however, is limited to auto cases and does not profess to relate to the situation in other areas of tort law, such as product liability. . . . [I]n Japan formal litigation against manufacturers is indeed uncommon. According to one survey of 194 major Japanese manufacturers, only 24 had been sued in Japan under product liability doctrines, and only 7 of these 24 had actually been subjected to judgments requiring compensation.

Apparently, however, these Japanese litigation rates are as low as they are in part because of the availability of alternative procedures for the resolution of disputes.[3] During a two-year period, for example, local consumer centers negotiated

---

3. An article in the New York Times, August 29, 1991, p.A4, col. 3, describes one such alternative process we are quite certain the author did not intend. The article reports that many would-be tort plaintiffs in Japan hire members of organized crime to collect damages for them, without ever hiring a lawyer or going to court. Like lawyers in the U.S., these "yakuza" are paid a percentage of the recovery.—EDS.

the outcome in more than 109 cases; personal injury damages were awarded in at least 34, with the largest award being about $20,000. The Japanese drug statute has been described above. Between 1980 and mid-1984, 270 claims were filed against the fund that this statute creates. Of these claims, 141 resulted in payments, averaging about $7,000. In addition, 54 products in Japan choose to carry an SG Seal. (The SG stands for Safety Goods; the 54 products are an odd assortment that includes baby carriages, swimming face-masks, mailboxes, bicycle helmets, and toilet-paper holders.) If a product marked with such a seal turns out to contain an injury-producing defect, the consumer can file a claim against the SG Association; if the claim is accepted, the largest allowable award is about $165,000. To cover the cost of all awards, the association buys product liability insurance with the help of fees it collects from the manufacturers who elect to use its seal. This voluntary program was authorized by 1973 consumer legislation. As it happens, that legislation can be read as indicating that the association should bear liability only under Japan's ordinary negligence principles. Nevertheless, for whatever reason the association has chosen to neglect its defense of no negligence and accept liability whenever the labeled product is demonstrably defective. Between 1973 and early 1986, 132 claims — more than half of all claims filed — resulted in payments to victims by the association. . . .

Systemic Differences

To identify those elements of the tort system that might explain the differences in liability patterns among countries, this section begins by considering ways in which civil procedures employed in American tort cases differ from the procedures relied on by other legal systems. I then look at how the American tort system provides for the remuneration of lawyers representing plaintiffs and defendants. Finally, I consider differences among countries in the calculation of damages in tort cases once liability has been affirmed.

Civil Procedure

A distinctive feature of American procedure is the availability of pretrial discovery. In American tort actions the plaintiff, seeking to acquire information that will support his case, can depose any potential witness and can subject the defendant to a series of written interrogatories. These are discovery techniques that are largely unavailable in European legal systems and in Japan as well. Discovery in its American form clearly makes it enormously more feasible for the plaintiff's lawyer to develop the facts of a complicated tort case. And claims in medical malpractice and product liability are usually complex. Indeed, an experienced Japanese lawyer is emphatic that the lack of discovery places the Japanese product liability plaintiff in a "very weak and difficult position." . . .

One distinctive feature of American procedure that clearly does make a major difference relates to the identity of the trier-of-fact. In the United States, tort cases are heard by a jury (under the supervision, to be sure, of a trial judge). But juries in tort cases are unknown in civil law countries like France and Germany; nor are juries now provided for in tort actions in Japan. In England personal injury cases were commonly heard by juries until 1883, when new rules of procedure were adopted that gave the trial judge the discretion to rule whether a jury trial is appropriate. The trial judge's discretion was reemphasized by a 1933 statute. However, judicial opinions subsequently interpreting that statute have declared that in personal injury cases jury trials should be ordered (if at all) only in exceptional circumstances. . . .

As for the battle of experts in product . . . cases, such battles are most likely in the United States and England, given the adversary system that is associated with the common law. By contrast, the civil law system that prevails in continental Europe assigns a far greater range of responsibilities to the judge. In the trial itself, it is the judge who will probably examine the expert; for that matter, the judge may well be the person who designates those experts who will testify. (For example, the Dutch judge hearing a product case involving the sleeping medication Halcion resolved to decide the case by arranging for a committee of three experts.) And even when a party is allowed to select his own expert, for that party's lawyer to interview the expert before trial might be regarded as an impropriety. For an American lawyer not to "prepare" the important witnesses in his case would be all but unthinkable; in civil law countries such preparation, far from being obligatory, is frequently just about forbidden. . . .

Financing Lawyers' Fees

This country's legal system differs considerably from legal systems elsewhere in how plaintiffs' lawyers and defendants' lawyers receive their compensation. As for the plaintiff's lawyer, in the United States the personal injury plaintiff routinely enters into a contingent fee arrangement with his lawyer pursuant to which the lawyer retains perhaps one-third of whatever recovery is eventually received but receives nothing if the claim is disposed of without any payment by the defendant. Contingent fee arrangements are regarded as unethical, however, by the legal systems in England and other European countries. In those legal systems, therefore, the middle-income victim who is thinking of filing a claim realizes that if his claim finally proves unsuccessful, he will be required to pay his own lawyer's fee. As for the fee of the defense counsel, the "American rule" specifies that, regardless of who finally wins the case, each side should bear its own legal costs. By contrast, the so-called English rule — which is also in effect in other European legal systems — specifies that the losing party must reimburse the prevailing party for the latter's attorney's fees. That is, the plaintiff who loses his case is required to pay not only his own lawyer's fee but also the fee of the defendant's lawyer. . . .

Damages

The American plaintiff who prevails on the issue of liability is likely . . . to receive a much larger damage award than the plaintiff in Europe or Japan who is similarly successful. In the American tort system, personal injury awards as large as $15 million are by no means unknown. In Japan, however, even the high-income professional who is totally disabled because of a defendant's clear negligence is able to recover no more than about $1,400,000. And Japanese awards are high relative to awards in Europe. In 1989 the largest personal injury award in France was about $700,000. As of the early 1980s the largest medical malpractice award in England was $775,000. Danzon has more recently reported that the mean payment for malpractice claims in England is currently only one-fourth of the mean payment for such claims in the United States. . . .

In some respects larger damage awards in the United States are due to distinctive attributes of the American economy. For example, since real American wages remain higher than real wages elsewhere, American awards for income losses will be higher than similar awards in other parts of the world. In other respects our larger damage awards are due to distinctive features in the American law of damages. For example, American wrongful death statutes, as interpreted by American judges, provide for a measure of recovery in wrongful death actions that often greatly surpasses the damages available in such actions in countries like England. Also, English damages for income losses are measured on an after-tax basis; most American courts, by contrast, are willing to afford compensation for pretax losses. Moreover, in Germany, France, and Japan, punitive damages are understood to be simply unavailable in tort actions for personal injuries. . . .

One can begin, then, with the legal point that the milder European version of the collateral source rule renders the rule inapplicable to benefits provided to the victim by social welfare programs. One can then blend in the public policy observation that disability programs in Europe — though of course far less than 100 percent — are much more generous than their American counterparts, and that England, France, Germany, and Japan all operate under systems of socialized medicine (which do cover most of the costs of medical treatment). In a country like England, tort awards include almost nothing for medical costs, and the compensation they provide for income losses is reduced to acknowledge important collateral sources; moreover, as noted, the pain-and-suffering damages that those awards include are measured conservatively. In all, then, it becomes easy to understand why personal injury awards in the United States are so much larger than those in legal systems elsewhere. . . .

Jane Stapleton's article, Bugs in Anglo-American Products Liability, 53 S.C. L. Rev. 1225 (2002), uses the example of pathogenically-infected products to highlight the differences between how the Third Restatement and the European Directive address products liability claims.

Hideyuki Kobayashi & Yoshimasa Furuta, Products Liability Act and Transnational Litigation in Japan
34 Tex. Int'l Law J. 93, 94-101 (1999)

I. Introduction

On July 1, 1994, the Diet of Japan announced the adoption of the Products Liability Act (PLA), which applies to products as defined therein, delivered on and after July 1, 1995. Since the PLA was implemented, six lawsuits have been filed in Japanese courts alleging liability under the PLA, but none have reached judgment on the merits yet. In this article, we will summarize the various features of the PLA. In addition, we will analyze several selected issues concerning the transnational litigation aspects of products liability lawsuits in Japan — namely, service of process, jurisdiction to adjudicate, parallel litigation, and the recognition of foreign judgments. While the new Code of Civil Procedure of Japan (CCP) took effect on January 1, 1998, superseding the previous version of the Code of Civil Procedure (Old CCP), no material amendment was made with respect to issues concerning transnational litigation. Accordingly, case law and scholarly discussions under the Old CCP are still relevant under the CCP.

II. Outline of The Products Liability Act

A. History

Prior to the passage of the PLA, there was no specific statute or body of law governing questions of products liability in Japan. Instead, the law traditionally dealt with products liability and related issues of consumer protection under the Civil Code of Japan (Civil Code). Almost two hundred cases dealing with products liability in Japanese jurisprudence have developed on the theory of liability in contract (when a contractual relationship of some type exists between a plaintiff and a defendant) or on the theory of liability in tort under the Civil Code (in those instances, when a contractual relationship does not exist between a plaintiff and a defendant). Under both theories, courts have generally required a finding of negligence to establish the defendant's liability. In cases where products liability is an issue, usually no contractual relationship exists, and therefore most cases are brought under the tort theory. However, in some cases based on tort theory, courts have imposed a very high duty of care on the defendant or have tentatively recognized a presumption of negligence. This especially occurs in cases involving food and medical products. Accordingly, the liability of the defendant in these cases has become akin to strict liability.

On December 10, 1993, the Economic Welfare Council, an auxiliary organ of the Economic Planning Agency of Japan, released its 14th Report (EWC Report), which recommended that the Japanese government enact a products liability act. The PLA, which is the result of numerous draft versions debated over many years, is modeled closely on the Directive on Liability for Defective Products that the European Union (formerly the European Community) adopted in 1985 (Products Liability Directive), rather than on the substantial body of products liability law that has developed in the United States.

B. General Features of the PLA

The primary purpose of the PLA is to protect consumers against injuries caused by defective products, and thereby, to improve the national living standard and the development of the economy generally. Key provisions include Article 2, which prescribes the range of products subject to the law, particularly manufactured or processed items of movable property, and Article 3, which establishes the standard of strict liability. Exemptions from liability are set forth in Article 4 and can be procured by proving that a product meets the "development risk" or "state-of-the-art" standard for such products, or that the product is a component or ingredient manufactured without negligence and according to specifications provided by the manufacturer of a product into which the components or ingredients are incorporated. Liability may also be limited under Article 5, which provides certain time limits within which a plaintiff must claim damages, and also stipulates special time limits for damages accumulated over long periods or that are discovered later. Finally, Article 6 provides that, in addition to the relief provided under the PLA, a plaintiff may seek relief under the provisions of the Civil Code. A detailed analysis of each provision of the PLA follows.

C. Individual Articles

1. Article 1: Purpose

The specific purposes of the PLA include the stable upgrading of the national quality of life and the proper development of the national economy through the protection of consumers. Article 1 provides only abstract purposes and is a general principle; therefore, it is not intended to apply to particular cases directly.

2. Article 2: Definitions

Article 2, a key provision of the PLA, defines the range of the manufactured products covered by the PLA as well as factors and criteria for determining defects and defining the persons who may be held liable for damages.

a. Manufactured Products. Paragraph 1 of Article 2 defines the products that the PLA designates as manufactured or processed movable items of property. The upshot of this definition is that the PLA does not apply to immovable property, energy, services, or unprocessed products, including unprocessed agricultural products. Parts and raw materials, however, are included in the definition of movable items of property to which the PLA does apply. There are several important points that should be noted with regard to this definition.

First, intangibles such as electricity or services, which are not regarded as movable items of property under the Civil Code, are outside the scope of the PLA. Thus, unlike tile Products Liability Directive, the PLA does not apply to electricity. However, a product such as software, which is generally regarded as an intangible, is not within the scope of the PLA, whereas a product incorporating software would be subject to it.

When an item of movable property is installed into immovable property after the movable property has been delivered, the movable parts or components will be subject to the PLA because they were items of movable property at the time of their delivery.

Unprocessed agricultural products are not included among movable items of property in principle, because they are products of nature and are not manufactured. However, in recent years numerous agricultural products have been produced artificially by using high technology (e.g., with the aid of biotechnology). Accordingly, the applicability of the PLA to such products is currently vague and uncertain and will likely remain so until clarified by the courts.

The most hotly debated issue in the drafting of this legislation was the application of the PLA to whole blood preparations and blood derivative preparations for use in transfusions in humans. The EWC Report took the position that, on the one hand, granulated blood plasma products, which are extracted from human blood and processed in a highly complicated manner, should be subject to the PLA because of the extensive processing required to produce them. On the other hand, whole blood preparations and blood derivative preparations, both of which are substances used for transfusion purposes and which are made from human tissue left intact and applied in natural form, should not be subject to the PLA, according to the EWC Report, because they are left in essentially their natural form. However, following various discussions and evaluations by relevant ministries and the government's project team, the government's present view is that both whole blood preparations and blood derivative preparations should be subject to the PLA on the basis that they are produced using coagulating agents. The Diet finally adopted the government's proposed treatment without any changes. However, opponents of the official version succeeded in passing a resolution providing that any defects in blood preparations should be evaluated in consideration of possible mitigating factors such as the need for the product in emergency situations, the inclusion of clear warnings about the side effects and risks from use, and demonstrated preparation in compliance with the highest safety standards.

The Economic Welfare Council maintains that raw vaccines should be outside the scope of the PLA, whereas inactivated vaccines such as the influenza vaccine or Hepatitis B vaccine should be subject to the PLA. However, the view of the government is that all vaccines, including raw vaccines, should be covered by the PLA.

Finally, secondhand goods are subject to the PLA, although waste products are not.

b. Defects. The level of safety that the relevant product is generally expected to meet will be judged according to the expectations of an ordinary person under normal circumstances. Paragraph 2 of Article 2 stipulates three factors to be considered in determining defects: (1) the characteristics of the product; (2) the manner of the expected use of the product; and (3) the presence of the defect at the time of the delivery of the product by the manufacturer. All of these factors are generally important and relevant to all products. In this regard, the PLA basically follows Article 6 of the Products Liability Directive.

c. Liable Entity. Paragraph 3 of Article 2 provides that a person who manufactures, processes, or imports a product—a "Manufacturer"—is an entity that, in principle, may be held liable for defective goods. Furthermore, a party that affixes to a product its name, trade name, trademark, or any other indication that it is the Manufacturer of the product—a "Represented Manufacturer"—is also an entity that may be held liable for defective goods. Finally, a person who affixes his or her name, trade name, trademark, or any other indication from which he or she may be deemed to be the substantial Manufacturer of the product is an entity that may be held liable for defective goods.

The PLA does not include a distributor as a party who can be held liable for defective goods, and in this regard the PLA differs significantly from the Products Liability Directive. However, if a distributor affixes its name to a product, it may be deemed to be a Manufacturer, and thus may become subject to the PLA. In the SUMON (Subacute Myelo Optico Neuropathy) cases, several Japanese courts ruled that a chemical company that indicated it was a distributor could be deemed to be a substantial Manufacturer and thus could be held liable for a defective product it distributed.

3. Article 3: Products Liability

Article 3 provides for the "strict liability" or "liability without fault" of the Manufacturer. As mentioned above, this is a dramatic departure from liability based on fault — i.e., negligence — recognized under the Civil Code.

It is important to note that the PLA does not cover pure economic loss. Instead, economic loss may be recovered under the Civil Code. In the event that economic loss occurs along with other damages, and those damages are attributable to a defective product, the economic loss can be recovered together with other damages under the PLA.

Because Article 3 does not exclude a businessperson's economic loss, various parties have criticized this provision because it can operate to protect against business losses under the theory of strict liability, and thereby, diverge from the intent of the law — namely, to protect consumers against damages to the person or property. The Economic Welfare Council maintains that economic losses of businesspersons should not be covered by the PLA because they can deal with manufacturers on an equal basis and because the purpose of the PLA is to protect consumers. However, the PLA has not adopted this distinction between businesspersons and consumers because the difference between these two groups is not always clear, as there are many small business operators in Japan. The Civil Code, which is not excluded by the PLA, also recognizes no such distinction. For example, in a recent case concerning fire damages caused by a defective television set, the Osaka District Court ruled in favor of the plaintiff who was not an individual consumer but a corporation.

4. Article 4: Exemptions

Item 1 of Article 4 is the so-called "state-of-the-art" or "development risk" exemption. Item 2 of Article 4 provides an exemption for manufacturers of components or ingredients used in a finished product that proves defective, or if the components are produced according to the specifications of another manufacturer that incorporates them into an end product, provided that the manufacturer of the components has not otherwise been negligent with respect to the relevant defect. Both of these provisions are based on similar exemptions in Article 7 of the Products Liability Directive.

The adoption of Item 1 was hotly debated. In particular, various industries insisted on the adoption of the "state-of-the-art" or "development risk" exemption to ensure that this legislation does not discourage development or innovation. On the other hand, if this exemption is interpreted too broadly, it may substantially result in a return to fault-based liability. Taking these considerations into account, the Economic Welfare Council has taken the position that scientific and technological knowledge must be judged against the highest standards of technology applicable at the time and not against the level applied by a specific manufacturer or the industry. Accordingly, many manufacturers may find it difficult to take advantage of this exemption.

5. Article 5: Limitations Period

Article 5 concerns the limitations period during which a plaintiff can bring a lawsuit under the PLA, and is based on the corresponding provision of the Products Liability Directive. The limitation of ten years from the date of the delivery of a product, in Paragraph 1 of Article 5, is in stark contrast to the twenty-year limitation from the commission of a tortious act that applies under the Civil Code. The drafters of the PLA determined that a ten-year limitations period is a reasonable term in which to settle legal disputes considering the normal life span of products, the preservation period of documents, and the application of insurance coverage. In addition, Paragraph 1 requires a plaintiff to commence an action within three years after the victim, or his or her legal representative, has discovered damages or injuries and identified the liable parties. Paragraph 2 of Article 5 provides for the calculation of the time period in which to identify damages that may have accumulated or delayed but that have not yet become apparent.

6. Article 6: Application of the Civil Code

Pursuant to Article 6, unless otherwise provided by the PLA, the Civil Code also applies to products liability lawsuits. This is significant because the Civil Code allows a defendant to limit liability by way of comparative damages. In addition, Article 6 permits a plaintiff to seek compensation for damages under both the PLA and the Civil Code to the extent that they are not overlapping. In this regard, the limitations period under the Civil Code is twenty years, enabling a plaintiff to seek relief even after the ten-year limitation under the PLA has expired, unless three years have elapsed since the victim first became aware of damages, injuries, or the liable parties.

D. Other Matters

The PLA does not provide presumptions for the existence of defects or for causality between defects and damages. The legislature chose not to include such presumptions because proof of the existence of defects or causality depends on the particular facts of each case; therefore, to recognize presumptions would go beyond the objectives of the PLA.

Other omissions in the PLA include provisions for the discovery of evidence, punitive damages, and limits on the amount of liability.

Finally, the Diet, with an aim toward lessening the burden of proof borne by the plaintiff, has adopted resolutions proposing that an ombudsperson-type of institute be established to monitor the causes of damages in products liability cases.

For a useful collection of articles on foreign products liability, see Symposium on Products Liability: Comparative Approaches & Transnational Litigation, 34 Tex. Int'l L.J. 1 (1999). See also Simon Taylor, The Harmonisation of European Product Liability Rules: French and English Law, 48 Int'l & Comp. L.Q. 419 (1999).

For an article suggesting that the new Japanese products liability law's strict liability has led to an increase in liability complaints and caused the Japanese and American practices to converge concerning product labeling, liability insurance, and attention to liability concerns in commercial contracts, see R. Daniel Kelemen & Eric C. Sibbitt, The Americanization of Japanese Law, 23 U. Pa. J. Int'l Econ. L. 269 (2002).

B. DOES THE AMERICAN LIABILITY SYSTEM PUT AMERICAN FIRMS AT A COMPETITIVE DISADVANTAGE?

American firms face at home a liability system that is much harsher than the systems in the EC or in Japan. Do these differences necessarily place American firms at a competitive disadvantage with their foreign counterparts? Many observers, both lay and academic, answer this question affirmatively. In an August 1991 address to the American Bar Association, Vice President Dan Quayle expressed discontent with the American liability system and its impact on our nation's world economic standing: "There are stumbling blocks that we can't make excuses for, because, quite frankly, they're our own fault. Our system of civil justice is, at times, a self-inflicted competitive disadvantage." Nonetheless, the effects of products liability laws on American producers are not altogether clear. Consider the following materials.

1. Effects of the American Liability System on Costs and Prices of American Products

There can be no doubt that the American products liability system imposes uniquely high costs on firms — predominantly American firms — distributing products in this country. Earlier in the chapter, we sketched some of the reasons in our discussion of the substantive and procedural differences between the products liability laws of the U.S. and its principal competitors. In sum, the scope of liability faced by U.S. firms is significantly greater than that burdening the EC and Japan. American manufacturers are also more likely to be held liable for injuries arising from older products already on the market not equipped with modern safety devices. International competitors will be less concerned with such liability since very few older products of foreign origin exist in the United States. See Randolph J. Stayin, The U.S. Product Liability System: A Competitive Advantage to Foreign Manufacturers, 14 Can.-U.S. L.J. 193, 199 (1988). In addition, suits can be instituted in the United States much more readily than in other nations. Stayin argues that the procedural ease with which lawsuits may be brought against domestic manufacturers

> confers an advantage upon foreign manufacturers which makes them less accountable than U.S. manufacturers to persons injured by their products, which results in unprotected American users of foreign products, lower insurance costs to be included in

the prices of foreign products and loss of market share for U.S. manufacturers. [Stayin at 204]

The higher costs borne by American manufacturers can also be attributed to non-legal factors such as divergent cultural attitudes. As one observer notes:

> . . . [T]here is also the overriding predisposition among European and Japanese [accident victims] against litigation, a phenomenon in stark contrast to the high level of litigation consciousness among the American population. The "deep pocket" expectation does not exist in these countries. In Japan, the injured worker would consider it improper to attempt to hold others responsible for his/her injury. Bringing a lawsuit would cause further "loss of face." [Stayin at 197]

Besides the costs of paying victorious plaintiffs, American firms must insure against liability to a much greater extent than their foreign counterparts. Indeed, a 1984 International Trade Administration study found that domestic machine manufacturers had products liability insurance costs 20 to 100 times greater in their respective home markets than did similar foreign firms in their respective home markets. A wealth of anecdotal evidence about rising insurance costs supplements such empirical studies. For example, a major manufacturer of lacrosse equipment was offered $1 million in coverage for a $200,000 annual premium payment. Members of the Woodworking Machinery Distributors Association received premium increases of up to 1,000 percent on only five days' notice. Even when competing in international markets, many American companies, by failing to purchase separate insurance for foreign coverage, do not reap the benefits of lower premium payments associated with foreign markets.

In addition to paying higher tort claims and insurance premiums, American firms are inundated by less obvious costs, such as deductible sums and awards above insurance policy limits. Other significant costs include legal expenses, settlement payments, and product safety testing expenditures. Firms also engage in socially wasteful behavior designed to evade liability, the costs of which are difficult to estimate.

Obviously American firms must be more attentive than foreign manufacturers to their potential liability. But what does this mean in terms of product costs and prices? Selected industries and municipalities are certainly hit hard because of the perceived risk associated with their goods and services. Indeed, even marginal increases in costs and prices can be very damaging to firms participating in highly competitive markets with relatively undifferentiated products. Furthermore, smaller businesses may suffer more than larger, diversified firms that are better able to absorb the costs of liability insurance. Peter Huber believes that the impact of products liability law on costs and prices is significant:

> [The $80 billion annual "liability tax"] is one of the most ubiquitous taxes we pay, now levied on virtually everything we buy, sell, and use. The tax accounts for 30 percent of the price of a stepladder and over 95 percent of the price of childhood vaccines. It is responsible for one-quarter of the price of a ride on a Long Island tour bus and one-third of the price of a small airplane. It will soon cost large municipalities as much as they spend on fire and sanitation services. . . .
>
> Because of the tax, you cannot use a sled in Denver city parks or a diving board in New York City schools. You cannot buy an American Motors "CJ" Jeep or a set of con-

struction plans for novel airplanes from Burt Rutan, the pioneering designer of the Voyager . . . [from Huber, Liability: The Legal Revolution and Its Consequences, (1988), pp.1-2]

But the aggregate effects of the liability system on product costs and prices may not be as significant as Huber suggests, despite the crippling impact of liability on certain individual products and industries. As Robert E. Litan notes, the "liability tax" on average comprises only 2 percent of the cost of all products and services sold within the United States. See Litan, The Liability Explosion and American Trade Performance: Myths and Realities, in Tort Law and the Public Interest: Competition, Innovation, and Consumer Welfare, Peter H. Schuck, ed. (1991). Moreover, Huber's $80 billion liability figure, which he seems to pull out of thin air, is only half the story. That estimate does not represent the net impact on U.S. living standards, which Litan contends is the appropriate measure of the competitive effect of the current products liability system. Benefits of the liability system include improved standards of quality control, safer products for consumers, healthier workplace environments, and an arguably more "just" distribution of wealth. Thus, the infrequency with which products cases are litigated in Japan is not necessarily desirable, given the fairness and efficiency goals served by the consistent imposition of strict liability. When considered in their entirety, Litan argues, these benefits could potentially outweigh the negative impact of increased liability costs.

Admittedly, little empirical evidence exists regarding the safety benefits accruing from the U.S. products liability scheme. Defenders of the system can point to the withdrawal of the Ford Pinto and the Dalkon Shield from the market as instances where the system presumably worked; but few conclusions can be drawn from such isolated occurrences. In an attempt to analyze these benefits empirically, George Priest found little evidence that increased liability promotes safety. See George Priest, Products Liability Law and the Accident Rate, pp.184-222, in Liability: Perspectives and Policy, Robert E. Litan and Clifford Winston, eds. (1988). Like any statistical survey on the subject, however, Priest's study failed to account for the inherent complexity of evaluating the impact of liability laws on safety and competitiveness. But even if Priest is mistaken and significant safety benefits exist, their value is certainly diminished by the high administrative costs of the tort liability system. Approximately half of all total awards and settlements are paid to insurers and attorneys for monitoring the claims process. See James S. Kakalik & Nicholas M. Pace, Costs and Compensation Paid in Tort Litigation, pp.ix-x (1986).

Additionally, the substantive and procedural differences between American and foreign products liability law may have relatively little effect upon international trade. After all, most foreign-country defendants who engage in business in the United States can be hauled into American courts and will have sufficient assets within this country to satisfy any judgment rendered against them. A leading U.S. Supreme Court case limiting jurisdiction against foreign corporations (Asahi Metal Industry Co. v. Superior Court of Calif., 480 U.S. 102 (1987)) is too uncertain and tenuous a decision to stand for the proposition that larger international manufacturers will be able to routinely escape the jurisdictional reach of the American legal system. Granted, potential jurisdictional and choice-of-law anomalies do exist. For example, foreign manufacturers sued in the United States may be subject to their own restrictive discovery rules, and victorious American plaintiffs may encounter some difficulties in executing judgments secured against foreign firms. Nonetheless, foreign defendants should continue to be held accountable for their commercial activities affecting the United States.

In cases involving foreign plaintiffs who sue in the United States on claims that should be brought elsewhere, judicial application of *forum non conveniens* will mitigate against unilateral advantages that injured foreigners may reap. Therefore, when foreign manufacturers serve American markets, theoretically they should be as amenable to service as domestic firms. And when U.S. manufacturers conduct business abroad, they should be subject to less demanding foreign products liability standards (assuming foreign courts apply forum law). Certain cases will be dismissed or considered by domestic courts, but as these suits are few in number their impact on American competitiveness should be slight.

Rather than draw "common sense" conclusions from examining the increasing trade deficit and the differences between the American, European Community, and Japanese products liability systems, Litan attempts to determine exactly what affects a country's "competitiveness." In order to assess the impact of the products liability system on a nation's competitiveness, he says, one must

> determine how its citizens' living standards are affected when its trade is balanced. Bangladesh may import no more than it exports, but it is hardly "competitive" with industrialized nations whose living standards are far higher. Conversely, nations such as the United States may enjoy rising living standards largely by running trade deficits and borrowing from abroad to do so. Only by measuring our rate of improvement in living standards relative to other countries *when our trade is balanced* can we know how competitive we truly are.
>
> The analytical distinction between competitiveness and trade performance has important implications for how one thinks about the international impact of the U.S. tort system. Perhaps most significant, it demonstrates that however adverse an impact liability trends may have on U.S. firms, *the tort system will not permanently affect the nation's overall trade deficit unless it also somehow affects domestic saving and investment.* [Litan at 130]

Noting that any effects of liability trends on savings and investment are minimal, Litan concludes that using the trade balance to assess the impact of liability trends is nonsensical. As was mentioned earlier, some firms and industries will bear a greater burden of the liability explosion:

> [T]he liability tax should encourage certain types of imports and discourage certain exports. But . . . this does *not* mean that the overall trade balance will be affected. Any initial negative effects on the trade balance will increase the supply of dollars on the world market, thereby reducing the value of the dollar. After some period of adjustment, other exports will rise and other imports will fall. The aggregate trade balance will remain unchanged. [Litan at 140]

To assume, by examining international trade statistics, that products liability contributes significantly to the plight of American manufacturers competing abroad thus ignores other relevant factors and cause-and-effect relationships. American firms certainly bear higher liability costs than their foreign counterparts. But the magnitude of this burden is difficult to assess in light of the dearth of statistical evidence on the subject. According to Litan, many factors, in addition to liability influencing firms' costs and pricing decisions, render inadequate any attempt to conclusively establish the tort system's effects.

2. Effects of the American Products Liability System on Product Innovation

Even if the direct costs of liability are relatively insignificant, products liability law may reduce America's competitiveness by discouraging product innovation. Many observers believe that the threat of liability has a stifling effect on the research and development of new products because of the unforeseen risks these products might pose. Rather than venture into untested waters, it is argued, manufacturers opt to continue producing older designs whose risks are typically knowable. As Stayin summarizes,

> [T]hrough the suspicious-looking glass of our product liability law, attorneys too often see the risks rather than the benefits. They advise their clients that the new development may be too risky, too new, with no precedent to follow in a broad area of technology. . . . This thinking leads to a status quoism that prefers staying with a proven product rather than taking a chance with something new, more advanced and more competitive. Adoption of a new, safer technology implicitly involves acknowledgement that the previous technology was not as safe as possible. There is a perception that it is safer to stay with an established product than risk lawsuits with an unknown product which may also stimulate lawsuits with respect to established product lines. [Stayin at 206]

Peter W. Huber echoes a similar sentiment, but focuses more on the capabilities and tendencies of jurors rather than the risk-averseness of corporate managers and the attorneys advising them:

> Jurors can make reasonably sensitive judgments about people—even about professionals—because we are all in the people-judging business every day of our lives. But jurors are not experts about technology itself, and intuition here is a terrible guide. When a juror is asked to categorize technologies—as distinct from their inventors and managers—as good, bad, or ugly, the answers follow a quite predictable pattern. Age, familiarity, and ubiquity are the most powerful legitimizing forces known to the layperson. The inexpert juror is predisposed at every turn to identify technologies that are novel, exotic, unfamiliar, or adventuresome as unwelcome and fraught with danger—in short, defective. [Huber at 157]

Evidence regarding the influence of liability on innovation is even more speculative and anecdotal than in the context of cost and price increases. The presence of many complex factors that affect the decision of whether or not to market a new product makes analyzing such developments particularly difficult. Moreover, assessing the consequences of the absence of action—that is, the failure to develop new products—is not currently feasible. Thus, much of the literature in the field is brimming with case studies of firms and trades, such as the pharmaceutical and textile industries, that have absorbed a disproportional impact of the liability explosion. Alfred W. Cortese and Kathleen L. Blaner, for example, list 30 instances of "anti-competitive effects" of American products liability law, including plant closings, discontinued product lines, decisions not to market new products, and discontinued research. Cortese & Blaner, The Anti-Competitive Impact of U.S. Product Liability Laws: Are Foreign Businesses Beating Us at Our Own Game?, 9 J. of L. & Comm. 167, 198-202 (1989). Their evidence seems to bear out Litan's previously mentioned observation that products liability law may affect the composition of trade. Most of Cortese and Blaner's examples involve either sporting goods, pharmaceuticals, or component parts in motor vehicles and aircraft.

Nonetheless, some empirical evidence on the link between products liability and innovation is available. A popular approach is to sample corporate managers to assess the effect of products liability on their decisions to introduce new goods. In one such survey, 19 percent of the respondents reported that they dropped a product line because of the high risks associated with it, while 16 percent said they decided against developing a new product because of liability fears. Another survey revealed that 57 percent of the managers polled agreed that all-important innovative technology is not being produced for fear of crippling lawsuits. See Stayin 204-205. Top-level corporate complaints, however, should be received with a certain skepticism, as the respondents may be quick to blame external forces for problems attributable to their own shortcomings.

Fortunately, more extensive statistical research exists. In Rationalizing the Relationship between Product Liability and Innovation, in Tort Law and the Public Interest (1991), Peter Schuck, ed., W. Kip Viscusi and Michael J. Moore compare products liability costs (the ratio of premiums per policy to industry sales) with various measures of innovation and new product introductions. Though they determine that increasing liability costs do dampen innovative strategies, the effect is not so devastating as the criticisms of corporate executives would lead one to believe. With guarded optimism, they conclude:

> The statistical evidence indicates that the relationships are much more complex than is generally believed. By most measures we have examined, innovators bear a larger share of the product liability burden. On the other hand, there is no evidence that their share is escalating dramatically. Moreover, product liability has increased incentives for introducing product design changes that outweigh liability's depressing effect on the introduction of products with new attributes other than those relating to safety. Id. at 123.

Another comprehensive project, edited by Huber and Litan, examines the link between liability law and safety and innovation in five selected contexts: motor vehicles, medical malpractice, prescription drugs, chemical development, and general aviation. See The Liability Maze, Peter W. Huber and Robert E. Litan, eds. (1991). Regarding safety, most of the authors in the study conclude that factors outside the tort system—such as regulation, industry-imposed standards, and bad publicity—are primarily responsible for influencing product safety. With respect to innovation, however, most of the authors find a positive correlation between sharply rising liability costs and diminished innovation. For example, general aviation manufacturers, long burdened by skyrocketing liability, have ceased new developments and, in some cases, production altogether. Though Huber and Litan make clear that tort law may reduce innovation in those particular industries hardest hit by liability, their study does not address products liability law's effect on American manufacturing in general. In the aggregate, the negative impact of liability would presumably be much less significant.

In a RAND study conducted for the Institute for Civil Justice, Peter Reuter found "surprisingly little evidence suggesting that liability currently hinders international competitiveness." See Peter Reuter, The Economic Consequences of Expanded Corporate Liability: An Exploratory Study (1988). In accordance with Huber and Litan's findings, however, Reuter's research suggests that certain industries (like sporting goods) do constitute exceptions.

Assuming that American products liability law influences corporate behavior and diminishes international competitiveness, one must be fully aware of the other factors that arguably have a much greater impact on American trade performance. Corporate managers may emphasize "the bottom line" without giving due regard to the long-term benefits of research and modernization. In addition, the American labor force may be less well-educated than foreign workers in some markets, which could result in increased outlays for training and less competitive products. The United States government also plays a relatively inactive role in supporting and protecting American industries. A frequent target of criticism is the allegedly unfair trade practices of our international competitors, primarily Japan. For example, the Japanese word processor industry was tagged with steep import duties after an investigation revealed that those firms "dumped" their products on U.S. markets, or sold them well below fair market value. See "Duty to Rise for Japanese Processors," N.Y. Times, Aug. 9, 1991, §D, at 1. Oligopolistic practices in some domestic Japanese industries, like the glass trade, render such markets virtually impenetrable by American firms, even those whose prices are lower than Japanese firms'. Close relationships between wholesalers and manufacturers, coupled with domination of the entire distributional scheme by a handful of firms, prompted one American business director to note: "We won't be able to compete in the 21st century [with Japanese glass manufacturers outside the United States and Japan] if they still have a cash sanctuary in Japan." See Japan Glass Market Proves Hard to Crack, Wall St. J., Aug. 7, 1991, at A8.

The effects of products liability law on innovation may be potentially more damaging to America's long-run competitive well-being than are marginal cost and price increases induced by exposure to tort liability. Once again, however, an absence of empirical research makes such conclusions difficult, if not impossible, to assess. Quantifying the countless other variables that affect product innovation — trade barriers, government involvement in and regulation of industry, consumer demand, unstable world financial markets, and so on — would be next to impossible. But if the criticisms and observations of corporate managers are sincere and accurately reflect their decision-making processes, then perhaps their shared perceptions of the products liability system are as important as the underlying reality.

For recent law review commentary on the product innovation question, see Cristoph Ann, Innovators in the Crossfire: A Policy Sketch for Unknowable Risks in European and United States Product Liability Law, 10 Tul. Eur. & Civ. L.F. 173 (1995); Bruce A. Thomas & Lawrence G. Theall, Product Liability and Innovation: A Canadian Perspective, 21 Can.-U.S. L.J. 313 (1995).

Table of Cases

Principal cases are in italics.

Abco Metals Corp. v. Equico Lessors, Inc., 58
Abco Metals Corp. v. J.W. Imports Co., 58
Acoba v. General Tire Co., 280
Adams v. Children's Mercy Hospital, 578
"Agent Orange" Product Liability Litigation, In re, 499, *683,* 688
Air Crash Disaster at Sioux City, In re, 379
Akins v. Glens Falls City School Dist., 484
Alden v. Maine, 446
Allenberg v. Bentley Hedges Travel Serv., Inc., 560
Amchem Prods. Inc. v. Windsor, 690
American Fire & Casualty Co. v. Ford Motor Co., 600
American Tobacco Co. v. Grinnel, 407
Anderson v. Klix Chem., 358
Anderson v. Owens-Corning Fiberglas Corp., 329, 334, 338
Andren v. White-Rodgers Co., 457, 485, 489
Andrews v. John E. Smith's Sons, Co., 674
Antcliff v. State Employees Credit Union, 324
Apgar v. Lederle Labs., 494
Armentrout v. FMC Corp., 542
Arnold v. Dow Chem. Co., 278
Arrell's Fine Jewelers, Inc. v. Honeywell, Inc., 602
Artiglio v. Superior Court, 542
Asavo v. Cardinal Glennon Memorial Hospital, 580
Ashi Metal Industry Co. v. Superior Court of Calif., 713
Auburn Mach. Works Co. v. Jones, 164
Ault v. International Harvester Co., 196
Austin v. Wil-Burt Co., 180

Ayala v. V. & O. Press Co., 46
Ayers v. Johnson & Johnson Baby Prods. Co., 797 P.2d 527 (Wash. Ct. App. 1990), 379, 380
Ayers v. Johnson & Johnson Baby Prods. Co., 818 P.2d 1337 (Wash. 1991), 380, 388, 393
Azzarello v. Black Bros. Co., 280-282

Badillo v. Am. Brands, Inc., 625
Bahlman v. Hudson Motor Co., 483
Baker v. Arbor Drug, 554
Barber Greene Co. v. Urbantes, 495
Barker v. Allied Supermarket, 56
Barker v. Lull Eng'g Co., 277, 280
Barnard v. Saturn Corp., 475
Barry v. Quality Steel Prods., Inc., 457
Bastian v. Wausau Homes Inc., 47
Baughn v. Honda Motor Co., 227
Baxter v. Ford Motor Co., 398
Beatie v. Martin Chevrolet-Buick, Inc., 56
Beatty v. Trailmaster Prods., Inc., 293
Beauchamp v. Dow Chem. Co., 98
Beaudoin v. Texaco, Inc., 456
Becker v. Baron Bros., 135
Becker v. IRM Corp., 64
Bednarski v. Hideout Homes & Realty Inc., 48
Bell v. Industrial Vangas, Inc., 107, 108
Bell v. Lollar, 435
Bell v. Poplar Bluff Physicians Group, Inc., 62
Bell v. Precision Airmotive Corp., 47
Benjamin v. Wal-Mart Stores, Inc., 358
Berg v. Jensen, 294
Berg Litigation, In re, 625
Berry v. Beech Aircraft Corp., 496
Beshada v. Johns-Manville Prods. Corp., 334, 335
Bickram v. Case I.H., 58
Bilotta v. Kelley Co., 255

Birmingham v. Fodor's Travel Publications, Inc., 52
Blanco v. American Telephone & Telegraph Co., 492
Blankenship v. Cincinnati Milacron Chem., Inc., 95-97
Blankenship v. CRT Tree, 488
Blankenship v. General Motors Corp., 678
Blazovic v. Andrich, 75
Block v. Wyeth, Inc., 391
Board of Education of City of Chicago v. A. C. and S., Inc., 601
Boatland of Houston, Inc. v. Bailey, 188
Boatmen's Trust Co. v. St. Paul Fire & Marine Ins. Co., 377
Bocci v. Rey Pharmaceuticals, Inc., 645
Bonnette v. Conoco Inc., 633
Borel v. Fibreboard Paper Prods. Corp., 343
Bovsun v. Sanperi, 580
Bowen v. Niagara Mohawk Power Corp., 48
Bower v. Westinghouse Elec. Corp, 617, 625
Bowserfield v. Suzuki Motor Corp., 226
Boyle v. United Tech. Corp., 499
Brady v. Safety-Kleen Corp., 97
Brannigan v. Usitalo, 578
Brannon v. Wood, 9
Breast Implant Prod. Liability Litigation, In re, 62
Breidenstein v. Ludlow Corp., 318
Brennaman v. R.M.I. Co., 497
Brenner v. American Cyanamid Co., 135
Bresnahan v. Chrysler Corp., 278
Brewer v. Harley Davidson, Inc., 323
Bridgestone/Firestone, Inc., In re, 601
Broussard v. Continental Oil Co., 368, 371
Brown v. Matthews Mortuary, Inc., 580
Brown v. Sears Roebuck & Co., 267
Brown v. Superior Court (Abbott Labs.), 534
Brown Forman Corp. v. Brune, 325
Bruce v. Martin-Marietta Corp., 200
Bryant v. Hoffman-LaRoche Inc., 553
Bryant v. Tri-County Elec. Membership Corp., 48
Budding v. SSM Healthcare Sys., 63, 75
Buongiovanni v. General Motors Corp., 180
Burgess v. Eli Lilly & Co., 497
Burke v. Spartanics, 324

Burt v. Makita USA, Inc., 367
Butler v. Flint Goodrich Hospital of Dillard University, 578
Butler v. Pittway Corp., 602
Butterfield v. Forrester, 454
Byrd v. Munsey Prods. of Tennessee, 108
Byrns v. Riddel, Inc., 164

Cacevic v. Simplimatic Eng'g Co., 180
Cafazzo v. Central Med. Health Servs., Inc., 62
Caldwell v. Yamaha Motor Co., 197
Campbell v. General Motors Corp., 253
Campbell Soup Co. v. Wentz, 562
Campo v. Scofield, 163, 164
Campos v. Firestone Tire & Rubber Co., 371
Carlin v. Superior Court, 334
Carrasquilla v. Mazda Motor Corp., 450
Carroll v. Owens-Corning Fiberglas Corp., 492, 610
Carroll Towing Co.; United States v., 4, 5, 169
Casebolt v. Cowan, 226
Castano v. American Tobacco Co., 435, 691
Castro v. United Container Mach. Group, Inc., 112
Catania v. Brown, 413
Caterpillar Tractor Co. v. Beck, 280
Cavanaugh v. Skil Corp., 195
Chaney v. Hobart Int'l, Inc., 349
Chestnut v. Ford Motor Co., 205
Chicago, City of v. Berretta U.S.A. Corp., 282
Chin, Estate of v. St. Barnabas Med. Ctr., 87
Chown v. USM Corp., 195
Cimino v. Raymark Indus., 512
Cincinnati v. Berretta U.S.A. Corp., 282
Cintrone v. Hertz Truck Leasing & Rental Serv., 56
Cipollone v. Liggett Group, Inc., 505 U.S. 504, 112 S. Ct. 2608, 120 L. Ed. 2d 407 (1992), 425, 434, 436, 437
Cipollone v. Liggett Group, Inc., 893 F.2d 541 (3d Cir. 1990), 401, 408, 424
City of. *See name of city*
Clay v. Ford Motor Co., 180, 226
Clime v. Dewey Beach Enter., 568
Cochran v. GAF Corp., 493
Cohen v. Steve's Ice Cream, 317

Table of Cases

Cohen v. Winnebago Ind., Inc., 178, 195
Coleman v. Thompson, 446
Collins v. Eli Lilly Co., 132-134, 136
Condos v. Muskoloskeletal Transplant Found., 54
Conley v. Boyle Drug Co., 133
Controltek, Inc. v. Kwikee Enters., Inc., 413
Cook v. Gran-Aire, Inc., 64
Corgan v. Muehling, 580
Costello v. Unipress Corp., 674
Cottam v. CVS Pharmacy, 554
Cotton v. Buckeye Gas Prods. Co., 366
Cover v. Cohen, 198
Coward v. Owens-Corning Fiberglas Corp., 382
Cowgill v. Raymark Indus., 492
Crandell v. Larkin & Jones Appliances Co., 556
Crippen v. Central Jersey Concrete Pipe Co., 107
Crocker v. Winthrop Labs., 415
Cronin v. J. B. E. Olson Corp., 33, 36, 39
Crowston v. Goodyear Tire & Rubber Co., 377
Cunningham v. Charles Pfizer & Co., 381, 522
Curtiss v. Northeast Utilities, 48
Cyr v. J.I. Case Co., 198

Daley v. McNeil Consumer Prods. Co., 573
Daly v. General Motors Corp., 474
D'Amario v. Ford Motor Co., 477
Dart v. Wiebe Mfg., Inc., 254
Data Processing v. L. H. Smith Oil Corp., 52
Daubert v. Merrell Dow Pharmaceuticals, Inc., 121-123, 128, 140, 183, 304, 305
Davis v. American Home Products, 691
Davis v. Munie, 489
Dawson v. Chrysler Corp., 234, 240, 241
Dekens v. Underwriters Labs. Inc., 58
Delaney v. Deere & Co., 253
Delaney v. Townmotor Corp., 56
Delgado v. Phelps Dodge Chino, 107
Denny v. Ford Motor Co., 257, 279
Denolf v. Frank L. Jursik Co., 198
Densberger v. United Tech. Corp., 500
Dentson v. Eddins & Lee Bus Sales, 294
De-Santis v. Frick Co., 377

Dewey v. R. J. Reynolds Tobacco Co., 424
Dhillon v. Crown Controls Corp., 305
D'Huyvetter v. A. O. Smith Harvestore Prods., 58
Dickie v. Farmers Union Oil Co., 497
Dillon v. Legg, 580
Dincher v. Marlin Firearms Co., 497
Doe v. *See name of opposing party*
Dole v. Dow Chem. Co., 112
Douglas v. E & J Gallo Winery, 107, 108
Dow Agrosciences v. Bastes, 437
Downs v. R.T.S. Security, Inc., 227
Downtowner, Inc. v. Acrometal Products, Inc., 674
Dreisonstok v. Volkswagenwerk, A.G., 231
Duchess v. Langston Corp., 198, 199
Dura-Stilts Co. v. Zachry, 131
Durden v. Hydro Flam Corp., 336

Eads v. R. D. Werner Co., 213
Eagle-Picher Indus., Inc. v. Liberty Mutual Ins. Co., 337
Easterly v. HSP of Texas, Inc., 62
East Penn Mfg. Co. v. Pineda, 77
East River Steamship Corp. v. Transamerica Delaval, Inc., 587, 600
Eckenrode v. Life of America Ins. Co., 579
Edmonds v. Compagnie Generale Transatlantique, 113
Elder v. Orluck, 456
Elderkin v. Gaster, 47
Elley v. Stephens, 65
Ellis v. C.R. Bard, Inc., 515
Ellsworth v. Sherrie Lingerie, Inc., 306
Emery v. Federated Foods, Inc., 380
Emory v. McDonnell Douglas Corp., 500
English v. General Elec. Co., 423
Erickson v. Whirlpool Corp., 457
Escola v. Coca Cola Bottling Co., 9, 13, 15, 16, 23, 25, 33
Estate of. *See name of party*
Evans v. General Motors Corp., 243
Evans ex rel. Kutch v. State, 635

Farm Bureau Mut. Ins. Co. v. Foote, 123
Feik v. Sieg Co., 64
Fein v. Permanente Medical Group, 578
Feldman v. Lederle Labs., 335, 435
Felle v. W. W. Grainger, Inc., 323, 324
Fenner v. Municipality of Anchorage, 107

Ferebee v. Chevron Chem. Co., 436
Feres v. United States, 499
Ferguson v. Winkler & Co., 306
Ferragamo v. Massachusetts Bay Transportation Authority, 560
Ferrari v. Grand Canyon Dories, 63
Ferris v. Gatke, 135
Fibreboard Corp. v. Fenton, 336
Fibreboard Corp., In re, 690
Firestone Steel Prods. Co. v. Barajas, 392
Fish v. Amsted Industries, 674
Fitzpatrick v. Madonna, 281
Flaminio v. Honda Motor Co., 196, 197, 379
Fleck v. KDI Sylvan Pools, Inc., 512
Fletcher v. Atex, Inc., 660
Florom v. Elliott Mfg., 674
FNS Mortgage Serv. Corp. v. Pacific Gen. Group, Inc., 58
Ford Motor Co. v. Ammerman, 226
Ford Motor Co. v. D'Amario, 477
Ford Motor Co. v. Eads, 155, 158
Ford Motor Co. v. Fulkerson, 197
Ford Motor Co. v. Moulton, 563
Ford Motor Co. v. Nuckolls, 198
Ford Motor Co. v. Tritt, 564
Forma Scientific, Inc. v. BioSera, 197, 199
Foster v. Cone-Blanchard Machine Co., 674
Francioni v. Gibsonia Truck Corp., 56
Franklin v. Mazda Motor Corp., 578
Fraust v. Swift & Co., 380
Frazer v. A.F. Munsterman, Inc., 76, 77
Frazier v. Materials Transp. Co., 353
Freeman v. Hoffman-LaRoche Inc., 552
Freightliner Corp. v. Myrick, 437
Frey v. Harley, 560
Friedrichs v. Huebner, 197
Fritchey v. Rhone-Poulenc, Inc., 281
Frye v. United States, 120, 123, 128

Garcia v. Kusan, Inc., 51
Garrett v. Hamilton Controls, Inc., 205
Geier v. American Honda Motor Co., 439, 450, 451
General Elec. Co. v. Joiner, 123
General Motors Corp. v. Harper, 180
General Motors Corp. v. Lahocki, 145
General Motors Corp. v. Moseley, 198
General Motors Corp. v. Sanchez, 304
General Motors type III Door Latch Lit v. General Motors Corp., In re, 601

George v. Jordan Marsh Co., 579
Gerow v. Mitch Crawford Holiday Motors, 243
Ghionis v. Deer Valley Resort Co., 56
Gianitsis v. American Brands, Inc., 227
Gibbs v. The O'Malley Lumber Co., 475
Giglio v. Saab-Scania of Am., Inc., 379
Godoy v. Abamaster of Miami, Inc., 76
Goeb v. Tharaldson, 123
Golec v. Metal Exch. Corp., 98
Golonka v. General Motors Corp., 205, *382*
Gonzalez v. Rutherford Corp., 560, 565
Gonzalez v. Volvo of Am. Corp., 353
Goodlin v. Medtronic, Inc., 439
Goss v. Oklahoma Blood Inst., 54
Gray v. Cannon, 379
Green v. BDI Pharmaceuticals, 575
Green v. Smith & Co., 253
Green v. Smith & Nephew AHP, Inc., 186
Greenman v. Yuba Power Products, Inc., 16, 19
Greenville, City of v. W.R. Grace & Co., 601
Greiten v. LaDow, 206
Griffin v. Kia Motors Corp., 243
Grundberg v. Upjohn Co., 542

Habecker v. Clark Equip. Co., 195
Hagans v. Oliver Mach. Co., 201
Halliday v. Sturm, Ruger & Co., 259, 268, 269
Hallmark v. Allied Products Cor., 198
Halphen v. Johns-Manville Sales Corp., 226
Hamilton v. Beretta U.S.A. Corp., 135, *295*
Hanberry v. Hearst Corp., 57
Hansen v. Baxter Healthcare Corp., 280
Hansen v. Mountain Fuel Supply Co., 627
Happel v. Wal-Mart Stores, Inc., 555
Harber v. Altec Industries Inc., 565
Harned v. Dura Corp., 293
Harris v. Great Dane Trailers, Inc., 451
Harris v. Jones, 579
Harris v. T. I., Inc., 674
Harris-Teeter, Inc. v. Burroughs, 568
Hartman v. Opelika Mach. Welding Co., 198
Hauenstein v. Loctite Corp., 316
Hauter v. Zogarts, 417
Hazine v. Montgomery Elevator Co., 497
Heath v. Sears, Roebuck & Co., 497
Heaton v. Ford Motor Co., 244, 256

Hempstead v. General Fire Extinguishing Corp., 57
Henley v. Philip Motors, Inc., 645
Henningsen v. Bloomfield Motors, Inc., 15, 16, 23, 343, 563
Henry v. Bridgestone/Firestone, Inc., 139
Herber v. Johnson Manville Corp., 616
Hernandez v. Nueces County Med. Soc'y Community Blood Bank, 54
Hernandez-Gomez v. Volkswagen of Am., 450
Herskovits v. Group Health Coop., 147
Hibbard v. Nelson Hardware, Inc., 560
Hilberg ex rel. Hilberg v. F.W. Woolworth Co., 226
Hill v. Searle Labs., 422
Hiner v. Bridgestone/Firestone, Inc., 382
Hiner v. Deer & Co., 377
Hodges v. S.C. Toof & Co., 634
Hoffman v. Houghton Chem. Corp., 354
Hoffman v. Sterling Drug, Inc., 522
Hollenbeck v. Selectone Corp., 157
Holley v. Burroughs Wellcome Co., 354, 522
Holm v. Sponco Mfg., Inc., 164
Holtz v. Schutt Pattern Works Co., 97
Hon v. Stroh Brewery Co., 325, 326
Honda of Am. Mfg., Inc. v. Norman, 179
Hood v. Ryobi N. Am., 367
Horner v. Spalitto, 554
Hou Tex, Inc. v. Landmark Graphics, 52
Hovenden v. Tenbush, 560
Hubbard-Hall Chem. Co. v. Silverman, 371
Huddell v. Levin, 147
Huffman v. Caterpillar Tractor Co., 474
Hufft v. Horowitz, 542
Hughes v. Magic Chef, Inc., 306
Hunter v. Werner Co., 378
Hurley v. Lederle Labs., 435
Hutton v. Globe Hoist Co., 323
Hyjek v. Anthony Indus., 198
Hymowitz v. Eli Lilly Co., 133, 134
Hyundai Motor Co. v. Rodriguez, 243

Ibarra v. Equipment Control, Inc., 112
In re. *See name of party*
Insurance Co. of N. Am. v. Forty-Eight Insulations, Inc., 337

Jackson v. General Motors Corp., 280
Jackson v. Johns-Manville Sales Corp., 688
Jackson v. L.A.W. Contracting Corp., 46
Jackson v. Nestle-Beich, Inc., 568
Jacobs v. Technical Chem. Co., 381
James v. Arms Tech., Inc., 282
James v. Mazda Motor Corp., 451
James v. Meow Media, Inc., 53
Jamieson v. Woodward & Lothrop, 319, 323, 394
Jarmco v. Polygard, Inc., 418
Jenkins v. Raymark Indus., Inc., 689
Jessop v. Angelo Benedetti, Inc., 108
Jimenez v. Sears, Roebuck & Co., 475
Jimenez v. The Superior Court, 595
Johnson v. Am. Nat'l Red Cross, 616
Johnson v. B.P. Chem., Inc., 97
Johnson v. Hannibal Mower Corp., 195
Johnson; United States v., 499
Johnson v. Walgreen, 554
Joint E. Dist. & S. Dist. Asbestos Litigation, In re, 199
Jonathan Woodner Co. v. Breedan, 634
Jones v. GMRI, Inc., 71
Jones v. Hittle Servs., Inc., 294
Jones v. NordicTrack, Inc., 178
Jordan v. Ravenswood Aluminum Corp., 674
Jordan v. Sunnyslope Appliance Propane & Plumbing Supplies Co., 560
Jurado v. Western Gear Works, 290, 306, 310, 475

Kaczorowska v. National Envelope Corp., 108
Kaempfe v. Lehn & Fink Products, 572
Kallio v. Ford Motor Co., 198
Kampen v. American Isuzu Motors, 213
Kasin v. Osco Drug, Inc., 555
Keen v. Dominick's Finer Foods, Inc., 64
Keene Corp. v. Insurance Co. of N. Am., 337
Kelly v. Rival Manufacturing Co., 267
Kemp v. Medotronic, Inc., 439
Kemp v. Miller, 56
Kennedy v. McKesson Co., 581, 585
Kim v. Ingersoll Rand Co., 131
Klages v. General Ordnance Equip. Corp., 417
Klootwyk v. Daimler-Chrysler Corp., 120
Knitz v. Minster Mach. Co., 280
Knott v. Liberty Jewelry & Loan Inc., 227
Knowles v. United States, 578
Kotecki v. Cyclops Welding Corp., 109, 112, 113
Kotler v. American Tobacco Co., 227

Krause v. American Aerolights, Inc., 198
Kumho Tire Co. v. Carmichael, 123
Kupetz v. Deere & Co., 281

Laaperi v. Sears, Roebuck & Co., 602
Labelle v. Phillip Morris Inc., 419
Lagano v. Chrysler Corp., 324
Lahocki v. Contee Sand & Gravel Co., 140, 145, 146
Laidlow v. Hariton Mach. Co., 99, 107
La Jolla Village Homeowners' Assn. v. Superior Court, 47
Lally v. Volkswagen Aktiengesellschaft, 147
Lambertson v. Cincinnati Corp., 112
Land v. Yamaha Motor Corp., 378
Landry v. Union Pacific R.R., 112
Lankford v. Sullivan, Long & Hagerty, 496
Lannom v. Kosco, 113
LaRosa v. Superior Court, 565
Larsen v. General Motors Corp., 243
Lasley v. Shrake's Country Club Pharmacy, 555
Lauzon v. Senco Prods., 304
Lawhon v. L.B.J. Inst. Supply, Inc., 493
Leaf v. Goodyear Tire & Rubber Co., 213, 304
Lear Siegler, Inc. v. Perez, 154, 155
Lecy v. Bayliner Marine Corp., 201
Lee v. Wolfson, 493
Leichtamer v. American Motors Corp., 394
Lenherr v. NRM Corp., 131
Levondsky v. Marina Assocs., 56
Lewis v. American Cyanamid Co., 213
Lewis v. Sea Ray Boats, Inc., 361
Lewis & Lambert Metal Contractors, Inc. v. Jackson, 418
Liebman v. BMC Inc., 45
Liggett Group Inc. v. Engle, 691
Linegar v. Armour of Am., Inc., 282, 289, 290
Linnen v. A.H. Robins Co., 524
Linthicum v. Nationwide Life Ins. Co., 634
Liriano v. Hobart Corp., 343
Little v. Brown & Williamson Tobacco Corp., 227
Livingston v. Isuzu Motors, Ltd., 206
Livingston v. Marie Callenders, Inc., 570
Lobianco v. Property Protection, Inc., 601
Loch v. Confair, 82

Lonasco v. A-Best Prods. Co., 381
Lopez v. Precision Papers Inc., 312, 313
Lorenz v. Celotex Corp., 294
Lougbridge v. Goodyear Tire & Rubber Co., 484
Lovick v. Wil-Rich, 373
Lowrie v. City of Evanston, 47
Lucas v. United States, 578
Lukaszewicz v. Ortho Pharm. Corp., 522
Lutz Farms v. Asgrow Seed Co., 407

Maake v. Ross Operating Valve Co., 353
MacDonald v. Ortho Pharmaceutical Corp., 435, 523
Maciag v. Strato Med. Corp., 87
Mack Trucks v. Conckle, 635
MacPherson v. Buick Motor Co., 7, 8, 13, 15
Magnante v. Pettibone-Wood Mfg. Co., 198
Magrine v. Krasnica, 59, 62, 63, 136
Maguire v. Pabst Brewing Co., 325
Mandolidis v. Elkins Indus Inc., 98
Marderosian v. Stroh Brewery Co., 82
Marshall v. Nugent, 154, 155
Martin v. Abbott Labs., 133, 134, *668*
Martin v. Hacker, 515, 521
Martin v. Michelin N. Am., 304
Martin v. Ortho Pharmaceutical Corp., 522
Martinez v. Callahan Mfg., Inc., 109
Martinez-Ferrer v. Richardson-Merrell, Inc., 492
Masaki v. General Motors Corp., 634
Mattis v. Carlon Elec. Prods., 358
Mattis v. Harrell Co., 358
Mauro v. Raymark Industries, Inc., 606
May v. Dafoe, 328, 329
McBride v. Gen. Motors Corp., 635
McCabe v. American Honda Motor Co., 278
McCarthy v. Olin Corp., 227
McCathern v. Toyota Motor Co., 254
McClain v. Chem-Lube Corp., 294
McCleary v. Armstrong World Indus., Inc., 616
McCollum v. Grove Mfg. Co., 164
McCoy v. American Suzuki Motor Corp., 156
McCullough v. General Motors Corp., 563
McCully v. Fuller Brush Co., 401
McFarland v. Bruno Mach. Corp., 197
McGuire v. Joseph E. Seagram & Sons, Inc., 326

McIntosh v. Melroe Co., 497
McKee v. American Home Products Corp., 554
McKisson v. Sales Affiliates, Inc., 56
McLennan v. American Eurocopter Corp., 377
McIntyre v. Balentine, 68
M'Cluny v. Silliman, 489
McQuiston v. K-Mart Corp., 56
Medtronic, Inc. v. Lohr, 438
Meis v. ELO Organization, LLC, 112
Menton v. Cavaney, 654
Merrill v. Navegar, 393, 395
Methyl Tertiary Butyl Ether (MTBE), In re, 135
Metro-North Commuter R.R. Co. v. Buckley, 610, 615, 625
Mexicali Rose v. Superior Court, 570
Micallef v. Miehle Co., 164, 290
Michalko v. Cooke Color & Chem. Corp., 47
Midwestern V.W. Corp. v. Ringley, 137
Milford v. Commercial Carriers, Inc., 46
Miller v. Pfizer Inc., 419
Mills v. Allegiance Healthcare Corp., 135
Mineer v. Atlas Tire Co., 82
Mine Safety Appliances Co. v. Stiles, 493
Mitchell v. BBB Servs. Co., 568
Mitchell v. TGI Friday's, 569
Mix v. Ingersoll Candy Co., 568, 570
Mobil Oil v. Bransford, 667
Modelski v. Navistar, 377
Moisan v. Loftus, 5
Moisenko v. Volkswagenwerk Aktiengesellschaft, 243
Moning v. Alfono, 393
Monroe v. Savannah Elec. & Power Co., 48
Montgomery Ward & Co. v. Gregg, 195
Moran v. Eastern Equip. Sales, Inc., 325
Morgan v. Wal-Mart Stores, Inc., 554
Morguson v. 3M Co., 307
Morson v. Superior Court, 187, 278, 542
Mosely; State v., 635
Motus v. Pfizer, Inc., 395
Mull v. Zeta Consumer Prods., 107
Murcia v. Textron, Inc., 108
Murphy v. Chestnut, 195
Murphy v. Edmonds, 578
Murphy v. E.R. Squibb & Sons, Inc., 554
Murray v. Fairbanks Morse, 463, 464, 474
Musser v. Vilsmeier Auction Co., 58
Myers v. Hearth Tech., Inc., 377

National Bank of Commerce of El Dorado, Arkansas v. Dow Chem. Co., 436
Nelson v. International Paint Co., 654
Nelson v. Nelson Hardware, Inc., 560
Netland v. Hess & Clark, 436
Newman v. Utility Trailer & Equip. Co., 305
Newmark v. Gimbel's Inc., 63
Nichols v. Nold, 82
Nissen Corp. v. Miller, 674
Nissen Trampoline Co. v. Terre Haute First Nat'l Bank, 381
Norfolk & Western R. Co. v. Ayers, 615
Norplant Contraceptive Products Liability Litigation, In re, 533
Northwest Arkansas Masonry Inc. v. Summit Specialty Products, Inc., 600

O'Brien v. Muskin Corp., 219, 226, 230, 240
Odenwalt v. Zaring, 457
Odom v. G.D. Searle & Co., 522
Ogletree v. Navistar Int'l Transp. Co., 164
Oliver v. Superior Court, 47
Olson v. Prosoco, Inc., 338
Order of Railroad Telegraphers v. Railway Express Agency, 489
Orear v. International Paint Co., 494
Ortho Pharmaceutical Corp. v. Health, 542
Ortiz v. Fibreboard Corp., 690
Osborn v. Irwin Memorial Blood Bank, 54
Osontoski v. Wal-Mart Stores, Inc., 324
Otte v. Dayton Power & Light Co., 48
Owens v. Truckstops of Am., Inc., 68
Owens-Illinois v. Zenobia, 634
Oxendine v. Merrell Dow Pharmaceuticals, Inc., 121

Pacaar, Inc. v. NHTSA, 438
Pace v. Parrish, 413
Pacific National Insurance Co. v. Gormsen Appliance Co., 560
Palmer v. Liggett Group, 424
Pan-Alaska Fisheries, Inc. v. Marine Constr. & Design Co., 464
Pancratz v. Monsanto Co., 674
Paoli Railroad Yard PCB Litigation, In re, 616
Papas v. Upjohn Co., 436
Parker v. St. Vincent Hospital, 554
Parks v. A.P. Green Indus., Inc., 492

Patin v. Thoroughbred Power Boats, Inc., 674
Patino v. Lockformer Co., 313
Patitucci v. Drelich, 47
Pavelich v. All Am. Homes, Inc., 113
Pavlik v. Lane Limited/Tobacco Exporters Int'l, 381
Payne v. Soft Sheen Prod., Inc., 336
Peck v. Bridgeport Mach., Inc., 178
Pelman v. McDonald's Corp., 571
Pennington v. Visitron Corp., 424
Perez v. Wyeth Labs. Inc., 354, *524*
Perkins v. F.I.E. Corp., 226
Persons v. Salomon N. Am., Inc., 349, 391
Peterson v. Idaho First National, 560
Peterson v. Lou Bachrodt Chevrolet Co., 561
Peterson v. Superior Court, 64, 560
Phillips v. Kimwood Mach. Co., 186
Phillips v. Ripley & Fletcher Co., 407
Pierce v. Johns-Manville Sales Corp., 492
Pike v. Frank G. Hough Co., 164
Port Authority of New York & New Jersey v. Arcadian Corp., 512
Potter v. Chicago Pneumatic Tool Co., 194, *248*
Potter v. Firestone Fire & Rubber Co., 627
Potts v. UAP-GA AG CHEM, Inc., 58
Powell v. Standard Brands Paint Co., 387
Presbrey v. Gillette Co., 573
Presto v. Sandoz, 533
Priest v. Brown, 48
Progressive Ins. Co. v. General Motors Corp., 600, 601
Promaulayko v. Johns Manville Sales Corp., 76
Pruitt v. General Motors Corp., 278
Prutch v. Ford Motor Co., 82
Pulley v. Pacific Coca-Cola Bottling Co., 21
Pullum v. Cincinnati, Inc., 498

Quintana-Ruiz v. Hyundai Motor Corp., 179

Radke v. H.C. Davis Sons' Mfg. Co., 498
Rahmig v. Mosley Mach. Co., 253
Raimbeault v. Takeuchi, 325
Ramirez v. Plough, Inc., 294
Rastelli v. Goodyear Tire & Rubber Co., 392, 661
Ray v. Alad Corp., 602
Raymond v. Eli Lilly & Co., 492
Realmuto v. Straub Motors, 560
Redfield v. Mead Johnson & Co., 494
Redland Soccer Club v. Dept. of the Army, 627
Reeves v. Cincinnati, Inc., 178
Regier; State v., 94
Reyes v. Wyeth Labs., Inc., 381, 522
Rhone-Poulenc Rorer, Inc., In re, 690, 691
Ridenhour v. Colson Caster Corp., 65
Rider v. Sandoz Pharmaceutical Corp., 123
Riley v. American Honda Motor Co., 382
Riordan v. International Armament Corp., 227
Ritter v. Custom Chemicides, Inc., 418
Rivera v. Mahogony Corp., 58
Rix v. General Motors Corp., 198
Robert Ford v. GACS Inc., 633
Robinson v. Reed-Prentice Div. of Package Mach. Co., 311-313
Rodriguez v. Suzuki Motor Corp., 634
Rogers v. Ingersoll-Rand Co., 213
Rogers ex rel. Rogers v. Cosco, Inc., 294
Roland v. Daimler-Chrysler Corp., 323
Rose v. XYZ Cable Co., 98
Rostocki v. Southwest Florida Blood Bank, Inc., 54
Roysdon v. R. J. Reynolds Tobacco Co., 424
RRX Indus., Inc. v. Lab-Con Inc., 52
Ruiz-Guzman v. Amvac Chemical Corp., 226
Russell v. Bishop, 325
Rutledge v. Dodenhoff, 47
Rypkema v. Time Mfg. Co., 305

Safeway Stores v. Nest Kart, 64
St. Jude Medical Inc. Silzone Heart Valves Prod. Liab. Litigation, In re, 627
Salvi v. Montgomery Ward & Co., 393
Samsel v. Wheeler Transport Services, 578
Samuel Friedland Family Enter. v. Amoroso, 56
Sanchez v. Hillerich, 487
Sanders v. Acclaim Entertainment, 53
Sanderson v. Steve Snyder Enters., 197
Sand Hill Energy, Inc. v. Ford Motor Co., 304
San Diego Hosp. Ass'n v. Superior Court, 554

Table of Cases 729

Santiago v. Sherwin Williams Co., 135
Saratoga Fishing Co. v. J.M. Martinac & Co., 593
Savage v. Scripto-Tokai Corp., 377
Scarangella v. Thomas Built Buses, Inc., 289, 290
Scheman-Gonzales v. Saber Mfg. Co., 392
Schipper v. Levitt & Sons, Inc., 47
Schmeiser v. Trus Joist, 358
Schneider National, Inc. v. Holland Hitch Co., 75, 77
Schump v. Firestone Tire & Rubber Co., 108
SCM Corp. v. Letterer, 82
Sease v. Taylor's Pets, Inc., 46
Seo v. All-Makes Overhead Doors, 317
September 11 Litig., In re, 300
Sharp ex rel. Gordon v. Case Corp., 206
Shea v. Kueffel & Esser of N.J., 492
Sheffield v. Eli Lilly & Co., 135
Shellman v. United States Lines, Inc., 113
Sherman v. Sea Ray Boats, Inc., 600, 601
Silicone Gel Breast Implants Product Liability Lit., In re, 512
Simmons v. Pacor, 616
Sindell v. Abbott Labs., 132, 134, 135
Skill v. Martinez, 522
Smith v. Ariens Co., 131
Smith v. Cutter Biological, Inc., 135
Smith v. Daimlerchrysler Corp., 377
Smith v. Department of Ins., 578
Smith v. Linn, 52
Smith v. Louis Berkman Co., 475
Smith v. Louisville Ladder Co., 172, 178, 182
Smith v. Monsanto Co., 98
Smith v. Smith, 454
Smith ex rel. Smith v. Bryco Arms, 475
Snell v. Bell Helicopter Texron, Inc., 500
Snider v. Bob Thibodeau Ford, Inc., 82
Snyder v. American Ass'n of Blood Banks, 55
Snyder v. Ortho-McNeil Pharmaceuticals, 278
Sofie v. Fibreboard Corp., 578
Sopha v. Owens-Corning Fiberglas Corp., 610
Soproni v. Polygon Apartment Partners, 293
Sorenson v. Allied Products Corp., 674
Soule v. General Motors Corp., 268, 277, 278, 280
Sours v. General Motors Corp., 293

Speller v. Sears, Roebuck & Co., 41
Spencer v. Baxter Int'l, Inc., 135
Sperry-New Holland v. Prestage, 164, 267
Sprietsong v. Mercury Marine, 451
Sprung v. MTR Ravenburg, Inc., 66
Stahl v. Novartis Pharmaceuticals Corp., 522
Standard Havens Prods., Inc. v. Benitez, 475
Stanley v. Aeroquip Corp., 324
Star Furniture Co. v. Pulaski Furniture Co., 474
State v. *See name of other party*
State Farm Mutual Automobile Ins. Co. v. Campbell, 636, 645, 646
State Farm Mutual Automobile Ins. Co. v. Ford Motor Co., 600
State Rubbish Collectors v. Siliznoff, 579
States v. R.D. Werner Co., 475
Steinter v. Ford Motor Co., 600
Stencel Aero Eng'g Corp. v. United States, 499
Sterling Drug, Inc. v. Yarrow, 516
Sternhagen v. Dow Co., 336
Stevens v. Parke, Davis & Co., 394
Stillie v. AM International, 561
Sturm Ruger & Co. v. Day, 195
Suburban Hosp., Inc. v. Kirson, 108
Suklijian v. Ross & Son Co., 66
Sullivan v. Boston Gas Co., 580
Suter v. San Angelo Foundry & Mach. Co., 474

Talley v. Danek Medical, Inc., 515
Tate v. Boeing Helicopters, 500
Tatum v. Medical Univ. of South Carolina, 108
Taylor v. Danek Med., Inc., 553
Temporomandibular Joint (TMJ) Implants Products Liability Litigation, In re, 512
Tenbarge v. Ames Taping Tool Sys. Inc., 381
Terhune v. A.H. Robins Co., 522
Tesmer v. Rich Ladder Co., 355
Thatcher v. Commonwealth Edison Co., 77
Thibault v. Sears, Roebuck & Co., 169
Thing v. LaChusa, 580
Thomas v. Amway Corp., 573
Thomas v. Winchester, 7
Thompson v. F. B. Cross & Sons, Inc., 317

Thompson v. Rockford Machine Tool Co., 560
Thongchoom v. Graco Children's Prods., Inc., 377
Thorpe v. Bullock, Inc., 56
Tillman v. Vance Equipment Co., 560, 565
Tobin v. Astra Pharmaceutical Products, Inc., 542
Todd v. Societe Bic, 277
Tolley v. ACF Indus., Inc., 108
Tomasovic v. American Honda Motor Co., 243
Toole v. Richardson-Merrell, Inc., 293
Torres v. Goodyear Tire & Rubber Co., 57
Torres v. Northwest Eng'g Co., 407, 484
Torres-Rios v. LPS Labs., 371
Torrington Co. v. Stutzman, 500
Trahan v. Trans-Louisiana Gas Co., 98
Travelers Indem. Co. v. Armstrong, 634
Travenol Labs.; Doe v., 54
Travis v. Dreis & Krump Mfg. Co., 98
Triangle Underwriters, Inc. v. Honeywell, Inc., 52
Troja v. Black & Decker Mfg. Co., 179
Truglio v. Hayes Construction Co., 46
Trull v. Volkswagon of Am., Inc., 206
Tucker v. Caterpillar, Inc., 198
Turcotte v. Fell, 485
Turner v. Bituminous Casualty Co., 674
Turner v. General Motors Corp., 254, 255
Turner v. International Harvester Co., 560
Tuttle v. Kelley-Springfield Tire Co., 564
Tuttle v. Raymond, 634
Tyler v. Pepsico, 57

Uloth v. City Tank Corp., 213
Union Pump Co. v. Allbritton, 149, 152, 153, 154, 155
Uniroyal Goodrich Tire Co. v. Martinez, 206
United Blood Services v. Quintana, 54
United States v. *See name of other party*
United States Lighting Serv. v. Llerrad Corp., 57

Vaccariello v. Smith & Nephew Richards, Inc., 515
Vassallo v. Baxter Healthcare Corp., 336
Vautour v. Body Masters Sports Indus., Inc., 213

Victorson v. Bock Laundry Mach. Co., 494
Vines v. Beloit Corp., 178
Vispisiano v. Ashland Chem. Co., 492
Vitolo v. Dow Corning Corp., 585
Voss v. Black & Decker Mfg. Co., 186
Vuono v. New York Blood Ctr., 54

Wagner v. Coronet Hotel, 64
Walker v. Clark Equip. Co., 580
Walkovszky v. Carlton, 654
Wallace v. Parks Corp., 580
Wallace v. Tesco Eng'g Inc., 281
Walsh v. Ford Motor Co., 564
Walt Disney World Co. v. Wood, 68
Wangen v. Ford Motor Co., 627, 634
Wanner v. Philip Carey Mfg. Co., 492
Ward v. Hobart Mfg. Co., 201
Warner v. Fruehauf Trailer Co. v. Boston, 254
Waterson v. General Motors Corp., 476
Watkins v. Ford Motor Co., 226
Watson v. Uniden Corp. of Am., 358
Way v. Boy Scouts of Am., 52
Webb v. Navistar Int'l 1994 Transp. Corp., 464, 474
Webster v. L. Romano Eng'g Corp., 413
Weiner v. American Honda Motor Co., 324
Welco Industries, Inc. v. Applied Companies, 674
West v. Searle & Co., 522
West Bend Mut. Ins. Co. v. Mulligan Masonry Co., 113
Wetmore v. American Guard Co., 97
Wheeler v. HO Sports, Inc., 253
White v. Caterpillar, Inc., 475
White v. R.J. Reynolds Tobacco Co., 420
White Consolidated Industries, Inc. v. Wilkerson, 580
Williams v. Dow Chem. Co., 417
Williams v. Phillip Morris, Inc., 419, 435
Williams v. Wilson, 634
Wilson v. Bradlees of New England, 382
Wilson v. Dover Skating Ctr., Ltd., 63
Wilson v. Johns-Manville Sales Corp., 492
Wilson v. Midway Games, Inc., 52
Wilson v. Piper Aircraft, 293
Wilson v. Piper Aircraft Corp., 179
Winter v. G. P. Putnam's Sons, 49, 51
Winterbottom v. Wright, 7

Wong v. Hawaiian Scenic Tours, Ltd., 456
Wood v. Wyeth-Ayerst Lab., 625
Woodill v. Parke Davis & Co., 336
Wooldridge v. Rowe, 48
Wright v. Brooke Group, Ltd., 178, 255, 434
Wright v. Louisiana Power & Light Co., 243
Wyatt v. A-Best Co., 491
Wynia v. Richard-Ewing Equipment Co., 561
Wyrulec Co. v. Schutt, 48

Yarusso v. International Sport Marketing, Inc., 408
Yeroshefsky v. Unisys Corp., 500
Young v. Key Pharms., 542

Zaza v. Marquess & Nell, Inc., 505
Zeller v. Cantu, 75
Ziegelmann v. Dailmer Chrysler Corp., 601

Table of Statutes and Other Authorities

UNITED STATES

Constitution

Art. III, §2	696

Statutes

Alcoholic Beverage Labeling Act of 1988 (27 U.S.C.A.)

§215	326
§216	326

Biomaterials Access Assurance Act (1998)	512

Common Sense Product Liability Legal Reform Act of 1996	681

Federal Cigarette Labeling & Advertising Act of 1965 (15 U.S.C.)

§§1331-1340	424

Federal Employers Liability Act (45 U.S.C.A.)

§53	455

Federal Insecticide, Fungicide, & Rodenticide Act (7 U.S.C.)

§§136-136y	435
§136v(a)	436
§136v(b)	436

Food and Drug Administration Act (1997)	575
§379	575
§379(e)	575

Mandatory Seat Belt Use Laws (MSLS)

625 ILCS 5/12-603.1	476

Medical Device Act (MDA) (21 U.S.C.)

§360k	438

Risk Retention Act of 1986 (Pub. L. 99–563)	682

ALABAMA

Code

§6-5-486	579
§6-11-20	634
§6-11-21	634

ALASKA

Statutes

§09.17.020	577, 634
§09.17.020(j)	635
§09.17.040	579

ARIZONA

Revised Statutes Annotated

§12-683(1)	195
§12-686	199
§12-701	635
§12-2501(D)	80
§32-1481(B)	54

ARKANSAS

Acts

649	634

CALIFORNIA

Civil Code

§3333.2	577

Liability Code		**ILLINOIS**	
§3602	108	*Comparative Laws Annotated*	
		§5/2-1115.1	577

COLORADO

Revised Statutes Annotated

INDIANA

Code Annotated

§13-21-102(1)(a)	634		
§13-21-102.5(3)(a)	577	§34-4-33-5(b)(4)	456
§13-21-111	456	§34-6-2.29	677
§13-21-111.5	70	§34-51-2-7	70
§13-21-111.6	578	§34-51-3-4	634
§13-21-403	293	§34-51-3-6(b)	635
§13-21-404	199		
§13-25-127(2)	634	**IOWA**	
§13-64-203	579	*Code Annotated*	
§42-4-437(7)	476	§321.445	476
		§668.12	195
DELAWARE		§668A.1	635
Code Annotated			
tit. 18 §7001	71	**KANSAS**	
		Statutes Annotated	
FLORIDA		§60-19a01	577
Statutes Annotated		§60-3304	293
§768.73	634	§60-3701	634
§768.78(1)(b)	579		
		KENTUCKY	
GEORGIA		*Revised Statutes Annotated*	
Code Annotated		§411.188	578
§51-12-5.1	634	§411.300	677
§51-12-5.1(e)(1)	635	§411.310(2)	195
HAWAII		**LOUISIANA**	
Revised Statutes		*Revised Statutes Annotated*	
§663-10.9	69	§9:2797	54
		§9:2800.56(1)	226
IDAHO			
Code		**MAINE**	
§6-801	457	*Revised Statutes*	
§6-1401	677	tit. 24, §2906	578
§6-1406(1)	199		
§6-1407	73	**MARYLAND**	
§6-1603	577	*Code Annotated*	
§6-1604	634	§11-108(b)	577

Table of Statutes and Other Authorities

MASSACHUSETTS

Laws Annotated

ch. 231, §60G	578

MICHIGAN

Comparative Laws Annotated

§257.710e(4)	476
§418.131(1)	98
§600.2946	635
§600.2946(3)	199
§600.2959	456

MINNESOTA

Statutes Annotated

§549.20(4)	635
§604.01	69, 457

MISSISSIPPI

Code Annotated

§11-1-65	634
§1454	455

MISSOURI

Annotated Statutes

§307.178	476
§537.675(3)	635

MONTANA

Code Annotated

§27-1-221(7)(a)	635

NEVADA

Revised Statutes Annotated

§2A:15-5.13	635
§42.005	634

NEW JERSEY

Statutes Annotated

§2A:15-5.1	456
§2A:15-5.3	69
§2A:15-5.14	634
§2A:58C-3	267
§2A:58C-3(1)	195
§2A:58C-3(b)(1)-(3)	226
§2A:58C-5	635
§2A:58C-8	73
§4:46-2	99
§34:15-8	98

NEW MEXICO

Statutes Annotated

§41-3a-1	69, 70

NEW YORK

Civil Practice Laws & Rules

§1411	474
§5035	579
§5041(e)	579
§5045	579

General Obligations Laws

§15-108(c)	80

Vehicle & Traffic Law

§1229-c	476

NORTH CAROLINA

General Statutes

§1D-1	634
§99B-2(a)	71

NORTH DAKOTA

Cent. Code

§32-03.2-11	634

OHIO

Revised Code Annotated

§2307.75(E)	73, 195, 268
§2307.78	73
§2307.80(C)	635
§2745.01	97
§4121.80	97
§4121.80(G)	96
§§4123.01-4123.94	96
§4123.95	96

OKLAHOMA

Statutes Annotated

tit. 23, §9.1	634

OREGON

Revised Statutes

§18.440(3)	80
§18.485	456
§18.590	476
§30.905	495
§30.907	495
§30.908(1)-(4)	495

TEXAS

Constitution

Art. 3, §66	578

Civil Practice & Remedies Code Annotated

§33.013	456
§41	635
§82.001	677
§82.005	173
§82.005(b)	174

Rules of Civil Evidence

§407(a)	197

UTAH

Code Annotated

§78-15-6(3)	293
§78-18-1(3)(a)	635
§78-18-2	635
§78-27-38	70

VIRGINIA

Code Annotated

§8.01-38.1	635
§8.01-581.15	577

WASHINGTON

Revised Statutes Annotated

§4.56.260	579
§7.72.010	677

WEST VIRGINIA

Code

§23-4-2	98
55-7B-8	577

WISCONSIN

Statutes Annotated

§895.045	69, 457

MODEL ACTS

Model Business Corporation Act

§6.22	651

Model Uniform Product Liability Act (MUPLA)

§101	679
§104	72
§104(D)	72
§105	71, 73, 74
§107	199
§114	113
§114(a)	114

RESTATEMENT (SECOND) OF TORTS

§310	413, 418
§311	418
§324A	58
§400	660
§402A	19, 20, 33, 36, 71, 82, 200, 209, 231, 232, 250, 353, 514, 522, 602
§402A(1)(a)	64
§402A, Comment *b*	20
§402A, Comment *f*	64
§402A, Comment *i*	250, 267, 277
§402A, Comment *j*	209, 213, 381, 573
§402A, Comment *k*	542
§402A, Comment *n*	454
§402B	414, 418, 419, 420
§402B, Comment *j*	420
§463	454
§464	454
§876	661
§876(b)	661

RESTATEMENT (THIRD) OF TORTS: PRODUCTS LIABILITY

§1	37, 40, 45, 169, 170, 218, 317
§2	37, 40, 169, 170, 178, 218, 512, 553, 569
§2(a)	38, 40, 218, 258, 559, 569, 570
§2(b)	178, 205, 212, 213, 218, 248, 258, 335, 543, 569, 572
§2(c)	218, 258, 316, 318, 335, 355, 543, 569, 574
§2, Comment c	37
§2, Comment d	164, 194, 195, 218
§2, Comment e	219, 227
§2, Comment f	170, 209, 212, 289, 304, 422
§2, Comment g	171, 254, 422
§2, Comment i	317, 354, 358, 360
§2, Comment j	324
§2, Comment l	212-13
§2, Comment m	186, 335, 336
§2, Comment n	257
§2, Comment o	317
§3	168, 559, 569
§3, Comment b	168
§4	291, 569
§4(b)	293
§4, Comment d	291
§4, Comment e	291, 294
§5	511
§6	515, 542, 553
§6(c)	553
§6, Comment b	543
§6, Comment e	534
§6, Comment h	553
§6(d)(2)	534
§6(e)	554
§7	569, 571, 572
§7, Comment a	569
§7, Comment b	569
§8	559, 566, 567
§9	378, 419, 420
§10	372, 511
§11	378
§12	674
§14, Comment d	57
§15	118
§16	145
§16(a)	146
§16(b)	145, 146
§16(c)	146
§16, Comment f	483
§16(d)	483
§17	463
§18	564
§19, Comment b	505, 513
§20	55
§20(b)	56
§21	594
§21, Comment e	594

RESTATEMENT (THIRD) OF TORTS: APPORTIONMENT OF LIABILITY

§1(b)	484
§16	79
§22	77
§23	78
§40(b)	78
§A18	68
§B18	68
§C21	69
§D19	69
§E18	69

RESTATEMENT (THIRD) OF TORTS: LIABILITY FOR PHYSICAL HARM (BASIC PRINCIPALS)

Tentative Draft No. 2

§26	118, 137
§26, Comment n	148
§29	118, 155
§29, Comment b	155
§31	157
§33	157

Tentative Draft No. 3

§29	156

UNIFORM ACTS

Uniform Commercial Code (UCC)

§2-103	52
§2-302	258, 398, 563, 564
§2-302(1)	562
§2-302(2)	562
§2-302, Comment 1	562
§2-313	258, 398, 410-11, 417
§2-313A	258, 411
§2-313B	411, 412, 421
§2-314	407
§2-314(2)(c)	15, 258
§2-315	258, 412
§2-316	15, 561, 563
§2-316, Comment 1	15, 561, 563
§2-318	16
§2-715	258
§2-715(2)(b)	258
§2-718	562

§2-719	562, 563
§2-719(1)	563
§2-719(1)(a)	563
§2-719(1)(b)	563
§2-719(2)	563
§2-719(3)	563
§2-719, Comment 3	563
§2-725	15, 494
§2-725(1)	586, 601
Art. 2	256-59, 397, 421

Uniform Comparative Fault Act

§6	78

Uniform Contribution Among Tortfeasors Act

§1	75
§2	75

MISCELLANEOUS

Comparative Negligence, Law, & Practice

§19.10	79

Federal Rules of Evidence

§407	196-99, 379

Model Code of Professional Responsibility

DR 4-101	94
DR 7-102	92
DR 7102(A)(4)	92

Model Rules of Professional Conduct

Rule 1.6(a)	94
Rule 3.3	92
Rule 3.3(a)(4)	94
Rule 3.3(c)	94

Index

Abnormally dangerous activities
   Restatement (Second) of Torts, 223
Abuse
   comparative fault and, 475-476
   defective design and, 305-313
Adjudicability of disputes
   strict liability and, 32, 166
Admiralty law, 696-698
   aircraft and, 697
   asbestos and, 697
   boats and, 697-698
Advertising
   express warranty based on, 422
Affirmative defenses, 453-501
   comparative fault. *See* Comparative fault
   conduct-based defenses, 453-489
      comparative fault. *See* Comparative fault
      contributory negligence, 454-455
      overview, 453-454
   contract-based defenses, 498
      government contractors, 499-501
   contributory negligence, 454-455
   government contractors, 499-501
   non-conduct-based defenses, 489-501
   sovereign immunity, 498-499
   statutes of limitations, 489-494
      causal connection, knowledge of triggering, 492-493
      defendant's identity, knowledge of triggering, 493-494
      injury, knowledge of triggering, 491-492
      in Japan, 712
   statutes of repose, 494-498
      constitutionality, 496-498
      motor vehicles and, 495-496
      post-sale warnings and, 377-378
      Uniform Commercial Code, 494
   time-based defenses
      statutes of limitations. *See* Statutes of limitations
      statutes of repose. *See* Statutes of repose
   workers' compensation, 498
Agent Orange
   federalism issues and, 683-688

Agitators
   workers' compensation and, 109-111
Airbags
   consumer expectations standard and, 248
   defective design
      two-prong standard and, 278
   preemption and, 439-451
Aircraft
   admiralty law and, 697
Alarms
   economic loss rule and, 601-603
   used products and, 566-568
Alcoholic beverages
   duty to warn, 325-327
Allocating liability, 67-115
   collective responsibility, 80-94
      medical devices and, 82-87
      medical providers, 87-88
      normal course of events, 81-82
      special circumstances, 82-94
      workplace accidents, 88-92
   comparative fault and, 68
   contribution. *See* Contribution
   distributors, between, 67-80
      contribution, 74-76
      indemnity, 76-78
      joint and several liability, 67-70
      release, 78-80
      retailers, letting out of litigation, 70-74
      "sealed container" doctrine, 70-71
      settlement, 78-80
      wholesalers, letting out of litigation, 70-74
   indemnity
      distributors, allocating liability between, 76-78
      members of distributive chain, allocating liability among, 76-78
      Restatement (Third) of Torts, 77-78
   joint and several liability, 67-70
   medical providers, collective responsibility, 87-88
   members of distributive chain, among, 67-80
      contribution, 74-76
      indemnity, 76-78
      joint and several liability, 67-70

Allocating liability (*continued*)
   release, 78-80
   settlement, 78-80
  Model Uniform Product Liability Act, 71-74
  retailers, letting out of litigation, 70-74
  several liability, 67-70
  Uniform Comparative Fault Act, 78-80
  Uniform Contribution Among Tortfeasors Act, 74-75
  vertical distributive chain, 80-81
  wholesalers, letting out of litigation, 70-74
  workplace accidents, 95-115
   collective responsibility, 88-92
   shared responsibility between employer and manufacturer, 109-115
    reduction of tort recovery, 113-115
   sole responsibility of employer, 95-109
    dual capacity doctrine, 107-109
    intentional tort by employer, 95-107
    workers' compensation, bar to product liability, 95
All-or-nothing causation, 137-140
  motor vehicles and, 137-139
All-terrain vehicles
  defective design, 280
Alteration
  comparative fault and, 475-476
  defective design and, 305-313
Anesthesia
  causation and, 136
Appliances
  defective design and, 41-44
  used products, 556-558
Asbestos
  admiralty law and, 697
  bankruptcy law and, 696
  component parts and, 512
  duty to warn and, 329-334, 341
  economic loss rule and, 601
  federalism issues and, 690
  informed choice warnings, 341
  integrated systems and, 512
  mass tort litigation, 690
  raw materials and, 512
  toxic torts litigation and, 606-616
Asset securitization
  corporate liability and, 664-667
Assumption of the risk
  athletic activities and, 487-488
  comparative fault and, 457, 484-489
  motor vehicles and, 488-489
  propane heaters and, 485-487
Athletic activities
  assumption of the risk and, 487-488
Attorneys
  ethics, 93-94
  economic loss rule and, 604-605

Attorneys' fees
  in foreign countries, 706
Auctioneers
  selling or otherwise distributing, exception, 58

Bailors
  selling or otherwise distributing, exception, 56-57
Bankruptcy law, 691-696
  asbestos and, 696
  mass tort litigation and, 692-696
Basis of the bargain
  express warranty and, 402-413
   cigarettes and, 401-407
   motorcycle helmets and, 408-410
   reliance, contrasted, 407-408, 410-412
   tobacco products and, 401-407
  Uniform Commercial Code, 401
BB guns
  defective marketing and, 393
Blood
  federalism issues and, 690-691
  mass tort litigation, 690-691
  as product, 53-55
Boats
  admiralty law and, 697-698
  economic loss rule and, 593-594
  preemption and, 451
  reasonable alternative design standard and, 188-194, 201-205
  sufficiency of warning and, 361-365
Bottles
  implied warranty and, 21-22
  res ipsa loquitur and, 9-14
Brakes
  preemption and, 437-438
Bulk supplier doctrine
  duty to warn and, 354
Bulletproof vests
  defective design and, 282-285
Burden of proof
  defective design
   duty, problems regarding, 305-306
   proximate cause, 306
   two-prong standard and, 278-280
But-for causation, 118-119
  cause in fact, 118-119
  defective design, 137
  general causation, 119
  proximate cause and, 152, 156
  specific causation, 119

Causation, 117-158
  all-or-nothing causation, 137-140
   motor vehicles and, 137-139

anesthesia, 136
but-for causation, 118-119
   cause in fact, 118-119
   defective design, 137
   general causation, 119
   proximate cause and, 152, 156
   specific causation, 119
cause in fact, 118-119
   proximate cause and, 154
defect causing harm, proving, 137-149
   all-or-nothing causation, 137-140
   enhanced injury, 140-147
      Restatement (Third) of Torts, 145-147
   loss-of-a-chance causation, 147-149
      medical devices, 148-149
      Restatement (Third) of Torts, 148
Diethylstilbestrol (DES), 131-134
elements, 117-118
enhanced injury, 140-147
   comparative fault and, 477-483
   motor vehicles and, 140-145
   Restatement (Third) of Torts, 145-147
expert witnesses, proving by, 119-131
   general causation, 120
   peer review, 122
   specific causation, 119-120
IUDs, 130-131
loss-of-a-chance causation, 147-149
   medical devices, 148-149
   Restatement (Third) of Torts, 148
overview, 117-118
product causing harm, proving, 118-131
proximate cause. *See* Proximate cause
rescuer doctrine, 156-157
Restatement (Third) of Torts and, 118
safety devices and measures and, 157-158
slip and fall, 139-140
supplying product, proving, 131-136
   identification of defendant, 131
   market share approach, 131-136
Cause in fact, 118-119
   proximate cause and, 154
Child ingestion cases
   duty to warn, 379-381
Cigarettes
   basis of the bargain and, 401-407
   Federal Cigarette Labeling and Advertising Act, 426-431
   federalism issues and, 691
   mass tort litigation, 691
   misrepresentation and, 419-420
   preemption and, 425-435
   Public Health Cigarette Smoking Act of 1969, 426-431
Circumstantial evidence
   defective design, Restatement (Third) of Torts, 40, 168-169

Class actions
   federalism issues, 689-691
"Clear and convincing evidence" standard
   punitive damages, 634
Collateral source rule
   compensatory damages and, 578
Common law
   federal common law, 683-689
   product category liability and, 233-234
Common Sense Product Liability Legal Reform Act of 1996
   federalism issues regarding, 681-682
Comparative fault, 455-489
   abuse and, 475-476
   allocating liability and, 68
   alteration and, 475-476
   assumption of the risk and, 457, 484-489
   defective design, compared, 463-489
      difficulty in comparison, 463-464
      risk-utility standard, 464
   enhanced injury and, 477-483
   express warranty and, 483-484
   farm equipment and, 464-474
   individual rule, 457
   last clear chance and, 457
   misuse and, 475-476
   modification and, 475-476
   modified unit rule, 456
   motor vehicles and, 477-483
   multiple defendants, 456-457
   Restatement (Third) of Torts, 455, 463
   seat belts and, 476
   superseding cause and, 457-462
   Uniform Comparative Fault Act, 78-80
   unit rule, 456
   workplace accidents and, 457-462
Compensatory damages, 577-579
   collateral source rule, 578
   noneconomic damages, limitations, 577-578
   periodic payments, 579
Component parts, 505-513
   asbestos and, 512
   Restatement (Third) of Torts, 505, 511-512
Computer equipment
   shareholder limited liability and, 660-661
Conduct-based defenses, 453-489
   comparative fault. *See* Comparative fault
   contributory negligence, 454-455
   overview, 453-454
Constitutionality
   punitive damages, limitations, 636-647
   statutes of repose, 496-498
Consumer expectations standard, 243-268
   airbags and, 248
   firearms and, 259-267
   food products and, 568-571
   minors and, 267-268

Consumer expectations standard (*continued*)
  motor vehicles and, 244-247, 255-256
  overview, 161, 243-244
  Restatement (Third) of Torts and, 254
  "shield" against liability, 259-268
  "sword" for imposing liability, 244-259
  Uniform Commercial Code and, 256-259
  workplace accidents and, 248-253
Contact lenses
  sufficiency of warning, 359-360
Contraceptive devices
  duty to warn and, 524-534
Contracts
  affirmative defenses, 498
    government contractors, 499-501
  privity of contract, decline of rule in connection with strict liability, 6-8
  unconscionability and used products, 562-564
Contribution
  distributors, allocating liability between, 74-76
  members of distributive chain, allocating liability among, 74-76
  Restatement (Third) of Torts, 75-76
  Uniform Contribution Among Tortfeasors Act, 74-75
  workplace accidents, shared responsibility between employer and manufacturer, 111-113
Contributory negligence, 454-455
  Restatement (Second) of Torts, 454
Corporate liability, 651-675
  asset securitization and, 664-667
  criminal sanctions and, 663-664
  "gatekeeper" liability and, 663-664
  manager liability and, 663-664
  proof of financial responsibility requirements and, 665-667
  shareholder limited liability, 651-668
    computer equipment and, 660-661
    electronic locks and, 661-662
    moral hazard and, 651, 662-663
    overview, 651-654
    paint and, 654-660
    "piercing the corporate veil," 651, 654
    several liability and, 652-653
  subsidiaries and, 664
  successor corporation liability, 668-675
    continuation of business enterprise rule, 674
    diethylstilbestrol (DES), 668-673
    prescription drugs, 668-673
    product line extension rule, 674
    Restatement (Third) of Torts, 674
  "virtual" companies and, 667-668
Cosmetics, 572-575
  Food and Drug Administration Modernization Act, 575
  Restatement (Second) of Torts, 573

Restatement (Third) of Torts, 574
Criminal sanctions
  corporate liability and, 663-664

Damages, 577-647
  collateral source rule, 578
  compensatory damages, 577-579
    collateral source rule, 578
    noneconomic damages, limitations, 577-578
    periodic payments, 579
  economic loss rule, 586-605
    alarms and, 601-603
    asbestos and, 601
    boats and, 593-594
    ethics and, 604-605
    hazardous substances and, 603-604
    oil tankers and, 587-593
    Restatement (Third) of Torts, 594-595
    windows and, 595-600
  emotional distress, 579-585
    medical providers, 581-585
    silicone breast implants, 585
    toxic torts litigation, 610-616
  in foreign countries, 706-707
  noneconomic damages, limitations, 577-578
  periodic payments, 579
  punitive damages, 627-647
    "clear and convincing evidence" standard, 634
    constitutional limitations, 636-647
    egregious behavior, 633
    monetary caps, 634-635
    motor vehicle insurance and, 636-645
    motor vehicles and, 627-633
    prescription drugs, exemptions, 635
    state limitations, 627-636
    wanton and reckless behavior, 633-634
  toxic torts litigation, 605-627
    asbestos and, 606-609, 610-616
    emotional distress, 610-616
    increased risk of future injury, 605-610
    medical monitoring costs, 616-627
    PCBs and, 616
Daubert doctrine
  expert witnesses and, 121-130
    challenges, 304-305
Defective design
  abuse and, 305-313
  alteration and, 305-313
  appliances and, 41-44
  bulletproof vests and, 282-285
  burden of proof
    duty, problems regarding, 305-306
    proximate cause, 306
    two-prong standard and, 278-280
  but-for causation, 137

Index

categories, Restatement (Third) of Torts, 37
causes other than defect, 41
circumstantial evidence of, 168-169
   Restatement (Third) of Torts, 40
comparative fault, compared, 463-489
   difficulty in comparison, 463-464
   risk-utility standard, 464
consumer expectations standard. *See* Consumer expectations standard
Daubert challenges, 304-305
duty, problems regarding, 282-303
   burden of proof, 305-306
   firearms and, 297-298
   September 11 litigation, 300-303
enterprise liability as alternative to, 164-167
   adjudicability of disputes, lack of, 166
   insurability of risk, lack of, 166-167
expert witnesses, proof by, 39-40, 304-305
external standards, necessity, 167-169
firearms
   duty, problems regarding, 297-298
   nuisance theory, 282
guarantor of safety, manufacturer as, 281
harm caused by defect, proving, 137-149
   all-or-nothing causation, 137-140
   enhanced injury, 140-147
      Restatement (Third) of Torts, 145-147
   loss-of-a-chance causation, 147-149
      medical devices, 148-149
      Restatement (Third) of Torts, 148
idiosyncratic standards, 280-282
inference of defect, 167-169
in Japan, 708
judicial review, necessity of, 163-164
liability for, overview, 1
manufacturing defects, 37-38
marketplace, deference to, 282-290
   Restatement (Third) of Torts, 289-290
medical devices and, 307-310, 534-553
   alternative safer design test, 550-552
   Restatement (Third) of Torts, 542-544
misuse and, 305-313
modification and, 305-313
motor vehicles and, 33-36
   two-prong standard and, 268-277
necessity of defect, 164-167
ordinary occurrence as result of product defect, 40
overview, 161-163
"patent danger rule," 163-164
polycentricity of, 161-163
preemption and, 437-451
   airbags and, 439-451
   boats and, 451
   brakes and, 437-438
   medical devices and, 438-439

prescription drugs and, 534-553
   alternative safer design test, 550-552
   differences between drugs and other products, 544-550
   Restatement (Third) of Torts, 542-544, 552-553
proof, 39-45
proximate cause, 306
reasonable alternative design standard. *See* Reasonable alternative design standard
regulations, deference to, 290-294
   compliance as conclusiveness of nondefectiveness, 293-294
   defect per se, 293
   Restatement (Third) of Torts, 291-292
res ipsa loquitur, 168
Restatement (Third) of Torts
   circumstantial evidence, 168-169
   marketplace, deference to, 289-290
   regulations, deference to, 291-292
   statutes, deference to, 291-292
risk-utility standard, 169-243
   balancing without reasonable alternative design, 213-218
   comparative fault, compared, 464
   product category liability, 218-243
      common law and, 233-234
      implementation problems, 229-230
      motor vehicles and, 234-243
      reasonable alternative design standard and, 226-227, 230-232
      Restatement (Third) of Torts, 218-219
      terminology, 227-229
reasonable alternative design standard. *See* Reasonable alternative design standard
safety devices and measures and, 311-313
school buses and, 285-289
seat belts, 44-45
slip and fall and, 139-140, 310-311
specific aspect of defect, proof of, 40-41
statutes, deference to, 290-294
   compliance as conclusiveness of nondefectiveness, 293-294
   defect per se, 293
   Restatement (Third) of Torts, 291-292
strict liability
   as alternative to, 164-167
      adjudicability of disputes, lack of, 166
      insurability of risk, lack of, 166-167
   centrality to, 33-45
sufficiency of warning, compared, 360-361
two-prong standard, 268-280
   airbags and, 278
   all-terrain vehicles and, 280
   burden of proof and, 278-280
   minors and, 277

Defective design (*continued*)
    motor vehicles and, 268-277
    "unreasonably dangerous" test, 277
  "unreasonably dangerous," construed, 33-37
Defective marketing
  BB guns and, 393
  duty to warn and, 393-395
    BB guns and, 393
    prescription drugs, 394-395
  prescription drugs and, 394-395
Defenses. *See* Affirmative defenses
Definitions
  "in the business of selling or distributing," 64-66
  product, 45-55
    Restatement (Third) of Torts, 46
  "selling or otherwise distributing," 55-64
    Restatement (Third) of Torts, 55
DES (Diethylstilbestrol), 131-134
  successor corporations, liability, 668-673
Disclaimers
  used products and, 561-568
    Restatement (Third) of Torts, 564
    unconscionability, 562-564
    Uniform Commercial Code, 561-563
Discovery
  in foreign countries, 705-706
Distributors, allocating liability between, 67-80
  contribution, 74-76
  indemnity, 76-78
  joint and several liability, 67-70
  release, 78-80
  retailers, letting out of litigation, 70-74
  "sealed container" doctrine, 70-71
  settlement, 78-80
  wholesalers, letting out of litigation, 70-74
Drills
  sufficiency of warning and, 368-371
Dual capacity doctrine
  tires and, 108
  workplace accidents, exception to workers' compensation bar to product liability, 107-109
Duty to warn, 315-395
  alcoholic beverages, 325-327
  asbestos and, 329-334, 341
  basic duty, 316-349
  bulk supplier doctrine, 354
  child ingestion cases, 379-381
  contraceptive devices and, 524-534
  cosmetics and, 572-575
    Restatement (Third) of Torts, 574
  defective marketing and, 393-395
    BB guns and, 393
    prescription drugs, 394-395
  "digging your own grave with the best of intentions," 328-329
  exercise equipment and, 319-323
  food products and, 571

  foreseeable users, 353-355
  generally known risks, 318-329
    alcoholic beverages, 325-327
    expertise of users, effect, 324-325
    Restatement (Third) of Torts, 318
  general rule, 316-318
  hazardous materials and, 338-340, 387-391
  heeding of warnings, likelihood, 379-387
  informed choice warnings, 340-349
    asbestos, 341
    hazardous materials, 342-343
    meat grinders and, 343-347
    prescription drugs, 340-341
    Restatement (Third) of Torts, 341-342
    risk reduction warnings, 340
    safety devices and measures, 349
  long-tail risks, 337-340
  medical devices and, 514-534
    contraceptive devices, 524-534
    medical providers, warnings to, 514-522
    patients, warnings to, 522-534
    Restatement (Second) of Torts, 514-515
    Restatement (Third) of Torts, 515-516, 534
  mismatch of product and user, 353-355, 393-395
  nonprescription drugs and, 572-575
    Restatement (Third) of Torts, 574
  obvious risks, 318-329
    alcoholic beverages, 325-327
    expertise of users, effect, 324-325
    Restatement (Third) of Torts, 318
  other products, harm caused by, 387-392
    combination of products, 391-392
    generic drugs, 391
    hazardous materials and, 387-391
  overview, 315-316
  persons required to warn or be warned, 317-318, 349-355
    bulk supplier doctrine, 354
    foreseeable users, 353-355
    skiing equipment, 349-352
    ultimate users, 353-355
  post-sale warnings, 372-379
    defects existing at time of sale, distinguished, 373
    duty to recall and, 378-379
    farm equipment and, 373-377
    Restatement (Third) of Torts, 372-373
    statutes of repose and, 377-378
  preemption and, 424-437
    cigarettes and, 425-435
    pesticides and, 435-437
    prescription drugs and, 435-437
    tobacco products and, 425-435
  prescription drugs and, 514-534
    generic drugs, 391
    informed choice warnings, 340-341

Index

medical providers, warnings to, 514-522
  negligence and, 516-521
  patients, warnings to, 522-534
  Restatement (Second) of Torts, 514-515
  Restatement (Third) of Torts, 515-516, 534
  strict liability and, 521-522
  unknowable risks, 334-335
proximate cause and, 379-393
  heeding of warnings, likelihood, 379-387
  motor vehicles and, 382-387
  other products, harm caused by, 387-392
  result within the risk, 156
  sort of harm warning would have prevented, 392-393
reasonable alternative design standard, as substitute for, 206-213
  Restatement (Third) of Torts, 212-213
Restatement (Second) of Torts
  medical devices and, 514-515
  prescription drugs and, 514-515
Restatement (Third) of Torts, 316-317
  cosmetics and, 574
  generally known risks, 318
  medical devices and, 515-516, 534
  nonprescription drugs and, 574
  obvious risks, 318
  prescription drugs and, 515-516, 534
  unknowable risks, 335-337
risk reduction warnings, 340
sort of harm warning would have prevented, 392-393
sufficiency of warning, 355-372
  boats and, 361-365
  contact lenses, 359-360
  defective design, compared, 360-361
  drills and, 368-371
  English language and, 371-372
  hazardous materials, 358
  jury instructions and, 361-367
  ladders and, 355-358
  motor vehicles, 371
  propane heaters, 358-359
  Restatement (Third) of Torts, 359
  safety devices and measures and, 367-372
  telephones, 358
swimming pools, 327-328
ultimate users, 353-355
unknowable risks, 329-340
  liability insurance and, 337-340
  prescription drugs, 334-335
  Restatement (Third) of Torts, 335-337

Economic loss rule, 586-605
  alarms and, 601-603
  asbestos and, 601
  boats and, 593-594
  ethics and, 604-605
  hazardous substances and, 603-604
  oil tankers and, 587-593
  Restatement (Third) of Torts, 594-595
  windows and, 595-600
Electrical power
  as product, 48
Electronic locks
  shareholder limited liability and, 661-662
Emotional distress, 579-585
  medical providers, 581-585
  silicone breast implants, 585
  toxic torts litigation, 610-616
English language
  sufficiency of warning and, 371-372
Enhanced injury, 140-147
  comparative fault and, 477-483
  motor vehicles and, 140-145
  Restatement (Third) of Torts, 145-147
Enterprise liability
  defective design, as alternative to, 164-167
    adjudicability of disputes, lack of, 166
    insurability of risk, lack of, 166-167
Ethics, 93-94
  economic loss rule and, 604-605
European Community, 699-707
  American firms, competitive disadvantages
    innovation, effect of products liability law on, 717-719
    price, effect of products liability law on, 713-717
  attorneys' fees in, 706
  damages in, 706-707
  discovery in, 705-706
Exercise equipment
  duty to warn and, 319-323
  reasonable alternative design standard and, 213-317
Expert witnesses
  causation, proving, 119-131
    general causation, 120
    peer review, 122
    specific causation, 119-120
  Daubert doctrine, 121-130
    challenges, 304-305
  defective design, proving, 39-40, 304-305
  IUDs, 130-131
  prescription drugs and, 123-129
Express warranty, 397-413
  advertising, based on, 422
  basis of the bargain, 402-413
    cigarettes and, 401-407
    motorcycle helmets and, 408-410
    reliance, contrasted, 407-408, 410-412
    tobacco products and, 401-407
    Uniform Commercial Code, 401
  comparative fault and, 483-484

Express warranty (*continued*)
  food products and, 400-401
  historical overview, 397
  law merchant, 397
  misrepresentation, relationship to, 417-418
  motor vehicles and, 398-400
  preemption and, 434-435
  reliance and, 402-413
    basis of the bargain, contrasted, 407-408, 410-412
  subject of warranty, 397-401
  Uniform Commercial Code, 397-398
  used products, disclaimers under, 561-563

Farm equipment
  comparative fault and, 464-474
  post-sale warnings and, 373-377
Federal Cigarette Labeling and Advertising Act
  preemption and, 426-431
Federal Insecticide, Fungicide, and Rodenticide Act
  preemption and, 435-437
Federalism issues, 677-698
  admiralty law, 696-698
    aircraft and, 697
    asbestos and, 697
    boats and, 697-698
  Agent Orange and, 683-688
  asbestos and, 690
  bankruptcy law, 691-696
    asbestos and, 696
    mass tort litigation and, 692-696
  blood and, 690-691
  cigarettes and, 691
  class actions, 689-691
  Common Sense Product Liability Legal Reform Act of 1996, 681-682
  federal common law, 683-689
  HIV and, 690-691
  judicial solutions, 682-691
  mass tort litigation, 689-691
    bankruptcy law and, 692-696
  Model Uniform Product Liability Act, 679-680
  patchwork nature of state statutes, 677-679
  preemption and, 689. *See also* Preemption
  Restatement (Third) of Torts and, 681
  Risk Retention Act, 682
  state statutes, patchwork nature of, 677-679
  tobacco products and, 691
  toxic torts litigation, 689-691
  uniform law approach, 679-680
Federal Rules of Evidence
  subsequent remedial measures under, 197
Firearms
  consumer expectations standard and, 259-267
  defective design
    duty, problems regarding, 297-298
    nuisance theory, 282
    market share approach and, 298-299
Fitness, implied warranty of, 412-413
  strict liability and, 15
Food and Drug Administration Modernization Act
  duty to warn under, 575
Food products, 568-572
  consumer expectations standard and, 568-571
  duty to warn and, 571
  express warranty and, 400-401
  foreign-natural test and, 568-571
  implied warranty and, 571
  misrepresentation and, 571
  Restatement (Third) of Torts, 569-570
  strict liability and, 568
Foreign countries. *See* International perspectives
Foreign-natural test
  food products and, 568-571

"Gatekeeper" liability
  corporate liability and, 663-664
Generic drugs
  duty to warn and, 391
Generic product risks
  defective design. *See* Defective design
  duty to warn. *See* Duty to warn
  overview, 159-160
Government contractors
  affirmative defenses, 499-501

Hazardous materials
  duty to warn and, 338-340, 387-391
  informed choice warnings, 342-343
  medical monitoring costs, 617-625
  sufficiency of warning, 358
HIV
  federalism issues and, 690-691
  mass tort litigation, 690-691
Human tissue
  as product, 53-55

Implied warranty
  bottles and, 21-22
  of fitness, 412-413
    strict liability and, 15
  food products and, 571
  of merchantability, 15-16
  power tools and, 16-19
  strict liability and, 14-19
  used products, disclaimers under, 561-563
Indemnity
  distributors, allocating liability between, 76-78

Index

members of distributive chain, allocating liability among, 76-78
Restatement (Third) of Torts, 77-78
Information
  as product, 51-53
Informed choice warnings, 340-349
  asbestos, 341
  hazardous materials, 342-343
  meat grinders and, 343-347
  prescription drugs, 340-341
  Restatement (Third) of Torts, 341-342
  risk reduction warnings, 340
  safety devices and measures, 349
Innovation
  effect of products liability law on, 717-719
Insurance
  Risk Retention Act, 680
  strict liability and insurability of risk, 32-33, 166-167
Integrated systems, 505-513
  asbestos and, 512
  Restatement (Third) of Torts, 505, 511-512
Intentional tort by employer
  rolling mills and, 99-106
  substantial certainty of injury, 97
  workers' compensation bar to product liability, exception to, 95-107
International perspectives, 699-719
  American firms, competitive disadvantages
    innovation, effect of products liability law on, 717-719
    price, effect of products liability law on, 713-717
  attorneys' fees, 706
  damages, 706-707
  discovery, 705-706
"In the business of selling or distributing"
  defined, 64-66
  retailers and, 64-66
  wholesalers and, 64-66
IUDs
  expert witnesses and, 130-131

Japan, 699-713
  American firms, competitive disadvantages
    innovation, effect of products liability law on, 717-719
    price, effect of products liability law on, 713-717
  attorneys' fees in, 706
  damages in, 706-707
  defective design in, 710
  discovery in, 705-706
  product, 709-710
  Products Liability Act, 707-712
  statutes of limitations, 712

Joint and several liability, 67-70
  market share approach, 134
Judicial review
  defective design, necessity in, 163-164
Jury instructions
  sufficiency of warning and, 361-367

Ladders
  reasonable alternative design standard and, 172-177
  sufficiency of warning and, 355-358
Last clear chance
  comparative fault and, 457
Law merchant
  express warranty and, 397
Liability insurance
  duty to warn of unknowable risks and, 337-340
Loss-of-a-chance causation, 147-149
  medical devices, 148-149
  Restatement (Third) of Torts, 148

Managers
  corporate liability and, 663-664
Manufacturing defects
  allocating liability. See Allocating liability
  causation. See Causation
  overview, 1
  strict liability. See Strict liability
Marketplace
  defective design, deference to, 282-290
    Restatement (Third) of Torts, 289-290
Market share approach, 131-136
  firearms and, 298-299
  joint and several liability, 134
Mass tort litigation
  bankruptcy law and, 692-696
  federalism issues, 689-691
Meat grinders
  informed choice warnings and, 343-347
Medical Device Act
  preemption and, 438-439
Medical devices, 514-556. See also Prescription drugs
  collective responsibility and, 82-87
  contraceptive devices
    duty to warn and, 524-534
  defective design and, 307-310, 534-553
    alternative safer design test, 550-552
    Restatement (Third) of Torts, 542-544
  distributors, liability, 553-556
    Restatement (Third) of Torts, 553-554
  duty to warn and, 514-534
    contraceptive devices, 524-534
    medical providers, warnings to, 514-522
    patients, warnings to, 522-534

Medical devices (*continued*)
    Restatement (Second) of Torts, 514-515
    Restatement (Third) of Torts, 515-516, 534
  loss-of-a-chance causation, 148-149
  preemption and, 438-439
  Restatement (Second) of Torts, duty to warn under, 514-515
  Restatement (Third) of Torts
    defective design under, 542-544
    duty to warn under, 515-516, 534
    liability of distributors under, 553-554
  "selling or otherwise distributing" and, 59-62
Medical providers
  collective responsibility, 87-88
  emotional distress, 581-585
  medical devices, duty to warn of, 514-522
  prescription drugs, duty to warn of, 514-522
  selling or otherwise distributing, exception, 62-63
Members of distributive chain
  allocating liability among, 67-80
    contribution, 74-76
    indemnity, 76-78
    joint and several liability, 67-70
    release, 78-80
    settlement, 78-80
Merchantability, implied warranty of
  strict liability and, 15-16
Minors
  consumer expectations standard and, 267-268
  defective design
    two-prong standard and, 277
Misrepresentation, 413-422
  cigarettes and, 419-420
  express warranty, relationship to, 417-418
  food products and, 571
  preemption and, 434-435
  prescription drugs and, 415-417, 419
  Restatement (Second) of Torts, 413-415
    negligent misrepresentation, 414
    sale of goods, 414-415
  Restatement (Third) of Torts, 418-419
  tobacco products and, 419-420
Misuse
  comparative fault and, 475-476
  defective design and, 305-313
Model Rules of Professional Conduct
  ethics and, 92-93
Model Uniform Product Liability Act, 679-680
  allocating liability under, 71-74
Modification
  comparative fault and, 475-476
  defective design and, 305-313
Moral hazard, 31-32
  shareholder limited liability and, 651, 662-663

Motorcycle helmets
  basis of the bargain and, 408-410
Motor vehicle insurance
  punitive damages and, 636-645
Motor vehicles
  all-or-nothing causation and, 137-139
  assumption of the risk and, 488-489
  comparative fault and, 477-483
  consumer expectations standard and, 244-247, 255-256
  crashworthiness, 477-483
  defective design and, 33-36
    two-prong standard and, 268-277
  duty to warn and, 382-387
  enhanced injury and, 140-145
  express warranty and, 398-400
  product category liability and, 234-243
  punitive damages and, 627-633
  reasonable alternative design standard and, 182-184
  statutes of repose and, 495-496
  sufficiency of warning, 371
Mushrooms
  product, information regarding as, 49-51

Negligence
  contributory negligence, 454-455
    Restatement (Second) of Torts, 454
  duty to warn and prescription drugs, 516-521
  economic test of negligence and strict liability, 4-5
  overview, 4-6
  strict liability
    public policy advantages of strict liability over negligence, 25-30
    role in, 4-14
  submitting claim on both grounds of negligence and strict liability, 201-206
Negligent misrepresentation
  Restatement (Second) of Torts, 414
Noneconomic damages
  limitations, 577-578
Nonprescription drugs, 572-575
  Food and Drug Administration Modernization Act, 575
  Restatement (Second) of Torts, 573
  Restatement (Third) of Torts, 574
Nuisance
  firearms, defective design, 282

Oil tankers
  economic loss rule and, 587-593

Index

Paint
  shareholder limited liability and, 654-660
"Patent danger rule"
  Restatement (Third) of Torts, 163-164
Patients
  medical devices, duty to warn of, 522-534
  prescription drugs, duty to warn of, 522-534
PCBs
  medical monitoring costs, 616
Perjury
  ethics and, 93-94
Pesticides
  preemption and, 435-437
Pharmacists
  prescription drugs, liability, 553-556
    Restatement (Third) of Torts, 553-554
Piercing the corporate veil, 651, 654
Playgrounds
  reasonable alternative design standard and, 181-182
Post-sale warnings, 372-379
  defects existing at time of sale, distinguished, 373
  duty to recall and, 378-379
  farm equipment and, 373-377
  Restatement (Third) of Torts, 372-373
  statutes of repose and, 377-378
Power tools
  implied warranty and, 16-19
Preemption, 423-451
  defective design and, 437-451
    airbags and, 439-451
    boats and, 451
    brakes and, 437-438
    medical devices and, 438-439
  duty to warn and, 424-437
    cigarettes and, 425-435
    pesticides and, 435-437
    prescription drugs and, 435-437
    tobacco products and, 425-435
  express warranty and, 434-435
  Federal Cigarette Labeling and Advertising Act and, 426-431
  Federal Insecticide, Fungicide, and Rodenticide Act and, 435-437
  federalism issues and, 689
  Medical Device Act and, 438-439
  misrepresentation and, 434-435
  overview, 423-424
  Public Health Cigarette Smoking Act of 1969 and, 426-431
Prescription drugs, 514-556. *See also* Medical devices
  defective design and, 534-553
    alternative safer design test, 550-552
    differences between drugs and other products, 544-550
    Restatement (Third) of Torts, 542-544, 552-553
  defective marketing and, 394-395
  distributors, liability, 542-544, 553-554
  duty to warn and, 514-534
    generic drugs, 391
    informed choice warnings, 340-341
    medical providers, warnings to, 514-522
    negligence and, 516-521
    patients, warnings to, 522-534
    Restatement (Second) of Torts, 514-515
    Restatement (Third) of Torts, 515-516, 534
    strict liability and, 521-522
    unknowable risks, 334-335
  expert witnesses and, 123-129
  generic drugs, 391
  informed choice warnings, 340-341
  medical monitoring costs, 625
  misrepresentation and, 415-417, 419
  pharmacists, liability, 553-556
    Restatement (Third) of Torts, 553-554
  preemption and, 435-437
  punitive damages, exemptions, 635
  Restatement (Second) of Torts, duty to warn under, 514-515
  Restatement (Third) of Torts
    distributors, liability under, 542-544, 553-554
    duty to warn under, 515-516, 534
    liability of pharmacists under, 553-554
  successor corporation liability, 668-673
  unknowable risks, duty to warn, 334-335
Prevention costs
  strict liability and, 6
Price
  effect of products liability law on, 713-717
Privity
  strict liability, decline of rule in connection with, 6-8
Product category liability, 218-243
  common law and, 233-234
  implementation problems, 229-230
  motor vehicles and, 234-243
  reasonable alternative design standard and, 226-227, 230-232
  Restatement (Third) of Torts, 218-219
  risk-utility standard, 218-243
    common law and, 233-234
    implementation problems, 229-230
    motor vehicles and, 234-243
    reasonable alternative design standard and, 226-227, 230-232
    Restatement (Third) of Torts, 218-219
    terminology, 227-229
  terminology, 227-229
Products
  blood as, 53-55

Products (*continued*)
  defined, 45-55
    Restatement (Third) of Torts, defined under, 46
  electrical power as, 48
  harm caused by product, proving, 118-131
  human tissue as, 53-55
  information as, 51-53
  innovation, effect of products liability law on, 717-719
  in Japan, 709-710
  mushrooms, information regarding as, 49-51
  price, effect of products liability law on, 713-717
  recipes as, 53
  Restatement (Third) of Torts, defined under, 46
  supplying product, proving, 131-136
    identification of defendant, 131
    market share approach, 131-136
  tangible property as, 46-48
Propane heaters
  assumption of the risk and, 485-487
  sufficiency of warning, 358-359
Proximate cause, 149-158
  but-for causation and, 152, 156
  cause in fact and, 154
  defective design
    burden of proof, 306
  duty to warn and, 379-393
    heeding of warnings, likelihood, 379-387
    motor vehicles and, 382-387
    other products, harm caused by, 387-392
    result within the risk, 156
    sort of harm warning would have prevented, 392-393
  pumps and, 149-151
  rescuer doctrine and, 156-157
  safety devices and measures and, 157-158
  tires and, 379, 382
Public Health Cigarette Smoking Act of 1969
  preemption and, 426-431
Public policy
  strict liability, 25-30
Pumps
  proximate cause and, 149-151
Punitive damages, 627-647
  "clear and convincing evidence" standard, 634
  constitutional limitations, 636-647
  egregious behavior, 633
  monetary caps, 634-635
  motor vehicle insurance and, 636-645
  motor vehicles and, 627-633
  prescription drugs, exemptions, 635
  state limitations, 627-636
  wanton and reckless behavior, 633-634
Pure economic loss. *See* Economic loss rule

Raw materials, 505-513
  asbestos and, 512
  Restatement (Third) of Torts, 505, 511-512
Reasonable alternative design standard, 169-213
  boats and, 188-194, 201-205
  defining the standard, 172-184
  duty to warn as substitute for, 206-213
    Restatement (Third) of Torts, 212-213
  exercise equipment and, 213-317
  expert witnesses, 304
  ladders and, 172-177
  medical devices and, 310
  motor vehicles and, 182-184
  negligence and strict liability, submitting claim on both grounds, 201-206
  overview, 161
  playgrounds and, 181-182
  product category liability and, 226-227, 230-232
  Restatement (Third) of Torts, 170-172
    expert witnesses, 304
    negligence and strict liability, submitting claim on both grounds, 205-206
    warnings as substitute for, 212-213
  risk-utility balancing without, 213-218
  "state of the art" defense, 187-195
  strict liability and negligence, submitting claim on both grounds, 201-206
  subsequent remedial measures, 195-199
  swimming pools and, 219-226
  time for applying standard, 184-201
    post-sale improvement in risk avoidance, responsibility for, 187-199
      "state of the art" defense, 187-195
      subsequent remedial measures, 195-199
    post-sale increase in knowledge of risk, responsibility for, 186-187
    post-sale shifts in public attitude toward risk, responsibility for, 199-201
    "state of the art" defense, 187-195
    subsequent remedial measures, 195-199
  tires and, 206-212
  warnings as substitute for, 206-213
    Restatement (Third) of Torts, 212-213
Recalls
  post-sale warnings and, 378-379
Recipes
  as product, 53
Regulations
  defective design, deference to, 290-294
    compliance as conclusiveness of nondefectiveness, 293-294
    defect per se, 293
    Restatement (Third) of Torts, 291-292
Release
  distributors, allocating liability between, 78-80

Index

members of distributive chain, allocating liability among, 78-80
Reliance
   basis of the bargain, contrasted, 407-408, 410-412
   express warranty and, 402-413
      basis of the bargain, contrasted, 407-408, 410-412
      Uniform Sales Act, 401
Rescuer doctrine
   proximate cause and, 156-157
Residual accident costs
   strict liability and, 5-6, 23, 28-30
Res ipsa loquitur
   bottles and, 9-14
   Restatement (Third) of Torts, 168
   Strict liability, rise of rule in connection with, 8-14
Restatement (Second) of Torts
   abnormally dangerous activities under, 223
   contributory negligence under, 454
   cosmetics and, 573
   duty to warn under
      medical devices and, 514-515
      prescription drugs and, 514-515
   misrepresentation under, 413-415
      negligent misrepresentation, 414
      sale of goods, 414-415
   nonprescription drugs and, 573
   prescription drugs and
      duty to warn under, 514-515
   strict liability under, 19-25
      history, 20-21
      practical implications, 23-24
      provisions, 20
Restatement (Third) of Torts
   categories of defects under, 37
   causation and, 118
   circumstantial evidence of defective design under, 40, 168-169
   comparative fault under, 455, 463
   component parts under, 505, 511-512
   consumer expectations standard and, 254
   contribution under, 75-76
   defective design under
      circumstantial evidence, 168-169
      marketplace, deference to, 289-290
      regulations, deference to, 291-292
      statutes, deference to, 291-292
   duty to warn under, 316-317
      cosmetics and, 574
      generally known risks, 318
      medical devices and, 515-516, 534
      nonprescription drugs and, 574
      obvious risks, 318
      prescription drugs and, 515-516, 534
      unknowable risks, 335-337
   economic loss rule under, 594-595
   enhanced injury under, 145-147
   federalism issues and, 681
   food products under, 569-570
   generally known risks, duty to warn under, 318
   indemnity under, 77-78
   informed choice warnings under, 341-342
   integrated systems under, 505, 511-512
   loss-of-a-chance causation under, 148
   medical devices
      defective design under, 542-544
      duty to warn under, 515-516, 534
      liability of distributors under, 553-554
   misrepresentation under, 418-419
   obvious risks, duty to warn under, 318
   "patent danger rule" under, 164
   post-sale warnings under, 372-373
   prescription drugs
      distributors, liability under, 542-544, 553-554
      duty to warn under, 515-516, 534
      liability of pharmacists under, 553-554
   "product," defined, 46
   product category liability under, 218-219
   raw materials under, 505, 511-512
   reasonable alternative design standard under, 170-172
      expert witnesses, 304
      negligence and strict liability, submitting claim on both grounds, 205-206
      warnings as substitute for, 212-213
   res ipsa loquitur under, 168
   "selling or otherwise distributing," defined, 55
   strict liability under, 37
   successor corporation liability under, 674
   sufficiency of warning under, 359
   unknowable risks, duty to warn under, 335-337
   used products under, 559
      disclaimers, 564
Retailers
   allocating liability, letting out of litigation, 70-74
   duty to warn, 317-318
   "in the business of selling or distributing," 64-66
   Model Uniform Product Liability Act, allocating liability under, 71-74
   "sealed container" doctrine, 70-71
   strict liability and, 23
Risk
   strict liability and insurability of risk, 32-33
Risk Retention Act
   federalism issues regarding, 682
Risk-utility standard, 169-243
   balancing without reasonable alternative design, 213-218

Risk-utility standard (*continued*)
  comparative fault, compared, 464
  product category liability, 218-243
    common law and, 233-234
    implementation problems, 229-230
    motor vehicles and, 234-243
    reasonable alternative design standard and, 226-227, 230-232
    Restatement (Third) of Torts, 218-219
    terminology, 227-229
  reasonable alternative design standard. *See* Reasonable alternative design standard
Rolling mills
  intentional tort by employer and, 99-106

Safety devices and measures
  defective design and, 311-313
  informed choice warnings, 349
  proximate cause and, 157-158
  sufficiency of warning and, 367-372
Sale of goods
  misrepresentation, Restatement (Second) of Torts, 414-415
Sales facilitators
  selling or otherwise distributing, exception, 57-59
School buses
  defective design and, 285-289
"Sealed container" doctrine
  distributors, allocating liability between, 70-71
Seat belts
  comparative fault and, 476
  defective design, 44-45
"Selling or otherwise distributing"
  auctioneers, exception, 58
  bailors, exception, 56-57
  defined, 55-64
    Restatement (Third) of Torts, 55
  medical devices and, 59-62
  medical providers, exception, 62-63
  Restatement (Third) of Torts, defined under, 55
  sales facilitators, exception, 57-59
  sales-services hybrids, 63-64
  trademark licensors, exception, 57
September 11 litigation
  defective design, problems regarding, 300-303
Settlement
  distributors, allocating liability between, 78-80
  members of distributive chain, allocating liability among, 78-80
Several liability, 67-70
  shareholder limited liability and, 652-653
Shareholder limited liability, 651-668
  computer equipment and, 660-661
  electronic locks and, 661-662

moral hazard and, 651, 662-663
  overview, 651-654
  paint and, 654-660
  "piercing the corporate veil," 651, 654
  several liability and, 652-653
Silicone breast implants
  emotional distress, 585
Skiing equipment
  persons required to warn or be warned, 349-352
Slip and fall
  defective design and, 139-140, 310-311
Sovereign immunity
  as affirmative defense, 498-499
Special problem areas
  corporate liability. *See* Corporate liability
  damages. *See* Damages
  federalism issues. *See* Federalism issues
  international perspectives. *See* International perspectives
"State of the art" defense
  reasonable alternative design standard and, 187-195
Statutes
  defective design, deference to, 290-294
    compliance as conclusiveness of nondefectiveness, 293-294
    defect per se, 293
    Restatement (Third) of Torts, 291-292
  federalism issues. *See* Federalism issues
  patchwork nature of, 677-679
  preemption. *See* Preemption
  punitive damages, limitations, 627-636
Statutes of limitations, 489-494
  causal connection, knowledge of triggering, 492-493
  defendant's identity, knowledge of triggering, 493-494
  injury, knowledge of triggering, 491-492
  in Japan, 712
Statutes of repose, 494-498
  constitutionality, 496-498
  motor vehicles and, 495-496
  post-sale warnings and, 377-378
  Uniform Commercial Code, 494
Strict liability
  adjudicability of disputes, 32, 166
  boundaries of doctrine, 45-66
    "in the business of selling or distributing," definition of, 64-66
    "product," definition of, 45-55
    "selling or otherwise distributing," definition of, 55-64
  claim on grounds of both strict liability and negligence, 201-206
  defective design
    as alternative to, 164-167

Index

adjudicability of disputes, lack of, 166
  insurability of risk, lack of, 166-167
centrality of, 33-45
duty to warn and
  prescription drugs and, 521-522
economic test of negligence and, 4-5
fitness, implied warranty of and, 15
food products and, 568
implied warranty and, 14-19
insurability of risk, 32-33, 166-167
"in the business of selling or distributing,"
  definition as boundary on doctrine,
  64-66
merchantability, implied warranty of and, 15-16
modern rule, 14-33
moral hazard and, 31-32
necessary conditions, 30-32
negligence
  public policy advantages of strict liability
    over negligence, 25-30
  role of, 4-14
overview, 3
prescription drugs and duty to warn, 521-522
prevention costs, 6
privity, decline of rule in connection with,
  6-8
"product," definition as boundary on doctrine,
  45-55
public policy, 25-30
residual accident costs, 5-6, 23, 28-30
res ipsa loquitur, rise of rule in connection
  with, 8-14
Restatement (Second) of Torts, 19-25
  history, 20-21
  practical implications, 23-24
  provisions, 20
Restatement (Third) of Torts, 37
retailers and, 23
"selling or otherwise distributing," definition
  as boundary on doctrine, 55-64
surgical implants and, 24-25
tires and, 57
used products and, 559-561
viability, 30-33
  adjudicability of disputes, 32
  insurability of risk, 32-33
  necessary conditions, 30-32
wholesalers and, 23
Subsequent remedial measures
  reasonable alternative design standard and, 195-199
Subsidiaries
  corporate liability and, 664
Successor corporation liability, 668-675
  continuation of business enterprise rule, 674
  diethylstilbestrol (DES), 668-673

prescription drugs, 668-673
product line extension rule, 674
Restatement (Third) of Torts, 674
Sufficiency of warning, 355-372
  boats and, 361-365
  contact lenses, 359-360
  defective design, compared, 360-361
  drills and, 368-371
  English language and, 371-372
  hazardous materials, 358
  jury instructions and, 361-367
  ladders and, 355-358
  motor vehicles, 371
  propane heaters, 358-359
  Restatement (Third) of Torts, 359
  safety devices and measures and, 367-372
  telephones, 358
Superseding cause
  comparative fault and, 457-462
  workplace accidents and, 457-462
Surgical implants
  strict liability and, 24-25
Swimming pools
  duty to warn, 327-328
  reasonable alternative design standard and, 219-226

Tangible property
  as product, 46-48
Telephones
  sufficiency of warning, 358
Time-based defenses
  statutes of limitations. *See* Statutes of limitations
  statutes of repose. *See* Statutes of repose
Tires
  dual capacity doctrine and, 108
  proximate cause and, 379, 382
  reasonable alternative design standard and, 206-212
  strict liability and, 57
Tobacco products
  basis of the bargain and, 401-407
  federalism issues and, 691
  mass tort litigation, 691
  misrepresentation and, 419-420
  preemption and, 425-435
Toxic torts litigation, 605-627
  asbestos and, 606-616
  emotional distress, 610-616
  federalism issues, 689-691
  increased risk of future injury, 605-610
  medical monitoring costs, 616-627
  PCBs and, 616
Trademark licensors
  selling or otherwise distributing, exception, 57

Unconscionability
  used products, disclaimers, 562-564
Uniform Commercial Code
  basis of the bargain under, 401
  consumer expectations standard and, 256-259
  express warranty under, 397-398
  implied warranty of fitness under, 412-413
  statutes of repose under, 494
  used products, disclaimers under, 561-563
    unconscionability, 562-564
Uniform Comparative Fault Act
  members of distributive chain, allocating liability among, 78-80
Uniform Contribution Among Tortfeasors Act
  allocating liability under, 74-75
Uniform Sales Act
  reliance under, 401
"Unreasonably dangerous"
  defective design, construed, 33-37
Used products, 556-568
  alarms and, 566-568
  appliances, 556-558
  disclaimers and, 561-568
    Restatement (Third) of Torts, 564
    unconscionability, 562-564
    Uniform Commercial Code, 561-563
  Restatement (Third) of Torts, 559
    disclaimers, 564
  strict liability and, 559-561
  Uniform Commercial Code, disclaimers under, 561-563
    unconscionability, 562-564

"Virtual" companies
  corporate liability and, 667-668

Warnings. *See* Duty to warn
Warranty
  express warranty. *See* Express warranty
  implied warranty. *See* Implied warranty

Wholesalers
  allocating liability, letting out of litigation, 70-74
  duty to warn, 317-318
  "in the business of selling or distributing," 64-66
  Model Uniform Product Liability Act, allocating liability under, 71-74
  "sealed container" doctrine, 70-71
  strict liability and, 23
Windows
  economic loss rule and, 595-600
Workers' compensation
  affirmative defenses, 498
  agitators and, 109-111
  bar to product liability, 95
    dual capacity doctrine, 107-109
    intentional tort by employer exception, 95-107
    substantial certainty of injury, 97
  shared responsibility between employer and manufacturer, 109-115
  reduction of tort recovery, 113-115
Workplace accidents
  allocating liability, 95-115
    collective responsibility, 88-92
    shared responsibility between employer and manufacturer, 109-115
      reduction of tort recovery, 113-115
    sole responsibility of employer, 95-109
      dual capacity doctrine, 107-109
      intentional tort by employer, 95-107
      workers' compensation, bar to product liability, 95
  consumer expectations standard and, 248-253
  intentional tort by employer, 95-107
    rolling mills and, 99-106
    substantial certainty of injury, 97
    workers' compensation bar to product liability, exception to, 95-107
  superseding cause and, 457-462